Visual C# 2010

HOW TO PROGRAM

FOURTH EDITION

Library of Congress Cataloging-in-Publication Data

```
Deitel, Paul J.
  Visual C# 2010 : how to program / P.J. Deitel, H.M. Deitel. -- 4th ed.
      p. cm.
  Rev. ed. of: Visual C# 2008 / P.J. Deitel, H.M. Deitel. 2009.
  Includes index.
  ISBN-13: 978-0-13-215142-9 (pbk.)
  ISBN-10: 0-13-215142-1 (pbk.)

1.  C# (Computer program language)  I. Deitel, Harvey M., 1945- II. Deitel, Paul J.
Visual C# 2008. III. Title.
  QA76.73.C154D46 2011
  005.13'3--dc22
```

                                                                    2010034739

Vice President and Editorial Director, ECS: *Marcia J. Horton*
Editor-in-Chief, Computer Science: *Michael Hirsch*
Associate Editor: *Carole Snyder*
Vice-President, Production: *Vince O'Brien*
Managing Editor: *Jeff Holcomb*
Associate Managing Editor: *Robert Engelhardt*
Art Director: *Kristine Carney*
Cover Photo Credit: *bamboo forest, Daryl Benson/Photographer's Choice RF/Getty Images*
Cover Design: *Abbey S. Deitel, Harvey M. Deitel, Kristine Carney*
Interior Design: *Harvey M. Deitel, Kristine Carney*
Manufacturing Manager: *Alexis Heydt-Long*
Manufacturing Buyer: *Lisa McDowell*
Marketing Manager, Computer Science: *Yezan Alayan*

Prentice Hall
is an imprint of

PEARSON

© 2011 by Pearson Education, Inc.
Upper Saddle River, New Jersey 07458

Pearson Education Ltd., *London*
Pearson Education Australia Pty. Ltd., *Sydney*
Pearson Education Singapore, Pte. Ltd.
Pearson Education North Asia Ltd., *Hong Kong*
Pearson Education Canada, Inc., *Toronto*
Pearson Educación de Mexico, S.A. de C.V.
Pearson Education–Japan, *Tokyo*
Pearson Education Malaysia, Pte. Ltd.
Pearson Education, Inc., *Upper Saddle River, New Jersey*

Visual C# 2010

HOW TO PROGRAM

FOURTH EDITION

P. J. Deitel
Deitel & Associates, Inc.

H. M. Deitel
Deitel & Associates, Inc.

Prentice Hall
is an imprint of

PEARSON

Upper Saddle River, New Jersey 07458

Trademarks

DEITEL, the double-thumbs-up bug and DIVE INTO are registered trademarks of Deitel and Associates, Inc.

Microsoft, Windows, Silverlight, SQL Server, Visual Studio, Visual C#, Visual Basic and Visual Web Developer are either registered trademarks or trademarks of Microsoft Corporation in the United States and/or other countries.

To Anders Hejlsberg,
   Chief Designer of Microsoft's
   C# Programming Language

Paul and Harvey Deitel

Contents

Chapters 24–31 and Appendices D–G are PDF documents posted online at the book's Companion Website (located at www.pearsonhighered.com/deitel/).

9   Introduction to LINQ and the List Collection   344

10   Classes and Objects: A Deeper Look   364

11   Object-Oriented Programming: Inheritance   398

14 Graphical User Interfaces with Windows Forms: Part 1   510

15 Graphical User Interfaces with Windows Forms: Part 2   561

16 Strings and Characters   630

17 Files and Streams   661

18 Databases and LINQ   707

21 Data Structures — 830

22 Generics — 873

23 Collections — 898

Chapters on the Web — 932

Chapters 24–31 and Appendices D–G are PDF documents posted online at the book's Companion Website (located at www.pearsonhighered.com/deitel/).

Preface

Welcome to the Visual C#® 2010 programming language and the world of Microsoft® Windows® and Internet programming with Microsoft's .NET platform!

This book focuses on software engineering best practices. At the heart of the book is the Deitel signature "live-code approach." Concepts are presented in the context of working programs, rather than in code snippets. Each code example is accompanied by sample executions. All the source code is available at www.deitel.com/books/vcsharp2010htp/ and at the book's Companion Website at www.pearsonhighered.com/deitel/.

As you read the book, if you have questions, send an e-mail to deitel@deitel.com; we'll respond promptly. For updates on this book and its supporting Visual C# software, visit www.deitel.com/books/vcsharp2010htp/, follow us on Twitter (@deitel) and Facebook (www.deitel.com/deitelfan), and subscribe to the *Deitel® Buzz Online* newsletter (www.deitel.com/newsletter/subscribe.html).

New and Updated Features

Here are the updates we've made for *Visual C#® 2010 How to Program, 4/e*:

- *Printed book contains core content; advanced chapters are online.* The printed book contains sufficient core content for most introductory Visual C# course sequences. Several online chapters are included for more advanced courses and for professionals. These are available in searchable PDF format on the book's password-protected Companion Website—see the access card in the front of this book.

- The book's Companion Website includes extensive *VideoNotes* in which co-author Paul Deitel explains in detail most of the programs in the core chapters.

- *Making a Difference exercises set.* We encourage you to use computers and the Internet to research and solve significant social problems. These new exercises are meant to increase awareness and discussion of important issues the world is facing. We hope you'll approach them with your own values, politics and beliefs.

- *Up-to-date with Visual C# 2010, C# 4, the Visual Studio 2010 IDE and .NET 4.* The C# language has been standardized internationally by ECMA and ISO. The latest version of that language is referred to as C# 4. Microsoft's implementation of this standard is referred to as Visual C# 2010.

- *New language features.* We cover new C# features, such as optional parameters, named parameters, covariance and contravariance.

- *Databases.* We use Microsoft's free SQL Server Express (which installs with the free Visual C# Express) to teach the fundamentals of database programming. Chapters 18, 19, 27 and 28 use database and LINQ fundamentals in the context of an address-book desktop application, a web-based guestbook, a bookstore and an airline reservation system.

- *ASP.NET 4.* Microsoft's .NET server-side technology, ASP.NET, enables you to create robust, scalable web-based applications. In Chapter 19, you'll build several applications, including a web-based guestbook application that uses ASP.NET, LINQ and a LinqDataSource to store data in a database and display data in a web page. The chapter also discusses the ASP.NET Development Server for testing your web applications on your local computer.

- *We removed generic methods* from Chapter 9 to make the code easier to understand.

- The code will run on *Windows 7, Windows Vista* and *Windows XP.* We'll post any issues on www.deitel.com/books/vcsharp2010htp/.

- *We introduce exception handling much earlier* (Chapter 8) and integrated it in subsequent chapters in which it had not been used previously. We also now throw exceptions for invalid data received in the set accessors of properties.

- *New design.* The book has a new interior design that graphically organizes, clarifies and highlights the information, and enhances the book's pedagogy. We used italics extensively to emphasize important words, phrases and points in the text.

- *We titled the programming exercises* to help instructors tailor assignments.

Other features of *Visual C# 2010 How to Program, 4/e* include:

- We've provide instructors with *solutions to the vast majority of the exercises.* There are a few large exercises marked "Project" for which solutions are not provided.

- *We use LINQ (Language Integrated Query) to query files, databases, XML and collections.* The introductory LINQ chapter, Chapter 9, in the core printed book is intentionally brief to encourage instructors to cover this important technology early. The online chapters continue the discussion of LINQ.

- *Local type inference.* When you initialize a local variable in its declaration, you can now omit the variable's type—the compiler infers it from the initializer value.

- *Object initializers.* For new objects, you can use object initializer syntax (similar to array initializer syntax) to assign values to the new object's public properties and public instance variables.

- *We emphasize the IDE's* IntelliSense *feature* that helps you write code faster and with fewer errors.

Our Text + Digital Approach to Content

We surveyed hundreds of instructors teaching Visual C# courses and learned that most want a book with content focused on their introductory courses. With that in mind, we moved various intermediate and advanced chapters to the web. Having this content in digital format makes it easily searchable, and gives us the ability to fix errata and add new content as appropriate. The book's Companion Website at

    www.pearsonhighered.com/deitel/

(see the access card at the front of the book) contains the following chapters in *searchable* PDF format:

- *WPF (Windows Presentation Foundation) GUI, graphics and multimedia.* We extend the core book's GUI coverage in Chapters 24–25 with an introduction to Windows Presentation Foundation (WPF)—Microsoft's new framework that integrates GUI, graphics and multimedia capabilities. We implement a painting application, a text editor, a color chooser, a book-cover viewer, a television video player, various animations, and speech synthesis and recognition applications.

- *ASP.NET 4 and ASP.NET AJAX.* Chapter 27 extends Chapter 19's ASP.NET discussion with a case study on building a password-protected, web-based bookstore application. We also introduce ASP.NET AJAX controls and use them to add AJAX functionality to web applications to improve their responsiveness.

- *WCF (Windows Communication Foundation) Web Services.* Web services enable you to package application functionality in a manner that turns the web into a library of reusable services. In Chapter 28, we include case studies on building an airline reservation web service, a blackjack web service and a math question generator web service that's called by a math tutor application.

- *Silverlight.* Chapter 29 introduces Silverlight, which enables you to create visually stunning, multimedia-intensive user interfaces for web applications. The chapter presents powerful multimedia applications, including a weather viewer, Flickr photo viewer, deep zoom book-cover collage and video viewer.

- *Visual C# XML capabilities.* Use of the Extensible Markup Language (XML) is exploding in the software-development industry and in e-business, and is pervasive throughout the .NET platform. In Chapter 26, we use show how to programmatically manipulate the elements of an XML document using LINQ to XML.

- *Optional Case Study: Using the UML to Develop an Object-Oriented Design and C# Implementation of an ATM.* The UML™ (Unified Modeling Language™) is the preferred graphical modeling language for designing object-oriented systems. This edition includes an optional online case study on object-oriented design using the UML (Chapters 30–31). We design and implement the software for a simple automated teller machine (ATM). We analyze a typical requirements document that specifies the system to be built. We determine the classes needed to implement that system, the attributes the classes need to have, the behaviors the classes need to exhibit and specify how the classes must interact with one another to meet the system requirements. From the design we produce a working Visual C# implementation. We've presented this case study to professional audiences in C#, Java, Visual Basic and C++. After seeing the case-study presentation, students report having a "light-bulb moment"—the case study "ties it all together" for them and helps them understand how objects in a larger system communicate with one another.

- *Index.* The online index includes the content from the printed book *and* the online content. The printed book index covers only the printed material.

Dependency Charts

The charts in Figs. 1–2 show the dependencies among the chapters to help instructors plan their syllabi. The printed book focuses on introductory course sequences (Fig. 1). The online chapters include intermediate and advanced content for more advanced courses (Fig. 2).

Dependency Chart for Print Chapters[1]

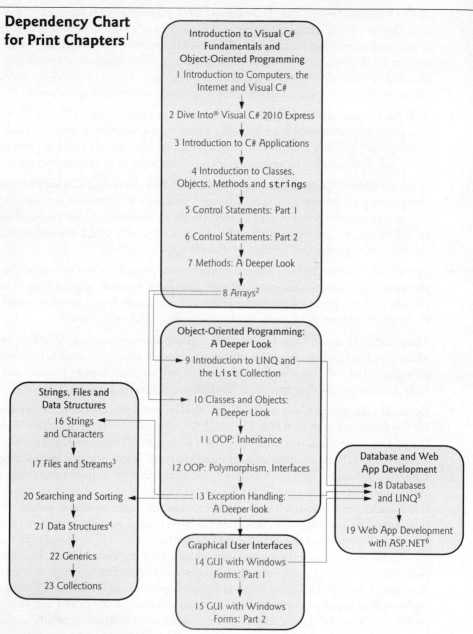

Introduction to Visual C# Fundamentals and Object-Oriented Programming

1 Introduction to Computers, the Internet and Visual C#

↓

2 Dive Into® Visual C# 2010 Express

↓

3 Introduction to C# Applications

↓

4 Introduction to Classes, Objects, Methods and `strings`

↓

5 Control Statements: Part 1

↓

6 Control Statements: Part 2

↓

7 Methods: A Deeper Look

↓

8 Arrays[2]

Object-Oriented Programming: A Deeper Look

9 Introduction to LINQ and the `List` Collection

↓

10 Classes and Objects: A Deeper Look

↓

11 OOP: Inheritance

↓

12 OOP: Polymorphism, Interfaces

↓

13 Exception Handling: A Deeper look

Strings, Files and Data Structures

16 Strings and Characters

↓

17 Files and Streams[3]

↓

20 Searching and Sorting

↓

21 Data Structures[4]

↓

22 Generics

↓

23 Collections

Database and Web App Development

18 Databases and LINQ[5]

↓

19 Web App Development with ASP.NET[6]

Graphical User Interfaces

14 GUI with Windows Forms: Part 1

↓

15 GUI with Windows Forms: Part 2

1. See Fig. 2 for the online chapters.
2. Chapter 8 introduces exception handling.
3. Requires Sections 14.1–14.5.
4. Requires Sections 14.1–14.5 and 15.6.
5. Requires Sections 14.1–14.6 and 15.8.
6. Requires general GUI and event-handling knowledge (Sections 14.1–14.3).

Fig. 1 | Chapter dependency chart for the chapters in the printed book.

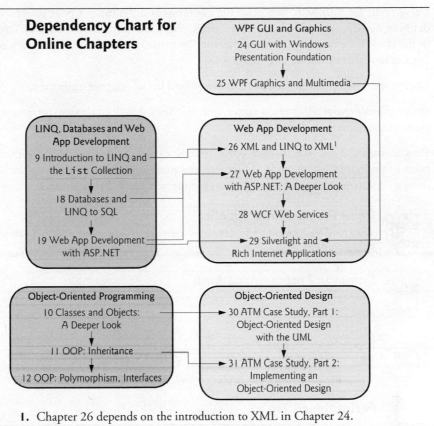

Dependency Chart for Online Chapters

1. Chapter 26 depends on the introduction to XML in Chapter 24.

Fig. 2 | Chapter dependency chart for the online chapters.

Teaching Approach

Visual C# 2010 How to Program, 4/e contains a rich collection of examples. We concentrate on building good software and stress program clarity.

Live-Code Approach. The book is loaded with "live-code" examples. Most new concepts are presented in the context of complete working Visual C# applications, followed by one or more executions showing program inputs and outputs. In the few cases where we use snippets, we tested them in complete working programs then copied the code from the program and pasted it into the book.

Syntax Shading. For readability, we syntax shade the code, similar to the way most integrated-development environments and code editors syntax color the code. Our syntax-shading conventions are:

```
comments appear like this
keywords appear like this
constants and literal values appear like this
all other code appears in black
```

Code Highlighting. We place gray rectangles around each program's key code.

Using Fonts for Emphasis. We place the key terms and the index's page reference for each defining occurrence in **bold** text for easy reference. We emphasize on-screen components in the **bold Helvetica** font (for example, the **File** menu) and Visual C# program text in the Lucida font (for example, int count = 5).

Objectives. The opening quotes are followed by a list of chapter objectives.

Illustrations/Figures. Abundant tables, line drawings, UML diagrams, programs and program outputs are included.

Programming Tips. We include programming tips to help you focus on important aspects of program development. These tips and practices represent the best we've gleaned from a combined seven decades of programming and teaching experience.

Good Programming Practice

The Good Programming Practices *call attention to techniques that will help you produce programs that are clearer, more understandable and more maintainable.*

Common Programming Error

Pointing out these Common Programming Errors *reduces the likelihood that you'll make them.*

Error-Prevention Tip

These tips contain suggestions for exposing and removing bugs from your programs; many of the tips describe aspects of Visual C# that prevent bugs from getting into programs.

Performance Tip

These tips highlight opportunities for making your programs run faster or minimizing the amount of memory that they occupy.

Portability Tip

The Portability Tips *help you write code that will run on a variety of platforms.*

Software Engineering Observation

The Software Engineering Observations *highlight architectural and design issues that affect the construction of software systems, especially large-scale systems.*

Look-and-Feel Observation

These observations help you design attractive, user-friendly graphical user interfaces that conform to industry norms.

Summary Bullets. We present a section-by-section, bullet-list summary of each chapter.

Terminology. We include an alphabetized list of the important terms defined in each chapter.

Self-Review Exercises and Answers. Extensive self-review exercises *and* answers are included for self-study.

Exercises. Each chapter concludes with additional exercises including:

- simple recall of important terminology and concepts
- What's wrong with this code?
- What does this code do?
- writing individual statements and small portions of methods and classes
- writing complete methods, classes and programs
- major projects.

Please do not write to us requesting access to the Pearson Instructor's Resource Center which contains the book's instructor supplements, including the exercise solutions. Access is limited strictly to college instructors teaching from the book. Instructors may obtain access only through their Pearson representatives. Solutions are *not* provided for "project" exercises. Check out our Programming Projects Resource Center for lots of additional exercise and project possibilities (www.deitel.com/ProgrammingProjects/).

Index. We've included an extensive index for reference. Defining occurrences of key terms are highlighted with a **bold** page number.

Student Resources and Software

This book includes the Microsoft® Visual Studio® 2010 Express Editions DVD, which contains the Visual C#® 2010 Express Edition (and other Microsoft development tools). These tools are also downloadable from

```
www.microsoft.com/express/Windows
```

We wrote *Visual C# 2010 How to Program* using Visual C#® Express Edition. You can learn more about Visual C#® at msdn.microsoft.com/vcsharp.

Deitel Online Resource Centers

Our website www.deitel.com provides Resource Centers on various topics of interest to our readers (www.deitel.com/ResourceCenters.html). We've found many exceptional resources online, including tutorials, documentation, software downloads, articles, blogs, podcasts, videos, code samples, books, e-books and more—most are free. Some of the Resource Centers you might find helpful while studying this book are Visual C#, ASP.NET, ASP.NET AJAX, LINQ, .NET, Silverlight, SQL Server, Web Services, Windows Communication Foundation, Windows Presentation Foundation, Windows 7, UML, Code Search Engines and Code Sites, Game Programming and Programming Projects.

Instructor Supplements

The following supplements are available to qualified instructors only through Pearson Education's Instructor Resource Center (www.pearsonhighered.com/irc):

- *Solutions Manual* with solutions to most of the end-of-chapter exercises.
- *Test Item File* of multiple-choice questions (approximately two per book section)
- *PowerPoint® slides* containing all the code and figures in the text, plus bulleted items that summarize key points.

If you're not a registered faculty member, contact your Pearson representative or visit www.pearsonhighered.com/educator/replocator/.

CourseSmart Web Books

Today's students and instructors have increasing demands on their time and money. Pearson has responded to that need by offering digital texts and course materials online through CourseSmart. CourseSmart allows faculty to review course materials online, saving time and costs. It is also environmentally sound and offers students a high-quality digital version of the text for as much as 50% off the cost of a print copy of the text. Students receive the same content offered in the print textbook enhanced by search, note-taking, and printing tools. For more information, visit www.coursesmart.com.

Microsoft Developer Network Academic Alliance (MSDNAA) and Microsoft DreamSpark

Microsoft Developer Network Academic Alliance (MSDNAA)—Free Microsoft Software for Academic and Research Purposes
The MSDNAA provides free software for academic and research purposes. For software direct to faculty, visit www.microsoft.com/faculty. For software for your department, visit www.msdnaa.com.

Microsoft DreamSpark—Professional Developer and Designer Tools for Students
Microsoft provides many of its developer tools to students for free via a program called DreamSpark (www.dreamspark.com). See the website for details on verifying your student status so you take advantage of this program.

Acknowledgments

We'd like to thank Abbey Deitel and Barbara Deitel of Deitel & Associates, Inc., who devoted long hours of research and writing to this book.

We are fortunate to have worked on this project with the dedicated team of publishing professionals at Pearson. We appreciate the guidance, savvy and energy of Michael Hirsch, Editor-in-Chief of Computer Science. Carole Snyder recruited the book's reviewers and managed the review process. Kristine Carney designed the book's cover. Bob Engelhardt and Jeffrey Holcomb managed the book's production.

Reviewers
We wish to acknowledge the efforts of our fourth edition reviewers. Adhering to a tight schedule, they scrutinized the text and the programs and provided countless suggestions for improving the presentation:

- Octavio Hernandez, Microsoft C# MVP, Advanced Bionics
- José Antonio González Seco, Parliament of Andalusia, Spain
- Zijiang Yang, Western Michigan University

Previous Edition Reviewers
Huanhui Hu (Microsoft Corporation), Narges Kasiri (Oklahoma State University), Charles Liu (University of Texas at San Antonio), Dr. Hamid R. Nemati (The University

of North Carolina at Greensboro), Jeffrey P. Scott (Blackhawk Technical College), José Antonio González Seco (Parliament of Andalusia, Spain), Douglas B. Bock (MCSD.NET, Southern Illinois University Edwardsville), Dan Crevier (Microsoft), Amit K. Ghosh (University of Texas at El Paso), Marcelo Guerra Hahn (Microsoft), Kim Hamilton (Software Design Engineer at Microsoft and co-author of *Learning UML 2.0*), James Edward Keysor (Florida Institute of Technology), Helena Kotas (Microsoft), Chris Lovett (Software Architect at Microsoft), Bashar Lulu (INETA Country Leader, Arabian Gulf), John McIlhinney (Spatial Intelligence; Microsoft MVP 2008 Visual Developer, Visual Basic), Ged Mead (Microsoft Visual Basic MVP, DevCity.net), Anand Mukundan (Architect, Polaris Software Lab Ltd.), Timothy Ng (Microsoft), Akira Onishi (Microsoft), Joe Stagner (Senior Program Manager, Developer Tools & Platforms), Erick Thompson (Microsoft) and Jesús Ubaldo Quevedo-Torrero (University of Wisconsin–Parkside, Department of Computer Science)

Well, there you have it! Visual C# 2010 is a powerful programming language that will help you write programs quickly and effectively. It scales nicely into the realm of enterprise-systems development to help organizations build their business-critical and mission-critical information systems. As you read the book, we'd appreciate your comments, criticisms, corrections and suggestions for improvement. Please address all correspondence to:

```
deitel@deitel.com
```

We'll respond promptly. We hope you enjoy working with *Visual C# 2010 How to Program, 4/e* as much as we enjoyed writing it!

Paul Deitel and Harvey Deitel
August 2010 Maynard, Massachusetts

About the Authors

Paul J. Deitel, CEO and Chief Technical Officer of Deitel & Associates, Inc., is a graduate of MIT, where he studied Information Technology. Through Deitel & Associates, Inc., he has delivered hundreds of C#, Visual Basic, Java, C++, C and Internet programming courses to industry clients, including Cisco, IBM, Sun Microsystems, Dell, Lucent Technologies, Fidelity, NASA at the Kennedy Space Center, the National Severe Storm Laboratory, White Sands Missile Range, Rogue Wave Software, Boeing, SunGard Higher Education, Stratus, Cambridge Technology Partners, One Wave, Hyperion Software, Adra Systems, Entergy, CableData Systems, Nortel Networks, Puma, iRobot, Invensys and many more. He and his co-author, Dr. Harvey M. Deitel, are the world's best-selling programming-language textbook authors.

Dr. Harvey M. Deitel, Chairman and Chief Strategy Officer of Deitel & Associates, Inc., has 49 years of experience in the computer field. Dr. Deitel earned B.S. and M.S. degrees from MIT and a Ph.D. from Boston University. He has extensive college teaching experience, including earning tenure and serving as the Chairman of the Computer Science Department at Boston College before founding Deitel & Associates, Inc., with his son, Paul J. Deitel. He and Paul are the co-authors of dozens of books and LiveLessons multimedia packages and they are writing many more. With translations published in Japanese, German, Russian, Chinese, Spanish, Korean, French, Polish, Italian, Portuguese, Greek, Urdu and Turkish, the Deitels' texts have earned international recognition. Dr.

Deitel has delivered hundreds of professional programming seminars to major corporations, academic institutions, government organizations and the military.

About Deitel & Associates, Inc.

Deitel & Associates, Inc., is an internationally recognized corporate training and authoring organization specializing in computer programming languages, Internet and web software technology, object-technology education and Android™ and iPhone® app development. The company provides instructor-led courses delivered at client sites worldwide on major programming languages and platforms, such as C++, Visual C++®, C, Java™, Visual C#®, Visual Basic®, XML®, Python®, object technology, Internet and web programming, Android and iPhone app development, and a growing list of additional programming and software-development courses. The founders of Deitel & Associates, Inc., are Paul J. Deitel and Dr. Harvey M. Deitel. The company's clients include many of the world's largest companies, government agencies, branches of the military, and academic institutions. Through its 34-year publishing partnership with Prentice Hall/Pearson, Deitel & Associates, Inc., publishes leading-edge programming textbooks, professional books, interactive multimedia *Cyber Classrooms*, and *LiveLessons* DVD-based and web-based video courses. Deitel & Associates, Inc., and the authors can be reached via e-mail at:

```
deitel@deitel.com
```

To learn more about Deitel & Associates, Inc., its publications and its *Dive Into® Series* Corporate Training curriculum delivered at client locations worldwide, visit:

```
www.deitel.com/training/
```

and subscribe to the free *Deitel® Buzz Online* e-mail newsletter at:

```
www.deitel.com/newsletter/subscribe.html
```

Individuals wishing to purchase Deitel books, and *LiveLessons* DVD and web-based training courses can do so through www.deitel.com. Bulk orders by corporations, the government, the military and academic institutions should be placed directly with Pearson. For more information, visit

```
www.prenhall.com/mischtm/support.html#order
```

Before You Begin

This section contains information you should review before using this book and instructions to ensure that your computer is set up properly for use with this book. We'll post updates to this Before You Begin section (if any) on the book's website:

> www.deitel.com/books/vcsharp2010htp/

Font and Naming Conventions

We use fonts to distinguish between features, such as menu names, menu items, and other elements that appear in the program-development environment. Our convention is to emphasize IDE features in a sans-serif bold Helvetica font (for example, **Properties** window) and to emphasize program text in a sans-serif Lucida font (for example, bool x = true).

A Note Regarding Software for the Book

This textbook includes a DVD which contains the Microsoft® Visual Studio® 2010 Express Edition integrated development environments for Visual C# 2010, Visual Basic 2010, Visual C++ 2010, Visual Web Developer 2010 and SQL Server 2008. The latest versions of these tools are also downloadable from www.microsoft.com/express. The Express Editions are fully functional, and there's no time limit for using the software. We discuss the setup of this software shortly. You do not need Visual Basic or Visual C++ for use with this book.

Hardware and Software Requirements for the Visual Studio 2010 Express Editions

To install and run the Visual Studio 2010 Express Editions, ensure that your system meets the minimum requirements specified at:

> http://www.microsoft.com/express/support/default.aspx

Desktop Theme Settings for Windows 7 Users

If you are using Windows 7, we assume that your theme is set to **Windows 7**. Follow these steps to set **Windows 7** as your desktop theme:

1. Right click the desktop, then click **Personalize**.
2. Select the **Windows 7** theme.

Desktop Theme Settings for Windows Vista Users

If you are using Windows Vista, we assume that your theme is set to **Windows Vista**. Follow these steps to set **Windows Vista** as your desktop theme:

1. Right click the desktop, then click **Personalize**.
2. Click the **Theme** item. Select **Windows Vista** from the **Theme:** drop-down list.
3. Click **Apply** to save the settings.

Desktop Theme Settings for Windows XP Users

If you are using Windows XP, the windows you see on the screen will look slightly different from the screen captures in the book. We assume that your theme is set to **Windows XP**. Follow these steps to set **Windows XP** as your desktop theme:

1. Right click the desktop, then click **Properties**.

2. Click the **Themes** tab. Select **Windows XP** from the **Theme:** drop-down list.

3. Click **OK** to save the settings.

Viewing File Extensions

Several screenshots in *Visual C# 2010 How to Program, 4/e* display file names with file-name extensions (e.g., `.txt`, `.cs` or `.png`). Your system's settings may need to be adjusted to display file-name extensions. Follow these steps to configure your computer:

1. In the **Start** menu, select **All Programs**, then **Accessories**, then **Windows Explorer**.

2. In Windows 7 and Windows Vista, press *Alt* to display the menu bar, then select **Folder Options…** from **Windows Explorer**'s **Tools** menu. In Windows XP, simply select **Folder Options…** from **Windows Explorer**'s **Tools** menu.

3. In the dialog that appears, select the **View** tab.

4. In the **Advanced settings:** pane, uncheck the box to the left of the text **Hide extensions for known file types**. [*Note*: If this item is already unchecked, no action needs to be taken.]

5. Click OK to apply the setting and close the dialog.

Notes to Windows XP Users Regarding the Segoe UI Font Used in Many Applications

To make user interfaces more readable, Microsoft recommends using the Segoe UI font in Windows 7 and Windows Vista. This font is not available by default on Windows XP, but it is installed with the following software products: Windows Live Messenger, Windows Live Mail, Microsoft Office 2007 and Microsoft Office 2010. You can download Windows Live Messenger from `explore.live.com/windows-live-messenger`. You can downloadS Windows Live Mail from `explore.live.com/windows-live-mail`.

You must also enable ClearType on your system; otherwise, the font will not display correctly. ClearType is a technology for smoothing the edges of fonts displayed on the screen. To enable ClearType, perform the following steps:

1. Right click your desktop and select **Properties…** from the popup menu to view the **Display Properties** dialog.

2. In the dialog, click the **Appearance** tab, then click the **Effects…** button to display the **Effects** dialog.

3. In the **Effects** dialog, ensure that the **Use the following method to smooth edges of screen fonts** checkbox is checked, then select **ClearType** from the combobox below the checkbox.

4. Click **OK** to close the **Effects** dialog. Click **OK** to close the **Display Properties** dialog.

Obtaining the Code Examples

The examples for *Visual C# 2010 How to Program, 4/e* are available for download at

    www.deitel.com/books/vcsharp2010htp/

If you're not already registered at our website, go to www.deitel.com and click the **Register** link below our logo in the upper-left corner of the page. Fill in your information. There's no charge to register, and we do not share your information with anyone. We send you only account-management e-mails unless you register separately for our free e-mail newsletter at www.deitel.com/newsletter/subscribe.html. *You must enter a valid email address.* After registering, you'll receive a confirmation e-mail with your verification code. Click the link in the confirmation email to go to www.deitel.com and sign in.

Next, go to www.deitel.com/books/vcsharp2010htp/. Click the **Examples** link to download the Examples.zip file to your computer. Write down the location where you choose to save the file on your computer.

We assume the examples are located at C:\Examples on your computer. Extract the contents of Examples.zip using a tool such as WinZip (www.winzip.com) or the built-in capabilities of Windows.

Installing the Software

Before you can run the applications in *Visual C# 2010 How to Program, 4/e* or build your own applications, you must install a development environment. We used Microsoft's free Visual C# 2010 Express Edition in the examples for most chapters and Visual Web Developer 2010 Express Edition for Chapters 19 and 27–29. Chapters 18, 27 and 28 also require SQL Server Express Edition. To install the Visual C# 2010 and Visual Web Developer 2010 Express Editions:

1. Insert the DVD that accompanies this book into your computer's DVD drive to launch the software installer. If the **Visual Studio 2010 Express Setup** window does not appear, use Windows Explorer to view the contents of the DVD drive and double click Setup.hta to launch the installer

2. In the **Visual Studio 2010 Express Setup** window, click **Visual C# 2010 Express** to display the **Visual C# 2010 Express Setup** window, then click **Next >**.

3. Carefully read the license agreement. Click the **I have read and accept the license terms** radio button to agree to the terms, then click **Next >**. [*Note:* If you do not accept the license agreement, the software will not install and you will not be able to create or execute Visual C# applications.]

4. Select the **MSDN Express Library for Visual Studio 2010, Microsoft SQL Server 2008 Express Edition (x86)** and **Microsoft Silverlight Runtime** options to install. Click **Next >**. [*Note:* Installing the MSDN documentation is not required but is highly recommended.]

5. Click **Next >**, then click **Finish >** to continue with the installation. The installer will now begin copying the files required by Visual C# 2010 Express Edition and SQL Server 2008 Express Edition. Wait for the installation to complete before proceeding—the installation process can be quite lengthy and might require you to reboot your computer. When the installation completes, click **Exit**.

6. In the **Visual Studio 2010 Express Setup** window, click **Visual Web Developer 2010 Express** to display the **Visual Web Developer 2010 Express Setup** window, then click **Next >**.

7. Carefully read the license agreement. Click the **I have read and accept the license terms** radio button to agree to the terms, then click **Next >**. [*Note:* If you do not accept the license agreement, the software will not install and you will not be able to create or execute web applications with Visual Web Developer.]

8. Click **Install >** to continue with the installation. The installer will now begin copying the files required by Visual Web Developer 2010 Express Edition. This portion of the install process should be much faster, since you've already installed most of the supporting software and files required by Visual Web Developer. When the installation completes, click **Exit**.

Miscellaneous Notes

- Some people like to change the workspace layout in the development tools. You can return the tools to their default layouts by selecting **Window > Reset Window Layout**.

- There are differences between the full Visual Studio 2010 products and the Express Edition products we use in this book, such as additional menu items. One key difference is that the **Database Explorer** we refer to in Chapters 18, 27 and 28 is called the **Server Explorer** in the full Visual Studio 2010 products.

- Many of the menu items we use in the book have corresponding icons shown with each menu item in the menus. Many of the icons also appear on one of the toolbars at the top of the development environment. As you become familiar with these icons, you can use the toolbars to help speed up your development time. Similarly, many of the menu items have keyboard shortcuts (also shown with each menu item in the menus) for accessing commands quickly.

You are now ready to begin your Visual C# studies with *Visual C# 2010 How to Program, 4/e.* We hope you enjoy the book!

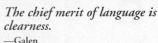

Introduction to Computers, the Internet and Visual C#

The chief merit of language is clearness.
—Galen

Our life is frittered away with detail. . . . Simplify, simplify.
—Henry David Thoreau

Man is still the most extraordinary computer of all.
—John F. Kennedy

Objectives

In this chapter you'll learn:

- Basic hardware and software concepts.

- The different types of programming languages.

- The history of the Visual C# programming language.

- Some basics of object technology.

- The history of the Internet and the World Wide Web.

- About Microsoft's .NET initiative, which involves the Internet in developing and using software systems.

- To test-drive a Visual C# 2010 drawing application.

1.1 Introduction

Welcome to Visual C# 2010 which, from this point forward, we'll refer to simply as C#. Computer use is increasing in almost every field. Computing costs have been decreasing dramatically due to rapid developments in hardware, software and communications technologies. Computing has become so economical that billions of computers are in use worldwide, helping people in business, industry and government, and in their personal lives.

Computers process **data**, using sets of instructions called **computer programs**. These programs guide computers through orderly sets of calculations and other actions that are specified by people known as **computer programmers**. Today's personal computers can perform billions of these calculations and actions per second. A person operating a desk calculator might require a lifetime to complete the same amount of work! Today's fastest **supercomputers** work so quickly that they can perform the equivalent of 150,000 actions and calculations per second for every person on the planet!

A computer consists of various devices referred to as **hardware** (for example, the keyboard, screen, mouse, hard drive, memory, DVD drives and processing units). The programs that run on a computer are referred to as **software** (for example, applications such as word processors, payroll systems, spreadsheets, e-mail systems, games, etc.).

Object-oriented programming (which models real-world objects with software counterparts), available in C# and other major programming languages, can greatly enhance your productivity. The core of this book emphasizes achieving program clarity through the proven techniques of object-oriented programming (OOP).

1.2 Computer Organization

Regardless of differences in physical appearance, virtually every computer can be envisioned as divided into various logical units or sections:

1. *Input unit*. This "receiving" section obtains information (data and computer programs) from **input devices** and places it at the disposal of the other units so that

it can be processed. Most information is entered into computers through keyboards and mouse devices. Information also can be entered in many other ways, including by speaking to your computer, scanning images and barcodes, reading from secondary storage devices (like hard drives, CD drives, DVD drives and USB drives—also called thumb drives, flash drives or memory sticks) and having your computer receive information from the Internet (such as when you download videos from YouTube™, e-books from Amazon, and the like).

2. *Output unit.* This "shipping" section takes information that the computer has processed and places it on various **output devices** to make it available for use outside the computer. Most information that is output from computers today is displayed on screens, printed on paper, played on audio players (such as Apple's popular iPods), or used to control other devices. Computers also can output their information to networks, such as the Internet.

3. *Memory unit.* This rapid-access, relatively low-capacity "warehouse" section retains information that has been entered through the input unit, making it immediately available for processing when needed. The memory unit also retains processed information until it can be placed on output devices by the output unit. Information in the memory unit is **volatile**—it's typically lost when the computer's power is turned off. The memory unit is often called either **memory** or **primary memory**.

4. *Arithmetic and logic unit (ALU).* This "manufacturing" section performs calculations, such as addition, subtraction, multiplication and division. It also contains the decision mechanisms that allow the computer, for example, to compare two items from the memory unit to determine whether they're equal. In today's systems, the ALU is usually implemented as part of the next logical unit, the CPU.

5. *Central processing unit (CPU).* This "administrative" section coordinates and supervises the operation of the other sections. The CPU tells the input unit when information should be read into the memory unit, tells the ALU when information from the memory unit should be used in calculations and tells the output unit when to send information from the memory unit to certain output devices. Many of today's computers have multiple CPUs and, hence, can perform many operations simultaneously—such computers are called **multiprocessors**. A **multicore processor** implements multiprocessing on a single integrated circuit chip—for example, a dual-core processor has two CPUs and a quad-core processor has four CPUs.

6. *Secondary storage unit.* This is the long-term, high-capacity "warehousing" section. Programs or data not actively being used by the other units normally are placed on secondary storage devices (for example, your hard drive) until they're needed again, possibly hours, days, months or even years later. Therefore, information on secondary storage devices is said to be **persistent**—it is preserved even when the computer's power is turned off. Secondary storage information takes much longer to access than information in primary memory, but the cost per unit of secondary storage is much less than that of primary memory. Examples of secondary storage devices include CDs, DVDs and USB drives, which can hold hundreds of millions to billions of characters.

1.3 Personal Computing, Distributed Computing and Client/Server Computing

In the early years of computing, computer systems were too large and expensive for individuals to own. In the 1970s, silicon chip technology made it possible for computers to be much smaller and so economical that individuals and small organizations could own these machines. In 1977, Apple Computer—creator of today's popular Mac personal computers, iPod digital music players and iPhones—popularized **personal computing**. In 1981, IBM, then the world's largest computer vendor, introduced the IBM Personal Computer, legitimizing personal computing in business, industry and government organizations.

These computers were "stand-alone" units—people transported disks back and forth between computers to share information (creating what was often called "sneakernet"). These machines could be linked together in computer networks, sometimes over telephone lines and sometimes in **local area networks** (**LANs**) within an organization. This led to the phenomenon of **distributed computing**, in which an organization's computing, instead of being performed only at some central computer installation, is distributed over networks to the geographically dispersed sites where the organization's work is performed.

Today's personal computers are as powerful as the million-dollar machines of a few decades ago; complete personal computer systems often sell for as little as a few hundred dollars. The most powerful desktop machines provide individual users with enormous capabilities. Information is shared easily across computer networks, where computers called **servers** offer a common data store and various services that may be used by **client** computers distributed throughout the network, hence the term **client/server computing**. In Chapter 19, Web App Development with ASP.NET, you'll learn how to build web apps; we'll talk about web servers (computers that distribute content over the web) and web clients (computers that request and receive the content offered up by web servers).

1.4 Hardware Trends

For decades, hardware costs have been falling rapidly. Every year or two, the computing power of computers has approximately doubled without any increase in price. This often is called **Moore's Law**, named after the person who first identified and explained the trend, Gordon Moore, co-founder of Intel—the company that manufactures the vast majority of the processors in today's personal computers. Moore's Law is especially true in relation to the amount of memory that computers have for programs and data, the amount of secondary storage (such as disk storage) they have, and their processor speeds—the speeds at which computers execute their programs (that is, do their work). Similar growth has occurred in the communications field, in which costs have plummeted as enormous demand for communications bandwidth has attracted intense competition. Such phenomenal improvement in the computing and communications fields is truly fostering the so-called Information Revolution.

1.5 Microsoft's Windows® Operating System

Microsoft became the dominant software company in the 1980s and 1990s. In the mid-1980s, Microsoft developed the **Windows operating system**, consisting of a graphical user interface built on top of DOS (a personal computer operating system that users interacted with by typing commands). The Windows operating system became incredibly popular after the 1993 release of Windows 3.1, whose successors, Windows 95 and Windows 98, virtually cornered the desktop operating systems market by the late 1990s. These operating systems, which borrowed from many concepts (such as icons, menus and windows) popularized by early Apple Macintosh operating systems, enabled users to work with multiple applications simultaneously. Microsoft entered the corporate operating systems market with the 1993 release of Windows NT. Windows XP was released in 2001 and combined Microsoft's corporate and consumer operating system lines. Windows Vista, released in 2007, offered the attractive new Aero user interface, many powerful enhancements and new applications. A key focus of Windows Vista was enhanced security. Windows 7 is Microsoft's latest operating system—its features include enhancements to the Aero user interface, faster startup times, further refinement of Vista's security features, touch screen and multi-touch support, and more. This book is intended for Windows XP, Windows Vista and Windows 7 users. Windows is by far the world's most widely used operating system.

1.6 Machine Languages, Assembly Languages and High-Level Languages

Although hundreds of computer languages are in use today, they can be divided into three general types:

1. Machine languages

2. Assembly languages

3. High-level languages

Machine Languages

A computer can directly understand only its own **machine language**, which is defined by the computer's hardware design. Machine languages generally consist of streams of numbers (ultimately represented in the computer as combinations of 1s and 0s) that instruct computers how to perform their most elementary operations. People normally work in the decimal number system with digits in the range 0–9. The number system with only 1s and 0s is called the binary number system. Machine-language programs are sometimes called "binaries" for that reason. Machine languages are *machine dependent*—a particular machine language can be used on only *one* type of computer. The following section of an early machine-language program, which adds *overtime pay* to *base pay* and stores the result in *gross pay*, demonstrates the incomprehensibility of machine language to humans:

```
+1300042774
+1400593419
+1200274027
```

Assembly Languages

As the popularity of computers increased, machine-language programming proved to be tedious and error prone. Instead of using the strings of numbers that computers could directly understand, programmers began using English-like abbreviations (called mnemonics) to represent the computer's basic operations. These abbreviations formed the basis of **assembly languages**. **Translator programs** called **assemblers** convert assembly-language programs to machine language at computer speeds. The following section of an assembly-language program also adds *overtime pay* to *base pay* and stores the result in *gross pay*, but the steps are clearer to humans than in the machine-language example:

```
LOAD    BASEPAY
ADD     OVERPAY
STORE   GROSSPAY
```

High-Level Languages

The speed at which programmers could write programs increased rapidly with the creation of assembly languages, but these languages still require many instructions to accomplish even simple tasks. To speed up the programming process, **high-level languages** (in which single program statements accomplish more substantial tasks) were developed. Translator programs called **compilers** convert high-level-language programs into machine language. High-level languages enable programmers to write instructions that look almost like everyday English and contain common mathematical notations. For example, a payroll application written in a high-level language might contain a statement such as

```
grossPay = basePay + overTimePay
```

From these examples, it's clear why programmers prefer high-level languages. The languages we discuss in the remainder of the chapter are all high-level languages. C# is one of the world's most popular high-level programming languages.

1.7 Visual Basic

Visual Basic evolved from **BASIC** (Beginner's All-purpose Symbolic Instruction Code), developed in the mid-1960s at Dartmouth College for introducing novices to fundamental programming techniques.

When Bill Gates founded Microsoft Corporation in the 1970s, he implemented BASIC on several early personal computers. In the late 1980s and the early 1990s, Microsoft developed the Microsoft Windows **graphical user interface (GUI)**—the *visual* part of the operating system with which users interact. With the creation of the Windows GUI, the natural evolution of BASIC was to **Visual Basic**, introduced by Microsoft in 1991 to make programming Windows applications easier.

Visual Basic and C# programs are created with the use of Microsoft's Visual Studio—a collection of software tools called an **Integrated Development Environment (IDE)**. With the **Visual Studio 2010** IDE, you can write, run, test and debug Visual Basic and C# programs quickly and conveniently.

1.8 C, C++, Objective-C and Java

The C programming language was developed in the early 1970s. C first gained widespread recognition as the development language of the UNIX operating system. C is a hardware-independent language, and, with careful design, it's possible to write C programs that are portable to most computers.

C++, developed in the early 1980s, provides several features that "spruce up" the C language, and, more importantly, capabilities for **object-oriented programming (OOP)**. **Objects** are reusable software **components** that model items in the real world. A modular, object-oriented approach to design and implementation can make software development groups much more *productive* than is possible using earlier programming techniques.

The **Objective-C** programming language, also developed in the early 1980s, added capabilities for object-oriented programming (OOP) to the C programming language. It eventually became the software development language for Apple's Macintosh. Its use has exploded as the app development language for Apple's wildly popular iPod, iPhone and iPad consumer devices.

Microprocessors are having a profound impact in intelligent consumer electronic devices. Recognizing this, Sun Microsystems in 1991 funded an internal corporate research project that resulted in the development of a C++-based language, which Sun eventually called **Java**. As the World Wide Web exploded in popularity in 1993, Sun saw the possibility of using Java to add **dynamic content** (for example, interactivity, animations and the like) to web pages. Sun announced the language in 1995. This generated immediate interest in the business community because of the commercial potential of the web. Java is now used to develop large-scale enterprise applications, to enhance the functionality of web servers (the computers that provide the content we see in our web browsers), to provide applications for consumer devices (such as cell phones, pagers and smartphones) and for many other purposes.

1.9 C#

In 2000, Microsoft announced the **C#** (pronounced "C-Sharp") programming language—created specifically for the .NET platform (discussed in Section 1.12). C# has roots in C, C++ and Java. Like Visual Basic, C# is object oriented and has access to the powerful **.NET Framework Class Library**—a vast collection of prebuilt components, enabling programmers to develop applications quickly. Both languages have similar capabilities to Java and are appropriate for the most demanding application development tasks, especially for building today's enterprise applications, and web-based and mobile applications.

C# is *object oriented*—you'll learn some basics of object technology shortly and will study a rich treatment later in the book. C# is **event driven**—you'll write programs that respond to user-initiated **events** such as mouse clicks, keystrokes and timer expirations. Microsoft's Visual C# is indeed a *visual programming language*—in addition to writing program statements to build portions of your applications, you'll also use Visual Studio's graphical user interface to conveniently drag and drop predefined objects like buttons and textboxes into place on your screen, and label and resize them. Visual Studio will write much of the GUI code for you.

C# has been standardized internationally, enabling other implementations of the language besides Microsoft's Visual C#, such as Mono (www.mono-project.com).

1.10 The Internet and the World Wide Web

In the late 1960s, ARPA—the Advanced Research Projects Agency of the Department of Defense—rolled out plans to network the main computer systems of some ARPA-funded universities and research institutions. Academic research was about to take a giant leap forward. ARPA proceeded to implement what quickly became known as the **ARPAnet**, the grandparent of today's **Internet**.

Things worked out differently from the original plan. Although the ARPAnet enabled researchers to network their computers, its main benefit proved to be the capability for quick and easy communication via what came to be known as electronic mail (e-mail). This is true even on today's Internet, with e-mail, instant messaging and file transfer allowing billions of people worldwide to communicate with each other.

Businesses rapidly realized that by using the Internet, they could improve their operations and offer new and better services to their clients. Companies started spending large amounts of money to develop and enhance their Internet presence. This generated fierce competition among communications carriers and hardware and software suppliers to meet the increased infrastructure demand. As a result, **bandwidth**—the information-carrying capacity of communications lines—on the Internet has increased tremendously, while hardware costs have plummeted.

The **World Wide Web** is a collection of hardware and software associated with the Internet that allows computer users to locate and view multimedia-based documents (documents with various combinations of text, graphics, animations, audios and videos) on almost any subject. In 1989, Tim Berners-Lee of CERN (the European Organization for Nuclear Research) began to develop a technology for sharing information over the Internet via "hyperlinked" text documents. Berners-Lee called his invention the **HyperText Markup Language (HTML)**. He also wrote communication protocols such as **HyperText Transfer Protocol (HTTP)** to form the backbone of his new hypertext information system, which he referred to as the World Wide Web—or simply "the web."

In 1994, Berners-Lee founded an organization, called the **World Wide Web Consortium (W3C**, www.w3.org), devoted to developing technologies for the World Wide Web. One of the W3C's primary goals is to make the web universally accessible to everyone regardless of disabilities, language or culture.

In the past, most computer applications ran on "stand-alone" computers (computers that were not connected to one another). Today's applications can be written with the aim of communicating among the world's computers via the Internet and the web. In fact, as you'll see, this is the focus of Microsoft's .NET strategy. Later in this book we discuss how to build web-based applications with C#.

1.11 Extensible Markup Language (XML)

As the popularity of the web exploded, HTML's limitations became apparent. HTML's lack of **extensibility** (the ability to change or add features) frustrated developers, and its ambiguous definition allowed erroneous HTML to proliferate. The need for a standardized, fully extensible and structurally strict language was apparent. As a result, XML was developed by the W3C.

Data independence, the separation of content from its presentation, is the essential characteristic of XML. Because XML documents describe data, any application conceivably can process them. Software developers are integrating XML into their applications to improve web functionality and interoperability.

XML isn't limited to web applications. For example, it's increasingly used in databases—an XML document's structure enables it to be integrated easily with database applications. As applications become more web enabled, it's likely that XML will become the universal technology for data representation. Applications employing XML would be able to communicate with one another, provided that they could understand their respective XML markup schemes, or **vocabularies**. Microsoft's .NET technologies use XML to mark up and transfer data over the Internet, and to enable software components to interoperate.

1.12 Introduction to Microsoft .NET

In 2000, Microsoft announced its **.NET initiative** (www.microsoft.com/net), a broad new vision for using the Internet and the web in the development, engineering, distribution and use of software. Rather than forcing developers to use a single programming language, the .NET initiative permits developers to create .NET applications in *any* .NET-compatible language (such as C#, Visual Basic, and others). Part of the initiative includes Microsoft's **ASP.NET** technology, which allows you to create web applications.

The .NET strategy extends the idea of **software reuse** to the Internet by allowing programmers to concentrate on their specialties without having to implement every component of every application. Visual programming (which you'll learn throughout this book) has become popular because it enables you to create Windows and web applications easily, using such prepackaged controls as **buttons**, **textboxes** and **scrollbars**.

The **.NET Framework** is at the heart of Microsoft's .NET strategy. This framework executes applications, includes the .NET Framework Class Library and provides many other programming capabilities that you'll use to build C# applications.

1.13 The .NET Framework and the Common Language Runtime

The details of the .NET Framework are found in the **Common Language Infrastructure (CLI)**, which contains information about the storage of data types (that is, data that has predefined characteristics such as a date, percentage or currency amount), objects and so on. The CLI has been standardized, making it easier to implement the .NET Framework for other platforms. This is like publishing the blueprints of the framework—anyone can build it by following the specifications.

The **Common Language Runtime (CLR)** is the central part of the .NET Framework—it executes .NET programs. Programs are compiled into machine-specific instructions in two steps. First, the program is compiled into **Microsoft Intermediate Language (MSIL)**, which defines instructions for the CLR. Code converted into MSIL from other languages and sources can be woven together by the CLR. The MSIL for an application's components is placed into the application's executable file. When the application executes, another compiler (known as the **just-in-time compiler** or **JIT compiler**) in the CLR translates the MSIL in the executable file into machine-language code (for a particular platform), then the machine-language code executes on that platform.

If the .NET Framework is installed on a platform, that platform can run any .NET program. A program's ability to run (without modification) across multiple platforms is known as **platform independence**. Code written once can be used on another type of computer without modification, saving time and money. Software can also target a wider audience—previously, companies had to decide whether converting their programs to different platforms (sometimes called **porting**) was worth the cost. With .NET, porting programs is no longer an issue (at least once .NET itself has been made available on the platforms).

The .NET Framework also provides a high level of **language interoperability**. Programs written in different languages (for example, C# and Visual Basic) are all compiled into MSIL—the different parts can be combined to create a single unified program. MSIL allows the .NET Framework to be **language independent**, because .NET programs are not tied to a particular programming language.

The .NET Framework Class Library can be used by any .NET language. The library contains a variety of reusable components, saving you the trouble of creating new components. This book explains how to develop .NET software with C#.

1.14 Test-Driving the Advanced Painter Application

In this section, you'll "test-drive" an existing application that enables you to draw on the screen using the mouse. The **Advanced Painter** application allows you to draw with different brush sizes and colors. The elements and functionality you see in this application are typical of what you'll learn to program in this text. The following steps show you how to test-drive the application. You'll run and interact with the working application.

1. *Checking your setup.* Confirm that you've set up your computer properly by reading the Before You Begin section located after the Preface.

2. *Locating the application directory.* Open a Windows Explorer window and navigate to the C:\examples\ch01 directory (Fig. 1.1)—we assume you placed the examples in the C:\examples folder.

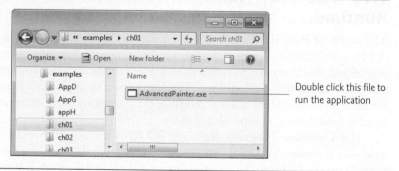

Double click this file to run the application

Fig. 1.1 | Contents of C:\examples\ch01.

3. *Running the Advanced Painter application.* Now that you're in the proper directory, double click the file name AdvancedPainter.exe (Fig. 1.1) to run the application (Fig. 1.2). [*Note:* Depending on your system configuration, Windows Explorer might not display file name extensions. To display file name extensions (like .exe in Fig. 1.1), type *Alt + T* in Windows Explorer to open the **Tools** menu, then select **Folder options....** In the **Folder Options** window, select the **View** tab, uncheck **Hide extensions for known file types** and click **OK.**]

Figure 1.2 labels several graphical elements—called **controls**. These include GroupBoxes, RadioButtons, a Panel and Buttons (these controls and many others are discussed in depth throughout the text). The application allows you to draw with a red, blue, green or black brush of small, medium or large size. You can also undo your previous operation or clear the drawing to start from scratch.

By using existing controls—which are objects—you can create powerful applications much faster than if you had to write all the code yourself.

The brush's properties, selected in the RadioButtons labeled **Black** and **Medium,** are *default settings*—the initial settings you see when you first run the

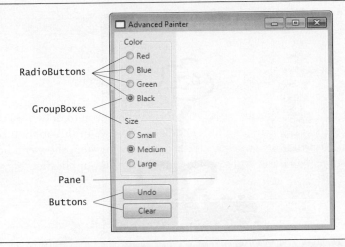

Fig. 1.2 | C# **Advanced Painter** application.

application. Programmers include default settings to provide reasonable choices that the application will use if the user chooses not to change the settings. Default settings also provide visual cues for users to choose their own settings. Now you'll choose your own settings as a user of this application.

4. *Changing the brush color and size.* Click the RadioButton labeled **Red** to change the color of the brush, then click **Small** to change the size of the brush. Position the mouse over the white Panel, then press and hold down the left mouse button to draw with the brush. Draw flower petals, as shown in Fig. 1.3.

Fig. 1.3 | Drawing with a new brush color.

5. *Changing the brush size.* Click the RadioButton labeled **Green** to change the color of the brush again. Then, click the RadioButton labeled **Large** to change the size of the brush. Draw grass and a flower stem, as shown in Fig. 1.4.

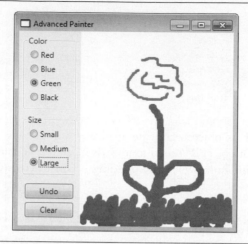

Fig. 1.4 | Drawing with a new brush size.

6. *Finishing the drawing.* Click the **Blue** and **Medium** RadioButtons. Draw raindrops, as shown in Fig. 1.5, to complete the drawing.

Fig. 1.5 | Finishing the drawing.

7. *Closing the application.* Close your running application by clicking its **close box**, (Fig. 1.5).

1.15 Introduction to Object Technology

When object-oriented programming became widely used in the 1980s and 1990s, it dramatically improved the software development process.

What are objects, and why are they special? **Object technology** is a packaging scheme for creating meaningful software units. There are date objects, time objects, paycheck objects, invoice objects, automobile objects, people objects, audio objects, video objects, file objects, record objects and so on. On your computer screen, there are button objects, textbox objects, menu objects and many more. In fact, almost any *noun* can be reasonably represented as a software object. Objects have **attributes** (also called **properties**), such as color, size, weight and speed; and perform **actions** (also called **methods** or **behaviors**), such as moving, sleeping or drawing.

Classes are types of related objects. For example, all cars belong to the "car" class, even though individual cars vary in make, model, color and options packages. A class specifies the general format of its objects, and the attributes and actions available to an object depend on its class. An object is related to its class in much the same way as a building is related to the blueprint from which the building is constructed. Contractors can build many buildings from the same blueprint; programmers can instantiate (create) many objects from the same class.

With object technology, properly designed classes can be *reused* on future projects. Some organizations report that another key benefit they get from object-oriented programming is the production of software that's better organized and has fewer maintenance requirements than software produced with earlier technologies.

Object orientation allows you to focus on the "big picture." Instead of worrying about the minute details of how reusable objects are implemented, you can focus on the behaviors and interactions of objects. A road map that showed every tree, house and driveway would be difficult, if not impossible, to read. When such details are removed and only the essential information (roads) remains, the map becomes easier to understand. In the same way, an application that is divided into objects is easy to understand, modify and update because it hides much of the detail.

It's clear that object-oriented programming will be the key programming methodology for the next several decades. C# is one of the world's most widely used object-oriented languages, especially in the Microsoft software development community.

Basic Object-Technology Concepts

Object-oriented design (OOD) models software in terms similar to those that people use to describe real-world objects. It takes advantage of class relationships, where objects of a certain class, such as a class of vehicles, have the same characteristics—cars, trucks, little red wagons and roller skates have much in common. OOD takes advantage of **inheritance** relationships, where new classes of objects are derived by absorbing characteristics of existing classes and adding unique characteristics of their own. An object of class "convertible" certainly has the characteristics of the more general class "automobile," but more specifically, the roof goes up and down.

Object-oriented design provides a natural and intuitive way to view the software design process—namely, modeling objects by their attributes, behaviors and interrelationships, just as we describe real-world objects. OOD also models communication between objects. Just as people send messages to one another (for example, a sergeant commands a soldier to stand at attention), objects also communicate via messages. A bank-account object may receive a message to decrease its balance by a certain amount because the customer is withdrawing that amount of money.

OOD **encapsulates** (that is, wraps) attributes and **operations** (behaviors) into objects—an object's attributes and operations are intimately tied together. Objects have the property of **information hiding**. This means that objects may know how to communicate with one another across well-defined **interfaces**, but normally they're not allowed to know how other objects are implemented—implementation details are hidden within the objects themselves. You can drive a car effectively, for example, without knowing the details of how engines, transmissions, brakes and exhaust systems work internally—as long as you know how to use the accelerator pedal, the brake pedal, the steering wheel and so on. Information hiding, as you'll see, is crucial to good software engineering.

Classes, Fields and Methods

As a C# programmer, you'll concentrate on creating your own classes. Each class contains data as well as the set of methods that manipulate that data and provide services to **clients** (that is, other classes that *use* the class). The data components of a class are called attributes or **fields**. For example, a bank account class might include an account number and a balance. The operation components of a class are called methods. For example, a bank-account class might include methods to make a deposit (increase the balance), make a withdrawal (decrease the balance) and inquire what the current balance is.

Classes are to objects as blueprints are to houses—a class is a "plan" for building objects of the class. Just as we can build many houses from one blueprint, we can instantiate (create) many objects from one class. You *cannot* cook meals in the kitchen of a blueprint, but you *can* cook meals in the kitchen of a house. Packaging software as classes makes it possible for future software systems to reuse the classes.

 Software Engineering Observation 1.1

Reuse of existing classes when building new classes and programs saves time, money and effort. Reuse also helps you build better systems, because existing classes and components often have gone through extensive testing, debugging and performance tuning.

You'll be *using existing classes and making objects of those classes* throughout the entire book. In Chapter 4, you'll begin building your own *customized* classes.

With object technology, you can build much of the new software you'll need by *combining existing classes*, just as automobile manufacturers combine *standardized interchangeable parts*. Each class you create will have the potential to become a valuable *software asset* that you and other programmers can reuse to speed future software development efforts.

Introduction to Object-Oriented Analysis and Design (OOAD)

Soon you'll be writing C# programs. How will you create the code for your programs? Perhaps, like many beginning programmers, you'll simply turn on your computer and start typing. This approach may work for small programs (like the ones we present in the early chapters of the book), but what if you were asked to create a software system to control thousands of automated teller machines for a major bank? Or what if you were asked to work on a team of thousands of software developers building the next generation of the U.S. air traffic control system? For projects so large and complex, you could not simply sit down and start writing programs.

To create the best solutions, you should follow a detailed process for determining your project's **requirements** (that is, *what* your system is supposed to do) and developing a **design** that satisfies them (that is, deciding *how* your system should do it). Ideally, you would go through this process and carefully review the design (and have your design reviewed by other software professionals) before writing any code. If this process involves analyzing and designing your system from an object-oriented point of view, it's called

object-oriented analysis and design (OOAD). Experienced programmers know that proper analysis and design can help avoid an ill-planned system development approach that has to be abandoned partway through its implementation, possibly wasting considerable time, money and effort. Although many different OOAD processes exist, a single graphical language known as the **UML (Unified Modeling Language)** for communicating the results of *any* OOAD process has come into wide use. We introduce some simple UML diagrams in the early chapters and present a richer treatment in the optional ATM OOD case study.

1.16 Wrap-Up

This chapter introduced basic hardware and software concepts and basic object-technology concepts, including classes, objects, attributes and behaviors. We discussed the different types of programming languages and some widely used languages. We presented a brief history of Microsoft's Windows operating system, and the Internet and the web. We discussed the history of the C# programming language and Microsoft's .NET initiative, which allows you to program Internet and web-based applications using C# (and other languages). You learned the steps for executing a C# application. You test-drove a sample C# application similar to the types of applications you'll learn to program in this book.

In the next chapter, you'll use the Visual Studio IDE (Integrated Development Environment) to create your first C# application, using the techniques of visual programming. You'll also become familiar with Visual Studio's help features.

1.17 Web Resources

The Internet and the web are extraordinary resources. This section includes links to interesting and informative websites.

www.deitel.com/books/csharp2010htp/
Visit this site for code downloads, updates, corrections and additional resources for *Visual C# 2010 How To Program*—such as links to our Resource Centers for C# and related Visual Studio 2010 technologies. Our Resource Centers provide links to downloads, tutorials, documentation, books, e-books, journals, articles, blogs and more that will help you develop C# applications.

www.pearsonhighered.com/deitel
The Deitel & Associates page on the Prentice Hall website contains information about our publications and code downloads for this book.

Summary

Section 1.1 Introduction
- Computers process data, using sets of instructions called computer programs.
- A computer consists of various devices referred to as hardware.
- The programs that run on a computer are referred to as software.

Section 1.2 Computer Organization
- The input unit obtains information (data and computer programs) from input devices and places it at the disposal of the other units so that it can be processed.
- The output unit takes information that the computer has processed and places it on various output devices to make it available for use outside the computer.

- The memory unit temporarily retains information that has been entered through the input unit, making it immediately available for processing when needed. The memory unit also retains processed information until it can be placed on output devices by the output unit.

- The arithmetic and logic unit (ALU) performs calculations and makes decisions.

- The central processing unit (CPU) is the "administrative" section of the computer, which coordinates and supervises the operation of the other sections.

- Many of today's computers have multiple CPUs and, hence, can perform many operations simultaneously—such computers are called multiprocessors.

- A multi-core processor implements multiprocessing on a single integrated circuit chip.

- The secondary storage unit is the long-term, high-capacity "warehousing" section. Programs or data not actively being used by the other units normally are placed on secondary storage devices (for example, your hard drive) until they're needed again. Information on secondary storage devices is persistent.

Section 1.3 Personal Computing, Distributed Computing and Client/Server Computing

- Silicon chip technology made it possible for computers to be much smaller and more economical—individuals and small organizations could own these machines.

- In 1977, Apple Computer—creator of today's popular Macintosh personal computers and iPod digital music players—popularized personal computing.

- In 1981, IBM, then the world's largest computer vendor, introduced the IBM Personal Computer, legitimizing personal computing in business, industry and government organizations.

- Personal computers could be linked together in computer networks, sometimes over telephone lines and sometimes in local area networks (LANs) within an organization. This led to the phenomenon of distributed computing, in which an organization's computing is distributed over networks to the geographically dispersed sites where the organization's work is performed.

- Information is shared easily across computer networks, where computers called file servers offer a common data store and various services that may be used by client computers distributed throughout the network, hence the term client/server computing.

Section 1.4 Hardware Trends

- Moore's Law states that the computing power of computers approximately doubles every year or two, without any increase in price. Similar growth has occurred in the communications field.

Section 1.5 Microsoft's Windows® Operating System

- In the mid-1980s, Microsoft developed the Windows operating system, a graphical user interface built on top of DOS (a personal computer operating system that users interacted with by typing commands).

- The Windows operating system became incredibly popular after the 1993 release of Windows 3.1, whose successors, Windows 95 and Windows 98, virtually cornered the desktop operating systems market by the late 1990s.

- Windows XP was released in 2001 and combined Microsoft's corporate and consumer operating system lines.

- Windows Vista, released in 2007, offered the attractive new Aero user interface, many powerful enhancements and new applications. A key focus of Windows Vista was enhanced security.

- Windows 7 is Microsoft's latest operating system. Some new features include enhancements to the Aero user interface, faster startup times, further refinement of Vista's security features, touch screen and multi-touch support, and much more.

Section 1.6 Machine Languages, Assembly Languages and High-Level Languages

- Computer languages can be divided into three general types—machine languages, assembly languages and high-level languages.

- A computer can directly understand only its own machine language, which is defined by the computer's hardware design.

- Machine languages generally consist of streams of numbers (ultimately represented in the computer as combnations of 1s and 0s) that instruct computers how to perform their most elementary operations.

- The number system with only 1s and 0s is called the binary number system. Machine-language programs are sometimes called "binaries" for that reason.

- A particular machine language can be used on only one type of computer.

- Programmers began using English-like abbreviations (mnemonics) to represent the computer's basic operations. These abbreviations formed the basis of assembly languages. Translator programs called assemblers convert assembly-language programs to machine language.

- High-level languages enable programmers to write instructions that look almost like everyday English and contain common mathematical notations. Translator programs called compilers convert high-level-language programs into machine language.

Section 1.7 Visual Basic

- BASIC was developed to teach novices fundamental programming techniques.

- Visual Basic made programming Windows applications easier.

- With Microsoft's Visual Studio Integrated Development Environment (IDE), you can write, run, test and debug Visual Basic programs quickly and conveniently.

- The Visual Studio IDE enables you to conveniently drag and drop predefined objects like buttons and textboxes into place on your screen, and label and resize them.

Section 1.8 C, C++, Objective-C and Java

- The C programming language was developed in the early 1970s and gained widespread recognition as the development language of the UNIX operating system.

- C++ provides a number of features that "spruce up" the C language and provides capabilities for object-oriented programming (OOP).

- The Objective-C programming language also added OOP capabilities to C. It became the software development language for Apple's Macintosh. Its use exploded as the app development language for Apple's iPod, iPhone and iPad consumer devices.

- Objects are reusable software components that model items in the real world.

- A modular, object-oriented approach to design and implementation can make software development groups much more productive.

- Sun Microsystems developed Java, a C++-based language, which is used to develop large-scale enterprise applications, to enhance the functionality of web servers, to provide applications for consumer devices and for many other purposes.

Section 1.9 C#

- C#, created by Microsoft specifically for the .NET platform, has roots in C, C++ and Java.

- C# is object oriented and has access to the powerful .NET Framework Class Library—a vast collection of prebuilt components, enabling you to develop applications quickly.

- C# is appropriate for the most demanding application development tasks, especially for building today's enterprise applications, and web-based and mobile applications.

- C# is event-driven—C# programs can respond to user-initiated events such as mouse clicks, keystrokes and timer expirations.
- Microsoft's Visual C# is indeed a visual programming language— you can use Visual Studio's graphical user interface to drag and drop predefined objects like buttons and textboxes into place on your screen, and label and resize them. Visual Studio will write much of the GUI code for you.

Section 1.10 The Internet and the World Wide Web

- In the late 1960s, ARPA—the Advanced Research Projects Agency of the Department of Defense—rolled out plans to network the main computer systems of some ARPA-funded universities and research institutions. This became known as the ARPAnet, the grandparent of the Internet.
- ARPAnet's main benefit proved to be the capability for quick and easy communication via what came to be known as electronic mail (e-mail).
- Bandwidth—the information-carrying capacity of communications lines—on the Internet has increased tremendously, while hardware costs have plummeted.
- The World Wide Web is a collection of hardware and software associated with the Internet that allows computer users to locate and view multimedia-based documents on almost any subject.
- HyperText Markup Language (HTML) is a technology for sharing information via "hyperlinked" text documents on the World Wide Web.
- The Internet and the web make information instantly and conveniently accessible to billions of people worldwide.

Section 1.11 Extensible Markup Language (XML)

- Data independence, the separation of content from its presentation, is the essential characteristic of XML.
- As applications become more web enabled, it is likely that XML will become the universal technology for data representation.

Section 1.12 Introduction to Microsoft .NET

- In 2000, Microsoft announced its .NET initiative, a broad new vision for using the Internet and the web in the development, engineering, distribution and use of software.
- You can create .NET applications in any .NET-compatible language.
- ASP.NET technology allows you to create web applications.
- The .NET strategy extends the idea of software reuse to the Internet by allowing programmers to concentrate on their specialties without having to implement every component of every application.
- The .NET Framework executes applications, contains the .NET Framework Class Library and provides many other programming capabilities that you'll use to build C# applications.

Section 1.13 The .NET Framework and the Common Language Runtime

- The details of the .NET Framework are found in the Common Language Infrastructure (CLI), which contains information about the storage of data types, objects and so on.
- The Common Language Runtime (CLR) executes .NET programs.
- Programs are compiled into machine-specific instructions in two steps. First, the program is compiled into Microsoft Intermediate Language (MSIL), which defines instructions for the CLR. When the application executes, a just-in-time (JIT) compiler in the CLR translates the MSIL in the executable file into machine-language code, then the machine-language code executes on that platform.
- If the .NET Framework exists (and is installed) for a platform, that platform can run any .NET program. The ability of a program to run (without modification) across multiple platforms is known as platform independence.

Section 1.14 Test-Driving the Advanced Painter Application

- You can use existing controls—which are objects—to get powerful applications running in C# much faster than if you had to write all of the code yourself.

- The default settings for controls are the initial settings you see when you first run the application. Programmers include default settings to provide reasonable choices that the application will use if the user chooses not to change the settings.

Section 1.15 Introduction to Object Technology

- Object technology is a packaging scheme for creating meaningful software units.

- Objects have attributes (also called properties) and perform actions (also called methods or behaviors).

- Classes are types of related objects. A class specifies the general format of its objects, and the attributes and actions available to an object depend on its class.

- Programmers can instantiate (create) many objects from the same class.

- Properly designed classes can be reused on future projects.

- An application that is divided into objects is easy to understand, modify and update because it hides much of the detail.

- Object-oriented design (OOD) models software in terms similar to those that people use to describe real-world objects. It takes advantage of class relationships, where objects of a certain class have the same characteristics.

- OOD takes advantage of inheritance relationships, where new classes of objects are derived by absorbing characteristics of existing classes and adding unique characteristics of their own.

- Object-oriented design provides a natural and intuitive way to view the software design process—namely, modeling objects by their attributes, behaviors and interrelationships, just as we describe real-world objects.

- OOD also models communication between objects.

- Objects have the property of information hiding—objects may know how to communicate with one another across well-defined interfaces, but normally they're not allowed to know how other objects are implemented.

- Languages like C# are object oriented. Programming in such a language is called object-oriented programming (OOP), and it allows you to conveniently implement an object-oriented design as a working software system.

- C# classes contain methods that implement operations, and data that implements attributes.

- C# is one of the most widely used object-oriented languages, especially in the Microsoft software development community.

- The data components of a class are called attributes or fields.

- The operation components of a class are called methods.

- With object technology, you can build much of the new software you'll need by combining existing classes.

Terminology

actions (verbs)
arithmetic and logic unit (ALU)
ARPAnet
ASP.NET

assembler
assembly language
attribute
bandwidth

BASIC (Beginner's All-purpose Symbolic Instruction Code)
behavior
button
C programming language
C# programming language
C++ programming language
central processing unit (CPU)
class
class library
client computer
client of a class
client/server computing
close box
Common Language Infrastructure (CLI)
Common Language Runtime (CLR)
compiler
component
computer program
computer programmer
controls
data
data independence
design
distributed computing
dynamic content
encapsulate
event
event driven
extensibility
field
graphical user interface (GUI)
hardware
high-level language
HyperText Markup Language(HTML)
HyperText Transfer Protocol (HTTP)
information hiding
inheritance
input device
input unit
Integrated Development Environment (IDE)
interface
Internet
just-in-time (JIT) compiler
language independent

language interoperability
local area network (LAN)
machine language
memory
memory unit
method
Microsoft Intermediate Language (MSIL)
Moore's Law
multi-core processor
multiprocessors
.NET Framework
.NET Framework Class Library
.NET Initiative
object (or instance)
object-oriented analysis and design (OOAD)
object-oriented design (OOD)
object-oriented programming (OOP)
object technology
Objective-C
operation
output device
output unit
persistent information
personal computer
platform independence
porting
primary memory
programmer
property of a class
requirements
scrollbars
server
software
software reuse
supercomputer
textbox
translator program
Unified Modeling Language (UML)
Visual Basic
Visual Studio 2010
volatile information
Windows operating system
World Wide Web (WWW)
World Wide Web Consortium (W3C)
XML (Extensible Markup Language) vocabulary

Self-Review Exercises

1.1 Fill in the blanks in each of the following statements:
 a) Computers can directly understand only their native _____ language, which is composed only of 1s and 0s.

b) Computers process data under the control of sets of instructions called computer _____.

c) The three types of computer programming languages discussed in the chapter are machine languages, _____ and _____.

d) Programs that translate high-level-language programs into machine language are called _____.

e) Visual Studio is a(n) _____ in which C# programs are developed.

f) C# is a(n) _____, event-driven language.

g) _____ is a programming language that was created by Microsoft specifically for the .NET platform.

h) _____ is a language for sharing information via "hyperlinked" text documents on the World Wide Web.

i) The _____ executes .NET programs.

j) Objects have _____ (also called properties) and perform actions (also called methods or _____).

k) _____ models software in terms similar to those that people use to describe real-world objects.

l) With _____, you can build much of the new software you'll need by combining existing classes.

1.2 State whether each of the following is *true* or *false*. If *false*, explain why.

a) The UML is used primarily to implement object-oriented systems.

b) C# is an object-oriented language.

c) C# is the only language available for programming .NET applications.

d) Computers can directly understand high-level languages.

e) MSIL is the common intermediate format to which all .NET programs compile, regardless of their original .NET language.

f) The .NET Framework is portable to non-Windows platforms.

Answers to Self-Review Exercises

1.1   a) machine. b) programs. c) assembly languages, high-level languages. d) compilers. e) IDE. f) object-oriented. g) C#. h) HyperText Markup Language (HTML). i) Common Language Runtime (CLR). j) attributes, behaviors. k) Object-oriented design (OOD). l) object technology.

1.2   a) False. The UML is used primarily for communicating the results of any OOAD process. b) True. c) False. C# is one of many .NET languages (another is Visual Basic). d) False. Computers can directly understand only their own machine languages. e) True. f) True.

Exercises

1.3   Categorize each of the following items as either hardware or software:

a) CPU

b) Compiler

c) Input unit

d) A word-processor program

e) A C# program

1.4   Translator programs, such as assemblers and compilers, convert programs from one language (referred to as the source language) to another language (referred to as the target language). Determine which of the following statements are *true* and which are *false*:

a) An assembler translates source-language programs into machine-language programs.

b) High-level languages are generally machine dependent.

      c) A machine-language program requires translation before it can be run on a computer.

      d) The C# compiler translates high-level-language programs into SMIL.

1.5   Expand each of the following acronyms:

      a) W3C

      b) XML

      c) OOP

      d) CLR

      e) CLI

      f) MSIL

      g) UML

      h) IDE

1.6   What are the key benefits of the .NET Framework and the CLR? What are the drawbacks?

1.7   What are the advantages to using object-oriented techniques?

1.8   You are probably wearing on your wrist one of the world's most common types of objects—a watch. Discuss how each of the following terms and concepts applies to the notion of a watch: object, attributes and behaviors.

1.9   What was the key reason that Visual Basic was developed as a special version of the BASIC programming language?

1.10   What is the key accomplishment of the UML?

1.11   What did the chief benefit of the early Internet prove to be?

1.12   What is the key capability of the web?

1.13   What is the key vision of Microsoft's .NET initiative?

1.14   How does the .NET Framework Class Library facilitate the development of .NET applications?

1.15   What is the key advantage of standardizing .NET's CLI (Common Language Infrastructure)?

1.16   Besides the obvious benefits of reuse made possible by OOP, what do many organizations report as another key benefit of OOP?

1.17   Why is XML so crucial to the development of future software systems?

Making a Difference Exercises

1.18   *(Test Drive: Carbon Footprint Calculator)* Some scientists believe that carbon emissions, especially from the burning of fossil fuels, contribute significantly to global warming and that this can be combatted if individuals take steps to limit their use of carbon-based fuels. Organizations and individuals are increasingly concerned about their "carbon footprints." Websites such as TerraPass

      `www.terrapass.com/carbon-footprint-calculator/`

and Carbon Footprint

      `www.carbonfootprint.com/calculator.aspx`

provide carbon footprint calculators. Test drive these calculators to determine your carbon footprint. Exercises in later chapters will ask you to program your own carbon footprint calculator. To prepare for this, use the web to research the formulas for calculating carbon footprints.

1.19   *(Test Drive: Body Mass Index Calculator)* By recent estimates, two-thirds of the people in the United States are overweight and about half of those are obese. This causes significant increases in illnesses such as diabetes and heart disease. To determine whether a person is overweight or obese, you can use a measure called the body mass index (BMI). The United States Department of Health and Human Services provides a BMI calculator at www.nhlbisupport.com/bmi/. Use it to calculate your own BMI. A forthcoming exercise will ask you to program your own BMI calculator. To prepare for this, use the web to research the formulas for calculating BMI.

1.20 *(Attributes of Hybrid Vehicles)* In this chapter you learned some basics of classes. Now you'll "flesh out" aspects of a class called "Hybrid Vehicle." Hybrid vehicles are becoming increasingly popular, because they often get much better mileage than purely gasoline-powered vehicles. Browse the web and study the features of four or five of today's popular hybrid cars, then list as many of their hybrid-related attributes as you can. Some common attributes include city-miles-per-gallon and highway-miles-per-gallon. Also list the attributes of the batteries (type, weight, etc.).

1.21 *(Gender Neutrality)* Many people want to eliminate sexism in all forms of communication. You've been asked to create a program that can process a paragraph of text and replace gender-specific words with gender-neutral ones. Assuming that you've been given a list of gender-specific words and their gender-neutral replacements (e.g., replace "wife" with "spouse," "man" with "person," "daughter" with "child" and so on), explain the procedure you'd use to read through a paragraph of text and manually perform these replacements. How might your procedure generate a strange term like "woperchild?" You'll soon learn that a more formal term for "procedure" is "algorithm," and that an algorithm specifies the steps to be performed and the order in which to perform them.

2

Dive Into® Visual C# 2010 Express

Seeing is believing.
—Proverb

Form ever follows function.
—Louis Henri Sullivan

Intelligence ... is the faculty of making artificial objects, especially tools to make tools.
—Henri-Louis Bergson

Objectives

In this chapter you'll learn:

- The basics of the Visual Studio Integrated Development Environment (IDE) that assists you in writing, running and debugging your Visual C# programs.

- Visual Studio's help features.

- Key commands contained in the IDE's menus and toolbars.

- The purpose of the various kinds of windows in the Visual Studio 2010 IDE.

- What visual programming is and how it simplifies and speeds program development.

- To create, compile and execute a simple Visual C# program that displays text and an image using the Visual Studio IDE and the technique of visual programming.

2.1 Introduction

Visual Studio 2010 is Microsoft's Integrated Development Environment (IDE) for creating, running and debugging programs (also called **applications**) written in various .NET programming languages. This chapter provides an overview of the Visual Studio 2010 IDE and shows how to create a simple Visual C# program by dragging and dropping predefined building blocks into place—a technique known as **visual programming**.

2.2 Overview of the Visual Studio 2010 IDE

There are several Visual Studio versions. This book's examples are based on the **Visual C# 2010 Express Edition**. See the Before You Begin section that follows the Preface for information on installing the software. We assume that you're familiar with Windows.

Introduction to Microsoft Visual C# 2010 Express Edition
We use the **>** character to indicate the selection of a menu item from a menu. For example, we use the notation **File > Open File...** to indicate that you should select the **Open File...** menu item from the **File** menu.

To start Microsoft Visual C# 2010 Express Edition, select **Start > All Programs > Microsoft Visual Studio 2010 Express > Microsoft Visual C# 2010 Express**. Once the Express Edition begins execution, the **Start Page** displays (Fig. 2.1). Depending on your version of Visual Studio, your **Start Page** may look different. The **Start Page** contains a list of links to Visual Studio 2010 IDE resources and web-based resources. At any time, you can return to the **Start Page** by selecting **View > Start Page**.

Links on the Start Page
The **Start Page** links are organized into sections—**Recent Projects**, **Get Started** and **Latest News**—that contain links to helpful programming resources. Clicking any link on the **Start Page** displays relevant information associated with the specific link. [*Note:* An Internet connection is required for the IDE to access some of this information.] We refer to single clicking with the left mouse button as selecting or clicking. We refer to double clicking with the left mouse button simply as double clicking.

The **Recent Projects** section contains information on projects you've recently created or modified. You can also open existing projects or create new ones by clicking the links above this section. The **Get Started** section focuses on using the IDE for creating programs and learning Visual C#.

New Project button   Start Page tab   Latest News tab   Solution Explorer (no projects open)

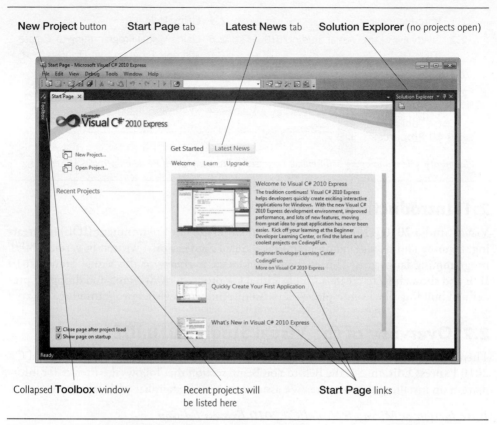

Collapsed **Toolbox** window   Recent projects will   **Start Page** links
                                      be listed here

Fig. 2.1 | **Start Page** in Visual C# 2010 Express Edition.

The **Latest News** tab provides links to the latest Visual C# developments (such as updates and bug fixes) and to information on advanced programming topics. To access more extensive information on Visual Studio, you can browse the **MSDN** (**Microsoft Developer Network**) library at msdn.microsoft.com/en-us/library/default.aspx. The MSDN site contains articles, downloads and tutorials on technologies of interest to Visual Studio developers. You can also browse the web from the IDE by selecting **View > Other Windows > Web Browser**. To request a web page, type its URL into the location bar (Fig. 2.2) and press the *Enter* key—your computer, of course, must be connected to the Internet. The web page that you wish to view appears as another tab in the IDE (Fig. 2.2).

Customizing the IDE and Creating a New Project
To begin programming in Visual C#, you must create a new project or open an existing one. Select either **File > New Project...** to create a new project or **File > Open Project...** to open an existing project. From the **Start Page**, above the **Recent Projects** section, you can also click the links **New Project...** or **Open Project....** A **project** is a group of related files, such as the Visual C# code and any images that might make up a program. Visual Studio 2010 organizes programs into projects and **solutions**, which contain one or more projects. Multiple-project solutions are used to create large-scale programs. Most of the programs we create in this book consist of a single project.

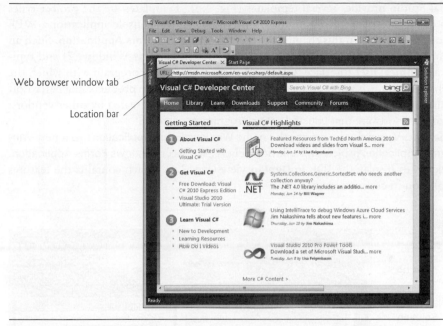

Fig. 2.2 | Displaying a web page in Visual Studio.

When you select **File > New Project...** or click the **New Project...** link on the **Start Page**, the **New Project dialog** (Fig. 2.3) displays. **Dialogs** are windows that facilitate user–computer communication.

Visual C# **Windows Forms Application** (selected)

Default project name (provided by Visual Studio)

Description of selected project (provided by Visual Studio)

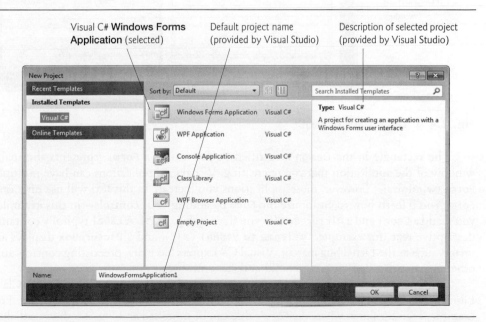

Fig. 2.3 | New Project dialog.

Visual Studio provides several templates (Fig. 2.3). **Templates** are the project types users can create in Visual C#—Windows Forms applications, console applications, WPF applications and others. In this chapter, we build a **Windows Forms Application**. Such an application executes within a Windows operating system (such as Windows 7) and typically has a **graphical user interface** (**GUI**)—the visual part of the program with which the user interacts. Windows applications include Microsoft software products like Microsoft Word, Internet Explorer and Visual Studio; software products created by other vendors; and customized software that you and other programmers create.

By default, Visual Studio assigns the name **WindowsFormsApplication1** to a new **Windows Forms Application** project and solution (Fig. 2.3). Select **Windows Forms Application**, then click **OK** to display the IDE in **Design** view (Fig. 2.4), which contains the features that enable you to create programs.

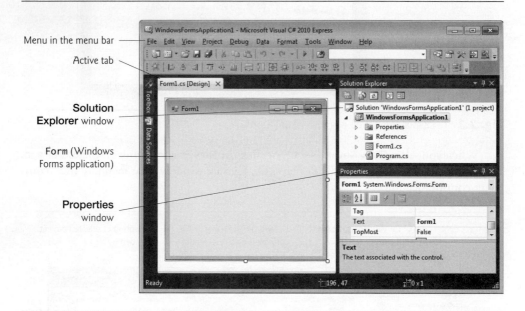

Fig. 2.4 | **Design** view of the IDE.

The rectangle in the **Design** area titled **Form1** (called a **Form**) represents the main window of the application that you're creating. Visual C# applications can have multiple Forms (windows)—however, most applications you'll create in this text will use only one Form. You'll learn how to customize the Form by adding GUI **controls**—in this example, you'll add a Label and a PictureBox (as you'll see in Fig. 2.25). A **Label** typically contains descriptive text (for example, "Welcome to Visual C#!"), and a **PictureBox** displays an image, such as the Deitel bug mascot. Visual C# Express has many preexisting controls and other components you can use to build and customize your programs.

In this chapter, you'll work with preexisting controls from the .NET Framework Class Library. As you place controls on the Form, you'll be able to modify their properties. For example, Fig. 2.5 shows where the Form's title can be modified and Fig. 2.6 shows a dialog in which a control's font properties can be modified.

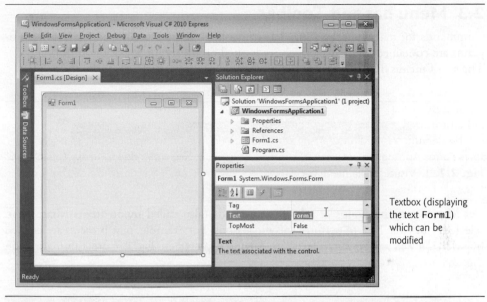

Textbox (displaying the text **Form1**) which can be modified

Fig. 2.5 | Textbox control for modifying a property in the Visual Studio IDE.

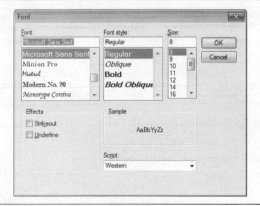

Fig. 2.6 | Dialog for modifying a control's font properties.

Collectively, the Form and controls make up the program's GUI. Users enter data (**inputs**) into the program by typing at the keyboard, by clicking the mouse buttons and in a variety of other ways. Programs use the GUI to display instructions and other information (**outputs**) for users to view. For example, the **New Project** dialog in Fig. 2.3 presents a GUI where the user clicks the mouse button to select a template type, then inputs a project name from the keyboard (the figure is still showing the default project name **WindowsFormsApplication1** supplied by Visual Studio).

Each open file name is listed on a tab. To view a document when multiple documents are open, click its tab. Tabs facilitate easy access to multiple open documents. The **active tab** (the tab of the currently displayed document) is highlighted in yellow (for example, **Form1.cs [Design]** in Fig. 2.4).

2.3 Menu Bar and Toolbar

Commands for managing the IDE and for developing, maintaining and executing programs are contained in **menus**, which are located on the **menu bar** of the IDE (Fig. 2.7). The set of menus displayed depends on what you're currently doing in the IDE.

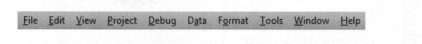

Fig. 2.7 | Visual Studio menu bar.

Menus contain groups of related commands (also called **menu items**) that, when selected, cause the IDE to perform specific actions. For example, new projects are created by selecting **File > New Project...**. The menus depicted in Fig. 2.7 are summarized in Fig. 2.8.

Menu	Description
File	Contains commands for opening, closing, adding and saving projects, as well as printing project data and exiting Visual Studio.
Edit	Contains commands for editing programs, such as cut, copy, paste, undo, redo, delete, find and select.
View	Contains commands for displaying IDE windows (for example, **Solution Explorer, Toolbox, Properties** window) and for adding toolbars to the IDE.
Project	Contains commands for managing projects and their files.
Debug	Contains commands for compiling, debugging (that is, identifying and correcting problems in programs) and running programs.
Data	Contains commands for interacting with databases (that is, organized collections of data stored on computers), which we discuss in Chapter 18, Databases and LINQ.
Format	Contains commands for arranging and modifying a **Form**'s controls. The **Format** menu appears only when a GUI component is selected in **Design** view.
Tools	Contains commands for accessing additional IDE tools and options for customizing the IDE.
Window	Contains commands for hiding, opening, closing and displaying IDE windows.
Help	Contains commands for accessing the IDE's help features.

Fig. 2.8 | Summary of Visual Studio 2010 IDE menus.

You can access many of the more common menu commands from the **toolbar** (Fig. 2.9), which contains graphics, called **icons**, that graphically represent commands. By default, the standard toolbar is displayed when you run Visual Studio for the first time—it contains icons for the most commonly used commands, such as opening a file, adding an item to a project, saving files and running applications (Fig. 2.9). The icons that appear on the standard toolbar may vary, depending on the version of Visual Studio you're using. Some commands are initially disabled (grayed out or unavailable to use). These commands are enabled by Visual Studio only when they're necessary. For example, Visual Studio enables the command for saving a file once you begin editing a file.

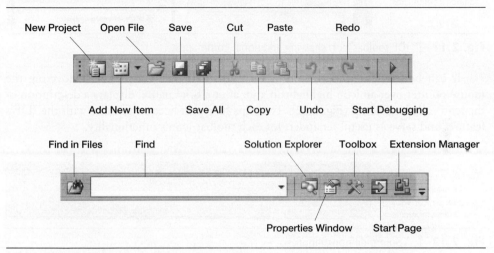

Fig. 2.9 | Standard Visual Studio toolbar.

You can customize the IDE's toolbars. Select **View > Toolbars** (Fig. 2.10). Each toolbar you select is displayed with the other toolbars at the top of the Visual Studio window. To execute a command via the toolbar, click its icon. Some icons contain a down arrow that you can click to display related commands, as shown in Fig. 2.11.

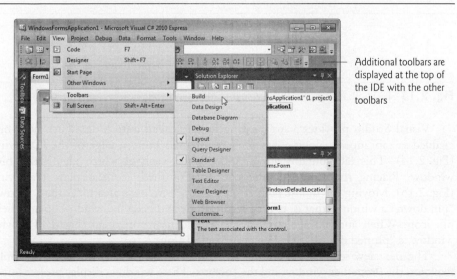

Additional toolbars are displayed at the top of the IDE with the other toolbars

Fig. 2.10 | Adding the **Build** toolbar to the IDE.

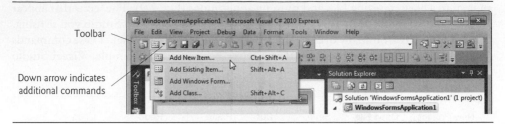

Fig. 2.11 | IDE toolbar icon showing additional commands.

It can be difficult to remember what each toolbar icon represents. Hovering the mouse pointer over an icon highlights it and, after a brief pause, displays a description of the icon called a tool tip (Fig. 2.12). **Tool tips** help you become familiar with the IDE's features and serve as useful reminders for each toolbar icon's functionality.

Fig. 2.12 | Tool tip demonstration.

2.4 Navigating the Visual Studio IDE

The IDE provides windows for accessing project files and customizing controls. This section introduces several windows that you'll use frequently when developing Visual C# programs. These windows can be accessed via the toolbar icons (Fig. 2.13) or by selecting the desired window's name from **View > Other Windows.**

Fig. 2.13 | Toolbar icons for three Visual Studio windows.

Visual Studio provides a space-saving feature called **auto-hide**. When auto-hide is enabled, a tab appears along either the left, right or bottom edge of the IDE window (Fig. 2.14). This tab contains one or more icons, each of which identifies a hidden window. Placing the mouse pointer over one of these icons displays that window (Fig. 2.15). Moving the mouse pointer outside the window's area hides the window. To "pin down" a window (that is, to disable auto-hide and keep the window open), click the pin icon. When auto-hide is enabled, the pin icon is horizontal (Fig. 2.15)—when a window is "pinned down," the pin icon is vertical (Fig. 2.16).

The next few sections cover three of Visual Studio's main windows—the **Solution Explorer,** the **Properties** window and the **Toolbox.** These windows display project information and include tools that help you build your programs.

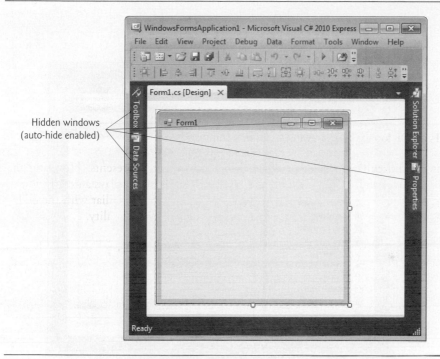

Fig. 2.14 | Auto-hide feature demonstration.

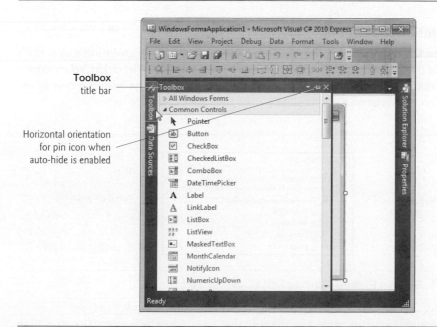

Fig. 2.15 | Displaying a hidden window when auto-hide is enabled.

Toolbox
"pinned down"

Vertical orientation for pin icon
when window is "pinned down"

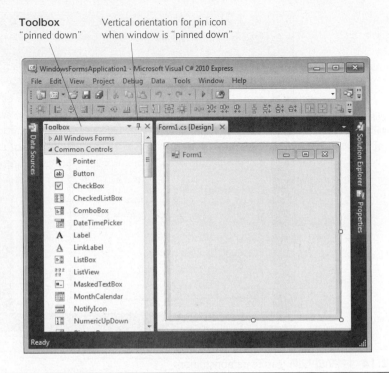

Fig. 2.16 | Disabling auto-hide ("pinning down" a window).

2.4.1 Solution Explorer

The **Solution Explorer** window (Fig. 2.17) provides access to all of a solution's files. If it's not shown in the IDE, click the **Solution Explorer** icon in the IDE (Fig. 2.13), select **View > Other Windows > Solution Explorer** or type *<Ctrl> <Alt> L*. When you open a new or existing solution, the **Solution Explorer** displays the solution's contents.

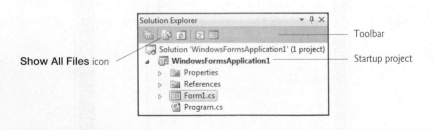

Show All Files icon

Toolbar

Startup project

Fig. 2.17 | **Solution Explorer** window with an open project.

The solution's **startup project** is the one that runs when you select **Debug > Start Debugging** (or press the *F5* key). For a single-project solution like the examples in this book, the startup project is the only project (in this case, **WindowsFormsApplication1**) and the project name appears in bold text in the **Solution Explorer** window. When you create an application for the first time, the **Solution Explorer** window lists entries for the project's **Properties** and **References**, and the files Form1.cs and Program.cs (Fig. 2.17). The Visual C# file that corresponds to the Form shown in Fig. 2.4 is named Form1.cs (selected in Fig. 2.17). Visual C# files use the .cs file-name extension.

By default, the IDE displays only files that you may need to edit—other files that the IDE generates are hidden. The **Solution Explorer** window includes a toolbar that contains several icons. Clicking the **Show All Files icon** (Fig. 2.17) displays all the solution's files, including those generated by the IDE. Clicking the arrows to the left of a file or folder expands or collapses the project tree's nodes. Try clicking the arrow to the left of **References** to display items grouped under that heading (Fig. 2.18). Click the arrow again to collapse the tree. Other Visual Studio windows also use this convention.

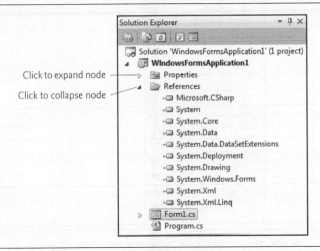

Fig. 2.18 | Solution Explorer with the References node expanded.

2.4.2 Toolbox

The **Toolbox** (**View > Other Windows > Toolbox**) contains icons representing controls used to customize Forms (Fig. 2.19). With visual programming, you can "drag and drop" controls onto the Form and the IDE will write the code that creates the controls for you. This is faster and simpler than writing this code yourself. Just as you do not need to know how to build an engine to drive a car, you do not need to know how to build controls to use them. Reusing preexisting controls saves time and money when you develop programs. You'll use the **Toolbox** when you create your first program later in the chapter.

The **Toolbox** groups the prebuilt controls into categories—**All Windows Forms, Common Controls, Containers, Menus & Toolbars, Data, Components, Printing, Dialogs, WPF Interoperability** and **General** are listed in Fig. 2.19. Again, note the use of arrows, which can expand or collapse a group of controls. We discuss many of the **Toolbox**'s controls and their functionality throughout the book.

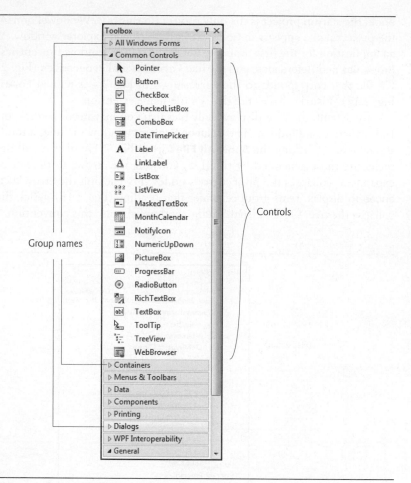

Fig. 2.19 | **Toolbox** window displaying controls for the **Common Controls** group.

2.4.3 Properties Window

To display the **Properties** window, select **View > Other Windows > Properties Window** or click the **Properties** window toolbar icon shown in Fig. 2.13. The **Properties window** displays the properties for the currently selected Form (Fig. 2.20), control or file in **Design** view. **Properties** specify information about the Form or control, such as its size, color and position. Each Form or control has its own set of properties—a property's description is displayed at the bottom of the **Properties** window whenever that property is selected.

Figure 2.20 shows Form1's **Properties** window. The left column lists the names of the Form's properties—the right column displays the current value of each property. You can sort the properties either alphabetically (by clicking the **Alphabetical** icon) or categorically (by clicking the **Categorized** icon). The properties can be sorted alphabetically from A to Z or Z to A—sorting by category groups the properties according to their use (that is, **Appearance**, **Behavior**, **Design**, etc.). Depending on the size of the **Properties** window, some of the properties may be hidden from view on the screen. Users can scroll through the list of properties by **dragging** the **scrollbox** up or down inside the **scrollbar**, or by

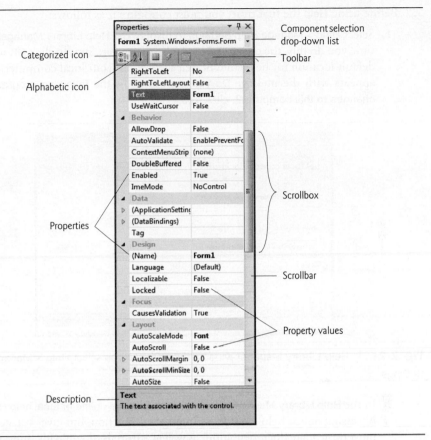

Component selection drop-down list

Categorized icon

Alphabetic icon

Toolbar

Scrollbox

Properties

Scrollbar

Property values

Description

Fig. 2.20 | **Properties** window.

clicking the arrows at the top and bottom of the scrollbar. We show how to set individual properties later in this chapter.

The **Properties** window is crucial to visual programming—it allows you to modify a control's properties visually, without writing code. You can see which properties are available for modification and, in many cases, can learn the range of acceptable values for a given property. The **Properties** window displays a brief description of the selected property, helping you understand its purpose. A property can be set quickly using this window, and no code needs to be written.

At the top of the **Properties** window is the **component selection drop-down list**, which allows you to select the Form or control whose properties you wish to display in the **Properties** window (Fig. 2.20). Using the component selection drop-down list is an alternative way to display a Form's or control's properties without clicking the actual Form or control in the GUI.

2.5 Using Help

Microsoft provides extensive help documentation via the **Help menu**. Using **Help** is an excellent way to get information quickly about Visual Studio, Visual C# and more.

Before using **Help** the first time, you must configure it as follows:

1. Select **Help > Manage Help Settings** to display the **Help Library Manager**. The first time you do this, the dialog in Fig. 2.21 will appear. Simply click **OK** to select the default location for help content that's stored on your local computer. If a dialog appears with the message **Do you want to allow the following program to make changes to this computer?**, click **Yes**.

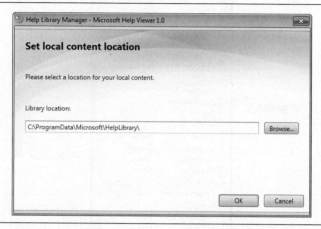

Fig. 2.21 | Help Library Manager window the first time you select **Help > Manage Help Settings**.

2. In the **Help Library Manager** window, click **Choose online or local help** (Fig. 2.22). Accessing online help requires an Internet connection, but gives you access to the most up-to-date documentation, as well as tutorials, downloads, support, forums and more. Accessing local help requires that you first download the help files, which can take considerable time and use a significant amount of disk space. If possible, we recommend that you use the online help.

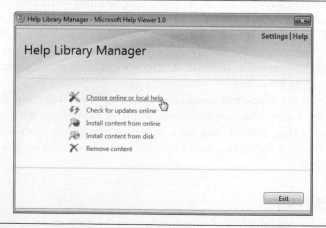

Fig. 2.22 | Preparing to select online or local help.

3. If it's not already selected, select **I want to use online help**, then click **OK**; otherwise, click **Cancel**. Next, click **Exit** in the **Help Library Manager** window. Your IDE is now configured to use online help.

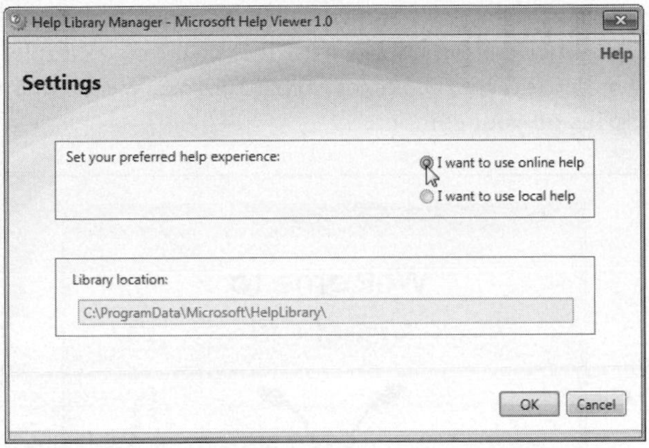

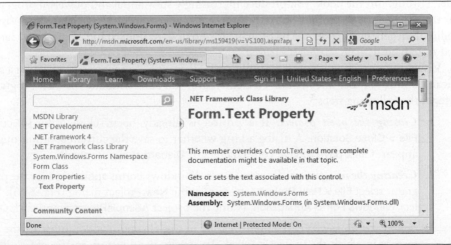

Fig. 2.23 | Selecting online help.

Context-Sensitive Help

Visual Studio provides **context-sensitive help** pertaining to the "current content" (that is, the items around the location of the mouse cursor). To use context-sensitive help, click an item, such as the Form, then press the *F1* key. The help documentation is displayed in a web browser window. To return to the IDE, either close the browser window or select the icon for the IDE in your Windows task bar. Figure 2.24 shows the help page for a Form's Text property. You can view this help by selecting the Form, clicking its Text property in the **Properties** window and pressing the *F1* key.

Fig. 2.24 | Using context-sensitive help.

2.6 Using Visual Programming to Create a Simple Program that Displays Text and an Image

Next, we create a program that displays the text "Welcome to Visual C#!" and an image of the Deitel & Associates bug mascot. The program consists of a single Form that uses a Label and a PictureBox. Figure 2.25 shows the result of the program as it executes. The program and the bug image are available with this chapter's examples, which you can download from www.deitel.com/books/csharp2010htp/. We assume the examples are located at C:\examples on your computer.

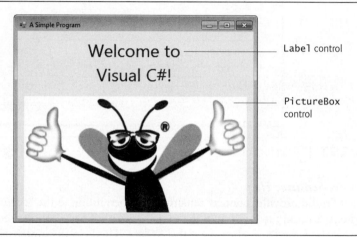

Fig. 2.25 | Simple program executing.

You won't write a single line of program code. Instead, you'll use visual programming techniques. Visual Studio processes your actions (such as mouse clicking, dragging and dropping) to generate program code. Chapter 3 begins our discussion of writing program code. Throughout the book, you produce increasingly substantial and powerful programs that usually include a combination of code written by you and code generated by Visual Studio. The generated code can be difficult for novices to understand—but you'll rarely need to look at it.

Visual programming is useful for building GUI-intensive programs that require a significant amount of user interaction. To create, save, run and terminate this first program, perform the following steps:

1. *Closing the open project.* If a project is already open, close it by selecting **File > Close Solution**. A dialog asking whether to save the current solution might appear. Click **Save** to save your changes or **Discard** to ignore them.

2. *Creating the new project.* To create a new Windows Forms application for the program, select **File > New Project...** to display the **New Project** dialog (Fig. 2.26). Select **Windows Forms Application**. Name the project **ASimpleProgram** and click **OK**.

3. *Saving the project.* We mentioned earlier in this chapter that you must set the directory in which the project is saved. To specify the directory in Visual C# 2010 Express, select **File > Save All** to display the **Save Project** dialog (Fig. 2.27). By de-

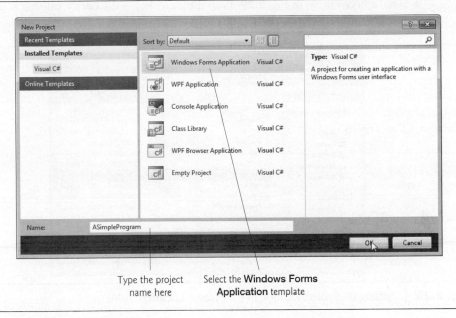

Type the project
name here

Select the **Windows Forms
Application** template

Fig. 2.26 | New Project dialog.

fault, projects are saved to your user directory in the folder My Documents\visual
studio 2010\Projects. To change the project location, click the **Browse...** button,
which opens the **Project Location** dialog (Fig. 2.28). Navigate through the directories, select one in which to place the project (in our example, we use the directory
C:\MyCSharpProjects) and click **Select Folder** to close the dialog. Click **Save** in the
Save Project dialog (Fig. 2.27) to save the project and close the dialog.

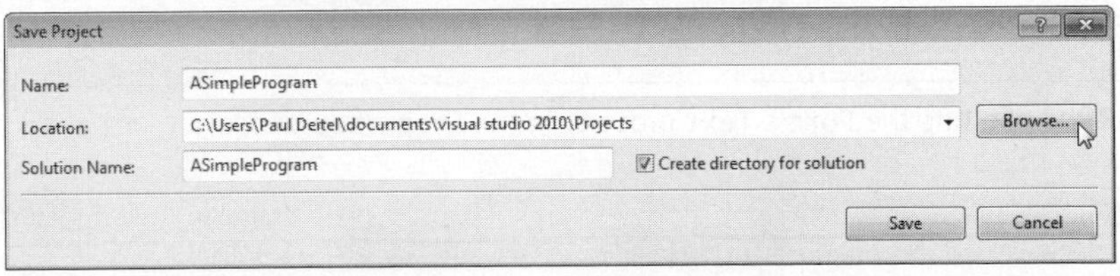

Fig. 2.27 | Save Project dialog.

When you first begin working in the IDE, it is in **design mode** (that is, the program
is being designed and is not executing). This provides access to all the environment windows (for example, **Toolbox**, **Properties**), menus and toolbars, as you'll see shortly.

4. *Setting the text in the Form's title bar.* The text in the Form's title bar is deter-
    mined by the Form's **Text property** (Fig. 2.29). If the **Properties** window is not
    open, click the properties icon in the toolbar or select **View > Other Windows >
    Properties Window**. Click anywhere in the Form to display the Form's properties
    in the **Properties** window. In the textbox to the right of the Text property, type

A Simple Program, as in Fig. 2.29. Press the *Enter* key—the Form's title bar is updated immediately (Fig. 2.30).

Selected project location

Click to set project location

Fig. 2.28 | Setting the project location in the **Project Location** dialog.

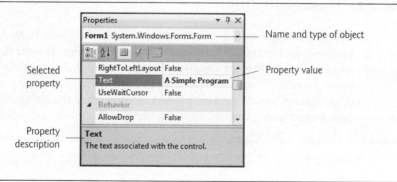

Name and type of object

Selected property

Property value

Property description

Fig. 2.29 | Setting the Form's Text property in the **Properties** window.

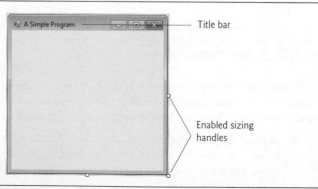

Title bar

Enabled sizing handles

Fig. 2.30 | Form with enabled sizing handles.

5. *Resizing the Form.* Click and drag one of the Form's enabled **sizing handles** (the small white squares that appear around the Form, as shown in Fig. 2.30). Using the mouse, select the bottom-right sizing handle and drag it down and to the right to make the Form larger (Fig. 2.31).

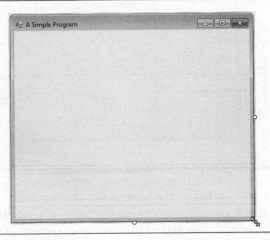

Fig. 2.31 | Resized Form.

6. *Changing the Form's background color.* The **BackColor property** specifies a Form's or control's background color. Clicking BackColor in the **Properties** window causes a down-arrow button to appear next to the value of the property (Fig. 2.32). When clicked, the down-arrow button displays other options, which vary depending on the property. In this case, the arrow displays tabs for **Custom**, **Web** and **System** (the default). Click the **Custom tab** to display the **palette** (a grid of colors). Select the box that represents light blue. Once you select the color, the palette closes and the Form's background color changes to light blue (Fig. 2.33).

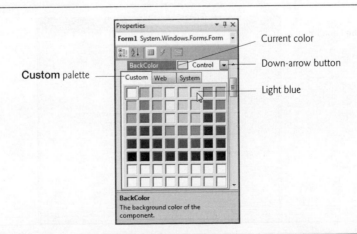

Fig. 2.32 | Changing the Form's BackColor property.

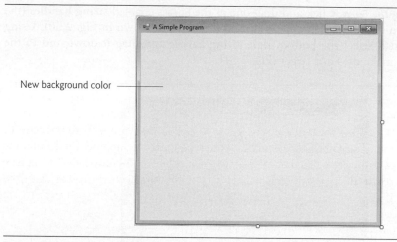

New background color

Fig. 2.33 | Form with new BackColor property applied.

7. **Adding a Label control to the Form.** If the **Toolbox** is not already open, select **View > Other Windows > Toolbox** to display the set of controls you'll use for creating your programs. For the type of program we're creating in this chapter, the typical controls we use are located in either the **All Windows Forms** group of the **Toolbox** or the **Common Controls** group. If either group name is collapsed, expand it by clicking the arrow to the left of the group name (the **All Windows Forms** and **Common Controls** groups are shown in Fig. 2.19). Next, double click the Label control in the **Toolbox**. This action causes a Label to appear in the upper-left corner of the Form (Fig. 2.34). [*Note:* If the Form is behind the **Toolbox**, you may need to hide the **Toolbox** to see the Label.] Although double clicking any **Toolbox** control places the control on the Form, you also can "drag" controls from the **Toolbox** to the Form—you may prefer dragging the control because you can position it wherever you want. The Label displays the text **label1** by default. The Label's

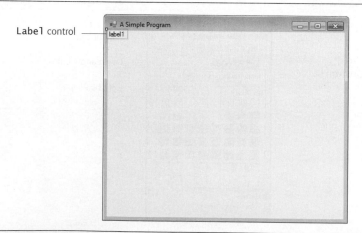

Label control

Fig. 2.34 | Adding a Label to the Form.

background color is the same as the Form's background color. When a control is added to the Form, its BackColor property is set to the Form's BackColor. You can change the Label's background color by changing its BackColor property.

8. *Customizing the Label's appearance.* Select the Label by clicking it. Its properties now appear in the **Properties** window. The Label's Text property determines the text (if any) that the Label displays. The Form and Label each have their own Text property—Forms and controls can have the same types of properties (such as Back-Color, Text, etc.) without conflict. Set the Label's Text property to Welcome to Visual C#!. The Label resizes to fit all the typed text on one line. By default, the **AutoSize property** of the Label is set to True, which allows the Label to update its size to fit all of the text if necessary. Set the AutoSize property to False (Fig. 2.35) so that you can resize the Label on your own. Resize the Label (using the sizing handles) so that the text fits. Move the Label to the top center of the Form by dragging it or by using the keyboard's left and right arrow keys to adjust its position (Fig. 2.36). Alternatively, when the Label is selected, you can center the Label control horizontally by selecting **Format > Center In Form > Horizontally**.

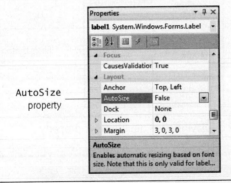

Fig. 2.35 | Changing the Label's AutoSize property to False.

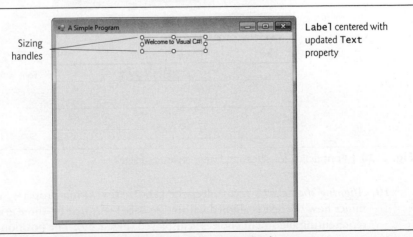

Fig. 2.36 | GUI after the Form and Label have been customized.

9. *Setting the Label's font size.* To change the font type and appearance of the Label's text, select the value of the **Font property**, which causes an **ellipsis button** to appear next to the value (Fig. 2.37). When the ellipsis button is clicked, a dialog that provides additional values—in this case, the **Font dialog** (Fig. 2.38)—is displayed. You can select the font name (the font options may be different, depending on your system), font style (**Regular, Italic, Bold,** etc.) and font size (**16, 18, 20,** etc.) in this dialog. The **Sample** text shows the selected font settings. Under Font, select **Segoe UI**, Microsoft's recommended font for user interfaces. Under Size, select **24** points and click **OK**. If the Label's text does not fit on a single line, it wraps to the next line. Resize the Label so that it appears as shown in Fig. 2.25 if it's not large enough to hold the text. You may need to center the Label horizontally again after resizing.

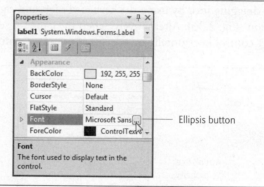

Fig. 2.37 | **Properties** window displaying the Label's Font property.

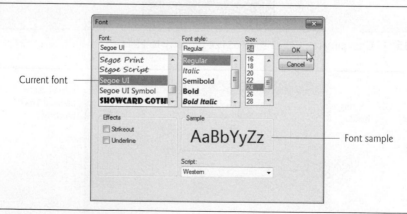

Fig. 2.38 | **Font** dialog for selecting fonts, styles and sizes.

10. *Aligning the Label's text.* Select the Label's **TextAlign** property, which determines how the text is aligned within the Label. A three-by-three grid of buttons representing alignment choices is displayed (Fig. 2.39). The position of each button corresponds to where the text appears in the Label. For this program, set the

`TextAlign` property to `MiddleCenter` in the three-by-three grid—this selection causes the text to appear centered in the middle of the `Label`, with equal spacing from the text to all sides of the `Label`. The other `TextAlign` values, such as `Top-Left`, `TopRight`, and `BottomCenter`, can be used to position the text anywhere within a `Label`. Certain alignment values may require that you resize the `Label` larger or smaller to better fit the text.

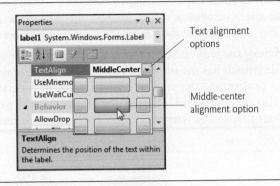

Text alignment options

Middle-center alignment option

Fig. 2.39 | Centering the `Label`'s text.

11. *Adding a **PictureBox** to the Form.* The `PictureBox` control displays images. The process involved in this step is similar to that of *Step 7*, in which we added a `Label` to the Form. Locate the `PictureBox` in the **Toolbox** (Fig. 2.19) and double click it to add it to the Form. When the `PictureBox` appears, move it underneath the `Label`, either by dragging it or by using the arrow keys (Fig. 2.40).

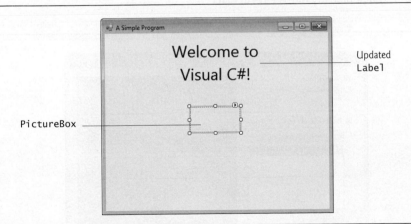

Updated `Label`

PictureBox

Fig. 2.40 | Inserting and aligning a `PictureBox`.

12. *Inserting an image.* Click the `PictureBox` to display its properties in the **Properties** window (Fig. 2.41). Locate the **Image property**, which displays a preview of

the selected image or **(none)** if no image is selected. Click the ellipsis button to display the **Select Resource** dialog (Fig. 2.42), which is used to import files, such as images, for use in a program. Click the **Import...** button to browse for an image to insert, select the image file and click **OK**. We used bug.png from this chapter's examples folder. The image is previewed in the **Select Resource** dialog (Fig. 2.43). Click **OK** to use the image. Supported image formats include PNG (Portable Network Graphics), GIF (Graphic Interchange Format), JPEG (Joint Photographic Experts Group) and BMP (Windows bitmap). To scale the image to the `PictureBox`'s size, change the **SizeMode** property to **StretchImage** (Fig. 2.44). Resize the `PictureBox`, making it larger (Fig. 2.45).

13. *Saving the project.* Select **File > Save All** to save the entire solution. The solution file (which has the file name extension .sln) contains the name and location of its project, and the project file (which has the file name extension .csproj) contains the names and locations of all the files in the project. If you want to reopen your project at a later time, simply open its .sln file.

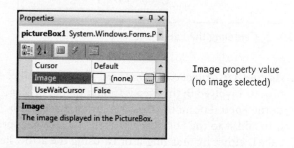

Fig. 2.41 | Image property of the `PictureBox`.

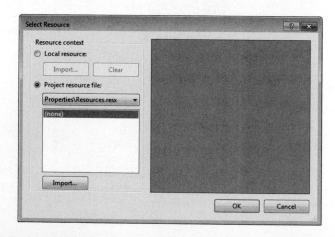

Fig. 2.42 | **Select Resource** dialog to select an image for the `PictureBox`.

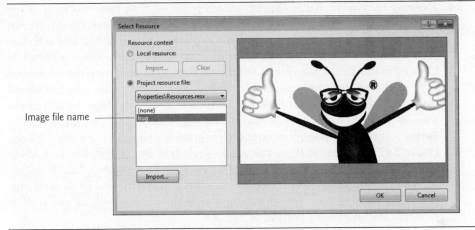

Image file name

Fig. 2.43 | **Select Resource** dialog displaying a preview of selected image.

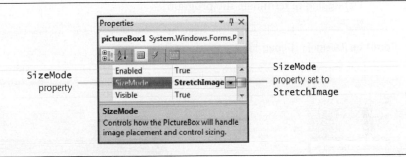

SizeMode property

SizeMode property set to StretchImage

Fig. 2.44 | Scaling an image to the size of the PictureBox.

Newly inserted image

Fig. 2.45 | PictureBox displaying an image.

14. *Running the project.* Recall that up to this point we have been working in the IDE design mode (that is, the program being created is not executing). In **run mode**, the program is executing, and you can interact with only a few IDE features—features that are not available are disabled (grayed out). The text **Form1.cs [Design]** in the project tab (Fig. 2.46) means that we're designing the Form visually rather than programmatically. If we had been writing code, the tab would have contained only the text **Form1.cs**. If there's an asterisk (*) at the end of the text in the tab, the file has been changed and should be saved. Select **Debug > Start Debugging** to execute the program (or you can press the *F5* key). Figure 2.47 shows the IDE in run mode (indicated by the title-bar text **ASimpleProgram (Running) – Microsoft Visual C# 2010 Express Edition**). Many toolbar icons and menus are disabled, since they cannot be used while the program is running. The running program appears in a separate window outside the IDE as shown in the lower-right portion of Fig. 2.47.

15. *Terminating execution.* Click the running program's close box (▣) in the top-right corner of the running program's window. This action stops the program's execution and returns the IDE to design mode. You can also select **Debug > Stop Debugging** to terminate the program.

Form1.cs [Design]   Debug menu

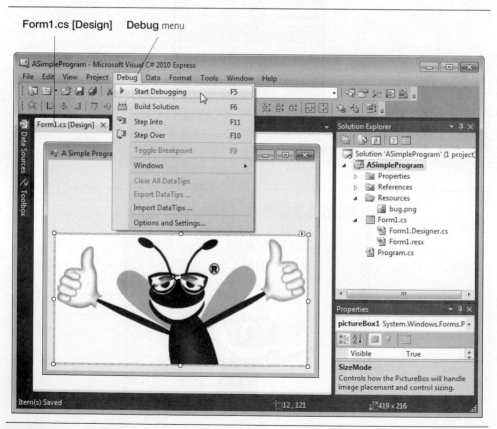

Fig. 2.46 | Debugging a solution.

IDE displays text **Running**, which
signifies that the program is executing

Close
box

`Form`

Running program

Fig. 2.47 | IDE in run mode, with the running program in the foreground.

2.7 Wrap-Up

In this chapter, we introduced key features of the Visual Studio Integrated Development Environment (IDE). You used the technique of visual programming to create a working Visual C# program without writing a single line of code. Visual C# programming is a mixture of the two styles: Visual programming allows you to develop GUIs easily and avoid tedious GUI programming. Conventional programming (which we introduce in Chapter 3) allows you to specify the behavior of your programs.

You created a Visual C# Windows Forms application with one `Form`. You worked with the **Solution Explorer, Toolbox** and **Properties** windows, which are essential to developing Visual C# programs. The **Solution Explorer** window allows you to manage your solution's files visually.

You explored Visual Studio's help features. You learned how to set **Help** options to display help resources internally or externally in a web browser. We also demonstrated context-sensitive help, which displays help topics related to selected controls or text.

You used visual programming to design the GUI portions of a program quickly and easily, by dragging and dropping controls (a `Label` and a `PictureBox`) onto a `Form` or by double clicking controls in the **Toolbox**.

In creating the **ASimpleProgram** program, you used the **Properties** window to set the Text and BackColor properties of the Form. You learned that Label controls display text and that PictureBoxes display images. You displayed text in a Label and added an image to a PictureBox. You also worked with the AutoSize, TextAlign and Font properties of a Label and the Image and SizeMode properties of a PictureBox.

In the next chapter, we discuss "nonvisual," or "conventional," programming—you'll create your first programs that contain Visual C# code that you write, instead of having Visual Studio write the code. You'll study console applications (programs that display only text and do not have a GUI). You'll also learn memory concepts, arithmetic, decision making and how to use a dialog to display a message.

2.8 Web Resources

Please take a moment to visit each of these sites briefly.

social.msdn.microsoft.com/forums/en-US/category/visualcsharp/
This site provides access to the Microsoft Visual C# forums, which you can use to get your Visual C# language and IDE questions answered.

www.deitel.com/VisualCSharp2010/
This site lists many of the key web resources we used as we were preparing to write this book. There's lots of great stuff here to help you become familiar with the world of Visual C# 2010.

msdn.microsoft.com/vstudio
This site is the home page for Microsoft Visual Studio. The site includes news, documentation, downloads and other resources.

msdn.microsoft.com/vcsharp
This site provides information on the newest release of Visual C#, including downloads, community information and resources.

Summary

Section 2.1 Introduction
- Visual Studio is Microsoft's Integrated Development Environment (IDE) for creating, running and debugging programs written in a variety of .NET programming languages.
- Creating simple programs by dragging and dropping predefined building blocks into place is called visual programming.

Section 2.2 Overview of the Visual Studio 2010 IDE
- The **Start Page** contains links to Visual Studio 2010 IDE resources and web-based resources.
- A project is a group of related files that compose a program.
- The Visual Studio 2010 IDE organizes programs into projects and solutions—a solution may contain one or more projects.
- Dialogs are windows that facilitate user–computer communication.
- Visual Studio provides templates for the project types you can create, including Windows Forms applications and console applications.
- A Form represents the main window of the Windows Forms application that you're creating.
- Collectively, the Form and controls constitute the program's graphical user interface (GUI), which is the visual part of the program with which the user interacts.

Section 2.3 Menu Bar and Toolbar

- Commands for managing the IDE and for developing, maintaining and executing programs are contained in the menus, which are located on the menu bar.
- Menus contain groups of commands (menu items) that, when selected, cause the IDE to perform actions (for example, open a window, save a file, print a file and execute a program).
- Tool tips help you become familiar with the IDE's features.

Section 2.4 Navigating the Visual Studio IDE

- The **Solution Explorer** window lists all the files in the solution.
- The **Toolbox** contains controls for customizing Forms.
- By using visual programming, you can place predefined controls onto the Form instead of writing the code yourself.
- Moving the mouse pointer over a hidden window's icon opens that window. Moving the mouse out of that window hides it. This feature is known as auto-hide. To "pin down" a window (that is, to disable auto-hide), click the pin icon.
- The **Properties** window displays the properties for a Form, control or file (in **Design** view). Properties are information about a Form or control, such as size, color and position. The **Properties** window allows you to modify Forms and controls visually, without writing code.
- Each control has properties. The **Properties** window shows the property names and values. The window's toolbar contains options for organizing properties alphabetically or categorically.

Section 2.5 Using Help

- Extensive help documentation is available via **Help** menu.
- Context-sensitive help brings up a list of relevant help articles. To use context-sensitive help, select an item and press the *F1* key.

Section 2.6 Using Visual Programming to Create a Simple Program that Displays Text and an Image

- Visual C# programming usually involves a combination of writing a portion of the program code and having Visual Studio generate the remaining code.
- The text that appears at the top of the Form (the title bar) is specified in the Form's Text property.
- To resize the Form, click and drag one of the Form's enabled sizing handles (the small squares around the Form). Enabled sizing handles appear as white boxes.
- The BackColor property specifies the background color of a Form. The Form's background color is the default background color for any controls added to the Form.
- Double clicking any **Toolbox** control icon places a control of that type on the Form. Alternatively, you can drag and drop controls from the **Toolbox** to the Form.
- The Label's Text property determines the text (if any) that the Label displays. The Form and Label each have their own Text property.
- A property's ellipsis button, when clicked, displays a dialog containing additional options.
- In the **Font** dialog, you can select the font for a Form's or Label's text.
- The TextAlign property determines how the text is aligned within a Label's boundaries.
- The PictureBox control displays images. The Image property specifies the image to display.
- Select **File > Save All** to save the entire solution, including all of its files.
- A program that is in design mode is not executing.

- In run mode, the program is executing—you can interact with only a few IDE features.
- When designing a program visually, the name of the Visual C# file appears in the project tab, followed by [Design].
- Terminate execution by clicking the close box.

Terminology

active tab
Alphabetical icon
application
auto-hide
AutoSize property of Label
BackColor property of Form
Categorized icon
component selection drop-down list
context-sensitive help
control
Custom tab
design mode
Design view
dialog
dragging
ellipsis button
Font dialog
Font property of Label
Form
graphical user interface (GUI)
Help menu
icon
Image property of PictureBox
input
Label
menu
menu bar in Visual Studio
menu item
MSDN (Microsoft Developers Network)
New Project dialog

output
palette
PictureBox
project
Project Location dialog
Properties window
property of a Form or control
run mode
Save Project dialog
scrollbar
scrollbox
Select Resource dialog
Show All Files icon
SizeMode property of PictureBox
sizing handle
solution
Solution Explorer in Visual Studio
Start Page
startup project
StretchImage value
templates for projects
Text property
TextAlign property of Label
tool tip
toolbar
Visual C# 2010 Express Edition
visual programming
Visual Studio 2010
Windows Forms application

Self-Review Exercises

2.1 Fill in the blanks in each of the following statements:

a) The technique of _____ allows you to create GUIs without writing any code.

b) A(n) _____ is a group of one or more projects that collectively form a Visual C# program.

c) The _____ feature hides a window when the mouse pointer is moved outside the window's area.

d) A(n) _____ appears when the mouse pointer hovers over an icon.

e) The _____ window allows you to browse solution files.

f) The properties in the **Properties** window can be sorted _____ or _____.

g) A Form's _____ property specifies the text displayed in the Form's title bar.

h) The _____ allows you to add controls to the Form in a visual manner.

i) Using _____ displays relevant help articles, based on the current context.

     j) The _____ property specifies how text is aligned within a `Label`'s boundaries.

2.2   State whether each of the following is *true* or *false*. If *false*, explain why.
    a) The title bar of the IDE displays the IDE's mode.
    b) The ▨ box toggles auto-hide.
    c) The toolbar icons represent various menu commands.
    d) The toolbar contains icons that represent controls you can drag onto a `Form`.
    e) Both `Form`s and `Label`s have a title bar.
    f) Control properties can be modified only by writing code.
    g) `PictureBox`es typically display images.
    h) C# files use the file extension `.csharp`.
    i) A `Form`'s background color is set using the `BackColor` property.

Answers to Self-Review Exercises

2.1   a) visual programming. b) solution. c) auto-hide. d) tool tip. e) **Solution Explorer.** f) alphabetically, categorically. g) `Text`. h) **Toolbox.** i) context-sensitive help. j) `TextAlign`.

2.2   a) True. b) False. The pin icon toggles auto-hide. The ▨ box closes a window. c) True. d) False. The **Toolbox** contains icons that represent such controls. e) False. `Form`s have a title bar but `Label`s do not (although they do have `Label` text). f) False. Control properties can be modified using the **Properties** window. g) True. h) False. C# files use the file extension `.cs`. i) True.

Exercises

2.3   Fill in the blanks in each of the following statements:
    a) When an ellipsis button is clicked, a(n) _____ is displayed.
    b) To save every file in a solution, select _____.
    c) Using _____ help immediately displays a relevant help article.
    d) GUI is an acronym for _____.

2.4   State whether each of the following is *true* or *false*. If *false*, explain why.
    a) You can add a control to a `Form` by double clicking its control icon in the **Toolbox**.
    b) The `Form`, `Label` and `PictureBox` have identical properties.
    c) If your machine is connected to the Internet, you can browse the Internet from the Visual Studio IDE.
    d) Visual C# programmers usually create complex programs without writing any code.
    e) Sizing handles are visible during execution.

2.5   Some features that appear throughout Visual Studio perform similar actions in different contexts. Explain and give examples of how the ellipsis buttons, down-arrow buttons and tool tips act in this manner. Why do you think the Visual Studio IDE was designed this way?

2.6   Fill in the blanks in each of the following statements:
    a) The _____ property specifies which image a `PictureBox` displays.
    b) The _____ menu contains commands for arranging and displaying windows.

2.7   Briefly describe each of the following terms:
    a) toolbar
    b) menu bar
    c) **Toolbox**
    d) control
    e) `Form`
    f) solution

[*Note:* In the following exercises, you're asked to create GUIs using controls that we have not yet discussed in this book. The exercises give you practice with visual programming only—the programs do not perform any actions. You place controls from the **Toolbox** on a Form to familiarize yourself with what each control looks like. We have provided step-by-step instructions for you. If you follow these, you should be able to replicate the screen images we provide.]

2.8 *(Notepad GUI)* Create the GUI for the notepad as shown in Fig. 2.48.

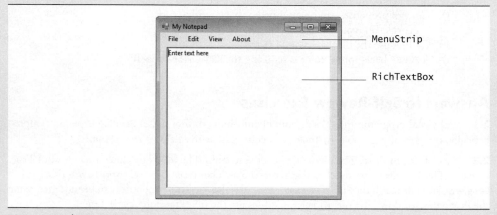

Fig. 2.48 | Notepad GUI.

a) *Manipulating the **Form**'s properties.* Change the Text property of the Form to My Notepad. Change the Font property to 9pt Segoe UI.

b) *Adding a **MenuStrip** control to the **Form**.* Add a MenuStrip to the Form. After inserting the MenuStrip, add items by clicking the **Type Here** section, typing a menu name (for example, **File**, **Edit**, **View** and **About**) and then pressing *Enter*.

c) *Adding a **RichTextBox** to the **Form**.* Drag this control onto the Form. Use the sizing handles to resize and position the RichTextBox as shown in Fig. 2.48. Change the Text property to Enter text here.

2.9 *(Calendar and Appointments GUI)* Create the GUI for the calendar as shown in Fig. 2.49.

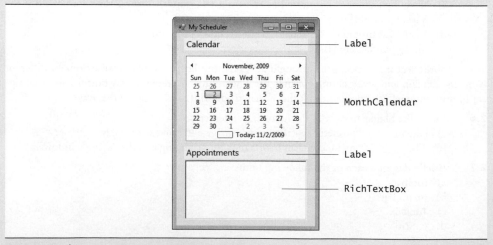

Fig. 2.49 | Calendar and appointments GUI.

a) *Manipulating the Form's properties.* Change the Text property of the Form to My Schedul-er. Change the Font property to 9pt Segoe UI. Set the Form's Size property to 275, 400.

b) *Adding Labels to the Form.* Add two Labels to the Form. Both should be of equal size (231, 23; remember to set the AutoSize property to False) and should be centered in the Form horizontally, as shown. Set the Label's Text properties to match Fig. 2.49. Use 12-point font size. Also, set the BackColor property to Yellow.

c) *Adding a MonthCalendar control to the Form.* Add this control to the Form and center it horizontally in the appropriate place between the two Labels.

d) *Adding a RichTextBox control to the Form.* Add a RichTextBox control to the Form and center it below the second Label. Resize the RichTextBox accordingly.

2.10 *(Calculator GUI)* Create the GUI for the calculator as shown in Fig. 2.50.

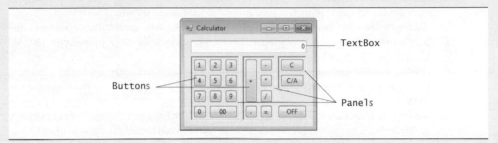

Fig. 2.50 | Calculator GUI.

a) *Manipulating the Form's properties.* Change the Text property of the Form to Calcula-tor. Change the Font property to 9pt Segoe UI. Change the Size property of the Form to 258, 210.

b) *Adding a TextBox to the Form.* Set the TextBox's Text property in the **Properties** window to 0. Stretch the TextBox and position it as shown in Fig. 2.50. Set the TextAlign property to Right—this right aligns text displayed in the TextBox.

c) *Adding the first Panel to the Form.* Panel controls are used to group other controls. Add a Panel to the Form. Change the Panel's BorderStyle property to Fixed3D to make the inside of the Panel appear recessed. Change the Size property to 90, 120. This Panel will contain the calculator's numeric keys.

d) *Adding the second Panel to the Form.* Change the Panel's BorderStyle property to Fixed3D. Change the Size property to 62, 120. This Panel will contain the calculator's operator keys.

e) *Adding the third (and last) Panel to the Form.* Change the Panel's BorderStyle property to Fixed3D. Change the Size property to 54, 62. This Panel contains the calculator's **C** (clear) and **C/A** (clear all) keys.

f) *Adding Buttons to the Form.* There are 20 Buttons on the calculator. Add a Button to the Panel by dragging and dropping it on the Panel. Change the Text property of each Button to the calculator key it represents. The value you enter in the Text property will appear on the face of the Button. Finally, resize the Buttons, using their Size properties. Each Button labeled 0–9, *, /, -, = and . should have a size of 23, 23. The **00** Button has size 52, 23. The **OFF** Button has size 54, 23. The **+** Button is sized 23, 81. The **C** (clear) and **C/A** (clear all) Buttons are sized 44, 23.

2.11 *(Alarm Clock GUI)* Create the GUI for the alarm clock as shown in Fig. 2.51.

a) *Manipulating the Form's properties.* Change the Text property of the Form to Alarm Clock. Change the Font property to 9pt Segoe UI. Change the Size property of the Form to 438, 170.

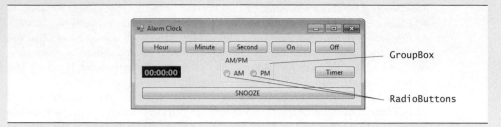

Fig. 2.51 | Alarm clock GUI.

b) *Adding **Buttons** to the **Form***. Add six Buttons to the Form. Change the Text property of each Button to the appropriate text. Align the Buttons as shown.

c) *Adding a **GroupBox** to the **Form***. GroupBoxes are like Panels, except that GroupBoxes display a title. Change the Text property to AM/PM, and set the Size property to 100, 50. Center the GroupBox horizontally on the Form.

d) *Adding **AM/PM** **RadioButtons** to the **GroupBox***. Place two RadioButtons in the GroupBox. Change the Text property of one RadioButton to AM and the other to PM. Align the RadioButtons as shown.

e) *Adding the time **Label** to the **Form***. Add a Label to the Form and change its Text property to 00:00:00. Change the BorderStyle property to Fixed3D and the BackColor to Black. Use the Font property to make the time bold and 12pt. Change the ForeColor to Silver (located in the **Web** tab) to make the time stand out against the black background. Position the Label as shown.

2.12 *(Radio GUI)* Create the GUI for the radio as shown in Fig. 2.52. [*Note:* The image used in this exercise is located in the examples folder for Chapter 2.]

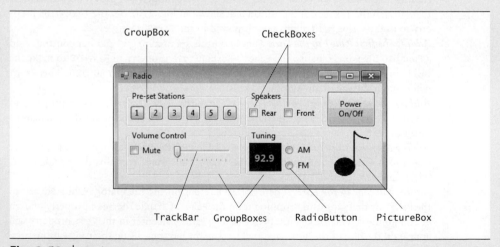

Fig. 2.52 | Radio GUI.

a) *Manipulating the **Form**'s properties*. Change the Font property to 9pt Segoe UI. Change the Form's Text property to Radio and the Size to 427, 194.

b) *Adding the **Pre-set Stations** **GroupBox** and **Buttons***. Set the GroupBox's Size to 180, 55 and its Text to Pre-set Stations. Add six Buttons to the GroupBox. Set each one's Size to 23, 23. Change the Buttons' Text properties to 1, 2, 3, 4, 5, 6, respectively.

c) *Adding the **Speakers** GroupBox and CheckBoxes.* Set the GroupBox's Size to 122, 55 and its Text to Speakers. Add two CheckBoxes to the GroupBox. Set the Text properties for the CheckBoxes to Rear and Front.

d) *Adding the **Power On/Off** Button.* Add a Button to the Form. Set its Text to Power On/Off and its Size to 75, 55.

e) *Adding the **Volume Control** GroupBox, the **Mute** CheckBox and the **Volume** TrackBar.* Add a GroupBox to the Form. Set its Text to Volume Control and its Size to 180, 70. Add a CheckBox to the GroupBox. Set its Text to Mute. Add a TrackBar (from the **Toolbox**'s **All Windows Forms** group) to the GroupBox.

f) *Adding the **Tuning** GroupBox, the radio station **Label** and the **AM/FM** RadioButtons.* Add a GroupBox to the Form. Set its Text to Tuning and its Size to 122, 70. Add a Label to the GroupBox. Set its AutoSize to False, its Size to 50, 44, its BackColor to Black, its ForeColor to Silver, its font to 12pt bold and its TextAlign to MiddleCenter. Set its Text to 92.9. Place the Label as shown in the figure. Add two RadioButtons to the GroupBox. Set the Text of one to AM and of the other to FM.

g) *Adding the image.* Add a PictureBox to the Form. Set its SizeMode to StretchImage and its Size to 55, 70. Set the Image property to MusicNote.gif (located in the examples folder for Chapter 2).

3

Introduction to C# Applications

What's in a name?
That which we call a rose
by any other name
would smell as sweet.
—William Shakespeare

When faced with a decision, I
always ask, "What would be the
most fun?"
—Peggy Walker

Objectives

In this chapter you'll learn:

- To write simple C# applications using code rather than visual programming.

- To input data from the keyboard and output data to the screen.

- To declare and use data of various types.

- To store and retrieve data from memory.

- To use arithmetic operators.

- To determine the order in which operators are applied.

- To write decision-making statements.

- To use relational and equality operators.

3.1 Introduction

We now introduce C# application programming. Most of the C# applications you'll study in this book process information and display results. In this chapter, we introduce **console applications**—these input and output text in a **console window**, which in Windows is known as the **Command Prompt**.

We begin with several examples that simply display messages on the screen. We then demonstrate an application that obtains two numbers from a user, calculates their sum and displays the result. You'll perform various arithmetic calculations and save the results for later use. Many applications contain logic that makes decisions—the last example in this chapter demonstrates decision-making fundamentals by showing you how to compare numbers and display messages based on the comparison results. For example, the application displays a message indicating that two numbers are equal only if they have the same value. We analyze each example one line at a time.

3.2 A Simple C# Application: Displaying a Line of Text

Let's consider a simple application that displays a line of text. The application and its output are shown in Fig. 3.1, which illustrates several important C# language features. Each program we present in this book includes line numbers, which are not part of actual C# code. In Section 3.3 we show how to display line numbers for your C# code in the IDE. We'll soon see that line 10 does the real work of the application—namely, displaying the phrase Welcome to C# Programming! on the screen. We now consider each line of the application—this is called a **code walkthrough**.

Line 1

```
// Fig. 3.1: Welcome1.cs
```

begins with //, indicating that the remainder of the line is a **comment**. Programmers insert comments to document applications and improve their readability. The C# compiler ignores comments, so they do not cause the computer to perform any action when the application is run. We begin every application with a comment indicating the figure number and the name of the file in which the application is stored.

```
 1   // Fig. 3.1: Welcome1.cs
 2   // Text-displaying application.
 3   using System;
 4
 5   public class Welcome1
 6   {
 7      // Main method begins execution of C# application
 8      public static void Main( string[] args )
 9      {
10         Console.WriteLine( "Welcome to C# Programming!" );
11      } // end Main
12   } // end class Welcome1
```

```
Welcome to C# Programming!
```

Fig. 3.1 | Text-displaying application.

A comment that begins with // is called a **single-line comment**, because it terminates at the end of the line on which it appears. A // comment also can begin in the middle of a line and continue until the end of that line (as in lines 7, 11 and 12).

Delimited comments such as

```
/* This is a delimited comment.
   It can be split over many lines */
```

can be spread over several lines. This type of comment begins with the delimiter /* and ends with the delimiter */. All text between the delimiters is ignored by the compiler.

Common Programming Error 3.1

*Forgetting one of the delimiters of a delimited comment is a syntax error. The **syntax** of a programming language specifies the rules for creating a proper application in that language. A **syntax** error occurs when the compiler encounters code that violates C#'s language rules. In this case, the compiler does not produce an executable file. Instead, it issues one or more error messages to help you identify and fix the incorrect code. Syntax errors are also called **compiler errors**, **compile-time errors** or **compilation errors**, because the compiler detects them during the compilation phase. You'll be unable to execute your application until you correct all the syntax errors in it.*

Line 2

```
// Text-displaying application.
```

is a single-line comment that describes the purpose of the application.

Line 3

```
using System;
```

is a **using directive** that tells the compiler where to look for a class that is used in this application. A great strength of Visual C# is its rich set of predefined classes that you can reuse rather than "reinventing the wheel." These classes are organized under **namespaces**—named collections of related classes. Collectively, .NET's namespaces are referred to as the **.NET Framework Class Library**. Each using directive identifies a namespace containing predefined classes that a C# application should be able to use. The using directive in line 3 indicates that this example uses classes from the System namespace, which contains the predefined Console class (discussed shortly) used in line 10, and many other useful classes.

Error-Prevention Tip 3.1

Forgetting to include a using *directive for a namespace that contains a class used in your application typically results in a compilation error, containing a message such as "The name 'Console' does not exist in the current context." When this occurs, check that you provided the proper* using *directives and that the names in the* using *directives are spelled correctly, including proper use of uppercase and lowercase letters.*

For each new .NET class we use, we indicate the namespace in which it's located. This information is important, because it helps you locate descriptions of each class in the **.NET documentation**. A web-based version of this documentation can be found at

```
msdn.microsoft.com/en-us/library/ms229335.aspx
```

This can also be accessed via the **Help** menu. You can also place the cursor on the name of any .NET class or method, then press the *F1* key to get more information.

Line 4 is simply a blank line. Blank lines and space characters make code easier to read. Together, blank lines, space characters and tab characters are known as **whitespace**. Space characters and tabs are known specifically as **whitespace characters**. Whitespace is ignored by the compiler.

Line 5

```
public class Welcome1
```

begins a **class declaration** for the class Welcome1. Every application consists of at least one class declaration that is defined by you—the programmer. These are known as **user-defined classes**. The **class keyword** introduces a class declaration and is immediately followed by the **class name** (Welcome1). Keywords (sometimes called **reserved words**) are reserved for use by C# and are always spelled with all lowercase letters. The complete list of C# keywords is shown in Fig. 3.2.

By convention, all class names begin with a capital letter and capitalize the first letter of each word they include (e.g., SampleClassName). This convention is known as **upper camel casing**. A class name is an **identifier**—a series of characters consisting of letters, digits and underscores (_) that does not begin with a digit and does not contain spaces. Some valid identifiers are Welcome1, identifier, _value and m_inputField1. The name 7button is not a valid identifier because it begins with a digit, and the name input field is not a valid identifier because it contains a space. Normally, an identifier that does not begin with a capital letter is not the name of a class. C# is **case sensitive**—that is, uppercase and lowercase letters are distinct, so a1 and A1 are different (but both valid) identifiers. Identifiers may also be preceded by the @ character. This indicates that a word should be interpreted as an identifier, even if it's a keyword (e.g., @int). This allows C# code to use code written in other .NET languages where an identifier might have the same name as a C# keyword. The **contextual keywords** in Fig. 3.2 can be used as identifiers outside the contexts in which they're keywords, but for clarity this is not recommended.

Good Programming Practice 3.1

By convention, always begin a class name's identifier with a capital letter and start each subsequent word in the identifier with a capital letter.

C# Keywords and contextual keywords				
abstract	as	base	bool	break
byte	case	catch	char	checked
class	const	continue	decimal	default
delegate	do	double	dynamic	else
enum	event	explicit	extern	false
finally	fixed	float	for	foreach
goto	if	implicit	in	int
interface	internal	is	lock	long
namespace	new	null	object	operator
out	override	params	private	protected
public	readonly	ref	return	sbyte
sealed	short	sizeof	stackalloc	static
string	struct	switch	this	throw
true	try	typeof	uint	ulong
unchecked	unsafe	ushort	using	virtual
void	volatile	while		
Contextual Keywords				
add	alias	ascending	by	descending
equals	from	get	global	group
into	join	let	on	orderby
partial	remove	select	set	value
var	where	yield		

Fig. 3.2 | C# keywords and contextual keywords.

Common Programming Error 3.2

C# is case sensitive. Not using the proper uppercase and lowercase letters for an identifier normally causes a compilation error.

In Chapters 3–9, every class we define begins with the keyword **public**. For now, we'll simply require this keyword. You'll learn more about public and non-public classes in Chapter 10. When you save your public class declaration in a file, the file name is usually the class name followed by the .cs file-name extension. For our application, the file name is Welcome1.cs.

Good Programming Practice 3.2

By convention, a file that contains a single public class should have a name that is identical to the class name (plus the .cs extension) in both spelling and capitalization. Naming your files in this way makes it easier for you and other programmers to determine where the classes of an application are located.

A **left brace** (in line 6 in Fig. 3.1), {, begins the **body** of every class declaration. A corresponding **right brace** (in line 12), }, must end each class declaration. Lines 7–11 are indented. This indentation is one of the spacing conventions mentioned earlier. We define each spacing convention as a *Good Programming Practice*.

Error-Prevention Tip 3.2

Whenever you type an opening left brace, {, in your application, immediately type the closing right brace, }, then reposition the cursor between the braces and indent to begin typing the body. This practice helps prevent errors due to missing braces.

Good Programming Practice 3.3

Indent the entire body of each class declaration one "level" of indentation between the left and right braces that delimit the body of the class. This format emphasizes the class declaration's structure and makes it easier to read. You can let the IDE format your code by selecting Edit > Advanced > Format Document.

Good Programming Practice 3.4

Set a convention for the indent size you prefer, then uniformly apply that convention. The **Tab** *key may be used to create indents, but tab stops vary among text editors. We recommend using three spaces to form each level of indentation. We show how to do this in Section 3.3.*

Common Programming Error 3.3

It is a syntax error if braces do not occur in matching pairs.

Line 7

```
// Main method begins execution of C# application
```

is a comment indicating the purpose of lines 8–11 of the application. Line 8

```
public static void Main( string[] args )
```

is the starting point of every application. The **parentheses** after the identifier `Main` indicate that it's an application building block called a method. Class declarations normally contain one or more methods. Method names usually follow the same capitalization conventions used for class names. For each application, one of the methods in a class must be called `Main` (which is typically defined as shown in line 8); otherwise, the application will not execute. Methods are able to perform tasks and return information when they complete their tasks. Keyword **void** (line 8) indicates that this method will not return any information after it completes its task. Later, we'll see that many methods do return information. You'll learn more about methods in Chapters 4 and 7. We discuss the contents of `Main`'s parentheses in Chapter 8. For now, simply mimic `Main`'s first line in your applications.

The left brace in line 9 begins the **body of the method declaration**. A corresponding right brace must end the method's body (line 11 of Fig. 3.1). Line 10 in the body of the method is indented between the braces.

Good Programming Practice 3.5

As with class declarations, indent the entire body of each method declaration one "level" of indentation between the left and right braces that define the method body.

Line 10

```
Console.WriteLine( "Welcome to C# Programming!" );
```

instructs the computer to **perform an action**—namely, to display the **string** of characters between the double quotation marks. A string is sometimes called a **character string**, a **message** or a **string literal**. We refer to characters between double quotation marks simply as strings. Whitespace characters in strings are *not* ignored by the compiler.

Class **Console** provides **standard input/output** capabilities that enable applications to read and display text in the console window from which the application executes. The **Console.WriteLine method** displays a line of text in the console window. The string in the parentheses in line 10 is the **argument** to the method. Method Console.WriteLine performs its task by displaying (also called outputting) its argument in the console window. When Console.WriteLine completes its task, it positions the **screen cursor** (the blinking symbol indicating where the next character will be displayed) at the beginning of the next line in the console window. (This movement of the cursor is similar to what happens when a user presses the *Enter* key while typing in a text editor—the cursor moves to the beginning of the next line in the file.)

The entire line 10, including Console.WriteLine, the parentheses, the argument "Welcome to C# Programming!" in the parentheses and the **semicolon** (**;**), is called a **statement**. Most statements end with a semicolon. When the statement in line 10 executes, it displays the message Welcome to C# Programming! in the console window. A method is typically composed of one or more statements that perform the method's task.

Error-Prevention Tip 3.3

When the compiler reports a syntax error, the error may not be in the line indicated by the error message. First, check the line for which the error was reported. If that line does not contain syntax errors, check several preceding lines.

Some programmers find it difficult when reading or writing an application to match the left and right braces ({ and }) that delimit the body of a class declaration or a method declaration. To help, you can include a comment after each closing right brace (}) that ends a method declaration and after each closing right brace that ends a class declaration. For example, line 11

```
      } // end Main
```

specifies the closing right brace of method Main, and line 12

```
   } // end class Welcome1
```

specifies the closing right brace of class Welcome1. Each of these comments indicates the method or class that the right brace terminates. Visual Studio can help you locate matching braces in your code. Simply place the cursor immediately in front of the left brace or immediately after the right brace, and Visual Studio will highlight both.

3.3 Creating a Simple Application in Visual C# Express

Now that we have presented our first console application (Fig. 3.1), we provide a step-by-step explanation of how to create, compile and execute it using Visual C# Express.

Creating the Console Application

After opening Visual C# 2010 Express, select **File > New Project...** to display the **New Project** dialog (Fig. 3.3), then select the **Console Application** template. In the dialog's **Name** field, type `Welcome1`. Click **OK** to create the project. The IDE now contains the open console application, as shown in Fig. 3.4. The editor window already contains some code provided by the IDE. Some of this code is similar to that of Fig. 3.1. Some is not, and uses features that we have not yet discussed. The IDE inserts this extra code to help organize the application and to provide access to some common classes in the .NET Framework Class Library—at this point in the book, this code is neither required nor relevant to the discussion of this application; delete all of it.

Fig. 3.3 | Creating a **Console Application** with the **New Project** dialog.

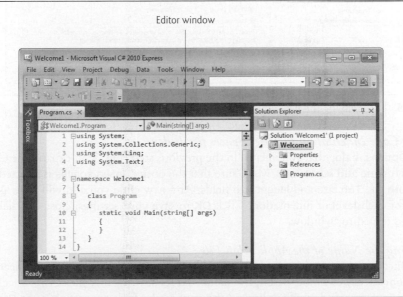

Fig. 3.4 | IDE with an open console application.

The code coloring scheme used by the IDE is called **syntax-color highlighting** and helps you visually differentiate application elements. For example, keywords appear in blue and comments appear in green. We syntax-shade our code similarly—bold for keywords, gray for comments, bold gray for literals and constants, and black for other text. One example of a literal is the string passed to `Console.WriteLine` in line 10 of Fig. 3.1. You can customize the colors shown in the code editor by selecting **Tools > Options...**. This displays the **Options** dialog. Then expand the **Environment** node and select **Fonts and Colors**. Here you can change the colors for various code elements.

Modifying the Editor Settings to Display Line Numbers

Visual C# Express provides many ways to personalize your coding experience. In this step, you'll change the settings so that your code matches that of this book. To have the IDE display line numbers, select **Tools > Options...**. In the dialog that appears (Fig. 3.5), click the **Show all settings** checkbox on the lower left of the dialog, then expand the **Text Editor** node in the left pane and select **All Languages**. On the right, check the **Line numbers** checkbox. Keep the **Options** dialog open.

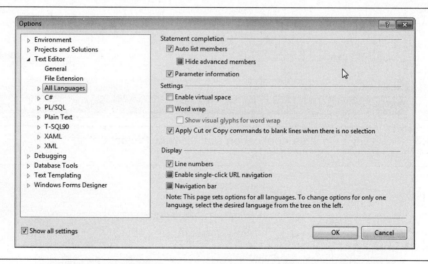

Fig. 3.5 | Modifying the IDE settings.

Setting Code Indentation to Three Spaces per Indent

In the **Options** dialog that you opened in the previous step (Fig. 3.5), expand the C# node in the left pane and select **Tabs**. Make sure that the option **Insert spaces** is selected. Enter **3** for both the **Tab size** and **Indent size** fields. Any new code you add will now use three spaces for each level of indentation. Click **OK** to save your settings, close the dialog and return to the editor window.

Changing the Name of the Application File

For applications we create in this book, we change the default name of the application file (i.e., `Program.cs`) to a more descriptive name. To rename the file, click `Program.cs` in the **Solution Explorer** window. This displays the application file's properties in the **Properties** window (Fig. 3.6). Change the **File Name property** to `Welcome1.cs`. This will display a

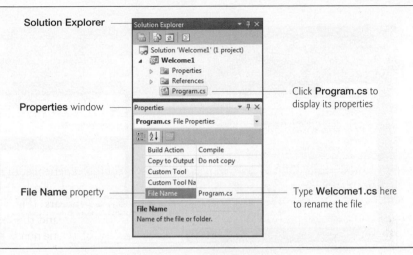

Fig. 3.6 | Renaming the program file in the **Properties** window.

dialog asking whether you'd like to rename all of the references in the project to the code element Program. Clicking **Yes** renames the class from Program to Welcome1 and ensures that the project is configured properly to execute the program.

Writing Code and Using IntelliSense

In the editor window (Fig. 3.4), replace the code generated by the IDE with the code from Fig. 3.1. As you begin typing the class name Console (line 10), an *IntelliSense* window is displayed (Fig. 3.7, part 1). As you type, *IntelliSense* lists various items that start with or contain the letters you've typed so far. *IntelliSense* also filters the list to show only the mem-

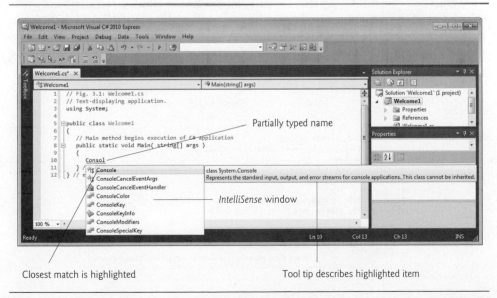

Fig. 3.7 | *IntelliSense* feature of Visual C# Express. (Part 1 of 2.)

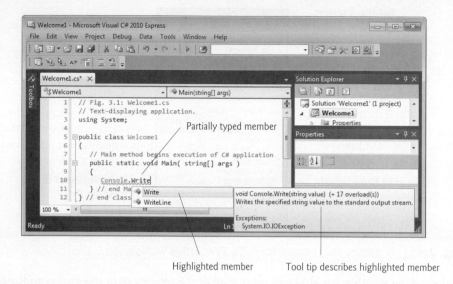

Partially typed member

Highlighted member   Tool tip describes highlighted member

Fig. 3.7 | *IntelliSense* feature of Visual C# Express. (Part 2 of 2.)

bers that match what you've typed, then displays a tool tip containing a description of the first matching item. You can either type the complete item name (e.g., `Console`), double click the item name in the member list or press the *Tab* key to complete the name. Once the complete name is provided, the *IntelliSense* window closes. While the *IntelliSense* window is displayed, pressing the *Ctrl* key makes the window transparent so you can see the code behind the window.

When you type the dot (.) after `Console`, the *IntelliSense* window reappears and shows only the members of class `Console` that can be used on the right side of the dot (Fig. 3.7, part 1). When you type the open parenthesis character, (, after `Console.WriteLine`, the *Parameter Info* window is displayed (Fig. 3.8). This window contains information about the

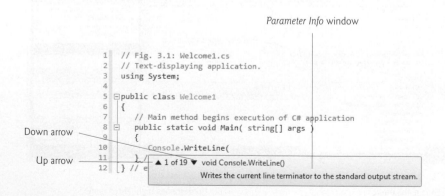

Fig. 3.8 | *Parameter Info* window.

method's parameters. As you'll learn in Chapter 7, there can be several versions of a method. That is, a class can define several methods that have the same name, as long as they have different numbers and/or types of parameters—a concept known as overloaded methods. These methods normally all perform similar tasks. The *Parameter Info* window indicates how many versions of the selected method are available and provides up and down arrows for scrolling through the different versions. For example, there are 19 versions of the WriteLine method—we use one of these 19 versions in our application. The *Parameter Info* window is one of many features provided by the IDE to facilitate application development. In the next several chapters, you'll learn more about the information displayed in these windows. The *Parameter Info* window is especially helpful when you want to see the different ways in which a method can be used. From the code in Fig. 3.1, we already know that we intend to display one string with WriteLine, so, because you know exactly which version of WriteLine you want to use, you can simply close the *Parameter Info* window by pressing the *Esc* key.

Saving the Application

Select **File > Save All** to display the **Save Project** dialog (Fig. 3.9). In the **Location** textbox, specify the directory where you want to save this project. We created and chose the directory MyProjects on the C: drive. Ensure that the **Create directory for solution** checkbox is checked to create a subdirectory containing all of the files for your program and click **Save**.

Fig. 3.9 | **Save Project** dialog.

Compiling and Running the Application

You're now ready to compile and execute your application. Depending on the project's type, the compiler may compile the code into files with the **.exe (executable) extension**, the **.dll (dynamically linked library) extension** or one of several other extensions. Such files are called **assemblies** and are the packaging units for compiled C# code. These assemblies contain the Microsoft Intermediate Language (MSIL) code for the application.

To compile the application, select **Debug > Build Solution**. If the application contains no syntax errors, this will compile your application and build it into an executable file (named Welcome1.exe, in one of the project's subdirectories). To execute it, type *Ctrl + F5*, which invokes the Main method (Fig. 3.1). If you attempt to run the application before building it, the IDE will build the application first, then run it only if there are no compilation errors. The statement in line 10 of Main displays Welcome to C# Programming!. Figure 3.10 shows the results of executing this application, displayed in a console (**Command Prompt**) window. Leave the application's project open in Visual C# Express; we'll go back to it later in this section. [*Note:* The console window normally has a black background and white text. We reconfigured it to have a white background and black text for readability. To do this, click the ■ icon in the upper-left corner of the console window, then select **Properties**. You can change the colors in the **Colors** tab of the dialog that appears.]

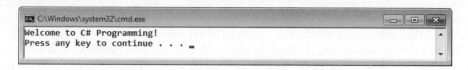

Fig. 3.10 | Executing the application shown in Fig. 3.1.

Running the Application from the Command Prompt
As we mentioned at the beginning of the chapter, you can execute applications outside the IDE in a **Command Prompt**. This is useful when you simply want to run an application rather than open it for modification. To open the **Command Prompt**, select **Start > All Programs > Accessories > Command Prompt**. The window (Fig. 3.11) displays copyright information, followed by a prompt that indicates the current directory. By default, the prompt specifies the current user's directory on the local machine. On your machine, the folder name Paul Deitel will be replaced with your username.

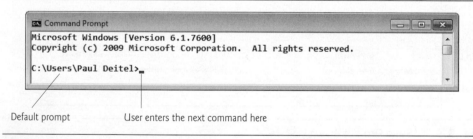

Default prompt   User enters the next command here

Fig. 3.11 | **Command Prompt** window when it's initially opened.

Enter the command cd (which stands for "change directory"), followed by the /d flag (to change drives if necessary), then the directory where the application's .exe file is located (i.e., your application's bin\Debug or bin\Release directory). For example, the command

```
cd /d C:\MyProjects\Welcome1\Welcome1\bin\Release
```

(Fig. 3.12) changes the current directory, to the Welcome1 application's Release directory on the C: drive. The next prompt displays the new directory. After changing to the proper directory, you can run the application by entering the name of the .exe file— Welcome1. The application will run to completion, then the prompt will display again, awaiting the next command. To close the **Command Prompt**, type exit (Fig. 3.12) and press *Enter*.

Visual C# 2010 Express maintains a Debug and a Release directory in each project's bin directory. The Debug directory contains a version of the application that can be used with the debugger (see Appendix G, Using the Visual C# 2010 Debugger). The Release directory contains an optimized version that you could provide to your customers. In the complete Visual Studio 2010, you can select the specific version you wish to build from the

Solution Configurations drop-down list in the toolbars at the top of the IDE. The default is the Release version. The Debug version is created if you run the program with **Debug > Start Debugging** (or by pressing F5 or the ▶ button on the IDE's toolbar).

Updated prompt showing   Type this to change to the
the new current directory   application's directory

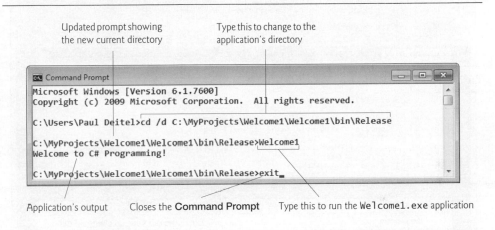

```
Command Prompt

Microsoft Windows [Version 6.1.7600]
Copyright (c) 2009 Microsoft Corporation.  All rights reserved.

C:\Users\Paul Deitel>cd /d C:\MyProjects\Welcome1\Welcome1\bin\Release

C:\MyProjects\Welcome1\Welcome1\bin\Release>Welcome1
Welcome to C# Programming!

C:\MyProjects\Welcome1\Welcome1\bin\Release>exit_
```

Application's output   Closes the **Command Prompt**   Type this to run the Welcome1.exe application

Fig. 3.12 | Executing the application shown in Fig. 3.1 from a **Command Prompt** window.

Syntax Errors, Error Messages and the Error List Window

Go back to the application in Visual C# Express. As you type code, the IDE responds either by applying syntax-color highlighting or by generating a **syntax error**, which indicates a violation of Visual C#'s rules for creating correct applications (i.e., one or more statements are not written correctly). Syntax errors occur for various reasons, such as missing parentheses and misspelled keywords.

When a syntax error occurs, the IDE underlines the error in red and provides a description of it in the **Error List** window (Fig. 3.13). If the **Error List** window is not visible in the IDE, select **View > Error List** to display it. In Figure 3.13, we intentionally omitted the comma between "Welcome to" and "C# Programming!" in line 10. The first error is simply indicating that line 10 is not a valid statement. The second error indicates that a right parenthesis is expected at character position 51 in the statement, because the compiler is confused by the unmatched left parenthesis from earlier in line 10. The third error has the text "**Invalid expression term ')'**", because the compiler thinks the closing right parenthesis should have appeared earlier in the line. The fourth error has the text "**; expected**", because the prior errors make the compiler think that the statement should have been terminated with a semicolon earlier in the line. Although we deleted only one comma in line 10, this caused the compiler to misinterpret several items in this line and to generate *four* error messages. You can double click an error message in the **Error List** to jump to the place in the code that caused the error.

> **Error-Prevention Tip 3.4**
> *One syntax error can lead to multiple entries in the* **Error List** *window. Each error that you address could eliminate several subsequent error messages when you recompile your application. So when you see an error you know how to fix, correct it and recompile—this may make several other error messages disappear.*

Error List window   Intentionally omitted comma character (syntax error)

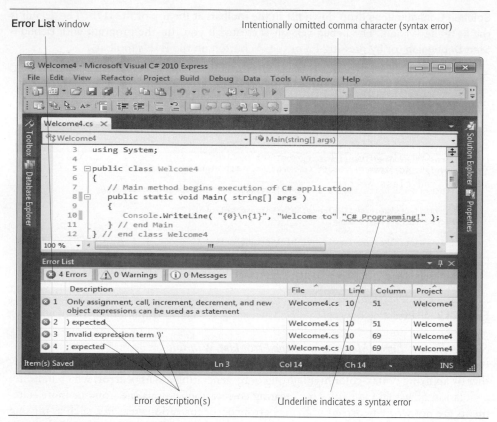

Error description(s)   Underline indicates a syntax error

Fig. 3.13 | Syntax errors indicated by the IDE.

3.4 Modifying Your Simple C# Application

This section continues our introduction to C# programming with two examples that modify the example of Fig. 3.1.

Displaying a Single Line of Text with Multiple Statements
Class Welcome2, shown in Fig. 3.14, uses two statements to produce the same output as that shown in Fig. 3.1. From this point forward, we highlight the new and key features in each code listing, as shown in lines 10–11 of Fig. 3.14.

The application is almost identical to Fig. 3.1. We discuss the changes here. Line 2

```
// Displaying one line of text with multiple statements.
```

states the purpose of this application. Line 5 begins the Welcome2 class declaration.
Lines 10–11 of method Main

```
Console.Write( "Welcome to " );
Console.WriteLine( "C# Programming!" );
```

display one line of text in the console window. The first statement uses Console's method **Write** to display a string. Unlike WriteLine, after displaying its argument, Write does not position the screen cursor at the beginning of the next line in the console window—the

```
 1    // Fig. 3.14: Welcome2.cs
 2    // Displaying one line of text with multiple statements.
 3    using System;
 4
 5    public class Welcome2
 6    {
 7       // Main method begins execution of C# application
 8       public static void Main( string[] args )
 9       {
10          Console.Write( "Welcome to " );
11          Console.WriteLine( "C# Programming!" );
12       } // end Main
13    } // end class Welcome2
```

```
Welcome to C# Programming!
```

Fig. 3.14 | Displaying one line of text with multiple statements.

next character the application displays will appear immediately after the last character that Write displays. Thus, line 11 positions the first character in its argument (the letter "C") immediately after the last character that line 10 displays (the space character before the string's closing double-quote character). Each Write statement resumes displaying characters from where the last Write statement displayed its last character.

Displaying Multiple Lines of Text with a Single Statement
A single statement can display multiple lines by using newline characters, which indicate to Console methods Write and WriteLine when they should position the screen cursor to the beginning of the next line in the console window. Like space characters and tab characters, newline characters are whitespace characters. The application of Fig. 3.15 outputs four lines of text, using newline characters to indicate when to begin each new line.

Most of the application is identical to the applications of Fig. 3.1 and Fig. 3.14, so we discuss only the changes here. Line 2

```
// Displaying multiple lines with a single statement.
```

states the purpose of this application. Line 5 begins the Welcome3 class declaration.

```
 1    // Fig. 3.15: Welcome3.cs
 2    // Displaying multiple lines with a single statement.
 3    using System;
 4
 5    public class Welcome3
 6    {
 7       // Main method begins execution of C# application
 8       public static void Main( string[] args )
 9       {
10          Console.WriteLine( "Welcome\nto\nC#\nProgramming!" );
11       } // end Main
12    } // end class Welcome3
```

Fig. 3.15 | Displaying multiple lines with a single statement. (Part 1 of 2.)

```
Welcome
to
C#
Programming!
```

Fig. 3.15 | Displaying multiple lines with a single statement. (Part 2 of 2.)

Line 10

```
Console.WriteLine( "Welcome\nto\nC#\nProgramming!" );
```

displays four separate lines of text in the console window. Normally, the characters in a string are displayed exactly as they appear in the double quotes. Note, however, that the two characters \ and n (repeated three times in the statement) do not appear on the screen. The **backslash** (\) is called an **escape character**. It indicates to C# that a "special character" is in the string. When a backslash appears in a string of characters, C# combines the next character with the backslash to form an **escape sequence**. The escape sequence \n represents the **newline character**. When a newline character appears in a string being output with Console methods, the newline character causes the screen cursor to move to the beginning of the next line in the console window. Figure 3.16 lists several common escape sequences and describes how they affect the display of characters in the console window.

Escape sequence	Description
\n	Newline. Positions the screen cursor at the beginning of the next line.
\t	Horizontal tab. Moves the screen cursor to the next tab stop.
\r	Carriage return. Positions the screen cursor at the beginning of the current line—does not advance the cursor to the next line. Any characters output after the carriage return overwrite the characters previously output on that line.
\\	Backslash. Used to place a backslash character in a string.
\"	Double quote. Used to place a double-quote character (") in a string—e.g., `Console.Write( "\"in quotes\"" );` displays `"in quotes"`.

Fig. 3.16 | Some common escape sequences.

3.5 Formatting Text with Console.Write and Console.WriteLine

Console methods Write and WriteLine also have the capability to display formatted data. Figure 3.17 outputs the strings "Welcome to" and "C# Programming!" with WriteLine.

Line 10

```
Console.WriteLine( "{0}\n{1}", "Welcome to", "C# Programming!" );
```

calls method Console.WriteLine to display the application's output. The method call specifies three arguments. When a method requires multiple arguments, the arguments are separated with **commas** (,)—this is known as a **comma-separated list**.

```
 1   // Fig. 3.17: Welcome4.cs
 2   // Displaying multiple lines of text with string formatting.
 3   using System;
 4
 5   public class Welcome4
 6   {
 7      // Main method begins execution of C# application
 8      public static void Main( string[] args )
 9      {
10         Console.WriteLine( "{0}\n{1}", "Welcome to", "C# Programming!" );
11      } // end Main
12   } // end class Welcome4
```

```
Welcome to
C# Programming!
```

Fig. 3.17 | Displaying multiple lines of text with string formatting.

Good Programming Practice 3.6

Place a space after each comma (,) in an argument list to make applications more readable.

Most statements end with a semicolon (;). Therefore, line 10 represents only one statement. Large statements can be split over many lines, but there are some restrictions.

Common Programming Error 3.4

Splitting a statement in the middle of an identifier or a string is a syntax error.

Method WriteLine's first argument is a **format string** that may consist of **fixed text** and **format items**. Fixed text is output by WriteLine, as in Fig. 3.1. Each format item is a placeholder for a value. Format items also may include optional formatting information.

Format items are enclosed in curly braces and contain characters that tell the method which argument to use and how to format it. For example, the format item {0} is a placeholder for the first additional argument (because C# starts counting from 0), {1} is a placeholder for the second, and so on. The format string in line 10 specifies that WriteLine should output two arguments and that the first one should be followed by a newline character. So this example substitutes "Welcome to" for the {0} and "C# Programming!" for the {1}. The output shows that two lines of text are displayed. Because braces in a formatted string normally indicate a placeholder for text substitution, you must type two left braces ({{) or two right braces (}}) to insert a single left or right brace into a formatted string, respectively. We introduce additional formatting features as they're needed in our examples.

3.6 Another C# Application: Adding Integers

Our next application reads (or inputs) two **integers** (whole numbers, like –22, 7, 0 and 1024) typed by a user at the keyboard, computes the sum of the values and displays the result. This application must keep track of the numbers supplied by the user for the calculation later in the application. Applications remember numbers and other data in the computer's memory and access that data through application elements called **variables**. The application of Fig. 3.18 demonstrates these concepts. In the sample output, we highlight data the user enters at the keyboard in bold.

```
1   // Fig. 3.18: Addition.cs
2   // Displaying the sum of two numbers input from the keyboard.
3   using System;
4
5   public class Addition
6   {
7      // Main method begins execution of C# application
8      public static void Main( string[] args )
9      {
10        int number1; // declare first number to add
11        int number2; // declare second number to add
12        int sum; // declare sum of number1 and number2
13
14        Console.Write( "Enter first integer: " ); // prompt user
15        // read first number from user
16        number1 = Convert.ToInt32( Console.ReadLine() );
17
18        Console.Write( "Enter second integer: " ); // prompt user
19        // read second number from user
20        number2 = Convert.ToInt32( Console.ReadLine() );
21
22        sum = number1 + number2; // add numbers
23
24        Console.WriteLine( "Sum is {0}", sum ); // display sum
25     } // end Main
26  } // end class Addition
```

```
Enter first integer: 45
Enter second integer: 72
Sum is 117
```

Fig. 3.18 | Displaying the sum of two numbers input from the keyboard.

Lines 1–2

```
// Fig. 3.18: Addition.cs
// Displaying the sum of two numbers input from the keyboard.
```

state the figure number, file name and purpose of the application.

Line 5

```
public class Addition
```

begins the declaration of class Addition. Remember that the body of each class declaration starts with an opening left brace (line 6) and ends with a closing right brace (line 26).

The application begins execution with Main (lines 8–25). The left brace (line 9) marks the beginning of Main's body, and the corresponding right brace (line 25) marks the end of Main's body. Method Main is indented one level within the body of class Addition and the code in the body of Main is indented another level for readability.

Line 10

```
int number1; // declare first number to add
```

is a **variable declaration statement** (also called a **declaration**) that specifies the name
(number1) and type of a variable (int) used in this application. A **variable** is a location in
the computer's memory where a value can be stored for use later in an application. Variables are typically declared with a **name** and a **type** before they're used. A variable's name
enables the application to access the value of the variable in memory—the name can be
any valid identifier. (See Section 3.2 for identifier naming requirements.) A variable's type
specifies what kind of information is stored at that location in memory. Like other statements, declaration statements end with a semicolon (;).

The declaration in line 10 specifies that the variable named number1 is of type **int**—
it will hold **integer** values (whole numbers such as 7, –11, 0 and 31914). The range of values
for an int is –2,147,483,648 (int.MinValue) to +2,147,483,647 (int.MaxValue). We'll
soon discuss types **float**, **double** and **decimal**, for specifying real numbers, and type **char**,
for specifying characters. Real numbers contain decimal points, as in 3.4, 0.0 and –11.19.
Variables of type float and double store approximations of real numbers in memory.
Variables of type decimal store real numbers precisely (to 28–29 significant digits), so decimal variables are often used with monetary calculations. Variables of type char represent
individual characters, such as an uppercase letter (e.g., A), a digit (e.g., 7), a special character
(e.g., * or %) or an escape sequence (e.g., the newline character, \n). Types such as int,
float, double, decimal and char are often called **simple types**. Simple-type names are
keywords and must appear in all lowercase letters. Appendix B summarizes the characteristics of the simple types (bool, byte, sbyte, char, short, ushort, int, uint, long, ulong,
float, double and decimal).

The variable declaration statements at lines 11–12

```
int number2; // declare second number to add
int sum; // declare sum of number1 and number2
```

similarly declare variables number2 and sum to be of type int.

Variable declaration statements can be split over several lines, with the variable names
separated by commas (i.e., a comma-separated list of variable names). Several variables of
the same type may be declared in one declaration or in multiple declarations. For example,
lines 10–12 can also be written as follows:

```
int number1, // declare first number to add
    number2, // declare second number to add
    sum; // declare sum of number1 and number2
```

Good Programming Practice 3.7

Declare each variable on a separate line. This format allows a comment to be easily inserted next to each declaration.

Good Programming Practice 3.8

*Choosing meaningful variable names helps code to be **self-documenting** (i.e., one can understand the code simply by reading it rather than by reading documentation manuals or viewing an excessive number of comments).*

Good Programming Practice 3.9

*By convention, variable-name identifiers begin with a lowercase letter, and every word in the name after the first word begins with a capital letter. This naming convention is known as **lower camel casing**.*

Line 14

```
Console.Write( "Enter first integer: " ); // prompt user
```

uses `Console.Write` to display the message `"Enter first integer: "`. This message is called a **prompt** because it directs the user to take a specific action.

Line 16

```
number1 = Convert.ToInt32( Console.ReadLine() );
```

works in two steps. First, it calls the `Console`'s **ReadLine** method. This method waits for the user to type a string of characters at the keyboard and press the *Enter* key. As we mentioned, some methods perform a task then return the result of that task. In this case, `Read-Line` returns the text the user entered. Then, the `string` is used as an argument to class **Convert**'s **ToInt32** method, which converts this sequence of characters into data of type `int`. In this case, method `ToInt32` returns the `int` representation of the user's input.

Technically, the user can type anything as the input value. `ReadLine` will accept it and pass it off to the `ToInt32` method. This method assumes that the string contains a valid integer value. In this application, if the user types a noninteger value, a runtime logic error called an exception will occur and the application will terminate. C# offers a technology called exception handling that will help you make your applications more robust by enabling them to handle exceptions and continue executing. This is also known as making your application **fault tolerant**. We introduce exception handling in Section 8.4, then use it again in Chapter 10. We take a deeper look at exception handling in Chapter 13.

In line 16, the result of the call to method `ToInt32` (an `int` value) is placed in variable `number1` by using the **assignment operator**, `=`. The statement is read as "`number1` gets the value returned by `Convert.ToInt32`." Operator `=` is a **binary operator**, because it works on two pieces of information. These are known as its **operands**—in this case, the operands are `number1` and the result of the method call `Convert.ToInt32`. This statement is called an **assignment statement**, because it assigns a value to a variable. Everything to the right of the assignment operator, `=`, is always evaluated before the assignment is performed.

Good Programming Practice 3.10

Place spaces on either side of a binary operator to make it stand out and make the code more readable.

Line 18

```
Console.Write( "Enter second integer: " ); // prompt user
```

prompts the user to enter the second integer. Line 20

```
number2 = Convert.ToInt32( Console.ReadLine() );
```

reads a second integer and assigns it to the variable `number2`.

Line 22

```
sum = number1 + number2; // add numbers
```

calculates the sum of `number1` and `number2` and assigns the result to variable `sum` by using the assignment operator, `=`. The statement is read as "sum gets the value of `number1` + `number2`." Most calculations are performed in assignment statements. When `number1` + `number2` is encountered, the values stored in the variables are used in the calculation. The addition operator is a binary operator—its two **operands** are `number1` and `number2`. Portions of statements that contain calculations are called **expressions**. In fact, an expression is any portion of a statement that has a value associated with it. For example, the value of the expression `number1` + `number2` is the sum of the numbers. Similarly, the value of the expression `Console.ReadLine()` is the string of characters typed by the user.

After the calculation has been performed, line 24

```
Console.WriteLine( "Sum is {0}", sum ); // display sum
```

uses method `Console.WriteLine` to display the `sum`. The format item `{0}` is a placeholder for the first argument after the format string. Other than the `{0}` format item, the remaining characters in the format string are all fixed text. So method `WriteLine` displays "Sum is ", followed by the value of `sum` (in the position of the `{0}` format item) and a newline.

Calculations can also be performed inside output statements. We could have combined the statements in lines 22 and 24 into the statement

```
Console.WriteLine( "Sum is {0}", ( number1 + number2 ) );
```

The parentheses around the expression `number1` + `number2` are not required—they're included to emphasize that the value of the expression `number1` + `number2` is output in the position of the `{0}` format item.

3.7 Memory Concepts

Variable names such as `number1`, `number2` and `sum` actually correspond to **locations** in the computer's memory. Every variable has a **name**, a **type**, a **size** (determined by the type) and a **value**.

In the addition application of Fig. 3.18, when the statement (line 16)

```
number1 = Convert.ToInt32( Console.ReadLine() );
```

executes, the number typed by the user is placed into a **memory location** to which the name `number1` has been assigned by the compiler. Suppose that the user enters 45. The computer places that integer value into location `number1`, as shown in Fig. 3.19. Whenever a value is placed in a memory location, the value replaces the previous value in that location, and the previous value is lost.

number1	45

Fig. 3.19 | Memory location showing the name and value of variable `number1`.

When the statement (line 20)

```
number2 = Convert.ToInt32( Console.ReadLine() );
```

executes, suppose that the user enters 72. The computer places that integer value into location `number2`. The memory now appears as shown in Fig. 3.20.

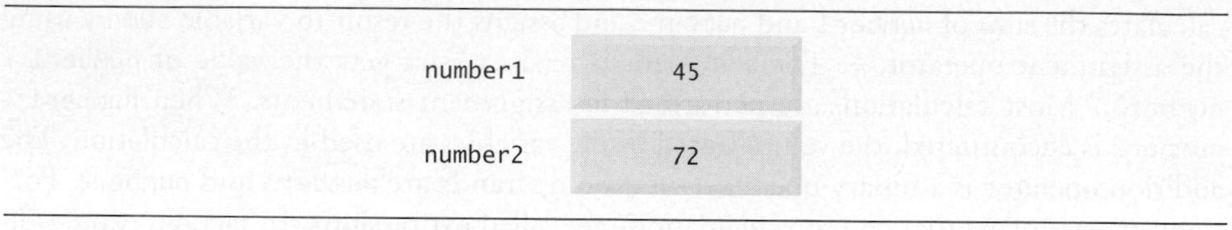

number1	45
number2	72

Fig. 3.20 | Memory locations after storing values for `number1` and `number2`.

After the application of Fig. 3.18 obtains values for `number1` and `number2`, it adds the values and places the sum into variable `sum`. The statement (line 22)

```
sum = number1 + number2; // add numbers
```

performs the addition, then replaces `sum`'s previous value. After `sum` has been calculated, memory appears as shown in Fig. 3.21. The values of `number1` and `number2` appear exactly as they did before they were used in the calculation of `sum`. These values were used, but not destroyed, as the computer performed the calculation—when a value is read from a memory location, the process is nondestructive.

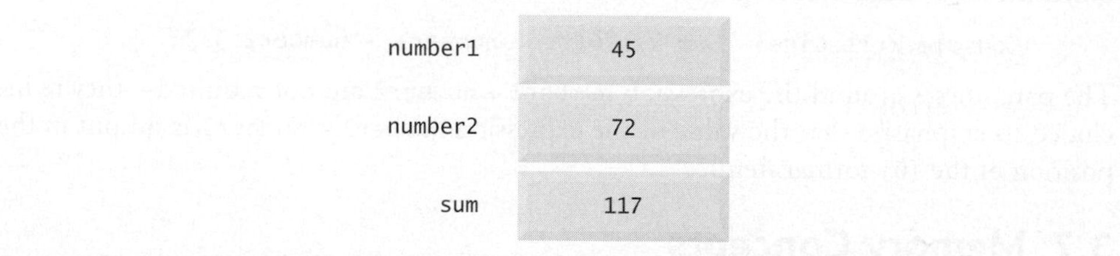

number1	45
number2	72
sum	117

Fig. 3.21 | Memory locations after calculating and storing the sum of `number1` and `number2`.

3.8 Arithmetic

Most applications perform arithmetic calculations. The **arithmetic operators** are summarized in Fig. 3.22. Note the various special symbols not used in algebra. The **asterisk (*)** indicates multiplication, and the **percent sign (%)** is the **remainder operator** (called modulus in some languages), which we'll discuss shortly. The arithmetic operators in Fig. 3.22 are binary operators—for example, the expression f + 7 contains the binary operator + and the two operands f and 7.

C# operation	Arithmetic operator	Algebraic expression	C# expression
Addition	+	$f + 7$	f + 7
Subtraction	−	$p - c$	p - c
Multiplication	*	$b \cdot m$	b * m
Division	/	x / y or $\frac{x}{y}$ or $x \div y$	x / y
Remainder	%	$r \bmod s$	r % s

Fig. 3.22 | Arithmetic operators.

If both operands of the division operator (/) are integers, **integer division** is performed and the result is an integer—for example, the expression 7 / 4 evaluates to 1, and the expression 17 / 5 evaluates to 3. Any fractional part in integer division is simply discarded (i.e., truncated)—no rounding occurs. C# provides the remainder operator, %, which yields the remainder after division. The expression x % y yields the remainder after x is divided by y. Thus, 7 % 4 yields 3, and 17 % 5 yields 2. This operator is most commonly used with integer operands but can also be used with floats, doubles, and decimals. In this chapter's exercises and in later chapters, we consider several interesting applications of the remainder operator, such as determining whether one number is a multiple of another.

Arithmetic expressions must be written in **straight-line form** to facilitate entering applications into the computer. Thus, expressions such as "a divided by b" must be written as a / b, so that all constants, variables and operators appear in a straight line. The following algebraic notation is generally not acceptable to compilers:

$$\frac{a}{b}$$

Parentheses are used to group terms in C# expressions in the same manner as in algebraic expressions. For example, to multiply a times the quantity b + c, we write

a * (b + c)

If an expression contains **nested parentheses**, such as

((a + b) * c)

the expression in the innermost set of parentheses (a + b in this case) is evaluated first.

C# applies the operators in arithmetic expressions in a precise sequence determined by the following **rules of operator precedence**, which are generally the same as those followed in algebra (Fig. 3.23). These rules enable C# to apply operators in the correct order.[1]

Operators	Operations	Order of evaluation (associativity)
Evaluated first		
*	Multiplication	If there are several operators of this type,
/	Division	they're evaluated from left to right.
%	Remainder	
Evaluated next		
+	Addition	If there are several operators of this type,
-	Subtraction	they're evaluated from left to right.

Fig. 3.23 | Precedence of arithmetic operators.

---

1. We discuss simple examples here to explain the order of evaluation of expressions. More subtle order of evaluation issues occur in the increasingly complex expressions you'll encounter later in the book. For more information, see the following blog posts from Microsoft's Eric Lippert: blogs.msdn.com/ericlippert/archive/2008/05/23/precedence-vs-associativity-vs-order.aspx and blogs.msdn.com/oldnewthing/archive/2007/08/14/4374222.aspx.

When we say that operators are applied from left to right, we're referring to their **associativity**. You'll see that some operators associate from right to left. Figure 3.23 summarizes these rules of operator precedence. The table will be expanded as additional operators are introduced. Appendix A provides the complete precedence chart.

Now let us consider several expressions in light of the rules of operator precedence. Each example lists an algebraic expression and its C# equivalent. The following is an example of an arithmetic mean (average) of five terms:

Algebra: $m = \dfrac{a + b + c + d + e}{5}$

C#:   m = (a + b + c + d + e) / 5;

The parentheses are required because division has higher precedence than addition. The entire quantity (a + b + c + d + e) is to be divided by 5. If the parentheses are erroneously omitted, we obtain a + b + c + d + e / 5, which evaluates as

$a + b + c + d + \dfrac{e}{5}$

The following is an example of the equation of a straight line:

Algebra: $y = mx + b$

C#:   y = m * x + b;

No parentheses are required. The multiplication operator is applied first, because multiplication has a higher precedence than addition. The assignment occurs last, because it has a lower precedence than multiplication or addition.

The following example contains remainder (%), multiplication, division, addition and subtraction operations:

Algebra: $z = pr\,\%q + w/x - y$

C#:   z = p * r % q + w / x - y;
        ⑥   ①   ②   ④   ③   ⑤

The circled numbers under the statement indicate the order in which C# applies the operators. The multiplication, remainder and division operations are evaluated first in left-to-right order (i.e., they associate from left to right), because they have higher precedence than addition and subtraction. The addition and subtraction operations are evaluated next. These operations are also applied from left to right.

To develop a better understanding of the rules of operator precedence, consider the evaluation of a second-degree polynomial ($y = ax^2 + bx + c$):

y = a * x * x + b * x + c;
       ⑥   ①   ②   ④   ③   ⑤

The circled numbers indicate the order in which C# applies the operators. The multiplication operations are evaluated first in left-to-right order (i.e., they associate from left to right), because they have higher precedence than addition. The addition operations are evaluated next and are applied from left to right. There's no arithmetic operator for exponentiation in C#, so x^2 is represented as x * x. Section 6.4 shows an alternative for performing exponentiation in C#.

Suppose that a, b, c and x in the preceding second-degree polynomial are initialized (given values) as follows: a = 2, b = 3, c = 7 and x = 5. Figure 3.24 illustrates the order in which the operators are applied.

Step 1.   y = 2 * 5 * 5 + 3 * 5 + 7;   *(Leftmost multiplication)*

2 * 5 is 10

Step 2.   y = 10 * 5 + 3 * 5 + 7;   *(Leftmost multiplication)*

10 * 5 is 50

Step 3.   y = 50 + 3 * 5 + 7;   *(Multiplication before addition)*

3 * 5 is 15

Step 4.   y = 50 + 15 + 7;   *(Leftmost addition)*

50 + 15 is 65

Step 5.   y = 65 + 7;   *(Last addition)*

65 + 7 is 72

Step 6.   y = 72   *(Last operation—place 72 in y)*

Fig. 3.24 | Order in which a second-degree polynomial is evaluated.

As in algebra, it's acceptable to place unnecessary parentheses in an expression to make the expression clearer. These are called **redundant parentheses**. For example, the preceding assignment statement might be parenthesized to highlight its terms as follows:

```
y = ( a * x * x ) + ( b * x ) + c;
```

3.9 Decision Making: Equality and Relational Operators

A **condition** is an expression that can be either **true** or **false**. This section introduces a simple version of C#'s **if statement** that allows an application to make a **decision** based on the value of a condition. For example, the condition "grade is greater than or equal to 60" determines whether a student passed a test. If the condition in an if statement is true, the body of the if statement executes. If the condition is false, the body does not execute. We'll see an example shortly.

Conditions in if statements can be formed by using the **equality operators** (== and !=) and **relational operators** (>, <, >= and <=) summarized in Fig. 3.25. The two equality operators (== and !=) each have the same level of precedence, the relational operators (>, <, >= and <=) each have the same level of precedence, and the equality operators have lower precedence than the relational operators. They all associate from left to right.

Standard algebraic equality and relational operators	C# equality or relational operator	Sample C# condition	Meaning of C# condition
Relational operators			
>	>	x > y	x is greater than y
<	<	x < y	x is less than y
≥	>=	x >= y	x is greater than or equal to y
≤	<=	x <= y	x is less than or equal to y
Equality operators			
=	==	x == y	x is equal to y
≠	!=	x != y	x is not equal to y

Fig. 3.25 | Relational and equality operators.

Common Programming Error 3.5

Confusing the equality operator, ==, with the assignment operator, =, can cause a logic error or a syntax error. The equality operator should be read as "is equal to," and the assignment operator should be read as "gets" or "gets the value of." To avoid confusion, some programmers read the equality operator as "double equals" or "equals equals."

Figure 3.26 uses six if statements to compare two integers entered by the user. If the condition in any of these if statements is true, the assignment statement associated with that if statement executes. The application uses class Console to prompt for and read two lines of text from the user, extracts the integers from that text with the ToInt32 method of class Convert, and stores them in variables number1 and number2. Then the application compares the numbers and displays the results of the comparisons that are true.

```
1   // Fig. 3.26: Comparison.cs
2   // Comparing integers using if statements, equality operators,
3   // and relational operators.
4   using System;
5
6   public class Comparison
7   {
8      // Main method begins execution of C# application
9      public static void Main( string[] args )
10     {
11        int number1; // declare first number to compare
12        int number2; // declare second number to compare
13
14        // prompt user and read first number
15        Console.Write( "Enter first integer: " );
16        number1 = Convert.ToInt32( Console.ReadLine() );
```

Fig. 3.26 | Comparing integers using if statements, equality operators and relational operators. (Part 1 of 2.)

```
17
18          // prompt user and read second number
19          Console.Write( "Enter second integer: " );
20          number2 = Convert.ToInt32( Console.ReadLine() );
21
22          if ( number1 == number2 )
23             Console.WriteLine( "{0} == {1}", number1, number2 );
24
25          if ( number1 != number2 )
26             Console.WriteLine( "{0} != {1}", number1, number2 );
27
28          if ( number1 < number2 )
29             Console.WriteLine( "{0} < {1}", number1, number2 );
30
31          if ( number1 > number2 )
32             Console.WriteLine( "{0} > {1}", number1, number2 );
33
34          if ( number1 <= number2 )
35             Console.WriteLine( "{0} <= {1}", number1, number2 );
36
37          if ( number1 >= number2 )
38             Console.WriteLine( "{0} >= {1}", number1, number2 );
39       } // end Main
40    } // end class Comparison
```

```
Enter first integer: 42
Enter second integer: 42
42 == 42
42 <= 42
42 >= 42
```

```
Enter first integer: 1000
Enter second integer: 2000
1000 != 2000
1000 < 2000
1000 <= 2000
```

```
Enter first integer: 2000
Enter second integer: 1000
2000 != 1000
2000 > 1000
2000 >= 1000
```

Fig. 3.26 | Comparing integers using if statements, equality operators and relational operators. (Part 2 of 2.)

The declaration of class Comparison begins at line 6

```
public class Comparison
```

The class's Main method (lines 9–39) begins the execution of the application.

Lines 11–12

```
int number1; // declare first number to compare
int number2; // declare second number to compare
```

declare the int variables used to store the values entered by the user.
Lines 14–16

```
// prompt user and read first number
Console.Write( "Enter first integer: " );
number1 = Convert.ToInt32( Console.ReadLine() );
```

prompt the user to enter the first integer and input the value. The input value is stored in variable number1. Lines 18–20

```
// prompt user and read second number
Console.Write( "Enter second integer: " );
number2 = Convert.ToInt32( Console.ReadLine() );
```

perform the same task, except that the input value is stored in variable number2.
Lines 22–23

```
if ( number1 == number2 )
    Console.WriteLine( "{0} == {1}", number1, number2 );
```

compare the values of the variables number1 and number2 to determine whether they're equal. An if statement always begins with keyword if, followed by a condition in parentheses. An if statement expects one statement in its body. The indentation of the body statement shown here is not required, but it improves the code's readability by emphasizing that the statement in line 23 is part of the if statement that begins in line 22. Line 23 executes only if the numbers stored in variables number1 and number2 are equal (i.e., the condition is true). The if statements in lines 25–26, 28–29, 31–32, 34–35 and 37–38 compare number1 and number2 with the operators !=, <, >, <= and >=, respectively. If the condition in any of the if statements is true, the corresponding body statement executes.

Common Programming Error 3.6

Omitting the left and/or right parentheses for the condition in an if statement is a syntax error—the parentheses are required.

Common Programming Error 3.7

Reversing the operators !=, >= and <=, as in =!, => and =<, can result in syntax or logic errors.

Common Programming Error 3.8

It is a syntax error if the operators ==, !=, >= and <= contain spaces between their symbols, as in = =, ! =, > = and < =, respectively.

Good Programming Practice 3.11

Indent an if statement's body to make it stand out and to enhance application readability.

There's no semicolon (;) at the end of the first line of each if statement. Such a semicolon would result in a logic error at execution time. For example,

```
if ( number1 == number2 ); // logic error
   Console.WriteLine( "{0} == {1}", number1, number2 );
```

would actually be interpreted by C# as

```
if ( number1 == number2 )
   ; // empty statement
Console.WriteLine( "{0} == {1}", number1, number2 );
```

where the semicolon in the line by itself—called the **empty statement**—is the statement to execute if the condition in the `if` statement is true. When the empty statement executes, no task is performed in the application. The application then continues with the output statement, which always executes, regardless of whether the condition is true or false, because the output statement is not part of the `if` statement.

Common Programming Error 3.9

Placing a semicolon immediately after the right parenthesis of the condition in an `if` statement is normally a logic error.

Note the use of whitespace in Fig. 3.26. Recall that whitespace characters, such as tabs, newlines and spaces, are normally ignored by the compiler. So statements may be split over several lines and may be spaced according to your preferences without affecting the meaning of an application. It's incorrect to split identifiers, strings, and multicharacter operators (like `>=`). Ideally, statements should be kept small, but this is not always possible.

Good Programming Practice 3.12

Place no more than one statement per line in an application. This format enhances readability.

Good Programming Practice 3.13

A lengthy statement can be spread over several lines. If a single statement must be split across lines, choose breaking points that make sense, such as after a comma in a comma-separated list, or after an operator in a lengthy expression. If a statement is split across two or more lines, indent all subsequent lines until the end of the statement.

Figure 3.27 shows the precedence of the operators introduced in this chapter. The operators are shown from top to bottom in decreasing order of precedence. All these operators, with the exception of the assignment operator, =, associate from left to right. Addition is left associative, so an expression like x + y + z is evaluated as if it had been written as (x + y) + z. The assignment operator, =, associates from right to left, so an expression like x = y = 0 is evaluated as if it had been written as x = (y = 0), which, as you'll soon see, first assigns the value 0 to variable y then assigns the result of that assignment, 0, to x.

Good Programming Practice 3.14

Refer to the operator precedence chart (the complete chart is in Appendix A) when writing expressions containing many operators. Confirm that the operations in the expression are performed in the order you expect. If you're uncertain about the order of evaluation in a complex expression, use parentheses to force the order, as you would do in algebraic expressions. Observe that some operators, such as assignment, =, associate from right to left rather than from left to right.

Operators			Associativity	Type
*	/	%	left to right	multiplicative
+	–		left to right	additive
<	<=	> >=	left to right	relational
==	!=		left to right	equality
=			right to left	assignment

Fig. 3.27 | Precedence and associativity of operations discussed.

3.10 Wrap-Up

You learned many important features of C# in this chapter, including displaying data on the screen in a **Command Prompt**, inputting data from the keyboard, performing calculations and making decisions. The applications presented here introduced you to basic programming concepts. As you'll see in Chapter 4, C# applications typically contain just a few lines of code in method Main—these statements normally create the objects that perform the work of the application. In Chapter 4, you'll learn how to implement your own classes and use objects of those classes in applications.

Summary

Section 3.2 A Simple C# Application: Displaying a Line of Text

- Programmers insert comments to document applications and improve their readability. The C# compiler ignores comments.
- A comment that begins with // is called a single-line comment, because it terminates at the end of the line on which it appears.
- Comments delimited by /* and */ can be spread over several lines.
- A programming language's syntax specifies rules for creating a proper application in that language.
- A using directive helps the compiler locate a class that is used in an application.
- C# provides a rich set of predefined classes that you can reuse rather than "reinventing the wheel." These classes are grouped into namespaces—named collections of classes.
- Collectively, C#'s predefined namespaces are referred to as the .NET Framework Class Library.
- Programmers use blank lines and space characters to make applications easier to read. Together, blank lines, space characters and tab characters are known as whitespace. Space characters and tabs are known specifically as whitespace characters. Whitespace is ignored by the compiler.
- Every application in C# consists of at least one class declaration that is defined by the programmer (also known as a user-defined class).
- Keywords are reserved for use by C# and are always spelled with all lowercase letters.
- Keyword class introduces a class declaration and is immediately followed by the class name.
- By convention, all class names in C# begin with a capital letter and capitalize the first letter of each word they include (e.g., SampleClassName). The is known as upper camel casing.
- A C# class name is an identifier—a series of characters consisting of letters, digits, and underscores (_) that does not begin with a digit and does not contain spaces.

- C# is case sensitive—that is, uppercase and lowercase letters are distinct.
- The body of every class declaration is delimited by braces, { and }.
- Method `Main` is the starting point of every C# application and is typically defined as:

  ```
  public static void Main( string[] args )
  ```

- Methods are able to perform tasks and can return information when they complete their tasks. Keyword `void` indicates that a method will perform a task but will not return any information.
- Statements instruct the computer to perform actions.
- A sequence of characters in double quotation marks is called a string, a character string, a message or a string literal.
- The `Console` class allows C# applications to read and display characters in the console window.
- Method `Console.WriteLine` displays its argument in the console window, followed by a newline character to position the screen cursor to the beginning of the next line.
- Most statements end with a semicolon.

Section 3.3 Creating a Simple Application in Visual C# Express
- Visual C# Express provides many ways to personalize your coding experience. You can modify the editor settings to display line numbers or set code indentation.
- As you type characters, in some contexts Visual C# Express highlights the first member that matches all the characters typed, then displays a tool tip containing a description of that member. This IDE feature is called *IntelliSense*.
- To execute an application, select **Debug > Start Without Debugging**.
- When you type a line of code and press *Enter*, the IDE either applies syntax-color highlighting or generates a syntax error.

Section 3.4 Modifying Your Simple C# Application
- `Console.Write` displays its argument and positions the screen cursor immediately after the last character displayed.
- C# combines a backslash (\) in a string with the next character in the string to form an escape sequence. The escape sequence \n (newline) positions the cursor on the next line.

Section 3.5 Formatting Text with `Console.Write` and `Console.WriteLine`
- The `Console.Write` and `Console.WriteLine` methods can also display formatted data.
- When a method requires multiple arguments, the arguments are separated with commas (,)—this is known as a comma-separated list.
- Method `Console.Write`'s first argument can be a format string that may consist of fixed text and format items. Fixed text is displayed normally. Each format item is a placeholder for a value.
- Format items are enclosed in curly braces and begin with a number that specifies an argument. The format item {0} is a placeholder for the first additional argument after the format string (because we start counting from 0), {1} is a placeholder for the second, and so on.

Section 3.6 Another C# Application: Adding Integers
- Integers are whole numbers, like –22, 7, 0 and 1024.
- A variable declaration statement specifies the name and type of a variable.
- A variable is a location in the computer's memory where a value can be stored for use later in an application. Variables are typically declared with a name and a type before they're used.

- A variable's name enables the application to access the value of the variable in memory. A variable name can be any valid identifier.

- Like other statements, variable declaration statements end with a semicolon (;).

- Type int is used to declare variables that will hold integer values. The range of values for an int is –2,147,483,648 to +2,147,483,647.

- Types float, double, and decimal specify real numbers, and type char specifies character data. Real numbers are numbers that may contain decimal points, such as 3.4, 0.0 and –11.19. Variables of type char data represent individual characters, such as an uppercase letter (e.g., A), a digit (e.g., 7), a special character (e.g., * or %) or an escape sequence (e.g., the newline character, \n).

- Types such as int, float, double, decimal, and char are often called simple types. Simple-type names are keywords; thus, they must appear in all lowercase letters.

- A prompt directs the user to take a specific action.

- Console method ReadLine obtains a line of text for use in an application.

- Convert method ToInt32 extracts an integer from a string of characters.

- The assignment operator, =, enables the application to give a value to a variable. Operator = is called a binary operator because it has two operands. An assignment statement uses an assignment operator to assign a value to a variable.

- Portions of statements that have values are called expressions.

Section 3.7 Memory Concepts
- Variable names correspond to locations in the computer's memory. Every variable has a name, a type, a size and a value.

- Whenever a value is placed in a memory location, the value replaces the previous value in that location. The previous value is lost.

Section 3.8 Arithmetic
- Most applications perform arithmetic calculations. The arithmetic operators are + (addition), - (subtraction), * (multiplication), / (division) and % (remainder).

- If both operands of the division operator (/) are integers, the result is an integer

- The remainder operator, %, yields the remainder after division.

- Arithmetic expressions in C# must be written in straight-line form.

- If an expression contains nested parentheses, the innermost set of parentheses is evaluated first.

- C# applies the operators in arithmetic expressions in a precise sequence determined by the rules of operator precedence.

- Associativity determines whether operators are applied from left to right or right to left.

- Redundant parentheses in an expression can make an expression clearer.

Section 3.9 Decision Making: Equality and Relational Operators
- A condition is an expression that can be either true or false. C#'s if statement allows an application to make a decision based on the value of a condition.

- Conditions in if statements can be formed by using the equality (== and !=) and relational (>, <, >= and <=) operators.

- An if statement always begins with keyword if, followed by a condition in parentheses, and expects one statement in its body.

- An empty statement is a statement that does not perform a task.

Terminology

addition operator (+)
application
argument
arithmetic operators (*, /, %, + and -)
assembly
assignment operator (=)
assignment statement
associativity of operators
backslash (\) escape character
binary operator
body of a class declaration
body of a method declaration
case sensitive
char simple type
character string
class declaration
class keyword
class name
code walkthrough
comma (,)
comma-separated list
Command Prompt
comment
compilation error
compiler error
compile-time error
condition
Console class
console window
Console.Write method
Console.WriteLine method
contextual keyword
Convert class
.cs file-name extension
decimal simple type
decision
delimited comment (/* */)
division operator (/)
.dll file-name extension
document an application
double simple type
dynamically linked library
empty statement (;)
equality operators
    == "is equal to"
    != "is not equal to"
Error List window
escape character
escape sequence

.exe file-name extension
executable
expressionS
fault tolerant
File Name property
fixed text in a format string
float simple type
format item
format string
Framework Class Library
identifier
if statement
int (integer) simple type
integer
integer division
Intellisense
left brace ({)
literal
location of a variable
lower camel casing
Main method
member of a class
memory location
message
method
multiplication operator (*)
namespace
nested parentheses
.NET documentation
.NET Framework Class Library
newline character (\n)
operand
operator precedence
Parameter Info window
parentheses ( )
perform an action
precedence of operators
prompt
public keyword
ReadLine method of class Console
redundant parentheses
relational operators
    < "is less than"
    <= "is less than or equal to"
    > "is greater than"
    >= "is greater than or equal to"
remainder operator (%)
reserved words
right brace (})

rules of operator precedence	**Tab** key
screen cursor	toInt32 method of Convert class
self-documenting program	upper camel casing
semicolon (;) statement terminator	user-defined class
simple type	using directive
single-line comment (//)	variable
standard input/output class (Console)	variable declaration
statement	variable declaration statement
straight-line form	variable name
string	variable size
string literal	variable type
subtraction operator (-)	variable value
syntax	void keyword
syntax color highlighting	whitespace
syntax error	whitespace characters

Self-Review Exercises

3.1 Fill in the blanks in each of the following statements:
  a) A(n) _____ begins the body of every method, and a(n) _____ ends the body of every method.
  b) Most statements end with a(n) _____.
  c) The _____ statement is used to make decisions.
  d) _____ begins a single-line comment.
  e) _____, _____ and _____ are called whitespace characters. Newline characters are also considered whitespace characters.
  f) _____ are reserved for use by C#.
  g) C# applications begin execution at method _____.
  h) Methods _____ and _____ display information in the console window.

3.2 State whether each of the following is *true* or *false*. If *false*, explain why.
  a) Comments cause the computer to display the text after the // on the screen when the application executes.
  b) C# considers the variables number and NuMbEr to be identical.
  c) The remainder operator (%) can be used only with integer operands.
  d) The arithmetic operators *, /, %, + and - all have the same level of precedence.

3.3 Write statements to accomplish each of the following tasks:
  a) Declare variables c, thisIsAVariable, q76354 and number to be of type int.
  b) Prompt the user to enter an integer.
  c) Input an integer and assign the result to int variable value.
  d) If the variable number is not equal to 7, display "The variable number is not equal to 7".
  e) Display "This is a C# application" on one line in the console window.
  f) Display "This is a C# application" on two lines in the console window. The first line should end with C#. Use method Console.WriteLine.
  g) Display "This is a C# application" on two lines in the console window. The first line should end with C#. Use method Console.WriteLine and two format items.

3.4 Identify and correct the errors in each of the following statements:
  a) if (c < 7);
        Console.WriteLine("c is less than 7");
  b) if (c => 7)
        Console.WriteLine("c is equal to or greater than 7");

3.5   Write declarations, statements or comments that accomplish each of the following tasks:

   a) State that an application will calculate the product of three integers.
   b) Declare the variables x, y, z and `result` to be of type `int`.
   c) Prompt the user to enter the first integer.
   d) Read the first integer from the user and store it in the variable x.
   e) Prompt the user to enter the second integer.
   f) Read the second integer from the user and store it in the variable y.
   g) Prompt the user to enter the third integer.
   h) Read the third integer from the user and store it in the variable z.
   i) Compute the product of the three integers contained in variables x, y and z, and assign the result to the variable `result`.
   j) Display the message `"Product is"`, followed by the value of the variable `result`.

3.6   Using the statements you wrote in Exercise 3.5, write a complete application that calculates and displays the product of three integers.

Answers to Self-Review Exercises

3.1   a) left brace ({), right brace (}). b) semicolon (;). c) `if`. d) `//`. e) Blank lines, space characters, tab characters. f) Keywords. g) `Main`. h) `Console.WriteLine` and `Console.Write`.

3.2   a) *False.* Comments do not cause any action to be performed when the application executes. They're used to document applications and improve their readability.
   b) *False.* C# is case sensitive, so these variables are distinct.
   c) *False.* The remainder operator also can be used with noninteger operands in C#.
   d) *False.* The operators *, / and % are on the same level of precedence, and the operators + and - are on a lower level of precedence.

3.3   a) `int c, thisIsAVariable, q76354, number;`
      or
      `int c;`
      `int thisIsAVariable;`
      `int q76354;`
      `int number;`
   b) `Console.Write( "Enter an integer: " );`
   c) `value = Convert.ToInt32( Console.ReadLine() );`
   d) `if ( number != 7 )`
      `    Console.WriteLine( "The variable number is not equal to 7" );`
   e) `Console.WriteLine( "This is a C# application" );`
   f) `Console.WriteLine( "This is a C#\napplication" );`
   g) `Console.WriteLine( "{0}\n{1}", "This is a C#", "application" );`

3.4   a) *Error:* Semicolon after the right parenthesis of the condition (c < 7) in the `if` statement.
      Correction: Remove the semicolon after the right parenthesis. [*Note*: As a result, the output statement will execute regardless of whether the condition in the `if` is true.]
   b) *Error:* The relational operator => is incorrect.
      Correction: Change => to >=.

3.5   a) `// Calculating the product of three integers`
   b) `int x, y, z, result;`
      or
      `int x;`
      `int y;`
      `int z;`
      `int result;`

c) Console.Write("Enter first integer: ");
d) x = Convert.ToInt32(Console.ReadLine());
e) Console.Write("Enter second integer: ");
f) y = Convert.ToInt32(Console.ReadLine());
g) Console.Write("Enter third integer: ");
h) z = Convert.ToInt32(Console.ReadLine());
i) result = x * y * z;
j) Console.WriteLine("Product is {0}", result);

3.6   The solution to Self-Review Exercise 3.6 is as follows:

```
1   // Exercise 3.6: Product.cs
2   // Calculating the product of three integers.
3   using System;
4
5   public class Product
6   {
7      public static void Main( string[] args )
8      {
9         int x; // stores first number to be entered by user
10        int y; // stores second number to be entered by user
11        int z; // stores third number to be entered by user
12        int result; // product of numbers
13
14        Console.Write( "Enter first integer: " ); // prompt for input
15        x = Convert.ToInt32( Console.ReadLine() ); // read first integer
16
17        Console.Write( "Enter second integer: " ); // prompt for input
18        y = Convert.ToInt32( Console.ReadLine() ); // read second integer
19
20        Console.Write( "Enter third integer: " ); // prompt for input
21        z = Convert.ToInt32( Console.ReadLine() ); // read third integer
22
23        result = x * y * z; // calculate the product of the numbers
24
25        Console.WriteLine( "Product is {0}", result );
26     } // end Main
27  } // end class Product
```

```
Enter first integer: 10
Enter second integer: 20
Enter third integer: 30
Product is 6000
```

Exercises

3.7   Fill in the blanks in each of the following statements:
a) _____ are used to document an application and improve its readability.
b) A decision can be made in a C# application with a(n) _____.
c) Calculations are normally performed by _____ statements.
d) The arithmetic operators with the same precedence as multiplication are _____ and
_____.
e) When parentheses in an arithmetic expression are nested, the _____ set of parentheses is evaluated first.
f) A location in the computer's memory that may contain different values at various times throughout the execution of an application is called a(n) _____.

3.8   Write C# statements that accomplish each of the following tasks:
  a) Display the message `"Enter an integer: "`, leaving the cursor on the same line.
  b) Assign the product of variables b and c to variable a.
  c) State that an application performs a simple payroll calculation (i.e., use text that helps to document an application).

3.9   State whether each of the following is *true* or *false*. If *false*, explain why.
  a) C# operators are evaluated from left to right.
  b) The following are all valid variable names: `_under_bar_`, `m928134`, `t5`, `j7`, `her_sales`, `his_account_total`, `a`, `b`, `c`, `z` and `z2`.
  c) A valid C# arithmetic expression with no parentheses is evaluated from left to right.
  d) The following are all invalid variable names: `3g`, `87`, `67h2`, `h22` and `2h`.

3.10   Assuming that x = 2 and y = 3, what does each of the following statements display?
  a) `Console.WriteLine( "x = {0}", x );`
  b) `Console.WriteLine( "Value of {0} + {0} is {1}", x, ( x + x ) );`
  c) `Console.Write( "x =" );`
  d) `Console.WriteLine( "{0} = {1}", ( x + y ), ( y + x ) );`

3.11   Which of the following C# statements contain variables whose values are modified?
  a) `p = i + j + k + 7;`
  b) `Console.WriteLine( "variables whose values are modified" );`
  c) `Console.WriteLine( "a = 5" );`
  d) `value = Convert.ToInt32( Console.ReadLine() );`

3.12   Given that $y = ax^3 + 7$, which of the following are correct C# statements for this equation?
  a) `y = a * x * x * x + 7;`
  b) `y = a * x * x * ( x + 7 );`
  c) `y = ( a * x ) * x * ( x + 7 );`
  d) `y = ( a * x ) * x * x + 7;`
  e) `y = a * ( x * x * x ) + 7;`
  f) `y = a * x * ( x * x + 7 );`

3.13   *(Order of Evaluation)* State the order of evaluation of the operators in each of the following C# statements and show the value of x after each statement is performed:
  a) `x = 7 + 3 * 6 / 2 - 1;`
  b) `x = 2 % 2 + 2 * 2 - 2 / 2;`
  c) `x = ( 3 * 9 * ( 3 + ( 9 * 3 / ( 3 ) ) ) );`

3.14   *(Printing)* Write an application that displays the numbers 1 to 4 on the same line, with each pair of adjacent numbers separated by one space. Write the application using the following techniques:
  a) Use one `Console.WriteLine` statement.
  b) Use four `Console.Write` statements.
  c) Use one `Console.WriteLine` statement with four format items.

3.15   *(Arithmetic)* Write an application that asks the user to enter two integers, obtains them from the user and displays their sum, product, difference and quotient (division). Use the techniques shown in Fig. 3.18.

3.16   *(Comparing Integers)* Write an application that asks the user to enter two integers, obtains them from the user and displays the larger number followed by the words `"is larger"`. If the numbers are equal, display the message `"These numbers are equal."` Use the techniques shown in Fig. 3.26.

3.17   *(Arithmetic, Smallest and Largest)* Write an application that inputs three integers from the user and displays the sum, average, product, and smallest and largest of the numbers. Use the techniques from Fig. 3.26. [*Note:* The average calculation in this exercise should result in an integer representation of the average. So, if the sum of the values is 7, the average should be 2, not 2.3333….]

3.18 *(Displaying Shapes with Asterisks)* Write an application that displays a box, an oval, an arrow and a diamond using asterisks (*), as follows:

```
*********        ***        *           *
*       *       *   *       *          * *
*       *      *     *    *****        *   *
*       *      *     *      *         *     *
*       *      *     *      *        *       *
*       *      *     *      *         *     *
*       *      *     *      *          *   *
*       *       *   *       *           * *
*********        ***        *            *
```

3.19 What does the following code display?

```
Console.WriteLine( "*\n**\n***\n****\n*****" );
```

3.20 What does the following code display?

```
Console.WriteLine( "*" );
Console.WriteLine( "***" );
Console.WriteLine( "*****" );
Console.WriteLine( "****" );
Console.WriteLine( "**" );
```

3.21 What does the following code display?

```
Console.Write( "*" );
Console.Write( "***" );
Console.Write( "*****" );
Console.Write( "****" );
Console.WriteLine( "**" );
```

3.22 What does the following code display?

```
Console.Write( "*" );
Console.WriteLine( "***" );
Console.WriteLine( "*****" );
Console.Write( "****" );
Console.WriteLine( "**" );
```

3.23 What does the following code display?

```
Console.WriteLine( "{0}\n{1}\n{2}", "*", "***", "*****" );
```

3.24 *(Odd or Even)* Write an application that reads an integer, then determines and displays whether it's odd or even. [*Hint:* Use the remainder operator. An even number is a multiple of 2. Any multiple of 2 leaves a remainder of 0 when divided by 2.]

3.25 *(Multiples)* Write an application that reads two integers, determines whether the first is a multiple of the second and displays the result. [*Hint:* Use the remainder operator.]

3.26 *(Diameter, Circumference and Area of a Circle)* Here's a peek ahead. In this chapter, you have learned about integers and the type int. C# can also represent floating-point numbers that contain decimal points, such as 3.14159. Write an application that inputs from the user the radius of a circle as an integer and displays the circle's diameter, circumference and area using the floating-point value 3.14159 for π. Use the techniques shown in Fig. 3.18. [*Note:* You may also use the predefined constant Math.PI for the value of π. This constant is more precise than the value 3.14159. Class Math is defined in namespace System]. Use the following formulas (*r* is the radius):

$$diameter = 2r$$
$$circumference = 2\pi r$$
$$area = \pi r^2$$

Don't store each calculation's result in a variable. Rather, specify each calculation as the value to be output in a `Console.WriteLine` statement. The values produced by the circumference and area calculations are floating-point numbers. You'll learn more about floating-point numbers in Chapter 4.

3.27 *(Integer Equivalent of a Character)* Here's another peek ahead. In this chapter, you have learned about integers and the type `int`. C# can also represent uppercase letters, lowercase letters and a considerable variety of special symbols. Every character has a corresponding integer representation. The set of characters a computer uses and the corresponding integer representations for those characters is called that computer's character set. You can indicate a character value in an application simply by enclosing that character in single quotes, as in `'A'`.

You can determine the integer equivalent of a character by preceding that character with `(int)`, as in

```
(int) 'A'
```

The keyword `int` in parentheses is known as a cast operator, and the entire expression is called a cast expression. (You'll learn about cast operators in Chapter 5.) The following statement outputs a character and its integer equivalent:

```
Console.WriteLine( "The character {0} has the value {1}",
    'A', ( ( int ) 'A' ) );
```

When the preceding statement executes, it displays the character A and the value 65 (from the Unicode® character set) as part of the string.

Using statements similar to the one shown earlier in this exercise, write an application that displays the integer equivalents of some uppercase letters, lowercase letters, digits and special symbols. Display the integer equivalents of the following: A B C a b c 0 1 2 $ * + / and the space character.

3.28 *(Digits of an Integer)* Write an application that inputs one number consisting of five digits from the user, separates the number into its individual digits and displays the digits separated from one another by three spaces each. For example, if the user types in the number 42339, the application should display

```
4   2   3   3   9
```

Assume that the user enters the correct number of digits. What happens when you execute the application and type a number with more than five digits? What happens when you execute the application and type a number with fewer than five digits? [*Hint:* It's possible to do this exercise with the techniques you learned in this chapter. You'll need to use both division and remainder operations to "pick off" each digit.]

3.29 *(Table of Squares and Cubes)* Using only the programming techniques you learned in this chapter, write an application that calculates the squares and cubes of the numbers from 0 to 10 and displays the resulting values in table format, as shown below. All calculations should be done in terms of a variable x. [*Note:* This application does not require any input from the user.]

```
number  square  cube
0       0       0
1       1       1
2       4       8
3       9       27
4       16      64
5       25      125
6       36      216
7       49      343
8       64      512
9       81      729
10      100     1000
```

3.30 *(Counting Negative, Positive and Zero Values)* Write an application that inputs five numbers and determines and displays the number of negative numbers input, the number of positive numbers input and the number of zeros input.

Making a Difference Exercises

3.31 *(Body Mass Index Calculator)* We introduced the body mass index (BMI) calculator in Exercise 1.19. The formulas for calculating the BMI are

$$BMI = \frac{weightInPounds \times 703}{heightInInches \times heightInInches}$$

or

$$BMI = \frac{weightInKilograms}{heightInMeters \times heightInMeters}$$

Create a BMI calculator application that reads the user's weight in pounds and height in inches (or, if you prefer, the user's weight in kilograms and height in meters), then calculates and displays the user's body mass index. The application should also display the following information from the Department of Health and Human Services/National Institutes of Health so the user can evaluate his/her BMI:

```
BMI VALUES
Underweight: less than 18.5
Normal:      between 18.5 and 24.9
Overweight:  between 25 and 29.9
Obese:       30 or greater
```

3.32 *(Car-Pool Savings Calculator)* Research several car-pooling websites. Create an application that calculates your daily driving cost, so that you can estimate how much money could be saved by car pooling, which also has other advantages such as reducing carbon emissions and reducing traffic congestion. The application should input the following information and display the user's cost per day of driving to work:

    a) Total miles driven per day.
    b) Cost per gallon of gasoline (in cents).
    c) Average miles per gallon.
    d) Parking fees per day (in cents).
    e) Tolls per day (in cents).

Introduction to Classes, Objects, Methods and **string**s

4

Nothing can have value without being an object of utility.
—Karl Marx

Your public servants serve you right.
—Adlai E. Stevenson

You'll see something new. Two things. And I call them Thing One and Thing Two.
—Dr. Theodor Seuss Geisel

Objectives

In this chapter you'll learn:

- How to declare a class and use it to create an object.

- How to implement a class's behaviors as methods.

- How to implement a class's attributes as instance variables and properties.

- How to call an object's methods to make them perform their tasks.

- What instance variables of a class and local variables of a method are.

- How to use a constructor to initialize an object's data.

4.1 Introduction

In this chapter, we begin by explaining the concept of classes using a real-world example. Then we present five complete working applications to demonstrate how to create and use your own classes. The first four begin our case study on developing a grade book class that instructors can use to maintain student test scores. The last example introduces the type decimal and uses it to declare monetary amounts in the context of a bank account class that maintains a customer's balance.

4.2 Classes, Objects, Methods, Properties and Instance Variables

Let's begin with a simple analogy to help you understand classes and their contents. Suppose you want to drive a car and make it go faster by pressing down on its accelerator pedal. What must happen before you can do this? Well, before you can drive a car, someone has to design it. A car typically begins as engineering drawings, similar to the blueprints used to design a house. These engineering drawings include the design for an accelerator pedal to make the car go faster. The pedal "hides" the complex mechanisms that actually make the car go faster, just as the brake pedal "hides" the mechanisms that slow the car and the steering wheel "hides" the mechanisms that turn the car. This enables people with little or no knowledge of how engines work to drive a car easily.

Unfortunately, you can't drive the engineering drawings of a car. Before you can drive a car, it must be built from the engineering drawings that describe it. A completed car will have an actual accelerator pedal to make the car go faster, but even that's not enough—the car will not accelerate on its own, so the driver must press the accelerator pedal.

Methods

Now let's use our car example to introduce the key programming concepts of this section. Performing a task in an application requires a method. The **method** describes the mechanisms that actually perform its tasks. The method hides from its user the complex tasks that it performs, just as the accelerator pedal of a car hides from the driver the complex mechanisms of making the car go faster.

Classes
In C#, we begin by creating an application unit called a **class** to house (among other things) a method, just as a car's engineering drawings house (among other things) the design of an accelerator pedal. In a class, you provide one or more methods that are designed to perform the class's tasks. For example, a class that represents a bank account might contain one method to deposit money in an account, another to withdraw money from an account and a third to inquire what the current account balance is.

Objects
Just as you cannot drive an engineering drawing of a car, you cannot "drive" a class. Just as someone has to build a car from its engineering drawings before you can actually drive it, you must build an **object** of a class before you can make an application perform the tasks the class describes. That's one reason C# is known as an object-oriented programming language.

Method Calls
When you drive a car, pressing its gas pedal sends a message to the car to perform a task— make the car go faster. Similarly, you send **messages** to an object—each message is known as a **method call** and tells a method of the object to perform its task.

Attributes
Thus far, we've used the car analogy to introduce classes, objects and methods. In addition to a car's capabilities, it also has many **attributes**, such as its color, the number of doors, the amount of gas in its tank, its current speed and its total miles driven (i.e., its odometer reading). Like the car's capabilities, these attributes are represented as part of a car's design in its engineering diagrams. As you drive a car, these attributes are always associated with the car. Every car maintains its own attributes. For example, each car knows how much gas is in its own gas tank, but not how much is in the tanks of other cars. Similarly, an object has attributes that are carried with the object as it's used in an application. These attributes are specified as part of the object's class. For example, a bank-account object has a balance attribute that represents the amount of money in the account. Each bank-account object knows the balance in the account it represents, but not the balances of the other accounts in the bank. Attributes are specified by the class's **instance variables**.

Properties, Get Accessors and Set Accessors
Notice that these attributes are not necessarily accessible directly. The car manufacturer does not want drivers to take apart the car's engine to observe the amount of gas in its tank. Instead, the driver can check the fuel gauge on the dashboard. The bank does not want its customers to walk into the vault to count the amount of money in an account. Instead, the customers talk to a bank teller or check personalized online bank accounts. Similarly, you do not need to have access to an object's instance variables in order to use them. You can use the **properties** of an object. Properties contain **get accessors** for reading the values of variables, and **set accessors** for storing values into them.

4.3 Declaring a Class with a Method and Instantiating an Object of a Class

We begin with an example that consists of classes GradeBook (Fig. 4.1) and GradeBook-Test (Fig. 4.2). Class GradeBook (declared in file GradeBook.cs) will be used to display a message on the screen (Fig. 4.2) welcoming the instructor to the grade-book application. Class GradeBookTest (declared in the file GradeBookTest.cs) is a testing class in which the Main method will create and use an object of class GradeBook. By convention, we declare classes GradeBook and GradeBookTest in separate files, such that each file's name matches the name of the class it contains.

To start, select **File > New Project...** to open the **New Project** dialog, then create a GradeBook **Console Application**. Rename the Program.cs file to GradeBook.cs. Delete all the code provided automatically by the IDE and replace it with the code in Fig. 4.1.

Class *GradeBook*

The GradeBook **class declaration** (Fig. 4.1) contains a DisplayMessage method (lines 8–11) that displays a message on the screen. Line 10 of the class displays the message. Recall that a class is like a blueprint—we need to make an object of this class and call its method to get line 10 to execute and display its message—we do this in Fig. 4.2.

```
1   // Fig. 4.1: GradeBook.cs
2   // Class declaration with one method.
3   using System;
4
5   public class GradeBook
6   {
7      // display a welcome message to the GradeBook user
8      public void DisplayMessage()
9      {
10         Console.WriteLine( "Welcome to the Grade Book!" );
11      } // end method DisplayMessage
12   } // end class GradeBook
```

Fig. 4.1 | Class declaration with one method.

The class declaration begins in line 5. The keyword public is an **access modifier**. Access modifiers determine the accessibility of an object's properties and methods to other methods in an application. For now, we simply declare every class public. Every class declaration contains keyword class followed by the class's name. Every class's body is enclosed in a pair of left and right braces ({ and }), as in lines 6 and 12 of class GradeBook.

In Chapter 3, each class we declared had one method named Main. Class GradeBook also has one method—DisplayMessage (lines 8–11). Recall that Main is a special method that's always called automatically when you execute an application. Most methods do not get called automatically. As you'll soon see, you must call method DisplayMessage to tell it to perform its task.

The method declaration begins with keyword public to indicate that the method is "available to the public"—that is, it can be called from outside the class declaration's body by methods of other classes. Keyword void—known as the method's **return type**—indicates that this method will *not* return (i.e., give back) any information to its **calling method** when it completes its task. When a method that specifies a return type other than void is called and completes its task, the method returns a result to its calling method. For example, when you go to an automated teller machine (ATM) and request your account balance, you expect the ATM to give you back a value that represents your balance. If you have a method Square that returns the square of its argument, you'd expect the statement

```
    int result = Square( 2 );
```

to return 4 from method Square and assign 4 to variable result. If you have a method Maximum that returns the largest of three integer arguments, you'd expect the statement

```
    int biggest = Maximum( 27, 114, 51 );
```

to return the value 114 from method Maximum and assign the value to variable biggest. You've already used methods that return information—for example, in Chapter 3 you used Console method ReadLine to input a string typed by the user at the keyboard. When ReadLine inputs a value, it *returns* that value for use in the application.

The name of the method, DisplayMessage, follows the return type (line 8). Generally, methods are named as *verbs* or *verb phrases* while classes are named as *nouns*. By convention, method names begin with an uppercase first letter, and all subsequent words in the name begin with an uppercase letter. This naming convention is referred to as Pascal case. The parentheses after the method name indicate that this is a method. An empty set of parentheses, as shown in line 8, indicates that this method does *not* require additional information to perform its task. Line 8 is commonly referred to as the **method header**. Every method's body is delimited by left and right braces, as in lines 9 and 11.

The body of a method contains statements that perform the method's task. In this case, the method contains one statement (line 10) that displays the message "Welcome to the Grade Book!", followed by a newline in the console window. After this statement executes, the method has completed its task.

Next, we'd like to use class GradeBook in an application. As you learned in Chapter 3, method Main begins the execution of every application. Class GradeBook cannot begin an application because it does not contain Main. This was not a problem in Chapter 3, because every class you declared had a Main method. To fix this problem for the Grade-Book, we must either declare a separate class that contains a Main method or place a Main method in class GradeBook. To help you prepare for the larger applications you'll encounter later in this book and in industry, we use a separate class (GradeBookTest in this example) containing method Main to test each new class we create in this chapter.

Adding a Class to a Visual C# Project

For each example in this chapter, you'll add a class to your console application. To do this, right click the project name in the **Solution Explorer** and select **Add > New Item...** from the pop-up menu. In the **Add New Item** dialog that appears, select **Code File**, enter the name of your new file (GradeBookTest.cs) then click the **Add** button. A new blank file will be added to your project. Add the code from Fig. 4.2 to this file.

Class *GradeBookTest*

The GradeBookTest class declaration (Fig. 4.2) contains the Main method that controls our application's execution. Any class that contains a Main method (as shown in line 6) can be used to execute an application. This class declaration begins in line 3 and ends in line 14. The class contains only a Main method, which is typical of many classes that simply begin an application's execution.

Lines 6–13 declare method Main. A key part of enabling the method Main to begin the application's execution is the static keyword (line 6), which indicates that Main is a static method. A static method is special because it can be called without first creating an object of the class (in this case, `GradeBookTest`) in which the method is declared. We explain `static` methods in Chapter 7, Methods: A Deeper Look.

```
 1   // Fig. 4.2: GradeBookTest.cs
 2   // Create a GradeBook object and call its DisplayMessage method.
 3   public class GradeBookTest
 4   {
 5      // Main method begins program execution
 6      public static void Main( string[] args )
 7      {
 8         // create a GradeBook object and assign it to myGradeBook
 9         GradeBook myGradeBook = new GradeBook();
10
11         // call myGradeBook's DisplayMessage method
12         myGradeBook.DisplayMessage();
13      } // end Main
14   } // end class GradeBookTest
```

```
Welcome to the Grade Book!
```

Fig. 4.2 | Create a `GradeBook` object and call its `DisplayMessage` method.

In this application, we'd like to call class `GradeBook`'s `DisplayMessage` method to display the welcome message in the console window. Typically, you cannot call a method that belongs to another class until you create an object of that class, as shown in line 9. We begin by declaring variable `myGradeBook`. The variable's type is `GradeBook`—the class we declared in Fig. 4.1. Each new class you create becomes a new type in C# that can be used to declare variables and create objects. New class types will be accessible to all classes in the same project. You can declare new class types as needed; this is one reason why C# is known as an **extensible language**.

Variable `myGradeBook` (line 9) is initialized with the result of the **object-creation expression** `new GradeBook()`. The new operator creates a new object of the class specified to the right of the keyword (i.e., `GradeBook`). The parentheses to the right of the Grade-Book are required. As you'll learn in Section 4.10, those parentheses in combination with a class name represent a call to a constructor, which is similar to a method, but is used only at the time an object is created to initialize the object's data. In that section you'll see that data can be placed in parentheses to specify initial values for the object's data. For now, we simply leave the parentheses empty.

We can now use `myGradeBook` to call its method `DisplayMessage`. Line 12 calls the method `DisplayMessage` (lines 8–11 of Fig. 4.1) using variable `myGradeBook` followed by a **member access (.) operator**, the method name `DisplayMessage` and an empty set of parentheses. This call causes the `DisplayMessage` method to perform its task. This method call differs from the method calls in Chapter 3 that displayed information in a console window—each of those method calls provided arguments that specified the data to display. At the beginning of line 12, "`myGradeBook.`" indicates that `Main` should use the `GradeBook` object that was created in line 9. The empty parentheses in line 8 of Fig. 4.1 indicate that method `DisplayMessage` does not require additional information to perform its task. For this reason, the method call (line 12 of Fig. 4.2) specifies an empty set of parentheses after the method name to indicate that no arguments are being passed to method DisplayMessage. When method DisplayMessage completes its task, method Main continues executing at line 13. This is the end of method Main, so the application terminates.

*UML Class Diagram for Class **GradeBook***

Figure 4.3 presents a **UML class diagram** for class GradeBook of Fig. 4.1. Recall from Section 1.15 that the UML is a graphical language used by programmers to represent their object-oriented systems in a standardized manner. In the UML, each class is modeled in a class diagram as a rectangle with three compartments. The top compartment contains the name of the class centered horizontally in boldface type. The middle compartment contains the class's attributes, which correspond to instance variables and properties in C#. In Fig. 4.3, the middle compartment is empty because the version of class GradeBook in Fig. 4.1 does not have any attributes. The bottom compartment contains the class's operations, which correspond to methods in C#. The UML models operations by listing the operation name followed by a set of parentheses. Class GradeBook has one method, DisplayMessage, so the bottom compartment of Fig. 4.3 lists one operation with this name. Method DisplayMessage does not require additional information to perform its tasks, so there are empty parentheses following DisplayMessage in the class diagram, just as they appeared in the method's declaration in line 8 of Fig. 4.1. The plus sign (+) in front of the operation name indicates that DisplayMessage is a public operation in the UML (i.e., a public method in C#). The plus sign is sometimes called the **public visibility symbol**. We'll often use UML class diagrams to summarize a class's attributes and operations.

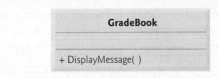

Fig. 4.3 | UML class diagram indicating that class GradeBook has a public DisplayMessage operation.

4.4 Declaring a Method with a Parameter

In our car analogy from Section 4.2, we discussed the fact that pressing a car's gas pedal sends a message to the car to perform a task—make the car go faster. But how fast should the car accelerate? As you know, the farther down you press the pedal, the faster the car accelerates. So the message to the car actually includes both the task to be performed and additional information that helps the car perform the task. This additional information is known as a **parameter**—the value of the parameter helps the car determine how fast to accelerate. Similarly, a method can require one or more parameters that represent additional information it needs to perform its task. A method call supplies values—called arguments—for each of the method's parameters. For example, the Console.WriteLine method requires an argument that specifies the data to be displayed in a console window. Similarly, to make a deposit into a bank account, a Deposit method specifies a parameter that represents the deposit amount. When the Deposit method is called, an argument value representing the deposit amount is assigned to the method's parameter. The method then makes a deposit of that amount, by increasing the account's balance.

Our next example declares class GradeBook (Fig. 4.4) with a `DisplayMessage` method that displays the course name as part of the welcome message. (See the sample execution in Fig. 4.5.) The new `DisplayMessage` method requires a parameter that represents the course name to output.

```
1   // Fig. 4.4: GradeBook.cs
2   // Class declaration with a method that has a parameter.
3   using System;
4
5   public class GradeBook
6   {
7      // display a welcome message to the GradeBook user
8      public void DisplayMessage( string courseName )
9      {
10         Console.WriteLine( "Welcome to the grade book for\n{0}!",
11            courseName );
12      } // end method DisplayMessage
13   } // end class GradeBook
```

Fig. 4.4 | Class declaration with a method that has a parameter.

Before discussing the new features of class GradeBook, let's see how the new class is used from the Main method of class GradeBookTest (Fig. 4.5). Line 12 creates an object of class GradeBook and assigns it to variable myGradeBook. Line 15 prompts the user to enter a course name. Line 16 reads the name from the user and assigns it to the variable nameOfCourse, using Console method ReadLine to perform the input. The user types the course name and presses *Enter* to submit the course name to the application. Pressing *Enter* inserts a newline character at the end of the characters typed by the user. Method ReadLine reads characters typed by the user until the newline character is encountered, then returns a string containing the characters up to, but not including, the newline. The newline character is discarded.

```
1   // Fig. 4.5: GradeBookTest.cs
2   // Create a GradeBook object and pass a string to
3   // its DisplayMessage method.
4   using System;
5
6   public class GradeBookTest
7   {
8      // Main method begins program execution
9      public static void Main( string[] args )
10      {
11         // create a GradeBook object and assign it to myGradeBook
12         GradeBook myGradeBook = new GradeBook();
13
```

Fig. 4.5 | Create GradeBook object and pass a string to its DisplayMessage method. (Part 1 of 2.)

```
14          // prompt for and input course name
15          Console.WriteLine( "Please enter the course name:" );
16          string nameOfCourse = Console.ReadLine(); // read a line of text
17          Console.WriteLine(); // output a blank line
18
19          // call myGradeBook's DisplayMessage method
20          // and pass nameOfCourse as an argument
21          myGradeBook.DisplayMessage( nameOfCourse );
22       } // end Main
23    } // end class GradeBookTest
```

```
Please enter the course name:
CS101 Introduction to C# Programming

Welcome to the grade book for
CS101 Introduction to C# Programming!
```

Fig. 4.5 | Create GradeBook object and pass a string to its DisplayMessage method. (Part 2 of 2.)

Line 21 calls myGradeBook's DisplayMessage method. The variable nameOfCourse in parentheses is the argument that's passed to method DisplayMessage so that the method can perform its task. Variable nameOfCourse's value in Main becomes the value of method DisplayMessage's parameter courseName in line 8 of Fig. 4.4. When you execute this application, notice that method DisplayMessage outputs as part of the welcome message the name you type (Fig. 4.5).

Software Engineering Observation 4.1

Normally, objects are created with new. One exception is a string literal that's contained in quotes, such as "hello". String literals are references to string objects that are implicitly created by C#.

More on Arguments and Parameters

When you declare a method, you must specify in the method's declaration whether the method requires data to perform its task. To do so, you place additional information in the method's **parameter list**, which is located in the parentheses that follow the method name. The parameter list may contain any number of parameters, including none at all. Each parameter is declared as a variable with a type and identifier in the parameter list. Empty parentheses following the method name (as in Fig. 4.1, line 8) indicate that a method does not require any parameters. In Fig. 4.4, DisplayMessage's parameter list (line 8) declares that the method requires one parameter. Each parameter must specify a type and an identifier. In this case, the type string and the identifier courseName indicate that method DisplayMessage requires a string to perform its task. At the time the method is called, the argument value in the call is assigned to the corresponding parameter (in this case, courseName) in the method header. Then, the method body uses the parameter courseName to access the value. Lines 10–11 of Fig. 4.4 display parameter courseName's value, using the {0} format item in WriteLine's first argument. The parameter variable's name (Fig. 4.4, line 8) can be the same or different from the argument variable's name (Fig. 4.5, line 21).

A method can specify multiple parameters by separating each parameter from the next with a comma. The number of arguments in a method call must match the number of required parameters in the parameter list of the called method's declaration. Also, the types of the arguments in the method call must be consistent with the types of the corresponding parameters in the method's declaration. (As you'll learn in subsequent chapters, an argument's type and its corresponding parameter's type are *not* always required to be identical.) In our example, the method call passes one argument of type `string` (`nameOfCourse` is declared as a `string` in line 16 of Fig. 4.5), and the method declaration specifies one parameter of type `string` (line 8 in Fig. 4.4). So the type of the argument in the method call exactly matches the type of the parameter in the method header.

Common Programming Error 4.1

A compilation error occurs if the number of arguments in a method call does not match the number of required parameters in the method declaration.

Common Programming Error 4.2

A compilation error occurs if the types of the arguments in a method call are not consistent with the types of the corresponding parameters in the method declaration.

Updated UML Class Diagram for Class GradeBook

The UML class diagram of Fig. 4.6 models class `GradeBook` of Fig. 4.4. Like Fig. 4.4, this `GradeBook` class contains `public` operation `DisplayMessage`. However, this version of `DisplayMessage` has a parameter. The UML models a parameter a bit differently from C# by listing the parameter name, followed by a colon and the parameter type in the parentheses following the operation name. The UML has several data types that are similar to the C# types. For example, UML types `String` and `Integer` correspond to C# types `string` and `int`, respectively. Unfortunately, the UML does not provide types that correspond to every C# type. For this reason, and to avoid confusion between UML types and C# types, *we use only C# types in our UML diagrams.* Class `Gradebook`'s method `DisplayMessage` (Fig. 4.4) has a `string` parameter named `courseName`, so Fig. 4.6 lists the parameter `courseName : string` between the parentheses following `DisplayMessage`.

GradeBook
+ DisplayMessage(courseName : string)

Fig. 4.6 | UML class diagram indicating that class `GradeBook` has a public `DisplayMessage` operation with a `courseName` parameter of type `string`.

Notes on using Directives

Notice the `using` directive in Fig. 4.5 (line 4). This indicates to the compiler that the application uses classes in the `System` namespace, like the `Console` class. Why do we need a `using` directive to use class `Console`, but not class `GradeBook`? There's a special relationship between classes that are compiled in the same project, like classes `GradeBook` and `GradeBookTest`. By default, such classes are considered to be in the same namespace. A using directive is not required when one class in a namespace uses another in the same namespace—such as when class GradeBookTest uses class GradeBook. For simplicity, our examples in this chapter do not declare a namespace. Any classes that are not *explicitly* placed in a namespace are *implicitly* placed in the so-called **global namespace**.

Actually, the using directive in line 4 is not required if we always refer to class Console as System.Console, which includes the full namespace and class name. This is known as the class's **fully qualified class name**. For example, line 15 could be written as

```
System.Console.WriteLine( "Please enter the course name:" );
```

Most C# programmers consider using fully qualified names to be cumbersome, and instead prefer to use using directives.

4.5 Instance Variables and Properties

In Chapter 3, we declared all of an application's variables in the application's Main method. Variables declared in the body of a method are known as **local variables** and can be used only in that method. When a method terminates, the values of its local variables are lost. Recall from Section 4.2 that an object has attributes that are carried with it as it's used in an application. Such attributes exist before a method is called on an object and after the method completes execution.

Attributes are represented as variables in a class declaration. Such variables are called **fields** and are declared *inside* a class declaration but *outside* the bodies of the class's method declarations. When each object of a class maintains its own copy of an attribute, the field that represents the attribute is also known as an instance variable—each object (instance) of the class has a separate instance of the variable. In Chapter 10, we discuss another type of field called a static variable, where all objects of the same class share one variable.

A class normally contains one or more properties that manipulate the attributes that belong to a particular object of the class. The example in this section demonstrates a GradeBook class that contains a courseName instance variable to represent a particular GradeBook object's course name, and a CourseName property to manipulate courseName.

GradeBook *Class with an Instance Variable and a Property*
In our next application (Figs. 4.7–4.8), class GradeBook (Fig. 4.7) maintains the course name as an instance variable so that it can be used or modified at any time during an application's execution. The class also contains one method—DisplayMessage (lines 24–30)—and one property—CourseName (line 11–21). Recall from Chapter 2 that properties are used to manipulate an object's attributes. For example, in that chapter, we used a Label's Text property to specify the text to display on the Label. In this example, we use a property in code rather than in the **Properties** window of the IDE. To do this, we first declare a property as a member of the GradeBook class. As you'll soon see, the GradeBook's CourseName property can be used to store a course name in a GradeBook (in instance variable courseName) or retrieve the GradeBook's course name (from instance variable courseName). Method DisplayMessage—which now specifies no parameters—still displays a welcome message that includes the course name. However, the method now uses the CourseName property to obtain the course name from instance variable courseName.

```
1   // Fig. 4.7: GradeBook.cs
2   // GradeBook class that contains a private instance variable, courseName,
3   // and a public property to get and set its value.
4   using System;
5
6   public class GradeBook
7   {
8      private string courseName; // course name for this GradeBook
9
10     // property to get and set the course name
11     public string CourseName
12     {
13        get
14        {
15           return courseName;
16        } // end get
17        set
18        {
19           courseName = value;
20        } // end set
21     } // end property CourseName
22
23     // display a welcome message to the GradeBook user
24     public void DisplayMessage()
25     {
26        // use property CourseName to get the
27        // name of the course that this GradeBook represents
28        Console.WriteLine( "Welcome to the grade book for\n{0}!",
29           CourseName ); // display property CourseName
30     } // end method DisplayMessage
31  } // end class GradeBook
```

Fig. 4.7 | GradeBook class that contains a `private` instance variable, `courseName`, and a `public` property to `get` and `set` its value.

A typical instructor teaches more than one course, each with its own course name. Line 8 declares `courseName` as a variable of type `string`. Line 8 is a declaration for an instance variable, because the variable is declared in the class's body (lines 7–31) but outside the bodies of the class's method (lines 24–30) and property (lines 11–21). Every instance (i.e., object) of class `GradeBook` contains one copy of each instance variable. For example, if there are two `GradeBook` objects, each object has its own copy of `courseName`. All the methods and properties of class `GradeBook` can directly manipulate its instance variable `courseName`, but it's considered good practice for methods of a class to use that class's properties to manipulate instance variables (as we do in line 29 of method `DisplayMessage`). The software engineering reasons for this will soon become clear.

Access Modifiers `public` and `private`
Most instance-variable declarations are preceded with the keyword `private` (as in line 8). Like `public`, keyword `private` is an access modifier. Variables, properties or methods declared with access modifier `private` are accessible *only* to properties and methods of the

class in which they're declared. Thus, variable `courseName` can be used *only* in property `CourseName` and method `DisplayMessage` of class `GradeBook`.

Software Engineering Observation 4.2

Precede every field and method declaration with an access modifier. Generally, instance variables should be declared `private` *and methods and properties should be declared* `public`. *If the access modifier is omitted before a member of a class, the member is implicitly declared* `private`. *We'll see that it's appropriate to declare certain methods* `private`, *if they will be accessed only by other methods of the class.*

Software Engineering Observation 4.3

Declaring the instance variables of a class as `private` *and the methods of the class as* `public` *facilitates debugging, because problems with data manipulations are localized to the class's methods and properties, since the* `private` *instance variables are accessible only to these methods and properties.*

Declaring instance variables with access modifier `private` is known as **information hiding**. When an application creates (instantiates) an object of class `GradeBook`, variable `courseName` is encapsulated (hidden) in the object and can be accessed only by methods and properties of the object's class.

Setting and Getting the Values of `private` *Instance Variables*
How can we allow a program to manipulate a class's `private` instance variables but ensure that they remain in a valid state? We need to provide controlled ways for programmers to "get" (i.e., retrieve) the value in an instance variable and "set" (i.e., modify) the value in an instance variable. Although you can define methods like `GetCourseName` and `SetCourseName`, C# properties provide a more elegant solution. Next, we show how to declare and use properties.

GradeBook Class with a Property
The `GradeBook` class's `CourseName` **property declaration** is located in lines 11–21 of Fig. 4.7. The property begins in line 11 with an access modifier (in this case, `public`), followed by the type that the property represents (`string`) and the property's name (`CourseName`). Properties use the same naming conventions as methods and classes.

Properties contain **accessors** that handle the details of returning and modifying data. A property declaration can contain a `get` accessor, a `set` accessor or both. The `get` accessor (lines 13–16) enables a client to read the value of `private` instance variable `courseName`; the `set` accessor (lines 17–20) enables a client to modify `courseName`.

After defining a property, you can use it like a variable in your code. For example, you can assign a value to a property using the = (assignment) operator. This executes the code in the property's `set` accessor to set the value of the corresponding instance variable. Similarly, referencing the property to use its value (for example, to display it on the screen) executes the code in the property's `get` accessor to obtain the corresponding instance variable's value. We show how to use properties shortly. By convention, we name each property with the capitalized name of the instance variable that it manipulates (e.g., `CourseName` is the property that represents instance variable `courseName`)—C# is case sensitive, so these are distinct identifiers.

get *and* set *Accessors*

Let us look more closely at property CourseName's get and set accessors (Fig. 4.7). The get accessor (lines 13–16) begins with the identifier **get** and its body is delimited by braces. The accessor's body contains a **return statement**, which consists of the keyword **return** followed by an expression. The expression's value is returned to the client code that uses the property. In this example, the value of courseName is returned when the property CourseName is referenced. For example, in the following statement

```
string theCourseName = gradeBook.CourseName;
```

the expression gradeBook.CourseName (where gradeBook is an object of class GradeBook) executes property CourseName's get accessor, which returns the value of instance variable courseName. That value is then stored in variable theCourseName. Property CourseName can be used as simply as if it were an instance variable. The property notation allows the client to think of the property as the underlying data. Again, the client cannot directly manipulate instance variable courseName because it's private.

The set accessor (lines 17–20) begins with the identifier **set** and its body is delimited by braces. When the property CourseName appears in an assignment statement, as in

```
gradeBook.CourseName = "CS100 Introduction to Computers";
```

the text "CS100 Introduction to Computers" is assigned to the set accessor's contextual keyword named **value** and the set accessor executes. Note that value is *implicitly* declared and initialized in the set accessor—it's a compilation error to declare a local variable value in this body. Line 19 stores the contents of value in instance variable courseName. A set accessor does not return any data when it completes its task.

The statements inside the property in lines 15 and 19 (Fig. 4.7) each access course-Name even though it was declared outside the property. We can use instance variable courseName in the methods and properties of class GradeBook, because courseName is an instance variable of the class.

*Using Property **CourseName** in Method **DisplayMessage***

Method DisplayMessage (lines 24–30 of Fig. 4.7) does not receive any parameters. Lines 28–29 output a welcome message that includes the value of instance variable courseName. We do not reference courseName directly. Instead, we access property CourseName (line 29), which executes the property's get accessor, returning the value of courseName.

GradeBookTest** Class That Demonstrates Class **GradeBook

Class GradeBookTest (Fig. 4.8) creates a GradeBook object and demonstrates property CourseName. Line 11 creates a GradeBook object and assigns it to local variable myGrade-Book. Lines 14–15 display the initial course name using the object's CourseName property—this executes the property's get accessor, which returns the value of courseName.

The first line of the output shows an empty name (marked by single quotes, ''). Unlike local variables, which are not automatically initialized, every field has a **default initial value**—a value provided by C# when you do not specify the initial value. Thus, fields are *not* required to be explicitly initialized before they're used in an application—unless they must be initialized to values other than their default values. The default value for an instance variable of type string (like courseName) is null. When you display a string variable that contains the value null, no text is displayed on the screen.

```
 1   // Fig. 4.8: GradeBookTest.cs
 2   // Create and manipulate a GradeBook object.
 3   using System;
 4
 5   public class GradeBookTest
 6   {
 7      // Main method begins program execution
 8      public static void Main( string[] args )
 9      {
10         // create a GradeBook object and assign it to myGradeBook
11         GradeBook myGradeBook = new GradeBook();
12
13         // display initial value of CourseName
14         Console.WriteLine( "Initial course name is: '{0}'\n",
15            myGradeBook.CourseName );
16
17         // prompt for and read course name
18         Console.WriteLine( "Please enter the course name:" );
19         myGradeBook.CourseName = Console.ReadLine(); // set CourseName
20         Console.WriteLine(); // output a blank line
21
22         // display welcome message after specifying course name
23         myGradeBook.DisplayMessage();
24      } // end Main
25   } // end class GradeBookTest
```

```
Initial course name is: ''

Please enter the course name:
CS101 Introduction to C# Programming

Welcome to the grade book for
CS101 Introduction to C# Programming!
```

Fig. 4.8 | Create and manipulate a GradeBook object.

Line 18 prompts the user to enter a course name. Line 19 assigns the course name entered by the user to object myGradeBook's CourseName property. When a value is assigned to CourseName, the value specified (which is returned by ReadLine in this case) is assigned to implicit parameter value of CourseName's set accessor (lines 17–20, Fig. 4.7). Then parameter value is assigned by the set accessor to instance variable courseName (line 19 of Fig. 4.7). Line 20 (Fig. 4.8) displays a blank line, then line 23 calls myGradeBook's DisplayMessage method to display the welcome message containing the course name.

4.6 UML Class Diagram with a Property

Figure 4.9 contains an updated UML class diagram for the version of class GradeBook in Fig. 4.7. We model properties in the UML as attributes—the property (in this case, CourseName) is listed as a public attribute—as indicated by the plus (+) sign—preceded by the word "property" in **guillemets** (« and »). Using descriptive words in guillemets (called **stereotypes** in the UML) helps distinguish properties from other attributes and operations. The UML indicates the type of the property by placing a colon and a type after the property name. The `get` and `set` accessors of the property are implied, so they're not listed in the UML diagram. Class `GradeBook` also contains one `public` method `Display-Message`, so the class diagram lists this operation in the third compartment. Recall that the plus (+) sign is the public visibility symbol.

A class diagram helps you design a class, so it's not required to show every implementation detail of the class. Since an instance variable that's manipulated by a property is really an implementation detail of that property, our class diagram does not show the `courseName` instance variable. A programmer implementing the `GradeBook` class based on this class diagram would create the instance variable `courseName` as part of the implementation process (as we did in Fig. 4.7).

In some cases, you may find it necessary to model the `private` instance variables of a class. Like properties, instance variables are attributes of a class and are modeled in the middle compartment of a class diagram. The UML represents instance variables as attributes by listing the attribute name, followed by a colon and the attribute type. To indicate that an attribute is `private`, a class diagram would list the **private visibility symbol**—a minus sign (–)—before the attribute's name. For example, the instance variable `course-Name` in Fig. 4.7 would be modeled as "`- courseName : string`" to indicate that it's a private attribute of type `string`.

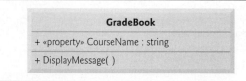

Fig. 4.9 | UML class diagram indicating that class `GradeBook` has a public `CourseName` property of type `string` and one public method.

4.7 Software Engineering with Properties and set and get Accessors

Using properties as described earlier in this chapter would seem to violate the notion of `private` data. Although providing a property with `get` and `set` accessors may appear to be the same as making its corresponding instance variable `public`, this is not the case. A `public` instance variable can be read or written by any property or method in the program. If an instance variable is `private`, the client code can access the instance variable only indirectly through the class's non-`private` properties or methods. This allows the class to control the manner in which the data is set or returned. For example, `get` and `set` accessors can translate between the format of the data stored in the `private` instance variable and the format of the data preferred by the client.

Consider a `Clock` class that represents the time of day as a `private int` instance variable `time`, containing the number of seconds since midnight. Suppose the class provides a `Time` property of type `string` to manipulate this instance variable. Although `get` accessors typically return data exactly as it's stored in an object, they need not expose the data in this "raw" format. When a client refers to a `Clock` object's `Time` property, the property's `get` accessor could use instance variable `time` to determine the number of hours, minutes and seconds since midnight, then return the time as a `string` of the form "`HH:MM:SS`". Similarly, suppose a Clock object's Time property is assigned a string of the form "HH:MM:SS". Using the string capabilities presented in Chapter 16, and the method Convert.ToInt32 presented in Section 3.6, the Time property's set accessor can convert this string to an int number of seconds since midnight and store the result in the Clock object's private instance variable time. The Time property's set accessor can also provide **data-validation** capabilities that scrutinize attempts to modify the instance variable's value to ensure that the value it receives represents a valid time (e.g., "12:30:45" is valid but "42:85:70" is not). We demonstrate data validation in Section 4.11. So, although a property's accessors enable clients to manipulate private data, they carefully control those manipulations, and the object's private data remains safely encapsulated (i.e., hidden) in the object. This is not possible with public instance variables, which can easily be set by clients to invalid values.

Properties of a class should also be used by the class's own methods to manipulate the class's private instance variables, even though the methods can directly access the private instance variables. Accessing an instance variable via a property's accessors—as in the body of method DisplayMessage (Fig. 4.7, lines 28–29)—creates a more robust class that's easier to maintain and less likely to malfunction. If we decide to change the representation of instance variable courseName in some way, the declaration of method DisplayMessage does not require modification—only the bodies of property CourseName's get and set accessors that directly manipulate the instance variable will need to change. For example, suppose we want to represent the course name as two separate instance variables—courseNumber (e.g., "CS101") and courseTitle (e.g., "Introduction to C# Programming"). The DisplayMessage method can still use property CourseName's get accessor to obtain the full course name to display as part of the welcome message. In this case, the get accessor would need to build and return a string containing the courseNumber, followed by the courseTitle. Method DisplayMessage would continue to display the complete course title "CS101 Introduction to C# Programming," because it's unaffected by the change to the class's instance variables.

4.8 Auto-Implemented Properties

In Fig. 4.7, we created a GradeBook class with a private courseName instance variable and a public property CourseName to enable client code to access the courseName. When you look at the CourseName property's definition (Fig. 4.7, lines 11–21), notice that the get accessor simply returns private instance variable courseName's value and the set accessor simply assigns a value to the instance variable—no other logic appears in the accessors. For such cases, C# provides **automatically implemented properties** (also known as **auto-implemented properties**). With an auto-implemented property, the C# compiler creates a private instance variable, and the get and set accessors for returning and modifying the private instance variable. Unlike a user-defined property, an auto-implemented property, must have both a get and a set accessor. This enables you to implement the property trivially, which is handy when you're first designing a class. If you later decide to include other logic in the get or set accessors, you can simply modify the property's implementation. To use an auto-implemented property in the GradeBook class of Fig. 4.7, you can replace the private instance variable at line 8 and the property at lines 11–21 with the following code:

```
public string CourseName { get; set; }
```

Code Snippets for Auto-implemented Properties

The IDE has a feature called **code snippets** that allows you to insert predefined code templates into your source code. One such snippet enables you to insert a `public` auto-implemented property by typing the word "prop" in the code window and pressing the *Tab* key twice. Certain pieces of the inserted code are highlighted for you to easily change the property's type and name. You can press the *Tab* key to move from one highlighted piece of text to the next in the inserted code. By default, the new property's type is `int` and its name is `MyProperty`. To get a list of all available code snippets, type *Ctrl + k, Ctrl + x*. This displays the **Insert Snippet** window in the code editor. You can navigate through the Visual C# snippet folders with the mouse to see the snippets. This feature can also be accessed by right clicking in the source code editor and selecting the **Insert Snippet...** menu item.

4.9 Value Types vs. Reference Types

Types in C# are divided into two categories—**value types** and **reference types**. C#'s simple types (like `int` and `double`) are all value types. A variable of a value type simply contains a *value* of that type. For example, Fig. 4.10 shows an `int` variable named `count` that contains the value 7. Values types are implemented as `struct`s, which are similar to classes and are discussed in more detail in Chapter 16.

By contrast, a variable of a reference type (sometimes called a **reference**) contains the *address* of a location in memory where the data referred to by that variable is stored. Such a variable is said to **refer to an object** in the program. Line 11 of Fig. 4.8 creates a Grade-Book object, places it in memory and stores the object's reference in variable `myGradeBook` of type `GradeBook` as shown in Fig. 4.11. The `GradeBook` object is shown with its `course-Name` instance variable.

Reference-type instance variables (such as `myGradeBook` in Fig. 4.11) are initialized by default to the value **null**. `string` is a reference type. For this reason, `string` variable `courseName` is shown in Fig. 4.11 with an empty box representing the `null`-valued variable. A `string` variable with the value `null` is *not* an empty string, which is represented by `""` or **string.Empty**. The value `null` represents a reference that does not refer to an object. The empty string is a `string` object with no characters in it.

A client of an object must use a variable that refers to the object to **invoke** (i.e., call) the object's methods and access the object's properties. In Fig. 4.8, the statements in `Main` use variable `myGradeBook`, which contains the `GradeBook` object's reference, to send messages to the `GradeBook` object. These messages are calls to methods (like `DisplayMessage`) or references to properties (like `CourseName`) that enable the program to interact with `GradeBook` objects. For example, the statement (in line 19 of Fig. 4.8)

```
myGradeBook.CourseName = Console.ReadLine(); // set CourseName
```

uses the reference `myGradeBook` to set the course name by assigning a value to property `CourseName`. This sends a message to the `GradeBook` object to invoke the `CourseName` property's *set* accessor. The message includes as an argument the value read from the user's input (in this case, `"CS101 Introduction to C# Programming"`) that `CourseName`'s *set* accessor requires to perform its task. The *set* accessor uses this information to set the `courseName` instance variable. In Section 7.16, we discuss value types and reference types in detail.

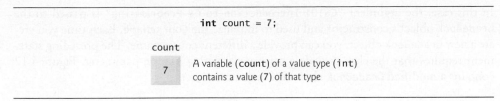

```
int count = 7;
```

count

| 7 | A variable (count) of a value type (int) contains a value (7) of that type |

Fig. 4.10 | Value-type variable.

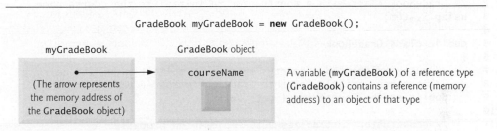

```
GradeBook myGradeBook = new GradeBook();
```

myGradeBook   GradeBook object

courseName

(The arrow represents the memory address of the GradeBook object)

A variable (myGradeBook) of a reference type (GradeBook) contains a reference (memory address) to an object of that type

Fig. 4.11 | Reference-type variable.

Software Engineering Observation 4.4

A variable's declared type (e.g., int, double or GradeBook) indicates whether the variable is of a value or a reference type. If a variable's type is not one of the simple types (Appendix B), or an enum or a struct type (which we discuss in Section 7.10 and Chapter 16, respectively), then it's a reference type. For example, Account account1 indicates that account1 is a variable that can refer to an Account object.

4.10 Initializing Objects with Constructors

As mentioned in Section 4.5, when a GradeBook (Fig. 4.7) object is created, its instance variable courseName is initialized to null by default. This is also true of the private instance variable that the compiler creates for the auto-implemented CourseName property discussed in Section 4.8. What if you want to provide a course name when you create a GradeBook object? Each class can provide a **constructor** that can be used to initialize an object of a class when the object is created. In fact, C# requires a constructor call for *every* object that's created. The new operator calls the class's constructor to perform the initialization. The constructor call is indicated by the class name, followed by parentheses. For example, line 11 of Fig. 4.8 first uses new to create a GradeBook object. The empty parentheses after "new GradeBook()" indicate a call without arguments to the class's constructor. The compiler provides a **public default constructor** with no parameters in any class that does not explicitly define a constructor, so *every* class has a constructor. The default constructor does not modify the default values of the instance variables.

When you declare a class, you can provide your own constructor (or several constructors, as you'll learn in Chapter 10) to specify custom initialization for objects of your class. For example, you might want to specify a course name for a GradeBook object when the object is created, as in

```
GradeBook myGradeBook =
    new GradeBook( "CS101 Introduction to C# Programming" );
```

In this case, the argument "CS101 Introduction to C# Programming" is passed to the GradeBook object's constructor and used to initialize the CourseName. Each time you create a new GradeBook object, you can provide a different course name. The preceding statement requires that the class provide a constructor with a string parameter. Figure 4.12 contains a modified GradeBook class with such a constructor.

```csharp
1  // Fig. 4.12: GradeBook.cs
2  // GradeBook class with a constructor to initialize the course name.
3  using System;
4
5  public class GradeBook
6  {
7     // auto-implemented property CourseName implicitly created an
8     // instance variable for this GradeBook's course name
9     public string CourseName { get; set; }
10
11    // constructor initializes auto-implemented property
12    // CourseName with string supplied as argument
13    public GradeBook( string name )
14    {
15       CourseName = name; // set CourseName to name
16    } // end constructor
17
18    // display a welcome message to the GradeBook user
19    public void DisplayMessage()
20    {
21       // use auto-implemented property CourseName to get the
22       // name of the course that this GradeBook represents
23       Console.WriteLine( "Welcome to the grade book for\n{0}!",
24          CourseName );
25    } // end method DisplayMessage
26 } // end class GradeBook
```

Fig. 4.12 | GradeBook class with a constructor to initialize the course name.

Lines 13–16 declare the constructor for class GradeBook. A constructor must have the same name as its class. Like a method, a constructor specifies in its parameter list the data it requires to perform its task. When you use new to create an object, you place this data in the parentheses that follow the class name. Unlike a method, a constructor doesn't specify a return type (not even void). Line 13 indicates that class GradeBook's constructor has a parameter called name of type string. In line 15, the name passed to the constructor is used to initialize auto-implemented property CourseName via its set accessor.

Figure 4.13 demonstrates initializing GradeBook objects using this constructor. Lines 12–13 create and initialize a GradeBook object. The constructor of class GradeBook is called with the argument "CS101 Introduction to C# Programming" to initialize the course name. The object-creation expression to the right of = in lines 12–13 returns a reference to the new object, which is assigned to variable gradeBook1. Lines 14–15 repeat this process for another GradeBook object, this time passing the argument "CS102 Data Structures in C#" to initialize the course name for gradeBook2. Lines 18–21 use each object's CourseName property to obtain the course names and show that they were indeed initialized when the objects were created. In Section 4.5, you learned that each instance (i.e., object) of a class contains its own copy of the class's instance variables. The output confirms that each GradeBook maintains its own course name.

```
1   // Fig. 4.13: GradeBookTest.cs
2   // GradeBook constructor used to specify the course name at the
3   // time each GradeBook object is created.
4   using System;
5
6   public class GradeBookTest
7   {
8      // Main method begins program execution
9      public static void Main( string[] args )
10     {
11        // create GradeBook object
12        GradeBook gradeBook1 = new GradeBook( // invokes constructor
13           "CS101 Introduction to C# Programming" );
14        GradeBook gradeBook2 = new GradeBook( // invokes constructor
15           "CS102 Data Structures in C#" );
16
17        // display initial value of courseName for each GradeBook
18        Console.WriteLine( "gradeBook1 course name is: {0}",
19           gradeBook1.CourseName );
20        Console.WriteLine( "gradeBook2 course name is: {0}",
21           gradeBook2.CourseName );
22     } // end Main
23  } // end class GradeBookTest
```

```
gradeBook1 course name is: CS101 Introduction to C# Programming
gradeBook2 course name is: CS102 Data Structures in C#
```

Fig. 4.13 | GradeBook constructor used to specify the course name at the time each GradeBook object is created.

Normally, constructors are declared public. If a class does not explicitly define a constructor, the class's instance variables are initialized to their default values—0 for numeric types, false for type bool and null for reference types. If you declare any constructors for a class, C# will *not* create a default constructor for that class.

Error-Prevention Tip 4.1

Unless default initialization of your class's instance variables is acceptable, provide a constructor to ensure that your class's instance variables are initialized with meaningful values when each new object of your class is created.

Adding the Constructor to Class GradeBook's UML Class Diagram

The UML class diagram of Fig. 4.14 models class GradeBook of Fig. 4.12, which has a constructor that has a name parameter of type string. Like operations, the UML models constructors in the third compartment of a class in a class diagram. To distinguish a constructor from a class's operations, the UML places the word "constructor" between guil-

lemets (« and ») before the constructor's name. It's customary to list constructors before
other operations in the third compartment.

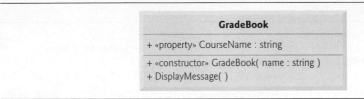

Fig. 4.14 | UML class diagram indicating that class `GradeBook` has a constructor with a
`name` parameter of type `string`.

4.11 Floating-Point Numbers and Type `decimal`

In our next application, we depart temporarily from our `GradeBook` case study to declare
a class called `Account` that maintains a bank account's balance. Most account balances are
not whole numbers (such as 0, –22 and 1024). For this reason, class `Account` represents
the account balance as a real number (i.e., a number with a decimal point, such as 7.33,
0.0975 or 1000.12345). C# provides three simple types for storing real numbers—`float`,
double, and `decimal`. Types `float` and `double` are called **floating-point** types. The primary difference between them and `decimal` is that `decimal` variables store a limited range
of real numbers *precisely*, whereas floating-point variables store only *approximations* of real
numbers, but across a much greater range of values. Also, `double` variables can store numbers with larger magnitude and finer detail (i.e., more digits to the right of the decimal
point—also known as the number's **precision**) than `float` variables. A key application of
type `decimal` is representing monetary amounts.

Real-Number Precision and Storage Requirements
Variables of type `float` represent **single-precision floating-point numbers** and have seven
significant digits. Variables of type `double` represent **double-precision floating-point
numbers**. These require twice as much storage as `float` variables and provide 15–16 significant digits—approximately double the precision of `float` variables. Furthermore, variables of type `decimal` require twice as much storage as `double` variables and provide 28–
29 significant digits. In some applications, even variables of type `double` and `decimal` will
be inadequate—such applications are beyond the scope of this book.

Most programmers represent floating-point numbers with type `double`. In fact, C#
treats *all* real numbers you type in an application's source code (such as 7.33 and 0.0975)
as `double` values by default. Such values in the source code are known as **floating-point
literals**. To type a **decimal literal**, you must type the letter "M" or "m" (which stands for
"money") at the end of a real number (for example, 7.33M is a `decimal` literal rather than
a `double`). Integer literals are implicitly converted into type `float`, `double` or `decimal`
when they're assigned to a variable of one of these types. See Appendix B for the ranges of
values for `float`s, `double`s, `decimal`s and all the other simple types.

Although floating-point numbers are not always 100% precise, they have numerous
applications. For example, when we speak of a "normal" body temperature of 98.6, we do
not need to be precise to a large number of digits. When we read the temperature on a

thermometer as 98.6, it may actually be 98.5999473210643. Calling this number simply 98.6 is fine for most applications involving body temperatures. Due to the imprecise nature of floating-point numbers, type `decimal` is preferred over the floating-point types whenever the calculations need to be exact, as with monetary calculations. In cases where approximation is enough, `double` is preferred over type `float` because `double` variables can represent floating-point numbers more accurately. For this reason, we use type `decimal` throughout the book for monetary amounts and type `double` for other real numbers.

Real numbers also arise as a result of division. In conventional arithmetic, for example, when we divide 10 by 3, the result is 3.3333333…, with the sequence of 3s repeating infinitely. The computer allocates only a fixed amount of space to hold such a value, so clearly the stored floating-point value can be only an approximation.

Common Programming Error 4.3

Using floating-point numbers in a manner that assumes they're represented precisely can lead to logic errors.

Account Class with an Instance Variable of Type `decimal`

Our next application (Figs. 4.15–4.16) contains a simple class named `Account` (Fig. 4.15) that maintains the balance of a bank account. A typical bank services many accounts, each with its own balance, so line 7 declares an instance variable named `balance` of type `decimal`. Variable `balance` is an instance variable because it's declared in the body of the class (lines 6–36) but outside the class's method and property declarations (lines 10–13, 16–19 and 22–35). Every instance (i.e., object) of class `Account` contains its own copy of `balance`.

```
 1   // Fig. 4.15: Account.cs
 2   // Account class with a constructor to
 3   // initialize instance variable balance.
 4
 5   public class Account
 6   {
 7      private decimal balance; // instance variable that stores the balance
 8
 9      // constructor
10      public Account( decimal initialBalance )
11      {
12         Balance = initialBalance; // set balance using property
13      } // end Account constructor
14
15      // credit (add) an amount to the account
16      public void Credit( decimal amount )
17      {
18         Balance = Balance + amount; // add amount to balance
19      } // end method Credit
20
21      // a property to get and set the account balance
22      public decimal Balance
23      {
```

Fig. 4.15 | Account class with a constructor to initialize instance variable `balance`. (Part 1 of 2.)

```
24          get
25          {
26              return balance;
27          } // end get
28          set
29          {
30              // validate that value is greater than or equal to 0;
31              // if it is not, balance is left unchanged
32              if ( value >= 0 )
33                  balance = value;
34          } // end set
35      } // end property Balance
36  } // end class Account
```

Fig. 4.15 | Account class with a constructor to initialize instance variable balance. (Part 2 of 2.)

```
1   // Fig. 4.16: AccountTest.cs
2   // Create and manipulate Account objects.
3   using System;
4
5   public class AccountTest
6   {
7       // Main method begins execution of C# application
8       public static void Main( string[] args )
9       {
10          Account account1 = new Account( 50.00M ); // create Account object
11          Account account2 = new Account( -7.53M ); // create Account object
12
13          // display initial balance of each object using a property
14          Console.WriteLine( "account1 balance: {0:C}",
15              account1.Balance ); // display Balance property
16          Console.WriteLine( "account2 balance: {0:C}\n",
17              account2.Balance ); // display Balance property
18
19          decimal depositAmount; // deposit amount read from user
20
21          // prompt and obtain user input
22          Console.Write( "Enter deposit amount for account1: " );
23          depositAmount = Convert.ToDecimal( Console.ReadLine() );
24          Console.WriteLine( "adding {0:C} to account1 balance\n",
25              depositAmount );
26          account1.Credit( depositAmount ); // add to account1 balance
27
28          // display balances
29          Console.WriteLine( "account1 balance: {0:C}",
30              account1.Balance );
31          Console.WriteLine( "account2 balance: {0:C}\n",
32              account2.Balance );
33
34          // prompt and obtain user input
35          Console.Write( "Enter deposit amount for account2: " );
36          depositAmount = Convert.ToDecimal( Console.ReadLine() );
```

Fig. 4.16 | Create and manipulate an Account object. (Part 1 of 2.)

```
37          Console.WriteLine( "adding {0:C} to account2 balance\n",
38             depositAmount );
39          account2.Credit( depositAmount ); // add to account2 balance
40
41          // display balances
42          Console.WriteLine( "account1 balance: {0:C}", account1.Balance );
43          Console.WriteLine( "account2 balance: {0:C}", account2.Balance );
44       } // end Main
45    } // end class AccountTest
```

```
account1 balance: $50.00
account2 balance: $0.00

Enter deposit amount for account1: 49.99
adding $49.99 to account1 balance

account1 balance: $99.99
account2 balance: $0.00

Enter deposit amount for account2: 123.21
adding $123.21 to account2 balance

account1 balance: $99.99
account2 balance: $123.21
```

Fig. 4.16 | Create and manipulate an Account object. (Part 2 of 2.)

Class Account contains a constructor, a method, and a property. Since it's common for someone opening an account to place money in the account immediately, the constructor (lines 10–13) receives a parameter initialBalance of type decimal that represents the account's starting balance. Line 12 assigns initialBalance to the property Balance, invoking Balance's set accessor to initialize the instance variable balance.

Method Credit (lines 16–19) doesn't return data when it completes its task, so its return type is void. The method receives one parameter named amount—a decimal value that's added to the property Balance. Line 18 uses both the get and set accessors of Balance. The expression Balance + amount invokes property Balance's get accessor to obtain the current value of instance variable balance, then adds amount to it. We then assign the result to instance variable balance by invoking the Balance property's set accessor (thus replacing the prior balance value).

Property Balance (lines 22–35) provides a get accessor, which allows clients of the class (i.e., other classes that use this class) to obtain the value of a particular Account object's balance. The property has type decimal (line 22). Balance also provides an enhanced set accessor.

In Section 4.5, we introduced properties whose set accessors allow clients of a class to modify the value of a private instance variable. In Fig. 4.7, class GradeBook defines property CourseName's set accessor to assign the value received in its parameter value to instance variable courseName (line 19). This CourseName property does not ensure that courseName contains only valid data.

The application of Figs. 4.15–4.16 enhances the set accessor of class Account's property Balance to perform this validation (also known as **validity checking**). Line 32 (Fig. 4.15) ensures that value is nonnegative. If the value is greater than or equal to 0, the amount stored in value is assigned to instance variable balance in line 33. Otherwise, balance is left unchanged.

AccountTest Class to Use Class Account

Class AccountTest (Fig. 4.16) creates two Account objects (lines 10–11) and initializes them respectively with 50.00M and -7.53M (the decimal literals representing the real numbers 50.00 and -7.53). The Account constructor (lines 10–13 of Fig. 4.15) references property Balance to initialize balance. In previous examples, the benefit of referencing the property in the constructor was not evident. Now, however, the constructor takes advantage of the validation provided by the set accessor of the Balance property. The constructor simply assigns a value to Balance rather than duplicating the set accessor's validation code. When line 11 of Fig. 4.16 passes an initial balance of -7.53 to the Account constructor, the constructor passes this value to the set accessor of property Balance, where the actual initialization occurs. This value is less than 0, so the set accessor does not modify balance, leaving this instance variable with its default value of 0.

Lines 14–17 in Fig. 4.16 output the balance in each Account by using the Account's Balance property. When Balance is used for account1 (line 15), the value of account1's balance is returned by the get accessor in line 26 of Fig. 4.15 and displayed by the Console.WriteLine statement (Fig. 4.16, lines 14–15). Similarly, when property Balance is called for account2 from line 17, the value of the account2's balance is returned from line 26 of Fig. 4.15 and displayed by the Console.WriteLine statement (Fig. 4.16, lines 16–17). The balance of account2 is 0 because the constructor ensured that the account could not begin with a negative balance. The value is output by WriteLine with the format item {0:C}, which formats the account balance as a monetary amount. The : after the 0 indicates that the next character represents a **format specifier**, and the C format specifier after the : specifies a monetary amount (C is for currency). The cultural settings on the user's machine determine the format for displaying monetary amounts. For example, in the United States, 50 displays as $50.00. In Germany, 50 displays as 50,00€. Figure 4.17 lists a few other format specifiers in addition to C.

Format specifier	Description
C or c	Formats the string as currency. Displays an appropriate currency symbol ($ in the U.S.) next to the number. Separates digits with an appropriate separator character (comma in the U.S.) and sets the number of decimal places to two by default.
D or d	Formats the string as a whole number. Displays number as an integer.
N or n	Formats the string with a thousands separator and a default of two decimal places.
E or e	Formats the number using scientific notation with a default of six decimal places.
F or f	Formats the string with a fixed number of decimal places (two by default).
G or g	Formats the number normally with decimal places or using scientific notation, depending on context. If a format item does not contain a format specifier, format G is assumed implicitly.
X or x	Formats the string as hexadecimal.

Fig. 4.17 | string format specifiers.

Line 19 declares local variable `depositAmount` to store each deposit amount entered by the user. Unlike the instance variable `balance` in class `Account`, the local variable `depositAmount` in `Main` is *not* initialized to 0 by default. Also, a local variable can be used only in the method in which it's declared. However, this variable does not need to be initialized here because its value will be determined by the user's input. The compiler does not allow a local variable's value to be read until it's initialized.

Line 22 prompts the user to enter a deposit amount for `account1`. Line 23 obtains the input from the user by calling the `Console` class's `ReadLine` method, then passing the `string` entered by the user to the `Convert` class's **`ToDecimal`** method, which returns the `decimal` value in this `string`. Lines 24–25 display the deposit amount. Line 26 calls object `account1`'s `Credit` method and supplies `depositAmount` as the method's argument. When the method is called, the argument's value is assigned to parameter `amount` of method `Credit` (lines 16–19 of Fig. 4.15), then method `Credit` adds that value to the `balance` (line 18 of Fig. 4.15). Lines 29–32 (Fig. 4.16) output the balances of both `Accounts` again to show that only `account1`'s balance changed.

Line 35 prompts the user to enter a deposit amount for `account2`. Line 36 obtains the input from the user by calling method `Console.ReadLine`, and passing the return value to the `Convert` class's `ToDecimal` method. Lines 37–38 display the deposit amount. Line 39 calls object `account2`'s `Credit` method and supplies `depositAmount` as the method's argument, then method `Credit` adds that value to the balance. Finally, lines 42–43 output the balances of both `Accounts` again to show that only `account2`'s balance changed.

set and get Accessors with Different Access Modifiers

By default, the `get` and `set` accessors of a property have the same access as the property—for example, for a `public` property, the accessors are `public`. It's possible to declare the `get` and `set` accessors with different access modifiers. In this case, one of the accessors must implicitly have the same access as the property and the other must be declared with a *more restrictive* access modifier than the property. For example, in a `public` property, the `get` accessor might be `public` and the `set` accessor might be `private`. We demonstrate this feature in Section 10.5.

Error-Prevention Tip 4.2

The benefits of data integrity are not automatic simply because instance variables are made `private`—you must provide appropriate validity checking and report the errors.

Error-Prevention Tip 4.3

`set` accessors that set the values of `private` data should verify that the intended new values are proper; if they're not, the `set` accessors should leave the instance variables unchanged and indicate an error. We demonstrate how to indicate errors in Chapter 10.

UML Class Diagram for Class Account

The UML class diagram in Fig. 4.18 models class `Account` of Fig. 4.15. The diagram models the `Balance` property as a UML attribute of type `decimal` (because the corresponding C# property had type `decimal`). The diagram models class `Account`'s constructor with a parameter `initialBalance` of type `decimal` in the third compartment of the class. The diagram models operation `Credit` in the third compartment with an `amount` parameter of type `decimal` (because the corresponding method has an `amount` parameter of C# type `decimal`).

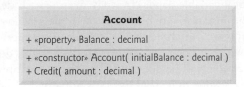

Fig. 4.18 | UML class diagram indicating that class `Account` has a `public Balance` property of type `decimal`, a constructor and a method.

4.12 Wrap-Up

In this chapter, you learned the basic object-oriented concepts of classes, objects, methods, instance variables and properties—these will be used in most substantial C# applications you create. You learned how to declare instance variables of a class to maintain data for each object of the class, how to declare methods that operate on that data, and how to declare properties to obtain and set that data. We demonstrated how to call a method to tell it to perform its task and how to pass information to methods as arguments. We discussed the difference between a local variable of a method and an instance variable of a class and that only instance variables are initialized automatically. We discussed the difference between a value type and a reference type. You learned how to create auto-implemented properties. You also learned how to use a class's constructor to specify the initial values for an object's instance variables. We discussed some of the differences between value types and reference types. You learned about the value types `float`, `double` and `decimal` for storing real numbers.

We showed how the UML can be used to create class diagrams that model the constructors, methods, properties and attributes of classes. You learned the value of declaring instance variables `private` and using `public` properties to manipulate them. For example, we demonstrated how `set` accessors in properties can be used to validate an object's data and ensure that the object is maintained in a consistent state. In the next chapter we begin our introduction to control statements, which specify the order in which an application's actions are performed. You'll use these in your methods to specify how they should perform their tasks.

Summary

Section 4.2 Classes, Objects, Methods, Properties and Instance Variables

- Methods perform tasks. Each method describes the mechanisms that actually perform its tasks. The method hides from its user the complex tasks that it performs.

- The application unit that houses a method is called a class. A class may contain one or more methods that are designed to perform the class's tasks.

- A method can perform a task and may return a result.

- An instance of a class is called an object.

- Each message sent to an object is a method call and tells that method to perform its task.

- Each method can specify parameters that represent additional information the method requires to perform its task correctly. A method call supplies arguments for the method's parameters.

- An object has attributes that are carried with the object as it's used in an application. These attributes are specified as part of the object's class. Attributes are specified in classes by fields.

- An object has properties for accessing attributes. Properties contain get accessors for reading attributes and set accessors for storing into them.

Section 4.3 Declaring a Class with a Method and Instantiating an Object of a Class

- Keyword public is an access modifier.

- Every class declaration contains keyword class followed immediately by the class's name.

- A method declaration that begins with keyword public indicates that the method is "available to the public"—that is, it can be called by other classes declared outside the class declaration.

- Keyword void indicates that a method will not return any information when it completes its task.

- By convention, method names begin with an uppercase first letter, and all subsequent words in the name begin with an uppercase first letter. This is called Pascal case.

- Empty parentheses following a method name indicate that the method does not require any parameters to perform its task.

- Every method's body is delimited by left and right braces ({ and }).

- The body of a method contains statements that perform the method's task. After the statements execute, the method has completed its task.

- When you attempt to execute an application, C# looks for a Main method to begin execution.

- Typically, you create an object of a class to call the class's methods.

- Object creation expressions begin with the new operator and create new objects.

- To call a method of an object, follow the variable name with a member access operator (.), the method name and a set of parentheses containing the method's arguments.

- In the UML, each class is modeled in a class diagram as a rectangle with three compartments. The top compartment contains the name of the class, centered horizontally in boldface. The middle compartment contains the class's attributes, which correspond to fields in C#. The bottom compartment contains the class's operations, which correspond to methods and constructors in C#.

- The UML models operations by listing the operation name, followed by a set of parentheses. A plus sign (+) in front of the operation name indicates that the operation is a public operation in the UML (i.e., a public method in C#). The plus sign is called the public visibility symbol.

Section 4.4 Declaring a Method with a Parameter

- Methods often require additional information to perform their tasks. Such additional information is provided to methods via arguments in method calls.

- Console method ReadLine reads characters until a newline character is encountered, then returns the characters as a string.

- A method that requires data to perform its task must specify this in its declaration by placing additional information in the method's parameter list.

- Each parameter must specify both a type and an identifier.

- At the time a method is called, its arguments are assigned to its parameters. Then the method body uses the parameter variables to access the argument values.

- A method can specify multiple parameters in a comma-separated parameter list.

- The number of arguments in the method call must match the number of required parameters in the method declaration's parameter list. Also, the argument types in the method call must be consistent with the types of the corresponding parameters in the method's declaration.

- The UML models a parameter of an operation by listing the parameter name, followed by a colon and the parameter type between the parentheses following the operation name.

- The UML does not provide types that correspond to every C# type. For this reason, and to avoid confusion between UML types and C# types, we use only C# types in our UML diagrams.

- There's a special relationship between classes that are compiled in the same project. By default, such classes are considered to be in the same namespace. A using directive is not required when one class in a namespace uses another in the same namespace.

- A using directive is not required if you always refer to a class with its fully qualified class name.

Section 4.5 Instance Variables and Properties

- Local variables can be used only in the method in which they're declared.

- A class normally contains methods that manipulate the attributes that belong to a particular object of the class. Attributes are represented as instance variables in a class declaration. Such variables are declared inside a class declaration but outside its method's bodies.

- Each object (instance) of a class has a separate copy of each instance variable.

- Most instance-variable declarations are preceded with the private access modifier. Variables, properties or methods declared with access modifier private are accessible only to methods (and properties) of the class in which they're declared.

- Declaring instance variables with access modifier private is known as information hiding.

- Properties contain accessors that handle the details of modifying and returning data.

- Properties provide a controlled way for programmers to "get" (i.e., retrieve) the value in an instance variable and "set" (i.e., modify) the value in an instance variable.

- A property declaration can contain a get accessor, a set accessor or both. The get accessor typically enables a client to read the value of a private instance variable. The set accessor typically enables a client to modify that instance variable's value.

- After defining a property, you can use it the same way as you use a variable.

- The default value for a field of type string is null.

Section 4.6 UML Class Diagram with a Property

- We model properties in the UML as attributes, preceded by the word "property" in guillemets (« and »). Using descriptive words in guillemets (called stereotypes in the UML) helps distinguish properties from other attributes.

- A class diagram helps you design a class, so it's not required to show every implementation detail of the class. Since an instance variable that's manipulated by a property is really an implementation detail of that property, our class diagrams do not show instance variables.

- private class members are preceded by the private visibility symbol (-) in the UML.

- The UML represents instance variables and properties as attributes by listing the attribute name, followed by a colon and the attribute type.

Section 4.7 Software Engineering with Properties and set and get Accessors

- Properties can scrutinize attempts to modify an instance variable's value (known as data validation), thus ensuring that the new value for that instance variable is valid.

- Using properties would seem to violate the notion of private data. However, a set accessor can provide data-validation capabilities to ensure that the value is set properly; get and set accessors can translate between the format of the data used by the client and the format used in the private instance variable.

- A benefit of fields over local variables is that all of a class's methods and properties can use the fields. Another distinction is that a field has a default initial value provided by C# when you do not specify the field's initial value, but a local variable does not.

Section 4.8 Auto-Implemented Properties
- With an auto-implemented property, the C# compiler automatically creates a `private` instance variable, and the `get` and `set` accessors for returning and modifying the `private` instance variable.
- Visual C# 2010 Express and Visual Studio 2010 have a feature called code snippets that allows you to insert predefined code templates into your source code. One such snippet enables you to insert a `public` auto-implemented property by typing the word "prop" in the code window and pressing the *Tab* key twice.
- Pieces of the inserted code are highlighted for you to easily change the property's type and name. Press the *Tab* key to move from one highlighted piece of text to the next in the inserted code.
- To get a list of all available code snippets, type *Ctrl* + *k*, *Ctrl* + *x*. This displays the **Insert Snippet** window in the code editor. This feature can also be accessed by right clicking in the source code editor and selecting the **Insert Snippet...** menu item.

Section 4.9 Value Types vs. Reference Types
- Types are divided into two categories—value types and reference types.
- A variable of a value type contains data of that type.
- A variable of a reference type (sometimes called a reference) contains the address of a location in memory where an object is stored.
- Reference-type instance variables are initialized by default to the value `null`.

Section 4.10 Initializing Objects with Constructors
- A constructor can be used to initialize an object of a class when the object is created.
- If no constructor is provided for a class, the compiler provides a `public` default constructor with no parameters that does not modify the instance variables' default values.
- Like operations, the UML models constructors in the third compartment of a class diagram. To distinguish a constructor from a class's operations, the UML places the word "constructor" between guillemets (« and ») before the constructor's name.
- Constructors can specify parameters but cannot specify return types.

Section 4.11 Floating-Point Numbers and Type `decimal`
- A real number is a number with a decimal point, such as 7.33, 0.0975 or 1000.12345. C# provides three simple types for storing real numbers—`float`, `double`, and `decimal`.
- Types `float` and `double` are called floating-point types. The primary difference between them and the `decimal` type is that `decimal` variables store a limited range of real numbers precisely, but floating-point variables store approximations of real numbers across a much greater range.
- Variables of type `float` represent single-precision floating-point numbers and have seven significant digits. Variables of type `double` represent double-precision floating-point numbers. These require twice as much storage as `float` variables and provide 15–16 significant digits—approximately double the precision of `float` variables. Furthermore, variables of type `decimal` require twice as much storage as `double` variables and provide 28–29 significant digits.
- Real number values that appear in source code are of type `double` by default.
- `Convert` method `ToDecimal` extracts a `decimal` value from a `string`.
- The `:` in a format item indicates that the next character represents a format specifier.
- The `C` format specifier specifies a monetary amount (`C` is for currency).

- It's possible to declare the `get` and `set` accessors of a property with different access modifiers. One accessor must implicitly have the same access as the property and the other must be declared with a more restrictive access modifier than the property; `private` is more restrictive than `public`.

Terminology

access modifier	local variable
attribute (UML)	member access (.) operator
auto-implemented property	message
automatically implemented property	method
`C` format specifier	method header
calling method	`new` operator
class	`null` keyword
class declaration	object (or instance)
`class` keyword	object-creation expression
client of an object or a class	operation (UML)
code snippet	parameter
compartment in a class diagram (UML)	parameter list
constructor	precision of a floating-point value
create an object	precision of a formatted floating-point number
`decimal` simple type	"prop" code snippet
default value	property
double-precision floating-point number	`private` access modifier
`double` simple type	`public` access modifier
field	`public` default constructor
`float` simple type	`public` method
floating-point number	`ReadLine` method of class `Console`
format specifier	refer to an object
fully qualified class name	reference
`get` accessor	reference type
global namespace	send a message
guillemets, « and » (UML)	`set` accessor
information hiding	single-precision floating-point number
instance of a class (object)	`ToDecimal` method of class `Convert`
instance variable	UML class diagram
instantiate (or create) an object	UML visibility symbol
invoke a method	`void` keyword

Self-Review Exercises

4.1   Fill in the blanks in each of the following:

   a) A house is to a blueprint as a(n) _____ is to a class.

   b) Every class declaration contains keyword _____ followed immediately by the class's name.

   c) Operator _____ creates an object of the class specified to the right of the keyword.

   d) Each parameter must specify both a(n) _____ and a(n) _____.

   e) By default, classes that are not explicitly declared in a namespace are implicitly placed in the _____.

   f) When each object of a class maintains its own copy of an attribute, the field that represents the attribute is also known as a(n) _____.

   g) C# provides three simple types for storing real numbers—_____, _____ and _____.

h) Variables of type `double` represent _____ floating-point numbers.

i) `Convert` method _____ returns a `decimal` value.

j) Keyword `public` is a(n) _____.

k) Return type _____ indicates that a method will not return any information when it completes its task.

l) `Console` method _____ reads characters until a newline character is encountered, then returns those characters (not including the newline) as a `string`.

m) A(n) _____ is not required if you always refer to a class with its fully qualified class name.

n) Variables of type `float` represent _____ floating-point numbers.

o) The format specifier _____ is used to display values in a monetary format.

p) Types are either _____ types or _____ types.

q) For a(n) _____, the compiler automatically generates a private instance variable and set and get accessors.

4.2 State whether each of the following is *true* or *false*. If *false*, explain why.

a) By convention, method names begin with a lowercase first letter and all subsequent words in the name begin with a capital first letter.

b) A property's `get` accessor enables a client to modify the value of the instance variable associated with the property.

c) A `using` directive is not required when one class in a namespace uses another in the same namespace.

d) Empty parentheses following a method name in a method declaration indicate that the method does not require any parameters to perform its task.

e) After defining a property, you can use it the same way you use a method, but with empty parentheses, because no arguments are passed to a property.

f) Variables or methods declared with access modifier `private` are accessible only to methods and properties of the class in which they're declared.

g) Variables declared in the body of a particular method are known as instance variables and can be used in all methods of the class.

h) A property declaration must contain both a `get` accessor and a `set` accessor.

i) The body of any method or property is delimited by left and right braces.

j) Local variables are initialized by default.

k) Reference-type instance variables are initialized by default to the value `null`.

l) Any class that contains `public static void Main( string[] args )` can be used to execute an application.

m) The number of arguments in the method call must match the number of required parameters in the method declaration's parameter list.

n) Real number values that appear in source code are known as floating-point literals and are of type `float` by default.

4.3 What is the difference between a local variable and an instance variable?

4.4 Explain the purpose of a method parameter. What is the difference between a parameter and an argument?

Answers to Self-Review Exercises

4.1 a) object. b) `class`. c) `new`. d) type, name. e) global namespace. f) instance variable. g) `float`, `double`, `decimal`. h) double-precision. i) `ToDecimal`. j) access modifier. k) `void`. l) `ReadLine`. m) `using` directive. n) single-precision. o) C. p) value, reference. q) auto-implemented property.

4.2 a) False. By convention, method names begin with an uppercase first letter and all subsequent words in the name begin with an uppercase first letter. b) False. A property's `get` accessor enables a client to retrieve the value of the instance variable associated with the property. A property's `set` accessor enables a client to modify the value of the instance variable associated with the property. c) True. d) True. e) False. After defining a property, you can use it the same way you use a variable. f) True. g) False. Such variables are called local variables and can be used only in the method in which they're declared. h) False. A property declaration can contain a `get` accessor, a `set` accessor or both. i) True. j) False. Instance variables are initialized by default. k) True. l) True. m) True. n) False. Such literals are of type `double` by default.

4.3 A local variable is declared in the body of a method and can be used only in the method in which it's declared. An instance variable is declared in a class, but not in the body of any of the class's methods. Every object (instance) of a class has a separate copy of the class's instance variables. Also, instance variables are accessible to all methods of the class. (We'll see an exception to this in Chapter 10, Classes and Objects: A Deeper Look.)

4.4 A parameter represents additional information that a method requires to perform its task. Each parameter required by a method is specified in the method's declaration. An argument is the actual value that's passed to a method parameter when a method is called.

Exercises

4.5 What is the purpose of operator `new`? Explain what happens when this keyword is used in an application.

4.6 What is a default constructor? How are an object's instance variables initialized if a class has only a default constructor?

4.7 Explain the purpose of an instance variable.

4.8 Explain how an application could use class `Console` without using a `using` directive.

4.9 Explain why a class might provide a property for an instance variable.

4.10 *(GradeBook Modification)* Modify class `GradeBook` (Fig. 4.12) as follows:
  a) Include a second `string` auto-implemented property that represents the name of the course's instructor.
  b) Modify the constructor to specify two parameters—one for the course name and one for the instructor's name.
  c) Modify method `DisplayMessage` such that it first outputs the welcome message and course name, then outputs "`This course is presented by:` ", followed by the instructor's name.

Use your modified class in a test application that demonstrates the class's new capabilities.

4.11 *(Account Modification)* Modify class `Account` (Fig. 4.15) to provide a method called `Debit` that withdraws money from an `Account`. Ensure that the debit amount doesn't exceed the balance. If it does, the balance should not be changed and the method should display a message indicating "`Debit amount exceeded account balance.`" Modify class `AccountTest` (Fig. 4.16) to test method `Debit`.

4.12 *(Invoice Class)* Create a class called `Invoice` that a hardware store might use to represent an invoice for an item sold at the store. An `Invoice` should include four pieces of information as either instance variables or automatic properties—a part number (type `string`), a part description (type `string`), a quantity of the item being purchased (type `int`) and a price per item (`decimal`). Your class should have a constructor that initializes the four values. Provide a property with a `get` and `set` accessor for any instance variables. For the `Quantity` and `PricePerItem` properties, if the value passed to the `set` accessor is negative, the value of the instance variable should be left unchanged. Also, provide a method named `GetInvoiceAmount` that calculates the invoice amount (i.e., multiplies the quantity by the price per item), then returns the amount as a `decimal` value. Write a test application named `InvoiceTest` that demonstrates class `Invoice`'s capabilities.

4.13   *(Employee Class)* Create a class called `Employee` that includes three pieces of information as either instance variables or automatic properties—a first name (type `string`), a last name (type `string`) and a monthly salary (`decimal`). Your class should have a constructor that initializes the three values. Provide a property with a `get` and `set` accessor for any instance variables. If the monthly salary is negative, the `set` accessor should leave the instance variable unchanged. Write a test application named `EmployeeTest` that demonstrates class `Employee`'s capabilities. Create two `Employee` objects and display each object's *yearly* salary. Then give each `Employee` a 10% raise and display each `Employee`'s yearly salary again.

4.14   *(Date Class)* Create a class called `Date` that includes three pieces of information as automatic properties—a month (type `int`), a day (type `int`) and a year (type `int`). Your class should have a constructor that initializes the three automatic properties and assumes that the values provided are correct. Provide a method `DisplayDate` that displays the month, day and year separated by forward slashes (/). Write a test application named `DateTest` that demonstrates class `Date`'s capabilities.

Making a Difference Exercises

4.15   *(Target-Heart-Rate Calculator)* While exercising, you can use a heart-rate monitor to see that your heart rate stays within a safe range suggested by your trainers and doctors. According to the American Heart Association (AHA) (`www.americanheart.org/presenter.jhtml?identifier=4736`), the formula for calculating your *maximum heart rate* in beats per minute is 220 minus your age in years. Your *target heart rate* is a range that is 50–85% of your maximum heart rate. [*Note:* These formulas are estimates provided by the AHA. Maximum and target heart rates may vary based on the health, fitness and gender of the individual. Always consult a physician or qualified health care professional before beginning or modifying an exercise program.] Create a class called `HeartRates`. The class attributes should include the person's first name, last name, year of birth and the current year. Your class should have a constructor that receives this data as parameters. For each attribute provide a property with `set` and `get` accessors. The class also should include a property that calculates and returns the person's age (in years), a property that calculates and returns the person's maximum heart rate and properties that calculate and return the person's minimum and maximim target heart rates. Write an application that prompts for the person's information, instantiates an object of class `HeartRates` and prints the information from that object—including the person's first name, last name and year of birth—then calculates and prints the person's age in (years), maximum heart rate and target-heart-rate range.

4.16   *(Computerization of Health Records)* A health care issue that has been in the news lately is the computerization of health records. This possibility is being approached cautiously because of sensitive privacy and security concerns, among others. [We address such concerns in later exercises.] Computerizing health records could make it easier for patients to share their health profiles and histories among their various health care professionals. This could improve the quality of health care, help avoid drug conflicts and erroneous drug prescriptions, reduce costs and, in emergencies, could save lives. In this exercise, you'll design a "starter" `HealthProfile` class for a person. The class attributes should include the person's first name, last name, gender, date of birth (consisting of separate attributes for the month, day and year of birth), height (in inches) and weight (in pounds). Your class should have a constructor that receives this data. For each attribute provide a property with `set` and `get` accessors. The class also should include methods that calculate and return the user's age in years, maximum heart rate and target-heart-rate range (see Exercise 4.15), and body mass index (BMI; see Exercise 3.31). Write an application that prompts for the person's information, instantiates an object of class `HealthProfile` for that person and prints the information from that object—including the person's first name, last name, gender, date of birth, height and weight—then calculates and prints the person's age in years, BMI, maximum heart rate and target-heart-rate range. It should also display the "BMI values" chart from Exercise 3.31.

5

Control Statements: Part 1

Let's all move one place on.
—Lewis Carroll

The wheel is come full circle.
—William Shakespeare

How many apples fell on Newton's head before he took the hint!
—Robert Frost

All the evolution we know of proceeds from the vague to the definite.
—Charles Sanders Peirce

Objectives

In this chapter you'll learn:

- Basic problem solving techniques.

- To develop algorithms through the process of top-down, stepwise refinement.

- To use the `if` and `if...else` selection statements to choose between actions.

- To use the `while` statement to execute statements in an application repeatedly.

- To use counter-controlled repetition and sentinel-controlled repetition.

- To use the increment, decrement and compound assignment operators.

5.1 Introduction

Before writing an application to solve a problem, we must have a thorough understanding of the problem and a carefully planned approach to solving it. When writing an application, we must understand the types of building blocks that are available and employ proven application-construction techniques. In this chapter and in Chapter 6, Control Statements: Part 2, we discuss these issues in our presentation of the theory and principles of structured programming. The concepts presented here are crucial to building classes and manipulating objects. We introduce C#'s if, if...else and while control statements, three of the building blocks that allow you to specify the logic required for methods to perform their tasks.

5.2 Algorithms

Any computing problem can be solved by executing a series of actions in a specific order. A **procedure** for solving a problem in terms of

1. the **actions** to execute and
2. the **order** in which these actions execute

is called an **algorithm**. The following example demonstrates that correctly specifying the order in which the actions execute is important.

Consider the "rise-and-shine algorithm" followed by one junior executive for getting out of bed and going to work: (1) get out of bed, (2) take off pajamas, (3) take a shower, (4) get dressed, (5) eat breakfast and (6) carpool to work. This routine prepares the executive for a productive day at the office.

However, suppose that the same steps are performed in a slightly different order: (1) get out of bed, (2) take off pajamas, (3) get dressed, (4) take a shower, (5) eat breakfast, (6) carpool to work. In this case, our junior executive shows up for work soaking wet.

Specifying the order in which statements (actions) execute in an application is called **program control**. This chapter investigates program control using C#'s **control statements**.

5.3 Pseudocode

Pseudocode is an informal language that helps you develop algorithms without having to worry about the strict details of C# language syntax. Pseudocode is useful for developing algorithms that will be converted to structured portions of C# applications. Pseudocode is similar to English—it's *not* a programming language.

Pseudocode does *not* execute on computers. Rather, it helps you "think out" an application before attempting to write it in C#. This chapter shows how to use pseudocode to develop C# applications.

You can create pseudocode using any text-editor application. A carefully prepared pseudocode application can easily be converted to a corresponding C# application. In many cases, this simply requires replacing pseudocode statements with C# equivalents.

Pseudocode normally describes only *actions*, such as input, output and calculations. We do not include variable declarations in our pseudocode, but some programmers do.

5.4 Control Structures

Normally, statements in an application are executed one after the other in the order in which they're written. This process is called **sequential execution**. Various C# statements enable you to specify that the next statement to execute is not necessarily the next one in sequence. This is called **transfer of control**.

During the 1960s, it became clear that the indiscriminate use of transfers of control was the root of much difficulty experienced by software development groups. The blame was pointed at the **goto statement** (used in most programming languages of the time), which allows programmers to specify a transfer of control to one of a wide range of possible destinations in an application (creating what is often called "spaghetti code"). The notion of so-called **structured programming** became almost synonymous with "goto elimination." We recommend that you avoid C#'s goto statement.

Research[1] had demonstrated that applications could be written without goto statements. The challenge of the era for programmers was to shift their styles to "goto-less programming." Not until the 1970s did programmers start taking structured programming seriously. The results were impressive because structured applications were clearer, easier to debug and modify, and more likely to be bug free in the first place.

Bohm and Jacopini's work demonstrated that all applications could be written in terms of only three control structures—the **sequence structure**, the **selection structure** and the **repetition structure**. When we introduce C#'s implementations of control structures, we'll refer to them in the terminology of the *C# Language Specification* as "control statements."

Sequence Structure in C#

The sequence structure is built into C#. Unless directed otherwise, the computer executes C# statements one after the other in the order in which they're written—that is, in sequence. The UML **activity diagram** in Fig. 5.1 illustrates a typical sequence structure in which two calculations are performed in order. C# lets you have as many actions as you want in a sequence structure.

---

1.   Bohm, C., and G. Jacopini, "Flow Diagrams, Turing Machines, and Languages with Only Two Formation Rules," *Communications of the ACM*, Vol. 9, No. 5, May 1966, pp. 336–371.

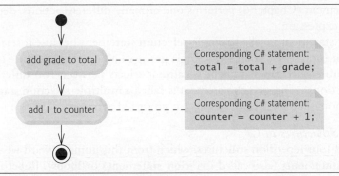

Fig. 5.1 | Sequence structure activity diagram.

An activity diagram models the **workflow** (also called the **activity**) of a portion of a software system. Such workflows may include a portion of an algorithm, such as the sequence structure in Fig. 5.1. Activity diagrams are composed of special-purpose symbols, such as **action-state symbols** (rectangles with their left and right sides replaced with arcs curving outward), **diamonds** and **small circles**. These symbols are connected by **transition arrows**, which represent the *flow* of the activity—that is, the order in which the actions should occur.

Like pseudocode, activity diagrams help you develop and represent algorithms, although many programmers prefer pseudocode. Activity diagrams clearly show how control structures operate.

Consider the activity diagram for the sequence structure in Fig. 5.1. It contains two **action states** that represent actions to perform. Each action state contains an **action expression**—for example, "add grade to total" or "add 1 to counter"—that specifies an action to perform. Other actions might include calculations or input/output operations. The arrows in the activity diagram represent **transitions**, which indicate the order in which the actions occur. The portion of the application that implements the activities illustrated by the diagram in Fig. 5.1 first adds grade to total, then adds 1 to counter.

The **solid circle** located at the top of the activity diagram represents the activity's **initial state**—the beginning of the workflow before the application performs the modeled actions. The **solid circle surrounded by a hollow circle** that appears at the bottom of the diagram represents the **final state**—the end of the workflow after the application performs its actions.

Figure 5.1 also includes rectangles with the upper-right corners folded over. These are UML **notes** (like comments in C#) that describe the purpose of symbols in the diagram. Figure 5.1 uses UML notes to show the C# code associated with each action state in the activity diagram. A **dotted line** connects each note with the element that the note describes. Activity diagrams normally do not show the C# code that implements the activity. We use notes for this purpose here to illustrate how the diagram relates to C# code.

Selection Structures in C#
C# has three types of selection structures, which from this point forward we shall refer to as **selection statements**. The **if statement** either performs (selects) an action if a condition is true or skips the action if the condition is false. The **if...else** statement performs an action if a condition is true or performs a different action if the condition is false. The

switch statement (Chapter 6) performs one of many different actions, depending on the value of an expression.

The if statement is called a **single-selection statement** because it selects or ignores a single action (or, as we'll soon see, a single group of actions). The if...else statement is called a **double-selection statement** because it selects between two different actions (or groups of actions). The switch statement is called a **multiple-selection statement** because it selects among many different actions (or groups of actions).

Repetition Structures in C#
C# provides four repetition structures, which from this point forward we shall refer to as **repetition statements** (also called **iteration statements** or **loops**). Repetition statements enable applications to perform statements repeatedly, depending on the value of a **loop-continuation condition**. The repetition statements are the while, do...while, for and foreach statements. (Chapter 6 presents the do...while and for statements. Chapter 8 discusses the foreach statement.) The while, for and foreach statements perform the action (or group of actions) in their bodies zero or more times—if the loop-continuation condition is initially false, the action (or group of actions) will not execute. The do...while statement performs the action (or group of actions) in its body one or more times. The words if, else, switch, while, do, for and foreach are C# keywords.

Summary of Control Statements in C#
C# has only three kinds of structured control statements: the sequence statement, selection statement (three types) and repetition statement (four types). We combine as many of each type of statement as necessary to make the program flow and work as required. As with the sequence statement in Fig. 5.1, we can model each control statement as an activity diagram. Each diagram contains one initial state and one final state that represent a control statement's entry point and exit point, respectively. **Single-entry/single-exit control statements** make it easy to build applications—the control statements are "attached" to one another by connecting the exit point of one to the entry point of the next. This procedure is similar to the way in which a child stacks building blocks, so we call it **control-statement stacking**. You'll learn that there's only one other way in which control statements may be connected: **control-statement nesting**, in which a control statement appears inside another control statement. Thus, algorithms in C# applications are constructed from only three kinds of structured control statements, combined in only two ways. This is the essence of simplicity.

5.5 if Single-Selection Statement

Applications use selection statements to choose among alternative courses of action. For example, suppose that the passing grade on an exam is 60. The pseudocode statement

```
if grade is greater than or equal to 60
    display "Passed"
```

determines whether the condition "grade is greater than or equal to 60" is true or false. If the condition is true, "Passed" is displayed, and the next pseudocode statement in order is "performed." (Remember that pseudocode is not a real programming language.) If the condition is false, the *display* statement is ignored, and the next pseudocode statement in order is performed. The indentation of the second line of this selection statement is optional, but recommended, because it emphasizes the inherent structure of structured applications.

The preceding pseudocode *if* statement may be written in C# as

```
if ( grade >= 60 )
    Console.WriteLine( "Passed" );
```

The C# code corresponds closely to the pseudocode. This is one of the characteristics of pseudocode that makes it such a useful application development tool.

Figure 5.2 illustrates the single-selection if statement. This activity diagram contains what is perhaps the most important symbol in an activity diagram—the diamond, or **decision symbol**, which indicates that a decision is to be made. The workflow will continue along a path determined by the symbol's associated **guard conditions**, which can be true or false. Each transition arrow emerging from a decision symbol has a guard condition (specified in square brackets next to the transition arrow). If a guard condition is true, the workflow enters the action state to which the transition arrow points. In Fig. 5.2, if the grade is greater than or equal to 60, the application displays "Passed," then transitions to the final state of this activity. If the grade is less than 60, the application immediately transitions to the final state without displaying a message.

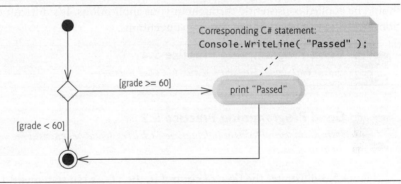

Fig. 5.2 | if single-selection statement UML activity diagram.

The if statement is a single-entry/single-exit control statement. You'll see that the activity diagrams for the remaining control statements also contain initial states, transition arrows, action states that indicate actions to perform and decision symbols (with associated guard conditions) that indicate decisions to be made, and final states. This is consistent with the **action/decision model of programming** we've been emphasizing.

Envision eight bins, each containing only one type of C# control statement. The control statements are all empty. Your task is to assemble an application from as many of each type of control statement as the algorithm demands, combining the control statements in only two possible ways (stacking or nesting), then filling in the action states and decisions with action expressions and guard conditions appropriate for the algorithm. We'll discuss in detail the variety of ways in which actions and decisions can be written.

5.6 if...else Double-Selection Statement

The if single-selection statement performs an indicated action only when the condition is true; otherwise, the action is skipped. The if...else double-selection statement allows you to specify an action to perform when the condition is true and a different action when the condition is false. For example, the pseudocode statement

> *if grade is greater than or equal to 60*
> > *display "Passed"*
> *else*
> > *display "Failed"*

displays "Passed" if the grade is greater than or equal to 60, but displays "Failed" if it's less than 60. In either case, after displaying occurs, the next pseudocode statement in sequence is "performed."

The preceding *if…else* pseudocode statement can be written in C# as

```
if ( grade >= 60 )
    Console.WriteLine( "Passed" );
else
    Console.WriteLine( "Failed" );
```

The body of the else part is also indented. Whatever indentation convention you choose should be applied consistently throughout your applications. It's difficult to read applications that do not obey uniform spacing conventions.

Good Programming Practice 5.1
Indent both body statements of an if…else statement.

Good Programming Practice 5.2
If there are several levels of indentation, each level should be indented the same additional amount of space.

Figure 5.3 illustrates the flow of control in the if…else statement. Imagine again a deep bin containing as many empty if…else statements as might be needed to build any C# application. Your job is to assemble these if…else statements (by stacking and nesting) with any other control statements required by the algorithm. You fill in the action states and decision symbols with action expressions and guard conditions appropriate for the algorithm you are developing.

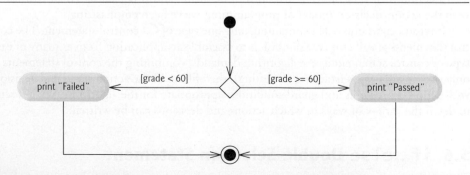

Fig. 5.3 | if…else double-selection statement UML activity diagram.

Conditional Operator (?:)

C# provides the **conditional operator** (?:), which can be used in place of an if...else statement. This is C#'s only **ternary operator**—this means that it takes three operands. Together, the operands and the ?: symbols form a **conditional expression**. The first operand (to the left of the ?) is a **boolean** expression (i.e., an expression that evaluates to a bool-type value—**true** or **false**), the second operand (between the ? and :) is the value of the conditional expression if the boolean expression is true and the third operand (to the right of the :) is the value of the conditional expression if the boolean expression is false. For example, the statement

```
Console.WriteLine( grade >= 60 ? "Passed" : "Failed" );
```

displays the value of WriteLine's conditional-expression argument. The conditional expression in the preceding statement evaluates to the string "Passed" if the boolean expression grade >= 60 is true and evaluates to the string "Failed" if the boolean expression is false. Thus, this statement with the conditional operator performs essentially the same function as the if...else statement shown earlier in this section, in which the boolean expression grade >= 60 was used as the if...else statement's condition. Actually, every control statement's condition must evaluate to the bool-type value true or false. You'll see that conditional expressions can be used in some situations where if...else statements cannot.

Good Programming Practice 5.3

When a conditional expression is inside a larger expression, it's good practice to parenthesize the conditional expression for clarity. Adding parentheses may also prevent operator-precedence problems that could cause syntax errors.

Nested if...else Statements

An application can test multiple cases by placing if...else statements inside other if...else statements to create **nested if...else statements**. For example, the following pseudocode represents a nested if...else statement that displays A for exam grades greater than or equal to 90, B for grades in the range 80 to 89, C for grades in the range 70 to 79, D for grades in the range 60 to 69 and F for all other grades:

> *if grade is greater than or equal to 90*
>   *display "A"*
> *else*
>   *if grade is greater than or equal to 80*
>   *display "B"*
>   *else*
>   *if grade is greater than or equal to 70*
>   *display "C"*
>   *else*
>   *if grade is greater than or equal to 60*
>   *display "D"*
>   *else*
>   *display "F"*

This pseudocode may be written in C# as

```csharp
if ( grade >= 90 )
    Console.WriteLine( "A" );
else
    if ( grade >= 80 )
        Console.WriteLine( "B" );
    else
        if ( grade >= 70 )
            Console.WriteLine( "C" );
        else
            if ( grade >= 60 )
                Console.WriteLine( "D" );
            else
                Console.WriteLine( "F" );
```

If grade is greater than or equal to 90, the first four conditions will be true, but only the statement in the if-part of the first if...else statement will execute. After that statement executes, the else-part of the "outermost" if...else statement is skipped. Most C# programmers prefer to write the preceding if...else statement as

```csharp
if ( grade >= 90 )
    Console.WriteLine( "A" );
else if ( grade >= 80 )
    Console.WriteLine( "B" );
else if ( grade >= 70 )
    Console.WriteLine( "C" );
else if ( grade >= 60 )
    Console.WriteLine( "D" );
else
    Console.WriteLine( "F" );
```

The two forms are identical except for the spacing and indentation, which the compiler ignores. The latter form is popular because it avoids deep indentation of the code to the right—such indentation often leaves little room on a line of code, forcing lines to be split and decreasing the readability of your code.

Dangling-else Problem

The C# compiler always associates an else with the immediately preceding if unless told to do otherwise by the placement of braces ({ and }). This behavior can lead to what is referred to as the **dangling-else problem**. For example,

```csharp
if ( x > 5 )
    if ( y > 5 )
        Console.WriteLine( "x and y are > 5" );
else
    Console.WriteLine( "x is <= 5" );
```

appears to indicate that if x is greater than 5, the nested if statement determines whether y is also greater than 5. If so, the string "x and y are > 5" is output. Otherwise, it appears that if x is not greater than 5, the else part of the if...else outputs the string "x is <= 5".

Beware! This nested if...else statement does not execute as it appears. The compiler actually interprets the statement as

```
if ( x > 5 )
   if ( y > 5 )
      Console.WriteLine( "x and y are > 5" );
   else
      Console.WriteLine( "x is <= 5" );
```

in which the body of the first if is a nested if…else. The outer if statement tests whether x is greater than 5. If so, execution continues by testing whether y is also greater than 5. If the second condition is true, the proper string—"x and y are > 5"—is displayed. However, if the second condition is false, the string "x is <= 5" is displayed, even though we know that x is greater than 5.

To force the nested if…else statement to execute as it was originally intended, we must write it as follows:

```
if ( x > 5 )
{
   if ( y > 5 )
      Console.WriteLine( "x and y are > 5" );
}
else
   Console.WriteLine( "x is <= 5" );
```

The braces ({}) indicate to the compiler that the second if statement is in the body of the first if and that the else is associated with the *first* if. Exercises 5.27–5.28 investigate the dangling-else problem further.

Blocks

The if statement expects only one statement in its body. To include several statements in the body of an if (or the body of an else for an if…else statement), enclose the statements in braces ({ and }). A set of statements contained within a pair of braces is called a **block**. A block can be placed anywhere in an application that a single statement can be placed.

The following example includes a block in the else-part of an if…else statement:

```
if ( grade >= 60 )
   Console.WriteLine( "Passed" );
else
{
   Console.WriteLine( "Failed" );
   Console.WriteLine( "You must take this course again." );
}
```

In this case, if grade is less than 60, the application executes both statements in the body of the else and displays

```
Failed.
You must take this course again.
```

Note the braces surrounding the two statements in the else clause. These braces are important. Without the braces, the statement

```
Console.WriteLine( "You must take this course again." );
```

would be outside the body of the else-part of the if…else statement and would execute regardless of whether the grade was less than 60.

Syntax errors are caught by the compiler. A **logic error** (e.g., when both braces in a block are left out of the application) has its effect at execution time. A **fatal logic error** causes an application to fail and terminate prematurely. A **nonfatal logic error** allows an application to continue executing, but causes it to produce incorrect results.

Good Programming Practice 5.4

Always using braces in an `if...else` (or other) statement helps prevent their accidental omission, especially when adding statements to the if-part or the else-part at a later time. To avoid omitting one or both of the braces, some programmers type the beginning and ending braces of blocks before typing the individual statements within them.

Just as a block can be placed anywhere a single statement can be placed, it's also possible to have an empty statement. Recall from Section 3.9 that the empty statement is represented by placing a semicolon (;) where a statement would normally be.

Common Programming Error 5.1

Placing a semicolon after the condition in an `if` or `if...else` statement leads to a logic error in single-selection `if` statements and a syntax error in double-selection `if...else` statements (when the if-part contains an actual body statement).

5.7 `while` Repetition Statement

A **repetition statement** allows you to specify that an application should repeat an action while some condition remains true. The pseudocode statement

> *while there are more items on my shopping list*
> *put next item in cart and cross it off my list*

describes the repetition that occurs during a shopping trip. The condition "there are more items on my shopping list" may be true or false. If it's true, then the action "Purchase next item and cross it off my list" is performed. This action will be performed repeatedly while the condition remains true. The statement(s) contained in the *while* repetition statement constitute the body of the *while* repetition statement, which may be a single statement or a block. Eventually, the condition will become false (when the last item on the shopping list has been purchased and crossed off the list). At this point, the repetition terminates, and the first statement after the repetition statement executes.

As an example of C#'s **while repetition statement**, consider a code segment designed to find the first power of 3 larger than 100. When the following `while` statement finishes executing, `product` contains the result:

```
int product = 3;
while ( product <= 100 )
   product = 3 * product;
```

When this `while` statement begins execution, the value of variable `product` is 3. Each repetition of the `while` statement multiplies `product` by 3, so `product` takes on the subsequent values 9, 27, 81 and 243 successively. When variable `product` becomes 243, the `while` statement condition—product <= 100—becomes false. This terminates the repetition, so the final value of `product` is 243. At this point, application execution continues with the next statement after the `while` statement.

> ### Common Programming Error 5.2
> *Not providing in the body of a* while *statement an action that eventually causes the condition in the* while *to become false normally results in a logic error called an* **infinite loop,** *in which the loop never terminates.*

The activity diagram in Fig. 5.4 illustrates the flow of control for the preceding while statement. This diagram also introduces the UML's **merge symbol.** The UML represents *both* the merge and decision symbols as diamonds. The merge symbol joins two flows of activity into one. In this diagram, the merge symbol joins the transitions from the initial state and the action state, so they both flow into the decision that determines whether the loop should begin (or continue) executing. The decision and merge symbols can be distinguished by the number of "incoming" and "outgoing" transition arrows. A decision symbol has one transition arrow pointing to the diamond and two or more transition arrows pointing out from the diamond to indicate possible transitions from that point. Each transition arrow pointing out of a decision symbol has a guard condition. A merge symbol has two or more transition arrows pointing to the diamond and only one transition arrow pointing from the diamond, to indicate multiple activity flows merging to continue the activity. None of the transition arrows associated with a merge have guard conditions.

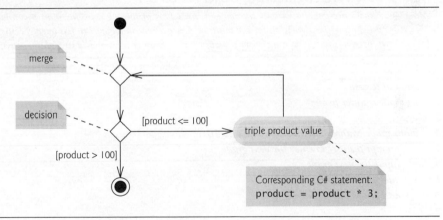

Fig. 5.4 | while repetition statement UML activity diagram.

Figure 5.4 clearly shows the repetition of the while statement discussed earlier in this section. The transition arrow emerging from the action state points back to the merge, from which program flow transitions back to the decision that is tested at the beginning of each repetition of the loop. The loop continues to execute until the guard condition product > 100 becomes true. Then the while statement exits (reaches its final state), and control passes to the next statement in sequence in the application.

5.8 Formulating Algorithms: Counter-Controlled Repetition

To illustrate how algorithms are developed, we modify the GradeBook class of Chapter 4 to solve two variations of a problem that averages student grades. Consider the following problem statement:

> *A class of 10 students took a quiz. The grades (integers in the range 0 to 100) for this quiz are available to you. Determine the class average on the quiz.*

The class average is equal to the sum of the grades divided by the number of students. The algorithm for solving this problem on a computer must input each grade, keep track of the total of all grades input, perform the averaging calculation and display the result.

Pseudocode Algorithm with Counter-Controlled Repetition

Let's use pseudocode to list the actions to execute and specify the order in which they should execute. We use **counter-controlled repetition** to input the grades one at a time. This technique uses a variable called a **counter** (or **control variable**) to control the number of times a set of statements will execute. Counter-controlled repetition is often called **definite repetition**, because the number of repetitions is known by the application before the loop begins executing. In this example, repetition terminates when the counter exceeds 10. This section presents a fully developed pseudocode algorithm (Fig. 5.5) and a version of class GradeBook (Fig. 5.6) that implements the algorithm in a C# method. The section then presents an application (Fig. 5.7) that demonstrates the algorithm in action. In Section 5.9, we demonstrate how to use pseudocode to develop such an algorithm from scratch.

Software Engineering Observation 5.1

Experience has shown that the most difficult part of solving a problem on a computer is developing the algorithm for the solution. Once a correct algorithm has been specified, the process of producing a working C# application from it is normally straightforward.

```
1    set total to zero
2    set grade counter to one
3
4    while grade counter is less than or equal to 10
5        prompt the user to enter the next grade
6        input the next grade
7        add the grade into the total
8        add one to the grade counter
9
10   set the class average to the total divided by 10
11   display the class average
```

Fig. 5.5 | Pseudocode algorithm that uses counter-controlled repetition to solve the class-average problem.

Note the references in the algorithm of Fig. 5.5 to a total and a counter. A **total** is a variable used to accumulate the sum of several values. A counter is a variable used to count—in this case, the grade counter indicates which of the 10 grades is about to be entered by the user. Variables used to store totals are normally initialized to zero before being used in an application.

Implementing Counter-Controlled Repetition in Class GradeBook

Class GradeBook (Fig. 5.6) contains a constructor (lines 12–15) that assigns a value to the instance variable created by auto-implemented property CourseName in line 9. Lines 18–

23 declare method `DisplayMessage`. Lines 26–52 declare method `DetermineClassAver-age`, which implements the class-averaging algorithm described by the pseudocode in Fig. 5.5.

```
 1   // Fig. 5.6: GradeBook.cs
 2   // GradeBook class that solves class-average problem using
 3   // counter-controlled repetition.
 4   using System;
 5
 6   public class GradeBook
 7   {
 8      // auto-implemented property CourseName
 9      public string CourseName { get; set; }
10
11      // constructor initializes CourseName property
12      public GradeBook( string name )
13      {
14         CourseName = name; // set CourseName to name
15      } // end constructor
16
17      // display a welcome message to the GradeBook user
18      public void DisplayMessage()
19      {
20         // property CourseName gets the name of the course
21         Console.WriteLine( "Welcome to the grade book for\n{0}!\n",
22            CourseName );
23      } // end method DisplayMessage
24
25      // determine class average based on 10 grades entered by user
26      public void DetermineClassAverage()
27      {
28         int total; // sum of the grades entered by user
29         int gradeCounter; // number of the grade to be entered next
30         int grade; // grade value entered by the user
31         int average; // average of the grades
32
33         // initialization phase
34         total = 0; // initialize the total
35         gradeCounter = 1; // initialize the loop counter
36
37         // processing phase
38         while ( gradeCounter <= 10 ) // loop 10 times
39         {
40            Console.Write( "Enter grade: " ); // prompt the user
41            grade = Convert.ToInt32( Console.ReadLine() ); // read grade
42            total = total + grade; // add the grade to total
43            gradeCounter = gradeCounter + 1; // increment the counter by 1
44         } // end while
45
46         // termination phase
47         average = total / 10; // integer division yields integer result
```

Fig. 5.6 | GradeBook class that solves the class-average problem using counter-controlled repetition. (Part 1 of 2.)

```
48
49          // display total and average of grades
50          Console.WriteLine( "\nTotal of all 10 grades is {0}", total );
51          Console.WriteLine( "Class average is {0}", average );
52       } // end method DetermineClassAverage
53    } // end class GradeBook
```

Fig. 5.6 | GradeBook class that solves the class-average problem using counter-controlled repetition. (Part 2 of 2.)

Lines 28–31 declare local variables total, gradeCounter, grade and average to be of type int. In this example, variable total accumulates the sum of the grades entered and gradeCounter counts the number of grades entered. Variable grade stores the most recent grade value entered (line 41). Variable average stores the average grade.

The declarations (in lines 28–31) appear in method DetermineClassAverage's body. Variables declared in a method body are local variables and can be used only from the line of their declaration to the closing right brace of the block in which they're declared. A local variable's declaration must appear before the variable is used in that method. A local variable cannot be accessed outside the method in which it's declared.

In the versions of class GradeBook in this chapter, we simply read and process a set of grades. The averaging calculation is performed in method DetermineClassAverage using local variables—we do not preserve any information about student grades in instance variables of the class. In later versions of the class (in Chapter 8), we store the grades using an instance variable that refers to a data structure known as an array. This allows a GradeBook object to perform various calculations on the same set of grades without requiring the user to enter the grades multiple times.

Good Programming Practice 5.5

Separate declarations from other statements in methods with a blank line for readability.

We say that a variable is **definitely assigned** when it's guaranteed to be assigned a value before it's used. Notice that each local variable declared in lines 28–31 is definitely assigned before it's used in calculations. The assignments (in lines 34–35) initialize total to 0 and gradeCounter to 1. Variables grade and average (for the user input and calculated average, respectively) need not be initialized here—their values are assigned as they're input or calculated later in the method.

Common Programming Error 5.3

Using the value of a local variable before it's definitely assigned results in a compilation error. All local variables must be definitely assigned before their values are used in expressions.

Error-Prevention Tip 5.1

Initialize each counter and total, either in its declaration or in an assignment statement. Totals are normally initialized to 0. Counters are normally initialized to 0 or 1, depending on how they're used (we'll show examples of each).

Line 38 indicates that the `while` statement should continue looping (also called **iterating**) as long as the value of `gradeCounter` is less than or equal to 10. While this condition remains true, the `while` statement repeatedly executes the statements between the braces that delimit its body (lines 39–44).

Line 40 displays the prompt `"Enter grade: "` in the console window. Line 41 reads the grade entered by the user and assigns it to variable `grade`. Then line 42 adds the new `grade` entered by the user to the `total` and assigns the result to `total`, which replaces its previous value.

Line 43 adds 1 to `gradeCounter` to indicate that the application has processed a grade and is ready to input the next grade from the user. Incrementing `gradeCounter` eventually causes `gradeCounter` to exceed 10. At that point the `while` loop terminates, because its condition (line 38) becomes false.

When the loop terminates, line 47 performs the averaging calculation and assigns its result to the variable `average`. Line 50 uses `Console`'s `WriteLine` method to display the text `"Total of all 10 grades is "` followed by variable `total`'s value. Line 51 then displays the text `"Class average is "` followed by variable `average`'s value. Method `DetermineClassAverage` returns control to the calling method (i.e., `Main` in `GradeBookTest` of Fig. 5.7) after reaching line 52.

Class *GradeBookTest*

Class `GradeBookTest` (Fig. 5.7) creates an object of class `GradeBook` (Fig. 5.6) and demonstrates its capabilities. Lines 9–10 of Fig. 5.7 create a new `GradeBook` object and assign it to variable `myGradeBook`. The `string` in line 10 is passed to the `GradeBook` constructor (lines 12–15 of Fig. 5.6). Line 12 calls `myGradeBook`'s `DisplayMessage` method to display a welcome message to the user. Line 13 then calls `myGradeBook`'s `DetermineClassAverage` method to allow the user to enter 10 grades, for which the method then calculates and displays the average—the method performs the algorithm shown in Fig. 5.5.

```
 1    // Fig. 5.7: GradeBookTest.cs
 2    // Create GradeBook object and invoke its DetermineClassAverage method.
 3    public class GradeBookTest
 4    {
 5       public static void Main( string[] args )
 6       {
 7          // create GradeBook object myGradeBook and
 8          // pass course name to constructor
 9          GradeBook myGradeBook = new GradeBook(
10             "CS101 Introduction to C# Programming" );
11
12          myGradeBook.DisplayMessage(); // display welcome message
13          myGradeBook.DetermineClassAverage(); // find average of 10 grades
14       } // end Main
15    } // end class GradeBookTest
```

```
Welcome to the grade book for
CS101 Introduction to C# Programming!
```

Fig. 5.7 | Create `GradeBook` object and invoke its `DetermineClassAverage` method. (Part 1 of 2.)

```
Enter grade: 88
Enter grade: 79
Enter grade: 95
Enter grade: 100
Enter grade: 48
Enter grade: 88
Enter grade: 92
Enter grade: 83
Enter grade: 90
Enter grade: 85

Total of all 10 grades is 848
Class average is 84
```

Fig. 5.7 | Create `GradeBook` object and invoke its `DetermineClassAverage` method. (Part 2 of 2.)

Notes on Integer Division and Truncation

The averaging calculation performed by method `DetermineClassAverage` in response to the method call at line 13 in Fig. 5.7 produces an integer result. The application's output indicates that the sum of the grade values in the sample execution is 848, which, when divided by 10, should yield the floating-point number 84.8. However, the result of the calculation `total / 10` (line 47 of Fig. 5.6) is the integer 84, because `total` and 10 are both integers. Dividing two integers results in **integer division**—any fractional part of the calculation is lost (i.e., **truncated**, not rounded). We'll see how to obtain a floating-point result from the averaging calculation in the next section.

Common Programming Error 5.4

Assuming that integer division rounds (rather than truncates) can lead to incorrect results. For example, 7 ÷ 4, which yields 1.75 in conventional arithmetic, truncates to 1 in integer arithmetic, rather than rounding to 2.

5.9 Formulating Algorithms: Sentinel-Controlled Repetition

Let us generalize Section 5.8's class-average problem. Consider the following problem:

> *Develop a class-averaging application that processes grades for an arbitrary number of students each time it's run.*

In the previous class-average example, the problem statement specified the number of students, so the number of grades (10) was known in advance. In this example, no indication is given of how many grades the user will enter during the application's execution. The application must process an arbitrary number of grades. How can it determine when to stop the input of grades? How will it know when to calculate and display the class average?

One way to solve this problem is to use a special value called a **sentinel value** (also called a **signal value**, a **dummy value** or a **flag value**) to indicate "end of data entry." This is called **sentinel-controlled repetition**. The user enters grades until all legitimate grades have been entered. The user then types the sentinel value to indicate that no more grades will be entered. Sentinel-controlled repetition is often called **indefinite repetition** because the number of repetitions is not known by the application before the loop begins executing.

Clearly, a sentinel value must be chosen that cannot be confused with an acceptable input value. Grades on a quiz are nonnegative integers, so –1 is an acceptable sentinel value for this problem. Thus, a run of the class-average application might process a stream of inputs such as 95, 96, 75, 74, 89 and –1. The application would then compute and display the class average for the grades 95, 96, 75, 74 and 89. Since –1 is the sentinel value, it should not enter into the averaging calculation.

Common Programming Error 5.5

Choosing a sentinel value that is also a legitimate data value is a logic error.

Developing the Pseudocode Algorithm with Top-Down, Stepwise Refinement: The Top and First Refinement

We approach the class-average application with a technique called **top-down, stepwise refinement**, which is essential to the development of well-structured applications. We begin with a pseudocode representation of the **top**—a single statement that conveys the overall function of the application:

determine the class average for the quiz

The top is, in effect, a *complete* representation of an application. Unfortunately, the top rarely conveys sufficient detail from which to write a C# application. So we now begin the refinement process. We divide the top into a series of smaller tasks and list these in the order in which they'll be performed. This results in the following **first refinement**:

initialize variables
input, sum and count the quiz grades
calculate and display the class average

This refinement uses only the sequence structure—the steps listed should execute in order, one after the other.

Software Engineering Observation 5.2

Each refinement, as well as the top itself, is a complete specification of the algorithm— only the level of detail varies.

Software Engineering Observation 5.3

Many applications can be divided logically into three phases: an initialization phase that initializes the variables; a processing phase that inputs data values and adjusts application variables (e.g., counters and totals) accordingly; and a termination phase that calculates and outputs the final results.

Proceeding to the Second Refinement

The preceding *Software Engineering Observation* is often all you need for the first refinement in the top-down process. To proceed to the next level, the **second refinement**, we specify individual variables. In this example, we need a running total of the numbers, a count of how many numbers have been processed, a variable to receive the value of each grade as it's input by the user and a variable to hold the calculated average. The pseudocode statement

> *initialize variables*

can be refined as follows:

> *initialize total to zero*
> *initialize counter to zero*

Only the variables *total* and *counter* need to be initialized before they're used. The variables *average* and *grade* (for the calculated average and the user input, respectively) need not be initialized, because their values will be replaced as they're calculated or input.

The pseudocode statement

> *input, sum and count the quiz grades*

requires a repetition statement that successively inputs each grade. We do not know in advance how many grades are to be processed, so we'll use sentinel-controlled repetition. The user enters grades one at a time. After entering the last grade, the user enters the sentinel value. The application tests for the sentinel value after each grade is input and terminates the loop when the user enters the sentinel value. The second refinement of the preceding pseudocode statement is then

> *prompt the user to enter the first grade*
> *input the first grade (possibly the sentinel)*
>
> *while the user has not yet entered the sentinel*
>   *add this grade into the running total*
>   *add one to the grade counter*
>   *prompt the user to enter the next grade*
>   *input the next grade (possibly the sentinel)*

In pseudocode, we do not use braces around the statements that form the body of the *while* structure. We simply indent the statements under the *while* to show that they belong to the *while*. Again, pseudocode is only an informal application-development aid.

The pseudocode statement

> *calculate and display the class average*

can be refined as follows:

> *if the counter is not equal to zero*
>   *set the average to the total divided by the counter*
>   *display the average*
> *else*
>   *display "No grades were entered"*

We're careful here to test for the possibility of division by zero—a logic error that, if undetected, would cause the application to fail or produce invalid output. The complete second refinement of the pseudocode for the class-average problem is shown in Fig. 5.8.

Error-Prevention Tip 5.2

When performing division by an expression whose value could be zero, explicitly test for this possibility and handle it appropriately in your application (e.g., by displaying an error message) rather than allowing the error to occur.

```
 1    initialize total to zero
 2    initialize counter to zero
 3
 4    prompt the user to enter the first grade
 5    input the first grade (possibly the sentinel)
 6
 7    while the user has not yet entered the sentinel
 8        add this grade into the running total
 9        add one to the grade counter
10        prompt the user to enter the next grade
11        input the next grade (possibly the sentinel)
12
13    if the counter is not equal to zero
14        set the average to the total divided by the counter
15        display the average
16    else
17        display "No grades were entered"
```

Fig. 5.8 | Class-average problem pseudocode algorithm with sentinel-controlled repetition.

In Fig. 5.5 and Fig. 5.8, we included some completely blank lines and indentation in the pseudocode to make it more readable. The blank lines separate the pseudocode algorithms into their various phases and set off control statements, and the indentation emphasizes the bodies of the control statements.

The pseudocode algorithm in Fig. 5.8 solves the more general class-averaging problem. This algorithm was developed after only two refinements. Sometimes more refinements are necessary.

Software Engineering Observation 5.4

Terminate the top-down, stepwise refinement process when you've specified the pseudocode algorithm in sufficient detail for you to convert the pseudocode to C#. Normally, implementing the C# application is then straightforward.

Software Engineering Observation 5.5

Some experienced programmers write applications without ever using application-development tools like pseudocode. They feel that their ultimate goal is to solve the problem on a computer and that writing pseudocode merely delays the production of final outputs. Although this method may work for simple and familiar problems, it can lead to serious errors and delays in large, complex projects.

Implementing Sentinel-Controlled Repetition in Class *GradeBook*

Figure 5.9 shows the C# class GradeBook containing method DetermineClassAverage that implements the pseudocode algorithm of Fig. 5.8. Although each grade is an integer, the averaging calculation is likely to produce a number with a decimal point—in other words, a real number or floating-point number. The type int cannot represent such a number, so this class uses type double to do so.

```
 1    // Fig. 5.9: GradeBook.cs
 2    // GradeBook class that solves class-average problem using
 3    // sentinel-controlled repetition.
 4    using System;
 5
 6    public class GradeBook
 7    {
 8       // auto-implemented property CourseName
 9       public string CourseName { get; set; }
10
11       // constructor initializes the CourseName property
12       public GradeBook( string name )
13       {
14          CourseName = name; // set CourseName to name
15       } // end constructor
16
17       // display a welcome message to the GradeBook user
18       public void DisplayMessage()
19       {
20          Console.WriteLine( "Welcome to the grade book for\n{0}!\n",
21             CourseName );
22       } // end method DisplayMessage
23
24       // determine the average of an arbitrary number of grades
25       public void DetermineClassAverage()
26       {
27          int total; // sum of grades
28          int gradeCounter; // number of grades entered
29          int grade; // grade value
30          double average; // number with decimal point for average
31
32          // initialization phase
33          total = 0; // initialize total
34          gradeCounter = 0; // initialize loop counter
35
36          // processing phase
37          // prompt for and read a grade from the user
38          Console.Write( "Enter grade or -1 to quit: " );
39          grade = Convert.ToInt32( Console.ReadLine() );
40
41          // loop until sentinel value is read from the user
42          while ( grade != -1 )
43          {
44             total = total + grade; // add grade to total
45             gradeCounter = gradeCounter + 1; // increment counter
46
47             // prompt for and read the next grade from the user
48             Console.Write( "Enter grade or -1 to quit: " );
49             grade = Convert.ToInt32( Console.ReadLine() );
50          } // end while
51
```

Fig. 5.9 | GradeBook class that solves the class-average problem using sentinel-controlled repetition. (Part 1 of 2.)

```
52          // termination phase
53          // if the user entered at least one grade...
54          if ( gradeCounter != 0 )
55          {
56              // calculate the average of all the grades entered
57              average = ( double ) total / gradeCounter;
58
59              // display the total and average (with two digits of precision)
60              Console.WriteLine( "\nTotal of the {0} grades entered is {1}",
61                  gradeCounter, total );
62              Console.WriteLine( "Class average is {0:F}", average );
63          } // end if
64          else // no grades were entered, so output error message
65              Console.WriteLine( "No grades were entered" );
66      } // end method DetermineClassAverage
67  } // end class GradeBook
```

Fig. 5.9 | GradeBook class that solves the class-average problem using sentinel-controlled repetition. (Part 2 of 2.)

In this example, we see that control statements may be stacked on top of one another (in sequence) just as a child stacks building blocks. The while statement (lines 42–50) is followed in sequence by an if...else statement (lines 54–65). Much of the code in this application is identical to the code in Fig. 5.6, so we concentrate on the new features and issues.

Line 30 declares double variable average. This variable allows us to store the calculated class average as a floating-point number. Line 34 initializes gradeCounter to 0, because no grades have been entered yet. Remember that this application uses sentinel-controlled repetition to input the grades from the user. To keep an accurate record of the number of grades entered, the application increments gradeCounter only when the user inputs a valid grade value.

Program Logic for Sentinel-Controlled Repetition vs. Counter-Controlled Repetition
Compare the program logic for sentinel-controlled repetition in this application with that for counter-controlled repetition in Fig. 5.6. In counter-controlled repetition, each repetition of the while statement (e.g., lines 38–44 of Fig. 5.6) reads a value from the user, for the specified number of repetitions. In sentinel-controlled repetition, the application reads the first value (lines 38–39 of Fig. 5.9) before reaching the while. This value determines whether the application's flow of control should enter the body of the while. If the condition of the while is false, the user entered the sentinel value, so the body of the while does not execute (because no grades were entered). If, on the other hand, the condition is true, the body begins execution, and the loop adds the grade value to the total (line 44) and adds 1 to gradeCounter (line 45). Then lines 48–49 in the loop's body input the next value from the user. Next, program control reaches the closing right brace of the body at line 50, so execution continues with the test of the while's condition (line 42). The condition uses the most recent grade input by the user to determine whether the loop's body should execute again. The value of variable grade is always input from the user immediately before the application tests the while condition. This allows the application to determine whether the value just input is the sentinel value *before* the application processes

that value (i.e., adds it to the `total`). If the sentinel value is input, the loop terminates; the application does *not* add –1 to the `total`.

Good Programming Practice 5.6

In a sentinel-controlled loop, the prompts requesting data entry should explicitly remind the user of the sentinel value.

Notice the `while` statement's block in Fig. 5.9 (lines 43–50). Without the braces, the loop would consider its body to be only the first statement, which adds the `grade` to the `total`. The last three statements in the block would fall outside the loop's body, causing the computer to interpret the code incorrectly as follows:

```
while ( grade != -1 )
    total = total + grade; // add grade to total
gradeCounter = gradeCounter + 1; // increment counter

// prompt for input and read next grade from user
Console.Write( "Enter grade or -1 to quit: " );
grade = Convert.ToInt32( Console.ReadLine() );
```

The preceding code would cause an infinite loop in the application if the user did not enter the sentinel –1 at line 39 (before the `while` statement).

Error-Prevention Tip 5.3

Omitting the braces that delimit a block can lead to logic errors, such as infinite loops. To prevent this problem, some programmers enclose the body of every control statement in braces even if the body contains only a single statement.

After the loop terminates, the `if...else` statement at lines 54–65 executes. The condition at line 54 determines whether any grades were input. If none were input, the `else` part (lines 64–65) of the `if...else` statement executes and displays the message "`No grades were entered`", and the method returns control to the calling method.

Explicitly and Implicitly Converting Between Simple Types

If at least one grade was entered, line 57 of Fig. 5.9 calculates the average of the grades. Recall from Fig. 5.6 that integer division yields an integer result. Even though variable `average` is declared as a `double` (line 30), the calculation

```
average = total / gradeCounter;
```

loses the division's fractional part before the result is assigned to `average`. This occurs because `total` and `gradeCounter` are both integers, and integer division yields an integer result. To perform a floating-point calculation with integer values, we must temporarily treat these values as floating-point numbers for use in the calculation. C# provides the **unary cast operator** to accomplish this task. Line 57 uses the **(double)** cast operator—which has higher precedence than the arithmetic operators—to create a *temporary* floating-point copy of its operand `total` (which appears to the right of the operator). Using a cast operator in this manner is called **explicit conversion**. The value stored in `total` is still an integer.

The calculation now consists of a floating-point value (the temporary `double` version of `total`) divided by the integer `gradeCounter`. C# knows how to evaluate only arithmetic expressions in which the operands' types are identical. To ensure that the operands are of the same type, C# performs an operation called **promotion** (or **implicit conversion**) on selected operands. For example, in an expression containing values of the types int and double, the int values are promoted to double values for use in the expression. In this example, the value of gradeCounter is promoted to type double, then floating-point division is performed and the result of the calculation is assigned to average. As long as the (double) cast operator is applied to any variable in the calculation, the calculation will yield a double result.

Common Programming Error 5.6

A cast operator can be used to convert between simple numeric types, such as int and double, and between related reference types (as we discuss in Chapter 12, OOP: Polymorphism, Interfaces and Operator Overloading). Casting to the wrong type may cause compilation or runtime errors.

Cast operators are available for all simple types. We'll discuss cast operators for reference types in Chapter 12. The cast operator is formed by placing parentheses around the name of a type. This operator is a **unary operator** (i.e., an operator that takes only one operand). In Chapter 3, we studied the binary arithmetic operators. C# also supports unary versions of the plus (+) and minus (–) operators, so you can write expressions like +5 or -7. Cast operators associate from right to left and have the same precedence as other unary operators, such as unary + and unary -. This precedence is one level higher than that of the **multiplicative operators** *, / and %. (See the operator precedence chart in Appendix A.) We indicate the cast operator with the notation (*type*) in our precedence charts, to indicate that any type name can be used to form a cast operator.

Line 62 outputs the class average. In this example, we decided that we'd like to display the class average rounded to the nearest hundredth and output the average with exactly two digits to the right of the decimal point. The format specifier F in WriteLine's format item (line 62) indicates that variable average's value should be displayed as a real number. By default, numbers output with F have two digits to the right of the decimal point. The number of decimal places to the right of the decimal point is also known as the number's **precision**. Any floating-point value output with F will be rounded to the hundredths position—for example, 123.457 will be rounded to 123.46, and 27.333 will be rounded to 27.33. In this application, the three grades entered during the sample execution of class GradeBookTest (Fig. 5.10) total 263, which yields the average 87.66666.... The format item rounds the average to the hundredths position, and the average is displayed as 87.67.

```
1   // Fig. 5.10: GradeBookTest.cs
2   // Create GradeBook object and invoke its DetermineClassAverage method.
3   public class GradeBookTest
4   {
5      public static void Main( string[] args )
6      {
7         // create GradeBook object myGradeBook and
8         // pass course name to constructor
9         GradeBook myGradeBook = new GradeBook(
10           "CS101 Introduction to C# Programming" );
```

Fig. 5.10 | Create GradeBook object and invoke DetermineClassAverage method. (Part 1 of 2.)

```
11
12          myGradeBook.DisplayMessage(); // display welcome message
13          myGradeBook.DetermineClassAverage(); // find average of grades
14      } // end Main
15  } // end class GradeBookTest
```

```
Welcome to the grade book for
CS101 Introduction to C# Programming!

Enter grade or -1 to quit: 96
Enter grade or -1 to quit: 88
Enter grade or -1 to quit: 79
Enter grade or -1 to quit: -1

Total of the 3 grades entered is 263
Class average is 87.67
```

Fig. 5.10 | Create GradeBook object and invoke DetermineClassAverage method. (Part 2 of 2.)

5.10 Formulating Algorithms: Nested Control Statements

For the next example, we once again formulate an algorithm by using pseudocode and top-down, stepwise refinement, and write a corresponding C# application. We've seen that control statements can be stacked on top of one another (in sequence). In this case study, we examine the only other structured way control statements can be connected, namely, by **nesting** one control statement within another.

Consider the following problem statement:

> *A college offers a course that prepares students for the state licensing exam for real estate brokers. Last year, 10 of the students who completed this course took the exam. The college wants to know how well its students did on the exam. You've been asked to write an application to summarize the results. You've been given a list of these 10 students. Next to each name is written a 1 if the student passed the exam or a 2 if the student failed.*

> *Your application should analyze the results of the exam as follows:*

>> *1. Input each test result (i.e., a 1 or a 2). Display the message "Enter result" on the screen each time the application requests another test result.*

>> *2. Count the number of test results of each type.*

>> *3. Display a summary of the test results indicating the number of students who passed and the number who failed.*

>> *4. If more than eight students passed the exam, display the message "Bonus to instructor!"*

After reading the problem statement, we make the following observations:

1. The application must process test results for 10 students. A counter-controlled loop can be used because the number of test results is known in advance.

2. Each test result has a numeric value—either a 1 or a 2. Each time the application reads a test result, the application must determine whether the number is a 1 or a 2. We test for a 1 in our algorithm. If the number is not a 1, we assume that it's a 2. (Exercise 5.24 considers the consequences of this assumption.)

3. Two counters are used to keep track of the exam results—one to count the number of students who passed the exam and one to count the number of students who failed the exam.

4. After the application has processed all the results, it must determine whether more than eight students passed the exam.

Let us proceed with top-down, stepwise refinement. We begin with a pseudocode representation of the top:

> *analyze exam results and decide whether the instructor should receive a bonus*

Once again, the top is a *complete* representation of the application, but several refinements are likely to be needed before the pseudocode can evolve naturally into a C# application.
Our first refinement is

> *initialize variables*
> *input the 10 exam results, and count passes and failures*
> *display a summary of the exam results and decide if the instructor should*
> *   receive a bonus*

Here, too, even though we have a complete representation of the entire application, further refinement is necessary. We now specify individual variables. Counters are needed to record the passes and failures, a counter will be used to control the looping process and a variable is needed to store the user input. The variable in which the user input will be stored is not initialized at the start of the algorithm, because its value is read from the user during each repetition of the loop.
The pseudocode statement

> *initialize variables*

can be refined as follows:

> *initialize passes to zero*
> *initialize failures to zero*
> *initialize student counter to one*

Notice that only the counters are initialized at the start of the algorithm.
The pseudocode statement

> *input the 10 exam results, and count passes and failures*

requires a loop that successively inputs the result of each exam. We know in advance that there are precisely 10 exam results, so counter-controlled looping is appropriate. Inside the loop (i.e., **nested** within the loop), a double-selection statement will determine whether each exam result is a pass or a failure and will increment the appropriate counter. The refinement of the preceding pseudocode statement is then

> *while student counter is less than or equal to 10*
>   *prompt the user to enter the next exam result*
>   *input the next exam result*
>
>   *if the student passed*
>   *add one to passes*
>   *else*
>   *add one to failures*
>
>   *add one to student counter*

We use blank lines to isolate the *if…else* control statement, which improves readability. The pseudocode statement

> *display a summary of the exam results and decide if the instructor should receive a bonus*

can be refined as follows:

> *display the number of passes*
> *display the number of failures*
>
> *if more than eight students passed*
>   *display "Bonus to instructor!"*

Complete Second Refinement of Pseudocode and Conversion to Class `Analysis`

The complete second refinement of the pseudocode appears in Fig. 5.11. Notice that blank lines are also used to set off the *while* statement for readability. This pseudocode is now sufficiently refined for conversion to C#. The program that implements the pseudocode algorithm and sample outputs are shown in Fig. 5.12.

---

1   *initialize passes to zero*
2   *initialize failures to zero*
3   *initialize student counter to one*
4
5   *while student counter is less than or equal to 10*
6   *prompt the user to enter the next exam result*
7   *input the next exam result*
8
9   *if the student passed*
10   *add one to passes*
11   *else*
12   *add one to failures*
13
14   *add one to student counter*
15

Fig. 5.11 | Pseudocode for the examination-results problem. (Part 1 of 2.)

```
16    display the number of passes
17    display the number of failures
18
19    if more than eight students passed
20        display "Bonus to instructor!"
```

Fig. 5.11 | Pseudocode for the examination-results problem. (Part 2 of 2.)

This example contains only one class, with method Main performing all the class's work. In this chapter and in Chapter 4, you've seen examples consisting of two classes—one class containing methods that perform useful tasks and one containing method Main, which creates an object of the other class and calls its methods. Occasionally, when it makes no sense to try to create a reusable class, we'll use a mechanical example contained entirely within the Main method of a single class.

Lines 10–13 of Fig. 5.12 declare the variables that method Main uses to process the examination results. Several of these declarations use C#'s ability to incorporate variable initialization into declarations (passes is assigned 0, failures is assigned 0 and student-Counter is assigned 1).

```
1     // Fig. 5.12: Analysis.cs
2     // Analysis of examination results, using nested control statements.
3     using System;
4
5     public class Analysis
6     {
7         public static void Main( string[] args )
8         {
9             // initialize variables in declarations
10            int passes = 0; // number of passes
11            int failures = 0; // number of failures
12            int studentCounter = 1; // student counter
13            int result; // one exam result from user
14
15            // process 10 students using counter-controlled repetition
16            while ( studentCounter <= 10 )
17            {
18                // prompt user for input and obtain a value from the user
19                Console.Write( "Enter result (1 = pass, 2 = fail): " );
20                result = Convert.ToInt32( Console.ReadLine() );
21
22                // if...else nested in while
23                if ( result == 1 ) // if result 1,
24                    passes = passes + 1; // increment passes
25                else // else result is not 1, so
26                    failures = failures + 1; // increment failures
27
28                // increment studentCounter so loop eventually terminates
29                studentCounter = studentCounter + 1;
30            } // end while
```

Fig. 5.12 | Analysis of examination results, using nested control statements. (Part 1 of 2.)

```
31
32          // termination phase; prepare and display results
33          Console.WriteLine( "Passed: {0}\nFailed: {1}", passes, failures );
34
35          // determine whether more than 8 students passed
36          if ( passes > 8 )
37              Console.WriteLine( "Bonus to instructor!" );
38      } // end Main
39  } // end class Analysis
```

```
Enter result (1 = pass, 2 = fail): 1
Enter result (1 = pass, 2 = fail): 2
Enter result (1 = pass, 2 = fail): 1
Enter result (1 = pass, 2 = fail): 1
Enter result (1 = pass, 2 = fail): 1
Enter result (1 = pass, 2 = fail): 1
Enter result (1 = pass, 2 = fail): 1
Enter result (1 = pass, 2 = fail): 1
Enter result (1 = pass, 2 = fail): 1
Enter result (1 = pass, 2 = fail): 1
Passed: 9
Failed: 1
Bonus to instructor!
```

```
Enter result (1 = pass, 2 = fail): 1
Enter result (1 = pass, 2 = fail): 2
Enter result (1 = pass, 2 = fail): 2
Enter result (1 = pass, 2 = fail): 2
Enter result (1 = pass, 2 = fail): 1
Enter result (1 = pass, 2 = fail): 1
Enter result (1 = pass, 2 = fail): 1
Enter result (1 = pass, 2 = fail): 1
Enter result (1 = pass, 2 = fail): 2
Enter result (1 = pass, 2 = fail): 2
Passed: 5
Failed: 5
```

Fig. 5.12 | Analysis of examination results, using nested control statements. (Part 2 of 2.)

The while statement (lines 16–30) loops 10 times. During each repetition, the loop inputs and processes one exam result. Notice that the if...else statement (lines 23–26) for processing each result is nested in the while statement. If the result is 1, the if...else statement increments passes; otherwise, it assumes the result is 2 and increments failures. Line 29 increments studentCounter before the loop condition is tested again at line 16. After 10 values have been input, the loop terminates and line 33 displays the number of passes and the number of failures. Lines 36–37 determine whether more than eight students passed the exam and, if so, outputs the message "Bonus to instructor!".

Figure 5.12 shows the input and output from two sample executions of the application. During the first sample execution, the condition at line 36 is true—more than eight students passed the exam, so the application outputs a message indicating that the instructor should receive a bonus.

Error-Prevention Tip 5.4

Initializing local variables when they're declared helps you avoid compilation errors that might arise from attempts to use uninitialized data. While C# does not require that local-variable initializations be incorporated into declarations, it does require that local variables be initialized before their values are used in an expression.

5.11 Compound Assignment Operators

C# provides several **compound assignment operators** for abbreviating assignment expressions. Any statement of the form

> *variable* = *variable   operator   expression*;

where *operator* is one of the binary operators +, -, *, / or % (or others we discuss later in the text) can be written in the form

> *variable   operator= expression*;

For example, you can abbreviate the statement

```
c = c + 3;
```

with the **addition compound assignment operator, +=,** as

```
c += 3;
```

The += operator adds the value of the expression on the right of the operator to the value of the variable on the left of the operator and stores the result in the variable on the left of the operator. Thus, the assignment expression c += 3 adds 3 to c. Figure 5.13 shows the arithmetic compound assignment operators, sample expressions using the operators and explanations of what the operators do.

Assignment operator	Sample expression	Explanation	Assigns
Assume: **int** c = 3, d = 5, e = 4, f = 6, g = 12;			
+=	c += 7	c = c + 7	10 to c
-=	d -= 4	d = d - 4	1 to d
*=	e *= 5	e = e * 5	20 to e
/=	f /= 3	f = f / 3	2 to f
%=	g %= 9	g = g % 9	3 to g

Fig. 5.13 | Arithmetic compound assignment operators.

5.12 Increment and Decrement Operators

C# provides two unary operators for adding 1 to or subtracting 1 from the value of a numeric variable. These are the unary **increment operator, ++,** and the unary **decrement operator, --,** respectively, which are summarized in Fig. 5.14. An application can increment by 1 the value of a variable called c using the increment operator, ++, rather than the expression c = c + 1 or c += 1. An increment or decrement operator that is prefixed to (placed before) a variable is referred to as the **prefix increment operator** or **prefix decrement operator**, respectively. An increment or decrement operator that is postfixed to (placed after) a variable is referred to as the **postfix increment operator** or **postfix decrement operator**, respectively.

Operator	Called	Sample expression	Explanation
++	prefix increment	++a	Increments a by 1, then uses the new value of a in the expression in which a resides.
++	postfix increment	a++	Uses the current value of a in the expression in which a resides, then increments a by 1.
--	prefix decrement	--b	Decrements b by 1, then uses the new value of b in the expression in which b resides.
--	postfix decrement	b--	Uses the current value of b in the expression in which b resides, then decrements b by 1.

Fig. 5.14 | Increment and decrement operators.

Incrementing (or decrementing) a variable with the prefix increment (or prefix decrement) operator causes it to be incremented (or decremented) by 1; then the new value of the variable is used in the expression in which it appears. Incrementing (or decrementing) the variable with the postfix increment (or postfix decrement) operator causes the variable's current value to be used in the expression in which it appears; then the variable's value is incremented (or decremented) by 1.

Good Programming Practice 5.7
Unlike binary operators, the unary increment and decrement operators should (by convention) be placed next to their operands, with no intervening spaces.

Figure 5.15 demonstrates the difference between the prefix increment and postfix increment versions of the ++ increment operator. The decrement operator (--) works similarly. In this example, we simply want to show the mechanics of the ++ operator, so we use only one class declaration containing method Main.

```
1   // Fig. 5.15: Increment.cs
2   // Prefix increment and postfix increment operators.
3   using System;
4
5   public class Increment
6   {
7      public static void Main( string[] args )
8      {
9         int c;
10
```

Fig. 5.15 | Prefix increment and postfix increment operators. (Part 1 of 2.)

```
11       // demonstrate postfix increment operator
12       c = 5; // assign 5 to c
13       Console.WriteLine( c ); // display 5
14       Console.WriteLine( c++ ); // display 5 again, then increment
15       Console.WriteLine( c ); // display 6
16
17       Console.WriteLine(); // skip a line
18
19       // demonstrate prefix increment operator
20       c = 5; // assign 5 to c
21       Console.WriteLine( c ); // display 5
22       Console.WriteLine( ++c ); // increment, then display
23       Console.WriteLine( c ); // display 6 again
24    } // end Main
25 } // end class Increment
```

```
5
5
6

5
6
6
```

Fig. 5.15 | Prefix increment and postfix increment operators. (Part 2 of 2.)

Line 12 initializes the variable c to 5, and line 13 outputs c's initial value. Line 14 outputs the value of the expression c++. This expression performs the postfix increment operation on the variable c, so c's original value (5) is output, then c's value is incremented. Thus, line 14 outputs c's initial value (5) again. Line 15 outputs c's new value (6) to prove that the variable's value was indeed incremented in line 14.

Line 20 resets c's value to 5, and line 21 outputs c's value. Line 22 outputs the value of the expression ++c. This expression performs the prefix increment operation on c, so its value is incremented; then the new value (6) is output. Line 23 outputs c's value again to show that the value of c is still 6 after line 22 executes.

The arithmetic compound assignment operators and the increment and decrement operators can be used to simplify statements. For example, the three assignment statements in Fig. 5.12 (lines 24, 26 and 29)

```
passes = passes + 1;
failures = failures + 1;
studentCounter = studentCounter + 1;
```

can be written more concisely with compound assignment operators as

```
passes += 1;
failures += 1;
studentCounter += 1;
```

and even more concisely with prefix increment operators as

```
++passes;
++failures;
++studentCounter;
```

or with postfix increment operators as

```
passes++;
failures++;
studentCounter++;
```

When incrementing or decrementing a variable in a statement by itself, the prefix increment and postfix increment forms have the same effect, and the prefix decrement and postfix decrement forms have the same effect. It's only when a variable appears in the context of a larger expression that the prefix increment and postfix increment have different effects (and similarly for the prefix decrement and postfix decrement).

 Common Programming Error 5.7

Attempting to use the increment or decrement operator on an expression other than one to which a value can be assigned is a syntax error. For example, writing ++(x + 1) is a syntax error, because (x + 1) is not an expression to which a value can be assigned.

Figure 5.16 shows the precedence and associativity of the operators we've introduced to this point. The operators are shown from top to bottom in decreasing order of precedence. The second column describes the associativity of the operators at each level of precedence. The conditional operator (?:); the unary operators prefix increment (++), prefix decrement (--), plus (+) and minus (-); the cast operators; and the assignment operators =, +=, -=, *=, /= and %= associate from right to left. All the other operators in the operator precedence chart in Fig. 5.16 associate from left to right. The third column names the groups of operators.

Operators				Associativity	Type
.	new	++*(postfix)*	--*(postfix)*	left to right	highest precedence
++	--	+	- (*type*)	right to left	unary prefix
*	/	%		left to right	multiplicative
+	-			left to right	additive
<	<=	>	>=	left to right	relational
==	!=			left to right	equality
?:				right to left	conditional
=	+=	-=	*= /= %=	right to left	assignment

Fig. 5.16 | Precedence and associativity of the operators discussed so far.

5.13 Simple Types

The table in Appendix B lists the 13 **simple types** in C#. Like its predecessor languages C and C++, C# requires all variables to have a type. For this reason, C# is referred to as a **strongly typed language**.

In C and C++, programmers frequently have to write separate versions of applications to support different computer platforms, because the simple types are *not* guaranteed to be identical from computer to computer. For example, an int value on one machine might be represented by 16 bits (2 bytes) of storage, while an `int` value on another machine might be represented by 32 bits (4 bytes) of storage. In C#, `int` values are always 32 bits (4 bytes). In fact, *all* C# numeric types have fixed sizes, as is shown in Appendix B.

Each type in Appendix B is listed with its size in bits (there are eight bits to a byte) and its range of values. Because the designers of C# want it to be maximally portable, they use internationally recognized standards for both character formats (Unicode; for more information, see Appendix F, Unicode®) and floating-point numbers (IEEE 754; for more information, visit `grouper.ieee.org/groups/754/`).

Recall from Section 4.5 that variables of simple types declared outside of a method as fields of a class are automatically assigned default values unless explicitly initialized. Instance variables of types `char`, `byte`, `sbyte`, `short`, `ushort`, `int`, `uint`, `long`, `ulong`, `float`, `double`, and `decimal` are all given the value 0 by default. Instance variables of type `bool` are given the value `false` by default. Similarly, reference-type instance variables are initialized by default to the value `null`.

5.14 Wrap-Up

This chapter presented basic problem-solving techniques that programmers use in building classes and developing methods for these classes. We demonstrated how to construct an algorithm (i.e., an approach to solving a problem), then how to refine the algorithm through several phases of pseudocode development, resulting in C# code that can be executed as part of a method. The chapter showed how to use top-down, stepwise refinement to plan out the specific actions that a method must perform and the order in which the method must perform these actions.

Only three types of control structures—sequence, selection and repetition—are needed to develop any algorithm. Specifically, we demonstrated the `if` single-selection statement, the `if...else` double-selection statement and the `while` repetition statement. These are some of the building blocks used to construct solutions to many problems. We used control-statement stacking to compute the total and the average of a set of student grades with counter- and sentinel-controlled repetition, and we used control-statement nesting to analyze and make decisions based on a set of exam results. We introduced C#'s compound assignment, unary cast, conditional (`?:`), increment and decrement operators. Finally, we discussed the simple types. In Chapter 6, we continue our discussion of control statements, introducing the `for`, `do...while` and `switch` statements.

Summary

Section 5.2 Algorithms
- An algorithm is a procedure for solving a problem in terms of the actions to execute and the order in which these actions execute.
- Specifying the order in which statements (actions) execute in an application is called program control.

Section 5.3 Pseudocode
- Pseudocode is an informal language that helps you develop algorithms without having to worry about the strict details of C# language syntax.

- Carefully prepared pseudocode can easily be converted to a corresponding C# application.

Section 5.4 Control Structures
- There are three types of control structures—sequence, selection and repetition.
- The sequence structure is built into C#. Unless directed otherwise, the computer executes C# statements one after the other in the order in which they're written.
- Activity diagrams are part of the UML. An activity diagram models the workflow of a portion of a software system.
- Activity diagrams are composed of special-purpose symbols, such as action-state symbols, diamonds and small circles. These symbols are connected by transition arrows, which represent the flow of the activity.
- Like pseudocode, activity diagrams help you develop and represent algorithms. Activity diagrams clearly show how control structures operate.
- Action-state symbols (rectangles with their left and right sides replaced with arcs curving outward) represent actions to perform.
- The arrows in an activity diagram represent transitions, which indicate the order in which the actions represented by the action states occur.
- The solid circle in an activity diagram represents the activity's initial state. The solid circle surrounded by a hollow circle represents the final state.
- Rectangles with the upper-right corners folded over are UML notes (like comments in C#)—explanatory remarks that describe the purpose of symbols in the diagram.
- C# has three types of selection statements: the `if` statement, the `if...else` statement and the `switch` statement.
- The `if` statement is called a single-selection statement because it selects or ignores a single action.
- The `if...else` statement is called a double-selection statement because it selects between two different actions (or groups of actions).
- The `switch` statement is called a multiple-selection statement because it selects among many different actions (or groups of actions).
- C# provides four repetition statements: the `while`, `do...while`, `for` and `foreach` statements.
- The `while`, `for` and `foreach` statements perform the actions in their bodies zero or more times.
- The `do...while` statement performs the actions in its body one or more times.
- Control statements may be connected in two ways: control-statement stacking and control-statement nesting.

Section 5.5 `if` Single-Selection Statement
- The `if` single-selection statement performs an indicated action (or group of actions) only when the condition is true; otherwise, the action is skipped.
- In an activity diagram, the diamond symbol indicates that a decision is to be made. The workflow will continue along a path determined by the symbol's associated guard conditions.
- When modelled by a UML activity diagram, all control statements contain initial states, transition arrows, action states and decision symbols.

Section 5.6 `if...else` Double-Selection Statement
- The `if...else` double-selection statement allows you to specify an action (or group of actions) to perform when the condition is true and a different action (or group of actions) when the condition is false.

- C# provides the conditional operator (?:), which can be used in place of an if...else statement. The conditional expression evaluates to the second operand if the first operand evaluates to true, and evaluates to the third operand if the first operand evaluates to false.

- To include several statements in the body of an if (or the body of an else for an if...else statement), enclose the statements in braces ({ and }).

- A set of statements contained within a pair of braces is called a block. A block can be placed anywhere in an application that a single statement can be placed.

Section 5.7 while *Repetition Statement*
- A repetition statement allows you to specify that an application should repeat an action while some condition remains true.

- The format for the while repetition statement is

      while (*condition*)
          statement

Section 5.8 *Formulating Algorithms: Counter-Controlled Repetition*
- Counter-controlled repetition is a technique that uses a variable called a counter to control the number of times a set of statements will execute.

- A variable is said to be definitely assigned when the variable is guaranteed to be assigned a value in every possible flow of control. Local variables must be definitely assigned before they're used in calculations.

- Dividing two integers results in integer division—any fractional part of the calculation is lost.

Section 5.9 *Formulating Algorithms: Sentinel-Controlled Repetition*
- Sentinel-controlled repetition is a technique that uses a special value called a sentinel value to indicate "end of data entry."

Section 5.10 *Formulating Algorithms: Nested Control Statements*
- The unary cast operator (double) creates a *temporary* floating-point copy of its operand. Using a cast operator in this manner is called explicit conversion.

- To ensure that both operands of a binary operator are of the same type, C# performs promotion on selected operands.

- The format specifier F indicates that a variable's value should be displayed as a real number.

Section 5.11 *Compound Assignment Operators*
- C# provides several compound assignment operators for abbreviating assignment expressions, including +=, -=, *=, /= and %=.

Section 5.12 *Increment and Decrement Operators*
- C# provides the unary increment operator, ++, and the unary decrement operator, --, for adding 1 to or subtracting 1 from the value of a numeric variable.

- Incrementing (or decrementing) a variable with the prefix increment (or prefix decrement) operator causes the variable to be incremented (decremented) by 1; then the new value of the variable is used in the expression in which it appears. Incrementing (or decrementing) the variable with the postfix increment (or postfix decrement) operator causes the current value of the variable to be used in the expression in which it appears; then the variable's value is incremented (decremented) by 1.

Section 5.13 Simple Types

- C# is a strongly typed language—it requires all variables to have a type.

- Variables of simple types declared outside a method as fields of a class are automatically assigned default values. Instance variables of types char, byte, sbyte, short, ushort, int, uint, long, ulong, float, double, and decimal are all given the value 0 by default. Instance variables of type bool are given the value false by default. Reference-type instance variables are initialized by default to the value null.

Terminology

-- operator
?: operator
++ operator
action
action/decision model of programming
action expression (in the UML)
action state (in the UML)
action-state symbol (in the UML)
activity (in the UML)
activity diagram (in the UML)
addition compound assignment operator (+=)
algorithm
arithmetic compound assignment operators:
    +=, -=, *=, /= and %=
block
body of a loop
bool simple type
boolean expression
cast operator, (*type*)
compound assignment operator
conditional expression
conditional operator (?:)
control statement
control-statement nesting
control-statement stacking
control structure
control variable
counter
counter-controlled repetition
dangling-else problem
decision
decision symbol (in the UML)
decrement operator (--)
definite assignment
definite repetition
diamond (in the UML)
dotted line
double-selection statement
dummy value
explicit conversion
false

fatal logic error
final state (in the UML)
flag value
goto statement
guard condition (in the UML)
if statement
if...else statement
implicit conversion
increment operator (++)
indefinite repetition
infinite loop
initial state (in the UML)
integer division
instantiate an object
iteration statement
logic error
loop
loop-continuation condition
merge symbol (in the UML)
multiple-selection statement
multiplicative operators
nested control statements
nested if...else statements
nonfatal logic error
note (in the UML)
order in which actions should execute
postfix decrement operator
postfix increment operator
prefix decrement operator
prefix increment operator
procedure
program control
promotion
pseudocode
refinement
repetition
repetition statement
selection statement
sentinel-controlled repetition
sentinel value
sequence structure

sequential execution
signal value
simple types
single-entry/single-exit control structures
single-selection statement
small circle (in the UML)
solid circle (in the UML)
solid circle surrounded by a hollow circle
    (in the UML)
stacked control statements
strongly typed language
structured programming
syntax error

ternary operator
top-down stepwise refinement
total
transfer of control
transition (in the UML)
transition arrow (in the UML)
true
truncate
unary cast operator
unary operator
while statement
workflow

Self-Review Exercises

5.1   Fill in the blanks in each of the following statements:

a) All applications can be written in terms of three types of control structures: _____, _____ and _____.

b) The _____ statement is used to execute one action when a condition is true and another when that condition is false.

c) Repeating a set of instructions a specific number of times is called _____ repetition.

d) When it's not known in advance how many times a set of statements will be repeated, a(n) _____ value can be used to terminate the repetition.

e) The _____ structure is built into C#—by default, statements execute in the order they appear.

f) Instance variables of type int are given the value _____ by default.

g) C# is a(n) _____ language—it requires all variables to have a type.

h) If the increment operator is _____ to a variable, the variable is incremented by 1 first, then its new value is used in the expression.

5.2   State whether each of the following is *true* or *false*. If *false*, explain why.

a) An algorithm is a procedure for solving a problem in terms of the actions to execute and the order in which these actions execute.

b) A set of statements contained within a pair of parentheses is called a block.

c) A selection statement specifies that an action is to be repeated while some condition remains true.

d) A nested control statement appears in the body of another control statement.

e) C# provides the arithmetic compound assignment operators +=, -=, *=, /= and %= for abbreviating assignment expressions.

f) Specifying the order in which statements (actions) execute in an application is called program control.

g) The unary cast operator (double) creates a temporary integer copy of its operand.

h) Instance variables of type bool are given the value true by default.

i) Pseudocode helps you think out an application before attempting to write it in a programming language.

5.3   Write four different C# statements that each add 1 to int variable x.

5.4   Write C# statements to accomplish each of the following tasks:

a) Assign the sum of x and y to z, and increment x by 1 after the calculation. Use only one statement.

b) Test whether variable count is greater than 10. If it is, display "Count is greater than 10".

    c) Decrement the variable x by 1, then subtract it from the variable `total`. Use only one statement.

    d) Calculate the remainder after q is divided by `divisor`, and assign the result to q. Write this statement in two different ways.

5.5   Write a C# statement to accomplish each of the following tasks:

    a) Declare variable `sum` to be of type `int`.

    b) Declare variable x to be of type `int`.

    c) Assign 1 to variable x.

    d) Assign 0 to variable `sum`.

    e) Add variable x to variable `sum`, and assign the result to variable `sum`.

    f) Display "The sum is: ", followed by the value of variable `sum`.

5.6   Combine the statements that you wrote in Exercise 5.5 into a C# application that calculates and displays the sum of the integers from 1 to 10. Use a `while` statement to loop through the calculation and increment statements. The loop should terminate when the value of x becomes 11.

5.7   Determine the values of the variables in the following statement after it executes. Assume that when the statement begins executing, all variables are type `int` and have the value 5.

```
product *= x++;
```

5.8   Identify and correct the errors in each of the following sets of code:

    a)
```
while ( c <= 5 )
   {
      product *= c;
      ++c;
```

    b)
```
if ( gender == 1 )
      Console.WriteLine( "Woman" );
   else;
      Console.WriteLine( "Man" );
```

5.9   What is wrong with the following `while` statement?

```
while ( z >= 0 )
   sum += z;
```

Answers to Self-Review Exercises

5.1   a) sequence, selection, repetition. b) `if...else`. c) counter-controlled (or definite). d) sentinel, signal, flag or dummy. e) sequence. f) 0 (zero). g) strongly typed. h) prefixed.

5.2   a) True. b) False. A set of statements contained within a pair of braces (`{` and `}`) is called a block. c) False. A repetition statement specifies that an action is to be repeated while some condition remains true. A selection statement determines whether an action is performed based on the truth or falsity of a condition. d) True. e) True. f) True. g) False. The unary cast operator (`double`) creates a temporary floating-point copy of its operand. h) False. Instance variables of type `bool` are given the value `false` by default. i) True.

5.3
```
x = x + 1;
x += 1;
++x;
x++;
```

5.4   a)
```
z = x++ + y;
```
    b)
```
if ( count > 10 )
      Console.WriteLine( "Count is greater than 10" );
```
    c)
```
total -= --x;
```

d) q %= divisor;
    q = q % divisor;

5.5 a) `int` sum;
       b) `int` x;
       c) x = 1;
       d) sum = 0;
       e) sum += x; or sum = sum + x;
       f) Console.WriteLine("The sum is: {0}", sum);

5.6 The application is as follows:

```
1    // Ex. 5.6: Calculate.cs
2    // Calculate the sum of the integers from 1 to 10
3    using System;
4
5    public class Calculate
6    {
7       public static void Main( string[] args )
8       {
9          int sum;
10         int x;
11
12         x = 1; // initialize x to 1 for counting
13         sum = 0; // initialize sum to 0 for totaling
14
15         while ( x <= 10 ) // while x is less than or equal to 10
16         {
17            sum += x; // add x to sum
18            ++x; // increment x
19         } // end while
20
21         Console.WriteLine( "The sum is: {0}", sum );
22      } // end Main
23   } // end class Calculate
```

```
The sum is: 55
```

5.7 product = 25, x = 6

5.8 a) *Error:* The closing right brace of the `while` statement's body is missing.
        Correction: Add a closing right brace after the statement ++c;.
       b) *Error:* The semicolon after `else` results in a logic error. The second output statement will always execute.
        Correction: Remove the semicolon after `else`.

5.9 The value of the variable z is never changed in the `while` statement. Therefore, an infinite loop occurs if the loop-continuation condition (z >= 0) is initially true. To prevent an infinite loop, z must be decremented so that it eventually becomes less than 0.

Exercises

5.10 Compare and contrast the `if` single-selection statement and the `while` repetition statement. How are these two statements similar? How are they different?

5.11 *(Integer Division)* Explain what happens when a C# application attempts to divide one integer by another. What happens to the fractional part of the calculation? How can you avoid that outcome?

5.12   *(Combining Control Statements)* Describe the two ways in which control statements can be combined.

5.13   *(Choosing Repetition Statements)* What type of repetition would be appropriate for calculating the sum of the first 100 positive integers? What type of repetition would be appropriate for calculating the sum of an arbitrary number of positive integers? Briefly describe how each of these tasks could be performed.

5.14   *(Prefix vs. Postfix Increment Operators)* What is the difference between the prefix increment operator and the postfix increment operator?

5.15   *(Find the Error)* Identify and correct the errors in each of the following pieces of code. [*Note:* There may be more than one error in each piece of code.]

a) ```
if (age >= 65);
    Console.WriteLine("Age greater than or equal to 65");
else
    Console.WriteLine("Age is less than 65)";
```

b) ```
int x = 1, total;
while ( x <= 10 )
{
    total += x;
    ++x;
}
```

c) ```
while (x <= 100)
    total += x;
    ++x;
```

d) ```
while ( y > 0 )
{
    Console.WriteLine( y );
    ++y;
```

5.16   *(What Does This Program Do?)* What does the following application display?

```
1   // Ex. 5.16: Mystery.cs
2   using System;
3
4   public class Mystery
5   {
6      public static void Main( string[] args )
7      {
8         int y;
9         int x = 1;
10        int total = 0;
11
12        while ( x <= 10 )
13        {
14           y = x * x;
15           Console.WriteLine( y );
16           total += y;
17           ++x;
18        } // end while
19
20        Console.WriteLine( "Total is {0}", total );
21     } // end Main
22  } // end class Mystery
```

For Exercises 5.17–5.20, perform each of the following steps:
    a) Read the problem statement.
    b) Formulate the algorithm using pseudocode and top-down, stepwise refinement.
    c) Write a C# application.
    d) Test, debug and execute the C# application.
    e) Process three complete sets of data.

5.17   *(Gas Mileage)* Drivers are concerned with the mileage their automobiles get. One driver has kept track of several tankfuls of gasoline by recording the miles driven and gallons used for each tankful. Develop a C# application that will input the miles driven and gallons used (both as integers) for each tankful. The application should calculate and display the miles per gallon obtained for each tankful and display the combined miles per gallon obtained for all tankfuls up to this point. All averaging calculations should produce floating-point results. Display the results rounded to the nearest hundredth. Use the `Console` class's `ReadLine` method and sentinel-controlled repetition to obtain the data from the user.

5.18   *(Credit Limit Calculator)* Develop a C# application that will determine whether any of several department-store customers has exceeded the credit limit on a charge account. For each customer, the following facts are available:
    a) account number
    b) balance at the beginning of the month
    c) total of all items charged by the customer this month
    d) total of all credits applied to the customer's account this month
    e) allowed credit limit.

The application should input all these facts as integers, calculate the new balance (= *beginning balance + charges − credits*), display the new balance and determine whether the new balance exceeds the customer's credit limit. For those customers whose credit limit is exceeded, the application should display the message `"Credit limit exceeded"`. Use sentinel-controlled repetition to obtain the data for each account.

5.19   *(Sales Commission Calculator)* A large company pays its salespeople on a commission basis. The salespeople receive $200 per week plus 9% of their gross sales for that week. For example, a salesperson who sells $5,000 worth of merchandise in a week receives $200 plus 9% of $5,000, or a total of $650. You've been supplied with a list of the items sold by each salesperson. The values of these items are as follows:

Item	Value
1	239.99
2	129.75
3	99.95
4	350.89

Develop a C# application that inputs one salesperson's items sold for the last week, then calculates and displays that salesperson's earnings. There's no limit to the number of items that can be sold by a salesperson.

5.20   *(Salary Calculator)* Develop a C# application that will determine the gross pay for each of three employees. The company pays straight time for the first 40 hours worked by each employee and time-and-a-half for all hours worked in excess of 40 hours. You are given a list of the three employees of the company, the number of hours each employee worked last week and the hourly rate of each employee. Your application should input this information for each employee, then should determine and display the employee's gross pay. Use the `Console` class's `ReadLine` method to input the data.

5.21   *(Find the Largest Number)* The process of finding the maximum value (i.e., the largest of a group of values) is used frequently in computer applications. For example, an application that determines the winner of a sales contest would input the number of units sold by each salesperson. The salesperson who sells the most units wins the contest. Write a pseudocode application, then a C# application that inputs a series of 10 integers, then determines and displays the largest integer. Your application should use at least the following three variables:

a) counter: A counter to count to 10 (i.e., to keep track of how many numbers have been input and to determine when all 10 numbers have been processed).

b) number: The integer most recently input by the user.

c) largest: The largest number found so far.

5.22   *(Tabular Output)* Write a C# application that uses looping to display the following table of values:

```
N       10*N    100*N   1000*N

1       10      100     1000
2       20      200     2000
3       30      300     3000
4       40      400     4000
5       50      500     5000
```

5.23   *(Find the Two Largest Numbers)* Using an approach similar to that for Exercise 5.21, find the *two* largest values of the 10 values entered. [*Note:* You may input each number only once.]

5.24   *(Validating User Input)* Modify the application in Fig. 5.12 to validate its inputs. For any input, if the value entered is other than 1 or 2, display the message "Invalid input," then keep looping until the user enters a correct value.

5.25   *(What Does This Program Do?)* What does the following application display?

```csharp
1  // Ex. 5.25: Mystery2.cs
2  using System;
3
4  public class Mystery2
5  {
6     public static void Main( string[] args )
7     {
8        int count = 1;
9
10       while ( count <= 10 )
11       {
12          Console.WriteLine( count % 2 == 1 ? "****" : "++++++++" );
13          ++count;
14       } // end while
15    } // end Main
16 } // end class Mystery2
```

5.26   *(What Does This Program Do?)* What does the following application display?

```csharp
1  // Ex. 5.26: Mystery3.cs
2  using System;
3
4  public class Mystery3
5  {
6     public static void Main( string[] args )
7     {
8        int row = 10;
9        int column;
```

```
10
11          while ( row >= 1 )
12          {
13            column = 1;
14
15            while ( column <= 10 )
16            {
17              Console.Write( row % 2 == 1 ? "<" : ">" );
18              ++column;
19            } // end while
20
21            --row;
22            Console.WriteLine();
23          } // end while
24        } // end Main
25      } // end class Mystery3
```

5.27 *(Dangling-else Problem)* Determine the output for each of the given sets of code when x is 9 and y, is 11 and when x is 11 and y is 9. The compiler ignores the indentation in a C# application. Also, the C# compiler always associates an else with the immediately preceding if unless told to do otherwise by the placement of braces ({}). On first glance, you may not be sure which if an else matches—this situation is referred to as the "dangling-else problem." We've eliminated the indentation from the following code to make the problem more challenging. [*Hint:* Apply the indentation conventions you've learned.]

a)
```
if ( x < 10 )
if ( y > 10 )
Console.WriteLine( "*****" );
else
Console.WriteLine( "#####" );
Console.WriteLine( "$$$$$" );
```

b)
```
if ( x < 10 )
{
if ( y > 10 )
Console.WriteLine( "*****" );
}
else
{
Console.WriteLine( "#####" );
Console.WriteLine( "$$$$$" );
}
```

5.28 *(Another Dangling-else Problem)* Modify the given code to produce the output shown in each part of the problem. Use proper indentation techniques. Make no changes other than inserting braces and changing the indentation of the code. The compiler ignores indentation in a C# application. We've eliminated the indentation from the given code to make the problem more challenging. [*Note:* It's possible that no modification is necessary for some of the parts.]

```
if ( y == 8 )
if ( x == 5 )
Console.WriteLine( "@@@@@" );
else
Console.WriteLine( "#####" );
Console.WriteLine( "$$$$$" );
Console.WriteLine( "&&&&&" );
```

a) Assuming that x = 5 and y = 8, the following output is produced:

```
@@@@@
$$$$$
&&&&&
```

b) Assuming that x = 5 and y = 8, the following output is produced:

```
@@@@@
```

c) Assuming that x = 5 and y = 8, the following output is produced:

```
@@@@@
&&&&&
```

d) Assuming that x = 5 and y = 7, the following output is produced.

```
#####
$$$$$
&&&&&
```

5.29   *(Square of Asterisks)* Write an application that prompts the user to enter the size of the side of a square, then displays a hollow square of that size made of asterisks. Your application should work for squares of all side lengths between 1 and 20. If the user enters a number less than 1 or greater than 20, your application should display a square of size 1 or 20, respectively.

5.30   *(Palindromes)* A palindrome is a sequence of characters that reads the same backward as forward. For example, each of the following five-digit integers is a palindrome: 12321, 55555, 45554 and 11611. Write an application that reads in a five-digit integer and determines whether it's a palindrome. If the number is not five digits long, display an error message and allow the user to enter a new value. [*Hint:* Use the remainder and division operators to pick off the number's digits one at a time, from right to left.]

5.31   *(Printing the Decimal Equivalent of a Binary Number)* Write an application that inputs an integer containing only 0s and 1s (i.e., a binary integer) and displays its decimal equivalent. [*Hint:* Picking the digits off a binary number is similar to picking the digits off a decimal number, which you did in Exercise 5.30. In the decimal number system, the rightmost digit has a positional value of 1 and the next digit to the left has a positional value of 10, then 100, then 1000 and so on. The decimal number 234 can be interpreted as 4 * 1 + 3 * 10 + 2 * 100. In the binary number system, the rightmost digit has a positional value of 1, the next digit to the left has a positional value of 2, then 4, then 8 and so on. The decimal equivalent of binary 1101 is 1 * 1 + 0 * 2 + 1 * 4 + 1 * 8, or 1 + 0 + 4 + 8, or 13.]

5.32   *(Checkerboard Pattern of Asterisks)* Write an application that uses only the output statements

```
Console.Write( "* " );
Console.Write( " " );
Console.WriteLine();
```

to display the checkerboard pattern that follows. A `Console.WriteLine` method call with no arguments outputs a single newline character. [*Hint:* Repetition statements are required.]

```
* * * * * * * *
 * * * * * * * *
* * * * * * * *
 * * * * * * * *
* * * * * * * *
 * * * * * * * *
* * * * * * * *
 * * * * * * * *
```

5.33   *(Multiples of 2)* Write an application that keeps displaying in the console window the powers of the integer 2—namely, 2, 4, 8, 16, 32, 64 and so on. Loop 40 times. What happens when you run this application?

5.34   *(What's Wrong with This Code?)* What is wrong with the following statement? Provide the correct statement to add 1 to the sum of x and y.

```
Console.WriteLine( ++(x + y) );
```

5.35   *(Sides of a Triangle)* Write an application that reads three nonzero values entered by the user, then determines and displays whether they could represent the sides of a triangle.

5.36   *(Sides of a Right Triangle)* Write an application that reads three nonzero integers, then determines and displays whether they could represent the sides of a right triangle.

5.37   *(Factorials)* The factorial of a nonnegative integer n is written as $n!$ (pronounced "n factorial") and is defined as follows:

$$n! = n \cdot (n-1) \cdot (n-2) \cdot \ldots \cdot 1 \quad \text{(for values of } n \text{ greater than or equal to 1)}$$

and

$$n! = 1 \quad \text{(for } n = 0\text{)}$$

For example, $5! = 5 \cdot 4 \cdot 3 \cdot 2 \cdot 1$, which is 120. Write an application that reads a nonnegative integer and computes and displays its factorial.

5.38   *(Infinite Series: Mathematical Constant **e**)* Write an application that estimates the value of the mathematical constant e by using the formula

$$e = 1 + \frac{1}{1!} + \frac{1}{2!} + \frac{1}{3!} + \cdots$$

The predefined constant `Math.E` (class `Math` is in the `System` namespace) provides a good approximation of e. Use the `WriteLine` method to output both your estimated value of e and `Math.E` for comparison.

5.39   *(Infinite Series: **e**^x^)* Write an application that computes the value of e^x by using the formula

$$e^x = 1 + \frac{x}{1!} + \frac{x^2}{2!} + \frac{x^3}{3!} + \cdots$$

Compare the result of your calculation to the return value of the method call

```
Math.Pow( Math.E, x )
```

[*Note:* The predefined method `Math.Pow` takes two arguments and raises the first argument to the power of the second. We discuss `Math.Pow` in Section 6.4.]

Making a Difference Exercises

5.40   *(World Population Growth)* World population has grown considerably over the centuries. Continued growth could eventually challenge the limits of breathable air, drinkable water, arable cropland and other limited resources. There's evidence that growth has been slowing in recent years and that world population could peak some time this century, then start to decline.

For this exercise, research world population growth issues online. *Be sure to investigate various viewpoints.* Get estimates for the current world population and its growth rate (the percentage by which it is likely to increase this year). Write a program that calculates world population growth each year for the next 75 years, *using the simplifying assumption that the current growth rate will stay constant.* When displaying the results, the first column should display the year from year 1 to year 75. The second column should display the anticipated world population at the end of that year. The third column should display the numerical increase in the world population that would occur that year. Using your results, determine the year in which the population would be double what it is today, if this year's growth rate were to persist. [*Hint:* Use double variables because int variables can store values only up to approximately two billion. Display the double values using the format F0.]

5.41 *(Enforcing Privacy with Cryptography)* The explosive growth of Internet communications and data storage on Internet-connected computers has greatly increased privacy concerns. The field of cryptography is concerned with coding data to make it difficult (and hopefully—with the most advanced schemes—impossible) for unauthorized users to read. In this exercise you'll investigate a simple scheme for encrypting and decrypting data. A company that wants to send data over the Internet has asked you to write a program that will encrypt it so that it may be transmitted more securely. All the data is transmitted as four-digit integers. Your application should read a four-digit integer entered by the user and encrypt it as follows: Replace each digit with the result of adding 7 to the digit and getting the remainder after dividing the new value by 10. Then swap the first digit with the third, and swap the second digit with the fourth. Then display the encrypted integer. Write a separate application that inputs an encrypted four-digit integer and decrypts it (by reversing the encryption scheme) to form the original number. Use the format specifier D4 to display the encrypted value in case the number starts with a 0.

6

Control Statements: Part 2

Not everything that can be counted counts, and not everything that counts can be counted.
—Albert Einstein

Who can control his fate?
—William Shakespeare

The used key is always bright.
—Benjamin Franklin

Every advantage in the past is judged in the light of the final issue.
—Demosthenes

Objectives

In this chapter you'll learn:

- The essentials of counter-controlled repetition.

- To use the `for` and `do...while` repetition statements.

- To use the `switch` multiple selection statement.

- To use the `break` and `continue` statements to alter the flow of control.

- To use the logical operators to form complex conditional expressions.

6.1 Introduction

In this chapter, we continue our presentation of the theory and principles of structured programming by introducing several of C#'s remaining control statements. (The foreach statement is introduced in Chapter 8, Arrays.) The control statements we study here and in Chapter 5 are helpful in building and manipulating objects.

Through a series of short examples using while and for, we explore the essentials of counter-controlled repetition. We create a version of class GradeBook that uses a switch statement to count the number of A, B, C, D and F grade equivalents in a set of numeric grades entered by the user. We introduce the break and continue program-control statements. We discuss C#'s logical operators, which enable you to use more complex conditional expressions in control statements. Finally, we summarize C#'s control statements and the proven problem-solving techniques presented in this chapter and Chapter 5.

6.2 Essentials of Counter-Controlled Repetition

This section uses the while **repetition statement** to formalize the elements required to perform counter-controlled repetition. Counter-controlled repetition requires

1. a **control variable** (or loop counter)
2. the **initial value** of the control variable
3. the **increment** (or **decrement**) by which the control variable is modified each time through the loop (also known as each **iteration of the loop**)
4. the **loop-continuation condition** that determines whether to continue looping.

To see these elements of counter-controlled repetition, consider the application of Fig. 6.1, which uses a loop to display the numbers from 1 through 10.

```
1   // Fig. 6.1: WhileCounter.cs
2   // Counter-controlled repetition with the while repetition statement.
3   using System;
4
5   public class WhileCounter
6   {
7      public static void Main( string[] args )
8      {
```

Fig. 6.1 | Counter-controlled repetition with the while repetition statement. (Part 1 of 2.)

```
9        int counter = 1; // declare and initialize control variable
10
11       while ( counter <= 10 ) // loop-continuation condition
12       {
13          Console.Write( "{0}  ", counter );
14          ++counter; // increment control variable
15       } // end while
16
17       Console.WriteLine(); // output a newline
18    } // end Main
19 } // end class WhileCounter
```

```
1  2  3  4  5  6  7  8  9  10
```

Fig. 6.1 | Counter-controlled repetition with the `while` repetition statement. (Part 2 of 2.)

In method `Main` (lines 7–18), the elements of counter-controlled repetition are defined in lines 9, 11 and 14. Line 9 declares the control variable (`counter`) as an `int`, reserves space for it in memory and sets its initial value to 1.

Line 13 in the `while` statement displays control variable `counter`'s value during each iteration of the loop. Line 14 increments the control variable by 1 for each iteration of the loop. The loop-continuation condition in the `while` (line 11) tests whether the value of the control variable is less than or equal to 10 (the final value for which the condition is `true`). The application performs the body of this `while` even when the control variable is 10. The loop terminates when the control variable exceeds 10 (i.e., `counter` becomes 11).

Common Programming Error 6.1

Because floating-point values may be approximate, controlling loops with floating-point variables may result in imprecise counter values and inaccurate termination tests.

Error-Prevention Tip 6.1

Control counting loops with integers.

The application in Fig. 6.1 can be made more concise by initializing `counter` to 0 in line 9 and incrementing `counter` in the `while` condition with the prefix increment operator as follows:

```
while ( ++counter <= 10 ) // loop-continuation condition
   Console.Write( "{0}  ", counter );
```

This code saves a statement (and eliminates the need for braces around the loop's body), because the `while` condition performs the increment before testing the condition. (Recall from Section 5.12 that the precedence of `++` is higher than that of `<=`.) Code written in such a condensed fashion might be more difficult to read, debug, modify and maintain.

Software Engineering Observation 6.1

"Keep it simple" is good advice for most of the code you'll write.

6.3 for Repetition Statement

Section 6.2 presented the essentials of counter-controlled repetition. The while statement can be used to implement any counter-controlled loop. C# also provides the **for repetition statement**, which specifies the elements of counter-controlled-repetition in a single line of code. In general, counter-controlled repetition should be implemented with a for statement. Figure 6.2 reimplements the application in Fig. 6.1 using the for statement.

```
1   // Fig. 6.2: ForCounter.cs
2   // Counter-controlled repetition with the for repetition statement.
3   using System;
4
5   public class ForCounter
6   {
7      public static void Main( string[] args )
8      {
9         // for statement header includes initialization,
10        // loop-continuation condition and increment
11        for ( int counter = 1; counter <= 10; counter++ )
12           Console.Write( "{0}  ", counter );
13
14        Console.WriteLine(); // output a newline
15     } // end Main
16  } // end class ForCounter
```

```
1  2  3  4  5  6  7  8  9  10
```

Fig. 6.2 | Counter-controlled repetition with the for repetition statement.

The application's Main method operates as follows: when the for statement (lines 11–12) begins executing, control variable counter is declared and initialized to 1. (Recall from Section 6.2 that the first two elements of counter-controlled repetition are the control variable and its initial value.) Next, the application checks the loop-continuation condition, counter <= 10, which is between the two required semicolons. Because the initial value of counter is 1, the condition initially is true. Therefore, the body statement (line 12) displays control variable counter's value, which is 1. After executing the loop's body, the application increments counter in the expression counter++, which appears to the right of the second semicolon. Then the loop-continuation test is performed again to determine whether the application should continue with the next iteration of the loop. At this point, the control-variable value is 2, so the condition is still true (the final value is not exceeded)—and the application performs the body statement again (i.e., the next iteration of the loop). This process continues until the numbers 1 through 10 have been displayed and the counter's value becomes 11, causing the loop-continuation test to fail and repetition to terminate (after 10 repetitions of the loop body at line 12). Then the application performs the first statement after the for—in this case, line 14.

Fig. 6.2 uses (in line 11) the loop-continuation condition counter <= 10. If you incorrectly specified counter < 10 as the condition, the loop would iterate only nine times—a common logic error called an **off-by-one error**.

Good Programming Practice 6.1

Using the final value in the condition of a while or for statement with the <= relational operator helps avoid off-by-one errors. For a loop that displays the values 1 to 10, the loop-continuation condition should be counter <= 10, rather than counter < 10 (which causes an off-by-one error) or counter < 11 (which is correct). Many programmers prefer so-called zero-based counting, in which, to count 10 times, counter would be initialized to zero and the loop-continuation test would be counter < 10.

Figure 6.3 takes a closer look at the for statement in Fig. 6.2. The for's first line (including the keyword for and everything in parentheses after for)—line 11 in Fig. 6.2—is sometimes called the **for statement header**, or simply the **for header**. The for header "does it all"—it specifies each of the items needed for counter-controlled repetition with a control variable. If there's more than one statement in the body of the for, braces are required to define the body of the loop.

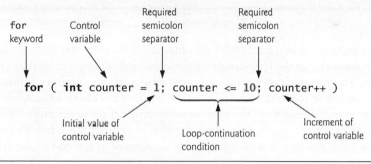

Fig. 6.3 | for statement header components.

The general format of the for statement is

> **for** (*initialization*; *loopContinuationCondition*; *increment*)
>   *statement*

where the *initialization* expression names the loop's control variable and provides its initial value, the *loopContinuationCondition* is the condition that determines whether looping should continue and the *increment* modifies the control variable's value (whether an increment or decrement), so that the loop-continuation condition eventually becomes false. The two semicolons in the for header are required. We don't include a semicolon after *statement*, because the semicolon is already assumed to be included in the notion of a *statement*.

In most cases, the for statement can be represented with an equivalent while statement as follows:

> *initialization*;
> **while** (*loopContinuationCondition*)
> {
>   *statement*
>   *increment*;
> }

In Section 6.7, we discuss a case in which a `for` statement cannot be represented with an equivalent `while` statement.

Typically, `for` statements are used for counter-controlled repetition, and `while` statements are used for sentinel-controlled repetition. However, `while` and `for` can each be used for either repetition type.

If the *initialization* expression in the `for` header declares the control variable (i.e., the control variable's type is specified before the variable name, as in Fig. 6.2), the control variable can be used only in that `for` statement—it will not exist outside it. This restricted use of the name of the control variable is known as the variable's **scope**. The scope of a variable defines where it can be used in an application. For example, a local variable can be used only in the method that declares the variable and only from the point of declaration through the end of the block in which the variable has been declared. Scope is discussed in detail in Chapter 7, Methods: A Deeper Look.

Common Programming Error 6.2

When a `for` statement's control variable is declared in the initialization section of the `for`'s header, using the control variable after the `for`'s body is a compilation error.

All three expressions in a `for` header are optional. If the *loopContinuationCondition* is omitted, C# assumes that the loop-continuation condition is always true, thus creating an infinite loop. You can omit the *initialization* expression if the application initializes the control variable before the loop—in this case, the scope of the control variable will not be limited to the loop. You can omit the *increment* expression if the application calculates the increment with statements in the loop's body or if no increment is needed. The increment expression in a `for` acts as if it were a stand-alone statement at the end of the `for`'s body. Therefore, the expressions

```
counter = counter + 1
counter += 1
++counter
counter++
```

are equivalent increment expressions in a `for` statement. Many programmers prefer `counter++` because it's concise and because a `for` loop evaluates its increment expression after its body executes—so the postfix increment form seems more natural. In this case, the variable being incremented does not appear in a larger expression, so the prefix and postfix increment operators have the same effect.

Performance Tip 6.1

There's a slight performance advantage to using the prefix increment operator, but if you choose the postfix increment operator because it seems more natural (as in a `for` header), optimizing compilers will generate MSIL code that uses the more efficient form anyway.

Good Programming Practice 6.2

In many cases, the prefix and postfix increment operators are both used to add 1 to a variable in a statement by itself. In these cases, the effect is exactly the same, except that the prefix increment operator has a slight performance advantage. Given that the compiler typically optimizes your code to help you get the best performance, use the idiom (prefix or postfix) with which you feel most comfortable in these situations.

Error-Prevention Tip 6.2
Infinite loops occur when the loop-continuation condition in a repetition statement never becomes false. To prevent this situation in a counter-controlled loop, ensure that the control variable is incremented (or decremented) during each iteration of the loop. In a sentinel-controlled loop, ensure that the sentinel value is eventually input.

The initialization, loop-continuation condition and increment portions of a for statement can contain arithmetic expressions. For example, assume that x = 2 and y = 10; if x and y are not modified in the body of the loop, then the statement

```
for ( int j = x; j <= 4 * x * y; j += y / x )
```

is equivalent to the statement

```
for ( int j = 2; j <= 80; j += 5 )
```

The increment of a for statement may also be negative, in which case it's a decrement, and the loop counts downward.

If the loop-continuation condition is initially false, the application does not execute the for statement's body. Instead, execution proceeds with the statement following the for.

Applications frequently display the control variable value or use it in calculations in the loop body, but this use is not required. The control variable is commonly used to control repetition without being mentioned in the body of the for.

Error-Prevention Tip 6.3
Although the value of the control variable can be changed in the body of a for loop, avoid doing so, because this can lead to subtle errors.

Figure 6.4 shows the activity diagram of the for statement in Fig. 6.2. The diagram makes it clear that initialization occurs *only once* before the loop-continuation test is eval-

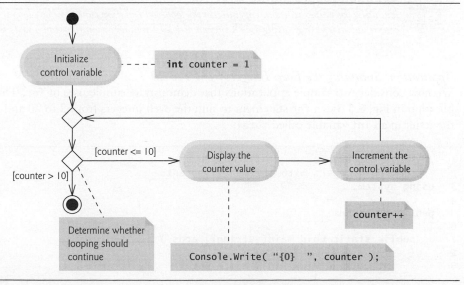

Fig. 6.4 | UML activity diagram for the for statement in Fig. 6.2.

uated the first time, and that incrementing occurs *each* time through the loop after the body statement executes.

6.4 Examples Using the for Statement

The following examples show techniques for varying the control variable in a for statement. In each case, we write the appropriate for header. Note the change in the relational operator for loops that decrement the control variable.

a) Vary the control variable from 1 to 100 in increments of 1.

```
for ( int i = 1; i <= 100; i++ )
```

b) Vary the control variable from 100 to 1 in decrements of 1.

```
for ( int i = 100; i >= 1; i-- )
```

c) Vary the control variable from 7 to 77 in increments of 7.

```
for ( int i = 7; i <= 77; i += 7 )
```

d) Vary the control variable from 20 to 2 in decrements of 2.

```
for ( int i = 20; i >= 2; i -= 2 )
```

e) Vary the control variable over the following sequence of values: 2, 5, 8, 11, 14, 17, 20.

```
for ( int i = 2; i <= 20; i += 3 )
```

f) Vary the control variable over the following sequence of values: 99, 88, 77, 66, 55, 44, 33, 22, 11, 0.

```
for ( int i = 99; i >= 0; i -= 11 )
```

 Common Programming Error 6.3
Not using the proper relational operator in the loop-continuation condition of a loop that counts downward (e.g., using i <= 1 instead of i >= 1 in a loop counting down to 1) is a logic error.

Application: Summing the Even Integers from 2 to 20

We now consider two sample applications that demonstrate simple uses of for. The application in Fig. 6.5 uses a for statement to sum the even integers from 2 to 20 and store the result in an int variable called total.

```
 1   // Fig. 6.5: Sum.cs
 2   // Summing integers with the for statement.
 3   using System;
 4
 5   public class Sum
 6   {
 7      public static void Main( string[] args )
 8      {
 9         int total = 0; // initialize total
```

Fig. 6.5 | Summing integers with the for statement. (Part 1 of 2.)

```
10
11            // total even integers from 2 through 20
12            for ( int number = 2; number <= 20; number += 2 )
13               total += number;
14
15            Console.WriteLine( "Sum is {0}", total ); // display results
16         } // end Main
17      } // end class Sum
```

```
Sum is 110
```

Fig. 6.5 | Summing integers with the for statement. (Part 2 of 2.)

The *initialization* and *increment* expressions can be comma-separated lists that enable you to use multiple initialization expressions or multiple increment expressions. For example, you could merge the body of the for statement in lines 12–13 of Fig. 6.5 into the increment portion of the for header by using a comma as follows:

```
for ( int number = 2; number <= 20; total += number, number += 2 )
   ; // empty statement
```

Application: Compound-Interest Calculations

The next application uses the for statement to compute compound interest. Consider the following problem:

> *A person invests $1,000 in a savings account yielding 5% interest, compounded yearly. Assuming that all the interest is left on deposit, calculate and display the amount of money in the account at the end of each year for 10 years. Use the following formula to determine the amounts:*
>
> $$a = p (1 + r)^n$$
>
> *where*
>
>> *p* is the original amount invested (i.e., the principal)
>> *r* is the annual interest rate (e.g., use 0.05 for 5%)
>> *n* is the number of years
>> *a* is the amount on deposit at the end of the *n*th year.

This problem involves a loop that performs the indicated calculation for each of the 10 years the money remains on deposit. The solution is the application shown in Fig. 6.6. Lines 9–11 in method Main declare decimal variables amount and principal, and double variable rate. Lines 10–11 also initialize principal to 1000 (i.e., $1000.00) and rate to 0.05. C# treats real-number constants like 0.05 as type double. Similarly, C# treats whole-number constants like 7 and 1000 as type int. When principal is initialized to 1000, the value 1000 of type int is promoted to a decimal type implicitly—no cast is required.

```
1   // Fig. 6.6: Interest.cs
2   // Compound-interest calculations with for.
3   using System;
```

Fig. 6.6 | Compound-interest calculations with for. (Part 1 of 2.)

```
4
5    public class Interest
6    {
7       public static void Main( string[] args )
8       {
9          decimal amount; // amount on deposit at end of each year
10         decimal principal = 1000; // initial amount before interest
11         double rate = 0.05; // interest rate
12
13         // display headers
14         Console.WriteLine( "Year{0,20}", "Amount on deposit" );
15
16         // calculate amount on deposit for each of ten years
17         for ( int year = 1; year <= 10; year++ )
18         {
19            // calculate new amount for specified year
20            amount = principal *
21               ( ( decimal ) Math.Pow( 1.0 + rate, year ) );
22
23            // display the year and the amount
24            Console.WriteLine( "{0,4}{1,20:C}", year, amount );
25         } // end for
26      } // end Main
27   } // end class Interest
```

```
Year    Amount on deposit
   1           $1,050.00
   2           $1,102.50
   3           $1,157.63
   4           $1,215.51
   5           $1,276.28
   6           $1,340.10
   7           $1,407.10
   8           $1,477.46
   9           $1,551.33
  10           $1,628.89
```

Fig. 6.6 | Compound-interest calculations with for. (Part 2 of 2.)

Line 14 outputs the headers for the application's two columns of output. The first column displays the year, and the second column displays the amount on deposit at the end of that year. We use the format item {0,20} to output the string "Amount on deposit". The integer 20 after the comma indicates that the value output should be displayed with a **field width** of 20—that is, WriteLine displays the value with at least 20 character positions. If the value to be output is less than 20 character positions wide (17 characters in this example), the value is **right justified** in the field by default (in this case the value is preceded by three blanks). If the year value to be output were more than four character positions wide, the field width would be extended to the right to accommodate the entire value—this would push the amount field to the right, upsetting the neat columns of our tabular output. To indicate that output should be **left justified**, simply use a negative field width.

The for statement (lines 17–25) executes its body 10 times, varying control variable year from 1 to 10 in increments of 1. This loop terminates when control variable year becomes 11. (year represents n in the problem statement.)

Classes provide methods that perform common tasks on objects. In fact, most methods must be called on a specific object. For example, to output a greeting in Fig. 4.2, we called method DisplayMessage on the myGradeBook object. Many classes also provide methods that perform common tasks and cannot be called on objects—they must be called using a class name. Such methods are called **static methods**. For example, C# does not include an exponentiation operator, so the designers of C#'s Math class defined static method Pow for raising a value to a power. You can call a static method by specifying the class name followed by the member access (.) operator and the method name, as in

ClassName.*methodName*(*arguments*)

Console methods Write and WriteLine are static methods. In Chapter 7, you'll learn how to implement static methods in your own classes.

We use static method Pow of class Math to perform the compound interest calculation in Fig. 6.6. Math.Pow(x, y) calculates the value of x raised to the yth power. The method receives two double arguments and returns a double value. Lines 20–21 perform the calculation $a = p (1 + r)^n$, where a is the amount, p is the principal, r is the rate and n is the year. Notice that, in this calculation, we need to multiply a decimal value (principal) by a double value (the return value of Math.Pow). C# will not implicitly convert double to a decimal type, or vice versa, because of the possible loss of information in either conversion, so line 21 contains a (decimal) cast operator that explicitly converts the double return value of Math.Pow to a decimal.

After each calculation, line 24 outputs the year and the amount on deposit at the end of that year. The year is output in a field width of four characters (as specified by {0,4}). The amount is output as a currency value with the format item {1,20:C}. The number 20 in the format item indicates that the value should be output right justified with a field width of 20 characters. The format specifier C specifies that the number should be formatted as currency.

Notice that we declared the variables amount and principal to be of type decimal rather than double. Recall that we introduced type decimal for monetary calculations in Section 4.11. We also use decimal in Fig. 6.6 for this purpose. You may be curious as to why we do this. We are dealing with fractional parts of dollars and thus need a type that allows decimal points in its values. Unfortunately, floating-point numbers of type double (or float) can cause trouble in monetary calculations. Two double dollar amounts stored in the machine could be 14.234 (which would normally be rounded to 14.23 for display purposes) and 18.673 (which would normally be rounded to 18.67 for display purposes). When these amounts are added, they produce the internal sum 32.907, which would normally be rounded to 32.91 for display purposes. Thus, your output could appear as

```
   14.23
 + 18.67
 -------
   32.91
```

but a person adding the individual numbers as displayed would expect the sum to be 32.90. You've been warned! For people who work with programming languages that do not support a type for precise monetary calculations, Exercise 6.18 explores the use of integers to perform such calculations.

Good Programming Practice 6.3

Do not use variables of type double *(or* float*) to perform precise monetary calculations; use type* decimal *instead. The imprecision of floating-point numbers can cause errors that will result in incorrect monetary values.*

The body of the for statement contains the calculation 1.0 + rate, which appears as an argument to the Math.Pow method. In fact, this calculation produces the same result each time through the loop, so repeating the calculation in every iteration of the loop is wasteful.

Performance Tip 6.2

In loops, avoid calculations for which the result never changes—such calculations should typically be placed before the loop. [Note: Optimizing compilers will typically place such calculations outside loops in the compiled code.]

6.5 do...while Repetition Statement

The **do...while repetition statement** is similar to the while statement. In the while, the application tests the loop-continuation condition at the beginning of the loop, before executing the loop's body. If the condition is false, the body never executes. The do...while statement tests the loop-continuation condition *after* executing the loop's body; therefore, the body always executes at least once. When a do...while statement terminates, execution continues with the next statement in sequence. Figure 6.7 uses a do...while (lines 11–15) to output the numbers 1–10.

```
1   // Fig. 6.7: DoWhileTest.cs
2   // do...while repetition statement.
3   using System;
4
5   public class DoWhileTest
6   {
7      public static void Main( string[] args )
8      {
9         int counter = 1; // initialize counter
10
11         do
12         {
13            Console.Write( "{0}  ", counter );
14            ++counter;
15         } while ( counter <= 10 ); // end do...while
16
17         Console.WriteLine(); // outputs a newline
18      } // end Main
19   } // end class DoWhileTest
```

```
1  2  3  4  5  6  7  8  9  10
```

Fig. 6.7 | do...while repetition statement.

Line 9 declares and initializes control variable counter. Upon entering the do...while statement, line 13 outputs counter's value, and line 14 increments counter. Then the application evaluates the loop-continuation test at the bottom of the loop (line 15). If the condition is true, the loop continues from the first body statement in the do...while (line 13). If the condition is false, the loop terminates, and the application continues with the next statement after the loop.

Figure 6.8 contains the UML activity diagram for the do...while statement. This diagram makes it clear that the loop-continuation condition is not evaluated until *after* the loop performs the action state *at least once*. Compare this activity diagram with that of the while statement (Fig. 5.4). It's not necessary to use braces in the do...while repetition statement if there's only one statement in the body. However, most programmers include the braces to avoid confusion between the while and do...while statements. For example,

```
while ( condition )
```

is normally the first line of a while statement. A do...while statement with no braces around a single-statement body appears as:

```
do
    statement
while ( condition );
```

which can be confusing. A reader may misinterpret the last line—while(*condition*);— as a while statement containing an empty statement (the semicolon by itself). To avoid confusion, a do...while statement with one body statement can be written as follows:

```
do
{
    statement
} while ( condition );
```

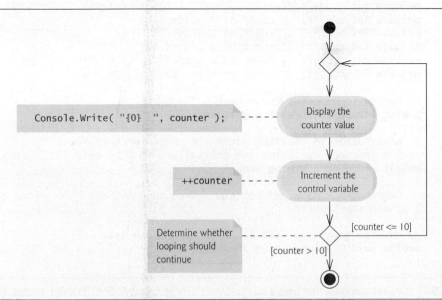

Fig. 6.8 | do...while repetition statement UML activity diagram.

6.6 switch Multiple-Selection Statement

We discussed the if single-selection statement and the if...else double-selection statement in Chapter 5. C# provides the **switch multiple-selection** statement to perform different actions based on the possible values of an expression. Each action is associated with the value of a **constant integral expression** or a **constant string expression** that the variable or expression on which the switch is based may assume. A constant integral expression is any expression involving character and integer constants that evaluates to an integer value—i.e., values of type sbyte, byte, short, ushort, int, uint, long, ulong and char, or a constant from an enum type (enum is discussed in Section 7.10). A constant string expression is any expression composed of string literals that always results in the same string.

***GradeBook* Class with *switch* Statement to Count A, B, C, D and F Grades.**
Figure 6.9 contains an enhanced version of the GradeBook class introduced in Chapter 4 and further developed in Chapter 5. The version of the class we now present not only calculates the average of a set of numeric grades entered by the user, but uses a switch statement to determine whether each grade is the equivalent of an A, B, C, D or F, then increments the appropriate grade counter. The class also displays a summary of the number of students who received each grade. Figure 6.10 shows sample input and output of the GradeBookTest application that uses class GradeBook to process a set of grades.

```
1   // Fig. 6.9: GradeBook.cs
2   // GradeBook class uses switch statement to count letter grades.
3   using System;
4
5   public class GradeBook
6   {
7      private int total; // sum of grades
8      private int gradeCounter; // number of grades entered
9      private int aCount; // count of A grades
10     private int bCount; // count of B grades
11     private int cCount; // count of C grades
12     private int dCount; // count of D grades
13     private int fCount; // count of F grades
14
15     // automatic property CourseName
16     public string CourseName { get; set; }
17
18     // constructor initializes automatic property CourseName;
19     // int instance variables are initialized to 0 by default
20     public GradeBook( string name )
21     {
22        CourseName = name; // set CourseName to name
23     } // end constructor
24
25     // display a welcome message to the GradeBook user
26     public void DisplayMessage()
27     {
```

Fig. 6.9 | GradeBook class that uses a switch statement to count A, B, C, D and F grades. (Part 1 of 3.)

```
28        // CourseName gets the name of the course
29        Console.WriteLine( "Welcome to the grade book for\n{0}!\n",
30           CourseName );
31     } // end method DisplayMessage
32
33     // input arbitrary number of grades from user
34     public void InputGrades()
35     {
36        int grade; // grade entered by user
37        string input; // text entered by the user
38
39        Console.WriteLine( "{0}\n{1}",
40           "Enter the integer grades in the range 0-100.",
41           "Type <Ctrl> z and press Enter to terminate input:" );
42
43        input = Console.ReadLine(); // read user input
44
45        // loop until user enters the end-of-file indicator (<Ctrl> z)
46        while ( input != null )
47        {
48           grade = Convert.ToInt32( input ); // read grade off user input
49           total += grade; // add grade to total
50           ++gradeCounter; // increment number of grades
51
52           // call method to increment appropriate counter
53           IncrementLetterGradeCounter( grade );
54
55           input = Console.ReadLine(); // read user input
56        } // end while
57     } // end method InputGrades
58
59     // add 1 to appropriate counter for specified grade
60     private void IncrementLetterGradeCounter( int grade )
61     {
62        // determine which grade was entered
63        switch ( grade / 10 )
64        {
65           case 9: // grade was in the 90s
66           case 10: // grade was 100
67              ++aCount; // increment aCount
68              break; // necessary to exit switch
69           case 8: // grade was between 80 and 89
70              ++bCount; // increment bCount
71              break; // exit switch
72           case 7: // grade was between 70 and 79
73              ++cCount; // increment cCount
74              break; // exit switch
75           case 6: // grade was between 60 and 69
76              ++dCount; // increment dCount
77              break; // exit switch
```

Fig. 6.9 | GradeBook class that uses a switch statement to count A, B, C, D and F grades. (Part 2 of 3.)

```
78              default: // grade was less than 60
79                 ++fCount; // increment fCount
80                 break; // exit switch
81           } // end switch
82        } // end method IncrementLetterGradeCounter
83
84        // display a report based on the grades entered by the user
85        public void DisplayGradeReport()
86        {
87           Console.WriteLine( "\nGrade Report:" );
88
89           // if user entered at least one grade...
90           if ( gradeCounter != 0 )
91           {
92              // calculate average of all grades entered
93              double average = ( double ) total / gradeCounter;
94
95              // output summary of results
96              Console.WriteLine( "Total of the {0} grades entered is {1}",
97                 gradeCounter, total );
98              Console.WriteLine( "Class average is {0:F}", average );
99              Console.WriteLine( "{0}A: {1}\nB: {2}\nC: {3}\nD: {4}\nF: {5}",
100                "Number of students who received each grade:\n",
101                aCount, // display number of A grades
102                bCount, // display number of B grades
103                cCount, // display number of C grades
104                dCount, // display number of D grades
105                fCount ); // display number of F grades
106          } // end if
107          else // no grades were entered, so output appropriate message
108             Console.WriteLine( "No grades were entered" );
109       } // end method DisplayGradeReport
110    } // end class GradeBook
```

Fig. 6.9 | GradeBook class that uses a switch statement to count A, B, C, D and F grades. (Part 3 of 3.)

Instance Variables

Class GradeBook (Fig. 6.9) declares instance variables total (line 7) and gradeCounter (line 8), which keep track of the sum of the grades entered by the user and the number of grades entered, respectively. Lines 9–13 declare counter variables for each grade category. Class GradeBook maintains total, gradeCounter and the five letter-grade counters as instance variables so that they can be used or modified in any of the class's methods.

Property *CourseName*, Method *DisplayMessage* and the Constructor

Like earlier versions of the class, class GradeBook declares automatic property CourseName (line 16) and method DisplayMessage (lines 26–31) to display a welcome message to the user. The class also contains a constructor (lines 20–23) that initializes the course name. The constructor sets only the course name—the remaining seven instance variables are ints and are initialized to 0 by default.

Methods *InputGrades* and *DisplayGradeReport*

Class GradeBook contains three additional methods—InputGrades, IncrementLetter-GradeCounter and DisplayGradeReport. Method InputGrades (lines 34–57) reads an arbitrary number of integer grades from the user using sentinel-controlled repetition and updates instance variables total and gradeCounter. Method InputGrades calls method IncrementLetterGradeCounter (lines 60–82) to update the appropriate letter-grade counter for each grade entered. Class GradeBook also contains method DisplayGradeReport (lines 85–109), which outputs a report containing the total of all grades entered, the average of the grades and the number of students who received each letter grade. Let's examine these methods in more detail.

Lines 36–37 in method InputGrades declare variables grade and input, which will first store the user's input as a string (in the variable input), then convert it to an int to store in the variable grade. Lines 39–41 prompt the user to enter integer grades and to type *Ctrl + z*, then press *Enter* to terminate the input. The notation *Ctrl + z* means to simultaneously press both the *Ctrl* key and the *z* key when typing in a **Command Prompt**. *Ctrl + z* is the Windows key sequence for typing the **end-of-file indicator**. This is one way to inform an application that there's no more data to input. If *Ctrl + z* is entered while the application is awaiting input with a ReadLine method, null is returned. (The end-of-file indicator is a system-dependent keystroke combination. On many non-Windows systems, end-of-file is entered by typing *Ctrl + d*.) In Chapter 17, Files and Streams, we'll see how the end-of-file indicator is used when an application reads its input from a file. [*Note:* Windows typically displays the characters ^Z in a **Command Prompt** when the end-of-file indicator is typed, as shown in the output of Fig. 6.10.]

Line 43 uses the ReadLine method to get the first line that the user entered and store it in variable input. The while statement (lines 46–56) processes this user input. The condition at line 46 checks whether the value of input is a null reference. The Console class's ReadLine method will return null only if the user typed an end-of-file indicator. As long as the end-of-file indicator has not been typed, input will not contain a null reference, and the condition will pass.

Line 48 converts the string in input to an int type. Line 49 adds grade to total. Line 50 increments gradeCounter. The class's DisplayGradeReport method uses these variables to compute the average of the grades. Line 53 calls the class's IncrementLetterGradeCounter method (declared in lines 60–82) to increment the appropriate letter-grade counter, based on the numeric grade entered.

Method *IncrementLetterGradeCounter*

Method IncrementLetterGradeCounter contains a switch statement (lines 63–81) that determines which counter to increment. In this example, we assume that the user enters a valid grade in the range 0–100. A grade in the range 90–100 represents A, 80–89 represents B, 70–79 represents C, 60–69 represents D and 0–59 represents F. The switch statement consists of a block that contains a sequence of **case labels** and an optional **default label**. These are used in this example to determine which counter to increment based on the grade.

When the flow of control reaches the switch statement, the application evaluates the expression in the parentheses (grade / 10) following keyword switch—this is called the **switch expression**. The application attempts to match the value of the switch expression with one of the case labels. The switch expression in line 63 performs integer division, which truncates the fractional part of the result. Thus, when we divide any value in the range 0–100 by 10, the result is always a value from 0 to 10. We use several of these values in our case labels. For example, if the user enters the integer 85, the switch expression evaluates to int value 8. If a match occurs between the switch expression and a case (case 8: at line 69), the application executes the statements for that case. For the integer 8, line 70 increments bCount, because a grade in the 80s is a B. The **break statement** (line 71) causes program control to proceed with the first statement after the switch—in this application, we reach the end of method IncrementLetterGradeCounter's body, so control returns to line 55 in method InputGrades (the first line after the call to IncrementLetterGradeCounter). This line uses the ReadLine method to read the next line entered by the user and assign it to the variable input. Line 56 marks the end of the body of the while statement that inputs grades (lines 46–56), so control flows to the while's condition (line 46) to determine whether the loop should continue executing based on the value just assigned to the variable input.

The cases in our switch explicitly test for the values 10, 9, 8, 7 and 6. Note the case labels at lines 65–66 that test for the values 9 and 10 (both of which represent the grade A). Listing case labels consecutively in this manner with no statements between them enables the cases to perform the same set of statements—when the switch expression evaluates to 9 or 10, the statements in lines 67–68 execute. The switch statement does not provide a mechanism for testing ranges of values, so every value to be tested must be listed in a separate case label. Each case can have multiple statements. The switch statement differs from other control statements in that it does *not* require braces around multiple statements in each case.

In C, C++, and many other programming languages that use the switch statement, the break statement *is not* required at the end of a case. Without break statements, each time a match occurs in the switch, the statements for that case and subsequent cases execute until a break statement or the end of the switch is encountered. This is often referred to as "falling through" to the statements in subsequent cases. This frequently leads to logic errors when you forget the break statement. For this reason, C# has a "no fall through" rule for cases in a switch—after the statements in a case, you are required to include a statement that terminates the case, such as a break, a return or a throw. (We discuss the throw statement in Chapter 13, Exception Handling: A Deeper Look.)

If no match occurs between the switch expression's value and a case label, the statements after the default label (lines 79–80) execute. We use the default label in this example to process all switch-expression values that are less than 6—that is, all failing grades. If no match occurs and the switch does not contain a default label, program control simply continues with the first statement (if there is one) after the switch statement.

GradeBookTest Class That Demonstrates Class GradeBook

Class GradeBookTest (Fig. 6.10) creates a GradeBook object (lines 10–11). Line 13 invokes the object's DisplayMessage method to output a welcome message to the user. Line 14 invokes the object's InputGrades method to read a set of grades from the user and keep track of the sum of all the grades entered and the number of grades. Recall that method InputGrades also calls method IncrementLetterGradeCounter to keep track of the number of students who received each letter grade. Line 15 invokes method DisplayGradeReport of class GradeBook, which outputs a report based on the grades entered. Line 90 of class GradeBook (Fig. 6.9) determines whether the user entered at least one grade—this avoids dividing by zero. If so, line 93 calculates the average of the grades. Lines 96–105 then output the total of all the grades, the class average and the number of students who received each letter grade. If no grades were entered, line 108 outputs an appropriate message. The output in Fig. 6.10 shows a sample grade report based on 9 grades.

```
1   // Fig. 6.10: GradeBookTest.cs
2   // Create GradeBook object, input grades and display grade report.
3
4   public class GradeBookTest
5   {
6      public static void Main( string[] args )
7      {
8         // create GradeBook object myGradeBook and
9         // pass course name to constructor
10        GradeBook myGradeBook = new GradeBook(
11           "CS101 Introduction to C# Programming" );
12
13        myGradeBook.DisplayMessage(); // display welcome message
14        myGradeBook.InputGrades(); // read grades from user
15        myGradeBook.DisplayGradeReport(); // display report based on grades
16     } // end Main
17  } // end class GradeBookTest
```

```
Welcome to the grade book for
CS101 Introduction to C# Programming!

Enter the integer grades in the range 0-100.
Type <Ctrl> z and press Enter to terminate input:
99
92
45
100
57
63
76
14
92
^Z

Grade Report:
Total of the 9 grades entered is 638
Class average is 70.89
Number of students who received each grade:
A: 4
B: 0
C: 1
D: 1
F: 3
```

Fig. 6.10 | Create GradeBook object, input grades and display grade report.

Class GradeBookTest (Fig. 6.10) does not directly call GradeBook method IncrementLetterGradeCounter (lines 60–82 of Fig. 6.9). This method is used exclusively by method InputGrades of class GradeBook to update the appropriate letter-grade counter as each new grade is entered by the user. Method `IncrementLetterGradeCounter` exists solely to support the operations of class `GradeBook`'s other methods and thus is declared `private`. Members of a class declared with access modifier `private` can be accessed only by members of the class in which the `private` members are declared. When a `private` member is a method, it's commonly referred to as a **utility method** or **helper method**, because it can be called *only* by other members of that class and is used to support the operation of those other members.

switch *Statement UML Activity Diagram*

Figure 6.11 shows the UML activity diagram for the general `switch` statement. Every set of statements after a `case` label normally ends its execution with a `break` or `return` statement to terminate the `switch` statement after processing the `case`. Typically, you'll use `break` statements. Figure 6.11 emphasizes this by including `break` statements in the activity diagram. The diagram makes it clear that the `break` statement at the end of a `case` causes control to exit the `switch` statement immediately.

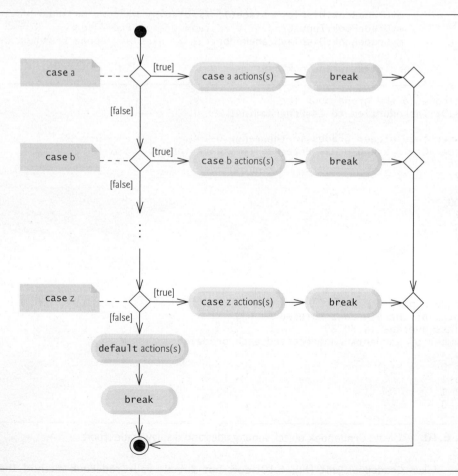

Fig. 6.11 | `switch` multiple-selection statement UML activity diagram with `break` statements.

Good Programming Practice 6.4

Although each case and the default *label in a switch can occur in any order, place the* default *label last for clarity.*

When using the switch statement, remember that the expression after each case can be only a constant integral expression or a constant string expression—that is, any combination of constants that evaluates to a constant value of an integral or string type. An integer constant is simply an integer value (e.g., –7, 0 or 221). In addition, you can use **character constants**—specific characters in single quotes, such as 'A', '7' or '$'—which represent the integer values of characters. (Appendix C shows the integer values of the characters in the ASCII character set, which is a popular subset of the Unicode character set used by C#.) A string constant (or string literal) is a sequence of characters in double quotes, such as "Welcome to C# Programming!". For strings, you can also use null.

The expression in each case also can be a **constant**—a value which does not change for the entire application. Constants are declared with the keyword const (discussed in Chapter 7). C# also has a feature called enumerations, which we also present in Chapter 7. Enumeration constants can also be used in case labels. In Chapter 12, we present a more elegant way to implement switch logic—we use a technique called polymorphism to create applications that are often clearer, easier to maintain and easier to extend than applications using switch logic.

6.7 break and continue Statements

In addition to selection and repetition statements, C# provides statements break and continue to alter the flow of control. The preceding section showed how break can be used to terminate a switch statement's execution. This section discusses how to use break to terminate any repetition statement.

break *Statement*
The break statement, when executed in a while, for, do...while, switch, or foreach, causes immediate exit from that statement. Execution typically continues with the first statement after the control statement—you'll see that there are other possibilities as you learn about additional statement types in C#. Common uses of the break statement are to escape early from a repetition statement or to skip the remainder of a switch (as in Fig. 6.9). Figure 6.12 demonstrates a break statement exiting a for.

```
1   // Fig. 6.12: BreakTest.cs
2   // break statement exiting a for statement.
3   using System;
4
5   public class BreakTest
6   {
7      public static void Main( string[] args )
8      {
9         int count; // control variable also used after loop terminates
10
```

Fig. 6.12 | break statement exiting a for statement. (Part 1 of 2.)

```
11          for ( count = 1; count <= 10; count++ ) // loop 10 times
12          {
13             if ( count == 5 ) // if count is 5,
14                break; // terminate loop
15
16             Console.Write( "{0} ", count );
17          } // end for
18
19          Console.WriteLine( "\nBroke out of loop at count = {0}", count );
20       } // end Main
21    } // end class BreakTest
```

```
1 2 3 4
Broke out of loop at count = 5
```

Fig. 6.12 | break statement exiting a for statement. (Part 2 of 2.)

When the if nested at line 13 in the for statement (lines 11–17) determines that count is 5, the break statement at line 14 executes. This terminates the for statement, and the application proceeds to line 19 (immediately after the for statement), which displays a message indicating the value of the control variable when the loop terminated. The loop fully executes its body only four times instead of 10 because of the break.

continue *Statement*

The **continue statement**, when executed in a while, for, do…while, or foreach, skips the remaining statements in the loop body and proceeds with the next iteration of the loop. In while and do…while statements, the application evaluates the loop-continuation test immediately after the continue statement executes. In a for statement, the increment expression normally executes next, then the application evaluates the loop-continuation test.

Figure 6.13 uses the continue statement in a for to skip the statement at line 14 when the nested if (line 11) determines that the value of count is 5. When the continue statement executes, program control continues with the increment of the control variable in the for statement (line 9).

```
1   // Fig. 6.13: ContinueTest.cs
2   // continue statement terminating an iteration of a for statement.
3   using System;
4
5   public class ContinueTest
6   {
7      public static void Main( string[] args )
8      {
9         for ( int count = 1; count <= 10; count++ ) // loop 10 times
10        {
11           if ( count == 5 ) // if count is 5,
12              continue; // skip remaining code in loop
13
14           Console.Write( "{0} ", count );
15        } // end for
```

Fig. 6.13 | continue statement terminating an iteration of a for statement. (Part 1 of 2.)

```
16
17          Console.WriteLine( "\nUsed continue to skip displaying 5" );
18      } // end Main
19   } // end class ContinueTest
```

```
1 2 3 4 6 7 8 9 10
Used continue to skip displaying 5
```

Fig. 6.13 | continue statement terminating an iteration of a for statement. (Part 2 of 2.)

In Section 6.3, we stated that the while statement can be used in most cases in place of for. One exception occurs when the increment expression in the while follows a continue statement. In this case, the increment does not execute before the application evaluates the repetition-continuation condition, so the while does not execute in the same manner as the for.

Software Engineering Observation 6.2

Some programmers feel that break and continue statements violate structured programming. Since the same effects are achievable with structured programming techniques, these programmers prefer not to use break or continue statements.

Software Engineering Observation 6.3

There's a tension between achieving quality software engineering and achieving the best-performing software. Often, one of these goals is achieved at the expense of the other. For all but the most performance-intensive situations, apply the following rule: First, make your code simple and correct; then make it fast, but only if necessary.

6.8 Logical Operators

The if, if...else, while, do...while and for statements each require a condition to determine how to continue an application's flow of control. So far, we've studied only **simple conditions**, such as count <= 10, number != sentinelValue and total > 1000. Simple conditions are expressed in terms of the relational operators >, <, >= and <=, and the equality operators == and !=. Each expression tests only one condition. To test multiple conditions in the process of making a decision, we performed these tests in separate statements or in nested if or if...else statements. Sometimes, control statements require more complex conditions to determine an application's flow of control.

C# provides **logical operators** to enable you to form more complex conditions by combining simple conditions. The logical operators are && (conditional AND), || (conditional OR), & (boolean logical AND), | (boolean logical inclusive OR), ^ (boolean logical exclusive OR) and ! (logical negation).

Conditional AND (&&) Operator

Suppose that we wish to ensure at some point in an application that two conditions are *both* true before we choose a certain path of execution. In this case, we can use the && (**conditional AND**) operator, as follows:

```
if ( gender == 'F' && age >= 65 )
    ++seniorFemales;
```

This `if` statement contains two simple conditions. The condition `gender == 'F'` determines whether a person is female. The condition `age >= 65` might be evaluated to determine whether a person is a senior citizen. The `if` statement considers the combined condition

```
gender == 'F' && age >= 65
```

which is true if and only if *both* simple conditions are true. If the combined condition is true, the `if` statement's body increments `seniorFemales` by 1. If either or both of the simple conditions are false, the application skips the increment. Some programmers find that the preceding combined condition is more readable when redundant parentheses are added, as in:

```
( gender == 'F' ) && ( age >= 65 )
```

The table in Fig. 6.14 summarizes the `&&` operator. The table shows all four possible combinations of `false` and `true` values for *expression1* and *expression2*. Such tables are called **truth tables**. C# evaluates all expressions that include relational operators, equality operators or logical operators to `bool` values—which are either `true` or `false`.

expression1	expression2	expression1 && expression2
false	false	false
false	true	false
true	false	false
true	true	true

Fig. 6.14 | `&&` (conditional AND) operator truth table.

Conditional OR (||) Operator

Now suppose we wish to ensure that *either or both* of two conditions are true before we choose a certain path of execution. In this case, we use the `||` (**conditional OR**) operator, as in the following application segment:

```
if ( ( semesterAverage >= 90 ) || ( finalExam >= 90 ) )
    Console.WriteLine ( "Student grade is A" );
```

This statement also contains two simple conditions. The condition `semesterAverage >= 90` is evaluated to determine whether the student deserves an A in the course because of a solid performance throughout the semester. The condition `finalExam >= 90` is evaluated to determine whether the student deserves an A in the course because of an outstanding performance on the final exam. The `if` statement then considers the combined condition

```
( semesterAverage >= 90 ) || ( finalExam >= 90 )
```

and awards the student an A if either or both of the simple conditions are true. The only time the message `"Student grade is A"` is *not* displayed is when both of the simple conditions are false. Figure 6.15 is a truth table for operator conditional OR (`||`). Operator `&&` has a higher precedence than operator `||`. Both operators associate from left to right.

expression1	expression2	expression1 || expression2
false	false	false
false	true	true
true	false	true
true	true	true

Fig. 6.15 | \|\| (conditional OR) operator truth table.

Short-Circuit Evaluation of Complex Conditions

The parts of an expression containing && or \|\| operators are evaluated *only* until it's known whether the condition is true or false. Thus, evaluation of the expression

```
( gender == 'F' ) && ( age >= 65 )
```

stops immediately if gender is not equal to 'F' (i.e., at that point, it's certain that the entire expression is false) and continues if gender *is* equal to 'F' (i.e., the entire expression could still be true if the condition age >= 65 is true). This feature of conditional AND and conditional OR expressions is called **short-circuit evaluation**.

Common Programming Error 6.4

In expressions using operator &&, a condition—which we refer to as the dependent condition—may require another condition to be true for the evaluation of the dependent condition to be meaningful. In this case, the dependent condition should be placed after the other condition, or an error might occur. For example, in the expression (i != 0) && (10 / i == 2), the second condition must appear after the first condition, or a divide-by-zero error might occur.

Boolean Logical AND (&) and Boolean Logical OR (|) Operators

The **boolean logical AND (&)** and **boolean logical inclusive OR (|)** operators work identically to the && (conditional AND) and \|\| (conditional OR) operators, with one exception—the boolean logical operators *always* evaluate both of their operands (i.e., they do not perform short-circuit evaluation). Therefore, the expression

```
( gender == 'F' ) & ( age >= 65 )
```

evaluates age >= 65 regardless of whether gender is equal to 'F'. This is useful if the right operand of the boolean logical AND or boolean logical inclusive OR operator has a required **side effect**—such as, a modification of a variable's value. For example, the expression

```
( birthday == true ) | ( ++age >= 65 )
```

guarantees that the condition ++age >= 65 will be evaluated. Thus, the variable age is incremented in the preceding expression, *regardless* of whether the overall expression is true or false.

Error-Prevention Tip 6.4

For clarity, avoid expressions with side effects in conditions. The side effects may look clever, but they can make it harder to understand code and can lead to subtle logic errors.

Boolean Logical Exclusive OR (^)

A complex condition containing the **boolean logical exclusive OR** (^) operator (also called the **logical XOR operator**) is true *if and only if one of its operands is* true *and the other is* false. If both operands are true or both are false, the entire condition is false. Figure 6.16 is a truth table for the boolean logical exclusive OR operator (^). This operator is also guaranteed to evaluate *both* of its operands.

expression1	expression2	expression1 ^ expression2
false	false	false
false	true	true
true	false	true
true	true	false

Fig. 6.16 | ^ (boolean logical exclusive OR) operator truth table.

Logical Negation (!) Operator

The **!** (**logical negation** or **not**) operator enables you to "reverse" the meaning of a condition. Unlike the logical operators &&, ||, &, | and ^, which are binary operators that combine two conditions, the logical negation operator is a unary operator that has only a single condition as an operand. The logical negation operator is placed before a condition to choose a path of execution if the original condition (without the logical negation operator) is false, as in the code segment

```
if ( ! ( grade == sentinelValue ) )
    Console.WriteLine( "The next grade is {0}", grade );
```

which executes the WriteLine call *only if* grade is not equal to sentinelValue. The parentheses around the condition grade == sentinelValue are needed because the logical negation operator has a higher precedence than the equality operator.

In most cases, you can avoid using logical negation by expressing the condition differently with an appropriate relational or equality operator. For example, the previous statement may also be written as follows:

```
if ( grade != sentinelValue )
    Console.WriteLine( "The next grade is {0}", grade );
```

This flexibility can help you express a condition in a more convenient manner. Figure 6.17 is a truth table for the logical negation operator.

expression	!expression
false	true
true	false

Fig. 6.17 | ! (logical negation) operator truth table.

Logical Operators Example

Figure 6.18 demonstrates the logical operators and boolean logical operators by producing their truth tables. The output shows the expression that was evaluated and the bool result of that expression. Lines 10–14 produce the truth table for && (conditional AND). Lines 17–21 produce the truth table for || (conditional OR). Lines 24–28 produce the truth table for & (boolean logical AND). Lines 31–36 produce the truth table for | (boolean logical inclusive OR). Lines 39–44 produce the truth table for ∧ (boolean logical exclusive OR). Lines 47–49 produce the truth table for ! (logical negation).

```
1   // Fig. 6.18: LogicalOperators.cs
2   // Logical operators.
3   using System;
4
5   public class LogicalOperators
6   {
7      public static void Main( string[] args )
8      {
9         // create truth table for && (conditional AND) operator
10        Console.WriteLine( "{0}\n{1}: {2}\n{3}: {4}\n{5}: {6}\n{7}: {8}\n",
11           "Conditional AND (&&)", "false && false", ( false && false ),
12           "false && true", ( false && true ),
13           "true && false", ( true && false ),
14           "true && true", ( true && true ) );
15
16        // create truth table for || (conditional OR) operator
17        Console.WriteLine( "{0}\n{1}: {2}\n{3}: {4}\n{5}: {6}\n{7}: {8}\n",
18           "Conditional OR (||)", "false || false", ( false || false ),
19           "false || true", ( false || true ),
20           "true || false", ( true || false ),
21           "true || true", ( true || true ) );
22
23        // create truth table for & (boolean logical AND) operator
24        Console.WriteLine( "{0}\n{1}: {2}\n{3}: {4}\n{5}: {6}\n{7}: {8}\n",
25           "Boolean logical AND (&)", "false & false", ( false & false ),
26           "false & true", ( false & true ),
27           "true & false", ( true & false ),
28           "true & true", ( true & true ) );
29
30        // create truth table for | (boolean logical inclusive OR) operator
31        Console.WriteLine( "{0}\n{1}: {2}\n{3}: {4}\n{5}: {6}\n{7}: {8}\n",
32           "Boolean logical inclusive OR (|)",
33           "false | false", ( false | false ),
34           "false | true", ( false | true ),
35           "true | false", ( true | false ),
36           "true | true", ( true | true ) );
37
38        // create truth table for ∧ (boolean logical exclusive OR) operator
39        Console.WriteLine( "{0}\n{1}: {2}\n{3}: {4}\n{5}: {6}\n{7}: {8}\n",
40           "Boolean logical exclusive OR (∧)",
41           "false ∧ false", ( false ∧ false ),
42           "false ∧ true", ( false ∧ true ),
```

Fig. 6.18 | Logical operators. (Part 1 of 2.)

```
43          "true ∧ false", ( true ∧ false ),
44          "true ∧ true", ( true ∧ true ) );
45
46      // create truth table for ! (logical negation) operator
47      Console.WriteLine( "{0}\n{1}: {2}\n{3}: {4}",
48          "Logical negation (!)", "!false", ( !false ),
49          "!true", ( !true ) );
50   } // end Main
51 } // end class LogicalOperators
```

```
Conditional AND (&&)
false && false: False
false && true: False
true && false: False
true && true: True

Conditional OR (||)
false || false: False
false || true: True
true || false: True
true || true: True

Boolean logical AND (&)
false & false: False
false & true: False
true & false: False
true & true: True

Boolean logical inclusive OR (|)
false | false: False
false | true: True
true | false: True
true | true: True

Boolean logical exclusive OR (^)
false ^ false: False
false ^ true: True
true ^ false: True
true ^ true: False

Logical negation (!)
!false: True
!true: False
```

Fig. 6.18 | Logical operators. (Part 2 of 2.)

Figure 6.19 shows the precedence and associativity of the C# operators introduced so far. The operators are shown from top to bottom in decreasing order of precedence.

Operators						Associativity	Type
.	new	++*(postfix)*	--*(postfix)*			left to right	highest precedence
++	--	+	-	!	*(type)*	right to left	unary prefix
*	/	%				left to right	multiplicative

Fig. 6.19 | Precedence/associativity of the operators discussed so far. (Part 1 of 2.)

Operators						Associativity	Type
+	-					left to right	additive
<	<=	>	>=			left to right	relational
==	!=					left to right	equality
&						left to right	boolean logical AND
^						left to right	boolean logical exclusive OR
|						left to right	boolean logical inclusive OR
&&						left to right	conditional AND
||						left to right	conditional OR
?:						right to left	conditional
=	+=	-=	*=	/=	%=	right to left	assignment

Fig. 6.19 | Precedence/associativity of the operators discussed so far. (Part 2 of 2.)

6.9 Structured-Programming Summary

Just as architects design buildings by employing the collective wisdom of their profession, so should programmers design applications. Our field is younger than architecture, and our collective wisdom is considerably sparser. We've learned that structured programming produces applications that are easier than unstructured applications to understand, test, debug, modify and even prove correct in a mathematical sense.

Figure 6.20 uses UML activity diagrams to summarize C#'s control statements. The initial and final states indicate the single entry point and the single exit point of each control statement. Arbitrarily connecting individual symbols in an activity diagram can lead to unstructured applications. Therefore, a limited set of control statements can be combined in only two simple ways to build structured applications.

For simplicity, only **single-entry/single-exit control statements** are used—there's *only one* way to enter and *only one* way to exit each control statement. Connecting control statements in sequence to form structured applications is simple. The final state of one control statement is connected to the initial state of the next—that is, the control statements are placed one after another in an application in sequence. We call this "control-statement stacking." The rules for forming structured applications also allow for control statements to be nested.

Figure 6.21 shows the rules for forming structured applications. The rules assume that action states may be used to indicate any action. The rules also assume that we begin with the simplest activity diagram (Fig. 6.22) consisting of only an initial state, an action state, a final state and transition arrows.

Applying the rules in Fig. 6.21 always results in a properly structured activity diagram with a neat, building-block appearance. For example, repeatedly applying Rule 2 to the simplest activity diagram results in an activity diagram containing many action states in sequence (Fig. 6.23). Rule 2 generates a stack of control statements, so let us call Rule 2 the **stacking rule**. [*Note:* The vertical dashed lines in Fig. 6.23 are not part of the UML—we use them to separate the four activity diagrams that demonstrate the application of Rule 2 of Fig. 6.21.]

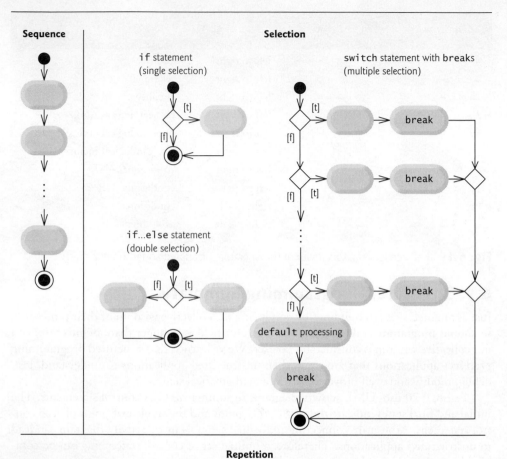

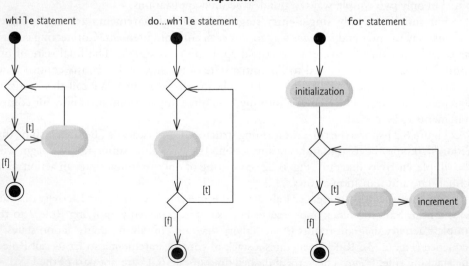

Fig. 6.20 | C#'s single-entry/single-exit sequence, selection and repetition statements.

Rules for forming structured applications

1   Begin with the simplest activity diagram (Fig. 6.22).
2   Any action state can be replaced by two action states in sequence.
3   Any action state can be replaced by any control statement (sequence of action states, `if`, `if...else`, `switch`, `while`, `do...while`, `for` or `foreach`, which we'll see in Chapter 8).
4   Rules 2 and 3 can be applied as often as necessary in any order.

Fig. 6.21 | Rules for forming structured applications.

Fig. 6.22 | Simplest activity diagram.

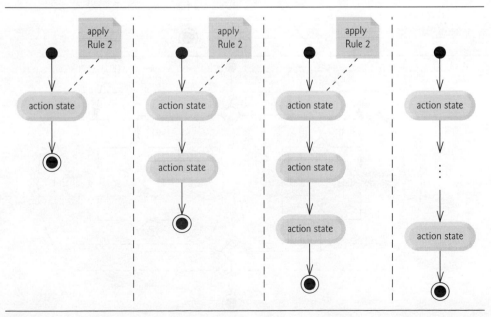

Fig. 6.23 | Repeatedly applying the stacking rule (Rule 2) of Fig. 6.21 to the simplest activity diagram.

Rule 3 is called the **nesting rule**. Repeatedly applying Rule 3 to the simplest activity diagram results in an activity diagram with neatly **nested control statements**. For example, in Fig. 6.24, the action state in the simplest activity diagram is replaced with a double-selection (if...else) statement. Then Rule 3 is applied again to the action states in the double-selection statement, replacing each of these action states with a double-selection statement. The dashed action-state symbols around each of the double-selection statements represent the action state that was replaced. [*Note:* The dashed arrows and dashed action-state symbols shown in Fig. 6.24 are not part of the UML. They're used here to illustrate that any action state can be replaced with any control statement.]

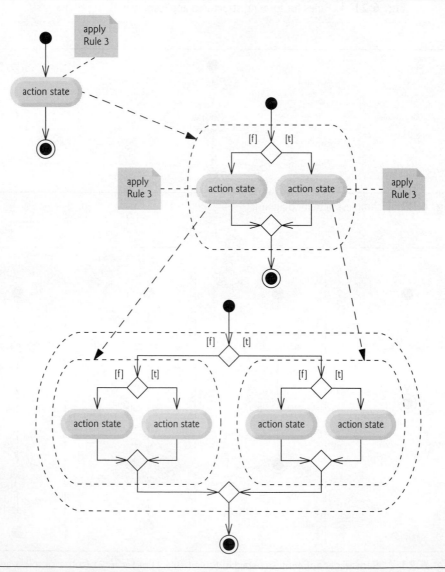

Fig. 6.24 | Repeatedly applying Rule 3 of Fig. 6.21 to the simplest activity diagram.

Rule 4 generates larger, more involved and more deeply nested statements. The diagrams that emerge from applying the rules in Fig. 6.21 constitute the set of all possible structured activity diagrams and hence the set of all possible structured applications. The beauty of the structured approach is that we use only eight simple single-entry/single-exit control statements (counting the `foreach` statement, which we introduce in Section 8.6) and assemble them in only two simple ways.

If the rules in Fig. 6.21 are followed, an "unstructured" activity diagram (like the one in Fig. 6.25) cannot be created. If you are uncertain about whether a particular diagram is structured, apply the rules of Fig. 6.21 in reverse to reduce the diagram to the simplest activity diagram. If you can reduce it, the original diagram is structured; otherwise, it's not.

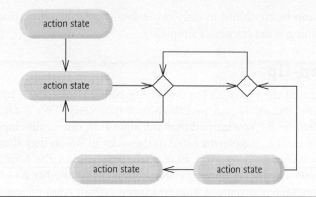

Fig. 6.25 | "Unstructured" activity diagram.

Structured programming promotes simplicity. Bohm and Jacopini have shown that only three forms of control are needed to implement any algorithm:

- sequence
- selection
- repetition

Sequence is trivial. Simply list the statements of the sequence in the order in which they should execute. Selection is implemented in one of three ways:

- `if` statement (single selection)
- `if...else` statement (double selection)
- `switch` statement (multiple selection)

In fact, it's straightforward to prove that the simple `if` statement is sufficient to provide any form of selection—everything that can be done with the `if...else` statement and the `switch` statement can be done by combining `if` statements (although perhaps not as clearly and efficiently).

Repetition is implemented in one of four ways:

- `while` statement
- `do...while`

- for statement
- foreach statement

It's straightforward to prove that the while statement is sufficient to provide any form of repetition. Everything that can be done with the do...while, for and foreach statements can be done with the while statement (although perhaps not as conveniently).

Combining these results illustrates that any form of control ever needed in a C# application can be expressed in terms of

- sequence structure
- if statement (selection)
- while statement (repetition)

and that these can be combined in only two ways—stacking and nesting. Indeed, structured programming is the essence of simplicity.

6.10 Wrap-Up

Chapter 5 discussed the if, if...else and while control statements. In this chapter, we discussed the for, do...while and switch control statements. (We'll discuss the foreach statement in Chapter 8.) You learned that any algorithm can be developed using combinations of sequence (i.e., statements listed in the order in which they should execute), the three selection statements—if, if...else and switch—and the four repetition statements—while, do...while, for and foreach. You saw that the for and do...while statements are simply more convenient ways to express certain types of repetition. Similarly, we showed that the switch statement is a convenient notation for multiple selection, rather than using nested if...else statements. We discussed how you can combine various control statements by stacking and nesting them. We showed how to use the break and continue statements to alter the flow of control in repetition statements. You learned about the logical operators, which enable you to use more complex conditional expressions in control statements.

In Chapter 4, we introduced the basic concepts of objects, classes and methods. Chapters 5 and 6 provided a thorough introduction to the control statements that you use to specify application logic in methods. In Chapter 7, we examine methods in greater depth.

Summary

Section 6.2 Essentials of Counter-Controlled Repetition
- Counter-controlled repetition requires a control variable, the initial value of the control variable, the increment (or decrement) by which the control variable is modified each time through the loop and the loop-continuation condition that determines whether looping should continue.

Section 6.3 for Repetition Statement
- The for header "does it all"—it specifies each of the items needed for counter-controlled repetition with a control variable. The general format of the for statement is

    for (*initialization*; *loopContinuationCondition*; *increment*)
       statement

where the *initialization* expression names the loop's control variable and provides its initial value, the *loopContinuationCondition* is the condition that determines whether looping should continue and the *increment* modifies the control variable's value so that the loop-continuation condition eventually becomes false.

- Typically, for statements are used for counter-controlled repetition, and while statements for sentinel-controlled repetition.

- The scope of a variable defines where it can be used in an application. For example, a local variable can be used only in the method that declares the variable and only from the point of declaration through the end of the block in which the variable is declared.

- The increment of a for statement may also be negative, in which case it's a decrement, and the loop counts downward.

- If the loop-continuation condition is initially false, the application does not execute the for statement's body.

Section 6.4 Examples Using the **for** Statement
- When a variable of type decimal is initialized to an int value, the value of type int is promoted to a decimal type implicitly—no cast is required.

- In a format item, an integer *n* after a comma indicates that the value output should be displayed with a field width of *n*—that is, Write (or WriteLine) displays the value with at least *n* character positions.

- Values are right justified in a field by default. To indicate that values should be output left justified, simply use a negative field width.

- Methods that must be called using a class name are called static methods.

- C# does not include an exponentiation operator. Instead, Math.Pow(x, y) calculates the value of *x* raised to the *y*th power. The method receives two double arguments and returns a double value.

- C# will not implicitly convert a double to a decimal type, or vice versa, because of the possible loss of information in either conversion. To perform this conversion, a cast operator is required.

- Floating-point numbers of type double (or float) can cause trouble in monetary calculations; use type decimal instead.

Section 6.5 **do...while** Repetition Statement
- The do...while statement tests the loop-continuation condition *after* executing the loop's body; therefore, the body always executes at least once.

- The do...while statement has the form:

```
do
{
    statement
} while ( condition );
```

Section 6.6 **switch** Multiple-Selection Statement
- The switch multiple-selection statement performs different actions based on the possible values of an expression.

- Method Console.ReadLine returns null when the end-of-file key sequence is encountered.

- The switch statement consists of a block that contains a sequence of case labels and an optional default label.

- The expression in parentheses following keyword switch is the switch expression. The application attempts to match the value of the switch expression to a case label. If a match occurs, the application executes the statements for that case.

- The switch statement does not provide a mechanism for testing ranges of values, so every value to be tested must be listed in a separate case label.

- After the statements in a case execute, you are required to include a statement that terminates the case, such as a break or a return.

- If no match occurs between the switch expression's value and a case label, the statements after the default label execute. If no match occurs and the switch does not contain a default label, program control typically continues with the first statement after the switch statement.

Section 6.7 **break** and **continue** Statements

- The break statement causes immediate exit from a while, for, do...while, switch or foreach statement. Execution typically continues with the first statement after the control statement.

- The continue statement, when executed in a while, for, do...while or foreach, skips the remaining statements in the loop body and proceeds with the next iteration of the loop. In a for statement, the increment is peformed before the loop-continuation condition is tested.

Section 6.8 Logical Operators

- Logical operators enable you to form more complex conditions by combining simple conditions. The logical operators are && (conditional AND), || (conditional OR), & (boolean logical AND), | (boolean logical inclusive OR), ∧ (boolean logical exclusive OR) and ! (logical negation).

- The && (conditional AND) operator ensures that two conditions are *both* true before we choose a certain path of execution.

- The || (conditional OR) operator ensures that *either or both* of two conditions are true before we choose a certain path of execution.

- The parts of an expression containing && or || operators are evaluated only until it's known whether the condition is true or false. This feature of conditional AND and conditional OR expressions is called short-circuit evaluation.

- The boolean logical AND (&) and boolean logical inclusive OR (|) operators work identically to the && (conditional AND) and || (conditional OR) operators, but the boolean logical operators always evaluate both of their operands (i.e., they do not perform short-circuit evaluation).

- A complex condition containing the boolean logical exclusive OR (∧) operator is true if and only if one of its operands is true and the other is false. If both operands are true or both are false, the entire condition is false.

- The ! (logical negation) operator enables you to "reverse" the meaning of a condition. The logical negation operator is placed before a condition to choose a path of execution if the original condition is false. In most cases, you can avoid using logical negation by expressing the condition differently with an appropriate relational or equality operator.

Section 6.9 Structured-Programming Summary

- Any form of control ever needed in a C# application can be expressed in terms of sequence, the if statement (selection) and the while statement (repetition). These can be combined in only two ways—stacking and nesting.

Terminology

!, logical negation operator
&, boolean logical AND operator
&&, conditional AND operator
|, boolean logical OR operator
||, conditional OR operator

∧, boolean logical exclusive OR operator
boolean logical AND (&)
boolean logical exclusive OR (∧)
boolean logical inclusive OR (|)
break statement

case label in switch	logical negation (!)
character constant	logical operators
conditional AND (&&)	logical OR operator (||)
conditional OR (||)	logical XOR operator (^)
const keyword	loop-continuation condition
constant	multiple-selection statement
constant integral expression	nested control statements
constant string expression	nesting rule
continue statement	off-by-one error
control variable	repetition statement
decrement a control variable	right justified
default label in switch	scope of a variable
do...while repetition statement	short-circuit evaluation
end-of-file indicator	side effect
field width	simple condition
for header	single-entry/single-exit control statements
for repetition statement	state machine diagram
for statement header	stacked control statements
helper method	stacking rule
increment a control variable	static method
initial value of a control variable	switch expression
iteration of a loop	switch multiple-selection statement
left justified	truth table
logical AND operator (&&)	utility method

Self-Review Exercises

6.1   Fill in the blanks in each of the following statements:

a) Typically, _____ statements are used for counter-controlled repetition and _____ statements are used for sentinel-controlled repetition.

b) The do...while statement tests the loop-continuation condition _____ executing the loop's body; therefore, the body always executes at least once.

c) The _____ statement selects among multiple actions based on the possible values of an integer variable or expression.

d) The _____ statement, when executed in a repetition statement, skips the remaining statements in the loop body and proceeds with the next iteration of the loop.

e) The _____ operator can be used to ensure that two conditions are *both* true before choosing a certain path of execution.

f) If the loop-continuation condition in a for header is initially _____, the for statement's body does not execute.

g) Methods that perform common tasks and do not need to be called on objects are called _____ methods.

6.2   State whether each of the following is *true* or *false*. If *false*, explain why.

a) The default label is required in the switch selection statement.

b) The break statement is required in every case of a switch statement.

c) The expression ((x > y) && (a < b)) is true if either (x > y) is true or (a < b) is true.

d) An expression containing the \|\| operator is true if either or both of its operands are true.

e) The integer after the comma (,) in a format item (e.g., {0,4}) indicates the field width of the displayed string.

    f) To test for a range of values in a switch statement, use a hyphen (–) between the start and end values of the range in a case label.

    g) Listing cases consecutively with no statements between them enables the cases to perform the same set of statements.

6.3 Write a C# statement or a set of C# statements to accomplish each of the following tasks:

    a) Sum the odd integers between 1 and 99, using a for statement. Assume that the integer variables sum and count have been declared.

    b) Calculate the value of 2.5 raised to the power of 3, using the Pow method.

    c) Display the integers from 1 to 20 using a while loop and the counter variable i. Assume that the variable i has been declared, but not initialized. Display only five integers per line. [*Hint:* Use the calculation i % 5. When the value of this expression is 0, display a newline character; otherwise, display a tab character. Use the Console.WriteLine() method to output the newline character, and use the Console.Write('\t') method to output the tab character.]

    d) Repeat part (c), using a for statement.

6.4 Find the error in each of the following code segments and explain how to correct it:

    a)
```
i = 1;
while ( i <= 10 );
   ++i;
}
```

    b)
```
for ( k = 0.1; k != 1.0; k += 0.1 )
    Console.WriteLine( k );
```

    c)
```
switch ( n )
{
   case 1:
      Console.WriteLine( "The number is 1" );
   case 2:
      Console.WriteLine( "The number is 2" );
      break;
   default:
      Console.WriteLine( "The number is not 1 or 2" );
      break;
} // end switch
```

    d) The following code should display the values 1 to 10:
```
n = 1;
while ( n < 10 )
    Console.WriteLine( n++ );
```

Answers to Self-Review Exercises

6.1 a) for, while. b) after. c) switch. d) continue. e) && (conditional AND) or & (boolean logical AND). f) false. g) static.

6.2 a) False. The default label is optional. If no default action is needed, then there's no need for a default label. b) False. You could terminate the case with other statements, such as a return. c) False. Both of the relational expressions must be true for this entire expression to be true when using the && operator. d) True. e) True. f) False. The switch statement does not provide a mechanism for testing ranges of values, so you must list every value to test in a separate case label. g) True.

6.3 a)
```
sum = 0;
for ( count = 1; count <= 99; count += 2 )
    sum += count;
```

b) **double** result = Math.Pow(2.5, 3);
c) i = 1;

```
while ( i <= 20 )
{
    Console.Write( i );

    if ( i % 5 == 0 )
        Console.WriteLine();
    else
        Console.Write( '\t' );

    ++i;
}
```
d)
```
for ( i = 1; i <= 20; i++ )
{
    Console.Write( i );

    if ( i % 5 == 0 )
        Console.WriteLine();
    else
        Console.Write( '\t' );
}
```

6.4 a) *Error:* The semicolon after the while header causes an infinite loop, and there's a missing left brace for the body of the while statement.
Correction: Remove the semicolon and add a { before the loop's body.
b) *Error:* Using a floating-point number to control a for statement may not work, because floating-point numbers are represented only approximately by most computers.
Correction: Use an integer, and perform the proper calculation in order to get the values you desire:

```
for ( k = 1; k < 10; k++ )
    Console.WriteLine( ( double ) k / 10 );
```

c) *Error:* case 1 cannot fall through into case 2.
Correction: Terminate the case in some way, such as adding a break statement at the end of the statements for the first case.
d) *Error:* An improper relational operator is used in the while repetition-continuation condition.
Correction: Use <= rather than <, or change 10 to 11.

Exercises

6.5   Describe the four basic elements of counter-controlled repetition.

6.6   Compare and contrast the while and for repetition statements.

6.7   Discuss a situation in which it would be more appropriate to use a do...while statement than a while statement. Explain why.

6.8   Compare and contrast the break and continue statements.

6.9   Find and correct the error(s) in each of the following segments of code:
a) **For** (i = 100, i >= 1, i++)
        Console.WriteLine(i);

b) The following code should display whether integer value is odd or even:

```
switch ( value % 2 )
{
   case 0:
      Console.WriteLine( "Even integer" );
   case 1:
      Console.WriteLine( "Odd integer" );
} // end switch
```

c) The following code should output the odd integers from 19 to 1:

```
for ( int i = 19; i >= 1; i += 2 )
   Console.WriteLine( i );
```

d) The following code should output the even integers from 2 to 100:

```
counter = 2;

do
{
   Console.WriteLine( counter );
   counter += 2;
} While ( counter < 100 );
```

6.10   *(What Does This Code Do?)* What does the following application do?

```
 1   // Exercise 6.10 Solution: Printing.cs
 2   using System;
 3
 4   public class Printing
 5   {
 6      public static void Main( string[] args )
 7      {
 8         for ( int i = 1; i <= 10; i++ )
 9         {
10            for ( int j = 1; j <= 5; j++ )
11               Console.Write( '@' );
12
13            Console.WriteLine();
14         } // end outer for
15      } // end Main
16   } // end class Printing
```

6.11   *(Find the Smallest Value)* Write an application that finds the smallest of several integers. Assume that the first value read specifies the number of values to input from the user.

6.12   *(Product of Odd Integers)* Write an application that calculates the product of the odd integers from 1 to 7.

6.13   *(Factorials)* *Factorials* are used frequently in probability problems. The factorial of a positive integer *n* (written *n!* and pronounced "*n* factorial") is equal to the product of the positive integers from 1 to *n*. Write an application that evaluates the factorials of the integers from 1 to 5. Display the results in tabular format. What difficulty might prevent you from calculating the factorial of 20?

6.14   *(Modified Compound Interest Program)* Modify the compound-interest application (Fig. 6.6) to repeat its steps for interest rates of 5, 6, 7, 8, 9 and 10%. Use a for loop to vary the rate.

6.15   *(Triangle Printing Program)* Write an application that displays the following patterns separately, one below the other. Use for loops to generate the patterns. All asterisks (*) should be displayed by a single statement of the form Console.Write('*'); which causes the asterisks to display side by side. A statement of the form Console.WriteLine(); can be used to move to the next line. A statement of the form Console.Write(' '); can be used to display a space for the last two patterns. There should be no other output statements in the application. [*Hint:* The last two patterns require that each line begin with an appropriate number of blank spaces.]

(a)	(b)	(c)	(d)
*	**********	**********	*
**	*********	*********	**
***	********	********	***
****	*******	*******	****
*****	******	******	*****
******	*****	*****	******
*******	****	****	*******
********	***	***	********
*********	**	**	*********
**********	*	*	**********

6.16   *(Bar Chart Printing)* One interesting application of computers is to display graphs and bar charts. Write an application that reads three numbers between 1 and 30. For each number that is read, your application should display the same number of adjacent asterisks. For example, if your application reads the number 7, it should display *******.

6.17   *(Calculating Sales)* A website sells three products whose retail prices are as follows: product 1, $2.98; product 2, $4.50; and product 3, $9.98. Write an application that reads a series of pairs of numbers as follows:

    a) product number
    b) quantity sold

Your application should use a `switch` statement to determine the retail price for each product. It should calculate and display the total retail value of all products sold. Use a sentinel-controlled loop to determine when the application should stop looping and display the final results.

6.18   *(Modified Compound Interest Program)* In the future, you may work with other programming languages that do not have a type like `decimal` which supports precise monetary calculations. In those languages, you should perform such calculations using integers. Modify the application in Fig. 6.6 to use only integers to calculate the compound interest. Treat all monetary amounts as integral numbers of pennies. Then break the result into its dollars and cents portions by using the division and remainder operations, respectively. Insert a period between the dollars and the cents portions when you display the results.

6.19   Assume that i = 1, j = 2, k = 3 and m = 2. What does each of the following statements display?
    a) `Console.WriteLine( i == 1 );`
    b) `Console.WriteLine( j == 3 );`
    c) `Console.WriteLine( ( i >= 1 ) && ( j < 4 ) );`
    d) `Console.WriteLine( ( m <= 99 ) & ( k < m ) );`
    e) `Console.WriteLine( ( j >= i ) || ( k == m ) );`
    f) `Console.WriteLine( ( k + m < j ) | ( 3 - j >= k ) );`
    g) `Console.WriteLine( !( k > m ) );`

6.20   *(Calculating the Value of π)* Calculate the value of π from the infinite series

$$\pi = 4 - \frac{4}{3} + \frac{4}{5} - \frac{4}{7} + \frac{4}{9} - \frac{4}{11} + \cdots$$

Display a table that shows the value of π approximated by computing one term of this series, by two terms, by three terms, and so on. How many terms of this series do you have to use before you first get 3.14? 3.141? 3.1415? 3.14159?

6.21   *(Pythagorean Triples)* A right triangle can have sides whose lengths are all integers. The set of three integer values for the lengths of the sides of a right triangle is called a Pythagorean triple.

The lengths of the three sides must satisfy the relationship that the sum of the squares of two of the sides is equal to the square of the hypotenuse. Write an application to find all Pythagorean triples for side1, side2 and the hypotenuse, all no larger than 500. Use a triple-nested for loop that tries all possibilities. This method is an example of "brute-force" computing. You'll learn in more advanced computer science courses that there are many interesting problems for which there's no known algorithmic approach other than using sheer brute force.

6.22 *(Modified Triangle Printing Program)* Modify Exercise 6.15 to combine your code from the four separate triangles of asterisks such that all four patterns display side by side. Make clever use of nested for loops.

6.23 *(Diamond Printing Program)* Write an application that displays the following diamond shape. You may use output statements that display a single asterisk (*), a single space or a single newline character. Maximize your use of repetition (with nested for statements) and minimize the number of output statements.

```
    *
   ***
  *****
 *******
*********
 *******
  *****
   ***
    *
```

6.24 *(Modified Diamond Printing Program)* Modify the application you wrote in Exercise 6.23 to read an odd number in the range 1 to 19 to specify the number of rows in the diamond. Your application should then display a diamond of the appropriate size.

6.25 *(Structured Equivalent of **break** Statement)* A criticism of the break statement and the continue statement is that each is unstructured. Actually, break and continue statements can always be replaced by structured statements, although doing so can be awkward. Describe in general how you would remove any break statement from a loop in an application and replace it with a structured equivalent. [*Hint:* The break statement exits a loop from the body of the loop. The other way to exit is by failing the loop-continuation test. Consider using in the loop-continuation test a second test that indicates "early exit because of a 'break' condition."] Use the technique you develop here to remove the break statement from the application in Fig. 6.12.

6.26 *(What Does This Code Do?)* What does the following code segment do?

```
for ( int i = 1; i <= 5; i++ )
{
   for ( int j = 1; j <= 3; j++ )
   {
      for ( int k = 1; k <= 4; k++ )
         Console.Write( '*' );

      Console.WriteLine();
   } // end middle for

   Console.WriteLine();
} // end outer for
```

6.27 *(Structured Equivalent of **continue** Statement)* Describe in general how you would remove any continue statement from a loop in an application and replace it with some structured equivalent. Use the technique you develop here to remove the continue statement from the application in Fig. 6.13.

Making a Difference Exercises

6.28   *(Global Warming Facts Quiz)* The controversial issue of global warming has been widely publicized by the film *An Inconvenient Truth*, featuring former Vice President Al Gore. Mr. Gore and a U.N. network of scientists, the Intergovernmental Panel on Climate Change, shared the 2007 Nobel Peace Prize in recognition of "their efforts to build up and disseminate greater knowledge about man-made climate change." Research *both* sides of the global warming issue online (you might want to search for phrases like "global warming skeptics"). Create a five-question multiple-choice quiz on global warming, each question having four possible answers (numbered 1–4). Be objective and try to fairly represent both sides of the issue. Next, write an application that administers the quiz, calculates the number of correct answers (zero through five) and returns a message to the user. If the user correctly answers five questions, print "Excellent"; if four, print "Very good"; if three or fewer, print "Time to brush up on your knowledge of global warming," and include a list of some of the websites where you found your facts.

6.29   *(Tax Plan Alternatives; The "FairTax")* There are many proposals to make taxation fairer. Check out the FairTax initiative in the United States at

```
www.fairtax.org/site/PageServer?pagename=calculator
```

Research how the proposed FairTax works. One suggestion is to eliminate income taxes and most other taxes in favor of a 23% consumption tax on all products and services that you buy. Some FairTax opponents question the 23% figure and say that because of the way the tax is calculated, it would be more accurate to say the rate is 30%—check this carefully. Write a program that prompts the user to enter expenses in various expense categories they have (e.g., housing, food, clothing, transportation, education, health care, vacations), then prints the estimated FairTax that person would pay.

7

Methods: A Deeper Look

E pluribus unum.
(One composed of many.)
—Virgil

O! call back yesterday, bid time return.
—William Shakespeare

Call me Ishmael.
—Herman Melville

Answer me in one word.
—William Shakespeare

There is a point at which methods devour themselves.
—Frantz Fanon

Objectives

In this chapter you'll learn:

- How **static** methods and variables are associated with classes rather than objects.

- How the method call/return mechanism is supported by the method-call stack.

- How to use random-number generation to implement game-playing applications.

- How the visibility of declarations is limited to specific parts of applications.

- How to create overloaded methods.

- How to use optional and named parameters.

- What recursive methods are.

- Passing method arguments by value and by reference.

7.1 Introduction

Most computer applications that solve real-world problems are much larger than the applications presented in this book's first few chapters. Experience has shown that the best way to develop and maintain a large application is to construct it from small, simple pieces. This technique is called **divide and conquer**. We introduced methods in Chapter 4. In this chapter we study methods in more depth. We emphasize how to declare and use methods to facilitate the design, implementation, operation and maintenance of large applications.

You'll see that it's possible for certain methods, called `static` methods, to be called without the need for an object of the class to exist. You'll learn how to declare a method with more than one parameter. You'll also learn how C# is able to keep track of which method is currently executing, how value-type and reference-type arguments are passed to methods, how local variables of methods are maintained in memory and how a method knows where to return after it completes execution.

We discuss **simulation** techniques with random-number generation and develop a version of the casino dice game called craps that uses most of the programming techniques you've learned to this point in the book. In addition, you'll learn to declare values that cannot change (i.e., constants). You'll also learn to write methods that call themselves—this is called **recursion**.

Many of the classes you'll use or create while developing applications will have more than one method of the same name. This technique, called method overloading, is used to implement methods that perform similar tasks but with different types and/or different numbers of arguments.

7.2 Packaging Code in C#

Common ways of packaging code are properties, methods, classes and namespaces. C# applications are written by combining new properties, methods and classes that you write with predefined properties, methods and classes available in the .NET Framework Class Library and in various other class libraries. Related classes are often grouped into namespaces and compiled into class libraries so that they can be reused in other applications. You'll learn how to create your own namespaces and class libraries in Chapter 15. The Framework Class Library provides many predefined classes that contain methods for performing common mathematical calculations, string manipulations, character manipulations, input/output operations, database operations, networking operations, file processing, error checking, web-application development and more.

Good Programming Practice 7.1

Familiarize yourself with the classes and methods provided by the Framework Class Library (msdn.microsoft.com/en-us/library/ms229335.aspx).

Software Engineering Observation 7.1

Don't try to "reinvent the wheel." When possible, reuse Framework Class Library classes and methods. This reduces application development time, avoids introducing programming errors and contributes to good application performance.

Methods (called **functions** or **procedures** in other programming languages) allow you to modularize an application by separating its tasks into self-contained units. You've declared methods in every application you've written. These methods are sometimes referred to as **user-defined methods.** The actual statements in the method bodies are written only once, can be reused from several locations in an application and are hidden from other methods.

There are several motivations for modularizing an application by means of methods. One is the "divide-and-conquer" approach, which makes application development more manageable by constructing applications from small, simple pieces. Another is **software reusability**—existing methods can be used as building blocks to create new applications. Often, you can create applications mostly by reusing existing methods rather than by building customized code. For example, in earlier applications, we did not have to define how to read data values from the keyboard—the Framework Class Library provides these capabilities in class Console. A third motivation is to avoid repeating code. Dividing an application into meaningful methods makes the application easier to debug and maintain.

Software Engineering Observation 7.2

To promote software reusability, every method should be limited to performing a single, well-defined task, and the name of the method should express that task effectively. Such methods make applications easier to write, debug, maintain and modify.

Software Engineering Observation 7.3

If you cannot choose a concise name that expresses a method's task, your method might be attempting to perform too many diverse tasks. It's usually best to break such a method into several smaller methods.

As you know, a method is invoked by a method call, and when the called method completes its task, it returns a result or simply returns control to the caller. The code that calls a method is also sometimes known as the client code—as it's a client of the method. An analogy to the method-call-and-return structure is the hierarchical form of management

(Figure 7.1). A boss (the caller) asks a worker (the called method) to perform a task and report back (i.e., return) the results after completing the task. The boss method does not know how the worker method performs its designated tasks. The worker may also call other worker methods, unbeknown to the boss. This "hiding" of implementation details promotes good software engineering. Figure 7.1 shows the boss method communicating with several worker methods in a hierarchical manner. The boss method divides the responsibilities among the various worker methods. Note that worker1 acts as a "boss method" to worker4 and worker5.

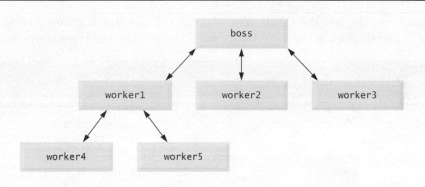

Fig. 7.1 | Hierarchical boss-method/worker-method relationship.

7.3 static Methods, static Variables and Class Math

Although most methods execute on specific objects in response to method calls, this is not always the case. Sometimes a method performs a task that does not depend on the contents of any object. Such a method applies to the class in which it's declared as a whole and is known as a static method. It's not uncommon for a class to contain a group of static methods to perform common tasks. For example, recall that we used static method Pow of class Math to raise a value to a power in Fig. 6.6. To declare a method as static, place the keyword static before the return type in the method's declaration. You call any static method by specifying the name of the class in which the method is declared, followed by the member access (.) operator and the method name, as in

ClassName.*MethodName*(*arguments*)

We use various methods of the Math class here to present the concept of static methods. Class Math (from the System namespace) provides a collection of methods that enable you to perform common mathematical calculations. For example, you can calculate the square root of 900.0 with the static method call

```
Math.Sqrt( 900.0 )
```

The preceding expression evaluates to 30.0. Method Sqrt takes an argument of type double and returns a result of type double. To output the value of the preceding method call in the console window, you might write the statement

```
Console.WriteLine( Math.Sqrt( 900.0 ) );
```

In this statement, the value that Sqrt returns becomes the argument to method Write-Line. We did not create a Math object before calling method Sqrt. Also, *all* of Math's methods are static—therefore, each is called by preceding the name of the method with the class name Math and the member access (.) operator. Similarly, Console method Write-Line is a static method of class Console, so we invoke the method by preceding its name with the class name Console and the member access (.) operator.

Method arguments may be constants, variables or expressions. If c = 13.0, d = 3.0 and f = 4.0, then the statement

```
Console.WriteLine( Math.Sqrt( c + d * f ) );
```

calculates and displays the square root of 13.0 + 3.0 * 4.0 = 25.0—namely, 5.0. Figure 7.2 summarizes several Math class methods. In the figure, *x* and *y* are of type double.

Method	Description	Example
Abs(*x*)	absolute value of *x*	Abs(23.7) is 23.7 Abs(0.0) is 0.0 Abs(-23.7) is 23.7
Ceiling(*x*)	rounds *x* to the smallest integer not less than *x*	Ceiling(9.2) is 10.0 Ceiling(-9.8) is -9.0
Cos(*x*)	trigonometric cosine of *x* (*x* in radians)	Cos(0.0) is 1.0
Exp(*x*)	exponential method e^x	Exp(1.0) is 2.71828 Exp(2.0) is 7.38906
Floor(*x*)	rounds *x* to the largest integer not greater than *x*	Floor(9.2) is 9.0 Floor(-9.8) is -10.0
Log(*x*)	natural logarithm of *x* (base *e*)	Log(Math.E) is 1.0 Log(Math.E * Math.E) is 2.0
Max(*x*, *y*)	larger value of *x* and *y*	Max(2.3, 12.7) is 12.7 Max(-2.3, -12.7) is -2.3
Min(*x*, *y*)	smaller value of *x* and *y*	Min(2.3, 12.7) is 2.3 Min(-2.3, -12.7) is -12.7
Pow(*x*, *y*)	*x* raised to the power *y* (i.e., x^y)	Pow(2.0, 7.0) is 128.0 Pow(9.0, 0.5) is 3.0
Sin(*x*)	trigonometric sine of *x* (*x* in radians)	Sin(0.0) is 0.0
Sqrt(*x*)	square root of *x*	Sqrt(900.0) is 30.0
Tan(*x*)	trigonometric tangent of *x* (*x* in radians)	Tan(0.0) is 0.0

Fig. 7.2 | Math class methods.

Math Class Constants PI and E
Class Math also declares two static constants that represent commonly used mathematical values: **Math.PI** and **Math.E**. The constant Math.PI (3.14159265358979323846) is the ratio of a circle's circumference to its diameter. The constant Math.E (2.7182818284590452354) is the base value for natural logarithms (calculated with static Math method Log). These constants are declared in class Math with the modifiers public and const. Making them public allows other programmers to use these variables

in their own classes. A constant is declared with the keyword **const**—its value cannot be changed after the constant is declared. Both PI and E are declared const because their values never change.

> ### Common Programming Error 7.1
> *Every constant declared in a class, but not inside a method of the class is implicitly* static, *so it's a syntax error to declare such a constant with keyword* static *explicitly.*

Because these constants are static, you can access them via the class name Math and the member access (.) operator, just like class Math's methods. Recall from Section 4.5 that when each object of a class maintains its own copy of an attribute, the variable that represents the attribute is also known as an instance variable—each object (instance) of the class has a separate instance of the variable. There are also variables for which each object of a class does *not* have a separate instance of the variable. That's the case with static variables. When objects of a class containing static variables are created, all the objects of that class share one copy of the class's static variables. Together the static variables and instance variables represent the **fields** of a class.

Why Is Method **Main** Declared **static?**

Why must Main be declared static? During application startup, when no objects of the class have been created, the Main method must be called to begin program execution. The Main method is sometimes called the application's **entry point**. Declaring Main as static allows the execution environment to invoke Main without creating an instance of the class. Method Main is often declared with the header:

```
public static void Main( string args[] )
```

When you execute your application from the command line, you type the application name, as in

ApplicationName argument1 argument2 ...

In the preceding command, *argument1* and *argument2* are the **command-line arguments** to the application that specify a list of strings (separated by spaces) the execution environment will pass to the Main method of your application. Such arguments might be used to specify options (e.g., a file name) to run the application. As you'll learn in Chapter 8, Arrays, your application can access those command-line arguments and use them to customize the application.

Additional Comments about Method **Main**

The header of a Main method does not need to appear exactly as we've shown. Applications that do not take command-line arguments may omit the string[] args parameter. The public keyword may also be omitted. In addition, you can declare Main with return type int (instead of void) to enable Main to return an error code with the return statement. A Main method declared with any one of these headers can be used as the application's entry point—but you can declare only one such Main method in each class.

In earlier chapters, most applications had one class that contained only Main, and some examples had a second class that was used by Main to create and manipulate objects. Actually, any class can contain a Main method. In fact, each of our two-class examples could have been implemented as one class. For example, in the application in Figs. 6.9 and

6.10, method Main (lines 6–16 of Fig. 6.10) could have been taken as is and placed in class GradeBook (Fig. 6.9). The application results would have been identical to those of the two-class version. You can place a Main method in every class you declare. Some programmers take advantage of this to build a small test application into each class they declare. However, if you declare more than one Main method among the classes of your project, you'll need to indicate to the IDE which one you would like to be the application's entry point. You can do this by selecting **Project > [ProjectName] Properties...** (where **[Project-Name]** is the name of your project) and selecting the class containing the Main method that should be the entry point from the **Startup object** list box.

7.4 Declaring Methods with Multiple Parameters

Methods often require more than one piece of information to perform their tasks. We now consider how to write your own methods with multiple parameters.

The application in Fig. 7.3 uses a user-defined method called Maximum to determine and return the largest of three double values that are input by the user. When the application begins execution, the Main method (lines 8–22) executes. Lines 11–15 prompt the user to enter three double values and read them from the user. Line 18 calls method Maximum (declared in lines 25–38) to determine the largest of the three double values passed as arguments to the method. When method Maximum returns the result to line 18, the application assigns Maximum's return value to local variable result. Then line 21 outputs result. At the end of this section, we'll discuss the use of operator + in line 21.

```
1   // Fig. 7.3: MaximumFinder.cs
2   // User-defined method Maximum.
3   using System;
4
5   public class MaximumFinder
6   {
7      // obtain three floating-point values and determine maximum value
8      public static void Main( string[] args )
9      {
10        // prompt for and input three floating-point values
11        Console.WriteLine( "Enter three floating-point values,\n"
12           + "  pressing 'Enter' after each one: " );
13        double number1 = Convert.ToDouble( Console.ReadLine() );
14        double number2 = Convert.ToDouble( Console.ReadLine() );
15        double number3 = Convert.ToDouble( Console.ReadLine() );
16
17        // determine the maximum value
18        double result = Maximum( number1, number2, number3 );
19
20        // display maximum value
21        Console.WriteLine( "Maximum is: " + result );
22     } // end Main
23
24     // returns the maximum of its three double parameters
25     public static double Maximum( double x, double y, double z )
26     {
```

Fig. 7.3 | User-defined method Maximum. (Part 1 of 2.)

```
27          double maximumValue = x; // assume x is the largest to start
28
29          // determine whether y is greater than maximumValue
30          if ( y > maximumValue )
31             maximumValue = y;
32
33          // determine whether z is greater than maximumValue
34          if ( z > maximumValue )
35             maximumValue = z;
36
37          return maximumValue;
38       } // end method Maximum
39    } // end class MaximumFinder
```

```
Enter three floating-point values,
  pressing 'Enter' after each one:
3.33
2.22
1.11
Maximum is: 3.33
```

```
Enter three floating-point values,
  pressing 'Enter' after each one:
2.22
3.33
1.11
Maximum is: 3.33
```

```
Enter three floating-point values,
  pressing 'Enter' after each one:
1.11
2.22
867.5309
Maximum is: 867.5309
```

Fig. 7.3 | User-defined method Maximum. (Part 2 of 2.)

The public and static Keywords

Method Maximum's declaration begins with keyword public to indicate that the method is "available to the public"—it can be called from methods of other classes. The keyword static enables the Main method (another static method) to call Maximum as shown in line 18 without qualifying the method name with the class name MaximumFinder—static methods in the same class can call each other directly. Any other class that uses Maximum must fully qualify the method name with the class name.

Method Maximum

Consider the declaration of method Maximum (lines 25–38). Line 25 indicates that the method returns a double value, that the method's name is Maximum and that the method requires three double parameters (x, y and z) to accomplish its task. When a method has more than one parameter, the parameters are specified as a comma-separated list. When Maximum is called in line 18, the parameter x is initialized with the value of the argument number1, the parameter y is initialized with the value of the argument number2 and the parameter z is initialized with the value of the argument number3. There must be one argument in the method call for each required parameter (sometimes called a **formal parameter**) in the method declaration. Also, each argument must be consistent with the type of the corresponding parameter. For example, a parameter of type double can receive values like 7.35 (a double), 22 (an int) or –0.03456 (a double), but not strings like "hello". Section 7.7 discusses the argument types that can be provided in a method call for each parameter of a simple type.

To determine the maximum value, we begin with the assumption that parameter x contains the largest value, so line 27 declares local variable maximumValue and initializes it with the value of parameter x. Of course, it's possible that parameter y or z contains the largest value, so we must compare each of these values with maximumValue. The if statement at lines 30–31 determines whether y is greater than maximumValue. If so, line 31 assigns y to maximumValue. The if statement at lines 34–35 determines whether z is greater than maximumValue. If so, line 35 assigns z to maximumValue. At this point, the largest of the three values resides in maximumValue, so line 37 returns that value to line 18. When program control returns to the point in the application where Maximum was called, Maximum's parameters x, y and z are no longer accessible. Methods can return at most one value; the returned value can be a value type that contains many values (implemented as a struct) or a reference to an object that contains many values.

Variable result is a local variable in method Main because it's declared in the block that represents the method's body. Variables should be declared as fields of a class (i.e., as either instance variables or static variables of the class) only if they're required for use in more than one method of the class or if the application should save their values between calls to the class's methods.

Common Programming Error 7.2

Declaring method parameters of the same type as float x, y instead of float x, float y is a syntax error—a type is required for each parameter in the parameter list.

Implementing Method Maximum by Reusing Method Math.Max

Recall from Fig. 7.2 that class Math has a Max method that can determine the larger of two values. The entire body of our maximum method could also be implemented with nested calls to Math.Max, as follows:

```
return Math.Max( x, Math.Max( y, z ) );
```

The leftmost call to Math.Max specifies arguments x and Math.Max(y, z). Before any method can be called, all its arguments must be evaluated to determine their values. If an argument is a method call, the method call must be performed to determine its return value. So, in the preceding statement, Math.Max(y, z) is evaluated first to determine the maximum of y and z. Then the result is passed as the second argument to the other call to Math.Max, which returns the larger of its two arguments. Using Math.Max in this manner is a good example of software reuse—we find the largest of three values by reusing Math.Max, which finds the larger of two values. Note how concise this code is compared to lines 27–37 of Fig. 7.3.

Assembling Strings with String Concatenation

C# allows string objects to be created by assembling smaller strings into larger strings using operator + (or the compound assignment operator +=). This is known as **string concatenation**. When both operands of operator + are string objects, operator + creates a new string object in which a copy of the characters of the right operand is placed at the end of a copy of the characters in the left operand. For example, the expression "hello " + "there" creates the string "hello there" without disturbing the original strings.

In line 21 of Fig. 7.3, the expression "Maximum is: " + result uses operator + with operands of types string and double. Every value of a simple type in C# has a string representation. When one of the + operator's operands is a string, the other is implicitly converted to a string, then the two are concatenated. In line 21, the double value is implicitly converted to its string representation and placed at the end of the string "Maximum is: ". If there are any trailing zeros in a double value, these will be discarded when the number is converted to a string. Thus, the number 9.3500 would be represented as 9.35 in the resulting string.

For values of simple types used in string concatenation, the values are converted to strings. If a bool is concatenated with a string, the bool is converted to the string "True" or "False" (each is capitalized). All objects have a ToString method that returns a string representation of the object. When an object is concatenated with a string, the object's ToString method is implicitly called to obtain the string representation of the object. If the object is null, an empty string is written.

Line 21 of Fig. 7.3 could also be written using string formatting as

```
Console.WriteLine( "Maximum is: {0}", result );
```

As with string concatenation, using a format item to substitute an object into a string implicitly calls the object's ToString method to obtain the object's string representation. You'll learn more about method ToString in Chapter 8.

When a large string literal is typed into an application's source code, you can break that string into several smaller strings and place them on multiple lines for readability. The strings can be reassembled using either string concatenation or string formatting. We discuss the details of strings in Chapter 16.

Common Programming Error 7.3

It's a syntax error to break a string literal across multiple lines in an application. If a string does not fit on one line, split the string into several smaller strings and use concatenation to form the desired string. C# also provides so-called verbatim string literals, which are preceded by the @ character. Such literals can be split over multiple lines and the characters in the literal are processed exactly as they appear in the literal.

Common Programming Error 7.4

Confusing the + operator used for string concatenation with the + operator used for addition can lead to strange results. The + operator is left-associative. For example, if integer variable y has the value 5, the expression "y + 2 = " + y + 2 results in the string "y + 2 = 52", not "y + 2 = 7", because first the value of y (5) is concatenated with the string "y + 2 = ", then the value 2 is concatenated with the new larger string "y + 2 = 5". The expression "y + 2 = " + (y + 2) produces the desired result "y + 2 = 7".

7.5 Notes on Declaring and Using Methods

You've seen three ways to call a method:

1. Using a method name by itself to call a method of the same class—such as `Maximum(number1, number2, number3)` in line 18 of Fig. 7.3.

2. Using a variable that contains a reference to an object, followed by the member access (.) operator and the method name to call a non-`static` method of the referenced object—such as the method call in line 13 of Fig. 6.10, `myGradeBook.DisplayMessage()`, which calls a method of class `GradeBook` from the `Main` method of `GradeBookTest`.

3. Using the class name and the member access (.) operator to call a `static` method of a class—such as `Convert.ToDouble(Console.ReadLine())` in lines 13–15 of Fig. 7.3 or `Math.Sqrt(900.0)` in Section 7.3.

A `static` method can call *only* other `static` methods of the same class directly (i.e., using the method name by itself) and can manipulate *only* `static` variables in the same class directly. To access the class's non-`static` members, a `static` method must use a reference to an object of the class. Recall that `static` methods relate to a class as a whole, whereas non-`static` methods are associated with a specific instance (object) of the class and may manipulate the instance variables of that object. Many objects of a class, each with its own copies of the instance variables, may exist at the same time. Suppose a `static` method were to invoke a non-`static` method directly. How would the method know which object's instance variables to manipulate? What would happen if no objects of the class existed at the time the non-`static` method was invoked? Thus, C# does not allow a `static` method to access non-`static` members of the same class directly.

There are three ways to return control to the statement that calls a method. If the method does not return a result, control returns when the program flow reaches the method-ending right brace or when the statement

```
return;
```

is executed. If the method returns a result, the statement

```
return expression;
```

evaluates the *expression*, then returns the result (and control) to the caller.

Common Programming Error 7.5
Declaring a method outside the body of a class declaration or inside the body of another method is a syntax error.

Common Programming Error 7.6
Omitting the return type in a method declaration is a syntax error.

Common Programming Error 7.7
Redeclaring a method parameter as a local variable in the method's body is a compilation error.

Common Programming Error 7.8

Forgetting to return a value from a method that should return one is a compilation error. If a return type other than void *is specified, the method must contain a* return *statement in each possible execution path through the method and each* return *statement must return a value consistent with the method's return type. Returning a value from a method whose return type has been declared* void *is a compilation error.*

7.6 Method-Call Stack and Activation Records

To understand how C# performs method calls, we first need to consider a data structure (i.e., collection of related data items) known as a **stack** (we discuss data structures in more detail in Chapters 20–23). You can think of a stack as analogous to a pile of dishes. When a dish is placed on the pile, it's normally placed at the top (referred to as **pushing** the dish onto the stack). Similarly, when a dish is removed from the pile, it's always removed from the top (referred to as **popping** the dish off the stack). Stacks are known as **last-in, first-out (LIFO) data structures**—the last item pushed (inserted) on the stack is the first item popped off (removed from) the stack.

When an application calls a method, the called method must know how to return to its caller, so the return address of the calling method is pushed onto the **program-execution stack** (sometimes referred to as the **method-call stack**). If a series of method calls occurs, the successive return addresses are pushed onto the stack in last-in, first-out order so that each method can return to its caller.

The program-execution stack also contains the memory for the local variables used in each invocation of a method during an application's execution. This data, stored as a portion of the program-execution stack, is known as the **activation record** or **stack frame** of the method call. When a method call is made, the activation record for it is pushed onto the program-execution stack. When the method returns to its caller, the activation record for this method call is popped off the stack, and those local variables are no longer known to the application. If a local variable holding a reference to an object is the only variable in the application with a reference to that object, when the activation record containing that local variable is popped off the stack, the object can no longer be accessed by the application and will eventually be deleted from memory during "garbage collection." We'll discuss garbage collection in Section 10.8.

Of course, the amount of memory in a computer is finite, so only a certain amount of memory can be used to store activation records on the program-execution stack. If more method calls occur than can have their activation records stored on the program-execution stack, an error known as a **stack overflow** occurs.

7.7 Argument Promotion and Casting

Another important feature of method calls is **argument promotion**—implicitly converting an argument's value to the type that the method expects to receive in its corresponding parameter. For example, an application can call Math method Sqrt with an integer argument even though the method expects to receive a double argument. The statement

```
Console.WriteLine( Math.Sqrt( 4 ) );
```

correctly evaluates `Math.Sqrt(4)` and displays the value `2.0`. `Sqrt`'s parameter list causes C# to convert the `int` value `4` to the `double` value `4.0` before passing the value to `Sqrt`. Such conversions may lead to compilation errors if C#'s **promotion rules** are not satisfied. The promotion rules specify which conversions are allowed—that is, which conversions can be performed without losing data. In the `Sqrt` example above, an `int` is converted to a `double` without changing its value. However, converting a `double` to an `int` truncates the fractional part of the `double` value—thus, part of the value is lost. Also, `double` variables can hold values much larger (and much smaller) than `int` variables, so assigning a `double` to an `int` can cause a loss of information when the `double` value doesn't fit in the `int`. Converting large integer types to small integer types (e.g., `long` to `int`) can also result in changed values.

The promotion rules apply to expressions containing values of two or more simple types and to simple-type values passed as arguments to methods. Each value is promoted to the appropriate type in the expression. (Actually, the expression uses a *temporary* copy of each value—the types of the original values remain unchanged.) Figure 7.4 lists the simple types alphabetically and the types to which each can be promoted. Values of all simple types can also be implicitly converted to type `object`. We demonstrate such implicit conversions in Chapter 21, Data Structures.

Type	Conversion types
bool	no possible implicit conversions to other simple types
byte	ushort, short, uint, int, ulong, long, decimal, float or double
char	ushort, int, uint, long, ulong, decimal, float or double
decimal	no possible implicit conversions to other simple types
double	no possible implicit conversions to other simple types
float	double
int	long, decimal, float or double
long	decimal, float or double
sbyte	short, int, long, decimal, float or double
short	int, long, decimal, float or double
uint	ulong, long, decimal, float or double
ulong	decimal, float or double
ushort	uint, int, ulong, long, decimal, float or double

Fig. 7.4 | Implicit conversions between simple types.

By default, C# does not allow you to implicitly convert values between simple types if the target type cannot represent the value of the original type (e.g., the `int` value 2000000 cannot be represented as a `short`, and any floating-point number with digits after its decimal point cannot be represented in an integer type such as `long`, `int` or `short`). Therefore, to prevent a compilation error in cases where information may be lost due to an implicit conversion between simple types, the compiler requires you to use a cast operator to explicitly force the conversion. This enables you to "take control" from the compiler. You essentially say, "I know this conversion might cause loss of information, but for my purposes here, that's fine." Suppose you create a method `Square` that calculates the square of an integer and thus requires an int argument. To call Square with the whole part of a double argument named doubleValue, you'd write Square((int) doubleValue). This method call explicitly casts (converts) the value of doubleValue to an integer for use in method Square. Thus, if doubleValue's value is 4.5, the method receives the value 4 and returns 16, not 20.25 (which does, unfortunately, result in the loss of information).

Common Programming Error 7.9

Converting a simple-type value to a value of another simple type may change the value if the promotion is not allowed. For example, converting a floating-point value to an integral value may introduce truncation errors (loss of the fractional part) in the result.

7.8 The .NET Framework Class Library

Many predefined classes are grouped into categories of related classes called namespaces. Together, these namespaces are referred to as the .NET Framework Class Library.

Throughout the text, using directives allow us to use library classes from the Framework Class Library without specifying their fully qualified names. For example, an application includes the declaration

```
using System;
```

in order to use the class names from the System namespace without fully qualifying their names. This allows you to use the **unqualified class name** Console, rather than the fully qualified class name System.Console, in your code. A great strength of C# is the large number of classes in the namespaces of the .NET Framework Class Library. Some key Framework Class Library namespaces are described in Fig. 7.5, which represents only a small portion of the reusable classes in the .NET Framework Class Library.

Namespace	Description
System.Windows.Forms	Contains the classes required to create and manipulate GUIs. (Various classes in this namespace are discussed in Chapter 14, Graphical User Interfaces with Windows Forms: Part 1, and Chapter 15, Graphical User Interfaces with Windows Forms: Part 2.)
System.Windows.Controls System.Windows.Input System.Windows.Media System.Windows.Shapes	Contain the classes of the Windows Presentation Foundation for GUIs, 2-D and 3-D graphics, multimedia and animation. (You'll learn more about these namespaces in Chapter 24, GUI with Windows Presentation Foundation, Chapter 25, WPF Graphics and Multimedia and Chapter 29, Silverlight and Rich Internet Applications.)
System.Linq	Contains the classes that support Language Integrated Query (LINQ). (You'll learn more about this namespace in Chapter 9, Introduction to LINQ and the List Collection, and several other chapters throughout the book.)

Fig. 7.5 | .NET Framework Class Library namespaces (a subset). (Part 1 of 2.)

Namespace	Description
`System.Data` `System.Data.Linq`	Contain the classes for manipulating data in databases (i.e., organized collections of data), including support for LINQ to SQL. (You'll learn more about these namespaces in Chapter 18, Databases and LINQ.)
`System.IO`	Contains the classes that enable programs to input and output data. (You'll learn more about this namespace in Chapter 17, Files and Streams.)
`System.Web`	Contains the classes used for creating and maintaining web applications, which are accessible over the Internet. (You'll learn more about this namespace in Chapter 19, Web App Development with ASP.NET.)
`System.Xml.Linq`	Contains the classes that support Language Integrated Query (LINQ) for XML documents. (You'll learn more about this namespace in Chapter 26, XML and LINQ to XML, and several other chapters throughout the book.)
`System.Xml`	Contains the classes for creating and manipulating XML data. Data can be read from or written to XML files. (You'll learn more about this namespace in Chapter 26.)
`System.Collections` `System.Collections.Generic`	Contain the classes that define data structures for maintaining collections of data. (You'll learn more about these namespaces in Chapter 23, Collections.)
`System.Text`	Contains the classes that enable programs to manipulate characters and strings. (You'll learn more about this namespace in Chapter 16, Strings and Characters.)

Fig. 7.5 | .NET Framework Class Library namespaces (a subset). (Part 2 of 2.)

The set of namespaces available in the .NET Framework Class Library is quite large. Besides those summarized in Fig. 7.5, the .NET Framework Class Library contains namespaces for complex graphics, advanced graphical user interfaces, printing, advanced networking, security, database processing, multimedia, accessibility (for people with disabilities) and many other capabilities—over 100 namespaces in all.

You can locate additional information about a predefined C# class's methods in the *.NET Framework Class Library* reference (`msdn.microsoft.com/en-us/library/ms229335.aspx`). When you visit this site, you'll see an alphabetical listing of all the namespaces in the Framework Class Library. Locate the namespace and click its link to see an alphabetical listing of all its classes, with a brief description of each. Click a class's link to see a more complete description of the class. Click the **Methods** link in the left-hand column to see a listing of the class's methods.

Good Programming Practice 7.2

The online .NET Framework documentation is easy to search and provides many details about each class. As you learn each class in this book, you should review the class in the online documentation for additional information.

7.9 Case Study: Random-Number Generation

In this and the next section, we develop a nicely structured game-playing application with multiple methods. The application uses most of the control statements presented thus far in the book and introduces several new programming concepts.

There's something in the air of a casino that invigorates people—from the high rollers at the plush mahogany-and-felt craps tables to the quarter poppers at the one-armed bandits. It's the **element of chance**, the possibility that luck will convert a pocketful of money into a mountain of wealth. The element of chance can be introduced in an application via an object of class Random (of namespace System). Objects of class **Random** can produce random byte, int and double values. In the next several examples, we use objects of class Random to produce random numbers.

A new random-number generator object can be created as follows:

```
Random randomNumbers = new Random();
```

The random-number generator object can then be used to generate random byte, int and double values—we discuss only random int values here.

Consider the following statement:

```
int randomValue = randomNumbers.Next();
```

Method **Next** of class Random generates a random int value in the range 0 to +2,147,483,646, inclusive. If the Next method truly produces values at random, then every value in that range should have an equal chance (or probability) of being chosen each time method Next is called. The values returned by Next are actually **pseudorandom numbers**—a sequence of values produced by a complex mathematical calculation. The calculation uses the current time of day (which, of course, changes constantly) to **seed** the random-number generator such that each execution of an application yields a different sequence of random values.

The range of values produced directly by method Next often differs from the range of values required in a particular C# application. For example, an application that simulates coin tossing might require only 0 for "heads" and 1 for "tails." An application that simulates the rolling of a six-sided die might require random integers in the range 1–6. A video game that randomly predicts the next type of spaceship (out of four possibilities) that will fly across the horizon might require random integers in the range 1–4. For cases like these, class Random provides other versions of method Next. One receives an int argument and returns a value from 0 up to, but not including, the argument's value. For example, you might use the statement

```
int randomValue = randomNumbers.Next( 6 );
```

which returns 0, 1, 2, 3, 4 or 5. The argument 6—called the **scaling factor**—represents the number of unique values that Next should produce (in this case, six—0, 1, 2, 3, 4 and 5). This manipulation is called **scaling** the range of values produced by Random method Next.

Suppose we wanted to simulate a six-sided die that has the numbers 1–6 on its faces, not 0–5. Scaling the range of values alone is not enough. So we **shift** the range of numbers produced. We could do this by adding a **shifting value**—in this case 1—to the result of method Next, as in

```
face = 1 + randomNumbers.Next( 6 );
```

The shifting value (1) specifies the first value in the desired set of random integers. The preceding statement assigns to face a random integer in the range 1–6.

The third alternative of method Next provides a more intuitive way to express both shifting and scaling. This method receives two int arguments and returns a value from the first argument's value up to, but not including, the second argument's value. We could use this method to write a statement equivalent to our previous statement, as in

```
face = randomNumbers.Next( 1, 7 );
```

Rolling a Six-Sided Die

To demonstrate random numbers, let's develop an application that simulates 20 rolls of a six-sided die and displays each roll's value. Figure 7.6 shows two sample outputs, which confirm that the results of the preceding calculation are integers in the range 1–6 and that each run of the application can produce a different sequence of random numbers. The using directive (line 3) enables us to use class Random without fully qualifying its name. Line 9 creates the Random object randomNumbers to produce random values. Line 16 executes 20 times in a loop to roll the die. The if statement (lines 21–22) starts a new line of output after every five numbers, so the results can be presented on multiple lines.

```
 1   // Fig. 7.6: RandomIntegers.cs
 2   // Shifted and scaled random integers.
 3   using System;
 4
 5   public class RandomIntegers
 6   {
 7      public static void Main( string[] args )
 8      {
 9         Random randomNumbers = new Random(); // random-number generator
10         int face; // stores each random integer generated
11
12         // loop 20 times
13         for ( int counter = 1; counter <= 20; counter++ )
14         {
15            // pick random integer from 1 to 6
16            face = randomNumbers.Next( 1, 7 );
17
18            Console.Write( "{0}  ", face ); // display generated value
19
20            // if counter is divisible by 5, start a new line of output
21            if ( counter % 5 == 0 )
22               Console.WriteLine();
23         } // end for
24      } // end Main
25   } // end class RandomIntegers
```

```
3  3  3  1  1
2  1  2  4  2
2  3  6  2  5
3  4  6  6  1
```

Fig. 7.6 | Shifted and scaled random integers. (Part 1 of 2.)

```
6   2   5   1   3
5   2   1   6   5
4   1   6   1   3
3   1   4   3   4
```

Fig. 7.6 | Shifted and scaled random integers. (Part 2 of 2.)

Rolling a Six-Sided Die 6000 Times

To show that the numbers produced by Next occur with approximately equal likelihood, let's simulate 6000 rolls of a die (Fig. 7.7). Each integer from 1 to 6 should appear approximately 1000 times.

```csharp
1   // Fig. 7.7: RollDie.cs
2   // Roll a six-sided die 6000 times.
3   using System;
4
5   public class RollDie
6   {
7      public static void Main( string[] args )
8      {
9         Random randomNumbers = new Random(); // random-number generator
10
11        int frequency1 = 0; // count of 1s rolled
12        int frequency2 = 0; // count of 2s rolled
13        int frequency3 = 0; // count of 3s rolled
14        int frequency4 = 0; // count of 4s rolled
15        int frequency5 = 0; // count of 5s rolled
16        int frequency6 = 0; // count of 6s rolled
17
18        int face; // stores most recently rolled value
19
20        // summarize results of 6000 rolls of a die
21        for ( int roll = 1; roll <= 6000; roll++ )
22        {
23           face = randomNumbers.Next( 1, 7 ); // number from 1 to 6
24
25           // determine roll value 1-6 and increment appropriate counter
26           switch ( face )
27           {
28              case 1:
29                 ++frequency1; // increment the 1s counter
30                 break;
31              case 2:
32                 ++frequency2; // increment the 2s counter
33                 break;
34              case 3:
35                 ++frequency3; // increment the 3s counter
36                 break;
```

Fig. 7.7 | Roll a six-sided die 6000 times. (Part 1 of 2.)

```
37              case 4:
38                 ++frequency4; // increment the 4s counter
39                 break;
40              case 5:
41                 ++frequency5; // increment the 5s counter
42                 break;
43              case 6:
44                 ++frequency6; // increment the 6s counter
45                 break;
46           } // end switch
47        } // end for
48
49        Console.WriteLine( "Face\tFrequency" ); // output headers
50        Console.WriteLine(
51           "1\t{0}\n2\t{1}\n3\t{2}\n4\t{3}\n5\t{4}\n6\t{5}", frequency1,
52           frequency2, frequency3, frequency4, frequency5, frequency6 );
53     } // end Main
54  } // end class RollDie
```

```
Face        Frequency
1           1039
2           994
3           991
4           970
5           978
6           1028
```

```
Face        Frequency
1           985
2           985
3           1001
4           1017
5           1002
6           1010
```

Fig. 7.7 | Roll a six-sided die 6000 times. (Part 2 of 2.)

As the two sample outputs show, the values produced by method Next enable the application to realistically simulate rolling a six-sided die. The application uses nested control statements (the switch is nested inside the for) to determine the number of times each side of the die occurred. The for statement (lines 21–47) iterates 6000 times. During each iteration, line 23 produces a random value from 1 to 6. This face value is then used as the switch expression (line 26) in the switch statement (lines 26–46). Based on the face value, the switch statement increments one of the six counter variables during each iteration of the loop. (In Section 8.4, we show an elegant way to replace the entire switch statement in this application with a single statement.) The switch statement has no default label because we have a case label for every possible die value that the expression in line 23 can produce. Run the application several times and observe the results. You'll see that every time you execute this application, it produces different results.

7.9.1 Scaling and Shifting Random Numbers

Previously, we demonstrated the statement

```
face = randomNumbers.Next( 1, 7 );
```

which simulates the rolling of a six-sided die. This statement always assigns to variable face an integer in the range $1 \leq$ face < 7. The width of this range (i.e., the number of consecutive integers in the range) is 6, and the starting number in the range is 1. Referring to the preceding statement, we see that the width of the range is determined by the difference between the two integers passed to Random method Next, and the starting number of the range is the value of the first argument. We can generalize this result as

```
number = randomNumbers.Next( shiftingValue, shiftingValue + scalingFactor );
```

where *shiftingValue* specifies the first number in the desired range of consecutive integers and *scalingFactor* specifies how many numbers are in the range.

It's also possible to choose integers at random from sets of values other than ranges of consecutive integers. For this purpose, it's simpler to use the version of the Next method that takes only one argument. For example, to obtain a random value from the sequence 2, 5, 8, 11 and 14, you could use the statement

```
number = 2 + 3 * randomNumbers.Next( 5 );
```

In this case, randomNumberGenerator.Next(5) produces values in the range 0–4. Each value produced is multiplied by 3 to produce a number in the sequence 0, 3, 6, 9 and 12. We then add 2 to that value to *shift* the range of values and obtain a value from the sequence 2, 5, 8, 11 and 14. We can generalize this result as

```
number = shiftingValue +
    differenceBetweenValues * randomNumbers.Next( scalingFactor );
```

where *shiftingValue* specifies the first number in the desired range of values, *differenceBetweenValues* represents the difference between consecutive numbers in the sequence and *scalingFactor* specifies how many numbers are in the range.

7.9.2 Random-Number Repeatability for Testing and Debugging

As we mentioned earlier in Section 7.9, the methods of class Random actually generate pseudorandom numbers based on complex mathematical calculations. Repeatedly calling any of Random's methods produces a sequence of numbers that appears to be random. The calculation that produces the pseudorandom numbers uses the time of day as a **seed value** to change the sequence's starting point. Each new Random object seeds itself with a value based on the computer system's clock at the time the object is created, enabling each execution of an application to produce a different sequence of random numbers.

When debugging an application, it's sometimes useful to repeat the exact same sequence of pseudorandom numbers during each execution of the application. This repeatability enables you to prove that your application is working for a specific sequence of random numbers before you test the application with different sequences of random numbers. When repeatability is important, you can create a Random object as follows:

```
Random randomNumbers = new Random( seedValue );
```

The seedValue argument (type int) seeds the random-number calculation. If the same seedValue is used every time, the Random object produces the same sequence of random numbers.

Error-Prevention Tip 7.1

While an application is under development, create the Random object with a specific seed value to produce a repeatable sequence of random numbers each time the application executes. If a logic error occurs, fix the error and test the application again with the same seed value—this allows you to reconstruct the same sequence of random numbers that caused the error. Once the logic errors have been removed, create the Random object without using a seed value, causing the Random object to generate a new sequence of random numbers each time the application executes.

7.10 Case Study: A Game of Chance (Introducing Enumerations)

One popular game of chance is the dice game known as "craps," which is played in casinos and back alleys throughout the world. The rules of the game are straightforward:

> *You roll two dice. Each die has six faces, which contain one, two, three, four, five and six spots, respectively. After the dice have come to rest, the sum of the spots on the two upward faces is calculated. If the sum is 7 or 11 on the first throw, you win. If the sum is 2, 3 or 12 on the first throw (called "craps"), you lose (i.e., "the house" wins). If the sum is 4, 5, 6, 8, 9 or 10 on the first throw, that sum becomes your "point." To win, you must continue rolling the dice until you "make your point" (i.e., roll that same point value). You lose by rolling a 7 before making your point.*

The application in Fig. 7.8 simulates the game of craps, using methods to define the logic of the game. The Main method (lines 24–70) calls the static RollDice method (lines 73–85) as needed to roll the two dice and compute their sum. The four sample outputs show winning on the first roll, losing on the first roll, winning on a subsequent roll and losing on a subsequent roll, respectively. Variable randomNumbers (line 8) is declared static so it can be created once during the program's execution and used in method RollDice.

```
1   // Fig. 7.8: Craps.cs
2   // Craps class simulates the dice game craps.
3   using System;
4
5   public class Craps
6   {
7      // create random-number generator for use in method RollDice
8      private static Random randomNumbers = new Random();
9
10     // enumeration with constants that represent the game status
11     private enum Status { CONTINUE, WON, LOST }
12
13     // enumeration with constants that represent common rolls of the dice
14     private enum DiceNames
15     {
```

Fig. 7.8 | Craps class simulates the dice game craps. (Part 1 of 3.)

```csharp
16          SNAKE_EYES = 2,
17          TREY = 3,
18          SEVEN = 7,
19          YO_LEVEN = 11,
20          BOX_CARS = 12
21       }
22
23       // plays one game of craps
24       public static void Main( string[] args )
25       {
26          // gameStatus can contain CONTINUE, WON or LOST
27          Status gameStatus = Status.CONTINUE;
28          int myPoint = 0; // point if no win or loss on first roll
29
30          int sumOfDice = RollDice(); // first roll of the dice
31
32          // determine game status and point based on first roll
33          switch ( ( DiceNames ) sumOfDice )
34          {
35             case DiceNames.SEVEN: // win with 7 on first roll
36             case DiceNames.YO_LEVEN: // win with 11 on first roll
37                gameStatus = Status.WON;
38                break;
39             case DiceNames.SNAKE_EYES: // lose with 2 on first roll
40             case DiceNames.TREY: // lose with 3 on first roll
41             case DiceNames.BOX_CARS: // lose with 12 on first roll
42                gameStatus = Status.LOST;
43                break;
44             default: // did not win or lose, so remember point
45                gameStatus = Status.CONTINUE; // game is not over
46                myPoint = sumOfDice; // remember the point
47                Console.WriteLine( "Point is {0}", myPoint );
48                break;
49          } // end switch
50
51          // while game is not complete
52          while ( gameStatus == Status.CONTINUE ) // game not WON or LOST
53          {
54             sumOfDice = RollDice(); // roll dice again
55
56             // determine game status
57             if ( sumOfDice == myPoint ) // win by making point
58                gameStatus = Status.WON;
59             else
60                // lose by rolling 7 before point
61                if ( sumOfDice == ( int ) DiceNames.SEVEN )
62                   gameStatus = Status.LOST;
63          } // end while
64
65          // display won or lost message
66          if ( gameStatus == Status.WON )
67             Console.WriteLine( "Player wins" );
```

Fig. 7.8 | Craps class simulates the dice game craps. (Part 2 of 3.)

```
68          else
69              Console.WriteLine( "Player loses" );
70      } // end Main
71
72      // roll dice, calculate sum and display results
73      public static int RollDice()
74      {
75          // pick random die values
76          int die1 = randomNumbers.Next( 1, 7 ); // first die roll
77          int die2 = randomNumbers.Next( 1, 7 ); // second die roll
78
79          int sum = die1 + die2; // sum of die values
80
81          // display results of this roll
82          Console.WriteLine( "Player rolled {0} + {1} = {2}",
83              die1, die2, sum );
84          return sum; // return sum of dice
85      } // end method RollDice
86  } // end class Craps
```

```
Player rolled 2 + 5 = 7
Player wins
```

```
Player rolled 2 + 1 = 3
Player loses
```

```
Player rolled 4 + 6 = 10
Point is 10
Player rolled 1 + 3 = 4
Player rolled 1 + 3 = 4
Player rolled 2 + 3 = 5
Player rolled 4 + 4 = 8
Player rolled 6 + 6 = 12
Player rolled 4 + 4 = 8
Player rolled 4 + 5 = 9
Player rolled 2 + 6 = 8
Player rolled 6 + 6 = 12
Player rolled 6 + 4 = 10
Player wins
```

```
Player rolled 2 + 4 = 6
Point is 6
Player rolled 3 + 1 = 4
Player rolled 5 + 5 = 10
Player rolled 6 + 1 = 7
Player loses
```

Fig. 7.8 | Craps class simulates the dice game craps. (Part 3 of 3.)

Method **RollDice**

In the rules of the game, the player must roll two dice on the first roll and must do the same on all subsequent rolls. We declare method RollDice (lines 73–85) to roll the dice and compute and display their sum. Method RollDice is declared once, but it's called from two places (lines 30 and 54) in method Main, which contains the logic for one complete game of craps. Method RollDice takes no arguments, so it has an empty parameter list. Each time it's called, RollDice returns the sum of the dice, so the return type int is indicated in the method header (line 73). Although lines 76 and 77 look the same (except for the die names), they do not necessarily produce the same result. Each of these statements produces a random value in the range 1–6. Variable randomNumbers (used in lines 76 and 77) is not declared in the method. Rather it's declared as a private static variable of the class and initialized in line 8. This enables us to create one Random object that's reused in each call to RollDice.

Method **Main**'s *Local Variables*

The game is reasonably involved. The player may win or lose on the first roll or may win or lose on any subsequent roll. Method Main (lines 24–70) uses local variable gameStatus (line 27) to keep track of the overall game status, local variable myPoint (line 28) to store the "point" if the player does not win or lose on the first roll and local variable sumOfDice (line 30) to maintain the sum of the dice for the most recent roll. Variable myPoint is initialized to 0 to ensure that the application will compile. If you do not initialize myPoint, the compiler issues an error, because myPoint is not assigned a value in every branch of the switch statement—thus, the application could try to use myPoint before it's definitely assigned a value. By contrast, gameStatus does not require initialization because it *is* assigned a value in every branch of the switch statement—thus, it's guaranteed to be initialized before it's used. However, as good programming practice, we initialize it anyway.

enum *Type* **Status**

Local variable gameStatus is declared to be of a new type called Status, which we declared in line 11. Type Status is declared as a private member of class Craps, because Status will be used only in that class. Status is a user-defined type called an **enumeration**, which declares a set of constants represented by identifiers. An enumeration is introduced by the keyword **enum** and a type name (in this case, Status). As with a class, braces ({ and }) delimit the body of an enum declaration. Inside the braces is a comma-separated list of **enumeration constants**. The enum constant names must be unique, but the value associated with each constant need not be.

> **Good Programming Practice 7.3**
>
> *Use only uppercase letters in the names of constants. This makes the constants stand out in an application and reminds you that enumeration constants are not variables.*

Variables of type Status should be assigned only one of the three constants declared in the enumeration. When the game is won, the application sets local variable gameStatus to Status.WON (lines 37 and 58). When the game is lost, the application sets local variable gameStatus to Status.LOST (lines 42 and 62). Otherwise, the application sets local variable gameStatus to Status.CONTINUE (line 45) to indicate that the dice must be rolled again.

> **Good Programming Practice 7.4**
>
> *Using enumeration constants (like* `Status.WON`*,* `Status.LOST` *and* `Status.CONTINUE`*) rather than literal integer values (such as 0, 1 and 2) can make code easier to read and maintain.*

Logic of the Main Method

Line 30 in method `Main` calls `RollDice`, which picks two random values from 1 to 6, displays the value of the first die, the value of the second die and the sum of the dice, and returns the sum of the dice. Method `Main` next enters the `switch` statement at lines 33–49, which uses the `sumOfDice` value from line 30 to determine whether the game has been won or lost, or whether it should continue with another roll.

The sums of the dice that would result in a win or loss on the first roll are declared in the `DiceNames` enumeration in lines 14–21. These are used in the `cases` of the `switch` statement. The identifier names use casino parlance for these sums. Notice that in the `DiceNames` enumeration, a value is explicitly assigned to each identifier name. When the `enum` is declared, each constant in the `enum` declaration is a constant value of type `int`. If you do not assign a value to an identifier in the `enum` declaration, the compiler will do so. If the first `enum` constant is unassigned, the compiler gives it the value 0. If any other `enum` constant is unassigned, the compiler gives it a value equal to one more than the value of the preceding `enum` constant. For example, in the `Status` enumeration, the compiler implicitly assigns 0 to `Status.WON`, 1 to `Status.CONTINUE` and 2 to `Status.LOST`.

You could also declare an `enum`'s underlying type to be `byte`, `sbyte`, `short`, `ushort`, `int`, `uint`, `long` or `ulong` by writing

```
private enum MyEnum : typeName { Constant1, Constant2, ... }
```

where *typeName* represents one of the integral simple types.

If you need to compare a simple integral type value to the underlying value of an enumeration constant, you must use a cast operator to make the two types match. In the `switch` statement at lines 33–49, we use the cast operator to convert the `int` value in `sumOfDice` to type `DiceNames` and compare it to each of the constants in `DiceNames`. Lines 35–36 determine whether the player won on the first roll with `SEVEN` (7) or `YO_LEVEN` (11). Lines 39–41 determine whether the player lost on the first roll with `SNAKE_EYES` (2), `TREY` (3) or `BOX_CARS` (12). After the first roll, if the game is not over, the `default` case (lines 44–48) saves `sumOfDice` in `myPoint` (line 46) and displays the point (line 47).

If we're still trying to "make our point" (i.e., the game is continuing from a prior roll), the loop in lines 52–63 executes. Line 54 rolls the dice again. If `sumOfDice` matches `myPoint` in line 57, line 58 sets `gameStatus` to `Status.WON`, and the loop terminates because the game is complete. In line 61, we use the cast operator (`int`) to obtain the underlying value of `DiceNames.SEVEN` so that we can compare it to `sumOfDice`. If `sumOfDice` is equal to `SEVEN` (7), line 62 sets `gameStatus` to `Status.LOST`, and the loop terminates because the game is over. When the game completes, lines 66–69 display a message indicating whether the player won or lost, and the application terminates.

Summary of the Craps Example

Note the use of the various program-control mechanisms we've discussed. The `Craps` class uses two methods—`Main` and `RollDice` (called twice from `Main`)—and the `switch`, `while`, `if...else` and nested `if` control statements. Also, notice that we use multiple case labels in the switch statement to execute the same statements for sums of SEVEN and YO_LEVEN (lines 35–36) and for sums of SNAKE_EYES, TREY and BOX_CARS (lines 39–41). To easily create a switch statement with all possible values for an enum type, you can use the switch code snippet. Type switch in the C# code then press *Tab* twice. If you enter an enum type into the switch statement's expression (the highlighted code of the snippet) and press *Enter*, a case for each enum constant will be generated automatically.

7.11 Scope of Declarations

You've seen declarations of C# entities, such as classes, methods, properties, variables and parameters. Declarations introduce names that can be used to refer to such C# entities. The **scope** of a declaration is the portion of the application that can refer to the declared entity by its unqualified name. Such an entity is said to be "in scope" for that portion of the application. This section introduces several important scope issues. The basic scope rules are as follows:

1. The scope of a parameter declaration is the body of the method in which the declaration appears.

2. The scope of a local-variable declaration is from the point at which the declaration appears to the end of the block containing the declaration.

3. The scope of a local-variable declaration that appears in the initialization section of a for statement's header is the body of the for statement and the other expressions in the header.

4. The scope of a method, property or field of a class is the entire body of the class. This enables non-static methods and properties of a class to use any of the class's fields, methods and properties, regardless of the order in which they're declared. Similarly, static methods and properties can use any of the static members of the class.

Any block may contain variable declarations. If a local variable or parameter in a method has the same name as a field, the field is hidden until the block terminates. In Chapter 10, we discuss how to access hidden fields. The application in Fig. 7.9 demonstrates scoping issues with fields and local variables.

Error-Prevention Tip 7.2

Use different names for fields and local variables to help prevent subtle logic errors that occur when a method is called and a local variable of the method hides a field of the same name in the class.

```
1   // Fig. 7.9: Scope.cs
2   // Scope class demonstrates static and local variable scopes.
3   using System;
4
5   public class Scope
6   {
```

Fig. 7.9 | Scope class demonstrates static and local variable scopes. (Part 1 of 3.)

```
 7      // static variable that is accessible to all methods of this class
 8      private static int x = 1;
 9
10      // Main creates and initializes local variable x
11      // and calls methods UseLocalVariable and UseStaticVariable
12      public static void Main( string[] args )
13      {
14         int x = 5; // method's local variable x hides static variable x
15
16         Console.WriteLine( "local x in method Main is {0}", x );
17
18         // UseLocalVariable has its own local x
19         UseLocalVariable();
20
21         // UseStaticVariable uses class Scope's static variable x
22         UseStaticVariable();
23
24         // UseLocalVariable reinitializes its own local x
25         UseLocalVariable();
26
27         // class Scope's static variable x retains its value
28         UseStaticVariable();
29
30         Console.WriteLine( "\nlocal x in method Main is {0}", x );
31      } // end Main
32
33      // create and initialize local variable x during each call
34      public static void UseLocalVariable()
35      {
36         int x = 25; // initialized each time UseLocalVariable is called
37
38         Console.WriteLine(
39            "\nlocal x on entering method UseLocalVariable is {0}", x );
40         ++x; // modifies this method's local variable x
41         Console.WriteLine(
42            "local x before exiting method UseLocalVariable is {0}", x );
43      } // end method UseLocalVariable
44
45      // modify class Scope's static variable x during each call
46      public static void UseStaticVariable()
47      {
48         Console.WriteLine( "\nstatic variable x on entering {0} is {1}",
49            "method UseStaticVariable", x );
50         x *= 10; // modifies class Scope's static variable x
51         Console.WriteLine( "static variable x before exiting {0} is {1}",
52            "method UseStaticVariable", x );
53      } // end method UseStaticVariable
54   } // end class Scope
```

```
local x in method Main is 5

local x on entering method UseLocalVariable is 25
local x before exiting method UseLocalVariable is 26
```

Fig. 7.9 | Scope class demonstrates static and local variable scopes. (Part 2 of 3.)

```
static variable x on entering method UseStaticVariable is 1
static variable x before exiting method UseStaticVariable is 10

local x on entering method UseLocalVariable is 25
local x before exiting method UseLocalVariable is 26

static variable x on entering method UseStaticVariable is 10
static variable x before exiting method UseStaticVariable is 100

local x in method Main is 5
```

Fig. 7.9 | Scope class demonstrates static and local variable scopes. (Part 3 of 3.)

Line 8 declares and initializes the static variable x to 1. This static variable is hidden in any block (or method) that declares local variable named x. Method Main (lines 12–31) declares local variable x (line 14) and initializes it to 5. This local variable's value is output to show that static variable x (whose value is 1) is hidden in method Main. The application declares two other methods—UseLocalVariable (lines 34–43) and UseStaticVariable (lines 46–53)—that each take no arguments and do not return results. Method Main calls each method twice (lines 19–28). Method UseLocalVariable declares local variable x (line 36). When UseLocalVariable is first called (line 19), it creates local variable x and initializes it to 25 (line 36), outputs the value of x (lines 38–39), increments x (line 40) and outputs the value of x again (lines 41–42). When UseLocalVariable is called a second time (line 25), it re-creates local variable x and reinitializes it to 25, so the output of each UseLocalVariable call is identical.

Method UseStaticVariable does not declare any local variables. Therefore, when it refers to x, static variable x (line 8) of the class is used. When method UseStaticVariable is first called (line 22), it outputs the value (1) of static variable x (lines 48–49), multiplies the static variable x by 10 (line 50) and outputs the value (10) of static variable x again (lines 51–52) before returning. The next time method UseStaticVariable is called (line 28), the static variable has its modified value, 10, so the method outputs 10, then 100. Finally, in method Main, the application outputs the value of local variable x again (line 30) to show that none of the method calls modified Main's local variable x, because the methods all referred to variables named x in other scopes.

7.12 Method Overloading

Methods of the same name can be declared in the same class, as long as they have different sets of parameters (determined by the number, types and order of the parameters). This is called **method overloading**. When an **overloaded method** is called, the C# compiler selects the appropriate method by examining the number, types and order of the arguments in the call. Method overloading is commonly used to create several methods with the *same name* that perform the same or similar tasks, but on *different types* or *different numbers of arguments*. For example, Math methods Min and Max (summarized in Section 7.3) are overloaded with 11 versions. These find the minimum and maximum, respectively, of two values of each of the 11 numeric simple types. Our next example demonstrates declaring and invoking overloaded methods. You'll see examples of overloaded constructors in Chapter 10.

Declaring Overloaded Methods

In class MethodOverload (Fig. 7.10), we include two overloaded versions of a method called Square—one that calculates the square of an int (and returns an int) and one that calculates the square of a double (and returns a double). Although these methods have the same name and similar parameter lists and bodies, you can think of them simply as *different* methods. It may help to think of the method names as "Square of int" and "Square of double," respectively.

```
 1   // Fig. 7.10: MethodOverload.cs
 2   // Overloaded method declarations.
 3   using System;
 4
 5   public class MethodOverload
 6   {
 7      // test overloaded square methods
 8      public static void Main( string[] args )
 9      {
10         Console.WriteLine( "Square of integer 7 is {0}", Square( 7 ) );
11         Console.WriteLine( "Square of double 7.5 is {0}", Square( 7.5 ) );
12      } // end Main
13
14      // square method with int argument
15      public static int Square( int intValue )
16      {
17         Console.WriteLine( "Called square with int argument: {0}",
18            intValue );
19         return intValue * intValue;
20      } // end method Square with int argument
21
22      // square method with double argument
23      public static double Square( double doubleValue )
24      {
25         Console.WriteLine( "Called square with double argument: {0}",
26            doubleValue );
27         return doubleValue * doubleValue;
28      } // end method Square with double argument
29   } // end class MethodOverload
```

```
Called square with int argument: 7
Square of integer 7 is 49
Called square with double argument: 7.5
Square of double 7.5 is 56.25
```

Fig. 7.10 | Overloaded method declarations.

Line 10 in Main invokes method Square with the argument 7. Literal integer values are treated as type int, so the method call in line 10 invokes the version of Square at lines 15–20 that specifies an int parameter. Similarly, line 11 invokes method Square with the argument 7.5. Literal real-number values are treated as type double, so the method call in line 11 invokes the version of Square at lines 23–28 that specifies a double parameter. Each method first outputs a line of text to prove that the proper method was called in each case.

Notice that the overloaded methods in Fig. 7.10 perform the same calculation, but with two different types. C#'s generics feature provides a mechanism for writing a single "generic method" that can perform the same tasks as an entire set of overloaded methods. We discuss generic methods in Chapter 22.

Distinguishing Between Overloaded Methods

The compiler distinguishes overloaded methods by their **signature**—a combination of the method's name and the number, types and order of its parameters. The signature also includes the way those parameters are passed, which can be modified by the ref and out keywords (discussed in Section 7.16). If the compiler looked only at method names during compilation, the code in Fig. 7.10 would be ambiguous—the compiler would not know how to distinguish between the Square methods (lines 15–20 and 23–28). Internally, the compiler uses signatures to determine whether a class's methods are unique in that class.

For example, in Fig. 7.10, the compiler will use the method signatures to distinguish between the "Square of int" method (the Square method that specifies an int parameter) and the "Square of double" method (the Square method that specifies a double parameter). If Method1's declaration begins as

```
void Method1( int a, float b )
```

then that method will have a different signature than the method declared beginning with

```
void Method1( float a, int b )
```

The *order* of the parameter types is important—the compiler considers the preceding two Method1 headers to be distinct.

Return Types of Overloaded Methods

In discussing the logical names of methods used by the compiler, we did not mention the return types of the methods. This is because method *calls* cannot be distinguished by return type. The application in Fig. 7.11 illustrates the compiler errors generated when two methods have the same signature but different return types. Overloaded methods can have the same or different return types if the methods have different parameter lists. Also, overloaded methods need not have the same number of parameters.

Common Programming Error 7.10

Declaring overloaded methods with identical parameter lists is a compilation error regardless of whether the return types are different.

```
1   // Fig. 7.11: MethodOverload.cs
2   // Overloaded methods with identical signatures
3   // cause compilation errors, even if return types are different.
4   public class MethodOverloadError
5   {
6      // declaration of method Square with int argument
7      public int Square( int x )
8      {
```

Fig. 7.11 | Overloaded methods with identical signatures cause compilation errors, even if return types are different. (Part 1 of 2.)

```
 9          return x * x;
10      } // end method Square
11
12      // second declaration of method Square with int argument
13      // causes compilation error even though return types are different
14      public double Square( int y )
15      {
16          return y * y;
17      } // end method Square
18  } // end class MethodOverloadError
```

Error List					
⊗ 1 Error	⚠ 0 Warnings	ⓘ 0 Messages			
	Description	File	Line	Column	Project
⊗ 1	Type 'MethodOverloadError' already defines a member called 'Square' with the same parameter types	MethodOverloadError	14	25	MethodOverloadError

Fig. 7.11 | Overloaded methods with identical signatures cause compilation errors, even if return types are different. (Part 2 of 2.)

7.13 Optional Parameters

As of Visual C# 2010, methods can have **optional parameters** that allow the calling method to vary the number of arguments to pass. An optional parameter specifies a **default value** that's assigned to the parameter if the optional argument is omitted.

You can create methods with one or more optional parameters. *All optional parameters must be placed to the right of the method's non-optional parameters*—that is, at the end of the parameter list.

Common Programming Error 7.11

Declaring a non-optional parameter to the right of an optional one is a compilation error.

When a parameter has a default value, the caller has the *option* of passing that particular argument. For example, the method header

```
public int Power( int baseValue, int exponentValue = 2)
```

specifies an optional second parameter. Any call to Power must pass at least an argument for the parameter baseValue, or a compilation error occurs. Optionally, a second argument (for the exponentValue parameter) can be passed to Power. Consider the following calls to Power:

```
Power()
Power(10)
Power(10, 3)
```

The first call generates a compilation error because this method requires a minimum of one argument. The second call is valid because one argument (10) is being passed—the optional exponentValue is not specified in the method call. The last call is also valid—10 is passed as the required argument and 3 is passed as the optional argument.

In the call that passes only one argument (10), parameter exponentValue defaults to 2, which is the default value specified in the method's header. Each optional parameter must specify a default value by using an equal (=) sign followed by the value. For example, the header for Power sets 2 as exponentValue's default value.

Figure 7.12 demonstrates an optional parameter. The program calculates the result of raising a base value to an exponent. Method Power (Fig. 7.12, lines 15–23) specifies that its second parameter is optional. In method DisplayPowers, lines 10–11 of Fig. 7.12 call method Power. Line 10 calls the method without the optional second argument. In this case, the compiler provides the second argument, 2, using the default value of the optional argument, which is not visible to you in the call.

```
1   // Fig. 7.12: Power.vb
2   // Optional argument demonstration with method Power.
3   using System;
4
5   class CalculatePowers
6   {
7       // call Power with and without optional arguments
8       public static void Main( string[] args )
9       {
10          Console.WriteLine( "Power(10) = {0}", Power( 10 ) ) ;
11          Console.WriteLine( "Power(2, 10) = {0}", Power( 2, 10 ) );
12      } // end Main
13
14      // use iteration to calculate power
15      public int Power( int baseValue, int exponentValue = 2 )
16      {
17          int result = 1; // initialize total
18
19          for ( int i = 1; i <= exponentValue; i++ )
20              result *= baseValue;
21
22          return result;
23      } // end method Power
24  } // end class CalculatePowers
```

```
Power(10) = 100
Power(2, 10) = 1024
```

Fig. 7.12 | Optional argument demonstration with method Power.

7.14 Named Parameters

Normally, when calling a method that has optional parameters, the argument values—in order—are assigned to the parameters from left to right in the parameter list. Consider a Time class that stores the time of day in 24-hour clock format as int values representing the hour (0–23), minute (0–59) and second (0–59). Such a class might provide a SetTime method with optional parameters like

```
public void SetTime( int hour = 0, int minute = 0, int second = 0 )
```

In the preceding method header, all of three of SetTime's parameters are optional. Assuming that we have a Time object named t, we can call SetTime as follows:

```
t.SetTime(); // sets the time to 12:00:00 AM
t.SetTime( 12 ); // sets the time to 12:00:00 PM
t.SetTime( 12, 30 ); // sets the time to 12:30:00 PM
t.SetTime( 12, 30, 22 ); // sets the time to 12:30:22 PM
```

In the first call, no arguments are specified, so the compiler assigns 0 to each parameter. In the second call, the compiler assigns the argument, 12, to the first parameter, hour, and assigns default values of 0 to the minute and second parameters. In the third call, the compiler assigns the two arguments, 12 and 30, to the parameters hour and minute, respectively, and assigns the default value 0 to the parameter second. In the last call, the compiler assigns the three arguments, 12, 30 and 22, to the parameters hour, minute and second, respectively.

What if you wanted to specify only arguments for the hour and second? You might think that you could call the method as follows:

```
t.SetTime( 12, , 22 ); // COMPILATION ERROR
```

Unlike some programming languages, C# doesn't allow you to skip an argument as shown in the preceding statement. However, Visual C# 2010 provides a new feature called **named parameters**, which enable you to call methods that receive optional parameters by providing only the optional arguments you wish to specify. To do so, you explicitly specify the parameter's name and value—separated by a colon (:)—in the argument list of the method call. For example, the preceding statement can be implemented in Visual C# 2010 as follows:

```
t.SetTime( hour: 12, second: 22 ); // sets the time to 12:00:22
```

In this case, the compiler assigns parameter hour the argument 12 and parameter second the argument 22. The parameter minute is not specified, so the compiler assigns it the default value 0. It's also possible to specify the arguments out of order when using named parameters. The arguments for the required parameters must always be supplied.

7.15 Recursion

The applications we've discussed thus far are generally structured as methods that call one another in a disciplined, hierarchical manner. For some problems, however, it's useful to have a method call itself. A **recursive method** is a method that calls itself, either directly or indirectly through another method.

We consider recursion conceptually first. Then we examine an application containing a recursive method. Recursive problem-solving approaches have a number of elements in common. When a recursive method is called to solve a problem, it actually is capable of solving only the simplest case(s), or **base case(s)**. If the method is called with a base case, it returns a result. If the method is called with a more complex problem, it divides the problem into two conceptual pieces: a piece that the method knows how to do and a piece that it does not know how to do. To make recursion feasible, the latter piece must resemble the original problem, but be a slightly simpler or slightly smaller version of it. Because this new problem looks like the original problem, the method calls a fresh copy of itself to work on the smaller problem; this is referred to as a **recursive call** and is also called the **recursion step**. The recursion step normally includes a return statement, because its result will be combined with the portion of the problem the method knew how to solve to form a result that will be passed back to the original caller.

The recursion step executes while the original call to the method is still active (i.e., while it has not finished executing). The recursion step can result in many more recursive calls, as the method divides each new subproblem into two conceptual pieces. For the recursion to terminate eventually, each time the method calls itself with a slightly simpler version of the original problem, the sequence of smaller and smaller problems must converge on the base case. At that point, the method recognizes the base case and returns a result to the previous copy of the method. A sequence of returns ensues until the original method call returns the result to the caller. This process sounds complex compared with the conventional problem solving we've performed to this point.

Recursive Factorial Calculations

As an example of recursion concepts at work, let's write a recursive application to perform a popular mathematical calculation. Consider the factorial of a nonnegative integer n, written $n!$ (and pronounced "n factorial"), which is the product

$$n \cdot (n - 1) \cdot (n - 2) \cdot \ldots \cdot 1$$

1! is equal to 1 and 0! is defined to be 1. For example, 5! is the product $5 \cdot 4 \cdot 3 \cdot 2 \cdot 1$, which is equal to 120.

The factorial of an integer, `number`, greater than or equal to 0 can be calculated iteratively (nonrecursively) using the `for` statement as follows:

```
factorial = 1;
for ( int counter = number; counter >= 1; counter-- )
   factorial *= counter;
```

A recursive declaration of the factorial method is arrived at by observing the following relationship:

$$n! = n \cdot (n - 1)!$$

For example, 5! is clearly equal to $5 \cdot 4!$, as is shown by the following equations:

$$5! = 5 \cdot 4 \cdot 3 \cdot 2 \cdot 1$$
$$5! = 5 \cdot (4 \cdot 3 \cdot 2 \cdot 1)$$
$$5! = 5 \cdot (4!)$$

The evaluation of 5! would proceed as shown in Fig. 7.13. Figure 7.13(a) shows how the succession of recursive calls proceeds until 1! is evaluated to be 1, which terminates the recursion. Figure 7.13(b) shows the values returned from each recursive call to its caller until the value is calculated and returned.

Figure 7.14 uses recursion to calculate and display the factorials of the integers from 0 to 10. The recursive method `Factorial` (lines 16–24) first tests to determine whether a terminating condition (line 19) is `true`. If `number` is less than or equal to 1 (the base case), `Factorial` returns 1, no further recursion is necessary and the method returns. If `number` is greater than 1, line 23 expresses the problem as the product of `number` and a recursive call to `Factorial` evaluating the factorial of `number - 1`, which is a slightly simpler problem than the original calculation, `Factorial( number )`.

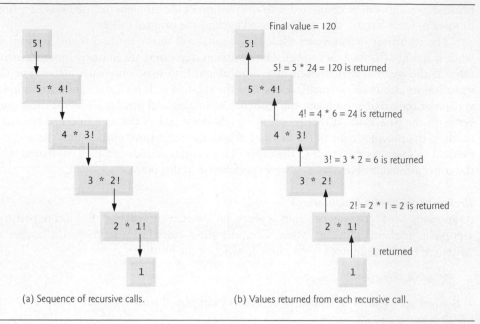

(a) Sequence of recursive calls.   (b) Values returned from each recursive call.

Fig. 7.13 | Recursive evaluation of 5!.

```
1   // Fig. 7.14: FactorialTest.cs
2   // Recursive Factorial method.
3   using System;
4
5   public class FactorialTest
6   {
7      public static void Main( string[] args )
8      {
9         // calculate the factorials of 0 through 10
10        for ( long counter = 0; counter <= 10; counter++ )
11           Console.WriteLine( "{0}! = {1}",
12              counter, Factorial( counter ) );
13     } // end Main
14
15     // recursive declaration of method Factorial
16     public static long Factorial( long number )
17     {
18        // base case
19        if ( number <= 1 )
20           return 1;
21        // recursion step
22        else
23           return number * Factorial( number - 1 );
24     } // end method Factorial
25  } // end class FactorialTest
```

Fig. 7.14 | Recursive Factorial method. (Part 1 of 2.)

```
0! = 1
1! = 1
2! = 2
3! = 6
4! = 24
5! = 120
6! = 720
7! = 5040
8! = 40320
9! = 362880
10! = 3628800
```

Fig. 7.14 | Recursive `Factorial` method. (Part 2 of 2.)

Method `Factorial` (lines 16–24) receives a parameter of type `long` and returns a result of type `long`. As you can see in Fig. 7.14, factorial values become large quickly. We chose type `long` (which can represent relatively large integers) so that the application could calculate factorials greater than 20!. Unfortunately, the `Factorial` method produces large values so quickly that factorial values soon exceed even the maximum value that can be stored in a `long` variable. Due to the restrictions on the integral types, variables of type `float`, `double` or `decimal` might ultimately be needed to calculate factorials of larger numbers. This situation points to a weakness in many programming languages—the languages are not easily extended to handle the unique requirements of various applications. As you know, C# allows you to create a type that supports arbitrarily large integers if you wish. For example, you could create a `HugeInteger` class (which we ask you to do in Exercise 10.10) that would enable an application to calculate the factorials of arbitrarily large numbers. You can also use the new type `BigInteger` from the .NET Framework's class library.

Common Programming Error 7.12

*Either omitting the base case or writing the recursion step incorrectly so that it does not converge on the base case will cause **infinite recursion**, eventually exhausting memory. This error is analogous to the problem of an infinite loop in an iterative (nonrecursive) solution.*

7.16 Passing Arguments: Pass-by-Value vs. Pass-by-Reference

Two ways to pass arguments to functions in many programming languages are **pass-by-value** and **pass-by-reference**. When an argument is passed by value (the default in C#), a *copy* of its value is made and passed to the called function. Changes to the copy do *not* affect the original variable's value in the caller. This prevents the accidental side effects that so greatly hinder the development of correct and reliable software systems. Each argument that has been passed in the programs in this chapter so far has been passed by value. When an argument is passed by reference, the caller gives the method the ability to access and modify the caller's original variable.

Software Engineering Observation 7.4

Pass-by-reference can weaken security, because the called function can corrupt the caller's data.

To pass an object by reference into a method, simply provide as an argument in the method call the variable that refers to the object. Then, in the method body, reference the object using the parameter name. The parameter refers to the original object in memory, so the called method can access the original object directly.

Previously, we discussed the difference between value types and reference types. A major difference between them is that *value-type variables store values*, so specifying a value-type variable in a method call passes a *copy* of that variable's value to the method. *Reference-type variables store references to objects*, so specifying a reference-type variable as an argument passes the method a copy of the actual reference that refers to the object. Even though the reference itself is passed by value, the method can still use the reference it receives to interact with—and possibly modify—the original object. Similarly, when returning information from a method via a `return` statement, the method returns a copy of the value stored in a value-type variable or a copy of the reference stored in a reference-type variable. When a reference is returned, the calling method can use that reference to interact with the referenced object.

ref *and* out *Parameters*

What if you would like to pass a variable by reference so the called method can modify the variable's value? To do this, C# provides keywords **ref** and **out**. Applying the `ref` keyword to a parameter declaration allows you to pass a variable to a method by reference—the called method will be able to modify the original variable in the caller. The `ref` keyword is used for variables that already have been initialized in the calling method. Normally, when a method call contains an uninitialized variable as an argument, the compiler generates an error. Preceding a parameter with keyword `out` creates an **output parameter**. This indicates to the compiler that the argument will be passed into the called method by reference and that the called method will assign a value to the original variable in the caller. If the method does not assign a value to the output parameter in every possible path of execution, the compiler generates an error. This also prevents the compiler from generating an error message for an uninitialized variable that's passed as an argument to a method. A method can return only one value to its caller via a return statement, but can return many values by specifying multiple output (`ref` and/or `out`) parameters.

You can also pass a reference-type variable by reference, which allows you to modify reference-type variable so that it refers to a new object. Passing a reference by reference is a tricky but powerful technique that we discuss in Section 8.8.

Demonstrating ref, out *and Value Parameters*

The application in Fig. 7.15 uses the `ref` and `out` keywords to manipulate integer values. The class contains three methods that calculate the square of an integer. Method Square-Ref (lines 37–40) multiplies its parameter x by itself and assigns the new value to x. SquareRef's parameter is declared as `ref int`, which indicates that the argument passed to this method must be an integer that's passed by reference. Because the argument is passed by reference, the assignment at line 39 modifies the original argument's value in the caller.

Method SquareOut (lines 44–48) assigns its parameter the value 6 (line 46), then squares that value. SquareOut's parameter is declared as `out int`, which indicates that the argument passed to this method must be an integer that's passed by reference and that the argument does not need to be initialized in advance.

```csharp
1    // Fig. 7.15: ReferenceAndOutputParameters.cs
2    // Reference, output and value parameters.
3    using System;
4
5    class ReferenceAndOutputParameters
6    {
7       // call methods with reference, output and value parameters
8       public static void Main( string[] args )
9       {
10         int y = 5; // initialize y to 5
11         int z; // declares z, but does not initialize it
12
13         // display original values of y and z
14         Console.WriteLine( "Original value of y: {0}", y );
15         Console.WriteLine( "Original value of z: uninitialized\n" );
16
17         // pass y and z by reference
18         SquareRef( ref y ); // must use keyword ref
19         SquareOut( out z ); // must use keyword out
20
21         // display values of y and z after they are modified by
22         // methods SquareRef and SquareOut, respectively
23         Console.WriteLine( "Value of y after SquareRef: {0}", y );
24         Console.WriteLine( "Value of z after SquareOut: {0}\n", z );
25
26         // pass y and z by value
27         Square( y );
28         Square( z );
29
30         // display values of y and z after they are passed to method Square
31         // to demonstrate that arguments passed by value are not modified
32         Console.WriteLine( "Value of y after Square: {0}", y );
33         Console.WriteLine( "Value of z after Square: {0}", z );
34      } // end Main
35
36      // uses reference parameter x to modify caller's variable
37      static void SquareRef( ref int x )
38      {
39         x = x * x; // squares value of caller's variable
40      } // end method SquareRef
41
42      // uses output parameter x to assign a value
43      // to an uninitialized variable
44      static void SquareOut( out int x )
45      {
46         x = 6; // assigns a value to caller's variable
47         x = x * x; // squares value of caller's variable
48      } // end method SquareOut
49
50      // parameter x receives a copy of the value passed as an argument,
51      // so this method cannot modify the caller's variable
52      static void Square( int x )
53      {
```

Fig. 7.15 | Reference, output and value parameters. (Part 1 of 2.)

```
54          x = x * x;
55      } // end method Square
56  } // end class ReferenceAndOutputParameters
```

```
Original value of y: 5
Original value of z: uninitialized

Value of y after SquareRef: 25
Value of z after SquareOut: 36

Value of y after Square: 25
Value of z after Square: 36
```

Fig. 7.15 | Reference, output and value parameters. (Part 2 of 2.)

Method Square (lines 52–55) multiplies its parameter x by itself and assigns the new value to x. When this method is called, a copy of the argument is passed to the parameter x. Thus, even though parameter x is modified in the method, the original value in the caller is not modified.

Method Main (lines 8–34) invokes methods SquareRef, SquareOut and Square. We begin by initializing variable y to 5 and declaring, but not initializing, variable z. Lines 18–19 call methods SquareRef and SquareOut. Notice that when you pass a variable to a method with a reference parameter, you must precede the argument with the same keyword (ref or out) that was used to declare the reference parameter. Lines 23–24 display the values of y and z after the calls to SquareRef and SquareOut. Notice that y has been changed to 25 and z has been set to 36.

Lines 27–28 call method Square with y and z as arguments. In this case, both variables are passed by value—only copies of their values are passed to Square. As a result, the values of y and z remain 25 and 36, respectively. Lines 32–33 output the values of y and z to show that they were not modified.

Common Programming Error 7.13

The ref and out arguments in a method call must match the parameters specified in the method declaration; otherwise, a compilation error occurs.

Software Engineering Observation 7.5

By default, C# does not allow you to choose whether to pass each argument by value or by reference. Value types are passed by value. Objects are not passed to methods; rather, references to objects are passed to methods. The references themselves are passed by value. When a method receives a reference to an object, the method can manipulate the object directly, but the reference value cannot be changed to refer to a new object. In Section 8.8, you'll see that references also can be passed by reference.

7.17 Wrap-Up

In this chapter, we discussed the difference between non-static and static methods, and we showed how to call static methods by preceding the method name with the name of the class in which it appears and the member access (.) operator. You saw that the Math class in the .NET Framework Class Library provides many `static` methods to perform mathematical calculations. We presented several commonly used Framework Class Library namespaces. You learned how to use operator + to perform `string` concatenations. You also learned how to declare constant values in two ways—with the `const` keyword and with `enum` types. We demonstrated simulation techniques and used class `Random` to generate sets of random numbers. We discussed the scope of fields and local variables in a class. You saw how to overload methods in a class by providing methods with the same name but different signatures. You learned how to use optional and named parameters. We discussed how recursive methods call themselves, breaking larger problems into smaller subproblems until eventually the original problem is solved. You learned the differences between value types and reference types with respect to how they're passed to methods, and how to use the `ref` and `out` keywords to pass arguments by reference.

In Chapter 8, you'll learn how to maintain lists and tables of data in arrays. You'll see a more elegant implementation of the application that rolls a die 6000 times and two enhanced versions of our `GradeBook` case study. You'll also learn how to access an application's command-line arguments that are passed to method `Main` when a console application begins execution.

Summary

Section 7.1 Introduction
- Experience has shown that the best way to develop and maintain a large application is to construct it from small, simple pieces. This technique is called divide and conquer.

Section 7.2 Packaging Code in C#
- Three common ways of packaging code are methods, classes and namespaces.
- Methods allow you to modularize an application by separating its tasks into self-contained units.
- Dividing an application into meaningful methods makes it easier to debug and maintain.

Section 7.3 `static` Methods, `static` Variables and Class `Math`
- You can call any `static` method by specifying the name of the class in which it's declared, followed by the member access (`.`) operator and the method name, as in

  ClassName.MethodName(*arguments*)

- Method arguments may be constants, variables or expressions.
- A constant is declared with the keyword `const`—its value cannot be changed after the constant is declared.
- Class `Math` declares constants `Math.PI` and `Math.E`. `Math.PI` (3.14159265358979323846) is the ratio of a circle's circumference to its diameter. `Math.E` (2.7182818284590452354) is the base value for natural logarithms.
- When each object of a class maintains its own copy of an attribute, each object (instance) of the class has a separate instance of the variable. When objects of a class containing `static` variables are created, all objects of that class share one copy of the class's `static` variables.
- Together the `static` variables and instance variables represent the fields of a class.
- When you execute your application, you can specify a list of `strings` (separated by spaces) as command-line arguments. The execution environment will pass these arguments to the `Main` method of your application.

- If you declare more than one `Main` method among all the classes of your project, you'll need to indicate which one you would like to be the application's entry point. You can do this by clicking the menu **Project > [ProjectName] Properties...** and selecting the class containing the `Main` method that should be the entry point from the **Startup object** list box.

Section 7.4 Declaring Methods with Multiple Parameters

- Multiple parameters are specified as a comma-separated list.

- When a method is called, each parameter is initialized with the value of the corresponding argument. There must be one argument in the method call for each required parameter in the method declaration. Each argument must be consistent with the type of the corresponding parameter.

- When program control returns to the point in the application where a method was called, the method's parameters are no longer accessible.

- Methods can return at most one value; the returned value can be a value type that contains many values (implemented as a `struct`) or a reference to an object that contains many values.

- C# allows `string` objects to be created by assembling smaller `strings` into larger `strings` using operator +. This is known as `string` concatenation.

- Every value of a simple type in C# has a `string` representation. When one of the + operator's operands is a `string`, the other is implicitly converted to a `string`, then the two are concatenated.

- All objects have a `ToString` method that returns a `string` representation of the object. When an object is concatenated with a `string`, the object's `ToString` method is implicitly called to obtain the `string` representation of the object.

Section 7.5 Notes on Declaring and Using Methods

- You've seen three ways to call a method—using a method name by itself to call another method of the same class; using a variable that contains a reference to an object, followed by the member access (.) operator and the method name to call a non-`static` method of the referenced object; and using the class name and the member access (.) operator to call a `static` method of a class.

- A `static` method can call only other `static` methods of the same class directly and can manipulate only `static` variables in the same class directly.

- There are three ways to return control to the statement that calls a method. If the method does not return a result, control returns when the program flow reaches the method-ending right brace or when the statement

      return;

  is executed. If the method returns a result, the statement

      return expression;

  evaluates the *expression*, then returns the result to the caller.

Section 7.6 Method-Call Stack and Activation Records

- Stacks are known as last-in, first-out (LIFO) data structures—the last item pushed (inserted) on the stack is the first item popped off (removed from) the stack.

- When an application calls a method, the called method must know how to return to its caller, so the return address of the calling method is pushed onto the program-execution stack. If a series of method calls occurs, the successive return addresses are pushed onto the stack in last-in, first-out order so that each method can return to its caller.

- The program-execution stack also contains the memory for the local variables used in each invocation of a method during an application's execution. This data, stored as a portion of the program-execution stack, is known as the activation record or stack frame of the method call.

- If a local variable holding a reference to an object is the only variable in the application with a reference to that object, when the activation record containing that local variable is popped off the stack, the object will eventually be deleted from memory during "garbage collection."

- The amount of memory in a computer is finite. If more method calls occur than can have their activation records stored on the program-execution stack, stack overflow occurs.

Section 7.7 Argument Promotion and Casting

- Another important feature of method calls is argument promotion—implicitly converting an argument's value to the type that the method expects to receive in its corresponding parameter.

- The argument-promotion rules apply to expressions containing values of two or more simple types and to simple-type values passed as arguments to methods.

- In cases where information may be lost due to conversion between simple types, the compiler requires you to use a cast operator to explicitly force the conversion.

Section 7.8 The .NET Framework Class Library

- Many predefined classes are grouped into categories of related classes called namespaces. Together, these namespaces are referred to as the .NET Framework Class Library.

Section 7.9 Case Study: Random-Number Generation

- Random method Next generates a random int value in the range 0 to +2,147,483,646, inclusive.

- Class Random provides other versions of method Next. One receives an int and returns a value from 0 up to, but not including, the argument's value. The other receives two ints and returns a value from the first argument's value up to, but not including, the second argument's value.

- The methods of class Random actually generate pseudorandom numbers based on complex mathematical calculations. The calculation that produces the pseudorandom numbers uses the time of day as a seed value to change the sequence's starting point.

- If the same seed value is used every time, the Random object produces the same sequence of random numbers.

Section 7.10 Case Study: A Game of Chance (Introducing Enumerations)

- An enumeration is introduced by the keyword enum and a type name. Braces delimit the body of an enum declaration. Inside the braces is a comma-separated list of enumeration constants.

- Variables of an enum type should be assigned only constants of that enum type.

- When an enum is declared, each constant in the enum declaration is a constant value of type int. If you do not assign a value to an identifier in the enum declaration, the compiler will do so. If the first enum constant is unassigned, the compiler gives it the value 0. If any other enum constant is unassigned, the compiler gives it a value equal to one more than the value of the preceding enum constant. The enum constant names must be unique, but their underlying values need not be.

- If you need to compare a simple integral type value to the underlying value of an enumeration constant, you must use a cast operator to make the two types match.

Section 7.11 Scope of Declarations

- The scope of a declaration is the portion of the application that can refer to the declared entity by its unqualified name.

- The scope of a parameter declaration is the body of the method in which the declaration appears.

- A local variable's scope is from the point at which the declaration appears to the end of that block.

- The scope of a local-variable declaration that appears in the initialization section of a for statement's header is the body of the for statement and the other expressions in the header.

- The scope of a method, property or field of a class is the entire body of the class.
- Any block may contain variable declarations. If a local variable or parameter in a method has the same name as a field, the field is hidden until the block terminates execution.

Section 7.12 Method Overloading

- Methods of the same name can be declared in the same class, as long as they have different sets of parameters. This is called method overloading. When an overloaded method is called, the C# compiler selects the appropriate method by examining the number, types and order of the arguments in the call.
- The compiler distinguishes overloaded methods by their signature—a combination of the method's name and the number, types and order of its parameters. The signature also includes the way those parameters are passed, which can be modified by the ref and out keywords.
- The compiler will generate an error when two methods have the same signature but different return types. Overloaded methods can have the same or different return types if the methods have different parameter lists.

Section 7.13 Optional Parameters

- As of Visual C# 2010, methods can have optional parameters, which allow the calling method to vary the number of arguments to pass. An optional parameter specifies a default value that's assigned to the parameter if the optional argument is omitted.
- Methods can have one or more optional parameters. All optional parameters must be placed to the right of the method's non-optional parameters.
- When a parameter has a default value, the caller has the option of passing that particular argument.

Section 7.14 Named Parameters

- Normally, when calling a method that has optional parameters, the argument values—in order—are assigned to the parameters from left to right in the parameter list.
- Visual C# 2010 provides a new feature called named parameters, which enable you to call methods that receive optional parameters by providing only the optional arguments you wish to specify. To do so, you explicitly specify the parameter's name and value—separated by a colon (:)—in the argument list of the method call.

Section 7.15 Recursion

- A recursive method calls itself, either directly or indirectly through another method.
- When a recursive method is called to solve a problem, the method actually is capable of solving only the simplest case(s), or base case(s). If the method is called with a base case, the method returns a result.
- If the method is called with a more complex problem, the method divides the problem into two conceptual pieces: a piece that the method knows how to do and a piece that it does not know how to do. Because this new problem looks like the original problem, the method calls a fresh copy of itself to work on the smaller problem; this procedure is referred to as a recursive call and is also called the recursion step.
- A recursive declaration of the factorial method is arrived at by observing the relationship:

$$n! = n \cdot (n - 1)!$$

Section 7.16 Passing Arguments: Pass-by-Value vs. Pass-by-Reference

- Two ways to pass arguments to functions in many programming languages are pass-by-value and pass-by-reference.

- When an argument is passed by value (the default), a *copy* of the argument's value is passed to the called function. Changes to the copy do not affect the original variable's value in the caller.
- When an argument is passed by reference, the caller gives the method the ability to access and modify the caller's original data directly.
- Value-type variables store values, so specifying a value-type variable in a method call passes a copy of that variable's value to the method. Reference-type variables store references to objects, so specifying a reference-type variable as an argument passes the method a copy of the actual reference that refers to the object.
- When returning information from a method via a `return` statement, the method returns a copy of the value stored in a value-type variable or a copy of the reference stored in a reference-type variable.
- C# provides the keywords `ref` and `out` to pass variables by reference.
- A `ref` parameter indicates that an argument will be passed to the method by reference—the called method will be able to modify the original variable in the caller.
- An `out` parameter indicates that a possibly uninitialized variable will be passed into the method by reference and that the called method will assign a value to the original variable in the caller.
- A method can return only one value to its caller via a return statement, but can return many values by specifying multiple output (`ref` and/or `out`) parameters.
- When a variable is passed to a method with a reference parameter, you must precede the variable with the same keyword (`ref` or `out`) that was used to declare the reference parameter.

Terminology

activation record
argument promotion
base case in recursion
block
command-line argument
const keyword
constant
default value
divide-and-conquer approach
element of chance
entry point of an application
enum keyword
enumeration
enumeration constant
field of a class
formal parameter
hierarchical boss-method/worker-method
   relationship
implicit conversion
infinite recursion
last-in, first-out (LIFO) data structure
local variable
Math.PI constant
Math.E constant
method-call stack
method overloading

modularizing an application with methods
named parameter
namespace
Next method of class Random
optional parameter
out keyword
output parameter
overloaded method
parameter list
pass by reference
pass by value
pop data from a stack
program-execution stack
promotion rules
push data onto a stack
pseudorandom number
Random class
random numbers
ref keyword
recursion
recursion step
recursive call
recursive method
reusable software components
scaling factor (with random numbers)
scope of a declaration

seed value (with random numbers)	stack
shift a range (with random numbers)	stack frame
shifting value (with random numbers)	stack overflow
signature of a method	string concatenation
simulation	unqualified class name
simple type promotions	user-defined method

Self-Review Exercises

7.1 Fill in the blanks in each of the following statements:

a) A method is invoked with a(n) _____.

b) A variable known only within the method in which it's declared is called a(n) _____.

c) The _____ statement in a called method can be used to pass the value of an expression back to the calling method.

d) The keyword _____ indicates that a method does not return a value.

e) Data can be added to or removed from only the _____ of a stack.

f) Stacks are known as _____ data structures—the last item pushed (inserted) on the stack is the first item popped off (removed from) the stack.

g) The three ways to return control from a called method to a caller are _____, _____ and _____.

h) An object of class _____ produces pseudorandom numbers.

i) The program-execution stack contains the memory for local variables on each invocation of a method during an application's execution. This data, stored as a portion of the program-execution stack, is known as the _____ or _____ of the method call.

j) If there are more method calls than can be stored on the program execution stack, an error known as a(n) _____ occurs.

k) The _____ of a declaration is the portion of an application that can refer to the entity in the declaration by its unqualified name.

l) It's possible to have several methods with the same name that each operate on different types or numbers of arguments. This feature is called method _____.

m) The program-execution stack is also referred to as the _____ stack.

n) A method that calls itself either directly or indirectly is a(n) _____ method.

o) A recursive method typically has two components: one that provides a means for the recursion to terminate by testing for a(n) _____ case and one that expresses the problem as a recursive call for a slightly simpler problem than does the original call.

7.2 For the class Craps in Fig. 7.8, state the scope of each of the following entities:

a) the variable randomNumbers.

b) the variable die1.

c) the method RollDice.

d) the method Main.

e) the variable sumOfDice.

7.3 Write an application that tests whether the examples of the Math class method calls shown in Fig. 7.2 actually produce the indicated results.

7.4 Give the method header for each of the following methods:

a) Method Hypotenuse, which takes two double-precision, floating-point arguments side1 and side2 and returns a double-precision, floating-point result.

b) Method Smallest, which takes three integers x, y and z and returns an integer.

c) Method Instructions, which does not take any arguments and does not return a value. [*Note:* Such methods are commonly used to display instructions to a user.]

d) Method IntToDouble, which takes integer argument number and returns a double value.

7.5   Find the error in each of the following code segments. Explain how to correct the error.

a) **void** G()
```
{
    Console.WriteLine( "Inside method G" );
    void H()
    {
        Console.WriteLine( "Inside method H" );
    }
}
```

b) **int** Sum(**int** x, **int** y)
```
{
    int result;
    result = x + y;
}
```

c) **void** F(**float** a);
```
{
    float a;
    Console.WriteLine( a );
}
```

d) **void** Product()
```
{
    int a = 6, b = 5, c = 4, result;
    result = a * b * c;
    Console.WriteLine( "Result is " + result );
    return result;
}
```

7.6   Write a complete C# application to prompt the user for the double radius of a sphere, and call method SphereVolume to calculate and display the volume of the sphere. Use the following statement to calculate the volume:

```
double volume = ( 4.0 / 3.0 ) * Math.PI * Math.Pow( radius, 3 )
```

Answers to Self-Review Exercises

7.1   a) method call. b) local variable. c) return. d) void. e) top. f) last-in-first-out (LIFO).
g) return; or return *expression*; or encountering the closing right brace of a method. h) Random.
i) activation record, stack frame. j) stack overflow. k) scope. l) overloading. m) method call.
n) recursive. o) base.

7.2   a) class body. b) block that defines method RollDice's body. c) class body. d) class body.
e) block that defines method Main's body.

7.3   The following solution demonstrates the Math class methods in Fig. 7.2:

```
1   // Exercise 7.3 Solution: MathTest.cs
2   // Testing the Math class methods.
3   using System;
4
5   public class MathTest
6   {
7       public static void Main( string[] args )
8       {
9           Console.WriteLine( "Math.Abs( 23.7 ) = {0}", Math.Abs( 23.7 ) );
10          Console.WriteLine( "Math.Abs( 0.0 ) = {0}", Math.Abs( 0.0 ) );
```

```
11        Console.WriteLine( "Math.Abs( -23.7 ) = {0}", Math.Abs( -23.7 ) );
12        Console.WriteLine( "Math.Ceiling( 9.2 ) = {0}",
13           Math.Ceiling( 9.2 ) );
14        Console.WriteLine( "Math.Ceiling( -9.8 ) = {0}",
15           Math.Ceiling( -9.8 ) );
16        Console.WriteLine( "Math.Cos( 0.0 ) = {0}", Math.Cos( 0.0 ) );
17        Console.WriteLine( "Math.Exp( 1.0 ) = {0}", Math.Exp( 1.0 ) );
18        Console.WriteLine( "Math.Exp( 2.0 ) = {0}", Math.Exp( 2.0 ) );
19        Console.WriteLine( "Math.Floor( 9.2 ) = {0}", Math.Floor( 9.2 ) );
20        Console.WriteLine( "Math.Floor( -9.8 ) = {0}",
21           Math.Floor( -9.8 ) );
22        Console.WriteLine( "Math.Log( Math.E ) = {0}",
23           Math.Log( Math.E ) );
24        Console.WriteLine( "Math.Log( Math.E * Math.E ) = {0}",
25           Math.Log( Math.E * Math.E ) );
26        Console.WriteLine( "Math.Max( 2.3, 12.7 ) = {0}",
27           Math.Max( 2.3, 12.7 ) );
28        Console.WriteLine( "Math.Max( -2.3, -12.7 ) = {0}",
29           Math.Max( -2.3, -12.7 ) );
30        Console.WriteLine( "Math.Min( 2.3, 12.7 ) = {0}",
31           Math.Min( 2.3, 12.7 ) );
32        Console.WriteLine( "Math.Min( -2.3, -12.7 ) = {0}",
33           Math.Min( -2.3, -12.7 ) );
34        Console.WriteLine( "Math.Pow( 2.0, 7.0 ) = {0}",
35           Math.Pow( 2.0, 7.0 ) );
36        Console.WriteLine( "Math.Pow( 9.0, 0.5 ) = {0}",
37           Math.Pow( 9.0, 0.5 ) );
38        Console.WriteLine( "Math.Sin( 0.0 ) = {0}", Math.Sin( 0.0 ) );
39        Console.WriteLine( "Math.Sqrt( 900.0 ) = {0}",
40           Math.Sqrt( 900.0 ) );
41        Console.WriteLine( "Math.Tan( 0.0 ) = {0}", Math.Tan( 0.0 ) );
42     } // end Main
43  } // end class MathTest
```

```
Math.Abs( 23.7 ) = 23.7
Math.Abs( 0.0 ) = 0
Math.Abs( -23.7 ) = 23.7
Math.Ceiling( 9.2 ) = 10
Math.Ceiling( -9.8 ) = -9
Math.Cos( 0.0 ) = 1
Math.Exp( 1.0 ) = 2.71828182845905
Math.Exp( 2.0 ) = 7.38905609893065
Math.Floor( 9.2 ) = 9
Math.Floor( -9.8 ) = -10
Math.Log( Math.E ) = 1
Math.Log( Math.E * Math.E ) = 2
Math.Max( 2.3, 12.7 ) = 12.7
Math.Max( -2.3, -12.7 ) = -2.3
Math.Min( 2.3, 12.7 ) = 2.3
Math.Min( -2.3, -12.7 ) = -12.7
Math.Pow( 2.0, 7.0 ) = 128
Math.Pow( 9.0, 0.5 ) = 3
Math.Sin( 0.0 ) = 0
Math.Sqrt( 900.0 ) = 30
Math.Tan( 0.0 ) = 0
```

7.4 a) **double** Hypotenuse(**double** side1, **double** side2)
    b) **int** Smallest(**int** x, **int** y, **int** z)
    c) **void** Instructions()
    d) **double** IntToDouble(**int** number)

7.5 a) *Error:* Method H is declared within method G.
 Correction: Move the declaration of H outside the declaration of G.

b) *Error:* The method is supposed to return an integer, but does not.
 Correction: Delete variable result and place the statement

```
return x + y;
```

in the method, or add the following statement at the end of the method body:

```
return result;
```

c) *Error:* The semicolon after the right parenthesis of the parameter list is incorrect, and the parameter a should not be redeclared in the method.
 Correction: Delete the semicolon after the right parenthesis of the parameter list, and delete the declaration float a;.

d) *Error:* The method returns a value when it's not supposed to.
 Correction: Change the return type from void to int.

7.6 The following solution calculates the volume of a sphere, using the radius entered by the user:

```csharp
1   // Exercise 7.6 Solution: Sphere.cs
2   // Calculate the volume of a sphere.
3   using System;
4
5   public class Sphere
6   {
7      // obtain radius from user and display volume of sphere
8      public static void Main( string[] args )
9      {
10        Console.Write( "Enter radius of sphere: " );
11        double radius = Convert.ToDouble( Console.ReadLine() );
12
13        Console.WriteLine( "Volume is {0:F3}", SphereVolume( radius ) );
14     } // end Main
15
16     // calculate and return sphere volume
17     public static double SphereVolume( double radius )
18     {
19        double volume = ( 4.0 / 3.0 ) * Math.PI * Math.Pow( radius, 3 );
20        return volume;
21     } // end method SphereVolume
22  } // end class Sphere
```

```
Enter radius of sphere: 4
Volume is 268.083
```

Exercises

7.7 What is the value of x after each of the following statements is executed?

a) x = Math.Abs(7.5);
b) x = Math.Floor(7.5);
c) x = Math.Abs(0.0);
d) x = Math.Ceiling(0.0);
e) x = Math.Abs(-6.4);
f) x = Math.Ceiling(-6.4);
g) x = Math.Ceiling(-Math.Abs(-8 + Math.Floor(-5.5)));

7.8 *(Parking Charges)* A parking garage charges a $2.00 minimum fee to park for up to three hours. The garage charges an additional $0.50 per hour for each hour *or part thereof* in excess of three hours. The maximum charge for any given 24-hour period is $10.00. Assume that no car parks for longer than 24 hours at a time. Write an application that calculates and displays the parking charges for each customer who parked in the garage yesterday. You should enter the hours parked for each customer. The application should display the charge for the current customer and should calculate and display the running total of yesterday's receipts. The application should use method Calculate-Charges to determine the charge for each customer.

7.9 *(Rounding to Nearest Integer)* An application of method Math.Floor is rounding a value to the nearest integer. The statement

```
y = Math.Floor( x + 0.5 );
```

will round the number x to the nearest integer and assign the result to y. Write an application that reads double values and uses the preceding statement to round each of the numbers to the nearest integer. For each number processed, display both the original number and the rounded number.

7.10 *(Rounding to a Specific Decimal Place)* Math.Floor may be used to round a number to a specific decimal place. The statement

```
y = Math.Floor( x * 10 + 0.5 ) / 10;
```

rounds x to the tenths position (i.e., the first position to the right of the decimal point). The statement

```
y = Math.Floor( x * 100 + 0.5 ) / 100;
```

rounds x to the hundredths position (i.e., the second position to the right of the decimal point). Write an application that defines four methods for rounding a number x in various ways:

a) RoundToInteger(number)
b) RoundToTenths(number)
c) RoundToHundredths(number)
d) RoundToThousandths(number)

For each value read, your application should display the original value, the number rounded to the nearest integer, the number rounded to the nearest tenth, the number rounded to the nearest hundredth and the number rounded to the nearest thousandth.

7.11 Answer each of the following questions:

a) What does it mean to choose numbers "at random"?
b) Why is the Random class useful for simulating games of chance?
c) Why is it often necessary to scale or shift the values produced by a Random object?
d) Why is computerized simulation of real-world situations a useful technique?

7.12 Write statements that assign random integers to the variable n in the following ranges. Assume Random randomNumbers = **new** Random() has been defined and use the two-parameter version of the method Random.Next.

a) $1 \leq n \leq 2$
b) $1 \leq n \leq 100$
c) $0 \leq n \leq 9$
d) $1000 \leq n \leq 1112$
e) $-1 \leq n \leq 1$
f) $-3 \leq n \leq 11$

7.13 For each of the following sets of integers, write a single statement that will display a number at random from the set. Assume Random randomNumbers = **new** Random() has been defined and use the one-parameter version of method Random.Next.

a) 2, 4, 6, 8, 10.
b) 3, 5, 7, 9, 11.
c) 6, 10, 14, 18, 22.

7.14 *(Exponentiation)* Write a method IntegerPower(base, exponent) that returns the value of
$$base^{\,exponent}$$

For example, IntegerPower(3, 4) calculates 3^4 (or 3 * 3 * 3 * 3). Assume that exponent is a positive integer and that base is an integer. Method IntegerPower should use a for or while loop to control the calculation. Do not use any Math-library methods. Incorporate this method into an application that reads integer values for base and exponent and performs the calculation with the IntegerPower method.

7.15 *(Hypotenuse of a Right Triangle)* Write method Hypotenuse that calculates the length of the hypotenuse of a right triangle when the lengths of the other two sides are given. The method should take two arguments of type double and return the hypotenuse as a double. Incorporate this method into an application that reads values for side1 and side2 and performs the calculation with the Hypotenuse method. Determine the length of the hypotenuse for each of the triangles in Fig. 7.16.

Triangle	Side 1	Side 2
1	3.0	4.0
2	5.0	12.0
3	8.0	15.0

Fig. 7.16 | Values for the sides of triangles in Exercise 7.15.

7.16 *(Multiples)* Write method Multiple that determines, for a pair of integers, whether the second integer is a multiple of the first. The method should take two integer arguments and return true if the second is a multiple of the first and false otherwise. Incorporate this method into an application that inputs a series of pairs of integers (one pair at a time) and determines whether the second value in each pair is a multiple of the first.

7.17 *(Even or Odd)* Write method IsEven that uses the remainder operator (%) to determine whether an integer is even. The method should take an integer argument and return true if the integer is even and false otherwise. Incorporate this method into an application that inputs a sequence of integers (one at a time) and determines whether each is even or odd.

7.18 *(Displaying a Square of Asterisks)* Write method SquareOfAsterisks that displays a solid square (the same number of rows and columns) of asterisks whose side length is specified in integer parameter side. For example, if side is 4, the method should display

```
****
****
****
****
```

Incorporate this method into an application that reads an integer value for side from the user and outputs the asterisks with the SquareOfAsterisks method.

7.19 *(Displaying a Square of Any Character)* Modify the method created in Exercise 7.18 to form the square out of whatever character is contained in character parameter FillCharacter. Thus, if side is 5 and FillCharacter is "#," the method should display

```
#####
#####
#####
#####
#####
```

[*Hint:* Use the expression Convert.ToChar(Console.Read()) to read a character from the user.]

7.20   *(Circle Area)* Write an application that prompts the user for the radius of a circle and uses method `CircleArea` to calculate the area of the circle.

7.21   *(Separating Digits)* Write code segments that accomplish each of the following tasks:
   a) Calculate the integer part of the quotient when integer a is divided by integer b.
   b) Calculate the integer remainder when integer a is divided by integer b.
   c) Use the application pieces developed in parts (a) and (b) to write a method `DisplayDigits` that receives an integer between 1 and 99999 and displays it as a sequence of digits, separating each pair of digits by two spaces. For example, the integer 4562 should appear as:
       4 5 6 2.
   d) Incorporate the method developed in part (c) into an application that inputs an integer and calls `DisplayDigits` by passing the method the integer entered. Display the results.

7.22   *(Temperature Conversions)* Implement the following integer methods:
   a) Method `Celsius` returns the Celsius equivalent of a Fahrenheit temperature, using the calculation

   $$c = 5.0 / 9.0 * (f - 32);$$

   b) Method `Fahrenheit` returns the Fahrenheit equivalent of a Celsius temperature, using the calculation

   $$f = 9.0 / 5.0 * c + 32;$$

   c) Use the methods from parts (a) and (b) to write an application that enables the user either to enter a Fahrenheit temperature and display the Celsius equivalent or to enter a Celsius temperature and display the Fahrenheit equivalent.

7.23   *(Find the Minimum)* Write a method `Minimum3` that returns the smallest of three floating-point numbers. Use the `Math.Min` method to implement `Minimum3`. Incorporate the method into an application that reads three values from the user, determines the smallest value and displays the result.

7.24   *(Perfect Numbers)* An integer number is said to be a *perfect number* if its factors, including 1 (but not the number itself), sum to the number. For example, 6 is a perfect number, because 6 = 1 + 2 + 3. Write method `Perfect` that determines whether parameter `value` is a perfect number. Use this method in an application that determines and displays all the perfect numbers between 2 and 1000. Display the factors of each perfect number to confirm that the number is indeed perfect.

7.25   *(Prime Numbers)* An integer is said to be *prime* if it's greater than 1 and divisible by only 1 and itself. For example, 2, 3, 5 and 7 are prime, but 4, 6, 8 and 9 are not.
   a) Write a method that determines whether a number is prime.
   b) Use this method in an application that displays all the prime numbers less than 10,000.
   c) Initially, you might think that $n/2$ is the upper limit for which you must test to see whether a number is prime, but you need only go as high as the square root of n. Rewrite the application, and run it both ways.

7.26   *(Reversing Digits)* Write a method that takes an integer value and returns the number with its digits reversed. For example, given the number 7631, the method should return 1367. Incorporate the method into an application that reads a value from the user and displays the result.

7.27   *(Greatest Common Divisor)* The *greatest common divisor* (*GCD*) of two integers is the largest integer that evenly divides each of the two numbers. Write method `Gcd` that returns the greatest common divisor of two integers. Incorporate the method into an application that reads two values from the user and displays the result.

7.28   *(Converting Grade Averages to a Four-Point Scale)* Write method `QualityPoints` that inputs a student's average and returns 4 if the student's average is 90–100, 3 if the average is 80–89, 2 if the average is 70–79, 1 if the average is 60–69 and 0 if the average is lower than 60. Incorporate the method into an application that reads a value from the user and displays the result.

7.29 *(Coin Tossing)* Write an application that simulates coin tossing. Let the application toss a coin each time the user chooses the "Toss Coin" menu option. Count the number of times each side of the coin appears. Display the results. The application should call a separate method Flip that takes no arguments and returns false for tails and true for heads. [*Note:* If the application realistically simulates coin tossing, each side of the coin should appear approximately half the time.]

7.30 *(Guess the Number Game)* Write an application that plays "guess the number" as follows: Your application chooses the number to be guessed by selecting a random integer in the range 1 to 1000. The application displays the prompt Guess a number between 1 and 1000. The player inputs a first guess. If the player's guess is incorrect, your application should display Too high. Try again. or Too low. Try again. to help the player "zero in" on the correct answer. The application should prompt the user for the next guess. When the user enters the correct answer, display Congratulations. You guessed the number! and allow the user to choose whether to play again. [*Note:* The guessing technique employed in this problem is similar to a binary search, which is discussed in Chapter 20.]

7.31 *(Enhanced Guess the Number Game)* Modify the application of Exercise 7.30 to count the number of guesses the player makes. If the number is 10 or fewer, display Either you know the secret or you got lucky! If the player guesses the number in 10 tries, display Aha! You know the secret! If the player makes more than 10 guesses, display You should be able to do better! Why should it take no more than 10 guesses? Well, with each "good guess," the player should be able to eliminate half of the numbers. Now show why any number from 1 to 1000 can be guessed in 10 or fewer tries.

7.32 *(Distance Between Two Points)* Write method Distance to calculate the distance between two points *(x1, y1)* and *(x2, y2)*. All numbers and return values should be of type double. Incorporate this method into an application that enables the user to enter the coordinates of the points.

7.33 *(Craps Game Modification)* Modify the craps application of Fig. 7.8 to allow wagering. Initialize variable balance to 1000 dollars. Prompt the player to enter a wager. Check that wager is less than or equal to balance, and if it's not, have the user reenter wager until a valid wager is entered. After a correct wager is entered, run one game of craps. If the player wins, increase balance by wager and display the new balance. If the player loses, decrease balance by wager, display the new balance, check whether balance has become zero and, if so, display the message "Sorry. You busted!"

7.34 *(Binary, Octal and Hexadecimal)* Write an application that displays a table of the binary, octal, and hexadecimal equivalents of the decimal numbers in the range 1–256. If you're not familiar with these number systems, read Appendix D first.

7.35 *(Recursive Power Calculation)* Write recursive method Power(base, exponent) that, when called, returns

$$base^{\,exponent}$$

For example, Power(3, 4) = 3 * 3 * 3 * 3. Assume that exponent is an integer greater than or equal to 1. The recursion step should use the relationship

$$base^{\,exponent} = base \cdot base^{\,exponent\,-\,1}$$

The terminating condition occurs when exponent is equal to 1, because

$$base^1 = base$$

Incorporate this method into an application that enables the user to enter the base and exponent.

7.36 *(Towers of Hanoi)* Every budding computer scientist must grapple with certain classic problems, and the *Towers of Hanoi* (see Fig. 7.17) is one of the most famous. Legend has it that in a temple in the Far East, priests are attempting to move a stack of disks from one peg to another. The initial stack has 64 disks threaded onto one peg and arranged from bottom to top by decreasing size. The priests are attempting to move the stack from this peg to a second peg under the constraints that exactly one disk is moved at a time and at no time may a larger disk be placed above a smaller disk. A third peg is available for temporarily holding disks. Supposedly, the world will end when the priests complete their task, so there's little incentive for us to facilitate their efforts.

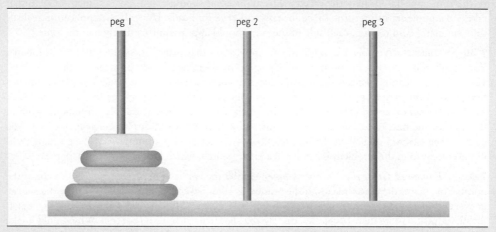

Fig. 7.17 | The Towers of Hanoi for the case with four disks.

Let's assume that the priests are attempting to move the disks from peg 1 to peg 3. We wish to develop an algorithm that will display the precise sequence of peg-to-peg disk transfers.

If we were to approach this problem with conventional methods, we would rapidly find ourselves hopelessly knotted up in managing the disks. Instead, if we attack the problem with recursion in mind, it immediately becomes tractable. Moving n disks can be viewed in terms of moving only $n - 1$ disks (hence the recursion) as follows:

   a) Move $n - 1$ disks from peg 1 to peg 2, using peg 3 as a temporary holding area.
   b) Move the last disk (the largest) from peg 1 to peg 3.
   c) Move the $n - 1$ disks from peg 2 to peg 3, using peg 1 as a temporary holding area.

The process ends when the last task involves moving $n = 1$ disk (i.e., the base case). This task is accomplished by simply moving the disk, without the need for a temporary holding area.

Write an application to solve the Towers of Hanoi problem. Allow the user to enter the number of disks. Use a recursive `Tower` method with four parameters:

   a) the number of disks to be moved,
   b) the peg on which these disks are initially threaded,
   c) the peg to which this stack of disks is to be moved, and
   d) the peg to be used as a temporary holding area.

Your application should display the precise instructions it will take to move the disks from the starting peg to the destination peg. For example, to move a stack of three disks from peg 1 to peg 3, your application should display the following series of moves:

```
1 --> 3 (This notation means "Move one disk from peg 1 to peg 3.")
1 --> 2
3 --> 2
1 --> 3
2 --> 1
2 --> 3
1 --> 3
```

7.37   *(What Does This Code Do?)* What does the following method do?

```
// Parameter b must be a positive to prevent infinite recursion
public static int Mystery( int a, int b )
{
```

```
      if ( b == 1 )
         return a;
      else
         return a + Mystery( a, b - 1 );
   }
```

7.38 *(Find the Error)* Find the error in the following recursive method, and explain how to correct it:

```
   public static int Sum( int n )
   {
      if ( n == 0 )
         return 0;
      else
         return n + Sum( n );
   }
```

Making a Difference Exercises

As computer costs decline, it becomes feasible for every student, regardless of economic circumstance, to have a computer and use it in school. This creates exciting possibilities for improving the educational experience of all students worldwide as suggested by the next two exercises. [*Note:* Check out initiatives such as the One Laptop Per Child Project (www.laptop.org). Also, research "green" laptops—and note the key "going green" characteristics of these devices. Look into the Electronic Product Environmental Assessment Tool (www.epeat.net) which can help you assess the "greenness" of desktops, notebooks and monitors to help you decide which products to purchase.]

7.39 *(Computer-Assisted Instruction)* The use of computers in education is referred to as *computer-assisted instruction* (*CAI*). Write a program that will help an elementary school student learn multiplication. Use a Random object to produce two positive one-digit integers. The program should then prompt the user with a question, such as

```
   How much is 6 times 7?
```

The student then inputs the answer. Next, the program checks the student's answer. If it's correct, display the message "Very good!" and ask another multiplication question. If the answer is wrong, display the message "No. Please try again." and let the student try the same question repeatedly until the student gets it right. A separate function should be used to generate each new question. This function should be called once when the application begins execution and each time the user answers the question correctly.

7.40 *(Computer-Assisted Instruction: Reducing Student Fatigue)* One problem in CAI environments is student fatigue. This can be reduced by varying the computer's responses to hold the student's attention. Modify the program of Exercise 7.39 so that various comments are displayed for each answer. Possible responses to a correct answer:

```
   Very good!
   Excellent!
   Nice work!
   Keep up the good work!
```

Possible responses to an incorrect answer:

```
   No. Please try again.
   Wrong. Try once more.
   Don't give up!
   No. Keep trying.
```

Use random-number generation to choose a number from 1 to 4 that will be used to select one of the four appropriate responses to each correct or incorrect answer. Use a switch statement to issue the responses.

8

Arrays

*Begin at the beginning, … and
go on till you come to the end:
then stop.*
—Lewis Carroll

*Now go, write it
before them in a table,
and note it in a book.*
—Isaiah 30:8

*To go beyond is as
wrong as to fall short.*
—Confucius

Objectives

In this chapter you'll learn:

- To use arrays to store data in and retrieve data from lists and tables of values.

- To declare arrays, initialize arrays and refer to individual elements of arrays.

- To use **foreach** to iterate through arrays.

- To use implicitly typed local variables.

- To pass arrays to methods.

- To declare and manipulate multidimensional arrays.

- To write methods that use variable-length argument lists.

- To read command-line arguments into an application.

8.1 Introduction

This chapter introduces the important topic of **data structures**—collections of related data items. **Arrays** are data structures consisting of related data items of the same type. Arrays are fixed-length entities—they remain the same length once they're created, although an array variable may be reassigned such that it refers to a new array of a different length.

After discussing how arrays are declared, created and initialized, we present examples that demonstrate several common array manipulations. We use arrays to simulate shuffling and dealing playing cards. The chapter demonstrates C#'s last structured control statement—the `foreach` repetition statement—which provides a concise notation for accessing data in arrays (and other data structures, as you'll see in Chapter 9 and later in the book). We enhance the `GradeBook` case study using arrays to enable the class to store a set of grades and analyze student grades from multiple exams.

8.2 Arrays

An array is a group of variables (called **elements**) containing values that all have the *same type*. Recall that types are divided into two categories—*value types* and *reference types*. Arrays are reference types. As you'll see, what we typically think of as an array is actually a reference to an array object. The elements of an array can be either value types or reference types, including other arrays. To refer to a particular element in an array, we specify the *name* of the reference to the array and the *position number* of the element in the array, which is known as the element's **index**.

Figure 8.1 shows a logical representation of an integer array called c. This array contains 12 elements. An application refers to any one of these elements with an **array-access expression** that includes the name of the array, followed by the index of the particular element in **square brackets** (`[]`). The first element in every array has **index zero** and is sometimes called the **zeroth element**. Thus, the elements of array c are c[0], c[1], c[2] and so on. The highest index in array c is 11, which is one less than the number of elements in the array, because indices begin at 0. Array names follow the same conventions as other variable names.

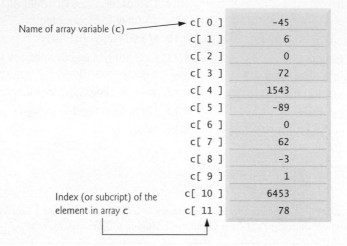

Fig. 8.1 | A 12-element array.

An index must be a nonnegative integer and can be an expression. For example, if we assume that variable a is 5 and variable b is 6, then the statement

```
c[ a + b ] += 2;
```

adds 2 to array element c[11]. An indexed array name is an array-access expression. Such expressions can be used on the left side of an assignment (i.e., an *lvalue*) to place a new value into an array element. The array index must be a value of type int, uint, long or ulong, or a value of a type that can be implicitly promoted to one of these types.

Let's examine array c in Fig. 8.1 more closely. The **name** of the variable that references the array is c. Every array instance knows its own length and provides access to this information with the Length property. For example, the expression c.Length uses array c's Length property to determine the length of the array (that is, 12). The Length property of an array *cannot* be changed, because it does not provide a set accessor. The array's 12 elements are referred to as c[0], c[1], c[2], ..., c[11]. Referring to elements outside of this range, such as c[-1] or c[12], is a runtime error (as we'll demonstrate in Fig. 8.8). The value of c[0] is -45, the value of c[1] is 6, the value of c[2] is 0, the value of c[7] is 62 and the value of c[11] is 78. To calculate the sum of the values contained in the first three elements of array c and store the result in variable sum, we would write

```
sum = c[ 0 ] + c[ 1 ] + c[ 2 ];
```

To divide the value of c[6] by 2 and assign the result to the variable x, we would write

```
x = c[ 6 ] / 2;
```

8.3 Declaring and Creating Arrays

Arrays occupy space in memory. Since they're objects, they're typically created with keyword new. To create an array object, you specify the type and the number of array elements as part of an **array-creation expression** that uses keyword new. Such an expression returns a reference that can be stored in an array variable. The following declaration and array-creation expression create an array object containing 12 int elements and store the array's reference in variable c:

```
int[] c = new int[ 12 ];
```

This expression can be used to create the array shown in Fig. 8.1 (but not the initial values in the array—we'll show how to initialize the elements of an array momentarily). This task also can be performed as follows:

```
int[] c; // declare the array variable
c = new int[ 12 ]; // create the array; assign to array variable
```

In the declaration, the square brackets following the type int indicate that c is a variable that will refer to an array of ints (i.e., c will store a reference to an array object). In the assignment statement, the array variable c receives the reference to a new array object of 12 int elements. The number of elements can also be specified as an expression that's calculated at execution time. When an array is created, each element of the array receives a default value—0 for the numeric simple-type elements, false for bool elements and null for references. As we'll soon see, we can provide specific, nondefault initial element values when we create an array.

Common Programming Error 8.1

In the declaration of a variable that will refer to an array, specifying the number of elements in the square brackets (e.g., int[12] c;) is a syntax error.

An application can create several arrays in a single declaration. The following statement reserves 100 elements for string array b and 27 elements for string array x:

```
string[] b = new string[ 100 ], x = new string[ 27 ];
```

In this statement, string[] applies to each variable. For readability and ease of commenting, we prefer to split the preceding statement into two statements, as in:

```
string[] b = new string[ 100 ]; // create string array b
string[] x = new string[ 27 ]; // create string array x
```

An application can declare variables that will refer to arrays of value-type elements or reference-type elements. For example, every element of an int array is an int value, and every element of a string array is a reference to a string object.

Resizing an Array

Though arrays are fixed-length entities, you can use the static Array method Resize, which takes two arguments—the array to be resized and the new length—to create a new array with the specified length. This method copies the contents of the old array into the new array and sets the variable it receives as its first argument to reference the new array. For example, consider the following statements:

```
int[] newArray = new int[ 5 ];
Array.Resize( ref newArray, 10 );
```

The variable newArray initially refers to a five-element array. The resize method sets newArray to refer to a new 10-element array. If the new array is smaller than the old array, any content that cannot fit into the new array is truncated without warning.

8.4 Examples Using Arrays

This section presents several examples that demonstrate declaring arrays, creating arrays, initializing arrays and manipulating array elements.

Creating and Initializing an Array
The application of Fig. 8.2 uses keyword new to create an array of five int elements that are initially 0 (the default for int variables).

```
1   // Fig. 8.2: InitArray.cs
2   // Creating an array.
3   using System;
4
5   public class InitArray
6   {
7      public static void Main( string[] args )
8      {
9         int[] array; // declare array named array
10
11        // create the space for array and initialize to default zeros
12        array = new int[ 5 ]; // 5 int elements
13
14        Console.WriteLine( "{0}{1,8}", "Index", "Value" ); // headings
15
16        // output each array element's value
17        for ( int counter = 0; counter < array.Length; counter++ )
18           Console.WriteLine( "{0,5}{1,8}", counter, array[ counter ] );
19     } // end Main
20  } // end class InitArray
```

```
Index   Value
    0       0
    1       0
    2       0
    3       0
    4       0
```

Fig. 8.2 | Creating an array.

Line 9 declares array—a variable capable of referring to an array of int elements. Line 12 creates the five-element array object and assigns its reference to variable array. Line 14 outputs the column headings. The first column contains the index (0–4) of each array element, and the second column contains the default value (0) of each array element right justified in a field width of 8.

The for statement in lines 17–18 outputs the index number (represented by counter) and the value (represented by array[counter]) of each array element. The loop-control variable counter is initially 0—index values start at 0, so using zero-based counting allows the loop to access *every* element of the array. The for statement's loop-continuation condition uses the property array.Length (line 17) to obtain the length of the array. In this example, the length of the array is 5, so the loop continues executing as long as the value of control variable counter is less than 5. The highest index value of a five-element array is 4, so using the less-than operator in the loop-continuation condition guarantees that the loop does not attempt to access an element beyond the end of the array (i.e., during the *final* iteration of the loop, counter is 4). We'll soon see what happens when an out-of-range index is encountered at execution time.

Using an Array Initializer

An application can create an array and initialize its elements with an **array initializer**, which is a comma-separated list of expressions (called an **initializer list**) enclosed in braces. In this case, the array length is determined by the number of elements in the initializer list. For example, the declaration

```
int[] n = { 10, 20, 30, 40, 50 };
```

creates a five-element array with index values 0, 1, 2, 3 and 4. Element n[0] is initialized to 10, n[1] is initialized to 20 and so on. This statement does *not* require new to create the array object. When the compiler encounters an array initializer list, it counts the number of initializers in the list to determine the array's size, then sets up the appropriate new operation "behind the scenes." The application in Fig. 8.3 initializes an integer array with 10 values (line 10) and displays the array in tabular format. The code for displaying the array elements (lines 15–16) is identical to that in Fig. 8.2 (lines 17–18).

```
 1   // Fig. 8.3: InitArray.cs
 2   // Initializing the elements of an array with an array initializer.
 3   using System;
 4
 5   public class InitArray
 6   {
 7      public static void Main( string[] args )
 8      {
 9         // initializer list specifies the value for each element
10         int[] array = { 32, 27, 64, 18, 95, 14, 90, 70, 60, 37 };
11
12         Console.WriteLine( "{0}{1,8}", "Index", "Value" ); // headings
13
14         // output each array element's value
15         for ( int counter = 0; counter < array.Length; counter++ )
16            Console.WriteLine( "{0,5}{1,8}", counter, array[ counter ] );
17      } // end Main
18   } // end class InitArray
```

```
Index   Value
    0      32
    1      27
    2      64
    3      18
    4      95
    5      14
    6      90
    7      70
    8      60
    9      37
```

Fig. 8.3 | Initializing the elements of an array with an array initializer.

Calculating a Value to Store in Each Array Element

Some applications calculate the value to be stored in each array element. The application in Fig. 8.4 creates a 10-element array and assigns to each element one of the even integers from 2 to 20 (2, 4, 6, ..., 20). Then the application displays the array in tabular format. The for statement at lines 13–14 calculates an array element's value by multiplying the current value of the for loop's control variable counter by 2, then adding 2.

```
1   // Fig. 8.4: InitArray.cs
2   // Calculating values to be placed into the elements of an array.
3   using System;
4
5   public class InitArray
6   {
7      public static void Main( string[] args )
8      {
9         const int ARRAY_LENGTH = 10; // create a named constant
10        int[] array = new int[ ARRAY_LENGTH ]; // create array
11
12        // calculate value for each array element
13        for ( int counter = 0; counter < array.Length; counter++ )
14           array[ counter ] = 2 + 2 * counter;
15
16        Console.WriteLine( "{0}{1,8}", "Index", "Value" ); // headings
17
18        // output each array element's value
19        for ( int counter = 0; counter < array.Length; counter++ )
20           Console.WriteLine( "{0,5}{1,8}", counter, array[ counter ] );
21     } // end Main
22  } // end class InitArray
```

```
Index    Value
    0        2
    1        4
    2        6
    3        8
    4       10
    5       12
    6       14
    7       16
    8       18
    9       20
```

Fig. 8.4 | Calculating values to be placed into the elements of an array.

Line 9 uses the modifier **const** to declare the constant ARRAY_LENGTH, whose value is 10. Constants must be initialized when they're declared and cannot be modified thereafter. We declare constants with all capital letters by convention to make them stand out in the code.

Common Programming Error 8.2

Assigning a value to a named constant after it's been initialized is a compilation error.

Common Programming Error 8.3
Attempting to declare a named constant without initializing it is a compilation error.

Good Programming Practice 8.1
*Constants also are called **named constants**. Applications using constants often are more readable than those that use literal values (e.g., 10)—a named constant such as ARRAY_LENGTH clearly indicates its purpose, whereas a literal value could have different meanings based on the context in which it's used. Another advantage to using named constants is that if the value of the constant must be changed, the change is necessary only in the declaration, thus reducing the cost of maintaining the code.*

Good Programming Practice 8.2
*Defining the size of an array as a constant variable instead of a literal constant makes programs clearer. This technique eliminates so-called **magic numbers**. For example, repeatedly mentioning the size 10 in array-processing code for a 10-element array gives the number 10 an artificial significance and can be confusing when the program includes other 10s that have nothing to do with the array size.*

Summing the Elements of an Array

Often, the elements of an array represent a series of values to be used in a calculation. For example, if the elements of an array represent exam grades, an instructor may wish to total the elements and use that total to calculate the class average for the exam. The GradeBook examples later in the chapter (Fig. 8.15 and Fig. 8.20) use this technique.

```
1   // Fig. 8.5: SumArray.cs
2   // Computing the sum of the elements of an array.
3   using System;
4
5   public class SumArray
6   {
7      public static void Main( string[] args )
8      {
9         int[] array = { 87, 68, 94, 100, 83, 78, 85, 91, 76, 87 };
10        int total = 0;
11
12        // add each element's value to total
13        for ( int counter = 0; counter < array.Length; counter++ )
14           total += array[ counter ];
15
16        Console.WriteLine( "Total of array elements: {0}", total );
17     } // end Main
18  } // end class SumArray
```

```
Total of array elements: 849
```

Fig. 8.5 | Computing the sum of the elements of an array.

The application in Fig. 8.5 sums the values contained in a 10-element integer array. The application creates and initializes the array at line 9. The `for` statement performs the calculations. [*Note:* The values supplied as array initializers are often read into an application, rather than specified in an initializer list. For example, an application could input the values from a user or from a file on disk (as discussed in Chapter 17, Files and Streams). Reading the data into an application makes the application more reusable, because it can be used with *different* sets of data.]

Using Bar Charts to Display Array Data Graphically

Many applications present data to users in a graphical manner. For example, numeric values are often displayed as bars in a bar chart. In such a chart, longer bars represent proportionally larger numeric values. One simple way to display numeric data graphically is with a bar chart that shows each numeric value as a bar of asterisks (*).

An instructor might graph the number of grades in each of several categories to visualize the grade distribution for an exam. Suppose the grades on an exam were 87, 68, 94, 100, 83, 78, 85, 91, 76 and 87. There was one grade of 100, two grades in the 90s, four grades in the 80s, two grades in the 70s, one grade in the 60s and no grades below 60. Our next application (Fig. 8.6) stores this grade distribution data in an array of 11 elements, each corresponding to a category of grades. For example, `array[0]` indicates the number of grades in the range 0–9, `array[7]` the number of grades in the range 70–79 and `array[10]` the number of 100 grades. The two versions of class `GradeBook` later in the chapter (Figs. 8.15 and 8.20) contain code that calculates these grade frequencies based on a set of grades. For now, we manually create `array` by examining the set of grades and initializing the elements of `array` to the number of values in each range (line 9).

```
 1   // Fig. 8.6: BarChart.cs
 2   // Bar chart displaying application.
 3   using System;
 4
 5   public class BarChart
 6   {
 7      public static void Main( string[] args )
 8      {
 9         int[] array = { 0, 0, 0, 0, 0, 0, 1, 2, 4, 2, 1 }; // distribution
10
11         Console.WriteLine( "Grade distribution:" );
12
13         // for each array element, output a bar of the chart
14         for ( int counter = 0; counter < array.Length; counter++ )
15         {
16            // output bar labels ( "00-09: ", ..., "90-99: ", "100: " )
17            if ( counter == 10 )
18               Console.Write( "  100: " );
19            else
20               Console.Write( "{0:D2}-{1:D2}: ",
21                  counter * 10, counter * 10 + 9 );
22
```

Fig. 8.6 | Bar chart displaying application. (Part 1 of 2.)

```
23              // display bar of asterisks
24              for ( int stars = 0; stars < array[ counter ]; stars++ )
25                Console.Write( "*" );
26
27              Console.WriteLine(); // start a new line of output
28          } // end outer for
29      } // end Main
30  } // end class BarChart
```

```
Grade distribution:
00-09:
10-19:
20-29:
30-39:
40-49:
50-59:
60-69: *
70-79: **
80-89: ****
90-99: **
  100: *
```

Fig. 8.6 | Bar chart displaying application. (Part 2 of 2.)

The application reads the numbers from the array and graphs the information as a bar chart. Each grade range is followed by a bar of asterisks indicating the number of grades in that range. To label each bar, lines 17–21 output a grade range (e.g., "70-79: ") based on the current value of counter. When counter is 10, line 18 outputs " 100: " to align the colon with the other bar labels. When counter is not 10, line 20 uses the format items {0:D2} and {1:D2} to output the label of the grade range. The format specifier D indicates that the value should be formatted as an integer, and the number after the D indicates how many digits this formatted integer must contain. The 2 indicates that values with fewer than two digits should begin with a **leading 0**.

The nested for statement (lines 24–25) outputs the bars. Note the loop-continuation condition at line 24 (stars < array[counter]). Each time the application reaches the inner for, the loop counts from 0 up to one less than array[counter], thus using a value in array to determine the number of asterisks to display. In this example, array[0]–array[5] contain 0s because no students received a grade below 60. Thus, the application displays no asterisks next to the first six grade ranges.

Using the Elements of an Array as Counters

Sometimes, applications use counter variables to summarize data, such as the results of a survey. In Fig. 7.7, we used separate counters in our die-rolling application to track the number of times each face of a six-sided die appeared as the application rolled the die 6000 times. An array version of the application in Fig. 7.7 is shown in Fig. 8.7.

Figure 8.7 uses array frequency (line 10) to count the occurrences of each side of the die. *The single statement in line 14 of this application replaces lines 26–46 of Fig. 7.7.* Line 14 uses the random value to determine which frequency element to increment during each iteration of the loop. The calculation in line 14 produces random numbers from 1 to 6, so array frequency must be large enough to store six counters. We use a seven-element array in which we ignore frequency[0]—it's more logical to have the face value 1 increment frequency[1] than frequency[0]. Thus, each face value is used as an index for array frequency. We also replaced lines 50–52 of Fig. 7.7 by looping through array frequency to output the results (Fig. 8.7, lines 19–20).

```
1   // Fig. 8.7: RollDie.cs
2   // Roll a six-sided die 6000 times.
3   using System;
4
5   public class RollDie
6   {
7      public static void Main( string[] args )
8      {
9         Random randomNumbers = new Random(); // random-number generator
10        int[] frequency = new int[ 7 ]; // array of frequency counters
11
12        // roll die 6000 times; use die value as frequency index
13        for ( int roll = 1; roll <= 6000; roll++ )
14           ++frequency[ randomNumbers.Next( 1, 7 ) ];
15
16        Console.WriteLine( "{0}{1,10}", "Face", "Frequency" );
17
18        // output each array element's value
19        for ( int face = 1; face < frequency.Length; face++ )
20           Console.WriteLine( "{0,4}{1,10}", face, frequency[ face ] );
21     } // end Main
22  } // end class RollDie
```

```
Face Frequency
   1       956
   2       981
   3      1001
   4      1030
   5      1035
   6       997
```

Fig. 8.7 | Roll a six-sided die 6000 times.

Using Arrays to Analyze Survey Results
Our next example uses arrays to summarize data collected in a survey. Consider the following problem statement:

> *Twenty students were asked to rate on a scale of 1 to 5 the quality of the food in the student cafeteria, with 1 being "awful" and 5 being "excellent." Place the 20 responses in an integer array and determine the frequency of each rating.*

This is a typical array-processing application (Fig. 8.8). We wish to summarize the number of responses of each type (that is, 1–5). Array responses (lines 10–11) is a 20-element integer array containing the students' survey responses. The last value in the array is intentionally an incorrect response (14). When a C# program executes, array element indices are checked for validity—all indices must be greater than or equal to 0 and less than the length of the array. Any attempt to access an element outside that range of indices results in a runtime error that is known as an IndexOutOfRangeException. At the end of this section, we'll discuss the invalid response value, demonstrate array **bounds checking** and introduce C#'s exception-handling mechanism, which can be used to detect and handle an IndexOutOfRangeException.

```csharp
1   // Fig. 8.8: StudentPoll.cs
2   // Poll analysis application.
3   using System;
4
5   public class StudentPoll
6   {
7      public static void Main( string[] args )
8      {
9         // student response array (more typically, input at run time)
10        int[] responses = { 1, 2, 5, 4, 3, 5, 2, 1, 3, 3, 1, 4, 3, 3, 3,
11           2, 3, 3, 2, 14 };
12        int[] frequency = new int[ 6 ]; // array of frequency counters
13
14        // for each answer, select responses element and use that value
15        // as frequency index to determine element to increment
16        for ( int answer = 0; answer < responses.Length; answer++ )
17        {
18           try
19           {
20              ++frequency[ responses[ answer ] ];
21           } // end try
22           catch ( IndexOutOfRangeException ex )
23           {
24              Console.WriteLine( ex.Message );
25              Console.WriteLine( "   responses({0}) = {1}\n",
26                 answer, responses[ answer ] );
27           } // end catch
28        } // end for
29
30        Console.WriteLine( "{0}{1,10}", "Rating", "Frequency" );
31
32        // output each array element's value
33        for ( int rating = 1; rating < frequency.Length; rating++ )
34           Console.WriteLine( "{0,6}{1,10}", rating, frequency[ rating ] );
35     } // end Main
36  } // end class StudentPoll
```

```
Index was outside the bounds of the array.
   responses(19) = 14

Rating Frequency
     1         3
     2         4
     3         8
     4         2
     5         2
```

Fig. 8.8 | Poll analysis application.

The *frequency* Array

We use the *six-element* array frequency (line 12) to count the number of occurrences of each response. Each element is used as a counter for one of the possible types of survey responses—frequency[1] counts the number of students who rated the food as 1, frequency[2] counts the number of students who rated the food as 2, and so on.

Summarizing the Results

The for statement (lines 16–28) reads the responses from the array responses one at a time and increments one of the counters frequency[1] to frequency[5]; we ignore frequency[0] because the survey responses are limited to the range 1–5. The key statement in the loop appears in line 20. This statement increments the appropriate frequency counter as determined by the value of responses[answer].

Let's step through the first few iterations of the for statement:

- When the counter answer is 0, responses[answer] is the value of responses[0] (that is, 1—see line 10). In this case, frequency[responses[answer]] is interpreted as frequency[1], and the counter frequency[1] is incremented by one. To evaluate the expression, we begin with the value in the *innermost* set of brackets (answer, currently 0). The value of answer is plugged into the expression, and the next set of brackets (responses[answer]) is evaluated. That value is used as the index for the frequency array to determine which counter to increment (in this case, frequency[1]).

- The next time through the loop answer is 1, responses[answer] is the value of responses[1] (that is, 2—see line 10), so frequency[responses[answer]] is interpreted as frequency[2], causing frequency[2] to be incremented.

- When answer is 2, responses[answer] is the value of responses[2] (that is, 5—see line 10), so frequency[responses[answer]] is interpreted as frequency[5], causing frequency[5] to be incremented, and so on.

Regardless of the number of responses processed in the survey, only a six-element array (in which we ignore element zero) is required to summarize the results, because all the correct response values are between 1 and 5, and the index values for a six-element array are 0–5. In the output in Fig. 8.8, the frequency column summarizes only 19 of the 20 values in the responses array—the last element of the array responses contains an incorrect response that was not counted.

Exception Handling: Processing the Incorrect Response

An **exception** indicates a problem that occurs while a program executes. The name "exception" suggests that the problem occurs infrequently—if the "rule" is that a statement normally executes correctly, then the problem represents the "exception to the rule." **Exception handling** enables you to create **fault-tolerant programs** that can resolve (or handle) exceptions. In many cases, this allows a program to continue executing as if no problems were encountered. For example, the **Student Poll** application still displays results (Fig. 8.8), even though one of the responses was out of range. More severe problems might prevent a program from continuing normal execution, instead requiring the program to notify the user of the problem, then terminate. When the runtime or a method detects a problem, such as an invalid array index or an invalid method argument, it **throws** an exception—that is, an exception occurs.

The **try** Statement

To handle an exception, place any code that might throw an exception in a **try statement** (lines 18–27). The **try block** (lines 18–21) contains the code that might *throw* an exception, and the **catch block** (lines 22–27) contains the code that *handles* the exception if one occurs. You can have many `catch` blocks to handle different types of exceptions that might be thrown in the corresponding `try` block. When line 20 correctly increments an element of the `frequency` array, lines 22–27 are ignored. The braces that delimit the bodies of the try and catch blocks are required.

Executing the **catch** Block

When the program encounters the value 14 in the `responses` array, it attempts to add 1 to `frequency[14]`, which does not exist—the `frequency` array has only six elements. Because array bounds checking is performed at execution time, the Common Language Runtime generates an exception—specifically line 20 throws an **IndexOutOfRange-Exception** to notify the program of this problem. At this point the `try` block terminates and the `catch` block begins executing—if you declared any variables in the `try` block, they're now out of scope and are not accessible in the `catch` block.

The `catch` block declares a type (`IndexOutOfRangeException`) and an exception parameter (`ex`). The `catch` block can handle exceptions of the specified type. Inside the catch block, you can use the parameter's identifier to interact with a caught exception object.

Error-Prevention Tip 8.1

When writing code to access an array element, ensure that the array index remains greater than or equal to 0 and less than the length of the array. This helps prevent IndexOutOf-RangeExceptions in your program.

Message Property of the Exception Parameter

When lines 22–27 *catch* the exception, the program displays a message indicating the problem that occurred. Line 24 uses the exception object's **Message property** to get the error message that is stored in the exception object and display it. Once the message is displayed in this example, the exception is considered handled and the program continues with the next statement after the `catch` block's closing brace. In this example, the end of the for statement is reached (line 28), so the program continues with the increment of the control variable in line 16. We use exception handling again in Chapter 10 and Chapter 13 presents a deeper look at exception handling.

8.5 Case Study: Card Shuffling and Dealing Simulation

So far, this chapter's examples have used arrays of value-type elements. This section uses random-number generation and an *array of reference-type elements*—namely, objects representing playing cards—to develop a class that simulates card shuffling and dealing. This class can then be used to implement applications that play card games. The exercises at the end of the chapter use the techniques developed here to build a poker application.

We first develop class `Card` (Fig. 8.9), which represents a playing card that has a face (e.g., "Ace", "Deuce", "Three", ..., "Jack", "Queen", "King") and a suit (e.g., "Hearts", "Diamonds", "Clubs", "Spades"). Next, we develop class `DeckOfCards` (Fig. 8.10), which creates a deck of 52 playing cards in which each element is a `Card` object. Then we build an application (Fig. 8.11) that uses class `DeckOfCards`'s card shuffling and dealing capabilities.

Class **Card**

Class Card (Fig. 8.9) contains two string instance variables—face and suit—that are used to store references to the *face value* and *suit name* for a specific Card. The constructor for the class (lines 9–13) receives two strings that it uses to initialize face and suit. Method ToString (lines 16–19) creates a string consisting of the face of the card, the string " of " and the suit of the card. Recall from Chapter 7 that the + operator can be used to concatenate (i.e., combine) several strings to form one larger string. Card's ToString method can be invoked *explicitly* to obtain a string representation of a Card object (e.g., "Ace of Spades"). The ToString method of an object is called *implicitly* in many cases when the object is used where a string is expected (e.g., when WriteLine outputs the object or when the object is concatenated to a string using the + operator). For this behavior to occur, ToString must be declared with the header exactly as shown in line 16 of Fig. 8.9. We'll explain the purpose of the override keyword in more detail when we discuss inheritance in Chapter 11.

```
1   // Fig. 8.9: Card.cs
2   // Card class represents a playing card.
3   public class Card
4   {
5      private string face; // face of card ("Ace", "Deuce", ...)
6      private string suit; // suit of card ("Hearts", "Diamonds", ...)
7
8      // two-parameter constructor initializes card's face and suit
9      public Card( string cardFace, string cardSuit )
10     {
11        face = cardFace; // initialize face of card
12        suit = cardSuit; // initialize suit of card
13     } // end two-parameter Card constructor
14
15     // return string representation of Card
16     public override string ToString()
17     {
18        return face + " of " + suit;
19     } // end method ToString
20  } // end class Card
```

Fig. 8.9 | Card class represents a playing card.

Class **DeckOfCards**

Class DeckOfCards (Fig. 8.10) declares an instance-variable named deck that will refer to an array of Card objects (line 7). Like simple-type array variable declarations, the declaration of a variable for an array of objects (e.g., Card[] deck) includes the type of the elements in the array, followed by square brackets and the name of the array variable. Class DeckOfCards also declares int instance variable currentCard (line 8), representing the next Card to be dealt from the deck array, and named constant NUMBER_OF_CARDS (line 9), indicating the number of Cards in the deck (52).

Class **DeckOfCards**: *Constructor*

The class's constructor instantiates the deck array (line 19) to be of size NUMBER_OF_CARDS. When first created, the elements of the deck array are null by default, so the constructor

```csharp
 1   // Fig. 8.10: DeckOfCards.cs
 2   // DeckOfCards class represents a deck of playing cards.
 3   using System;
 4
 5   public class DeckOfCards
 6   {
 7      private Card[] deck; // array of Card objects
 8      private int currentCard; // index of next Card to be dealt (0-51)
 9      private const int NUMBER_OF_CARDS = 52; // constant number of Cards
10      private Random randomNumbers; // random-number generator
11
12      // constructor fills deck of Cards
13      public DeckOfCards()
14      {
15         string[] faces = { "Ace", "Deuce", "Three", "Four", "Five", "Six",
16            "Seven", "Eight", "Nine", "Ten", "Jack", "Queen", "King" };
17         string[] suits = { "Hearts", "Diamonds", "Clubs", "Spades" };
18
19         deck = new Card[ NUMBER_OF_CARDS ]; // create array of Card objects
20         currentCard = 0; // set currentCard so deck[ 0 ] is dealt first
21         randomNumbers = new Random(); // create random-number generator
22
23         // populate deck with Card objects
24         for ( int count = 0; count < deck.Length; count++ )
25            deck[ count ] =
26               new Card( faces[ count % 13 ], suits[ count / 13 ] );
27      } // end DeckOfCards constructor
28
29      // shuffle deck of Cards with one-pass algorithm
30      public void Shuffle()
31      {
32         // after shuffling, dealing should start at deck[ 0 ] again
33         currentCard = 0; // reinitialize currentCard
34
35         // for each Card, pick another random Card and swap them
36         for ( int first = 0; first < deck.Length; first++ )
37         {
38            // select a random number between 0 and 51
39            int second = randomNumbers.Next( NUMBER_OF_CARDS );
40
41            // swap current Card with randomly selected Card
42            Card temp = deck[ first ];
43            deck[ first ] = deck[ second ];
44            deck[ second ] = temp;
45         } // end for
46      } // end method Shuffle
47
48      // deal one Card
49      public Card DealCard()
50      {
51         // determine whether Cards remain to be dealt
52         if ( currentCard < deck.Length )
53            return deck[ currentCard++ ]; // return current Card in array
```

Fig. 8.10 | DeckOfCards class represents a deck of playing cards. (Part 1 of 2.)

```
54            else
55               return null; // indicate that all Cards were dealt
56      } // end method DealCard
57   } // end class DeckOfCards
```

Fig. 8.10 | DeckOfCards class represents a deck of playing cards. (Part 2 of 2.)

uses a for statement (lines 24–26) to fill the deck array with Cards. The for statement initializes control variable count to 0 and loops while count is less than deck.Length, causing count to take on each integer value from 0 to 51 (the indices of the deck array). Each Card is instantiated and initialized with two strings—one from the faces array (which contains the strings "Ace" through "King") and one from the suits array (which contains the strings "Hearts", "Diamonds", "Clubs" and "Spades"). The calculation count % 13 always results in a value from 0 to 12 (the 13 indices of the faces array in lines 15–16), and the calculation count / 13 always results in a value from 0 to 3 (the four indices of the suits array in line 17). When the deck array is initialized, it contains the Cards with faces "Ace" through "King" in order for each suit.

Class *DeckOfCards: Shuffle Method*
Method Shuffle (lines 30–46) shuffles the Cards in the deck. The method loops through all 52 Cards (array indices 0 to 51). For each Card, a number between 0 and 51 is picked randomly to select another Card. Next, the current Card object and the randomly selected Card object are swapped in the array. This exchange is performed by the three assignments in lines 42–44. The extra variable temp temporarily stores one of the two Card objects being swapped. *The swap cannot be performed with only the two statements*

```
deck[ first ] = deck[ second ];
deck[ second ] = deck[ first ];
```

If deck[first] is the "Ace" of "Spades" and deck[second] is the "Queen" of "Hearts", then after the first assignment, both array elements contain the "Queen" of "Hearts", and the "Ace" of "Spades" is lost—hence, the extra variable temp is needed. After the for loop terminates, the Card objects are randomly ordered. Only 52 swaps are made in a single pass of the entire array, and the array of Card objects is shuffled. [*Note:* It's recommended that you use a so-called unbiased shuffling algorithm for real card games. Such an algorithm ensures that all possible shuffled card sequences are equally likely to occur. A popular unbiased shuffling algorithm is the Fisher-Yates algorithm—en.wikipedia.org/wiki/Fisher%E2%80%93Yates_shuffle. This page also shows how to implement the algorithm in several programming languages.]

Class *DeckOfCards: DealCard Method*
Method DealCard (lines 49–56) deals one Card in the array. Recall that currentCard indicates the index of the next Card to be dealt (i.e., the Card at the top of the deck). Thus, line 52 compares currentCard to the length of the deck array. If the deck is not empty (i.e., currentCard is less than 52), line 53 returns the top Card and increments currentCard to prepare for the next call to DealCard—otherwise, null is returned.

Shuffling and Dealing Cards

The application of Fig. 8.11 demonstrates the card shuffling and dealing capabilities of class DeckOfCards (Fig. 8.10). Line 10 creates a DeckOfCards object named myDeckOf-Cards. Recall that the DeckOfCards constructor creates the deck with the 52 Card objects in order by suit and face. Line 11 invokes myDeckOfCards's Shuffle method to rearrange the Card objects. The for statement in lines 14–20 deals all 52 Cards in the deck and displays them in four columns of 13 Cards each. Line 16 deals and displays a Card object by invoking myDeckOfCards's DealCard method. When Console.Write outputs a Card with string formatting, the Card's ToString method (declared in lines 16–19 of Fig. 8.9) is invoked implicitly. Because the field width is *negative*, the result is output *left* justified in a field of width 19.

```csharp
1   // Fig. 8.11: DeckOfCardsTest.cs
2   // Card shuffling and dealing application.
3   using System;
4
5   public class DeckOfCardsTest
6   {
7      // execute application
8      public static void Main( string[] args )
9      {
10        DeckOfCards myDeckOfCards = new DeckOfCards();
11        myDeckOfCards.Shuffle(); // place Cards in random order
12
13        // display all 52 Cards in the order in which they are dealt
14        for ( int i = 0; i < 52; i++ )
15        {
16           Console.Write( "{0,-19}", myDeckOfCards.DealCard() );
17
18           if ( ( i + 1 ) % 4 == 0 )
19              Console.WriteLine();
20        } // end for
21     } // end Main
22  } // end class DeckOfCardsTest
```

Eight of Clubs	Ten of Clubs	Ten of Spades	Four of Spades
Ace of Spades	Jack of Spades	Three of Spades	Seven of Spades
Three of Diamonds	Five of Clubs	Eight of Spades	Five of Hearts
Ace of Hearts	Ten of Hearts	Deuce of Hearts	Deuce of Clubs
Jack of Hearts	Nine of Spades	Four of Hearts	Seven of Clubs
Queen of Spades	Seven of Diamonds	Five of Diamonds	Ace of Clubs
Four of Clubs	Ten of Diamonds	Jack of Clubs	Six of Diamonds
Eight of Diamonds	King of Hearts	Three of Clubs	King of Spades
King of Diamonds	Six of Spades	Deuce of Spades	Five of Spades
Queen of Clubs	King of Clubs	Queen of Hearts	Seven of Hearts
Ace of Diamonds	Deuce of Diamonds	Four of Diamonds	Nine of Clubs
Queen of Diamonds	Jack of Diamonds	Six of Hearts	Nine of Diamonds
Nine of Hearts	Three of Hearts	Six of Clubs	Eight of Hearts

Fig. 8.11 | Card shuffling and dealing application.

8.6 foreach Statement

In previous examples, we demonstrated how to use counter-controlled for statements to iterate through the elements in an array. In this section, we introduce the **foreach statement**, which iterates through the elements of an entire array or collection. This section discusses how to use the foreach statement to loop through an array. We show how to use it with collections in Chapter 23. The syntax of a foreach statement is:

```
foreach ( type identifier in arrayName )
    statement
```

where *type* and *identifier* are the type and name (e.g., int number) of the **iteration variable**, and *arrayName* is the array through which to iterate. The type of the iteration variable must be consistent with the type of the elements in the array. As the next example illustrates, the iteration variable represents successive values in the array on successive iterations of the foreach statement.

Figure 8.12 uses the foreach statement (lines 13–14) to calculate the sum of the integers in an array of student grades. The type specified is int, because array contains int values—therefore, the loop will select one int value from the array during each iteration. The foreach statement iterates through successive values in the array one by one. The foreach header can be read concisely as "for each iteration, assign the next element of array to int variable number, then execute the following statement." Thus, for each iteration, identifier number represents the next int value in the array. Lines 13–14 are equivalent to the following counter-controlled repetition used in lines 13–14 of Fig. 8.5 to total the integers in array:

```
for ( int counter = 0; counter < array.Length; counter++ )
    total += array[ counter ];
```

Common Programming Error 8.4

The foreach statement can be used only to access array elements—it cannot be used to modify elements. Any attempt to change the value of the iteration variable in the body of a foreach statement will cause a compilation error.

```
 1   // Fig. 8.12: ForEachTest.cs
 2   // Using the foreach statement to total integers in an array.
 3   using System;
 4
 5   public class ForEachTest
 6   {
 7      public static void Main( string[] args )
 8      {
 9         int[] array = { 87, 68, 94, 100, 83, 78, 85, 91, 76, 87 };
10         int total = 0;
11
12         // add each element's value to total
13         foreach ( int number in array )
14            total += number;
15
```

Fig. 8.12 | Using the foreach statement to total integers in an array. (Part 1 of 2.)

```
16          Console.WriteLine( "Total of array elements: {0}", total );
17      } // end Main
18  } // end class ForEachTest
```

```
Total of array elements: 849
```

Fig. 8.12 | Using the foreach statement to total integers in an array. (Part 2 of 2.)

The foreach statement can be used in place of the for statement whenever code looping through an array does not require access to the counter indicating the index of the current array element. For example, totaling the integers in an array requires access only to the element values—the index of each element is irrelevant. However, if an application must use a counter for some reason other than simply to loop through an array (e.g., to display an index number next to each array element value, as in the examples earlier in this chapter), use the for statement.

8.7 Passing Arrays and Array Elements to Methods

To pass an array argument to a method, specify the name of the array *without any brackets*. For example, if hourlyTemperatures is declared as

```
double[] hourlyTemperatures = new double[ 24 ];
```

then the method call

```
ModifyArray( hourlyTemperatures );
```

passes the reference of array hourlyTemperatures to method ModifyArray. Every array object "knows" its own length (and makes it available via its Length property). Thus, when we pass an array object's reference to a method, we need not pass the array length as an additional argument.

For a method to receive an array reference through a method call, the method's parameter list must specify an array parameter. For example, the method header for method ModifyArray might be written as

```
void ModifyArray( double[] b )
```

indicating that ModifyArray receives the reference of an array of doubles in parameter b. The method call passes array hourlyTemperature's reference, so when the called method uses the array variable b, it refers to the same array object as hourlyTemperatures in the calling method.

When an argument to a method is an entire array or an individual array element of a reference type, the called method receives a *copy of the reference*. However, when an argument to a method is an individual array element of a value type, the called method receives a *copy of the element's value*. To pass an individual array element to a method, use the indexed name of the array as an argument in the method call. If you want to pass a value-type array element to a method by reference, you must use the ref keyword as shown in Section 7.16.

Figure 8.13 demonstrates the difference between passing an entire array and passing a value-type array element to a method. The foreach statement at lines 17–18 outputs the five elements of array (an array of int values). Line 20 invokes method ModifyArray, passing array as an argument. Method ModifyArray (lines 37–41) receives a copy of array's reference and uses the reference to multiply each of array's elements by 2. To prove that array's elements (in Main) were modified, the foreach statement at lines 24–25 outputs the five elements of array again. As the output shows, method ModifyArray doubled the value of each element.

```
1   // Fig. 8.13: PassArray.cs
2   // Passing arrays and individual array elements to methods.
3   using System;
4
5   public class PassArray
6   {
7      // Main creates array and calls ModifyArray and ModifyElement
8      public static void Main( string[] args )
9      {
10        int[] array = { 1, 2, 3, 4, 5 };
11
12        Console.WriteLine(
13           "Effects of passing reference to entire array:\n" +
14           "The values of the original array are:" );
15
16        // output original array elements
17        foreach ( int value in array )
18           Console.Write( "   {0}", value );
19
20        ModifyArray( array ); // pass array reference
21        Console.WriteLine( "\n\nThe values of the modified array are:" );
22
23        // output modified array elements
24        foreach ( int value in array )
25           Console.Write( "   {0}", value );
26
27        Console.WriteLine(
28           "\n\nEffects of passing array element value:\n" +
29           "array[3] before ModifyElement: {0}", array[ 3 ] );
30
31        ModifyElement( array[ 3 ] ); // attempt to modify array[ 3 ]
32        Console.WriteLine(
33           "array[3] after ModifyElement: {0}", array[ 3 ] );
34     } // end Main
35
36     // multiply each element of an array by 2
37     public static void ModifyArray( int[] array2 )
38     {
39        for ( int counter = 0; counter < array2.Length; counter++ )
40           array2[ counter ] *= 2;
41     } // end method ModifyArray
42
43     // multiply argument by 2
44     public static void ModifyElement( int element )
45     {
46        element *= 2;
```

Fig. 8.13 | Passing arrays and individual array elements to methods. (Part 1 of 2.)

```
47         Console.WriteLine(
48            "Value of element in ModifyElement: {0}", element );
49      } // end method ModifyElement
50    } // end class PassArray
```

```
Effects of passing reference to entire array:
The values of the original array are:
   1   2   3   4   5

The values of the modified array are:
   2   4   6   8   10

Effects of passing array element value:
array[3] before ModifyElement: 8
Value of element in ModifyElement: 16
array[3] after ModifyElement: 8
```

Fig. 8.13 | Passing arrays and individual array elements to methods. (Part 2 of 2.)

Figure 8.13 next demonstrates that when a copy of an individual value-type array element is passed to a method, modifying the copy in the called method does *not* affect the original value of that element in the calling method's array. To show the value of array[3] before invoking method ModifyElement, lines 27–29 output the value of array[3], which is 8. Line 31 calls method ModifyElement and passes array[3] as an argument. Remember that array[3] is actually one int value (8) in array. Therefore, the application passes a copy of the value of array[3]. Method ModifyElement (lines 44–49) multiplies the value received as an argument by 2, stores the result in its parameter element, then outputs the value of element (16). Since method parameters, like local variables, cease to exist when the method in which they're declared completes execution, the method parameter element is destroyed when method ModifyElement terminates. Thus, when the application returns control to Main, lines 32–33 output the unmodified value of array[3] (i.e., 8).

8.8 Passing Arrays by Value and by Reference

In C#, a variable that "stores" an object, such as an array, does not actually store the object itself. Instead, such a variable stores a reference to the object. The distinction between reference-type variables and value-type variables raises some subtle issues that you must understand to create secure, stable programs.

As you know, when an application passes an argument to a method, the called method receives a copy of that argument's value. Changes to the local copy in the called method do *not* affect the original variable in the caller. If the argument is of a reference type, the method makes a copy of the reference, not a copy of the actual object that's referenced. The local copy of the reference also refers to the original object, which means that changes to the object in the called method affect the original object.

Performance Tip 8.1

Passing references to arrays and other objects makes sense for performance reasons. If arrays were passed by value, a copy of each element would be passed. For large, frequently passed arrays, this would waste time and consume considerable storage for the copies of the arrays.

In Section 7.16, you learned that C# allows variables to be passed by reference with keyword ref. You can also use keyword ref to pass a *reference-type variable* by reference, which allows the called method to modify the original variable in the caller and make that variable refer to a different object. This is a subtle capability, which, if misused, can lead to problems. For instance, when a reference-type object like an array is passed with ref, the called method actually gains control over the reference itself, allowing the called method to replace the original reference in the caller with a reference to a different object, or even with null. Such behavior can lead to unpredictable effects, which can be disastrous in mission-critical applications. The application in Fig. 8.14 demonstrates the subtle difference between passing a reference by value and passing a reference by reference with keyword ref.

Lines 11 and 14 declare two integer array variables, firstArray and firstArrayCopy. Line 11 initializes firstArray with the values 1, 2 and 3. The assignment statement at line 14 copies the reference stored in firstArray to variable firstArrayCopy, causing these variables to reference the same array object. We make the copy of the reference so that we can determine later whether reference firstArray gets overwritten. The for statement at lines 23–24 displays the contents of firstArray before it's passed to method FirstDouble (line 27) so that we can verify that the called method indeed changes the array's contents.

```
1   // Fig. 8.14: ArrayReferenceTest.cs
2   // Testing the effects of passing array references
3   // by value and by reference.
4   using System;
5
6   public class ArrayReferenceTest
7   {
8      public static void Main( string[] args )
9      {
10        // create and initialize firstArray
11        int[] firstArray = { 1, 2, 3 };
12
13        // copy the reference in variable firstArray
14        int[] firstArrayCopy = firstArray;
15
16        Console.WriteLine(
17           "Test passing firstArray reference by value" );
18
19        Console.Write( "\nContents of firstArray " +
20           "before calling FirstDouble:\n\t" );
21
22        // display contents of firstArray
23        for ( int i = 0; i < firstArray.Length; i++ )
24           Console.Write( "{0} ", firstArray[ i ] );
25
26        // pass variable firstArray by value to FirstDouble
27        FirstDouble( firstArray );
28
29        Console.Write( "\n\nContents of firstArray after " +
30           "calling FirstDouble\n\t" );
```

Fig. 8.14 | Passing an array reference by value and by reference. (Part 1 of 3.)

```
31
32        // display contents of firstArray
33        for ( int i = 0; i < firstArray.Length; i++ )
34           Console.Write( "{0} ", firstArray[ i ] );
35
36        // test whether reference was changed by FirstDouble
37        if ( firstArray == firstArrayCopy )
38           Console.WriteLine(
39              "\n\nThe references refer to the same array" );
40        else
41           Console.WriteLine(
42              "\n\nThe references refer to different arrays" );
43
44        // create and initialize secondArray
45        int[] secondArray = { 1, 2, 3 };
46
47        // copy the reference in variable secondArray
48        int[] secondArrayCopy = secondArray;
49
50        Console.WriteLine( "\nTest passing secondArray " +
51           "reference by reference" );
52
53        Console.Write( "\nContents of secondArray " +
54           "before calling SecondDouble:\n\t" );
55
56        // display contents of secondArray before method call
57        for ( int i = 0; i < secondArray.Length; i++ )
58           Console.Write( "{0} ", secondArray[ i ] );
59
60        // pass variable secondArray by reference to SecondDouble
61        SecondDouble( ref secondArray );
62
63        Console.Write( "\n\nContents of secondArray " +
64           "after calling SecondDouble:\n\t" );
65
66        // display contents of secondArray after method call
67        for ( int i = 0; i < secondArray.Length; i++ )
68           Console.Write( "{0} ", secondArray[ i ] );
69
70        // test whether reference was changed by SecondDouble
71        if ( secondArray == secondArrayCopy )
72           Console.WriteLine(
73              "\n\nThe references refer to the same array" );
74        else
75           Console.WriteLine(
76              "\n\nThe references refer to different arrays" );
77     } // end Main
78
79     // modify elements of array and attempt to modify reference
80     public static void FirstDouble( int[] array )
81     {
```

Fig. 8.14 | Passing an array reference by value and by reference. (Part 2 of 3.)

```
82            // double each element's value
83            for ( int i = 0; i < array.Length; i++ )
84               array[ i ] *= 2;
85
86            // create new object and assign its reference to array
87            array = new int[] { 11, 12, 13 };
88         } // end method FirstDouble
89
90         // modify elements of array and change reference array
91         // to refer to a new array
92         public static void SecondDouble( ref int[] array )
93         {
94            // double each element's value
95            for ( int i = 0; i < array.Length; i++ )
96               array[ i ] *= 2;
97
98            // create new object and assign its reference to array
99            array = new int[] { 11, 12, 13 };
100        } // end method SecondDouble
101     } // end class ArrayReferenceTest
```

```
Test passing firstArray reference by value

Contents of firstArray before calling FirstDouble:
      1 2 3

Contents of firstArray after calling FirstDouble
      2 4 6

The references refer to the same array

Test passing secondArray reference by reference

Contents of secondArray before calling SecondDouble:
      1 2 3

Contents of secondArray after calling SecondDouble:
      11 12 13

The references refer to different arrays
```

Fig. 8.14 | Passing an array reference by value and by reference. (Part 3 of 3.)

The for statement in method FirstDouble (lines 83–84) multiplies the values of all the elements in the array by 2. Line 87 creates a new array containing the values 11, 12 and 13, and assigns the array's reference to parameter array in an attempt to overwrite reference firstArray in the caller—this, of course, does not happen, because the reference was passed by value. After method FirstDouble executes, the for statement at lines 33–34 displays the contents of firstArray, demonstrating that the values of the elements have been changed by the method. The if...else statement at lines 37–42 uses the == operator to compare references firstArray (which we just attempted to overwrite) and firstArray-Copy. The expression in line 37 evaluates to true if the operands of operator == reference the same object. In this case, the object represented by firstArray is the array created in line 11—not the array created in method FirstDouble (line 87)—so the original reference stored in firstArray was not modified.

Lines 45–76 perform similar tests, using array variables secondArray and second-ArrayCopy, and method SecondDouble (lines 92–100). Method SecondDouble performs the same operations as FirstDouble, but receives its array argument using keyword ref. In this case, the reference stored in secondArray after the method call is a reference to the array created in line 99 of SecondDouble, demonstrating that a variable passed with keyword ref can be modified by the called method so that the variable in the caller actually points to a *different* object—in this case, an array created in SecondDouble. The if...else statement in lines 71–76 confirms that secondArray and secondArrayCopy no longer refer to the same array.

Software Engineering Observation 8.1

When a method receives a reference-type parameter by value, a copy of the object's reference is passed. This prevents a method from overwriting references passed to that method. In the vast majority of cases, protecting the caller's reference from modification is the desired behavior. If you encounter a situation where you truly want the called procedure to modify the caller's reference, pass the reference-type parameter using keyword ref—but, again, such situations are rare.

Software Engineering Observation 8.2

In C#, references to objects (including arrays) are passed to called methods. A called method receiving a reference to an object in a caller can interact with, and possibly change, the caller's object.

8.9 Case Study: Class GradeBook Using an Array to Store Grades

This section further evolves class GradeBook, introduced in Chapter 4 and expanded in Chapters 5–6. Recall that this class represents a grade book used by an instructor to store and analyze a set of student grades. Previous versions of the class process a set of grades entered by the user, but do not maintain the individual grade values in instance variables of the class. Thus, repeat calculations require the user to re-enter the same grades. One way to solve this problem would be to store each grade entered in an individual instance of the class. For example, we could create instance variables grade1, grade2, ..., grade10 in class GradeBook to store 10 student grades. However, the code to total the grades and determine the class average would be cumbersome, and the class would not be able to process any more than 10 grades at a time. In this section, we solve this problem by storing grades in an array.

Storing Student Grades in an Array in Class *GradeBook*
The version of class GradeBook (Fig. 8.15) presented here uses an array of integers to store the grades of several students on a single exam. This eliminates the need to repeatedly input the same set of grades. Variable grades (which will refer to an array of ints) is declared as an instance variable in line 7—therefore, each GradeBook object maintains its own set of grades. The class's constructor (lines 14–18) has two parameters—the name of the course and an array of grades. When an application (e.g., class GradeBookTest in Fig. 8.16) creates a GradeBook object, the application passes an existing int array to the constructor, which assigns the array's reference to instance variable grades (line 17). The size of array grades is determined by the class that passes the array to the constructor.

Thus, a GradeBook object can process a variable number of grades—as many as are in the array in the caller. The grade values in the passed array could have been input from a user at the keyboard or read from a file on disk (as discussed in Chapter 17). In our test application, we simply initialize an array with a set of grade values (Fig. 8.16, line 9). Once the grades are stored in instance variable grades of class GradeBook, all the class's methods can access the elements of grades as needed to perform various calculations.

```csharp
1   // Fig. 8.15: GradeBook.cs
2   // Grade book using an array to store test grades.
3   using System;
4
5   public class GradeBook
6   {
7      private int[] grades; // array of student grades
8
9      // auto-implemented property CourseName
10     public string CourseName { get; set; }
11
12     // two-parameter constructor initializes
13     // auto-implemented property CourseName and grades array
14     public GradeBook( string name, int[] gradesArray )
15     {
16        CourseName = name; // set CourseName to name
17        grades = gradesArray; // initialize grades array
18     } // end two-parameter GradeBook constructor
19
20     // display a welcome message to the GradeBook user
21     public void DisplayMessage()
22     {
23        // auto-implemented property CourseName gets the name of course
24        Console.WriteLine( "Welcome to the grade book for\n{0}!\n",
25           CourseName );
26     } // end method DisplayMessage
27
28     // perform various operations on the data
29     public void ProcessGrades()
30     {
31        // output grades array
32        OutputGrades();
33
34        // call method GetAverage to calculate the average grade
35        Console.WriteLine( "\nClass average is {0:F}", GetAverage() );
36
37        // call methods GetMinimum and GetMaximum
38        Console.WriteLine( "Lowest grade is {0}\nHighest grade is {1}\n",
39           GetMinimum(), GetMaximum() );
40
41        // call OutputBarChart to display grade distribution chart
42        OutputBarChart();
43     } // end method ProcessGrades
44
```

Fig. 8.15 | Grade book using an array to store test grades. (Part 1 of 3.)

```
45      // find minimum grade
46      public int GetMinimum()
47      {
48         int lowGrade = grades[ 0 ]; // assume grades[ 0 ] is smallest
49
50         // loop through grades array
51         foreach ( int grade in grades )
52         {
53            // if grade lower than lowGrade, assign it to lowGrade
54            if ( grade < lowGrade )
55               lowGrade = grade; // new lowest grade
56         } // end for
57
58         return lowGrade; // return lowest grade
59      } // end method GetMinimum
60
61      // find maximum grade
62      public int GetMaximum()
63      {
64         int highGrade = grades[ 0 ]; // assume grades[ 0 ] is largest
65
66         // loop through grades array
67         foreach ( int grade in grades )
68         {
69            // if grade greater than highGrade, assign it to highGrade
70            if ( grade > highGrade )
71               highGrade = grade; // new highest grade
72         } // end for
73
74         return highGrade; // return highest grade
75      } // end method GetMaximum
76
77      // determine average grade for test
78      public double GetAverage()
79      {
80         int total = 0; // initialize total
81
82         // sum grades for one student
83         foreach ( int grade in grades )
84            total += grade;
85
86         // return average of grades
87         return ( double ) total / grades.Length;
88      } // end method GetAverage
89
90      // output bar chart displaying grade distribution
91      public void OutputBarChart()
92      {
93         Console.WriteLine( "Grade distribution:" );
94
95         // stores frequency of grades in each range of 10 grades
96         int[] frequency = new int[ 11 ];
97
```

Fig. 8.15 | Grade book using an array to store test grades. (Part 2 of 3.)

```
98          // for each grade, increment the appropriate frequency
99          foreach ( int grade in grades )
100            ++frequency[ grade / 10 ];
101
102         // for each grade frequency, display bar in chart
103         for ( int count = 0; count < frequency.Length; count++ )
104         {
105            // output bar label ( "00-09: ", ..., "90-99: ", "100: " )
106            if ( count == 10 )
107               Console.Write( "  100: " );
108            else
109               Console.Write( "{0:D2}-{1:D2}: ",
110                  count * 10, count * 10 + 9 );
111
112            // display bar of asterisks
113            for ( int stars = 0; stars < frequency[ count ]; stars++ )
114               Console.Write( "*" );
115
116            Console.WriteLine(); // start a new line of output
117         } // end outer for
118      } // end method OutputBarChart
119
120      // output the contents of the grades array
121      public void OutputGrades()
122      {
123         Console.WriteLine( "The grades are:\n" );
124
125         // output each student's grade
126         for ( int student = 0; student < grades.Length; student++ )
127            Console.WriteLine( "Student {0,2}: {1,3}",
128               student + 1, grades[ student ] );
129      } // end method OutputGrades
130   } // end class GradeBook
```

Fig. 8.15 | Grade book using an array to store test grades. (Part 3 of 3.)

Method ProcessGrades (lines 29–43) contains a series of method calls that result in the output of a report summarizing the grades. Line 32 calls method OutputGrades to display the contents of array grades. Lines 126–128 in method OutputGrades use a for statement to output the student grades. A for statement, rather than a foreach, must be used in this case, because lines 127–128 use counter variable student's value to output each grade next to a particular student number (see Fig. 8.16). Although array indices start at 0, an instructor would typically number students starting at 1. Thus, lines 127–128 output student + 1 as the student number to produce grade labels "Student 1: ", "Student 2: " and so on.

Method ProcessGrades next calls method GetAverage (line 35) to obtain the average of the grades in the array. Method GetAverage (lines 78–88) uses a foreach statement to total the values in array grades before calculating the average. The iteration variable in the foreach's header (e.g., int grade) indicates that for each iteration, int variable grade takes on a value in array grades. The averaging calculation in line 87 uses grades.Length to determine the number of grades being averaged.

Lines 38–39 in method ProcessGrades call methods GetMinimum and GetMaximum to determine the lowest and highest grades of any student on the exam, respectively. Each of these methods uses a foreach statement to loop through array grades. Lines 51–56 in method GetMinimum loop through the array, and lines 54–55 compare each grade to lowGrade. If a grade is less than lowGrade, lowGrade is set to that grade. When line 58 executes, lowGrade contains the lowest grade in the array. Method GetMaximum (lines 62–75) works the same way as method GetMinimum.

Finally, line 42 in method ProcessGrades calls method OutputBarChart to display a distribution chart of the grade data, using a technique similar to that in Fig. 8.6. In that example, we manually calculated the number of grades in each category (i.e., 0–9, 10–19, ..., 90–99 and 100) by simply looking at a set of grades. In this example, lines 99–100 use a technique similar to that in Figs. 8.7 and 8.8 to calculate the frequency of grades in each category. Line 96 declares variable frequency and initializes it with an array of 11 ints to store the frequency of grades in each grade category. For each grade in array grades, lines 99–100 increment the appropriate element of the frequency array. To determine which element to increment, line 100 divides the current grade by 10, using integer division. For example, if grade is 85, line 100 increments frequency[8] to update the count of grades in the range 80–89. Lines 103–117 next display the bar chart (see Fig. 8.6) based on the values in array frequency. Like lines 24–25 of Fig. 8.6, lines 113–114 of Fig. 8.15 use a value in array frequency to determine the number of asterisks to display in each bar.

Class *GradeBookTest* That Demonstrates Class *GradeBook*

The application of Fig. 8.16 creates an object of class GradeBook (Fig. 8.15) using int array gradesArray (declared and initialized in line 9). Lines 11–12 pass a course name and gradesArray to the GradeBook constructor. Line 13 displays a welcome message, and line 14 invokes the GradeBook object's ProcessGrades method. The output reveals the summary of the 10 grades in myGradeBook.

Software Engineering Observation 8.3

A test harness (or test application) is responsible for creating an object of the class being tested and providing it with data. This data could come from any of several sources. Test data can be placed directly into an array with an array initializer, it can come from the user at the keyboard or it can come from a file (as you'll see in Chapter 17). After passing this data to the class's constructor to instantiate the object, the test harness should call the object to test its methods and manipulate its data. Gathering data in the test harness like this allows the class to manipulate data from several sources.

```
1   // Fig. 8.16: GradeBookTest.cs
2   // Create GradeBook object using an array of grades.
3   public class GradeBookTest
4   {
5      // Main method begins application execution
6      public static void Main( string[] args )
7      {
8         // one-dimensional array of student grades
9         int[] gradesArray = { 87, 68, 94, 100, 83, 78, 85, 91, 76, 87 };
```

Fig. 8.16 | Create a GradeBook object using an array of grades. (Part 1 of 2.)

```
10
11          GradeBook myGradeBook = new GradeBook(
12             "CS101 Introduction to C# Programming", gradesArray );
13          myGradeBook.DisplayMessage();
14          myGradeBook.ProcessGrades();
15       } // end Main
16    } // end class GradeBookTest
```

```
Welcome to the grade book for
CS101 Introduction to C# Programming!

The grades are:

Student  1:   87
Student  2:   68
Student  3:   94
Student  4:  100
Student  5:   83
Student  6:   78
Student  7:   85
Student  8:   91
Student  9:   76
Student 10:   87


Class average is 84.90
Lowest grade is 68
Highest grade is 100

Grade distribution:
00-09:
10-19:
20-29:
30-39:
40-49:
50-59:
60-69: *
70-79: **
80-89: ****
90-99: **
  100: *
```

Fig. 8.16 | Create a GradeBook object using an array of grades. (Part 2 of 2.)

8.10 Multidimensional Arrays

Multidimensional arrays with two dimensions are often used to represent **tables of values** consisting of information arranged in **rows** and **columns**. To identify a particular table element, we must specify two indices. By convention, the first identifies the element's row and the second its column. Arrays that require two indices to identify a particular element are called **two-dimensional arrays**. (Multidimensional arrays can have more than two dimensions, but such arrays are beyond the scope of this book.) C# supports two types of two-dimensional arrays—**rectangular arrays** and **jagged arrays**.

Rectangular Arrays

Rectangular arrays are used to represent tables of information in the form of rows and columns, where each row has the same number of columns. Figure 8.17 illustrates a rectangular array named a containing three rows and four columns—a three-by-four array. In general, an array with *m* rows and *n* columns is called an ***m*-by-*n* array**.

Every element in array a is identified in Fig. 8.17 by an array-access expression of the form a[*row, column*]; a is the name of the array, and *row* and *column* are the indices that uniquely identify each element in array a by row and column number. The names of the elements in row 0 all have a first index of 0, and the names of the elements in column 3 all have a second index of 3.

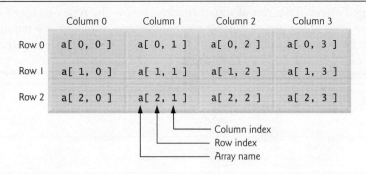

Fig. 8.17 | Rectangular array with three rows and four columns.

Like one-dimensional arrays, multidimensional arrays can be initialized with array initializers in declarations. A rectangular array b with two rows and two columns could be declared and initialized with **nested array initializers** as follows:

```
int[ , ] b = { { 1, 2 }, { 3, 4 } };
```

The initializer values are grouped by row in braces. So 1 and 2 initialize b[0, 0] and b[0, 1], respectively, and 3 and 4 initialize b[1, 0] and b[1, 1], respectively. The compiler counts the number of nested array initializers (represented by sets of two inner braces within the outer braces) in the initializer list to determine the number of rows in array b. The compiler counts the initializer values in the nested array initializer for a row to determine the number of columns (two) in that row. The compiler will generate an error if the number of initializers in each row is not the same, because every row of a rectangular array must have the same length.

Jagged Arrays

A jagged array is maintained as a one-dimensional array in which each element refers to a one-dimensional array. The manner in which jagged arrays are represented makes them quite flexible, because the lengths of the rows in the array need not be the same. For example, jagged arrays could be used to store a single student's exam grades across multiple classes, where the number of exams may vary from class to class.

We can access the elements in a jagged array by an array-access expression of the form *arrayName*[*row*] [*column*]—similar to the array-access expression for rectangular arrays, but with a separate set of square brackets for each dimension. A jagged array with three rows of different lengths could be declared and initialized as follows:

```
int[][] jagged = { new int[] { 1, 2 },
                   new int[] { 3 },
                   new int[] { 4, 5, 6 } };
```

In this statement, 1 and 2 initialize jagged[0][0] and jagged[0][1], respectively; 3 initializes jagged[1][0]; and 4, 5 and 6 initialize jagged[2][0], jagged[2][1] and jagged[2][2], respectively. Therefore, array jagged in the preceding declaration is actually composed of four separate one-dimensional arrays—one that represents the rows, one containing the values in the first row ({1, 2}), one containing the value in the second row ({3}) and one containing the values in the third row ({4, 5, 6}). Thus, array jagged itself is an array of three elements, each a reference to a one-dimensional array of int values.

Observe the differences between the array-creation expressions for rectangular arrays and for jagged arrays. Two sets of square brackets follow the type of jagged, indicating that this is an array of int arrays. Furthermore, in the array initializer, C# requires the keyword new to create an array object for each row. Figure 8.18 illustrates the array reference jagged after it's been declared and initialized.

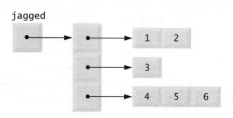

Fig. 8.18 | Jagged array with three rows of different lengths.

Creating Two-Dimensional Arrays with Array-Creation Expressions

A rectangular array can be created with an array-creation expression. For example, the following lines declare variable b and assign it a reference to a three-by-four rectangular array:

```
int[ , ] b;
b = new int[ 3, 4 ];
```

In this case, we use the literal values 3 and 4 to specify the number of rows and number of columns, respectively, but this is not required—applications can also use variables and expressions to specify array dimensions. As with one-dimensional arrays, the elements of a rectangular array are initialized when the array object is created.

A jagged array cannot be completely created with a single array-creation expression. The following statement is a syntax error:

```
int[][] c = new int[ 2 ][ 5 ]; // error
```

Instead, each one-dimensional array in the jagged array must be initialized separately. A jagged array can be created as follows:

```
int[][] c;
c = new int[ 2 ][ ]; // create 2 rows
c[ 0 ] = new int[ 5 ]; // create 5 columns for row 0
c[ 1 ] = new int[ 3 ]; // create 3 columns for row 1
```

The preceding statements create a jagged array with two rows. Row 0 has five columns, and row 1 has three columns.

Two-Dimensional Array Example: Displaying Element Values
Figure 8.19 demonstrates initializing rectangular and jagged arrays with array initializers and using nested for loops to **traverse** the arrays (i.e., visit every element of each array).

```
 1   // Fig. 8.19: InitArray.cs
 2   // Initializing rectangular and jagged arrays.
 3   using System;
 4
 5   public class InitArray
 6   {
 7      // create and output rectangular and jagged arrays
 8      public static void Main( string[] args )
 9      {
10         // with rectangular arrays,
11         // every row must be the same length.
12         int[ , ] rectangular = { { 1, 2, 3 }, { 4, 5, 6 } };
13
14         // with jagged arrays,
15         // we need to use "new int[]" for every row,
16         // but every row does not need to be the same length.
17         int[][] jagged = { new int[] { 1, 2 },
18                            new int[] { 3 },
19                            new int[] { 4, 5, 6 } };
20
21         OutputArray( rectangular ); // displays array rectangular by row
22         Console.WriteLine(); // output a blank line
23         OutputArray( jagged ); // displays array jagged by row
24      } // end Main
25
26      // output rows and columns of a rectangular array
27      public static void OutputArray( int[ , ] array )
28      {
29         Console.WriteLine( "Values in the rectangular array by row are" );
30
31         // loop through array's rows
32         for ( int row = 0; row < array.GetLength( 0 ); row++ )
33         {
34            // loop through columns of current row
35            for ( int column = 0; column < array.GetLength( 1 ); column++ )
36               Console.Write( "{0}  ", array[ row, column ] );
37
38            Console.WriteLine(); // start new line of output
39         } // end outer for
40      } // end method OutputArray
41
42      // output rows and columns of a jagged array
43      public static void OutputArray( int[][] array )
44      {
45         Console.WriteLine( "Values in the jagged array by row are" );
```

Fig. 8.19 | Initializing jagged and rectangular arrays. (Part 1 of 2.)

```
46
47            // loop through each row
48            foreach ( int[] row in array )
49            {
50               // loop through each element in current row
51               foreach ( int element in row )
52                  Console.Write( "{0}  ", element );
53
54               Console.WriteLine(); // start new line of output
55            } // end outer foreach
56      } // end method OutputArray
57   } // end class InitArray
```

```
Values in the rectangular array by row are
1  2  3
4  5  6

Values in the jagged array by row are
1  2
3
4  5  6
```

Fig. 8.19 | Initializing jagged and rectangular arrays. (Part 2 of 2.)

Class InitArray's Main method creates two arrays. Line 12 uses nested array initializers to initialize variable rectangular with an array in which row 0 has the values 1, 2 and 3, and row 1 has the values 4, 5 and 6. Lines 17–19 uses nested initializers of different lengths to initialize variable jagged. In this case, the initializer uses the keyword new to create a one-dimensional array for each row. Row 0 is initialized to have two elements with values 1 and 2, respectively. Row 1 is initialized to have one element with value 3. Row 2 is initialized to have three elements with the values 4, 5 and 6, respectively.

Method OutputArray has been overloaded with two versions. The first version (lines 27–40) specifies the array parameter as int[,] array to indicate that it takes a rectangular array. The second version (lines 43–56) takes a jagged array, because its array parameter is listed as int[][] array.

Line 21 invokes method OutputArray with argument rectangular, so the version of OutputArray at lines 27–40 is called. The nested for statement (lines 32–39) outputs the rows of a rectangular array. The loop-continuation condition of each for statement (lines 32 and 35) uses the rectangular array's GetLength method to obtain the length of each dimension. Dimensions are numbered starting from 0, so the method call GetLength(0) on array returns the size of the first dimension of the array (the number of rows), and the call GetLength(1) returns the size of the second dimension (the number of columns).

Line 23 invokes method OutputArray with argument jagged, so the version of OutputArray at lines 43–56 is called. The nested foreach statement (lines 48–55) outputs the rows of a jagged array. The inner foreach statement (lines 51–52) iterates through each element in the current row of the array. This allows the loop to determine the exact number of columns in each row. Since the jagged array is created as an array of arrays, we can use nested foreach statements to output the elements in the console window. The outer loop iterates through the elements of array, which are references to one-dimensional arrays of int values that represent each row. The inner loop iterates through the elements of the current row. A foreach statement can also iterate through all the elements in a rectangular array. In this case, foreach iterates through all the rows and columns starting from row 0, as if the elements were in a one-dimensional array.

Common Multidimensional-Array Manipulations Performed with* for *Statements
Many common array manipulations use for statements. As an example, the following for statement sets all the elements in row 2 of rectangular array a in Fig. 8.17 to 0:

```
for ( int column = 0; column < a.GetLength( 1 ); column++)
   a[ 2, column ] = 0;
```

We specified row 2; therefore, we know that the first index is always 2 (0 is the first row, and 1 is the second row). This for loop varies only the second index (i.e., the **column index**). The preceding for statement is equivalent to the assignment statements

```
a[ 2, 0 ] = 0;
a[ 2, 1 ] = 0;
a[ 2, 2 ] = 0;
a[ 2, 3 ] = 0;
```

The following nested for statement totals the values of all the elements in array a:

```
int total = 0;

for ( int row = 0; row < a.GetLength( 0 ); row++ )
{
   for ( int column = 0; column < a.GetLength( 1 ); column++ )
      total += a[ row, column ];
} // end outer for
```

These nested for statements total the array elements one row at a time. The outer for statement begins by setting the row index to 0 so that row 0's elements can be totaled by the inner for statement. The outer for then increments row to 1 so that row 1's elements can be totaled. Then the outer for increments row to 2 so that row 2's elements can be totaled. The variable total can be displayed when the outer for statement terminates. In the next example, we show how to process a rectangular array in a more concise manner using foreach statements.

8.11 Case Study: Class GradeBook Using a Rectangular Array

In Section 8.9, we presented class GradeBook (Fig. 8.15), which used a one-dimensional array to store student grades on a single exam. In most courses, students take several exams. Instructors are likely to want to analyze grades across the entire course, both for a single student and for the class as a whole.

***Storing Student Grades in a Rectangular Array in Class* GradeBook**
Figure 8.20 contains a version of class GradeBook that uses a rectangular array grades to store the grades of a number of students on multiple exams. Each row of the array represents a single student's grades for the entire course, and each column represents the grades for the whole class on one of the exams the students took during the course. An application

such as GradeBookTest (Fig. 8.21) passes the array as an argument to the GradeBook constructor. In this example, we use a 10-by-3 array containing 10 students' grades on three exams. Five methods perform array manipulations to process the grades. Each method is similar to its counterpart in the earlier one-dimensional-array version of class GradeBook (Fig. 8.15). Method GetMinimum (lines 44–58) determines the lowest grade of any student for the semester. Method GetMaximum (lines 61–75) determines the highest grade of any student for the semester. Method GetAverage (lines 78–90) determines a particular student's semester average. Method OutputBarChart (lines 93–122) outputs a bar chart of the distribution of all student grades for the semester. Method OutputGrades (lines 125–149) outputs the two-dimensional array in tabular format, along with each student's semester average.

```csharp
1   // Fig. 8.20: GradeBook.cs
2   // Grade book using rectangular array to store grades.
3   using System;
4
5   public class GradeBook
6   {
7      private int[ , ] grades; // rectangular array of student grades
8
9      // auto-implemented property CourseName
10     public string CourseName { get; set; }
11
12     // two-parameter constructor initializes
13     // auto-implemented property CourseName and grades array
14     public GradeBook( string name, int[ , ] gradesArray )
15     {
16        CourseName = name; // set CourseName to name
17        grades = gradesArray; // initialize grades array
18     } // end two-parameter GradeBook constructor
19
20     // display a welcome message to the GradeBook user
21     public void DisplayMessage()
22     {
23        // auto-implemented property CourseName gets the name of course
24        Console.WriteLine( "Welcome to the grade book for\n{0}!\n",
25           CourseName );
26     } // end method DisplayMessage
27
28     // perform various operations on the data
29     public void ProcessGrades()
30     {
31        // output grades array
32        OutputGrades();
33
34        // call methods GetMinimum and GetMaximum
35        Console.WriteLine( "\n{0} {1}\n{2} {3}\n",
36           "Lowest grade in the grade book is", GetMinimum(),
37           "Highest grade in the grade book is", GetMaximum() );
38
```

Fig. 8.20 | Grade book using a rectangular array to store grades. (Part 1 of 4.)

```
39         // output grade distribution chart of all grades on all tests
40         OutputBarChart();
41      } // end method ProcessGrades
42
43      // find minimum grade
44      public int GetMinimum()
45      {
46         // assume first element of grades array is smallest
47         int lowGrade = grades[ 0, 0 ];
48
49         // loop through elements of rectangular grades array
50         foreach ( int grade in grades )
51         {
52            // if grade less than lowGrade, assign it to lowGrade
53            if ( grade < lowGrade )
54               lowGrade = grade;
55         } // end foreach
56
57         return lowGrade; // return lowest grade
58      } // end method GetMinimum
59
60      // find maximum grade
61      public int GetMaximum()
62      {
63         // assume first element of grades array is largest
64         int highGrade = grades[ 0, 0 ];
65
66         // loop through elements of rectangular grades array
67         foreach ( int grade in grades )
68         {
69            // if grade greater than highGrade, assign it to highGrade
70            if ( grade > highGrade )
71               highGrade = grade;
72         } // end foreach
73
74         return highGrade; // return highest grade
75      } // end method GetMaximum
76
77      // determine average grade for particular student
78      public double GetAverage( int student )
79      {
80         // get the number of grades per student
81         int amount = grades.GetLength( 1 );
82         int total = 0; // initialize total
83
84         // sum grades for one student
85         for ( int exam = 0; exam < amount; exam++ )
86            total += grades[ student, exam ];
87
88         // return average of grades
89         return ( double ) total / amount;
90      } // end method GetAverage
91
```

Fig. 8.20 | Grade book using a rectangular array to store grades. (Part 2 of 4.)

```
 92       // output bar chart displaying overall grade distribution
 93       public void OutputBarChart()
 94       {
 95          Console.WriteLine( "Overall grade distribution:" );
 96
 97          // stores frequency of grades in each range of 10 grades
 98          int[] frequency = new int[ 11 ];
 99
100          // for each grade in GradeBook, increment the appropriate frequency
101          foreach ( int grade in grades )
102          {
103             ++frequency[ grade / 10 ];
104          } // end foreach
105
106          // for each grade frequency, display bar in chart
107          for ( int count = 0; count < frequency.Length; count++ )
108          {
109             // output bar label ( "00-09: ", ..., "90-99: ", "100: " )
110             if ( count == 10 )
111                Console.Write( "  100: " );
112             else
113                Console.Write( "{0:D2}-{1:D2}: ",
114                   count * 10, count * 10 + 9 );
115
116             // display bar of asterisks
117             for ( int stars = 0; stars < frequency[ count ]; stars++ )
118                Console.Write( "*" );
119
120             Console.WriteLine(); // start a new line of output
121          } // end outer for
122       } // end method OutputBarChart
123
124       // output the contents of the grades array
125       public void OutputGrades()
126       {
127          Console.WriteLine( "The grades are:\n" );
128          Console.Write( "              " ); // align column heads
129
130          // create a column heading for each of the tests
131          for ( int test = 0; test < grades.GetLength( 1 ); test++ )
132             Console.Write( "Test {0}  ", test + 1 );
133
134          Console.WriteLine( "Average" ); // student average column heading
135
136          // create rows/columns of text representing array grades
137          for ( int student = 0; student < grades.GetLength( 0 ); student++ )
138          {
139             Console.Write( "Student {0,2}", student + 1 );
140
141             // output student's grades
142             for ( int grade = 0; grade < grades.GetLength( 1 ); grade++ )
143                Console.Write( "{0,8}", grades[ student, grade ] );
144
```

Fig. 8.20 | Grade book using a rectangular array to store grades. (Part 3 of 4.)

```
145                // call method GetAverage to calculate student's average grade;
146                // pass row number as the argument to GetAverage
147                Console.WriteLine( "{0,9:F}", GetAverage( student ) );
148            } // end outer for
149        } // end method OutputGrades
150    } // end class GradeBook
```

Fig. 8.20 | Grade book using a rectangular array to store grades. (Part 4 of 4.)

Methods GetMinimum, GetMaximum and OutputBarChart each loop through array grades using the foreach statement—for example, the foreach statement from method GetMinimum (lines 50–55). To find the lowest overall grade, this foreach statement iterates through rectangular array grades and compares each element to variable lowGrade. If a grade is less than lowGrade, lowGrade is set to that grade.

When the foreach statement traverses the elements of array grades, it looks at each element of the first row in order by index, then each element of the second row in order by index and so on. The foreach statement in lines 50–55 traverses the elements of grade in the same order as the following equivalent code, expressed with nested for statements:

```
for ( int row = 0; row < grades.GetLength( 0 ); row++ )
   for ( int column = 0; column < grades.GetLength( 1 ); column++ )
   {
      if ( grades[ row, column ] < lowGrade )
         lowGrade = grades[ row, column ];
   }
```

When the foreach statement completes, lowGrade contains the lowest grade in the rectangular array. Method GetMaximum works similarly to method GetMinimum.

Method OutputBarChart (lines 93–122) displays the grade distribution as a bar chart. The syntax of the foreach statement (lines 101–104) is identical for one-dimensional and two-dimensional arrays.

Method OutputGrades (lines 125–149) uses nested for statements to output values of the array grades, in addition to each student's semester average. The output in Fig. 8.21 shows the result, which resembles the tabular format of an instructor's physical grade book. Lines 131–132 display the column headings for each test. We use the for statement rather than the foreach statement here so that we can identify each test with a number. Similarly, the for statement in lines 137–148 first outputs a row label using a counter variable to identify each student (line 139). Although array indices start at 0, lines 132 and 139 output test + 1 and student + 1, respectively, to produce test and student numbers starting at 1 (see Fig. 8.21). The inner for statement in lines 142–143 uses the outer for statement's counter variable student to loop through a specific row of array grades and output each student's test grade. Finally, line 147 obtains each student's semester average by passing the row index of grades (i.e., student) to method Get-Average.

Method GetAverage (lines 78–90) takes one argument—the row index for a particular student. When line 147 calls GetAverage, the argument is int value student, which specifies the particular row of rectangular array grades. Method GetAverage calculates the sum of the array elements on this row, divides the total by the number of test results and returns the floating-point result as a double value (line 89).

Class **GradeBookTest** *That Demonstrates Class* **GradeBook**

The application in Fig. 8.21 creates an object of class GradeBook (Fig. 8.20) using the two-dimensional array of ints that gradesArray references (lines 9–18). Lines 20–21 pass a course name and gradesArray to the GradeBook constructor. Lines 22–23 then invoke myGradeBook's DisplayMessage and ProcessGrades methods to display a welcome message and obtain a report summarizing the students' grades for the semester, respectively.

```
 1   // Fig. 8.21: GradeBookTest.cs
 2   // Create GradeBook object using a rectangular array of grades.
 3   public class GradeBookTest
 4   {
 5      // Main method begins application execution
 6      public static void Main( string[] args )
 7      {
 8         // rectangular array of student grades
 9         int[ , ] gradesArray = { { 87, 96, 70 },
10                                  { 68, 87, 90 },
11                                  { 94, 100, 90 },
12                                  { 100, 81, 82 },
13                                  { 83, 65, 85 },
14                                  { 78, 87, 65 },
15                                  { 85, 75, 83 },
16                                  { 91, 94, 100 },
17                                  { 76, 72, 84 },
18                                  { 87, 93, 73 } };
19
20         GradeBook myGradeBook = new GradeBook(
21            "CS101 Introduction to C# Programming", gradesArray );
22         myGradeBook.DisplayMessage();
23         myGradeBook.ProcessGrades();
24      } // end Main
25   } // end class GradeBookTest
```

```
Welcome to the grade book for
CS101 Introduction to C# Programming!

The grades are:

            Test 1  Test 2  Test 3  Average
Student  1      87      96      70    84.33
Student  2      68      87      90    81.67
Student  3      94     100      90    94.67
Student  4     100      81      82    87.67
Student  5      83      65      85    77.67
Student  6      78      87      65    76.67
Student  7      85      75      83    81.00
Student  8      91      94     100    95.00
Student  9      76      72      84    77.33
Student 10      87      93      73    84.33

Lowest grade in the grade book is 65
Highest grade in the grade book is 100
```

Fig. 8.21 | Create a GradeBook object using a rectangular array of grades. (Part 1 of 2.)

```
Overall grade distribution:
00-09:
10-19:
20-29:
30-39:
40-49:
50-59:
60-69: ***
70-79: ******
80-89: ***********
90-99: *******
  100: ***
```

Fig. 8.21 | Create a `GradeBook` object using a rectangular array of grades. (Part 2 of 2.)

8.12 Variable-Length Argument Lists

Variable-length argument lists allow you to create methods that receive an arbitrary number of arguments. A one-dimensional array-type argument preceded by the keyword **params** in a method's parameter list indicates that the method receives a variable number of arguments with the type of the array's elements. This use of a `params` modifier can occur only in the last entry of the parameter list. While you can use method overloading and array passing to accomplish much of what is accomplished with variable-length argument lists, using the `params` modifier is more concise.

Figure 8.22 demonstrates method `Average` (lines 8–17), which receives a variable-length sequence of `doubles` (line 8). C# treats the variable-length argument list as a one-dimensional array whose elements are all of the same type. Hence, the method body can manipulate the parameter `numbers` as an array of `doubles`. Lines 13–14 use the `foreach` loop to walk through the array and calculate the total of the `doubles` in the array. Line 16 accesses `numbers.Length` to obtain the size of the `numbers` array for use in the averaging calculation. Lines 31, 33 and 35 in `Main` call method `Average` with two, three and four arguments, respectively. Method `Average` has a variable-length argument list, so it can average as many `double` arguments as the caller passes. The output reveals that each call to method `Average` returns the correct value.

Common Programming Error 8.5

The params modifier may be used only with the last parameter of the parameter list.

```
1   // Fig. 8.22: ParamArrayTest.cs
2   // Using variable-length argument lists.
3   using System;
4
5   public class ParamArrayTest
6   {
7      // calculate average
8      public static double Average( params double[] numbers )
9      {
```

Fig. 8.22 | Using variable-length argument lists. (Part 1 of 2.)

```
10          double total = 0.0; // initialize total
11
12          // calculate total using the foreach statement
13          foreach ( double d in numbers )
14             total += d;
15
16          return total / numbers.Length;
17       } // end method Average
18
19       public static void Main( string[] args )
20       {
21          double d1 = 10.0;
22          double d2 = 20.0;
23          double d3 = 30.0;
24          double d4 = 40.0;
25
26          Console.WriteLine(
27             "d1 = {0:F1}\nd2 = {1:F1}\nd3 = {2:F1}\nd4 = {3:F1}\n",
28             d1, d2, d3, d4 );
29
30          Console.WriteLine( "Average of d1 and d2 is {0:F1}",
31             Average( d1, d2 ) );
32          Console.WriteLine( "Average of d1, d2 and d3 is {0:F1}",
33             Average( d1, d2, d3 ) );
34          Console.WriteLine( "Average of d1, d2, d3 and d4 is {0:F1}",
35             Average( d1, d2, d3, d4 ) );
36       } // end Main
37    } // end class ParamArrayTest
```

```
d1 = 10.0
d2 = 20.0
d3 = 30.0
d4 = 40.0

Average of d1 and d2 is 15.0
Average of d1, d2 and d3 is 20.0
Average of d1, d2, d3 and d4 is 25.0
```

Fig. 8.22 | Using variable-length argument lists. (Part 2 of 2.)

8.13 Using Command-Line Arguments

On many systems, it's possible to pass arguments from the command line (these are known as **command-line arguments**) to an application by including a parameter of type string[] (i.e., an array of strings) in the parameter list of Main, exactly as we have done in every application in the book. By convention, this parameter is named args (Fig. 8.23, line 7). When an application is executed from the **Command Prompt**, the execution environment passes the command-line arguments that appear after the application name to the application's Main method as strings in the one-dimensional array args. The number of arguments passed from the command line is obtained by accessing the array's Length property. For example, the command "MyApplication a b" passes two command-line arguments to application MyApplication. Command-line arguments are separated by white space, not commas. When the preceding command executes, the Main method entry point receives the two-element array args (i.e., args.Length is 2) in which args[0] contains the string "a" and args[1] contains the string "b". Common uses of command-line arguments include passing options and file names to applications.

```csharp
1   // Fig. 8.23: InitArray.cs
2   // Using command-line arguments to initialize an array.
3   using System;
4
5   public class InitArray
6   {
7      public static void Main( string[] args )
8      {
9         // check number of command-line arguments
10        if ( args.Length != 3 )
11           Console.WriteLine(
12              "Error: Please re-enter the entire command, including\n" +
13              "an array size, initial value and increment." );
14        else
15        {
16           // get array size from first command-line argument
17           int arrayLength = Convert.ToInt32( args[ 0 ] );
18           int[] array = new int[ arrayLength ]; // create array
19
20           // get initial value and increment from command-line argument
21           int initialValue = Convert.ToInt32( args[ 1 ] );
22           int increment = Convert.ToInt32( args[ 2 ] );
23
24           // calculate value for each array element
25           for ( int counter = 0; counter < array.Length; counter++ )
26              array[ counter ] = initialValue + increment * counter;
27
28           Console.WriteLine( "{0}{1,8}", "Index", "Value" );
29
30           // display array index and value
31           for ( int counter = 0; counter < array.Length; counter++ )
32              Console.WriteLine( "{0,5}{1,8}", counter, array[ counter ] );
33        } // end else
34     } // end Main
35  } // end class InitArray
```

```
C:\Examples\ch08\fig08_23>InitArray.exe
Error: Please re-enter the entire command, including
an array size, initial value and increment.
```

```
C:\Examples\ch08\fig08_23>InitArray.exe 5 0 4
Index    Value
    0        0
    1        4
    2        8
    3       12
    4       16
```

Fig. 8.23 | Using command-line arguments to initialize an array. (Part 1 of 2.)

```
C:\Examples\ch08\fig08_23>InitArray.exe 10 1 2
Index   Value
    0       1
    1       3
    2       5
    3       7
    4       9
    5      11
    6      13
    7      15
    8      17
    9      19
```

Fig. 8.23 | Using command-line arguments to initialize an array. (Part 2 of 2.)

Figure 8.23 uses three command-line arguments to initialize an array. When the application executes, if args.Length is not 3, the application displays an error message and terminates (lines 10–13). Otherwise, lines 16–32 initialize and display the array based on the values of the command-line arguments.

The command-line arguments become available to Main as strings in args. Line 17 gets args[0]—a string that specifies the array size—and converts it to an int value, which the application uses to create the array in line 18. The static method ToInt32 of class Convert converts its string argument to an int.

Lines 21–22 convert the args[1] and args[2] command-line arguments to int values and store them in initialValue and increment, respectively. Lines 25–26 calculate the value for each array element.

The first sample execution indicates that the application received an insufficient number of command-line arguments. The second sample execution uses command-line arguments 5, 0 and 4 to specify the size of the array (5), the value of the first element (0) and the increment of each value in the array (4), respectively. The corresponding output indicates that these values create an array containing the integers 0, 4, 8, 12 and 16. The output from the third sample execution illustrates that the command-line arguments 10, 1 and 2 produce an array whose 10 elements are the nonnegative odd integers from 1 to 19.

8.14 Wrap-Up

This chapter began our introduction to data structures, exploring the use of arrays to store data in and retrieve data from lists and tables of values. The chapter examples demonstrated how to declare array variables, initialize arrays and refer to individual elements of arrays. The chapter introduced the foreach statement as an additional means (besides the for statement) for iterating through arrays. We showed how to pass arrays to methods and how to declare and manipulate multidimensional arrays. Finally, the chapter showed how to write methods that use variable-length argument lists and how to read arguments passed to an application from the command line.

We continue our coverage of data structures in Chapter 9, where we discuss the List collection, which is a dynamically resizable array-based collection. Chapter 20 discusses searching and sorting algorithms. Chapter 21 introduces dynamic data structures, such as lists, queues, stacks and trees, that can grow and shrink as applications execute. Chapter 22 presents generics, which provide the means to create general models of methods and classes that can be declared once, but used with many different data types. Chapter 23 introduces the data structure classes provided by the .NET Framework, some of which use generics to allow you to specify the exact types of objects that a particular data structure will store. You can use these predefined data structures instead of building your own. Chapter 23 discusses many data-structure classes that can grow and shrink in response to an application's changing storage requirements. The .NET Framework also provides class Array, which contains utility methods for array manipulation. Chapter 23 uses several static methods of class Array to perform such manipulations as sorting and searching the data in an array.

We've now introduced the basic concepts of classes, objects, control statements, methods and arrays. In Chapter 9 we introduce Language Integrated Query (LINQ), which enables you to write expressions that can retrieve information from a wide variety of data sources, such as arrays. You'll see how to search, sort and filter data using LINQ.

If you're in a course which either skips LINQ or defers coverage until later in the book when it's needed to support other more advanced C# features, you can proceed to Chapter 10 in which we take a deeper look at classes and objects.

Summary

Section 8.1 Introduction

- Arrays are data structures consisting of related data items of the same type. Arrays are fixed-length entities—they remain the same length once they're created.

Section 8.2 Arrays

- Arrays are reference types. What we typically think of as an array is actually a reference to an array object. The elements of an array can be either value types or reference types (including other arrays).

- To refer to a particular element in an array, we specify the name of the reference to the array and the index (i.e., the position number) of the element in the array.

- An application refers to an array element with an array-access expression that includes the name of the array, followed by the index of the particular element in square brackets ([]).

- The first element in every array has index zero and is sometimes called the zeroth element.

- An array's Length property returns the number of elements in the array.

Section 8.3 Declaring and Creating Arrays

- To create an array instance, you specify the type and the number of array elements as part of an array-creation expression that uses keyword new. The following declaration and array-creation expression create an array object containing 12 int elements:

  ```
  int[] a = new int[ 12 ];
  ```

- When an array is created, each element of the array receives a default value—0 for the numeric simple-type elements, false for bool elements and null for references.

- An application can declare variables that reference arrays of any type. Every element of a value-type array contains a value of the array's declared type. In an array of a reference type, every element is a reference to an object of the array's declared type or null.

Section 8.4 Examples Using Arrays

- An application can create an array and initialize its elements with an array initializer, which is a comma-separated list of expressions (called an initializer list) enclosed in braces.

- Constants must be initialized when they're declared and cannot be modified thereafter.

- In a format item, a D format specifier indicates that the value should be formatted as an integer, and the number after the D indicates how many digits this formatted integer must contain.

- When a program is executed, array element indices are checked for validity—all indices must be greater than or equal to 0 and less than the length of the array. If an attempt is made to use an invalid index to access an element, an IndexOutOfRangeException exception occurs.

- An exception indicates a problem that occurs while a program executes. The name "exception" suggests that the problem occurs infrequently—if the "rule" is that a statement normally executes correctly, then the problem represents the "exception to the rule."

- Exception handling enables you to create fault-tolerant programs that can resolve exceptions.

- To handle an exception, place any code that might throw an exception in a try statement.

- The try block contains the code that might throw an exception, and the catch block contains the code that handles the exception if one occurs.

- You can have many catch blocks to handle different types of exceptions that might be thrown in the corresponding try block.

- When a try block terminates any variables declared in the try block go out of scope.

- A catch block declares a type and an exception parameter. Inside the catch block, you can use the parameter's identifier to interact with a caught exception object.

- An exception object's Message property returns the exception's error message.

Section 8.5 Case Study: Card Shuffling and Dealing Simulation
- The ToString method of an object is called implicitly in many cases when the object is used where a string is expected.

Section 8.6 foreach Statement
- The foreach statement iterates through the elements of an entire array or collection. The syntax of a foreach statement is:

    foreach (*type identifier* **in** *arrayName*)
    statement

where *type* and *identifier* are the type and name of the iteration variable, and *arrayName* is the array through which to iterate.

- The foreach header can be read concisely as "for each iteration, assign the next element of the array to the iteration variable, then execute the following statement."

- The foreach statement can be used only to access array elements, but it cannot be used to modify elements. Any attempt to change the value of the iteration variable in the body of a foreach statement will cause a compilation error.

Section 8.7 Passing Arrays and Array Elements to Methods
- When an argument to a method is an entire array or an individual array element of a reference type, the called method receives a copy of the reference. However, when an argument to a method is an individual array element of a value type, the called method receives a copy of the element's value.

Section 8.8 Passing Arrays by Value and by Reference
- When a reference-type object is passed with ref, the called method actually gains control over the reference itself, allowing the called method to replace the original reference in the caller with a different object or even with null.

- If you encounter a situation where you truly want the called procedure to modify the caller's reference, pass the reference-type parameter using keyword ref—but such situations are rare.

Section 8.10 Multidimensional Arrays

- Two-dimensional arrays are often used to represent tables of values consisting of information arranged in rows and columns. To identify a particular table element, we must specify two indices.

- C# supports two types of two-dimensional arrays—rectangular arrays and jagged arrays.

- Rectangular arrays are used to represent tables of information in the form of rows and columns, where each row has the same number of columns.

- Elements in rectangular array a are identified by an expression of the form a[row, column].

- A rectangular array could be declared and initialized with array initializers of the form:

  arrayType[,] *arrayName* = { {*row0 initializer*}, {*row1 initializer*}, ... };

  provided that each row of the rectangular array must have the same length.

- A rectangular array can be created with an array-creation expression of the form

  arrayType[,] *arrayName* = **new** *arrayType*[*numRows*, *numColumns*];

- A jagged array is maintained as a one-dimensional array in which each element refers to a one-dimensional array.

- The lengths of the rows in a jagged array need not be the same.

- We can access the elements in a jagged array *arrayName* by an array-access expression of the form *arrayName*[*row*][*column*].

- A jagged array can be declared and initialized in the form:

  arrayType[][] *arrayName* = { **new** *arrayType*[] {*row0 initializer*},
                        new *arrayType*[] {*row1 initializer*}, ... };

Section 8.11 Case Study: Class GradeBook Using a Rectangular Array

- When the foreach statement traverses a rectangular array's elements, it looks at each element of the first row in order by index, then each element of the second row in order by index and so on.

Section 8.12 Variable-Length Argument Lists

- A one-dimensional array parameter preceded by params in a method's parameter list indicates that the method receives a variable number of arguments with the type of the array's elements.

- The params modifier can appear only in the last entry of the parameter list.

- C# treats a variable-length argument list as a one-dimensional array.

Section 8.13 Using Command-Line Arguments

- When an application is executed from the **Command Prompt**, the execution environment passes the command-line arguments that appear after the application name to the application's Main method as strings in a one-dimensional array.

Terminology

array	const keyword
array-access expression	element of an array
array-creation expression	exception
array initializer	exception handling
bounds checking	fault-tolerant program
catch block	foreach statement
column index	index
column of an array	index zero
command-line arguments	IndexOutOfRangeException

initializer list	params modifier
iteration variable	rectangular array
jagged array	row index
leading 0	row of an array
`Length` property of an array	square brackets, `[]`
m-by-*n* array	table of values
magic number	test harness
`Message` property of an exception	traverse an array
multidimensional array	try statement
name of an array	two-dimensional array
named constant	variable-length argument list
nested array initializers	zeroth element

Self-Review Exercises

8.1   Fill in the blank(s) in each of the following statements:

a) Lists and tables of values can be stored in _____.

b) An array is a group of _____ (called elements) containing values that all have the same _____.

c) The _____ statement allows you to iterate through the elements in an array without using a counter.

d) The number that refers to a particular array element is called the element's _____.

e) An array that uses two indices is referred to as a(n) _____ array.

f) Use the `foreach` header _____ to iterate through `double` array `numbers`.

g) Command-line arguments are stored in _____.

h) Use the expression _____ to receive the total number of arguments in a command line. Assume that command-line arguments are stored in `string[] args`.

i) Given the command `MyApplication test`, the first command-line argument is _____.

j) A(n) _____ in the parameter list of a method indicates that the method can receive a variable number of arguments.

8.2   Determine whether each of the following is *true* or *false*. If *false*, explain why.

a) A single array can store values of many different types.

b) An array index should normally be of type `float`.

c) An individual array element that's passed to a method and modified in that method will contain the modified value when the called method completes execution.

d) Command-line arguments are separated by commas.

8.3   Perform the following tasks for an array called `fractions`:

a) Declare constant `ARRAY_SIZE` initialized to 10.

b) Declare variable `fractions` which will reference an array with `ARRAY_SIZE` elements of type `double`. Initialize the elements to 0.

c) Name the element of the array with index 3.

d) Assign the value `1.667` to the array element with index 9.

e) Assign the value `3.333` to the array element with index 6.

f) Sum all the elements of the array, using a `for` statement. Declare integer variable `x` as a control variable for the loop.

8.4   Perform the following tasks for an array called `table`:

a) Declare the variable and initialize it with a rectangular integer array that has three rows and three columns. Assume that constant `ARRAY_SIZE` has been declared to be 3.

b) How many elements does the array contain?

c) Use a `for` statement to initialize each element of the array to the sum of its indices.

8.5   Find and correct the error in each of the following code segments:

a) ```
const int ARRAY_SIZE = 5;
ARRAY_SIZE = 10;
```

b) Assume ```int[] b = new int[ 10 ];```
```
for (int i = 0; i <= b.Length; i++)
   b[i] = 1;
```

c) Assume ```int[ , ] a = { { 1, 2 }, { 3, 4 } };```
```
a[1][1] = 5;
```

## Answers to Self-Review Exercises

**8.1**    a) arrays. b) variables, type. c) foreach. d) index (or position number). e) two-dimensional. f) foreach ( double d in numbers ). g) an array of strings, usually called args. h) args.Length. i) test. j) params modifier.

**8.2**    a) False. An array can store only values of the same type.

b) False. An array index must be an integer or an integer expression.

c) For individual value-type elements of an array: False. A called method receives and manipulates a copy of the value of such an element, so modifications do not affect the original value. If the reference of an array is passed to a method, however, modifications to the array elements made in the called method are indeed reflected in the original. For individual elements of a reference type: True. A called method receives a copy of the reference of such an element, and changes to the referenced object will be reflected in the original array element.

d) False. Command-line arguments are separated by whitespace.

**8.3**    a) ```const int ARRAY_SIZE = 10;```

b) ```double[] fractions = new double[ ARRAY_SIZE ];```

c) ```fractions[ 3 ]```

d) ```fractions[ 9 ] = 1.667;```

e) ```fractions[ 6 ] = 3.333;```

f) ```double total = 0.0;```
```
for (int x = 0; x < fractions.Length; x++)
   total += fractions[x];
```

**8.4**    a) ```int[ , ] table = new int[ ARRAY_SIZE, ARRAY_SIZE ];```

b) Nine.

c) ```
for ( int x = 0; x < table.GetLength( 0 ); x++ )
   for ( int y = 0; y < table.GetLength( 1 ); y++ )
      table[ x, y ] = x + y;
```

8.5   a) *Error:* Assigning a value to a constant after it's been initialized.
Correction: Assign the correct value to the constant in the const declaration.

b) *Error:* Referencing an array element outside the bounds of the array (b[10]).
Correction: Change the <= operator to <.

c) *Error:* Array indexing is performed incorrectly.
Correction: Change the statement to a[1, 1] = 5;.

Exercises

8.6   Fill in the blanks in each of the following statements:

a) One-dimensional array p contains four elements. The names of those elements are _____, _____, _____ and _____.

b) Naming an array's variable, stating its type and specifying the number of dimensions in the array is called _____ the array.

c) In a two-dimensional array, the first index identifies the _____ of an element and the second index identifies the _____ of an element.

d) An *m*-by-*n* array contains _____ rows, _____ columns and _____ elements.

e) The name of the element in row 3 and column 5 of jagged array d is _____.

8.7   Determine whether each of the following is *true* or *false*. If *false*, explain why.

a) To refer to a particular location or element within an array, we specify the name of the array's variable and the value of the particular element.

b) The declaration of a variable that references an array reserves memory for the array.

c) To indicate that 100 locations should be reserved for integer array p, the programmer writes the declaration p[100];

d) An application that initializes the elements of a 15-element array to 0 must contain at least one for statement.

e) To total the elements of a two-dimensional array you must use nested for statements.

8.8   Write C# statements to accomplish each of the following tasks:

a) Display the value of the element of character array f with index 6.

b) Initialize each of the five elements of one-dimensional integer array g to 8.

c) Total the 100 elements of floating-point array c.

d) Copy 11-element array a into the first portion of array b, which contains 34 elements.

e) Determine and display the smallest and largest values contained in 99-element floating-point array w.

8.9   Consider the tw'o-by-three rectangular integer array t.

a) Write a statement that declares t and creates the array.

b) How many rows does t have?

c) How many columns does t have?

d) How many elements does t have?

e) Write the names of all the elements in row 1 of t.

f) Write the names of all the elements in column 2 of t.

g) Write a single statement that sets the element of t in row 0 and column 1 to zero.

h) Write a sequence of statements that initializes each element of t to 1. Do not use a repetition statement.

i) Write a nested for statement that initializes each element of t to 3.

j) Write a nested for statement that inputs values for the elements of t from the user.

k) Write a sequence of statements that determines and displays the smallest value in t.

l) Write a statement that displays the elements of row 0 of t.

m) Write a statement that totals the elements of column 2 of t.

n) Write a sequence of statements that displays the contents of t in tabular format. List the column indices as headings across the top, and list the row indices at the left of each row.

8.10   *(Sales Commissions)* Use a one-dimensional array to solve the following problem: A company pays its salespeople on a commission basis. The salespeople receive $200 per week plus 9% of their gross sales for that week. For example, a salesperson who grosses $5000 in sales in a week receives $200 plus 9% of $5000, or a total of $650. Write an application (using an array of counters) that determines how many of the salespeople earned salaries in each of the following ranges (assume that each salesperson's salary is an integer). Summarize the results in tabular format.

a) $200–299

b) $300–399

c) $400–499

d) $500–599

    e) $600–699

    f) $700–799

    g) $800–899

    h) $900–999

    i) $1000 and over

8.11   *(Array Manipulations)* Write statements that perform the following one-dimensional-array operations:

    a) Set the three elements of integer array `counts` to 0.

    b) Add 1 to each of the four elements of integer array `bonus`.

    c) Display the five values of integer array `bestScores` in column format.

8.12   *(Duplicate Elimination)* Use a one-dimensional array to solve the following problem: Write an application that inputs five numbers, each of which is between 10 and 100, inclusive. As each number is read, display it only if it's not a duplicate of a number already read. Provide for the "worst case," in which all five numbers are different. Use the smallest possible array to solve this problem. Display the complete set of unique values input after the user inputs each new value.

8.13   *(Jagged Arrays)* List the elements of the three-by-five jagged array `sales` in the order in which they're set to 0 by the following code segment:

```
for ( int row = 0; row < sales.Length; row++ )
{
    for ( int col = 0; col < sales[row].Length; col++ )
    {
        sales[ row ][ col ] = 0;
    }
}
```

8.14   *(Variable-Length Argument List)* Write an application that calculates the product of a series of integers that are passed to method `product` using a variable-length argument list. Test your method with several calls, each with a different number of arguments.

8.15   *(Command-Line Arguments)* Rewrite Fig. 8.2 so that the array's size is specified by the first command-line argument. If no command-line argument is supplied, use 10 as the default size.

8.16   *(Using the `foreach` Statement)* Write an application that uses a `foreach` statement to sum the `double` values passed by the command-line arguments. [*Hint:* Use `static` method `ToDouble` of class `Convert` to convert a `string` to a `double` value.]

8.17   *(Dice Rolling)* Write an application to simulate the rolling of two dice. The application should use an object of class `Random` once to roll the first die and again to roll the second die. The sum of the two values should then be calculated. Each die can show an integer value from 1 to 6, so the sum of the values will vary from 2 to 12, with 7 being the most frequent sum and 2 and 12 the least frequent sums. Figure 8.24 shows the 36 possible combinations of the two dice. Your application should roll the dice 36,000 times. Use a one-dimensional array to tally the number of times each possible sum appears. Display the results in tabular format. Determine whether the totals are reasonable (e.g., there are six ways to roll a 7, so approximately one-sixth of the rolls should be 7).

8.18   *(Game of Craps)* Write an application that runs 1000 games of craps (Fig. 7.8) and answers the following questions:

    a) How many games are won on the first roll, second roll, ..., twentieth roll and after the twentieth roll?

    b) How many games are lost on the first roll, second roll, ..., twentieth roll and after the twentieth roll?

    c) What are the chances of winning at craps? [*Note:* You should discover that craps is one of the fairest casino games.]

    d) What is the average length of a game of craps?

	1	2	3	4	5	6
1	2	3	4	5	6	7
2	3	4	5	6	7	8
3	4	5	6	7	8	9
4	5	6	7	8	9	10
5	6	7	8	9	10	11
6	7	8	9	10	11	12

Fig. 8.24 | The 36 possible sums of two dice.

8.19   *(Airline Reservations System)* A small airline has just purchased a computer for its new automated reservations system. You have been asked to develop the new system. You're to write an application to assign seats on each flight of the airline's only plane (capacity: 10 seats).

Display the following alternatives: `Please type 1 for First Class` and `Please type 2 for Economy`. If the user types `1`, your application should assign a seat in the first-class section (seats 1–5). If the user types `2`, your application should assign a seat in the economy section (seats 6–10).

Use a one-dimensional array of type `bool` to represent the seating chart of the plane. Initialize all the elements of the array to `false` to indicate that all the seats are empty. As each seat is assigned, set the corresponding element of the array to `true` to indicate that the seat is no longer available.

Your application should never assign a seat that has already been assigned. When the economy section is full, your application should ask the person if it's acceptable to be placed in the first-class section (and vice versa). If yes, make the appropriate seat assignment. If no, display the message `"Next flight leaves in 3 hours."`

8.20   *(Total Sales)* Use a rectangular array to solve the following problem: A company has three salespeople (1 to 3) who sell five different products (1 to 5). Once a day, each salesperson passes in a slip for each type of product sold. Each slip contains the following:

a) The salesperson number

b) The product number

c) The total dollar value of that product sold that day

Thus, each salesperson passes in between 0 and 5 sales slips per day. Assume that the information from all of the slips for last month is available. Write an application that will read all the information for last month's sales and summarize the total sales by salesperson and by product. All totals should be stored in rectangular array `sales`. After processing all the information for last month, display the results in tabular format, with each column representing a particular salesperson and each row representing a particular product. Cross-total each row to get the total sales of each product for last month. Cross-total each column to get the total sales by salesperson for last month. Your tabular output should include these cross-totals to the right of the totaled rows and below the totaled columns.

8.21   *(Turtle Graphics)* The Logo language made the concept of *turtle graphics* famous. Imagine a mechanical turtle that walks around the room under the control of a C# application. The turtle holds a pen in one of two positions—up or down. While the pen is down, the turtle traces out shapes as it moves, and while the pen is up, the turtle moves about freely without writing anything. In this problem, you'll simulate the operation of the turtle and create a computerized sketchpad.

Use a 20-by-20 rectangular array `floor` that's initialized to 0. Read commands from an array that contains them. Keep track at all times of the current position of the turtle and whether the pen is currently up or down. Assume that the turtle always starts at position (0, 0) of the floor with its pen up. The set of turtle commands your application must process are shown in Fig. 8.25.

Suppose that the turtle is somewhere near the center of the floor. The following "application" would draw and display a 12-by-12 square, leaving the pen in the up position:

```
2
5,12
3
5,12
3
5,12
3
5,12
1
6
9
```

As the turtle moves with the pen down, set the appropriate elements of array `floor` to 1s. When the 6 command (display the array) is given, wherever there's a 1 in the array, display an asterisk or any character you choose. Wherever there's a 0, display a blank.

Write an application to implement the turtle graphics capabilities discussed here. Write several turtle graphics applications to draw interesting shapes. Add other commands to increase the power of your turtle graphics language.

Command	Meaning
1	Pen up
2	Pen down
3	Turn right
4	Turn left
5,10	Move forward 10 spaces (replace 10 for a different number of spaces)
6	Display the 20-by-20 array
9	End of data (sentinel)

Fig. 8.25 | Turtle graphics commands.

8.22   *(Knight's Tour)* One of the more interesting puzzlers for chess buffs is the Knight's Tour problem, originally proposed by the mathematician Euler. Can the chess piece called the knight move around an empty chessboard and touch each of the 64 squares once and only once? We study this intriguing problem in depth here.

The knight makes only L-shaped moves (two spaces in one direction and one space in a perpendicular direction). Thus, as shown in Fig. 8.26, from a square near the middle of an empty chessboard, the knight (labeled K) can make eight different moves (numbered 0 through 7).

a) Draw an eight-by-eight chessboard on a sheet of paper, and attempt a Knight's Tour by hand. Put a 1 in the starting square, a 2 in the second square, a 3 in the third and so on. Before starting the tour, estimate how far you think you'll get, remembering that a full tour consists of 64 moves. How far did you get? Was this close to your estimate?

b) Now let's develop an application that will move the knight around a chessboard. The board is represented by an eight-by-eight rectangular array `board`. Each square is initialized to zero. We describe each of the eight possible moves in terms of their horizontal and vertical components. For example, a move of type 0, as shown in Fig. 8.26, consists of moving two squares horizontally to the right and one square vertically upward. A move of type 2 consists of moving one square horizontally to the left and two squares vertically upward. Horizontal moves to the left and vertical moves upward are indicated with negative numbers. The eight moves may be described by two one-dimensional arrays, `horizontal` and `vertical`, as follows:

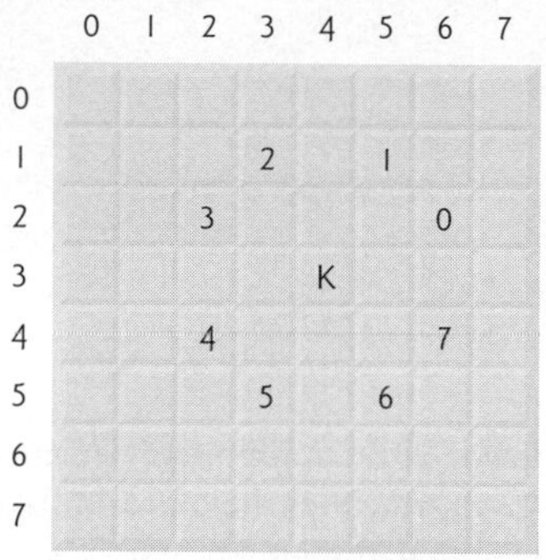

Fig. 8.26 | The eight possible moves of the knight.

```
horizontal[ 0 ] = 2      vertical[ 0 ] = -1
horizontal[ 1 ] = 1      vertical[ 1 ] = -2
horizontal[ 2 ] = -1     vertical[ 2 ] = -2
horizontal[ 3 ] = -2     vertical[ 3 ] = -1
horizontal[ 4 ] = -2     vertical[ 4 ] = 1
horizontal[ 5 ] = -1     vertical[ 5 ] = 2
horizontal[ 6 ] = 1      vertical[ 6 ] = 2
horizontal[ 7 ] = 2      vertical[ 7 ] = 1
```

Let variables currentRow and currentColumn indicate the row and column, respectively, of the knight's current position. To make a move of type moveNumber, where moveNumber is between 0 and 7, your application should use the statements

```
currentRow += vertical[ moveNumber ];
currentColumn += horizontal[ moveNumber ];
```

Write an application to move the knight around the chessboard. Keep a counter that varies from 1 to 64. Record the latest count in each square the knight moves to. Test each potential move to see if the knight has already visited that square. Test every potential move to ensure that the knight does not land off the chessboard. Run the application. How many moves did the knight make?

c) After attempting to write and run a Knight's Tour application, you have probably developed some valuable insights. We'll use these insights to develop a *heuristic* for moving the knight. Heuristics do not guarantee success, but a carefully developed heuristic greatly improves the chance of success. You may have observed that the outer squares are more troublesome than the squares nearer the center of the board. In fact, the most troublesome and inaccessible squares are the four corners.

Intuition may suggest that you should attempt to move the knight to the most troublesome squares first and leave open those that are easiest to get to, so that when the board gets congested near the end of the tour, there will be a greater chance of success.

We could develop an "accessibility heuristic" by classifying each of the squares according to how accessible it is and always moving the knight (using the knight's L-shaped moves) to the most inaccessible square. We label two-dimensional array accessibility with numbers indicating from how many squares each particular square is accessible. On a blank chessboard, each of the 16 squares nearest the center is rated as 8, each corner square is rated as 2, and the other squares have accessibility numbers of 3, 4 or 6 as follows:

```
2  3  4  4  4  4  3  2
3  4  6  6  6  6  4  3
4  6  8  8  8  8  6  4
4  6  8  8  8  8  6  4
4  6  8  8  8  8  6  4
4  6  8  8  8  8  6  4
3  4  6  6  6  6  4  3
2  3  4  4  4  4  3  2
```

Write a new version of the Knight's Tour, using the accessibility heuristic. The knight should always move to the square with the lowest accessibility number. In case of a tie, the knight may move to any of the tied squares. Therefore, the tour may begin in any of the four corners. [*Note:* As the knight moves around the chessboard as more squares become occupied, your application should reduce the accessibility numbers. In this way, at any given time during the tour, each available square's accessibility number will remain equal to precisely the number of squares from which that square may be reached.] Run this version of your application. Did you get a full tour? Modify the application to run 64 tours, one starting from each square of the chessboard. How many full tours did you get?

d) Write a version of the Knight's Tour application that, when encountering a tie between two or more squares, decides what square to choose by looking ahead to those squares reachable from the "tied" squares. Your application should move to the tied square for which the next move would arrive at the square with the lowest accessibility number.

8.23 *(Knight's Tour: Brute-Force Approaches)* In *Part c* of Exercise 8.22, we developed a solution to the Knight's Tour problem. The approach used, called the "accessibility heuristic," generates many solutions and executes efficiently.

As computers continue to increase in power, we'll be able to solve more problems with sheer computer power and relatively unsophisticated algorithms. Let's call this approach "brute-force" problem solving.

a) Use random-number generation to enable the knight to walk around the chessboard (in its legitimate L-shaped moves) at random. Your application should run one tour and display the final chessboard. How far did the knight get?

b) Most likely, the application in *Part a* produced a relatively short tour. Now modify your application to attempt 1000 tours. Use a one-dimensional array to keep track of the number of tours of each length. When your application finishes attempting the 1000 tours, it should display this information in neat tabular format. What was the best result?

c) Most likely, the application in *Part b* gave you some "respectable" tours, but no full tours. Now let your application run until it produces a full tour. Once again, keep a table of the number of tours of each length, and display this table when the first full tour is found. How many tours did your application attempt before producing a full tour?

d) Compare the brute-force version of the Knight's Tour with the accessibility-heuristic version. Which required a more careful study of the problem? Which algorithm was more difficult to develop? Which required more computer power? Could we be certain (in advance) of obtaining a full tour with the accessibility-heuristic approach? Could we be certain (in advance) of obtaining a full tour with the brute-force approach? Argue the pros and cons of brute-force problem solving in general.

8.24 *(Eight Queens)* Another puzzler for chess buffs is the Eight Queens problem, which asks: Is it possible to place eight queens on an empty chessboard so that no queen is "attacking" any other (i.e., no two queens are in the same row, in the same column or along the same diagonal)? Use the thinking developed in Exercise 8.22 to formulate a heuristic for solving the Eight Queens problem. Run your application. [*Hint:* It's possible to assign a value to each square of the chessboard to indicate how many squares of an empty chessboard are "eliminated" if a queen is placed in that square. Each of the corners would be assigned the value 22, as demonstrated by Fig. 8.27. Once these "elimination numbers" are placed in all 64 squares, an appropriate heuristic might be as follows: Place the next queen in the square with the smallest elimination number. Why is this strategy intuitively appealing?]

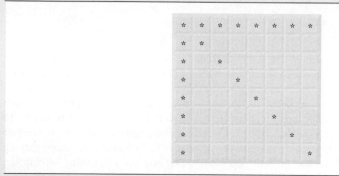

Fig. 8.27 | The 22 squares eliminated by placing a queen in the upper left corner.

8.25 *(Eight Queens: Brute-Force Approaches)* In this exercise, you'll develop several brute-force approaches to solving the Eight Queens problem introduced in Exercise 8.24.

    a) Use the random brute-force technique developed in Exercise 8.23 to solve the Eight Queens problem.

    b) Use an exhaustive technique (i.e., try all possible combinations of eight queens on the chessboard) to solve the Eight Queens problem.

8.26 *(Knight's Tour: Closed-Tour Test)* In the Knight's Tour (Exercise 8.22), a full tour occurs when the knight makes 64 moves, touching each square of the chessboard once and only once. A closed tour occurs when the 64th move is one move away from the square in which the tour started. Modify the application you wrote in Exercise 8.22 to test for a closed tour if a full tour has occurred.

8.27 *(Sieve of Eratosthenes)* A prime number is any integer greater than 1 that's evenly divisible only by itself and 1. The Sieve of Eratosthenes finds prime numbers. It operates as follows:

    a) Create a simple type bool array with all elements initialized to true. Array elements with prime indices will remain true. All other array elements will eventually be set to false.

    b) Starting with array index 2, determine whether a given element is true. If so, loop through the remainder of the array and set to false every element whose index is a multiple of the index for the element with value true. Then continue the process with the next element with value true. For array index 2, all elements beyond element 2 in the array with indices that are multiples of 2 (indices 4, 6, 8, 10, etc.) will be set to false; for array index 3, all elements beyond element 3 in the array with indices that are multiples of 3 (indices 6, 9, 12, 15, etc.) will be set to false; and so on.

When this process completes, the array elements that are still true indicate that the index is a prime number. These indices can be displayed. Write an application that uses an array of 1000 elements to determine and display the prime numbers between 2 and 999. Ignore elements 0 and 1.

8.28 *(Simulation: The Tortoise and the Hare)* You'll now re-create the classic race of the tortoise and the hare. You'll use random-number generation to develop a simulation of this memorable event.

    Our contenders begin the race at square 1 of 70 squares. Each square represents a possible position along the race course. The finish line is at square 70. The first contender to reach or pass square 70 is rewarded with a pail of fresh carrots and lettuce. The course weaves its way up the side of a slippery mountain, so occasionally the contenders lose ground.

    A clock ticks once per second. With each tick of the clock, your application should adjust the position of the animals according to the rules in Fig. 8.28. Use variables to keep track of the

Animal	Move type	Percentage of the time	Actual move
Tortoise	Fast plod	50%	3 squares to the right
	Slip	20%	6 squares to the left
	Slow plod	30%	1 square to the right
Hare	Sleep	20%	No move at all
	Big hop	20%	9 squares to the right
	Big slip	10%	12 squares to the left
	Small hop	30%	1 square to the right
	Small slip	20%	2 squares to the left

Fig. 8.28 | Rules for adjusting the positions of the tortoise and the hare.

positions of the animals (i.e., position numbers are 1–70). Start each animal at position 1 (the "starting gate"). If an animal slips left before square 1, move it back to square 1.

Generate the percentages in Fig. 8.28 by producing a random integer i in the range $1 \leq i \leq 10$. For the tortoise, perform a "fast plod" when $1 \leq i \leq 5$, a "slip" when $6 \leq i \leq 7$ or a "slow plod" when $8 \leq i \leq 10$. Use a similar technique to move the hare.

Begin the race by displaying

```
ON YOUR MARK, GET SET
BANG !!!!!
AND THEY'RE OFF !!!!!
```

Then, for each tick of the clock (i.e., each repetition of a loop), display a 70-position line showing the letter T in the position of the tortoise and the letter H in the position of the hare. Occasionally, the contenders will land on the same square. In this case, the tortoise bites the hare, and your application should display OUCH!!! beginning at that position. All output positions other than the T, the H or the OUCH!!! (in case of a tie) should be blank.

After each line is displayed, test for whether either animal has reached or passed square 70. If so, display the winner and terminate the simulation. If the tortoise wins, display TORTOISE WINS!!! YAY!!! If the hare wins, display Hare wins. Yuch. If both animals win on the same tick of the clock, you may want to favor the tortoise (the "underdog"), or you may want to display It's a tie. If neither animal wins, perform the loop again to simulate the next tick of the clock. When you're ready to run your application, assemble a group of fans to watch the race. You'll be amazed at how involved your audience gets!

8.29 *(Card Shuffling and Dealing)* Modify the application of Fig. 8.11 to deal a five-card poker hand. Then modify class DeckOfCards of Fig. 8.10 to include methods that determine whether a hand contains

    a) a pair
    b) two pairs
    c) three of a kind (e.g., three jacks)
    d) four of a kind (e.g., four aces)
    e) a flush (i.e., all five cards of the same suit)
    f) a straight (i.e., five cards of consecutive face values)
    g) a full house (i.e., two cards of one face value and three cards of another face value)

[*Hint:* Add methods GetFace and GetSuit to class Card of Fig. 8.9.]

8.30 *(Card Shuffling and Dealing)* Use the methods developed in Exercise 8.29 to write an application that deals two five-card poker hands, evaluates each hand and determines which is better.

Special Section: Building Your Own Computer

In the next several problems, we take a temporary diversion from the world of high-level language programming to "peel open" a computer and look at its internal structure. We introduce machine-language programming and write several machine-language programs. To make this an especially valuable experience, we then build a computer (through the technique of software-based simulation) on which you can execute your machine-language programs.

8.31 (*Machine-Language Programming*) Let's create a computer called the Simpletron. As its name implies, it's a simple machine, but powerful. The Simpletron runs programs written in the only language it directly understands: Simpletron Machine Language, or SML for short.

The Simpletron contains an *accumulator*—a special register into which information is put before the Simpletron uses it in calculations or examines it in various ways. All the information in the Simpletron is handled in terms of *words*. A word is a signed four-digit decimal number, such as +3364, -1293, +0007 and -0001. The Simpletron is equipped with a 100-word memory, and these words are referenced by their location numbers 00, 01, ..., 99.

Before running an SML program, we must *load*, or place, the code into memory. The first instruction (or statement) of every SML program is always placed in location 00. The simulator will start executing at this location.

Each instruction written in SML occupies one word of the Simpletron's memory (hence, instructions are signed four-digit decimal numbers). We shall assume that the sign of an SML instruction is always plus, but the sign of a data word may be either plus or minus. Each location in the Simpletron's memory may contain an instruction, a data value used by a program or an unused (and hence undefined) area of memory. The first two digits of each SML instruction are the *operation code* specifying the operation to be performed. SML operation codes are summarized in Fig. 8.29.

Operation code	Meaning
Input/output operations:	
`const int READ = 10;`	Read a word from the keyboard into a specific location in memory.
`const int WRITE = 11;`	Write a word from a specific location in memory to the screen.
Load/store operations:	
`const int LOAD = 20;`	Load a word from a specific location in memory into the accumulator.
`const int STORE = 21;`	Store a word from the accumulator into a specific location in memory.
Arithmetic operations:	
`const int ADD = 30;`	Add a word from a specific location in memory to the word in the accumulator (leave the result in the accumulator).
`const int SUBTRACT = 31;`	Subtract a word from a specific location in memory from the word in the accumulator (leave the result in the accumulator).
`const int DIVIDE = 32;`	Divide a word from a specific location in memory into the word in the accumulator (leave result in the accumulator).
`const int MULTIPLY = 33;`	Multiply a word from a specific location in memory by the word in the accumulator (leave the result in the accumulator).

Fig. 8.29 | Simpletron Machine Language (SML) operation codes. (Part 1 of 2.)

Operation code	Meaning
Transfer of control operations:	
const int BRANCH = 40;	Branch to a specific location in memory.
const int BRANCHNEG = 41;	Branch to a specific location in memory if the accumulator is negative.
const int BRANCHZERO = 42;	Branch to a specific location in memory if the accumulator is zero.
const int HALT = 43;	Halt. The program has completed its task.

Fig. 8.29 | Simpletron Machine Language (SML) operation codes. (Part 2 of 2.)

The last two digits of an SML instruction are the *operand*—the address of the memory location containing the word to which the operation applies. Let's consider several simple SML programs. The first SML program (Fig. 8.30) reads two numbers from the keyboard, then computes and displays their sum. The instruction +1007 reads the first number from the keyboard and places it into location 07 (which has been initialized to 0). Then instruction +1008 reads the next number into location 08. The *load* instruction, +2007, puts the first number into the accumulator, and the *add* instruction, +3008, adds the second number to the number in the accumulator. *All SML arithmetic instructions leave their results in the accumulator.* The *store* instruction, +2109, places the result in memory location 09, from which the *write* instruction, +1109, takes the number and displays it (as a signed four-digit decimal number). The *halt* instruction, +4300, terminates execution.

The second SML program (Fig. 8.31) reads two numbers from the keyboard and determines and displays the larger value. Note the use of the instruction +4107 as a conditional transfer of control, much the same as C#'s if statement.

Now write SML programs to accomplish each of the following tasks:

a) Use a sentinel-controlled loop to read positive numbers and compute and display their sum. Terminate input when a negative number is entered.

b) Use a counter-controlled loop to read seven numbers, some positive and some negative, then compute and display their average.

c) Read a series of numbers, then determine and display the largest number. The first number read indicates how many numbers should be processed.

Location	Number	Instruction
00	+1007	(Read A)
01	+1008	(Read B)
02	+2007	(Load A)
03	+3008	(Add B)
04	+2109	(Store C)
05	+1109	(Write C)
06	+4300	(Halt)
07	+0000	(Variable A)
08	+0000	(Variable B)
09	+0000	(Result C)

Fig. 8.30 | SML program that reads two integers and computes their sum.

Location	Number	Instruction
00	+1009	(Read A)
01	+1010	(Read B)
02	+2009	(Load A)
03	+3110	(Subtract B)
04	+4107	(Branch negative to 07)
05	+1109	(Write A)
06	+4300	(Halt)
07	+1110	(Write B)
08	+4300	(Halt)
09	+0000	(Variable A)
10	+0000	(Variable B)

Fig. 8.31 | SML program that reads two integers and determines the larger.

8.32 *(Computer Simulator)* In this problem, you're going to build your own computer. No, you'll not be soldering components together. Rather, you'll use the powerful technique of *software-based simulation* to create an object-oriented *software model* of the Simpletron of Exercise 8.31. Your Simpletron simulator will turn the computer you're using into a Simpletron, and you'll actually be able to run, test and debug the SML programs you wrote in Exercise 8.31.

When you run your Simpletron simulator, it should begin by displaying:

```
*** Welcome to Simpletron! ***
*** Please enter your program one instruction ***
*** ( or data word ) at a time into the input ***
*** text field. I will display the location   ***
*** number and a question mark (?). You then   ***
*** type the word for that location. Enter     ***
*** -99999 to stop entering your program.      ***
```

Your application should simulate the memory of the Simpletron with one-dimensional array memory of 100 elements. Now assume that the simulator is running, and let's examine the dialog as we enter the program of Fig. 8.31 (Exercise 8.31):

```
00 ? +1009
01 ? +1010
02 ? +2009
03 ? +3110
04 ? +4107
05 ? +1109
06 ? +4300
07 ? +1110
08 ? +4300
09 ? +0000
10 ? +0000
11 ? -99999
```

Your program should display the memory location followed by a question mark. Each of the values to the right of a question mark is input by the user. When the sentinel value -99999 is input, the program should display the following:

```
*** Program loading completed ***
*** Program execution begins  ***
```

The SML program has now been placed (or loaded) in array memory. Now the Simpletron executes the SML program. Execution begins with the instruction in location 00 and, as in C#, continues sequentially, unless directed to some other part of the program by a transfer of control.

Use variable accumulator to represent the accumulator register. Use variable instructionCounter to keep track of the location in memory that contains the instruction being performed. Use variable operationCode to indicate the operation currently being performed (i.e., the left two digits of the instruction word). Use variable operand to indicate the memory location on which the current instruction operates. Thus, operand is the rightmost two digits of the instruction currently being performed. Do not execute instructions directly from memory. Rather, transfer the next instruction to be performed from memory to a variable called instructionRegister. Then "pick off" the left two digits and place them in operationCode, and "pick off" the right two digits and place them in operand. When the Simpletron begins execution, the special registers are all initialized to zero.

Now, let's "walk through" execution of the first SML instruction, +1009 in memory location 00. This procedure is called an *instruction execution cycle.*

The instructionCounter tells us the location of the next instruction to be performed. We *fetch* the contents of that location from memory by using the C# statement

```
instructionRegister = memory[ instructionCounter ];
```

The operation code and the operand are extracted from the instruction register by the statements

```
operationCode = instructionRegister / 100;
operand = instructionRegister % 100;
```

Now the Simpletron must determine that the operation code is actually a *read* (versus a *write*, a *load*, or whatever). A switch differentiates among the 12 operations of SML. In the switch statement, the behavior of various SML instructions is simulated as shown in Fig. 8.32. We discuss branch instructions shortly and leave the others to you.

Instruction	Description
read:	Display the prompt "Enter an integer", then input the integer and store it in location memory[operand].
load:	accumulator = memory[operand];
add:	accumulator += memory[operand];
halt:	This instruction displays the message *** Simpletron execution terminated ***

Fig. 8.32 | Behavior of several SML instructions in the Simpletron.

When the SML program completes execution, the name and contents of each register, as well as the complete contents of memory, should be displayed. Such a printout is often called a memory dump. To help you program your dump method, a sample dump format is shown in Fig. 8.33. A dump after executing a Simpletron program would show the actual values of instructions and data values at the moment execution terminated.

Let's proceed with the execution of our program's first instruction—namely, the +1009 in location 00. As we have indicated, the switch statement simulates this task by prompting the user to enter a value, reading the value and storing it in memory location memory[operand]. The value is then read into location 09.

At this point, simulation of the first instruction is completed. All that remains is to prepare the Simpletron to execute the next instruction. Since the instruction just performed was not a transfer of control, we need merely increment the instructionCounter.

```
REGISTERS:
accumulator            +0000
instructionCounter        00
instructionRegister    +0000
operationCode             00
operand                   00

MEMORY:
        0      1      2      3      4      5      6      7      8      9
 0  +0000  +0000  +0000  +0000  +0000  +0000  +0000  +0000  +0000  +0000
10  +0000  +0000  +0000  +0000  +0000  +0000  +0000  +0000  +0000  +0000
20  +0000  +0000  +0000  +0000  +0000  +0000  +0000  +0000  +0000  +0000
30  +0000  +0000  +0000  +0000  +0000  +0000  +0000  +0000  +0000  +0000
40  +0000  +0000  +0000  +0000  +0000  +0000  +0000  +0000  +0000  +0000
50  +0000  +0000  +0000  +0000  +0000  +0000  +0000  +0000  +0000  +0000
60  +0000  +0000  +0000  +0000  +0000  +0000  +0000  +0000  +0000  +0000
70  +0000  +0000  +0000  +0000  +0000  +0000  +0000  +0000  +0000  +0000
80  +0000  +0000  +0000  +0000  +0000  +0000  +0000  +0000  +0000  +0000
90  +0000  +0000  +0000  +0000  +0000  +0000  +0000  +0000  +0000  +0000
```

Fig. 8.33 | A sample memory dump.

This action completes the simulated execution of the first instruction. The entire process (i.e., the instruction execution cycle) begins anew with the fetch of the next instruction to execute.

Now let's consider how the branching instructions—the transfers of control—are simulated. All we need to do is adjust the value in the instruction counter appropriately. Therefore, the unconditional branch instruction (40) is simulated within the switch as

```
instructionCounter = operand;
```

The conditional "branch if accumulator is zero" instruction is simulated as

```
if ( accumulator == 0 )
    instructionCounter = operand;
```

At this point, you should implement your Simpletron simulator and run each of the SML programs you wrote in Exercise 8.31. If you desire, you may embellish SML with additional features and provide for these features in your simulator.

Your simulator should check for various types of errors. During the program-loading phase, for example, each number the user types into the Simpletron's memory must be in the range -9999 to +9999. Your simulator should test that each number entered is in this range and, if not, keep prompting the user to re-enter the number until the user enters a correct number.

During the execution phase, your simulator should check for various serious errors, such as attempts to divide by zero, attempts to execute invalid operation codes and accumulator overflows (i.e., arithmetic operations resulting in values larger than +9999 or smaller than -9999). Such serious errors are called *fatal errors*. When a fatal error is detected, your simulator should display an error message, such as

```
*** Attempt to divide by zero ***
*** Simpletron execution abnormally terminated ***
```

and should display a full computer dump in the format we discussed previously. This treatment will help the user locate the error in the program.

8.33 *(Project: Simpletron Simulator Modifications)* In Exercise 8.32, you wrote a software simulation of a computer that executes programs written in Simpletron Machine Language (SML). In this exercise, we propose several modifications and enhancements to the Simpletron Simulator.

a) Extend the Simpletron Simulator's memory to contain 1000 memory locations to enable the Simpletron to handle larger programs.

b) Allow the simulator to perform remainder calculations. This modification requires an additional SML instruction.

c) Allow the simulator to perform exponentiation calculations. This modification requires an additional SML instruction.

d) Modify the simulator to use hexadecimal values rather than integer values to represent SML instructions.

e) Modify the simulator to allow output of a newline. This modification requires an additional SML instruction.

f) Modify the simulator to process floating-point values in addition to integer values.

g) Modify the simulator to handle string input. [*Hint:* Each Simpletron word can be divided into two groups, each holding a two-digit integer. Each two-digit integer represents the ASCII (see Appendix C) decimal equivalent of an uppercase character. Add a machine-language instruction that will input a string and store the string beginning at a specific Simpletron memory location. The first half of the word at that location will be a count of the number of characters in the string (i.e., the length of the string). Each succeeding half-word contains one ASCII character expressed as two decimal digits. The machine-language instruction converts each character into its ASCII equivalent and assigns it to a half-word.]

h) Modify the simulator to handle output of uppercase strings stored in the format of *Part g*. [*Hint:* Add a machine-language instruction that will display a string beginning at a certain Simpletron memory location. The first half of the word at that location is a count of the number of characters in the string (i.e., the length of the string). Each succeeding half-word contains one ASCII character expressed as two decimal digits. The machine-language instruction checks the length and displays the string by translating each two-digit number into its equivalent character.]

Making a Difference Exercise

8.34   *(Polling)* The Internet and the web are enabling more people to network, join a cause, voice opinions, and so on. The presidential candidates in 2008 used the Internet intensively to get out their messages and raise money for their campaigns. In this exercise, you'll write a simple polling program that allows users to rate five social-consciousness issues from 1 (least important) to 10 (most important). Pick five causes that are important to you (for example, political issues, global environmental issues). Use a one-dimensional array topics (of type String) to store the five causes. To summarize the survey responses, use a 5-row, 10-column two-dimensional array responses (of type Integer), each row corresponding to an element in the topics array. When the program runs, it should ask the user to rate each issue. Have your friends and family respond to the survey. Then have the program display a summary of the results, including:

a) A tabular report with the five topics down the left side and the 10 ratings across the top, listing in each column the number of ratings received for each topic.

b) To the right of each row, show the average of the ratings for that issue.

c) Which issue received the highest point total? Display both the issue and the point total.

d) Which issue received the lowest point total? Display both the issue and the point total.

9

Introduction to LINQ and the **List** Collection

To write it, it took three months; to conceive it three minutes; to collect the data in it—all my life.
—F. Scott Fitzgerald

Science is feasible when the variables are few and can be enumerated ...
—Paul Valéry

You shall listen to all sides and filter them from your self.
—Walt Whitman

The portraitist can select one tiny aspect of everything shown at a moment to incorporate into the final painting.
—Robert Nozick

List, list, O, list!
—William Shakespeare

Objectives

In this chapter you'll learn:

- Basic LINQ concepts.

- How to query an array using LINQ.

- Basic .NET collections concepts.

- How to create and use a generic **List** collection.

- How to query a generic **List** collection using LINQ.

9.1 Introduction

The preceding chapter introduced arrays—simple data structures used to store data items of a specific type. Although commonly used, arrays have limited capabilities. For instance, you must specify an array's size, and if at execution time, you wish to modify it, you must do so manually by creating a new array or by using the Array class's Resize method, which creates a new array and copies the existing elements into the new array for you.

Here, we introduce a set of *prepackaged* data structures—the .NET Framework's collection classes—that offer greater capabilities than traditional arrays. They're reusable, reliable, powerful and efficient and have been carefully designed and tested to ensure quality and performance. This chapter focuses on the List collection. Lists are similar to arrays but provide additional functionality, such as **dynamic resizing**—they automatically increase their size at execution time to accommodate additional elements. We use the List collection to implement several examples similar to those used in the preceding chapter.

Large amounts of data are often stored in a database—an organized collection of data. (We discuss databases in detail in Chapter 18.) A database management system (DBMS) provides mechanisms for storing, organizing, retrieving and modifying data in the database. A language called SQL—pronounced "sequel"—is the international standard used to perform **queries** (i.e., to request information that satisfies given criteria) and to manipulate data. For years, programs accessing a relational database passed SQL queries to the database management system, then processed the results. This chapter introduces C#'s new **LINQ (Language Integrated Query)** capabilities. LINQ allows you to write **query expressions**, similar to SQL queries, that retrieve information from a wide variety of data sources, not just databases. We use **LINQ to Objects** in this chapter to query arrays and Lists, selecting elements that satisfy a set of conditions—this is known as **filtering**. Figure 9.1 shows where and how we use LINQ throughout the book to retrieve information from many data sources.

Chapter	Used to
Chapter 9, Introduction to LINQ and the List Collection	Query arrays and Lists.
Chapter 16, Strings and Characters	Select GUI controls in a Windows Forms application.
Chapter 17, Files and Streams	Search a directory and manipulate text files.

Fig. 9.1 | LINQ usage throughout the book. (Part 1 of 2.)

Chapter	Used to
Chapter 18, Databases and LINQ	Retrieve information from a database.
Chapter 19, Web App Development with ASP.NET	Retrieve information from a database to be used in a web-based application.
Chapter 26, XML and LINQ to XML	Query an XML document.
Chapter 28, Windows Communication Foundation (WCF) Web Services	Query and update a database. Process XML returned by WCF services.
Chapter 29, Silverlight and Rich Internet Applications	Process XML returned by web services to a Silverlight application.

Fig. 9.1 | LINQ usage throughout the book. (Part 2 of 2.)

LINQ Providers
The syntax of LINQ is built into C#, but LINQ queries may be used in many different contexts because of libraries known as providers. A **LINQ provider** is a set of classes that implement LINQ operations and enable programs to interact with data sources to perform tasks such as sorting, grouping and filtering elements.

In this book, we discuss LINQ to SQL and LINQ to XML, which allow you to query databases and XML documents using LINQ. These providers, along with LINQ to Objects, mentioned above, are included with Visual Studio and the .NET Framework. There are many providers that are more specialized, allowing you to interact with a specific website or data format. An extensive list of available providers is located at:

```
blogs.msdn.com/charlie/archive/2006/10/05/Links-to-LINQ.aspx
```

9.2 Querying an Array of int Values Using LINQ

Figure 9.2 demonstrates querying an array of integers using LINQ. Repetition statements that filter arrays focus on the process of getting the results—iterating through the elements and checking whether they satisfy the desired criteria. LINQ specifies the conditions that selected elements must satisfy. This is known as **declarative programming**—as opposed to **imperative programming** (which we've been doing so far) in which you specify the actual steps to perform a task. The query in lines 20–22 specifies that the results should consist of all the ints in the values array that are greater than 4. It *does not* specify *how* those results are obtained—the C# compiler generates all the necessary code automatically, which is one of the great strengths of LINQ. To use LINQ to Objects, you must import the System.Linq namespace (line 4).

```
1   // Fig. 9.2: LINQWithSimpleTypeArray.cs
2   // LINQ to Objects using an int array.
3   using System;
4   using System.Linq;
```

Fig. 9.2 | LINQ to Objects using an int array. (Part 1 of 3.)

```
5
6   class LINQWithSimpleTypeArray
7   {
8      public static void Main( string[] args )
9      {
10        // create an integer array
11        int[] values = { 2, 9, 5, 0, 3, 7, 1, 4, 8, 5 };
12
13        // display original values
14        Console.Write( "Original array:" );
15        foreach ( var element in values )
16           Console.Write( " {0}", element );
17
18        // LINQ query that obtains values greater than 4 from the array
19        var filtered =
20           from value in values
21           where value > 4
22           select value;
23
24        // display filtered results
25        Console.Write( "\nArray values greater than 4:" );
26        foreach ( var element in filtered )
27           Console.Write( " {0}", element );
28
29        // use orderby clause to sort original array in ascending order
30        var sorted =
31           from value in values
32           orderby value
33           select value;
34
35        // display sorted results
36        Console.Write( "\nOriginal array, sorted:" );
37        foreach ( var element in sorted )
38           Console.Write( " {0}", element );
39
40        // sort the filtered results into descending order
41        var sortFilteredResults =
42           from value in filtered
43           orderby value descending
44           select value;
45
46        // display the sorted results
47        Console.Write(
48           "\nValues greater than 4, descending order (separately):" );
49        foreach ( var element in sortFilteredResults )
50           Console.Write( " {0}", element );
51
52        // filter original array and sort in descending order
53        var sortAndFilter =
54           from value in values
55           where value > 4
56           orderby value descending
57           select value;
```

Fig. 9.2 | LINQ to Objects using an int array. (Part 2 of 3.)

```
58
59          // display the filtered and sorted results
60          Console.Write(
61             "\nValues greater than 4, descending order (one query):" );
62          foreach ( var element in sortAndFilter )
63             Console.Write( " {0}", element );
64
65          Console.WriteLine();
66       } // end Main
67    } // end class LINQWithSimpleTypeArray
```

```
Original array: 2 9 5 0 3 7 1 4 8 5
Array values greater than 4: 9 5 7 8 5
Original array, sorted: 0 1 2 3 4 5 5 7 8 9
Values greater than 4, descending order (separately): 9 8 7 5 5
Values greater than 4, descending order (one query): 9 8 7 5 5
```

Fig. 9.2 | LINQ to Objects using an int array. (Part 3 of 3.)

The *from* Clause and Implicitly Typed Local Variables

A LINQ query begins with a **from clause** (line 20), which specifies a **range variable** (value) and the data source to query (values). The range variable represents each item in the data source (one at a time), much like the control variable in a foreach statement. We do not specify the range variable's type. Since it is assigned one element at a time from the array values, which is an int array, the compiler determines that the range variable value should be of type int. This is a C# feature called **implicitly typed local variables**, which enables the compiler to *infer* a local variable's type based on the context in which it's used.

Introducing the range variable in the from clause at the beginning of the query allows the IDE to provide *IntelliSense* while you write the rest of the query. The IDE knows the range variable's type, so when you enter the range variable's name followed by a dot (.) in the code editor, the IDE can display the range variable's methods and properties.

The *var* Keyword and Implicitly Typed Local Variables

You can also declare a local variable and let the compiler infer the variable's type based on the variable's initializer. To do so, the **var keyword** is used in place of the variable's type when declaring the variable. Consider the declaration

```
var x = 7;
```

Here, the compiler *infers* that the variable x should be of type int, because the compiler assumes that whole-number values, like 7, are of type int. Similarly, in the declaration

```
var y = -123.45;
```

the compiler infers that y should be of type double, because the compiler assumes that floating-point number values, like -123.45, are of type double. Typically, implicitly typed local variables are used for more complex types, such as the collections of data returned by LINQ queries. We use this feature in lines 19, 30, 41 and 53 to enable the compiler to determine the type of each variable that stores the results of a LINQ query. We also use this feature to declare the control variable in the foreach statements at lines 15–16, 26–27, 37–38, 49–50 and 62–63. In each case, the compiler infers that the control variable is of type int because the array values and the LINQ query results all contain int values.

The where Clause

If the condition in the **where clause** (line 21) evaluates to `true`, the element is *selected*—i.e., it's included in the results. Here, the `int`s in the array are included only if they're greater than 4. An expression that takes an element of a collection and returns `true` or `false` by testing a condition on that element is known as a **predicate**.

The select Clause

For each item in the data source, the **select clause** (line 22) determines what value appears in the results. In this case, it's the `int` that the range variable currently represents. A LINQ query typically ends with a `select` clause.

Iterating Through the Results of the LINQ Query

Lines 26–27 use a `foreach` statement to display the query results. As you know, a `foreach` statement can iterate through the contents of an array, allowing you to process each element in the array. Actually, the `foreach` statement can iterate through the contents arrays, collections and the results of LINQ queries. The `foreach` statement in lines 26–27 iterates over the query result `filtered`, displaying each of its items.

LINQ vs. Repetition Statements

It would be simple to display the integers greater than 4 using a repetition statement that tests each value before displaying it. However, this would intertwine the code that selects elements and the code that displays them. With LINQ, these are kept separate, making the code easier to understand and maintain.

The orderby Clause

The **orderby clause** (line 32) sorts the query results in ascending order. Lines 43 and 56 use the **descending** modifier in the `orderby` clause to sort the results in descending order. An **ascending** modifier also exists but isn't normally used, because it's the default. Any value that can be compared with other values of the same type may be used with the `orderby` clause. A value of a simple type (e.g., `int`) can always be compared to another value of the same type; we'll say more about comparing values of reference types in Chapter 12.

The queries in lines 42–44 and 54–57 generate the same results, but in different ways. The first query uses LINQ to sort the results of the query from lines 20–22. The second query uses both the `where` and `orderby` clauses. Because queries can operate on the results of other queries, it's possible to build a query one step at a time, and pass the results of queries between methods for further processing.

More on Implicitly Typed Local Variables

Implicitly typed local variables can also be used to initialize arrays without explicitly giving their type. For example, the following statement creates an array of `int` values:

```
var array = new[] { 32, 27, 64, 18, 95, 14, 90, 70, 60, 37 };
```

Note that there are no square brackets on the left side of the assignment operator, and that `new[]` is used to specify that the variable is an array.

An Aside: Interface IEnumerable<T>

As we mentioned, the `foreach` statement can iterate through the contents of arrays, collections and LINQ query results. Actually, `foreach` iterates over any so-called `IEnumerable<T>` object, which just happens to be what a LINQ query returns.

IEnumerable<T> is an **interface**. Interfaces define and standardize the ways in which people and systems can interact with one another. For example, the controls on a radio serve as an interface between radio users and the radio's internal components. The controls allow users to perform a limited set of operations (e.g., changing the station, adjusting the volume, and choosing between AM and FM), and different radios may implement the controls in different ways (e.g., using push buttons, dials or voice commands). The interface specifies *what* operations a radio permits users to perform but does not specify *how* the operations are implemented. Similarly, the interface between a driver and a car with a manual transmission includes the steering wheel, the gear shift, the clutch, the gas pedal and the brake pedal. This same interface is found in nearly all manual-transmission cars, enabling someone who knows how to drive one manual-transmission car to drive another.

Software objects also communicate via interfaces. A C# interface describes a set of methods that can be called on an object—to tell the object, for example, to perform some task or return some piece of information. The IEnumerable<T> interface describes the functionality of any object that can be iterated over and thus offers methods to access each element. A class that implements an interface must define each method in the interface with a signature identical to the one in the interface definition. Implementing an interface is like signing a contract with the compiler that states, "I will declare all the methods specified by the interface." Chapter 12 covers use of interfaces in more detail, as well as how to define your own interfaces.

Arrays are IEnumerable<T> objects, so a foreach statement can iterate over an array's elements. Similarly, each LINQ query returns an IEnumerable<T> object. Therefore, you can use a foreach statement to iterate over the results of any LINQ query. The notation <T> indicates that the interface is a generic interface that can be used with any type of data (for example, ints, strings or Employees). You'll learn more about the <T> notation in Section 9.4. You'll learn more about interfaces in Section 12.7.

9.3 Querying an Array of Employee Objects Using LINQ

LINQ is not limited to querying arrays of primitive types such as ints. It can be used with most data types, including strings and user-defined classes. It cannot be used when a query does not have a defined meaning—for example, you cannot use orderby on objects that are not comparable. Comparable types in .NET are those that implement the IComparable interface, which is discussed in Section 22.4. All built-in types, such as string, int and double implement IComparable. Figure 9.3 presents the Employee class. Figure 9.4 uses LINQ to query an array of Employee objects.

```
1   // Fig. 9.3: Employee.cs
2   // Employee class with FirstName, LastName and MonthlySalary properties.
3   public class Employee
4   {
5       private decimal monthlySalaryValue; // monthly salary of employee
6
7       // auto-implemented property FirstName
8       public string FirstName { get; set; }
9
```

Fig. 9.3 | Employee class. (Part 1 of 2.)

```
10        // auto-implemented property LastName
11        public string LastName { get; set; }
12
13        // constructor initializes first name, last name and monthly salary
14        public Employee( string first, string last, decimal salary )
15        {
16           FirstName = first;
17           LastName = last;
18           MonthlySalary = salary;
19        } // end constructor
20
21        // property that gets and sets the employee's monthly salary
22        public decimal MonthlySalary
23        {
24           get
25           {
26              return monthlySalaryValue;
27           } // end get
28           set
29           {
30              if ( value >= 0M ) // if salary is nonnegative
31              {
32                 monthlySalaryValue = value;
33              } // end if
34           } // end set
35        } // end property MonthlySalary
36
37        // return a string containing the employee's information
38        public override string ToString()
39        {
40           return string.Format( "{0,-10} {1,-10} {2,10:C}",
41              FirstName, LastName, MonthlySalary );
42        } // end method ToString
43     } // end class Employee
```

Fig. 9.3 | Employee class. (Part 2 of 2.)

```
1    // Fig. 9.4: LINQWithArrayOfObjects.cs
2    // LINQ to Objects using an array of Employee objects.
3    using System;
4    using System.Linq;
5
6    public class LINQWithArrayOfObjects
7    {
8       public static void Main( string[] args )
9       {
10          // initialize array of employees
11          Employee[] employees = {
12             new Employee( "Jason", "Red", 5000M ),
13             new Employee( "Ashley", "Green", 7600M ),
14             new Employee( "Matthew", "Indigo", 3587.5M ),
```

Fig. 9.4 | LINQ to Objects using an array of Employee objects. (Part 1 of 3.)

```
15              new Employee( "James", "Indigo", 4700.77M ),
16              new Employee( "Luke", "Indigo", 6200M ),
17              new Employee( "Jason", "Blue", 3200M ),
18              new Employee( "Wendy", "Brown", 4236.4M ) }; // end init list
19
20         // display all employees
21         Console.WriteLine( "Original array:" );
22         foreach ( var element in employees )
23            Console.WriteLine( element );
24
25         // filter a range of salaries using && in a LINQ query
26         var between4K6K =
27            from e in employees
28            where e.MonthlySalary >= 4000M && e.MonthlySalary <= 6000M
29            select e;
30
31         // display employees making between 4000 and 6000 per month
32         Console.WriteLine( string.Format(
33            "\nEmployees earning in the range {0:C}-{1:C} per month:",
34            4000, 6000 ) );
35         foreach ( var element in between4K6K )
36            Console.WriteLine( element );
37
38         // order the employees by last name, then first name with LINQ
39         var nameSorted =
40            from e in employees
41            orderby e.LastName, e.FirstName
42            select e;
43
44         // header
45         Console.WriteLine( "\nFirst employee when sorted by name:" );
46
47         // attempt to display the first result of the above LINQ query
48         if ( nameSorted.Any() )
49            Console.WriteLine( nameSorted.First() );
50         else
51            Console.WriteLine( "not found" );
52
53         // use LINQ to select employee last names
54         var lastNames =
55            from e in employees
56            select e.LastName;
57
58         // use method Distinct to select unique last names
59         Console.WriteLine( "\nUnique employee last names:" );
60         foreach ( var element in lastNames.Distinct() )
61            Console.WriteLine( element );
62
63         // use LINQ to select first and last names
64         var names =
65            from e in employees
66            select new { e.FirstName, Last = e.LastName };
67
```

Fig. 9.4 | LINQ to Objects using an array of Employee objects. (Part 2 of 3.)

```
68          // display full names
69          Console.WriteLine( "\nNames only:" );
70          foreach ( var element in names )
71             Console.WriteLine( element );
72
73          Console.WriteLine();
74       } // end Main
75    } // end class LINQWithArrayOfObjects
```

```
Original array:
Jason       Red         $5,000.00
Ashley      Green       $7,600.00
Matthew     Indigo      $3,587.50
James       Indigo      $4,700.77
Luke        Indigo      $6,200.00
Jason       Blue        $3,200.00
Wendy       Brown       $4,236.40

Employees earning in the range $4,000.00-$6,000.00 per month:
Jason       Red         $5,000.00
James       Indigo      $4,700.77
Wendy       Brown       $4,236.40

First employee when sorted by name:
Jason       Blue        $3,200.00

Unique employee last names:
Red
Green
Indigo
Blue
Brown

Names only:
{ FirstName = Jason, Last = Red }
{ FirstName = Ashley, Last = Green }
{ FirstName = Matthew, Last = Indigo }
{ FirstName = James, Last = Indigo }
{ FirstName = Luke, Last = Indigo }
{ FirstName = Jason, Last = Blue }
{ FirstName = Wendy, Last = Brown }
```

Fig. 9.4 | LINQ to Objects using an array of Employee objects. (Part 3 of 3.)

Accessing the Properties of a LINQ Query's Range Variable

Line 28 of Fig. 9.4 shows a where clause that accesses the properties of the range variable. In this example, the compiler infers that the range variable is of type Employee based on its knowledge that employees was defined as an array of Employee objects (lines 11–18). Any bool expression can be used in a where clause. Line 28 uses the conditional AND (&&) operator to combine conditions. Here, only employees that have a salary between $4,000 and $6,000 per month, inclusive, are included in the query result, which is displayed in lines 35–36.

Sorting a LINQ Query's Results By Multiple Properties

Line 41 uses an orderby clause to sort the results according to multiple properties—specified in a comma-separated list. In this query, the employees are sorted alphabetically by last name. Each group of Employees that have the same last name is then sorted within the group by first name.

Any, First and Count Extension Methods

Line 48 introduces the query result's **Any** method, which returns true if there's at least one element, and false if there are no elements. The query result's **First** method (line 49) returns the first element in the result. You should check that the query result is not empty (line 48) before calling First.

We've not specified the class that defines methods First and Any. Your intuition probably tells you they're methods declared in the IEnumerable<T> interface, but they aren't. They're actually extension methods, but they can be used as if they were methods of IEnumerable<T>.

LINQ defines many more extension methods, such as **Count**, which returns the number of elements in the results. Rather than using Any, we could have checked that Count was nonzero, but it's more efficient to determine whether there's at least one element than to count all the elements. The LINQ query syntax is actually transformed by the compiler into extension method calls, with the results of one method call used in the next. It's this design that allows queries to be run on the results of previous queries, as it simply involves passing the result of a method call to another method.

Selecting a Portion of an Object

Line 56 uses the select clause to select the range variable's LastName property rather than the range variable itself. This causes the results of the query to consist of only the last names (as strings), instead of complete Employee objects. Lines 60–61 display the unique last names. The **Distinct extension method** (line 60) removes duplicate elements, causing all elements in the result to be unique.

Creating New Types in the select Clause of a LINQ Query

The last LINQ query in the example (lines 65–66) selects the properties FirstName and LastName. The syntax

```
new { e.FirstName, Last = e.LastName }
```

creates a new object of an **anonymous type** (a type with no name), which the compiler generates for you based on the properties listed in the curly braces ({}). In this case, the anonymous type consists of properties for the first and last names of the selected Employee. The LastName property is assigned to the property Last in the select clause. This shows how you can specify a new name for the selected property. If you don't specify a new name, the property's original name is used—this is the case for FirstName in this example. The preceding query is an example of a **projection**—it performs a transformation on the data. In this case, the transformation creates new objects containing only the FirstName and Last properties. Transformations can also manipulate the data. For example, you could give all employees a 10% raise by multiplying their MonthlySalary properties by 1.1.

When creating a new anonymous type, you can select any number of properties by specifying them in a comma-separated list within the curly braces ({}) that delineate the anonymous type definition. In this example, the compiler automatically creates a new class having properties FirstName and Last, and the values are copied from the Employee objects. These selected properties can then be accessed when iterating over the results.

Implicitly typed local variables allow you to use anonymous types because you do not have to explicitly state the type when declaring such variables.

When the compiler creates an anonymous type, it automatically generates a ToString method that returns a string representation of the object. You can see this in the program's output—it consists of the property names and their values, enclosed in braces. Anonymous types are discussed in more detail in Chapter 18.

9.4 Introduction to Collections

The .NET Framework Class Library provides several classes, called collections, used to store groups of related objects. These classes provide efficient methods that organize, store and retrieve your data without requiring knowledge of how the data is being stored. This reduces application-development time.

You've used arrays to store sequences of objects. Arrays do not automatically change their size at execution time to accommodate additional elements—you must do so manually by creating a new array or by using the Array class's Resize method.

The collection class **List<T>** (from namespace System.Collections.Generic) provides a convenient solution to this problem. The T is a placeholder—when declaring a new List, replace it with the type of elements that you want the List to hold. This is similar to specifying the type when declaring an array. For example,

```
List< int > list1;
```

declares list1 as a List collection that can store only int values, and

```
List< string > list2;
```

declares list2 as a List of strings. Classes with this kind of placeholder that can be used with any type are called **generic classes**. Generic classes and additional generic collection classes are discussed in Chapters 22 and 23, respectively. Figure 23.2 provides a table of collection classes. Figure 9.5 shows some common methods and properties of class List<T>.

Method or property	Description
Add	Adds an element to the end of the List.
Capacity	Property that gets or sets the number of elements a List can store without resizing.
Clear	Removes all the elements from the List.
Contains	Returns true if the List contains the specified element; otherwise, returns false.
Count	Property that returns the number of elements stored in the List.
IndexOf	Returns the index of the first occurrence of the specified value in the List.
Insert	Inserts an element at the specified index.
Remove	Removes the first occurrence of the specified value.

Fig. 9.5 | Some methods and properties of class List<T>. (Part 1 of 2.)

Method or property	Description
RemoveAt	Removes the element at the specified index.
RemoveRange	Removes a specified number of elements starting at a specified index.
Sort	Sorts the List.
TrimExcess	Sets the Capacity of the List to the number of elements the List currently contains (Count).

Fig. 9.5 | Some methods and properties of class List<T>. (Part 2 of 2.)

Figure 9.6 demonstrates dynamically resizing a List object. The Add and Insert methods add elements to the List (lines 13–14). The **Add** method appends its argument to the end of the List. The **Insert** method inserts a new element at the specified position. The first argument is an index—as with arrays, collection indices start at zero. The second argument is the value that's to be inserted at the specified index. All elements at the specified index and above are shifted up by one position. This is usually slower than adding an element to the end of the List.

```
 1   // Fig. 9.6: ListCollection.cs
 2   // Generic List collection demonstration.
 3   using System;
 4   using System.Collections.Generic;
 5
 6   public class ListCollection
 7   {
 8      public static void Main( string[] args )
 9      {
10         // create a new List of strings
11         List< string > items = new List< string >();
12
13         items.Add( "red" ); // append an item to the List
14         items.Insert( 0, "yellow" ); // insert the value at index 0
15
16         // display the colors in the list
17         Console.Write(
18            "Display list contents with counter-controlled loop:" );
19         for ( int i = 0; i < items.Count; i++ )
20            Console.Write( " {0}", items[ i ] );
21
22         // display colors using foreach
23         Console.Write(
24            "\nDisplay list contents with foreach statement:" );
25         foreach ( var item in items )
26            Console.Write( " {0}", item );
27
28         items.Add( "green" ); // add "green" to the end of the List
29         items.Add( "yellow" ); // add "yellow" to the end of the List
30
```

Fig. 9.6 | Generic List<T> collection demonstration. (Part 1 of 2.)

```
31          // display the List
32          Console.Write( "\nList with two new elements:" );
33          foreach ( var item in items )
34             Console.Write( " {0}", item );
35
36          items.Remove( "yellow" ); // remove the first "yellow"
37
38          // display the List
39          Console.Write( "\nRemove first instance of yellow:" );
40          foreach ( var item in items )
41             Console.Write( " {0}", item );
42
43          items.RemoveAt( 1 ); // remove item at index 1
44
45          // display the List
46          Console.Write( "\nRemove second list element (green):" );
47          foreach ( var item in items )
48             Console.Write( " {0}", item );
49
50          // check if a value is in the List
51          Console.WriteLine( "\n\"red\" is {0}in the list",
52             items.Contains( "red" ) ? string.Empty : "not " );
53
54          // display number of elements in the List
55          Console.WriteLine( "Count: {0}", items.Count );
56
57          // display the capacity of the List
58          Console.WriteLine( "Capacity: {0}", items.Capacity );
59       } // end Main
60    } // end class ListCollection
```

```
Display list contents with counter-controlled loop: yellow red
Display list contents with foreach statement: yellow red
List with two new elements: yellow red green yellow
Remove first instance of yellow: red green yellow
Remove second list element (green): red yellow
"red" is in the list
Count: 2
Capacity: 4
```

Fig. 9.6 | Generic List<T> collection demonstration. (Part 2 of 2.)

Lines 19–20 display the items in the List. The **Count** property returns the number of elements currently in the List. Lists can be indexed like arrays by placing the index in square brackets after the List variable's name. The indexed List expression can be used to modify the element at the index. Lines 25–26 output the List by using a foreach statement. More elements are then added to the List, and it's displayed again (lines 28–34).

The **Remove** method is used to remove the *first* element with a specific value (line 36). If no such element is in the List, Remove does nothing. A similar method, **RemoveAt**, removes the element at the specified index (line 43). When an element is removed through either of these methods, all elements above that index are shifted down by one—the opposite of the Insert method.

Line 52 uses the **Contains** method to check if an item is in the List. The Contains method returns true if the element is found in the List, and false otherwise. The method compares its argument to each element of the List in order until the item is found, so using Contains on a large List is inefficient.

Lines 55 and 58 display the List's Count and Capacity. Recall that the Count property (line 55) indicates the number of items in the List. The **Capacity** property (line 58) indicates how many items the List can hold without growing. List is implemented using an array behind the scenes. When the List grows, it must create a larger internal array and copy each element to the new array. This is a time-consuming operation. It would be inefficient for the List to grow each time an element is added. Instead, the List grows only when an element is added *and* the Count and Capacity properties are equal—there's no space for the new element.

9.5 Querying a Generic Collection Using LINQ

You can use LINQ to Objects to query Lists just as arrays. In Fig. 9.7, a List of strings is converted to uppercase and searched for those that begin with "R".

```
1   // Fig. 9.7: LINQWithListCollection.cs
2   // LINQ to Objects using a List< string >.
3   using System;
4   using System.Linq;
5   using System.Collections.Generic;
6
7   public class LINQWithListCollection
8   {
9      public static void Main( string[] args )
10     {
11        // populate a List of strings
12        List< string > items = new List< string >();
13        items.Add( "aQua" ); // add "aQua" to the end of the List
14        items.Add( "RusT" ); // add "RusT" to the end of the List
15        items.Add( "yElLow" ); // add "yElLow" to the end of the List
16        items.Add( "rEd" ); // add "rEd" to the end of the List
17
18        // convert all strings to uppercase; select those starting with "R"
19        var startsWithR =
20           from item in items
21           let uppercaseString = item.ToUpper()
22           where uppercaseString.StartsWith( "R" )
23           orderby uppercaseString
24           select uppercaseString;
25
26        // display query results
27        foreach ( var item in startsWithR )
28           Console.Write( "{0} ", item );
29
30        Console.WriteLine(); // output end of line
```

Fig. 9.7 | LINQ to Objects using a List<string>. (Part 1 of 2.)

```
31
32          items.Add( "rUbY" ); // add "rUbY" to the end of the List
33          items.Add( "SaFfRon" ); // add "SaFfRon" to the end of the List
34
35          // display updated query results
36          foreach ( var item in startsWithR )
37             Console.Write( "{0} ", item );
38
39          Console.WriteLine(); // output end of line
40       } // end Main
41    } // end class LINQWithListCollection
```

```
RED RUST
RED RUBY RUST
```

Fig. 9.7 | LINQ to Objects using a List<string>. (Part 2 of 2.)

Line 21 uses LINQ's **let clause** to create a new range variable. This is useful if you need to store a temporary result for use later in the LINQ query. Typically, let declares a new range variable to which you assign the result of an expression that operates on the query's original range variable. In this case, we use string method **ToUpper** to convert each item to uppercase, then store the result in the new range variable uppercaseString. We then use the new range variable uppercaseString in the where, orderby and select clauses. The where clause (line 22) uses string method **StartsWith** to determine whether uppercaseString starts with the character "R". Method StartsWith performs a case-sensitive comparison to determine whether a string starts with the string received as an argument. If uppercaseString starts with "R", method StartsWith returns true, and the element is included in the query results. More powerful string matching can be done using the regular-expression capabilities introduced in Chapter 16, Strings and Characters.

The query is created only once (lines 20–24), yet iterating over the results (lines 27–28 and 36–37) gives two different lists of colors. This demonstrates LINQ's **deferred execution**—the query executes only when you access the results—such as iterating over them or using the Count method—not when you define the query. This allows you to create a query once and execute it many times. Any changes to the data source are reflected in the results each time the query executes.

There may be times when you do not want this behavior, and want to retrieve a collection of the results immediately. LINQ provides extension methods ToArray and ToList for this purpose. These methods execute the query on which they're called and give you the results as an array or List<T>, respectively. These methods can also improve efficiency if you'll be iterating over the results multiple times, as you execute the query only once.

C# has a feature called **collection initializers**, which provide a convenient syntax (similar to array initializers) for initializing a collection. For example, lines 12–16 of Fig. 9.7 could be replaced with the following statement:

```
List< string > items =
   new List< string > { "aQua", "RusT", "yElLow", "rEd" };
```

9.6 Wrap-Up

This chapter introduced LINQ (Language Integrated Query), a powerful feature for querying data. We showed how to filter an array or collection using LINQ's where clause, and how to sort the query results using the orderby clause. We used the select clause to select specific properties of an object, and the let clause to introduce a new range variable to make writing queries more convenient. The StartsWith method of class string was used to filter strings starting with a specified character or series of characters. We used several LINQ extension methods to perform operations not provided by the query syntax—the Distinct method to remove duplicates from the results, the Any method to determine if the results contain any items, and the First method to retrieve the first element in the results.

We introduced the List<T> generic collection, which provides all the functionality of arrays, along with other useful capabilities such as dynamic resizing. We used method Add to append new items to the end of the List, method Insert to insert new items into specified locations in the List, method Remove to remove the first occurrence of a specified item, method RemoveAt to remove an item at a specified index and method Contains to determine if an item was in the List. We used property Count to get the number of items in the List, and property Capacity to get the size the List can grow to without reallocating the internal array. In Chapter 10 we take a deeper look at classes and objects.

9.7 Deitel LINQ Resource Center

We use more advanced features of LINQ in later chapters. We've also created a LINQ Resource Center (www.deitel.com/LINQ/) that contains many links to additional information, including blogs by Microsoft LINQ team members, books, sample chapters, FAQs, tutorials, videos, webcasts and more. We encourage you to browse the LINQ Resource Center to learn more about this powerful technology.

Summary

Section 9.1 Introduction

- .NET's collection classes provide reusable data structures that are reliable, powerful and efficient.

- Lists automatically increase their size to accommodate additional elements.

- Large amounts of data are often stored in a database—an organized collection of data. Today's most popular database systems are relational databases. SQL is the international standard language used almost universally with relational databases to perform queries (i.e., to request information that satisfies given criteria).

- LINQ allows you to write query expressions (similar to SQL queries) that retrieve information from a wide variety of data sources. You can query arrays and Lists, selecting elements that satisfy a set of conditions—this is known as filtering.

- A LINQ provider is a set of classes that implement LINQ operations and enable programs to interact with data sources to perform tasks such as sorting, grouping and filtering elements.

Section 9.2 Querying an Array of int Values Using LINQ

- Repetition statements focus on the process of iterating through elements and checking whether they satisfy the desired criteria. LINQ specifies the conditions that selected elements must satisfy, not the steps necessary to get the results.

- The System.Linq namespace contains the classes for LINQ to Objects.
- A from clause specifies a range variable and the data source to query. The range variable represents each item in the data source (one at a time), much like the control variable in a foreach statement.
- If the condition in the where clause evaluates to true for an element, it's included in the results.
- The select clause determines what value appears in the results.
- A C# interface describes a set of methods and properties that can be used to interact with an object.
- The IEnumerable<T> interface describes the functionality of any object that's capable of being iterated over and thus offers methods to access each element in some order.
- A class that implements an interface must define each method in the interface.
- Arrays and collections implement the IEnumerable<T> interface.
- A foreach statement can iterate over any object that implements the IEnumerable<T> interface.
- A LINQ query returns an object that implements the IEnumerable<T> interface.
- The orderby clause sorts query results in ascending order by default. Results can also be sorted in descending order using the descending modifier.
- C# provides implicitly typed local variables, which enable the compiler to infer a local variable's type based on the variable's initializer.
- To distinguish such an initialization from a simple assignment statement, the var keyword is used in place of the variable's type.
- You can use local type inference with control variables in the header of a for or foreach statement.
- Implicitly typed local variables can be used to initialize arrays without explicitly giving their type. To do so, use new[] to specify that the variable is an array.

Section 9.3 Querying an Array of *Employee* Objects Using LINQ
- LINQ can be used with collections of most data types.
- Any boolean expression can be used in a where clause.
- An orderby clause can sort the results according to multiple properties specified in a comma-separated list.
- Method Any returns true if there's at least one element in the result; otherwise, it returns false.
- The First method returns the first element in the query result. You should check that the query result is not empty before calling First.
- The Count method returns the number of elements in the query result.
- The Distinct method removes duplicate values from query results.
- You can select any number of properties in a select clause by specifying them in a comma-separated list in braces after the **new** keyword. The compiler automatically creates a new class having these properties—called an anonymous type.

Section 9.4 Introduction to Collections
- The .NET collection classes provide efficient methods that organize, store and retrieve data without requiring knowledge of how the data is being stored.
- Class List<T> is similar to an array but provides richer functionality, such as dynamic resizing.
- The Add method appends an element to the end of a List.
- The Insert method inserts a new element at a specified position in the List.
- The Count property returns the number of elements currently in a List.
- Lists can be indexed like arrays by placing the index in square brackets after the List object's name.

- The Remove method is used to remove the first element with a specific value.
- The RemoveAt method removes the element at the specified index.
- The Contains method returns true if the element is found in the List, and false otherwise.
- The Capacity property indicates how many items a List can hold without growing.

Section 9.5 Querying a Generic Collection Using LINQ
- LINQ to Objects can query Lists.
- LINQ's let clause creates a new range variable. This is useful if you need to store a temporary result for use later in the LINQ query.
- The StartsWith method of the string class determines whether a string starts with the string passed to it as an argument.
- A LINQ query uses deferred execution—it executes only when you access the results, not when you create the query.

Terminology

Add method of class List<T>	Insert method of class List<T>
anonymous type	interface
Any extension method for IEnumerable<T>	let clause of a LINQ query
ascending modifier of the orderby clause	LINQ (Language Integrated Query)
Capacity property of class List<T>	LINQ provider
collection initializer	LINQ to Objects
Contains method of class List<T>	List<T> collection class
Count extension method for IEnumerable<T>	orderby clause of a LINQ query
Count property of class List<T>	predicate
declarative programming	projection
deferred execution	query expression
descending modifier of the orderby clause	query using LINQ
Distinct extension method for IEnumerable<T>	range variable
dynamic resizing	Remove method of class List<T>
filtering a collection with LINQ	RemoveAt method of class List<T>
First extension method for IEnumerable<T>	select clause of a LINQ query
from clause of a LINQ query	StartsWith method of class string
IEnumerable<T> interface	ToUpper method of class string
imperative programming	var keyword
implicitly typed local variable	where clause of a LINQ query

Self-Review Exercises

9.1 Fill in the blanks in each of the following statements:
a) Use the _____ property of the List class to find the number of elements in the List.
b) The LINQ _____ clause is used for filtering.
c) _____ are classes specifically designed to store groups of objects and provide methods that organize, store and retrieve those objects.
d) To add an element to the end of a List, use the _____ method.
e) To get only unique results from a LINQ query, use the _____ method.

9.2 State whether each of the following is *true* or *false*. If *false*, explain why.
a) The orderby clause in a LINQ query can sort only in ascending order.
b) LINQ queries can be used on both arrays and collections.
c) The Remove method of the List class removes an element at a specific index.

Answers to Self-Review Exercises

9.1 a) Count. b) where. c) Collections. d) Add. e) Distinct.

9.2 a) False. The descending modifier is used to make orderby sort in descending order. b) True. c) False. Remove removes the first element equal to its argument. RemoveAt removes the element at a specific index.

Exercises

9.3 *(Querying an Array of Invoice Objects)* Use the class Invoice provided in the ex09_03 folder with this chapter's examples to create an array of Invoice objects. Use the sample data shown in Fig. 9.8. Class Invoice includes four properties—a PartNumber (type int), a PartDescription (type string), a Quantity of the item being purchased (type int) and a Price (type decimal). Perform the following queries on the array of Invoice objects and displays the results:
  a) Use LINQ to sort the Invoice objects by PartDescription.
  b) Use LINQ to sort the Invoice objects by Price.
  c) Use LINQ to select the PartDescription and Quantity and sort the results by Quantity.
  d) Use LINQ to select from each Invoice the PartDescription and the value of the Invoice (i.e., Quantity * Price). Name the calculated column InvoiceTotal. Order the results by Invoice value. [*Hint:* Use let to store the result of Quantity * Price in a new range variable total.]
  e) Using the results of the LINQ query in *Part d*, select the InvoiceTotals in the range $200 to $500.

Part number	Part description	Quantity	Price
83	Electric sander	7	57.98
24	Power saw	18	99.99
7	Sledge hammer	11	21.50
77	Hammer	76	11.99
39	Lawn mower	3	79.50
68	Screwdriver	106	6.99
56	Jig saw	21	11.00
3	Wrench	34	7.50

Fig. 9.8 | Sample data for Exercise 9.3.

9.4 *(Duplicate Word Removal)* Write a console application that inputs a sentence from the user (assume no punctuation), then determines and displays the nonduplicate words in alphabetical order. Treat uppercase and lowercase letters the same. [*Hint:* You can use string method Split with no arguments, as in sentence.Split(), to break a sentence into an array of strings containing the individual words. By default, Split uses spaces as delimiters. Use string method ToLower in the select and orderby clauses of your LINQ query to obtain the lowercase version of each word.]

9.5 *(Sorting Letters and Removing Duplicates)* Write a console application that inserts 30 random letters into a List< char >. Perform the following queries on the List and display your results: [*Hint:* Strings can be indexed like arrays to access a character at a specific index.]
  a) Use LINQ to sort the List in ascending order.
  b) Use LINQ to sort the List in descending order.
  c) Display the List in ascending order with duplicates removed.

10

Classes and Objects:
A Deeper Look

*But what, to serve
our private ends,
Forbids the cheating
of our friends?*
—Charles Churchill

*This above all: to thine own self
be true.*
—William Shakespeare.

Objectives

In this chapter you'll learn:

- Encapsulation and data hiding.

- To use keyword **this**.

- To use **static** variables and methods.

- To use **readonly** fields.

- To take advantage of C#'s memory-management features.

- To use the IDEs **Class View** and **Object Browser** windows.

- To use object initializers to create an object and initialize it in the same statement.

10.1 Introduction

In this chapter, we take a deeper look at building classes, controlling access to members of a class and creating constructors. We discuss composition—a capability that allows a class to have references to objects of other classes as members. We reexamine the use of properties. The chapter also discusses static class members and readonly instance variables in detail. We investigate issues such as software reusability, data abstraction and encapsulation. We also discuss several miscellaneous topics related to defining classes.

10.2 Time Class Case Study

Time1 *Class Declaration*

Our first example consists of two classes—Time1 (Fig. 10.1) and Time1Test (Fig. 10.2). Class Time1 represents the time of day. Class Time1Test is a testing class in which the Main method creates an object of class Time1 and invokes its methods. The output of this application appears in Fig. 10.2.

Class Time1 contains three private instance variables of type int (Fig. 10.1, lines 7–9)—hour, minute and second—that represent the time in universal-time format (24-hour clock format, in which hours are in the range 0–23). Class Time1 contains public methods SetTime (lines 13–25), ToUniversalString (lines 28–32) and ToString (lines 35–40). These are the **public services** or the **public interface** that the class provides to its clients.

```
1   // Fig. 10.1: Time1.cs
2   // Time1 class declaration maintains the time in 24-hour format.
3   using System; // namespace containing ArgumentOutOfRangeException
4
5   public class Time1
6   {
7       private int hour; // 0 - 23
8       private int minute; // 0 - 59
9       private int second; // 0 - 59
```

Fig. 10.1 | Time1 class declaration maintains the time in 24-hour format. (Part 1 of 2.)

```
10
11    // set a new time value using universal time; throw an
12    // exception if the hour, minute or second is invalid
13    public void SetTime( int h, int m, int s )
14    {
15       // validate hour, minute and second
16       if ( ( h >= 0 && h < 24 ) && ( m >= 0 && m < 60 ) &&
17          ( s >= 0 && s < 60 ) )
18       {
19          hour = h;
20          minute = m;
21          second = s;
22       } // end if
23       else
24          throw new ArgumentOutOfRangeException();
25    } // end method SetTime
26
27    // convert to string in universal-time format (HH:MM:SS)
28    public string ToUniversalString()
29    {
30       return string.Format( "{0:D2}:{1:D2}:{2:D2}",
31          hour, minute, second );
32    } // end method ToUniversalString
33
34    // convert to string in standard-time format (H:MM:SS AM or PM)
35    public override string ToString()
36    {
37       return string.Format( "{0}:{1:D2}:{2:D2} {3}",
38          ( ( hour == 0 || hour == 12 ) ? 12 : hour % 12 ),
39          minute, second, ( hour < 12 ? "AM" : "PM" ) );
40    } // end method ToString
41 } // end class Time1
```

Fig. 10.1 | Time1 class declaration maintains the time in 24-hour format. (Part 2 of 2.)

In this example, class Time1 does not declare a constructor, so the class has a default constructor that is supplied by the compiler. Each instance variable implicitly receives the default value 0 for an int. When instance variables are declared in the class body, they can be initialized using the same initialization syntax as a local variable.

Method SetTime and Throwing Exceptions

Method SetTime (lines 13–25) is a public method that declares three int parameters and uses them to set the time. Lines 16–17 tests each argument to determine whether the value is in the proper range, and, if so, lines 19–21 assign the values to the hour, minute and second instance variables. The hour value (line 13) must be greater than or equal to 0 and less than 24, because universal-time format represents hours as integers from 0 to 23 (e.g., 1 PM is hour 13 and 11 PM is hour 23; midnight is hour 0 and noon is hour 12). Similarly, both minute and second values must be greater than or equal to 0 and less than 60. For values outside these ranges, SetTime **throws an exception** of type **ArgumentOutOfRangeException** (lines 23–24), which notifies the client code that an invalid argument was passed to the method. As you learned in Chapter 8, you can use try...catch to catch exceptions and attempt to recover from them, which we'll do in Fig. 10.2. The **throw statement** (line

24) creates a new object of type `ArgumentOutOfRangeException`. The parentheses following the class name indicate a call to the `ArgumentOutOfRangeException` constructor. After the exception object is created, the `throw` statement immediately terminates method `Set-Time` and the exception is returned to the code that attempted to set the time.

Method *ToUniversalString*

Method `ToUniversalString` (lines 28–32) takes no arguments and returns a `string` in universal-time format, consisting of six digits—two for the hour, two for the minute and two for the second. For example, if the time were 1:30:07 PM, method `ToUniversal-String` would return 13:30:07. The `return` statement (lines 30–31) uses `static` method **Format** of class `string` to return a `string` containing the formatted `hour`, `minute` and `second` values, each with two digits and, where needed, a leading 0 (specified with the `D2` format specifier—which pads the integer with leading 0s if it has less than two digits). Method `Format` is similar to the `string` formatting in method `Console.Write`, except that `Format` returns a formatted `string` rather than displaying it in a console window. The formatted `string` is returned by method `ToUniversalString`.

Method *ToString*

Method `ToString` (lines 35–40) takes no arguments and returns a `string` in standard-time format, consisting of the `hour`, `minute` and `second` values separated by colons and followed by an AM or PM indicator (e.g., 1:27:06 PM). Like method `ToUniversalString`, method `ToString` uses `static string` method `Format` to format the `minute` and `second` as two-digit values with leading 0s, if necessary. Line 38 uses a conditional operator (`?:`) to determine the value for `hour` in the string—if the `hour` is 0 or 12 (AM or PM), it appears as 12—otherwise, it appears as a value from 1 to 11. The conditional operator in line 39 determines whether AM or PM will be returned as part of the `string`.

Recall from Section 7.4 that all objects in C# have a `ToString` method that returns a `string` representation of the object. We chose to return a `string` containing the time in standard-time format. Method `ToString` is called *implicitly* when an object's value is output with a format item in a call to `Console.Write`. Remember that to enable objects to be converted to their `string` representations, we need to declare method `ToString` with keyword `override`—the reason for this will become clear when we discuss inheritance in Chapter 11.

Using Class *Time1*

As you learned in Chapter 4, each class you declare represents a new *type* in C#. Therefore, after declaring class `Time1`, we can use it as a type in declarations such as

```
Time1 sunset; // sunset can hold a reference to a Time1 object
```

The `Time1Test` application class (Fig. 10.2) uses class `Time1`. Line 10 creates a `Time1` object and assigns it to local variable `time`. Operator new invokes class `Time1`'s default constructor, since `Time1` does not declare any constructors. Lines 13–17 output the time, first in universal-time format (by invoking `time`'s `ToUniversalString` method in line 14), then in standard-time format (by explicitly invoking `time`'s `ToString` method in line 16) to confirm that the `Time1` object was initialized properly. Line 20 invokes method `SetTime` of the `time` object to change the time. Then lines 21–25 output the time again in both formats to confirm that the time was set correctly.

```csharp
1   // Fig. 10.2: Time1Test.cs
2   // Time1 object used in an application.
3   using System;
4
5   public class Time1Test
6   {
7      public static void Main( string[] args )
8      {
9         // create and initialize a Time1 object
10        Time1 time = new Time1(); // invokes Time1 constructor
11
12        // output string representations of the time
13        Console.Write( "The initial universal time is: " );
14        Console.WriteLine( time.ToUniversalString() );
15        Console.Write( "The initial standard time is: " );
16        Console.WriteLine( time.ToString() );
17        Console.WriteLine(); // output a blank line
18
19        // change time and output updated time
20        time.SetTime( 13, 27, 6 );
21        Console.Write( "Universal time after SetTime is: " );
22        Console.WriteLine( time.ToUniversalString() );
23        Console.Write( "Standard time after SetTime is: " );
24        Console.WriteLine( time.ToString() );
25        Console.WriteLine(); // output a blank line
26
27        // attempt to set time with invalid values
28        try
29        {
30           time.SetTime( 99, 99, 99 );
31        } // end try
32        catch ( ArgumentOutOfRangeException ex )
33        {
34           Console.WriteLine( ex.Message + "\n" );
35        } // end catch
36
37        // display time after attempt to set invalid values
38        Console.WriteLine( "After attempting invalid settings:" );
39        Console.Write( "Universal time: " );
40        Console.WriteLine( time.ToUniversalString() );
41        Console.Write( "Standard time: " );
42        Console.WriteLine( time.ToString() );
43     } // end Main
44  } // end class Time1Test
```

```
The initial universal time is: 00:00:00
The initial standard time is: 12:00:00 AM

Universal time after SetTime is: 13:27:06
Standard time after SetTime is: 1:27:06 PM

Specified argument was out of the range of valid values.
```

Fig. 10.2 | Time1 object used in an application. (Part 1 of 2.)

```
After attempting invalid settings:
Universal time: 13:27:06
Standard time: 1:27:06 PM
```

Fig. 10.2 | Time1 object used in an application. (Part 2 of 2.)

Calling Time Method SetTime with Invalid Values
To illustrate that method SetTime validates its arguments, line 30 calls method SetTime with invalid arguments of 99 for the hour, minute and second. This statement is placed in a try block (lines 28–31) in case SetTime throws an ArgumentOutOfRangeException, which it will do since the arguments are all invalid. When this occurs, the exception is caught at lines 32–35 and the exception's Message property is displayed. Lines 38–42 output the time again in both formats to confirm that SetTime did not change the time when invalid arguments were supplied.

Notes on the Time1 Class Declaration
Consider several issues of class design with respect to class Time1. The instance variables hour, minute and second are each declared private. The actual data representation used within the class is of no concern to the class's clients. For example, it would be perfectly reasonable for Time1 to represent the time internally as the number of seconds since midnight or the number of minutes and seconds since midnight. Clients could use the same public methods and properties to get the same results without being aware of this. (Exercise 10.4 asks you to represent the time as the number of seconds since midnight and show that indeed no change is visible to the clients of the class.)

Software Engineering Observation 10.1
Classes simplify programming because the client can use only the public members exposed by the class. Such members are usually client oriented rather than implementation oriented. Clients are neither aware of, nor involved in, a class's implementation. Clients generally care about what the class does but not how the class does it. Clients do, of course, care that the class operates correctly and efficiently.

Software Engineering Observation 10.2
Interfaces change less frequently than implementations. When an implementation changes, implementation-dependent code must change accordingly. Hiding the implementation reduces the possibility that other application parts become dependent on class-implementation details.

10.3 Controlling Access to Members

The access modifiers public and private control access to a class's variables, methods and properties. (In Chapter 11, we'll introduce the additional access modifier protected.) As we stated in Section 10.2, the primary purpose of public methods is to present to the class's clients a view of the services the class provides (that is, the class's public interface). Clients of the class need not be concerned with how the class accomplishes its tasks. For this reason, a class's `private` variables, properties and methods (i.e., the class's implementation details) are not directly accessible to the class's clients.

Figure 10.3 demonstrates that `private` class members are not directly accessible outside the class. Lines 9–11 attempt to directly access `private` instance variables `hour`, `minute` and `second` of `Time1` object `time`. When this application is compiled, the compiler generates error messages stating that these `private` members are not accessible. [*Note:* This application uses the `Time1` class from Fig. 10.1.]

```
 1   // Fig. 10.3: MemberAccessTest.cs
 2   // Private members of class Time1 are not accessible outside the class.
 3   public class MemberAccessTest
 4   {
 5      public static void Main( string[] args )
 6      {
 7         Time1 time = new Time1(); // create and initialize Time1 object
 8
 9         time.hour = 7; // error: hour has private access in Time1
10         time.minute = 15; // error: minute has private access in Time1
11         time.second = 30; // error: second has private access in Time1
12      } // end Main
13   } // end class MemberAccessTest
```

	Description	File	Line	Column	Project
1	'Time1.hour' is inaccessible due to its protection level	MemberAccessTest.cs	9	12	MemberAccessTest
2	'Time1.minute' is inaccessible due to its protection level	MemberAccessTest.cs	10	12	MemberAccessTest
3	'Time1.second' is inaccessible due to its protection level	MemberAccessTest.cs	11	12	MemberAccessTest

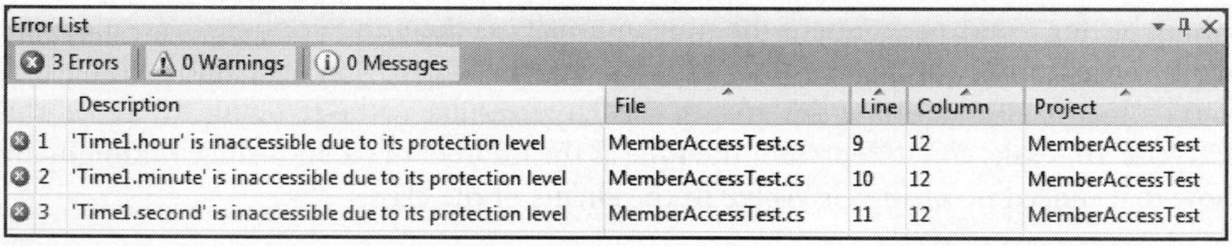

Error List — 3 Errors — 0 Warnings — 0 Messages

Fig. 10.3 | Private members of class `Time1` are not accessible outside the class.

Notice that members of a class—for instance, properties, methods and instance variables—do not need to be explicitly declared `private`. If a class member is not declared with an access modifier, it has `private` access *by default*. For clarity, we always explicitly declare `private` members.

10.4 Referring to the Current Object's Members with the `this` Reference

Every object can access a reference to itself with keyword **`this`** (also called the **`this` reference**). When a non-`static` method is called for a particular object, the method's body implicitly uses keyword `this` to refer to the object's instance variables and other methods. As you'll see in Fig. 10.4, you can also use keyword `this` *explicitly* in a non-`static` method's body. Section 10.5 shows a more interesting use of keyword `this`. Section 10.9 explains why keyword `this` cannot be used in a `static` method.

We now demonstrate implicit and explicit use of the `this` reference to enable class `ThisTest`'s `Main` method to display the `private` data of a class `SimpleTime` object (Fig. 10.4). For the sake of brevity, we declare two classes in one file—class `ThisTest` is declared in lines 5–12, and class `SimpleTime` is declared in lines 15–48.

```csharp
 1   // Fig. 10.4: ThisTest.cs
 2   // this used implicitly and explicitly to refer to members of an object.
 3   using System;
 4
 5   public class ThisTest
 6   {
 7      public static void Main( string[] args )
 8      {
 9         SimpleTime time = new SimpleTime( 15, 30, 19 );
10         Console.WriteLine( time.BuildString() );
11      } // end Main
12   } // end class ThisTest
13
14   // class SimpleTime demonstrates the "this" reference
15   public class SimpleTime
16   {
17      private int hour; // 0-23
18      private int minute; // 0-59
19      private int second; // 0-59
20
21      // if the constructor uses parameter names identical to
22      // instance-variable names, the "this" reference is
23      // required to distinguish between names
24      public SimpleTime( int hour, int minute, int second )
25      {
26         this.hour = hour; // set "this" object's hour instance variable
27         this.minute = minute; // set "this" object's minute
28         this.second = second; // set "this" object's second
29      } // end SimpleTime constructor
30
31      // use explicit and implicit "this" to call ToUniversalString
32      public string BuildString()
33      {
34         return string.Format( "{0,24}: {1}\n{2,24}: {3}",
35            "this.ToUniversalString()", this.ToUniversalString(),
36            "ToUniversalString()", ToUniversalString() );
37      } // end method BuildString
38
39      // convert to string in universal-time format (HH:MM:SS)
40      public string ToUniversalString()
41      {
42         // "this" is not required here to access instance variables,
43         // because method does not have local variables with same
44         // names as instance variables
45         return string.Format( "{0:D2}:{1:D2}:{2:D2}",
46            this.hour, this.minute, this.second );
47      } // end method ToUniversalString
48   } // end class SimpleTime
```

```
this.ToUniversalString(): 15:30:19
   ToUniversalString(): 15:30:19
```

Fig. 10.4 | this used implicitly and explicitly to refer to members of an object.

Class SimpleTime declares three private instance variables—hour, minute and second (lines 17–19). The constructor (lines 24–29) receives three int arguments to initialize a SimpleTime object. For the constructor we used parameter names that are identical to the class's instance-variable names (lines 17–19). We don't recommend this practice, but we intentionally did it here to hide the corresponding instance variables so that we could illustrate explicit use of the this reference. Recall from Section 7.11 that if a method contains a local variable with the same name as a field, that method will refer to the local variable rather than the field. In this case, the parameter hides the field in the method's scope. However, the method can use the this reference to refer to the hidden instance variable explicitly, as shown in lines 26–28 for SimpleTime's hidden instance variables.

Method BuildString (lines 32–37) returns a string created by a statement that uses the this reference explicitly and implicitly. Line 35 uses the this reference *explicitly* to call method ToUniversalString. Line 36 uses the this reference *implicitly* to call the same method. Programmers typically do not use the this reference explicitly to reference other methods in the current object. Also, line 46 in method ToUniversalString explicitly uses the this reference to access each instance variable. This is not necessary here, because the method does not have any local variables that hide the instance variables of the class.

Common Programming Error 10.1

It's often a logic error when a method contains a parameter or local variable that has the same name as an instance variable of the class. In such a case, use reference this if you wish to access the instance variable of the class—otherwise, the method parameter or local variable will be referenced.

Error-Prevention Tip 10.1

Avoid method-parameter names or local-variable names that conflict with field names. This helps prevent subtle, hard-to-locate bugs.

Class ThisTest (Fig. 10.4, lines 5–12) demonstrates class SimpleTime. Line 9 creates an instance of class SimpleTime and invokes its constructor. Line 10 invokes the object's BuildString method, then displays the results.

Performance Tip 10.1

C# conserves memory by maintaining only one copy of each method per class—this method is invoked by every object of the class. Each object, on the other hand, has its own copy of the class's instance variables (i.e., non-static variables). Each method of the class implicitly uses the this reference to determine the specific object of the class to manipulate.

10.5 Time Class Case Study: Overloaded Constructors

As you know, you can declare your own constructor to specify how objects of a class should be initialized. Next, we demonstrate a class with several **overloaded constructors** that enable objects of that class to be initialized in different ways. To overload constructors, simply provide multiple constructor declarations with different signatures.

Class *Time2* with Overloaded Constructors

By default, instance variables hour, minute and second of class Time1 (Fig. 10.1) are initialized to their default values of 0—midnight in universal time. Class Time1 doesn't enable the class's clients to initialize the time with specific nonzero values. Class Time2 (Fig. 10.5) contains overloaded constructors for conveniently initializing its objects in a variety of ways. In this application, one constructor invokes the other constructor, which in turn calls SetTime to set the hour, minute and second. The compiler invokes the appropriate Time2 constructor by matching the number and types of the arguments specified in the constructor call with the number and types of the parameters specified in each constructor declaration.

```csharp
1   // Fig. 10.5: Time2.cs
2   // Time2 class declaration with overloaded constructors.
3   using System; // for class ArgumentOutOfRangeException
4
5   public class Time2
6   {
7      private int hour; // 0 - 23
8      private int minute; // 0 - 59
9      private int second; // 0 - 59
10
11     // constructor can be called with zero, one, two or three arguments
12     public Time2( int h = 0, int m = 0, int s = 0 )
13     {
14        SetTime( h, m, s ); // invoke SetTime to validate time
15     } // end Time2 three-argument constructor
16
17     // Time2 constructor: another Time2 object supplied as an argument
18     public Time2( Time2 time )
19        : this( time.Hour, time.Minute, time.Second ) { }
20
21     // set a new time value using universal time; ensure that
22     // the data remains consistent by setting invalid values to zero
23     public void SetTime( int h, int m, int s )
24     {
25        Hour = h; // set the Hour property
26        Minute = m; // set the Minute property
27        Second = s; // set the Second property
28     } // end method SetTime
29
30     // property that gets and sets the hour
31     public int Hour
32     {
33        get
34        {
35           return hour;
36        } // end get
37        set
38        {
39           if ( value >= 0 && value < 24 )
40              hour = value;
41           else
42              throw new ArgumentOutOfRangeException(
43                 "Hour", value, "Hour must be 0-23" );
44        } // end set
45     } // end property Hour
```

Fig. 10.5 | Time2 class declaration with overloaded constructors. (Part 1 of 2.)

```
46
47      // property that gets and sets the minute
48      public int Minute
49      {
50         get
51         {
52            return minute;
53         } // end get
54         set
55         {
56            if ( value >= 0 && value < 60 )
57               minute = value;
58            else
59               throw new ArgumentOutOfRangeException(
60                  "Minute", value, "Minute must be 0-59" );
61         } // end set
62      } // end property Minute
63
64      // property that gets and sets the second
65      public int Second
66      {
67         get
68         {
69            return second;
70         } // end get
71         set
72         {
73            if ( value >= 0 && value < 60 )
74               second = value;
75            else
76               throw new ArgumentOutOfRangeException(
77                  "Second", value, "Second must be 0-59" );
78         } // end set
79      } // end property Second
80
81      // convert to string in universal-time format (HH:MM:SS)
82      public string ToUniversalString()
83      {
84         return string.Format(
85            "{0:D2}:{1:D2}:{2:D2}", Hour, Minute, Second );
86      } // end method ToUniversalString
87
88      // convert to string in standard-time format (H:MM:SS AM or PM)
89      public override string ToString()
90      {
91         return string.Format( "{0}:{1:D2}:{2:D2} {3}",
92            ( ( Hour == 0 || Hour == 12 ) ? 12 : Hour % 12 ),
93            Minute, Second, ( Hour < 12 ? "AM" : "PM" ) );
94      } // end method ToString
95   } // end class Time2
```

Fig. 10.5 | Time2 class declaration with overloaded constructors. (Part 2 of 2.)

Class Time2's Constructors

Lines 12–15 declare a constructor with three default parameters. This constructor is also considered to be the class's **parameterless constructor**—a constructor invoked without arguments—because you can call the constructor without arguments and the compiler will automatically provide the default parameter values. This constructor can also be called with one argument for the hour, two arguments for the hour and minute, or three arguments for the hour, minute and second. This constructor calls SetTime to set the time.

Common Programming Error 10.2

A constructor can call methods of its class. Be aware that the instance variables might not yet be initialized, because the constructor is in the process of initializing the object. Using instance variables before they have been initialized properly is a logic error.

Lines 18–19 declare a Time2 constructor that receives a reference to a Time2 object. In this case, the values from the Time2 argument are passed to the three-parameter constructor at lines 12–15 to initialize the hour, minute and second. In this constructor, we use this in a manner that is allowed *only* in the constructor's header. In line 19, the usual constructor header is followed by a colon (:), then the keyword this. The this reference is used in method-call syntax (along with the three int arguments) to invoke the Time2 constructor that takes three int arguments (lines 12–15). The constructor passes the values of the time argument's Hour, Minute and Second properties to set the hour, minute and second of the Time2 object being constructed. Additional initialization code can be placed in this constructor's body and it will execute after the other constructor is called.

The use of the this reference as shown in line 19 is called a **constructor initializer**. Constructor initializers are a popular way to reuse initialization code provided by one of the class's constructors rather than defining similar code in another constructor's body. This syntax makes the class easier to maintain, because one constructor reuses the other. If we needed to change how objects of class Time2 are initialized, only the constructor at lines 12–15 would need to be modified. Even that constructor might not need modification—it simply calls the SetTime method to perform the actual initialization, so it's possible that the changes the class might require would be localized to this method.

Line 19 could have directly accessed instance variables hour, minute and second of the constructor's time argument with the expressions time.hour, time.minute and time.second—even though they're declared as private variables of class Time2.

Software Engineering Observation 10.3

When one object of a class has a reference to another object of the same class, the first object can access all the second object's data and methods (including those that are private).

Class Time2's SetTime Method

Method SetTime (lines 23–28) invokes the set accessors of the new properties Hour (lines 31–45), Minute (lines 48–62) and Second (lines 65–79), which ensure that the value supplied for hour is in the range 0 to 23 and that the values for minute and second are each in the range 0 to 59. If a value is out of range, each set accessor throws an ArgumentOutOfRangeException (lines 42–43, 59–60 and 76–77). In this example, we use the ArgumentOutOfRangeException constructor that receives three arguments—the name of the item that was out of range, the value that was supplied for that item and an error message.

Notes Regarding Class *Time2's* Methods, Properties and Constructors

Time2's properties are accessed throughout the class's body. Method SetTime assigns values to properties Hour, Minute and Second in lines 25–27, and methods ToUniversalString and ToString use properties Hour, Minute and Second in line 85 and lines 92–93, respectively. These methods could have accessed the class's private data directly. However, consider changing the representation of the time from three int values (requiring 12 bytes of memory) to a single int value representing the total number of seconds that have elapsed since midnight (requiring only 4 bytes of memory). If we make such a change, only the bodies of the methods that access the private data directly would need to change—in particular, the individual properties Hour, Minute and Second. There would be no need to modify the bodies of methods SetTime, ToUniversalString or ToString, because they do not access the private data directly. Designing the class in this manner reduces the likelihood of programming errors when altering the class's implementation.

Similarly, each constructor could be written to include a copy of the appropriate statements from method SetTime. Doing so may be slightly more efficient, because the extra constructor call and the call to SetTime are eliminated. However, duplicating statements in multiple methods or constructors makes changing the class's internal data representation more difficult and error-prone. Having one constructor call the other or even call SetTime directly requires any changes to SetTime's implementation to be made only once.

Software Engineering Observation 10.4

When implementing a method of a class, use the class's properties to access the class's private data. This simplifies code maintenance and reduces the likelihood of errors.

Using Class *Time2's* Overloaded Constructors

Class Time2Test (Fig. 10.6) creates six Time2 objects (lines 9–13 and 42) to invoke the overloaded Time2 constructors. Lines 9–13 demonstrate passing arguments to the Time2 constructors. C# invokes the appropriate overloaded constructor by matching the number and types of the arguments specified in the constructor call with the number and types of the parameters specified in each constructor declaration. Lines 9–12 each invoke the constructor at lines 12–15 of Fig. 10.5. Line 9 invokes the constructor with no arguments, which causes the compiler to supply the default value 0 for each of the three parameters. Line 10 invokes the constructor with one argument that represents the hour—the compiler supplies the default value 0 for the minute and second. Line 11 invokes the constructor with two arguments that represent the hour and minute—the compiler supplies the default value 0 for the second. Line 12 invoke the constructor with values for all three parameters. Line 13 invokes the constructor at lines 18–19 of Fig. 10.5. Lines 16–37 display the string representation of each initialized Time2 object to confirm that each was initialized properly.

```
1   // Fig. 10.6: Time2Test.cs
2   // Overloaded constructors used to initialize Time2 objects.
3   using System;
4
5   public class Time2Test
6   {
```

Fig. 10.6 | Overloaded constructors used to initialize Time2 objects. (Part 1 of 3.)

```
 7      public static void Main( string[] args )
 8      {
 9         Time2 t1 = new Time2(); // 00:00:00
10         Time2 t2 = new Time2( 2 ); // 02:00:00
11         Time2 t3 = new Time2( 21, 34 ); // 21:34:00
12         Time2 t4 = new Time2( 12, 25, 42 ); // 12:25:42
13         Time2 t5 = new Time2( t4 ); // 12:25:42
14         Time2 t6; // initialized later in the program
15
16         Console.WriteLine( "Constructed with:\n" );
17         Console.WriteLine( "t1: all arguments defaulted" );
18         Console.WriteLine( "   {0}", t1.ToUniversalString() ); // 00:00:00
19         Console.WriteLine( "   {0}\n", t1.ToString() ); // 12:00:00 AM
20
21         Console.WriteLine(
22            "t2: hour specified; minute and second defaulted" );
23         Console.WriteLine( "   {0}", t2.ToUniversalString() ); // 02:00:00
24         Console.WriteLine( "   {0}\n", t2.ToString() ); // 2:00:00 AM
25
26         Console.WriteLine(
27            "t3: hour and minute specified; second defaulted" );
28         Console.WriteLine( "   {0}", t3.ToUniversalString() ); // 21:34:00
29         Console.WriteLine( "   {0}\n", t3.ToString() ); // 9:34:00 PM
30
31         Console.WriteLine( "t4: hour, minute and second specified" );
32         Console.WriteLine( "   {0}", t4.ToUniversalString() ); // 12:25:42
33         Console.WriteLine( "   {0}\n", t4.ToString() ); // 12:25:42 PM
34
35         Console.WriteLine( "t5: Time2 object t4 specified" );
36         Console.WriteLine( "   {0}", t5.ToUniversalString() ); // 12:25:42
37         Console.WriteLine( "   {0}", t5.ToString() ); // 12:25:42 PM
38
39         // attempt to initialize t6 with invalid values
40         try
41         {
42            t6 = new Time2( 27, 74, 99 ); // invalid values
43         } // end try
44         catch ( ArgumentOutOfRangeException ex )
45         {
46            Console.WriteLine( "\nException while initializing t6:" );
47            Console.WriteLine( ex.Message );
48         } // end catch
49      } // end Main
50   } // end class Time2Test
```

```
Constructed with:

t1: all arguments defaulted
   00:00:00
   12:00:00 AM

t2: hour specified; minute and second defaulted
   02:00:00
   2:00:00 AM
```

Fig. 10.6 | Overloaded constructors used to initialize Time2 objects. (Part 2 of 3.)

```
t3: hour and minute specified; second defaulted
   21:34:00
   9:34:00 PM

t4: hour, minute and second specified
   12:25:42
   12:25:42 PM

t5: Time2 object t4 specified
   12:25:42
   12:25:42 PM

Exception while initializing t6:
hour must be 0-23
Parameter name: hour
Actual value was 27.
```

Fig. 10.6 | Overloaded constructors used to initialize Time2 objects. (Part 3 of 3.)

Line 42 attempts to intialize t6 by creating a new Time2 object and passing three invalid values to the constructor. When the constructor attempts to use the invalid hour value to initialize the object's Hour property, an ArgumentOutOfRangeException occurs. We catch this exception at line 44 and display its Message property, which results in the last three lines of the output in Fig. 10.6. Because we used the three-argument Argument-OutOfRangeException constructor when the exception object was created, the exception's Message property also includes the information about the out-of-range value.

10.6 Default and Parameterless Constructors

Every class must have at least one constructor. Recall from Section 4.10 that if you do not provide any constructors in a class's declaration, the compiler creates a *default constructor* that takes no arguments when it's invoked. In Section 11.4.1, you'll learn that the default constructor implicitly performs a special task.

The compiler will *not* create a default constructor for a class that *explicitly* declares at least one constructor. In this case, if you want to be able to invoke the constructor with no arguments, you must declare a *parameterless constructor*—as in line 12 of Fig. 10.5. Like a default constructor, a parameterless constructor is invoked with empty parentheses. The Time2 parameterless constructor explicitly initializes a Time2 object by passing to the three-parameter constructor 0 for each parameter. Since 0 is the default value for int instance variables, the parameterless constructor in this example could actually omit the constructor initializer. In this case, each instance variable would receive its default value when the object is created. If we omit the parameterless constructor, clients of this class would not be able to create a Time2 object with the expression new Time2().

Common Programming Error 10.3

If a class has constructors, but none of the public constructors are parameterless constructors, and an attempt is made to call a parameterless constructor to initialize an object of the class, a compilation error occurs. A constructor can be called with no arguments only if the class does not have any constructors (in which case the default constructor is called) or if the class has a visible parameterless constructor.

10.7 Composition

A class can have references to objects of other classes as members. This is called **composition** and is sometimes referred to as a *has-a* relationship. For example, an object of class AlarmClock needs to know the current time *and* the time when it's supposed to sound its alarm, so it's reasonable to include *two* references to Time objects in an AlarmClock object.

> **Software Engineering Observation 10.5**
>
> *One form of software reuse is composition, in which a class has as members references to objects of other classes.*

Class **Date**

Our example of composition contains three classes—Date (Fig. 10.7), Employee (Fig. 10.8) and EmployeeTest (Fig. 10.9). Class Date (Fig. 10.7) declares instance variables month and day (lines 7–8) and auto-implemented property Year (line 11) to represent a date. The constructor receives three int parameters. Line 17 invokes the set accessor of property Month (lines 24–38) to validate the month—if the value is out-of-range the accessor throws an exception. Line 18 uses property Year to set the year. Since Year is an auto-implemented property, we're assuming in this example that the value for Year is correct. Line 19 uses property Day (lines 41–63), which validates and assigns the value for day based on the current month and Year (by using properties Month and Year in turn to obtain the values of month and Year). The order of initialization is important, because the set accessor of property Day validates the value for day based on the assumption that month and Year are correct. Line 53 determines whether the day is correct based on the number of days in the particular Month. If the day is not correct, lines 56–57 determine whether the Month is February, the day is 29 and the Year is a leap year. Otherwise, if the parameter value does not contain a correct value for day, the set accessor throws an exception. Line 20 in the constructor outputs the this reference as a string. Since this is a reference to the current Date object, the object's ToString method (lines 66–69) is called *implicitly* to obtain the object's string representation.

```
1   // Fig. 10.7: Date.cs
2   // Date class declaration.
3   using System;
4
5   public class Date
6   {
7      private int month; // 1-12
8      private int day; // 1-31 based on month
9
10     // auto-implemented property Year
11     public int Year { get; private set; }
12
13     // constructor: use property Month to confirm proper value for month;
14     // use property Day to confirm proper value for day
15     public Date( int theMonth, int theDay, int theYear )
16     {
17        Month = theMonth; // validate month
```

Fig. 10.7 | Date class declaration. (Part 1 of 2.)

```
18          Year = theYear; // could validate year
19          Day = theDay; // validate day
20          Console.WriteLine( "Date object constructor for date {0}", this );
21      } // end Date constructor
22
23      // property that gets and sets the month
24      public int Month
25      {
26          get
27          {
28              return month;
29          } // end get
30          private set // make writing inaccessible outside the class
31          {
32              if ( value > 0 && value <= 12 ) // validate month
33                  month = value;
34              else // month is invalid
35                  throw new ArgumentOutOfRangeException(
36                      "Month", value, "Month must be 1-12" );
37          } // end set
38      } // end property Month
39
40      // property that gets and sets the day
41      public int Day
42      {
43          get
44          {
45              return day;
46          } // end get
47          private set // make writing inaccessible outside the class
48          {
49              int[] daysPerMonth = { 0, 31, 28, 31, 30, 31, 30,
50                                     31, 31, 30, 31, 30, 31 };
51
52              // check if day in range for month
53              if ( value > 0 && value <= daysPerMonth[ Month ] )
54                  day = value;
55              // check for leap year
56              else if ( Month == 2 && value == 29 &&
57                  ( Year % 400 == 0 || ( Year % 4 == 0 && Year % 100 != 0 ) ) )
58                  day = value;
59              else // day is invalid
60                  throw new ArgumentOutOfRangeException(
61                      "Day", value, "Day out of range for current month/year" );
62          } // end set
63      } // end property Day
64
65      // return a string of the form month/day/year
66      public override string ToString()
67      {
68          return string.Format( "{0}/{1}/{2}", Month, Day, Year );
69      } // end method ToString
70  } // end class Date
```

Fig. 10.7 | Date class declaration. (Part 2 of 2.)

Class *Date's private set Accessors*

Class Date uses access modifiers to ensure that *clients* of the class must use the appropriate methods and properties to access private data. In particular, the properties Year, Month and Day declare private set accessors (lines 11, 30 and 47, respectively) to restrict the use of the set accessors to members of the class. We declare these private for the same reasons that we declare the instance variables private—to simplify code maintenance and control access to the class's data. Although the constructor, method and properties in class Date still have all the advantages of using the set accessors to perform validation, clients of the class must use the class's constructor to initialize the data in a Date object. The get accessors of properties Year, Month and Day are implicitly declared public because their properties are declared public—when there's no access modifier before a get or set accessor, the accessor inherits the access modifier preceding the property name.

Class *Employee*

Class Employee (Fig. 10.8) has public auto-implemented properties FirstName, LastName, BirthDate and HireDate. BirthDate and HireDate (lines 7–8) manipulate Date objects, demonstrating that *a class can have references to objects of other classes as members.* This, of course, is also true of the properties FirstName and LastName, which manipulate String objects. The Employee constructor (lines 11–18) takes four parameters—first, last, dateOfBirth and dateOfHire. The objects referenced by parameters dateOfBirth and dateOfHire are assigned to the Employee object's BirthDate and HireDate properties, respectively. When class Employee's ToString method is called, it returns a string containing the string representations of the two Date objects. Each of these strings is obtained with an implicit call to the Date class's ToString method.

```
1   // Fig. 10.8: Employee.cs
2   // Employee class with references to other objects.
3   public class Employee
4   {
5      public string FirstName { get; private set; }
6      public string LastName { get; private set; }
7      public Date BirthDate { get; private set; }
8      public Date HireDate { get; private set; }
9
10     // constructor to initialize name, birth date and hire date
11     public Employee( string first, string last,
12        Date dateOfBirth, Date dateOfHire )
13     {
14        firstName = first;
15        lastName = last;
16        birthDate = dateOfBirth;
17        hireDate = dateOfHire;
18     } // end Employee constructor
19
20     // convert Employee to string format
21     public override string ToString()
22     {
```

Fig. 10.8 | Employee class with references to other objects. (Part I of 2.)

```
23          return string.Format( "{0}, {1}  Hired: {2}  Birthday: {3}",
24             lastName, firstName, hireDate, birthDate );
25       } // end method ToString
26    } // end class Employee
```

Fig. 10.8 | Employee class with references to other objects. (Part 2 of 2.)

Class EmployeeTest

Class EmployeeTest (Fig. 10.9) creates two Date objects (lines 9–10) to represent an Employee's birthday and hire date, respectively. Line 11 creates an Employee and initializes its instance variables by passing to the constructor two strings (representing the Employee's first and last names) and two Date objects (representing the birthday and hire date). Line 13 implicitly invokes the Employee's ToString method to display the values of its instance variables and demonstrate that the object was initialized properly.

```
1    // Fig. 10.9: EmployeeTest.cs
2    // Composition demonstration.
3    using System;
4
5    public class EmployeeTest
6    {
7       public static void Main( string[] args )
8       {
9          Date birth = new Date( 7, 24, 1949 );
10         Date hire = new Date( 3, 12, 1988 );
11         Employee employee = new Employee( "Bob", "Blue", birth, hire );
12
13         Console.WriteLine( employee );
14      } // end Main
15   } // end class EmployeeTest
```

```
Date object constructor for date 7/24/1949
Date object constructor for date 3/12/1988
Blue, Bob  Hired: 3/12/1988  Birthday: 7/24/1949
```

Fig. 10.9 | Composition demonstration.

10.8 Garbage Collection and Destructors

Every object you create uses various system resources, such as memory. In many programming languages, these system resources are reserved for the object's use until they're explicitly released by the programmer. If all the references to the object that manages the resource are lost before the resource is explicitly released, the application can no longer access the resource to release it. This is known as a **resource leak**.

We need a disciplined way to give resources back to the system when they're no longer needed, thus avoiding resource leaks. The Common Language Runtime (CLR) performs automatic memory management by using a **garbage collector** to reclaim the memory occupied by objects that are no longer in use, so the memory can be used for other objects. When there are no more references to an object, the object becomes **eligible for destruction**. Every object has a special member, called a **destructor**, that is invoked by the garbage collector to perform **termination housekeeping** on an object before the garbage collector reclaims the object's memory. A destructor is declared like a parameterless constructor, except that its name is the class name, preceded by a tilde (~), and it has no access modifier in its header. After the garbage collector calls the object's destructor, the object becomes **eligible for garbage collection**. The memory for such an object can be reclaimed by the garbage collector. With .NET 4, Microsoft has introduced a new background garbage collector that manages memory more efficiently than the garbage collectors in earlier .NET versions.

Memory leaks, which are common in other languages such as C and C++ (because memory is not automatically reclaimed in those languages), are less likely in C# (but some can still happen in subtle ways). Other types of resource leaks can occur. For example, an application could open a file on disk to modify its contents. If the application does not close the file, no other application can modify (or possibly even use) the file until the application that opened it terminates.

A problem with the garbage collector is that it doesn't guarantee that it will perform its tasks at a specified time. Therefore, the garbage collector may call the destructor any time after the object becomes eligible for destruction, and may reclaim the memory any time after the destructor executes. In fact, it's possible that neither will happen before the application terminates. Thus, it's unclear whether, or when, the destructor will be called. For this reason, destructors are rarely used.

Software Engineering Observation 10.6

A class that uses system resources, such as files on disk, should provide a method to eventually release the resources. Many Framework Class Library classes provide Close or Dispose methods for this purpose. Section 13.5 introduces the Dispose method, which is then used in many later examples. Close methods are typically used with objects that are associated with files (Chapter 17) and other types of so-called streams of data.

10.9 static Class Members

Every object has its own copy of all the instance variables of the class. In certain cases, only one copy of a particular variable should be *shared* by all objects of a class. A **static variable** is used in such cases. A static variable represents **classwide information**—all objects of the class share the same piece of data. The declaration of a static variable begins with the keyword static.

Let's motivate static data with an example. Suppose that we have a video game with Martians and other space creatures. Each Martian tends to be brave and willing to attack other space creatures when it's aware that there are at least four other Martians present. If fewer than five Martians are present, each Martian becomes cowardly. Thus each Martian needs to know the martianCount. We could endow class Martian with martianCount as an instance variable. If we do this, every Martian will have a separate copy of the instance variable, and every time we create a new Martian, we'll have to update the instance variable martianCount in every Martian. This wastes space on redundant copies, wastes time updating the separate copies and is error prone. Instead, we declare martianCount to be static, making martianCount classwide data. Every Martian can access the martian-Count as if it were an instance variable of class Martian, but only one copy of the static martianCount is maintained. This saves space. We save time by having the Martian constructor increment the `static` `martianCount`—there's only one copy, so we do not have to increment separate copies of `martianCount` for each `Martian` object.

Software Engineering Observation 10.7

Use a `static` variable when all objects of a class must use the same copy of the variable.

The scope of a `static` variable is the body of its class. A class's `public` `static` members can be accessed by qualifying the member name with the class name and the member access (.) operator, as in `Math.PI`. A class's `private` `static` class members can be accessed only through the methods and properties of the class. Actually, `static` class members exist even when no objects of the class exist—they're available as soon as the class is loaded into memory at execution time. To access a `private` `static` member from outside its class, a `public` `static` method or property can be provided.

Common Programming Error 10.4

It's a compilation error to access or invoke a `static` member by referencing it through an instance of the class, like a non-static member.

Software Engineering Observation 10.8

Static variables, methods and properties exist, and can be used, even if no objects of that class have been instantiated.

Class *Employee*

Our next application declares two classes—`Employee` (Fig. 10.10) and `EmployeeTest` (Fig. 10.11). Class `Employee` declares `private` `static` auto-implemented property `Count`. We declare `Count`'s `set` accessor `private`, because we don't want clients of the class to be able to modify the property's value. The compiler automatically creates a `private` `static` variable that property `Count` will manage. If a `static` variable is not initialized, the compiler assigns a default value to the variable—in this case, the `static` variable for the auto-implemented `Count` property is initialized to 0, the default value for type `int`. Property `Count` maintains a count of the number of objects of class `Employee` that have been created.

When `Employee` objects exist, `Count` can be used in any method of an `Employee` object—this example increments `Count` in the constructor (line 22). Client code can access the `Count` with the expression `Employee.Count`, which evaluates to the number of `Employee` objects currently in memory.

```
1   // Fig. 10.10: Employee.cs
2   // Static variable used to maintain a count of the number of
3   // Employee objects that have been created.
4   using System;
5
6   public class Employee
7   {
```

Fig. 10.10 | `static` property used to maintain a count of the number of `Employee` objects that have been created. (Part 1 of 2.)

```
 8        public static int Count { get; private set; } // objects in memory
 9
10        // read-only auto-implemented property FirstName
11        public string FirstName { get; private set; }
12
13        // read-only auto-implemented property LastName
14        public string LastName { get; private set; }
15
16        // initialize employee, add 1 to static Count and
17        // output string indicating that constructor was called
18        public Employee( string first, string last )
19        {
20           FirstName = first;
21           LastName = last;
22           ++Count; // increment static count of employees
23           Console.WriteLine( "Employee constructor: {0} {1}; Count = {2}",
24              FirstName, LastName, Count );
25        } // end Employee constructor
26     } // end class Employee
```

Fig. 10.10 | static property used to maintain a count of the number of Employee objects that have been created. (Part 2 of 2.)

Class EmployeeTest

EmployeeTest method Main (Fig. 10.11) instantiates two Employee objects (lines 14–15). When each Employee object's constructor is invoked, lines 20–21 of Fig. 10.10 assign the Employee's first name and last name to properties FirstName and LastName. These two statements do *not* make copies of the original string arguments. Actually, string objects in C# are **immutable**—they cannot be modified after they're created. Therefore, it's safe to have many references to one string object. This is not normally the case for objects of most other classes in C#. If string objects are immutable, you might wonder why we're able to use operators + and += to concatenate string objects. String-concatenation operations actually result in a new string object containing the concatenated values. The original string objects are not modified.

```
 1    // Fig. 10.11: EmployeeTest.cs
 2    // Static member demonstration.
 3    using System;
 4
 5    public class EmployeeTest
 6    {
 7       public static void Main( string[] args )
 8       {
 9          // show that Count is 0 before creating Employees
10          Console.WriteLine( "Employees before instantiation: {0}",
11             Employee.Count );
12
13          // create two Employees; Count should become 2
14          Employee e1 = new Employee( "Susan", "Baker" );
```

Fig. 10.11 | static member demonstration. (Part 1 of 2.)

```
15         Employee e2 = new Employee( "Bob", "Blue" );
16
17         // show that Count is 2 after creating two Employees
18         Console.WriteLine( "\nEmployees after instantiation: {0}",
19            Employee.Count );
20
21         // get names of Employees
22         Console.WriteLine( "\nEmployee 1: {0} {1}\nEmployee 2: {2} {3}\n",
23            e1.FirstName, e1.LastName,
24            e2.FirstName, e2.LastName );
25
26         // in this example, there is only one reference to each Employee,
27         // so the following statements cause the CLR to mark each
28         // Employee object as being eligible for garbage collection
29         e1 = null; // good practice: mark object e1 no longer needed
30         e2 = null; // good practice: mark object e2 no longer needed
31      } // end Main
32   } // end class EmployeeTest
```

```
Employees before instantiation: 0
Employee constructor: Susan Baker; Count = 1
Employee constructor: Bob Blue; Count = 2

Employees after instantiation: 2

Employee 1: Susan Baker
Employee 2: Bob Blue
```

Fig. 10.11 | static member demonstration. (Part 2 of 2.)

Lines 18–19 display the updated Count. When Main has finished using the two Employee objects, references e1 and e2 are set to null at lines 29–30, so they no longer refer to the objects that were instantiated in lines 14–15. The objects become "eligible for destruction" because there are no more references to them in the application. After the objects' destructors are called, the objects become "eligible for garbage collection."

Eventually, the garbage collector might reclaim the memory for these objects (or the operating system will reclaim the memory when the application terminates). C# does not guarantee when, or even whether, the garbage collector will execute. When the garbage collector does run, it's possible that no objects or only a subset of the eligible objects will be collected.

A method declared static cannot access non-static class members directly, because a static method can be called even when no objects of the class exist. For the same reason, the this reference cannot be used in a static method—the this reference must refer to a specific object of the class, and when a static method is called, there might not be any objects of its class in memory.

10.10 readonly Instance Variables

The **principle of least privilege** is fundamental to good software engineering. In the context of an application, the principle states that *code should be granted the amount of privilege* *and access needed to accomplish its designated task, but no more.* Let's see how this principle applies to instance variables.

Some instance variables need to be modifiable, and some do not. In Section 8.4, we used keyword const for declaring constants. These constants must be initialized to a constant value when they're declared. Suppose, however, we want to initialize a constant belonging to an object in the object's constructor. C# provides keyword **readonly** to specify that an instance variable of an object is not modifiable and that any attempt to modify it after the object is constructed is an error. For example,

```
private readonly int INCREMENT;
```

declares readonly instance variable INCREMENT of type int. Like constants, readonly variables are declared with all capital letters by convention. Although readonly instance variables can be initialized when they're declared, this isn't required. Readonly variables should be initialized *by each* of the class's constructors. Each constructor can assign values to a readonly instance variable multiple times—the variable doesn't become unmodifiable until after the constructor completes execution. A constructor does not initialize the readonly variable, the variable receives the same default value as any other instance variable (0 for numeric simple types, false for bool type and null for reference types), and the compiler generates a warning.

Software Engineering Observation 10.9

Declaring an instance variable as readonly helps enforce the principle of least privilege. If an instance variable should not be modified after the object is constructed, declare it to be readonly to prevent modification.

Members that are declared as const must be assigned values at compile time. Therefore, const members can be initialized *only* with other constant values, such as integers, string literals, characters and other const members. Constant members with values that cannot be determined at compile time must be declared with keyword readonly, so they can be initialized at *execution time*. Variables that are readonly can be initialized with more complex expressions, such as an array initializer or a method call that returns a value or a reference to an object.

Common Programming Error 10.5

Attempting to modify a readonly instance variable anywhere but in its declaration or the object's constructors is a compilation error.

Error-Prevention Tip 10.2

Attempts to modify a readonly instance variable are caught at compilation time rather than causing execution-time errors. It's always preferable to get bugs out at compile time, if possible, rather than allowing them to slip through to execution time (where studies have found that repairing bugs is often many times more costly).

Software Engineering Observation 10.10

If a readonly instance variable is initialized to a constant only in its declaration, it's not necessary to have a separate copy of the instance variable for every object of the class. The variable should be declared const instead. Constants declared with const are implicitly static, so there will only be one copy for the entire class.

10.11 Data Abstraction and Encapsulation

Classes normally hide the details of their implementation from their clients. This is called **information hiding**. As an example, let's consider the **stack data structure** introduced in Section 7.6. Recall that a stack is a **last-in, first-out (LIFO)** data structure—the last item pushed (inserted) on the stack is the first item popped (removed) off the stack.

Stacks can be implemented with arrays and with other data structures, such as linked lists. (We discuss stacks and linked lists in Chapters 21 and 23.) A client of a stack class need not be concerned with the stack's implementation. The client knows only that when data items are placed in the stack, they'll be recalled in last-in, first-out order. The client cares about *what* functionality a stack offers, not about *how* that functionality is implemented. This concept is referred to as **data abstraction**. Even if you know the details of a class's implementation, you shouldn't write code that depends on these details as they may later change. This enables a particular class (such as one that implements a stack and its *push* and *pop* operations) to be replaced with another version—perhaps one that runs faster or uses less memory—without affecting the rest of the system. As long as the public services of the class do not change (i.e., every original method still has the same name, return type and parameter list in the new class declaration), the rest of the system is not affected.

Earlier non-object-oriented programming languages like C emphasize actions. In these languages, data exists to support the actions that applications must take. Data is "less interesting" than actions. Data is "crude." Only a few simple types exist, and it's difficult for programmers to create their own types. C# and the object-oriented style of programming elevate the importance of data. The primary activities of object-oriented programming in C# are creating types (e.g., classes) and expressing the interactions among objects of those types. To create languages that emphasize data, the programming-languages community needed to formalize some notions about data. The formalization we consider here is the notion of **abstract data types (ADTs)**, which improve the application-development process.

Consider the type int, which most people associate with an integer in mathematics. Actually, an int is an *abstract representation of an integer*. Unlike mathematical integers, computer ints are *fixed* in size. Type int in C# is limited to the range –2,147,483,648 to +2,147,483,647. If the result of a calculation falls *outside* this range, an error occurs, and the computer responds in some appropriate manner. It might "quietly" produce an incorrect result, such as a value too large to fit in an int variable—commonly called **arithmetic overflow**. It also might throw an exception, called an OverflowException. (We show how to deal with arithmetic overflow in Section 13.8.) *Mathematical* integers do not have this problem. Therefore, the computer int is only an *approximation* of the real-world integer. Simple types like int, double, and char are all examples of abstract data types—*representations of real-world concepts to some satisfactory level of precision within a computer system.*

An ADT actually captures two notions: a **data representation** and the **operations** that can be performed on that data. For example, in C#, an int contains an integer value (data) and provides addition, subtraction, multiplication, division and remainder operations—division by zero is undefined.

Software Engineering Observation 10.11

Programmers create types through the class mechanism. New types can be designed to be as convenient to use as the simple types. Although the language is easy to extend via new types, you cannot alter the base language itself.

Another ADT we discuss is a **queue**, which is similar to a "waiting line." Computer systems use many queues internally. A queue offers well-understood behavior to its clients: Clients place items in a queue one at a time via an *enqueue* operation, then retrieve them one at a time via a *dequeue* operation. A queue returns items in **first-in, first-out (FIFO)** order—the first item inserted in a queue is the first removed. Conceptually, a queue can become infinitely long, but real queues are finite.

The queue hides an internal data representation that keeps track of the items currently waiting in line, and it offers *enqueue* and *dequeue* operations to its clients. The clients are not concerned about the implementation of the queue—they simply depend on the queue to operate "as advertised." When a client enqueues an item, the queue should accept that item and place it in some kind of internal FIFO data structure. Similarly, when the client wants the next item from the front of the queue, the queue should remove the item from its internal representation and deliver it in FIFO order—the item that has been in the queue the longest should be returned by the next dequeue operation.

The queue ADT guarantees the integrity of its internal data structure. Clients cannot manipulate this data structure directly—only the queue ADT has access to its internal data. Clients are able to perform only allowable operations on the data representation—the ADT rejects operations that its public interface does not provide. We'll discuss stacks and queues in greater depth in Chapter 21, Data Structures.

10.12 Class View and Object Browser

Now that we have introduced key concepts of object-oriented programming, we present two features that Visual Studio provides to facilitate the design of object-oriented applications—**Class View** and **Object Browser**.

Using the *Class View Window*

The **Class View** displays the fields, methods and properties for all classes in a project. To access this feature, you must first enable the IDE's "expert features." To do so, select **Tools > Settings > Expert Settings**. Next, select **View > Class View**. Figure 10.12 shows the **Class View** for the Time1 project of Fig. 10.1 (class Time1) and Fig. 10.2 (class Time1Test). The view follows a hierarchical structure, positioning the project name (Time1) as the *root* and including a series of nodes that represent the classes, variables, methods and properties in the project. If a ▷ appears to the left of a node, that node can be expanded to show other nodes. If a ◢ appears to the left of a node, that node can be collapsed. According to the **Class View**, project Time1 contains class Time1 and class Time1Test as children. When class Time1 is selected, the class's members appear in the lower half of the window. Class Time1 contains methods SetTime, ToString and ToUniversalString (indicated by purple boxes, ◖) and instance variables hour, minute and second (indicated by blue boxes, ◢). The lock icons to the left of the blue box icons for the instance variables specify that the variables are private. Both class Time1 and class Time1Test contain the **Base Types** node. If you expand this node, you'll see class Object in each case, because each class *inherits* from class System.Object (discussed in Chapter 11).

Using the *Object Browser*

Visual C# Express's **Object Browser** lists all classes in the C# library. You can use the **Object Browser** to learn about the functionality provided by a specific class. To open the **Object**

Fig. 10.12 | **Class View** of class Time1 (Fig. 10.1) and class Time1Test (Fig. 10.2).

Browser, select **Other Windows** from the **View** menu and click **Object Browser.** Figure 10.13 depicts the **Object Browser** when the user navigates to the Math class in namespace System. To do this, we expanded the node for mscorlib (Microsoft Core Library) in the upper-left pane of the **Object Browser,** then expanded its subnode for System. [*Note:* The most common classes from the System namespace, such as System.Math, are in mscorlib.]

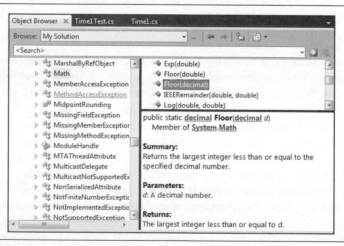

Fig. 10.13 | **Object Browser** for class Math.

The **Object Browser** lists all methods provided by class Math in the upper-right frame—this offers you "instant access" to information regarding the functionality of various objects. If you click the name of a member in the upper-right frame, a description of that member appears in the lower-right frame. The **Object Browser** lists all the classes of the Framework Class Library. The **Object Browser** can be a quick mechanism to learn about a class or one of its methods. Remember that you can also view the complete description of a class or a method in the online documentation available through the **Help** menu in Visual C# Express.

10.13 Object Initializers

Visual C# provides **object initializers** that allow you to create an object and initialize its `public` properties (and `public` instance variables, if any) in the same statement. This can be useful when a class does not provide an appropriate constructor to meet your needs, but does provide properties that you can use to manipulate the class's data. The following statements demonstrate object initializers using the class `Time2` from Fig. 10.5.

```
// create a Time2 object and initialize its properties
Time2 aTime = new Time2 { Hour = 14, Minute = 30, Second = 12 };

// create a Time2 object and initialize only its Minute property
Time2 anotherTime = new Time2 { Minute = 45 };
```

The first statement creates a `Time2` object (`aTime`), initializes it with class `Time2`'s constructor that can be called with no arguments, then uses an object initializer to set its `Hour`, `Minute` and `Second` properties. Notice that `new Time2` is immediately followed by an **object-initializer list**—a comma-separated list in curly braces ({ }) of properties and their values. Each property name can appear only once in the object-initializer list. The object initializer executes the property initializers in the order in which they appear.

The second statement creates a new `Time2` object (`anotherTime`), initializes it with class `Time2`'s constructor that can be called with no arguments, then sets only its `Minute` property using an object initializer. When the `Time2` constructor is called with no arguments, it initializes the time to midnight. The object initializer then sets each specified property to the supplied value. In this case, the `Minute` property is set to 45. The `Hour` and `Second` properties retain their default values, because no values are specified for them in the object initializer.

10.14 Wrap-Up

In this chapter, we discussed additional class concepts. The `Time` class case study presented a complete class declaration consisting of `private` data, overloaded `public` constructors for initialization flexibility, properties for manipulating the class's data and methods that returned `string` representations of a `Time` object in two different formats. You learned that every class can declare a `ToString` method that returns a `string` representation of an object of the class and that this method is invoked implicitly when an object of a class is output as a `string` or concatenated with a `string`.

You learned that the `this` reference is used implicitly in a class's non-`static` methods to access the class's instance variables and other non-`static` methods. You saw explicit uses of the `this` reference to access the class's members (including hidden fields) and learned how to use keyword `this` in a constructor to call another constructor of the class.

You saw that composition enables a class to have references to objects of other classes as members. You learned about C#'s garbage-collection capability and how it reclaims the memory of objects that are no longer used. We explained the motivation for `static` variables in a class and demonstrated how to declare and use `static` variables and methods in your own classes. You also learned how to declare and initialize `readonly` variables.

We also showed how to use Visual Studio's **Class View** and **Object Browser** windows to navigate the classes of the Framework Class Library and your own applications to discover information about those classes. Finally, you learned how to initialize an object's properties as you create it with an object-initializer list.

In the next chapter, you'll learn about inheritance. You'll see that all classes in C# are related directly or indirectly to the object class and begin to understand how inheritance enables you to build more powerful applications faster.

Summary

Section 10.2 Time Class Case Study

- The public methods of a class are the public services or the public interface that the class provides to its clients.
- Methods and properties that modify the values of private variables should verify that the intended new values are valid.
- A class's methods and properties can throw exceptions to indicate invalid data.
- The actual data representation used within the class is of no concern to the class's clients. This allows you to change the implementation of the class. Clients could use the same public methods and properties to get the same results without being aware of this change.
- Clients are neither aware of, nor involved in, a class's implementation. Clients generally care about *what* the class does but not *how* the class does it.

Section 10.3 Controlling Access to Members

- Access modifiers public and private control access to a class's variables, methods and properties. A class's private variables, methods and properties are not directly accessible to the class's clients.
- If a client attempts to use the private members of another class, the compiler generates error messages stating that these private members are not accessible.
- If a class member is not declared with an access modifier, it has private access by default.

Section 10.4 Referring to the Current Object's Members with the this Reference

- Every object can access a reference to itself with keyword this. When a non-static method is called for a particular object, the method's body implicitly uses keyword this to refer to the object's instance variables, other methods and properties.
- If a method contains a local variable with the same name as a field, that method will refer to the local variable rather than the field. However, a non-static method can use the this reference to refer to a hidden instance variable explicitly.
- Avoid method-parameter names or local-variable names that conflict with field names. This helps prevent subtle, hard-to-locate bugs.

Section 10.5 Time Class Case Study: Overloaded Constructors

- To overload constructors, provide multiple constructor declarations with different signatures.
- Following the constructor header with the constructor initializer : this (*args*) invokes the matching overloaded constructor in the same class.
- Constructor initializers are a popular way to reuse initialization code provided by one of the class's constructors rather than defining similar code in another constructor's body.
- When one object of a class has a reference to another object of the same class, the first object can access all the second object's data and methods (including those that are private).
- When implementing a method of a class, use the class's properties to access the class's private data. This simplifies code maintenance and reduces the likelihood of errors.

- The `ArgumentOutOfRangeException` constructor with three arguments lets you specify the name of the item that is out of range, the value that was out of range and an error message.

Section 10.6 Default and Parameterless Constructors

- Every class must have at least one constructor. If there are no constructors in a class's declaration, the compiler creates a default constructor for the class.

- The compiler will not create a default constructor for a class that explicitly declares at least one constructor. In this case, if you want to be able to invoke the constructor with no arguments, you must declare a parameterless constructor.

Section 10.7 Composition

- A class can have references to objects of other classes as members. Such a capability is called composition and is sometimes referred to as a *has-a* relationship.

Section 10.8 Garbage Collection and Destructors

- Every object you create uses various system resources, such as memory. The CLR performs automatic memory management by using a garbage collector to reclaim the memory occupied by objects that are no longer in use.

- The destructor is invoked by the garbage collector to perform termination housekeeping on an object before the garbage collector reclaims the object's memory.

- Memory leaks, which are common in other languages like C and C++ (because memory is not automatically reclaimed in those languages), are less likely in C#.

- A problem with the garbage collector is that it's not guaranteed to perform its tasks at a specified time. Therefore, the garbage collector may call the destructor any time after the object becomes eligible for destruction, making it unclear when, or whether, the destructor will be called.

Section 10.9 `static` Class Members

- A `static` variable represents classwide information—all objects of the class share the variable.

- The scope of a `static` variable is the body of its class. A class's `public static` members can be accessed by qualifying the member name with the class name and the member access (.) operator.

- Static class members exist even when no objects of the class exist—they're available as soon as the class is loaded into memory at execution time.

- String objects in C# are immutable—they cannot be modified after they're created. Therefore, it's safe to have many references to one `string` object.

- It's possible that no objects or only a subset of the eligible objects will be collected.

- A method declared `static` cannot access non-`static` class members directly, because a `static` method can be called even when no objects of the class exist. For the same reason, the `this` reference cannot be used in a `static` method.

Section 10.10 `readonly` Instance Variables

- The principle of least privilege is fundamental to good software engineering. In the context of an application, the principle states that code should be granted only the amount of privilege and access needed to accomplish its designated task, but no more.

- Any attempt to modify a `readonly` instance variable after its object is constructed is an error.

- Although `readonly` instance variables can be initialized when they're declared, this is not required. A `readonly` variable can be initialized by each of the class's constructors.

- Members that are declared as `const` must be assigned values at compile time. Constant members with values that cannot be determined at compile time must be declared with keyword `readonly`, so they can be initialized at execution time.

Section 10.11 Data Abstraction and Encapsulation

- Classes use information hiding to hide the details of their implementation from their clients.

- The client cares about what functionality a class offers, not about how that functionality is implemented. This is referred to as data abstraction. Programmers should not write code that depends on these details as the details may later change.

- The primary activities of object-oriented programming in C# are the creation of types (e.g., classes) and the expression of the interactions among objects of those types.

- Types like int, double, and char are all examples of abstract data types. They're representations of real-world notions to some satisfactory level of precision within a computer system.

- An ADT actually captures two notions: a data representation and the operations that can be performed on that data.

Section 10.12 Class View and Object Browser

- The **Class View** displays the variables, methods and properties for all classes in a project. The view follows a hierarchical structure, positioning the project name as the root and including a series of nodes that represent the classes, variables, methods and properties in the project.

- The **Object Browser** lists all classes of the Framework Class Library. The **Object Browser** can be a quick mechanism to learn about a class or method of a class.

Section 10.13 Object Initializers

- Object initializers allow you to create an object and initialize its public properties (and public instance variables, if any) in the same statement.

- An object-initializer list is a comma-separated list in curly braces ({}) of properties and their values.

- Each property and instance variable name can appear only once in the object-initializer list.

- An object initializer first calls the class's constructor, then sets the value of each property and variable specified in the object-initializer list.

Terminology

abstract data type (ADT)	memory leak
ArgumentOutOfRangeException class	**Object Browser**
arithmetic overflow	object initializer
attribute (in the UML)	object-initializer list
Class View	overloaded constructors
classwide information	parameterless constructor
composition	principle of least privilege
constructor initializer	public interface
data abstraction	public service
data representation	queue data structure
destructor	readonly instance variable
eligible for destruction	resource leak
eligible for garbage collection	service of a class
first-in, first-out (FIFO) data structure	simple name of a class, field or method
Format method of class string	static variable
garbage collector	stack data structure
has-a relationship	termination housekeeping
immutable	this keyword
information hiding	throw an exception
last-in, first-out (LIFO) data structure	unmodifiable variable

Self-Review Exercises

10.1 Fill in the blanks in each of the following statements:
   a) `string` class `static` method _____ is similar to method `Console.Write`, but returns a formatted `string` rather than displaying a `string` in a console window.
   b) If a method contains a local variable with the same name as one of its class's fields, the local variable _____ the field in that method's scope.
   c) The _____ is called by the garbage collector before it reclaims an object's memory.
   d) If a class declares constructors, the compiler will not create a(n) _____.
   e) An object's _____ method can be called implicitly when an object appears in code where a `string` is needed.
   f) Composition is sometimes referred to as a(n) _____ relationship.
   g) A(n) _____ variable represents classwide information that is shared by all the objects of the class.
   h) The _____ states that code should be granted only the amount of access needed to accomplish its designated task.
   i) Declaring an instance variable with keyword _____ specifies that the variable is not modifiable.
   j) A(n) _____ consists of a data representation and the operations that can be performed on the data.
   k) The `public` methods of a class are also known as the class's _____ or _____.

10.2 Suppose class `Book` defines properties `Title`, `Author` and `Year`. Use an object initializer to create an object of class `Book` and initialize its properties.

Answers to Self-Review Exercises

10.1 a) `Format`. b) hides. c) destructor. d) default constructor. e) `ToString`. f) *has-a*. g) `static`. h) principle of least privilege. i) `readonly`. j) abstract data type (ADT). k) public services, public interface.

10.2 `new` Book { Title = "Visual C# 2010 HTP",
        Author = "Deitel", Year = 2010 }

Exercises

10.3 *(Rectangle Class)* Create class `Rectangle`. The class has attributes `length` and `width`, each of which defaults to 1. It has read-only properties that calculate the `Perimeter` and the `Area` of the rectangle. It has properties for both `length` and `width`. The set accessors should verify that `length` and `width` are each floating-point numbers greater than 0.0 and less than 20.0. Write an application to test class `Rectangle`.

10.4 *(Modifying the Internal Data Representation of a Class)* It would be perfectly reasonable for the `Time2` class of Fig. 10.5 to represent the time internally as the number of seconds since midnight rather than the three integer values `hour`, `minute` and `second`. Clients could use the same public methods and properties to get the same results. Modify the `Time2` class of Fig. 10.5 to implement the `Time2` as the number of seconds since midnight and show that no change is visible to the clients of the class by using the same test application from Fig. 10.6.

10.5 *(Savings-Account Class)* Create the class `SavingsAccount`. Use the `static` variable `annualInterestRate` to store the annual interest rate for all account holders. Each object of the class contains a `private` instance variable `savingsBalance`, indicating the amount the saver currently has on deposit. Provide method `CalculateMonthlyInterest` to calculate the monthly interest by multiplying the `savingsBalance` by `annualInterestRate` divided by 12—this interest should be added to `savingsBal-`

ance. Provide static method `ModifyInterestRate` to set the `annualInterestRate` to a new value. Write an application to test class `SavingsAccount`. Create two `savingsAccount` objects, saver1 and saver2, with balances of $2000.00 and $3000.00, respectively. Set `annualInterestRate` to 4%, then calculate the monthly interest and display the new balances for both savers. Then set the `annualInterestRate` to 5%, calculate the next month's interest and display the new balances for both savers.

10.6 *(Enhancing Class Date)* Modify class `Date` of Fig. 10.7 to perform error checking on the initializer values for instance variables `month`, `day` and `year` (class `Date` currently validates only the month and day). You'll need to convert the auto-implemented property `Year` into instance variable `year` with an associated `Year` property. Provide method `NextDay` to increment the day by 1. The `Date` object should always maintain valid data and throw exceptions when attempts are made to set invalid values. Write an application that tests the `NextDay` method in a loop that displays the date during each iteration of the loop to illustrate that the `NextDay` method works correctly. Test the following cases:

   a) incrementing to the next month and
   b) incrementing to the next year.

10.7 *(Complex Numbers)* Create a class called `Complex` for performing arithmetic with complex numbers. Complex numbers have the form *realPart* + *imaginaryPart* * *i* where *i* is $\sqrt{-1}$. Write an application to test your class. Use floating-point variables to represent the private data of the class. Provide a constructor that enables an object of this class to be initialized when it's declared. Provide a parameterless constructor with default values in case no initializers are provided. Provide public methods that perform the following operations:

   a) Add two `Complex` numbers: The real parts are added together and the imaginary parts are added together.
   b) Subtract two `Complex` numbers: The real part of the right operand is subtracted from the real part of the left operand, and the imaginary part of the right operand is subtracted from the imaginary part of the left operand.
   c) Return a `string` representation of a `Complex` number in the form (a, b), where a is the real part and b is the imaginary part.

10.8 *(Set of Integers)* Create class `IntegerSet`. Each `IntegerSet` object can hold integers in the range 0–100. The set is represented by an array of bools. Array element a[i] is true if integer *i* is in the set. Array element a[j] is false if integer *j* is not in the set. The parameterless constructor initializes the array to the "empty set" (i.e., a set whose array representation contains all false values).

   Provide the following methods:

   a) Method `Union` creates a third set that is the set-theoretic union of two existing sets (i.e., an element of the third set's array is set to true if that element is true in either or both of the existing sets—otherwise, the element of the third set is set to false).
   b) Method `Intersection` creates a third set which is the set-theoretic intersection of two existing sets (i.e., an element of the third set's array is set to false if that element is false in either or both of the existing sets—otherwise, the element of the third set is set to true).
   c) Method `InsertElement` inserts a new integer *k* into a set (by setting a[k] to true).
   d) Method `DeleteElement` deletes integer *m* (by setting a[m] to false).
   e) Method `ToString` returns a string containing a set as a list of numbers separated by spaces. Include only those elements that are present in the set. Use --- to represent an empty set.
   f) Method `IsEqualTo` determines whether two sets are equal.

   Write an application to test class `IntegerSet`. Instantiate several `IntegerSet` objects. Test that all your methods work properly.

10.9 *(Rational Numbers)* Create a class called `Rational` for performing arithmetic with fractions. Write an application to test your class. Use integer variables to represent the private instance variables of the class—the numerator and the denominator. Provide a constructor that enables an object of this class to be initialized when it's declared. The constructor should store the fraction in reduced form. The fraction

> 2/4

is equivalent to 1/2 and would be stored in the object as 1 in the numerator and 2 in the denominator. Provide a parameterless constructor with default values in case no initializers are provided. Provide `public` methods that perform each of the following operations (all calculation results should be stored in a reduced form):

a) Add two Rational numbers.
b) Subtract two Rational numbers.
c) Multiply two Rational numbers.
d) Divide two Rational numbers.
e) Display Rational numbers in the form a/b, where a is the numerator and b is the denominator.
f) Display Rational numbers in floating-point format. (Consider providing formatting capabilities that enable the user of the class to specify the number of digits of precision to the right of the decimal point.)

10.10   *(HugeInteger Class)* Create a class HugeInteger which uses a 40-element array of digits to store integers as large as 40 digits each. Provide methods Input, ToString, Add and Subtract. For comparing HugeInteger objects, provide the following methods: IsEqualTo, IsNotEqualTo, IsGreaterThan, IsLessThan, IsGreaterThanOrEqualTo and IsLessThanOrEqualTo. Each of these is a method that returns true if the relationship holds between the two HugeInteger objects and returns false if the relationship does not hold. Provide method IsZero. If you feel ambitious, also provide methods Multiply, Divide and Remainder. In the Input method, use the string method ToCharArray to convert the input string into an array of characters, then iterate through these characters to create your HugeInteger. [*Note:* The .NET Framework Class Library now includes type BigInteger for arbitrary sized integer values.]

10.11   *(Tic-Tac-Toe)* Create class TicTacToe that will enable you to write a complete application to play the game of Tic-Tac-Toe. The class contains a private 3-by-3 rectangular array of integers. The constructor should initialize the empty board to all 0s. Allow two human players. Wherever the first player moves, place a 1 in the specified square, and place a 2 wherever the second player moves. Each move must be to an empty square. After each move, determine whether the game has been won and whether it's a draw. If you feel ambitious, modify your application so that the computer makes the moves for one of the players. Also, allow the player to specify whether he or she wants to go first or second. If you feel exceptionally ambitious, develop an application that will play three-dimensional Tic-Tac-Toe on a 4-by-4-by-4 board.

10.12   What happens when a return type, even void, is specified for a constructor?

11

Object-Oriented Programming: Inheritance

Say not you know another entirely, till you have divided an inheritance with him.
—Johann Kasper Lavater

This method is to define as the number of a class the class of all classes similar to the given class.
—Bertrand Russell

Objectives

In this chapter you'll learn:

- How inheritance promotes software reusability.

- To create a derived class that inherits attributes and behaviors from a base class.

- To use access modifier **protected** to give derived-class methods access to base-class members.

- To access base-class members with **base**.

- How constructors are used in inheritance hierarchies.

- The methods of class **object**, the direct or indirect base class of all classes.

11.1 Introduction

This chapter continues our discussion of object-oriented programming (OOP) by introducing one of its primary features—**inheritance**, a form of software reuse in which a new class is created by absorbing an existing class's members and enhancing them with new or modified capabilities. Inheritance lets you save time during application development by reusing proven and debugged high-quality software. This also increases the likelihood that a system will be implemented effectively.

The existing class from which a new class inherits members is called the **base class**, and the new class is the **derived class.** Each derived class can become the base class for future derived classes.

A derived class normally adds its own fields and methods. Therefore, it's more specific than its base class and represents a more specialized group of objects. Typically, the derived class exhibits the behaviors of its base class and additional ones that are specific to itself.

The **direct base class** is the base class from which the derived class explicitly inherits. An **indirect base class** is any class above the direct base class in the **class hierarchy**, which defines the inheritance relationships among classes. The class hierarchy begins with class **object** (which is the C# alias for System.Object in the Framework Class Library), which *every* class directly or indirectly **extends** (or "inherits from"). Section 11.7 lists the methods of class object, which *every* other class inherits. In the case of **single inheritance,** a class is derived from one direct base class. C#, unlike C++, does not support multiple inheritance (which occurs when a class is derived from more than one direct base class). In Chapter 12, OOP: Polymorphism, Interfaces and Operator Overloading, we explain how you can use interfaces to realize many of the benefits of multiple inheritance while avoiding the associated problems.

Experience in building software systems indicates that significant amounts of code deal with closely related special cases. When you're preoccupied with special cases, the details can obscure the big picture. With object-oriented programming, you can, when appropriate, focus on the commonalities among objects in the system rather than the special cases.

We distinguish between the *is-a* **relationship** and the *has-a* **relationship.** *Is-a* represents inheritance. In an *is-a* relationship, an object of a derived class can also be treated as an object of its base class. For example, a car *is a* vehicle, and a truck *is a* vehicle. By contrast, *has-a* represents composition (see Chapter 10). In a *has-a* relationship, an object contains as members references to other objects. For example, a car *has a* steering wheel, and a car object *has a* reference to a steering-wheel object.

New classes can inherit from classes in **class libraries**. Organizations develop their own class libraries and can take advantage of others available worldwide. Some day, most new software likely will be constructed from **standardized reusable components**, just as automobiles and most computer hardware are constructed today. This will facilitate the development of more powerful, abundant and economical software.

11.2 Base Classes and Derived Classes

Often, an object of one class *is an* object of another class as well. For example, in geometry, a rectangle *is a* quadrilateral (as are squares, parallelograms and trapezoids). Thus, class Rectangle can be said to inherit from class Quadrilateral. In this context, class Quadrilateral is a base class and class Rectangle is a derived class. A rectangle *is a* specific type of quadrilateral, but it's incorrect to claim that every quadrilateral *is a* rectangle—the quadrilateral could be a parallelogram or some other shape. Figure 11.1 lists several simple examples of base classes and derived classes—base classes tend to be "more general," and derived classes tend to be "more specific."

Base class	Derived classes
Student	GraduateStudent, UndergraduateStudent
Shape	Circle, Triangle, Rectangle
Loan	CarLoan, HomeImprovementLoan, MortgageLoan
Employee	Faculty, Staff, HourlyWorker, CommissionWorker
BankAccount	CheckingAccount, SavingsAccount

Fig. 11.1 | Inheritance examples.

Because every derived-class object *is an* object of its base class, and one base class can have many derived classes, the set of objects represented by a base class is typically larger than the set of objects represented by any of its derived classes. For example, the base class Vehicle represents all vehicles—cars, trucks, boats, bicycles and so on. By contrast, derived class Car represents a smaller, more specific subset of vehicles.

Inheritance relationships form treelike hierarchical structures (Figs. 11.2 and 11.3). A base class exists in a hierarchical relationship with its derived classes. When classes participate in inheritance relationships, they become "affiliated" with other classes. A class becomes either a base class, supplying members to other classes, or a derived class, inheriting its members from another class. Sometimes, a class is both a base and a derived class.

Let us develop a sample class hierarchy, also called an **inheritance hierarchy** (Fig. 11.2). The UML class diagram of Fig. 11.2 shows a university community that has many types of members, including employees, students and alumni. Employees are either faculty members or staff members. Faculty members are either administrators (such as deans and department chairpersons) or teachers. The hierarchy could contain many other classes. For example, students can be graduate or undergraduate students. Undergraduate students can be freshmen, sophomores, juniors or seniors.

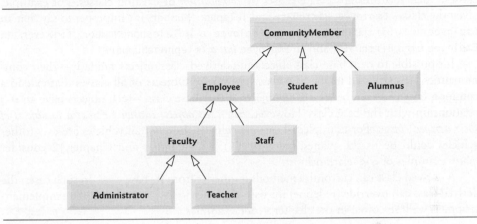

Fig. 11.2 | UML class diagram showing an inheritance hierarchy for university CommunityMembers.

Each arrow with a hollow triangular arrowhead in the hierarchy diagram represents an *is-a* relationship. As we follow the arrows, we can state, for instance, that "an Employee *is a* CommunityMember" and "a Teacher *is a* Faculty member." CommunityMember is the *direct* base class of Employee, Student and Alumnus and is an *indirect* base class of all the other classes in the diagram. Starting from the bottom, the reader can follow the arrows and apply the *is-a* relationship up to the topmost base class. For example, an Administrator *is a* Faculty member, *is an* Employee and *is a* CommunityMember.

Now consider the Shape hierarchy in Fig. 11.3, which begins with base class Shape. This class is extended by derived classes TwoDimensionalShape and ThreeDimensionalShape—a Shape is either a TwoDimensionalShape or a ThreeDimensionalShape. The third level of this hierarchy contains specific TwoDimensionalShapes and ThreeDimensionalShapes. We can follow the arrows from the bottom to the topmost base class in this hierarchy to identify the *is-a* relationships. For instance, a Triangle *is a* TwoDimensionalShape and *is a* Shape, while a Sphere *is a* ThreeDimensionalShape and *is a* Shape. This hierarchy could contain many other classes. For example, ellipses and trapezoids also are TwoDimensionalShapes.

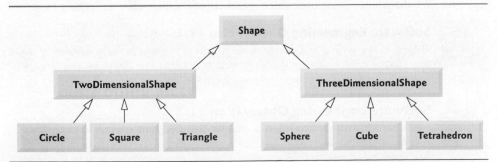

Fig. 11.3 | UML class diagram showing an inheritance hierarchy for Shapes.

Not every class relationship is an inheritance relationship. In Chapter 10 we discussed the *has-a* relationship, in which classes have members that are references to objects of other classes. Such relationships create classes by *composition* of existing classes. For example, given the classes Employee, BirthDate and TelephoneNumber, it's improper to say that an Employee *is a* BirthDate or that an Employee *is a* TelephoneNumber. However, an Employee *has a* BirthDate, and an Employee *has a* TelephoneNumber.

It's possible to treat base-class objects and derived-class objects similarly—their commonalities are expressed in the base class's members. Objects of all classes that extend a common base class can be treated as objects of that base class—such objects have an *is-a* relationship with the base class. However, *base-class objects cannot be treated as objects of their derived classes*. For example, all cars are vehicles, but not all vehicles are cars (other vehicles could be trucks, planes, bicycles, etc.). This chapter and Chapter 12 consider many examples of *is-a* relationships.

A derived class can customize methods it inherits from its base class. In such cases, the derived class can **override** (redefine) the base-class method with an appropriate implementation, as we'll see often in the chapter's code examples.

11.3 protected Members

Chapter 10 discussed access modifiers public and private. A class's public members are accessible wherever the application has a reference to an object of that class or one of its derived classes. A class's private members are accessible *only* within the class itself. A base class's private members *are* inherited by its derived classes, but are *not* directly accessible by derived-class methods and properties. In this section, we introduce access modifier protected. Using protected access offers an intermediate level of access between public and private. A base class's protected members can be accessed by members of that base class *and* by members of its derived classes.

All non-private base-class members retain their original access modifier when they become members of the derived class—public members of the base class become public members of the derived class, and protected members of the base class become protected members of the derived class.

Derived-class methods can refer to public and protected members inherited from the base class simply by using the member names. When a derived-class method overrides a base-class method, the base-class version can be accessed from the derived class by preceding the base-class method name with the keyword base and the member access (.) operator. We discuss accessing overridden members of the base class in Section 11.4.

Software Engineering Observation 11.1

Properties and methods of a derived class cannot directly access private members of the base class. A derived class can change the state of private base-class fields only through non-private methods and properties provided in the base class.

Software Engineering Observation 11.2

Declaring private fields in a base class helps you test, debug and correctly modify systems. If a derived class could access its base class's private fields, classes that inherit from that base class could access the fields as well. This would propagate access to what should be private fields, and the benefits of information hiding would be lost.

11.4 Relationship between Base Classes and Derived Classes

In this section, we use an inheritance hierarchy containing types of employees in a company's payroll application to discuss the relationship between a base class and its derived classes. In this company, commission employees (who will be represented as objects of a base class) are paid a percentage of their sales, while base-salaried commission employees (who will be represented as objects of a derived class) receive a base salary *plus* a percentage of their sales.

We divide our discussion of the relationship between commission employees and base-salaried commission employees into five examples:

1. The first example creates class CommissionEmployee, which directly inherits from class object and declares as private instance variables a first name, last name, social security number, commission rate and gross (i.e., total) sales amount.

2. The second example declares class BasePlusCommissionEmployee, which also directly inherits from class object and declares as private instance variables a first name, last name, social security number, commission rate, gross sales amount *and* base salary. We create the latter class by writing *every* line of code the class requires—we'll soon see that it's much more efficient to create this class by inheriting from class CommissionEmployee.

3. The third example declares a separate BasePlusCommissionEmployee class that extends class CommissionEmployee (i.e., a BasePlusCommissionEmployee *is a* CommissionEmployee who also has a base salary). We show that base-class methods must be explicitly declared virtual if they're to be overridden by methods in derived classes. BasePlusCommissionEmployee attempts to access class CommissionEmployee's private members, but this results in compilation errors because a derived class cannot access its base class's private instance variables.

4. The fourth example shows that if base class CommissionEmployee's instance variables are declared as protected, a BasePlusCommissionEmployee class that inherits from class CommissionEmployee can access that data directly. For this purpose, we declare class CommissionEmployee with protected instance variables.

5. After we discuss the convenience of using protected instance variables, we create the fifth example, which sets the CommissionEmployee instance variables back to private in class CommissionEmployee to enforce good software engineering. Then we show how a separate BasePlusCommissionEmployee class, which inherits from class CommissionEmployee, can use CommissionEmployee's public methods to manipulate CommissionEmployee's private instance variables.

11.4.1 Creating and Using a CommissionEmployee Class

We begin by declaring class CommissionEmployee (Fig. 11.4). Line 5 begins the class declaration. The colon (:) followed by class name object at the end of the declaration header indicates that class CommissionEmployee extends (i.e., inherits from) class object (System.Object in the Framework Class Library). C# programmers use inheritance to create classes from existing classes. In fact, every class in C# (except object) extends an existing class. Because class CommissionEmployee extends class object, class CommissionEmployee inherits the methods of class object—class object has no fields. Every C# class directly or indirectly inherits object's methods. If a class does not specify that it inherits from another class, the new class implicitly inherits from object. For this reason, you typically do not include ": object" in your code—we do so in this example for demonstration purposes.

Software Engineering Observation 11.3

The compiler sets the base class of a class to object when the class declaration does not explicitly extend a base class.

```csharp
1   // Fig. 11.4: CommissionEmployee.cs
2   // CommissionEmployee class represents a commission employee.
3   using System;
4
5   public class CommissionEmployee : object
6   {
7      private string firstName;
8      private string lastName;
9      private string socialSecurityNumber;
10     private decimal grossSales; // gross weekly sales
11     private decimal commissionRate; // commission percentage
12
13     // five-parameter constructor
14     public CommissionEmployee( string first, string last, string ssn,
15        decimal sales, decimal rate )
16     {
17        // implicit call to object constructor occurs here
18        firstName = first;
19        lastName = last;
20        socialSecurityNumber = ssn;
21        GrossSales = sales; // validate gross sales via property
22        CommissionRate = rate; // validate commission rate via property
23     } // end five-parameter CommissionEmployee constructor
24
25     // read-only property that gets commission employee's first name
26     public string FirstName
27     {
28        get
29        {
30           return firstName;
31        } // end get
32     } // end property FirstName
33
34     // read-only property that gets commission employee's last name
35     public string LastName
36     {
37        get
38        {
39           return lastName;
40        } // end get
41     } // end property LastName
```

Fig. 11.4 | CommissionEmployee class represents a commission employee. (Part 1 of 3.)

```
42
43     // read-only property that gets
44     // commission employee's social security number
45     public string SocialSecurityNumber
46     {
47        get
48        {
49           return socialSecurityNumber;
50        } // end get
51     } // end property SocialSecurityNumber
52
53     // property that gets and sets commission employee's gross sales
54     public decimal GrossSales
55     {
56        get
57        {
58           return grossSales;
59        } // end get
60        set
61        {
62           if ( value >= 0 )
63              grossSales = value;
64           else
65              throw new ArgumentOutOfRangeException(
66                 "GrossSales", value, "GrossSales must be >= 0" );
67        } // end set
68     } // end property GrossSales
69
70     // property that gets and sets commission employee's commission rate
71     public decimal CommissionRate
72     {
73        get
74        {
75           return commissionRate;
76        } // end get
77        set
78        {
79           if ( value > 0 && value < 1 )
80              commissionRate = value;
81           else
82              throw new ArgumentOutOfRangeException( "CommissionRate",
83                 value, "CommissionRate must be > 0 and < 1" );
84        } // end set
85     } // end property CommissionRate
86
87     // calculate commission employee's pay
88     public decimal Earnings()
89     {
90        return commissionRate * grossSales;
91     } // end method Earnings
92
```

Fig. 11.4 | CommissionEmployee class represents a commission employee. (Part 2 of 3.)

```
93      // return string representation of CommissionEmployee object
94      public override string ToString()
95      {
96         return string.Format(
97            "{0}: {1} {2}\n{3}: {4}\n{5}: {6:C}\n{7}: {8:F2}",
98            "commission employee", FirstName, LastName,
99            "social security number", SocialSecurityNumber,
100           "gross sales", GrossSales, "commission rate", CommissionRate );
101     } // end method ToString
102  } // end class CommissionEmployee
```

Fig. 11.4 | CommissionEmployee class represents a commission employee. (Part 3 of 3.)

CommissionEmployee Class Overview

CommissionEmployee's public services include a constructor (lines 14–23), methods Earnings (lines 88–91) and ToString (lines 94–101), and the public properties (lines 26–85) for manipulating the class's instance variables firstName, lastName, socialSecurityNumber, grossSales and commissionRate (declared in lines 7–11). Each of its instance variable is private, so objects of other classes cannot directly access these variables. Declaring instance variables as private and providing public properties to manipulate and validate them helps enforce good software engineering. The set accessors of properties GrossSales and CommissionRate, for example, *validate* their arguments before assigning the values to instance variables grossSales and commissionRate, respectively.

CommissionEmployee Constructor

Constructors are *not* inherited, so class CommissionEmployee does not inherit class object's constructor. However, class CommissionEmployee's constructor calls class object's constructor implicitly. In fact, before executing the code in its own body, the derived class's constructor calls its direct base class's constructor, either explicitly or implicitly (if no constructor call is specified), to ensure that the instance variables inherited from the base class are initialized properly. The syntax for calling a base-class constructor explicitly is discussed in Section 11.4.3. If the code does not include an explicit call to the base-class constructor, the compiler generates an implicit call to the base class's default or parameterless constructor. The comment in line 17 indicates where the implicit call to the base class object's default constructor is made (you do not write the code for this call). Class object's default (empty) constructor does nothing. Even if a class does not have constructors, the default constructor that the compiler implicitly declares for the class will call the base class's default or parameterless constructor. Class object is the *only* class that does not have a base class.

After the implicit call to object's constructor occurs, lines 18–22 in the constructor assign values to the class's instance variables. We do *not* validate the values of arguments first, last and ssn before assigning them to the corresponding instance variables. We certainly could validate the first and last names—perhaps by ensuring that they're of a reasonable length. Similarly, a social security number could be validated to ensure that it contains nine digits, with or without dashes (e.g., 123-45-6789 or 123456789).

CommissionEmployee Method Earnings

Method Earnings (lines 88–91) calculates a CommissionEmployee's earnings. Line 90 multiplies the commissionRate by the grossSales and returns the result.

CommissionEmployee Method ToString

Method ToString (lines 94–101) is special—it's one of the methods that every class inherits directly or indirectly from class object, which is the root of the C# class hierarchy. Section 11.7 summarizes class object's methods. Method ToString returns a string representing an object. It's called implicitly by an application whenever an object must be converted to a string representation, such as in Console's Write method or string method Format using a format item. Class object's ToString method returns a string that includes the name of the object's class. It's primarily a placeholder that can be (and typically should be) overridden by a derived class to specify an appropriate string representation of the data in a derived class object. Method ToString of class CommissionEmployee overrides (redefines) class object's ToString method. When invoked, CommissionEmployee's ToString method uses string method Format to return a string containing information about the CommissionEmployee. We use the format specifier C to format grossSales as currency and the format specifier F2 to format the commissionRate with two digits of precision to the right of the decimal point. To override a base-class method, a derived class must declare a method with keyword **override** and with the same signature (method name, number of parameters and parameter types) *and* return type as the base-class method—object's ToString method takes no parameters and returns type string, so CommissionEmployee declares ToString with no parameters and returns type string.

Common Programming Error 11.1

It's a compilation error to override a method with one that has a different access modifier. Overriding a method with a more restrictive access modifier would break the is-a relationship. If a public method could be overridden as a protected or private method, the derived-class objects would not be able to respond to the same method calls as base-class objects. Once a method is declared in a base class, the method must have the same access modifier for all that class's direct and indirect derived classes.

Class CommissionEmployeeTest

Figure 11.5 tests class CommissionEmployee. Lines 10–11 create a CommissionEmployee object and invoke its constructor (lines 14–23 of Fig. 11.4) to initialize it. We append the M suffix to the gross sales amount and the commission rate to indicate that the compiler should treat these as decimal literals, rather than doubles. Lines 16–22 use CommissionEmployee's properties to retrieve the object's instance-variable values for output. Line 23 outputs the amount calculated by the Earnings method. Lines 25–26 invoke the set accessors of the object's GrossSales and CommissionRate properties to change the values of instance variables grossSales and commissionRate. Lines 28–29 output the string representation of the updated CommissionEmployee. When an object is output using a format item, the object's ToString method is invoked implicitly to obtain the object's string representation. Line 30 outputs the earnings again.

```
1   // Fig. 11.5: CommissionEmployeeTest.cs
2   // Testing class CommissionEmployee.
3   using System;
4
```

Fig. 11.5 | Testing class CommissionEmployee. (Part 1 of 2.)

```
 5   public class CommissionEmployeeTest
 6   {
 7      public static void Main( string[] args )
 8      {
 9         // instantiate CommissionEmployee object
10         CommissionEmployee employee = new CommissionEmployee( "Sue",
11            "Jones", "222-22-2222", 10000.00M, .06M );
12
13         // display commission-employee data
14         Console.WriteLine(
15            "Employee information obtained by properties and methods: \n" );
16         Console.WriteLine( "First name is {0}", employee.FirstName );
17         Console.WriteLine( "Last name is {0}", employee.LastName );
18         Console.WriteLine( "Social security number is {0}",
19            employee.SocialSecurityNumber );
20         Console.WriteLine( "Gross sales are {0:C}", employee.GrossSales );
21         Console.WriteLine( "Commission rate is {0:F2}",
22            employee.CommissionRate );
23         Console.WriteLine( "Earnings are {0:C}", employee.Earnings() );
24
25         employee.GrossSales = 5000.00M; // set gross sales
26         employee.CommissionRate = .1M; // set commission rate
27
28         Console.WriteLine( "\n{0}:\n\n{1}",
29            "Updated employee information obtained by ToString", employee );
30         Console.WriteLine( "earnings: {0:C}", employee.Earnings() );
31      } // end Main
32   } // end class CommissionEmployeeTest
```

```
Employee information obtained by properties and methods:

First name is Sue
Last name is Jones
Social security number is 222-22-2222
Gross sales are $10,000.00
Commission rate is 0.06
Earnings are $600.00

Updated employee information obtained by ToString:

commission employee: Sue Jones
social security number: 222-22-2222
gross sales: $5,000.00
commission rate: 0.10
earnings: $500.00
```

Fig. 11.5 | Testing class CommissionEmployee. (Part 2 of 2.)

11.4.2 Creating a BasePlusCommissionEmployee Class without Using Inheritance

We now discuss the second part of our introduction to inheritance by declaring and testing the (completely new and independent) class BasePlusCommissionEmployee (Fig. 11.6), which contains a first name, last name, social security number, gross sales amount, commission rate *and* base salary. Class BasePlusCommissionEmployee's public services include a BasePlusCommissionEmployee constructor (lines 16–26), methods Earnings (lines 113–116) and ToString (lines 119–127), and public properties (lines 30–110) for the class's private instance variables firstName, lastName, socialSecurityNumber, grossSales, commissionRate and baseSalary (declared in lines 8–11). These variables, properties and methods encapsulate all the necessary features of a base-salaried commission employee. Note the similarity between this class and class CommissionEmployee (Fig. 11.4)—in this example, *we do not yet exploit that similarity*.

```
1   // Fig. 11.6: BasePlusCommissionEmployee.cs
2   // BasePlusCommissionEmployee class represents an employee that receives
3   // a base salary in addition to a commission.
4   using System;
5
6   public class BasePlusCommissionEmployee
7   {
8      private string firstName;
9      private string lastName;
10     private string socialSecurityNumber;
11     private decimal grossSales; // gross weekly sales
12     private decimal commissionRate; // commission percentage
13     private decimal baseSalary; // base salary per week
14
15     // six-parameter constructor
16     public BasePlusCommissionEmployee( string first, string last,
17        string ssn, decimal sales, decimal rate, decimal salary )
18     {
19        // implicit call to object constructor occurs here
20        firstName = first;
21        lastName = last;
22        socialSecurityNumber = ssn;
23        GrossSales = sales; // validate gross sales via property
24        CommissionRate = rate; // validate commission rate via property
25        BaseSalary = salary; // validate base salary via property
26     } // end six-parameter BasePlusCommissionEmployee constructor
27
28     // read-only property that gets
29     // BasePlusCommissionEmployee's first name
30     public string FirstName
31     {
32        get
33        {
34           return firstName;
35        } // end get
36     } // end property FirstName
37
38     // read-only property that gets
39     // BasePlusCommissionEmployee's last name
40     public string LastName
41     {
```

Fig. 11.6 | BasePlusCommissionEmployee class represents an employee that receives a base salary in addition to a commission. (Part 1 of 3.)

```csharp
42          get
43          {
44             return lastName;
45          } // end get
46       } // end property LastName
47
48       // read-only property that gets
49       // BasePlusCommissionEmployee's social security number
50       public string SocialSecurityNumber
51       {
52          get
53          {
54             return socialSecurityNumber;
55          } // end get
56       } // end property SocialSecurityNumber
57
58       // property that gets and sets
59       // BasePlusCommissionEmployee's gross sales
60       public decimal GrossSales
61       {
62          get
63          {
64             return grossSales;
65          } // end get
66          set
67          {
68             if ( value >= 0 )
69                grossSales = value;
70             else
71                throw new ArgumentOutOfRangeException(
72                   "GrossSales", value, "GrossSales must be >= 0" );
73          } // end set
74       } // end property GrossSales
75
76       // property that gets and sets
77       // BasePlusCommissionEmployee's commission rate
78       public decimal CommissionRate
79       {
80          get
81          {
82             return commissionRate;
83          } // end get
84          set
85          {
86             if ( value > 0 && value < 1 )
87                commissionRate = value;
88             else
89                throw new ArgumentOutOfRangeException( "CommissionRate",
90                   value, "CommissionRate must be > 0 and < 1" );
91          } // end set
92       } // end property CommissionRate
```

Fig. 11.6 | BasePlusCommissionEmployee class represents an employee that receives a base salary in addition to a commission. (Part 2 of 3.)

```
 93
 94     // property that gets and sets
 95     // BasePlusCommissionEmployee's base salary
 96     public decimal BaseSalary
 97     {
 98        get
 99        {
100           return baseSalary;
101        } // end get
102        set
103        {
104           if ( value >= 0 )
105              baseSalary = value;
106           else
107              throw new ArgumentOutOfRangeException( "BaseSalary",
108                 value, "BaseSalary must be >= 0" );
109        } // end set
110     } // end property BaseSalary
111
112     // calculate earnings
113     public decimal Earnings()
114     {
115        return baseSalary + ( commissionRate * grossSales );
116     } // end method earnings
117
118     // return string representation of BasePlusCommissionEmployee
119     public override string ToString()
120     {
121        return string.Format(
122           "{0}: {1} {2}\n{3}: {4}\n{5}: {6:C}\n{7}: {8:F2}\n{9}: {10:C}",
123           "base-salaried commission employee", firstName, lastName,
124           "social security number", socialSecurityNumber,
125           "gross sales", grossSales, "commission rate", commissionRate,
126           "base salary", baseSalary );
127     } // end method ToString
128  } // end class BasePlusCommissionEmployee
```

Fig. 11.6 | BasePlusCommissionEmployee class represents an employee that receives a base salary in addition to a commission. (Part 3 of 3.)

Class BasePlusCommissionEmployee does not specify that it extends object with the syntax ": object" in line 6, so the class *implicitly* extends object. Also, like class CommissionEmployee's constructor (lines 14–23 of Fig. 11.4), class BasePlusCommissionEmployee's constructor invokes class object's default constructor implicitly, as noted in the comment in line 19 of Fig. 11.6.

Class BasePlusCommissionEmployee's Earnings method (lines 113–116) computes the earnings of a base-salaried commission employee. Line 115 adds the employee's base salary to the product of the commission rate and the gross sales, and returns the result.

Class BasePlusCommissionEmployee overrides object method ToString to return a string containing the BasePlusCommissionEmployee's information (lines 119–127). Once again, we use format specifier C to format the gross sales and base salary as currency and format specifier F2 to format the commission rate with two digits of precision to the right of the decimal point (line 122).

Class *BasePlusCommissionEmployeeTest*

Figure 11.7 tests class BasePlusCommissionEmployee. Lines 10–12 instantiate a Base-PlusCommissionEmployee object and pass "Bob", "Lewis", "333-33-3333", 5000.00M, .04M and 300.00M to the constructor as the first name, last name, social security number, gross sales, commission rate and base salary, respectively. Lines 17–25 use BasePlusCommissionEmployee's properties and methods to retrieve the values of the object's instance variables and calculate the earnings for output. Line 27 invokes the object's BaseSalary property to *change* the base salary. Property BaseSalary's set accessor (Fig. 11.6, lines 102–109) ensures that instance variable baseSalary is not assigned a negative value, because an employee's base salary cannot be negative. Lines 29–30 of Fig. 11.7 invoke the object's ToString method implicitly to get the object's string representation.

```csharp
1   // Fig. 11.7: BasePlusCommissionEmployeeTest.cs
2   // Testing class BasePlusCommissionEmployee.
3   using System;
4
5   public class BasePlusCommissionEmployeeTest
6   {
7      public static void Main( string[] args )
8      {
9         // instantiate BasePlusCommissionEmployee object
10        BasePlusCommissionEmployee employee =
11           new BasePlusCommissionEmployee( "Bob", "Lewis",
12           "333-33-3333", 5000.00M, .04M, 300.00M );
13
14        // display BasePlusCommissionEmployee's data
15        Console.WriteLine(
16           "Employee information obtained by properties and methods: \n" );
17        Console.WriteLine( "First name is {0}", employee.FirstName );
18        Console.WriteLine( "Last name is {0}", employee.LastName );
19        Console.WriteLine( "Social security number is {0}",
20           employee.SocialSecurityNumber );
21        Console.WriteLine( "Gross sales are {0:C}", employee.GrossSales );
22        Console.WriteLine( "Commission rate is {0:F2}",
23           employee.CommissionRate );
24        Console.WriteLine( "Earnings are {0:C}", employee.Earnings() );
25        Console.WriteLine( "Base salary is {0:C}", employee.BaseSalary );
26
27        employee.BaseSalary = 1000.00M; // set base salary
28
29        Console.WriteLine( "\n{0}:\n\n{1}",
30           "Updated employee information obtained by ToString", employee );
31        Console.WriteLine( "earnings: {0:C}", employee.Earnings() );
32     } // end Main
33  } // end class BasePlusCommissionEmployeeTest
```

Fig. 11.7 | Testing class BasePlusCommissionEmployee. (Part 1 of 2.)

```
Employee information obtained by properties and methods:

First name is Bob
Last name is Lewis
Social security number is 333-33-3333
Gross sales are $5,000.00
Commission rate is 0.04
Earnings are $500.00
Base salary is $300.00

Updated employee information obtained by ToString:

base-salaried commission employee: Bob Lewis
social security number: 333-33-3333
gross sales: $5,000.00
commission rate: 0.04
base salary: $1,000.00
earnings: $1,200.00
```

Fig. 11.7 | Testing class `BasePlusCommissionEmployee`. (Part 2 of 2.)

Much of the code for class `BasePlusCommissionEmployee` (Fig. 11.6) is similar, if not identical, to the code for class `CommissionEmployee` (Fig. 11.4). For example, in class `BasePlusCommissionEmployee`, private instance variables `firstName` and `lastName` and properties `FirstName` and `LastName` are identical to those of class `CommissionEmployee`. Classes `CommissionEmployee` and `BasePlusCommissionEmployee` also both contain `private` instance variables `socialSecurityNumber`, `commissionRate` and `grossSales`, as well as properties to manipulate these variables. In addition, the `BasePlusCommissionEmployee` constructor is almost identical to that of class `CommissionEmployee`, except that `BasePlusCommissionEmployee`'s constructor also sets the `baseSalary`. The other additions to class `BasePlusCommissionEmployee` are `private` instance variable `baseSalary` and property `BaseSalary`. Class `BasePlusCommissionEmployee`'s `Earnings` method is nearly identical to that of class `CommissionEmployee`, except that `BasePlusCommissionEmployee`'s also adds the `baseSalary`. Similarly, class `BasePlusCommissionEmployee`'s `ToString` method is nearly identical to that of class `CommissionEmployee`, except that `BasePlusCommissionEmployee`'s `ToString` also formats the value of instance variable `baseSalary` as currency.

We literally *copied* the code from class `CommissionEmployee` and *pasted* it into class `BasePlusCommissionEmployee`, then modified class `BasePlusCommissionEmployee` to include a base salary and methods and properties that manipulate the base salary. This "copy-and-paste" approach is often error prone and time consuming. Worse yet, it can spread many physical copies of the same code throughout a system, creating a code-maintenance nightmare. Is there a way to "absorb" the members of one class in a way that makes them part of other classes without copying code? In the next several examples we answer this question, using a more elegant approach to building classes—namely, inheritance.

Error-Prevention Tip 11.1

Copying and pasting code from one class to another can spread errors across multiple source-code files. To avoid duplicating code (and possibly errors) in situations where you want one class to "absorb" the members of another class, use inheritance rather than the "copy-and-paste" approach.

Software Engineering Observation 11.4

With inheritance, the common members of all the classes in the hierarchy are declared in a base class. When changes are required for these common features, you need to make the changes only in the base class—derived classes then inherit the changes. Without inheritance, changes would need to be made to all the source-code files that contain a copy of the code in question.

11.4.3 Creating a CommissionEmployee–BasePlusCommissionEmployee Inheritance Hierarchy

Now we declare class BasePlusCommissionEmployee (Fig. 11.8), which extends class CommissionEmployee (Fig. 11.4). A BasePlusCommissionEmployee object *is a* CommissionEmployee (because inheritance passes on the capabilities of class CommissionEmployee), but class BasePlusCommissionEmployee also has instance variable baseSalary (Fig. 11.8, line 7). The colon (:) in line 5 of the class declaration indicates inheritance. As a derived class, BasePlusCommissionEmployee inherits the members of class CommissionEmployee and can access those members that are non-private. The constructor of class CommissionEmployee is *not* inherited. Thus, the public services of BasePlusCommissionEmployee include its constructor (lines 11–16), public methods and properties inherited from class CommissionEmployee, property BaseSalary (lines 20–34), method Earnings (lines 37–41) and method ToString (lines 44–53).

```
 1   // Fig. 11.8: BasePlusCommissionEmployee.cs
 2   // BasePlusCommissionEmployee inherits from class CommissionEmployee.
 3   using System;
 4
 5   public class BasePlusCommissionEmployee : CommissionEmployee
 6   {
 7      private decimal baseSalary; // base salary per week
 8
 9      // six-parameter derived-class constructor
10      // with call to base class CommissionEmployee constructor
11      public BasePlusCommissionEmployee( string first, string last,
12         string ssn, decimal sales, decimal rate, decimal salary )
13         : base( first, last, ssn, sales, rate )
14      {
15         BaseSalary = salary; // validate base salary via property
16      } // end six-parameter BasePlusCommissionEmployee constructor
17
18      // property that gets and sets
19      // BasePlusCommissionEmployee's base salary
20      public decimal BaseSalary
21      {
22         get
23         {
24            return baseSalary;
25         } // end get
```

Fig. 11.8 | BasePlusCommissionEmployee inherits from class CommissionEmployee. (Part 1 of 2.)

```
26          set
27          {
28              if ( value >= 0 )
29                  baseSalary = value;
30              else
31                  throw new ArgumentOutOfRangeException( "BaseSalary",
32                      value, "BaseSalary must be >= 0" );
33          } // end set
34      } // end property BaseSalary
35
36      // calculate earnings
37      public override decimal Earnings()
38      {
39          // not allowed: commissionRate and grossSales private in base class
40          return baseSalary + ( commissionRate * grossSales );
41      } // end method Earnings
42
43      // return string representation of BasePlusCommissionEmployee
44      public override string ToString()
45      {
46          // not allowed: attempts to access private base-class members
47          return string.Format(
48              "{0}: {1} {2}\n{3}: {4}\n{5}: {6:C}\n{7}: {8:F2}\n{9}: {10:C}",
49              "base-salaried commission employee", firstName, lastName,
50              "social security number", socialSecurityNumber,
51              "gross sales", grossSales, "commission rate", commissionRate,
52              "base salary", baseSalary );
53      } // end method ToString
54  } // end class BasePlusCommissionEmployee
```

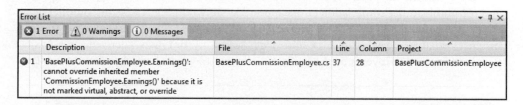

	Description	File	Line	Column	Project
1	'BasePlusCommissionEmployee.Earnings()': cannot override inherited member 'CommissionEmployee.Earnings()' because it is not marked virtual, abstract, or override	BasePlusCommissionEmployee.cs	37	28	BasePlusCommissionEmployee

Fig. 11.8 | BasePlusCommissionEmployee inherits from class CommissionEmployee. (Part 2 of 2.)

A Derived Class's Constructor Must Call Its Base Class's Constructor

Each derived-class constructor *must* implicitly or explicitly call its base-class constructor to ensure that the instance variables inherited from the base class are initialized properly. BasePlusCommissionEmployee's six-parameter constructor explicitly calls class CommissionEmployee's five-parameter constructor to initialize the base-class portion of a BasePlusCommissionEmployee object—that is, the instance variables firstName, lastName, socialSecurityNumber, grossSales and commissionRate. Line 13 in the header of BasePlusCommissionEmployee's six-parameter constructor invokes the CommissionEmployee's five-parameter constructor (declared at lines 14–23 of Fig. 11.4) by using a constructor initializer. In Section 10.5, we used constructor initializers with keyword this to call overloaded constructors in the same class. In line 13 of Fig. 11.8, we use a constructor initializer with keyword **base** to invoke the base-class constructor. The arguments `first`, `last`, `ssn`, `sales` and `rate` are used to initialize base-class members `firstName`, `lastName`, `socialSecurityNumber`, `grossSales` and `commissionRate`, respectively. If `BasePlus-CommissionEmployee`'s constructor did not invoke `CommissionEmployee`'s constructor explicitly, C# would attempt to invoke class `CommissionEmployee`'s parameterless or default constructor—but the class does not have such a constructor, so the compiler would issue an error. When a base class contains a parameterless constructor, you can use `base()` in the constructor initializer to call that constructor explicitly, but this is rarely done.

Common Programming Error 11.2

A compilation error occurs if a derived-class constructor calls one of its base-class constructors with arguments that do not match the number and types of parameters specified in one of the base-class constructor declarations.

BasePlusCommissionEmployee Method Earnings

Lines 37–41 of Fig. 11.8 declare method `Earnings` using keyword `override` to override the `CommissionEmployee`'s `Earnings` method, as we did with method `ToString` in previous examples. Line 37 causes a compilation error indicating that we cannot override the base class's `Earnings` method because it was not explicitly "marked virtual, abstract, or override." The **virtual** and abstract keywords indicate that a base-class method can be overridden in derived classes. (As you'll learn in Section 12.4, abstract methods are implicitly `virtual`.) The override modifier declares that a derived-class method overrides a `virtual` or abstract base-class method. This modifier also implicitly declares the derived-class method `virtual` and allows it to be overridden in derived classes further down the inheritance hierarchy.

If we add the keyword `virtual` to the declaration of method `Earnings` in Fig. 11.4 and recompile, other compilation errors appear. As shown in Fig. 11.9, the compiler generates additional errors for line 40 of Fig. 11.8 because base class `CommissionEmployee`'s instance variables `commissionRate` and `grossSales` are private—derived class `BasePlusCommissionEmployee`'s methods are not allowed to access base class `CommissionEm-`

	Description	File	Line	Column	Project
1	'CommissionEmployee.commissionRate' is inaccessible due to its protection level	BasePlusCommissionEmployee.cs	40	29	BasePlusCommissionEmployee
2	'CommissionEmployee.grossSales' is inaccessible due to its protection level	BasePlusCommissionEmployee.cs	40	46	BasePlusCommissionEmployee
3	'CommissionEmployee.firstName' is inaccessible due to its protection level	BasePlusCommissionEmployee.cs	49	47	BasePlusCommissionEmployee
4	'CommissionEmployee.lastName' is inaccessible due to its protection level	BasePlusCommissionEmployee.cs	49	58	BasePlusCommissionEmployee
5	'CommissionEmployee.socialSecurityNumber' is inaccessible due to its protection level	BasePlusCommissionEmployee.cs	50	36	BasePlusCommissionEmployee
6	'CommissionEmployee.grossSales' is inaccessible due to its protection level	BasePlusCommissionEmployee.cs	51	25	BasePlusCommissionEmployee
7	'CommissionEmployee.commissionRate' is inaccessible due to its protection level	BasePlusCommissionEmployee.cs	51	56	BasePlusCommissionEmployee

Error List — 7 Errors — 0 Warnings — 0 Messages

Fig. 11.9 | Compilation errors generated by `BasePlusCommissionEmployee` (Fig. 11.8) after declaring the `Earnings` method in Fig. 11.4 with keyword `virtual`.

ployee's private instance variables. The compiler issues additional errors at lines 49–51 of BasePlusCommissionEmployee's ToString method for the same reason. The errors in BasePlusCommissionEmployee could have been prevented by using the public properties inherited from class CommissionEmployee. For example, line 40 could have invoked the get accessors of properties CommissionRate and GrossSales to access CommissionEmployee's private instance variables commissionRate and grossSales, respectively. Lines 49–51 also could have used appropriate properties to retrieve the values of the base class's instance variables.

11.4.4 CommissionEmployee–BasePlusCommissionEmployee Inheritance Hierarchy Using protected Instance Variables

To enable class BasePlusCommissionEmployee to directly access base-class instance variables firstName, lastName, socialSecurityNumber, grossSales and commissionRate, we can declare those members as protected in the base class. As we discussed in Section 11.3, a base class's protected members *are* inherited by all derived classes of that base class. Class CommissionEmployee in this example is a modification of the version from Fig. 11.4 that declares its instance variables firstName, lastName, socialSecurityNumber, grossSales and commissionRate as protected rather than private. We also declare the Earnings method virtual as in

```
public virtual decimal Earnings()
```

so that BasePlusCommissionEmployee can override the method. The rest of the class declaration in this example is identical to that of Fig. 11.4. The complete source code for class CommissionEmployee is included in this example's project.

public vs. protected Data

We could have declared base class CommissionEmployee's instance variables firstName, lastName, socialSecurityNumber, grossSales and commissionRate as public to enable derived class BasePlusCommissionEmployee to access the base-class instance variables. However, declaring public instance variables is poor software engineering, because it allows unrestricted access to the instance variables, greatly increasing the chance of errors. With protected instance variables, the derived class gets access to the instance variables, but classes that are not derived from the base class cannot access its variables directly.

Class BasePlusCommissionEmployee

Class BasePlusCommissionEmployee (Fig. 11.10) in this example extends the version of class CommissionEmployee with protected data rather than the one with private data in Fig. 11.4. Each BasePlusCommissionEmployee object inherits CommissionEmployee's protected instance variables firstName, lastName, socialSecurityNumber, grossSales and commissionRate—all these variables are now protected members of BasePlusCommissionEmployee. As a result, the compiler does not generate errors when compiling line 40 of method Earnings and lines 48–50 of method ToString. If another class extends BasePlusCommissionEmployee, the new derived class also inherits the protected members.

Class BasePlusCommissionEmployee does *not* inherit class CommissionEmployee's constructor. However, class BasePlusCommissionEmployee's six-parameter constructor (lines 12–17) calls class CommissionEmployee's five-parameter constructor with a constructor initializer. BasePlusCommissionEmployee's six-parameter constructor must explicitly call the five-parameter constructor of class CommissionEmployee, because CommissionEmployee does not provide a parameterless constructor that could be invoked implicitly.

```csharp
 1   // Fig. 11.10: BasePlusCommissionEmployee.cs
 2   // BasePlusCommissionEmployee inherits from CommissionEmployee and has
 3   // access to CommissionEmployee's protected members.
 4   using System;
 5
 6   public class BasePlusCommissionEmployee : CommissionEmployee2
 7   {
 8      private decimal baseSalary; // base salary per week
 9
10      // six-parameter derived-class constructor
11      // with call to base class CommissionEmployee constructor
12      public BasePlusCommissionEmployee( string first, string last,
13         string ssn, decimal sales, decimal rate, decimal salary )
14         : base( first, last, ssn, sales, rate )
15      {
16         BaseSalary = salary; // validate base salary via property
17      } // end six-parameter BasePlusCommissionEmployee constructor
18
19      // property that gets and sets
20      // BasePlusCommissionEmployee's base salary
21      public decimal BaseSalary
22      {
23         get
24         {
25            return baseSalary;
26         } // end get
27         set
28         {
29            if ( value >= 0 )
30               baseSalary = value;
31            else
32               throw new ArgumentOutOfRangeException( "BaseSalary",
33                  value, "BaseSalary must be >= 0" );
34         } // end set
35      } // end property BaseSalary
36
37      // calculate earnings
38      public override decimal Earnings()
39      {
40         return baseSalary + ( commissionRate * grossSales );
41      } // end method Earnings
42
43      // return string representation of BasePlusCommissionEmployee
44      public override string ToString()
45      {
46         return string.Format(
47            "{0}: {1} {2}\n{3}: {4}\n{5}: {6:C}\n{7}: {8:F2}\n{9}: {10:C}",
48            "base-salaried commission employee", firstName, lastName,
```

Fig. 11.10 | BasePlusCommissionEmployee inherits from CommissionEmployee and has access to CommissionEmployee's protected members. (Part 1 of 2.)

```
49          "social security number", socialSecurityNumber,
50          "gross sales", grossSales, "commission rate", commissionRate,
51          "base salary", baseSalary );
52    } // end method ToString
53  } // end class BasePlusCommissionEmployee
```

Fig. 11.10 | BasePlusCommissionEmployee inherits from CommissionEmployee and has access to CommissionEmployee's **protected** members. (Part 2 of 2.)

Class *BasePlusCommissionEmployeeTest*

Figure 11.11 uses a BasePlusCommissionEmployee object to perform the same tasks that Fig. 11.7 performed on the version of the class from Fig. 11.6. The outputs of the two applications are identical. Although we declared the version of the class in Fig. 11.6 without using inheritance and declared the version in Fig. 11.10 using inheritance, both classes provide the same functionality. The source code in Fig. 11.10 (which is 53 lines) is considerably shorter than version in Fig. 11.6 (which is 128 lines), because the new class inherits most of its functionality from CommissionEmployee, whereas the version in Fig. 11.6 inherits only class object's functionality. Also, there's now only one copy of the commission-employee functionality declared in class CommissionEmployee. This makes the code easier to maintain, modify and debug, because the code related to a commission employee exists only in class CommissionEmployee.

```
1   // Fig. 11.11: BasePlusCommissionEmployee.cs
2   // Testing class BasePlusCommissionEmployee.
3   using System;
4
5   public class BasePlusCommissionEmployeeTest
6   {
7       public static void Main( string[] args )
8       {
9           // instantiate BasePlusCommissionEmployee object
10          BasePlusCommissionEmployee basePlusCommissionEmployee =
11              new BasePlusCommissionEmployee( "Bob", "Lewis",
12              "333-33-3333", 5000.00M, .04M, 300.00M );
13
14          // display BasePlusCommissionEmployee's data
15          Console.WriteLine(
16              "Employee information obtained by properties and methods: \n" );
17          Console.WriteLine( "First name is {0}",
18              basePlusCommissionEmployee.FirstName );
19          Console.WriteLine( "Last name is {0}",
20              basePlusCommissionEmployee.LastName );
21          Console.WriteLine( "Social security number is {0}",
22              basePlusCommissionEmployee.SocialSecurityNumber );
23          Console.WriteLine( "Gross sales are {0:C}",
24              basePlusCommissionEmployee.GrossSales );
25          Console.WriteLine( "Commission rate is {0:F2}",
26              basePlusCommissionEmployee.CommissionRate );
```

Fig. 11.11 | Testing class BasePlusCommissionEmployee. (Part 1 of 2.)

```
27        Console.WriteLine( "Earnings are {0:C}",
28            basePlusCommissionEmployee.Earnings() );
29        Console.WriteLine( "Base salary is {0:C}",
30            basePlusCommissionEmployee.BaseSalary );
31
32        basePlusCommissionEmployee.BaseSalary = 1000.00M; // set base salary
33
34        Console.WriteLine( "\n{0}:\n\n{1}",
35            "Updated employee information obtained by ToString",
36            basePlusCommissionEmployee );
37        Console.WriteLine( "earnings: {0:C}",
38            basePlusCommissionEmployee.Earnings() );
39    } // end Main
40 } // end class BasePlusCommissionEmployee
```

```
Employee information obtained by properties and methods:

First name is Bob
Last name is Lewis
Social security number is 333-33-3333
Gross sales are $5,000.00
Commission rate is 0.04
Earnings are $500.00
Base salary is $300.00

Updated employee information obtained by ToString:

base-salaried commission employee: Bob Lewis
social security number: 333-33-3333
gross sales: $5,000.00
commission rate: 0.04
base salary: $1,000.00
earnings: $1,200.00
```

Fig. 11.11 | Testing class `BasePlusCommissionEmployee`. (Part 2 of 2.)

In this example, we declared base-class instance variables as `protected` so that derived classes could access them. Inheriting `protected` instance variables enables you to directly access the variables in the derived class without invoking the `set` or `get` accessors of the corresponding property. In most cases, however, it's better to use `private` instance variables to encourage proper software engineering. Your code will be easier to maintain, modify and debug.

Using `protected` instance variables creates several potential problems. First, the derived-class object can set an inherited variable's value directly without using a property's set accessor. Therefore, a derived-class object can assign an invalid value to the variable. For example, if we were to declare `CommissionEmployee`'s instance variable `grossSales` as `protected`, a derived-class object (e.g., `BasePlusCommissionEmployee`) could then assign a negative value to `grossSales`. The second problem with using `protected` instance variables is that derived-class methods are more likely to be written to depend on the base class's data implementation. In practice, derived classes should depend only on the base-class services (i.e., non-`private` methods and properties) and not on the base-class data implementation. With `protected` instance variables in the base class, we may need to modify all the derived classes of the base class if the base-class implementation changes. For example, if for some reason we were to change the names of instance variables first-Name and lastName to first and last, then we would have to do so for all occurrences in which a derived class directly references base-class instance variables firstName and last-Name. In such a case, the software is said to be **fragile** or **brittle**, because a small change in the base class can "break" derived-class implementation. You should be able to change the base-class implementation while still providing the same services to the derived classes. Of course, if the base-class services change, we must reimplement our derived classes.

Software Engineering Observation 11.5

Declaring base-class instance variables private *(as opposed to* protected*) enables the base-class implementation of these instance variables to change without affecting derived-class implementations.*

11.4.5 CommissionEmployee–BasePlusCommissionEmployee Inheritance Hierarchy Using private Instance Variables

We now reexamine our hierarchy once more, this time using the best software engineering practices. Class CommissionEmployee (Fig. 11.12) declares instance variables firstName, lastName, socialSecurityNumber, grossSales and commissionRate as private (lines 7–11) and provides public properties FirstName, LastName, SocialSecurityNumber, GrossSales and GrossSales for manipulating these values. Methods Earnings (lines 88–91) and ToString (lines 94–101) use the class's properties to obtain the values of its instance variables. If we decide to change the instance-variable names, the Earnings and ToString declarations will not require modification—only the bodies of the properties that directly manipulate the instance variables will need to change. These changes occur solely within the base class—no changes to the derived class are needed. Localizing the effects of changes like this is a good software engineering practice. Derived class BasePlusCommissionEmployee (Fig. 11.13) inherits from CommissionEmployee's and can access the private base-class members via the inherited public properties.

```
1   // Fig. 11.12: CommissionEmployee.cs
2   // CommissionEmployee class represents a commission employee.
3   using System;
4
5   public class CommissionEmployee
6   {
7      private string firstName;
8      private string lastName;
9      private string socialSecurityNumber;
10     private decimal grossSales; // gross weekly sales
11     private decimal commissionRate; // commission percentage
12
13     // five-parameter constructor
14     public CommissionEmployee( string first, string last, string ssn,
15        decimal sales, decimal rate )
16     {
```

Fig. 11.12 | CommissionEmployee class represents a commission employee. (Part 1 of 3.)

```
17              // implicit call to object constructor occurs here
18              firstName = first;
19              lastName = last;
20              socialSecurityNumber = ssn;
21              GrossSales = sales; // validate gross sales via property
22              CommissionRate = rate; // validate commission rate via property
23          } // end five-parameter CommissionEmployee constructor
24
25          // read-only property that gets commission employee's first name
26          public string FirstName
27          {
28              get
29              {
30                  return firstName;
31              } // end get
32          } // end property FirstName
33
34          // read-only property that gets commission employee's last name
35          public string LastName
36          {
37              get
38              {
39                  return lastName;
40              } // end get
41          } // end property LastName
42
43          // read-only property that gets
44          // commission employee's social security number
45          public string SocialSecurityNumber
46          {
47              get
48              {
49                  return socialSecurityNumber;
50              } // end get
51          } // end property SocialSecurityNumber
52
53          // property that gets and sets commission employee's gross sales
54          public decimal GrossSales
55          {
56              get
57              {
58                  return grossSales;
59              } // end get
60              set
61              {
62                  if ( value >= 0 )
63                      grossSales = value;
64                  else
65                      throw new ArgumentOutOfRangeException(
66                          "GrossSales", value, "GrossSales must be >= 0" );
67              } // end set
68          } // end property GrossSales
69
```

Fig. 11.12 | CommissionEmployee class represents a commission employee. (Part 2 of 3.)

```
70      // property that gets and sets commission employee's commission rate
71      public decimal CommissionRate
72      {
73         get
74         {
75            return commissionRate;
76         } // end get
77         set
78         {
79            if ( value > 0 && value < 1 )
80               commissionRate = value;
81            else
82               throw new ArgumentOutOfRangeException( "CommissionRate",
83                  value, "CommissionRate must be > 0 and < 1" );
84         } // end set
85      } // end property CommissionRate
86
87      // calculate commission employee's pay
88      public virtual decimal Earnings()
89      {
90         return CommissionRate * GrossSales;
91      } // end method Earnings
92
93      // return string representation of CommissionEmployee object
94      public override string ToString()
95      {
96         return string.Format(
97            "{0}: {1} {2}\n{3}: {4}\n{5}: {6:C}\n{7}: {8:F2}",
98            "commission employee", FirstName, LastName,
99            "social security number", SocialSecurityNumber,
100           "gross sales", GrossSales, "commission rate", CommissionRate );
101     } // end method ToString
102 } // end class CommissionEmployee
```

Fig. 11.12 | CommissionEmployee class represents a commission employee. (Part 3 of 3.)

Class BasePlusCommissionEmployee (Fig. 11.13) has several changes to its method implementations that distinguish it from the version in Fig. 11.10. Methods Earnings (Fig. 11.13, lines 39–42) and ToString (lines 45–49) each invoke property BaseSalary's get accessor to obtain the base-salary value, rather than accessing baseSalary directly. If we decide to rename instance variable baseSalary, only the body of property BaseSalary will need to change.

```
1   // Fig. 11.13: BasePlusCommissionEmployee.cs
2   // BasePlusCommissionEmployee inherits from CommissionEmployee and has
3   // access to CommissionEmployee's private data via
4   // its public properties.
5   using System;
6
```

Fig. 11.13 | BasePlusCommissionEmployee inherits from CommissionEmployee and has access to CommissionEmployee's private data via its public properties. (Part 1 of 2.)

```
 7   public class BasePlusCommissionEmployee : CommissionEmployee
 8   {
 9      private decimal baseSalary; // base salary per week
10
11      // six-parameter derived class constructor
12      // with call to base class CommissionEmployee constructor
13      public BasePlusCommissionEmployee( string first, string last,
14         string ssn, decimal sales, decimal rate, decimal salary )
15         : base( first, last, ssn, sales, rate )
16      {
17         BaseSalary = salary; // validate base salary via property
18      } // end six-parameter BasePlusCommissionEmployee constructor
19
20      // property that gets and sets
21      // BasePlusCommissionEmployee's base salary
22      public decimal BaseSalary
23      {
24         get
25         {
26            return baseSalary;
27         } // end get
28         set
29         {
30            if ( value >= 0 )
31               baseSalary = value;
32            else
33               throw new ArgumentOutOfRangeException( "BaseSalary",
34                  value, "BaseSalary must be >= 0" );
35         } // end set
36      } // end property BaseSalary
37
38      // calculate earnings
39      public override decimal Earnings()
40      {
41         return BaseSalary + base.Earnings();
42      } // end method Earnings
43
44      // return string representation of BasePlusCommissionEmployee
45      public override string ToString()
46      {
47         return string.Format( "base-salaried {0}\nbase salary: {1:C}",
48            base.ToString(), BaseSalary );
49      } // end method ToString
50   } // end class BasePlusCommissionEmployee
```

Fig. 11.13 | BasePlusCommissionEmployee inherits from CommissionEmployee and has access to CommissionEmployee's private data via its public properties. (Part 2 of 2.)

BasePlusCommissionEmployee *Method* Earnings

Class BasePlusCommissionEmployee's Earnings method (Fig. 11.13, lines 39–42) overrides class CommissionEmployee's Earnings method (Fig. 11.12, lines 88–91) to calculate the earnings of a BasePlusCommissionEmployee. The new version obtains the portion of the employee's earnings based on commission alone by calling CommissionEmployee's

Earnings method with the expression base.Earnings() (Fig. 11.13, line 41), then adds the base salary to this value to calculate the total earnings of the employee. Note the syntax used to invoke an overridden base-class method from a derived class—place the keyword base and the member access (.) operator before the base-class method name. This method invocation is a good software engineering practice—by having BasePlusCommissionEmployee's Earnings method invoke CommissionEmployee's Earnings method to calculate part of a BasePlusCommissionEmployee object's earnings, we avoid duplicating the code and reduce code-maintenance problems.

Common Programming Error 11.3

When a base-class method is overridden in a derived class, the derived-class version often calls the base-class version to do a portion of the work. Failure to prefix the base-class method name with the keyword base and the member access (.) operator when referencing the base class's method from the derived-class version causes the derived-class method to call itself, creating infinite recursion.

BasePlusCommissionEmployee Method ToString

Similarly, BasePlusCommissionEmployee's ToString method (Fig. 11.13, lines 45–49) overrides class CommissionEmployee's ToString method (Fig. 11.12, lines 94–101) to return a string representation that's appropriate for a base-salaried commission employee. The new version creates part of a BasePlusCommissionEmployee object's string representation (i.e., the string "commission employee" and the values of class CommissionEmployee's private instance variables) by calling CommissionEmployee's ToString method with the expression base.ToString() (Fig. 11.13, line 48). The derived class's ToString method then outputs the remainder of the object's string representation (i.e., the value of class BasePlusCommissionEmployee's base salary).

Class BasePlusCommissionEmployeeTest

Figure 11.14 performs the same manipulations on a BasePlusCommissionEmployee object as did Figs. 11.7 and 11.11, respectively. Although each "base-salaried commission employee" class behaves identically, the BasePlusCommissionEmployee in this example is the best engineered. By using inheritance and by using properties that hide the data and ensure consistency, we have efficiently and effectively constructed a well-engineered class.

```
1   // Fig. 11.14: BasePlusCommissionEmployeeTest.cs
2   // Testing class BasePlusCommissionEmployee.
3   using System;
4
5   public class BasePlusCommissionEmployeeTest
6   {
7      public static void Main( string[] args )
8      {
9         // instantiate BasePlusCommissionEmployee object
10        BasePlusCommissionEmployee employee =
11           new BasePlusCommissionEmployee( "Bob", "Lewis",
12           "333-33-3333", 5000.00M, .04M, 300.00M );
13
```

Fig. 11.14 | Testing class BasePlusCommissionEmployee. (Part 1 of 2.)

```
14          // display BasePlusCommissionEmployee's data
15          Console.WriteLine(
16              "Employee information obtained by properties and methods: \n" );
17          Console.WriteLine( "First name is {0}", employee.FirstName );
18          Console.WriteLine( "Last name is {0}", employee.LastName );
19          Console.WriteLine( "Social security number is {0}",
20              employee.SocialSecurityNumber );
21          Console.WriteLine( "Gross sales are {0:C}", employee.GrossSales );
22          Console.WriteLine( "Commission rate is {0:F2}",
23              employee.CommissionRate );
24          Console.WriteLine( "Earnings are {0:C}", employee.Earnings() );
25          Console.WriteLine( "Base salary is {0:C}", employee.BaseSalary );
26
27          employee.BaseSalary = 1000.00M; // set base salary
28
29          Console.WriteLine( "\n{0}:\n\n{1}",
30              "Updated employee information obtained by ToString", employee );
31          Console.WriteLine( "earnings: {0:C}", employee.Earnings() );
32      } // end Main
33  } // end class BasePlusCommissionEmployeeTest
```

```
Employee information obtained by properties and methods:

First name is Bob
Last name is Lewis
Social security number is 333-33-3333
Gross sales are $5,000.00
Commission rate is 0.04
Earnings are $500.00
Base salary is $300.00

Updated employee information obtained by ToString:

base-salaried commission employee: Bob Lewis
social security number: 333-33-3333
gross sales: $5,000.00
commission rate: 0.04
base salary: $1,000.00
earnings: $1,200.00
```

Fig. 11.14 | Testing class BasePlusCommissionEmployee. (Part 2 of 2.)

In this section, you saw an evolutionary set of examples that was carefully designed to teach key capabilities for good software engineering with inheritance. You learned how to create a derived class using inheritance, how to use protected base-class members to enable a derived class to access inherited base-class instance variables and how to override base-class methods to provide versions that are more appropriate for derived-class objects. In addition, you applied software engineering techniques from Chapter 4, Chapter 10 and this chapter to create classes that are easy to maintain, modify and debug.

11.5 Constructors in Derived Classes

As we explained in the preceding section, instantiating a derived-class object begins a chain of constructor calls. The derived-class constructor, before performing its own tasks, invokes its direct base class's constructor either explicitly (via a constructor initializer with the base reference) or implicitly (calling the base class's default constructor or parameter-less constructor). Similarly, if the base class is derived from another class (as every class except object is), the base-class constructor invokes the constructor of the next class up in the hierarchy, and so on. The last constructor called in the chain is always the constructor for class object. The original derived-class constructor's body finishes executing last. Each base class's constructor manipulates the base-class instance variables that the derived-class object inherits. For example, consider again the CommissionEmployee–BasePlusCommissionEmployee hierarchy from Figs. 11.12 and 11.13. When an application creates a BasePlusCommissionEmployee object, the BasePlusCommissionEmployee constructor is called. That constructor immediately calls CommissionEmployee's constructor, which in turn immediately calls object's constructor implicitly. Class object's constructor has an empty body, so it immediately returns control to CommissionEmployee's constructor, which then initializes the private instance variables of CommissionEmployee that are part of the BasePlusCommissionEmployee object. When CommissionEmployee's constructor completes execution, it returns control to BasePlusCommissionEmployee's constructor, which initializes the BasePlusCommissionEmployee object's baseSalary.

11.6 Software Engineering with Inheritance

This section discusses customizing existing software with inheritance. When a new class extends an existing class, the new class inherits the members of the existing class. We can customize the new class to meet our needs by including additional members and by overriding base-class members. Doing this does not require the derived-class programmer to change the base class's source code. C# simply requires access to the compiled base-class code, so it can compile and execute any application that uses or extends the base class. This powerful capability is attractive to independent software vendors (ISVs), who can develop proprietary classes for sale or license and make them available to users in class libraries. Users then can derive new classes from these library classes rapidly, without accessing the ISVs' proprietary source code.

Software Engineering Observation 11.6

Although inheriting from a class does not require access to the class's source code, developers often insist on seeing the source code to understand how the class is implemented. They may, for example, want to ensure that they're extending a class that performs well and is implemented securely.

Students sometimes have difficulty appreciating the scope of the problems faced by designers who work on large-scale software projects in industry. People experienced with such projects say that effective software reuse improves the software-development process. Object-oriented programming facilitates software reuse, potentially shortening development time. The availability of substantial and useful class libraries delivers the maximum benefits of software reuse through inheritance.

Software Engineering Observation 11.7

At the design stage in an object-oriented system, the designer often finds that certain classes are closely related. The designer should "factor out" common members and place them in a base class. Then the designer should use inheritance to develop derived classes, specializing them with capabilities beyond those inherited from the base class.

Software Engineering Observation 11.8

Declaring a derived class does not affect its base class's source code. Inheritance preserves the integrity of the base class.

Reading derived-class declarations can be confusing, because inherited members are not declared explicitly in the derived classes, but are nevertheless present in them. A similar problem exists in documenting derived-class members.

11.7 Class object

As we discussed earlier in this chapter, all classes inherit directly or indirectly from the object class (System.Object in the Framework Class Library), so its seven methods are inherited by all other classes. Figure 11.15 summarizes object's methods. You can learn more about object's methods at:

msdn.microsoft.com/en-us/library/system.object_members.aspx

Method	Description
Equals	This method compares two objects for equality and returns true if they're equal and false otherwise. It takes any object as an argument. When objects of a particular class must be compared for equality, the class should override method Equals to compare the *contents* of the two objects. The method's implementation should meet the following requirements: • It should return false if the argument is null. • It should return true if an object is compared to itself, as in object1.Equals(object1). • It should return true only if both object1.Equals(object2) and object2.Equals(object1) would return true. • For three objects, if object1.Equals(object2) returns true and object2.Equals(object3) returns true, then object1.Equals(object3) should also return true. • A class that overrides the method Equals should also override the method GetHashCode to ensure that equal objects have identical hashcodes. The default Equals implementation determines only whether two references *refer to the same object.*
Finalize	This method cannot be explicitly declared or called. When a class contains a destructor, the compiler implicitly renames it to override the protected method Finalize, which is called only by the garbage collector before it reclaims an object's memory. The garbage collector is not guaranteed to reclaim an object, thus it's not guaranteed that an object's Finalize method will execute. When a derived class's Finalize method executes, it performs its task, then invokes the base class's Finalize method. In general, you should avoid using Finalize.

Fig. 11.15 | object methods that are inherited directly or indirectly by all classes. (Part 1 of 2.)

Method	Description
GetHashCode	A hashtable data structure relates one object, called the key, to another object, called the value. We discuss Hashtable in Chapter 23, Collections. When a value is initially inserted in a hashtable, the key's GetHashCode method is called. The value returned is used by the hashtable to determine the location at which to insert the corresponding value. The key's hashcode is also used by the hashtable to locate the key's corresponding value.
GetType	Every object knows its own type at execution time. Method GetType (used in Section 12.5) returns an object of class Type (namespace System) that contains information about the object's type, such as its class name (obtained from Type property FullName).
Memberwise-Clone	This protected method, which takes no arguments and returns an object reference, makes a copy of the object on which it's called. The implementation of this method performs a **shallow copy**—instance-variable values in one object are copied into another object of the same type. For reference types, only the references are copied.
Reference-Equals	This static method receives two objects and returns true if two they're the same instance or if they're null references. Otherwise, it returns false.
ToString	This method (introduced in Section 7.4) returns a string representation of an object. The default implementation of this method returns the namespace followed by a dot and the class name of the object's class.

Fig. 11.15 | object methods that are inherited directly or indirectly by all classes. (Part 2 of 2.)

11.8 Wrap-Up

This chapter introduced inheritance—the ability to create classes by absorbing an existing class's members and enhancing them with new capabilities. You learned the notions of base classes and derived classes and created a derived class that inherits members from a base class. The chapter introduced access modifier protected; derived-class members can access protected base-class members. You learned how to access base-class members with base. You also saw how constructors are used in inheritance hierarchies. Finally, you learned about the methods of class object, the direct or indirect base class of *all* classes.

In Chapter 12, we build on our discussion of inheritance by introducing polymorphism—an object-oriented concept that enables us to write applications that handle, in a more general manner, objects of a wide variety of classes related by inheritance. After studying Chapter 12, you'll be familiar with classes, objects, encapsulation, inheritance and polymorphism—the most essential aspects of object-oriented programming.

Summary

Section 11.1 Introduction

- Inheritance is a form of software reuse in which a new class is created by absorbing an existing class's members and enhancing them with new or modified capabilities. With inheritance, you save time during application development by reusing proven and debugged high-quality software.

- A derived class is more specific than its base class and represents a more specialized group of objects.

- The *is-a* relationship represents inheritance. In an *is-a* relationship, an object of a derived class can also be treated as an object of its base class.

Section 11.2 Base Classes and Derived Classes

- Inheritance relationships form treelike hierarchical structures. A base class exists in a hierarchical relationship with its derived classes.

- Objects of all classes that extend a common base class can be treated as objects of that base class. However, base-class objects cannot be treated as objects of their derived classes.

- When a base-class method is inherited by a derived class, that derived class often needs a customized version of the method. In such cases, the derived class can override the base-class method with an appropriate implementation.

Section 11.3 protected Members

- Using protected access offers an intermediate level of access between public and private. A base class's protected members can be accessed by members of that base class *and* by members of its derived classes.

- Base-class members retain their original access modifier when they become members of the derived class.

- Methods of a derived class cannot directly access private members of the base class.

Section 11.4.1 Creating and Using a CommissionEmployee Class

- A colon (:) followed by a base-class name at the end of a class declaration header indicates that the declared class extends the base class.

- If a class does not specify that it inherits from another class, the class implicitly inherits from object.

- The first task of any derived class's constructor is to call its direct base class's constructor, either explicitly or implicitly (if no constructor call is specified).

- Constructors are not inherited. Even if a class does not have constructors, the default constructor that the compiler implicitly declares for the class will call the base class's default or parameterless constructor.

- Method ToString is one of the methods that every class inherits directly or indirectly from class object, which is the root of the C# class hierarchy.

- To override a base-class method, a derived class must declare a method with keyword override and with the same signature (method name, number of parameters and parameter types) and return type as the base-class method.

- It's a compilation error to override a method with a different access modifier.

Section 11.4.2 Creating a BasePlusCommissionEmployee Class without Using Inheritance

- Copying and pasting code from one class to another can spread errors across multiple source-code files. To avoid duplicating code (and possibly errors) in situations where you want one class to "absorb" the members of another class, use inheritance.

Section 11.4.3 Creating a CommissionEmployee–BasePlusCommissionEmployee Inheritance Hierarchy

- The virtual and abstract keywords indicate that a base-class property or method can be overridden in derived classes.

- The override modifier declares that a derived-class method overrides a virtual or abstract base-class method. This modifier also implicitly declares the derived-class method virtual.

- When a base class's members are private, a derived class's members are not allowed to access them.

Section 11.4.4 CommissionEmployee–BasePlusCommissionEmployee Inheritance Hierarchy Using protected Instance Variables

- Inheriting protected instance variables enables you to directly access the variables in the derived class without invoking the set or get accessors of the corresponding property.

- Software is said to be fragile or brittle when a small change in the base class can "break" derived-class implementation. You should be able to change the base-class implementation while still providing the same services to the derived classes.

- Declaring base-class instance variables private enables the base-class implementation of these instance variables to change without affecting derived-class implementations.

Section 11.4.5 CommissionEmployee–BasePlusCommissionEmployee Inheritance Hierarchy Using private Instance Variables

- Place the keyword base and the member access (.) operator before the base-class method name to invoke an overridden base-class method from a derived class.

- Failure to prefix the base-class method name with the keyword base and the member access (.) operator when referencing the base class's method causes the derived-class method to call itself, creating an error called infinite recursion.

Section 11.5 Constructors in Derived Classes

- Instantiating a derived-class object begins a chain of constructor calls. The last constructor called in the chain is always the constructor for class object. The original derived class constructor's body finishes executing last.

Section 11.6 Software Engineering with Inheritance

- We can customize new classes to meet our needs by including additional members and by overriding base-class members.

Section 11.7 Class object

- All classes in C# inherit directly or indirectly from the object class, so its seven methods are inherited by all other classes. These methods are Equals, Finalize, GetHashCode, GetType, MemberwiseClone, ReferenceEquals and ToString.

Terminology

base class
base-class constructor
base-class constructor call syntax
base-class parameterless constructor
base keyword
brittle software
class hierarchy
class library
composition
derived class
derived-class constructor
direct base class

Equals method of class object
extend a base class
Finalize method of class object
fragile software
GetHashCode method of class object
GetType method of class object
has-a relationship
hierarchical relationship
hierarchy diagram
indirect base class
inheritance
inheritance hierarchy

inherited member
inherited method
invoke a base-class constructor
invoke a base-class method
is-a relationship
`MemberwiseClone` method of class `object`
`object` class
object of a derived class
object of a base class
`override` keyword
override (redefine) a base-class method

`private` base-class member
`protected` base-class member
`protected` access modifier
`public` base-class member
`ReferenceEquals` method of class `object`
single inheritance
shallow copy
software reuse
standardized reusable components
`ToString` method of class `object`
`virtual` keyword

Self-Review Exercises

11.1 Fill in the blanks in each of the following statements:

a) _____ is a form of software reusability in which new classes acquire the members of existing classes and enhance those classes with new capabilities.

b) A base class's _____ members can be accessed only in the base-class declaration and in derived-class declarations.

c) In a(n) _____ relationship, an object of a derived class can also be treated as an object of its base class.

d) In a(n) _____ relationship, a class object has references to objects of other classes as members.

e) In single inheritance, a base class exists in a(n) _____ relationship with its derived classes.

f) A base class's _____ members are accessible anywhere that the application has a reference to an object of that base class or to an object of any of its derived classes.

g) When an object of a derived class is instantiated, a base class _____ is called implicitly or explicitly.

h) Derived-class constructors can call base class constructors via the _____ keyword.

11.2 State whether each of the following is *true* or *false*. If a statement is *false*, explain why.

a) Base-class constructors are not inherited by derived classes.

b) A *has-a* relationship is implemented via inheritance.

c) A `Car` class has *is-a* relationships with the `SteeringWheel` and `Brakes` classes.

d) Inheritance encourages the reuse of proven high-quality software.

e) When a derived class redefines a base-class method by using the same signature and return type, the derived class is said to overload that base-class method.

Answers to Self-Review Exercises

11.1 a) Inheritance. b) `protected`. c) *is-a* or inheritance. d) *has-a* or composition. e) hierarchical. f) `public`. g) constructor. h) `base`.

11.1 a) True. b) False. A *has-a* relationship is implemented via composition. An *is-a* relationship is implemented via inheritance. c) False. These are examples of *has-a* relationships. Class `Car` has an *is-a* relationship with class `Vehicle`. d) True. e) False. This is known as overriding, not overloading.

Exercises

11.2 *(Composition vs. Inheritance)* Many applications written with inheritance could be written with composition instead, and vice versa. Rewrite class `BasePlusCommissionEmployee` (Fig. 11.13) of the `CommissionEmployee`–`BasePlusCommissionEmployee` hierarchy to use composition rather than inheritance.

11.3 *(Inheritance and Software Reuse)* Discuss the ways in which inheritance promotes software reuse, saves time during application development and helps prevent errors.

11.4 *(Student Inheritance Hierarchy)* Draw a UML class diagram for an inheritance hierarchy for students at a university similar to the hierarchy shown in Fig. 11.2. Use Student as the base class of the hierarchy, then extend Student with classes UndergraduateStudent and GraduateStudent. Continue to extend the hierarchy as deeply (i.e., as many levels) as possible. For example, Freshman, Sophomore, Junior and Senior might extend UndergraduateStudent, and DoctoralStudent and MastersStudent might be derived classes of GraduateStudent. After drawing the hierarchy, discuss the relationships that exist between the classes. [*Note:* You do not need to write any code for this exercise.]

11.5 *(Shape Inheritance Hierarchy)* The world of shapes is much richer than the shapes included in the inheritance hierarchy of Fig. 11.3. Write down all the shapes you can think of—both two-dimensional and three-dimensional—and form them into a more complete Shape hierarchy with as many levels as possible. Your hierarchy should have class Shape at the top. Class TwoDimensionalShape and class ThreeDimensionalShape should extend Shape. Add additional derived classes, such as Quadrilateral and Sphere, at their correct locations in the hierarchy as necessary.

11.6 *(Protected vs. Private Access)* Some programmers prefer not to use protected access, because they believe it breaks the encapsulation of the base class. Discuss the relative merits of using protected access vs. using private access in base classes.

11.7 *(Quadrilateral Inheritance Hierarchy)* Write an inheritance hierarchy for classes Quadrilateral, Trapezoid, Parallelogram, Rectangle and Square. Use Quadrilateral as the base class of the hierarchy. Make the hierarchy as deep (i.e., as many levels) as possible. Specify the instance variables, properties and methods for each class. The private instance variables of Quadrilateral should be the *x–y* coordinate pairs for the four endpoints of the Quadrilateral. Write an application that instantiates objects of your classes and outputs each object's area (except Quadrilateral).

11.8 *(Package Inheritance Hierarchy)* Package-delivery services, such as FedEx®, DHL® and UPS®, offer a number of different shipping options, each with specific costs associated. Create an inheritance hierarchy to represent various types of packages. Use Package as the base class of the hierarchy, then include classes TwoDayPackage and OvernightPackage that derive from Package. Base class Package should include the name, address, city, state and zip code for the package's sender and recipient, and instance variables that store the weight (in ounces) and cost per ounce to ship the package. Package's constructor should initialize these private instance variables with public properties. Ensure that the weight and cost per ounce contain positive values. Package should provide a public method CalculateCost that returns a decimal indicating the cost associated with shipping the package. Package's CalculateCost method should determine the cost by multiplying the weight by the cost per ounce. Derived class TwoDayPackage should inherit the functionality of base class Package, but also include an instance variable that represents a flat fee the shipping company charges for two-day delivery service. TwoDayPackage's constructor should receive a value to initialize this instance variable. TwoDayPackage should redefine method CalculateCost so that it computes the shipping cost by adding the flat fee to the weight-based cost calculated by base class Package's CalculateCost method. Class OvernightPackage should inherit directly from class Package and contain an instance variable representing an additional fee per ounce charged for overnight delivery service. OvernightPackage should redefine method CalculateCost so that it adds the additional fee per ounce to the standard cost per ounce before calculating the shipping cost. Write a test application that creates objects of each type of Package and tests method CalculateCost.

11.9 *(Account Inheritance Hierarchy)* Create an inheritance hierarchy that a bank might use to represent customers' bank accounts. All customers at this bank can deposit (i.e., credit) money into their accounts and withdraw (i.e., debit) money from their accounts. More specific types of accounts also exist. Savings accounts, for instance, earn interest on the money they hold. Checking accounts, on the other hand, charge a fee per transaction.

Create base class `Account` and derived classes `SavingsAccount` and `CheckingAccount` that inherit from class `Account`. Base class `Account` should include one `private` instance variable of type `decimal` to represent the account balance. The class should provide a constructor that receives an initial balance and uses it to initialize the instance variable with a `public` property. The property should validate the initial balance to ensure that it's greater than or equal to `0.0`; if not, throw an exception. The class should provide two `public` methods. Method `Credit` should add an amount to the current balance. Method `Debit` should withdraw money from the `Account` and ensure that the debit amount does not exceed the `Account`'s balance. If it does, the balance should be left unchanged, and the method should print the message `"Debit amount exceeded account balance."` The class should also provide a `get` accessor in property `Balance` that returns the current balance.

Derived class `SavingsAccount` should inherit the functionality of an `Account`, but also include a `decimal` instance variable indicating the interest rate (percentage) assigned to the `Account`. SavingsAccount's constructor should receive the initial balance, as well as an initial value for the interest rate. `SavingsAccount` should provide `public` method `CalculateInterest` that returns a `decimal` indicating the amount of interest earned by an account. Method `CalculateInterest` should determine this amount by multiplying the interest rate by the account balance. [*Note:* `SavingsAccount` should inherit methods `Credit` and `Debit` without redefining them.]

Derived class `CheckingAccount` should inherit from base class `Account` and include a `decimal` instance variable that represents the fee charged per transaction. CheckingAccount's constructor should receive the initial balance, as well as a parameter indicating a fee amount. Class `CheckingAccount` should redefine methods `Credit` and `Debit` so that they subtract the fee from the account balance whenever either transaction is performed successfully. CheckingAccount's versions of these methods should invoke the base-class `Account` version to perform the updates to an account balance. CheckingAccount's `Debit` method should charge a fee only if money is actually withdrawn (i.e., the debit amount does not exceed the account balance). [*Hint:* Define Account's `Debit` method so that it returns a `bool` indicating whether money was withdrawn. Then use the return value to determine whether a fee should be charged.]

After defining the classes in this hierarchy, write an application that creates objects of each class and tests their methods. Add interest to the `SavingsAccount` object by first invoking its `CalculateInterest` method, then passing the returned interest amount to the object's `Credit` method.

OOP: Polymorphism, Interfaces and Operator Overloading

12

Objectives

In this chapter you'll learn:

- How polymorphism enables you to "program in the general" and make systems extensible.

- To use overridden methods to effect polymorphism.

- To create abstract classes and methods.

- To determine an object's type at execution time.

- To create `sealed` methods and classes.

- To declare and implement interfaces.

- To overload operators to enable them to manipulate objects.

12.1 Introduction

We now continue our study of object-oriented programming by explaining and demonstrating **polymorphism** with inheritance hierarchies. Polymorphism enables us to "program in the general" rather than "program in the specific." In particular, polymorphism enables us to write applications that process objects that share the same base class in a class hierarchy as if they were all objects of the base class.

Let's consider a polymorphism example. Suppose we create an application that simulates moving several types of animals for a biological study. Classes Fish, Frog and Bird represent the types of animals under investigation. Imagine that each class extends base class Animal, which contains a method Move and maintains an animal's current location as *x–y–z* coordinates. Each derived class implements method Move. Our application maintains an array of references to objects of the various Animal-derived classes. To simulate an animal's movements, the application sends each object the *same* message once per second—namely, Move. Each specific type of Animal responds to a Move message in a unique way—a Fish might swim three feet, a Frog might jump five feet and a Bird might fly 10 feet. The application issues the Move message to each animal object generically, but each object modifies its *x–y–z* coordinates appropriately for its specific type of movement. Relying on each object to know how to "do the right thing" in response to the *same* method call is the key concept of polymorphism. The *same* message (in this case, Move) sent to a variety of objects has "many forms" of results—hence the term polymorphism.

Systems Are Easy to Extend

With polymorphism, we can design and implement systems that are easily extensible—new classes can be added with little or no modification to the general portions of the application, as long as the new classes are part of the inheritance hierarchy that the application processes generically. The only parts of an application that must be altered to accommodate new classes are those that require direct knowledge of the new classes that you add to the hierarchy. For example, if we extend class Animal to create class Tortoise (which might respond to a Move message by crawling one inch), we need to write only the Tortoise class and the part of the simulation that instantiates a Tortoise object. The portions of the simulation that process each Animal generically can remain the same.

This chapter has several parts. First, we discuss common examples of polymorphism. We then provide a live-code example demonstrating polymorphic behavior. As you'll soon see, you'll use base-class references to manipulate both base-class objects and derived-class objects polymorphically.

Polymorphic *Employee* Inheritance Hierarchy

We then present a case study that revisits the employee hierarchy of Section 11.4.5. We develop a simple payroll application that polymorphically calculates the weekly pay of several different types of employees using each employee's Earnings method. Though the earnings of each type of employee are calculated in a specific way, polymorphism allows us to process the employees "in the general." In the case study, we enlarge the hierarchy to include two new classes—SalariedEmployee (for people paid a fixed weekly salary) and HourlyEmployee (for people paid an hourly salary and "time-and-a-half" for overtime). We declare a *common set of functionality* for all the classes in the updated hierarchy in an "abstract" class, Employee, from which classes SalariedEmployee, HourlyEmployee and CommissionEmployee *inherit directly* and class BasePlusCommissionEmployee *inherits indirectly*. As you'll soon see, when we invoke each employee's Earnings method off a base-class Employee reference, the correct earnings calculation is performed due to C#'s polymorphic capabilities.

Determining the Type of an Object at Execution Time

Occasionally, when performing polymorphic processing, we need to program "in the specific." Our Employee case study demonstrates that an application can determine the type of an object at execution time and act on that object accordingly. In the case study, we use these capabilities to determine whether a particular employee object *is a* BasePlus-CommissionEmployee. If so, we increase that employee's base salary by 10%.

Interfaces

The chapter continues with an introduction to C# interfaces. An interface describes a set of methods and properties that can be called on an object, but does not provide concrete implementations for them. You can declare classes that **implement** (i.e., provide concrete implementations for the methods and properties of) one or more interfaces. Each interface member must be defined for all the classes that implement the interface. Once a class implements an interface, all objects of that class have an *is-a* relationship with the interface type, and all objects of the class are guaranteed to provide the functionality described by the interface. This is true of all derived classes of that class as well.

Interfaces are particularly useful for assigning common functionality to possibly unrelated classes. This allows objects of unrelated classes to be processed polymorphically— objects of classes that implement the same interface can respond to the same method calls. To demonstrate creating and using interfaces, we modify our payroll application to create a general accounts-payable application that can calculate payments due for the earnings of company employees and for invoice amounts to be billed for purchased goods. As you'll see, interfaces enable polymorphic capabilities similar to those enabled by inheritance.

Operator Overloading

This chapter ends with an introduction to operator overloading. In previous chapters, we declared our own classes and used methods to perform tasks on objects of those classes. Operator overloading allows us to define the behavior of the built-in operators, such as +, – and <, when used on objects of our own classes. This provides a much more convenient notation than calling methods for performing tasks on objects.

12.2 Polymorphism Examples

We now consider several additional examples of polymorphism.

Quadrilateral *Inheritance Hierachy*

If class `Rectangle` is derived from class `Quadrilateral` (a four-sided shape), then a `Rectangle` *is a* more specific version of a `Quadrilateral`. Any operation (e.g., calculating the perimeter or the area) that can be performed on a `Quadrilateral` object can also be performed on a `Rectangle` object. These operations also can be performed on other `Quadrilaterals`, such as `Squares`, `Parallelograms` and `Trapezoids`. The polymorphism occurs when an application invokes a method through a base-class variable—at execution time, the correct derived-class version of the method is called, based on the type of the referenced object. You'll see a simple code example that illustrates this process in Section 12.3.

Video Game `SpaceObject` *Inheritance Hierarchy*

As another example, suppose we design a video game that manipulates objects of many different types, including objects of classes `Martian`, `Venusian`, `Plutonian`, `SpaceShip` and `LaserBeam`. Imagine that each class inherits from the common base class `SpaceObject`, which contains method `Draw`. Each derived class implements this method. A screen-manager application maintains a collection (e.g., a `SpaceObject` array) of references to objects of the various classes. To refresh the screen, the screen manager periodically sends each object the *same message*—namely, `Draw`. However, each object responds in a unique way. For example, a `Martian` object might *draw itself* in red with the appropriate number of antennae. A `SpaceShip` object might *draw itself* as a bright silver flying saucer. A `LaserBeam` object might *draw itself* as a bright red beam across the screen. Again, the *same message* (in this case, `Draw`) sent to a variety of objects has *many forms* of results.

A polymorphic screen manager might use polymorphism to facilitate adding new classes to a system with minimal modifications to the system's code. Suppose we want to add `Mercurian` objects to our video game. To do so, we must build a `Mercurian` class that extends `SpaceObject` and provides its own `Draw` method implementation. When objects of class `Mercurian` appear in the `SpaceObject` collection, the screen-manager code invokes method `Draw`, exactly as it does for every other object in the collection, *regardless of its type*, so the new `Mercurian` objects simply "plug right in" without any modification of the screen-manager code by the programmer. Thus, without modifying the system (other than to build new classes and modify the code that creates new objects), you can use polymorphism to include additional types that might not have been envisioned when the system was created.

Software Engineering Observation 12.1

Polymorphism promotes extensibility: Software that invokes polymorphic behavior is independent of the object types to which messages are sent. New object types that can respond to existing method calls can be incorporated into a system without requiring modification of the base system. Only client code that instantiates new objects must be modified to accommodate new types.

12.3 Demonstrating Polymorphic Behavior

Section 11.4 created a commission-employee class hierarchy, in which class BasePlusCommissionEmployee inherited from class CommissionEmployee. The examples in that section manipulated CommissionEmployee and BasePlusCommissionEmployee objects by using references to them to invoke their methods. We aimed base-class references at base-class objects and derived-class references at derived-class objects. These assignments are natural and straightforward—base-class references are intended to refer to base-class objects, and derived-class references are intended to refer to derived-class objects. However, other assignments are possible.

In the next example, we aim a base-class reference at a derived-class object. We then show how invoking a method on a derived-class object via a base-class reference can invoke the derived-class functionality—*the type of the actual referenced object, not the type of the reference, determines which method is called.* This example demonstrates the key concept that an object of a derived class can be treated as an object of its base class. This enables various interesting manipulations. An application can create an array of base-class references that refer to objects of many derived-class types. This is allowed because each derived-class object *is an* object of its base class. For instance, we can assign the reference of a BasePlusCommissionEmployee object to a base-class CommissionEmployee variable because a BasePlusCommissionEmployee *is a* CommissionEmployee—so we can treat a BasePlusCommissionEmployee as a CommissionEmployee.

A base-class object is not an object of any of its derived classes. For example, we cannot directly assign the reference of a CommissionEmployee object to a derived-class BasePlusCommissionEmployee variable, because a CommissionEmployee *is not* a BasePlusCommissionEmployee—a CommissionEmployee does not, for example, have a baseSalary instance variable and does not have a BaseSalary property. The *is-a* relationship applies from a derived class to its direct and indirect base classes, but not vice versa.

The compiler allows the assignment of a base-class reference to a derived-class variable *if* we explicitly cast the base-class reference to the derived-class type—a technique we discuss in greater detail in Section 12.5.6. Why would we ever want to perform such an assignment? *A base-class reference can be used to invoke only the methods declared in the base class*—attempting to invoke derived-class-only methods through a base-class reference results in compilation errors. If an application needs to perform a derived-class-specific operation on a derived-class object referenced by a base-class variable, the application must first cast the base-class reference to a derived-class reference through a technique known as **downcasting**. This enables the application to invoke derived-class methods that are not in the base class. We present an example of downcasting in Section 12.5.6.

Figure 12.1 demonstrates three ways to use base-class and derived-class variables to store references to base-class and derived-class objects. The first two are straightforward— as in Section 11.4, we assign a base-class reference to a base-class variable, and we assign a derived class reference to a derived class variable. Then we demonstrate the relationship between derived classes and base classes (i.e., the *is-a* relationship) by assigning a derived-class reference to a base-class variable. [*Note:* This application uses classes CommissionEmployee and BasePlusCommissionEmployee from Fig. 11.12 and Fig. 11.13, respectively.]

```csharp
 1   // Fig. 12.1: PolymorphismTest.cs
 2   // Assigning base-class and derived-class references to base-class and
 3   // derived-class variables.
 4   using System;
 5
 6   public class PolymorphismTest
 7   {
 8      public static void Main( string[] args )
 9      {
10         // assign base-class reference to base-class variable
11         CommissionEmployee commissionEmployee = new CommissionEmployee(
12            "Sue", "Jones", "222-22-2222", 10000.00M, .06M );
13
14         // assign derived-class reference to derived-class variable
15         BasePlusCommissionEmployee basePlusCommissionEmployee =
16            new BasePlusCommissionEmployee( "Bob", "Lewis",
17            "333-33-3333", 5000.00M, .04M, 300.00M );
18
19         // invoke ToString and Earnings on base-class object
20         // using base-class variable
21         Console.WriteLine( "{0} {1}:\n\n{2}\n{3}: {4:C}\n",
22            "Call CommissionEmployee's ToString and Earnings methods ",
23            "with base-class reference to base class object",
24            commissionEmployee.ToString(),
25            "earnings", commissionEmployee.Earnings() );
26
27         // invoke ToString and Earnings on derived-class object
28         // using derived-class variable
29         Console.WriteLine( "{0} {1}:\n\n{2}\n{3}: {4:C}\n",
30            "Call BasePlusCommissionEmployee's ToString and Earnings ",
31            "methods with derived class reference to derived-class object",
32            basePlusCommissionEmployee.ToString(),
33            "earnings", basePlusCommissionEmployee.Earnings() );
34
35         // invoke ToString and Earnings on derived-class object
36         // using base-class variable
37         CommissionEmployee commissionEmployee2 =
38            basePlusCommissionEmployee;
39         Console.WriteLine( "{0} {1}:\n\n{2}\n{3}: {4:C}",
40            "Call BasePlusCommissionEmployee's ToString and Earnings ",
41            "with base class reference to derived-class object",
42            commissionEmployee2.ToString(), "earnings",
43            commissionEmployee2.Earnings() );
44      } // end Main
45   } // end class PolymorphismTest
```

Fig. 12.1 | Assigning base-class and derived-class references to base-class and derived-class variables. (Part 1 of 2.)

```
Call CommissionEmployee's ToString and Earnings methods with base class refer-
ence to base class object:

commission employee: Sue Jones
social security number: 222-22-2222
gross sales: $10,000.00
commission rate: 0.06
earnings: $600.00

Call BasePlusCommissionEmployee's ToString and Earnings methods with derived
class reference to derived class object:

base-salaried commission employee: Bob Lewis
social security number: 333-33-3333
gross sales: $5,000.00
commission rate: 0.04
base salary: $300.00
earnings: $500.00

Call BasePlusCommissionEmployee's ToString and Earnings methods with base
class reference to derived class object:

base-salaried commission employee: Bob Lewis
social security number: 333-33-3333
gross sales: $5,000.00
commission rate: 0.04
base salary: $300.00
earnings: $500.00
```

Fig. 12.1 | Assigning base-class and derived-class references to base-class and derived-class variables. (Part 2 of 2.)

In Fig. 12.1, lines 11–12 create a new CommissionEmployee object and assign its reference to a CommissionEmployee variable. Lines 15–17 create a new BasePlusCommissionEmployee object and assign its reference to a BasePlusCommissionEmployee variable. These assignments are *natural*—for example, a CommissionEmployee variable's primary purpose is to hold a reference to a CommissionEmployee object. Lines 21–25 use the reference commissionEmployee to invoke methods ToString and Earnings. Because commissionEmployee refers to a CommissionEmployee object, *base class* CommissionEmployee's version of the methods are called. Similarly, lines 29–33 use the reference basePlusCommissionEmployee to invoke the methods ToString and Earnings on the BasePlusCommissionEmployee object. This invokes *derived class* BasePlusCommissionEmployee's version of the methods.

Lines 37–38 then assign the reference to derived-class object basePlusCommissionEmployee to a base-class CommissionEmployee variable, which lines 39–43 use to invoke methods ToString and Earnings. *A base-class variable that contains a reference to a derived-class object and is used to call a virtual method actually calls the overriding derived-class version of the method.* Hence, commissionEmployee2.ToString() in line 42 actually calls *derived* class BasePlusCommissionEmployee's ToString method. The compiler allows this "crossover" because an object of a derived class *is an* object of its base class (but not vice versa). When the compiler encounters a method call made through a variable, the compiler determines if the method can be called by checking the *variable's* class type. If that class contains the proper method declaration (or inherits one), the compiler allows the call to be compiled. At execution time, *the type of the object to which the variable refers* determines the actual method to use.

12.4 Abstract Classes and Methods

When we think of a class type, we assume that applications will create objects of that type. In some cases, however, it's useful to declare *classes for which you never intend to instantiate objects*. Such classes are called **abstract classes**. Because they're used only as base classes in inheritance hierarchies, we refer to them as **abstract base classes**. These classes cannot be used to instantiate objects, because, as you'll soon see, abstract classes are *incomplete*—derived classes must define the "missing pieces." We demonstrate abstract classes in Section 12.5.1.

The purpose of an abstract class is primarily to provide an appropriate base class from which other classes can inherit, and thus share a common design. In the Shape hierarchy of Fig. 11.3, for example, derived classes inherit the notion of what it means to be a Shape—common attributes such as location, color and borderThickness, and behaviors such as Draw, Move, Resize and ChangeColor. Classes that can be used to instantiate objects are called **concrete classes**. Such classes provide implementations of *every* method they declare (some of the implementations can be inherited). For example, we could derive concrete classes Circle, Square and Triangle from abstract base class TwoDimensionalShape. Similarly, we could derive concrete classes Sphere, Cube and Tetrahedron from abstract base class ThreeDimensionalShape. Abstract base classes are *too general* to create real objects—they specify only what is common among derived classes. We need to be more *specific* before we can create objects. For example, if you send the Draw message to abstract class TwoDimensionalShape, the class knows that two-dimensional shapes should be drawable, but it does not know what *specific* shape to draw, so it cannot implement a real Draw method. *Concrete* classes provide the *specifics* that make it reasonable to instantiate objects.

Not all inheritance hierarchies contain abstract classes. However, you'll often write client code that uses only abstract base-class types to reduce client code's dependencies on a range of specific derived-class types. For example, you can write a method with a parameter of an abstract base-class type. When called, such a method can be passed an object of any concrete class that directly or indirectly extends the base class specified as the parameter's type.

Abstract classes sometimes constitute several levels of the hierarchy. For example, the Shape hierarchy of Fig. 11.3 begins with abstract class Shape. On the next level of the hierarchy are two more abstract classes, TwoDimensionalShape and ThreeDimensionalShape. The next level of the hierarchy declares concrete classes for TwoDimensionalShapes (Circle, Square and Triangle) and for ThreeDimensionalShapes (Sphere, Cube and Tetrahedron).

You make a class abstract by declaring it with the keyword **abstract**. An abstract class normally contains one or more **abstract methods**. An abstract method is one with keyword abstract in its declaration, as in

```
public abstract void Draw(); // abstract method
```

Abstract methods are implicitly virtual and do not provide implementations. A class that contains abstract methods must be declared as an abstract class even if it contains some concrete (nonabstract) methods. Each concrete derived class of an abstract base class also must provide concrete implementations of the base class's abstract methods. We show an example of an abstract class with an abstract method in Fig. 12.4.

Properties can also be declared `abstract` or `virtual`, then overridden in derived classes with the `override` keyword, just like methods. This allows an abstract base class to specify common properties of its derived classes. Abstract property declarations have the form:

```
public abstract PropertyType MyProperty
{
    get;
    set;
} // end abstract property
```

The semicolons after the `get` and `set` keywords indicate that we provide *no implementation* for these accessors. An abstract property may omit implementations for the `get` accessor or the `set` accessor. Concrete derived classes must provide implementations for *every* accessor declared in the abstract property. When both `get` and `set` accessors are specified, every concrete derived class must implement both. If one accessor is omitted, the derived class is not allowed to implement that accessor. Doing so causes a compilation error.

Constructors and `static` methods cannot be declared `abstract`. Constructors are not inherited, so an `abstract` constructor could never be implemented. Similarly, derived classes cannot override `static` methods, so an `abstract` `static` method could never be implemented.

Software Engineering Observation 12.2

An abstract class declares common attributes and behaviors of the various classes that inherit from it, either directly or indirectly, in a class hierarchy. An abstract class typically contains one or more abstract methods or properties that concrete derived classes must override. The instance variables, concrete methods and concrete properties of an abstract class are subject to the normal rules of inheritance.

Common Programming Error 12.1

Attempting to instantiate an object of an abstract class is a compilation error.

Common Programming Error 12.2

Failure to implement a base class's abstract methods and properties in a derived class is a compilation error unless the derived class is also declared `abstract`

Although we cannot instantiate objects of abstract base classes, you'll soon see that we *can* use abstract base classes to declare variables that can hold references to objects of any concrete classes derived from those abstract classes. Applications typically use such variables to manipulate derived-class objects polymorphically. Also, you can use abstract base-class names to invoke `static` methods declared in those abstract base classes.

Polymorphism and Device Drivers
Polymorphism is particularly effective for implementing so-called *layered software systems*. In operating systems, for example, each type of physical device could operate quite differently from the others. Even so, common commands can read or write data from and to the devices. For each device, the operating system uses a piece of software called a *device driver* to control all communication between the system and the device. The write message

sent to a device driver object needs to be interpreted specifically in the context of that driver and how it manipulates a specific device. However, the write call itself really is no different from the write to any other device in the system: Place some number of bytes from memory onto that device. An object-oriented operating system might use an abstract base class to provide an "interface" appropriate for all device drivers. Then, through inheritance from that abstract base class, derived classes are formed that all behave similarly. The device-driver methods are declared as abstract methods in the abstract base class. The implementations of these abstract methods are provided in the derived classes that correspond to the specific types of device drivers. New devices are always being developed, often long after the operating system has been released. When you buy a new device, it comes with a device driver provided by the device vendor. The device is immediately operational after you connect it to your computer and install the device driver. This is another elegant example of how polymorphism makes systems extensible.

Iterators

It's common in object-oriented programming to declare an **iterator class** that can traverse all the objects in a collection, such as an array (Chapter 8) or a List (Chapter 9). For example, an application can print a List of objects by creating an iterator object and using it to obtain the next list element each time the iterator is called. Iterators often are used in polymorphic programming to traverse a collection that contains references to objects of various classes in an inheritance hierarchy. (Chapters 22–23 present a thorough treatment of C#'s "generics" capabilities and iterators.) A List of references to objects of class TwoDimensionalShape, for example, could contain references to objects from derived classes Square, Circle, Triangle and so on. Calling method Draw for each TwoDimensionalShape object off a TwoDimensionalShape variable would polymorphically draw each object correctly on the screen.

12.5 Case Study: Payroll System Using Polymorphism

This section reexamines the CommissionEmployee-BasePlusCommissionEmployee hierarchy that we explored throughout Section 11.4. Now we use an abstract method and polymorphism to perform payroll calculations based on the type of employee. We create an enhanced employee hierarchy to solve the following problem:

> *A company pays its employees on a weekly basis. The employees are of four types: Salaried employees are paid a fixed weekly salary regardless of the number of hours worked, hourly employees are paid by the hour and receive "time-and-a-half" overtime pay for all hours worked in excess of 40 hours, commission employees are paid a percentage of their sales, and salaried-commission employees receive a base salary plus a percentage of their sales. For the current pay period, the company has decided to reward salaried-commission employees by adding 10% to their base salaries. The company wants to implement a C# application that performs its payroll calculations polymorphically.*

We use abstract class Employee to represent the general concept of an employee. The classes that extend Employee are SalariedEmployee, CommissionEmployee and HourlyEmployee. Class BasePlusCommissionEmployee—which extends CommissionEmployee—represents the last employee type. The UML class diagram in Fig. 12.2 shows the inheritance hierarchy for our polymorphic employee payroll application. Abstract class Employee is *italicized*, as per the convention of the UML.

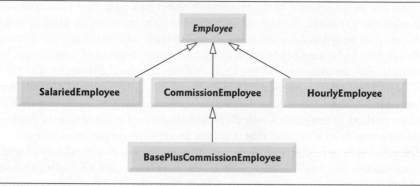

Fig. 12.2 | `Employee` hierarchy UML class diagram.

Abstract base class `Employee` declares the "interface" to the hierarchy—that is, the set of methods that an application can invoke on all `Employee` objects. We use the term "interface" here in a general sense to refer to the various ways applications can communicate with objects of any `Employee` derived class. Be careful not to confuse the general notion of an "interface" with the formal notion of a C# interface, the subject of Section 12.7. Each employee, regardless of the way his or her earnings are calculated, has a first name, a last name and a social security number, so those pieces of data appear in abstract base class `Employee`.

Software Engineering Observation 12.3

*A derived class can inherit "interface" or "implementation" from a base class. Hierarchies designed for **implementation inheritance** tend to have their functionality high in the hierarchy—each new derived class inherits one or more methods that were implemented in a base class, and the derived class uses the base-class implementations. Hierarchies designed for **interface inheritance** tend to have their functionality lower in the hierarchy—a base class specifies one or more abstract methods that must be declared for each concrete class in the hierarchy, and the individual derived classes override these methods to provide derived-class-specific implementations.*

The following sections implement the `Employee` class hierarchy. The first section implements `abstract` base class `Employee`. The next four sections each implement one of the concrete classes. The sixth section implements a test application that builds objects of all these classes and processes those objects polymorphically.

12.5.1 Creating Abstract Base Class Employee

Class `Employee` (Fig. 12.4) provides methods `Earnings` and `ToString`, in addition to the auto-implemented properties that manipulate `Employee`'s data. An `Earnings` method certainly applies generically to all employees. But each earnings calculation depends on the employee's class. So we declare `Earnings` as `abstract` in base class `Employee`, because a default implementation does not make sense for that method—there's not enough information to determine what amount `Earnings` should return. Each derived class overrides `Earnings` with an appropriate implementation. To calculate an employee's earnings, the application assigns a reference to the employee's object to a base class `Employee` variable, then invokes the `Earnings` method on that variable. We maintain an array of `Employee` variables, each of which holds a reference to an `Employee` object (of course, there *cannot* be `Employee` objects because `Employee` is an *abstract* class—because of inheritance, however-er, all objects of all derived classes of `Employee` may nevertheless be thought of as `Employee` objects). The application iterates through the array and calls method `Earnings` for each `Employee` object. C# processes these method calls polymorphically. Including `Earnings` as an abstract method in `Employee` forces every directly derived *concrete* class of `Employee` to override `Earnings` with a method that performs an appropriate pay calculation.

Method `ToString` in class `Employee` returns a `string` containing the employee's first name, last name and social security number. Each derived class of `Employee` overrides method `ToString` to create a string representation of an object of that class containing the employee's type (e.g., `"salaried employee:"`), followed by the rest of the employee's information.

The diagram in Fig. 12.3 shows each of the five classes in the hierarchy down the left side and methods `Earnings` and `ToString` across the top. For each class, the diagram shows the desired results of each method. [*Note:* We do not list base class `Employee`'s prop-erties because they're not overridden in any of the derived classes—each of these properties is inherited and used "as is" by each of the derived classes.]

	Earnings	ToString
Employee	abstract	*firstName lastName* `social security number:` *SSN*
Salaried-Employee	weeklySalary	`salaried employee:` *firstName lastName* `social security number:` *SSN* `weekly salary:` *weeklysalary*

Hourly-Employee	*If hours <= 40*
	    `wage * hours`
	If hours > 40
	    `40 * wage +`
	    `( hours - 40 ) *`
	    `wage * 1.5`
		`hourly employee:` *firstName lastName*
		`social security number:` *SSN*
		`hourly wage:` *wage*
		`hours worked:` *hours*

Commission-Employee	commissionRate * grossSales	`commission employee:` *firstName lastName* `social security number:` *SSN* `gross sales:` *grossSales* `commission rate:` *commissionRate*
BasePlus-Commission-Employee	(commissionRate * grossSales) + baseSalary	`base salaried commission employee:` *firstName lastName* `social security number:` *SSN* `gross sales:` *grossSales* `commission rate:` *commissionRate* `base salary:` *baseSalary*

Fig. 12.3 | Polymorphic interface for the `Employee` hierarchy classes.

Let's consider class Employee's declaration (Fig. 12.4). The class includes a constructor that takes the first name, last name and social security number as arguments (lines 15–20); read-only properties for obtaining the first name, last name and social security number (lines 6, 9 and 12, respectively); method ToString (lines 23–27), which uses properties to return the string representation of the Employee; and abstract method Earnings (line 30), which *must* be implemented by *concrete* derived classes. The Employee constructor does not validate the social security number in this example. Normally, such validation should be provided.

```
1   // Fig. 12.4: Employee.cs
2   // Employee abstract base class.
3   public abstract class Employee
4   {
5      // read-only property that gets employee's first name
6      public string FirstName { get; private set; }
7
8      // read-only property that gets employee's last name
9      public string LastName { get; private set; }
10
11     // read-only property that gets employee's social security number
12     public string SocialSecurityNumber { get; private set; }
13
14     // three-parameter constructor
15     public Employee( string first, string last, string ssn )
16     {
17        FirstName = first;
18        LastName = last;
19        SocialSecurityNumber = ssn;
20     } // end three-parameter Employee constructor
21
22     // return string representation of Employee object, using properties
23     public override string ToString()
24     {
25        return string.Format( "{0} {1}\nsocial security number: {2}",
26           FirstName, LastName, SocialSecurityNumber );
27     } // end method ToString
28
29     // abstract method overridden by derived classes
30     public abstract decimal Earnings(); // no implementation here
31  } // end abstract class Employee
```

Fig. 12.4 | Employee abstract base class.

Why did we declare Earnings as an abstract method? As explained earlier, it simply does not make sense to provide an implementation of this method in class Employee. We cannot calculate the earnings for a general Employee—we first must know the *specific* Employee type to determine the appropriate earnings calculation. By declaring this method abstract, we indicate that each *concrete* derived class *must* provide an appropriate Earnings implementation and that an application will be able to use base-class Employee variables to invoke method Earnings polymorphically for *any* type of Employee.

12.5.2 Creating Concrete Derived Class SalariedEmployee

Class SalariedEmployee (Fig. 12.5) extends class Employee (line 5) and overrides Earnings (lines 34–37), which makes SalariedEmployee a concrete class. The class includes a constructor (lines 10–14) that takes a first name, a last name, a social security number and a weekly salary as arguments; property WeeklySalary (lines 17–31) to manipulate instance variable weeklySalary, including a set accessor that ensures we assign only nonnegative values to weeklySalary; method Earnings (lines 34–37) to calculate a SalariedEmployee's earnings; and method ToString (lines 40–44), which returns a string including the employee's type, namely, "salaried employee: ", followed by employee-specific information produced by base class Employee's ToString method and SalariedEmployee's WeeklySalary property. Class SalariedEmployee's constructor passes the first name, last name and social security number to the Employee constructor (line 11) via a constructor initializer to initialize the base class's data. Method Earnings overrides Employee's abstract method Earnings to provide a concrete implementation that returns the SalariedEmployee's weekly salary. If we do not implement Earnings, class SalariedEmployee must be declared abstract—otherwise, a compilation error occurs (and, of course, we want SalariedEmployee to be a concrete class).

```
1   // Fig. 12.5: SalariedEmployee.cs
2   // SalariedEmployee class that extends Employee.
3   using System;
4
5   public class SalariedEmployee : Employee
6   {
7      private decimal weeklySalary;
8
9      // four-parameter constructor
10     public SalariedEmployee( string first, string last, string ssn,
11        decimal salary ) : base( first, last, ssn )
12     {
13        WeeklySalary = salary; // validate salary via property
14     } // end four-parameter SalariedEmployee constructor
15
16     // property that gets and sets salaried employee's salary
17     public decimal WeeklySalary
18     {
19        get
20        {
21           return weeklySalary;
22        } // end get
23        set
24        {
25           if ( value >= 0 ) // validation
26              weeklySalary = value;
27           else
28              throw new ArgumentOutOfRangeException( "WeeklySalary",
29                 value, "WeeklySalary must be >= 0" );
30        } // end set
31     } // end property WeeklySalary
```

Fig. 12.5 | SalariedEmployee class that extends Employee. (Part 1 of 2.)

```
32
33        // calculate earnings; override abstract method Earnings in Employee
34        public override decimal Earnings()
35        {
36           return WeeklySalary;
37        } // end method Earnings
38
39        // return string representation of SalariedEmployee object
40        public override string ToString()
41        {
42           return string.Format( "salaried employee: {0}\n{1}: {2:C}",
43              base.ToString(), "weekly salary", WeeklySalary );
44        } // end method ToString
45     } // end class SalariedEmployee
```

Fig. 12.5 | SalariedEmployee class that extends Employee. (Part 2 of 2.)

SalariedEmployee method ToString (lines 40–44) overrides Employee's version. If class SalariedEmployee did not override ToString, SalariedEmployee would have inherited the Employee version. In that case, SalariedEmployee's ToString method would simply return the employee's full name and social security number, which does not adequately represent a SalariedEmployee. To produce a complete string representation of a SalariedEmployee, the derived class's ToString method returns "salaried employee: ", followed by the base-class Employee-specific information (i.e., first name, last name and social security number) obtained by invoking the base class's ToString (line 43)—this is a nice example of code reuse. The string representation of a SalariedEmployee also contains the employee's weekly salary, obtained by using the class's WeeklySalary property.

12.5.3 Creating Concrete Derived Class HourlyEmployee

Class HourlyEmployee (Fig. 12.6) also extends class Employee (line 5). The class includes a constructor (lines 11–17) that takes as arguments a first name, a last name, a social security number, an hourly wage and the number of hours worked. Lines 20–34 and 37–51 declare properties Wage and Hours for instance variables wage and hours, respectively. The set accessor in property Wage ensures that wage is nonnegative, and the set accessor in property Hours ensures that hours is in the range 0–168 (the total number of hours in a week) inclusive. The class overrides method Earnings (lines 54–60) to calculate an HourlyEmployee's earnings and method ToString (lines 63–68) to return the employee's string representation. The HourlyEmployee constructor, similarly to the SalariedEmployee constructor, passes the first name, last name and social security number to the base-class Employee constructor (line 13) to initialize the base class's data. Also, method ToString calls base-class method ToString (line 67) to obtain the Employee-specific information (i.e., first name, last name and social security number.

```
1    // Fig. 12.6: HourlyEmployee.cs
2    // HourlyEmployee class that extends Employee.
3    using System;
4
```

Fig. 12.6 | HourlyEmployee class that extends Employee. (Part 1 of 3.)

```csharp
 5   public class HourlyEmployee : Employee
 6   {
 7      private decimal wage; // wage per hour
 8      private decimal hours; // hours worked for the week
 9
10      // five-parameter constructor
11      public HourlyEmployee( string first, string last, string ssn,
12         decimal hourlyWage, decimal hoursWorked )
13         : base( first, last, ssn )
14      {
15         Wage = hourlyWage; // validate hourly wage via property
16         Hours = hoursWorked; // validate hours worked via property
17      } // end five-parameter HourlyEmployee constructor
18
19      // property that gets and sets hourly employee's wage
20      public decimal Wage
21      {
22         get
23         {
24            return wage;
25         } // end get
26         set
27         {
28            if ( value >= 0 ) // validation
29               wage = value;
30            else
31               throw new ArgumentOutOfRangeException( "Wage",
32                  value, "Wage must be >= 0" );
33         } // end set
34      } // end property Wage
35
36      // property that gets and sets hourly employee's hours
37      public decimal Hours
38      {
39         get
40         {
41            return hours;
42         } // end get
43         set
44         {
45            if ( value >= 0 && value <= 168 ) // validation
46               hours = value;
47            else
48               throw new ArgumentOutOfRangeException( "Hours",
49                  value, "Hours must be >= 0 and <= 168" );
50         } // end set
51      } // end property Hours
52
53      // calculate earnings; override Employee's abstract method Earnings
54      public override decimal Earnings()
55      {
56         if ( Hours <= 40 ) // no overtime
57            return Wage * Hours;
```

Fig. 12.6 | HourlyEmployee class that extends Employee. (Part 2 of 3.)

```
58        else
59           return ( 40 * Wage ) + ( ( Hours - 40 ) * Wage * 1.5M );
60     } // end method Earnings
61
62     // return string representation of HourlyEmployee object
63     public override string ToString()
64     {
65        return string.Format(
66           "hourly employee: {0}\n{1}: {2:C}; {3}: {4:F2}",
67           base.ToString(), "hourly wage", Wage, "hours worked", Hours );
68     } // end method ToString
69  } // end class HourlyEmployee
```

Fig. 12.6 | HourlyEmployee class that extends Employee. (Part 3 of 3.)

12.5.4 Creating Concrete Derived Class CommissionEmployee

Class CommissionEmployee (Fig. 12.7) extends class Employee (line 5). The class includes a constructor (lines 11–16) that takes a first name, a last name, a social security number, a sales amount and a commission rate; properties (lines 19–33 and 36–50) for instance variables grossSales and commissionRate, respectively; method Earnings (lines 53–56) to calculate a CommissionEmployee's earnings; and method ToString (lines 59–64), which returns the employee's string representation. The CommissionEmployee's constructor also passes the first name, last name and social security number to the Employee constructor (line 12) to initialize Employee's data. Method ToString calls base-class method ToString (line 62) to obtain the Employee-specific information (i.e., first name, last name and social security number).

```
1   // Fig. 12.7: CommissionEmployee.cs
2   // CommissionEmployee class that extends Employee.
3   using System;
4
5   public class CommissionEmployee : Employee
6   {
7      private decimal grossSales; // gross weekly sales
8      private decimal commissionRate; // commission percentage
9
10     // five-parameter constructor
11     public CommissionEmployee( string first, string last, string ssn,
12        decimal sales, decimal rate ) : base( first, last, ssn )
13     {
14        GrossSales = sales; // validate gross sales via property
15        CommissionRate = rate; // validate commission rate via property
16     } // end five-parameter CommissionEmployee constructor
17
18     // property that gets and sets commission employee's gross sales
19     public decimal GrossSales
20     {
21        get
22        {
```

Fig. 12.7 | CommissionEmployee class that extends Employee. (Part 1 of 2.)

```
23            return grossSales;
24         } // end get
25         set
26         {
27            if ( value >= 0 )
28               grossSales = value;
29            else
30               throw new ArgumentOutOfRangeException(
31                  "GrossSales", value, "GrossSales must be >= 0" );
32         } // end set
33      } // end property GrossSales
34
35      // property that gets and sets commission employee's commission rate
36      public decimal CommissionRate
37      {
38         get
39         {
40            return commissionRate;
41         } // end get
42         set
43         {
44            if ( value > 0 && value < 1 )
45               commissionRate = value;
46            else
47               throw new ArgumentOutOfRangeException( "CommissionRate",
48                  value, "CommissionRate must be > 0 and < 1" );
49         } // end set
50      } // end property CommissionRate
51
52      // calculate earnings; override abstract method Earnings in Employee
53      public override decimal Earnings()
54      {
55         return CommissionRate * GrossSales;
56      } // end method Earnings
57
58      // return string representation of CommissionEmployee object
59      public override string ToString()
60      {
61         return string.Format( "{0}: {1}\n{2}: {3:C}\n{4}: {5:F2}",
62            "commission employee", base.ToString(),
63            "gross sales", GrossSales, "commission rate", CommissionRate );
64      } // end method ToString
65   } // end class CommissionEmployee
```

Fig. 12.7 | CommissionEmployee class that extends Employee. (Part 2 of 2.)

12.5.5 Creating Indirect Concrete Derived Class BasePlusCommissionEmployee

Class BasePlusCommissionEmployee (Fig. 12.8) extends class CommissionEmployee (line 5) and therefore is an *indirect* derived class of class Employee. Class BasePlusCommission-Employee has a constructor (lines 10–15) that takes as arguments a first name, a last name, a social security number, a sales amount, a commission rate and a base salary. It then passes the first name, last name, social security number, sales amount and commission rate to the

CommissionEmployee constructor (line 12) to initialize the base class's data. BasePlusCommissionEmployee also contains property BaseSalary (lines 19–33) to manipulate instance variable baseSalary. Method Earnings (lines 36–39) calculates a BasePlusCommissionEmployee's earnings. Line 38 in method Earnings calls base class CommissionEmployee's Earnings method to calculate the commission-based portion of the employee's earnings. Again, this shows the benefits of code reuse. BasePlusCommissionEmployee's ToString method (lines 42–46) creates a string representation of a BasePlusCommissionEmployee that contains "base-salaried", followed by the string obtained by invoking base class CommissionEmployee's ToString method (another example of code reuse), then the base salary. The result is a string beginning with "base-salaried commission employee", followed by the rest of the BasePlusCommissionEmployee's information. Recall that CommissionEmployee's ToString method obtains the employee's first name, last name and social security number by invoking the ToString method of *its* base class (i.e., Employee)—a further demonstration of code reuse. BasePlusCommissionEmployee's ToString initiates a chain of method calls that spans all three levels of the Employee hierarchy.

```csharp
1   // Fig. 12.8: BasePlusCommissionEmployee.cs
2   // BasePlusCommissionEmployee class that extends CommissionEmployee.
3   using System;
4
5   public class BasePlusCommissionEmployee : CommissionEmployee
6   {
7      private decimal baseSalary; // base salary per week
8
9      // six-parameter constructor
10     public BasePlusCommissionEmployee( string first, string last,
11        string ssn, decimal sales, decimal rate, decimal salary )
12        : base( first, last, ssn, sales, rate )
13     {
14        BaseSalary = salary; // validate base salary via property
15     } // end six-parameter BasePlusCommissionEmployee constructor
16
17     // property that gets and sets
18     // base-salaried commission employee's base salary
19     public decimal BaseSalary
20     {
21        get
22        {
23           return baseSalary;
24        } // end get
25        set
26        {
27           if ( value >= 0 )
28              baseSalary = value;
29           else
30              throw new ArgumentOutOfRangeException( "BaseSalary",
31                 value, "BaseSalary must be >= 0" );
32        } // end set
33     } // end property BaseSalary
```

Fig. 12.8 | BasePlusCommissionEmployee class that extends CommissionEmployee. (Part 1 of 2.)

```
34
35    // calculate earnings; override method Earnings in CommissionEmployee
36    public override decimal Earnings()
37    {
38       return BaseSalary + base.Earnings();
39    } // end method Earnings
40
41    // return string representation of BasePlusCommissionEmployee object
42    public override string ToString()
43    {
44       return string.Format( "base-salaried {0}; base salary: {1:C}",
45          base.ToString(), BaseSalary );
46    } // end method ToString
47 } // end class BasePlusCommissionEmployee
```

Fig. 12.8 | BasePlusCommissionEmployee class that extends CommissionEmployee. (Part 2 of 2.)

12.5.6 Polymorphic Processing, Operator is and Downcasting

To test our Employee hierarchy, the application in Fig. 12.9 creates an object of each of the four concrete classes SalariedEmployee, HourlyEmployee, CommissionEmployee and BasePlusCommissionEmployee. The application manipulates these objects, first via variables of each object's own type, then polymorphically, using an array of Employee variables. While processing the objects polymorphically, the application increases the base salary of each BasePlusCommissionEmployee by 10% (this, of course, requires determining the object's type at execution time). Finally, the application polymorphically determines and outputs the type of each object in the Employee array. Lines 10–20 create objects of each of the four concrete Employee derived classes. Lines 24–32 output the string representation and earnings of each of these objects. Each object's ToString method is called implicitly by WriteLine when the object is output as a string with format items.

Assigning Derived-Class Objects to Base-Class References
Line 35 declares employees and assigns it an array of four Employee variables. Lines 38–41 assign a SalariedEmployee object, an HourlyEmployee object, a CommissionEmployee object and a BasePlusCommissionEmployee object to employees[0], employees[1], employees[2] and employees[3], respectively. Each assignment is allowed, because a SalariedEmployee *is an* Employee, an HourlyEmployee *is an* Employee, a CommissionEmployee *is an* Employee and a BasePlusCommissionEmployee *is an* Employee. Therefore, we can assign the references of SalariedEmployee, HourlyEmployee, CommissionEmployee and BasePlusCommissionEmployee objects to base-class Employee variables, even though Employee is an abstract class.

```
1    // Fig. 12.9: PayrollSystemTest.cs
2    // Employee hierarchy test application.
3    using System;
4
```

Fig. 12.9 | Employee hierarchy test application. (Part 1 of 4.)

```
 5   public class PayrollSystemTest
 6   {
 7      public static void Main( string[] args )
 8      {
 9         // create derived-class objects
10         SalariedEmployee salariedEmployee =
11            new SalariedEmployee( "John", "Smith", "111-11-1111", 800.00M );
12         HourlyEmployee hourlyEmployee =
13            new HourlyEmployee( "Karen", "Price",
14            "222-22-2222", 16.75M, 40.0M );
15         CommissionEmployee commissionEmployee =
16            new CommissionEmployee( "Sue", "Jones",
17            "333-33-3333", 10000.00M, .06M );
18         BasePlusCommissionEmployee basePlusCommissionEmployee =
19            new BasePlusCommissionEmployee( "Bob", "Lewis",
20            "444-44-4444", 5000.00M, .04M, 300.00M );
21
22         Console.WriteLine( "Employees processed individually:\n" );
23
24         Console.WriteLine( "{0}\nearned: {1:C}\n",
25            salariedEmployee, salariedEmployee.Earnings() );
26         Console.WriteLine( "{0}\nearned: {1:C}\n",
27            hourlyEmployee, hourlyEmployee.Earnings() );
28         Console.WriteLine( "{0}\nearned: {1:C}\n",
29            commissionEmployee, commissionEmployee.Earnings() );
30         Console.WriteLine( "{0}\nearned: {1:C}\n",
31            basePlusCommissionEmployee,
32            basePlusCommissionEmployee.Earnings() );
33
34         // create four-element Employee array
35         Employee[] employees = new Employee[ 4 ];
36
37         // initialize array with Employees of derived types
38         employees[ 0 ] = salariedEmployee;
39         employees[ 1 ] = hourlyEmployee;
40         employees[ 2 ] = commissionEmployee;
41         employees[ 3 ] = basePlusCommissionEmployee;
42
43         Console.WriteLine( "Employees processed polymorphically:\n" );
44
45         // generically process each element in array employees
46         foreach ( Employee currentEmployee in employees )
47         {
48            Console.WriteLine( currentEmployee ); // invokes ToString
49
50            // determine whether element is a BasePlusCommissionEmployee
51            if ( currentEmployee is BasePlusCommissionEmployee )
52            {
53               // downcast Employee reference to
54               // BasePlusCommissionEmployee reference
55               BasePlusCommissionEmployee employee =
56                  ( BasePlusCommissionEmployee ) currentEmployee;
57
```

Fig. 12.9 | Employee hierarchy test application. (Part 2 of 4.)

```
58              employee.BaseSalary *= 1.10M;
59              Console.WriteLine(
60                 "new base salary with 10% increase is: {0:C}",
61                 employee.BaseSalary );
62          } // end if
63
64          Console.WriteLine(
65             "earned {0:C}\n", currentEmployee.Earnings() );
66       } // end foreach
67
68       // get type name of each object in employees array
69       for ( int j = 0; j < employees.Length; j++ )
70          Console.WriteLine( "Employee {0} is a {1}", j,
71             employees[ j ].GetType() );
72    } // end Main
73 } // end class PayrollSystemTest
```

```
Employees processed individually:

salaried employee: John Smith
social security number: 111-11-1111
weekly salary: $800.00
earned: $800.00

hourly employee: Karen Price
social security number: 222-22-2222
hourly wage: $16.75; hours worked: 40.00
earned: $670.00

commission employee: Sue Jones
social security number: 333-33-3333
gross sales: $10,000.00
commission rate: 0.06
earned: $600.00

base-salaried commission employee: Bob Lewis
social security number: 444-44-4444
gross sales: $5,000.00
commission rate: 0.04; base salary: $300.00
earned: $500.00


Employees processed polymorphically:

salaried employee: John Smith
social security number: 111-11-1111
weekly salary: $800.00
earned $800.00

hourly employee: Karen Price
social security number: 222-22-2222
hourly wage: $16.75; hours worked: 40.00
earned $670.00
```

Fig. 12.9 | Employee hierarchy test application. (Part 3 of 4.)

```
commission employee: Sue Jones
social security number: 333-33-3333
gross sales: $10,000.00
commission rate: 0.06
earned $600.00

base-salaried commission employee: Bob Lewis
social security number: 444-44-4444
gross sales: $5,000.00
commission rate: 0.04; base salary: $300.00
new base salary with 10% increase is: $330.00
earned $530.00

Employee 0 is a SalariedEmployee
Employee 1 is a HourlyEmployee
Employee 2 is a CommissionEmployee
Employee 3 is a BasePlusCommissionEmployee
```

Fig. 12.9 | Employee hierarchy test application. (Part 4 of 4.)

Polymorphically Processing Employees

Lines 46–66 iterate through array employees and invoke methods ToString and Earnings with Employee variable currentEmployee, which is assigned the reference to a different Employee during each iteration. The output illustrates that the appropriate methods for each class are indeed invoked. All calls to virtual methods ToString and Earnings are resolved at execution time, based on the type of the object to which currentEmployee refers. This process is known as **dynamic binding** or **late binding**. For example, line 48 implicitly invokes method ToString of the object to which currentEmployee refers. Only the methods of class Employee can be called via an Employee variable—and Employee includes class object's methods, such as ToString. (Section 11.7 discussed the methods that all classes inherit from class object.) A base-class reference can be used to invoke only methods of the base class.

Giving BasePlusCommissionEmployees 10% Raises

We perform special processing on BasePlusCommissionEmployee objects—as we encounter them, we increase their base salary by 10%. When processing objects polymorphically, we typically do not need to worry about the "specifics," but to adjust the base salary, we do have to determine the specific type of each Employee object at execution time. Line 51 uses the is operator to determine whether a particular Employee object's type is Base-PlusCommissionEmployee. The condition in line 51 is true if the object referenced by currentEmployee *is a* BasePlusCommissionEmployee. This would also be true for any object of a BasePlusCommissionEmployee derived class (if there were any), because of the *is-a* relationship a derived class has with its base class. Lines 55–56 downcast currentEmployee from type Employee to type BasePlusCommissionEmployee—this cast is allowed only if the object has an *is-a* relationship with BasePlusCommissionEmployee. The condition at line 51 ensures that this is the case. This cast is required if we are to use derived class BasePlusCommissionEmployee's BaseSalary property on the current Employee object—*attempting to invoke a derived-class-only method directly on a base class reference is a compilation error.*

Common Programming Error 12.3

Assigning a base-class variable to a derived-class variable (without an explicit downcast) is a compilation error.

Software Engineering Observation 12.4

If at execution time the reference to a derived-class object has been assigned to a variable of one of its direct or indirect base classes, it's acceptable to cast the reference stored in that base-class variable back to a reference of the derived-class type. Before performing such a cast, use the is operator to ensure that the object is indeed an object of an appropriate derived-class type.

When downcasting an object, an InvalidCastException (of namespace *System*) occurs if at execution time the object does not have an *is a* relationship with the type specified in the cast operator. An object can be cast only to its own type or to the type of one of its base classes. You can avoid a potential InvalidCastException by using the **as** operator to perform a downcast rather than a cast operator. For example, in the statement

```
BasePlusCommissionEmployee employee =
    currentEmployee as BasePlusCommissionEmployee;
```

employee is assigned a reference to an object that *is a* BasePlusCommissionEmployee, or the value null if currentEmployee is not a BasePlusCommissionEmployee. You can then compare employee with null to determine whether the cast succeeded.

If the is expression in line 51 is true, the if statement (lines 51–62) performs the special processing required for the BasePlusCommissionEmployee object. Using Base-PlusCommissionEmployee variable employee, line 58 accesses the derived-class-only property BaseSalary to retrieve and update the employee's base salary with the 10% raise.

Lines 64–65 invoke method Earnings on currentEmployee, which calls the appropriate derived-class object's Earnings method polymorphically. Obtaining the earnings of the SalariedEmployee, HourlyEmployee and CommissionEmployee polymorphically in lines 64–65 produces the same result as obtaining these employees' earnings individually in lines 24–29. However, the earnings amount obtained for the BasePlusCommissionEmployee in lines 64–65 is higher than that obtained in lines 30–32, due to the 10% increase in its base salary.

Every Object Knows Its Own Type

Lines 69–71 display each employee's type as a string. Every object in C# knows its own type and can access this information through method **GetType**, which all classes inherit from class object. Method GetType returns an object of class Type (of namespace System), which contains information about the object's type, including its class name, the names of its methods, and the name of its base class. Line 71 invokes method GetType on the object to get its runtime class (i.e., a Type object that represents the object's type). Then method ToString is implicitly invoked on the object returned by GetType. The Type class's ToString method returns the class name.

Avoiding Compilation Errors with Downcasting

In the previous example, we avoid several compilation errors by downcasting an Employee variable to a BasePlusCommissionEmployee variable in lines 55–56. If we remove the cast operator (BasePlusCommissionEmployee) from line 56 and attempt to assign Employee variable currentEmployee directly to BasePlusCommissionEmployee variable employee, we receive a "Cannot implicitly convert type" compilation error. This error indicates that the attempt to assign the reference of base-class object commissionEmployee to derived-class variable basePlusCommissionEmployee is not allowed without an appropriate cast operator. The compiler prevents this assignment, because a CommissionEmployee is *not* a BasePlusCommissionEmployee—again, the *is-a* relationship applies only between the derived class and its base classes, not vice versa.

Similarly, if lines 58 and 61 use base-class variable currentEmployee, rather than derived-class variable employee, to use derived-class-only property BaseSalary, we receive an "'Employee' does not contain a definition for 'BaseSalary'" compilation error on each of these lines. *Attempting to invoke derived-class-only methods on a base-class reference is not allowed.* While lines 58 and 61 execute only if is in line 51 returns true to indicate that currentEmployee has been assigned a reference to a BasePlusCommissionEmployee object, we cannot attempt to use derived-class BasePlusCommissionEmployee property BaseSalary with base-class Employee reference currentEmployee. The compiler would generate errors in lines 58 and 61, because BaseSalary is not a base-class member and cannot be used with a base-class variable. Although the actual method that's called depends on the object's type at execution time, *a variable can be used to invoke only those methods that are members of that variable's type*, which the compiler verifies. Using a base-class Employee variable, we can invoke only methods and properties found in class Employee—methods Earnings and ToString, and properties FirstName, LastName and SocialSecurityNumber—and method methods inherited from class object.

12.5.7 Summary of the Allowed Assignments Between Base-Class and Derived-Class Variables

Now that you've seen a complete application that processes diverse derived-class objects polymorphically, we summarize what you can and cannot do with base-class and derived-class objects and variables. Although a derived-class object also *is a* base-class object, the two are nevertheless different. As discussed previously, derived-class objects can be treated as if they were base-class objects. However, the derived class can have additional derived-class-only members. For this reason, assigning a base-class reference to a derived-class variable is not allowed without an explicit cast—such an assignment would leave the derived-class members undefined for a base-class object.

We've discussed four ways to assign base-class and derived-class references to variables of base-class and derived-class types:

1. Assigning a base-class reference to a base-class variable is straightforward.

2. Assigning a derived-class reference to a derived-class variable is straightforward.

3. Assigning a derived-class reference to a base-class variable is safe, because the derived-class object *is an* object of its base class. However, this reference can be used to refer *only* to base-class members. If this code refers to derived-class-only members through the base-class variable, the compiler reports errors.

4. Attempting to assign a base-class reference to a derived-class variable is a compilation error. To avoid this error, the base-class reference must be cast to a derived-class type explicitly or must be converted using the as operator. At execution

time, if the object to which the reference refers is *not* a derived-class object, an exception will occur. The is operator can be used to ensure that such a cast is performed *only* if the object is a derived-class object.

12.6 sealed Methods and Classes

Only methods declared virtual, override or abstract can be overridden in derived classes. A method declared **sealed** in a base class cannot be overridden in a derived class. Methods that are declared private are implicitly sealed, because it's impossible to override them in a derived class (though the derived class can declare a new method with the same signature as the private method in the base class). Methods that are declared static also are implicitly sealed, because static methods cannot be overridden either. A derived-class method declared both override and sealed can override a base-class method, but cannot be overridden in derived classes further down the inheritance hierarchy.

A sealed method's declaration can never change, so all derived classes use the same method implementation, and calls to sealed methods are resolved at compile time—this is known as **static binding**. Since the compiler knows that sealed methods cannot be overridden, it can often optimize code by removing calls to sealed methods and replacing them with the expanded code of their declarations at each method-call location—a technique known as **inlining the code**.

Performance Tip 12.1
The compiler can decide to inline a sealed method call and will do so for small, simple sealed methods. Inlining does not violate encapsulation or information hiding, but does improve performance, because it eliminates the overhead of making a method call.

A class that's declared sealed cannot be a base class (i.e., a class cannot extend a sealed class). All methods in a sealed class are implicitly sealed. Class string is a sealed class. This class cannot be extended, so applications that use strings can rely on the functionality of string objects as specified in the Framework Class Library.

Common Programming Error 12.4
Attempting to declare a derived class of a sealed class is a compilation error.

12.7 Case Study: Creating and Using Interfaces

Our next example (Figs. 12.11–12.15) reexamines the payroll system of Section 12.5. Suppose that the company involved wishes to perform several accounting operations in a single accounts-payable application—in addition to calculating the payroll earnings that must be paid to each employee, the company must also calculate the payment due on each of several invoices (i.e., bills for goods purchased). Though applied to unrelated things (i.e., employees and invoices), both operations have to do with calculating some kind of payment amount. For an employee, the payment refers to the employee's earnings. For an invoice, the payment refers to the total cost of the goods listed on the invoice. Can we calculate such different things as the payments due for employees and invoices polymorphically in a single application? Does C# offer a capability that requires that *unrelated* classes implement a set of common methods (e.g., a method that calculates a payment amount)? C# interfaces offer exactly this capability.

Interfaces define and standardize the ways in which people and systems can interact with one another. For example, the controls on a radio serve as an interface between a radio's users and its internal components. The controls allow users to perform a limited set of operations (e.g., changing the station, adjusting the volume, choosing between AM and FM), and different radios may implement the controls in different ways (e.g., using push buttons, dials, voice commands). The interface specifies *what* operations a radio must permit users to perform but does not specify *how* they're performed. Similarly, the interface between a driver and a car with a manual transmission includes the steering wheel, the gear shift, the clutch pedal, the gas pedal and the brake pedal. This same interface is found in nearly all manual-transmission cars, enabling someone who knows how to drive one particular manual-transmission car to drive just about any other. The components of each car may look a bit different, but the general purpose is the same—to allow people to drive the car.

Software objects also communicate via interfaces. A C# interface describes a set of methods and properties that can be called on an object—to tell it, for example, to perform some task or return some piece of information. The next example introduces an interface named `IPayable` that describes the functionality of any object that must be capable of being paid and thus must offer a method to determine the proper payment amount due. An **interface declaration** begins with the keyword **interface** and can contain only abstract methods, properties, indexers and events (events are discussed in Chapter 14, Graphical User Interfaces with Windows Forms: Part 1.) All interface members are implicitly declared both `public` and `abstract`. In addition, each interface can extend one or more other interfaces to create a more elaborate interface that other classes can implement.

Common Programming Error 12.5

It's a compilation error to declare an interface member `public` or `abstract` explicitly, because they're redundant in interface-member declarations. It's also a compilation error to specify any implementation details, such as concrete method declarations, in an interface.

To use an interface, a class must specify that it **implements** the interface by listing the interface after the colon (`:`) in the class declaration. This is the same syntax used to indicate inheritance from a base class. A concrete class implementing the interface must declare each member of the interface with the signature specified in the interface declaration. A class that implements an interface but does not implement all its members is an abstract class—it must be declared `abstract` and must contain an `abstract` declaration for each unimplemented member of the interface. Implementing an interface is like signing a contract with the compiler that states, "I will provide an implementation for all the members specified by the interface, or I will declare them `abstract`."

Common Programming Error 12.6

Failing to define or declare any member of an interface in a class that implements the interface results in a compilation error.

An interface is typically used when unrelated classes need to share common methods. This allows objects of unrelated classes to be processed polymorphically—objects of classes that implement the same interface can respond to the same method calls. You can create an interface that describes the desired functionality, then implement this interface in any classes requiring that functionality. For example, in the accounts-payable application developed in this section, we implement interface IPayable in any class that must be able to calculate a payment amount (e.g., Employee, Invoice).

An interface often is used in place of an abstract class when there's no default implementation to inherit—that is, no fields and no default method implementations. Like abstract classes, interfaces are typically public types, so they're normally declared in files by themselves with the same name as the interface and the .cs file-name extension.

12.7.1 Developing an IPayable Hierarchy

To build an application that can determine payments for employees and invoices alike, we first create an interface named IPayable. Interface IPayable contains method GetPaymentAmount that returns a decimal amount to be paid for an object of any class that implements the interface. Method GetPaymentAmount is a general-purpose version of method Earnings of the Employee hierarchy—method Earnings calculates a payment amount specifically for an Employee, while GetPaymentAmount can be applied to a broad range of unrelated objects. After declaring interface IPayable, we introduce class Invoice, which implements interface IPayable. We then modify class Employee such that it also implements interface IPayable. Finally, we update Employee derived class SalariedEmployee to "fit" into the IPayable hierarchy (i.e., we rename SalariedEmployee method Earnings as GetPaymentAmount).

Good Programming Practice 12.1

By convention, the name of an interface begins with "I". This helps distinguish interfaces from classes, improving code readability.

Good Programming Practice 12.2

When declaring a method in an interface, choose a name that describes the method's purpose in a general manner, because the method may be implemented by a broad range of unrelated classes.

Classes Invoice and Employee both represent things for which the company must be able to calculate a payment amount. Both classes implement IPayable, so an application can invoke method GetPaymentAmount on Invoice objects and Employee objects alike. This enables the polymorphic processing of Invoices and Employees required for our company's accounts-payable application.

The UML class diagram in Fig. 12.10 shows the interface and class hierarchy used in our accounts-payable application. The hierarchy begins with interface IPayable. The UML distinguishes an interface from a class by placing the word "interface" in guillemets (« and ») above the interface name. The UML expresses the relationship between a class and an interface through a **realization**. A class is said to "realize," or implement, an interface. A class diagram models a realization as a dashed arrow with a hollow arrowhead pointing from the implementing class to the interface. The diagram in Fig. 12.10 indicates that classes Invoice and Employee each realize (i.e., implement) interface IPayable. As in the class diagram of Fig. 12.2, class Employee appears in italics, indicating that it's an abstract class. Concrete class SalariedEmployee extends Employee and inherits its base class's realization relationship with interface IPayable.

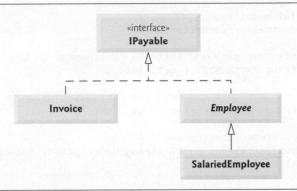

Fig. 12.10 | IPayable interface and class hierarchy UML class diagram.

12.7.2 Declaring Interface IPayable

The declaration of interface IPayable begins in Fig. 12.11 at line 3. Interface IPayable contains public abstract method GetPaymentAmount (line 5). The method cannot be *explicitly* declared public or abstract. Interfaces can have any number of members and interface methods can have parameters.

```
1   // Fig. 12.11: IPayable.cs
2   // IPayable interface declaration.
3   public interface IPayable
4   {
5       decimal GetPaymentAmount(); // calculate payment; no implementation
6   } // end interface IPayable
```

Fig. 12.11 | IPayable interface declaration.

12.7.3 Creating Class Invoice

We now create class Invoice (Fig. 12.12) to represent a simple invoice that contains billing information for one kind of part. The class contains properties PartNumber (line 11), PartDescription (line 14), Quantity (lines 27–41) and PricePerItem (lines 44–58) that indicate the part number, the description of the part, the quantity of the part ordered and the price per item. Class Invoice also contains a constructor (lines 17–24) and a ToString method (lines 61–67) that returns a string representation of an Invoice object. The set accessors of properties Quantity and PricePerItem ensure that quantity and pricePerItem are assigned only nonnegative values.

```
1   // Fig. 12.12: Invoice.cs
2   // Invoice class implements IPayable.
3   using System;
4
5   public class Invoice : IPayable
6   {
```

Fig. 12.12 | Invoice class implements IPayable. (Part I of 3.)

```
7       private int quantity;
8       private decimal pricePerItem;
9
10      // property that gets and sets the part number on the invoice
11      public string PartNumber { get; set; }
12
13      // property that gets and sets the part description on the invoice
14      public string PartDescription { get; set; }
15
16      // four-parameter constructor
17      public Invoice( string part, string description, int count,
18         decimal price )
19      {
20         PartNumber = part;
21         PartDescription = description;
22         Quantity = count; // validate quantity via property
23         PricePerItem = price; // validate price per item via property
24      } // end four-parameter Invoice constructor
25
26      // property that gets and sets the quantity on the invoice
27      public int Quantity
28      {
29         get
30         {
31            return quantity;
32         } // end get
33         set
34         {
35            if ( value >= 0 ) // validate quantity
36               quantity = value;
37            else
38               throw new ArgumentOutOfRangeException( "Quantity",
39                  value, "Quantity must be >= 0" );
40         } // end set
41      } // end property Quantity
42
43      // property that gets and sets the price per item
44      public decimal PricePerItem
45      {
46         get
47         {
48            return pricePerItem;
49         } // end get
50         set
51         {
52            if ( value >= 0 ) // validate price
53               quantity = value;
54            else
55               throw new ArgumentOutOfRangeException( "PricePerItem",
56                  value, "PricePerItem must be >= 0" );
57         } // end set
58      } // end property PricePerItem
59
```

Fig. 12.12 | Invoice class implements IPayable. (Part 2 of 3.)

```
60      // return string representation of Invoice object
61      public override string ToString()
62      {
63          return string.Format(
64              "{0}: \n{1}: {2} ({3}) \n{4}: {5} \n{6}: {7:C}",
65              "invoice", "part number", PartNumber, PartDescription,
66              "quantity", Quantity, "price per item", PricePerItem );
67      } // end method ToString
68
69      // method required to carry out contract with interface IPayable
70      public decimal GetPaymentAmount()
71      {
72          return Quantity * PricePerItem; // calculate total cost
73      } // end method GetPaymentAmount
74  } // end class Invoice
```

Fig. 12.12 | Invoice class implements IPayable. (Part 3 of 3.)

Line 5 of Fig. 12.12 indicates that class Invoice implements interface IPayable. Like all classes, class Invoice also implicitly inherits from class object. *C# does not allow derived classes to inherit from more than one base class, but it does allow a class to inherit from a base class and implement* any *number of interfaces.* All objects of a class that implement multiple interfaces have the *is-a* relationship with each implemented interface type. To implement more than one interface, use a comma-separated list of interface names after the colon (:) in the class declaration, as in:

public class *ClassName* : *BaseClassName*, *FirstInterface*, *SecondInterface*, ...

When a class inherits from a base class and implements one or more interfaces, the class declaration *must* list the base-class name before any interface names.

Class Invoice implements the one method in interface IPayable—method GetPaymentAmount is declared in lines 70–73. The method calculates the amount required to pay the invoice. The method multiplies the values of quantity and pricePerItem (obtained through the appropriate properties) and returns the result (line 72). This method satisfies the implementation requirement for the method in interface IPayable—we've fulfilled the interface contract with the compiler.

12.7.4 Modifying Class Employee to Implement Interface IPayable

We now modify class Employee to implement interface IPayable. Figure 12.13 contains the modified Employee class. This class declaration is identical to that of Fig. 12.4 with two exceptions. First, line 3 of Fig. 12.13 indicates that class Employee now implements interface IPayable. Because of this, we must rename Earnings to GetPaymentAmount throughout the Employee hierarchy. As with method Earnings in the version of class Employee in Fig. 12.4, however, it does not make sense to implement method GetPayment-Amount in class Employee, because we cannot calculate the earnings payment owed to a *general* Employee—first, we must know the *specific* type of Employee. In Fig. 12.4, we declared method Earnings as abstract for this reason, and as a result, class Employee had to be declared abstract. This forced each Employee derived class to override Earnings with a concrete implementation.

```
1   // Fig. 12.13: Employee.cs
2   // Employee abstract base class.
3   public abstract class Employee : IPayable
4   {
5      // read-only property that gets employee's first name
6      public string FirstName { get; private set; }
7
8      // read-only property that gets employee's last name
9      public string LastName { get; private set; }
10
11     // read-only property that gets employee's social security number
12     public string SocialSecurityNumber { get; private set; }
13
14     // three-parameter constructor
15     public Employee( string first, string last, string ssn )
16     {
17        FirstName = first;
18        LastName = last;
19        SocialSecurityNumber = ssn;
20     } // end three-parameter Employee constructor
21
22     // return string representation of Employee object
23     public override string ToString()
24     {
25        return string.Format( "{0} {1}\nsocial security number: {2}",
26           FirstName, LastName, SocialSecurityNumber );
27     } // end method ToString
28
29     // Note: We do not implement IPayable method GetPaymentAmount here, so
30     // this class must be declared abstract to avoid a compilation error.
31     public abstract decimal GetPaymentAmount();
32  } // end abstract class Employee
```

Fig. 12.13 | Employee abstract base class.

In Fig. 12.13, we handle this situation the same way. Recall that when a class implements an interface, the class makes a contract with the compiler stating that the class either will implement *each* of the methods in the interface *or* will declare them abstract. If the latter option is chosen, we must also declare the class abstract. As we discussed in Section 12.4, any concrete derived class of the abstract class must implement the abstract methods of the base class. If the derived class does not do so, it too must be declared abstract. As indicated by the comments in lines 29–30, class Employee of Fig. 12.13 does not implement method GetPaymentAmount, so the class is declared abstract.

12.7.5 Modifying Class SalariedEmployee for Use with IPayable

Figure 12.14 contains a modified version of class SalariedEmployee that extends Employee and implements method GetPaymentAmount. This version of SalariedEmployee is identical to that of Fig. 12.5 with the exception that the version here implements method GetPaymentAmount (lines 35–38) instead of method Earnings. The two methods contain the same functionality but have different names. Recall that the IPayable version of the method has a more general name to be applicable to possibly disparate classes. The remaining Employee derived classes (e.g., HourlyEmployee, CommissionEmployee and BasePlusCommissionEmployee) also must be modified to contain method GetPaymentAmount in place of Earnings to reflect the fact that Employee now implements IPayable. We leave these modifications as an exercise and use only SalariedEmployee in our test application in this section.

```
1   // Fig. 12.14: SalariedEmployee.cs
2   // SalariedEmployee class that extends Employee.
3   using System;
4
5   public class SalariedEmployee : Employee
6   {
7      private decimal weeklySalary;
8
9      // four-parameter constructor
10     public SalariedEmployee( string first, string last, string ssn,
11        decimal salary ) : base( first, last, ssn )
12     {
13        WeeklySalary = salary; // validate salary via property
14     } // end four-parameter SalariedEmployee constructor
15
16     // property that gets and sets salaried employee's salary
17     public decimal WeeklySalary
18     {
19        get
20        {
21           return weeklySalary;
22        } // end get
23        set
24        {
25           if ( value >= 0 ) // validation
26              weeklySalary = value;
27           else
28              throw new ArgumentOutOfRangeException( "WeeklySalary",
29                 value, "WeeklySalary must be >= 0" );
30        } // end set
31     } // end property WeeklySalary
32
33     // calculate earnings; implement interface IPayable method
34     // that was abstract in base class Employee
35     public override decimal GetPaymentAmount()
36     {
37        return WeeklySalary;
38     } // end method GetPaymentAmount
39
40     // return string representation of SalariedEmployee object
41     public override string ToString()
42     {
43        return string.Format( "salaried employee: {0}\n{1}: {2:C}",
44           base.ToString(), "weekly salary", WeeklySalary );
45     } // end method ToString
46  } // end class SalariedEmployee
```

Fig. 12.14 | SalariedEmployee class that extends Employee.

When a class implements an interface, the same *is-a* relationship provided by inheritance applies. Class `Employee` implements `IPayable`, so we can say that an `Employee` *is an* `IPayable`, as are any classes that extend `Employee`. As such, `SalariedEmployee` objects are `IPayable` objects. An object of a class that implements an interface may be thought of as an object of the interface type. Objects of any classes derived from the class that implements the interface can also be thought of as objects of the interface type. Thus, just as we can assign the reference of a `SalariedEmployee` object to a base-class `Employee` variable, we can assign the reference of a `SalariedEmployee` object to an interface `IPayable` variable. `Invoice` implements `IPayable`, so an `Invoice` object also *is an* `IPayable` object, and we can assign the reference of an `Invoice` object to an `IPayable` variable.

Software Engineering Observation 12.5

Inheritance and interfaces are similar in their implementation of the is-a *relationship. An object of a class that implements an interface may be thought of as an object of that interface type. An object of any derived classes of a class that implements an interface also can be thought of as an object of the interface type.*

Software Engineering Observation 12.6

The is-a *relationship that exists between base classes and derived classes, and between interfaces and the classes that implement them, holds when passing an object to a method. When a method parameter receives an argument of a base class or interface type, the method polymorphically processes the object received as an argument.*

12.7.6 Using Interface IPayable to Process Invoices and Employees Polymorphically

`PayableInterfaceTest` (Fig. 12.15) illustrates that interface `IPayable` can be used to process a set of `Invoice`s and `Employee`s polymorphically in a single application. Line 10 declares `payableObjects` and assigns it an array of four `IPayable` variables. Lines 13–14 assign the references of `Invoice` objects to the first two elements of `payableObjects`. Lines 15–18 assign the references of `SalariedEmployee` objects to the remaining two elements of `payableObjects`. These assignments are allowed because an `Invoice` *is an* `IPayable`, a `SalariedEmployee` *is an* `Employee` and an `Employee` *is an* `IPayable`. Lines 24–29 use a foreach statement to process each `IPayable` object in `payableObjects` polymorphically, printing the object as a `string`, along with the payment due. Lines 27–28 implicitly invokes method `ToString` off an `IPayable` interface reference, even though `ToString` is not declared in interface `IPayable`—all references (including those of interface types) refer to objects that extend `object` and therefore have a `ToString` method. Line 28 invokes `IPayable` method `GetPaymentAmount` to obtain the payment amount for each object in `payableObjects`, regardless of the actual type of the object. The output reveals that the method calls in lines 27–28 invoke the appropriate class's implementation of methods `ToString` and `GetPaymentAmount`. For instance, when `currentPayable` refers to an `Invoice` during the first iteration of the foreach loop, class `Invoice`'s `ToString` and `GetPaymentAmount` methods execute.

Software Engineering Observation 12.7

All methods of class object can be called by using a reference of an interface type—the reference refers to an object, and all objects inherit the methods of class object.

```
1    // Fig. 12.15: PayableInterfaceTest.cs
2    // Tests interface IPayable with disparate classes.
3    using System;
4
5    public class PayableInterfaceTest
6    {
7       public static void Main( string[] args )
8       {
9          // create four-element IPayable array
10         IPayable[] payableObjects = new IPayable[ 4 ];
11
12         // populate array with objects that implement IPayable
13         payableObjects[ 0 ] = new Invoice( "01234", "seat", 2, 375.00M );
14         payableObjects[ 1 ] = new Invoice( "56789", "tire", 4, 79.95M );
15         payableObjects[ 2 ] = new SalariedEmployee( "John", "Smith",
16            "111-11-1111", 800.00M );
17         payableObjects[ 3 ] = new SalariedEmployee( "Lisa", "Barnes",
18            "888-88-8888", 1200.00M );
19
20         Console.WriteLine(
21            "Invoices and Employees processed polymorphically:\n" );
22
23         // generically process each element in array payableObjects
24         foreach ( var currentPayable in payableObjects )
25         {
26            // output currentPayable and its appropriate payment amount
27            Console.WriteLine( "payment due {0}: {1:C}\n",
28               currentPayable, currentPayable.GetPaymentAmount() );
29         } // end foreach
30      } // end Main
31   } // end class PayableInterfaceTest
```

```
Invoices and Employees processed polymorphically:

invoice:
part number: 01234 (seat)
quantity: 2
price per item: $375.00
payment due: $750.00

invoice:
part number: 56789 (tire)
quantity: 4
price per item: $79.95
payment due: $319.80

salaried employee: John Smith
social security number: 111-11-1111
weekly salary: $800.00
payment due: $800.00

salaried employee: Lisa Barnes
social security number: 888-88-8888
weekly salary: $1,200.00
payment due: $1,200.00
```

Fig. 12.15 | Tests interface IPayable with disparate classes.

12.7.7 Common Interfaces of the .NET Framework Class Library

In this section, we overview several common interfaces defined in the .NET Framework Class Library. These interfaces are implemented and used in the same manner as those you create (e.g., interface IPayable in Section 12.7.2). The Framework Class Library's interfaces enable you to extend many important aspects of C# with your own classes. Figure 12.16 overviews several commonly used Framework Class Library interfaces.

Interface	Description
IComparable	As you learned in Chapter 3, C# contains several comparison operators (e.g., <, <=, >, >=, ==, !=) that allow you to compare simple-type values. In Section 12.8 you'll see that these operators can be defined to compare two objects. Interface IComparable can also be used to allow objects of a class that implements the interface to be compared to one another. The interface contains one method, CompareTo, that compares the object that calls the method to the object passed as an argument to the method. Classes must implement CompareTo to return a value indicating whether the object on which it's invoked is less than (negative integer return value), equal to (0 return value) or greater than (positive integer return value) the object passed as an argument, using any criteria you specify. For example, if class Employee implements IComparable, its CompareTo method could compare Employee objects by their earnings amounts. Interface IComparable is commonly used for ordering objects in a collection such as an array. We use IComparable in Chapter 22, Generics, and Chapter 23, Collections.
IComponent	Implemented by any class that represents a component, including Graphical User Interface (GUI) controls (such as buttons or labels). Interface IComponent defines the behaviors that components must implement. We discuss IComponent and many GUI controls that implement this interface in Chapter 14, Graphical User Interfaces with Windows Forms: Part 1, and Chapter 15, Graphical User Interfaces with Windows Forms: Part 2.
IDisposable	Implemented by classes that must provide an explicit mechanism for releasing resources. Some resources can be used by only one program at a time. In addition, some resources, such as files on disk, are unmanaged resources that, unlike memory, cannot be released by the garbage collector. Classes that implement interface IDisposable provide a Dispose method that can be called to explicitly release resources. We discuss IDisposable briefly in Chapter 13, Exception Handling: A Deeper Look. You can learn more about this interface at msdn.microsoft.com/en-us/library/system.idisposable.aspx. The MSDN article *Implementing a Dispose Method* at msdn.microsoft.com/en-us/library/fs2xkftw.aspx discusses the proper implementation of this interface in your classes.
IEnumerator	Used for iterating through the elements of a collection (such as an array) one element at a time. Interface IEnumerator contains method MoveNext to move to the next element in a collection, method Reset to move to the position before the first element and property Current to return the object at the current location. We use IEnumerator in Chapter 23.

Fig. 12.16 | Common interfaces of the .NET Framework Class Library.

12.8 Operator Overloading

Object manipulations are accomplished by sending messages (in the form of method calls) to the objects. This method-call notation is cumbersome for certain kinds of classes, especially mathematical classes. For these classes, it would be convenient to use C#'s rich set of built-in operators to specify object manipulations. In this section, we show how to enable these operators to work with class objects—via a process called **operator overloading**.

C# enables you to overload most operators to make them sensitive to the context in which they're used. Some operators are overloaded more frequently than others, especially the various arithmetic operators, such as + and -, where operator notation often is more natural. Figures 12.17 and 12.18 provide an example of using operator overloading with a ComplexNumber class. For a list of overloadable operators, see msdn.microsoft.com/en-us/library/8edha89s.aspx.

Class ComplexNumber (Fig. 12.17) overloads the plus (+), minus (-) and multiplication (*) operators to enable programs to add, subtract and multiply instances of class ComplexNumber using common mathematical notation. Lines 9 and 12 define properties for the Real and Imaginary components of the complex number.

```
1   // Fig. 12.17: ComplexNumber.cs
2   // Class that overloads operators for adding, subtracting
3   // and multiplying complex numbers.
4   using System;
5
6   public class ComplexNumber
7   {
8      // read-only property that gets the real component
9      public double Real { get; private set; }
10
11     // read-only property that gets the imaginary component
12     public double Imaginary { get; private set; }
13
14     // constructor
15     public ComplexNumber( double a, double b )
16     {
17        Real = a;
18        Imaginary = b;
19     } // end constructor
20
21     // return string representation of ComplexNumber
22     public override string ToString()
23     {
24        return string.Format( "({0} {1} {2}i)",
25           Real, ( Imaginary < 0 ? "-" : "+" ), Math.Abs( Imaginary ) );
26     } // end method ToString
27
28     // overload the addition operator
29     public static ComplexNumber operator+ (
30        ComplexNumber x, ComplexNumber y )
31     {
```

Fig. 12.17 | Class that overloads operators for adding, subtracting and multiplying complex numbers. (Part 1 of 2.)

```
32          return new ComplexNumber( x.Real + y.Real,
33             x.Imaginary + y.Imaginary );
34       } // end operator +
35
36       // overload the subtraction operator
37       public static ComplexNumber operator- (
38          ComplexNumber x, ComplexNumber y )
39       {
40          return new ComplexNumber( x.Real - y.Real,
41             x.Imaginary - y.Imaginary );
42       } // end operator -
43
44       // overload the multiplication operator
45       public static ComplexNumber operator* (
46          ComplexNumber x, ComplexNumber y )
47       {
48          return new ComplexNumber(
49             x.Real * y.Real - x.Imaginary * y.Imaginary,
50             x.Real * y.Imaginary + y.Real * x.Imaginary );
51       } // end operator *
52    } // end class ComplexNumber
```

Fig. 12.17 | Class that overloads operators for adding, subtracting and multiplying complex numbers. (Part 2 of 2.)

Lines 29–34 overload the plus operator (+) to perform addition of ComplexNumbers. Keyword **operator**, followed by an operator symbol, indicates that a method overloads the specified operator. Methods that overload binary operators must take two arguments. The first argument is the left operand, and the second argument is the right operand. Class ComplexNumber's overloaded plus operator takes two ComplexNumber references as arguments and returns a ComplexNumber that represents the sum of the arguments. This method is marked public and static, which is required for overloaded operators. The body of the method (lines 32–33) performs the addition and returns the result as a new ComplexNumber. Notice that we do not modify the contents of either of the original operands passed as arguments x and y. This matches our intuitive sense of how this operator should behave—adding two numbers does not modify either of the original numbers. Lines 37–51 provide similar overloaded operators for subtracting and multiplying ComplexNumbers.

Software Engineering Observation 12.8

Overload operators to perform the same function or similar functions on class objects as the operators perform on objects of simple types. Avoid nonintuitive use of operators.

Software Engineering Observation 12.9

At least one parameter of an overloaded operator method must be a reference to an object of the class in which the operator is overloaded. This prevents you from changing how operators work on simple types.

Class ComplexTest (Fig. 12.18) demonstrates the overloaded ComplexNumber operators +, - and *. Lines 14–27 prompt the user to enter two complex numbers, then use this input to create two ComplexNumbers and assign them to variables x and y.

```
 1    // Fig. 12.18: OperatorOverloading.cs
 2    // Overloading operators for complex numbers.
 3    using System;
 4
 5    public class ComplexTest
 6    {
 7       public static void Main( string[] args )
 8       {
 9          // declare two variables to store complex numbers
10          // to be entered by user
11          ComplexNumber x, y;
12
13          // prompt the user to enter the first complex number
14          Console.Write( "Enter the real part of complex number x: " );
15          double realPart = Convert.ToDouble( Console.ReadLine() );
16          Console.Write(
17             "Enter the imaginary part of complex number x: " );
18          double imaginaryPart = Convert.ToDouble( Console.ReadLine() );
19          x = new ComplexNumber( realPart, imaginaryPart );
20
21          // prompt the user to enter the second complex number
22          Console.Write( "\nEnter the real part of complex number y: " );
23          realPart = Convert.ToDouble( Console.ReadLine() );
24          Console.Write(
25             "Enter the imaginary part of complex number y: " );
26          imaginaryPart = Convert.ToDouble( Console.ReadLine() );
27          y = new ComplexNumber( realPart, imaginaryPart );
28
29          // display the results of calculations with x and y
30          Console.WriteLine();
31          Console.WriteLine( "{0} + {1} = {2}", x, y, x + y );
32          Console.WriteLine( "{0} - {1} = {2}", x, y, x - y );
33          Console.WriteLine( "{0} * {1} = {2}", x, y, x * y );
34       } // end method Main
35    } // end class ComplexTest
```

```
Enter the real part of complex number x: 2
Enter the imaginary part of complex number x: 4

Enter the real part of complex number y: 4
Enter the imaginary part of complex number y: -2

(2 + 4i) + (4 - 2i) = (6 + 2i)
(2 + 4i) - (4 - 2i) = (-2 + 6i)
(2 + 4i) * (4 - 2i) = (16 + 12i)
```

Fig. 12.18 | Overloading operators for complex numbers.

Lines 31–33 add, subtract and multiply x and y with the overloaded operators, then output the results. In line 31, we perform the addition by using the plus operator with ComplexNumber operands x and y. Without operator overloading, the expression x + y wouldn't make sense—the compiler wouldn't know how two objects of class Complex-Number should be added. This expression makes sense here because we've defined the plus operator for two ComplexNumbers in lines 29–34 of Fig. 12.17. When the two Complex-

Numbers are "added" in line 31 of Fig. 12.18, this invokes the operator+ declaration, passing the left operand as the first argument and the right operand as the second argument. When we use the subtraction and multiplication operators in lines 32–33, their respective overloaded operator declarations are invoked similarly.

Each calculation's result is a reference to a new ComplexNumber object. When this new object is passed to the Console class's WriteLine method, its ToString method (Fig. 12.17, lines 22–26) is implicitly invoked. Line 31 of Fig. 12.18 could be rewritten to explicitly invoke the ToString method of the object created by the overloaded plus operator, as in:

```
Console.WriteLine( "{0} + {1} = {2}", x, y, ( x + y ).ToString() );
```

12.9 Wrap-Up

This chapter introduced polymorphism—the ability to process objects that share the same base class in a class hierarchy as if they were all objects of the base class. The chapter discussed how polymorphism makes systems extensible and maintainable, then demonstrated how to use overridden methods to effect polymorphic behavior. We introduced the notion of an abstract class, which allows you to provide an appropriate base class from which other classes can inherit. You learned that an abstract class can declare abstract methods that each derived class must implement to become a concrete class, and that an application can use variables of an abstract class to invoke derived class implementations of abstract methods polymorphically. You also learned how to determine an object's type at execution time. We showed how to create sealed methods and classes. The chapter discussed declaring and implementing an interface as another way to achieve polymorphic behavior, often among objects of different classes. Finally, you learned how to define the behavior of the built-in operators on objects of your own classes with operator overloading.

You should now be familiar with classes, objects, encapsulation, inheritance, interfaces and polymorphism—the most essential aspects of object-oriented programming. Next, we take a deeper look at using exception handling to deal with runtime errors.

Summary

Section 12.1 Introduction

- With polymorphism, we can design and implement systems that are easily extensible—new classes can be added with little or no modification to the general portions of the application.

Section 12.2 Polymorphism Examples

- With polymorphism, the same method name and signature can be used to cause different actions to occur, depending on the type of object on which the method is invoked.

- Polymorphism promotes extensibility: Software that invokes polymorphic behavior is independent of the object types to which messages are sent. New object types that can respond to existing method calls can be incorporated in a system without requiring modification of the base system.

Section 12.3 Demonstrating Polymorphic Behavior

- Invoking a method on a derived-class object via a base-class reference invokes the derived-class functionality—the type of the referenced object determines which method is called.

- A base-class reference can be used to invoke only the methods declared in the base class. If an application needs to perform a derived-class-specific operation on a derived-class object referenced by a base-class variable, the application must first downcast the base-class reference to a derived-class reference.

Section 12.4 Abstract Classes and Methods
- Abstract base classes are incomplete classes for which you never intend to instantiate objects.
- The purpose of an abstract class is primarily to provide an appropriate base class from which other classes can inherit, and thus share a common design.
- Classes that can be used to instantiate objects are called concrete classes.
- You make a class abstract by declaring it with keyword abstract.
- Each concrete derived class of an abstract base class must provide concrete implementations of the base class's abstract methods and properties.
- Failure to implement a base class's abstract methods and properties in a derived class is a compilation error unless the derived class is also declared abstract.
- Although we cannot instantiate objects of abstract base classes, we can use them to declare variables that can hold references to objects of any concrete class derived from those abstract classes.

Section 12.5 Case Study: Payroll System Using Polymorphism
- By declaring a method abstract, we indicate that each concrete derived class must provide an appropriate implementation.
- All virtual method calls are resolved at execution time, based on the type of the object to which the reference-type variable refers. This process is known as dynamic binding or late binding.
- The is operator determines whether the type of the object in the left operand matches the type specified by the right operand and returns true if the two have an *is-a* relationship.
- The as operator performs a downcast that returns a reference to the appropriate object if the downcast is successful and returns null if the downcast fails.
- Every object in C# knows its own type and can access this information through method GetType, which all classes inherit from class object.
- Assigning a base-class reference to a derived-class variable is not allowed without an explicit cast or without using the as operator. The is operator can be used to ensure that such a cast is performed only if the object is a derived-class object.

Section 12.6 sealed Methods and Classes
- A method that's declared sealed in a base class cannot be overridden in a derived class.
- A class that's declared sealed cannot be a base class (i.e., a class cannot extend a sealed class). All methods in a sealed class are implicitly sealed.

Section 12.7 Case Study: Creating and Using Interfaces
- Interfaces define and standardize the ways in which things such as people and systems can interact with one another.
- An interface declaration begins with keyword interface and can contain only abstract methods, properties, indexers and events.
- All interface members are implicitly declared both public and abstract. They do not specify any implementation details, such as concrete method declarations.
- Each interface can extend one or more other interfaces to create a more elaborate interface that other classes can implement.
- To use an interface, a class must specify that it implements the interface by listing it after the colon (:) in the class declaration.

- A class that implements an interface but doesn't implement all the interface's members must be declared `abstract` and contain an abstract declaration of each unimplemented interface member.
- The UML expresses the relationship between a class and an interface through a realization. A class is said to "realize," or implement, an interface.
- To implement more than one interface, use a comma-separated list of interface names after the colon (:) in the class declaration.
- Inheritance and interfaces are similar in their implementation of the *is-a* relationship. An object of a class that implements an interface may be thought of as an object of that interface type.
- All methods of class `object` can be called by using a reference of an interface type—the reference refers to an object, and all objects inherit the methods of class `object`.

Section 12.8 Operator Overloading
- Method-call notation is cumbersome for certain kinds of classes, especially mathematical classes. Sometimes, it's convenient to use C#'s built-in operators to specify object manipulations.
- Keyword `operator`, followed by an operator, indicates that a method overloads the specified operator. Methods that overload binary operators must be declared `static` and must take two arguments. The first argument is the left operand, and the second is the right operand.
- Overload operators to perform the same function or similar functions on class objects as the operators perform on objects of simple types. Avoid nonintuitive use of operators.

Terminology

abstract base class	interface declaration
abstract class	interface inheritance
abstract keyword	`interface` keyword
abstract method	*is a* relationship
abstract operation	`is` operator
as operator	iterator class
base-class reference	late binding
concrete class	`operator` keyword
derived-class reference	operator overloading
downcasting	polymorphism
dynamic binding	realization
generalization in the UML	sealed class
`GetType` method of class `object`	sealed method
implement an interface	static binding
inlining code	Type class

Self-Review Exercises

12.1 Fill in the blanks in each of the following statements:
  a) If a class contains at least one abstract method, it must be declared as a(n) _____ class.
  b) Classes from which objects can be instantiated are called _____ classes.
  c) _____ involves using a base-class variable to invoke methods on base-class and derived-class objects, enabling you to "program in the general."
  d) Methods in a class that do not provide implementations must be declared using keyword _____.
  e) Casting a reference stored in a base-class variable to a derived-class type is called _____.

12.2 State whether each of the statements that follows is *true* or *false*. If *false*, explain why.
  a) It's possible to treat base-class objects and derived-class objects similarly.

    b) All methods in an abstract class must be declared as abstract methods.

    c) Attempting to invoke a derived-class-only method through a base-class variable is an error.

    d) If a base class declares an abstract method, a derived class must implement that method.

    e) An object of a class that implements an interface may be thought of as an object of that interface type.

Answers to Self-Review Exercises

12.1 a) abstract. b) concrete. c) Polymorphism. d) abstract. e) downcasting.

12.2 a) True. b) False. An abstract class can include methods with implementations and abstract methods. c) True. d) False. Only a concrete derived class must implement the method. e) True.

Exercises

12.3 *(Programming in the General)* How does polymorphism enable you to program "in the general" rather than "in the specific"? Discuss the key advantages of programming "in the general."

12.4 *(Inheriting Interface vs. Inheriting Implementation)* A derived class can inherit "interface" or "implementation" from a base class. How do inheritance hierarchies designed for inheriting interface differ from those designed for inheriting implementation?

12.5 *(Abstract Methods)* What are abstract methods? Describe the circumstances in which an abstract method would be appropriate.

12.6 *(Polymorphism and Extensibility)* How does polymorphism promote extensibility?

12.7 *(Assigning Base Class and Derived Class References)* Discuss four ways in which you can assign base-class and derived-class references to variables of base-class and derived-class types.

12.8 *(Abstract Classes vs. Interfaces)* Compare and contrast abstract classes and interfaces. Why would you use an abstract class? Why would you use an interface?

12.9 *(Payroll System Modification)* Modify the payroll system of Figs. 12.4–12.9 to include private instance variable birthDate in class Employee. Use class Date of Fig. 10.7 to represent an employee's birthday. Assume that payroll is processed once per month. Create an array of Employee variables to store references to the various employee objects. In a loop, calculate the payroll for each Employee (polymorphically), and add a $100.00 bonus to the person's payroll amount if the current month is the month in which the Employee's birthday occurs.

12.10 *(Shape Hierarchy)* Implement the Shape hierarchy of Fig. 11.3. Omit the Triangle and Tetrahedron classes. Each TwoDimensionalShape should contain read-only abstract property Area to calculate the area of the two-dimensional shape. Each ThreeDimensionalShape should have read-only abstract properties Area and Volume to calculate the surface area and volume, respectively, of the three-dimensional shape. Create an application that uses an array of Shape references to objects of each concrete class in the hierarchy. Print a text description of the object to which each array element refers. Also, in the loop that processes all the shapes in the array, determine whether each shape is a TwoDimensionalShape or a ThreeDimensionalShape. If a shape is a TwoDimensionalShape, display its area. If a shape is a ThreeDimensionalShape, display its area and volume.

12.11 *(Payroll System Modification)* Modify the payroll system of Figs. 12.4–12.9 to include an additional Employee derived class, PieceWorker, that represents an employee whose pay is based on the number of pieces of merchandise produced. Class PieceWorker should contain private instance variables wage (to store the employee's wage per piece) and pieces (to store the number of pieces produced). Provide a concrete implementation of method Earnings in class PieceWorker that calculates the employee's earnings by multiplying the number of pieces produced by the wage per piece. Create an array of Employee variables to store references to objects of each concrete class in the new Employee hierarchy. Display each Employee's string representation and earnings.

12.12 *(Accounts Payable System Modification)* In this exercise, we modify the accounts payable application of Figs. 12.11–12.15 to include the complete functionality of the payroll application of Figs. 12.4–12.9. The application should still process two Invoice objects, but now should process one object of each of the four Employee derived classes. If the object currently being processed is a BasePlusCommissionEmployee, the application should increase the BasePlusCommissionEmployee's base salary by 10%. Finally, the application should output the payment amount for each object. Complete the following steps to create the new application:

    a) Modify classes HourlyEmployee (Fig. 12.6) and CommissionEmployee (Fig. 12.7) to place them in the IPayable hierarchy as derived classes of the version of Employee (Fig. 12.13) that implements IPayable. [*Hint:* Change the name of method Earnings to GetPaymentAmount in each derived class.]

    b) Modify class BasePlusCommissionEmployee (Fig. 12.8) such that it extends the version of class CommissionEmployee created in *Part a*.

    c) Modify PayableInterfaceTest (Fig. 12.15) to polymorphically process two Invoices, one SalariedEmployee, one HourlyEmployee, one CommissionEmployee and one Base-PlusCommissionEmployee. First, output a string representation of each IPayable object. Next, if an object is a BasePlusCommissionEmployee, increase its base salary by 10%. Finally, output the payment amount for each IPayable object.

12.13 *(Package Inheritance Hierarchy)* Use the Package inheritance hierarchy created in Exercise 11.8 to create an application that displays the address information and calculates the shipping costs for several Packages. The application should contain an array of Package objects of classes TwoDayPackage and OvernightPackage. Loop through the array to process the Packages polymorphically. For each Package, use properties to obtain the address information of the sender and the recipient, then print the two addresses as they would appear on mailing labels. Also, call each Package's CalculateCost method and print the result. Keep track of the total shipping cost for all Packages in the array, and display this total when the loop terminates.

12.14 *(Polymorphic Banking Program Using Account Hierarchy)* Develop a polymorphic banking application using the Account hierarchy created in Exercise 11.9. Create an array of Account references to SavingsAccount and CheckingAccount objects. For each Account in the array, allow the user to specify an amount of money to withdraw from the Account using method Debit and an amount of money to deposit into the Account using method Credit. As you process each Account, determine its type. If an Account is a SavingsAccount, calculate the amount of interest owed to the Account using method CalculateInterest, then add the interest to the account balance using method Credit. After processing an Account, print the updated account balance obtained by using base-class property Balance.

Making a Difference Exercise

12.15 *(CarbonFootprint Interface: Polymorphism)* Using interfaces, as you learned in this chapter, you can specify similar behaviors for possibly disparate classes. Governments and companies worldwide are becoming increasingly concerned with carbon footprints (annual releases of carbon dioxide into the atmosphere) from buildings burning various types of fuels for heat, vehicles burning fuels for power, and the like. Many scientists blame these greenhouse gases for the phenomenon called global warming. Create three small classes unrelated by inheritance—classes Building, Car and Bicycle. Write an interface ICarbonFootprint with a GetCarbonFootprint method. Have each of your classes implement that interface, so that its GetCarbonFootprint method calculates an appropriate carbon footprint for that class (check out a few websites that explain how to calculate carbon footprints). Write an application that creates objects of each of the three classes, places references to those objects in List<CarbonFootprint>, then iterates through the List, polymorphically invoking each object's GetCarbonFootprint method.

Exception Handling:
A Deeper Look

It is common sense to take a method and try it. If it fails, admit it frankly and try another. But above all, try something.
—Franklin Delano Roosevelt

O! throw away the worser part of it, And live the purer with the other half.
—William Shakespeare

If they're running and they don't look where they're going I have to come out from somewhere and catch them.
—J. D. Salinger

Objectives

In this chapter you'll learn:

- What exceptions are and how they're handled.

- When to use exception handling.

- To use **try** blocks to delimit code in which exceptions might occur.

- To **throw** exceptions to indicate a problem.

- To use **catch** blocks to specify exception handlers.

- To use the **finally** block to release resources.

- The .NET exception class hierarchy.

- **Exception** properties.

- To create user-defined exceptions.

13.1 Introduction

In this chapter, we take a deeper look at **exception handling**. As you know from Section 8.4, an **exception** indicates that a problem occurred during a program's execution. The name "exception" comes from the fact that, although the problem can occur, it occurs infrequently. If the "rule" is that a statement normally executes correctly, then the occurrence of a problem represents the "exception to the rule." As we showed in Section 8.4 and in Chapter 10, exception handling enables you to create applications that can handle exceptions—in many cases allowing a program to continue executing as if no problems were encountered. More severe problems may prevent a program from continuing normal execution, instead requiring the program to notify the user of the problem, then terminate in a controlled manner. The features presented in this chapter enable you to write clear, **robust** and more **fault-tolerant programs** (i.e., programs that are able to deal with problems that may arise and continue executing). The style and details of C# exception handling are based in part on the work of Andrew Koenig and Bjarne Stroustrup. "Best practices" for exception handling in Visual C# are specified in the Visual Studio documentation.[1]

After reviewing exception-handling concepts and basic exception-handling techniques, we overview .NET's exception-handling class hierarchy. Programs typically request and release resources (such as files on disk) during program execution. Often, the supply of these resources is limited, or the resources can be used by only one program at a time. We demonstrate a part of the exception-handling mechanism that enables a program to use a resource, then guarantee that it will be released for use by other programs, even if an exception occurs. We show several properties of class System.Exception (the base class of all exception classes) and discuss how you can create and use your own exception classes.

13.2 Example: Divide by Zero without Exception Handling

Let's revisit what happens when errors arise in a console application that does not use exception handling. Figure 13.1 inputs two integers from the user, then divides the first in-

---

1. "Best Practices for Handling Exceptions [C#]," *.NET Framework Developer's Guide*, Visual Studio .NET Online Help. Available at msdn.microsoft.com/en-us/library/seyhszts.aspx.

teger by the second using integer division to obtain an int result. In this example, an exception is **thrown** (i.e., an exception occurs) when a method detects a problem and is unable to handle it.

Running the Application

In most of our examples, the application appears to run the same with or without debugging. As we discuss shortly, the example in Fig. 13.1 might cause errors, depending on the user's input. If you run this application using the **Debug > Start Debugging** menu option, the program pauses at the line where an exception occurs, displays the Exception Assistant and allows you to analyze the current state of the program and debug it. We discuss the Exception Assistant in Section 13.3.3. We discuss debugging in detail in Appendix G.

In this example, we do not wish to debug the application; we simply want to see what happens when errors arise. For this reason, we execute this application from a **Command**

```
 1   // Fig. 13.1: DivideByZeroNoExceptionHandling.cs
 2   // Integer division without exception handling.
 3   using System;
 4
 5   class DivideByZeroNoExceptionHandling
 6   {
 7      static void Main()
 8      {
 9         // get numerator and denominator
10         Console.Write( "Please enter an integer numerator: " );
11         int numerator = Convert.ToInt32( Console.ReadLine() );
12         Console.Write( "Please enter an integer denominator: " );
13         int denominator = Convert.ToInt32( Console.ReadLine() );
14
15         // divide the two integers, then display the result
16         int result = numerator / denominator;
17         Console.WriteLine( "\nResult: {0:D} / {1:D} = {2:D}",
18            numerator, denominator, result );
19      } // end Main
20   } // end class DivideByZeroNoExceptionHandling
```

```
Please enter an integer numerator: 100
Please enter an integer denominator: 7

Result: 100 / 7 = 14
```

```
Please enter an integer numerator: 100
Please enter an integer denominator: 0

Unhandled Exception: System.DivideByZeroException:
   Attempted to divide by zero.
   at DivideByZeroNoExceptionHandling.Main()
      in C:\examples\ch13\Fig13_01\DivideByZeroNoExceptionHandling\
      DivideByZeroNoExceptionHandling\
      DivideByZeroNoExceptionHandling.cs:line 16
```

Fig. 13.1 | Integer division without exception handling. (Part 1 of 2.)

```
Please enter an integer numerator: 100
Please enter an integer denominator: hello

Unhandled Exception: System.FormatException:
   Input string was not in a correct format.
   at System.Number.StringToNumber(String str, NumberStyles options,
      NumberBuffer& number, NumberFormatInfo info, Boolean parseDecimal)
   at System.Number.ParseInt32(String s, NumberStyles style,
      NumberFormatInfo info)
   at DivideByZeroNoExceptionHandling.Main()
      in C:\examples\ch13\Fig13_01\DivideByZeroNoExceptionHandling\
      DivideByZeroNoExceptionHandling\
      DivideByZeroNoExceptionHandling.cs:line 13
```

Fig. 13.1 | Integer division without exception handling. (Part 2 of 2.)

Prompt window. Select **Start > All Programs > Accessories > Command Prompt** to open a **Command Prompt** window, then use the cd command to change to the application's Debug directory. For example, if this application resides in the directory C:\examples\ ch13\Fig13_01\DivideByZeroNoExceptionHandling on your system, you will type

```
cd /d C:\examples\ch13\Fig13_01\DivideByZeroNoExceptionHandling\
   DivideByZeroNoExceptionHandling\bin\Debug
```

in the **Command Prompt**, then press *Enter* to change to the application's Debug directory. To execute the application, type

```
DivideByZeroNoExceptionHandling.exe
```

in the **Command Prompt**, then press *Enter*. If an error arises during execution, a dialog is displayed indicating that the application encountered a problem and needs to close. In Windows Vista and Windows 7, the system tries to find a solution to the problem, then asks you to choose between looking online for a solution to the problem and closing the program. [*Note:* On some systems a **Just-In-Time Debugging** dialog is displayed instead. If this occurs, simply click the **No** button to dismiss the dialog.] At this point, an error message describing the problem is displayed in the **Command Prompt**. We formatted the error messages in Fig. 13.1 for readability. [*Note:* Selecting **Debug > Start Without Debugging** (or *<Ctrl> F5*) to run the application from Visual Studio executes the application's so-called release version. The error messages produced by this version of the application may differ from those shown in Fig. 13.1, because of optimizations that the compiler performs to create an application's release version.]

Analyzing the Results

The first sample execution shows a successful division. In the second, the user enters 0 as the denominator. Several lines of information are displayed in response to the invalid input. This information—known as a **stack trace**—includes the name of the exception class (System.DivideByZeroException) in a message indicating the problem that occurred and the path of execution that led to the exception, method by method. This information helps you debug a program. The first line of the error message specifies that a DivideByZeroException occurred. When a program divides an integer by 0, the CLR throws a **DivideByZeroException** (namespace System). The text after the name of the exception,

"`Attempted to divide by zero`," indicates why this exception occurred. Division by zero is not allowed in integer arithmetic. [*Note:* Division by zero with floating-point values *is* allowed and results in the value infinity—represented by either constant **Double.PositiveInfinity** or constant **Double.NegativeInfinity**, depending on whether the numerator is positive or negative. These values are displayed as `Infinity` or `-Infinity`. If both the numerator and denominator are zero, the result of the calculation is the constant **Double.NaN** ("not a number"), which is returned when a calculation's result is undefined.]

Each "at" line in a stack trace indicates a line of code in the particular method that was executing when the exception occurred. The "at" line contains the namespace, class and method in which the exception occurred (`DivideByZeroNoExceptionHandling.Main`), the location and name of the file containing the code (`C:\examples\ch13\Fig13_01\DivideByZeroNoExceptionHandling\DivideByZeroNoExceptionHandling\DivideByZeroNoExceptionHandling.cs`) and the line number (`:line 16`) where the exception occurred. In this case, the stack trace indicates that the `DivideByZeroException` occurred when the program was executing line 16 of method `Main`. The first "at" line in the stack trace indicates the exception's **throw point**—the initial point at which the exception occurred (i.e., line 16 in `Main`). This information makes it easy for you to see where the exception originated, and what method calls were made to get to that point in the program.

In the third sample execution, the user enters the string `"hello"` as the denominator. This causes a `FormatException`, and another stack trace is displayed. Our earlier examples that read numeric values from the user assumed that the user would input an integer value, but a noninteger value could be entered. A **FormatException** (namespace `System`) occurs, for example, when `Convert` method `ToInt32` receives a string that does not represent a valid integer. Starting from the last "at" line in the stack trace, we see that the exception was detected in line 13 of method `Main`. The stack trace also shows the other methods that led to the exception being thrown. To perform its task, `Convert.ToInt32` calls method `Number.ParseInt32`, which in turn calls `Number.StringToNumber`. The throw point occurs in `Number.StringToNumber`, as indicated by the first "at" line in the stack trace. Method `Convert.ToInt32` is not in the stack trace because the compiler optimized this call out of the code—all it does forward its arguments to `Number.ParseInt32`.

In the sample executions in Fig. 13.1, the program terminates when exceptions occur and stack traces are displayed. This does not always happen—sometimes a program may continue executing even though an exception has occurred and a stack trace has been printed. In such cases, the application may produce incorrect results. The next section demonstrates how to handle exceptions to enable the program to run to normal completion.

13.3 Example: Handling `DivideByZeroExceptions` and `FormatExceptions`

Now, let's consider a simple example of exception handling. The application in Fig. 13.2 uses exception handling to process any `DivideByZeroExceptions` and `FormatExceptions` that might arise. The application reads two integers from the user (lines 18–21). Assuming that the user provides integers as input and does not specify 0 as the denominator for the division, line 25 performs the division and lines 28–29 display the result. However, if the user inputs a noninteger value or supplies 0 as the denominator, an exception occurs. This program demonstrates how to **catch** and **handle** such exceptions—in this case, displaying an error message and allowing the user to enter another set of values.

```
1   // Fig. 13.2: DivideByZeroExceptionHandling.cs
2   // FormatException and DivideByZeroException handlers.
3   using System;
4
5   class DivideByZeroExceptionHandling
6   {
7      static void Main( string[] args )
8      {
9         bool continueLoop = true; // determines whether to keep looping
10
11        do
12        {
13           // retrieve user input and calculate quotient
14           try
15           {
16              // Convert.ToInt32 generates FormatException
17              // if argument cannot be converted to an integer
18              Console.Write( "Enter an integer numerator: " );
19              int numerator = Convert.ToInt32( Console.ReadLine() );
20              Console.Write( "Enter an integer denominator: " );
21              int denominator = Convert.ToInt32( Console.ReadLine() );
22
23              // division generates DivideByZeroException
24              // if denominator is 0
25              int result = numerator / denominator;
26
27              // display result
28              Console.WriteLine( "\nResult: {0} / {1} = {2}",
29                 numerator, denominator, result );
30              continueLoop = false;
31           } // end try
32           catch ( FormatException formatException )
33           {
34              Console.WriteLine( "\n" + formatException.Message );
35              Console.WriteLine(
36                 "You must enter two integers. Please try again.\n" );
37           } // end catch
38           catch ( DivideByZeroException divideByZeroException )
39           {
40              Console.WriteLine( "\n" + divideByZeroException.Message );
41              Console.WriteLine(
42                 "Zero is an invalid denominator. Please try again.\n" );
43           } // end catch
44        } while ( continueLoop ); // end do...while
45     } // end Main
46  } // end class DivideByZeroExceptionHandling
```

```
Please enter an integer numerator: 100
Please enter an integer denominator: 7

Result: 100 / 7 = 14
```

Fig. 13.2 | FormatException and DivideByZeroException handlers. (Part 1 of 2.)

```
Enter an integer numerator: 100
Enter an integer denominator: 0

Attempted to divide by zero.
Zero is an invalid denominator. Please try again.

Enter an integer numerator: 100
Enter an integer denominator: 7

Result: 100 / 7 = 14
```

```
Enter an integer numerator: 100
Enter an integer denominator: hello

Input string was not in a correct format.
You must enter two integers. Please try again.

Enter an integer numerator: 100
Enter an integer denominator: 7

Result: 100 / 7 = 14
```

Fig. 13.2 | FormatException and DivideByZeroException handlers. (Part 2 of 2.)

Sample Outputs

Before we discuss the details of the program, let's consider the sample outputs in Fig. 13.2. The first sample output shows a successful calculation in which the user enters the numerator 100 and the denominator 7. The result (14) is an int, because integer division always yields an int result. The second sample output demonstrates the result of an attempt to divide by zero. In integer arithmetic, the CLR tests for division by zero and generates a DivideByZeroException if the denominator is zero. The program detects the exception and displays an error message indicating the attempt to divide by zero. The last sample output depicts the result of inputting a non-int value—in this case, the user enters "hello" as the denominator. The program attempts to convert the input strings to ints using method Convert.ToInt32 (lines 19 and 21). If an argument cannot be converted to an int, the method throws a FormatException. The program catches the exception and displays an error message indicating that the user must enter two ints.

Another Way to Convert Strings to Integers

Another way to validate the input is to use the **Int32.TryParse** method, which converts a string to an int value if possible. All of the numeric types have TryParse methods. The method requires two arguments—one is the string to parse and the other is the variable in which the converted value is to be stored. The method returns a bool value that's true only if the string was parsed successfully. If the string could not be converted, the value 0 is assigned to the second argument, which is passed by reference so its value can be modified in the calling method. Method TryParse can be used to validate input in code rather than allowing the code to throw an exception.

13.3.1 Enclosing Code in a try Block

Now we consider the user interactions and flow of control that yield the results shown in the sample output windows. Lines 14–31 define a **try block** enclosing the code that might throw exceptions, as well as the code that's skipped when an exception occurs. For example, the program should not display a new result (lines 28–29) unless the calculation in line 25 completes successfully.

The user inputs values that represent the numerator and denominator. The two statements that read the ints (lines 19 and 21) call method `Convert.ToInt32` to convert strings to int values. This method throws a `FormatException` if it cannot convert its string argument to an int. If lines 19 and 21 convert the values properly (i.e., no exceptions occur), then line 25 divides the numerator by the denominator and assigns the result to variable result. If denominator is 0, line 25 causes the CLR to throw a `DivideByZero-Exception`. If line 25 does not cause an exception to be thrown, then lines 28–29 display the result of the division.

13.3.2 Catching Exceptions

Exception-handling code appears in a **catch block**. In general, when an exception occurs in a try block, a corresponding catch block catches the exception and handles it. The try block in this example is followed by two catch blocks—one that handles a `Format-Exception` (lines 32–37) and one that handles a `DivideByZeroException` (lines 38–43). A catch block specifies an exception parameter representing the exception that the catch block can handle. The catch block can use the parameter's identifier (which you choose) to interact with a caught exception object. If there's no need to use the exception object in the catch block, the exception parameter's identifier can be omitted. The type of the catch's parameter is the type of the exception that the catch block handles. Optionally, you can include a catch block that does not specify an exception type—such a catch block (known as a **general catch clause**) catches all exception types. At least one catch block and/or a **finally block** (discussed in Section 13.5) must immediately follow a try block.

In Fig. 13.2, the first catch block catches `FormatExceptions` (thrown by method `Convert.ToInt32`), and the second catch block catches `DivideByZeroExceptions` (thrown by the CLR). If an exception occurs, the program executes only the first matching catch block. Both exception handlers in this example display an error-message dialog. After either catch block terminates, program control continues with the first statement after the last catch block (the end of the method, in this example). We'll soon take a deeper look at how this flow of control works in exception handling.

13.3.3 Uncaught Exceptions

An **uncaught exception** (or **unhandled exception**) is an exception for which there's no matching catch block. You saw the results of uncaught exceptions in the second and third outputs of Fig. 13.1. Recall that when exceptions occur in that example, the application terminates early (after displaying the exception's stack trace). The result of an uncaught exception depends on how you execute the program—Fig. 13.1 demonstrated the results of an uncaught exception when an application is executed in a **Command Prompt**. If you run the application from Visual Studio with debugging, and the runtime environment detects an uncaught exception, the application pauses, and a window called the **Exception Assistant** appears indicating where the exception occurred, the type of the exception and links to helpful information on handling the exception. Figure 13.3 shows the Exception Assistant that's displayed if the user attempts to divide by zero in the application of Fig. 13.1.

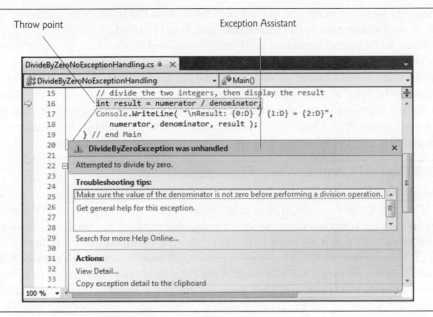

Throw point   Exception Assistant

Fig. 13.3 | Exception Assistant.

13.3.4 Termination Model of Exception Handling

When a method called in a program or the CLR detects a problem, the method or the CLR throws an exception. Recall that the point in the program at which an exception occurs is called the throw point—this is an important location for debugging purposes (as we demonstrate in Section 13.7). If an exception occurs in a try block (such as a FormatException being thrown as a result of the code in lines 19 and 21 in Fig. 13.2), the try block terminates immediately, and program control transfers to the first of the following catch blocks in which the exception parameter's type matches the type of the thrown exception. In Fig. 13.2, the first catch block catches FormatExceptions (which occur if input of an invalid type is entered); the second catch block catches DivideByZeroExceptions (which occur if an attempt is made to divide by zero). After the exception is handled, program control does not return to the throw point because the try block has expired (which also causes any of its local variables to go out of scope). Rather, control resumes after the last catch block. This is known as the **termination model of exception handling**. [*Note:* Some languages use the **resumption model of exception handling**, in which, after an exception is handled, control resumes just after the throw point.]

If no exceptions occur in the try block, the program of Fig. 13.2 successfully completes the try block by ignoring the catch blocks in lines 32–37 and 38–43, and passing line 43. Then the program executes the first statement following the try and catch blocks. In this example, the program reaches the end of the do...while loop (line 44), so the method terminates, and the program awaits the next user interaction.

The try block and its corresponding catch and finally blocks together form a **try statement**. It's important not to confuse the terms "try block" and "try statement"—the term "try block" refers to the block of code following the keyword try (but before any catch or finally blocks), while the term "try statement" includes all the code from the opening `try` keyword to the end of the last `catch` or `finally` block. This includes the `try` block, as well as any associated `catch` blocks and `finally` block.

When a `try` block terminates, local variables defined in the block go out of scope. If a `try` block terminates due to an exception, the CLR searches for the first `catch` block that can process the type of exception that occurred. The CLR locates the matching `catch` by comparing the type of the thrown exception to each `catch`'s parameter type. A match occurs if the types are identical or if the thrown exception's type is a derived class of the `catch`'s parameter type. Once an exception is matched to a `catch` block, the code in that block executes and the other `catch` blocks in the `try` statement are ignored.

13.3.5 Flow of Control When Exceptions Occur

In the third sample output of Fig. 13.2, the user inputs `hello` as the denominator. When line 21 executes, `Convert.ToInt32` cannot convert this `string` to an `int`, so the method throws a `FormatException` object to indicate that the method was unable to convert the `string` to an `int`. When the exception occurs, the `try` block expires (terminates). Next, the CLR attempts to locate a matching `catch` block. A match occurs with the `catch` block in line 32, so the exception handler displays the exception's `Message` property (to retrieve the error message associated with the exception) and the program ignores all other exception handlers following the `try` block. Program control then continues with line 44.

Common Programming Error 13.1

Specifying a comma-separated list of parameters in a `catch` *block is a syntax error. A* `catch` *block can have at most one parameter.*

In the second sample output of Fig. 13.2, the user inputs 0 as the denominator. When the division in line 25 executes, a `DivideByZeroException` occurs. Once again, the `try` block terminates, and the program attempts to locate a matching `catch` block. In this case, the first `catch` block does not match—the exception type in the `catch`-handler declaration is not the same as the type of the thrown exception, and `FormatException` is not a base class of `DivideByZeroException`. Therefore the program continues to search for a matching `catch` block, which it finds in line 38. Line 40 displays the exception's `Message` property. Again, program control then continues with line 44.

13.4 .NET Exception Hierarchy

In C#, the exception-handling mechanism allows only objects of class **Exception** (namespace `System`) and its derived classes to be thrown and caught. Note, however, that C# programs may interact with software components written in other .NET languages (such as C++) that do not restrict exception types. The general `catch` clause can be used to catch such exceptions.

This section overviews several of the .NET Framework's exception classes and focuses exclusively on exceptions that derive from class `Exception`. In addition, we discuss how to determine whether a particular method throws exceptions.

13.4.1 Class `SystemException`

Class `Exception` (namespace `System`) is the base class of .NET's exception class hierarchy. An important derived class is **SystemException**. The CLR generates `SystemExceptions`.

Many of these can be avoided if applications are coded properly. For example, if a program attempts to access an **out-of-range array index**, the CLR throws an exception of type **IndexOutOfRangeException** (a derived class of SystemException). Similarly, an exception occurs when a program uses a reference-type variable to call a method when the reference has a value of null. This causes a **NullReferenceException** (another derived class of SystemException). You saw earlier in this chapter that a DivideByZeroException occurs in integer division when a program attempts to divide by zero.

Other exceptions thrown by the CLR include **OutOfMemoryException**, **StackOverflowException** and **ExecutionEngineException**, which are thrown when something goes wrong that causes the CLR to become unstable. Sometimes such exceptions cannot even be caught. It's best to simply log such exceptions, then terminate your application.

A benefit of the exception class hierarchy is that a catch block can catch exceptions of a particular type or—because of the *is-a* relationship of inheritance—can use a base-class type to catch exceptions in a hierarchy of related exception types. For example, Section 13.3.2 discussed the catch block with no parameter, which catches exceptions of all types (including those that are not derived from Exception). A catch block that specifies a parameter of type Exception can catch all exceptions that derive from Exception, because Exception is the base class of all exception classes. The advantage of this approach is that the exception handler can access the caught exception's information via the parameter in the catch. We'll say more about accessing exception information in Section 13.7.

Using inheritance with exceptions enables an catch block to catch related exceptions using a concise notation. A set of exception handlers could catch each derived-class exception type individually, but catching the base-class exception type is more concise. However, this technique makes sense only if the handling behavior is the same for a base class and all derived classes. Otherwise, catch each derived-class exception individually.

Common Programming Error 13.2

The compiler issues an error if a catch block that catches a base-class exception is placed before a catch block for any of that class's derived-class types. In this case, the base-class catch block would catch all base-class and derived-class exceptions, so the derived-class exception handler would never execute.

13.4.2 Determining Which Exceptions a Method Throws

How do we determine that an exception might occur in a program? For methods contained in the .NET Framework classes, read the detailed descriptions of the methods in the online documentation. If a method throws an exception, its description contains a section called **Exceptions** that specifies the types of exceptions the method throws and briefly describes what causes them. For an example, search for "Convert.ToInt32 method" in the Visual Studio online documentation. The **Exceptions** section of this method's web page indicates that method Convert.ToInt32 throws two exception types—FormatException and OverflowException—and describes the reason why each might occur. [*Note:* You can also find this information in the **Object Browser** described in Section 10.12.]

Software Engineering Observation 13.1

If a method throws exceptions, statements that invoke the method directly or indirectly should be placed in try blocks, and those exceptions should be caught and handled.

It's more difficult to determine when the CLR throws exceptions. Such information appears in the *C# Language Specification* (available from `bit.ly/CSharp4Spec`). This document defines C#'s syntax and specifies cases in which exceptions are thrown.

13.5 `finally` Block

Programs frequently request and release resources dynamically (i.e., at execution time). For example, a program that reads a file from disk first makes a file-open request (as we'll see in Chapter 17, Files and Streams). If that request succeeds, the program reads the contents of the file. Operating systems typically prevent more than one program from manipulating a file at once. Therefore, when a program finishes processing a file, the program should close the file (i.e., release the resource) so other programs can use it. If the file is not closed, a **resource leak** occurs. In such a case, the file resource is not available to other programs, possibly because a program using the file has not closed it.

In programming languages such as C and C++, in which the programmer is responsible for dynamic memory management, the most common type of resource leak is a **memory leak**. A memory leak occurs when a program allocates memory (as C# programmers do via keyword `new`), but does not deallocate the memory when it's no longer needed. Normally, this is not an issue in C#, because the CLR performs garbage collection of memory that's no longer needed by an executing program (Section 10.8). However, other kinds of resource leaks (such as unclosed files) can occur.

Error-Prevention Tip 13.1
The CLR does not completely eliminate memory leaks. The CLR will not garbage collect an object until the program contains no more references to that object, and even then there may be a delay until the memory is required. Thus, memory leaks can occur if you inadvertently keep references to unwanted objects.

Moving Resource-Release Code to a `finally` Block

Typically, exceptions occur when processing resources that require explicit release. For example, a program that processes a file might receive `IOExceptions` during the processing. For this reason, file-processing code normally appears in a `try` block. Regardless of whether a program experiences exceptions while processing a file, the program should close the file when it's no longer needed. Suppose a program places all resource-request and resource-release code in a `try` block. If no exceptions occur, the `try` block executes normally and releases the resources after using them. However, if an exception occurs, the `try` block may expire before the resource-release code can execute. We could duplicate all the resource-release code in each of the `catch` blocks, but this would make the code more difficult to modify and maintain. We could also place the resource-release code after the `try` statement; however, if the `try` block terminated due to a return statement, code following the `try` statement would never execute.

To address these problems, C#'s exception-handling mechanism provides the `finally` block, which is guaranteed to execute regardless of whether the `try` block executes successfully or an exception occurs. This makes the `finally` block an ideal location in which to place resource-release code for resources that are acquired and manipulated in the corresponding `try` block. If the `try` block executes successfully, the `finally` block executes immediately after the `try` block terminates. If an exception occurs in the `try` block, the finally block executes immediately after a catch block completes. If the exception is not caught by a catch block associated with the try block, or if a catch block associated with the try block throws an exception itself, the finally block executes before the exception is processed by the next enclosing try block, which could be in the calling method. By placing the resource-release code in a finally block, we ensure that even if the program terminates due to an uncaught exception, the resource will be deallocated. Local variables in a try block cannot be accessed in the corresponding finally block. For this reason, variables that must be accessed in both a try block, and its corresponding finally block should be declared before the try block.

Error-Prevention Tip 13.2

A finally block typically contains code to release resources acquired in the corresponding try block, which makes the finally block an effective mechanism for eliminating resource leaks.

Performance Tip 13.1

As a rule, resources should be released as soon as they're no longer needed in a program. This makes them available for reuse promptly.

If one or more catch blocks follow a try block, the finally block is optional. However, if no catch blocks follow a try block, a finally block must appear immediately after the try block. If any catch blocks follow a try block, the finally block (if there is one) appears *after* the last catch block. Only whitespace and comments can separate the blocks in a try statement.

Demonstrating the finally Block

The application in Fig. 13.4 demonstrates that the finally block always executes, regardless of whether an exception occurs in the corresponding try block. The program consists of method Main (lines 8–47) and four other methods that Main invokes to demonstrate finally. These methods are DoesNotThrowException (lines 50–67), ThrowException-WithCatch (lines 70–89), ThrowExceptionWithoutCatch (lines 92–108) and ThrowExceptionCatchRethrow (lines 111–136).

```
 1  // Fig. 13.4: UsingExceptions.cs
 2  // Using finally blocks.
 3  // finally blocks always execute, even when no exception occurs.
 4  using System;
 5
 6  class UsingExceptions
 7  {
 8     static void Main()
 9     {
10        // Case 1: No exceptions occur in called method
11        Console.WriteLine( "Calling DoesNotThrowException" );
12        DoesNotThrowException();
13
14        // Case 2: Exception occurs and is caught in called method
15        Console.WriteLine( "\nCalling ThrowExceptionWithCatch" );
```

Fig. 13.4 | finally blocks always execute, even when no exception occurs. (Part 1 of 4.)

```
16              ThrowExceptionWithCatch();
17
18              // Case 3: Exception occurs, but is not caught in called method
19              // because there is no catch block.
20              Console.WriteLine( "\nCalling ThrowExceptionWithoutCatch" );
21
22              // call ThrowExceptionWithoutCatch
23              try
24              {
25                  ThrowExceptionWithoutCatch();
26              } // end try
27              catch
28              {
29                  Console.WriteLine( "Caught exception from " +
30                      "ThrowExceptionWithoutCatch in Main" );
31              } // end catch
32
33              // Case 4: Exception occurs and is caught in called method,
34              // then rethrown to caller.
35              Console.WriteLine( "\nCalling ThrowExceptionCatchRethrow" );
36
37              // call ThrowExceptionCatchRethrow
38              try
39              {
40                  ThrowExceptionCatchRethrow();
41              } // end try
42              catch
43              {
44                  Console.WriteLine( "Caught exception from " +
45                      "ThrowExceptionCatchRethrow in Main" );
46              } // end catch
47          } // end method Main
48
49          // no exceptions thrown
50          static void DoesNotThrowException()
51          {
52              // try block does not throw any exceptions
53              try
54              {
55                  Console.WriteLine( "In DoesNotThrowException" );
56              } // end try
57              catch
58              {
59                  Console.WriteLine( "This catch never executes" );
60              } // end catch
61              finally
62              {
63                  Console.WriteLine( "finally executed in DoesNotThrowException" );
64              } // end finally
65
66              Console.WriteLine( "End of DoesNotThrowException" );
67          } // end method DoesNotThrowException
68
```

Fig. 13.4 | finally blocks always execute, even when no exception occurs. (Part 2 of 4.)

```
69      // throws exception and catches it locally
70      static void ThrowExceptionWithCatch()
71      {
72         // try block throws exception
73         try
74         {
75            Console.WriteLine( "In ThrowExceptionWithCatch" );
76            throw new Exception( "Exception in ThrowExceptionWithCatch" );
77         } // end try
78         catch ( Exception exceptionParameter )
79         {
80            Console.WriteLine( "Message: " + exceptionParameter.Message );
81         } // end catch
82         finally
83         {
84            Console.WriteLine(
85               "finally executed in ThrowExceptionWithCatch" );
86         } // end finally
87
88         Console.WriteLine( "End of ThrowExceptionWithCatch" );
89      } // end method ThrowExceptionWithCatch
90
91      // throws exception and does not catch it locally
92      static void ThrowExceptionWithoutCatch()
93      {
94         // throw exception, but do not catch it
95         try
96         {
97            Console.WriteLine( "In ThrowExceptionWithoutCatch" );
98            throw new Exception( "Exception in ThrowExceptionWithoutCatch" );
99         } // end try
100        finally
101        {
102           Console.WriteLine( "finally executed in " +
103              "ThrowExceptionWithoutCatch" );
104        } // end finally
105
106        // unreachable code; logic error
107        Console.WriteLine( "End of ThrowExceptionWithoutCatch" );
108     } // end method ThrowExceptionWithoutCatch
109
110     // throws exception, catches it and rethrows it
111     static void ThrowExceptionCatchRethrow()
112     {
113        // try block throws exception
114        try
115        {
116           Console.WriteLine( "In ThrowExceptionCatchRethrow" );
117           throw new Exception( "Exception in ThrowExceptionCatchRethrow" );
118        } // end try
119        catch ( Exception exceptionParameter )
120        {
121           Console.WriteLine( "Message: " + exceptionParameter.Message );
```

Fig. 13.4 | finally blocks always execute, even when no exception occurs. (Part 3 of 4.)

```
122
123            // rethrow exception for further processing
124            throw;
125
126            // unreachable code; logic error
127         } // end catch
128         finally
129         {
130            Console.WriteLine( "finally executed in " +
131               "ThrowExceptionCatchRethrow" );
132         } // end finally
133
134         // any code placed here is never reached
135         Console.WriteLine( "End of ThrowExceptionCatchRethrow" );
136      } // end method ThrowExceptionCatchRethrow
137   } // end class UsingExceptions
```

```
Calling DoesNotThrowException
In DoesNotThrowException
finally executed in DoesNotThrowException
End of DoesNotThrowException

Calling ThrowExceptionWithCatch
In ThrowExceptionWithCatch
Message: Exception in ThrowExceptionWithCatch
finally executed in ThrowExceptionWithCatch
End of ThrowExceptionWithCatch

Calling ThrowExceptionWithoutCatch
In ThrowExceptionWithoutCatch
finally executed in ThrowExceptionWithoutCatch
Caught exception from ThrowExceptionWithoutCatch in Main

Calling ThrowExceptionCatchRethrow
In ThrowExceptionCatchRethrow
Message: Exception in ThrowExceptionCatchRethrow
finally executed in ThrowExceptionCatchRethrow
Caught exception from ThrowExceptionCatchRethrow in Main
```

Fig. 13.4 | `finally` blocks always execute, even when no exception occurs. (Part 4 of 4.)

Line 12 of Main invokes method DoesNotThrowException. This method's try block outputs a message (line 55). Because the try block does not throw any exceptions, program control ignores the catch block (lines 57–60) and executes the finally block (lines 61–64), which outputs a message. At this point, program control continues with the first statement after the close of the finally block (line 66), which outputs a message indicating that the end of the method has been reached. Then, program control returns to Main.

Throwing Exceptions Using the throw Statement

Line 16 of Main invokes method ThrowExceptionWithCatch (lines 70–89), which begins in its try block (lines 73–77) by outputting a message. Next, the try block creates an Exception object and uses a **throw statement** to throw it (line 76). Executing the throw statement indicates that a problem has occurred in the code. As you've seen in earlier chapters, you can throw exceptions by using the throw statement. Just as with exceptions thrown by the Framework Class Library's methods and the CLR, this indicates to client applications that an error has occurred. A throw statement specifies an object to be thrown. The operand of a throw statement can be of type Exception or of any type derived from class Exception.

The string passed to the constructor becomes the exception object's error message. When a throw statement in a try block executes, the try block expires immediately, and program control continues with the first matching catch block (lines 78–81) following the try block. In this example, the type thrown (Exception) matches the type specified in the catch, so line 80 outputs a message indicating the exception that occurred. Then, the finally block (lines 82–86) executes and outputs a message. At this point, program control continues with the first statement after the close of the finally block (line 88), which outputs a message indicating that the end of the method has been reached. Program control then returns to Main. In line 80, we use the exception object's Message property to retrieve the error message associated with the exception (i.e., the message passed to the Exception constructor). Section 13.7 discusses several properties of class Exception.

Lines 23–31 of Main define a try statement in which Main invokes method Throw-ExceptionWithoutCatch (lines 92–108). The try block enables Main to catch any exceptions thrown by ThrowExceptionWithoutCatch. The try block in lines 95–99 of ThrowExceptionWithoutCatch begins by outputting a message. Next, the try block throws an Exception (line 98) and expires immediately.

Normally, program control would continue at the first catch following this try block. However, this try block does not have any catch blocks. Therefore, the exception is not caught in method ThrowExceptionWithoutCatch. Program control proceeds to the finally block (lines 100–104), which outputs a message. At this point, program control returns to Main—any statements appearing after the finally block (e.g., line 107) do not execute. In this example, such statements could cause logic errors, because the exception thrown in line 98 is not caught. In Main, the catch block in lines 27–31 catches the exception and displays a message indicating that the exception was caught in Main.

Rethrowing Exceptions

Lines 38–46 of Main define a try statement in which Main invokes method Throw-ExceptionCatchRethrow (lines 111–136). The try statement enables Main to catch any exceptions thrown by ThrowExceptionCatchRethrow. The try statement in lines 114–132 of ThrowExceptionCatchRethrow begins by outputting a message. Next, the try block throws an Exception (line 117). The try block expires immediately, and program control continues at the first catch (lines 119–127) following the try block. In this example, the type thrown (Exception) matches the type specified in the catch, so line 121 outputs a message indicating where the exception occurred. Line 124 uses the throw statement to **rethrow** the exception. This indicates that the catch block performed partial processing of the exception and now is throwing the exception again (in this case, back to the method Main) for further processing. In general, it's considered better practice to throw a new exception and pass the original one to the new exception's constructor. This maintains all of the stack-trace information from the original exception. Rethrowing an exception loses the original exception's stack-trace information.

You can also rethrow an exception with a version of the throw statement which takes an operand that is the reference to the exception that was caught. It's important to note, however, that this form of throw statement resets the throw point, so the original throw point's stack-trace information is lost. Section 13.7 demonstrates using a throw statement with an operand from a catch block. In that section, you'll see that after an exception is caught, you can create and throw a different type of exception object from the catch block and you can include the original exception as part of the new exception object. Class library designers often do this to customize the exception types thrown from methods in their class libraries or to provide additional debugging information.

The exception handling in method ThrowExceptionCatchRethrow does not complete, because the throw statement in line 124 immediately terminates the catch block—if there were any code between line 124 and the end of the block, it would not execute. When line 124 executes, method ThrowExceptionCatchRethrow terminates and returns control to Main. Once again, the finally block (lines 128–132) executes and outputs a message before control returns to Main. When control returns to Main, the catch block in lines 42–46 catches the exception and displays a message indicating that the exception was caught. Then the program terminates.

Returning After a *finally* Block
The next statement to execute after a finally block terminates depends on the exception-handling state. If the try block successfully completes, or if a catch block catches and handles an exception, the program continues its execution with the next statement after the finally block. However, if an exception is not caught, or if a catch block rethrows an exception, program control continues in the next enclosing try block. The enclosing try could be in the calling method or in one of its callers. It also is possible to nest a try statement in a try block; in such a case, the outer try statement's catch blocks would process any exceptions that were not caught in the inner try statement. If a try block executes and has a corresponding finally block, the finally block executes even if the try block terminates due to a return statement. The return occurs after the execution of the finally block.

Common Programming Error 13.3
If an uncaught exception is awaiting processing when the finally block executes, and the finally block throws a new exception that's not caught in the finally block, the first exception is lost, and the new exception is passed to the next enclosing try block.

Error-Prevention Tip 13.3
When placing code that can throw an exception in a finally block, always enclose the code in a try statement that catches the appropriate exception types. This prevents the loss of any uncaught and rethrown exceptions that occur before the finally block executes.

Software Engineering Observation 13.2
Do not place try blocks around every statement that might throw an exception—this can make programs difficult to read. Instead, place one try block around a significant portion of code, and follow this try block with catch blocks that handle each possible exception. Then follow the catch blocks with a single finally block. Use separate try blocks to distinguish between multiple statements that can throw the same exception type.

13.6 The using Statement
Typically resource-release code should be placed in a finally block to ensure that a resource is released, regardless of whether there were exceptions when the resource was used

in the corresponding `try` block. An alternative notation—the **using** statement (not to be confused with the `using` directive for using namespaces)—simplifies writing code in which you obtain a resource, use the resource in a `try` block and release the resource in a corresponding `finally` block. For example, a file-processing application (Chapter 17) could process a file with a `using` statement to ensure that the file is closed properly when it's no longer needed. The resource must be an object that implements the `IDisposable` interface and therefore has a `Dispose` method. The general form of a `using` statement is

```
using ( ExampleObject exampleObject = new ExampleObject() )
{
    exampleObject.SomeMethod();
}
```

where `ExampleObject` is a class that implements the `IDisposable` interface. This code creates an object of type `ExampleObject` and uses it in a statement, then calls its `Dispose` method to release any resources used by the object. The `using` statement implicitly places the code in its body in a `try` block with a corresponding `finally` block that calls the object's `Dispose` method. For instance, the preceding code is equivalent to

```
{
    ExampleObject exampleObject = new ExampleObject();

    try
    {
        exampleObject.SomeMethod();
    }
    finally
    {
        if ( exampleObject != null )
            ( ( IDisposable ) exampleObject ).Dispose();
    }
}
```

The `if` statement ensures that `exampleObject` still references an object; otherwise, a `NullReferenceException` might occur.

13.7 Exception Properties

As we discussed in Section 13.4, exception types derive from class `Exception`, which has several properties. These frequently are used to formulate error messages indicating a caught exception. Two important properties are `Message` and **StackTrace**. Property `Message` stores the error message associated with an `Exception` object. This message can be a default message associated with the exception type or a customized message passed to an `Exception` object's constructor when the `Exception` object is thrown. Property `StackTrace` contains a `string` that represents the **method-call stack**. Recall that the runtime environment at all times keeps a list of open method calls that have been made but have not yet returned. The `StackTrace` represents the series of methods that have not finished processing at the time the exception occurs. If the debugging information that is generated by the compiler for the method is accessible to the IDE, the stack trace also includes line numbers; the first line number indicates the throw point, and subsequent line numbers indicate the locations from which the methods in the stack trace were called. PDB files are created by the IDE to maintain the debugging information for your projects.

Property *InnerException*

Another property used frequently by class-library programmers is **InnerException**. Typically, class library programmers "wrap" exception objects caught in their code so that they then can throw new exception types that are specific to their libraries. For example, a programmer implementing an accounting system might have some account-number processing code in which account numbers are input as strings but represented as ints in the code. Recall that a program can convert strings to int values with Convert.ToInt32, which throws a FormatException when it encounters an invalid number format. When an invalid account-number format occurs, the accounting-system programmer might wish to employ a different error message than the default message supplied by FormatException or might wish to indicate a new exception type, such as InvalidAccountNumberFormat-Exception. In such cases, you would provide code to catch the FormatException, then create an appropriate type of Exception object in the catch block and pass the original exception as one of the constructor arguments. The original exception object becomes the InnerException of the new exception object. When an InvalidAccountNumberFormat-Exception occurs in code that uses the accounting system library, the catch block that catches the exception can obtain a reference to the original exception via property Inner-Exception. Thus the exception indicates both that the user specified an invalid account number and that the problem was an invalid number format. If the InnerException property is null, this indicates that the exception was not caused by another exception.

Other *Exception* Properties

Class Exception provides other properties, including **HelpLink**, **Source** and **TargetSite**. Property HelpLink specifies the location of the help file that describes the problem that occurred. This property is null if no such file exists. Property Source specifies the name of the application or object that caused the exception. Property TargetSite specifies the method where the exception originated.

Demonstrating *Exception* Properties and Stack Unwinding

Our next example (Fig. 13.5) demonstrates properties Message, StackTrace and Inner-Exception of class Exception. In addition, the example introduces **stack unwinding**—when an exception is thrown but not caught in a particular scope, the method-call stack is "unwound," and an attempt is made to catch the exception in the next outer try block. We keep track of the methods on the call stack as we discuss property StackTrace and the stack-unwinding mechanism. To see the proper stack trace, you should execute this program using steps similar to those presented in Section 13.2.

```
1   // Fig. 13.5: Properties.cs
2   // Stack unwinding and Exception class properties.
3   // Demonstrates using properties Message, StackTrace and InnerException.
4   using System;
5
6   class Properties
7   {
8      static void Main()
9      {
```

Fig. 13.5 | Stack unwinding and Exception class properties. (Part 1 of 3.)

```
10          // call Method1; any Exception generated is caught
11          // in the catch block that follows
12          try
13          {
14              Method1();
15          } // end try
16          catch ( Exception exceptionParameter )
17          {
18              // output the string representation of the Exception, then output
19              // properties Message, StackTrace and InnerException
20              Console.WriteLine( "exceptionParameter.ToString: \n{0}\n",
21                  exceptionParameter );
22              Console.WriteLine( "exceptionParameter.Message: \n{0}\n",
23                  exceptionParameter.Message );
24              Console.WriteLine( "exceptionParameter.StackTrace: \n{0}\n",
25                  exceptionParameter.StackTrace );
26              Console.WriteLine( "exceptionParameter.InnerException: \n{0}\n",
27                  exceptionParameter.InnerException );
28          } // end catch
29      } // end method Main
30
31      // calls Method2
32      static void Method1()
33      {
34          Method2();
35      } // end method Method1
36
37      // calls Method3
38      static void Method2()
39      {
40          Method3();
41      } // end method Method2
42
43      // throws an Exception containing an InnerException
44      static void Method3()
45      {
46          // attempt to convert string to int
47          try
48          {
49              Convert.ToInt32( "Not an integer" );
50          } // end try
51          catch ( FormatException formatExceptionParameter )
52          {
53              // wrap FormatException in new Exception
54              throw new Exception( "Exception occurred in Method3",
55                  formatExceptionParameter );
56          } // end catch
57      } // end method Method3
58  } // end class Properties
```

```
exceptionParameter.ToString:
System.Exception: Exception occurred in Method3 --->
   System.FormatException: Input string was not in a correct format.
```

Fig. 13.5 | Stack unwinding and Exception class properties. (Part 2 of 3.)

```
    at System.Number.StringToNumber(String str, NumberStyles options,
        NumberBuffer& number, NumberFormatInfo info, Boolean parseDecimal)
    at System.Number.ParseInt32(String s, NumberStyles style,
        NumberFormatInfo info)
    at Properties.Method3() in C:\examples\ch13\Fig13_05\Properties\
        Properties\Properties.cs:line 49
    --- End of inner exception stack trace ---
    at Properties.Method3() in C:\examples\ch13\Fig13_05\Properties\
        Properties\Properties.cs:line 54
    at Properties.Method2() in C:\examples\ch13\Fig13_05\Properties\
        Properties\Properties.cs:line 40
    at Properties.Method1() in C:\examples\ch13\Fig13_05\Properties\
        Properties\Properties.cs:line 34
    at Properties.Main() in C:\examples\ch13\Fig13_05\Properties\
        Properties\Properties.cs:line 14

exceptionParameter.Message:
Exception occurred in Method3

exceptionParameter.StackTrace:
    at Properties.Method3() in C:\examples\ch13\Fig13_05\Properties\
        Properties\Properties.cs:line 54
    at Properties.Method2() in C:\examples\ch13\Fig13_05\Properties\
        Properties\Properties.cs:line 40
    at Properties.Method1() in C:\examples\ch13\Fig13_05\Properties\
        Properties\Properties.cs:line 34
    at Properties.Main() in C:\examples\ch13\Fig13_05\Properties\
        Properties\Properties.cs:line 14

exceptionParameter.InnerException:
System.FormatException: Input string was not in a correct format.
    at System.Number.StringToNumber(String str, NumberStyles options,
        NumberBuffer& number, NumberFormatInfo info, Boolean parseDecimal)
    at System.Number.ParseInt32(String s, NumberStyles style,
        NumberFormatInfo info)
    at Properties.Method3() in C:\examples\ch13\Fig13_05\Properties\
        Properties\Properties.cs:line 49
```

Fig. 13.5 | Stack unwinding and `Exception` class properties. (Part 3 of 3.)

Program execution begins with `Main`, which becomes the first method on the method-call stack. Line 14 of the `try` block in `Main` invokes `Method1` (declared in lines 32–35), which becomes the second method on the stack. If `Method1` throws an exception, the `catch` block in lines 16–28 handles the exception and outputs information about the exception that occurred. Line 34 of `Method1` invokes `Method2` (lines 38–41), which becomes the third method on the stack. Then line 40 of `Method2` invokes `Method3` (lines 44–57), which becomes the fourth method on the stack.

At this point, the method-call stack (from top to bottom) for the program is:

```
    Method3
    Method2
    Method1
    Main
```

The method called most recently (`Method3`) appears at the top of the stack; the first method called (`Main`) appears at the bottom. The `try` statement (lines 47–56) in `Method3` invokes method `Convert.ToInt32` (line 49), which attempts to convert a `string` to an `int`. At this point, `Convert.ToInt32` becomes the fifth and final method on the call stack.

Throwing an Exception with an InnerException

Because the argument to `Convert.ToInt32` is not in `int` format, line 49 throws a `Format-Exception` that's caught in line 51 of `Method3`. The exception terminates the call to `Convert.ToInt32`, so the method is removed (or unwound) from the method-call stack. The `catch` block in `Method3` then creates and throws an `Exception` object. The first argument to the `Exception` constructor is the custom error message for our example, "Exception occurred in Method3." The second argument is the `InnerException`—the `Format-Exception` that was caught. The `StackTrace` for this new exception object reflects the point at which the exception was thrown (lines 54–55). Now `Method3` terminates, because the exception thrown in the `catch` block is not caught in the method body. Thus, control returns to the statement that invoked `Method3` in the prior method in the call stack (`Method2`). This removes, or **unwinds**, `Method3` from the method-call stack.

When control returns to line 40 in `Method2`, the CLR determines that line 40 is not in a `try` block. Therefore the exception cannot be caught in `Method2`, and `Method2` terminates. This unwinds `Method2` from the call stack and returns control to line 34 in `Method1`.

Here again, line 34 is not in a `try` block, so `Method1` cannot catch the exception. The method terminates and is unwound from the call stack, returning control to line 14 in `Main`, which *is* located in a `try` block. The `try` block in `Main` expires and the `catch` block (lines 16–28) catches the exception. The `catch` block uses properties `Message`, `StackTrace` and `InnerException` to create the output. Stack unwinding continues until a `catch` block catches the exception or the program terminates.

Displaying Information About the Exception

The first block of output (which we reformatted for readability) in Fig. 13.5 contains the exception's `string` representation, which is returned from an implicit call to method `To-String`. The `string` begins with the name of the exception class followed by the `Message` property value. The next four items present the stack trace of the `InnerException` object. The remainder of the block of output shows the `StackTrace` for the exception thrown in `Method3`. The `StackTrace` represents the state of the method-call stack at the throw point of the exception, rather than at the point where the exception eventually is caught. Each `StackTrace` line that begins with "at" represents a method on the call stack. These lines indicate the method in which the exception occurred, the file in which the method resides and the line number of the throw point in the file. The inner-exception information includes the inner-exception stack trace.

Error-Prevention Tip 13.4

When catching and rethrowing an exception, provide additional debugging information in the rethrown exception. To do so, create an `Exception` object containing more specific debugging information, then pass the original caught exception to the new exception object's constructor to initialize the `InnerException` property.

The next block of output (two lines) simply displays the `Message` property's value (`Exception occurred in Method3`) of the exception thrown in `Method3`.

The third block of output displays the `StackTrace` property of the exception thrown in `Method3`. This `StackTrace` property contains the stack trace starting from line 54 in

Method3, because that's the point at which the Exception object was created and thrown. The stack trace always begins from the exception's throw point.

Finally, the last block of output displays the string representation of the Inner-Exception property, which includes the namespace and class name of the exception object, as well as its Message and StackTrace properties.

13.8 User-Defined Exception Classes

In many cases, you can use existing exception classes from the .NET Framework Class Library to indicate exceptions that occur in your programs. In some cases, however, you might wish to create new exception classes specific to the problems that occur in your programs. **User-defined exception classes** should derive directly or indirectly from class Exception of namespace System. When you create code that throws exceptions, they should be well documented, so that other developers who use your code will know how to handle them.

Good Programming Practice 13.1
Associating each type of malfunction with an appropriately named exception class improves program clarity.

Software Engineering Observation 13.3
Before creating a user-defined exception class, investigate the existing exceptions in the .NET Framework Class Library to determine whether an appropriate exception type already exists.

Class *NegativeNumberException*

Figures 13.6–13.7 demonstrate a user-defined exception class. NegativeNumberException (Fig. 13.6) represents exceptions that occur when a program performs an illegal operation on a negative number, such as attempting to calculate its square root.

```
1   // Fig. 13.6: NegativeNumberException.cs
2   // NegativeNumberException represents exceptions caused by
3   // illegal operations performed on negative numbers.
4   using System;
5
6   class NegativeNumberException : Exception
7   {
8      // default constructor
9      public NegativeNumberException()
10        : base( "Illegal operation for a negative number" )
11     {
12        // empty body
13     } // end default constructor
14
15     // constructor for customizing error message
16     public NegativeNumberException( string messageValue )
17        : base( messageValue )
18     {
```

Fig. 13.6 | NegativeNumberException represents exceptions caused by illegal operations performed on negative numbers. (Part 1 of 2.)

```
19          // empty body
20      } // end one-argument constructor
21
22      // constructor for customizing the exception's error
23      // message and specifying the InnerException object
24      public NegativeNumberException( string messageValue,
25          Exception inner )
26          : base( messageValue, inner )
27      {
28          // empty body
29      } // end two-argument constructor
30  } // end namespace SquareRootTest
```

Fig. 13.6 | NegativeNumberException represents exceptions caused by illegal operations performed on negative numbers. (Part 2 of 2.)

According to Microsoft's docuemtn on "Best Practices for Handling Exceptions" (bit.ly/ExceptionsBestPractices), user-defined exceptions should typically extend class Exception, have a class name that ends with "Exception" and define three constructors: a parameterless constructor; a constructor that receives a string argument (the error message); and a constructor that receives a string argument and an Exception argument (the error message and the inner-exception object). Defining these three constructors makes your exception class more flexible, allowing other programmers to easily use and extend it.

NegativeNumberExceptions most frequently occur during arithmetic operations, so it seems logical to derive class NegativeNumberException from class ArithmeticException. However, class ArithmeticException derives from class SystemException—the category of exceptions thrown by the CLR. Per Microsoft's best practices for exception handling, user-defined exception classes should inherit from Exception rather than SystemException. In this case, we could have used the built-in ArgumentException class, which is recommended in the best practices for invalid argument values. We create our own exception type here simply for demonstration purposes.

Class NegativeNumberException

Class SquareRootTest (Fig. 13.7) demonstrates our user-defined exception class. The application enables the user to input a numeric value, then invokes method SquareRoot (lines 40–48) to calculate the square root of that value. To perform this calculation, SquareRoot invokes class Math's Sqrt method, which receives a double value as its argument. Normally, if the argument is negative, method Sqrt returns NaN. In this program, we'd like to prevent the user from calculating the square root of a negative number. If the numeric value that the user enters is negative, method SquareRoot throws a NegativeNumberException (lines 44–45). Otherwise, SquareRoot invokes class Math's method Sqrt to compute the square root (line 47).

When the user inputs a value, the try statement (lines 14–34) attempts to invoke SquareRoot using the value input by the user. If the user input is not a number, a FormatException occurs, and the catch block in lines 25–29 processes the exception. If the user inputs a negative number, method SquareRoot throws a NegativeNumberException (lines 44–45); the catch block in lines 30–34 catches and handles this type of exception.

```csharp
1   // Fig. 13.7: SquareRootTest.cs
2   // Demonstrating a user-defined exception class.
3   using System;
4
5   class SquareRootTest
6   {
7      static void Main( string[] args )
8      {
9         bool continueLoop = true;
10
11        do
12        {
13           // catch any NegativeNumberException thrown
14           try
15           {
16              Console.Write(
17                 "Enter a value to calculate the square root of: " );
18              double inputValue = Convert.ToDouble( Console.ReadLine() );
19              double result = SquareRoot( inputValue );
20
21              Console.WriteLine( "The square root of {0} is {1:F6}\n",
22                 inputValue, result );
23              continueLoop = false;
24           } // end try
25           catch ( FormatException formatException )
26           {
27              Console.WriteLine( "\n" + formatException.Message );
28              Console.WriteLine( "Please enter a double value.\n" );
29           } // end catch
30           catch ( NegativeNumberException negativeNumberException )
31           {
32              Console.WriteLine( "\n" + negativeNumberException.Message );
33              Console.WriteLine( "Please enter a non-negative value.\n" );
34           } // end catch
35        } while ( continueLoop );
36     } // end Main
37
38     // computes square root of parameter; throws
39     // NegativeNumberException if parameter is negative
40     public static double SquareRoot( double value )
41     {
42        // if negative operand, throw NegativeNumberException
43        if ( value < 0 )
44           throw new NegativeNumberException(
45              "Square root of negative number not permitted" );
46        else
47           return Math.Sqrt( value ); // compute square root
48     } // end method SquareRoot
49  } // end class SquareRootTest
```

```
Enter a value to calculate the square root of: 30
The square root of 30 is 5.477226
```

Fig. 13.7 | Demonstrating a user-defined exception class. (Part 1 of 2.)

```
Enter a value to calculate the square root of: hello

Input string was not in a correct format.
Please enter a double value.

Enter a value to calculate the square root of: 25
The square root of 25 is 5.000000
```

```
Enter a value to calculate the square root of: -2

Square root of negative number not permitted
Please enter a non-negative value.

Enter a value to calculate the square root of: 2
The square root of 2 is 1.414214
```

Fig. 13.7 | Demonstrating a user-defined exception class. (Part 2 of 2.)

13.9 Wrap-Up

In this chapter, you learned how to use exception handling to deal with errors in an application. We demonstrated that exception handling enables you to remove error-handling code from the "main line" of the program's execution. You saw exception handling in the context of a divide-by-zero example. You learned how to use try blocks to enclose code that may throw an exception, and how to use catch blocks to deal with exceptions that may arise. We explained the termination model of exception handling, in which, after an exception is handled, program control does not return to the throw point. We discussed several important classes of the .NET Exception hierarchy, including Exception (from which user-defined exception classes are derived) and SystemException. Next you learned how to use the finally block to release resources whether or not an exception occurs, and how to throw and rethrow exceptions with the throw statement. We showed how the using statement can be used to automate the process of releasing a resource. You then learned how to obtain information about an exception using Exception properties Message, StackTrace and InnerException, and method ToString. You learned how to create your own exception classes. In the next two chapters, we present an in-depth treatment of graphical user interfaces. In these chapters and throughout the rest of the book, we use exception handling to make our examples more robust, while demonstrating new features of the language.

Summary

Section 13.1 Introduction
- An exception is an indication of a problem that occurs during a program's execution.
- Exception handling enables you to create applications that can resolve (or handle) exceptions.

Section 13.2 Example: Divide by Zero without Exception Handling
- An exception is thrown when a method or the CLR detects a problem and is unable to handle it.
- A stack trace includes the name of the exception in a descriptive message that indicates the problem that occurred and the complete method-call stack at the time the exception occurred.
- Division by zero is not allowed in integer arithmetic.

- Division by zero is allowed with floating-point values. Such a calculation results in the value infinity, which is represented by `Double.PositiveInfinity` or `Double.NegativeInfinity`, depending on whether the numerator is positive or negative. If both the numerator and denominator are zero, the result of the calculation is `Double.NaN`.

- When division by zero occurs in integer arithmetic, a `DivideByZeroException` is thrown.

- A `FormatException` occurs when `Convert` method `ToInt32` receives a string that does not represent a valid integer.

Section 13.3 Example: Handling `DivideByZeroException`s and `FormatException`s

- A `try` block encloses the code that might throw exceptions, as well as the code that should not execute if an exception occurs.

- A `catch` block can specify an identifier representing the exception that the `catch` block can handle. A general `catch` clause catches all exception types, but cannot access exception information.

- At least one `catch` block and/or a `finally` block must immediately follow the `try` block.

- An uncaught exception is an exception that occurs for which there's no matching `catch` block.

- When a method called in a program detects an exception, or when the CLR detects a problem, the method or the CLR throws an exception.

- The point in the program at which an exception occurs is called the throw point.

- If an exception occurs in a `try` block, the `try` block terminates immediately, and program control transfers to the first of the following `catch` blocks in which the exception parameter's type matches the type of the thrown exception.

- After an exception is handled, program control does not return to the throw point, because the `try` block has expired. Instead, control resumes after the `try` statement's last `catch` block. This is known as the termination model of exception handling.

- The `try` block and its corresponding `catch` and `finally` blocks together form a `try` statement.

- The CLR locates the matching `catch` by comparing the thrown exception's type to each `catch`'s exception-parameter type. A match occurs if the types are identical or if the thrown exception's type is a derived class of the exception-parameter type.

- Once an exception is matched to a `catch` block, the other `catch` blocks are ignored.

Section 13.4 .NET `Exception` Hierarchy

- The C# exception-handling mechanism allows objects only of class `Exception` and its derived classes to be thrown and caught.

- Class `Exception` of namespace `System` is the base class of the .NET Framework Class Library exception class hierarchy.

- The CLR generates `SystemException`s, which can occur at any point during the execution of the program. Many of these exceptions can be avoided if applications are coded properly.

- A benefit of using the exception class hierarchy is that a `catch` block can catch exceptions of a particular type or—because of the *is-a* relationship of inheritance—can use a base-class type to catch exceptions in a hierarchy of related exception types.

- A `catch` block that specifies an exception parameter of type `Exception` can catch all exceptions that derive from `Exception`, because `Exception` is the base class of all exception classes.

- Using inheritance with exceptions enables an exception handler to catch related exceptions.

Section 13.5 `finally` Block

- The most common type of resource leak is a memory leak.

- A memory leak occurs when a program allocates memory but does not deallocate it when it's no longer needed. Normally, this is not an issue in C#, because the CLR performs garbage collection of memory that's no longer needed by an executing program.

- C#'s exception-handling mechanism provides the `finally` block, which is guaranteed to execute if program control enters the corresponding `try` block.

- The `finally` block executes regardless of whether the corresponding `try` block executes successfully or an exception occurs. This makes the `finally` block an ideal location in which to place resource-release code for resources acquired and manipulated in the corresponding `try` block.

- If a `try` block executes successfully, the `finally` block executes immediately after the `try` block terminates. If an exception occurs in the `try` block, the `finally` block executes immediately after a `catch` block completes.

- If the exception is not caught by a `catch` block associated with the `try` block, or if a `catch` block associated with the `try` block throws an exception, the `finally` block executes before the exception is processed by the next enclosing `try` block (if there is one).

- A `throw` statement can rethrow an exception, indicating that a `catch` block performed partial processing of the exception and now is throwing the exception again for further processing.

- If a `try` block executes and has a corresponding `finally` block, the `finally` block always executes. The `return` occurs after the execution of the `finally` block.

Section 13.6 The *using* Statement
- The `using` statement simplifies writing code in which you obtain a resource, use the resource in a `try` block and release the resource in a corresponding `finally` block.

Section 13.7 *Exception Properties*
- Property `Message` of class `Exception` stores the error message associated with an `Exception` object.

- Property `StackTrace` of class `Exception` contains a `string` that represents the method-call stack.

- Another `Exception` property used frequently by class library programmers is `InnerException`. Typically, you use this property to "wrap" exception objects caught in your code, so that you then can throw new exception types specific to your libraries.

- When an exception is thrown but not caught in a particular scope, stack unwinding occurs and an attempt is made to catch the exception in the next outer `try` block.

Section 13.8 *User-Defined Exception Classes*
- User-defined exception classes should derive directly or indirectly from class `Exception` of namespace `System`.

- User-defined exceptions should typically extend `Exception`, have a class name that ends with "Exception" and define a parameterless constructor, a constructor that receives a `string` argument (the error message), and a constructor that receives a `string` argument and an `Exception` argument (the error message and the inner-exception object).

Terminology

catch an exception
catch block
divide by zero
DivideByZeroException class
error-processing code
exception
Exception Assistant

Exception class
exception handling
fault-tolerant program
finally block
FormatException class
general catch clause
handle an exception

HelpLink property of class Exception
IndexOutOfRangeException class
InnerException property of class Exception
memory leak
method-call stack
NullReferenceException class
out-of-range array index
resource leak
resumption model of exception handling
rethrow an exception
robust program
Source property of class Exception
stack trace
stack unwinding
StackTrace property of class Exception

SystemException class
TargetSite property of class Exception
termination model of exception handling
throw an exception
throw point
throw statement
try block
try statement
TryParse method of structure Int32
uncaught exception
unhandled exception
unwind a method from call stack
user-defined exception class
using statement

Self-Review Exercises

13.1 Fill in the blanks in each of the following statements:
a) A method is said to _____ an exception when it detects that a problem has occurred.
b) When present, the _____ block associated with a try block always executes.
c) Exception classes are derived from class _____.
d) The statement that throws an exception is called the _____ of the exception.
e) C# uses the _____ model of exception handling as opposed to the _____ model of exception handling.
f) An uncaught exception in a method causes the method to _____ from the method-call stack.
g) Method Convert.ToInt32 can throw a(n) _____ exception if its argument is not a valid integer value.

13.2 State whether each of the following is *true* or *false*. If *false*, explain why.
a) Exceptions always are handled in the method that initially detects the exception.
b) User-defined exception classes should extend class SystemException.
c) Accessing an out-of-bounds array index causes the CLR to throw an exception.
d) A finally block is optional after a try block that does not have any corresponding catch blocks.
e) A finally block is guaranteed to execute.
f) It's possible to return to the throw point of an exception using keyword return.
g) Exceptions can be rethrown.
h) Property Message of class Exception returns a string indicating the method from which the exception was thrown.

Answers to Self-Review Exercises

13.1 a) throw. b) finally. c) Exception. d) throw point. e) termination, resumption. f) unwind. g) FormatException.

13.2 a) False. Exceptions can be handled by other methods on the method-call stack. b) False. User-defined exception classes should typically extend class Exception. c) True. d) False. A try block that does not have any catch blocks requires a finally block. e) False. The finally block executes only if program control enters the corresponding try block. f) False. return causes control to return to the caller. g) True. h) False. Property Message of class Exception returns a string representing the error message.

Exercises

13.3 *(Exception Base Classes and Derived Classes)* Use inheritance to create an exception base class and various exception-derived classes. Write a program to demonstrate that the catch specifying the base class catches derived-class exceptions.

13.4 *(Catching Exceptions)* Write a program that demonstrates how various exceptions are caught with

```
catch ( Exception ex )
```

13.5 *(Order of Exception Handlers)* To demonstrate the importance of the order of exception handlers, write two programs, one with correct ordering of catch blocks (i.e., place the base-class exception handler after all derived-class exception handlers) and another with improper ordering (i.e., place the base-class exception handler before the derived-class exception handlers). What happens when you attempt to compile the second program?

13.6 *(Constructor Failure)* Exceptions can be used to indicate problems that occur when an object is being constructed. Write a program that shows a constructor passing information about constructor failure to an exception handler. The exception thrown also should contain the arguments sent to the constructor.

13.7 *(Rethrowing and Exception)* Write a program that demonstrates rethrowing an exception.

13.8 *(Not Catching Every Exception)* Write a program demonstrating that a method with its own try block does not have to catch every possible exception that occurs within the try block—some exceptions can slip through to, and be handled in, other scopes.

13.9 *(Exception from a Deeply Nested Method)* Write a program that throws an exception from a deeply nested method. The catch block should follow the try block that encloses the call chain. The exception caught should be one you defined yourself. In catching the exception, display the exception's message and stack trace.

13.10 *(FormatExceptions)* Create an application that inputs miles driven and gallons used, and calculates miles per gallon. The example should use exception handling to process the FormatExceptions that occur when converting the input strings to doubles. If invalid data is entered, display a message informing the user.

Graphical User Interfaces with Windows Forms: Part 1

14

... the wisest prophets make sure of the event first.
—Horace Walpole

...The user should feel in control of the computer; not the other way around. This is achieved in applications that embody three qualities: responsiveness, permissiveness, and consistency.
—Inside Macintosh, Volume 1
Apple Computer, Inc. 1985

All the better to see you with my dear.
—The Big Bad Wolf to Little Red Riding Hood

Objectives

In this chapter you'll learn:

- Design principles of graphical user interfaces (GUIs).

- How to create graphical user interfaces.

- How to process events in response to user interactions with GUI controls.

- The namespaces that contain the classes for GUI controls and event handling.

- How to create and manipulate various controls.

- How to add descriptive `ToolTip`s to GUI controls.

- How to process mouse and keyboard events.

14.1 Introduction

A graphical user interface (GUI) allows a user to interact visually with a program. A GUI (pronounced "GOO-ee") gives a program a distinctive "look" and "feel." Providing different applications with a consistent set of intuitive user-interface components enables users to become productive with each application faster.

 Look-and-Feel Observation 14.1
Consistent user interfaces enable a user to learn new applications more quickly because the applications have the same "look" and "feel."

As an example of a GUI, consider Fig. 14.1, which shows a Visual C# Express Edition window containing various GUI controls. Near the top of the window, there's a menu bar containing the menus **File**, **Edit**, **View**, **Project**, **Build**, **Debug**, **Data**, **Tools**, **Window**, and **Help**. Below the menu bar is a tool bar of buttons, each with a defined task, such as creating

Button   Tabs   Menu   Title bar   Menu bar   Tool bar

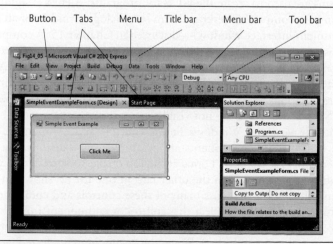

Fig. 14.1 | GUI controls in the Visual C# IDE window.

a new project or opening an existing project. There are two tabs below the tool bar—these present information in a tabbed view and allow users to switch between them. These controls form a user-friendly interface through which you have been interacting with the IDE.

GUIs are built from GUI controls (which are sometimes called **components** or **widgets**—short for **window gadgets**). GUI controls are objects that can display information on the screen or enable users to interact with an application via the mouse, keyboard or some other form of input (such as voice commands). Several common GUI controls are listed in Fig. 14.2—in the sections that follow and in Chapter 15, we discuss each of these in detail. Chapter 15 also explores the features and properties of additional GUI controls.

Control	Description
Label	Displays images or uneditable text.
TextBox	Enables the user to enter data via the keyboard. It can also be used to display editable or uneditable text.
Button	Triggers an event when clicked with the mouse.
CheckBox	Specifies an option that can be selected (checked) or unselected (not checked).
ComboBox	Provides a drop-down list of items from which the user can make a selection either by clicking an item in the list or by typing in a box.
ListBox	Provides a list of items from which the user can make a selection by clicking one or more items.
Panel	A container in which controls can be placed and organized.
NumericUpDown	Enables the user to select from a range of numeric input values.

Fig. 14.2 | Some basic GUI controls.

14.2 Windows Forms

Windows Forms are used to create the GUIs for programs. A Form is a graphical element that appears on your computer's desktop; it can be a dialog, a window or an **MDI window** (**multiple document interface window**)—discussed in Chapter 15. A component is an instance of a class that implements the **IComponent interface**, which defines the behaviors that components must implement, such as how the component is loaded. A control, such as a Button or Label, has a graphical representation at runtime. Some components lack graphical representations (e.g., class Timer of namespace System.Windows.Forms—see Chapter 15). Such components are not visible at run time.

Figure 14.3 displays the Windows Forms controls and components from the C# **Toolbox**. The controls and components are organized into categories by functionality. Selecting the category **All Windows Forms** at the top of the **Toolbox** allows you to view all the controls and components from the other tabs in one list (as shown in Fig. 14.3). In this chapter and the next, we discuss many of these controls and components. To add a control or component to a Form, select that control or component from the **Toolbox** and drag it on the Form. To deselect a control or component, select the **Pointer** item in the **Toolbox** (the icon at the top of the list). When the **Pointer** item is selected, you cannot accidentally add a new control to the Form.

Display all controls and components

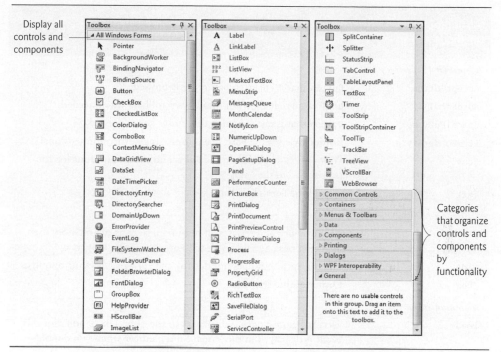

Categories that organize controls and components by functionality

Fig. 14.3 | Components and controls for Windows Forms.

When there are several windows on the screen, the **active window** is the frontmost and has a highlighted title bar. A window becomes the active window when the user clicks somewhere inside it. The active window is said to "have the **focus**." For example, in Visual Studio the active window is the **Toolbox** when you're selecting an item from it, or the **Properties** window when you're editing a control's properties.

A Form is a **container** for controls and components. When you drag items from the **Toolbox** onto the Form, Visual Studio generates code that creates the object and sets its basic properties. This code is updated when the control or component's properties are modified in the IDE. Removing a control or component from the Form deletes the corresponding generated code. The IDE maintains the generated code in a separate file using **partial classes**—classes that are split among multiple files and assembled into a single class by the compiler. We could write this code ourselves, but it's much easier to allow Visual Studio to handle the details. We introduced visual programming concepts in Chapter 2. In this chapter and the next, we use visual programming to build more substantial GUIs.

Each control or component we present in this chapter is located in namespace System.Windows.Forms. To create a Windows application, you generally create a Windows Form, set its properties, add controls to the Form, set their properties and implement event handlers (methods) that respond to events generated by the controls. Figure 14.4 lists common Form properties, methods and a common event.

When we create controls and event handlers, Visual Studio generates much of the GUI-related code. In visual programming, the IDE maintains GUI-related code and you write the bodies of the event handlers to indicate what actions the program should take when particular events occur.

Form properties, methods and an event	Description
Common Properties	
AcceptButton	Button that is clicked when *Enter* is pressed.
AutoScroll	bool value that allows or disallows scrollbars when needed.
CancelButton	Button that is clicked when the *Escape* key is pressed.
FormBorderStyle	Border style for the Form (e.g., none, single, three-dimensional).
Font	Font of text displayed on the Form, and the default font for controls added to the Form.
Text	Text in the Form's title bar.
Common Methods	
Close	Closes a Form and releases all resources, such as the memory used for the Form's contents. A closed Form cannot be reopened.
Hide	Hides a Form, but does not destroy the Form or release its resources.
Show	Displays a hidden Form.
Common Event	
Load	Occurs before a Form is displayed to the user. The handler for this event is displayed in the Visual Studio editor when you double click the Form in the Visual Studio designer.

Fig. 14.4 | Common Form properties, methods and an event.

14.3 Event Handling

Normally, a user interacts with an application's GUI to indicate the tasks that the application should perform. For example, when you write an e-mail in an e-mail application, clicking the **Send** button tells the application to send the e-mail to the specified e-mail addresses. GUIs are **event driven**. When the user interacts with a GUI component, the interaction—known as an **event**—drives the program to perform a task. Common events (user interactions) that might cause an application to perform a task include clicking a Button, typing in a TextBox, selecting an item from a menu, closing a window and moving the mouse. All GUI controls have events associated with them. Objects of other types can also have associated events as well. A method that performs a task in response to an event is called an **event handler**, and the overall process of responding to events is known as **event handling**.

14.3.1 A Simple Event-Driven GUI

The Form in the application of Fig. 14.5 contains a Button that a user can click to display a MessageBox. In line 6, notice the namespace declaration, which is inserted for every class you create. We've been removing these from earlier simple examples because they were unnecessary. Namespaces organize groups of related classes. Each class's name is actually a combination of its namespace name, a dot (.) and the class name. This is known as the class's **fully qualified class name**. You can use the class's **simple name** (the unqualified class name—SimpleEventExample) in the application. If you were to reuse this class in another application, you'd use the fully qualified name or write a using directive so that you could refer to the class by its simple name. We'll use namespaces like this in Chapters 15 and Chapters 21. If another namespace also contains a class with the same name, the fully qualified class names can be used to distinguish between the classes in the application and prevent a **name conflict** (also called a **name collision**).

```
1   // Fig. 14.5: SimpleEventExampleForm.cs
2   // Simple event handling example.
3   using System;
4   using System.Windows.Forms;
5
6   namespace SimpleEventExample
7   {
8      // Form that shows a simple event handler
9      public partial class SimpleEventExampleForm : Form
10     {
11        // default constructor
12        public SimpleEventExampleForm()
13        {
14           InitializeComponent();
15        } // end constructor
16
17        // handles click event of Button clickButton
18        private void clickButton_Click( object sender, EventArgs e )
19        {
20           MessageBox.Show( "Button was clicked." );
21        } // end method clickButton_Click
22     } // end class SimpleEventExampleForm
23  } // end namespace SimpleEventExample
```

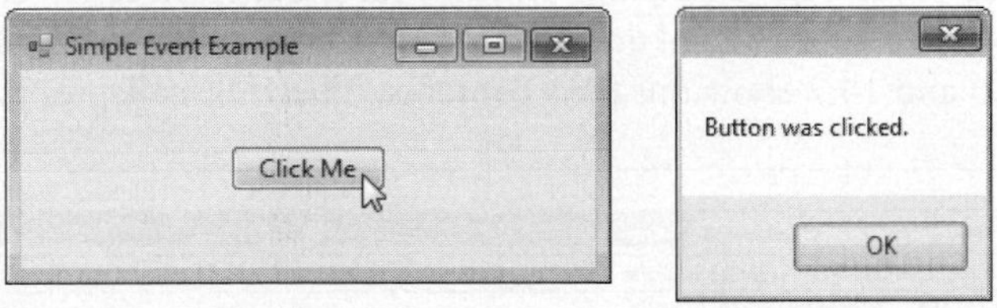

Fig. 14.5 | Simple event-handling example.

Using the techniques presented in Chapter 2, create a Form containing a Button. First, create a new Windows application. Next, rename the Form1.cs file to SimpleEventExample.cs in the **Solution Explorer**. Click the Form in the designer, then use the **Properties** window to set the Form's Text property to "Simple Event Example". Set the Form's Font property to Segoe UI, 9pt. To do so, select the Font property in the **Properties** window, then click the ellipsis (...) button in the property's value field to display a font dialog.

Drag a Button from the **Toolbox** onto the Form. In the **Properties** window for the Button, set the (Name) property to clickButton and the Text property to Click Me. You'll notice that we use a convention in which each variable name we create for a control ends with the control's type. For example, in the variable name clickButton, "Button" is the control's type.

When the user clicks the Button in this example, we want the application to respond by displaying a MessageBox. To do this, you must create an event handler for the Button's Click event. You can create this event handler by double clicking the Button on the Form, which declares the following empty event handler in the program code:

```
private void clickButton_Click( object sender, EventArgs e )
{
}
```

By convention, the IDE names the event-handler method as *objectName_eventName* (e.g., clickButton_Click). The clickButton_Click event handler executes when the user clicks the clickButton control.

Each event handler receives two parameters when it's called. The first—an object reference typically named sender—is a reference to the object that generated the event. The second is a reference to an event arguments object of type EventArgs (or one of its derived classes), which is typically named e. This object contains additional information about the event that occurred. EventArgs is the base class of all classes that represent event information.

To display a MessageBox in response to the event, insert the statement

```
MessageBox.Show( "Button was clicked." );
```

in the event handler's body. The resulting event handler appears in lines 18–21 of Fig. 14.5. When you execute the application and click the Button, a MessageBox appears displaying the text "Button was clicked".

14.3.2 Visual Studio Generated GUI Code

Visual Studio places the auto-generated GUI code in the Designer.cs file of the Form (SimpleEventExampleForm.Designer.cs in this example). You can open this file by expanding the node in the **Solution Explorer** window for the file you're currently working in (SimpleEventExampleForm.cs) and double clicking the file name that ends with Designer.cs. Figs. 14.6 and 14.7 show this file's contents. The IDE collapses the code in lines

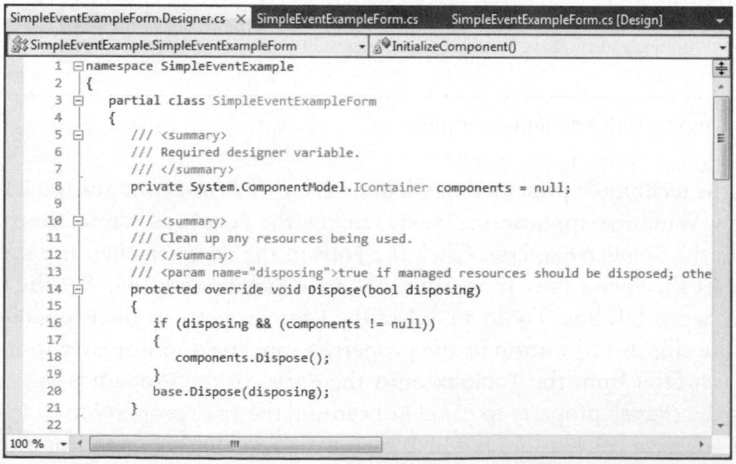

Fig. 14.6 | First half of the Visual Studio generated code file.

```
SimpleEventExampleForm.Designer.cs ×  Program.cs      SimpleEventExampleForm.cs

SimpleEventExample.SimpleEventExampleForm          ▼  components

23 ⊟        #region Windows Form Designer generated code
24
25 ⊟        /// <summary>
26          /// Required method for Designer support - do not modify
27          /// the contents of this method with the code editor.
28          /// </summary>
29 ⊟        private void InitializeComponent()
30          {
31              this.clickButton = new System.Windows.Forms.Button();
32              this.SuspendLayout();
33              //
34              // clickButton
35              //
36              this.clickButton.Location = new System.Drawing.Point(104, 37);
37              this.clickButton.Name = "clickButton";
38              this.clickButton.Size = new System.Drawing.Size(75, 23);
39              this.clickButton.TabIndex = 0;
40              this.clickButton.Text = "Click Me";
41              this.clickButton.UseVisualStyleBackColor = true;
42              this.clickButton.Click += new System.EventHandler(this.clickButton_Click);
43              //
44              // SimpleEventExampleForm
45              //
46              this.AutoScaleDimensions = new System.Drawing.SizeF(7F, 15F);
47              this.AutoScaleMode = System.Windows.Forms.AutoScaleMode.Font;
48              this.ClientSize = new System.Drawing.Size(282, 97);
49              this.Controls.Add(this.clickButton);
50              this.Font = new System.Drawing.Font("Segoe UI", 9F, System.Drawing.FontStyl
51              this.Name = "SimpleEventExampleForm";
52              this.Text = "Simple Event Example";
53              this.ResumeLayout(false);
54
55          }
56
57          #endregion
58
59          private System.Windows.Forms.Button clickButton;
60          }
61  }
100 %  ▼ ◀                        III                                        ▶
```

Fig. 14.7 | Second half of the Visual Studio generated code file.

23–57 of Fig. 14.7 by default—you can click the + icon next to line 23 to expand the code, then click the – icon next to that line to collapse it.

Now that you have studied classes and objects in detail, this code will be easier to understand. Since this code is created and maintained by Visual Studio, you generally don't need to look at it. In fact, you do not need to understand most of the code shown here to build GUI applications. However, we now take a closer look to help you understand how GUI applications work.

The auto-generated code that defines the GUI is actually part of the Form's class—in this case, SimpleEventExample. Line 3 of Fig. 14.6 (and line 9 of Fig. 14.5) uses the partial modifier, which allows this class to be split among multiple files, including the files that contain auto-generated code and those in which you write your own code. Line 59 of Fig. 14.7 declares the clickButton that we created in **Design** mode. It's declared as an instance variable of class SimpleEventExampleForm. By default, all variable declarations for controls created through C#'s design window have a private access modifier. The code also includes the Dispose method for releasing resources (lines 14–21) and method InitializeComponent (lines 29–55), which contains the code that creates the Button, then sets some of the Button's and the Form's properties. The property values correspond to the values set in the **Properties** window for each control. Visual Studio adds comments to the code that it generates, as in lines 33–35. Line 42 was generated when we created the event handler for the Button's Click event.

Method `InitializeComponent` is called when the `Form` is created, and establishes such properties as the `Form` title, the `Form` size, control sizes and text. Visual Studio also uses the code in this method to create the GUI you see in design view. Changing the code in `InitializeComponent` may prevent Visual Studio from displaying the GUI properly.

Error-Prevention Tip 14.1

*The code generated by building a GUI in **Design** mode is not meant to be modified directly, which is why this code is placed in a separate file. Modifying this code can prevent the GUI from being displayed correctly in **Design** mode and might cause an application to function incorrectly. Modify control properties only through the **Properties** window.*

14.3.3 Delegates and the Event-Handling Mechanism

The control that generates an event is known as the **event sender**. An event-handling method—known as the event handler—responds to a particular event that a control generates. When the event occurs, the event sender calls its event handler to perform a task (i.e., to "handle the event").

The .NET event-handling mechanism allows you to choose your own names for event-handling methods. However, each event-handling method must declare the proper parameters to receive information about the event that it handles. Since you can choose your own method names, an event sender such as a `Button` cannot know in advance which method will respond to its events. So, we need a mechanism to indicate which method is the event handler for an event.

Delegates

Event handlers are connected to a control's events via special objects called **delegates**. A delegate object holds a reference to a method with a signature that is specified by the delegate type's declaration. GUI controls have predefined delegates that correspond to every event they can generate. For example, the delegate for a `Button`'s `Click` event is of type `EventHandler` (namespace `System`). If you look at this type in the online help documentation, you'll see that it's declared as follows:

```
public delegate void EventHandler( object sender, EventArgs e );
```

This uses the **delegate** keyword to declare a delegate type named `EventHandler`, which can hold references to methods that return `void` and receive two parameters—one of type `object` (the event sender) and one of type `EventArgs`. If you compare the delegate declaration with `clickButton_Click`'s header (Fig. 14.5, line 18), you'll see that this event handler indeed meets the requirements of the `EventHandler` delegate. The preceding declaration actually creates an entire class for you. The details of this special class's declaration are handled by the compiler.

Indicating the Method that a Delegate Should Call

An event sender calls a delegate object like a method. Since each event handler is declared as a delegate, the event sender can simply call the appropriate delegate when an event occurs—a `Button` calls the `EventHandler` delegate that corresponds to its `Click` event in response to a click. The delegate's job is to invoke the appropriate method. To enable the `clickButton_Click` method to be called, Visual Studio assigns `clickButton_Click` to the delegate, as shown in line 42 of Fig. 14.7. This code is added by Visual Studio when you double click the `Button` control in **Design** mode. The expression

```
new System.EventHandler(this.clickButton_Click);
```

creates an `EventHandler` delegate object and initializes it with the `clickButton_Click` method. Line 42 uses the `+=` operator to add the delegate to the `Button`'s `Click` event. This indicates that `clickButton_Click` will respond when a user clicks the `Button`. The `+=` operator is overloaded by the delegate class that is created by the compiler.

You can actually specify that several different methods should be invoked in response to an event by adding other delegates to the `Button`'s `Click` event with statements similar to line 42 of Fig. 14.7. Event delegates are **multicast**—they represent a set of delegate objects that all have the same signature. Multicast delegates enable several methods to be called in response to a single event. When an event occurs, the event sender calls every method referenced by the multicast delegate. This is known as **event multicasting**. Event delegates derive from class **MulticastDelegate**, which derives from class **Delegate** (both from namespace `System`).

14.3.4 Another Way to Create Event Handlers

For the GUI application in Fig. 14.5, you double clicked the `Button` control on the `Form` to create its event handler. This technique creates an event handler for a control's **default event**—the event that is most frequently used with that control. Controls can generate many different events, and each one can have its own event handler. For instance, your application can also provide an event handler for a `Button`'s `MouseHover` event, which occurs when the mouse pointer remains positioned over the `Button` for a short period of time. We now discuss how to create an event handler for an event that is not a control's default event.

Using the Properties Window to Create Event Handlers
You can create additional event handlers through the **Properties** window. If you select a control on the `Form`, then click the **Events** icon (the lightning bolt icon in Fig. 14.8) in the **Properties** window, all the events for that control are listed in the window. You can double click an event's name to display the event handler in the editor, if the event handler already exists, or to create the event handler. You can also select an event, then use the drop-down list to its right to choose an existing method that should be used as the event handler for that event. The methods that appear in this drop-down list are the `Form` class's methods that have the proper signature to be an event handler for the selected event. You can return to viewing the properties of a control by selecting the **Properties** icon (Fig. 14.8).

A single method can handle multiple events from multiple controls. For example, the `Click` events of three `Button`s could all be handled by the same method. You can specify an event handler for multiple events by selecting multiple controls and selecting a single method in the **Properties** window. If you create a new event handler this way, you should rename it appropriately. You could also select each control individually and specify the same method for each one's event.

14.3.5 Locating Event Information

Read the Visual Studio documentation to learn about the different events raised by each control. To do this, select a control in the IDE and press the *F1* key to display that control's online help (Fig. 14.9). The web page that is displayed contains basic information

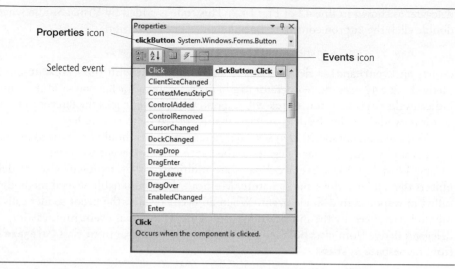

Fig. 14.8 | Viewing events for a `Button` control in the **Properties** window.

about the control's class. In the left column of the page are several links to more information about the class—**Members**, **Constructor**, **Methods**, **Properties** and **Events**. This list may vary by class. The **Members** link displays a complete list of the class's members. This list includes the events that the class can generate. Each of the other links displays a subset of the class's members. Click the link to the list of events for that control (**Button Events** in this case) to display the supported events for that control.

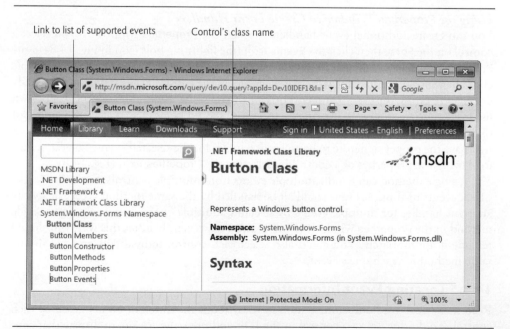

Fig. 14.9 | List of `Button` events.

Next, click the name of an event to view its description and examples of its use. We selected the Click event to display the information in Fig. 14.10. The Click event is a member of class Control, an indirect base class of class Button. The **Remarks** section of the page discusses the details of the selected event. Alternatively, you could use the **Object Browser** to look up this information. The **Object Browser** shows only the members originally defined in a given class. The Click event is originally defined in class Control and inherited into Button. For this reason, you must look at class Control in the **Object Browser** to see the documentation for the Click event. See Section 10.12 for more information regarding the **Object Browser**.

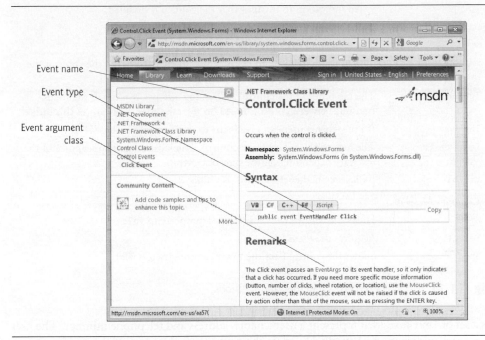

Fig. 14.10 | Click event details.

14.4 Control Properties and Layout

This section overviews properties that are common to many controls. Controls derive from class **Control** (namespace System.Windows.Forms). Figure 14.11 lists some of class Control's properties and methods. The properties shown here can be set for many controls. For example, the Text property specifies the text that appears on a control. The location of this text varies depending on the control. In a Form, the text appears in the title bar, but the text of a Button appears on its face.

The **Select** method transfers the focus to a control and makes it the **active control**. When you press the *Tab* key in an executing Windows application, controls receive the focus in the order specified by their **TabIndex** property. This property is set by Visual Studio based on the order in which controls are added to a Form, but you can change the tabbing order. TabIndex is helpful for users who enter information in many controls, such

Class `Control` properties and methods	Description
Common Properties	
BackColor	The control's background color.
BackgroundImage	The control's background image.
Enabled	Specifies whether the control is enabled (i.e., if the user can interact with it). Typically, portions of a disabled control appear "grayed out" as a visual indication to the user that the control is disabled.
Focused	Indicates whether the control has the focus.
Font	The `Font` used to display the control's text.
ForeColor	The control's foreground color. This usually determines the color of the text in the `Text` property.
TabIndex	The tab order of the control. When the *Tab* key is pressed, the focus transfers between controls based on the tab order. You can set this order.
TabStop	If `true`, then a user can give focus to this control via the *Tab* key.
Text	The text associated with the control. The location and appearance of the text vary depending on the type of control.
Visible	Indicates whether the control is visible.
Common Methods	
Hide	Hides the control (sets the `Visible` property to `false`).
Select	Acquires the focus.
Show	Shows the control (sets the `Visible` property to `true`).

Fig. 14.11 | Class `Control` properties and methods.

as a set of `TextBox`es that represent a user's name, address and telephone number. The user can enter information, then quickly select the next control by pressing the *Tab* key.

The **Enabled** property indicates whether the user can interact with a control to generate an event. Often, if a control is disabled, it's because an option is unavailable to the user at that time. For example, text editor applications often disable the "paste" command until the user copies some text. In most cases, a disabled control's text appears in gray (rather than in black). You can also hide a control from the user without disabling the control by setting the `Visible` property to `false` or by calling method `Hide`. In each case, the control still exists but is not visible on the `Form`.

Anchoring and Docking

You can use anchoring and docking to specify the layout of controls inside a container (such as a `Form`). **Anchoring** causes controls to remain at a fixed distance from the sides of the container even when the container is resized. Anchoring enhances the user experience. For example, if the user expects a control to appear in a particular corner of the application, anchoring ensures that the control will always be in that corner—even if the user resizes the `Form`. **Docking** attaches a control to a container such that the control stretches across an entire side or fills an entire area. For example, a button docked to the top of a container stretches across the entire top of that container, regardless of the width of the container.

When parent containers are resized, anchored controls are moved (and possibly resized) so that the distance from the sides to which they're anchored does not vary. By default, most controls are anchored to the top-left corner of the Form. To see the effects of anchoring a control, create a simple Windows application that contains two Buttons. Anchor one control to the right and bottom sides by setting the **Anchor** property as shown in Fig. 14.12. Leave the other control with its default anchoring (top, left). Execute the application and enlarge the Form. Notice that the Button anchored to the bottom-right corner is always the same distance from the Form's bottom-right corner (Fig. 14.13), but that the other control stays its original distance from the top-left corner of the Form.

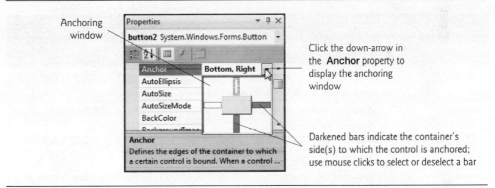

Fig. 14.12 | Manipulating the **Anchor** property of a control.

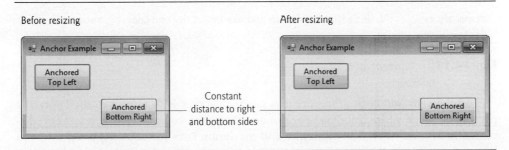

Fig. 14.13 | Anchoring demonstration.

Sometimes, it's desirable for a control to span an entire side of the Form, even when the Form is resized. For example, a control such as a status bar typically should remain at the bottom of the Form. Docking allows a control to span an entire side (left, right, top or bottom) of its parent container or to fill the entire container. When the parent control is resized, the docked control resizes as well. In Fig. 14.14, a Button is docked at the top of the Form (spanning the top portion). When the Form is resized, the Button is resized to the Form's new width. Forms have a **Padding** property that specifies the distance between the docked controls and the Form edges. This property specifies four values (one for each side), and each value is set to 0 by default. Some common control layout properties are summarized in Fig. 14.15.

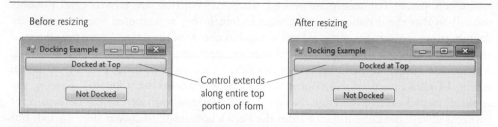

Fig. 14.14 | Docking a Button to the top of a Form.

Control layout properties	Description
Anchor	Causes a control to remain at a fixed distance from the side(s) of the container even when the container is resized.
Dock	Allows a control to span one side of its container or to fill the remaining space in the container.
Padding	Sets the space between a container's edges and docked controls. The default is 0, causing the control to appear flush with the container's sides.
Location	Specifies the location (as a set of coordinates) of the upper-left corner of the control, in relation to its container's upper-left corner.
Size	Specifies the size of the control in pixels as a Size object, which has properties Width and Height.
MinimumSize, MaximumSize	Indicates the minimum and maximum size of a Control, respectively.

Fig. 14.15 | Control layout properties.

The Anchor and Dock properties of a Control are set with respect to the Control's parent container, which could be a Form or another parent container (such as a Panel; discussed in Section 14.6). The minimum and maximum Form (or other Control) sizes can be set via properties **MinimumSize** and **MaximumSize**, respectively. Both are of type **Size**, which has properties **Width** and **Height** to specify the size of the Form. Properties MinimumSize and MaximumSize allow you to design the GUI layout for a given size range. The user cannot make a Form smaller than the size specified by property MinimumSize and cannot make a Form larger than the size specified by property MaximumSize. To set a Form to a fixed size (where the Form cannot be resized by the user), set its minimum and maximum size to the same value.

Look-and-Feel Observation 14.2

For resizable Forms, ensure that the GUI layout appears consistent across various Form sizes.

Using Visual Studio To Edit a GUI's Layout

Visual Studio helps you with GUI layout. When you drag a control across a Form, blue **snap lines** appear to help you position the control with respect to others (Fig. 14.16) and the Form's edges. This feature makes the control you're dragging appear to "snap into place" alongside other controls. Visual Studio also provides the **Format** menu, which contains options for modifying your GUI's layout. The **Format** menu does not appear in the IDE unless you select one or more controls in design view. When you select multiple controls, you can align them with the **Format** menu's **Align** submenu. The **Format** menu also enables you to modify the space between controls or to center a control on the Form.

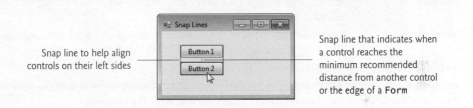

Snap line to help align controls on their left sides

Snap line that indicates when a control reaches the minimum recommended distance from another control or the edge of a Form

Fig. 14.16 | Snap lines for aligning controls.

14.5 Labels, TextBoxes and Buttons

Labels provide text information (as well as optional images) and are defined with class Label (a derived class of Control). A Label displays text that the user cannot directly modify. A Label's text can be changed programmatically by modifying the Label's Text property. Figure 14.17 lists common Label properties.

Common Label properties	Description
Font	The font of the text on the Label.
Text	The text on the Label.
TextAlign	The alignment of the Label's text on the control—horizontally (left, center or right) and vertically (top, middle or bottom). The default is top, left.

Fig. 14.17 | Common Label properties.

A textbox (class TextBox) is an area in which either text can be displayed by a program or the user can type text via the keyboard. A **password TextBox** is a TextBox that hides the information entered by the user. As the user types characters, the password TextBox masks the user input by displaying a password character. If you set the property **UseSystemPasswordChar** to true, the TextBox becomes a password TextBox. Users often encounter both types of TextBoxes, when logging into a computer or website—the username TextBox allows users to input their usernames; the password TextBox allows users to enter their passwords. Figure 14.18 lists the common properties and a common event of TextBoxes.

TextBox properties and an event	Description
Common Properties	
AcceptsReturn	If true in a multiline TextBox, pressing *Enter* in the TextBox creates a new line. If false (the default), pressing *Enter* is the same as pressing the default Button on the Form. The default Button is the one assigned to a Form's AcceptButton property.
Multiline	If true, the TextBox can span multiple lines. The default value is false.
ReadOnly	If true, the TextBox has a gray background, and its text cannot be edited. The default value is false.
ScrollBars	For multiline textboxes, this property indicates which scrollbars appear (None—the default, Horizontal, Vertical or Both).
Text	The TextBox's text content.
UseSystem-PasswordChar	When true, the TextBox becomes a password TextBox, and the system-specified character masks each character the user types.
Common Event	
TextChanged	Generated when the text changes in a TextBox (i.e., when the user adds or deletes characters). When you double click the TextBox control in **Design** mode, an empty event handler for this event is generated.

Fig. 14.18 | TextBox properties and an event.

A button is a control that the user clicks to trigger a specific action or to select an option in a program. As you'll see, a program can use several types of buttons, such as **checkboxes** and **radio buttons**. All the button classes derive from class **ButtonBase** (namespace System.Windows.Forms), which defines common button features. In this section, we discuss class Button, which typically enables a user to issue a command to an application. Figure 14.19 lists common properties and a common event of class Button.

Button properties and an event	Description
Common Properties	
Text	Specifies the text displayed on the Button face.
FlatStyle	Modifies a Button's appearance—attribute Flat (for the Button to display without a three-dimensional appearance), Popup (for the Button to appear flat until the user moves the mouse pointer over the Button), Standard (three-dimensional) and System, where the Button's appearance is controlled by the operating system. The default value is Standard.
Common Event	
Click	Generated when the user clicks the Button. When you double click a Button in design view, an empty event handler for this event is created.

Fig. 14.19 | Button properties and an event.

Figure 14.20 uses a TextBox, a Button and a Label. The user enters text into a password box and clicks the Button, causing the text input to be displayed in the Label. Normally, we would not display this text—the purpose of password TextBoxes is to hide the text being entered by the user. When the user clicks the **Show Me** Button, this application retrieves the text that the user typed in the password TextBox and displays it in a Label.

```
1   // Fig. 14.20: LabelTextBoxButtonTestForm.cs
2   // Using a TextBox, Label and Button to display
3   // the hidden text in a password TextBox.
4   using System;
5   using System.Windows.Forms;
6
7   namespace LabelTextBoxButtonTest
8   {
9      // Form that creates a password TextBox and
10     // a Label to display TextBox contents
11     public partial class LabelTextBoxButtonTestForm : Form
12     {
13        // default constructor
14        public LabelTextBoxButtonTestForm()
15        {
16           InitializeComponent();
17        } // end constructor
18
19        // display user input in Label
20        private void displayPasswordButton_Click(
21           object sender, EventArgs e )
22        {
23           // display the text that the user typed
24           displayPasswordLabel.Text = inputPasswordTextBox.Text;
25        } // end method displayPasswordButton_Click
26     } // end class LabelTextBoxButtonTestForm
27  } // end namespace LabelTextBoxButtonTest
```

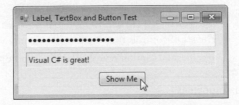

Fig. 14.20 | Program to display hidden text in a password box.

First, create the GUI by dragging the controls (a TextBox, a Button and a Label) on the Form. Once the controls are positioned, change their names in the **Properties** window from the default values—textBox1, button1 and label1—to the more descriptive displayPasswordLabel, displayPasswordButton and inputPasswordTextBox. The (Name) property in the **Properties** window enables us to change the variable name for a control. Visual Studio creates the necessary code and places it in method InitializeComponent of the partial class in the file LabelTextBoxButtonTestForm.Designer.cs.

We set displayPasswordButton's Text property to "Show Me" and clear the Text of displayPasswordLabel so that it's blank when the program begins executing. The BorderStyle property of displayPasswordLabel is set to Fixed3D, giving our Label a three-dimensional appearance. We also changed its TextAlign property to MiddleLeft so that the Label's text is displayed centered between its top and bottom. The password character for inputPasswordTextBox is determined by the user's system settings when you set UseSystemPasswordChar to true. This property accepts only one character.

We create an event handler for displayPasswordButton by double clicking this control in **Design** mode. We added line 24 to the event handler's body. When the user clicks the **Show Me** Button in the executing application, line 24 obtains the text entered by the user in inputPasswordTextBox and displays the text in displayPasswordLabel.

14.6 GroupBoxes and Panels

GroupBoxes and **Panels** arrange controls on a GUI. GroupBoxes and Panels are typically used to group several controls of similar functionality or several controls that are related in a GUI. All of the controls in a GroupBox or Panel move together when the GroupBox or Panel is moved. Furthermore, a GroupBoxes and Panels can also be used to show or hide a set of controls at once. When you modify a container's Visible property, it toggles the visibility of all the controls within it.

The primary difference between these two controls is that GroupBoxes can display a caption (i.e., text) and do not include scrollbars, whereas Panels can include scrollbars and do not include a caption. GroupBoxes have thin borders by default; Panels can be set so that they also have borders by changing their BorderStyle property. Figures 14.21–14.22 list the common properties of GroupBoxes and Panels, respectively.

 Look-and-Feel Observation 14.3
Panels and GroupBoxes can contain other Panels and GroupBoxes for more complex layouts.

GroupBox properties	Description
Controls	The set of controls that the GroupBox contains.
Text	Specifies the caption text displayed at the top of the GroupBox.

Fig. 14.21 | GroupBox properties.

Panel properties	Description
AutoScroll	Indicates whether scrollbars appear when the Panel is too small to display all of its controls. The default value is false.
BorderStyle	Sets the border of the Panel. The default value is None; other options are Fixed3D and FixedSingle.
Controls	The set of controls that the Panel contains.

Fig. 14.22 | Panel properties.

Look-and-Feel Observation 14.4

You can organize a GUI by anchoring and docking controls inside a GroupBox or Panel. The GroupBox or Panel then can be anchored or docked inside a Form. This divides controls into functional "groups" that can be arranged easily.

To create a GroupBox, drag its icon from the **Toolbox** onto a Form. Then, drag new controls from the **Toolbox** into the GroupBox. These controls are added to the GroupBox's **Controls** property and become part of the GroupBox. The GroupBox's Text property specifies the caption.

To create a Panel, drag its icon from the **Toolbox** onto the Form. You can then add controls directly to the Panel by dragging them from the **Toolbox** onto the Panel. To enable the scrollbars, set the Panel's AutoScroll property to true. If the Panel is resized and cannot display all of its controls, scrollbars appear (Fig. 14.23). The scrollbars can be used to view all the controls in the Panel—both at design time and at execution time. In Fig. 14.23, we set the Panel's BorderStyle property to FixedSingle so that you can see the Panel in the Form.

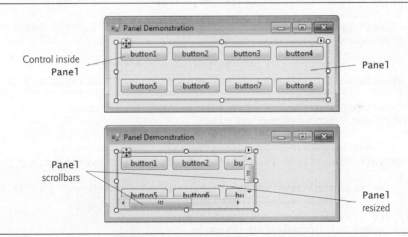

Fig. 14.23 | Creating a Panel with scrollbars.

Look-and-Feel Observation 14.5

Use Panels with scrollbars to avoid cluttering a GUI and to reduce the GUI's size.

The program in Fig. 14.24 uses a GroupBox and a Panel to arrange Buttons. When these Buttons are clicked, their event handlers change the text on a Label.

```
1   // Fig. 14.24: GroupboxPanelExampleForm.cs
2   // Using GroupBoxes and Panels to arrange Buttons.
3   using System;
4   using System.Windows.Forms;
```

Fig. 14.24 | Using GroupBoxes and Panels to arrange Buttons. (Part 1 of 2.)

```
5
6   namespace GroupBoxPanelExample
7   {
8      // Form that displays a GroupBox and a Panel
9      public partial class GroupBoxPanelExampleForm : Form
10     {
11        // default constructor
12        public GroupBoxPanelExampleForm()
13        {
14           InitializeComponent();
15        } // end constructor
16
17        // event handler for Hi Button
18        private void hiButton_Click( object sender, EventArgs e )
19        {
20           messageLabel.Text = "Hi pressed"; // change text in Label
21        } // end method hiButton_Click
22
23        // event handler for Bye Button
24        private void byeButton_Click( object sender, EventArgs e )
25        {
26           messageLabel.Text = "Bye pressed"; // change text in Label
27        } // end method byeButton_Click
28
29        // event handler for Far Left Button
30        private void leftButton_Click( object sender, EventArgs e )
31        {
32           messageLabel.Text = "Far left pressed"; // change text in Label
33        } // end method leftButton_Click
34
35        // event handler for Far Right Button
36        private void rightButton_Click( object sender, EventArgs e )
37        {
38           messageLabel.Text = "Far right pressed"; // change text in Label
39        } // end method rightButton_Click
40     } // end class GroupBoxPanelExampleForm
41  } // end namespace GroupBoxPanelExample
```

Fig. 14.24 | Using GroupBoxes and Panels to arrange Buttons. (Part 2 of 2.)

The mainGroupBox has two Buttons—hiButton (which displays the text **Hi**) and bye-Button (which displays the text **Bye**). The Panel (named mainPanel) also has two Buttons, leftButton (which displays the text **Far Left**) and rightButton (which displays the text **Far Right**). The mainPanel has its AutoScroll property set to true, allowing scrollbars to appear when the contents of the Panel require more space than the Panel's visible area. The Label (named messageLabel) is initially blank. To add controls to mainGroupBox or mainPanel, Visual Studio calls method Add of each container's Controls property. This code is placed in the partial class located in the file GroupBoxPanelExample.Designer.cs.

The event handlers for the four Buttons are located in lines 18–39. Lines 20, 26, 32 and 38 change the text of messageLabel to indicate which Button the user pressed.

14.7 CheckBoxes and RadioButtons

C# has two types of **state buttons** that can be in the on/off or true/false states—**CheckBoxes** and **RadioButtons**. Like class Button, classes CheckBox and RadioButton are derived from class ButtonBase.

CheckBoxes

A CheckBox is a small square that either is blank or contains a check mark. When the user clicks a CheckBox to select it, a check mark appears in the box. If the user clicks the Check-Box again to deselect it, the check mark is removed. You can also configure a CheckBox to toggle between three states (checked, unchecked and indeterminate) by setting its **Three-State** property to true. Any number of CheckBoxes can be selected at a time. A list of common CheckBox properties and events appears in Fig. 14.25.

CheckBox properties and events	Description
Common Properties	
Appearance	By default, this property is set to Normal, and the CheckBox displays as a traditional checkbox. If it's set to Button, the CheckBox displays as a Button that looks pressed when the CheckBox is checked.
Checked	Indicates whether the CheckBox is checked (contains a check mark) or unchecked (blank). This property returns a bool value. The default is false (unchecked).
CheckState	Indicates whether the CheckBox is checked or unchecked with a value from the CheckState enumeration (Checked, Unchecked or Indeterminate). Indeterminate is used when it's unclear whether the state should be Checked or Unchecked. When CheckState is set to Indeterminate, the CheckBox is usually shaded.
Text	Specifies the text displayed to the right of the CheckBox.
ThreeState	When this property is true, the CheckBox has three states—checked, unchecked and indeterminate. By default, this property is false and the CheckBox has only two states—checked and unchecked.
Common Events	
CheckedChanged	Generated when the Checked property changes. This is a CheckBox's default event. When a user double clicks the CheckBox control in design view, an empty event handler for this event is generated.
CheckStateChanged	Generated when the CheckState property changes.

Fig. 14.25 | CheckBox properties and events.

The program in Fig. 14.26 allows the user to select CheckBoxes to change a Label's font style. The event handler for one CheckBox applies bold and the event handler for the other applies italic. If both CheckBoxes are selected, the font style is set to bold and italic. Initially, neither CheckBox is checked.

```csharp
 1  // Fig. 14.26: CheckBoxTestForm.cs
 2  // Using CheckBoxes to toggle italic and bold styles.
 3  using System;
 4  using System.Drawing;
 5  using System.Windows.Forms;
 6
 7  namespace CheckBoxTest
 8  {
 9     // Form contains CheckBoxes to allow the user to modify sample text
10     public partial class CheckBoxTestForm : Form
11     {
12        // default constructor
13        public CheckBoxTestForm()
14        {
15           InitializeComponent();
16        } // end constructor
17
18        // toggle the font style between bold and
19        // not bold based on the  current setting
20        private void boldCheckBox_CheckedChanged(
21           object sender, EventArgs e )
22        {
23           outputLabel.Font = new Font( outputLabel.Font,
24              outputLabel.Font.Style ^ FontStyle.Bold );
25        } // end method boldCheckBox_CheckedChanged
26
27        // toggle the font style between italic and
28        // not italic based on the current setting
29        private void italicCheckBox_CheckedChanged(
30           object sender, EventArgs e )
31        {
32           outputLabel.Font = new Font( outputLabel.Font,
33              outputLabel.Font.Style ^ FontStyle.Italic );
34        } // end method italicCheckBox_CheckedChanged
35     } // end class CheckBoxTestForm
36  } // end namespace CheckBoxTest
```

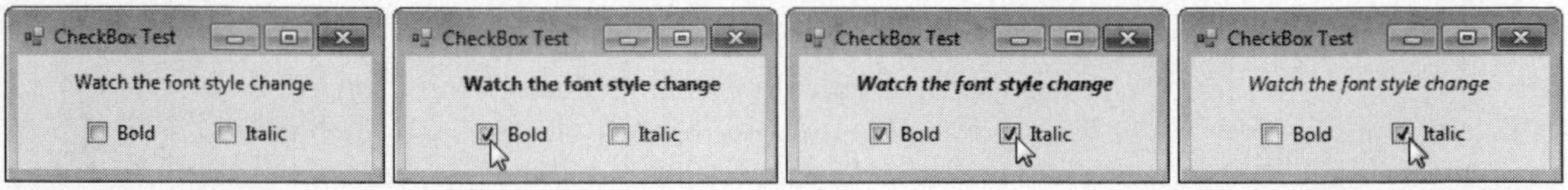

Fig. 14.26 | Using CheckBoxes to change font styles.

The boldCheckBox has its Text property set to Bold. The italicCheckBox has its Text property set to Italic. The Text property of outputLabel is set to Watch the font style change. After creating the controls, we define their event handlers. Double clicking the CheckBoxes at design time creates empty CheckedChanged event handlers.

To change a Label's font style, set its Font property to a new **Font object** (lines 23–24 and 32–33). Class Font is in the System.Drawing namespace. The Font constructor that we use here takes the current font and new style as arguments. The first argument—output-Label.Font—uses outputLabel's original font name and size. The style is specified with a member of the **FontStyle enumeration**, which contains Regular, Bold, Italic, Strikeout and Underline. (The Strikeout style displays text with a line through it.) A Font object's **Style** property is read-only, so it can be set only when the Font object is created.

Combining Font Styles with Bitwise Operators

Styles can be combined via **bitwise operators**—operators that perform manipulation on bits of information. Recall from Chapter 1 that all data is represented in the computer as combinations of 0s and 1s. Each 0 or 1 represents a bit. The FontStyle (namespace System.Drawing) is represented as a set of bits that are selected in a way that allows us to combine different FontStyle elements to create compound styles, using bitwise operators. These styles are not mutually exclusive, so we can combine different styles and remove them without affecting the combination of previous FontStyle elements. We can combine these various font styles, using either the logical OR (|) operator or the logical exclusive OR (∧) operator (also called XOR). When the logical OR operator is applied to two bits, if at least one bit of the two has the value 1, then the result is 1. Combining styles using the logical OR operator works as follows. Assume that FontStyle.Bold is represented by bits 01 and that FontStyle.Italic is represented by bits 10. When we use the logical OR (|) to combine the styles, we obtain the bits 11.

```
01  =  Bold
10  =  Italic
--
11  =  Bold and Italic
```

The logical OR operator helps create style combinations. However, what happens if we want to undo a style combination, as we did in Fig. 14.26?

The logical exclusive OR operator enables us to combine styles and to undo existing style settings. When logical exclusive OR is applied to two bits, if both bits have the same value, then the result is 0. If both bits are different, then the result is 1.

Combining styles using logical exclusive OR works as follows. Assume, again, that FontStyle.Bold is represented by bits 01 and that FontStyle.Italic is represented by bits 10. When we use logical exclusive OR (∧) on both styles, we obtain the bits 11.

```
01  =  Bold
10  =  Italic
--
11  =  Bold and Italic
```

Now, suppose that we would like to remove the FontStyle.Bold style from the previous combination of FontStyle.Bold and FontStyle.Italic. The easiest way to do so is to reapply the logical exclusive OR (∧) operator to the compound style and Font-Style.Bold.

```
11  =  Bold and Italic
01  =  Bold
--
10  =  Italic
```

This is a simple example. The advantages of using bitwise operators to combine `FontStyle` values become more evident when we consider that there are five `FontStyle` values (`Bold`, `Italic`, `Regular`, `Strikeout` and `Underline`), resulting in 16 `FontStyle` combinations. Using bitwise operators to combine font styles greatly reduces the amount of code required to check all possible font combinations.

In Fig. 14.26, we need to set the `FontStyle` so that the text appears in bold if it was not bold originally, and vice versa. Line 24 uses the bitwise logical exclusive OR operator to do this. If `outputLabel.Font.Style` is bold, then the resulting style is not bold. If the text is originally italic, the resulting style is bold and italic, rather than just bold. The same applies for `FontStyle.Italic` in line 33.

If we didn't use bitwise operators to compound `FontStyle` elements, we'd have to test for the current style and change it accordingly. In `boldCheckBox_CheckedChanged`, we could test for the regular style and make it bold; test for the bold style and make it regular; test for the italic style and make it bold italic; and test for the italic bold style and make it italic. This is cumbersome because, for every new style we add, we double the number of combinations. Adding a `CheckBox` for underline would require testing eight additional styles. Adding a `CheckBox` for strikeout would require testing 16 additional styles.

RadioButtons

Radio buttons (defined with class `RadioButton`) are similar to `CheckBoxes` in that they also have two states—**selected** and **not selected** (also called **deselected**). However, `RadioButtons` normally appear as a **group**, in which only one `RadioButton` can be selected at a time. Selecting one `RadioButton` in the group forces all the others to be deselected. Therefore, `RadioButtons` are used to represent a set of **mutually exclusive** options (i.e., a set in which multiple options cannot be selected at the same time).

Look-and-Feel Observation 14.6
Use RadioButtons when the user should choose only one option in a group.

Look-and-Feel Observation 14.7
Use CheckBoxes when the user should be able to choose multiple options in a group.

All `RadioButtons` added to a container become part of the same group. To divide `RadioButtons` into several groups, they must be added to separate containers, such as `GroupBoxes` or `Panels`. The common properties and a common event of class `RadioButton` are listed in Fig. 14.27.

RadioButton properties and an event	Description
Common Properties	
Checked	Indicates whether the `RadioButton` is checked.
Text	Specifies the `RadioButton`'s text.

Fig. 14.27 | `RadioButton` properties and an event. (Part 1 of 2.)

RadioButton properties and an event	Description
Common Event	
CheckedChanged	Generated every time the RadioButton is checked or unchecked. When you double click a RadioButton control in design view, an empty event handler for this event is generated.

Fig. 14.27 | RadioButton properties and an event. (Part 2 of 2.)

Software Engineering Observation 14.1

Forms, GroupBoxes, and Panels can act as logical groups for RadioButtons. The RadioButtons within each group are mutually exclusive to each other, but not to RadioButtons in different logical groups.

The program in Fig. 14.28 uses RadioButtons to enable users to select options for a MessageBox. After selecting the desired attributes, the user presses the **Display** Button to display the MessageBox. A Label in the lower-left corner shows the result of the MessageBox (i.e., which Button the user clicked—**Yes**, **No**, **Cancel**, etc.).

To store the user's choices, we create and initialize the iconType and buttonType objects (lines 13–14). Object iconType is of type MessageBoxIcon, and can have values Asterisk, Error, Exclamation, Hand, Information, None, Question, Stop and Warning. The sample output shows only Error, Exclamation, Information and Question icons.

Object buttonType is of type MessageBoxButtons, and can have values AbortRetryIgnore, OK, OKCancel, RetryCancel, YesNo and YesNoCancel. The name indicates the options that are presented to the user in the MessageBox. The sample output windows show MessageBoxes for all of the MessageBoxButtons enumeration values.

```
1   // Fig. 14.28: RadioButtonsTestForm.cs
2   // Using RadioButtons to set message window options.
3   using System;
4   using System.Windows.Forms;
5
6   namespace RadioButtonsTest
7   {
8      // Form contains several RadioButtons--user chooses one
9      // from each group to create a custom MessageBox
10     public partial class RadioButtonsTestForm : Form
11     {
12        // create variables that store the user's choice of options
13        private MessageBoxIcon iconType;
14        private MessageBoxButtons buttonType;
15
16        // default constructor
17        public RadioButtonsTestForm()
18        {
```

Fig. 14.28 | Using RadioButtons to set message-window options. (Part 1 of 4.)

```
19              InitializeComponent();
20         } // end constructor
21
22         // change Buttons based on option chosen by sender
23         private void buttonType_CheckedChanged(
24             object sender, EventArgs e )
25         {
26             if ( sender == okRadioButton ) // display OK Button
27                 buttonType = MessageBoxButtons.OK;
28
29             // display OK and Cancel Buttons
30             else if ( sender == okCancelRadioButton )
31                 buttonType = MessageBoxButtons.OKCancel;
32
33             // display Abort, Retry and Ignore Buttons
34             else if ( sender == abortRetryIgnoreRadioButton )
35                 buttonType = MessageBoxButtons.AbortRetryIgnore;
36
37             // display Yes, No and Cancel Buttons
38             else if ( sender == yesNoCancelRadioButton )
39                 buttonType = MessageBoxButtons.YesNoCancel;
40
41             // display Yes and No Buttons
42             else if ( sender == yesNoRadioButton )
43                 buttonType = MessageBoxButtons.YesNo;
44
45             // only on option left--display Retry and Cancel Buttons
46             else
47                 buttonType = MessageBoxButtons.RetryCancel;
48         } // end method buttonType_CheckedChanged
49
50         // change Icon based on option chosen by sender
51         private void iconType_CheckedChanged( object sender, EventArgs e )
52         {
53             if ( sender == asteriskRadioButton ) // display asterisk Icon
54                 iconType = MessageBoxIcon.Asterisk;
55
56             // display error Icon
57             else if ( sender == errorRadioButton )
58                 iconType = MessageBoxIcon.Error;
59
60             // display exclamation point Icon
61             else if ( sender == exclamationRadioButton )
62                 iconType = MessageBoxIcon.Exclamation;
63
64             // display hand Icon
65             else if ( sender == handRadioButton )
66                 iconType = MessageBoxIcon.Hand;
67
68             // display information Icon
69             else if ( sender == informationRadioButton )
70                 iconType = MessageBoxIcon.Information;
```

Fig. 14.28 | Using RadioButtons to set message-window options. (Part 2 of 4.)

```
71
72              // display question mark Icon
73              else if ( sender == questionRadioButton )
74                 iconType = MessageBoxIcon.Question;
75
76              // display stop Icon
77              else if ( sender == stopRadioButton )
78                 iconType = MessageBoxIcon.Stop;
79
80              // only one option left--display warning Icon
81              else
82                 iconType = MessageBoxIcon.Warning;
83           } // end method iconType_CheckedChanged
84
85           // display MessageBox and Button user pressed
86           private void displayButton_Click( object sender, EventArgs e )
87           {
88              // display MessageBox and store
89              // the value of the Button that was pressed
90              DialogResult result = MessageBox.Show(
91                 "This is your Custom MessageBox.", "Custom MessageBox",
92                 buttonType, iconType );
93
94              // check to see which Button was pressed in the MessageBox
95              // change text displayed accordingly
96              switch (result)
97              {
98                 case DialogResult.OK:
99                    displayLabel.Text = "OK was pressed.";
100                    break;
101                 case DialogResult.Cancel:
102                    displayLabel.Text = "Cancel was pressed.";
103                    break;
104                 case DialogResult.Abort:
105                    displayLabel.Text = "Abort was pressed.";
106                    break;
107                 case DialogResult.Retry:
108                    displayLabel.Text = "Retry was pressed.";
109                    break;
110                 case DialogResult.Ignore:
111                    displayLabel.Text = "Ignore was pressed.";
112                    break;
113                 case DialogResult.Yes:
114                    displayLabel.Text = "Yes was pressed.";
115                    break;
116                 case DialogResult.No:
117                    displayLabel.Text = "No was pressed.";
118                    break;
119              } // end switch
120           } // end method displayButton_Click
121        } // end class RadioButtonsTestForm
122     } // end namespace RadioButtonsTest
```

Fig. 14.28 | Using RadioButtons to set message-window options. (Part 3 of 4.)

Fig. 14.28 | Using RadioButtons to set message-window options. (Part 4 of 4.)

We created two GroupBoxes, one for each set of enumeration values. The GroupBox captions are **Button Type** and **Icon**. The GroupBoxes contain RadioButtons for the corresponding enumeration options, and the RadioButtons' Text properties are set appropriately. Because the RadioButtons are grouped, only one RadioButton can be selected from each GroupBox. There's also a Button (displayButton) labeled **Display**. When a user clicks this Button, a customized MessageBox is displayed. A Label (displayLabel) displays which Button the user pressed within the MessageBox.

The event handler for the RadioButtons handles the CheckedChanged event of each RadioButton. When a RadioButton contained in the **Button Type** GroupBox is checked, the corresponding event handler sets buttonType to the appropriate value. Lines 23–48 contain the event handling for these RadioButtons. Similarly, when the user checks the RadioButtons belonging to the **Icon** GroupBox, the corresponding event handler associated with these events (lines 51–83) sets iconType to the appropriate value.

The Click event handler for displayButton (lines 86–120) creates a MessageBox (lines 90–93). The MessageBox options are specified with the values stored in iconType and buttonType. When the user clicks one of the MessageBox's buttons, the result of the message box is returned to the application. This result is a value from the **DialogResult enumeration** that contains Abort, Cancel, Ignore, No, None, OK, Retry or Yes. The switch statement in lines 96–119 tests for the result and sets displayLabel.Text appropriately.

14.8 PictureBoxes

A PictureBox displays an image. The image can be one of several formats, such as bitmap, GIF (Graphics Interchange Format) and JPEG. A PictureBox's Image property specifies the image that is displayed, and the SizeMode property indicates how the image is displayed (Normal, StretchImage, Autosize, CenterImage or Zoom). Figure 14.29 describes common PictureBox properties and a common event.

PictureBox properties and an event	Description
Common Properties	
Image	Sets the image to display in the PictureBox.
SizeMode	Enumeration that controls image sizing and positioning. Values are Normal (default), StretchImage, AutoSize, CenterImage, and Zoom. Normal places the image in the PictureBox's top-left corner, and CenterImage puts the image in the middle. These two options truncate the image if it's too large. StretchImage resizes the image to fit in the PictureBox. AutoSize resizes the PictureBox to hold the image. Zoom resizes the image to to fit the PictureBox but maintains the original aspect ratio.
Common Event	
Click	Occurs when the user clicks a control. When you double click this control in the designer, an event handler is generated for this event.

Fig. 14.29 | PictureBox properties and an event.

Figure 14.30 uses a PictureBox named imagePictureBox to display one of three bitmap images—image0.bmp, image1.bmp or image2.bmp. These images are provided in the Images subdirectory of this chapter's examples directory. Whenever a user clicks the **Next Image** Button, the image changes to the next image in sequence. When the last image is displayed and the user clicks the **Next Image** Button, the first image is displayed again.

```
 1  // Fig. 14.30: PictureBoxTestForm.cs
 2  // Using a PictureBox to display images.
 3  using System;
 4  using System.Drawing;
 5  using System.Windows.Forms;
 6
 7  namespace PictureBoxTest
 8  {
 9     // Form to display different images when PictureBox is clicked
10     public partial class PictureBoxTestForm : Form
11     {
12        private int imageNum = -1; // determines which image is displayed
13
14        // default constructor
15        public PictureBoxTestForm()
16        {
17           InitializeComponent();
18        } // end constructor
19
20        // change image whenever Next Button is clicked
21        private void nextButton_Click( object sender, EventArgs e )
22        {
23           imageNum = ( imageNum + 1 ) % 3; // imageNum cycles from 0 to 2
24
25           // retrieve image from resources and load into PictureBox
26           imagePictureBox.Image = ( Image )
27              ( Properties.Resources.ResourceManager.GetObject(
28              string.Format( "image{0}", imageNum ) ) );
29        } // end method nextButton_Click
30     } // end class PictureBoxTestForm
31  } // end namespace PictureBoxTest
```

Fig. 14.30 | Using a PictureBox to display images.

Using Resources Programmatically

In this example, we added the images to the project as **resources**. This causes the compiler to embed the images in the application's executable file and enables the application to access the images through the project's Properties namespace. By embedding the images in the application, you don't need to worry about wrapping the images with the application when you move it to another location or computer.

If you're creating a new project, use the following steps to add images to the project as resources:

1. After creating your project, right click the project's **Properties** node in the **Solution Explorer** and select **Open** to display the project's properties.

2. From the tabs on the left, click the **Resources** tab.

3. At the top of the **Resources** tab, click the down arrow next to **Add Resource** and select **Add Existing File...** to display the **Add existing file to resources** dialog.

4. Locate the image files you wish to add as resources and click the **Open** button. We provided three sample images in the Images folder with this chapter's examples.

5. Save your project.

The files now appear in a folder named **Resources** in the **Solution Explorer**. We'll use this technique in most examples that use images going forward.

A project's resources are stored in its **Resources** class (of the project's Properties namespace). The Resources class contains a **ResourceManager** object for interacting with the resources programmatically. To access an image, you can use the method **GetObject**, which takes as an argument the resource name as it appears in the **Resources** tab (e.g., "image0") and returns the resource as an Object. Lines 27–28 invoke GetObject with the result of the expression

```
string.Format( "image{0}", imageNum )
```

which builds the name of the resource by placing the index of the next picture (imageNum, which was obtained earlier in line 23) at the end of the word "image". You must convert this Object to type Image (namespace System.Drawing) to assign it to the PictureBox's Image property (line 26).

The Resources class also provides direct access to the resources you define with expressions of the form Resources.*resourceName*, where *resourceName* is the name you provided to the resource when you created it. When using such an expression, the resource returned already has the appropriate type. For example, Properties.Resources.image0 is an Image object representing the first image.

14.9 ToolTips

In Chapter 2, we demonstrated tool tips—the helpful text that appears when the mouse hovers over an item in a GUI. Recall that the tool tips displayed in Visual Studio help you become familiar with the IDE's features and serve as useful reminders for each toolbar icon's functionality. Many programs use tool tips to remind users of each control's purpose. For example, Microsoft Word has tool tips that help users determine the purpose of the application's icons. This section demonstrates how to use the **ToolTip** component to add tool tips to your applications. Figure 14.31 describes common properties and a common event of class `ToolTip`.

ToolTip properties and an event	Description
Common Properties	
AutoPopDelay	The amount of time (in milliseconds) that the tool tip appears while the mouse is over a control.
InitialDelay	The amount of time (in milliseconds) that a mouse must hover over a control before a tool tip appears.
ReshowDelay	The amount of time (in milliseconds) between which two different tool tips appear (when the mouse is moved from one control to another).
Common Event	
Draw	Raised when the tool tip is displayed. This event allows programmers to modify the appearance of the tool tip.

Fig. 14.31 | `ToolTip` properties and an event.

When you add a `ToolTip` component from the **Toolbox**, it appears in the **component tray**—the gray region below the `Form` in **Design** mode. Once a `ToolTip` is added to a `Form`, a new property appears in the **Properties** window for the `Form`'s other controls. This property appears in the **Properties** window as **ToolTip on**, followed by the name of the `ToolTip` component. For instance, if our `Form`'s `ToolTip` were named `helpfulToolTip`, you would set a control's **ToolTip on helpfulToolTip** property value to specify the control's tool tip text. Figure 14.32 demonstrates the `ToolTip` component. For this example, we create a GUI containing two `Label`s, so we can demonstrate different tool tip text for each `Label`. To make the sample outputs clearer, we set the `BorderStyle` property of each `Label` to `FixedSingle`, which displays a solid border. Since there's no event-handling code in this example, we did not show the code for the `Form` class.

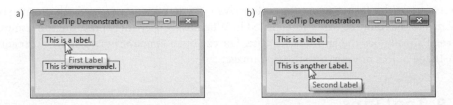

Fig. 14.32 | Demonstrating the `ToolTip` component.

In this example, we named the `ToolTip` component `labelsToolTip`. Figure 14.33 shows the `ToolTip` in the component tray. We set the tool tip text for the first `Label` to `"First Label"` and the tool tip text for the second `Label` to `"Second Label"`. Figure 14.34 demonstrates setting the tool tip text for the first `Label`.

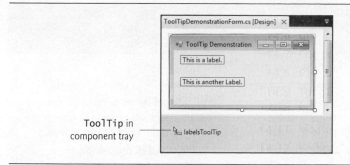

Fig. 14.33 | Demonstrating the component tray.

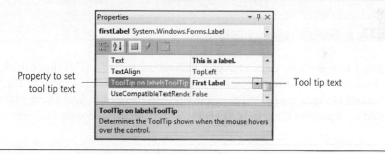

Fig. 14.34 | Setting a control's tool tip text.

14.10 NumericUpDown Control

At times, you'll want to restrict a user's input choices to a specific range of numeric values. This is the purpose of the **NumericUpDown control**. This control appears as a TextBox, with two small Buttons on the right side—one with an up arrow and one with a down arrow. By default, a user can type numeric values into this control as if it were a TextBox or click the up and down arrows to increase or decrease the value in the control, respectively. The largest and smallest values in the range are specified with the **Maximum** and **Minimum** properties, respectively (both of type decimal). The **Increment** property (also of type decimal) specifies by how much the current value changes when the user clicks the arrows. Property **DecimalPlaces** specifies the number of decimal places that the control should display as an integer. Figure 14.35 describes common NumericUpDown properties and an event.

NumericUpDown properties and an event	Description
Common Properties	
DecimalPlaces	Specifies how many decimal places to display in the control.
Increment	Specifies by how much the current number in the control changes when the user clicks the control's up and down arrows.

Fig. 14.35 | NumericUpDown properties and an event. (Part 1 of 2.)

NumericUpDown properties and an event	Description
Maximum	Largest value in the control's range.
Minimum	Smallest value in the control's range.
UpDownAlign	Modifies the alignment of the up and down Buttons on the NumericUpDown control. This property can be used to display these Buttons either to the left or to the right of the control.
Value	The numeric value currently displayed in the control.
Common Event	
ValueChanged	This event is raised when the value in the control is changed. This is the default event for the NumericUpDown control.

Fig. 14.35 | NumericUpDown properties and an event. (Part 2 of 2.)

Figure 14.36 demonstrates a NumericUpDown control in a GUI that calculates interest rate. The calculations performed in this application are similar to those in Fig. 6.6. Text-Boxes are used to input the principal and interest rate amounts, and a NumericUpDown control is used to input the number of years for which we want to calculate interest.

```
1   // Fig. 14.36: InterestCalculatorForm.cs
2   // Demonstrating the NumericUpDown control.
3   using System;
4   using System.Windows.Forms;
5
6   namespace NumericUpDownTest
7   {
8      public partial class InterestCalculatorForm : Form
9      {
10        // default constructor
11        public InterestCalculatorForm()
12        {
13           InitializeComponent();
14        } // end constructor
15
16        private void calculateButton_Click(
17           object sender, EventArgs e )
18        {
19           // declare variables to store user input
20           decimal principal; // store principal
21           double rate; // store interest rate
22           int year; // store number of years
23           decimal amount; // store amount
24           string output; // store output
25
26           // retrieve user input
27           principal = Convert.ToDecimal( principalTextBox.Text );
```

Fig. 14.36 | Demonstrating the NumericUpDown control. (Part 1 of 2.)

```
28            rate = Convert.ToDouble( interestTextBox.Text );
29            year = Convert.ToInt32( yearUpDown.Value );
30
31            // set output header
32            output = "Year\tAmount on Deposit\r\n";
33
34            // calculate amount after each year and append to output
35            for ( int yearCounter = 1; yearCounter <= year;  yearCounter++ )
36            {
37               amount =  principal * ( ( decimal )
38                  Math.Pow( ( 1 + rate / 100 ), yearCounter ) );
39               output += ( yearCounter + "\t" +
40                  string.Format( "{0:C}", amount ) + "\r\n" );
41            } // end for
42
43            displayTextBox.Text = output; // display result
44         } // end method calculateButton_Click
45      } // end class InterestCalculatorForm
46   } // end namespace NumericUpDownTest
```

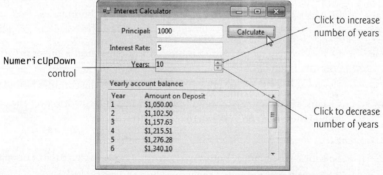

Fig. 14.36 | Demonstrating the NumericUpDown control. (Part 2 of 2.)

For the NumericUpDown control named yearUpDown, we set the Minimum property to 1 and the Maximum property to 10. We left the Increment property set to 1, its default value. These settings specify that users can enter a number of years in the range 1 to 10 in increments of 1. If we had set the Increment to 0.5, we could also input values such as 1.5 or 2.5. If you don't modify the DecimalPlaces property (0 by default), 1.5 and 2.5 display as 2 and 3, respectively. We set the NumericUpDown's **ReadOnly property** to true to indicate that the user cannot type a number into the control to make a selection. Thus, the user must click the up and down arrows to modify the value in the control. By default, the ReadOnly property is set to false, but the IDE changes this to true when you drag a NumericUpDown onto the Form. The output for this application is displayed in a multiline read-only TextBox with a vertical scrollbar, so the user can scroll through the entire output.

14.11 Mouse-Event Handling

This section explains how to handle **mouse events**, such as **clicks** and **moves**, which are generated when the user interacts with a control via the mouse. Mouse events can be handled for any control that derives from class System.Windows.Forms.Control. For most mouse events, information about the event is passed to the event-handling method through an object of class **MouseEventArgs**, and the delegate used to create the mouse-event handlers is **MouseEventHandler**. Each mouse-event-handling method for these events requires an object and a MouseEventArgs object as arguments.

Class MouseEventArgs contains information related to the mouse event, such as the mouse pointer's x- and y-coordinates, the mouse button pressed (Right, Left or Middle) and the number of times the mouse was clicked. The x- and y-coordinates of the MouseEventArgs object are relative to the control that generated the event—i.e., point *(0,0)* represents the upper-left corner of the control where the mouse event occurred. Several common mouse events and event arguments are described in Fig. 14.37.

Mouse events and event arguments	
Mouse Events with Event Argument of Type EventArgs	
MouseEnter	Occurs when the mouse cursor enters the control's boundaries.
MouseHover	Occurs when the mouse cursor hovers within the control's boundaries.
MouseLeave	Occurs when the mouse cursor leaves the control's boundaries.
Mouse Events with Event Argument of Type MouseEventArgs	
MouseDown	Occurs when a mouse button is pressed while the mouse cursor is within a control's boundaries.
MouseMove	Occurs when the mouse cursor is moved while in the control's boundaries.
MouseUp	Occurs when a mouse button is released when the cursor is over the control's boundaries.
Class MouseEventArgs Properties	
Button	Specifies which mouse button was pressed (Left, Right, Middle or None).
Clicks	The number of times that the mouse button was clicked.
X	The x-coordinate within the control where the event occurred.
Y	The y-coordinate within the control where the event occurred.

Fig. 14.37 | Mouse events and event arguments.

Figure 14.38 uses mouse events to draw on a Form. Whenever the user drags the mouse (i.e., moves the mouse while a mouse button is pressed), small circles appear on the Form at the position where each mouse event occurs during the drag operation.

```
1   // Fig. 14.38: PainterForm.cs
2   // Using the mouse to draw on a Form.
3   using System;
4   using System.Drawing;
5   using System.Windows.Forms;
6
7   namespace Painter
8   {
```

Fig. 14.38 | Using the mouse to draw on a Form. (Part 1 of 2.)

```
 9      // creates a Form that is a drawing surface
10      public partial class PainterForm : Form
11      {
12         bool shouldPaint = false; // determines whether to paint
13
14         // default constructor
15         public PainterForm()
16         {
17            InitializeComponent();
18         } // end constructor
19
20         // should paint when mouse button is pressed down
21         private void PainterForm_MouseDown(
22            object sender, MouseEventArgs e )
23         {
24            // indicate that user is dragging the mouse
25            shouldPaint = true;
26         } // end method PainterForm_MouseDown
27
28         // stop painting when mouse button is released
29         private void PainterForm_MouseUp( object sender, MouseEventArgs e )
30         {
31            // indicate that user released the mouse button
32            shouldPaint = false;
33         } // end method PainterForm_MouseUp
34
35         // draw circle whenever mouse moves with its button held down
36         private void PainterForm_MouseMove(
37            object sender, MouseEventArgs e )
38         {
39            if ( shouldPaint ) // check if mouse button is being pressed
40            {
41               // draw a circle where the mouse pointer is present
42               using ( Graphics graphics = CreateGraphics() )
43               {
44                  graphics.FillEllipse(
45                     new SolidBrush( Color.BlueViolet ), e.X, e.Y, 4, 4 );
46               } // end using; calls graphics.Dispose()
47            } // end if
48         } // end method PainterForm_MouseMove
49      } // end class PainterForm
50   } // end namespace Painter
```

Fig. 14.38 | Using the mouse to draw on a Form. (Part 2 of 2.)

In line 12, the program declares variable shouldPaint, which determines whether to draw on the Form. We want the program to draw only while the mouse button is pressed (i.e., held down). Thus, when the user clicks or holds down a mouse button, the system generates a MouseDown event, and the event handler (lines 21–26) sets shouldPaint to true. When the user releases the mouse button, the system generates a MouseUp event, shouldPaint is set to false in the PainterForm_MouseUp event handler (lines 29–33) and the program stops drawing. Unlike MouseMove events, which occur continuously as the user moves the mouse, the system generates a MouseDown event only when a mouse button is first pressed and generates a MouseUp event only when a mouse button is released.

Whenever the mouse moves over a control, the MouseMove event for that control occurs. Inside the PainterForm_MouseMove event handler (lines 36–48), the program draws only if shouldPaint is true (i.e., a mouse button is pressed). In the using statement, line 42 calls inherited Form method CreateGraphics to create a **Graphics** object that allows the program to draw on the Form. Class Graphics provides methods that draw various shapes. For example, lines 44–45 use method **FillEllipse** to draw a circle. The first parameter to method FillEllipse in this case is an object of class **SolidBrush**, which specifies the solid color that will fill the shape. The color is provided as an argument to class SolidBrush's constructor. Type **Color** contains numerous predefined color constants—we selected Color.BlueViolet. FillEllipse draws an oval in a bounding rectangle that is specified by the *x*- and *y*-coordinates of its upper-left corner, its width and its height—the final four arguments to the method. The *x*- and *y*-coordinates represent the location of the mouse event and can be taken from the mouse-event arguments (e.X and e.Y). To draw a circle, we set the width and height of the bounding rectangle so that they're equal—in this example, both are 4 pixels. Graphics, SolidBrush and Color are all part of the namespace System.Drawing. Recall from Chapter 13 that the using statement automatically calls Dispose on the object that was created in the parentheses following keyword using. This is important because Graphics objects are a limited resource. Calling Dispose on a Graphics object ensures that its resources are returned to the system for reuse.

14.12 Keyboard-Event Handling

Key events occur when keyboard keys are pressed and released. Such events can be handled for any control that inherits from System.Windows.Forms.Control. There are three key events—KeyPress, KeyUp and KeyDown. The **KeyPress** event occurs when the user presses a key that represents an ASCII character. The specific key can be determined with property **KeyChar** of the event handler's **KeyPressEventArgs** argument. ASCII is a 128-character set of alphanumeric symbols, a full listing of which can be found in Appendix C.

The KeyPress event does not indicate whether **modifier keys** (e.g., *Shift*, *Alt* and *Ctrl*) were pressed when a key event occurred. If this information is important, the **KeyUp** or **KeyDown** events can be used. The **KeyEventArgs** argument for each of these events contains information about modifier keys. Figure 14.39 lists important key event information. Several properties return values from the **Keys enumeration**, which provides constants that specify the various keys on a keyboard. Like the FontStyle enumeration (Section 14.7), the Keys enumeration is represented with a set of bits, so the enumeration's constants can be combined to indicate multiple keys pressed at the same time.

Keyboard events and event arguments	
Key Events with Event Arguments of Type `KeyEventArgs`	
KeyDown	Generated when a key is initially pressed.
KeyUp	Generated when a key is released.
Key Event with Event Argument of Type `KeyPressEventArgs`	
KeyPress	Generated when a key is pressed. Raised after `KeyDown` and before `KeyUp`.
Class `KeyPressEventArgs` *Properties*	
KeyChar	Returns the ASCII character for the key pressed.
Class `KeyEventArgs` *Properties*	
Alt	Indicates whether the *Alt* key was pressed.
Control	Indicates whether the *Ctrl* key was pressed.
Shift	Indicates whether the *Shift* key was pressed.
KeyCode	Returns the key code for the key as a value from the `Keys` enumeration. This does not include modifier-key information. It's used to test for a specific key.
KeyData	Returns the key code for a key combined with modifier information as a `Keys` value. This property contains all information about the pressed key.
KeyValue	Returns the key code as an `int`, rather than as a value from the `Keys` enumeration. This property is used to obtain a numeric representation of the pressed key. The `int` value is known as a Windows virtual key code.
Modifiers	Returns a `Keys` value indicating any pressed modifier keys (*Alt*, *Ctrl* and *Shift*). This property is used to determine modifier-key information only.

Fig. 14.39 | Keyboard events and event arguments.

Figure 14.40 demonstrates the use of the key-event handlers to display a key pressed by a user. The program is a `Form` with two `Label`s that displays the pressed key on one `Label` and modifier key information on the other.

```
1    // Fig. 14.40: KeyDemo.cs
2    // Displaying information about the key the user pressed.
3    using System;
4    using System.Windows.Forms;
5
6    namespace KeyDemo
7    {
8       // Form to display key information when key is pressed
9       public partial class KeyDemo : Form
10      {
11         // default constructor
12         public KeyDemo()
13         {
```

Fig. 14.40 | Demonstrating keyboard events. (Part 1 of 2.)

```
14              InitializeComponent();
15       } // end constructor
16
17       // display the character pressed using KeyChar
18       private void KeyDemo_KeyPress(
19           object sender, KeyPressEventArgs e )
20       {
21           charLabel.Text = "Key pressed: " + e.KeyChar;
22       } // end method KeyDemo_KeyPress
23
24       // display modifier keys, key code, key data and key value
25       private void KeyDemo_KeyDown( object sender, KeyEventArgs e )
26       {
27           keyInfoLabel.Text =
28               "Alt: " + ( e.Alt ? "Yes" : "No" ) + '\n' +
29               "Shift: " + ( e.Shift ? "Yes" : "No" ) + '\n' +
30               "Ctrl: " + ( e.Control ? "Yes" : "No" ) + '\n' +
31               "KeyCode: " + e.KeyCode + '\n' +
32               "KeyData: " + e.KeyData + '\n' +
33               "KeyValue: " + e.KeyValue;
34       } // end method KeyDemo_KeyDown
35
36       // clear Labels when key released
37       private void KeyDemo_KeyUp( object sender, KeyEventArgs e )
38       {
39           charLabel.Text = "";
40           keyInfoLabel.Text = "";
41       } // end method KeyDemo_KeyUp
42   } // end class KeyDemo
43 } // end namespace KeyDemo
```

a) *H* pressed   b) *F7* pressed   c) *$* pressed   d) *Tab* pressed

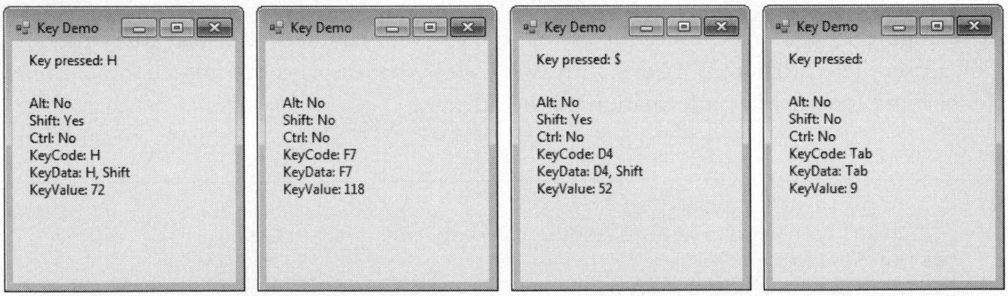

Fig. 14.40 | Demonstrating keyboard events. (Part 2 of 2.)

Control charLabel displays the character value of the key pressed, whereas keyInfo-Label displays information relating to the pressed key. Because the KeyDown and KeyPress events convey different information, the Form (KeyDemo) handles both.

The KeyPress event handler (lines 18–22) accesses the KeyChar property of the Key-PressEventArgs object. This returns the pressed key as a char, which we then display in charLabel (line 21). If the pressed key is not an ASCII character, then the KeyPress event will not occur, and charLabel will not display any text. ASCII is a common encoding format for letters, numbers, punctuation marks and other characters. It does not support keys such as the **function keys** (like *F1*) or the modifier keys (*Alt*, *Ctrl* and *Shift*).

The `KeyDown` event handler (lines 25–34) displays information from its `KeyEventArgs` object. The event handler tests for the *Alt*, *Shift* and *Ctrl* keys by using the `Alt`, `Shift` and `Control` properties, each of which returns a `bool` value—`true` if the corresponding key is pressed and `false` otherwise. The event handler then displays the `KeyCode`, `KeyData` and `KeyValue` properties.

The `KeyCode` property returns a `Keys` enumeration value (line 31). The `KeyCode` property returns the pressed key, but does not provide any information about modifier keys. Thus, both a capital and a lowercase "a" are represented as the *A* key.

The `KeyData` property (line 32) also returns a `Keys` enumeration value, but this property includes data about modifier keys. Thus, if "A" is input, the `KeyData` shows that both the *A* key and the *Shift* key were pressed. Lastly, `KeyValue` (line 33) returns an `int` representing a pressed key. This `int` is the **key code**. The key code is useful when testing for non-ASCII keys like *F12*.

The `KeyUp` event handler (lines 37–41) clears both `Label`s when the key is released. As we can see from the output, non-ASCII keys are not displayed in `charLabel`, because the `KeyPress` event is not generated. For example, `charLabel` does not display any text when you press the *F7* or *Tab* keys, as shown in Fig. 14.40(b) and (d). However, the `KeyDown` event still is generated, and `keyInfoLabel` displays information about the key that is pressed. The `Keys` enumeration can be used to test for specific keys by comparing the key pressed to a specific `KeyCode`.

Software Engineering Observation 14.2

To cause a control to react when a particular key is pressed (such as Enter*), handle a key event and test for the pressed key. To cause a* Button *to be clicked when the* Enter *key is pressed on a* Form*, set the* Form's AcceptButton *property.*

By default, a keyboard event is handled by the control that currently has the focus. Sometimes it's appropriate to have the `Form` handle these events. This can be accomplished by setting the `Form`'s `KeyPreview` property to `true`, which makes the `Form` receive keyboard events before they're passed to another control. For example, a key press would raise the `Form`'s `KeyPress`, even if a control within the `Form` has the focus instead of the `Form` itself.

14.13 Wrap-Up

This chapter introduced several common GUI controls. We discussed event handling in detail, and showed how to create event handlers. We also discussed how delegates are used to connect event handlers to the events of specific controls. You learned how to use a control's properties and Visual Studio to specify the layout of your GUI. We then demonstrated several controls, beginning with `Label`s, `Button`s and `TextBox`es. You learned how to use `GroupBox`es and `Panel`s to organize other controls. We then demonstrated `CheckBox`es and `RadioButton`s, which are state buttons that allow users to select among several options. We displayed images in `PictureBox` controls, displayed helpful text on a GUI with `ToolTip` components and specified a range of numeric input values for users with a `NumericUpDown` control. We then demonstrated how to handle mouse and keyboard events. The next chapter introduces additional GUI controls. You'll learn how to add menus to your GUIs and create Windows applications that display multiple `Form`s.

Summary

Section 14.1 Introduction

- A graphical user interface (GUI) allows a user to interact visually with a program.

- By providing different applications with a consistent set of intuitive user-interface components, GUIs enable users to become productive with each application faster.

- GUIs are built from GUI controls.

- GUI controls are objects that can display information on the screen or enable users to interact with an application via the mouse, keyboard or some other form of input.

Section 14.2 Windows Forms

- Windows Forms are used to create the GUIs for programs.

- A Form is a graphical element that appears on the desktop; it can be a dialog, a window or an MDI (multiple document interface) window.

- A component is an instance of a class that implements the IComponent interface, which defines the behaviors that components must implement, such as how the component is loaded.

- A control has a graphical representation at runtime.

- Some components lack graphical representations (e.g., class Timer of namespace System.Windows.Forms). Such components are not visible at runtime.

- When there are several windows on the screen, the active window is the frontmost and has a highlighted title bar. A window becomes the active window when the user clicks somewhere inside it.

- The active window is said to "have the focus."

- A Form is a container for controls and components.

Section 14.3 Event Handling

- Normally, a user interacts with an application's GUI to indicate the tasks that the application should perform.

- GUIs are event driven.

- When the user interacts with a GUI component, the interaction—known as an event—drives the program to perform a task. Common events include clicking a Button, typing in a TextBox, selecting an item from a menu, closing a window and moving the mouse.

- A method that performs a task in response to an event is called an event handler, and the overall process of responding to events is known as event handling.

Section 14.3.1 A Simple Event-Driven GUI

- An event handler executes only when the user performs the specific event.

- Each event handler receives two parameters when it's called. The first—an object reference typically named sender—is a reference to the object that generated the event. The second is a reference to an event arguments object of type EventArgs (or one of its derived classes), which is typically named e. This object contains additional information about the event that occurred.

- EventArgs is the base class of all classes that represent event information.

Section 14.3.2 Visual Studio Generated GUI Code

- Visual Studio generates the code that creates and initializes the GUI that you build in the GUI design window. This auto-generated code is placed in the Designer.cs file of the Form.

- The auto-generated code that defines the GUI is part of the Form's class. The use of the partial modifier in the class declaration allows the class to be split among multiple files.

- The Designer.cs file declares the controls you create in **Design** mode. By default, all variable declarations for controls created through C#'s design window have a private access modifier.

- The Designer.cs file includes the Dispose method for releasing resources and method InitializeComponent, which sets the properties of the Form and its controls.

- Visual Studio uses the code in InitializeComponent to create the GUI you see in design view. Changing the code in this method may prevent Visual Studio from displaying the GUI properly.

Section 14.3.3 Delegates and the Event-Handling Mechanism
- The control that generates an event is known as the event sender.

- An event-handling method—known as the event handler—responds to a particular event that a control generates.

- When an event occurs, the event sender calls its event handler to perform a task.

- The .NET event-handling mechanism allows you to choose your own names for event-handling methods. However, each event-handling method must declare the proper parameters to receive information about the event that it handles.

- Event handlers are connected to a control's events via special objects called delegates.

- A delegate object holds a reference to a method with a signature specified by the delegate type's declaration.

- GUI controls have predefined delegates that correspond to every event they can generate.

- An event sender calls a delegate object like a method.

- Since each event handler is declared as a delegate, the event sender can simply call the appropriate delegate when an event occurs. The delegate's job is to invoke the appropriate method.

- Event delegates represent a set of delegate objects that all have the same signature.

- When an event occurs, its sender calls every method referenced by a multicast delegate. Multicast delegates enable several methods to be called in response to a single event.

- Event delegates derive from class MulticastDelegate, which derives from class Delegate (both from namespace System).

Section 14.3.4 Another Way to Create Event Handlers
- Double-clicking a control on the Form in the designer creates an event handler for a control's default event.

- Typically, controls can generate many different events, and each can have its own event handler.

- You can create additional event handlers through the **Properties** window.

- If you select a control on the Form, then click the **Events** icon (the lightning bolt icon) in the **Properties** window, all the events for that control are listed in the window. You can double click an event's name to display the event handler in the editor, if the event handler already exists, or to create the corresponding event handler.

- You can select an event, then use the drop-down list to its right to choose an existing method that should be used as the event handler for that event. The methods that appear in this drop-down list are the Form class's methods that have the proper signature to be an event handler for the selected event.

- A single event handler can handle multiple events from multiple controls.

Section 14.3.5 Locating Event Information
- Read the Visual Studio documentation to learn about the different events raised by each control. To do this, select a control in the IDE and press the *F1* key to display that control's online help.

The web page that is displayed contains basic information about the control's class. Click the link to the list of events for that control to display the supported events for that control.

Section 14.4 Control Properties and Layout

- Controls derive from class `Control` (of namespace `System.Windows.Forms`).

- The `Select` method transfers the focus to a control and makes it the active control.

- The `Enabled` property indicates whether the user can interact with a control to generate an event.

- A programmer can hide a control from the user without disabling the control by setting the `Visible` property to `false` or by calling method `Hide`.

- Anchoring causes controls to remain at a fixed distance from the sides of the container even when the control is resized.

- Docking attaches a control to a container such that the control stretches across an entire side or fills all the remaining space.

- `Forms` have a `Padding` property that specifies the distance between the docked controls and the `Form` edges.

- The `Anchor` and `Dock` properties of a `Control` are set with respect to the `Control`'s parent container, which could be a `Form` or other parent container (such as a `Panel`).

- The minimum and maximum `Form` (or other `Control`) sizes can be set via properties `MinimumSize` and `MaximumSize`, respectively.

- When dragging a control across a `Form`, blue lines (known as snap lines) appear to help you position the control with respect to other controls and the `Form`'s edges.

- Visual Studio also provides the **Format** menu, which contains several options for modifying your GUI's layout.

Section 14.5 Labels, TextBoxes and Buttons

- Labels provide text information (as well as optional images) that the user cannot directly modify.

- A textbox (class `TextBox`) is an area in which text either can be displayed by a program or in which the user can type text via the keyboard.

- A password `TextBox` is a `TextBox` that hides the information entered by the user. As the user types, the password `TextBox` masks the user input by displaying a password character (usually *). If you set the `UseSystemPasswordChar` property to `true`, the `TextBox` becomes a password `TextBox`.

- A button is a control that the user clicks to trigger an action in a program or to select an option.

- All the button classes derive from class `ButtonBase` (namespace `System.Windows.Forms`), which defines common button features.

Section 14.6 GroupBoxes and Panels

- `GroupBoxes` and `Panels` arrange controls on a GUI.

- `GroupBoxes` and `Panels` are typically used to group several controls of similar functionality or several controls that are related in a GUI.

- `GroupBoxes` can display a caption (i.e., text) and do not include scrollbars, whereas `Panels` can include scrollbars and do not include a caption.

- `GroupBoxes` have thin borders by default; `Panels` can be set so that they also have borders, by changing their `BorderStyle` property.

- The controls of a `GroupBox` or `Panel` are added to the container's `Controls` property.

- To enable a `Panel`'s scrollbars, set the `Panel`'s `AutoScroll` property to `true`. If the `Panel` is resized and cannot display all of its controls, scrollbars appear.

Section 14.7 *CheckBoxes* and *RadioButtons*

- CheckBoxes and RadioButtons can be in the on/off or true/false states.

- Classes CheckBox and RadioButton are derived from class ButtonBase.

- A CheckBox is a small square that either is blank or contains a check mark. When a CheckBox is selected, a check mark appears in the box. Any number of CheckBoxes can be selected at a time.

- A CheckBox can be configured to have three states—checked, unchecked, and indeterminate—by setting its ThreeState property to true.

- Font styles can be combined via bitwise operators, such as the logical OR (|) operator or the logical exclusive OR (^) operator.

- RadioButtons (defined with class RadioButton) are similar to CheckBoxes in that they also have two states: selected and not selected (also called deselected).

- RadioButtons normally appear as a group, in which only one RadioButton can be selected at a time. The selection of one RadioButton in the group forces all the others to be deselected. Therefore, RadioButtons are used to represent a set of mutually exclusive options.

- All RadioButtons added to a container become part of the same group.

Section 14.8 *PictureBoxes*

- A PictureBox displays an image.

- The Image property specifies the image that is displayed

- The SizeMode property indicates how the image is displayed (Normal, StretchImage, Autosize, CenterImage, or Zoom).

- You can embed images into a project as resources.

- Embedded image files appear in a folder named **Resources** in the **Solution Explorer**.

- The Resources class (of a project's properties namespace) stores a project's resources.

- Class ResourceManager provides methods for programmatically accessing a project's resources.

- To access an image (or any other resource) in the project's resources, you use the method Get-Object of class ResourceManager, which takes as an argument the resource name as it appears in the **Resources** tab and returns the resource as an Object.

- The Resources class also provides direct access to the resources you define with expressions of the form Resources.*resourceName*, where *resourceName* is the name you provided to the resource when you created it. When using such an expression, the resource returned already has the appropriate type.

Section 14.9 *ToolTips*

- Tool tips help you become familiar with a Form's features and serve as useful reminders for each control's functionality. In the **Properties** window, you can specify a tool tip for a control by setting the **ToolTip on** *componentName* entry, where *componentName* is the name of the ToolTip component.

- The ToolTip component can be used to add tool tips to your application.

- The component tray is the gray region below the Form in **Design** mode.

Section 14.10 *NumericUpDown Control*

- At times you'll want to restrict a user's input choices to a specific range of numeric values. This is the purpose of the NumericUpDown control.

- The NumericUpDown control appears as a TextBox, with two small Buttons on the right side, one with an up arrow and one with a down arrow. By default, a user can type numeric values into this control as if it were a TextBox or click the up and down arrows to increase or decrease the value in the control, respectively.

- The largest and smallest values in the range are specified with the Maximum and Minimum properties, respectively (both are of type decimal).

- The Increment property (of type decimal) specifies by how much the current number in the control changes when the user clicks the control's up and down arrows.

- Setting a NumericUpDown control's ReadOnly property to true specifies that the user can only use the up and down arrows to modify the value in the NumericUpDown control.

Section 14.11 Mouse-Event Handling
- Mouse events, such as clicks and moves, are generated when the mouse interacts with a control.

- Mouse events can be handled for any subclass of System.Windows.Forms.Control.

- Class MouseEventArgs contains information related to the mouse event, such as the *x*- and *y*-coordinates of the mouse pointer, the mouse button pressed (Right, Left or Middle) and the number of times the mouse was clicked.

- Whenever the user clicks or holds down a mouse button, the system generates a MouseDown event.

- When the user releases the mouse button (to complete a "click" operation), the system generates a single MouseUp event.

- Whenever the mouse moves over a control, the MouseMove event for that control is raised.

Section 14.12 Keyboard-Event Handling
- Key events occur when keys on the keyboard are pressed and released.

- There are three key events—KeyPress, KeyUp and KeyDown.

- The KeyPress event occurs when the user presses a key that represents an ASCII character. The specific key can be determined with property KeyChar of the event handler's KeyPressEventArgs argument.

- The KeyPress event does not indicate whether modifier keys were pressed when a key event occurred. If this information is important, the KeyUp or KeyDown events can be used.

Terminology

active control
active window
anchor a control
bitwise operator
Button properties and events
Button property of class MouseEventArgs
ButtonBase class
checkbox
CheckBox class
Checked property of class CheckBox
Checked property of class RadioButton
CheckedChanged event of class CheckBox
CheckedChanged event of class RadioButton
CheckState property of class CheckBox
CheckStateChanged event of class CheckBox
Color structure
component

component tray
container
Control class
Controls property of a container
DecimalPlaces property of class NumericUpDown
default event
delegate
delegate class
delegate keyword
deselected state
DialogResult enumeration
dock a control
Dock property of class Control
Enabled property of class Control
event
event-driven programming
event handler

event handling
event multicasting
event handler
event sender
FillEllipse method of class Graphics
FlatStyle property of class Button
focus
Font class
FontStyle enumeration
GetObject method of class ResourceManager
Graphics class
Height property of structure Size
IComponent interface
Increment property of class NumericUpDown
key code
key event
KeyChar property of class KeyPressEventArgs
KeyCode property of class KeyEventArgs
KeyData property of class KeyEventArgs
KeyDown event of class Control
KeyEventArgs class
KeyPress event of class Control
KeyPressEventArgs class
Keys enumeration
KeyUp event of class Control
KeyValue property of class KeyEventArgs
Maximum property of class NumericUpDown
MaximumSize property of class Control
Minimum property of class NumericUpDown
MinimumSize property of class Control
modifier key
mouse click
mouse event
mouse move
mouse press
MouseDown event of class Control
MouseEventArgs class
MouseEventHandler delegate
MouseMove event of class Control

MouseUp event of class Control
multicast delegate
MulticastDelegate class
multiple document interface (MDI) window
mutual exclusion
"not-selected" state
NumericUpDown class
Padding property of class Control
Panel class
partial class
password TextBox
radio button
radio button group
RadioButton class
ReadOnly property of class NumericUpDown
ResourceManager class
Resources class
Select method of class Control
selected state
Size property of class Control
Size structure
snap line
SolidBrush class
state button
Style property of class Font
TabIndex property of class Control
TabStop property of class Control
ToolTip class
ThreeState property of class CheckBox
UseSystemPasswordChar property of class
    TextBox
UpDownAlign property of class NumericUpDown
Value property of class NumericUpDown
Visible property of class Control
widget
Width property of structure Size
window gadget
Windows Form

Self-Review Exercises

14.1 State whether each of the following is *true* or *false*. If *false*, explain why.
   a) The KeyData property includes data about modifier keys.
   b) A Form is a container.
   c) All Forms, components and controls are classes.
   d) CheckBoxes are used to represent a set of mutually exclusive options.
   e) A Label displays text that a user running an application can edit.
   f) Button presses generate events.
   g) All mouse events use the same event arguments class.
   h) Visual Studio can register an event and create an empty event handler.

i) The `NumericUpDown` control is used to specify a range of input values.

j) A control's tool tip text is set with the `ToolTip` property of class `Control`.

14.2 Fill in the blanks in each of the following statements:

a) The active control is said to have the _____.

b) The `Form` acts as a(n) _____ for the controls that are added.

c) GUIs are _____ driven.

d) Every method that handles the same event must have the same _____.

e) A(n) _____ `TextBox` masks user input with a character used repeatedly.

f) Class _____ and class _____ help arrange controls on a GUI and provide logical groups for radio buttons.

g) Typical mouse events include _____ and _____.

h) _____ events are generated when a key on the keyboard is pressed or released.

i) The modifier keys are _____, _____ and _____.

j) A(n) _____ event or delegate can be used to call multiple methods.

Answers To Self-Review Exercises

14.1 a) True. b) True. c) True. d) False. `RadioButtons` are used to represent a set of mutually exclusive options. e) False. A `Label`'s text cannot be edited by the user. f) True. g) False. Some mouse events use `EventArgs`, others use `MouseEventArgs`. h) True. i) True. j) False. A control's tool tip text is set using a `ToolTip` component that must be added to the application.

14.2 a) focus. b) container. c) event. d) signature. e) password. f) `GroupBox`, `Panel`. g) mouse clicks, mouse moves. h) `Key`. i) *Shift, Ctrl, Alt*. j) multicast.

Exercises

14.3 Extend the program in Fig. 14.26 to include a `CheckBox` for every font-style option. [*Hint:* Use logical exclusive OR (^) rather than testing for every bit explicitly.]

14.4 Create the GUI in Fig. 14.41 (you do not have to provide functionality).

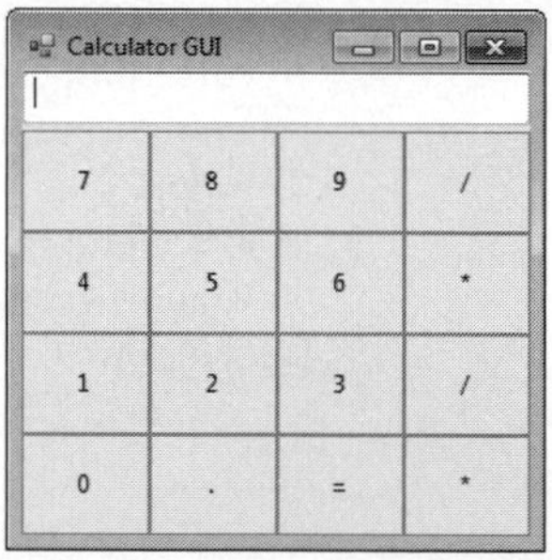

Fig. 14.41 | Calculator GUI.

14.5 Create the GUI in Fig. 14.42 (you do not have to provide functionality).

14.6 *(Temperature Conversions)* Write a temperature conversion program that converts from Fahrenheit to Celsius. The Fahrenheit temperature should be entered from the keyboard (via a `TextBox`). A `Label` should be used to display the converted temperature. Use the following formula for the conversion:

$$Celsius = (5 / 9) \times (Fahrenheit - 32)$$

Fig. 14.42 | Printer GUI.

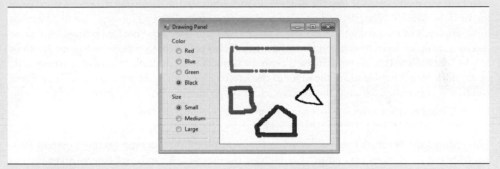

Fig. 14.43 | Drawing Panel GUI.

14.7 *(Enhanced Painter)* Extend the program of Fig. 14.38 to include options for changing the size and color of the lines drawn. Create a GUI similar to Fig. 14.43. The user should be able to draw on the application's Panel. To retrieve a Graphics object for drawing, call method *panelName*.CreateGraphics(), substituting in the name of your Panel.

14.8 *(Guess the Number Game)* Write a program that plays "guess the number" as follows: Your program chooses the number to be guessed by selecting an int at random in the range 1–1000. The program then displays the following text in a label:

```
I have a number between 1 and 1000--can you guess my number?
Please enter your first guess.
```

A TextBox should be used to input the guess. As each guess is input, the background color should change to red or blue. Red indicates that the user is getting "warmer," blue that the user is getting "colder." A Label should display either "Too High" or "Too Low," to help the user zero in on the correct answer. When the user guesses the correct answer, display "Correct!" in a message box, change the Form's background color to green and disable the TextBox. Recall that a TextBox (like other controls) can be disabled by setting the control's Enabled property to false. Provide a Button that allows the user to play the game again. When the Button is clicked, generate a new random number, change the background to the default color and enable the TextBox.

14.9 *(Fuzzy Dice Order Form)* Write an application that allows users to process orders for fuzzy dice. The application should calculate the total price of the order, including tax and shipping. TextBoxes for inputting the order number, the customer name and the shipping address are provided. Initially, these fields contain text that describes their purpose. Provide CheckBoxes for selecting the fuzzy-dice color and TextBoxes for inputting the quantities of fuzzy dice to order. The application should update the total cost, tax and shipping when the user changes any one of the three **Quantity** fields' values. The application should also contain a Button that when clicked, returns all fields to their original values. Use 5% for the tax rate. Shipping charges are $1.50 for up to 20 pairs of dice. If more than 20 pairs of dice are ordered, shipping is free. All fields must be filled out, and an item must be checked for the user to enter a quantity for that item.

Making a Difference Exercises

14.10   *(Ecofont)* Ecofont (www.ecofont.eu/ecofont_en.html)—developed by SPRANQ (a Netherlands-based company)—is a free, open-source computer font designed to reduce by as much as 20% the amount of ink used for printing, thus reducing also the number of ink cartridges used and the environmental impact of the manufacturing and shipping processes (using less energy, less fuel for shipping, and so on). The font, based on sans-serif Verdana, has small circular "holes" in the letters that are not visible in smaller sizes—such as the 9- or 10-point type frequently used. Download Ecofont, then install the font file ecofont_vera_sans_regular.ttf using the instructions from the Ecofont website. Next, develop a GUI-based program that allows you to type text in a TextBox to be displayed in the Ecofont. Create **Increase Font Size** and **Decrease Font Size** buttons that allow you to scale up or down by one point at a time. Set the TextBox's Font property to 9 point Ecofont. Set the TextBox's MultiLine property to true so the user can enter multiple lines of text. As you scale up the font, you'll be able to see the holes in the letters more clearly. As you scale down, the holes will be less apparent. To change the TextBox's font programmatically, use a statement of the form:

```
inputTextBox.Font = new Font( inputTextBox.Font.FontFamily,
    inputTextBox.Font.SizeInPoints + 1 );
```

This changes the TextBox's Font property to a new Font object that uses the TextBox's current font, but adds 1 to its SizeInPoints property to increase the font size. A similar statement can be used to decrease the font size. What is the smallest font size at which you begin to notice the holes?

14.11   *(Project: Typing Tutor—Tuning a Crucial Skill in the Computer Age)* Typing quickly and correctly is an essential skill for working effectively with computers and the Internet. In this exercise, you'll build an application that can help users learn to "touch type" (i.e., type correctly without looking at the keyboard). The application should display a *virtual keyboard* that mimics the one on your computer and should allow the user to watch what he or she is typing on the screen without looking at the *actual keyboard*. Use Buttons to represent the keys. As the user presses each key, the application highlights the corresponding Button and adds the character to a TextBox that shows what the user has typed so far. [*Hint:* To highlight a Button, use its BackColor property to change its background color. When the key is released, reset its original background color.]

You can test your program by typing a pangram—a phrase that contains every letter of the alphabet at least once—such as "The quick brown fox jumped over a lazy dog." You can find other pangrams on the web.

To make the program more interesting you could monitor the user's accuracy. You could have the user type specific phrases that you've prestored in your program and that you display on the screen above the virtual keyboard. You could keep track of how many keystrokes the user types correctly and how many are typed incorrectly. You could also keep track of which keys the user is having difficulty with and display a report showing those keys.

Graphical User Interfaces with Windows Forms: Part 2

15

I claim not to have controlled events, but confess plainly that events have controlled me.
—Abraham Lincoln

Capture its reality in paint!
—Paul Cézanne

An actor entering through the door, you've got nothing. But if he enters through the window, you've got a situation.
—Billy Wilder

But, soft! what light through yonder window breaks?
It is the east, and Juliet is the sun!
—William Shakespeare

Objectives

In this chapter you'll learn:

- To create menus, tabbed windows and multiple document interface (MDI) programs.

- To use the `ListView` and `TreeView` controls for displaying information.

- To create hyperlinks using the `LinkLabel` control.

- To display lists of information in `ListBox` and `ComboBox` controls.

- To input date and time data with the `DateTimePicker`.

- To create custom controls.

15.1 Introduction

This chapter continues our study of GUIs. We start with menus, which present users with logically organized commands (or options). We show how to develop menus with the tools provided by Visual Studio. Next, we discuss how to input and display dates and times using the MonthCalendar and DateTimePicker controls. We also introduce LinkLabels—powerful GUI components that enable the user to access one of several destinations, such as a file on the current machine or a web page, by simply clicking the mouse.

We demonstrate how to manipulate a list of values via a ListBox and how to combine several checkboxes in a CheckedListBox. We also create drop-down lists using ComboBoxes and display data hierarchically with a TreeView control. You'll learn two other important GUI elements—tab controls and multiple document interface (MDI) windows. These components enable you to create real-world programs with sophisticated GUIs.

Visual Studio provides many GUI components, several of which are discussed in this (and the previous) chapter. You can also design custom controls and add them to the **ToolBox**, as we demonstrate in this chapter's last example. The techniques presented here form the groundwork for creating more substantial GUIs and custom controls.

15.2 Menus

Menus provide groups of related commands for Windows applications. Although these commands depend on the program, some—such as **Open** and **Save**—are common to many applications. Menus are an integral part of GUIs, because they organize commands without "cluttering" the GUI.

In Fig. 15.1, an expanded menu from the Visual C# IDE lists various commands (called **menu items**), plus **submenus** (menus within a menu). The top-level menus appear in the left portion of the figure, whereas any submenus or menu items are displayed to the right. The menu that contains a menu item is called that menu item's **parent menu**. A menu item that contains a submenu is considered to be the parent of that submenu.

Menus can have *Alt* key shortcuts (also called **access shortcuts**, **keyboard shortcuts** or **hotkeys**), which are accessed by pressing *Alt* and the underlined letter—for example, *Alt F* typically expands the **File** menu. Menu items can have shortcut keys as well (combinations of *Ctrl*, *Shift*, *Alt*, *F1*, *F2*, letter keys, and so on). Some menu items display checkmarks, usually indicating that multiple options on the menu can be selected at once.

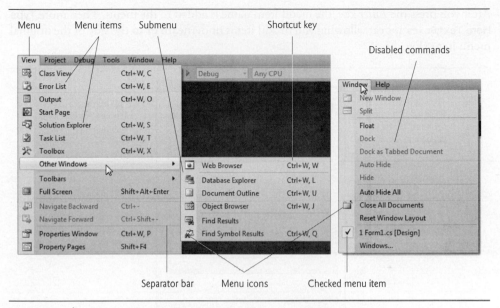

Fig. 15.1 | Menus, submenus and menu items.

To create a menu, open the **Toolbox** and drag a **MenuStrip** control onto the Form. This creates a menu bar across the top of the Form (below the title bar) and places a MenuStrip icon in the component tray. To select the MenuStrip, click this icon. You can now use **Design** mode to create and edit menus for your application. Menus, like other controls, have properties and events, which can be accessed through the **Properties** window.

To add menu items to the menu, click the **Type Here** TextBox (Fig. 15.2) and type the menu item's name. This action adds an entry to the menu of type **ToolStripMenuItem**.

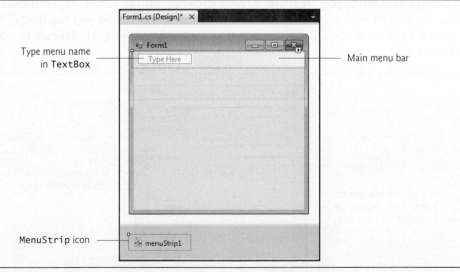

Fig. 15.2 | Editing menus in Visual Studio.

After you press the *Enter* key, the menu item name is added to the menu. Then more **Type Here** TextBoxes appear, allowing you to add items underneath or to the side of the original menu item (Fig. 15.3).

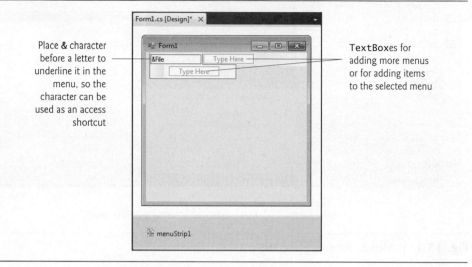

Place & character before a letter to underline it in the menu, so the character can be used as an access shortcut

TextBoxes for adding more menus or for adding items to the selected menu

Fig. 15.3 │ Adding `ToolStripMenuItems` to a `MenuStrip`.

To create an access shortcut, type an ampersand (&) before the character to be underlined. For example, to create the **File** menu item with the letter **F** underlined, type &File. To display an ampersand, type &&. To add other shortcut keys (e.g., *<Ctrl> F9*) for menu items, set the **ShortcutKeys** property of the appropriate `ToolStripMenuItems`. To do this, select the down arrow to the right of this property in the **Properties** window. In the window that appears (Fig. 15.4), use the CheckBoxes and drop-down list to select the shortcut keys. When you are finished, click elsewhere on the screen. You can hide the shortcut keys by setting property **ShowShortcutKeys** to `false`, and you can modify how the shortcut keys are displayed in the menu item by modifying property **ShortcutKeyDisplayString**.

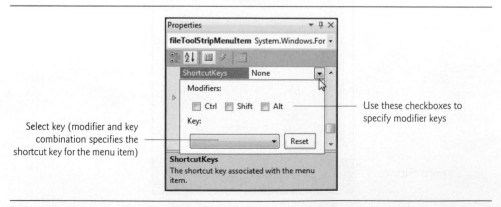

Select key (modifier and key combination specifies the shortcut key for the menu item)

Use these checkboxes to specify modifier keys

Fig. 15.4 │ Setting a menu item's shortcut keys.

Look-and-Feel Observation 15.1

Buttons can have access shortcuts. Place the & symbol immediately before the desired character in the Button's text. To press the button by using its access key in the running application, the user presses Alt and the underlined character. If the underline is not visible when the application runs, press the Alt key to display the underlines.

You can remove a menu item by selecting it with the mouse and pressing the *Delete* key. Menu items can be grouped logically by **separator bars**, which are inserted by right clicking the menu and selecting **Insert > Separator** or by typing "-" for the text of a menu item.

In addition to text, Visual Studio allows you to easily add TextBoxes and ComboBoxes (drop-down lists) as menu items. When adding an item in **Design** mode, you may have noticed that before you enter text for a new item, you are provided with a drop-down list. Clicking the down arrow (Fig. 15.5) allows you to select the type of item to add—**MenuItem** (of type ToolStripMenuItem, the default), **ComboBox** (of type ToolStripComboBox) and **TextBox** (of type ToolStripTextBox). We focus on ToolStripMenuItems. [*Note:* If you view this drop-down list for menu items that are not on the top level, a fourth option appears, allowing you to insert a separator bar.]

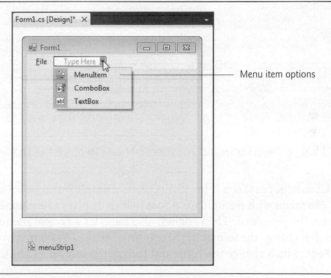

Fig. 15.5 | Menu-item options.

ToolStripMenuItems generate a **Click** event when selected. To create an empty Click event handler, double click the menu item in **Design** mode. Common actions in response to these events include displaying dialogs and setting properties. Common menu properties and a common event are summarized in Fig. 15.6.

Look-and-Feel Observation 15.2

*It is a convention to place an ellipsis (...) after the name of a menu item (e.g., **Save As...**) that requires the user to provide more information—typically through a dialog. A menu item that produces an immediate action without prompting the user for more information (e.g., **Save**) should not have an ellipsis following its name.*

MenuStrip and ToolStripMenuItem properties and an event	Description
MenuStrip Properties	
RightToLeft	Causes text to display from right to left. This is useful for languages that are read from right to left.
ToolStripMenuItem Properties	
Checked	Indicates whether a menu item is checked. The default value is false, meaning that the menu item is unchecked.
CheckOnClick	Indicates that a menu item should appear checked or unchecked as it is clicked.
ShortcutKey-DisplayString	Specifies text that should appear beside a menu item for a shortcut key. If left blank, the key names are displayed. Otherwise, the text in this property is displayed for the shortcut key.
ShortcutKeys	Specifies the shortcut key for the menu item (e.g., *<Ctrl>-F9* is equivalent to clicking a specific item).
ShowShortcutKeys	Indicates whether a shortcut key is shown beside menu item text. The default is true, which displays the shortcut key.
Text	Specifies the menu item's text. To create an *Alt* access shortcut, precede a character with **&** (e.g., &File to specify a menu named **File** with the letter **F** underlined).
Common ToolStripMenuItem Event	
Click	Generated when an item is clicked or a shortcut key is used. This is the default event when the menu is double clicked in the designer.

Fig. 15.6 | MenuStrip and ToolStripMenuItem properties and an event.

Class MenuTestForm (Fig. 15.7) creates a simple menu on a Form. The Form has a top-level **File** menu with menu items **About** (which displays a MessageBox) and **Exit** (which terminates the program). The program also includes a **Format** menu, which contains menu items that change the format of the text on a Label. The **Format** menu has submenus **Color** and **Font**, which change the color and font of the text on a Label.

Create the GUI
To create this GUI, begin by dragging the MenuStrip from the **ToolBox** onto the Form. Then use **Design** mode to create the menu structure shown in the sample outputs. The **File** menu (fileToolStripMenuItem) has menu items **About** (aboutToolStripMenuItem) and **Exit** (exitToolStripMenuItem); the **Format** menu (formatToolStripMenuItem) has two submenus. The first submenu, **Color** (colorToolStripMenuItem), contains menu items **Black** (blackToolStripMenuItem), **Blue** (blueToolStripMenuItem), **Red** (redToolStrip-MenuItem) and **Green** (greenToolStripMenuItem). The second submenu, **Font** (fontTool-StripMenuItem), contains menu items **Times New Roman** (timesToolStripMenuItem), **Courier** (courierToolStripMenuItem), **Comic Sans** (comicToolStripMenuItem), a separator bar (dashToolStripMenuItem), **Bold** (boldToolStripMenuItem) and **Italic** (italic-ToolStripMenuItem).

```
 1   // Fig. 15.7: MenuTestForm.cs
 2   // Using Menus to change font colors and styles.
 3   using System;
 4   using System.Drawing;
 5   using System.Windows.Forms;
 6
 7   namespace MenuTest
 8   {
 9      // our Form contains a Menu that changes the font color
10      // and style of the text displayed in Label
11      public partial class MenuTestForm : Form
12      {
13         // constructor
14         public MenuTestForm()
15         {
16            InitializeComponent();
17         } // end constructor
18
19         // display MessageBox when About ToolStripMenuItem is selected
20         private void aboutToolStripMenuItem_Click(
21            object sender, EventArgs e )
22         {
23            MessageBox.Show( "This is an example\nof using menus.", "About",
24               MessageBoxButtons.OK, MessageBoxIcon.Information );
25         } // end method aboutToolStripMenuItem_Click
26
27         // exit program when Exit ToolStripMenuItem is selected
28         private void exitToolStripMenuItem_Click(
29            object sender, EventArgs e )
30         {
31            Application.Exit();
32         } // end method exitToolStripMenuItem_Click
33
34         // reset checkmarks for Color ToolStripMenuItems
35         private void ClearColor()
36         {
37            // clear all checkmarks
38            blackToolStripMenuItem.Checked = false;
39            blueToolStripMenuItem.Checked = false;
40            redToolStripMenuItem.Checked = false;
41            greenToolStripMenuItem.Checked = false;
42         } // end method ClearColor
43
44         // update Menu state and color display black
45         private void blackToolStripMenuItem_Click(
46            object sender, EventArgs e )
47         {
48            // reset checkmarks for Color ToolStripMenuItems
49            ClearColor();
50
51            // set color to Black
52            displayLabel.ForeColor = Color.Black;
```

Fig. 15.7 | Menus for changing text font and color. (Part 1 of 4.)

```
53          blackToolStripMenuItem.Checked = true;
54       } // end method blackToolStripMenuItem_Click
55
56       // update Menu state and color display blue
57       private void blueToolStripMenuItem_Click(
58          object sender, EventArgs e )
59       {
60          // reset checkmarks for Color ToolStripMenuItems
61          ClearColor();
62
63          // set color to Blue
64          displayLabel.ForeColor = Color.Blue;
65          blueToolStripMenuItem.Checked = true;
66       } // end method blueToolStripMenuItem_Click
67
68       // update Menu state and color display red
69       private void redToolStripMenuItem_Click(
70          object sender, EventArgs e )
71       {
72          // reset checkmarks for Color ToolStripMenuItems
73          ClearColor();
74
75          // set color to Red
76          displayLabel.ForeColor = Color.Red;
77          redToolStripMenuItem.Checked = true;
78       } // end method redToolStripMenuItem_Click
79
80       // update Menu state and color display green
81       private void greenToolStripMenuItem_Click(
82          object sender, EventArgs e )
83       {
84          // reset checkmarks for Color ToolStripMenuItems
85          ClearColor();
86
87          // set color to Green
88          displayLabel.ForeColor = Color.Green;
89          greenToolStripMenuItem.Checked = true;
90       } // end method greenToolStripMenuItem_Click
91
92       // reset checkmarks for Font ToolStripMenuItems
93       private void ClearFont()
94       {
95          // clear all checkmarks
96          timesToolStripMenuItem.Checked = false;
97          courierToolStripMenuItem.Checked = false;
98          comicToolStripMenuItem.Checked = false;
99       } // end method ClearFont
100
101      // update Menu state and set Font to Times New Roman
102      private void timesToolStripMenuItem_Click(
103         object sender, EventArgs e )
104      {
105         // reset checkmarks for Font ToolStripMenuItems
```

Fig. 15.7 | Menus for changing text font and color. (Part 2 of 4.)

```
106              ClearFont();
107
108              // set Times New Roman font
109              timesToolStripMenuItem.Checked = true;
110              displayLabel.Font = new Font( "Times New Roman", 14,
111                  displayLabel.Font.Style );
112          } // end method timesToolStripMenuItem_Click
113
114          // update Menu state and set Font to Courier
115          private void courierToolStripMenuItem_Click(
116              object sender, EventArgs e )
117          {
118              // reset checkmarks for Font ToolStripMenuItems
119              ClearFont();
120
121              // set Courier font
122              courierToolStripMenuItem.Checked = true;
123              displayLabel.Font = new Font( "Courier", 14,
124                  displayLabel.Font.Style );
125          } // end method courierToolStripMenuItem_Click
126
127          // update Menu state and set Font to Comic Sans MS
128          private void comicToolStripMenuItem_Click(
129              object sender, EventArgs e )
130          {
131              // reset checkmarks for Font ToolStripMenuItems
132              ClearFont();
133
134              // set Comic Sans font
135              comicToolStripMenuItem.Checked = true;
136              displayLabel.Font = new Font( "Comic Sans MS", 14,
137                  displayLabel.Font.Style );
138          } // end method comicToolStripMenuItem_Click
139
140          // toggle checkmark and toggle bold style
141          private void boldToolStripMenuItem_Click(
142              object sender, EventArgs e )
143          {
144              // toggle checkmark
145              boldToolStripMenuItem.Checked = !boldToolStripMenuItem.Checked;
146
147              // use Xor to toggle bold, keep all other styles
148              displayLabel.Font = new Font( displayLabel.Font
149                  displayLabel.Font.Style ^ FontStyle.Bold );
150          } // end method boldToolStripMenuItem_Click
151
152          // toggle checkmark and toggle italic style
153          private void italicToolStripMenuItem_Click(
154              object sender, EventArgs e )
155          {
156              // toggle checkmark
157              italicToolStripMenuItem.Checked =
158                  !italicToolStripMenuItem.Checked;
```

Fig. 15.7 | Menus for changing text font and color. (Part 3 of 4.)

```
159
160            // use Xor to toggle italic, keep all other styles
161            displayLabel.Font = new Font( displayLabel.Font
162               displayLabel.Font.Style ^ FontStyle.Italic );
163         } // end method italicToolStripMenuItem_Click
164      } // end class MenuTestForm
165   } // end namespace MenuTest
```

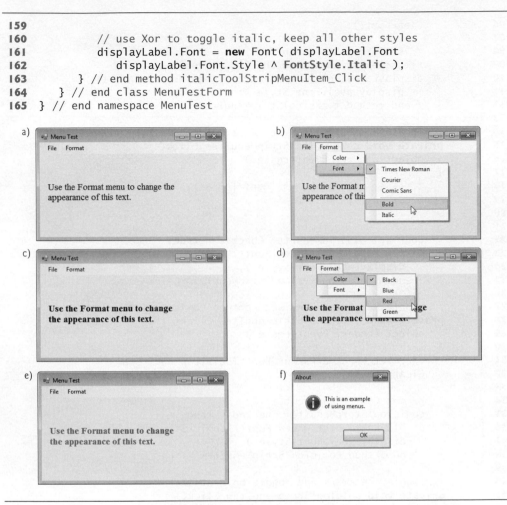

Fig. 15.7 | Menus for changing text font and color. (Part 4 of 4.)

Handling the *Click* Events for the *About* and *Exit* Menu Items

The **About** menu item in the **File** menu displays a MessageBox when clicked (lines 20–25). The **Exit** menu item closes the application through static method **Exit** of class **Application** (line 31). Class Application's static methods control program execution. Method Exit causes our application to terminate.

Color Submenu Events

We made the items in the **Color** submenu (**Black**, **Blue**, **Red** and **Green**) mutually exclusive—the user can select only one at a time (we explain how we did this shortly). To indicate that a menu item is selected, we will set each **Color** menu item's **Checked** property to true. This causes a check to appear to the left of a menu item.

Each **Color** menu item has its own Click event handler. The method handler for color **Black** is blackToolStripMenuItem_Click (lines 45–54). Similarly, the event handlers for colors **Blue**, **Red** and **Green** are `blueToolStripMenuItem_Click` (lines 57–66), `redTool-StripMenuItem_Click` (lines 69–78) and `greenToolStripMenuItem_Click` (lines 81–90), respectively. Each **Color** menu item must be mutually exclusive, so each event handler calls method `ClearColor` (lines 35–42) before setting its corresponding `Checked` property to `true`. Method `ClearColor` sets the `Checked` property of each color `ToolStripMenuItem` to `false`, effectively preventing more than one menu item from being selected at a time. In the designer, we initially set the **Black** menu item's `Checked` property to `true`, because at the start of the program, the text on the `Form` is black.

> **Software Engineering Observation 15.1**
>
> *The mutual exclusion of menu items is not enforced by the `MenuStrip`, even when the Checked property is true. You must program this behavior.*

Font Submenu Events

The **Font** menu contains three menu items for fonts (**Courier**, **Times New Roman** and **Comic Sans**) and two menu items for font styles (**Bold** and **Italic**). We added a separator bar between the font and font-style menu items to indicate that these are separate options. A `Font` object can specify only one font at a time but can set multiple styles at once (e.g., a font can be both bold and italic). We set the font menu items to display checks. As with the **Color** menu, we must enforce mutual exclusion of these items in our event handlers.

Event handlers for font menu items **Times New Roman**, **Courier** and **Comic Sans** are `timesToolStripMenuItem_Click` (lines 102–112), `courierToolStripMenuItem_Click` (lines 115–125) and `comicToolStripMenuItem_Click` (lines 128–138), respectively. These event handlers behave in a manner similar to that of the event handlers for the **Color** menu items. Each event handler clears the `Checked` properties for all font menu items by calling method `ClearFont` (lines 93–99), then sets the `Checked` property of the menu item that raised the event to `true`. This enforces the mutual exclusion of the font menu items. In the designer, we initially set the **Times New Roman** menu item's `Checked` property to `true`, because this is the original font for the text on the `Form`. The event handlers for the **Bold** and **Italic** menu items (lines 141–163) use the bitwise logical exclusive OR (∧) operator to combine font styles, as we discussed in Chapter 14.

15.3 MonthCalendar Control

Many applications must perform date and time calculations. The .NET Framework provides two controls that allow an application to retrieve date and time information—the `MonthCalendar` and `DateTimePicker` (Section 15.4) controls.

The **MonthCalendar** (Fig. 15.8) control displays a monthly calendar on the `Form`. The user can select a date from the currently displayed month or can use the provided arrows to navigate to another month. When a date is selected, it is highlighted. Multiple dates can be selected by clicking dates on the calendar while holding down the *Shift* key. The default event for this control is the **DateChanged** event, which is generated when a new date is selected. Properties are provided that allow you to modify the appearance of the calendar, how many dates can be selected at once, and the minimum date and maximum date that may be selected. `MonthCalendar` properties and a common `MonthCalendar` event are summarized in Fig. 15.9.

Fig. 15.8 | MonthCalendar control.

MonthCalendar properties and an event	Description
MonthCalendar Properties	
FirstDayOfWeek	Sets which day of the week is the first displayed for each week in the calendar.
MaxDate	The last date that can be selected.
MaxSelectionCount	The maximum number of dates that can be selected at once.
MinDate	The first date that can be selected.
MonthlyBoldedDates	An array of dates that will displayed in bold in the calendar.
SelectionEnd	The last of the dates selected by the user.
SelectionRange	The dates selected by the user.
SelectionStart	The first of the dates selected by the user.
Common MonthCalendar Event	
DateChanged	Generated when a date is selected in the calendar.

Fig. 15.9 | MonthCalendar properties and an event.

15.4 DateTimePicker Control

The **DateTimePicker** control (see output of Fig. 15.11) is similar to the MonthCalendar control but displays the calendar when a down arrow is selected. The DateTimePicker can be used to retrieve date and time information from the user. A DateTimePicker's **Value** property stores a DateTime object, which always contains both date and time information. You can retrieve the date information from the DateTime object by using property **Date**, and you can retrieve only the time information by using the **TimeOfDay** property.

The DateTimePicker is also more customizable than a MonthCalendar control—more properties are provided to edit the look and feel of the drop-down calendar. Property **Format** specifies the user's selection options using the **DateTimePickerFormat** enumeration. The values in this enumeration are Long (displays the date in long format, as in **Thursday, July 10, 2010**), Short (displays the date in short format, as in **7/10/2010**), Time (displays a time value, as in **5:31:02 PM**) and Custom (indicates that a custom format will be used). If value Custom is used, the display in the DateTimePicker is specified using property **CustomFormat**. The default event for this control is **ValueChanged**, which occurs when the selected value (whether a date or a time) is changed. DateTimePicker properties and a common event are summarized in Fig. 15.10.

DateTimePicker properties and an event	Description
DateTimePicker Properties	
CalendarForeColor	Sets the text color for the calendar.
CalendarMonth-Background	Sets the calendar's background color.
CustomFormat	Sets the custom format string for the user's options.
Format	Sets the format of the date and/or time used for the user's options.
MaxDate	The maximum date and time that can be selected.
MinDate	The minimum date and time that can be selected.
ShowCheckBox	Indicates if a CheckBox should be displayed to the left of the selected date and time.
ShowUpDown	Indicates whether the control displays up and down Buttons. Helpful when the DateTimePicker is used to select a time—the Buttons can be used to increase or decrease hour, minute and second.
Value	The data selected by the user.
Common DateTimePicker Event	
ValueChanged	Generated when the Value property changes, including when the user selects a new date or time.

Fig. 15.10 | DateTimePicker properties and an event.

Figure 15.11 demonstrates using a DateTimePicker to select an item's drop-off time. Many companies use such functionality—several online DVD rental companies specify the day a movie is sent out and the estimated time that it will arrive at your home. The user selects a drop-off day, then an estimated arrival date is displayed. The date is always two days after drop-off, three days if a Sunday is reached (mail is not delivered on Sunday).

```
1   // Fig. 15.11: DateTimePickerForm.cs
2   // Using a DateTimePicker to select a drop-off time.
3   using System;
4   using System.Windows.Forms;
5
6   namespace DateTimePickerTest
7   {
```

Fig. 15.11 | Demonstrating DateTimePicker. (Part 1 of 3.)

```
8      // Form lets user select a drop-off date using a DateTimePicker
9      // and displays an estimated delivery date
10     public partial class DateTimePickerForm : Form
11     {
12        // constructor
13        public DateTimePickerForm()
14        {
15           InitializeComponent();
16        } // end constructor
17
18        private void dateTimePickerDropOff_ValueChanged(
19           object sender, EventArgs e )
20        {
21           DateTime dropOffDate = dateTimePickerDropOff.Value;
22
23           // add extra time when items are dropped off around Sunday
24           if ( dropOffDate.DayOfWeek == DayOfWeek.Friday ||
25              dropOffDate.DayOfWeek == DayOfWeek.Saturday ||
26              dropOffDate.DayOfWeek == DayOfWeek.Sunday )
27
28              //estimate three days for delivery
29              outputLabel.Text =
30                 dropOffDate.AddDays( 3 ).ToLongDateString();
31           else
32              // otherwise estimate only two days for delivery
33              outputLabel.Text =
34                 dropOffDate.AddDays( 2 ).ToLongDateString();
35        } // end method dateTimePickerDropOff_ValueChanged
36
37        private void DateTimePickerForm_Load( object sender, EventArgs e )
38        {
39           // user cannot select days before today
40           dateTimePickerDropOff.MinDate = DateTime.Today;
41
42           // user can only select days of this year
43           dateTimePickerDropOff.MaxDate = DateTime.Today.AddYears( 1 );
44        } // end method DateTimePickerForm_Load
45     } // end class DateTimePickerForm
46  } // end namespace DateTimePickerTest
```

Fig. 15.11 | Demonstrating DateTimePicker. (Part 2 of 3.)

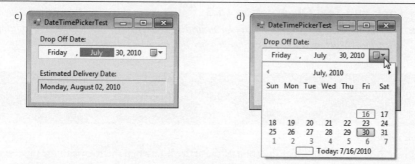

Fig. 15.11 | Demonstrating DateTimePicker. (Part 3 of 3.)

The DateTimePicker (dropOffDateTimePicker) has its Format property set to Long, so the user can select a date and not a time in this application. When the user selects a date, the ValueChanged event occurs. The event handler for this event (lines 18–35) first retrieves the selected date from the DateTimePicker's Value property (line 21). Lines 24–26 use the DateTime structure's **DayOfWeek** property to determine the day of the week on which the selected date falls. The day values are represented using the **DayOfWeek** enumeration. Lines 29–30 and 33–34 use DateTime's **AddDays** method to increase the date by three days or two days, respectively. The resulting date is then displayed in Long format using method **ToLongDateString**.

In this application, we do not want the user to be able to select a drop-off day before the current day, or one that is more than a year into the future. To enforce this, we set the DateTimePicker's **MinDate** and **MaxDate** properties when the Form is loaded (lines 40 and 43). Property Today returns the current day, and method **AddYears** (with an argument of 1) is used to specify a date one year in the future.

Let's take a closer look at the output. This application begins by displaying the current date (Fig. 15.11(a)). In Fig. 15.11(b), we selected the 30th of July. In Fig. 15.11(c), the estimated arrival date is displayed as the 2nd of August. Figure 15.11(d) shows that the 30th, after it is selected, is highlighted in the calendar.

15.5 LinkLabel Control

The **LinkLabel** control displays links to other resources, such as files or web pages (Fig. 15.12). A LinkLabel appears as underlined text (colored blue by default). When the mouse moves over the link, the pointer changes to a hand; this is similar to the behavior of a hyperlink in a web page. The link can change color to indicate whether it is not yet visited, previously visited or active. When clicked, the LinkLabel generates a **LinkClicked** event (see Fig. 15.13). Class LinkLabel is derived from class Label and therefore inherits all of class Label's functionality.

LinkLabel on a Form ——————————

Hand image displays when mouse moves over LinkLabel

Fig. 15.12 | LinkLabel control in running program.

Look-and-Feel Observation 15.3

A LinkLabel is the preferred control for indicating that the user can click a link to jump to a resource such as a web page, though other controls can perform similar tasks.

LinkLabel properties and an event	Description
Common Properties	
ActiveLinkColor	Specifies the color of the active link when the user is in the process of clicking the link. The default color (typically red) is set by the system.
LinkArea	Specifies which portion of text in the LinkLabel is part of the link.
LinkBehavior	Specifies the link's behavior, such as how the link appears when the mouse is placed over it.
LinkColor	Specifies the original color of the link before it's been visited. The default color (typically blue) is set by the system.
LinkVisited	If true, the link appears as though it has been visited (its color is changed to that specified by property VisitedLinkColor). The default value is false.
Text	Specifies the control's text.
UseMnemonic	If true, the & character in the Text property acts as a shortcut (similar to the *Alt* shortcut in menus).
VisitedLinkColor	Specifies the color of a visited link. The default color (typically purple) is set by the system.
Common Event	*(Event arguments LinkLabelLinkClickedEventArgs)*
LinkClicked	Generated when the link is clicked. This is the default event when the control is double clicked in **Design** mode.

Fig. 15.13 | LinkLabel properties and an event.

Class LinkLabelTestForm (Fig. 15.14) uses three LinkLabels to link to the C: drive, the Deitel website (www.deitel.com) and the Notepad application, respectively. The Text properties of the LinkLabel's cDriveLinkLabel, deitelLinkLabel and notepadLinkLabel describe each link's purpose.

```
1   // Fig. 15.14: LinkLabelTestForm.cs
2   // Using LinkLabels to create hyperlinks.
3   using System;
4   using System.Windows.Forms;
5
6   namespace LinkLabelTest
7   {
8      // Form using LinkLabels to browse the C:\ drive,
9      // load a web page and run Notepad
10     public partial class LinkLabelTestForm : Form
11     {
```

Fig. 15.14 | LinkLabels used to link to a drive, a web page and an application. (Part 1 of 3.)

```
12          // constructor
13          public LinkLabelTestForm()
14          {
15              InitializeComponent();
16          } // end constructor
17
18          // browse C:\ drive
19          private void cDriveLinkLabel_LinkClicked( object sender,
20              LinkLabelLinkClickedEventArgs e )
21          {
22              // change LinkColor after it has been clicked
23              driveLinkLabel.LinkVisited = true;
24
25              System.Diagnostics.Process.Start( @"C:\" );
26          } // end method cDriveLinkLabel_LinkClicked
27
28          // load www.deitel.com in web browser
29          private void deitelLinkLabel_LinkClicked( object sender,
30              LinkLabelLinkClickedEventArgs e )
31          {
32              // change LinkColor after it has been clicked
33              deitelLinkLabel.LinkVisited = true;
34
35              System.Diagnostics.Process.Start( "http://www.deitel.com" );
36          } // end method deitelLinkLabel_LinkClicked
37
38          // run application Notepad
39          private void notepadLinkLabel_LinkClicked( object sender,
40              LinkLabelLinkClickedEventArgs e )
41          {
42              // change LinkColor after it has been clicked
43              notepadLinkLabel.LinkVisited = true;
44
45              // program called as if in run
46              // menu and full path not needed
47              System.Diagnostics.Process.Start( "notepad" );
48          } // end method driveLinkLabel_LinkClicked
49      } // end class LinkLabelTestForm
50  } // end namespace LinkLabelTest
```

Click first LinkLabel to
look at contents of C: drive

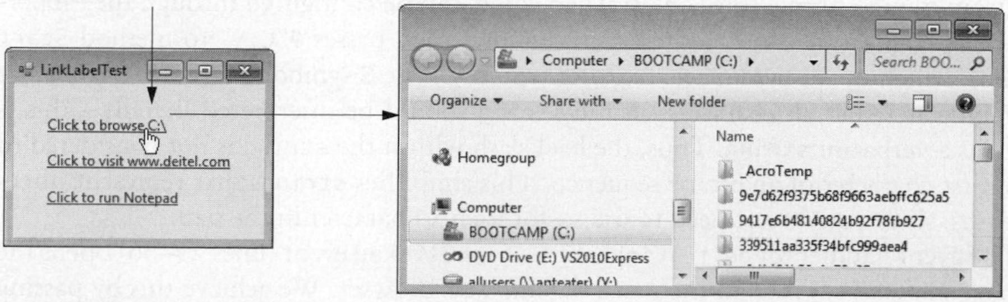

Fig. 15.14 | LinkLabels used to link to a drive, a web page and an application. (Part 2 of 3.)

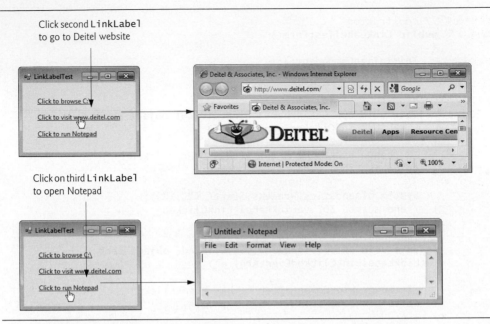

Click second `LinkLabel` to go to Deitel website

Click on third `LinkLabel` to open Notepad

Fig. 15.14 | `LinkLabel`s used to link to a drive, a web page and an application. (Part 3 of 3.)

The event handlers for the `LinkLabel`s call method **Start** of class **Process** (namespace **System.Diagnostics**), which allows you to execute other programs, or load documents or web sites from an application. Method `Start` can take one argument, the file to open, or two arguments, the application to run and its command-line arguments. Method `Start`'s arguments can be in the same form as if they were provided for input to the Windows **Run** command (**Start > Run...**). For applications that are known to Windows, full path names are not needed, and the file extension often can be omitted. To open a file of a type that Windows recognizes (and knows how to handle), simply use the file's full path name. For example, if you a pass the method a `.doc` file, Windows will open it in Microsoft Word (or whatever program is registered to open .doc files, if any). The Windows operating system must be able to use the application associated with the given file's extension to open the file.

The event handler for `cDriveLinkLabel`'s `LinkClicked` event browses the C: drive (lines 19–26). Line 23 sets the `LinkVisited` property to `true`, which changes the link's color from blue to purple (the `LinkVisited` colors can be configured through the **Properties** window in Visual Studio). The event handler then passes `@"C:\"` to method `Start` (line 25), which opens a **Windows Explorer** window. The @ symbol that we placed before `"C:\"` indicates that all characters in the `string` should be interpreted literally—this is known as a **verbatim string**. Thus, the backslash within the `string` is not considered to be the first character of an escape sequence. This simplifies `string`s that represent directory paths, since you do not need to use `\\` for each `\` character in the path.

The event handler for `deitelLinkLabel`'s `LinkClicked` event (lines 29–36) opens the web page www.deitel.com in the user's default web browser. We achieve this by passing the web-page address as a `string` (line 35), which opens the web page in a new web browser window or tab. Line 33 sets the `LinkVisited` property to `true`.

The event handler for notepadLinkLabel's LinkClicked event (lines 39–48) opens the Notepad application. Line 43 sets the LinkVisited property to true so that the link appears as a visited link. Line 47 passes the argument "notepad" to method Start, which runs notepad.exe. In line 47, neither the full path nor the .exe extension is required—Windows automatically recognizes the argument given to method Start as an executable file.

15.6 ListBox Control

The **ListBox** control allows the user to view and select from multiple items in a list. List-Boxes are static GUI entities, which means that users cannot directly edit the list of items. The user can be provided with TextBoxes and Buttons with which to specify items to be added to the list, but the actual additions must be performed in code. The **CheckedList-Box** control (Section 15.7) extends a ListBox by including CheckBoxes next to each item in the list. This allows users to place checks on multiple items at once, as is possible with CheckBox controls. (Users also can select multiple items from a ListBox by setting the ListBox's **SelectionMode** property, which is discussed shortly.) Figure 15.15 displays a ListBox and a CheckedListBox. In both controls, scrollbars appear if the number of items exceeds the ListBox's viewable area.

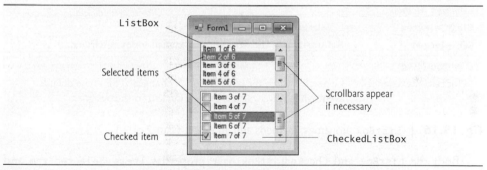

Fig. 15.15 | ListBox and CheckedListBox on a Form.

Figure 15.16 lists common ListBox properties and methods and a common event. The SelectionMode property determines the number of items that can be selected. This property has the possible values None, One, MultiSimple and MultiExtended (from the **SelectionMode** enumeration)—the differences among these settings are explained in Fig. 15.16. The **SelectedIndexChanged** event occurs when the user selects a new item.

ListBox properties, methods and an event	Description
Common Properties	
Items	The collection of items in the ListBox.
MultiColumn	Indicates whether the ListBox can display multiple columns. Multiple columns eliminate vertical scrollbars from the display.

Fig. 15.16 | ListBox properties, methods and an event. (Part 1 of 2.)

ListBox properties, methods and an event	Description
SelectedIndex	Returns the index of the selected item. If no items have been selected, the property returns -1. If the user selects multiple items, this property returns only one of the selected indices. If multiple items are selected, use property SelectedIndices.
SelectedIndices	Returns a collection containing the indices for all selected items.
SelectedItem	Returns a reference to the selected item. If multiple items are selected, it returns the item with the lowest index number.
SelectedItems	Returns a collection of the selected item(s).
SelectionMode	Determines the number of items that can be selected and the means through which multiple items can be selected. Values None, One (the default), MultiSimple (multiple selection allowed) or MultiExtended (multiple selection allowed using a combination of arrow keys or mouse clicks and *Shift* and *Ctrl* keys).
Sorted	Indicates whether items are sorted alphabetically. Setting this property's value to true sorts the items. The default value is false.
Common Methods	
ClearSelected	Deselects every item.
GetSelected	Returns true if the item at the specified index is selected.
Common Event	
SelectedIndexChanged	Generated when the selected index changes. This is the default event when the control is double clicked in the designer.

Fig. 15.16 | ListBox properties, methods and an event. (Part 2 of 2.)

Both the ListBox and CheckedListBox have properties Items, SelectedItem and SelectedIndex. Property **Items** returns a collection of the list items. Collections are a common way to manage lists of objects in the .NET framework. Many .NET GUI components (e.g., ListBoxes) use collections to expose lists of internal objects (e.g., items in a ListBox). We discuss collections further in Chapter 23. The collection returned by property Items is represented as an object of type ListBox.ObjectCollection. Property **SelectedItem** returns the ListBox's currently selected item. If the user can select multiple items, use collection **SelectedItems** to return all the selected items as a ListBox.SelectedObjectColection. Property **SelectedIndex** returns the index of the selected item—if there could be more than one, use property **SelectedIndices**, which returns a ListBox.SelectedIndexColection. If no items are selected, property SelectedIndex returns -1. Method **GetSelected** takes an index and returns true if the corresponding item is selected.

Adding Items to ListBoxes and CheckedListBoxes

To add items to a ListBox or to a CheckedListBox, we must add objects to its Items collection. This can be accomplished by calling method Add to add a string to the ListBox's or CheckedListBox's Items collection. For example, we could write

```
myListBox.Items.Add( myListItem );
```

to add string *myListItem* to ListBox *myListBox*. To add multiple objects, you can either call method Add multiple times or call method AddRange to add an array of objects. Classes ListBox and CheckedListBox each call the submitted object's ToString method to determine the Label for the corresponding object's entry in the list. This allows you to add different objects to a ListBox or a CheckedListBox that later can be returned through properties SelectedItem and SelectedItems.

Alternatively, you can add items to ListBoxes and CheckedListBoxes visually by examining the Items property in the **Properties** window. Clicking the ellipsis button opens the **String Collection Editor**, which contains a text area for adding items; each item appears on a separate line (Fig. 15.17). Visual Studio then writes code to add these strings to the Items collection inside method InitializeComponent.

Fig. 15.17 | String Collection Editor.

Figure 15.18 uses class ListBoxTestForm to add, remove and clear items from ListBox displayListBox. Class ListBoxTestForm uses TextBox inputTextBox to allow the user to type in a new item. When the user clicks the **Add** Button, the new item appears in displayListBox. Similarly, if the user selects an item and clicks **Remove**, the item is deleted. When clicked, **Clear** deletes all entries in displayListBox. The user terminates the application by clicking **Exit**.

The addButton_Click event handler (lines 20–24) calls method Add of the Items collection in the ListBox. This method takes a string as the item to add to displayListBox. In this case, the string used is the user input from the inputTextBox (line 22). After the item is added, inputTextBox.Text is cleared (line 23).

```
1   // Fig. 15.18: ListBoxTestForm.cs
2   // Program to add, remove and clear ListBox items
3   using System;
4   using System.Windows.Forms;
5
6   namespace ListBoxTest
7   {
8      // Form uses a TextBox and Buttons to add,
9      // remove, and clear ListBox items
10     public partial class ListBoxTestForm : Form
11     {
```

Fig. 15.18 | Program that adds, removes and clears ListBox items. (Part 1 of 3.)

```
12          // constructor
13          public ListBoxTestForm()
14          {
15              InitializeComponent();
16          } // end constructor
17
18          // add new item to ListBox (text from input TextBox)
19          // and clear input TextBox
20          private void addButton_Click( object sender, EventArgs e )
21          {
22              displayListBox.Items.Add( inputTextBox.Text );
23              inputTextBox.Clear();
24          } // end method addButton_Click
25
26          // remove item if one is selected
27          private void removeButton_Click( object sender, EventArgs e )
28          {
29              // check whether item is selected, remove if
30              if ( displayListBox.SelectedIndex != -1 )
31                  displayListBox.Items.RemoveAt(
32                      displayListBox.SelectedIndex );
33          } // end method removeButton_Click
34
35          // clear all items in ListBox
36          private void clearButton_Click( object sender, EventArgs e )
37          {
38              displayListBox.Items.Clear();
39          } // end method clearButton_Click
40
41          // exit application
42          private void exitButton_Click( object sender, EventArgs e )
43          {
44              Application.Exit();
45          } // end method exitButton_Click
46      } // end class ListBoxTestForm
47  } // end namespace ListBoxTest
```

Fig. 15.18 | Program that adds, removes and clears ListBox items. (Part 2 of 3.)

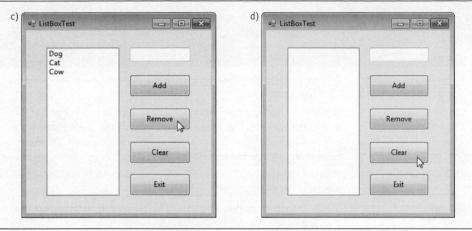

Fig. 15.18 | Program that adds, removes and clears ListBox items. (Part 3 of 3.)

The removeButton_Click event handler (lines 27–33) uses method RemoveAt to remove an item from the ListBox. Event handler removeButton_Click first uses property SelectedIndex to determine which index is selected. If SelectedIndex is not -1 (i.e., an item is selected), lines 31–32 remove the item that corresponds to the selected index.

The clearButton_Click event handler (lines 36–39) calls method Clear of the Items collection (line 38). This removes all the entries in displayListBox. Finally, event handler exitButton_Click (lines 42–45) terminates the application by calling method Application.Exit (line 44).

15.7 CheckedListBox Control

The CheckedListBox control derives from ListBox and displays a CheckBox with each item. Items can be added via methods Add and AddRange or through the **String Collection Editor**. CheckedListBoxes allow multiple items to be checked, but item selection is more restrictive. The only values for the SelectionMode property are None and One. One allows a single selection, whereas None allows no selections. Because an item must be selected to be checked, you must set the SelectionMode to be One if you wish to allow users to check items. Thus, toggling property SelectionMode between One and None effectively switches between enabling and disabling the user's ability to check list items. Common properties, a method and an event of CheckedListBoxes appear in Fig. 15.19.

Common Programming Error 15.1

*The IDE displays an error message if you attempt to set the SelectionMode property to MultiSimple or MultiExtended in the **Properties** window of a CheckedListBox. If this value is set programmatically, a runtime error occurs.*

Event **ItemCheck** occurs whenever a user checks or unchecks a CheckedListBox item. Event-argument properties CurrentValue and NewValue return CheckState values for the current and new state of the item, respectively. A comparison of these values allows you to determine whether the CheckedListBox item was checked or unchecked. The Checked-ListBox control retains the SelectedItems and SelectedIndices properties (it inherits

CheckedListBox properties, a method and an event	Description
Common Properties	*(All the ListBox properties, methods and events are inherited by CheckedListBox.)*
CheckedItems	Returns the collection of items that are checked as a CheckedListBox.CheckedItemCollection. This is distinct from the selected item, which is highlighted (but not necessarily checked). [*Note:* There can be at most one selected item at any given time.]
CheckedIndices	Returns indices for all checked items as a CheckedListBox.CheckedIndexCollection.
CheckOnClick	When true and the user clicks an item, the item is both selected and checked or unchecked. By default, this property is false, which means that the user must select an item, then click it again to check or uncheck it.
SelectionMode	Determines whether items can be selected and checked. The possible values are One (the default; allows multiple checks to be placed) or None (does not allow any checks to be placed).
Common Method	
GetItemChecked	Takes an index and returns true if the corresponding item is checked.
Common Event	*(Event arguments ItemCheckEventArgs)*
ItemCheck	Generated when an item is checked or unchecked.
ItemCheckEventArgs Properties	
CurrentValue	Indicates whether the current item is checked or unchecked. Possible values are Checked, Unchecked and Indeterminate.
Index	Returns the zero-based index of the item that changed.
NewValue	Specifies the new state of the item.

Fig. 15.19 | CheckedListBox properties, a method and an event.

them from class ListBox). However, it also includes properties CheckedItems and CheckedIndices, which return information about the checked items and indices.

In Fig. 15.20, class CheckedListBoxTestForm uses a CheckedListBox and a ListBox to display a user's selection of books. The CheckedListBox allows the user to select multiple titles. In the **String Collection Editor**, items were added for some Deitel books: C, C++, Java™, Internet & WWW, VB 2008, Visual C++ and Visual C# 2008 (the acronym HTP stands for "How to Program"). The ListBox (named displayListBox) displays the user's selection. In the screenshots accompanying this example, the CheckedListBox appears to the left, the ListBox on the right.

When the user checks or unchecks an item in itemCheckedListBox_ItemCheck, an ItemCheck event occurs and event handler itemCheckedListBox_ItemCheck (lines 19–31) executes. An if...else statement (lines 27–30) determines whether the user checked or unchecked an item in the CheckedListBox. Line 27 uses the NewValue property to deter-

```
 1   // Fig. 15.20: CheckedListBoxTestForm.cs
 2   // Using a CheckedListBox to add items to a display ListBox
 3   using System;
 4   using System.Windows.Forms;
 5
 6   namespace CheckedListBoxTest
 7   {
 8      // Form uses a checked ListBox to add items to a display ListBox
 9      public partial class CheckedListBoxTestForm : Form
10      {
11         // constructor
12         public CheckedListBoxTestForm()
13         {
14            InitializeComponent();
15         } // end constructor
16
17         // item about to change
18         // add or remove from display ListBox
19         private void itemCheckedListBox_ItemCheck(
20            object sender, ItemCheckEventArgs e )
21         {
22            // obtain reference of selected item
23            string item = itemCheckedListBox.SelectedItem.ToString();
24
25            // if item checked, add to ListBox
26            // otherwise remove from ListBox
27            if ( e.NewValue == CheckState.Checked )
28               displayListBox.Items.Add( item );
29            else
30               displayListBox.Items.Remove( item );
31         } // end method itemCheckedListBox_ItemCheck
32      } // end class CheckedListBoxTestForm
33   } // end namespace CheckedListBoxTest
```

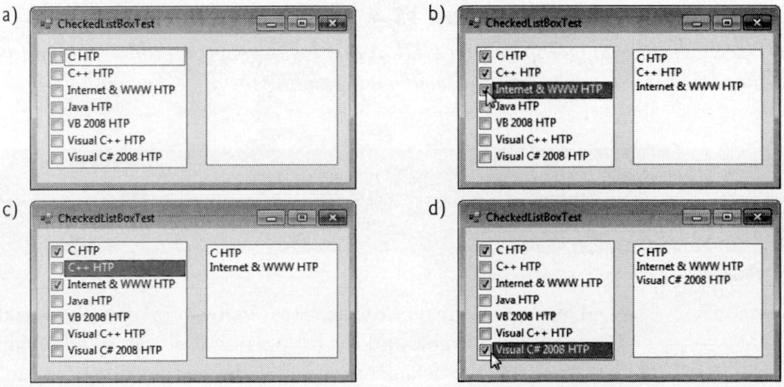

Fig. 15.20 | CheckedListBox and ListBox used in a program to display a user selection.

mine whether the item is being checked (CheckState.Checked). If the user checks an item, line 28 adds the checked entry to the ListBox displayListBox. If the user unchecks an item, line 30 removes the corresponding item from displayListBox. This event handler was created by selecting the `CheckedListBox` in **Design** mode, viewing the control's events in the **Properties** window and double clicking the `ItemCheck` event. The default event for a `CheckedListBox` is a `SelectedIndexChanged` event.

15.8 ComboBox Control

The **ComboBox** control combines `TextBox` features with a **drop-down list**—a GUI component that contains a list from which a value can be selected. A `ComboBox` usually appears as a `TextBox` with a down arrow to its right. By default, the user can enter text into the `TextBox` or click the down arrow to display a list of predefined items. If a user chooses an element from this list, that element is displayed in the `TextBox`. If the list contains more elements than can be displayed in the drop-down list, a scrollbar appears. The maximum number of items that a drop-down list can display at one time is set by property **MaxDropDownItems**. Figure 15.21 shows a sample `ComboBox` in three different states.

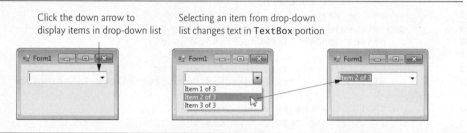

Fig. 15.21 | ComboBox demonstration.

As with the `ListBox` control, you can add objects to collection `Items` programmatically, using methods `Add` and `AddRange`, or visually, with the **String Collection Editor**. Figure 15.22 lists common properties and a common event of class `ComboBox`.

 Look-and-Feel Observation 15.4

Use a ComboBox to save space on a GUI. A disadvantage is that, unlike with a ListBox, the user cannot see available items without expanding the drop-down list.

ComboBox properties and an event	Description
Common Properties	
`DropDownStyle`	Determines the type of `ComboBox`. Value `Simple` means that the text portion is editable and the list portion is always visible. Value `DropDown` (the default) means that the text portion is editable but the user must click an arrow button to see the list portion. Value `DropDownList` means that the text portion is not editable and the user must click the arrow button to see the list portion.
`Items`	The collection of items in the `ComboBox` control.

Fig. 15.22 | ComboBox properties and an event. (Part 1 of 2.)

ComboBox properties and an event	Description
MaxDropDownItems	Specifies the maximum number of items (between 1 and 100) that the drop-down list can display. If the number of items exceeds the maximum number of items to display, a scrollbar appears.
SelectedIndex	Returns the index of the selected item, or -1 if none are selected.
SelectedItem	Returns a reference to the selected item.
Sorted	Indicates whether items are sorted alphabetically. Setting this property's value to true sorts the items. The default is false.
Common Event	
SelectedIndexChanged	Generated when the selected index changes (such as when a different item is selected). This is the default event when control is double clicked in the designer.

Fig. 15.22 | ComboBox properties and an event. (Part 2 of 2.)

Property **DropDownStyle** determines the type of ComboBox and is represented as a value of the **ComboBoxStyle** enumeration, which contains values Simple, DropDown and DropDownList. Option Simple does not display a drop-down arrow. Instead, a scrollbar appears next to the control, allowing the user to select a choice from the list. The user also can type in a selection. Style DropDown (the default) displays a drop-down list when the down arrow is clicked (or the down arrow key is pressed). The user can type a new item in the ComboBox. The last style is DropDownList, which displays a drop-down list but does not allow the user to type in the TextBox.

The ComboBox control has properties **Items** (a collection), **SelectedItem** and **SelectedIndex**, which are similar to the corresponding properties in ListBox. There can be at most one selected item in a ComboBox. If no items are selected, then SelectedIndex is -1. When the selected item changes, a **SelectedIndexChanged** event occurs.

Class ComboBoxTestForm (Fig. 15.23) allows users to select a shape to draw—circle, ellipse, square or pie (in both filled and unfilled versions)—by using a ComboBox. The ComboBox in this example is uneditable, so the user cannot type in the TextBox.

Look-and-Feel Observation 15.5
Make lists (such as ComboBoxes) editable only if the program is designed to accept user-submitted elements. Otherwise, the user might try to enter a custom item that is improper for the purposes of your application.

```
1   // Fig. 15.23: ComboBoxTestForm.cs
2   // Using ComboBox to select a shape to draw.
3   using System;
4   using System.Drawing;
5   using System.Windows.Forms;
```

Fig. 15.23 | ComboBox used to draw a selected shape. (Part 1 of 3.)

```
6
7    namespace ComboBoxTest
8    {
9       // Form uses a ComboBox to select different shapes to draw
10      public partial class ComboBoxTestForm : Form
11      {
12         // constructor
13         public ComboBoxTestForm()
14         {
15            InitializeComponent();
16         } // end constructor
17
18         // get index of selected shape, draw shape
19         private void imageComboBox_SelectedIndexChanged(
20            object sender, EventArgs e )
21         {
22            // create graphics object, Pen and SolidBrush
23            Graphics myGraphics = base.CreateGraphics();
24
25            // create Pen using color DarkRed
26            Pen myPen = new Pen( Color.DarkRed );
27
28            // create SolidBrush using color DarkRed
29            SolidBrush mySolidBrush = new SolidBrush( Color.DarkRed );
30
31            // clear drawing area, setting it to color white
32            myGraphics.Clear( Color.White );
33
34            // find index, draw proper shape
35            switch ( imageComboBox.SelectedIndex )
36            {
37               case 0: // case Circle is selected
38                  myGraphics.DrawEllipse( myPen, 50, 50, 150, 150 );
39                  break;
40               case 1: // case Rectangle is selected
41                  myGraphics.DrawRectangle( myPen, 50, 50, 150, 150 );
42                  break;
43               case 2: // case Ellipse is selected
44                  myGraphics.DrawEllipse( myPen, 50, 85, 150, 115 );
45                  break;
46               case 3: // case Pie is selected
47                  myGraphics.DrawPie( myPen, 50, 50, 150, 150, 0, 45 );
48                  break;
49               case 4: // case Filled Circle is selected
50                  myGraphics.FillEllipse( mySolidBrush, 50, 50, 150, 150 );
51                  break;
52               case 5: // case Filled Rectangle is selected
53                  myGraphics.FillRectangle( mySolidBrush, 50, 50, 150,
54                     150 );
55                  break;
56               case 6: // case Filled Ellipse is selected
57                  myGraphics.FillEllipse( mySolidBrush, 50, 85, 150, 115 );
58                  break;
```

Fig. 15.23 | ComboBox used to draw a selected shape. (Part 2 of 3.)

```
59              case 7: // case Filled Pie is selected
60                  myGraphics.FillPie( mySolidBrush, 50, 50, 150, 150, 0,
61                      45 );
62                  break;
63          } // end switch
64
65          myGraphics.Dispose(); // release the Graphics object
66      } // end method imageComboBox_SelectedIndexChanged
67  } // end class ComboBoxTestForm
68 } // end namespace ComboBoxTest
```

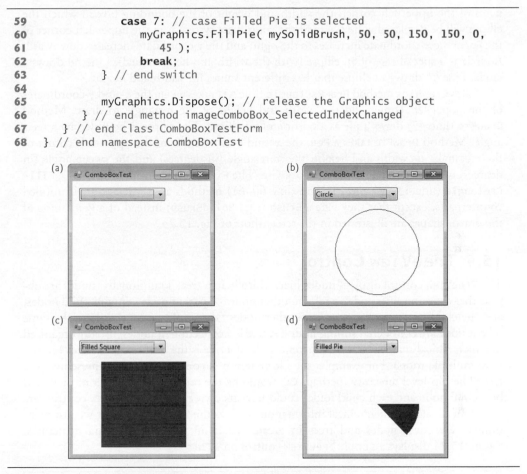

Fig. 15.23 | ComboBox used to draw a selected shape. (Part 3 of 3.)

After creating ComboBox imageComboBox, make it uneditable by setting its DropDown-Style to DropDownList in the **Properties** window. Next, add items Circle, Square, Ellipse, Pie, Filled Circle, Filled Square, Filled Ellipse and Filled Pie to the Items collection using the **String Collection Editor**. Whenever the user selects an item from imageComboBox, a SelectedIndexChanged event occurs and event handler imageCombo-Box_SelectedIndexChanged (lines 19–66) executes. Lines 23–29 create a Graphics object, a Pen and a SolidBrush, which are used to draw on the Form. The Graphics object (line 23) allows a pen or brush to draw on a component, using one of several Graphics methods. The Pen object (line 26) is used by methods DrawEllipse, DrawRectangle and DrawPie (lines 38, 41, 44 and 47) to draw the outlines of their corresponding shapes. The SolidBrush object (line 29) is used by methods FillEllipse, FillRectangle and FillPie (lines 50, 53–54, 57 and 60–61) to fill their corresponding solid shapes. Line 32 colors the entire Form White, using Graphics method **Clear**.

The application draws a shape based on the selected item's index. The switch statement (lines 35–63) uses imageComboBox.SelectedIndex to determine which item the user selected. Graphics method **DrawEllipse** (line 38) takes a Pen, and the x- and y-coordinates of the upper-left corner, the width and height of the bounding box in which the ellipse will be displayed. The origin of the coordinate system is in the upper-left corner of the Form; the *x*-coordinate increases to the right, and the *y*-coordinate increases downward. A circle is a special case of an ellipse (with the width and height equal). Line 38 draws a circle. Line 44 draws an ellipse that has different values for width and height.

Class Graphics method **DrawRectangle** (line 41) takes a Pen, the *x*- and *y*-coordinates of the upper-left corner and the width and height of the rectangle to draw. Method **DrawPie** (line 47) draws a pie as a portion of an ellipse. The ellipse is bounded by a rectangle. Method DrawPie takes a Pen, the *x*- and *y*-coordinates of the upper-left corner of the rectangle, its width and height, the start angle (in degrees) and the sweep angle (in degrees) of the pie. Angles increase clockwise. The **FillEllipse** (lines 50 and 57), **FillRectangle** (line 53–54) and **FillPie** (line 60–61) methods are similar to their unfilled counterparts, except that they take a Brush (e.g., SolidBrush) instead of a Pen. Some of the drawn shapes are illustrated in the screenshots of Fig. 15.23.

15.9 TreeView Control

The **TreeView** control displays **nodes** hierarchically in a **tree**. Traditionally, nodes are objects that contain values and can refer to other nodes. A **parent node** contains **child nodes**, and the child nodes can be parents to other nodes. Two child nodes that have the same parent node are considered **sibling nodes**. A tree is a collection of nodes, usually organized in a hierarchical manner. The first parent node of a tree is the **root** node (a TreeView can have multiple roots). For example, the file system of a computer can be represented as a tree. The top-level directory (perhaps C:) would be the root, each subfolder of C: would be a child node and each child folder could have its own children. TreeView controls are useful for displaying hierarchical information, such as the file structure that we just mentioned. We cover nodes and trees in greater detail in Chapter 21, Data Structures. Figure 15.24 displays a sample TreeView control on a Form.

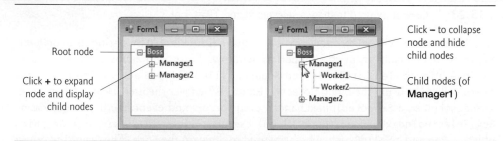

Fig. 15.24 | TreeView displaying a sample tree.

A parent node can be expanded or collapsed by clicking the plus box or minus box to its left. Nodes without children do not have these boxes.

The nodes in a TreeView are instances of class **TreeNode**. Each TreeNode has a **Nodes collection** (type **TreeNodeCollection**), which contains a list of other TreeNodes—known as its children. The Parent property returns a reference to the parent node (or null if the node is a root node). Figure 15.25 and Fig. 15.26 list the common properties of TreeViews and TreeNodes, common TreeNode methods and a common TreeView event.

TreeView properties and an event	Description
Common Properties	
CheckBoxes	Indicates whether CheckBoxes appear next to nodes. A value of true displays CheckBoxes. The default value is false.
ImageList	Specifies an ImageList object containing the node icons. An **Image-List** object is a collection that contains Image objects.
Nodes	Returns the collection of TreeNodes in the control as a TreeNodeCollection. It contains methods Add (adds a TreeNode object), Clear (deletes the entire collection) and Remove (deletes a specific node). Removing a parent node deletes all of its children.
SelectedNode	The selected node.
*Common Event (Event arguments **TreeViewEventArgs**)*	
AfterSelect	Generated after selected node changes. This is the default event when the control is double clicked in the designer.

Fig. 15.25 | TreeView properties and an event.

TreeNode properties and methods	Description
Common Properties	
Checked	Indicates whether the TreeNode is checked (CheckBoxes property must be set to true in the parent TreeView).
FirstNode	Specifies the first node in the Nodes collection (i.e., the first child in the tree).
FullPath	Indicates the path of the node, starting at the root of the tree.
ImageIndex	Specifies the index in the TreeView's ImageList of the image shown when the node is deselected.
LastNode	Specifies the last node in the Nodes collection (i.e., the last child in the tree).
NextNode	Next sibling node.
Nodes	Collection of TreeNodes contained in the current node (i.e., all the children of the current node). It contains methods Add (adds a TreeNode object), Clear (deletes the entire collection) and Remove (deletes a specific node). Removing a parent node deletes all of its children.
PrevNode	Previous sibling node.
SelectedImageIndex	Specifies the index in the TreeView's ImageList of the image to use when the node is selected.
Text	Specifies the TreeNode's text.
Common Methods	
Collapse	Collapses a node.

Fig. 15.26 | TreeNode properties and methods. (Part 1 of 2.)

TreeNode properties and methods	Description
Expand	Expands a node.
ExpandAll	Expands all the children of a node.
GetNodeCount	Returns the number of child nodes.

Fig. 15.26 | TreeNode properties and methods. (Part 2 of 2.)

To add nodes to the TreeView visually, click the ellipsis next to the Nodes property in the **Properties** window. This opens the **TreeNode Editor** (Fig. 15.27), which displays an empty tree representing the TreeView. There are Buttons to create a root and to add or delete a node. To the right are the properties of current node. Here you can rename the node.

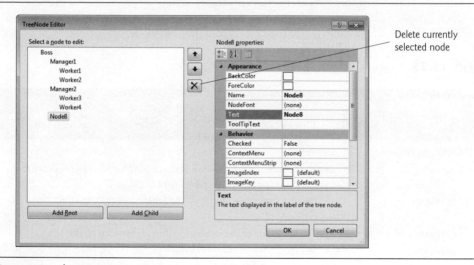

Fig. 15.27 | TreeNode Editor.

To add nodes programmatically, first create a root node. Create a new TreeNode object and pass it a string to display. Then call method Add to add this new TreeNode to the TreeView's Nodes collection. Thus, to add a root node to TreeView *myTreeView*, write

> *myTreeView*.Nodes.Add(**new** TreeNode(*rootLabel*));

where *myTreeView* is the TreeView to which we are adding nodes, and *rootLabel* is the text to display in *myTreeView*. To add children to a root node, add new TreeNodes to its Nodes collection. We select the appropriate root node from the TreeView by writing

> *myTreeView*.Nodes[*myIndex*]

where *myIndex* is the root node's index in *myTreeView*'s Nodes collection. We add nodes to child nodes through the same process by which we added root nodes to *myTreeView*. To add a child to the root node at index *myIndex*, write

> *myTreeView*.Nodes[*myIndex*].Nodes.Add(**new** TreeNode(*ChildLabel*));

Class TreeViewDirectoryStructureForm (Fig. 15.28) uses a TreeView to display the
contents of a directory chosen by the user. A TextBox and a Button are used to specify the
directory. First, enter the full path of the directory you want to display. Then click the
Button to set the specified directory as the root node in the TreeView. Each subdirectory
of this directory becomes a child node. This layout is similar to that used in **Windows
Explorer**. Folders can be expanded or collapsed by clicking the plus or minus boxes that
appear to their left.

When the user clicks the enterButton, all the nodes in directoryTreeView are
cleared (line 68). Then, if the directory exists (line 73), the path entered in inputTextBox
is used to create the root node. Line 76 adds the directory to directoryTreeView as the
root node, and lines 79–80 call method PopulateTreeView (lines 21–62), which takes a
directory (a string) and a parent node. Method PopulateTreeView then creates child
nodes corresponding to the subdirectories of the directory it receives as an argument.

```
1   // Fig. 15.28: TreeViewDirectoryStructureForm.cs
2   // Using TreeView to display directory structure.
3   using System;
4   using System.Windows.Forms;
5   using System.IO;
6
7   namespace TreeViewDirectoryStructure
8   {
9      // Form uses TreeView to display directory structure
10     public partial class TreeViewDirectoryStructureForm : Form
11     {
12        string substringDirectory; // store last part of full path name
13
14        // constructor
15        public TreeViewDirectoryStructureForm()
16        {
17           InitializeComponent();
18        } // end constructor
19
20        // populate current node with subdirectories
21        public void PopulateTreeView(
22           string directoryValue, TreeNode parentNode )
23        {
24           // array stores all subdirectories in the directory
25           string[] directoryArray =
26              Directory.GetDirectories( directoryValue );
27
28           // populate current node with subdirectories
29           try
30           {
31              // check to see if any subdirectories are present
32              if ( directoryArray.Length != 0 )
33              {
34                 // for every subdirectory, create new TreeNode,
35                 // add as a child of current node and recursively
36                 // populate child nodes with subdirectories
```

Fig. 15.28 | TreeView used to display directories. (Part 1 of 3.)

```
37                        foreach ( string directory in directoryArray )
38                        {
39                           // obtain last part of path name from the full path
40                           // name by calling the GetFileNameWithoutExtension
41                           // method of class Path
42                           substringDirectory =
43                              Path.GetFileNameWithoutExtension( directory );
44
45                           // create TreeNode for current directory
46                           TreeNode myNode = new TreeNode( substringDirectory );
47
48                           // add current directory node to parent node
49                           parentNode.Nodes.Add( myNode );
50
51                           // recursively populate every subdirectory
52                           PopulateTreeView( directory, myNode );
53                        } // end foreach
54                     } // end if
55               } //end try
56
57               // catch exception
58               catch ( UnauthorizedAccessException )
59               {
60                  parentNode.Nodes.Add( "Access denied" );
61               } // end catch
62            } // end method PopulateTreeView
63
64            // handles enterButton click event
65            private void enterButton_Click( object sender, EventArgs e )
66            {
67               // clear all nodes
68               directoryTreeView.Nodes.Clear();
69
70               // check if the directory entered by user exists
71               // if it does, then fill in the TreeView,
72               // if not, display error MessageBox
73               if ( Directory.Exists( inputTextBox.Text ) )
74               {
75                  // add full path name to directoryTreeView
76                  directoryTreeView.Nodes.Add( inputTextBox.Text );
77
78                  // insert subfolders
79                  PopulateTreeView(
80                     inputTextBox.Text, directoryTreeView.Nodes[ 0 ] );
81               }
82               // display error MessageBox if directory not found
83               else
84                  MessageBox.Show( inputTextBox.Text + " could not be found.",
85                     "Directory Not Found", MessageBoxButtons.OK,
86                     MessageBoxIcon.Error );
87            } // end method enterButton_Click
88         } // end class TreeViewDirectoryStructureForm
89      } // end namespace TreeViewDirectoryStructure
```

Fig. 15.28 | TreeView used to display directories. (Part 2 of 3.)

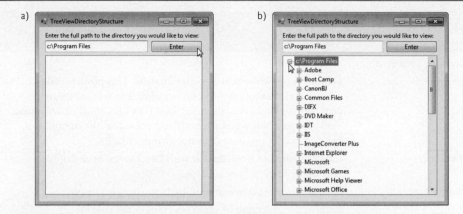

Fig. 15.28 | TreeView used to display directories. (Part 3 of 3.)

Method `PopulateTreeView` (lines 21–62) obtains a list of subdirectories, using method **GetDirectories** of class `Directory` (namespace `System.IO`) in lines 25–26. Method `GetDirectories` takes a `string` (the current directory) and returns an array of `strings` (the subdirectories). If a directory is not accessible for security reasons, an `UnauthorizedAccessException` is thrown. Lines 58–61 catch this exception and add a node containing "`Access denied`" instead of displaying the subdirectories.

If there are accessible subdirectories, lines 42–43 use method `GetFileNameWithoutExtension` of class `Path` to increase readability by shortening the full path name to just the directory name. The **Path** class provides functionality for working with `strings` that are file or directory paths. Next, each `string` in the `directoryArray` is used to create a new child node (line 46). We use method `Add` (line 49) to add each child node to the parent. Then method `PopulateTreeView` is called recursively on every subdirectory (line 52), which eventually populates the `TreeView` with the entire directory structure. Our recursive algorithm may cause a delay when the program loads large directories. However, once the folder names are added to the appropriate `Nodes` collection, they can be expanded and collapsed without delay. In the next section, we present an alternate algorithm to solve this problem.

15.10 ListView Control

The **ListView** control is similar to a `ListBox` in that both display lists from which the user can select one or more items (an example of a `ListView` can be found in Fig. 15.31). `ListView` is more versatile and can display items in different formats. For example, a `ListView` can display icons next to the list items (controlled by its `SmallImageList`, `LargeImageList` or `StateImageList` properties) and show the details of items in columns. Property **Multi-Select** (a `bool`) determines whether multiple items can be selected. `CheckBoxes` can be included by setting property **CheckBoxes** (a `bool`) to true, making the `ListView`'s appearance similar to that of a `CheckedListBox`. The **View** property specifies the layout of the `ListBox`. Property **Activation** determines the method by which the user selects a list item. The details of these properties and the `ItemActivate` event are explained in Fig. 15.29.

`ListView` allows you to define the images used as icons for `ListView` items. To display images, an `ImageList` component is required. Create one by dragging it to a `Form` from

`ListView` properties and events	Description
Common Properties	
`Activation`	Determines how the user activates an item. This property takes a value in the `ItemActivation` enumeration. Possible values are `OneClick` (single-click activation), `TwoClick` (double-click activation, item changes color when selected) and `Standard` (the default; double-click activation, item does not change color).
`CheckBoxes`	Indicates whether items appear with `CheckBoxes`. `true` displays `CheckBoxes`. The default is `false`.
`LargeImageList`	Specifies the `ImageList` containing large icons for display.
`Items`	Returns the collection of `ListViewItems` in the control.
`MultiSelect`	Determines whether multiple selection is allowed. The default is `true`, which enables multiple selection.
`SelectedItems`	Returns the collection of selected items as a `ListView.SelectedListViewItemCollection`.
`SmallImageList`	Specifies the `ImageList` containing small icons for display.
`View`	Determines appearance of `ListViewItems`. Possible values are `LargeIcon` (the default; large icon displayed, items can be in multiple columns), `SmallIcon` (small icon displayed, items can be in multiple columns), `List` (small icons displayed, items appear in a single column), `Details` (like `List`, but multiple columns of information can be displayed per item) and `Tile` (large icons displayed, information provided to right of icon; valid only in Windows XP or later).
Common Events	
`Click`	Generated when an item is clicked. This is the default event.
`ItemActivate`	Generated when an item in the `ListView` is activated (clicked or double clicked). Does not contain the specifics of which item is activated.

Fig. 15.29 | `ListView` properties and events.

the **ToolBox**. Then, select the **Images** property in the **Properties** window to display the **Image Collection Editor** (Fig. 15.30). Here you can browse for images that you wish to add to the `ImageList`, which contains an array of `Images`. Adding images this way embeds them into the application (like resources), so they do not need to be included separately with the published application. They're not however part of the project. In this example, we added images to the `ImageList` programmatically rather than using the **Image Collection Editor** so that we could use image resources. After creating an empty `ImageList`, add the file and folder icon images to the project as resources. Next, set property `SmallImageList` of the `ListView` to the new `ImageList` object. Property **SmallImageList** specifies the image list for the small icons. Property **LargeImageList** sets the `ImageList` for large icons. The items in a `ListView` are each of type **ListViewItem**. Icons for the `ListView` items are selected by setting the item's **ImageIndex** property to the appropriate index.

Class `ListViewTestForm` (Fig. 15.31) displays files and folders in a `ListView`, along with small icons representing each file or folder. If a file or folder is inaccessible because of

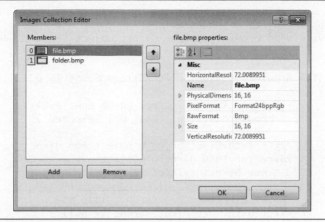

Fig. 15.30 | Image Collection Editor window for an ImageList component.

permission settings, a MessageBox appears. The program scans the contents of the directory as it browses, rather than indexing the entire drive at once.

Method ListViewTestForm_Load

Method ListViewTestForm_Load (lines 114–123) handles the Form's Load event. When the application loads, the folder and file icon images are added to the Images collection of fileFolderImageList (lines 117–118). Since the ListView's SmallImageList property is set to this ImageList, the ListView can display these images as icons for each item. Because the folder icon was added first, it has array index 0, and the file icon has array index 1. The application also loads its home directory (obtained at line 14) into the ListView when it first loads (line 121) and displays the directory path (line 122).

```
1   // Fig. 15.31: ListViewTestForm.cs
2   // Displaying directories and their contents in ListView.
3   using System;
4   using System.Windows.Forms;
5   using System.IO;
6
7   namespace ListViewTest
8   {
9      // Form contains a ListView which displays
10     // folders and files in a directory
11     public partial class ListViewTestForm : Form
12     {
13        // store current directory
14        string currentDirectory = Directory.GetCurrentDirectory();
15
16        // constructor
17        public ListViewTestForm()
18        {
19           InitializeComponent();
20        } // end constructor
```

Fig. 15.31 | ListView displaying files and folders. (Part 1 of 4.)

```
21
22      // browse directory user clicked or go up one level
23      private void browserListView_Click( object sender, EventArgs e )
24      {
25         // ensure an item is selected
26         if ( browserListView.SelectedItems.Count != 0 )
27         {
28            // if first item selected, go up one level
29            if ( browserListView.Items[ 0 ].Selected )
30            {
31               // create DirectoryInfo object for directory
32               DirectoryInfo directoryObject =
33                  new DirectoryInfo( currentDirectory );
34
35               // if directory has parent, load it
36               if ( directoryObject.Parent != null )
37               {
38                  LoadFilesInDirectory(
39                     directoryObject.Parent.FullName );
40               } // end if
41            } // end if
42
43            // selected directory or file
44            else
45            {
46               // directory or file chosen
47               string chosen = browserListView.SelectedItems[ 0 ].Text;
48
49               // if item selected is directory, load selected directory
50               if ( Directory.Exists(
51                  Path.Combine( currentDirectory, chosen ) ) )
52               {
53                  LoadFilesInDirectory(
54                     Path.Combine( currentDirectory, chosen ) );
55               } // end if
56            } // end else
57
58            // update displayLabel
59            displayLabel.Text = currentDirectory;
60         } // end if
61      } // end method browserListView_Click
62
63      // display files/subdirectories of current directory
64      public void LoadFilesInDirectory( string currentDirectoryValue )
65      {
66         // load directory information and display
67         try
68         {
69            // clear ListView and set first item
70            browserListView.Items.Clear();
71            browserListView.Items.Add( "Go Up One Level" );
72
```

Fig. 15.31 | ListView displaying files and folders. (Part 2 of 4.)

```
 73                    // update current directory
 74                    currentDirectory = currentDirectoryValue;
 75                    DirectoryInfo newCurrentDirectory =
 76                       new DirectoryInfo( currentDirectory );
 77
 78                    // put files and directories into arrays
 79                    DirectoryInfo[] directoryArray =
 80                       newCurrentDirectory.GetDirectories();
 81                    FileInfo[] fileArray = newCurrentDirectory.GetFiles();
 82
 83                    // add directory names to ListView
 84                    foreach ( DirectoryInfo dir in directoryArray )
 85                    {
 86                       // add directory to ListView
 87                       ListViewItem newDirectoryItem =
 88                          browserListView.Items.Add( dir.Name );
 89
 90                       newDirectoryItem.ImageIndex = 0;   // set directory image
 91                    } // end foreach
 92
 93                    // add file names to ListView
 94                    foreach ( FileInfo file in fileArray )
 95                    {
 96                       // add file to ListView
 97                       ListViewItem newFileItem =
 98                          browserListView.Items.Add( file.Name );
 99
100                       newFileItem.ImageIndex = 1;   // set file image
101                    } // end foreach
102             } // end try
103
104             // access denied
105             catch ( UnauthorizedAccessException )
106             {
107                MessageBox.Show( "Warning: Some fields may not be " +
108                   "visible due to permission settings",
109                   "Attention", 0, MessageBoxIcon.Warning );
110             } // end catch
111          } // end method LoadFilesInDirectory
112
113          // handle load event when Form displayed for first time
114          private void ListViewTestForm_Load( object sender, EventArgs e )
115          {
116             // add icon images to ImageList
117             fileFolderImageList.Images.Add( Properties.Resources.folder );
118             fileFolderImageList.Images.Add( Properties.Resources.file );
119
120             // load current directory into browserListView
121             LoadFilesInDirectory( currentDirectory );
122             displayLabel.Text = currentDirectory;
123          } // end method ListViewTestForm_Load
124       } // end class ListViewTestForm
125    } // end namespace ListViewTest
```

Fig. 15.31 | ListView displaying files and folders. (Part 3 of 4.)

Fig. 15.31 | `ListView` displaying files and folders. (Part 4 of 4.)

Method `LoadFilesInDirectory`

The `LoadFilesInDirectory` method (lines 64–111) populates `browserListView` with the directory passed to it (`currentDirectoryValue`). It clears `browserListView` and adds the element `"Go Up One Level"`. When the user clicks this element, the program attempts to move up one level (we see how shortly). The method then creates a `DirectoryInfo` object initialized with the `string` `currentDirectory` (lines 75–76). If permission is not given to browse the directory, an exception is thrown (and caught in line 105). Method `Load-FilesInDirectory` works differently from method `PopulateTreeView` in the previous program (Fig. 15.28). Instead of loading all the folders on the hard drive, method `Load-FilesInDirectory` loads only the folders in the current directory.

Class **`DirectoryInfo`** (namespace `System.IO`) enables us to browse or manipulate the directory structure easily. Method **`GetDirectories`** (line 80) returns an array of `Directory-Info` objects containing the subdirectories of the current directory. Similarly, method **`GetFiles`** (line 81) returns an array of class **`FileInfo`** objects containing the files in the current directory. Property **`Name`** (of both class `DirectoryInfo` and class `FileInfo`) contains only the directory or file name, such as `temp` instead of `C:\myfolder\temp`. To access the full name, use property **`FullName`**.

Lines 84–91 and lines 94–101 iterate through the subdirectories and files of the current directory and add them to browserListView. Lines 90 and 100 set the ImageIndex properties of the newly created items. If an item is a directory, we set its icon to a directory icon (index 0); if an item is a file, we set its icon to a file icon (index 1).

Method browserListView_Click

Method browserListView_Click (lines 23–61) responds when the user clicks control browserListView. Line 26 checks whether anything is selected. If a selection has been made, line 29 determines whether the user chose the first item in browserListView. The first item in browserListView is always **Go Up One Level**; if it is selected, the program attempts to go up a level. Lines 32–33 create a DirectoryInfo object for the current directory. Line 36 tests property Parent to ensure that the user is not at the root of the directory tree. Property **Parent** indicates the parent directory as a DirectoryInfo object; if no parent directory exists, Parent returns the value null. If a parent directory does exist, lines 38–39 pass the parent directory's full name to LoadFilesInDirectory.

If the user did not select the first item in browserListView, lines 44–56 allow the user to continue navigating through the directory structure. Line 47 creates string chosen and assigns it the text of the selected item (the first item in collection SelectedItems). Lines 50–51 determine whether the user selected a valid directory (rather than a file). Using the Combine method of class Path, the program combines strings currentDirectory and chosen to form the new directory path. The Combine method automatically adds a backslash (\), if necessary, between the two pieces. This value is passed to the **Exists** method of class Directory. Method Exists returns true if its string parameter is a valid directory. If so, the program passes the string to method LoadFilesInDirectory (lines 53–54). Finally, displayLabel is updated with the new directory (line 59).

This program loads quickly, because it indexes only the files in the current directory. A small delay may occur when a new directory is loaded. In addition, changes in the directory structure can be shown by reloading a directory. The previous program (Fig. 15.28) may have a large initial delay, as it loads an entire directory structure. This type of trade-off is typical in the software world.

Software Engineering Observation 15.2

When designing applications that run for long periods of time, you might choose a large initial delay to improve performance throughout the rest of the program. However, in applications that run for only short periods, developers often prefer fast initial loading times and small delays after each action.

15.11 TabControl Control

The **TabControl** creates tabbed windows, such as those in Visual Studio (Fig. 15.32). This enables you to specify more information in the same space on a Form and group displayed data logically. TabControls contain **TabPage** objects, which are similar to Panels and GroupBoxes in that TabPages also can contain controls. You first add controls to the TabPage objects, then add the TabPages to the TabControl. Only one TabPage is displayed at a time. To add objects to the TabPage and the TabControl, write

```
myTabPage.Controls.Add( myControl );
myTabControl.TabPages.Add( myTabPage );
```

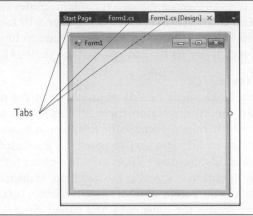

Fig. 15.32 | Tabbed windows in Visual Studio.

The preceding statements call method Add of the Controls collection and method Add of the TabPages collection. The example adds TabControl *myControl* to TabPage *myTab-Page*, then adds *myTabPage* to *myTabControl*. Alternatively, we can use method AddRange to add an array of TabPages or controls to a TabControl or TabPage, respectively. Figure 15.33 depicts a sample TabControl.

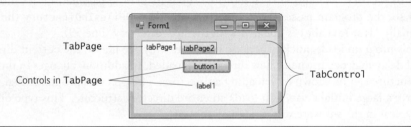

Fig. 15.33 | TabControl with TabPages example.

You can add TabControls visually by dragging and dropping them onto a Form in **Design** mode. To add TabPages in **Design** mode, right click the TabControl and select **Add Tab** (Fig. 15.34). Alternatively, click the **TabPages** property in the **Properties** window and add tabs in the dialog that appears. To change a tab label, set the **Text** property of the TabPage. Clicking the tabs selects the TabControl—to select the TabPage, click the control area underneath the tabs. You can add controls to the TabPage by dragging and dropping items from the **ToolBox**. To view different TabPages, click the appropriate tab (in either design or run mode). Common properties and a common event of TabControls are described in Fig. 15.35.

Each TabPage generates a Click event when its tab is clicked. Event handlers for this event can be created by double clicking the body of the TabPage.

Class UsingTabsForm (Fig. 15.36) uses a TabControl to display various options relating to the text on a label (**Color**, **Size** and **Message**). The last TabPage displays an **About** message, which describes the use of TabControls.

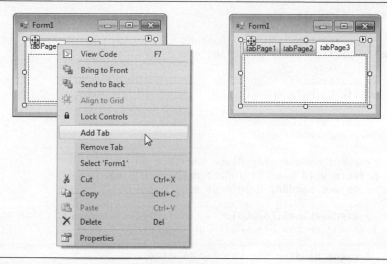

Fig. 15.34 | TabPages added to a TabControl.

TabControl properties and an event	Description
Common Properties	
ImageList	Specifies images to be displayed on tabs.
ItemSize	Specifies the tab size.
Multiline	Indicates whether multiple rows of tabs can be displayed.
SelectedIndex	Index of the selected TabPage.
SelectedTab	The selected TabPage.
TabCount	Returns the number of tab pages.
TabPages	Returns the collection of TabPages within the TabControl as a TabControl.TabPageCollection.
Common Event	
SelectedIndexChanged	Generated when SelectedIndex changes (i.e., another TabPage is selected).

Fig. 15.35 | TabControl properties and an event.

```
1   // Fig. 15.36: UsingTabsForm.cs
2   // Using TabControl to display various font settings.
3   using System;
4   using System.Drawing;
5   using System.Windows.Forms;
6
```

Fig. 15.36 | TabControl used to display various font settings. (Part 1 of 3.)

```
7   namespace UsingTabs
8   {
9      // Form uses Tabs and RadioButtons to display various font settings
10     public partial class UsingTabsForm : Form
11     {
12        // constructor
13        public UsingTabsForm()
14        {
15           InitializeComponent();
16        } // end constructor
17
18        // event handler for Black RadioButton
19        private void blackRadioButton_CheckedChanged(
20           object sender, EventArgs e )
21        {
22           displayLabel.ForeColor = Color.Black; // change color to black
23        } // end method blackRadioButton_CheckedChanged
24
25        // event handler for Red RadioButton
26        private void redRadioButton_CheckedChanged(
27           object sender, EventArgs e )
28        {
29           displayLabel.ForeColor = Color.Red; // change color to red
30        } // end method redRadioButton_CheckedChanged
31
32        // event handler for Green RadioButton
33        private void greenRadioButton_CheckedChanged(
34           object sender, EventArgs e )
35        {
36           displayLabel.ForeColor = Color.Green; // change color to green
37        } // end method greenRadioButton_CheckedChanged
38
39        // event handler for 12 point RadioButton
40        private void size12RadioButton_CheckedChanged(
41           object sender, EventArgs e )
42        {
43           // change font size to 12
44           displayLabel.Font = new Font( displayLabel.Font.Name, 12 );
45        } // end method size12RadioButton_CheckedChanged
46
47        // event handler for 16 point RadioButton
48        private void size16RadioButton_CheckedChanged(
49           object sender, EventArgs e )
50        {
51           // change font size to 16
52           displayLabel.Font = new Font( displayLabel.Font.Name, 16 );
53        } // end method size16RadioButton_CheckedChanged
54
55        // event handler for 20 point RadioButton
56        private void size20RadioButton_CheckedChanged(
57           object sender, EventArgs e )
58        {
```

Fig. 15.36 | TabControl used to display various font settings. (Part 2 of 3.)

```
59              // change font size to 20
60              displayLabel.Font = new Font( displayLabel.Font.Name, 20 );
61          } // end method size20RadioButton_CheckedChanged
62
63          // event handler for Hello! RadioButton
64          private void helloRadioButton_CheckedChanged(
65              object sender, EventArgs e )
66          {
67              displayLabel.Text = "Hello!"; // change text to Hello!
68          } // end method helloRadioButton_CheckedChanged
69
70          // event handler for Goodbye! RadioButton
71          private void goodbyeRadioButton_CheckedChanged(
72              object sender, EventArgs e )
73          {
74              displayLabel.Text = "Goodbye!"; // change text to Goodbye!
75          } // end method goodbyeRadioButton_CheckedChanged
76      } // end class UsingTabsForm
77  } // end namespace UsingTabs
```

Fig. 15.36 | TabControl used to display various font settings. (Part 3 of 3.)

The textOptionsTabControl and the colorTabPage, sizeTabPage, messageTabPage and aboutTabPage are created in the designer (as described previously). The colorTabPage contains three RadioButtons for the colors black (blackRadioButton), red (red-RadioButton) and green (greenRadioButton). This TabPage is displayed in Fig. 15.36(a). The CheckedChanged event handler for each RadioButton updates the color of the text in displayLabel (lines 22, 29 and 36). The sizeTabPage (Fig. 15.36(b)) has three RadioButtons, corresponding to font sizes 12 (size12RadioButton), 16 (size16RadioButton) and 20 (size20RadioButton), which change the font size of displayLabel—lines 44, 52 and 60, respectively. The messageTabPage (Fig. 15.36(c)) contains two RadioButtons for the messages **Hello!** (helloRadioButton) and **Goodbye!** (goodbyeRadioButton). The two RadioButtons determine the text on displayLabel (lines 67 and 74, respectively). The aboutTabPage (Fig. 15.36(d)) contains a Label (messageLabel) describing the purpose of TabControls.

> **Software Engineering Observation 15.3**
>
> *A TabPage can act as a container for a single logical group of RadioButtons, enforcing their mutual exclusivity. To place multiple RadioButton groups inside a single TabPage, you should group RadioButtons within Panels or GroupBoxes contained within the TabPage.*

15.12 Multiple Document Interface (MDI) Windows

In previous chapters, we have built only **single document interface** (SDI) applications. Such programs (including Microsoft's Notepad and Paint) can support only one open window or document at a time. SDI applications usually have limited abilities—Paint and Notepad, for example, have limited image- and text-editing features. To edit multiple documents, the user must execute another instance of the SDI application.

Many complex applications are **multiple document interface** (MDI) programs, which allow users to edit multiple documents at once (e.g., Microsoft Office products). MDI programs also tend to be more complex—Paint Shop Pro and Photoshop have a greater number of image-editing features than does Paint.

An MDI program's main window is called the **parent window**, and each window inside the application is referred to as a **child window**. Although an MDI application can have many child windows, each has only one parent window. Furthermore, a maximum of one child window can be active at once. Child windows cannot be parents themselves and cannot be moved outside their parent. Otherwise, a child window behaves like any other window (with regard to closing, minimizing, resizing, and so on). A child window's functionality can differ from that of other child windows of the parent. For example, one child window might allow the user to edit images, another might allow the user to edit text and a third might display network traffic graphically, but all could belong to the same MDI parent. Figure 15.37 depicts a sample MDI application with two child windows.

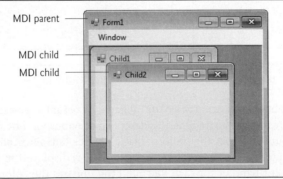

Fig. 15.37 | MDI parent window and MDI child windows.

To create an MDI Form, create a new Form and set its **IsMdiContainer** property to true. The Form changes appearance, as in Fig. 15.38. Next, create a child Form class to be added to the Form. To do this, right click the project in the **Solution Explorer**, select **Project > Add Windows Form...** and name the file. Edit the Form as you like. To add the

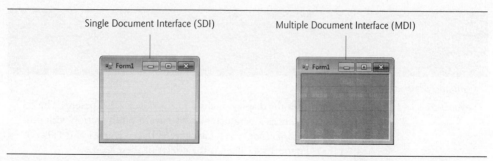

Fig. 15.38 | SDI and MDI forms.

child Form to the parent, we must create a new child Form object, set its **MdiParent** property to the parent Form and call the child Form's Show method. In general, to add a child Form to a parent, write

```
ChildFormClass childForm = New ChildFormClass();
childForm.MdiParent = parentForm;
childForm.Show();
```

In most cases, the parent Form creates the child, so the *parentForm* reference is this. The code to create a child usually lies inside an event handler, which creates a new window in response to a user action. Menu selections (such as **File**, followed by a submenu option of **New**, followed by a submenu option of **Window**) are common techniques for creating new child windows.

Class Form property **MdiChildren** returns an array of child Form references. This is useful if the parent window wants to check the status of all its children (for example, ensuring that all are saved before the parent closes). Property **ActiveMdiChild** returns a reference to the active child window; it returns null if there are no active child windows. Other features of MDI windows are described in Fig. 15.39.

MDI Form properties, a method and an event	Description
Common MDI Child Properties	
IsMdiChild	Indicates whether the Form is an MDI child. If true, Form is an MDI child (read-only property).
MdiParent	Specifies the MDI parent Form of the child.
Common MDI Parent Properties	
ActiveMdiChild	Returns the Form that is the currently active MDI child (returns null if no children are active).
IsMdiContainer	Indicates whether a Form can be an MDI parent. If true, the Form can be an MDI parent. The default value is false.
MdiChildren	Returns the MDI children as an array of Forms.

Fig. 15.39 | MDI parent and MDI child properties, a method and an event. (Part 1 of 2.)

MDI Form properties, a method and an event	Description
Common Method	
LayoutMdi	Determines the display of child forms on an MDI parent. The method takes as a parameter an MdiLayout enumeration with possible values ArrangeIcons, Cascade, TileHorizontal and TileVertical. Figure 15.42 depicts the effects of these values.
Common Event	
MdiChildActivate	Generated when an MDI child is closed or activated.

Fig. 15.39 | MDI parent and MDI child properties, a method and an event. (Part 2 of 2.)

Child windows can be minimized, maximized and closed independently of the parent window. Figure 15.40 shows two images: one containing two minimized child windows and a second containing a maximized child window. When the parent is minimized or closed, the child windows are minimized or closed as well. Notice that the title bar in Fig. 15.40(b) is **Form1 - [Child1]**. When a child window is maximized, its title-bar text is inserted into the parent window's title bar. When a child window is minimized or maximized, its title bar displays a restore icon, which can be used to return the child window to its previous size (its size before it was minimized or maximized).

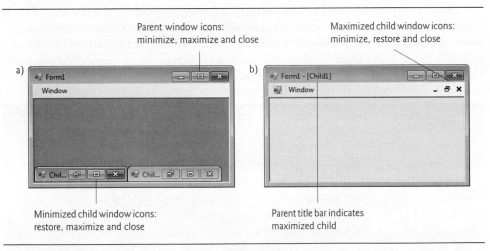

Fig. 15.40 | Minimized and maximized child windows.

C# provides a property that helps track which child windows are open in an MDI container. Property **MdiWindowListItem** of class MenuStrip specifies which menu, if any, displays a list of open child windows that the user can select to bring the corresponding window to the foreground. When a new child window is opened, an entry is added to the end of the list (Fig. 15.41). If ten or more child windows are open, the list includes the option **More Windows...**, which allows the user to select a window from a list in a dialog.

Good Programming Practice 15.1

When creating MDI applications, include a menu that displays a list of the open child windows. This helps the user select a child window quickly, rather than having to search for it in the parent window.

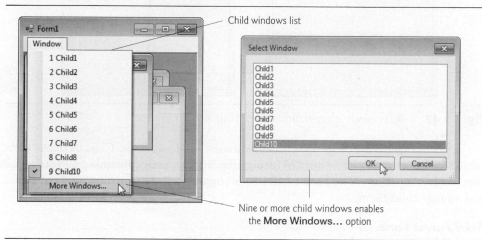

Fig. 15.41 | MenuStrip property MdiWindowListItem example.

MDI containers allow you to organize the placement of its child windows. The child windows in an MDI application can be arranged by calling method **LayoutMdi** of the parent Form. Method LayoutMdi takes an **MdiLayout** enumeration, which can have values Arrange-Icons, Cascade, TileHorizontal and TileVertical. **Tiled windows** completely fill the parent and do not overlap; such windows can be arranged horizontally (value TileHorizontal) or vertically (value TileVertical). **Cascaded windows** (value Cascade) overlap—each is the same size and displays a visible title bar, if possible. Value ArrangeIcons arranges the icons for any minimized child windows. If minimized windows are scattered around the parent window, value ArrangeIcons orders them neatly at the bottom-left corner of the parent window. Figure 15.42 illustrates the values of the MdiLayout enumeration.

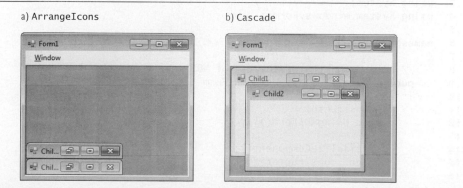

Fig. 15.42 | MdiLayout enumeration values. (Part 1 of 2.)

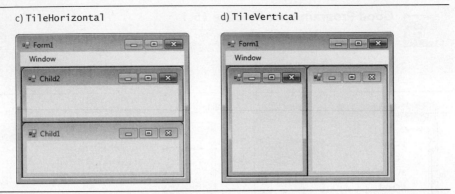

Fig. 15.42 | `MdiLayout` enumeration values. (Part 2 of 2.)

Class `UsingMDIForm` (Fig. 15.43) demonstrates MDI windows. Class `UsingMDIForm` uses three instances of child `Form` `ChildForm` (Fig. 15.44), each containing a `PictureBox` that displays an image. The parent MDI `Form` contains a menu enabling users to create and arrange child `Form`s.

MDI Parent Form
Figure 15.43 presents class `UsingMDIForm`—the application's MDI parent `Form`. This `Form`, which is created first, contains two top-level menus. The first of these menus, **File** (`fileToolStripMenuItem`), contains both an **Exit** item (`exitToolStripMenuItem`) and a **New** submenu (`newToolStripMenuItem`) consisting of items for each child window. The second menu, **Window** (`windowToolStripMenuItem`), provides options for laying out the MDI children, plus a list of the active MDI children.

In the **Properties** window, we set the `Form`'s `IsMdiContainer` property to `true`, making the `Form` an MDI parent. In addition, we set the `MenuStrip`'s `MdiWindowListItem` property to `windowToolStripMenuItem`. This enables the **Window** menu to contain the list of child MDI windows.

```
1   // Fig. 15.43: UsingMDIForm.cs
2   // Demonstrating use of MDI parent and child windows.
3   using System;
4   using System.Windows.Forms;
5
6   namespace UsingMDI
7   {
8      // Form demonstrates the use of MDI parent and child windows
9      public partial class UsingMDIForm : Form
10     {
11        // constructor
12        public UsingMDIForm()
13        {
14           InitializeComponent();
15        } // end constructor
16
```

Fig. 15.43 | MDI parent-window class. (Part 1 of 3.)

```
17          // create Lavender Flowers image window
18          private void lavenderToolStripMenuItem_Click(
19             object sender, EventArgs e )
20          {
21             // create new child
22             ChildForm child = new ChildForm(
23                "Lavender Flowers", "lavenderflowers" );
24             child.MdiParent = this; // set parent
25             child.Show(); // display child
26          } // end method lavenderToolStripMenuItem_Click
27
28          // create Purple Flowers image window
29          private void purpleToolStripMenuItem_Click(
30             object sender, EventArgs e )
31          {
32             // create new child
33             ChildForm child = new ChildForm(
34                "Purple Flowers", "purpleflowers" );
35             child.MdiParent = this; // set parent
36             child.Show(); // display child
37          } // end method purpleToolStripMenuItem_Click
38
39          // create Yellow Flowers image window
40          private void yellowToolStripMenuItem_Click(
41             object sender, EventArgs e )
42          {
43             // create new child
44             Child child = new ChildForm(
45                "Yellow Flowers", "yellowflowers" );
46             child.MdiParent = this; // set parent
47             child.Show(); // display child
48          } // end method yellowToolStripMenuItem_Click
49
50          // exit application
51          private void exitToolStripMenuItem_Click(
52             object sender, EventArgs e )
53          {
54             Application.Exit();
55          } // end method exitToolStripMenuItem_Click
56
57          // set Cascade layout
58          private void cascadeToolStripMenuItem_Click(
59             object sender, EventArgs e )
60          {
61             this.LayoutMdi( MdiLayout.Cascade );
62          } // end method cascadeToolStripMenuItem_Click
63
64          // set TileHorizontal layout
65          private void tileHorizontalToolStripMenuItem_Click(
66             object sender, EventArgs e )
67          {
68             this.LayoutMdi( MdiLayout.TileHorizontal );
69          } // end method tileHorizontalToolStripMenuItem
```

Fig. 15.43 | MDI parent-window class. (Part 2 of 3.)

```
70
71          // set TileVertical layout
72          private void tileVerticalToolStripMenuItem_Click(
73             object sender, EventArgs e )
74          {
75             this.LayoutMdi( MdiLayout.TileVertical );
76          } // end method tileVerticalToolStripMenuItem_Click
77       } // end class UsingMDIForm
78    } // end namespace UsingMDI
```

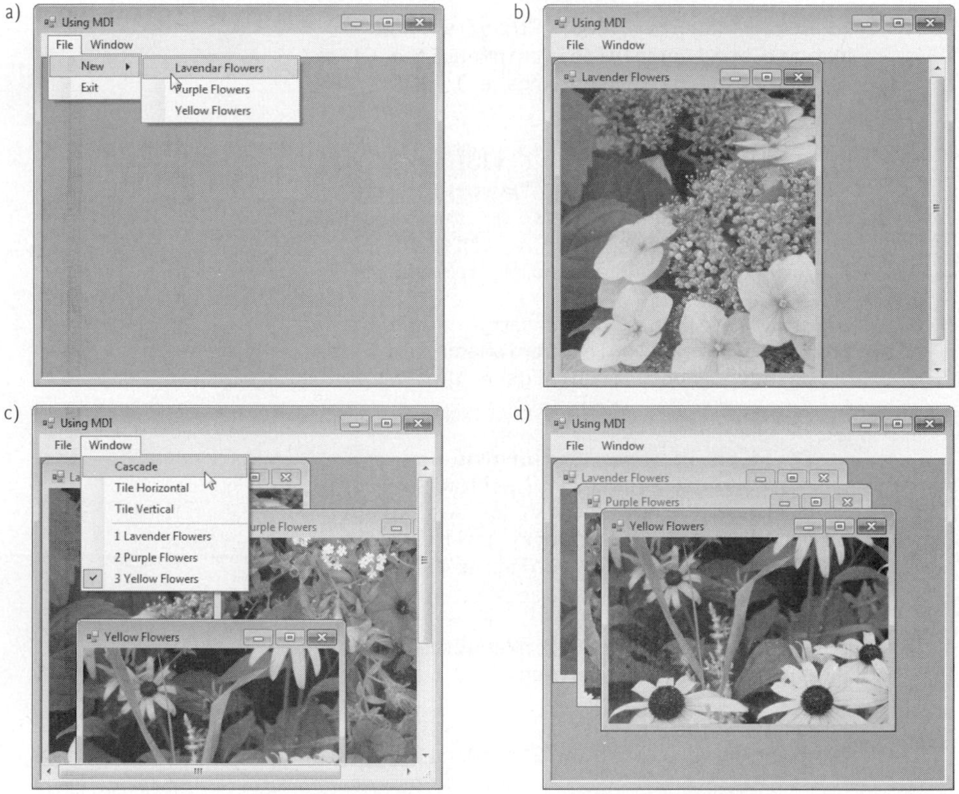

Fig. 15.43 | MDI parent-window class. (Part 3 of 3.)

The **Cascade** menu item (cascadeToolStripMenuItem) has an event handler (cascadeToolStripMenuItem_Click, lines 58–62) that arranges the child windows in a cascading manner. The event handler calls method LayoutMdi with the argument Cascade from the MdiLayout enumeration (line 61).

The **Tile Horizontal** menu item (tileHorizontalToolStripMenuItem) has an event handler (tileHorizontalToolStripMenuItem_Click, lines 65–69) that arranges the child windows in a horizontal manner. The event handler calls method LayoutMdi with the argument TileHorizontal from the MdiLayout enumeration (line 68).

Finally, the **Tile Vertical** menu item (tileVerticalToolStripMenuItem) has an event handler (tileVerticalToolStripMenuItem_Click, lines 72–76) that arranges the child windows in a vertical manner. The event handler calls method LayoutMdi with the argument TileVertical from the MdiLayout enumeration (line 75).

MDI Child Form

At this point, the application is still incomplete—we must define the MDI child class. To do this, right click the project in the **Solution Explorer** and select **Add > Windows Form....** Then name the new class in the dialog as ChildForm (Fig. 15.44). Next, we add a PictureBox (displayPictureBox) to ChildForm. In ChildForm's constructor, line 16 sets the title-bar text. Lines 19–21 retrieve the appropriate image resource, cast it to an Image and set displayPictureBox's Image property. The images that are used can be found in the Images subfolder of this chapter's examples directory.

```
1   // Fig. 15.44: ChildForm.cs
2   // Child window of MDI parent.
3   using System;
4   using System.Drawing;
5   using System.Windows.Forms;
6
7   namespace UsingMDI
8   {
9      public partial class ChildForm : Form
10     {
11        public ChildForm( string title, string resourceName )
12        {
13           // Required for Windows Form Designer support
14           InitializeComponent();
15
16           Text = title; // set title text
17
18           // set image to display in PictureBox
19           displayPictureBox.Image =
20              ( Image ) ( Properties.Resources.ResourceManager.GetObject(
21                 resourceName );
22        } // end constructor
23     } // end class ChildForm
24  } // end namespace UsingMDI
```

Fig. 15.44 | MDI child ChildForm.

After the MDI child class is defined, the parent MDI Form (Fig. 15.43) can create new child windows. The event handlers in lines 18–48 create a new child Form corresponding to the menu item clicked. Lines 22–23, 33–34 and 44–45 create new instances of ChildForm. Lines 24, 35 and 46 set each Child's MdiParent property to the parent Form. Lines 25, 36 and 47 call method Show to display each child Form.

15.13 Visual Inheritance

Chapter 11 discussed how to create classes by inheriting from other classes. We have also used inheritance to create Forms that display a GUI, by deriving our new Form classes from class System.Windows.Forms.Form. This is an example of **visual inheritance**. The derived Form class contains the functionality of its Form base class, including any base-class properties, methods, variables and controls. The derived class also inherits all visual aspects— such as sizing, component layout, spacing between GUI components, colors and fonts— from its base class.

Visual inheritance enables you to achieve visual consistency across applications. For example, you could define a base Form that contains a product's logo, a specific background color, a predefined menu bar and other elements. You then could use the base Form throughout an application for uniformity and branding. You can also create controls that inherit from other controls. For example, you might create a custom UserControl (discussed in Section 15.14) that is derived from an existing control.

Creating a Base **Form**
Class VisualInheritanceBaseForm (Fig. 15.45) derives from Form. The output depicts the workings of the program. The GUI contains two Labels with text **Bugs, Bugs, Bugs** and **Copyright 2010, by Deitel & Associates, Inc.**, as well as one Button displaying the text **Learn More**. When a user presses the **Learn More** Button, method learnMoreButton_Click (lines 18–24) is invoked. This method displays a MessageBox that provides some informative text.

```
1   // Fig. 15.45: VisualInheritanceBaseForm.cs
2   // Base Form for use with visual inheritance.
3   using System;
4   using System.Windows.Forms;
5
6   namespace VisualInheritanceBase
7   {
8      // base Form used to demonstrate visual inheritance
9      public partial class VisualInheritanceBaseForm : Form
10     {
11        // constructor
12        public VisualInheritanceForm()
13        {
14           InitializeComponent();
15        } // end constructor
16
17        // display MessageBox when Button is clicked
18        private void learnMoreButton_Click( object sender, EventArgs e )
19        {
20           MessageBox.Show(
21              "Bugs, Bugs, Bugs is a product of deitel.com",
22              "Learn More", MessageBoxButtons.OK,
23              MessageBoxIcon.Information );
24        } // end method learnMoreButton_Click
25     } // end class VisualInheritanceBaseForm
26  } // end namespace VisualInheritanceBase
```

Fig. 15.45 | Class VisualInheritanceBaseForm, which inherits from class Form, contains a Button (**Learn More**). (Part 1 of 2.)

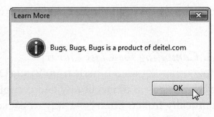

Fig. 15.45 | Class `VisualInheritanceBaseForm`, which inherits from class `Form`, contains a `Button` (**Learn More**). (Part 2 of 2.)

Steps for Declaring and Using a Reusable Class

Before a `Form` (or any class) can be used in multiple applications, it must be placed in a class library to make it reusable. The steps for creating a reusable class are:

1. Declare a `public` class. If the class is not `public`, it can be used only by other classes in the same assembly—that is, compiled into the same DLL or EXE file.

2. Choose a namespace name and add a `namespace` declaration to the source-code file for the reusable class declaration.

3. Compile the class into a class library.

4. Add a reference to the class library in an application.

5. Use the class.

Let's take a look at these steps in the context of this example

Step 1: Creating a `public` Class

For *Step 1* in this discussion, we use the `public` class `VisualInheritanceBaseForm` declared in Fig. 15.45. By default, every new `Form` class you create is declares as a public class.

Step 2: Adding the `namespace` Declaration

For *Step 2*, we use the `namespace` declaration that was created for us by the IDE. By default, every new class you define is placed in a `namespace` with the same name as the project. In almost every example in the text, we've seen that classes from preexisting libraries, such as the .NET Framework Class Library, can be imported into a C# application. Each class belongs to a namespace that contains a group of related classes. As applications become more complex, namespaces help you manage the complexity of application components. Class libraries and namespaces also facilitate software reuse by enabling applications to add classes from other namespaces (as we've done in most examples). We removed the namespace declarations in earlier chapters because they were not necessary.

Placing a class inside a `namespace` declaration indicates that the class is part of the specified namespace. The `namespace` name is part of the fully qualified class name, so the name of class `VisualInheritanceTestForm` is actually `VisualInheritanceBase.VisualInheritanceBaseForm`. You can use this fully qualified name in your applications, or you can write a `using` directive and use the class's simple name (the unqualified class name—

VisualInheritanceBaseForm) in the application. If another namespace also contains a class with the same name, the fully qualified class names can be used to distinguish between the classes in the application and prevent a name conflict (also called a name collision).

Step 3: Compiling the Class Library

To allow other Forms to inherit from VisualInheritanceForm, we must package Visual-InheritanceForm as a class library and compile it into a **.dll file**. Such as file is known as a **dynamically linked library**—a way to package classes that you can reference from other applications. Right click the project name in the **Solution Explorer** and select **Properties**, then choose the **Application** tab. In the **Output type** drop-down list, change **Windows Application** to **Class Library**. Building the project produces the .dll. You can configure a project to be a class library when you first create it by selecting the **Class Library** template in the **New Project** dialog. [*Note:* A class library cannot execute as a stand-alone application. The screen captures in Fig. 15.45 were taken before changing the project to a class library.]

Step 4: Adding a Reference to the Class Library

Once the class is compiled and stored in the class library file, the library can be referenced from any application by indicating to the Visual C# Express IDE where to find the class library file. To visually inherit from VisualInheritanceBaseForm, first create a new Windows application. Right-click the project name in the **Solution Explorer** window and select **Add Reference...** from the pop-up menu that appears. The dialog box that appears will contain a list of class libraries from the .NET Framework. Some class libraries, like the one containing the System namespace, are so common that they're added to your application by the IDE. The ones in this list are not.

In the **Add Reference...** dialog box, click the **Browse** tab. When you build a class library, Visual C# places the .dll file in the project's bin\Release folder. In the **Browse** tab, you can navigate to the directory containing the class library file you created in *Step 3*, as shown in Fig. 15.46. Select the .dll file and click **OK**.

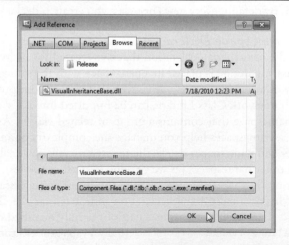

Fig. 15.46 | Adding a reference.

Step 5: Using the Class—Deriving From a Base **Form**

Open the file that defines the new application's GUI and modify the line that defines the class to indicate that the application's Form should inherit from class VisualInheritance-BaseForm. The class-declaration line should now appear as follows:

```
public partial class VisualInheritanceTestForm :
    VisualInheritanceBase.VisualInheritanceBaseForm
```

Unless you specify namespace VisualInheritanceBase in a using directive, you must use the fully qualified name VisualInheritanceBase.VisualInheritanceBaseForm. In **Design** view, the new application's Form should now display the controls inherited from the base Form (Fig. 15.47). We can now add more components to the Form.

Fig. 15.47 | Form demonstrating visual inheritance.

Class *VisualInheritanceTestForm*

Class VisualInheritanceTestForm (Fig. 15.48) is a derived class of VisualInheritance-BaseForm. The output illustrates the functionality of the program. The components, their layouts and the functionality of base class VisualInheritanceBaseForm (Fig. 15.45) are inherited by VisualInheritanceTestForm. We added an additional Button with text **About this Program**. When a user presses this Button, method aboutButton_Click (lines 19–25) is invoked. This method displays another MessageBox providing different informative text (lines 21–24).

```
1   // Fig. 15.48: VisualInheritanceTestForm.cs
2   // Derived Form using visual inheritance.
3   using System;
4   using System.Windows.Forms;
5
6   namespace VisualInheritanceTest
7   {
8      // derived form using visual inheritance
9      public partial class VisualInheritanceTestForm :
10        VisualInheritanceBase.VisualInheritanceBaseForm
11     {
```

Fig. 15.48 | Class VisualInheritanceTestForm, which inherits from class VisualInheritanceBaseForm, contains an additional Button. (Part 1 of 2.)

```
12          // constructor
13          public VisualInheritanceTestForm()
14          {
15              InitializeComponent();
16          } // end constructor
17
18          // display MessageBox when Button is clicked
19          private void aboutButton_Click(object sender, EventArgs e)
20          {
21              MessageBox.Show(
22                  "This program was created by Deitel & Associates.",
23                  "About This Program", MessageBoxButtons.OK,
24                  MessageBoxIcon.Information );
25          } // end method aboutButton_Click
26      } // end class VisualInheritanceTestForm
27  } // end namespace VisualInheritanceTest
```

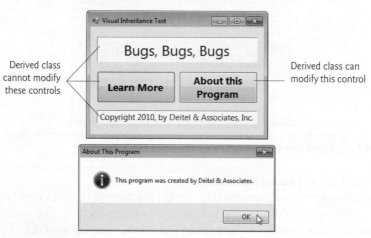

Fig. 15.48 | Class VisualInheritanceTestForm, which inherits from class VisualInheritanceBaseForm, contains an additional Button. (Part 2 of 2.)

If a user clicks the **Learn More** button, the event is handled by the base-class event handler learnMoreButton_Click. Because VisualInheritanceBaseForm uses a private access modifier to declare its controls, VisualInheritanceTestForm cannot modify the controls inherited from class VisualInheritanceBaseForm visually or programmatically. You can, however, add event handlers for the inherited controls. The IDE displays a small icon at the top left of the visually inherited controls to indicate that they're inherited and cannot be altered.

15.14 User-Defined Controls

The .NET Framework allows you to create **custom controls**. These custom controls appear in the user's **Toolbox** and can be added to Forms, Panels or GroupBoxes in the same way that we add Buttons, Labels and other predefined controls. The simplest way to create a custom control is to derive a class from an existing control, such as a Label. This is useful if you want to add functionality to an existing control, rather than replacing it with one that provides the desired functionality. For example, you can create a new type of Label that behaves like a normal Label but has a different appearance. You accomplish this by inheriting from class Label and overriding method OnPaint.

Method OnPaint

All controls have an **OnPaint** method, which the system calls when a component must be redrawn (such as when the component is resized). The method receives a **PaintEventArgs** object, which contains graphics information—property **Graphics** is the graphics object used to draw, and property **ClipRectangle** defines the rectangular boundary of the control. Whenever the system raises a Paint event to draw the control on the screen, the control catches the event and calls its OnPaint method. The base class's OnPaint should be called explicitly from an overridden OnPaint implementation before executing custom-paint code. In most cases, you want to do this to ensure that the original painting code executes in addition to the code you define in the custom control's class. Alternately, if we do not wish to let the base-class OnPaint method execute, we do not call it.

Creating New Controls

To create a new control composed of existing controls, use class **UserControl**. Controls added to a custom control are called **constituent controls**. For example, a programmer could create a UserControl composed of a Button, a Label and a TextBox, each associated with some functionality (for example, the Button setting the Label's text to that contained in the TextBox). The UserControl acts as a container for the controls added to it. The UserControl contains constituent controls, but it does not determine how these constituent controls are displayed. To control the appearance of each constituent control, you can handle each control's Paint event or override OnPaint. Both the Paint event handler and OnPaint are passed a PaintEventArgs object, which can be used to draw graphics (lines, rectangles, and so on) on the constituent controls.

Using another technique, a programmer can create a brand-new control by inheriting from class Control. This class does not define any specific behavior; that's left to you. Instead, class Control handles the items associated with all controls, such as events and sizing handles. Method OnPaint should contain a call to the base class's OnPaint method, which calls the Paint event handlers. You add code that draws custom graphics inside the overridden OnPaint method. This technique allows for the greatest flexibility but also requires the most planning. All three approaches are summarized in Fig. 15.49.

Custom-control techniques and PaintEventArgs properties	Description
Custom-Control Techniques	
Inherit from Windows Forms control	You can do this to add functionality to a preexisting control. If you override method OnPaint, call the base class's OnPaint method. You only can add to the original control's appearance, not redesign it.

Fig. 15.49 | Custom-control creation. (Part 1 of 2.)

Custom-control techniques and PaintEventArgs properties	Description
Create a UserControl	You can create a UserControl composed of multiple preexisting controls (e.g., to combine their functionality). You place drawing code in a Paint event handler or overridden OnPaint method.
Inherit from class Control	Define a brand new control. Override method OnPaint, then call base-class method OnPaint and include methods to draw the control. With this method you can customize control appearance and functionality.
PaintEventArgs Properties	
Graphics	The control's graphics object. It is used to draw on the control.
ClipRectangle	Specifies the rectangle indicating the boundary of the control.

Fig. 15.49 | Custom-control creation. (Part 2 of 2.)

Clock Control
We create a "clock" control in Fig. 15.50. This is a UserControl composed of a Label and a Timer—whenever the Timer raises an event (once per second in this example), the Label is updated to reflect the current time.

```
1   // Fig. 15.50: ClockUserControl.cs
2   // User-defined control with a timer and a Label.
3   using System;
4   using System.Windows.Forms;
5
6   namespace ClockExample
7   {
8      // UserControl that displays the time on a Label
9      public partial class ClockUserControl : UserControl
10     {
11        // constructor
12        public ClockUserControl()
13        {
14           InitializeComponent();
15        } // end constructor
16
17        // update Label at every tick
18        private void clockTimer_Tick(object sender, EventArgs e)
19        {
20           // get current time (Now), convert to string
21           displayLabel.Text = DateTime.Now.ToLongTimeString();
22        } // end method clockTimer_Tick
23     } // end class ClockUserControl
24  } // end namespace ClockExample
```

Fig. 15.50 | UserControl-defined clock. (Part 1 of 2.)

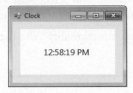
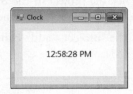

Fig. 15.50 | `UserControl`-defined clock. (Part 2 of 2.)

Timers
`Timers` (`System.Windows.Forms` namespace) are non-visual components that generate `Tick` events at a set interval. This interval is set by the `Timer`'s **Interval** property, which defines the number of milliseconds (thousandths of a second) between events. By default, timers are disabled and do not generate events.

Adding a User Control
This application contains a user control (`ClockUserControl`) and a `Form` that displays the user control. Create a Windows application, then create a `UserControl` class by selecting **Project > Add User Control...**. This displays a dialog from which we can select the type of control to add—user controls are already selected. We then name the file (and the class) `ClockUserControl`. Our empty `ClockUserControl` is displayed as a grey rectangle.

Designing the User Control
You can treat this control like a Windows Form, meaning that you can add controls using the **ToolBox** and set properties using the **Properties** window. However, instead of creating an application, you are simply creating a new control composed of other controls. Add a `Label` (`displayLabel`) and a `Timer` (`clockTimer`) to the `UserControl`. Set the `Timer` interval to 1000 milliseconds and set `displayLabel`'s text with each `Tick` event (lines 18–22). To generate events, `clockTimer` must be enabled by setting property `Enabled` to `true` in the **Properties** window.

Structure **DateTime** (namespace `System`) contains property **Now**, which returns the current time. Method **ToLongTimeString** converts `Now` to a `string` containing the current hour, minute and second (along with AM or PM, depending on your locale). We use this to set the time in `displayLabel` in line 21.

Once created, our clock control appears as an item on the **ToolBox** in the section titled *ProjectName* **Components**, where *ProjectName* is your project's name. *You may need to switch to the application's Form before the item appears in the **ToolBox***. To use the control, simply drag it to the `Form` and run the Windows application. We gave the `ClockUserControl` object a white background to make it stand out in the `Form`. Figure 15.50 shows the output of `Clock`, which contains our `ClockUserControl`. There are no event handlers in `Clock`, so we show only the code for `ClockUserControl`.

Sharing Custom Controls with Other Developers
Visual Studio allows you to share custom controls with other developers. To create a `UserControl` that can be exported to other solutions, do the following:

1. Create a new **Class Library** project.
2. Delete `Class1.cs`, initially provided with the application.

3. Right click the project in the **Solution Explorer** and select **Add > User Control....** In the dialog that appears, name the user-control file and click **Add**.

4. Inside the project, add controls and functionality to the `UserControl` (Fig. 15.51).

Fig. 15.51 | Custom-control creation.

5. Build the project. Visual Studio creates a `.dll` file for the `UserControl` in the output directory (`bin/Release`). The file is not executable; class libraries are used to define classes that are reused in other executable applications.

6. Create a new Windows application.

7. In the new Windows application, right click the **ToolBox** and select **Choose Items....** In the **Choose Toolbox Items** dialog that appears, click **Browse....** Browse for the `.dll` file from the class library created in *Steps 1–5*. The item will then appear in the **Choose Toolbox Items** dialog (Fig. 15.52). If it is not already checked, check this item. Click **OK** to add the item to the **Toolbox**. This control can now be added to the `Form` as if it were any other control.

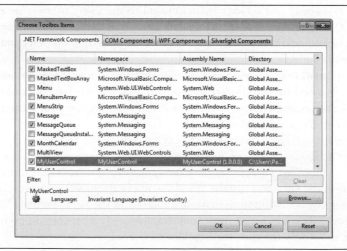

Fig. 15.52 | Custom control added to the **ToolBox**.

15.15 Wrap-Up

Many of today's commercial applications provide GUIs that are easy to use and manipulate. Because of this demand for user-friendly GUIs, the ability to design sophisticated

GUIs is an essential programming skill. Visual Studio's IDE makes GUI development quick and easy. In Chapters 14 and 15, we presented basic Windows Forms GUI development techniques. In Chapter 15, we demonstrated how to create menus, which provide users easy access to an application's functionality. You learned the DateTimePicker and MonthCalendar controls, which allow users to input date and time values. We demonstrated LinkLabels, which are used to link the user to an application or a web page. You used several controls that provide lists of data to the user—ListBoxes, CheckedListBoxes and ListViews. We used the ComboBox control to create drop-down lists, and the TreeView control to display data in hierarchical form. We then introduced complex GUIs that use tabbed windows and multiple document interfaces. The chapter concluded with demonstrations of visual inheritance and creating custom controls. In Chapter 16, we introduce string and character processing.

Summary

Section 15.2 Menus
- Menus provide groups of related commands for Windows applications.
- An expanded menu lists menu items and submenus.
- A menu that contains a menu item is called that menu item's parent menu. A menu item that contains a submenu is considered to be the parent of that submenu.
- All menus and menu items can have shortcut keys.
- Some menu items display checkmarks, indicating that multiple options on the menu can be selected at once.
- The MenuStrip control is used to create menus in a GUI.
- Top-level menus and their menu items are represented using type ToolStripMenuItem.
- To create an access shortcut, type an ampersand (&) before the character to be underlined.
- To add other shortcut keys, set the ShortcutKeys property of the ToolStripMenuItem.
- You can hide shortcut keys by setting property ShowShortcutKeys to false. You can modify how shortcut keys are displayed in the menu item by modifying property ShortcutKeyDisplayString.
- A menu item's Checked property is used to display a check to the left of the menu item.

Section 15.3 MonthCalendar Control
- The MonthCalendar control displays a monthly calendar.
- The user can select a date from the currently displayed month or navigate to another month.
- A MonthCalendar's DateChanged event occurs when a new date is selected.

Section 15.4 DateTimePicker Control
- The DateTimePicker control can be used to retrieve date and/or time information from the user.
- Property Format of class DateTimePicker specifies the user's selection options.
- The DateTimePicker's ValueChanged event is raised when the selected value is changed.

Section 15.5 LinkLabel Control
- The LinkLabel control displays links to other resources, such as files or web pages.
- A LinkLabel appears as underlined text (colored blue by default). When the mouse moves over the link, the pointer changes to a hand; this is similar to a hyperlink in a web page.

- The link can change color to indicate whether the link is new, previously visited or active.
- When clicked, the LinkLabel generates a LinkClicked event.

Section 15.6 ListBox Control

- The ListBox control allows the user to view and select items in a list.
- ListBox property SelectionMode determines the number of items that can be selected.
- The SelectedIndexChanged event of class ListBox occurs when the user selects a new item.
- Property Items returns all the list items as a collection.
- Property SelectedItem returns the currently selected item.
- Use method Add to add an item to the ListBox's Items collection.
- You can add items to ListBoxes and CheckedListBoxes visually by using the Items property in the **Properties** window.

Section 15.7 CheckedListBox Control

- The CheckedListBox control extends a ListBox by including a checkbox next to each item.
- Items can be added via methods Add and AddRange or through the **String Collection Editor**.
- CheckedListBoxes imply that multiple items can be checked.
- CheckedListBox event ItemCheck occurs when a user checks or unchecks a CheckedListBox item.

Section 15.8 ComboBox Control

- The ComboBox control combines TextBox features with a drop-down list.
- Property MaxDropDownItems specifies the maximum number of items that can display at one time.
- You can add objects to collection Items programmatically, using methods Add and AddRange, or visually, with the **String Collection Editor**.
- Property DropDownStyle determines the type of ComboBox and is represented as a value of the ComboBoxStyle enumeration, which contains values Simple, DropDown and DropDownList.
- There can be at most one selected item in a ComboBox (if none, then SelectedIndex is -1).
- When the selected item changes in a ComboBox, a SelectedIndexChanged event occurs.

Section 15.9 TreeView Control

- The TreeView control displays nodes hierarchically in a tree.
- Traditionally, nodes are objects that contain values and can refer to other nodes.
- A parent node contains child nodes, and the child nodes can be parents to other nodes.
- Two child nodes that have the same parent node are considered sibling nodes.
- A tree is a collection of nodes, usually organized in a hierarchical manner. The first parent node of a tree is the root node.
- TreeView controls are useful for displaying hierarchical information.
- In a TreeView, a parent node can be expanded or collapsed by clicking the plus box or minus box to its left. Nodes without children do not have these boxes.
- The nodes displayed in a TreeView are instances of class TreeNode.
- Each TreeNode has a Nodes collection (type TreeNodeCollection), containing a list of TreeNodes.
- To add nodes to a TreeView visually, click the ellipsis next to property Nodes in the **Properties** window. This opens the **TreeNode Editor**, which displays an empty tree representing the TreeView.
- To add nodes programmatically, you must create a root TreeNode object and pass it a string to display. Then call method Add to add this new TreeNode to the TreeView's Nodes collection.

Section 15.10 `ListView` *Control*

- The `ListView` control is similar to a `ListBox` in that both display lists from which the user can select one or more items. `ListView` is more flexible and can display items in different formats.

- Property `MultiSelect` (a `bool`) determines whether multiple items can be selected.

- To display images, an `ImageList` component is required.

- Property `SmallImageList` of class `ListView` sets the `ImageList` for the small icons.

- Property `LargeImageList` of class `ListView` sets the `ImageList` for large icons.

- The items in a `ListView` are each of type `ListViewItem`.

Section 15.11 `TabControl` *Control*

- The `TabControl` control creates tabbed windows.

- `TabControl`s contain `TabPage` objects. Only one `TabPage` is displayed at a time.

- You can add `TabControl`s visually by dragging and dropping them on a `Form` in **Design** mode.

- To add `TabPage`s in **Design** mode, right click the `TabControl` and select **Add Tab**, or click the Tab-Pages property in the **Properties** window, and add tabs in the dialog that appears.

- Each `TabPage` raises a `Click` event when its tab is clicked.

Section 15.12 Multiple Document Interface (MDI) Windows

- The application window of a Multiple document interface (MDI) program is called the parent window, and each window inside the application is referred to as a child window.

- Child windows cannot be parents themselves and cannot be moved outside their parent.

- To create an MDI `Form`, create a new `Form` and set its `IsMdiContainer` property to `true`.

- To add a child `Form` to the parent, create a new child `Form` object, set its `MdiParent` property to the parent `Form` and call the child `Form`'s `Show` method.

- Property `MdiWindowListItem` of class `MenuStrip` specifies which menu, if any, displays a list of open child windows.

- MDI containers allow you to organize the placement of child windows. The child windows in an MDI application can be arranged by calling method `LayoutMdi` of the parent `Form`.

Section 15.13 Visual Inheritance

- Visual inheritance allows you to create a new `Form` by inheriting from an existing `Form`. The derived `Form` class contains the functionality of its base class.

- Visual inheritance can also be applied with other controls as well.

- Visual inheritance enables you to achieve visual consistency across applications by reusing code.

- A reusable class is typically placed in a class library.

- When you compile a class library, the compiler will create a `.dll` file, known as a dynamically linked library—a way to package classes that you can reference from other applications.

Section 15.14 User-Defined Controls

- The .NET Framework allows you to create custom controls.

- Custom controls can appear in the user's **Toolbox** and can be added to `Form`s, `Panel`s or Group-Boxes in the same way that `Button`s, `Label`s and other predefined controls are added.

- The simplest way to create a custom control is to derive a class from an existing control, such as a `Label`. This is useful if you want to add functionality to an existing control, rather than replacing it with one that provides the desired functionality.

- To create a new control composed of existing controls, use class UserControl.
- Controls added to a custom control are called constituent controls.
- A programmer can create a brand-new control by inheriting from class Control. This class does not define any specific behavior; that task is left to you.
- Timers are non-visual components that generate Tick events at a set interval. This interval is set by the Timer's Interval property, which defines the number of milliseconds (thousandths of a second) between events.

Terminology

access shortcut
Activation property of class ListView
ActiveMdiChild property of class Form
AddDays method of struct DateTime
AddYears method of struct DateTime
Application class
cascaded window
CheckBoxes property of class ListView
Checked property of class ToolStripMenuItem
CheckedListBox class
child node
child window
Clear method of class Graphics
Click event of class ToolStripMenuItem
ClipRectangle property of class
    PaintEventArgs
ComboBox class
ComboBoxStyle enumeration
constituent controls
CustomFormat property of class DateTimePicker
Date property of struct DateTime
DateChanged event of class MonthCalendar
DateTime struct
DateTimePicker class
DateTimePickerFormat enumeration
DayOfWeek enumeration
DayOfWeek property of struct DateTime
DirectoryInfo class
.dll file
DrawEllipse method of class Graphics
DrawPie method of class Graphics
DrawRectangle method of class Graphics
DropDownStyle property of class ComboBox
dynamically linked library
Exists method of class Directory
Exit method of class Application
FileInfo class
FillEllipse method of class Graphics
FillPie method of class Graphics
FillRectangle method of class Graphics

Format property of class DateTimePicker
FullName property of class DirectoryInfo
FullName property of class FileInfo
GetDirectories method of class DirectoryInfo
GetFiles method of class DirectoryInfo
GetSelected method of class ListBox
Graphics property of class PaintEventArgs
hotkey
ImageIndex property of class ListViewItem
ImageList class
Images property of class ImageList
Interval property of class Timer
IsMdiContainer property of class Form
ItemCheck event of class CheckedListBox
Items property of class ComboBox
Items property of class ListBox
keyboard shortcut
LargeImageList property of class ListView
LinkLabel class
ListBox class
ListView class
ListViewItem class
MaxDate property of class DateTimePicker
MaxDropDownItems property of class ComboBox
MdiChildren property of class Form
MdiParent property of class Form
MdiWindowListItem property of class MenuStrip
MenuStrip class
MinDate property of class DateTimePicker
MonthCalendar class
multiple document interface (MDI)
MultiSelect property of class ListView
Name property of class DirectoryInfo
Name property of class FileInfo
node
Nodes collection
Now property of struct DateTime
ObjectCollection class
OnPaint method of class Control
PaintEventArgs class

Self-Review Exercises

15.1 State whether each of the following is *true* or *false*. If *false*, explain why.
    a) Menus provide groups of related classes.
    b) Menu items can display `ComboBox`es, checkmarks and access shortcuts.
    c) The `ListBox` control allows only single selection (like a `RadioButton`).
    d) A `ComboBox` control typically has a drop-down list.
    e) Deleting a parent node in a `TreeView` control deletes its child nodes.
    f) The user can select only one item in a `ListView` control.
    g) A `TabPage` can act as a container for `RadioButton`s.
    h) An MDI child window can have MDI children.
    i) MDI child windows can be moved outside the boundaries of their parent window.
    j) There are two basic ways to create a customized control.

15.2 Fill in the blanks in each of the following statements:
    a) Method _____ of class `Process` can open files and web pages, similar to the **Run...** command in Windows.
    b) If more elements appear in a `ComboBox` than can fit, a(n) _____ appears.
    c) The top-level node in a `TreeView` is the _____ node.
    d) A(n) _____ and a(n) _____ can display icons contained in an `ImageList` control.
    e) The _____ property allows a menu to display a list of active child windows.
    f) Class _____ allows you to combine several controls into a single, custom control.
    g) The _____ saves space by layering `TabPage`s on top of each other.
    h) The _____ window layout option makes all MDI windows the same size and layers them so every title bar is visible (if possible).
    i) _____ are typically used to display hyperlinks to other resources, files or web pages.

Answers to Self-Review Exercises

15.1   a) False. Menus provide groups of related commands. b) True. c) False. It can have single or multiple selection. d) True. e) True. f) False. The user can select one or more items. g) True. h) False. Only an MDI parent window can have MDI children. An MDI parent window cannot be an MDI child. i) False. MDI child windows cannot be moved outside their parent window. j) False. There are three ways: 1) Derive from an existing control, 2) use a UserControl or 3) derive from Control and create a control from scratch.

15.2   a) Start. b) scrollbar. c) root. d) ListView, TreeView. e) MdiWindowListItem. f) UserControl. g) TabControl. h) Cascade. i) LinkLabels.

Exercises

15.3   *(Using ComboBoxes)* Write a program that displays the names of 15 states in a ComboBox. When an item is selected from the ComboBox, remove it.

15.4   *(Using ComboBoxes and ListBoxes)* Modify your solution to the previous exercise to add a ListBox. When the user selects an item from the ComboBox, remove the item from the ComboBox and add it to the ListBox. Your program should check to ensure that the ComboBox contains at least one item. If it does not, print a message, using a message box, then terminate program execution when the user dismisses the message box.

15.5   *(Sorting Strings)* Write a program that allows the user to enter strings in a TextBox. Each string input is added to a ListBox. As each string is added to the ListBox, ensure that the strings are in sorted order. [*Note:* Use property Sorted.]

15.6   *(File Browser)* Create a file browser (similar to Windows Explorer) based on the programs in Figs. 15.14, 15.28 and 15.31. The file browser should have a TreeView, which allows the user to browse directories. There should also be a ListView, which displays the contents (all subdirectories and files) of the directory being browsed. Double clicking a file in the ListView should open it, and double clicking a directory in either the ListView or the TreeView should browse it. If a file or directory cannot be accessed because of its permission settings, notify the user.

15.7   *(MDI Text Editor)* Create an MDI text editor. Each child window should contain a multi-line RichTextBox. The MDI parent should have a **Format** menu, with submenus to control the size, font and color of the text in the active child window. Each submenu should have at least three options. In addition, the parent should have a **File** menu, with menu items **New** (create a new child), **Close** (close the active child) and **Exit** (exit the application). The parent should have a **Window** menu to display a list of the open child windows and their layout options.

15.8   *(Login User Control)* Create a UserControl called LoginPasswordUserControl that contains a Label (loginLabel) that displays string "Login:", a TextBox (loginTextBox), where the user inputs a login name, a Label (passwordLabel) that displays the string "Password:" and, finally, a TextBox (passwordTextBox) where a user inputs a password (set property PasswordChar to "*" in the TextBox's **Properties** window). LoginPasswordUserControl must provide public read-only properties Login and Password that allow an application to retrieve the user input from loginTextBox and passwordTextBox. The UserControl must be exported to an application that displays the values input by the user in LoginPasswordUserControl.

15.9   *(Restaurant Bill Calculator)* A restaurant wants an application that calculates a table's bill. The application should display all the menu items from Fig. 15.53 in four ComboBoxes. Each ComboBox should contain a category of food offered by the restaurant (Beverage, Appetizer, Main Course and Dessert). The user can choose from one of these ComboBoxes to add an item to a table's bill. As each item is selected in the ComboBoxes, add the price of that item to the bill. The user can click the **Clear Bill** Button to restore the **Subtotal:**, **Tax:** and **Total:** fields to $0.00.

Name	Category	Price	Name	Category	Price
Soda	Beverage	$1.95	Chicken Alfredo	Main Course	$13.95
Tea	Beverage	$1.50	Chicken Picatta	Main Course	$13.95
Coffee	Beverage	$1.25	Turkey Club	Main Course	$11.95
Mineral Water	Beverage	$2.95	Lobster Pie	Main Course	$19.95
Juice	Beverage	$2.50	Prime Rib	Main Course	$20.95
Milk	Beverage	$1.50	Shrimp Scampi	Main Course	$18.95
Buffalo Wings	Appetizer	$5.95	Turkey Dinner	Main Course	$13.95
Buffalo Fingers	Appetizer	$6.95	Stuffed Chicken	Main Course	$14.95
Potato Skins	Appetizer	$8.95	Apple Pie	Dessert	$5.95
Nachos	Appetizer	$8.95	Sundae	Dessert	$3.95
Mushroom Caps	Appetizer	$10.95	Carrot Cake	Dessert	$5.95
Shrimp Cocktail	Appetizer	$12.95	Mud Pie	Dessert	$4.95
Chips and Salsa	Appetizer	$6.95	Apple Crisp	Dessert	$5.95
Seafood Alfredo	Main Course	$15.95			

Fig. 15.53 | Food items and prices.

15.10 *(Using TabPages)* Create an application that contains three TabPages. On the first TabPage, place a CheckedListBox with six items. On the second TabPage, place six TextBoxes. On the last TabPage, place six LinkLabels. The user's selections on the first TabPage should specify which of the six LinkLabels will be displayed. To hide or display a LinkLabel's value, use its Visible property. Use the second TabPage to modify the web page that is opened by the LinkLabels.

15.11 *(MDI Drawing Programs)* Create an MDI application with child windows that each have a Panel for drawing. Add menus to the MDI application that allow the user to modify the size and color of the paintbrush. When running this application, be aware that if one of the windows overlaps another, the Panel will be cleared.

16

Strings and Characters

The chief defect of Henry King
Was chewing little bits of string.
—Hilaire Belloc

The difference between the
almost-right word and the right
word is really a large matter—
it's the difference between the
lightning bug and the lightning.
—Mark Twain

Objectives

In this chapter you'll learn:

- To create and manipulate immutable character-string objects of class `string` and mutable character-string objects of class `StringBuilder`.

- To manipulate character objects of `struct Char`.

- To use regular-expression classes `Regex` and `Match`.

- To iterate through matches to a regular expression.

- To use character classes to match any character from a set of characters.

- To use quantifiers to match a pattern multiple times.

- To search for patterns in text using regular expressions.

- To validate data using regular expressions and LINQ.

- To modify `string`s using regular expressions and class `Regex`.

16.1 Introduction

This chapter introduces the .NET Framework Class Library's string- and character-processing capabilities and demonstrates how to use regular expressions to search for patterns in text. The techniques it presents can be employed in text editors, word processors, page-layout software, computerized typesetting systems and other kinds of text-processing software. Previous chapters presented some basic string-processing capabilities. Now we discuss in detail the text-processing capabilities of class `string` and type `char` from the `System` namespace and class `StringBuilder` from the `System.Text` namespace.

We begin with an overview of the fundamentals of characters and strings in which we discuss character constants and string literals. We then provide examples of class `string`'s many constructors and methods. The examples demonstrate how to determine the length of strings, copy strings, access individual characters in strings, search strings, obtain substrings from larger strings, compare strings, concatenate strings, replace characters in strings and convert strings to uppercase or lowercase letters.

Next, we introduce class `StringBuilder`, which is used to build strings dynamically. We demonstrate `StringBuilder` capabilities for determining and specifying the size of a `StringBuilder`, as well as appending, inserting, removing and replacing characters in a `StringBuilder` object. We then introduce the character-testing methods of struct `Char` that enable a program to determine whether a character is a digit, a letter, a lowercase letter, an uppercase letter, a punctuation mark or a symbol other than a punctuation mark. Such methods are useful for validating individual characters in user input. In addition, type `Char` provides methods for converting a character to uppercase or lowercase.

We provide an online section that discusses regular expressions. We present classes `Regex` and `Match` from the `System.Text.RegularExpressions` namespace as well as the symbols that are used to form regular expressions. We then demonstrate how to find patterns in a string, match entire strings to patterns, replace characters in a string that match a pattern and split strings at delimiters specified as a pattern in a regular expression.

16.2 Fundamentals of Characters and Strings

Characters are the fundamental building blocks of C# source code. Every program is composed of characters that, when grouped together meaningfully, create a sequence that the compiler interprets as instructions describing how to accomplish a task. In addition to normal characters, a program also can contain **character constants**. A character constant is a character that's represented as an integer value, called a *character code*. For example, the integer value 122 corresponds to the character constant 'z'. The integer value 10 corresponds to the newline character '\n'. Character constants are established according to the **Unicode character set**, an international character set that contains many more symbols and letters than does the ASCII character set (listed in Appendix C). To learn more about Unicode, see Appendix F.

A string is a series of characters treated as a unit. These characters can be uppercase letters, lowercase letters, digits and various **special characters**: +, -, *, /, $ and others. A string is an object of class string in the System namespace.[1] We write **string literals**, also called **string constants**, as sequences of characters in double quotation marks, as follows:

```
"John Q. Doe"
"9999 Main Street"
"Waltham, Massachusetts"
"(201) 555-1212"
```

A declaration can assign a string literal to a string reference. The declaration

```
string color = "blue";
```

initializes string reference color to refer to the string literal object "blue".

Performance Tip 16.1

If there are multiple occurrences of the same string literal object in an application, a single copy of it will be referenced from each location in the program that uses that string literal. It's possible to share the object in this manner, because string literal objects are implicitly constant. Such sharing conserves memory.

On occasion, a string will contain multiple backslash characters (this often occurs in the name of a file). To avoid excessive backslash characters, it's possible to exclude escape sequences and interpret all the characters in a string literally, using the @ character. Backslashes within the double quotation marks following the @ character are not considered escape sequences, but rather regular backslash characters. Often this simplifies programming and makes the code easier to read. For example, consider the string "C:\MyFolder\MySubFolder\MyFile.txt" with the following assignment:

```
string file = "C:\\MyFolder\\MySubFolder\\MyFile.txt";
```

Using the verbatim string syntax, the assignment can be altered to

```
string file = @"C:\MyFolder\MySubFolder\MyFile.txt";
```

This approach also has the advantage of allowing string literals to span multiple lines by preserving all newlines, spaces and tabs.

---

1. C# provides the string keyword as an alias for class String. In this book, we use the term string.

16.3 string Constructors

Class string provides eight constructors for initializing strings in various ways. Figure 16.1 demonstrates three of the constructors.

```
1   // Fig. 16.1: StringConstructor.cs
2   // Demonstrating string class constructors.
3   using System;
4
5   class StringConstructor
6   {
7      public static void Main( string[] args )
8      {
9         // string initialization
10        char[] characterArray =
11           { 'b', 'i', 'r', 't', 'h', ' ', 'd', 'a', 'y' };
12        string originalString = "Welcome to C# programming!";
13        string string1 = originalString;
14        string string2 = new string( characterArray );
15        string string3 = new string( characterArray, 6, 3 );
16        string string4 = new string( 'C', 5 );
17
18        Console.WriteLine( "string1 = " + "\"" + string1 + "\"\n" +
19           "string2 = " + "\"" + string2 + "\"\n" +
20           "string3 = " + "\"" + string3 + "\"\n" +
21           "string4 = " + "\"" + string4 + "\"\n" );
22     } // end Main
23  } // end class StringConstructor
```

```
string1 = "Welcome to C# programming!"
string2 = "birth day"
string3 = "day"
string4 = "CCCCC"
```

Fig. 16.1 | string constructors.

Lines 10–11 allocate the char array characterArray, which contains nine characters. Lines 12–16 declare the strings originalString, string1, string2, string3 and string4. Line 12 assigns string literal "Welcome to C# programming!" to string reference originalString. Line 13 sets string1 to reference the same string literal.

Line 14 assigns to string2 a new string, using the string constructor with a character array argument. The new string contains a copy of the array's characters.

Line 15 assigns to string3 a new string, using the string constructor that takes a char array and two int arguments. The second argument specifies the starting index position (the *offset*) from which characters in the array are to be copied. The third argument specifies the number of characters (the *count*) to be copied from the specified starting position in the array. The new string contains a copy of the specified characters in the array. If the specified offset or count indicates that the program should access an element outside the bounds of the character array, an ArgumentOutOfRangeException is thrown.

Line 16 assigns to string4 a new string, using the string constructor that takes as arguments a character and an int specifying the number of times to repeat that character in the string.

Software Engineering Observation 16.1

In most cases, it's not necessary to make a copy of an existing string. All strings are immutable—their character contents cannot be changed after they're created. Also, if there are one or more references to a string (or any object for that matter), the object cannot be reclaimed by the garbage collector.

16.4 string Indexer, Length Property and CopyTo Method

The application in Fig. 16.2 presents the string indexer, which facilitates the retrieval of any character in the string, and the string property Length, which returns the length of the string. The string method CopyTo copies a specified number of characters from a string into a char array.

```
 1    // Fig. 16.2: StringMethods.cs
 2    // Using the indexer, property Length and method CopyTo
 3    // of class string.
 4    using System;
 5
 6    class StringMethods
 7    {
 8       public static void Main( string[] args )
 9       {
10          string string1 = "hello there";
11          char[] characterArray = new char[ 5 ];
12
13          // output string1
14          Console.WriteLine( "string1: \"" + string1 + "\"" );
15
16          // test Length property
17          Console.WriteLine( "Length of string1: " + string1.Length );
18
19          // loop through characters in string1 and display reversed
20          Console.Write( "The string reversed is: " );
21
22          for ( int i = string1.Length - 1; i >= 0; i-- )
23             Console.Write( string1[ i ] );
24
25          // copy characters from string1 into characterArray
26          string1.CopyTo( 0, characterArray, 0, characterArray.Length );
27          Console.Write( "\nThe character array is: " );
28
29          for ( int i = 0; i < characterArray.Length; i++ )
30             Console.Write( characterArray[ i ] );
31
32          Console.WriteLine( "\n" );
33       } // end Main
34    } // end class StringMethods
```

Fig. 16.2 | string indexer, Length property and CopyTo method. (Part 1 of 2.)

```
string1: "hello there"
Length of string1: 11
The string reversed is: ereht olleh
The character array is: hello
```

Fig. 16.2 | string indexer, Length property and CopyTo method. (Part 2 of 2.)

This application determines the length of a string, displays its characters in reverse order and copies a series of characters from the string to a character array. Line 17 uses string property Length to determine the number of characters in string1. Like arrays, strings always know their own size.

Lines 22–23 write the characters of string1 in reverse order using the string indexer. The string indexer treats a string as an array of chars and returns each character at a specific position in the string. The indexer receives an integer argument as the *position number* and returns the character at that position. As with arrays, the first element of a string is considered to be at position 0.

Common Programming Error 16.1

Attempting to access a character that's outside a string's bounds results in an Index-OutOfRangeException.

Line 26 uses string method CopyTo to copy the characters of string1 into a character array (characterArray). The first argument given to method CopyTo is the index from which the method begins copying characters in the string. The second argument is the character array into which the characters are copied. The third argument is the index specifying the starting location at which the method begins placing the copied characters into the character array. The last argument is the number of characters that the method will copy from the string. Lines 29–30 output the char array contents one character at a time.

16.5 Comparing strings

The next two examples demonstrate various methods for comparing strings. To understand how one string can be "greater than" or "less than" another, consider the process of alphabetizing a series of last names. The reader would, no doubt, place "Jones" before "Smith", because the first letter of "Jones" comes before the first letter of "Smith" in the alphabet. The alphabet is more than just a set of 26 letters—it's an ordered list of characters in which each letter occurs in a specific position. For example, Z is more than just a letter of the alphabet; it's specifically the twenty-sixth letter of the alphabet. Computers can order characters alphabetically because they're represented internally as Unicode numeric codes.

*Comparing Strings with **Equals**, **CompareTo** and the Equality Operator (==)*
Class string provides several ways to compare strings. The application in Fig. 16.3 demonstrates the use of method Equals, method CompareTo and the equality operator (==).

The condition in line 21 uses string method Equals to compare string1 and literal string "hello" to determine whether they're equal. Method Equals (inherited from object and overridden in string) tests any two objects for equality (i.e., checks whether the objects have identical contents). The method returns true if the objects are equal and false otherwise. In this case, the condition returns true, because string1 references string literal object "hello". Method Equals uses word sorting rules that depend on your system's currently selected culture. Comparing "hello" with "HELLO" would return false, because the lowercase letters are different from the those of corresponding upper-case letters.

```
1    // Fig. 16.3: StringCompare.cs
2    // Comparing strings
3    using System;
4
5    class StringCompare
6    {
7       public static void Main( string[] args )
8       {
9          string string1 = "hello";
10         string string2 = "good bye";
11         string string3 = "Happy Birthday";
12         string string4 = "happy birthday";
13
14         // output values of four strings
15         Console.WriteLine( "string1 = \"" + string1 + "\"" +
16            "\nstring2 = \"" + string2 + "\"" +
17            "\nstring3 = \"" + string3 + "\"" +
18            "\nstring4 = \"" + string4 + "\"\n" );
19
20         // test for equality using Equals method
21         if ( string1.Equals( "hello" ) )
22            Console.WriteLine( "string1 equals \"hello\"" );
23         else
24            Console.WriteLine( "string1 does not equal \"hello\"" );
25
26         // test for equality with ==
27         if ( string1 == "hello" )
28            Console.WriteLine( "string1 equals \"hello\"" );
29         else
30            Console.WriteLine( "string1 does not equal \"hello\"" );
31
32         // test for equality comparing case
33         if ( string.Equals( string3, string4 ) ) // static method
34            Console.WriteLine( "string3 equals string4" );
35         else
36            Console.WriteLine( "string3 does not equal string4" );
37
38         // test CompareTo
39         Console.WriteLine( "\nstring1.CompareTo( string2 ) is " +
40            string1.CompareTo( string2 ) + "\n" +
41            "string2.CompareTo( string1 ) is " +
42            string2.CompareTo( string1 ) + "\n" +
43            "string1.CompareTo( string1 ) is " +
44            string1.CompareTo( string1 ) + "\n" +
45            "string3.CompareTo( string4 ) is " +
```

Fig. 16.3 | string test to determine equality. (Part 1 of 2.)

```
46                string3.CompareTo( string4 ) + "\n" +
47                "string4.CompareTo( string3 ) is " +
48                string4.CompareTo( string3 ) + "\n\n" );
49      } // end Main
50   } // end class StringCompare
```

```
string1 = "hello"
string2 = "good bye"
string3 = "Happy Birthday"
string4 = "happy birthday"

string1 equals "hello"
string1 equals "hello"
string3 does not equal string4

string1.CompareTo( string2 ) is 1
string2.CompareTo( string1 ) is -1
string1.CompareTo( string1 ) is 0
string3.CompareTo( string4 ) is 1
string4.CompareTo( string3 ) is -1
```

Fig. 16.3 | string test to determine equality. (Part 2 of 2.)

The condition in line 27 uses the overloaded equality operator (==) to compare string string1 with the literal string "hello" for equality. In C#, the equality operator also compares the contents of two strings. Thus, the condition in the if statement evaluates to true, because the values of string1 and "hello" are equal.

Line 33 tests whether string3 and string4 are equal to illustrate that comparisons are indeed case sensitive. Here, static method Equals is used to compare the values of two strings. "Happy Birthday" does not equal "happy birthday", so the condition of the if statement fails, and the message "string3 does not equal string4" is output (line 36).

Lines 40–48 use string method CompareTo to compare strings. Method CompareTo returns 0 if the strings are equal, a negative value if the string that invokes CompareTo is less than the string that's passed as an argument and a positive value if the string that invokes CompareTo is greater than the string that's passed as an argument.

Notice that CompareTo considers string3 to be greater than string4. The only difference between these two strings is that string3 contains two uppercase letters in positions where string4 contains lowercase letters.

Determining Whether a String Begins or Ends with a Specified String

Figure 16.4 shows how to test whether a string instance begins or ends with a given string. Method StartsWith determines whether a string instance starts with the string text passed to it as an argument. Method EndsWith determines whether a string instance ends with the string text passed to it as an argument. Class stringStartEnd's Main method defines an array of strings (called strings), which contains "started", "starting", "ended" and "ending". The remainder of method Main tests the elements of the array to determine whether they start or end with a particular set of characters.

Line 13 uses method StartsWith, which takes a string argument. The condition in the if statement determines whether the string at index i of the array starts with the characters "st". If so, the method returns true, and strings[i] is output along with a message.

```
1    // Fig. 16.4: StringStartEnd.cs
2    // Demonstrating StartsWith and EndsWith methods.
3    using System;
4
5    class StringStartEnd
6    {
7       public static void Main( string[] args )
8       {
9          string[] strings = { "started", "starting", "ended", "ending" };
10
11         // test every string to see if it starts with "st"
12         for ( int i = 0; i < strings.Length; i++ )
13            if ( strings[ i ].StartsWith( "st" ) )
14               Console.WriteLine( "\"" + strings[ i ] + "\"" +
15                  " starts with \"st\"" );
16
17         Console.WriteLine();
18
19         // test every string to see if it ends with "ed"
20         for ( int i = 0; i < strings.Length; i++ )
21            if ( strings[ i ].EndsWith( "ed" ) )
22               Console.WriteLine( "\"" + strings[ i ] + "\"" +
23                  " ends with \"ed\"" );
24
25         Console.WriteLine();
26      } // end Main
27   } // end class StringStartEnd
```

```
"started" starts with "st"
"starting" starts with "st"

"started" ends with "ed"
"ended" ends with "ed"
```

Fig. 16.4 | StartsWith and EndsWith methods.

Line 21 uses method EndsWith to determine whether the string at index i of the array ends with the characters "ed". If so, the method returns true, and strings[i] is displayed along with a message.

16.6 Locating Characters and Substrings in strings

In many applications, it's necessary to search for a character or set of characters in a string. For example, a programmer creating a word processor would want to provide capabilities for searching through documents. The application in Fig. 16.5 demonstrates some of the many versions of string methods IndexOf, IndexOfAny, LastIndexOf and LastIndexOfAny, which search for a specified character or substring in a string. We perform all searches in this example on the string letters (initialized with "abcdefghijklmabcdefghijklm") located in method Main of class StringIndexMethods.

Lines 14, 16 and 18 use method IndexOf to locate the first occurrence of a character or substring in a string. If it finds a character, IndexOf returns the index of the specified

```
 1   // Fig. 16.5: StringIndexMethods.cs
 2   // Using string-searching methods.
 3   using System;
 4
 5   class StringIndexMethods
 6   {
 7      public static void Main( string[] args )
 8      {
 9         string letters = "abcdefghijklmabcdefghijklm";
10         char[] searchLetters = { 'c', 'a', '$' };
11
12         // test IndexOf to locate a character in a string
13         Console.WriteLine( "First 'c' is located at index " +
14            letters.IndexOf( 'c' ) );
15         Console.WriteLine( "First 'a' starting at 1 is located at index " +
16            letters.IndexOf( 'a', 1 ) );
17         Console.WriteLine( "First '$' in the 5 positions starting at 3 " +
18            "is located at index " + letters.IndexOf( '$', 3, 5 ) );
19
20         // test LastIndexOf to find a character in a string
21         Console.WriteLine( "\nLast 'c' is located at index " +
22            letters.LastIndexOf( 'c' ) );
23         Console.WriteLine( "Last 'a' up to position 25 is located at " +
24            "index " + letters.LastIndexOf( 'a', 25 ) );
25         Console.WriteLine( "Last '$' in the 5 positions starting at 15 " +
26            "is located at index " + letters.LastIndexOf( '$', 15, 5 ) );
27
28         // test IndexOf to locate a substring in a string
29         Console.WriteLine( "\nFirst \"def\" is located at index " +
30            letters.IndexOf( "def" ) );
31         Console.WriteLine( "First \"def\" starting at 7 is located at " +
32            "index " + letters.IndexOf( "def", 7 ) );
33         Console.WriteLine( "First \"hello\" in the 15 positions " +
34            "starting at 5 is located at index " +
35            letters.IndexOf( "hello", 5, 15 ) );
36
37         // test LastIndexOf to find a substring in a string
38         Console.WriteLine( "\nLast \"def\" is located at index " +
39            letters.LastIndexOf( "def" ) );
40         Console.WriteLine( "Last \"def\" up to position 25 is located " +
41            "at index " + letters.LastIndexOf( "def", 25 ) );
42         Console.WriteLine( "Last \"hello\" in the 15 positions " +
43            "ending at 20 is located at index " +
44            letters.LastIndexOf( "hello", 20, 15 ) );
45
46         // test IndexOfAny to find first occurrence of character in array
47         Console.WriteLine( "\nFirst 'c', 'a' or '$' is " +
48            "located at index " + letters.IndexOfAny( searchLetters ) );
49         Console.WriteLine("First 'c', 'a' or '$' starting at 7 is " +
50            "located at index " + letters.IndexOfAny( searchLetters, 7 ) );
51         Console.WriteLine( "First 'c', 'a' or '$' in the 5 positions " +
52            "starting at 7 is located at index " +
53            letters.IndexOfAny( searchLetters, 7, 5 ) );
```

Fig. 16.5 | Searching for characters and substrings in strings. (Part 1 of 2.)

```
54
55          // test LastIndexOfAny to find last occurrence of character
56          // in array
57          Console.WriteLine( "\nLast 'c', 'a' or '$' is " +
58             "located at index " + letters.LastIndexOfAny( searchLetters ) );
59          Console.WriteLine( "Last 'c', 'a' or '$' up to position 1 is " +
60             "located at index " +
61             letters.LastIndexOfAny( searchLetters, 1 ) );
62          Console.WriteLine( "Last 'c', 'a' or '$' in the 5 positions " +
63             "ending at 25 is located at index " +
64             letters.LastIndexOfAny( searchLetters, 25, 5 ) );
65       } // end Main
66    } // end class StringIndexMethods
```

```
First 'c' is located at index 2
First 'a' starting at 1 is located at index 13
First '$' in the 5 positions starting at 3 is located at index -1

Last 'c' is located at index 15
Last 'a' up to position 25 is located at index 13
Last '$' in the 5 positions starting at 15 is located at index -1

First "def" is located at index 3
First "def" starting at 7 is located at index 16
First "hello" in the 15 positions starting at 5 is located at index -1

Last "def" is located at index 16
Last "def" up to position 25 is located at index 16
Last "hello" in the 15 positions ending at 20 is located at index -1

First 'c', 'a' or '$' is located at index 0
First 'c', 'a' or '$' starting at 7 is located at index 13
First 'c', 'a' or '$' in the 5 positions starting at 7 is located at index -1

Last 'c', 'a' or '$' is located at index 15
Last 'c', 'a' or '$' up to position 1 is located at index 0
Last 'c', 'a' or '$' in the 5 positions ending at 25 is located at index -1
```

Fig. 16.5 | Searching for characters and substrings in `strings`. (Part 2 of 2.)

character in the `string`; otherwise, `IndexOf` returns –1. The expression in line 16 uses a version of method `IndexOf` that takes two arguments—the character to search for and the starting index at which the search of the `string` should begin. The method does not examine any characters that occur prior to the starting index (in this case, 1). The expression in line 18 uses another version of method `IndexOf` that takes three arguments—the character to search for, the index at which to start searching and the number of characters to search.

Lines 22, 24 and 26 use method `LastIndexOf` to locate the last occurrence of a character in a `string`. Method `LastIndexOf` performs the search from the end of the `string` to the beginning of the `string`. If it finds the character, `LastIndexOf` returns the index of the specified character in the `string`; otherwise, `LastIndexOf` returns –1. There are three versions of method `LastIndexOf`. The expression in line 22 uses the version that takes as an argument the character for which to search. The expression in line 24 uses the version that takes two arguments—the character for which to search and the highest index from which to begin searching backward for the character. The expression in line 26 uses a third version of method LastIndexOf that takes three arguments—the character for which to search, the starting index from which to start searching backward and the number of characters (the portion of the string) to search.

     Lines 29–44 use versions of IndexOf and LastIndexOf that take a string instead of a character as the first argument. These versions of the methods perform identically to those described above except that they search for sequences of characters (or substrings) that are specified by their string arguments.

     Lines 47–64 use methods IndexOfAny and LastIndexOfAny, which take an array of characters as the first argument. These versions of the methods also perform identically to those described above, except that they return the index of the first occurrence of any of the characters in the character-array argument.

Common Programming Error 16.2

In the overloaded methods LastIndexOf *and* LastIndexOfAny *that take three parameters, the second argument must be greater than or equal to the third. This might seem counterintuitive, but remember that the search moves from the end of the string toward the start of the string.*

16.7 Extracting Substrings from strings

Class string provides two Substring methods, which create a new string by copying part of an existing string. Each method returns a new string. The application in Fig. 16.6 demonstrates the use of both methods.

```
1   // Fig. 16.6: SubString.cs
2   // Demonstrating the string Substring method.
3   using System;
4
5   class SubString
6   {
7      public static void Main( string[] args )
8      {
9         string letters = "abcdefghijklmabcdefghijklm";
10
11        // invoke Substring method and pass it one parameter
12        Console.WriteLine( "Substring from index 20 to end is \"" +
13           letters.Substring( 20 ) + "\"" );
14
15        // invoke Substring method and pass it two parameters
16        Console.WriteLine( "Substring from index 0 of length 6 is \"" +
17           letters.Substring( 0, 6 ) + "\"" );
18     } // end method Main
19  } // end class SubString
```

```
Substring from index 20 to end is "hijklm"
Substring from index 0 of length 6 is "abcdef"
```

Fig. 16.6 | Substrings generated from strings.

The statement in line 13 uses the Substring method that takes one int argument. The argument specifies the starting index from which the method copies characters in the original string. The substring returned contains a copy of the characters from the starting index to the end of the string. If the index specified in the argument is outside the bounds of the string, the program throws an ArgumentOutOfRangeException.

The second version of method Substring (line 17) takes two int arguments. The first argument specifies the starting index from which the method copies characters from the original string. The second argument specifies the length of the substring to copy. The substring returned contains a copy of the specified characters from the original string. If the supplied length of the substring is too large (i.e., the substring tries to retrieve characters past the end of the original string), an ArgumentOutOfRangeException is thrown.

16.8 Concatenating strings

The + operator is not the only way to perform string concatenation. The static method Concat of class string (Fig. 16.7) concatenates two strings and returns a new string containing the combined characters from both original strings. Line 16 appends the characters from string2 to the end of a copy of string1, using method Concat. The statement in line 16 does not modify the original strings.

```
1   // Fig. 16.7: SubConcatenation.cs
2   // Demonstrating string class Concat method.
3   using System;
4
5   class StringConcatenation
6   {
7      public static void Main( string[] args )
8      {
9         string string1 = "Happy ";
10        string string2 = "Birthday";
11
12        Console.WriteLine( "string1 = \"" + string1 + "\"\n" +
13           "string2 = \"" + string2 + "\"" );
14        Console.WriteLine(
15           "\nResult of string.Concat( string1, string2 ) = " +
16           string.Concat( string1, string2 ) );
17        Console.WriteLine( "string1 after concatenation = " + string1 );
18     } // end Main
19  } // end class StringConcatenation
```

```
string1 = "Happy "
string2 = "Birthday"

Result of string.Concat( string1, string2 ) = Happy Birthday
string1 after concatenation = Happy
```

Fig. 16.7 | Concat static method.

16.9 Miscellaneous string Methods

Class string provides several methods that return modified copies of strings. The application in Fig. 16.8 demonstrates the use of these methods, which include string methods Replace, ToLower, ToUpper and Trim.

```
1   // Fig. 16.8: StringMethods2.cs
2   // Demonstrating string methods Replace, ToLower, ToUpper, Trim,
3   // and ToString.
4   using System;
5
6   class StringMethods2
7   {
8      public static void Main( string[] args )
9      {
10        string string1 = "cheers!";
11        string string2 = "GOOD BYE ";
12        string string3 = "   spaces   ";
13
14        Console.WriteLine( "string1 = \"" + string1 + "\"\n" +
15           "string2 = \"" + string2 + "\"\n" +
16           "string3 = \"" + string3 + "\"" );
17
18        // call method Replace
19        Console.WriteLine(
20           "\nReplacing \"e\" with \"E\" in string1: \"" +
21           string1.Replace( 'e', 'E' ) + "\"" );
22
23        // call ToLower and ToUpper
24        Console.WriteLine( "\nstring1.ToUpper() = \"" +
25           string1.ToUpper() + "\"\nstring2.ToLower() = \"" +
26           string2.ToLower() + "\"" );
27
28        // call Trim method
29        Console.WriteLine( "\nstring3 after trim = \"" +
30           string3.Trim() + "\"" );
31
32        Console.WriteLine( "\nstring1 = \"" + string1 + "\"" );
33     } // end Main
34  } // end class StringMethods2
```

```
string1 = "cheers!"
string2 = "GOOD BYE "
string3 = "   spaces   "

Replacing "e" with "E" in string1: "chEErs!"

string1.ToUpper() = "CHEERS!"
string2.ToLower() = "good bye "

string3 after trim = "spaces"

string1 = "cheers!"
```

Fig. 16.8 | string methods Replace, ToLower, ToUpper and Trim.

Line 21 uses string method Replace to return a new string, replacing every occurrence in string1 of character 'e' with 'E'. Method Replace takes two arguments—a char for which to search and another char with which to replace all matching occurrences of the first argument. The original string remains unchanged. If there are no occurrences of the first argument in the string, the method returns the original string. An overloaded version of this method allows you to provide two strings as arguments.

The string method ToUpper generates a new string (line 25) that replaces any lowercase letters in string1 with their uppercase equivalents. The method returns a new string containing the converted string; the original string remains unchanged. If there are no characters to convert, the original string is returned. Line 26 uses string method ToLower to return a new string in which any uppercase letters in string2 are replaced by their lowercase equivalents. The original string is unchanged. As with ToUpper, if there are no characters to convert to lowercase, method ToLower returns the original string.

Line 30 uses string method Trim to remove all whitespace characters that appear at the beginning and end of a string. Without otherwise altering the original string, the method returns a new string that contains the string, but omits leading and trailing whitespace characters. This method is particularly useful for retrieving user input (i.e., via a TextBox). Another version of method Trim takes a character array and returns a copy of the string that does not begin or end with any of the characters in the array argument.

16.10 Class StringBuilder

The string class provides many capabilities for processing strings. However a string's contents can never change. Operations that seem to concatenate strings are in fact assigning string references to newly created strings (e.g., the += operator creates a new string and assigns the initial string reference to the newly created string).

The next several sections discuss the features of class StringBuilder (namespace System.Text), used to create and manipulate dynamic string information—i.e., mutable strings. Every StringBuilder can store a certain number of characters that's specified by its capacity. Exceeding the capacity of a StringBuilder causes the capacity to expand to accommodate the additional characters. As we'll see, members of class StringBuilder, such as methods Append and AppendFormat, can be used for concatenation like the operators + and += for class string. StringBuilder is particularly useful for manipulating in place a large number of strings, as it's much more efficient than creating individual immutable strings.

Performance Tip 16.2

Objects of class string are immutable (i.e., constant strings), whereas objects of class StringBuilder are mutable. C# can perform certain optimizations involving strings (such as the sharing of one string among multiple references), because it knows these objects will not change.

Class StringBuilder provides six overloaded constructors. Class StringBuilderConstructor (Fig. 16.9) demonstrates three of these overloaded constructors.

Line 10 employs the no-parameter StringBuilder constructor to create a StringBuilder that contains no characters and has an implementation-specific default initial capacity. Line 11 uses the StringBuilder constructor that takes an int argument to create a StringBuilder that contains no characters and has the initial capacity specified in the int argument (i.e., 10). Line 12 uses the StringBuilder constructor that takes a string argument to create a StringBuilder containing the characters of the string argument. Lines 14–16 implicitly use StringBuilder method ToString to obtain string representations of the StringBuilders' contents.

```
1    // Fig. 16.9: StringBuilderConstructor.cs
2    // Demonstrating StringBuilder class constructors.
3    using System;
4    using System.Text;
5
6    class StringBuilderConstructor
7    {
8       public static void Main( string[] args )
9       {
10         StringBuilder buffer1 = new StringBuilder();
11         StringBuilder buffer2 = new StringBuilder( 10 );
12         StringBuilder buffer3 = new StringBuilder( "hello" );
13
14         Console.WriteLine( "buffer1 = \"" + buffer1 + "\"" );
15         Console.WriteLine( "buffer2 = \"" + buffer2 + "\"" );
16         Console.WriteLine( "buffer3 = \"" + buffer3 + "\"" );
17      } // end Main
18   } // end class StringBuilderConstructor
```

```
buffer1 = ""
buffer2 = ""
buffer3 = "hello"
```

Fig. 16.9 | StringBuilder class constructors.

16.11 Length and Capacity Properties, EnsureCapacity Method and Indexer of Class StringBuilder

Class StringBuilder provides the Length and Capacity properties to return the number of characters currently in a StringBuilder and the number of characters that a StringBuilder can store without allocating more memory, respectively. These properties also can increase or decrease the length or the capacity of the StringBuilder. Method EnsureCapacity allows you to reduce the number of times that a StringBuilder's capacity must be increased. The method ensures that the StringBuilder's capacity is at least the specified value. The program in Fig. 16.10 demonstrates these methods and properties.

```
1    // Fig. 16.10: StringBuilderFeatures.cs
2    // Demonstrating some features of class StringBuilder.
3    using System;
4    using System.Text;
5
6    class StringBuilderFeatures
7    {
```

Fig. 16.10 | StringBuilder size manipulation. (Part 1 of 2.)

```
 8      public static void Main( string[] args )
 9      {
10         StringBuilder buffer =
11            new StringBuilder( "Hello, how are you?" );
12
13         // use Length and Capacity properties
14         Console.WriteLine( "buffer = " + buffer +
15            "\nLength = " + buffer.Length +
16            "\nCapacity = " + buffer.Capacity );
17
18         buffer.EnsureCapacity( 75 ); // ensure a capacity of at least 75
19         Console.WriteLine( "\nNew capacity = " +
20            buffer.Capacity );
21
22         // truncate StringBuilder by setting Length property
23         buffer.Length = 10;
24         Console.Write( "\nNew length = " +
25            buffer.Length + "\nbuffer = " );
26
27         // use StringBuilder indexer
28         for ( int i = 0; i < buffer.Length; i++ )
29            Console.Write( buffer[ i ] );
30
31         Console.WriteLine( "\n" );
32      } // end Main
33   } // end class StringBuilderFeatures
```

```
buffer = Hello, how are you?
Length = 19
Capacity = 19
New length = 10
buffer = Hello, how
```

Fig. 16.10 | StringBuilder size manipulation. (Part 2 of 2.)

The program contains one StringBuilder, called buffer. Lines 10–11 of the program use the StringBuilder constructor that takes a string argument to instantiate the StringBuilder and initialize its value to "Hello, how are you?". Lines 14–16 output the content, length and capacity of the StringBuilder.

Line 18 expands the capacity of the StringBuilder to a minimum of 75 characters. If new characters are added to a StringBuilder so that its length exceeds its capacity, the capacity grows to accommodate the additional characters in the same manner as if method EnsureCapacity had been called.

Line 23 uses property Length to set the length of the StringBuilder to 10. If the specified length is less than the current number of characters in the StringBuilder, the contents of the StringBuilder are truncated to the specified length. If the specified length is greater than the number of characters currently in the StringBuilder, null characters are appended to the StringBuilder until the total number of characters in the StringBuilder is equal to the specified length.

16.12 Append and AppendFormat Methods of Class StringBuilder

Class StringBuilder provides 19 overloaded Append methods that allow various types of values to be added to the end of a StringBuilder. The Framework Class Library provides versions for each of the simple types and for character arrays, strings and objects. (Remember that method ToString produces a string representation of any object.) Each method takes an argument, converts it to a string and appends it to the StringBuilder. Figure 16.11 demonstrates the use of several Append methods.

```
1    // Fig. 16.11: StringBuilderAppend.cs
2    // Demonstrating StringBuilder Append methods.
3    using System;
4    using System.Text;
5
6    class StringBuilderAppend
7    {
8       public static void Main( string[] args )
9       {
10         object objectValue = "hello";
11         string stringValue = "good bye";
12         char[] characterArray = { 'a', 'b', 'c', 'd', 'e', 'f' };
13         bool booleanValue = true;
14         char characterValue = 'Z';
15         int integerValue = 7;
16         long longValue = 1000000;
17         float floatValue = 2.5F; // F suffix indicates that 2.5 is a float
18         double doubleValue = 33.333;
19         StringBuilder buffer = new StringBuilder();
20
21         // use method Append to append values to buffer
22         buffer.Append( objectValue );
23         buffer.Append( " " );
24         buffer.Append( stringValue );
25         buffer.Append( " " );
26         buffer.Append( characterArray );
27         buffer.Append( " ");
28         buffer.Append( characterArray, 0, 3 );
29         buffer.Append( " " );
30         buffer.Append( booleanValue );
31         buffer.Append( " " );
32         buffer.Append( characterValue );
33         buffer.Append( " " );
34         buffer.Append( integerValue );
35         buffer.Append( " " );
36         buffer.Append( longValue );
37         buffer.Append( " " );
38         buffer.Append( floatValue );
39         buffer.Append( " " );
40         buffer.Append( doubleValue );
41
```

Fig. 16.11 | Append methods of StringBuilder. (Part 1 of 2.)

```
42              Console.WriteLine( "buffer = " + buffer.ToString() + "\n" );
43        } // end Main
44   } // end class StringBuilderAppend
```

```
buffer = hello  good bye  abcdef  abc  True  Z  7  1000000  2.5  33.333
```

Fig. 16.11 | Append methods of `StringBuilder`. (Part 2 of 2.)

Lines 22–40 use 10 different overloaded Append methods to attach the string representations of objects created in lines 10–18 to the end of the `StringBuilder`.

Class `StringBuilder` also provides method `AppendFormat`, which converts a string to a specified format, then appends it to the `StringBuilder`. The example in Fig. 16.12 demonstrates the use of this method.

```
1    // Fig. 16.12: StringBuilderAppendFormat.cs
2    // Demonstrating method AppendFormat.
3    using System;
4    using System.Text;
5
6    class StringBuilderAppendFormat
7    {
8       public static void Main( string[] args )
9       {
10          StringBuilder buffer = new StringBuilder();
11
12          // formatted string
13          string string1 = "This {0} costs: {1:C}.\n";
14
15          // string1 argument array
16          object[] objectArray = new object[ 2 ];
17
18          objectArray[ 0 ] = "car";
19          objectArray[ 1 ] = 1234.56;
20
21          // append to buffer formatted string with argument
22          buffer.AppendFormat( string1, objectArray );
23
24          // formatted string
25          string string2 = "Number:{0:d3}.\n" +
26             "Number right aligned with spaces:{0, 4}.\n" +
27             "Number left aligned with spaces:{0, -4}.";
28
29          // append to buffer formatted string with argument
30          buffer.AppendFormat( string2, 5 );
31
32          // display formatted strings
33          Console.WriteLine( buffer.ToString() );
34       } // end Main
35   } // end class StringBuilderAppendFormat
```

Fig. 16.12 | `StringBuilder`'s `AppendFormat` method. (Part 1 of 2.)

```
This car costs: $1,234.56.
Number:005.
Number right aligned with spaces:     5.
Number left aligned with spaces:5     .
```

Fig. 16.12 | StringBuilder's AppendFormat method. (Part 2 of 2.)

Line 13 creates a string that contains formatting information. The information enclosed in braces specifies how to format a specific piece of data. Formats have the form {X[,Y][:FormatString]}, where X is the number of the argument to be formatted, counting from zero. Y is an optional argument, which can be positive or negative, indicating how many characters should be in the result. If the resulting string is less than the number Y, it will be padded with spaces to make up for the difference. A positive integer aligns the string to the right; a negative integer aligns it to the left. The optional Format-String applies a particular format to the argument—currency, decimal or scientific, among others. In this case, "{0}" means the first argument will be printed out. "{1:C}" specifies that the second argument will be formatted as a currency value.

Line 22 shows a version of AppendFormat that takes two parameters—a string specifying the format and an array of objects to serve as the arguments to the format string. The argument referred to by "{0}" is in the object array at index 0.

Lines 25–27 define another string used for formatting. The first format "{0:d3}", specifies that the first argument will be formatted as a three-digit decimal, meaning that any number having fewer than three digits will have leading zeros placed in front to make up the difference. The next format, "{0, 4}", specifies that the formatted string should have four characters and be right aligned. The third format, "{0, -4}", specifies that the strings should be aligned to the left.

Line 30 uses a version of AppendFormat that takes two parameters—a string containing a format and an object to which the format is applied. In this case, the object is the number 5. The output of Fig. 16.12 displays the result of applying these two versions of AppendFormat with their respective arguments.

16.13 Insert, Remove and Replace Methods of Class StringBuilder

Class StringBuilder provides 18 overloaded Insert methods to allow various types of data to be inserted at any position in a StringBuilder. The class provides versions for each of the simple types and for character arrays, strings and objects. Each method takes its second argument, converts it to a string and inserts the string into the StringBuilder in front of the character in the position specified by the first argument. The index specified by the first argument must be greater than or equal to 0 and less than the length of the StringBuilder; otherwise, the program throws an ArgumentOutOfRangeException.

Class StringBuilder also provides method Remove for deleting any portion of a StringBuilder. Method Remove takes two arguments—the index at which to begin deletion and the number of characters to delete. The sum of the starting index and the number of characters to be deleted must always be less than the length of the StringBuilder; otherwise, the program throws an ArgumentOutOfRangeException. The Insert and Remove methods are demonstrated in Fig. 16.13.

```
 1   // Fig. 16.13: StringBuilderInsertRemove.cs
 2   // Demonstrating methods Insert and Remove of the
 3   // StringBuilder class.
 4   using System;
 5   using System.Text;
 6
 7   class StringBuilderInsertRemove
 8   {
 9      public static void Main( string[] args )
10      {
11         object objectValue = "hello";
12         string stringValue = "good bye";
13         char[] characterArray = { 'a', 'b', 'c', 'd', 'e', 'f' };
14         bool booleanValue = true;
15         char characterValue = 'K';
16         int integerValue = 7;
17         long longValue = 10000000;
18         float floatValue = 2.5F; // F suffix indicates that 2.5 is a float
19         double doubleValue = 33.333;
20         StringBuilder buffer = new StringBuilder();
21
22         // insert values into buffer
23         buffer.Insert( 0, objectValue );
24         buffer.Insert( 0, "   " );
25         buffer.Insert( 0, stringValue );
26         buffer.Insert( 0, "   " );
27         buffer.Insert( 0, characterArray );
28         buffer.Insert( 0, "   " );
29         buffer.Insert( 0, booleanValue );
30         buffer.Insert( 0, "   " );
31         buffer.Insert( 0, characterValue );
32         buffer.Insert( 0, "   " );
33         buffer.Insert( 0, integerValue );
34         buffer.Insert( 0, "   " );
35         buffer.Insert( 0, longValue );
36         buffer.Insert( 0, "   " );
37         buffer.Insert( 0, floatValue );
38         buffer.Insert( 0, "   " );
39         buffer.Insert( 0, doubleValue );
40         buffer.Insert( 0, "   " );
41
42         Console.WriteLine( "buffer after Inserts: \n" + buffer + "\n" );
43
44         buffer.Remove( 10, 1 ); // delete 2 in 2.5
45         buffer.Remove( 4, 4 );  // delete .333 in 33.333
46
47         Console.WriteLine( "buffer after Removes:\n" + buffer );
48      } // end Main
49   } // end class StringBuilderInsertRemove
```

```
buffer after Inserts:
  33.333  2.5  10000000  7  K  True  abcdef  good bye  hello
```

Fig. 16.13 | StringBuilder text insertion and removal. (Part 1 of 2.)

```
buffer after Removes:
  33  .5  10000000  7  K  True  abcdef  good bye  hello
```

Fig. 16.13 | StringBuilder text insertion and removal. (Part 2 of 2.)

Another useful method included with StringBuilder is Replace. Replace searches for a specified string or character and substitutes another string or character in its place. Figure 16.14 demonstrates this method.

```
1   // Fig. 16.14: StringBuilderReplace.cs
2   // Demonstrating method Replace.
3   using System;
4   using System.Text;
5
6   class StringBuilderReplace
7   {
8      public static void Main( string[] args )
9      {
10        StringBuilder builder1 =
11           new StringBuilder( "Happy Birthday Jane" );
12        StringBuilder builder2 =
13           new StringBuilder( "good bye greg" );
14
15        Console.WriteLine( "Before replacements:\n" +
16           builder1.ToString() + "\n" + builder2.ToString() );
17
18        builder1.Replace( "Jane", "Greg" );
19        builder2.Replace( 'g', 'G', 0, 5 );
20
21        Console.WriteLine( "\nAfter replacements:\n" +
22           builder1.ToString() + "\n" + builder2.ToString() );
23     } // end Main
24  } // end class StringBuilderReplace
```

```
Before Replacements:
Happy Birthday Jane
good bye greg

After replacements:
Happy Birthday Greg
Good bye greg
```

Fig. 16.14 | StringBuilder text replacement.

Line 18 uses method Replace to replace all instances "Jane" with the "Greg" in builder1. Another overload of this method takes two characters as parameters and replaces each occurrence of the first character with the second. Line 19 uses an overload of Replace that takes four parameters, of which the first two are characters and the second two are ints. The method replaces all instances of the first character with the second character, beginning at the index specified by the first int and continuing for a count specified by the second int. Thus, in this case, Replace looks through only five characters, starting with the character at index 0. As the output illustrates, this version of Replace replaces g with G in the word "good", but not in "greg". This is because the gs in "greg" are not in the range indicated by the int arguments (i.e., between indexes 0 and 4).

16.14 Char Methods

C# provides a concept called a **struct** (short for "structure") that's similar to a class. Although structs and classes are comparable, structs represent value types. Like classes, structs can have methods and properties, and can use the access modifiers public and private. Also, struct members are accessed via the member access operator (.).

The simple types are actually aliases for struct types. For instance, an int is defined by struct System.Int32, a long by System.Int64 and so on. All struct types derive from class **ValueType**, which derives from object. Also, all struct types are implicitly sealed, so they do not support virtual or abstract methods, and their members cannot be declared protected or protected internal.

In the struct **Char**,[2] which is the struct for characters, most methods are static, take at least one character argument and perform either a test or a manipulation on the character. We present several of these methods in the next example. Figure 16.15 demonstrates static methods that test characters to determine whether they're of a specific character type and static methods that perform case conversions on characters.

```
 1   // Fig. 16.15: StaticCharMethods.cs
 2   // Demonstrates static character-testing and case-conversion methods
 3   // from Char struct
 4   using System;
 5
 6   class StaticCharMethods
 7   {
 8      static void Main( string[] args )
 9      {
10         Console.Write( "Enter a character: " );
11         char character = Convert.ToChar( Console.ReadLine() );
12
13         Console.WriteLine( "is digit: {0}", Char.IsDigit( character ) );
14         Console.WriteLine( "is letter: {0}", Char.IsLetter( character )  );
15         Console.WriteLine( "is letter or digit: {0}",
16            Char.IsLetterOrDigit( character ) );
17         Console.WriteLine( "is lower case: {0}",
18            Char.IsLower( character ) );
19         Console.WriteLine( "is upper case: {0}",
20            Char.IsUpper( character ) );
21         Console.WriteLine( "to upper case: {0}",
22            Char.ToUpper( character ) );
23         Console.WriteLine( "to lower case: {0}",
24            Char.ToLower( character ) );
```

Fig. 16.15 | Char's static character-testing and case-conversion methods. (Part 1 of 3.)

---

2. Just as keyword string is an alias for class String, keyword char is an alias for struct Char. In this text, we use the term Char when calling a static method of struct Char and the term char elsewhere.

```
25          Console.WriteLine( "is punctuation: {0}",
26             Char.IsPunctuation( character ) );
27          Console.WriteLine( "is symbol: {0}", Char.IsSymbol( character ) );
28       } // end Main
29    } // end class StaticCharMethods
```

```
Enter a character: A
is digit: False
is letter: True
is letter or digit: True
is lower case: False
is upper case: True
to upper case: A
to lower case: a
is punctuation: False
is symbol: False
```

```
Enter a character: 8
is digit: True
is letter: False
is letter or digit: True
is lower case: False
is upper case: False
to upper case: 8
to lower case: 8
is punctuation: False
is symbol: False
```

```
Enter a character: @
is digit: False
is letter: False
is letter or digit: False
is lower case: False
is upper case: False
to upper case: @
to lower case: @
is punctuation: True
is symbol: False
```

```
Enter a character: m
is digit: False
is letter: True
is letter or digit: True
is lower case: True
is upper case: False
to upper case: M
to lower case: m
is punctuation: False
is symbol: False
```

Fig. 16.15 | Char's static character-testing and case-conversion methods. (Part 2 of 3.)

```
Enter a character: +
is digit: False
is letter: False
is letter or digit: False
is lower case: False
is upper case: False
to upper case: +
to lower case: +
is punctuation: False
is symbol: True
```

Fig. 16.15 | Char's static character-testing and case-conversion methods. (Part 3 of 3.)

After the user enters a character, lines 13–27 analyze it. Line 13 uses Char method IsDigit to determine whether character is defined as a digit. If so, the method returns true; otherwise, it returns false (note again that bool values are output capitalized). Line 14 uses Char method IsLetter to determine whether character character is a letter. Line 16 uses Char method IsLetterOrDigit to determine whether character character is a letter or a digit.

Line 18 uses Char method IsLower to determine whether character character is a lowercase letter. Line 20 uses Char method IsUpper to determine whether character character is an uppercase letter. Line 22 uses Char method ToUpper to convert character character to its uppercase equivalent. The method returns the converted character if the character has an uppercase equivalent; otherwise, the method returns its original argument. Line 24 uses Char method ToLower to convert character character to its lowercase equivalent. The method returns the converted character if the character has a lowercase equivalent; otherwise, the method returns its original argument.

Line 26 uses Char method IsPunctuation to determine whether character is a punctuation mark, such as "!", ":" or ")". Line 27 uses Char method IsSymbol to determine whether character character is a symbol, such as "+", "=" or "^".

Structure type Char also contains other methods not shown in this example. Many of the static methods are similar—for instance, IsWhiteSpace is used to determine whether a certain character is a whitespace character (e.g., newline, tab or space). The struct also contains several public instance methods; many of these, such as methods ToString and Equals, are methods that we have seen before in other classes. This group includes method CompareTo, which is used to compare two character values with one another.

16.15 (Online) Introduction to Regular Expressions

This online section is available via the book's Companion Website at

www.pearsonhighered.com/deitel

In this section, we introduce **regular expressions**—specially formatted strings used to find patterns in text. They can be used to ensure that data is in a particular format. For example, a U.S. zip code must consist of five digits, or five digits followed by a dash followed by four more digits. Compilers use regular expressions to validate program syntax. If the program code does not match the regular expression, the compiler indicates that there's a syntax error. We discuss classes Regex and Match from the System.Text.RegularExpressions namespace as well as the symbols used to form regular expressions. We then demonstrate how to find patterns in a string, match entire strings to patterns, replace characters in a string that match a pattern and split strings at delimiters specified as a pattern in a regular expression.

16.16 Wrap-Up

In this chapter, you learned about the Framework Class Library's string- and character-processing capabilities. We overviewed the fundamentals of characters and strings. You saw how to determine the length of strings, copy strings, access the individual characters in strings, search strings, obtain substrings from larger strings, compare strings, concatenate strings, replace characters in strings and convert strings to uppercase or lowercase letters.

We showed how to use class `StringBuilder` to build strings dynamically. You learned how to determine and specify the size of a `StringBuilder` object, and how to append, insert, remove and replace characters in a `StringBuilder` object. We then introduced the character-testing methods of type `Char` that enable a program to determine whether a character is a digit, a letter, a lowercase letter, an uppercase letter, a punctuation mark or a symbol other than a punctuation mark, and the methods for converting a character to uppercase or lowercase.

Finally, we discussed classes `Regex`, `Match` and `MatchCollection` from namespace `System.Text.RegularExpressions` and the symbols that are used to form regular expressions. You learned how to find patterns in a `string` and match entire `strings` to patterns with `Regex` methods `Match` and `Matches`, how to replace characters in a `string` with `Regex` method `Replace` and how to split `strings` at delimiters with `Regex` method `Split`. In the next chapter, you'll learn how to read data from and write data to files.

Summary

Section 16.2 Fundamentals of Characters and Strings

- Characters are the fundamental building blocks of C# program code. Every program is composed of a sequence of characters that's interpreted by the compiler as a series of instructions used to accomplish a task.

- A `string` is a series of characters treated as a single unit. A `string` may include letters, digits and the various special characters: +, -, *, /, $ and others.

Section 16.3 string Constructors

- Class `string` provides eight constructors.

- All `strings` are immutable—their character contents cannot be changed after they're created.

Section 16.4 string Indexer, Length Property and CopyTo Method

- Property `Length` determines the number of characters in a `string`.

- The `string` indexer receives an integer argument as the *position number* and returns the character at that position. The first element of a `string` is considered to be at position 0.

- Attempting to access a character that's outside a `string`'s bounds results in an `IndexOutOfRange-Exception`.

- Method `CopyTo` copies a specified number of characters from a `string` into a char array.

Section 16.5 Comparing `strings`

- When the computer compares two `strings`, it uses word sorting rules that depend on the computer's currently selected culture.
- Method `Equals` and the overloaded equality operator (`==`) can each be used to compare the contents of two `strings`.
- Method `CompareTo` returns `0` if the `strings` are equal, a negative number if the `string` that invokes `CompareTo` is less than the `string` passed as an argument and a positive number if the `string` that invokes `CompareTo` is greater than the `string` passed as an argument.
- `string` methods `StartsWith` and `EndsWith` determine whether a `string` starts or ends with the characters specified as an argument, respectively.

Section 16.6 Locating Characters and Substrings in `strings`

- `string` method `IndexOf` locates the first occurrence of a character or a substring in a `string`. Method `LastIndexOf` locates the last occurrence of a character or a substring in a `string`.

Section 16.7 Extracting Substrings from `strings`

- Class `string` provides two `Substring` methods to enable a new `string` to be created by copying part of an existing `string`.

Section 16.8 Concatenating `strings`

- The `static` method `Concat` of class `string` concatenates two `strings` and returns a new `string` containing the characters from both original `strings`.

Section 16.10 Class `StringBuilder`

- Once a `string` is created, its contents can never change. Class `StringBuilder` (namespace `System.Text`) is available for creating and manipulating `strings` that can change.

Section 16.11 `Length` and `Capacity` Properties, `EnsureCapacity` Method and Indexer of Class `StringBuilder`

- Class `StringBuilder` provides `Length` and `Capacity` properties to return, respectively, the number of characters currently in a `StringBuilder` and the number of characters that can be stored in a `StringBuilder` without allocating more memory. These properties also can be used to increase or decrease the length or the capacity of the `StringBuilder`.
- Method `EnsureCapacity` allows you to guarantee that a `StringBuilder` has a minimum capacity.

Section 16.12 `Append` and `AppendFormat` Methods of Class `StringBuilder`

- Class `StringBuilder` provides `Append` methods to allow various types of values to be added to the end of a `StringBuilder`.
- Formats have the form `{X[,Y][:FormatString]}`. `X` is the number of the argument to be formatted, counting from zero. `Y` is an optional positive or negative argument that indicates how many characters should be in the result of formatting. If the resulting `string` has fewer characters than this number, it will be padded with spaces. A positive integer means the `string` will be right aligned; a negative one means the `string` will be left aligned. The optional `FormatString` indicates other formatting to apply—currency, decimal or scientific, among others.

Section 16.13 `Insert`, `Remove` and `Replace` Methods of Class `StringBuilder`

- Class `StringBuilder` provides 18 overloaded `Insert` methods to allow various types of values to be inserted at any position in a `StringBuilder`. Versions are provided for each of the simple types and for character arrays, `strings` and `Objects`.
- Class `StringBuilder` also provides method `Remove` for deleting any portion of a `StringBuilder`.

- `StringBuilder` method `Replace` searches for a specified `string` or character and substitutes another in its place.

Section 16.14 *Char Methods*
- C# provides a concept called a `struct` (short for structure) that's similar to a class.
- `struct`s represent value types.
- `struct`s can have methods and properties and can use the access modifiers `public` and `private`.
- `struct` members are accessed via the member-access operator (`.`).
- The simple types are actually aliases for `struct` types.
- All `struct` types derive from class `ValueType`, which in turn derives from `object`.
- All `struct` types are implicitly `sealed`, so they do not support `virtual` or `abstract` methods, and their members cannot be declared `protected` or `protected internal`.
- `Char` is a struct that represents characters.
- Method `Char.IsDigit` determines whether a character is a defined Unicode digit.
- Method `Char.IsLetter` determines whether a character is a letter.
- Method `Char.IsLetterOrDigit` determines whether a character is a letter or a digit.
- Method `Char.IsLower` determines whether a character is a lowercase letter.
- Method `Char.IsUpper` determines whether a character is an uppercase letter.
- Method `Char.ToUpper` converts a lowercase character to its uppercase equivalent.
- Method `Char.ToLower` converts an uppercase character to its lowercase equivalent.
- Method `Char.IsPunctuation` determines whether a character is a punctuation mark.
- Method `Char.IsSymbol` determines whether a character is a symbol.
- Method `Char.IsWhiteSpace` determines whether a character is a whitespace character.
- Method `Char.CompareTo` compares two character values.

Terminology

@ verbatim string character
+ operator
+= concatenation operator
== equality operator
alphabetizing
Append method of class `StringBuilder`
AppendFormat method of class `StringBuilder`
Capacity property of `StringBuilder`
char array
Char struct
character
character constant
CompareTo method of class `string`
CompareTo method of struct `Char`
Concat method of class `string`
CopyTo method of class `string`
EndsWith method of class `string`
EnsureCapacity method of class `StringBuilder`
Equals method of class `string`
Equals method of struct `Char`

format string
immutable string
IndexOf method of class `string`
IndexOfAny method of class `string`
Insert method of class `StringBuilder`
IsDigit method of struct `Char`
IsLetter method of struct `Char`
IsLetterOrDigit method of struct `Char`
IsLower method of struct `Char`
IsPunctuation method of struct `Char`
IsSymbol method of struct `Char`
IsUpper method of struct `Char`
IsWhiteSpace method of struct `Char`
LastIndexOf method of class `string`
LastIndexOfAny method of class `string`
Length property of class `string`
Length property of class `StringBuilder`
let clause of a LINQ query
random-number generation
Remove method of class `StringBuilder`

Replace method of class string	ToLower method of class string
Replace method of class StringBuilder	ToLower method of struct Char
StartsWith method of class string	ToString method of class string
string class	ToString method of StringBuilder
string literal	ToUpper method of class string
string reference	ToUpper method of struct Char
StringBuilder class	trailing whitespace characters
struct keyword	Trim method of class string
Substring method of class string	Unicode character set
System namespace	ValueType class
System.Text namespace	verbatim string syntax

Self-Review Exercises

16.1 State whether each of the following is *true* or *false*. If *false*, explain why.
  a) When strings are compared with ==, the result is true if the strings contain the same values.
  b) A string can be modified after it's created.
  c) StringBuilder method EnsureCapacity sets the StringBuilder instance's length to the argument's value.
  d) Method Equals and the equality operator work the same for strings.
  e) Method Trim removes all whitespace at the beginning and the end of a string.
  f) It's always better to use strings, rather than StringBuilders, because strings containing the same value will reference the same object.
  g) string method ToUpper creates a new string with the first letter capitalized.

16.2 Fill in the blanks in each of the following statements:
  a) To concatenate strings, use operator _____, StringBuilder method _____ or string method _____.
  b) StringBuilder method _____ first formats the specified string, then concatenates it to the end of the StringBuilder.
  c) If the arguments to a Substring method call are out of range, a(n) _____ exception is thrown.
  d) A C in a format string means to output the number as _____.

Answers to Self-Review Exercises

16.1 a) True. b) False. strings are immutable; they cannot be modified after they're created. StringBuilder objects can be modified after they're created. c) False. EnsureCapacity simply ensures that the current capacity is at least the value specified in the method call. d) True. e) True. f) False. StringBuilder should be used if the string is to be modified. g) False. string method ToUpper creates a new string with all of its letters capitalized.

16.2 a) +, Append, Concat. b) AppendFormat c) ArgumentOutOfRangeException. d) currency.

Exercises

16.3 *(Comparing strings)* Write an application that uses string method CompareTo to compare two strings input by the user. Output whether the first string is less than, equal to or greater than the second.

16.4 *(Random Sentences and Story Writer)* Write an application that uses random-number generation to create sentences. Use four arrays of strings, called article, noun, verb and preposition. Create a sentence by selecting a word at random from each array in the following order: article, noun, verb, preposition, article, noun. As each word is picked, concatenate it to the previous words in the sentence. The words should be separated by spaces. When the sentence is output, it should start with a capital letter and end with a period. The program should generate 10 sentences and output them to a text box.

The arrays should be filled as follows: The article array should contain the articles "the", "a", "one", "some" and "any"; the noun array should contain the nouns "boy", "girl", "dog", "town" and "car"; the verb array should contain the past-tense verbs "drove", "jumped", "ran", "walked" and "skipped"; and the preposition array should contain the prepositions "to", "from", "over", "under" and "on".

After the preceding program is written, modify the program to produce a short story consisting of several of these sentences. (How about the possibility of a random term-paper writer!)

16.5   *(Pig Latin)* Write an application that encodes English-language phrases into pig Latin. Pig Latin is a form of coded language often used for amusement. Many variations exist in the methods used to form pig Latin phrases. For simplicity, use the following algorithm:

To translate each English word into a pig Latin word, place the first letter of the English word at the end of the word and add the letters "ay." Thus, the word "jump" becomes "umpjay," the word "the" becomes "hetay" and the word "computer" becomes "omputercay." Blanks between words remain blanks. Assume the following: The English phrase consists of words separated by blanks, there are no punctuation marks and all words have two or more letters. Enable the user to input a sentence. Use techniques discussed in this chapter to divide the sentence into separate words. Method GetPigLatin should translate a single word into pig Latin. Keep a running display of all the converted sentences in a text box.

16.6   *(All Possible Three-Letter Words from a Five-Letter Word)* Write a program that reads a five-letter word from the user and produces all possible three-letter combinations that can be derived from the letters of the five-letter word. For example, the three-letter words produced from the word "bathe" include the commonly used words "ate," "bat," "bet," "tab," "hat," "the" and "tea," and the 3-letter combinations "bth," "eab," etc.

16.7   *(Capitalizing Words)* Write a program that uses regular expressions to convert the first letter of every word to uppercase. Have it do this for an arbitrary string input by the user.

Making a Difference Exercises

16.8   *(Project: Cooking with Healthier Ingredients)* Obesity in the United States is increasing at an alarming rate. Check the map from the Centers for Disease Control and Prevention (CDC) at www.cdc.gov/nccdphp/dnpa/Obesity/trend/maps/index.htm, which shows obesity trends in the United States over the last 20 years. As obesity increases, so do occurrences of related problems (e.g., heart disease, high blood pressure, high cholesterol, type 2 diabetes). Write a program that helps users choose healthier ingredients when cooking, and helps those allergic to certain foods (e.g., nuts, gluten) find substitutes. The program should read a recipe from the user and suggest healthier replacements for some of the ingredients. For simplicity, your program should assume the recipe has no abbreviations for measures such as teaspoons, cups, and tablespoons, and uses numerical digits for quantities (e.g., 1 egg, 2 cups) rather than spelling them out (one egg, two cups). Some common substitutions are shown in Fig. 16.16. Your program should display a warning such as, "Always consult your physician before making significant changes to your diet."

Your program should take into consideration that replacements are not always one-for-one. For example, if a cake recipe calls for three eggs, it might reasonably use six egg whites instead. Conversion data for measurements and substitutes can be obtained at websites such as:

```
chinesefood.about.com/od/recipeconversionfaqs/f/usmetricrecipes.htm
www.pioneerthinking.com/eggsub.html
www.gourmetsleuth.com/conversions.htm
```

Ingredient	Substitution
1 cup sour cream	1 cup yogurt
1 cup milk	1/2 cup evaporated milk and 1/2 cup water
1 teaspoon lemon juice	1/2 teaspoon vinegar
1 cup sugar	1/2 cup honey, 1 cup molasses or 1/4 cup agave nectar
1 cup butter	1 cup margarine or yogurt
1 cup flour	1 cup rye or rice flour
1 cup mayonnaise	1 cup cottage cheese or 1/8 cup mayonnaise and 7/8 cup yogurt
1 egg	2 tablespoons cornstarch, arrowroot flour or potato starch or 2 egg whites or 1/2 of a large banana (mashed)
1 cup milk	1 cup soy milk
1/4 cup oil	1/4 cup applesauce
white bread	whole-grain bread
1 cup sour cream	1 cup yogurt

Fig. 16.16 | Common ingredient substitutions.

Your program should consider the user's health concerns, such as high cholesterol, high blood pressure, weight loss, gluten allergy, and so on. For high cholesterol, the program should suggest substitutes for eggs and dairy products; if the user wishes to lose weight, low-calorie substitutes for ingredients such as sugar should be suggested.

16.9 *(Project: Spam Scanner)* Spam (or junk e-mail) costs U.S. organizations billions of dollars a year in spam-prevention software, equipment, network resources, bandwidth, and lost productivity. Research online some of the most common spam e-mail messages and words, and check your own junk e-mail folder. Create a list of 30 words and phrases commonly found in spam messages. Write an application in which the user enters an e-mail message. Then, scan the message for each of the 30 keywords or phrases. For each occurrence of one of these within the message, add a point to the message's "spam score." Next, rate the likelihood that the message is spam, based on the number of points it received.

16.10 *(Project: SMS Language)* Short Message Service (SMS) is a communications service that allows sending text messages of 160 or fewer characters between mobile phones. With the proliferation of mobile phone use worldwide, SMS is being used in many developing nations for political purposes (e.g., voicing opinions and opposition), reporting news about natural disasters, and so on. For example, check out comunica.org/radio2.0/archives/87. Since the length of SMS messages is limited, SMS Language—abbreviations of common words and phrases in mobile text messages, e-mails, instant messages, etc.—is often used. For example, "in my opinion" is "IMO" in SMS Language. Research SMS Language online. Write a program in which the user can enter a message using SMS Language, then the program should translate it into English (or your own language). Also provide a mechanism to translate text written in English (or your own language) into SMS Language. One potential problem is that one SMS abbreviation could expand into a variety of phrases. For example, IMO (as used above) could also stand for "International Maritime Organization," "in memory of," etc.

Files and Streams

I can only assume that a "Do Not File" document is filed in a "Do Not File" file.
—Senator Frank Church
Senate Intelligence Subcommittee Hearing, 1975

Consciousness ... does not appear to itself chopped up in bits. ... A "river" or a "stream" are the metaphors by which it is most naturally described.
—William James

I read part of it all the way through.
—Samuel Goldwyn

Objectives

In this chapter you'll learn:

- To create, read, write and update files.

- To use classes `File` and `Directory` to obtain information about files and directories on your computer.

- To use LINQ to search through directories.

- To become familiar with sequential-access file processing.

- To use classes `FileStream`, `StreamReader` and `StreamWriter` to read text from and write text to files.

- To use classes `FileStream` and `BinaryFormatter` to read objects from and write objects to files.

17.1 Introduction

Variables and arrays offer only temporary storage of data—the data is lost when a local variable "goes out of scope" or when the program terminates. By contrast, **files** (and databases, which we cover in Chapter 18) are used for long-term retention of large amounts of data, even after the program that created the data terminates. Data maintained in files often is called **persistent data**. Computers store files on **secondary storage devices**, such as magnetic disks, optical disks, flash memory and magnetic tapes. In this chapter, we explain how to create, update and process data files in C# programs.

We begin with an overview of the data hierarchy from bits to files. Next, we overview some of the Framework Class Library's file-processing classes. We then present two examples that show how you can determine information about the files and directories on your computer. The remainder of the chapter shows how to write to and read from text files that are human readable and binary files that store entire objects in binary format.

17.2 Data Hierarchy

Ultimately, all data items that computers process are reduced to combinations of 0s and 1s. This occurs because it's simple and economical to build electronic devices that can assume two stable states—one state represents 0 and the other represents 1. It's remarkable that the impressive functions performed by computers involve only the most fundamental manipulations of 0s and 1s.

Bits

The smallest data item that computers support is called a **bit** (short for "**binary digit**"—a digit that can assume one of two values). Each bit can assume either the value 0 or the value 1. Computer circuitry performs various simple **bit manipulations**, such as examining the value of a bit, setting the value of a bit and reversing a bit (from 1 to 0 or from 0 to 1).

Characters

Programming with data in the low-level form of bits is cumbersome. It's preferable to program with data in forms such as **decimal digits** (i.e., 0, 1, 2, 3, 4, 5, 6, 7, 8 and 9), **letters** (i.e., A–Z and a–z) and **special symbols** (i.e., $, @, %, &, *, (,), -, +, ", :, ?, / and many others). Digits, letters and special symbols are referred to as **characters**. The set of all characters used to write programs and represent data items on a particular computer is called that computer's **character set**. Because computers can process only 0s and 1s, every character in a computer's character set is represented as a pattern of 0s and 1s. **Bytes** are composed of eight bits. C# uses the **Unicode®** **character set** (www.unicode.org) in which characters are composed of 2 bytes. Programmers create programs and data items with characters; computers manipulate and process these characters as patterns of bits.

Fields

Just as characters are composed of bits, fields are composed of characters. A **field** is a group of characters that conveys meaning. For example, a field consisting of uppercase and lowercase letters can represent a person's name.

Data items processed by computers form a **data hierarchy** (Fig. 17.1), in which data items become larger and more complex in structure as we progress from bits to characters to fields to larger data aggregates.

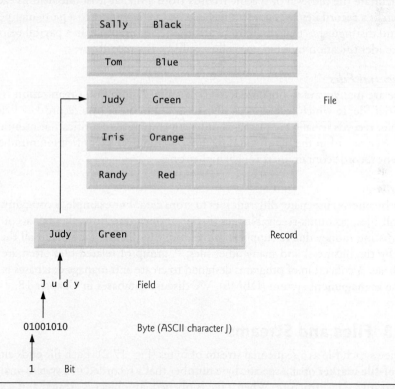

Fig. 17.1 | Data hierarchy.

Records and Files

Typically, a **record** (which can be represented as a class) is composed of several related fields. In a payroll system, for example, a record for a particular employee might include the following fields:

1. Employee identification number
2. Name

3. Address

4. Hourly pay rate

5. Number of exemptions claimed

6. Year-to-date earnings

7. Amount of taxes withheld

In the preceding example, each field is associated with the same employee. A file is a group of related records.[1] A company's payroll file normally contains one record for each employee. A payroll file for a small company might contain only 22 records, whereas one for a large company might contain 100,000. It's not unusual for a company to have many files, some containing millions, billions or even trillions of characters of information.

Record Key

To facilitate the retrieval of specific records from a file, at least one field in each record is chosen as a **record key**, which identifies a record as belonging to a particular person or entity and distinguishes that record from all others. For example, in a payroll record, the employee identification number normally would be the record key.

Sequential Files

There are many ways to organize records in a file. A common organization is called a **sequential file,** in which records typically are stored in order by a record-key field. In a payroll file, records usually are placed in order by employee identification number. The first employee record in the file contains the lowest employee identification number, and subsequent records contain increasingly higher ones.

Databases

Most businesses use many different files to store data. For example, a company might have payroll files, accounts-receivable files (listing money due from clients), accounts-payable files (listing money due to suppliers), inventory files (listing facts about all the items handled by the business) and many other files. A group of related files often are stored in a **database.** A collection of programs designed to create and manage databases is called a **database management system (DBMS).** We discuss databases in Chapter 18.

17.3 Files and Streams

C# views each file as a sequential **stream** of bytes (Fig. 17.2). Each file ends either with an **end-of-file marker** or at a specific byte number that's recorded in a system-maintained administrative data structure. When a file is opened, an object is created and a stream is associated with the object. When a console application executes, the runtime environment creates three stream objects that are accessible via properties **Console.Out**, **Console.In** and **Console.Error**, respectively. These objects facilitate communication between a program and a particular file or device. Console.In refers to the **standard input stream ob-**

---

1. Generally, a file can contain arbitrary data in arbitrary formats. In some operating systems, a file is viewed as nothing more than a collection of bytes, and any organization of the bytes in a file (such as organizing the data into records) is a view created by the application programmer.

ject, which enables a program to input data from the keyboard. Console.Out refers to the **standard output stream object**, which enables a program to output data to the screen. Console.Error refers to the **standard error stream object**, which enables a program to output error messages to the screen. We have been using Console.Out and Console.In in our console applications, Console methods Write and WriteLine use Console.Out to perform output, and Console methods Read and ReadLine use Console.In to perform input.

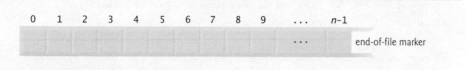

Fig. 17.2 | C#'s view of an n-byte file.

There are many file-processing classes in the Framework Class Library. The **System.IO namespace** includes stream classes such as **StreamReader** (for text input from a file), **StreamWriter** (for text output to a file) and **FileStream** (for both input from and output to a file). These stream classes inherit from abstract classes **TextReader**, **TextWriter** and Stream, respectively. Actually, properties Console.In and Console.Out are of type TextReader and TextWriter, respectively. The system creates objects of TextReader and TextWriter derived classes to initialize Console properties Console.In and Console.Out.

Abstract class **Stream** provides functionality for representing streams as bytes. Classes FileStream, **MemoryStream** and **BufferedStream** (all from namespace System.IO) inherit from class Stream. Class FileStream can be used to write data to and read data from files. Class MemoryStream enables the transfer of data directly to and from memory—this is much faster than reading from and writing to external devices. Class BufferedStream uses **buffering** to transfer data to or from a stream. Buffering is an I/O performance-enhancement technique, in which each output operation is directed to a region in memory, called a **buffer**, that's large enough to hold the data from many output operations. Then actual transfer to the output device is performed in one large **physical output operation** each time the buffer fills. The output operations directed to the output buffer in memory often are called **logical output operations**. Buffering can also be used to speed input operations by initially reading more data than is required into a buffer, so subsequent reads get data from memory rather than an external device.

In this chapter, we use key stream classes to implement file-processing programs that create and manipulate sequential-access files.

17.4 Classes File and Directory

Information is stored in files, which are organized in directories (also called folders). Classes File and Directory enable programs to manipulate files and directories on disk. Class **File** can determine information about files and can be used to open files for reading or writing. We discuss techniques for writing to and reading from files in subsequent sections.

Figure 17.3 lists several of class File's static methods for manipulating and determining information about files. We demonstrate several of these methods in Fig. 17.5.

static Method	Description
AppendText	Returns a StreamWriter that appends text to an existing file or creates a file if one does not exist.
Copy	Copies a file to a new file.
Create	Creates a file and returns its associated FileStream.
CreateText	Creates a text file and returns its associated StreamWriter.
Delete	Deletes the specified file.
Exists	Returns true if the specified file exists and false otherwise.
GetCreationTime	Returns a DateTime object representing when the file was created.
GetLastAccessTime	Returns a DateTime object representing when the file was last accessed.
GetLastWriteTime	Returns a DateTime object representing when the file was last modified.
Move	Moves the specified file to a specified location.
Open	Returns a FileStream associated with the specified file and equipped with the specified read/write permissions.
OpenRead	Returns a read-only FileStream associated with the specified file.
OpenText	Returns a StreamReader associated with the specified file.
OpenWrite	Returns a write FileStream associated with the specified file.

Fig. 17.3 | File class static methods (partial list).

Class **Directory** provides capabilities for manipulating directories. Figure 17.4 lists some of class Directory's static methods for directory manipulation. Figure 17.5 demonstrates several of these methods, as well. The **DirectoryInfo** object returned by method **CreateDirectory** contains information about a directory. Much of the information contained in class DirectoryInfo also can be accessed via the methods of class Directory.

static Method	Description
CreateDirectory	Creates a directory and returns its associated DirectoryInfo object.
Delete	Deletes the specified directory.
Exists	Returns true if the specified directory exists and false otherwise.
GetDirectories	Returns a string array containing the names of the subdirectories in the specified directory.
GetFiles	Returns a string array containing the names of the files in the specified directory.
GetCreationTime	Returns a DateTime object representing when the directory was created.
GetLastAccessTime	Returns a DateTime object representing when the directory was last accessed.
GetLastWriteTime	Returns a DateTime object representing when items were last written to the directory.
Move	Moves the specified directory to a specified location.

Fig. 17.4 | Directory class static methods.

*Demonstrating Classes **File** and **Directory***

Class FileTestForm (Fig. 17.5) uses File and Directory methods to access file and directory information. This Form contains the control inputTextBox, in which the user enters a file or directory name. For each key that the user presses while typing in the TextBox, the program calls event handler inputTextBox_KeyDown (lines 19–75). If the user presses the *Enter* key (line 22), this method displays either the file's or directory's contents, depending on the text the user input. (If the user does not press the *Enter* key, this method returns without displaying any content.) Line 28 uses File method Exists to determine whether the user-specified text is the name of an existing file. If so, line 31 invokes private method GetInformation (lines 79–97), which calls File methods GetCreationTime (line 88), GetLastWriteTime (line 92) and GetLastAccessTime (line 96) to access file information. When method GetInformation returns, line 38 instantiates a StreamReader for reading text from the file. The StreamReader constructor takes as an argument a string containing the name of the file to open. Line 40 calls StreamReader method ReadToEnd to read the entire contents of the file as a string, then appends the string to outputTextBox. Once the file has been read, the using block terminates, closes the file and disposes of the corresponding object.

```csharp
1    // Fig. 17.5: FileTestForm.cs
2    // Using classes File and Directory.
3    using System;
4    using System.Windows.Forms;
5    using System.IO;
6
7    namespace FileTest
8    {
9       // displays contents of files and directories
10      public partial class FileTestForm : Form
11      {
12         // parameterless constructor
13         public FileTestForm()
14         {
15            InitializeComponent();
16         } // end constructor
17
18         // invoked when user presses key
19         private void inputTextBox_KeyDown( object sender, KeyEventArgs e )
20         {
21            // determine whether user pressed Enter key
22            if ( e.KeyCode == Keys.Enter )
23            {
24               // get user-specified file or directory
25               string fileName = inputTextBox.Text;
26
27               // determine whether fileName is a file
28               if ( File.Exists( fileName ) )
29               {
30                  // get file's creation date, modification date, etc.
31                  GetInformation( fileName );
32                  StreamReader stream = null; // declare StreamReader
33
```

Fig. 17.5 | Using classes File and Directory. (Part 1 of 3.)

```
34                  // display file contents through StreamReader
35                  try
36                  {
37                      // obtain reader and file contents
38                      using ( stream = new StreamReader( fileName ) )
39                      {
40                          outputTextBox.AppendText( stream.ReadToEnd() );
41                      } // end using
42                  } // end try
43                  catch ( IOException )
44                  {
45                      MessageBox.Show( "Error reading from file",
46                          "File Error", MessageBoxButtons.OK,
47                          MessageBoxIcon.Error );
48                  } // end catch
49              } // end if
50              // determine whether fileName is a directory
51              else if ( Directory.Exists( fileName ) )
52              {
53                  // get directory's creation date,
54                  // modification date, etc.
55                  GetInformation( fileName );
56
57                  // obtain file/directory list of specified directory
58                  string[] directoryList =
59                      Directory.GetDirectories( fileName );
60
61                  outputTextBox.AppendText( "Directory contents:\n" );
62
63                  // output directoryList contents
64                  foreach ( var directory in directoryList )
65                      outputTextBox.AppendText( directory + "\n" );
66              } // end else if
67              else
68              {
69                  // notify user that neither file nor directory exists
70                  MessageBox.Show( inputTextBox.Text +
71                      " does not exist", "File Error",
72                      MessageBoxButtons.OK, MessageBoxIcon.Error );
73              } // end else
74          } // end if
75      } // end method inputTextBox_KeyDown
76
77      // get information on file or directory,
78      // and output it to outputTextBox
79      private void GetInformation( string fileName )
80      {
81          outputTextBox.Clear();
82
83          // output that file or directory exists
84          outputTextBox.AppendText( fileName + " exists\n" );
85
```

Fig. 17.5 | Using classes `File` and `Directory`. (Part 2 of 3.)

```
86              // output when file or directory was created
87              outputTextBox.AppendText( "Created: " +
88                  File.GetCreationTime( fileName ) + "\n" );
89
90              // output when file or directory was last modified
91              outputTextBox.AppendText( "Last modified: " +
92                  File.GetLastWriteTime( fileName ) + "\n" );
93
94              // output when file or directory was last accessed
95              outputTextBox.AppendText( "Last accessed: " +
96                  File.GetLastAccessTime( fileName ) + "\n" );
97          } // end method GetInformation
98      } // end class FileTestForm
99  } // end namespace FileTest
```

a) Viewing the contents of file "quotes.txt"

b) Viewing all files in directory C:\Program Files\

c) User gives invalid input

d) Error message is displayed

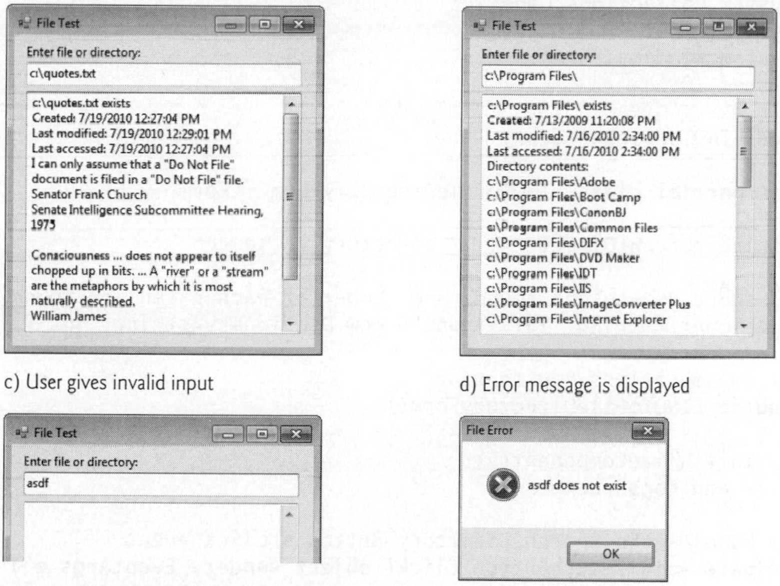

Fig. 17.5 | Using classes File and Directory. (Part 3 of 3.)

If line 28 determines that the user-specified text is not a file, line 51 determines whether it's a directory using Directory method **Exists**. If the user specified an existing directory, line 55 invokes method GetInformation to access the directory information. Line 59 calls Directory method **GetDirectories** to obtain a string array containing the names of subdirectories in the specified directory. Lines 64–65 display each element in the string array. Note that, if line 51 determines that the user-specified text is not a directory name, lines 70–72 notify the user (via a MessageBox) that the name the user entered does not exist as a file or directory.

Searching Directories with LINQ

We now consider another example that uses file- and directory-manipulation capabilities. Class LINQToFileDirectoryForm (Fig. 17.6) uses LINQ with classes File, Path and

Directory to report the number of files of each file type that exist in the specified directory path. The program also serves as a "clean-up" utility—when it finds a file that has the .bak file-name extension (i.e., a backup file), the program displays a MessageBox asking the user whether that file should be removed, then responds appropriately to the user's input. This example also uses LINQ to Objects to help delete the backup files.

When the user clicks **Search Directory**, the program invokes searchButton_Click (lines 25–65), which searches recursively through the directory path specified by the user. If the user inputs text in the TextBox, line 29 calls Directory method Exists to determine whether that text is a valid directory. If it's not, lines 32–33 notify the user of the error.

```csharp
1   // Fig. 17.6: LINQToFileDirectoryForm.cs
2   // Using LINQ to search directories and determine file types.
3   using System;
4   using System.Collections.Generic;
5   using System.Linq;
6   using System.Windows.Forms;
7   using System.IO;
8
9   namespace LINQToFileDirectory
10  {
11     public partial class LINQToFileDirectoryForm : Form
12     {
13        string currentDirectory; // directory to search
14
15        // store extensions found, and number of each extension found
16        Dictionary<string, int> found = new Dictionary<string, int>();
17
18        // parameterless constructor
19        public LINQToFileDirectoryForm()
20        {
21           InitializeComponent();
22        } // end constructor
23
24        // handles the Search Directory Button's Click event
25        private void searchButton_Click( object sender, EventArgs e )
26        {
27           // check whether user specified path exists
28           if ( pathTextBox.Text != string.Empty &&
29              !Directory.Exists( pathTextBox.Text ) )
30           {
31              // show error if user does not specify valid directory
32              MessageBox.Show( "Invalid Directory", "Error",
33                 MessageBoxButtons.OK, MessageBoxIcon.Error );
34           } // end if
35           else
36           {
37              // use current directory if no directory is specified
38              if ( pathTextBox.Text == string.Empty )
39                 currentDirectory = Directory.GetCurrentDirectory();
```

Fig. 17.6 | Using LINQ to search directories and determine file types. (Part 1 of 4.)

```
40              else
41                  currentDirectory = pathTextBox.Text;
42
43              directoryTextBox.Text = currentDirectory; // show directory
44
45              // clear TextBoxes
46              pathTextBox.Clear();
47              resultsTextBox.Clear();
48
49              SearchDirectory( currentDirectory ); // search the directory
50
51              // allow user to delete .bak files
52              CleanDirectory( currentDirectory );
53
54              // summarize and display the results
55              foreach ( var current in found.Keys )
56              {
57                  // display the number of files with current extension
58                  resultsTextBox.AppendText( string.Format(
59                      "* Found {0} {1} files.\r\n",
60                      found[ current ], current ) );
61              } // end foreach
62
63              found.Clear(); // clear results for new search
64          } // end else
65      } // end method searchButton_Click
66
67      // search directory using LINQ
68      private void SearchDirectory( string folder )
69      {
70          // files contained in the directory
71          string[] files = Directory.GetFiles( folder );
72
73          // subdirectories in the directory
74          string[] directories = Directory.GetDirectories( folder );
75
76          // find all file extensions in this directory
77          var extensions =
78              ( from file in files
79                select Path.GetExtension( file ) ).Distinct();
80
81          // count the number of files using each extension
82          foreach ( var extension in extensions )
83          {
84              var temp = extension;
85
86              // count the number of files with the extension
87              var extensionCount =
88                  ( from file in files
89                    where Path.GetExtension( file ) == temp
90                    select file ).Count();
91
```

Fig. 17.6 | Using LINQ to search directories and determine file types. (Part 2 of 4.)

```
92              // if the Dictionary already contains a key for the extension
93              if ( found.ContainsKey( extension ) )
94                  found[ extension ] += extensionCount; // update the count
95              else
96                  found.Add( extension, extensionCount ); // add new count
97          } // end foreach
98
99          // recursive call to search subdirectories
100         foreach ( var subdirectory in directories )
101             SearchDirectory( subdirectory );
102     } // end method SearchDirectory
103
104     // allow user to delete backup files (.bak)
105     private void CleanDirectory( string folder )
106     {
107         // files contained in the directory
108         string[] files = Directory.GetFiles( folder );
109
110         // subdirectories in the directory
111         string[] directories = Directory.GetDirectories( folder );
112
113         // select all the backup files in this directory
114         var backupFiles =
115             from file in files
116             where Path.GetExtension( file ) == ".bak"
117             select file;
118
119         // iterate over all backup files (.bak)
120         foreach ( var backup in backupFiles )
121         {
122             DialogResult result = MessageBox.Show( "Found backup file " +
123                 Path.GetFileName( backup ) + ". Delete?", "Delete Backup",
124                 MessageBoxButtons.YesNo, MessageBoxIcon.Question );
125
126             // delete file if user clicked 'yes'
127             if ( result == DialogResult.Yes )
128             {
129                 File.Delete( backup ); // delete backup file
130                 --found[ ".bak" ]; // decrement count in Dictionary
131
132                 // if there are no .bak files, delete key from Dictionary
133                 if ( found[ ".bak" ] == 0 )
134                     found.Remove( ".bak" );
135             } // end if
136         } // end foreach
137
138         // recursive call to clean subdirectories
139         foreach ( var subdirectory in directories )
140             CleanDirectory( subdirectory );
141     } // end method CleanDirectory
142 } // end class LINQToFileDirectoryForm
143 } // end namespace LINQToFileDirectory
```

Fig. 17.6 | Using LINQ to search directories and determine file types. (Part 3 of 4.)

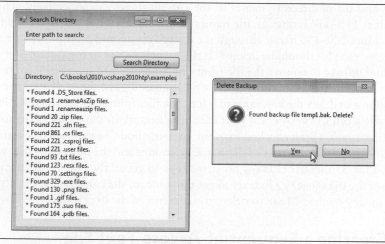

Fig. 17.6 | Using LINQ to search directories and determine file types. (Part 4 of 4.)

Method SearchDirectory

Lines 38–41 get the current directory (if the user did not specify a path) or the specified directory. Line 49 passes the directory name to recursive method SearchDirectory (lines 68–102). Line 71 calls Directory method **GetFiles** to get a string array containing file names in the specified directory. Line 74 calls Directory method GetDirectories to get a string array containing the subdirectory names in the specified directory.

Lines 78–79 use LINQ to get the Distinct file-name extensions in the files array. **Path** method **GetExtension** obtains the extension for the specified file name. For each file-name extension returned by the LINQ query, lines 82–97 determine the number of occurrences of that extension in the files array. The LINQ query at lines 88–90 compares each file-name extension in the files array with the current extension being processed (line 89). All matches are included in the result. We then use LINQ method Count to determine the total number of files that matched the current extension.

Class LINQToFileDirectoryForm uses a Dictionary (declared in line 16) to store each file-name extension and the corresponding number of file names with that extension. A **Dictionary** (namespace System.Collections.Generic) is a collection of key/value pairs, in which each key has a corresponding value. Class Dictionary is a generic class like class List (presented in Section 9.4). Line 16 indicates that the Dictionary found contains pairs of strings and ints, which represent the file-name extensions and the number of files with those extensions, respectively. Line 93 uses Dictionary method **ContainsKey** to determine whether the specified file-name extension has been placed in the Dictionary previously. If this method returns true, line 94 adds the extensionCount determined in lines 88–90 to the current total for that extension that's stored in the Dictionary. Otherwise, line 96 uses Dictionary method **Add** to insert a new key/value pair into the Dictionary for the new file-name extension and its extensionCount. Lines 100–101 recursively call SearchDirectory for each subdirectory in the current directory.

Method CleanDirectory

When method SearchDirectory returns, line 52 calls CleanDirectory (defined at lines 105–141) to search for all files with extension .bak. Lines 108 and 111 obtain the list of file names and list of directory names in the current directory, respectively. The LINQ query in lines 115–117 locates all file names in the current directory that have the .bak extension. Lines 120–136 iterate through the query's results and prompt the user to determine whether each file should be deleted. If the user clicks **Yes** in the dialog, line 129 uses File method **Delete** to remove the file from disk, and line 130 subtracts 1 from the total number of .bak files. If the number of .bak files remaining is 0, line 134 uses Dictionary method **Remove** to delete the key/value pair for .bak files from the Dictionary. Lines 139–140 recursively call CleanDirectory for each subdirectory in the current directory. After each subdirectory has been checked for .bak files, method CleanDirectory returns, and lines 55–61 display the summary of file-name extensions and the number of files with each extension. Line 55 uses Dictionary property **Keys** to get all the keys in the Dictionary. Line 60 uses the Dictionary's indexer to get the value for the current key. Finally, line 63 uses Dictionary method **Clear** to delete the contents of the Dictionary.

17.5 Creating a Sequential-Access Text File

C# imposes no structure on files. Thus, the concept of a "record" does not exist in C# files. This means that you must structure files to meet the requirements of your applications. The next few examples use text and special characters to organize our own concept of a "record."

Class *BankUIForm*

The following examples demonstrate file processing in a bank-account maintenance application. These programs have similar user interfaces, so we created reusable class BankUIForm (Fig. 17.7) to encapsulate a base-class GUI (see the screen capture in Fig. 17.7). Class BankUIForm contains four Labels and four TextBoxes. Methods ClearTextBoxes (lines 28–40), SetTextBoxValues (lines 43–64) and GetTextBoxValues (lines 67–78) clear, set the values of and get the values of the text in the TextBoxes, respectively.

```
1    // Fig. 17.7: BankUIForm.cs
2    // A reusable Windows Form for the examples in this chapter.
3    using System;
4    using System.Windows.Forms;
5
6    namespace BankLibrary
7    {
8       public partial class BankUIForm : Form
9       {
10          protected int TextBoxCount = 4; // number of TextBoxes on Form
11
12          // enumeration constants specify TextBox indices
13          public enum TextBoxIndices
14          {
15             ACCOUNT,
16             FIRST,
17             LAST,
18             BALANCE
19          } // end enum
20
```

Fig. 17.7 | Base class for GUIs in our file-processing applications. (Part 1 of 3.)

```
21        // parameterless constructor
22        public BankUIForm()
23        {
24           InitializeComponent();
25        } // end constructor
26
27        // clear all TextBoxes
28        public void ClearTextBoxes()
29        {
30           // iterate through every Control on form
31           foreach ( Control guiControl in Controls )
32           {
33              // determine whether Control is TextBox
34              if ( guiControl is TextBox )
35              {
36                 // clear TextBox
37                 ( ( TextBox ) guiControl ).Clear();
38              } // end if
39           } // end for
40        } // end method ClearTextBoxes
41
42        // set text box values to string-array values
43        public void SetTextBoxValues( string[] values )
44        {
45           // determine whether string array has correct length
46           if ( values.Length != TextBoxCount )
47           {
48              // throw exception if not correct length
49              throw ( new ArgumentException( "There must be " +
50                 ( TextBoxCount + 1 ) + " strings in the array" ) );
51           } // end if
52           // set array values if array has correct length
53           else
54           {
55              // set array values to TextBox values
56              accountTextBox.Text =
57                 values[ ( int ) TextBoxIndices.ACCOUNT ];
58              firstNameTextBox.Text =
59                 values[ ( int ) TextBoxIndices.FIRST ];
60              lastNameTextBox.Text = values[ ( int ) TextBoxIndices.LAST ];
61              balanceTextBox.Text =
62                 values[ ( int ) TextBoxIndices.BALANCE ];
63           } // end else
64        } // end method SetTextBoxValues
65
66        // return TextBox values as string array
67        public string[] GetTextBoxValues()
68        {
69           string[] values = new string[ TextBoxCount ];
70
71           // copy TextBox fields to string array
72           values[ ( int ) TextBoxIndices.ACCOUNT ] = accountTextBox.Text;
73           values[ ( int ) TextBoxIndices.FIRST ] = firstNameTextBox.Text;
```

Fig. 17.7 | Base class for GUIs in our file-processing applications. (Part 2 of 3.)

```
74            values[ ( int ) TextBoxIndices.LAST ] = lastNameTextBox.Text;
75            values[ ( int ) TextBoxIndices.BALANCE ] = balanceTextBox.Text;
76
77            return values;
78        } // end method GetTextBoxValues
79    } // end class BankUIForm
80 } // end namespace BankLibrary
```

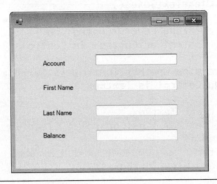

Fig. 17.7 | Base class for GUIs in our file-processing applications. (Part 3 of 3.)

Using visual inheritance (Section 15.13), you can extend this class to create the GUIs for several examples in this chapter. Recall that to reuse class BankUIForm, you must compile the GUI into a class library, then add a reference to the new class library in each project that will reuse it. This library (BankLibrary) is provided with the code for this chapter. You might need to re-add the references to this library in our examples when you copy them to your system, since the library most likely will reside in a different location on your system.

Class *Record*
Figure 17.8 contains class Record that Figs. 17.9, 17.11 and 17.12 use for maintaining the information in each record that's written to or read from a file. This class also belongs to the BankLibrary DLL, so it's located in the same project as class BankUIForm.

```
1  // Fig. 17.8: Record.cs
2  // Class that represents a data record.
3
4  namespace BankLibrary
5  {
6     public class Record
7     {
8        // auto-implemented Account property
9        public int Account { get; set; }
10
11       // auto-implemented FirstName property
12       public string FirstName { get; set; }
13
14       // auto-implemented LastName property
15       public string LastName { get; set; }
```

Fig. 17.8 | Record for sequential-access file-processing applications. (Part 1 of 2.)

```
16
17          // auto-implemented Balance property
18          public decimal Balance { get; set; }
19
20          // parameterless constructor sets members to default values
21          public Record()
22             : this( 0, string.Empty, string.Empty, 0M )
23          {
24          } // end constructor
25
26          // overloaded constructor sets members to parameter values
27          public Record( int accountValue, string firstNameValue,
28             string lastNameValue, decimal balanceValue )
29          {
30             Account = accountValue;
31             FirstName = firstNameValue;
32             LastName = lastNameValue;
33             Balance = balanceValue;
34          } // end constructor
35       } // end class Record
36    } // end namespace BankLibrary
```

Fig. 17.8 | Record for sequential-access file-processing applications. (Part 2 of 2.)

Class `Record` contains auto-implemented properties for instance variables `Account`, `FirstName`, `LastName` and `Balance` (lines 9–18), which collectively represent all the information for a record. The parameterless constructor (lines 21–24) sets these members by calling the four-argument constructor with 0 for the account number, `string.Empty` for the first and last name and `0.0M` for the balance. The four-argument constructor (lines 27–34) sets these members to the specified parameter values.

Using a Character Stream to Create an Output File

Class `CreateFileForm` (Fig. 17.9) uses instances of class `Record` to create a sequential-access file that might be used in an accounts-receivable system—i.e., a program that organizes data regarding money owed by a company's credit clients. For each client, the program obtains an account number and the client's first name, last name and balance (i.e., the amount of money that the client owes to the company for previously received goods and services). The data obtained for each client constitutes a record for that client. In this application, the account number is used as the record key—files are created and maintained in account-number order. This program assumes that the user enters records in account-number order. However, a comprehensive accounts-receivable system would provide a sorting capability, so the user could enter the records in any order.

```
1    // Fig. 17.9: CreateFileForm.cs
2    // Creating a sequential-access file.
3    using System;
4    using System.Windows.Forms;
5    using System.IO;
```

Fig. 17.9 | Creating and writing to a sequential-access file. (Part 1 of 5.)

```
 6    using BankLibrary;
 7
 8    namespace CreateFile
 9    {
10       public partial class CreateFileForm : BankUIForm
11       {
12          private StreamWriter fileWriter; // writes data to text file
13
14          // parameterless constructor
15          public CreateFileForm()
16          {
17             InitializeComponent();
18          } // end constructor
19
20          // event handler for Save Button
21          private void saveButton_Click( object sender, EventArgs e )
22          {
23             // create and show dialog box enabling user to save file
24             DialogResult result; // result of SaveFileDialog
25             string fileName; // name of file containing data
26
27             using ( SaveFileDialog fileChooser = new SaveFileDialog() )
28             {
29                fileChooser.CheckFileExists = false; // let user create file
30                result = fileChooser.ShowDialog();
31                fileName = fileChooser.FileName; // name of file to save data
32             } // end using
33
34             // ensure that user clicked "OK"
35             if ( result == DialogResult.OK )
36             {
37                // show error if user specified invalid file
38                if ( fileName == string.Empty )
39                   MessageBox.Show( "Invalid File Name", "Error",
40                      MessageBoxButtons.OK, MessageBoxIcon.Error );
41                else
42                {
43                   // save file via FileStream if user specified valid file
44                   try
45                   {
46                      // open file with write access
47                      FileStream output = new FileStream( fileName,
48                         FileMode.OpenOrCreate, FileAccess.Write );
49
50                      // sets file to where data is written
51                      fileWriter = new StreamWriter( output );
52
53                      // disable Save button and enable Enter button
54                      saveButton.Enabled = false;
55                      enterButton.Enabled = true;
56                   } // end try
57                   // handle exception if there is a problem opening the file
```

Fig. 17.9 | Creating and writing to a sequential-access file. (Part 2 of 5.)

```
 58                        catch ( IOException )
 59                        {
 60                            // notify user if file does not exist
 61                            MessageBox.Show( "Error opening file", "Error",
 62                                MessageBoxButtons.OK, MessageBoxIcon.Error );
 63                        } // end catch
 64                    } // end else
 65                } // end if
 66            } // end method saveButton_Click
 67
 68            // handler for enterButton Click
 69            private void enterButton_Click( object sender, EventArgs e )
 70            {
 71                // store TextBox values string array
 72                string[] values = GetTextBoxValues();
 73
 74                // Record containing TextBox values to output
 75                Record record = new Record();
 76
 77                // determine whether TextBox account field is empty
 78                if ( values[ ( int ) TextBoxIndices.ACCOUNT ] != string.Empty )
 79                {
 80                    // store TextBox values in Record and output it
 81                    try
 82                    {
 83                        // get account-number value from TextBox
 84                        int accountNumber = Int32.Parse(
 85                            values[ ( int ) TextBoxIndices.ACCOUNT ] );
 86
 87                        // determine whether accountNumber is valid
 88                        if ( accountNumber > 0 )
 89                        {
 90                            // store TextBox fields in Record
 91                            record.Account = accountNumber;
 92                            record.FirstName = values[ ( int )
 93                                TextBoxIndices.FIRST ];
 94                            record.LastName = values[ ( int )
 95                                TextBoxIndices.LAST ];
 96                            record.Balance = Decimal.Parse(
 97                                values[ ( int ) TextBoxIndices.BALANCE ] );
 98
 99                            // write Record to file, fields separated by commas
100                            fileWriter.WriteLine(
101                                record.Account + "," + record.FirstName + "," +
102                                record.LastName + "," + record.Balance );
103                        } // end if
104                        else
105                        {
106                            // notify user if invalid account number
107                            MessageBox.Show( "Invalid Account Number", "Error",
108                                MessageBoxButtons.OK, MessageBoxIcon.Error );
109                        } // end else
110                    } // end try
```

Fig. 17.9 | Creating and writing to a sequential-access file. (Part 3 of 5.)

```
111            // notify user if error occurs during the output operation
112            catch ( IOException )
113            {
114               MessageBox.Show( "Error Writing to File", "Error",
115                  MessageBoxButtons.OK, MessageBoxIcon.Error );
116            } // end catch
117            // notify user if error occurs regarding parameter format
118            catch ( FormatException )
119            {
120               MessageBox.Show( "Invalid Format", "Error",
121                  MessageBoxButtons.OK, MessageBoxIcon.Error );
122            } // end catch
123         } // end if
124
125         ClearTextBoxes(); // clear TextBox values
126      } // end method enterButton_Click
127
128      // handler for exitButton Click
129      private void exitButton_Click( object sender, EventArgs e )
130      {
131         // determine whether file exists
132         if ( fileWriter != null )
133         {
134            try
135            {
136               // close StreamWriter and underlying file
137               fileWriter.Close();
138            } // end try
139            // notify user of error closing file
140            catch ( IOException )
141            {
142               MessageBox.Show( "Cannot close file", "Error",
143                  MessageBoxButtons.OK, MessageBoxIcon.Error );
144            } // end catch
145         } // end if
146
147         Application.Exit();
148      } // end method exitButton_Click
149   } // end class CreateFileForm
150 } // end namespace CreateFile
```

a) BankUI graphical user interface with three additional controls

Fig. 17.9 | Creating and writing to a sequential-access file. (Part 4 of 5.)

b) Save File dialog

Files and directories

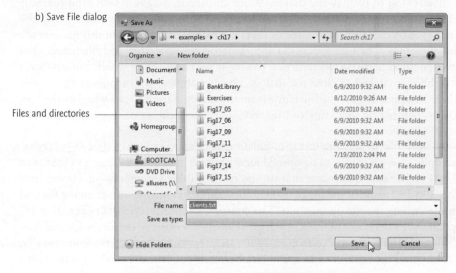

c) Account 100, "Nancy Brown", saved with a balance of -25.54

Fig. 17.9 | Creating and writing to a sequential-access file. (Part 5 of 5.)

Class CreateFileForm either creates or opens a file (depending on whether one exists), then allows the user to write records to it. The using directive in line 6 enables us to use the classes of the BankLibrary namespace; this namespace contains class BankUI-Form, from which class CreateFileForm inherits (line 10). Class CreateFileForm's GUI enhances that of class BankUIForm with buttons **Save As**, **Enter** and **Exit**.

Method saveButton_Click
When the user clicks the **Save As** button, the program invokes the event handler saveButton_Click (lines 21–66). Line 27 instantiates an object of class **SaveFileDialog** (namespace System.Windows.Forms). By placing this object in a using statement (lines 27–32), we can ensure that the dialog's Dispose method is called to release its resources as soon as the program has retrieved user input from it. SaveFileDialog objects are used for selecting files (see the second screen in Fig. 17.9). Line 29 indicates that the dialog should not check if the file name specified by the user already exists. Line 30 calls SaveFileDialog

method ShowDialog to display the dialog. When displayed, a SaveFileDialog prevents the user from interacting with any other window in the program until the user closes the SaveFileDialog by clicking either **Save** or **Cancel**. Dialogs that behave in this manner are called **modal dialogs**. The user selects the appropriate drive, directory and file name, then clicks **Save**. Method **ShowDialog** returns a DialogResult specifying which button (**Save** or **Cancel**) the user clicked to close the dialog. This is assigned to DialogResult variable result (line 30). Line 31 gets the file name from the dialog. Line 35 tests whether the user clicked **OK** by comparing this value to DialogResult.OK. If the values are equal, method saveButton_Click continues.

You can open files to perform text manipulation by creating objects of class FileStream. In this example, we want the file to be opened for output, so lines 47–48 create a FileStream object. The FileStream constructor that we use receives three arguments—a string containing the path and name of the file to open, a constant describing how to open the file and a constant describing the file permissions. The constant FileMode.OpenOrCreate (line 48) indicates that the FileStream object should open the file if it exists or create the file if it does not exist. Note that the contents of an existing file are overwritten by the StreamWriter. To preserve the original contents of a file, use FileMode.Append. There are other FileMode constants describing how to open files; we introduce these constants as we use them in examples. The constant FileAccess.Write indicates that the program can perform only write operations with the FileStream object. There are two other constants for the third constructor parameter—FileAccess.Read for read-only access and FileAccess.ReadWrite for both read and write access. Line 58 catches an **IOException** if there's a problem opening the file or creating the StreamWriter. If so, the program displays an error message (lines 61–62). If no exception occurs, the file is open for writing.

Good Programming Practice 17.1

When opening files, use the **FileAccess** *enumeration to control user access to these files.*

Common Programming Error 17.1

Failure to open a file before attempting to use it in a program is a logic error.

Method enterButton_Click

After typing information into each TextBox, the user clicks the **Enter** button, which calls event handler enterButton_Click (lines 69–126) to save the data from the TextBoxes into the user-specified file. If the user entered a valid account number (i.e., an integer greater than zero), lines 91–97 store the TextBox values in an object of type Record (created at line 75). If the user entered invalid data in one of the TextBoxes (such as nonnumeric characters in the **Balance** field), the program throws a FormatException. The catch block in lines 118–122 handles such exceptions by notifying the user (via a MessageBox) of the improper format.

If the user entered valid data, lines 100–102 write the record to the file by invoking method WriteLine of the StreamWriter object that was created at line 51. Method WriteLine writes a sequence of characters to a file. The StreamWriter object is constructed with a FileStream argument that specifies the file to which the StreamWriter will output text. Class StreamWriter belongs to the System.IO namespace.

Method **exitButton_Click**

When the user clicks **Exit**, exitButton_Click (lines 129–148) executes. Line 137 closes the **StreamWriter**, which automatically closes the **FileStream**. Then, line 147 terminates the program. Note that method **Close** is called in a **try** block. Method **Close** throws an **IOException** if the file or stream cannot be closed properly. In this case, it's important to notify the user that the information in the file or stream might be corrupted.

Performance Tip 17.1

Close each file explicitly when the program no longer needs to use it. This can reduce resource usage in programs that continue executing long after they finish using a specific file. The practice of explicitly closing files also improves program clarity.

Performance Tip 17.2

Releasing resources explicitly when they're no longer needed makes them immediately available for reuse by other programs, thus improving resource utilization.

Sample Data

To test the program, we entered information for the accounts shown in Fig. 17.10. The program does not depict how the data records are stored in the file. To verify that the file has been created successfully, we create a program in the next section to read and display the file. Since this is a text file, you can actually open it in any text editor to see its contents.

Account number	First name	Last name	Balance
100	Nancy	Brown	-25.54
200	Stacey	Dunn	314.33
300	Doug	Barker	0.00
400	Dave	Smith	258.34
500	Sam	Stone	34.98

Fig. 17.10 | Sample data for the program of Fig. 17.9.

17.6 Reading Data from a Sequential-Access Text File

The previous section demonstrated how to create a file for use in sequential-access applications. In this section, we discuss how to read (or retrieve) data sequentially from a file.

Class ReadSequentialAccessFileForm (Fig. 17.11) reads records from the file created by the program in Fig. 17.9, then displays the contents of each record. Much of the code in this example is similar to that of Fig. 17.9, so we discuss only the unique aspects of the application.

```
1    // Fig. 17.11: ReadSequentialAccessFileForm.cs
2    // Reading a sequential-access file.
3    using System;
```

Fig. 17.11 | Reading sequential-access files. (Part 1 of 4.)

```
 4    using System.Windows.Forms;
 5    using System.IO;
 6    using BankLibrary;
 7
 8    namespace ReadSequentialAccessFile
 9    {
10       public partial class ReadSequentialAccessFileForm : BankUIForm
11       {
12          private StreamReader fileReader; // reads data from a text file
13
14          // parameterless constructor
15          public ReadSequentialAccessFileForm()
16          {
17             InitializeComponent();
18          } // end constructor
19
20          // invoked when user clicks the Open button
21          private void openButton_Click( object sender, EventArgs e )
22          {
23             // create and show dialog box enabling user to open file
24             DialogResult result; // result of OpenFileDialog
25             string fileName; // name of file containing data
26
27             using ( OpenFileDialog fileChooser = new OpenFileDialog() )
28             {
29                result = fileChooser.ShowDialog();
30                fileName = fileChooser.FileName; // get specified name
31             } // end using
32
33             // ensure that user clicked "OK"
34             if ( result == DialogResult.OK )
35             {
36                ClearTextBoxes();
37
38                // show error if user specified invalid file
39                if ( fileName == string.Empty )
40                   MessageBox.Show( "Invalid File Name", "Error",
41                      MessageBoxButtons.OK, MessageBoxIcon.Error );
42                else
43                {
44                   try
45                   {
46                      // create FileStream to obtain read access to file
47                      FileStream input = new FileStream(
48                         fileName, FileMode.Open, FileAccess.Read );
49
50                      // set file from where data is read
51                      fileReader = new StreamReader( input );
52
53                      openButton.Enabled = false; // disable Open File button
54                      nextButton.Enabled = true; // enable Next Record button
55                   } // end try
```

Fig. 17.11 | Reading sequential-access files. (Part 2 of 4.)

```
56                      catch ( IOException )
57                      {
58                          MessageBox.Show( "Error reading from file",
59                              "File Error", MessageBoxButtons.OK,
60                              MessageBoxIcon.Error );
61                      } // end catch
62                  } // end else
63              } // end if
64          } // end method openButton_Click
65
66          // invoked when user clicks Next button
67          private void nextButton_Click( object sender, EventArgs e )
68          {
69              try
70              {
71                  // get next record available in file
72                  string inputRecord = fileReader.ReadLine();
73                  string[] inputFields; // will store individual pieces of data
74
75                  if ( inputRecord != null )
76                  {
77                      inputFields = inputRecord.Split( ',' );
78
79                      Record record = new Record(
80                          Convert.ToInt32( inputFields[ 0 ] ), inputFields[ 1 ],
81                          inputFields[ 2 ],
82                          Convert.ToDecimal( inputFields[ 3 ] ) );
83
84                      // copy string-array values to TextBox values
85                      SetTextBoxValues( inputFields );
86                  } // end if
87                  else
88                  {
89                      // close StreamReader and underlying file
90                      fileReader.Close();
91                      openButton.Enabled = true; // enable Open File button
92                      nextButton.Enabled = false; // disable Next Record button
93                      ClearTextBoxes();
94
95                      // notify user if no records in file
96                      MessageBox.Show( "No more records in file", string.Empty,
97                          MessageBoxButtons.OK, MessageBoxIcon.Information );
98                  } // end else
99              } // end try
100             catch ( IOException )
101             {
102                 MessageBox.Show( "Error Reading from File", "Error",
103                     MessageBoxButtons.OK, MessageBoxIcon.Error );
104             } // end catch
105         } // end method nextButton_Click
106     } // end class ReadSequentialAccessFileForm
107 } // end namespace ReadSequentialAccessFile
```

Fig. 17.11 | Reading sequential-access files. (Part 3 of 4.)

a) BankUI graphical user interface with an Open File button

b) `OpenFileDialog` window

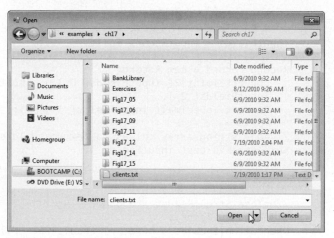

c) Reading account 100

d) User is shown a messagebox when all records have been read

Fig. 17.11 | Reading sequential-access files. (Part 4 of 4.)

Method **openButton_Click**

When the user clicks the **Open File** button, the program calls event handler open-Button_Click (lines 21–64). Line 27 creates an **OpenFileDialog**, and line 29 calls its ShowDialog method to display the **Open** dialog (see the second screenshot in Fig. 17.11). The behavior and GUI for the **Save** and **Open** dialog types are identical, except that **Save** is replaced by **Open**. If the user selects a valid file name, lines 47–48 create a FileStream object and assign it to reference input. We pass constant FileMode.Open as the second argument to the FileStream constructor to indicate that the FileStream should open the file if it exists or throw a **FileNotFoundException** if it does not. (In this example, the FileStream constructor will *not* throw a FileNotFoundException, because the OpenFile-Dialog is configured to check that the file exists.) In the last example (Fig. 17.9), we wrote text to the file using a FileStream object with write-only access. In this example (Fig. 17.11), we specify read-only access to the file by passing constant FileAccess.Read as the third argument to the FileStream constructor. This FileStream object is used to create a StreamReader object in line 51. The FileStream object specifies the file from which the StreamReader object will read text.

Error-Prevention Tip 17.1

Open a file with the FileAccess.Read file-open mode if its contents should not be modified. This prevents unintentional modification of the contents.

Method **nextButton_Click**

When the user clicks the **Next Record** button, the program calls event handler nextButton_Click (lines 67–104), which reads the next record from the user-specified file. (The user must click **Next Record** after opening the file to view the first record.) Line 72 calls StreamReader method ReadLine to read the next record. If an error occurs while reading the file, an IOException is thrown (caught at line 99), and the user is notified (lines 101–102). Otherwise, line 75 determines whether StreamReader method ReadLine returned null (i.e., there's no more text in the file). If not, line 77 uses method Split of class string to separate the stream of characters that was read from the file into strings that represent the Record's properties. These properties are then stored by constructing a Record object using the properties as arguments (lines 79–81). Line 84 displays the Record values in the TextBoxes. If ReadLine returns null, the program closes the StreamReader object (line 90), automatically closing the FileStream object, then notifies the user that there are no more records (lines 96–97).

17.7 Case Study: Credit Inquiry Program

To retrieve data sequentially from a file, programs normally start from the beginning of the file, reading consecutively until the desired data is found. It sometimes is necessary to process a file sequentially several times (from the beginning of the file) during the execution of a program. A FileStream object can reposition its **file-position pointer** (which contains the byte number of the next byte to be read from or written to the file) to any position in the file. When a FileStream object is opened, its file-position pointer is set to byte position 0 (i.e., the beginning of the file)

We now present a program that builds on the concepts employed in Fig. 17.11. Class CreditInquiryForm (Fig. 17.12) is a credit-inquiry program that enables a credit manager to search for and display account information for those customers with credit balances (i.e., customers to whom the company owes money), zero balances (i.e., customers who do not owe the company money) and debit balances (i.e., customers who owe the company money for previously received goods and services). We use a RichTextBox in the program to display the account information. RichTextBoxes provide more functionality than regular TextBoxes—for example, RichTextBoxes offer method Find for searching individual strings and method LoadFile for displaying file contents. Classes RichTextBox and TextBox both inherit from abstract class System.Windows.Forms.TextBoxBase. In this example, we chose a RichTextBox, because it displays multiple lines of text by default, whereas a regular TextBox displays only one. Alternatively, we could have specified that a TextBox object display multiple lines of text by setting its Multiline property to true.

The program displays buttons that enable a credit manager to obtain credit information. The **Open File** button opens a file for gathering data. The **Credit Balances** button displays a list of accounts that have credit balances, the **Debit Balances** button displays a list of accounts that have debit balances and the **Zero Balances** button displays a list of accounts that have zero balances. The **Done** button exits the application.

```
1    // Fig. 17.12: CreditInquiryForm.cs
2    // Read a file sequentially and display contents based on
3    // account type specified by user ( credit, debit or zero balances ).
4    using System;
5    using System.Windows.Forms;
6    using System.IO;
7    using BankLibrary;
8
9    namespace CreditInquiry
10   {
11      public partial class CreditInquiryForm : Form
12      {
13         private FileStream input; // maintains the connection to the file
14         private StreamReader fileReader; // reads data from text file
15
16         // name of file that stores credit, debit and zero balances
17         private string fileName;
18
19         // parameterless constructor
20         public CreditInquiryForm()
21         {
22            InitializeComponent();
23         } // end constructor
24
25         // invoked when user clicks Open File button
26         private void openButton_Click( object sender, EventArgs e )
27         {
28            // create dialog box enabling user to open file
29            DialogResult result;
30
31            using ( OpenFileDialog fileChooser = new OpenFileDialog() )
32            {
```

Fig. 17.12 | Credit-inquiry program. (Part 1 of 5.)

```
33              result = fileChooser.ShowDialog();
34              fileName = fileChooser.FileName;
35          } // end using
36
37          // exit event handler if user clicked Cancel
38          if ( result == DialogResult.OK )
39          {
40              // show error if user specified invalid file
41              if ( fileName == string.Empty )
42                  MessageBox.Show( "Invalid File Name", "Error",
43                      MessageBoxButtons.OK, MessageBoxIcon.Error );
44              else
45              {
46                  // create FileStream to obtain read access to file
47                  input = new FileStream( fileName,
48                      FileMode.Open, FileAccess.Read );
49
50                  // set file from where data is read
51                  fileReader = new StreamReader( input );
52
53                  // enable all GUI buttons, except for Open File button
54                  openButton.Enabled = false;
55                  creditButton.Enabled = true;
56                  debitButton.Enabled = true;
57                  zeroButton.Enabled = true;
58              } // end else
59          } // end if
60      } // end method openButton_Click
61
62      // invoked when user clicks credit balances,
63      // debit balances or zero balances button
64      private void getBalances_Click( object sender, System.EventArgs e )
65      {
66          // convert sender explicitly to object of type button
67          Button senderButton = ( Button ) sender;
68
69          // get text from clicked Button, which stores account type
70          string accountType = senderButton.Text;
71
72          // read and display file information
73          try
74          {
75              // go back to the beginning of the file
76              input.Seek( 0, SeekOrigin.Begin );
77
78              displayTextBox.Text = "The accounts are:\r\n";
79
80              // traverse file until end of file
81              while ( true )
82              {
83                  string[] inputFields; // stores individual pieces of data
84                  Record record; // store each Record as file is read
85                  decimal balance; // store each Record's balance
```

Fig. 17.12 | Credit-inquiry program. (Part 2 of 5.)

```
86
87                   // get next Record available in file
88                   string inputRecord = fileReader.ReadLine();
89
90                   // when at the end of file, exit method
91                   if ( inputRecord == null )
92                      return;
93
94                   inputFields = inputRecord.Split( ',' ); // parse input
95
96                   // create Record from input
97                   record = new Record(
98                      Convert.ToInt32( inputFields[ 0 ] ), inputFields[ 1 ],
99                      inputFields[ 2 ], Convert.ToDecimal(inputFields[ 3 ]));
100
101                  // store record's last field in balance
102                  balance = record.Balance;
103
104                  // determine whether to display balance
105                  if ( ShouldDisplay( balance, accountType ) )
106                  {
107                     // display record
108                     string output = record.Account + "\t" +
109                        record.FirstName + "\t" + record.LastName + "\t";
110
111                     // display balance with correct monetary format
112                     output += String.Format( "{0:F}", balance ) + "\r\n";
113
114                     // copy output to screen
115                     displayTextBox.AppendText( output );
116                  } // end if
117               } // end while
118            } // end try
119            // handle exception when file cannot be read
120            catch ( IOException )
121            {
122               MessageBox.Show( "Cannot Read File", "Error",
123                  MessageBoxButtons.OK, MessageBoxIcon.Error );
124            } // end catch
125      } // end method getBalances_Click
126
127      // determine whether to display given record
128      private bool ShouldDisplay( decimal balance, string accountType )
129      {
130         if ( balance > 0M )
131         {
132            // display credit balances
133            if ( accountType == "Credit Balances" )
134               return true;
135         } // end if
136         else if ( balance < 0M )
137         {
```

Fig. 17.12 | Credit-inquiry program. (Part 3 of 5.)

```
138                 // display debit balances
139                 if ( accountType == "Debit Balances" )
140                     return true;
141             } // end else if
142         else // balance == 0
143         {
144             // display zero balances
145             if ( accountType == "Zero Balances" )
146                 return true;
147         } // end else
148
149         return false;
150     } // end method ShouldDisplay
151
152     // invoked when user clicks Done button
153     private void doneButton_Click( object sender, EventArgs e )
154     {
155         if ( input != null )
156         {
157             // close file and StreamReader
158             try
159             {
160                 // close StreamReader and underlying file
161                 fileReader.Close();
162             } // end try
163             // handle exception if FileStream does not exist
164             catch ( IOException )
165             {
166                 // notify user of error closing file
167                 MessageBox.Show( "Cannot close file", "Error",
168                     MessageBoxButtons.OK, MessageBoxIcon.Error );
169             } // end catch
170         } // end if
171
172         Application.Exit();
173     } // end method doneButton_Click
174 } // end class CreditInquiryForm
175 } // end namespace CreditInquiry
```

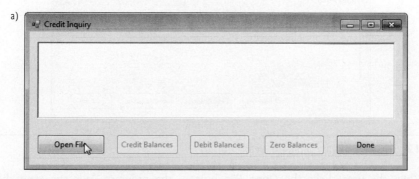

Fig. 17.12 | Credit-inquiry program. (Part 4 of 5.)

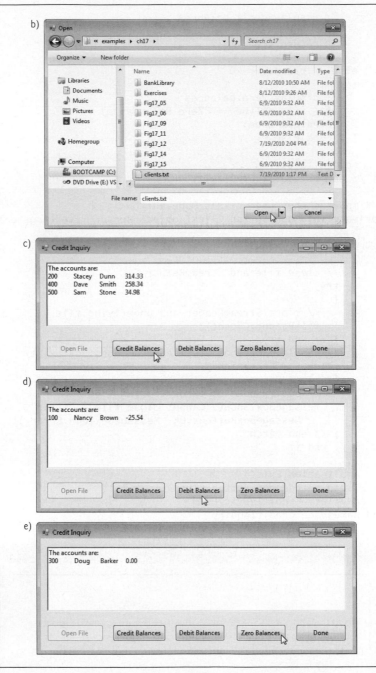

Fig. 17.12 | Credit-inquiry program. (Part 5 of 5.)

When the user clicks the **Open File** button, the program calls the event handler openButton_Click (lines 26–60). Line 31 creates an OpenFileDialog, and line 33 calls its ShowDialog method to display the **Open** dialog, in which the user selects the file to open.

Lines 47–48 create a `FileStream` object with read-only file access and assign it to reference input. Line 51 creates a `StreamReader` object that we use to read text from the `FileStream`.

When the user clicks **Credit Balances**, **Debit Balances** or **Zero Balances**, the program invokes method `getBalances_Click` (lines 64–125). Line 67 casts the `sender` parameter, which is an `object` reference to the control that generated the event, to a `Button` object. Line 70 extracts the `Button` object's text, which the program uses to determine which type of accounts to display. Line 76 uses `FileStream` method **Seek** to reset the file-position pointer back to the beginning of the file. `FileStream` method Seek allows you to reset the file-position pointer by specifying the number of bytes it should be offset from the file's beginning, end or current position. The part of the file you want to be offset from is chosen using constants from the **SeekOrigin** enumeration. In this case, our stream is offset by 0 bytes from the file's beginning (`SeekOrigin.Begin`). Lines 81–117 define a `while` loop that uses `private` method `ShouldDisplay` (lines 128–150) to determine whether to display each record in the file. The `while` loop obtains each record by repeatedly calling `StreamReader` method `ReadLine` (line 88) and splitting the text into tokens (line 94) that are used to initialize object `record` (lines 97–99). Line 91 determines whether the file-position pointer has reached the end of the file, in which case `ReadLine` returns `null`. If so, the program returns from method `getBalances_Click` (line 92).

17.8 Serialization

Section 17.5 demonstrated how to write the individual fields of a `Record` object to a text file, and Section 17.6 demonstrated how to read those fields from a file and place their values in a `Record` object in memory. In the examples, `Record` was used to aggregate the information for one record. When the instance variables for a `Record` were output to a disk file, certain information was lost, such as the type of each value. For instance, if the value `"3"` is read from a file, there's no way to tell if the value came from an `int`, a `string` or a `decimal`. We have only data, not type information, on disk. If the program that's going to read this data "knows" what object type the data corresponds to, then the data can be read directly into objects of that type. For example, in Fig. 17.11, we know that we are inputting an `int` (the account number), followed by two `string`s (the first and last name) and a `decimal` (the balance). We also know that these values are separated by commas, with only one record on each line. So, we are able to parse the strings and convert the account number to an `int` and the balance to a `decimal`. Sometimes it would be easier to read or write entire objects. C# provides such a mechanism, called **object serialization**. A **serialized object** is an object represented as a sequence of bytes that includes the object's data, as well as information about the object's type and the types of data stored in the object. After a serialized object has been written to a file, it can be read from the file and **deserialized**—that is, the type information and bytes that represent the object and its data can be used to recreate the object in memory.

Class **BinaryFormatter** (namespace **System.Runtime.Serialization.Formatters.Binary**) enables entire objects to be written to or read from a stream. `BinaryFormatter` method **Serialize** writes an object's representation to a file. `BinaryFormatter` method **Deserialize** reads this representation from a file and reconstructs the original object. Both methods throw a **SerializationException** if an error occurs during serialization or deserialization. Both methods require a `Stream` object (e.g., the `FileStream`) as a parameter so that the `BinaryFormatter` can access the correct stream.

In Sections 17.9–17.10, we create and manipulate sequential-access files using object serialization. Object serialization is performed with byte-based streams, so the sequential files created and manipulated will be binary files. Binary files are not human readable. For this reason, we write a separate application that reads and displays serialized objects.

17.9 Creating a Sequential-Access File Using Object Serialization

We begin by creating and writing serialized objects to a sequential-access file. In this section, we reuse much of the code from Section 17.5, so we focus only on the new features.

Defining the *RecordSerializable* Class

Let's begin by modifying our Record class (Fig. 17.8) so that objects of this class can be serialized. Class RecordSerializable (Fig. 17.13) is marked with the **[Serializable]** attribute (line 7), which indicates to the CLR that objects of class RecordSerializable can be serialized. The classes for objects that we wish to write to or read from a stream must include this attribute in their declarations or must implement interface **ISerializable**.

```
1    // Fig. 17.13: RecordSerializable.cs
2    // Serializable class that represents a data record.
3    using System;
4
5    namespace BankLibrary
6    {
7       [Serializable]
8       public class RecordSerializable
9       {
10          // automatic Account property
11          public int Account { get; set; }
12
13          // automatic FirstName property
14          public string FirstName { get; set; }
15
16          // automatic LastName property
17          public string LastName { get; set; }
18
19          // automatic Balance property
20          public decimal Balance { get; set; }
21
22          // default constructor sets members to default values
23          public RecordSerializable()
24             : this( 0, string.Empty, string.Empty, 0M )
25          {
26          } // end constructor
27
28          // overloaded constructor sets members to parameter values
29          public RecordSerializable( int accountValue, string firstNameValue,
30             string lastNameValue, decimal balanceValue )
31          {
32             Account = accountValue;
```

Fig. 17.13 | RecordSerializable class for serializable objects. (Part 1 of 2.)

```
33                  FirstName = firstNameValue;
34                  LastName = lastNameValue;
35                  Balance = balanceValue;
36           } // end constructor
37        } // end class RecordSerializable
38     } // end namespace BankLibrary
```

Fig. 17.13 | RecordSerializable class for serializable objects. (Part 2 of 2.)

In a class that's marked with the [Serializable] attribute or that implements interface ISerializable, you must ensure that every instance variable of the class is also serializable. All simple-type variables and strings are serializable. For variables of reference types, you must check the class declaration (and possibly its base classes) to ensure that the type is serializable. By default, array objects are serializable. However, if the array contains references to other objects, those objects may or may not be serializable.

Using a Serialization Stream to Create an Output File

Next, we'll create a sequential-access file with serialization (Fig. 17.14). To test this program, we used the sample data from Fig. 17.10 to create a file named clients.ser. Since the sample screen captures are the same as Fig. 17.9, they are not shown here. Line 15 creates a BinaryFormatter for writing serialized objects. Lines 53–54 open the FileStream to which this program writes the serialized objects. The string argument that's passed to the FileStream's constructor represents the name and path of the file to be opened. This specifies the file to which the serialized objects will be written.

This program assumes that data is input correctly and in the proper record-number order. Event handler enterButton_Click (lines 72–127) performs the write operation. Line 78 creates a RecordSerializable object, which is assigned values in lines 94–100. Line 103 calls method Serialize to write the RecordSerializable object to the output file. Method Serialize takes the FileStream object as the first argument so that the BinaryFormatter can write its second argument to the correct file. Only one statement is required to write the entire object. If a problem occurs during serialization, a SerializationException occurs—we catch this exception in lines 113–117.

In the sample execution for the program in Fig. 17.14, we entered information for five accounts—the same information shown in Fig. 17.10. The program does not show how the data records actually appear in the file. Remember that we are now using binary files, which are not human readable. To verify that the file was created successfully, the next section presents a program to read the file's contents.

```
1    // Fig. 17.14: CreateFileForm.cs
2    // Creating a sequential-access file using serialization.
3    using System;
4    using System.Windows.Forms;
5    using System.IO;
6    using System.Runtime.Serialization.Formatters.Binary;
7    using System.Runtime.Serialization;
8    using BankLibrary;
9
```

Fig. 17.14 | Sequential file created using serialization. (Part 1 of 4.)

```
10    namespace CreateFile
11    {
12        public partial class CreateFileForm : BankUIForm
13        {
14            // object for serializing RecordSerializables in binary format
15            private BinaryFormatter formatter = new BinaryFormatter();
16            private FileStream output; // stream for writing to a file
17
18            // parameterless constructor
19            public CreateFileForm()
20            {
21                InitializeComponent();
22            } // end constructor
23
24            // handler for saveButton_Click
25            private void saveButton_Click( object sender, EventArgs e )
26            {
27                // create and show dialog box enabling user to save file
28                DialogResult result;
29                string fileName; // name of file to save data
30
31                using ( SaveFileDialog fileChooser = new SaveFileDialog() )
32                {
33                    fileChooser.CheckFileExists = false; // let user create file
34
35                    // retrieve the result of the dialog box
36                    result = fileChooser.ShowDialog();
37                    fileName = fileChooser.FileName; // get specified file name
38                } // end using
39
40                // ensure that user clicked "OK"
41                if ( result == DialogResult.OK )
42                {
43                    // show error if user specified invalid file
44                    if ( fileName == string.Empty )
45                        MessageBox.Show( "Invalid File Name", "Error",
46                            MessageBoxButtons.OK, MessageBoxIcon.Error );
47                    else
48                    {
49                        // save file via FileStream if user specified valid file
50                        try
51                        {
52                            // open file with write access
53                            output = new FileStream( fileName,
54                                FileMode.OpenOrCreate, FileAccess.Write );
55
56                            // disable Save button and enable Enter button
57                            saveButton.Enabled = false;
58                            enterButton.Enabled = true;
59                        } // end try
60                        // handle exception if there is a problem opening the file
61                        catch ( IOException )
62                        {
```

Fig. 17.14 | Sequential file created using serialization. (Part 2 of 4.)

```
63                          // notify user if file could not be opened
64                          MessageBox.Show( "Error opening file", "Error",
65                              MessageBoxButtons.OK, MessageBoxIcon.Error );
66                      } // end catch
67                  } // end else
68              } // end if
69          } // end method saveButton_Click
70
71          // handler for enterButton Click
72          private void enterButton_Click( object sender, EventArgs e )
73          {
74              // store TextBox values string array
75              string[] values = GetTextBoxValues();
76
77              // RecordSerializable containing TextBox values to serialize
78              RecordSerializable record = new RecordSerializable();
79
80              // determine whether TextBox account field is empty
81              if ( values[ ( int ) TextBoxIndices.ACCOUNT ] != string.Empty )
82              {
83                  // store TextBox values in RecordSerializable and serialize it
84                  try
85                  {
86                      // get account-number value from TextBox
87                      int accountNumber = Int32.Parse(
88                          values[ ( int ) TextBoxIndices.ACCOUNT ] );
89
90                      // determine whether accountNumber is valid
91                      if ( accountNumber > 0 )
92                      {
93                          // store TextBox fields in RecordSerializable
94                          record.Account = accountNumber;
95                          record.FirstName = values[ ( int )
96                              TextBoxIndices.FIRST ];
97                          record.LastName = values[ ( int )
98                              TextBoxIndices.LAST ];
99                          record.Balance = Decimal.Parse( values[
100                             ( int ) TextBoxIndices.BALANCE ] );
101
102                         // write RecordSerializable to FileStream
103                         formatter.Serialize( output, record );
104                     } // end if
105                     else
106                     {
107                         // notify user if invalid account number
108                         MessageBox.Show( "Invalid Account Number", "Error",
109                             MessageBoxButtons.OK, MessageBoxIcon.Error );
110                     } // end else
111                 } // end try
112                 // notify user if error occurs in serialization
113                 catch ( SerializationException )
114                 {
```

Fig. 17.14 | Sequential file created using serialization. (Part 3 of 4.)

```
115              MessageBox.Show( "Error Writing to File", "Error",
116                 MessageBoxButtons.OK, MessageBoxIcon.Error );
117           } // end catch
118           // notify user if error occurs regarding parameter format
119           catch ( FormatException )
120           {
121              MessageBox.Show( "Invalid Format", "Error",
122                 MessageBoxButtons.OK, MessageBoxIcon.Error );
123           } // end catch
124        } // end if
125
126        ClearTextBoxes(); // clear TextBox values
127     } // end method enterButton_Click
128
129     // handler for exitButton Click
130     private void exitButton_Click( object sender, EventArgs e )
131     {
132        // determine whether file exists
133        if ( output != null )
134        {
135           // close file
136           try
137           {
138              output.Close(); // close FileStream
139           } // end try
140           // notify user of error closing file
141           catch ( IOException )
142           {
143              MessageBox.Show( "Cannot close file", "Error",
144                 MessageBoxButtons.OK, MessageBoxIcon.Error );
145           } // end catch
146        } // end if
147
148        Application.Exit();
149     } // end method exitButton_Click
150  } // end class CreateFileForm
151 } // end namespace CreateFile
```

Fig. 17.14 | Sequential file created using serialization. (Part 4 of 4.)

17.10 Reading and Deserializing Data from a Binary File

The preceding section showed how to create a sequential-access file using object serialization. In this section, we discuss how to read serialized objects sequentially from a file.

Figure 17.15 reads and displays the contents of the clients.ser file created by the program in Fig. 17.14. The sample screen captures are identical to those of Fig. 17.11, so they are not shown here. Line 15 creates the BinaryFormatter that will be used to read objects. The program opens the file for input by creating a FileStream object (lines 49–50). The name of the file to open is specified as the first argument to the FileStream constructor.

The program reads objects from a file in event handler nextButton_Click (lines 59–92). We use method Deserialize (of the BinaryFormatter created in line 15) to read the data (lines 65–66). Note that we cast the result of Deserialize to type RecordSerializable (line 66)—this cast is necessary, because Deserialize returns a reference of type object and we need to access properties that belong to class RecordSerializable. If an error occurs during deserialization, a SerializationException is thrown, and the FileStream object is closed (line 82).

```csharp
1   // Fig. 17.15: ReadSequentialAccessFileForm.cs
2   // Reading a sequential-access file using deserialization.
3   using System;
4   using System.Windows.Forms;
5   using System.IO;
6   using System.Runtime.Serialization.Formatters.Binary;
7   using System.Runtime.Serialization;
8   using BankLibrary;
9
10  namespace ReadSequentialAccessFile
11  {
12     public partial class ReadSequentialAccessFileForm : BankUIForm
13     {
14        // object for deserializing RecordSerializable in binary format
15        private BinaryFormatter reader = new BinaryFormatter();
16        private FileStream input; // stream for reading from a file
17
18        // parameterless constructor
19        public ReadSequentialAccessFileForm()
20        {
21           InitializeComponent();
22        } // end constructor
23
24        // invoked when user clicks the Open button
25        private void openButton_Click( object sender, EventArgs e )
26        {
27           // create and show dialog box enabling user to open file
28           DialogResult result; // result of OpenFileDialog
29           string fileName; // name of file containing data
30
31           using ( OpenFileDialog fileChooser = new OpenFileDialog() )
32           {
33              result = fileChooser.ShowDialog();
34              fileName = fileChooser.FileName; // get specified name
35           } // end using
36
37           // ensure that user clicked "OK"
38           if ( result == DialogResult.OK )
39           {
40              ClearTextBoxes();
41
42              // show error if user specified invalid file
43              if ( fileName == string.Empty )
44                 MessageBox.Show( "Invalid File Name", "Error",
45                    MessageBoxButtons.OK, MessageBoxIcon.Error );
46              else
47              {
```

Fig. 17.15 | Sequential file read using deserialization. (Part 1 of 2.)

```
48              // create FileStream to obtain read access to file
49              input = new FileStream(
50                 fileName, FileMode.Open, FileAccess.Read );
51
52              openButton.Enabled = false; // disable Open File button
53              nextButton.Enabled = true;  // enable Next Record button
54           } // end else
55        } // end if
56     } // end method openButton_Click
57
58        // invoked when user clicks Next button
59        private void nextButton_Click( object sender, EventArgs e )
60        {
61           // deserialize RecordSerializable and store data in TextBoxes
62           try
63           {
64              // get next RecordSerializable available in file
65              RecordSerializable record =
66                 ( RecordSerializable ) reader.Deserialize( input );
67
68              // store RecordSerializable values in temporary string array
69              string[] values = new string[] {
70                 record.Account.ToString(),
71                 record.FirstName.ToString(),
72                 record.LastName.ToString(),
73                 record.Balance.ToString()
74              };
75
76              // copy string-array values to TextBox values
77              SetTextBoxValues( values );
78           } // end try
79           // handle exception when there are no RecordSerializables in file
80           catch ( SerializationException )
81           {
82              input.Close(); // close FileStream
83              openButton.Enabled = true; // enable Open File button
84              nextButton.Enabled = false; // disable Next Record button
85
86              ClearTextBoxes();
87
88              // notify user if no RecordSerializables in file
89              MessageBox.Show( "No more records in file", string.Empty,
90                 MessageBoxButtons.OK, MessageBoxIcon.Information );
91           } // end catch
92        } // end method nextButton_Click
93     } // end class ReadSequentialAccessFileForm
94  } // end namespace ReadSequentialAccessFile
```

Fig. 17.15 | Sequential file read using deserialization. (Part 2 of 2.)

17.11 Wrap-Up

In this chapter, you learned how to use file processing to manipulate persistent data. You learned that data is stored in computers as 0s and 1s, and that combinations of these values are used to form bytes, fields, records and eventually files. We overviewed several file-processing classes from the `System.IO` namespace. You used class `File` to manipulate files, and classes `Directory` and `DirectoryInfo` to manipulate directories. Next, you learned how to use sequential-access file processing to manipulate records in text files. We then discussed the differences between text-file processing and object serialization, and used serialization to store entire objects in and retrieve entire objects from files.

In Chapter 18, we begin our discussion of databases, which organize data in such a way that the data can be selected and updated quickly. We introduce Structured Query Language (SQL) for writing simple database queries. We then introduce LINQ to SQL, which allows you to write LINQ queries that are automatically converted into SQL queries. These SQL queries are then used to query the database.

Summary

Section 17.1 Introduction
- Files are used for long-term retention of large amounts of data.
- Data stored in files often is called persistent data.
- Computers store files on secondary storage devices.

Section 17.2 Data Hierarchy
- All data items that computers process are reduced to combinations of 0s and 1s.
- The smallest data item that computers support is called a bit and can assume the value 0 or 1.
- Digits, letters and special symbols are referred to as characters. The set of all characters used to write programs and represent data items on a particular computer is that computer's character set.
- Bytes are composed of eight bits
- C# uses the Unicode character set which uses two bytes to represent each character.
- A field is a group of characters that conveys meaning. Typically, a record is composed of several related fields.
- A file is a group of related records.
- At least one field in each record is chosen as a record key, which identifies a record as belonging to a particular person or entity and distinguishes that record from all others.
- The most common type of file organization is a sequential file, in which records typically are stored in order by record-key field.

Section 17.3 Files and Streams
- C# views each file as a sequential stream of bytes.
- Files are opened by creating an object that has a stream associated with it.
- Streams provide communication channels between files and programs.
- To perform file processing in C#, the `System.IO` namespace must be imported.
- Class `Stream` provides functionality for representing streams as bytes. This class is `abstract`, so objects of this class cannot be instantiated.
- Classes `FileStream`, `MemoryStream` and `BufferedStream` inherit from class `Stream`.
- Class `FileStream` can be used to read data to and write data from sequential-access files.
- Class `MemoryStream` enables the transfer of data directly to and from memory—this is much faster than other types of data transfer (e.g., to and from disk).

- Class BufferedStream uses buffering to transfer data to or from a stream. Buffering enhances I/O performance by directing each output operation to a buffer that's large enough to hold the data from many outputs. Then the actual transfer to the output device is performed in one large physical output operation each time the buffer fills. Buffering can also be used to speed input operations.

Section 17.4 Classes *File and Directory*

- Information on computers is stored in files, which are organized in directories. Classes File and Directory enable programs to manipulate files and directories on disk.

- Class File provides static methods for determining information about files and can be used to open files for reading or writing.

- Class Directory provides static methods for manipulating directories.

- The DirectoryInfo object returned by Directory method CreateDirectory contains information about a directory. Much of the information contained in class DirectoryInfo also can be accessed via the methods of class Directory.

- File method Exists determines whether a string is the name and path of an existing file.

- A StreamReader reads text from a file. Its constructor takes a string containing the name of the file to open and its path. StreamReader method ReadToEnd reads the entire contents of a file.

- Directory method Exists determines whether a string is the name of an existing directory.

- Directory method GetDirectories obtains a string array containing the names of subdirectories in the specified directory.

- Directory method GetFiles returns a string array containing file names in the specified directory.

- Path method GetExtension obtains the extension for the specified file name.

- A Dictionary (namespace System.Collections.Generic) is a collection of key/value pairs, in which each key has a corresponding value. Class Dictionary is a generic class like class List.

- Dictionary method ContainsKey determines whether the specified key exists in the Dictionary.

- Dictionary method Add inserts a key/value pair into a Dictionary.

- File method Delete removes the specified file from disk.

- Dictionary property Keys returns all the keys in a Dictionary.

- Dictionary method Clear deletes the contents of a Dictionary.

Section 17.5 *Creating a Sequential-Access Text File*

- C# imposes no structure on files. You must structure files to meet your application's requirements.

- A SaveFileDialog is a modal dialog.

- A StreamWriter's constructor receives a FileStream that specifies the file in which to write text.

Section 17.6 *Reading Data from a Sequential-Access Text File*

- Data is stored in files so that it can be retrieved for processing when it's needed.

- To retrieve data sequentially from a file, programs normally start from the beginning of the file, reading consecutively until the desired data is found. It sometimes is necessary to process a file sequentially several times during the execution of a program.

- An OpenFileDialog allows a user to select files to open. Method ShowDialog displays the dialog.

Section 17.7 *Case Study: Credit Inquiry Program*

- Stream method Seek moves the file-position pointer in a file. You specify the number of bytes it should be offset from the file's beginning, end or current position. The part of the file you want to be offset from is chosen using constants from the SeekOrigin enumeration.

Section 17.8 Serialization

- A serialized object is represented as a sequence of bytes that includes the object's data, as well as information about the object's type and the types of data stored in the object.

- After a serialized object has been written to a file, it can be read from the file and deserialized (recreated in memory).

- Class `BinaryFormatter` (namespace `System.Runtime.Serialization.Formatters.Binary`), which supports the `ISerializable` interface, enables entire objects to be read from or written to a stream.

- `BinaryFormatter` methods `Serialize` and `Deserialize` write objects to and read objects from streams, respectively.

- Both method `Serialize` and method `Deserialize` require a `Stream` object (e.g., the `FileStream`) as a parameter so that the `BinaryFormatter` can access the correct file.

Section 17.9 Creating a Sequential-Access File Using Object Serialization

- Classes that are marked with the `Serializable` attribute or implement the `iSerializable` interface indicate to the CLR that objects of the class can be serialized. Objects that we wish to write to or read from a stream must include this attribute or implement the `iSerializable` interface in their class definitions.

- In a serializable class, you must ensure that every instance variable of the class is also serializable. By default, all simple-type variables are serializable. For reference-type variables, you must check the declaration of the class (and possibly its superclasses) to ensure that the type is serializable.

Section 17.10 Reading and Deserializing Data from a Binary File

- Method `Deserialize` (of class `BinaryFormatter`) reads a serialized object from a stream and reforms the object in memory.

- Method `Deserialize` returns a reference of type `object` which must be cast to the appropriate type to manipulate the object.

- If an error occurs during deserialization, a `SerializationException` is thrown.

Terminology

Add method of class `Dictionary`
binary digit (bit)
`BinaryFormatter` class
bit manipulation
buffer
`BufferedStream` class
buffering
`Close` method of class `StreamWriter`
closing a file
`ContainsKey` method of class `Dictionary`
`Copy` method of class `File`
`Create` method of class `File`
`CreateDirectory` method of class `Directory`
`CreateText` method of class `File`
data hierarchy
database
database management system (DBMS)
`Delete` method of class `Directory`
`Delete` method of class `File`

`Deserialize` method of class `BinaryFormatter`
deserialized object
`Dictionary` class
`Directory` class
`DirectoryInfo` class
end-of-file marker
`Error` property of class `Console`
`Exists` method of class `Directory`
field
file
`File` class
file-processing programs
`FileAccess` enumeration
`FileNotFoundException` class
file-position pointer
`FileStream` class
fixed-length records
`GetCreationTime` method of class `Directory`
`GetCreationTime` method of class `File`

GetDirectories method of class Directory
GetExtension method of class Path
GetFiles method of class Directory
GetLastAccessTime method of class Directory
GetLastAccessTime method of class File
GetLastWriteTime method of class Directory
GetLastWriteTime method of class File
In property of class Console
IOException
ISerializable interface
logical output operator
MemoryStream class
modal dialog
Move method of class Directory
Move method of class File
object serialization
Open method of class File
OpenFileDialog class
OpenRead method of class File
OpenText method of class File
OpenWrite method of class File
Out property of class Console
Path class
persistent data
physical output operation
Read method of class Console
ReadLine method of class Console

ReadLine method of class StreamReader
record
record key
SaveFileDialog class
Seek method of class Stream
SeekOrigin enumeration
sequential-access file
Serializable attribute
SerializationException
Serialize method of class BinaryFormatter
ShowDialog method of class SaveFileDialog
standard error stream object
standard input stream object
standard output stream object
Stream class
stream of bytes
StreamReader class
StreamWriter class
System.IO namespace
System.Runtime.Serialization.
    Formatters.Binary namespace
TextReader class
TextWriter class
transaction-processing system
Write method of class StreamWriter
WriteLine method of class StreamWriter

Self-Review Exercises

17.1 State whether each of the following is *true* or *false*. If *false*, explain why.
a) Creating instances of classes File and Directory is impossible.
b) Typically, a sequential file stores records in order by the record-key field.
c) Class StreamReader inherits from class Stream.
d) Any class can be serialized to a file.
e) Method Seek of class FileStream always seeks relative to the beginning of a file.
f) Classes StreamReader and StreamWriter are used with sequential-access files.
g) You cannot instantiate objects of type Stream.

17.2 Fill in the blanks in each of the following statements:
a) Ultimately, all data items processed by a computer are reduced to combinations of _____ and _____.
b) The smallest data item a computer can process is called a(n) _____.
c) A(n) _____ is a group of related records.
d) Digits, letters and special symbols are collectively referred to as _____.
e) A group of related files is called a(n) _____.
f) StreamReader method _____ reads a line of text from a file.
g) StreamWriter method _____ writes a line of text to a file.
h) Method Serialize of class BinaryFormatter takes a(n) _____ and a(n) _____ as arguments.
i) The _____ namespace contains most of C#'s file-processing classes.
j) The _____ namespace contains the BinaryFormatter class.

Answers to Self-Review Exercises

17.1   a) True. b) True. c) False. Class `StreamReader` inherits from class `TextReader`. d) False. Only classes that implement interface `ISerializable` or are declared with the `Serializable` attribute can be serialized. e) False. It seeks relative to the `SeekOrigin` enumeration member that's passed as one of the arguments. f) True. g) True.

17.2   a) 0s, 1s. b) bit. c) file. d) characters. e) database. f) `ReadLine`. g) `WriteLine`. h) `Stream`, object. i) `System.IO`. j) `System.Runtime.Serialization.Formatters.Binary`.

Exercises

17.3   *(File of Student Grades)* Create a program that stores student grades in a text file. The file should contain the name, ID number, class taken and grade of every student. Allow the user to load a grade file and display its contents in a read-only `TextBox`. The entries should be displayed in the following format:

```
LastName, FirstName:  ID#  Class  Grade
```

We list some sample data below:

```
Jones, Bob: 1 "Introduction to Computer Science" "A-"
Johnson, Sarah: 2 "Data Structures" "B+"
Smith, Sam: 3 "Data Structures" "C"
```

17.4   *(Serializing and Deserializing)* Modify the previous program to use objects of a class that can be serialized to and deserialized from a file.

17.5   *(Extending `StreamReader` and `StreamWriter`)* Extend classes `StreamReader` and `StreamWriter`. Make the class that derives from `StreamReader` have methods `ReadInteger`, `ReadBoolean` and `ReadString`. Make the class that derives from `StreamWriter` have methods `WriteInteger`, `WriteBoolean` and `WriteString`. Think about how to design the writing methods so that the reading methods will be able to read what was written. Design `WriteInteger` and `WriteBoolean` to write strings of uniform size so that `ReadInteger` and `ReadBoolean` can read those values accurately. Make sure `ReadString` and `WriteString` use the same character(s) to separate `strings`.

17.6   *(Reading and Writing Account Information)* Create a program that combines the ideas of Fig. 17.9 and Fig. 17.11 to allow a user to write records to and read records from a file. Add an extra field of type `bool` to the record to indicate whether the account has overdraft protection.

17.7   *(Telephone-Number Word Generator)* Standard telephone keypads contain the digits zero through nine. The numbers two through nine each have three letters associated with them (Fig. 17.16). Many people find it difficult to memorize phone numbers, so they use the correspondence between digits and letters to develop seven-letter words that correspond to their phone numbers. For example, a person whose telephone number is 686-2377 might use the correspondence indicated in Fig. 17.16 to develop the seven-letter word "NUMBERS." Every seven-letter word corresponds to exactly one seven-digit telephone number. A restaurant wishing to increase its takeout business could surely do so with the number 825-3688 (i.e., "TAKEOUT").

Every seven-letter phone number corresponds to many different seven-letter words. Unfortunately, most of these words represent unrecognizable juxtapositions of letters. It's possible, however, that the owner of a barbershop would be pleased to know that the shop's telephone number, 424-7288, corresponds to "HAIRCUT." The owner of a liquor store would no doubt be delighted to find that the store's number, 233-7226, corresponds to "BEERCAN." A veterinarian with the phone number 738-2273 would be pleased to know that the number corresponds to the letters "PETCARE." An automotive dealership would be pleased to know that its phone number, 639-2277, corresponds to "NEWCARS."

Digit	Letter	Digit	Letter
2	A B C	6	M N O
3	D E F	7	P R S
4	G H I	8	T U V
5	J K L	9	W X Y Z

Fig. 17.16 | Letters that correspond to the numbers on a telephone keypad .

Write a GUI program that, given a seven-digit number, uses a `StreamWriter` object to write to a file every possible seven-letter word combination corresponding to that number. There are 2,187 (3^7) such combinations. Avoid phone numbers with the digits 0 and 1.

17.8 *(Student Poll)* Figure 8.8 contains an array of survey responses that's hard-coded into the program. Suppose we wish to process survey results that are stored in a file. First, create a Windows `Form` that prompts the user for survey responses and outputs each response to a file. Use `StreamWriter` to create a file called `numbers.txt`. Each integer should be written using method `Write`. Then add a `TextBox` that will output the frequency of survey responses. You should modify the code in Fig. 8.8 to read the survey responses from `numbers.txt`. The responses should be read from the file by using a `StreamReader`. Class `string`'s `split` method should be used to split the input string into separate responses, then each response should be converted to an integer. The program should continue to read responses until it reaches the end of file. The results should be output to the `TextBox`.

Making a Difference Exercise

17.9 *(Phishing Scanner)* Phishing is a form of identity theft in which, in an e-mail, a sender posing as a trustworthy source attempts to acquire private information, such as your user names, passwords, credit-card numbers and social security number. Phishing e-mails claiming to be from popular banks, credit-card companies, auction sites, social networks and online payment services may look quite legitimate. These fraudulent messages often provide links to spoofed (fake) websites where you're asked to enter sensitive information.

Visit McAfee® (www.mcafee.com/us/threat_center/anti_phishing/phishing_top10.html), Security Extra (www.securityextra.com/), www.snopes.com and other websites to find lists of the top phishing scams. Also check out the Anti-Phishing Working Group (www.antiphishing.org/), and the FBI's Cyber Investigations website (www.fbi.gov/cyberinvest/cyberhome.htm), where you'll find information about the latest scams and how to protect yourself.

Create a list of 30 words, phrases and company names commonly found in phishing messages. Assign a point value to each based on your estimate of its likeliness to be in a phishing message (e.g., one point if it's somewhat likely, two points if moderately likely, or three points if highly likely). Write a program that scans a file of text for these terms and phrases. For each occurrence of a keyword or phrase within the text file, add the assigned point value to the total points for that word or phrase. For each keyword or phrase found, output one line with the word or phrase, the number of occurrences and the point total. Then show the point total for the entire message. Does your program assign a high point total to some actual phishing e-mails you've received? Does it assign a high point total to some legitimate e-mails you've received? [*Note:* If you search online for "sample phishing emails," you'll find many examples of text that you can test with this program.]

Databases and LINQ

*Now go, write it before them in
a table, and note it in a book,
that it may be for the time to
come for ever and ever.*
—Isaiah 30:8

*It is a capital mistake to
theorize before one has data.*
—Arthur Conan Doyle

Objectives

In this chapter you'll learn:

- The relational database model.

- To use LINQ to retrieve and manipulate data from a database.

- To add data sources to projects.

- To use the Object Relational Designer to create LINQ to SQL classes.

- To use the IDE's drag-and-drop capabilities to display database tables in applications.

- To use data binding to move data seamlessly between GUI controls and databases.

- To create Master/Detail views that enable you to select a record and display its details.

18.1 Introduction

A **database** is an organized collection of data. A **database management system (DBMS)** provides mechanisms for storing, organizing, retrieving and modifying data. Today's most popular DBMSs manage relational databases, which organize data simply as tables with *rows* and *columns*.

Some popular proprietary DBMSs are Microsoft SQL Server, Oracle, Sybase and IBM DB2. PostgreSQL and MySQL are popular *open-source* DBMSs that can be downloaded and used *freely* by anyone. In this chapter, we use Microsoft's free **SQL Server Express**, which is installed with Visual C# Express and Visual Studio. It can also be downloaded separately from Microsoft (www.microsoft.com/express/sql).

SQL Server Express provides many features of Microsoft's full (fee-based) SQL Server product, but has some limitations, such as a maximum database size. A SQL Server Express database can be easily migrated to a full version of SQL Server—we did this with our deitel.com website once our database became too large for SQL Server Express. You can learn more about the SQL Server versions at bit.ly/SQLServerEditions.

Today's most popular database systems are relational databases. A language called **Structured Query Language (SQL)**—pronounced "sequel"—is an international standard used with relational databases to perform **queries** (that is, to request information that satisfies given criteria) and to manipulate data. For years, programs that accessed a relational database passed SQL queries as Strings to the database management system, then processed the results.

A logical extension of querying and manipulating data in databases is to perform similar operations on any sources of data, such as arrays, collections (like the Items collection of a ListBox) and files. Chapter 9 introduced LINQ to Objects and used it to to manipulate data stored in arrays. **LINQ to SQL** allows you to manipulate data stored in a *SQL Server* or *SQL Server Express* relational database. The SQL in LINQ to SQL stands for *SQL Server, not Structured Query Language*. As with LINQ to Objects, the IDE provides *IntelliSense* for your LINQ to SQL queries.

This chapter introduces general concepts of relational databases, then explores LINQ to SQL and the IDE's tools for working with databases. In later chapters, you'll see other practical database and LINQ to SQL applications, such as a web-based bookstore and a web-based airline reservation service. Databases are at the heart of almost all "industrial strength" applications.

[*Note:* In previous editions of this book, this chapter included an introduction to Structured Query Language (SQL). We now perform all of the database interactions in this chapter using LINQ, so we've moved the introduction to SQL to this book's website at www.deitel.com/books/csharphtp4/.]

18.2 Relational Databases

A **relational database** organizes data simply in **tables**. Figure 18.1 illustrates a sample Employees table that might be used in a personnel system. The table stores the attributes of employees. Tables are composed of **rows** (also called records) and **columns** (also called **fields**) in which values are stored. This table consists of six rows (one per employee) and five columns (one per attribute). The attributes are the employee's ID, name, department, salary and location. The ID column of each row is the table's **primary key**—a column (or group of columns) requiring a *unique* value that cannot be duplicated in other rows. This guarantees that each primary key value can be used to identify *one* row. A primary key composed of two or more columns is known as a **composite key**. Good examples of primary-key columns in other applications are a book's ISBN number in a book information system or a part number in an inventory system—values in each of these columns must be unique. LINQ to SQL *requires every table to have a primary key* to support updating the data in tables. The rows in Fig. 18.1 are displayed in ascending order by primary key. But they could be listed in decreasing (descending) order or in no particular order at all.

Table Employees

	ID	Name	Department	Salary	Location
	23603	Jones	413	1100	New Jersey
	24568	Kerwin	413	2000	New Jersey
Row	34589	Larson	642	1800	Los Angeles
	35761	Myers	611	1400	Orlando
	47132	Neumann	413	9000	New Jersey
	78321	Stephens	611	8500	Orlando

Primary key   Column

Fig. 18.1 | Employees table sample data.

Each *column* represents a different data *attribute*. Some column values may be duplicated between rows. For example, three different rows in the Employees table's Department column contain the number 413, indicating that these employees work in the same department.

You can use LINQ to SQL to define queries that select subsets of the data from a table. For example, a program might select data from the Employees table to create a query result that shows where each department is located, in increasing order by Department number (Fig. 18.2).

Department	Location
413	New Jersey
611	Orlando
642	Los Angeles

Fig. 18.2 | Distinct Department and Location data from the Employees table.

18.3 A Books Database

We now consider a simple Books database that stores information about some Deitel publications. First, we overview the database's tables. A database's tables, their fields and the relationships among them are collectively known as a **database schema**. LINQ to SQL uses a database's schema to define classes that enable you to interact with the database. Next, we show how to use LINQ to SQL to retrieve information from the Books database. The database file—Books.mdf—is provided with this chapter's examples. SQL Server database files have the .mdf ("master data file") file-name extension.

Authors *Table of the* **Books** *Database*
The database consists of three tables: Authors, Titles and AuthorISBN. The Authors table (described in Fig. 18.3) consists of three columns that maintain each author's unique ID number, first name and last name, respectively. Figure 18.4 contains the data from the Authors table.

Column	Description
AuthorID	Author's ID number in the database. In the Books database, this integer column is defined as an **identity** column, also known as an **autoincremented** column—for each row inserted in the table, the AuthorID value is increased by 1 automatically to ensure that each row has a unique AuthorID. This is the *primary key*.
FirstName	Author's first name (a string).
LastName	Author's last name (a string).

Fig. 18.3 | Authors table of the Books database.

AuthorID	FirstName	LastName
1	Harvey	Deitel
2	Paul	Deitel
3	Greg	Ayer
4	Dan	Quirk

Fig. 18.4 | Data from the Authors table of the Books database.

Titles *Table of the* Books *Database*

The Titles table (described in Fig. 18.5) consists of four columns that maintain information about each book in the database, including its ISBN, title, edition number and copyright year. Figure 18.6 contains the data from the Titles table.

Column	Description
ISBN	ISBN of the book (a string). The table's primary key. ISBN is an abbreviation for "International Standard Book Number"—a numbering scheme that publishers worldwide use to give every book a *unique* identification number.
Title	Title of the book (a string).
EditionNumber	Edition number of the book (an integer).
Copyright	Copyright year of the book (a string).

Fig. 18.5 | Titles table of the Books database.

ISBN	Title	Edition-Number	Copy-right
0131752421	Internet & World Wide Web How to Program	4	2008
0132222205	Java How to Program	7	2007
0132404168	C How to Program	5	2007
0136053033	Simply Visual Basic 2008	3	2009
013605305X	Visual Basic 2008 How to Program	4	2009
013605322X	Visual C# 2008 How to Program	3	2009
0136151574	Visual C++ 2008 How to Program	2	2008
0136152503	C++ How to Program	6	2008

Fig. 18.6 | Data from the Titles table of the Books database.

AuthorISBN *Table of the* Books *Database*

The AuthorISBN table (described in Fig. 18.7) consists of two columns that maintain ISBNs for each book and their corresponding authors' ID numbers. This table associates authors with their books. The AuthorID column is a **foreign key**—a column in this table that matches the primary-key column in another table (that is, AuthorID in the Authors table). The ISBN column is also a foreign key—it matches the primary-key column (that is, ISBN) in the Titles table. Together the AuthorID and ISBN columns in this table form a *composite primary key*. Every row in this table uniquely matches one author to one book's ISBN. Figure 18.8 contains the data from the AuthorISBN table of the Books database.

Foreign Keys

A database might consist of many tables. A goal when designing a database is to minimize the amount of duplicated data among the database's tables. Foreign keys, which are specified when a database table is created, link the data in multiple tables.

Column	Description
AuthorID	The author's ID number, a foreign key to the Authors table.
ISBN	The ISBN for a book, a foreign key to the Titles table.

Fig. 18.7 | AuthorISBN table of the Books database.

AuthorID	ISBN	AuthorID	ISBN
1	0131752421	*(continued)*	
1	0132222205	2	0132222205
1	0132404168	2	0132404168
1	0136053033	2	0136053033
1	013605305X	2	013605305X
1	013605322X	2	013605322X
1	0136151574	2	0136151574
1	0136152503	2	0136152503
2	0131752421	3	0136053033
(continued)		4	0136151574

Fig. 18.8 | Data from the AuthorISBN table of the Books database.

Every foreign-key value must appear as another table's primary-key value so the DBMS can ensure that the foreign key value is valid. For example, the DBMS ensures that the AuthorID value for a particular row of the AuthorISBN table (Fig. 18.8) is valid by checking that there is a row in the Authors table with that AuthorID as the primary key.

Foreign keys also allow related data in multiple tables to be selected from those tables—this is known as **joining** the data. There is a **one-to-many relationship** between a primary key and a corresponding foreign key (for example, one author can write many books and one book can be written by many authors). This means that a foreign key can appear *many* times in its own table but only *once* (as the primary key) in another table. For example, the ISBN 0131450913 can appear in several rows of AuthorISBN (because this book has several authors) but only once in Titles, where ISBN is the primary key.

Entity-Relationship Diagram for the Books Database

Figure 18.9 is an **entity-relationship (ER) diagram** for the Books database. This diagram shows the tables in the database and the relationships among them. The first compartment in each box contains the table's name. The names in italic font are primary keys— *AuthorID* in the Authors table, AuthorID and ISBN in the AuthorISBN table, and ISBN in the Titles table. Every row *must* have a value in the primary-key column (or group of columns), and the value of the key must be *unique* in the table; otherwise, the DBMS will report an error. The names AuthorID and ISBN in the AuthorISBN table are *both* italic— together these form a *composite primary key* for the AuthorISBN table.

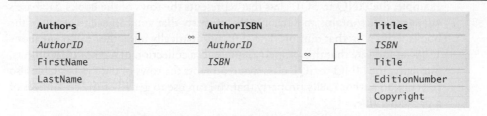

Fig. 18.9 | Entity-relationship diagram for the `Books` database.

The lines connecting the tables in Fig. 18.9 represent the relationships among the tables. Consider the line between the `Authors` and `AuthorISBN` tables. On the `Authors` end of the line, there's a `1`, and on the `AuthorISBN` end, an infinity symbol (∞). This indicates a one-to-many relationship—for *each* author in the `Authors` table, there can be an *arbitrary number* of ISBNs for books written by that author in the `AuthorISBN` table (that is, an author can write any number of books). Note that the relationship line links the `AuthorID` column in the `Authors` table (where `AuthorID` is the primary key) to the `AuthorID` column in the `AuthorISBN` table (where `AuthorID` is a foreign key)—the line between the tables links the primary key to the matching foreign key.

The line between the `Titles` and `AuthorISBN` tables illustrates a one-to-many relationship—one book can be written by many authors. Note that the line between the tables links the primary key `ISBN` in table `Titles` to the corresponding foreign key in table `AuthorISBN`. The relationships in Fig. 18.9 illustrate that the sole purpose of the `AuthorISBN` table is to provide a **many-to-many relationship** between the `Authors` and `Titles` tables—an author can write *many* books, and a book can have *many* authors.

18.4 LINQ to SQL

LINQ to SQL enables you to access data in *SQL Server databases* using the same LINQ syntax introduced in Chapter 9. You interact with the database via classes that are automatically generated from the database schema by the IDE's **LINQ to SQL Designer**. For each table in the database, the IDE creates two classes:

- A class that represents a row of the table: This class contains properties for each column in the table. LINQ to SQL creates objects of this class—called **row objects**—to store the data from individual rows of the table.

- A class that represents the table: LINQ to SQL creates an object of this class to store a collection of row objects that correspond to all of the rows in the table.

Relationships between tables are also taken into account in the generated classes:

- In a row object's class, an additional property is created for each foreign key. This property returns the row object of the corresponding primary key in another table. For example, the class that represents the rows of the `Books` database's `AuthorISBN` table also contains an `Author` property and a `Title` property—from any `AuthorISBN` row object, you can access the full author and title information.

- In the class for a row object, an additional property is created for the collection of row objects with foreign-keys that reference the row object's primary key. For example, the LINQ to SQL class that represents the rows of the Books database's Authors table contains an AuthorISBNs property that you can use to get all of the books written by that author. The IDE automatically adds the "s" to "Author-ISBN" to indicate that this property represents a collection of AuthorISBN objects. Similarly, the LINQ to SQL class that represents the rows of the Titles table also contains an AuthorISBNs property that you can use to get all of the co-authors of a particular title.

Once generated, the LINQ to SQL classes have full *IntelliSense* support in the IDE. Section 18.7 demonstrates queries that use the relationships among the Books database's tables to join data.

IQueryable *Interface*
LINQ to SQL works through the **IQueryable interface**, which inherits from the IEnumerable interface introduced in Chapter 9. When a LINQ to SQL query on an IQueryable object executes against the database, the results are loaded into objects of the corresponding LINQ to SQL classes for convenient access in your code.

DataContext *Class*
All LINQ to SQL queries occur via a **DataContext class**, which controls the flow of data between the program and the database. A specific DataContext derived class, which inherits from the class System.Data.Linq.DataContext, is created when the LINQ to SQL classes representing each row of the table are generated by the IDE. This derived class has properties for each table in the database, which can be used as data sources in LINQ queries. Any changes made to the DataContext can be saved back to the database using the DataContext's **SubmitChanges method**, so with LINQ to SQL you can modify the database's contents.

18.5 Querying a Database with LINQ

In this section, we demonstrate how to *connect* to a database, *query* it and *display* the results of the query. There is little code in this section—the IDE provides *visual programming* tools and *wizards* that simplify accessing data in applications. These tools establish database connections and create the objects necessary to view and manipulate the data through Windows Forms GUI controls—a technique known as **data binding**.

Our first example performs a simple query on the Books database from Section 18.3. We retrieve the entire Authors table and use data binding to display its data in a **DataGridView**—a control from namespace System.Windows.Forms that can display data from a data source in tabular format. The basic steps we'll perform are:

- Connect to the Books database.
- Create the LINQ to SQL classes required to use the database.
- Add the Authors table as a data source.
- Drag the Authors table data source onto the **Design** view to create a GUI for displaying the table's data.
- Add a few statements to the program to allow it to interact with the database.

The GUI for the program is shown in Fig. 18.10. All of the controls in this GUI are automatically generated when we drag a data source that represents the Authors table onto the Form in **Design** view. The BindingNavigator at the top of the window is a collection of controls that allow you to navigate through the records in the DataGridView that fills the rest of the window. The BindingNavigator controls also allow you to add records, delete records and save your changes to the database. If you add a new record, note that empty values are not allowed in the Books database, so attempting to save a new record without specifying a value for each field will cause an error.

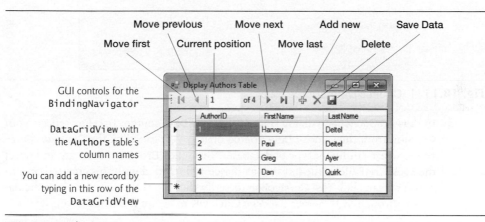

Fig. 18.10 | GUI for the **Display Authors Table** application.

18.5.1 Creating LINQ to SQL Classes

This section presents the steps required to create LINQ to SQL classes for a database.

Step 1: Creating the Project
Create a new **Windows Forms Application** named DisplayTable. Change the name of the source file to DisplayAuthorsTable.cs. The IDE updates the Form's class name to match the source file. Set the Form's **Text** property to Display Authors Table.

Step 2: Adding a Database to the Project and Connecting to the Database
To interact with a database, you must create a **connection** to the database. This will also give you the option of copying the database file to your project.

1. In Visual C# 2010 Express, select **View > Other Windows > Database Explorer** to display the **Database Explorer** window. By default, it appears on the left side of the IDE. If you're using a full version of Visual Studio, select **View > Server Explorer** to display the **Server Explorer**. From this point forward, we'll refer to the **Database Explorer**. If you have a full version of Visual Studio, substitute **Server Explorer** for **Database Explorer** in the steps.

2. Click the **Connect to Database** icon ( ) at the top of the **Database Explorer**. If the **Choose Data Source** dialog appears (Fig. 18.11), select **Microsoft SQL Server Database File** from the **Data source:** list. If you check the **Always use this selection** CheckBox, the IDE will use this type of database file by default when you connect to databases in the future. Click **Continue** to display the **Add Connection** dialog.

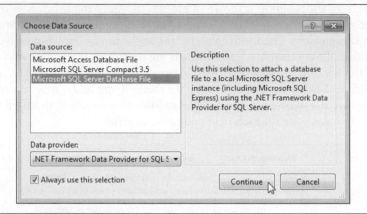

Fig. 18.11 | **Choose Data Source** dialog.

3. In the **Add Connection** dialog (Fig. 18.12), the **Data source:** TextBox reflects your selection from the **Choose Data Source** dialog. You can click the **Change...** Button to select a different type of database. Next, click **Browse...** to locate and select the Books.mdf file in the Databases directory included with this chapter's examples. You can click **Test Connection** to verify that the IDE can connect to the database through SQL Server Express. Click **OK** to create the connection.

Error-Prevention Tip 18.1

Ensure that no other program is using the database file before you attempt to add it to the project. Connecting to the database requires exclusive access.

Fig. 18.12 | **Add Connection** dialog.

Step 3: Generating the LINQ to SQL classes
After adding the database, you must select the database tables from which the LINQ to SQL classes will be created. LINQ to SQL uses the database's schema to help define the classes.

1. Right click the project name in the **Solution Explorer** and select **Add > New Item...** to display the **Add New Item** dialog. Select the **LINQ to SQL Classes** template, name the new item Books.dbml and click the **Add** button. The **Object Relational Designer** window will appear (Fig. 18.13). You can also double click the Books.dbml file in the **Solution Explorer** to open the **Object Relational Designer**.

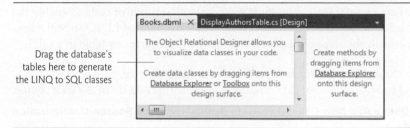

Drag the database's tables here to generate the LINQ to SQL classes

Fig. 18.13 | **Object Relational Designer** window.

2. Expand the Books.mdf database node in the **Database Explorer**, then expand the **Tables** node. Drag the Authors, Titles and AuthorISBN tables onto the **Object Relational Designer**. The IDE prompts whether you want to copy the database to the project directory. Select **Yes**. The **Object Relational Designer** will display the tables that you dragged from the **Database Explorer** (Fig. 18.14). Notice that the **Object Relational Designer** named the class that represents items from the Authors table as Author, and named the class that represents the Titles table as Title. This is because one object of the Author class represents one author—a single row from the Authors table. Similarly, one object of the Title class represents one book—a single row from the Titles table. Because the class name Title conflicts with one of the column names in the Titles table, the IDE renames that column's property in the Title class as Title1.

3. Save the Books.dbml file.

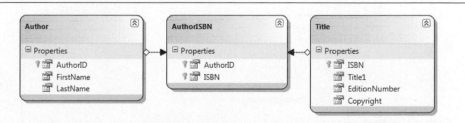

Fig. 18.14 | **Object Relational Designer** window showing the selected tables from the Books database and their relationships.

When you save Books.dbml, the IDE generates the LINQ to SQL classes that you can use to interact with the database. These include a class for each table you selected from the database and a derived class of DataContext named BooksDataContext that enables you to programmatically interact with the database.

Error-Prevention Tip 18.2

Be sure to save the file in the Object Relational Designer before trying to use the LINQ to SQL classes in code. The IDE does not generate the classes until you save the file.

18.5.2 Data Bindings Between Controls and the LINQ to SQL Classes

The IDE's automatic data binding capabilities simplify creating applications that can view and modify the data in a database. You must write a small amount of code to enable the autogenerated data-binding classes to interact with the autogenerated LINQ to SQL classes. You'll now perform the steps to display the contents of the Authors table in a GUI.

Step 1: Adding the **Author** LINQ to SQL Class as a Data Source
To use the LINQ to SQL classes for data binding, you must first add them as a data source.

1. Select Data > Add New Data Source... to display the **Data Source Configuration Wizard**.

2. The LINQ to SQL classes are used to create objects representing the tables in the database, so we'll use an **Object** data source. In the dialog, select **Object** and click **Next >**. Expand the tree view as shown in Fig. 18.15 and ensure that **Author** is checked. An object of this class will be used as the data source.

3. Click **Finish**.

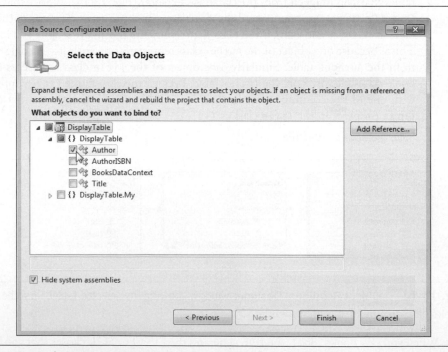

Fig. 18.15 | Selecting the Author LINQ to SQL class as the data source.

The Authors table in the database is now a data source that can be used by the bindings. Open the **Data Sources window** (Fig. 18.16) by selecting **Data > Show Data Sources**—the window is displayed at the left side of the IDE. You can see the Author class that you added in the previous step. The columns of the database's Authors table should appear below it, as well as an AuthorISBNs entry representing the relationship between the database's Authors and AuthorISBN tables.

Fig. 18.16 | **Data Sources** window showing the Author class as a data source.

Step 2: Creating GUI Elements
Next, you'll use the **Design** view to create a GUI control that can display the Authors table's data.

1. Switch to **Design** view for the DisplayAuthorsTable class.

2. Click the **Author** node in the **Data Sources** window—it should change to a drop-down list. Open the drop-down by clicking the down arrow and ensure that the DataGridView option is selected—this is the GUI control that will be used to display and interact with the data.

3. Drag the **Author** node from the **Data Sources** window onto the Form in **Design** view.

The IDE creates a DataGridView (Fig. 18.17) with the correct column names and a **BindingNavigator** (authorBindingNavigator) that contains Buttons for moving between entries, adding entries, deleting entries and saving changes to the database. The IDE also generates a **BindingSource** (authorBindingSource), which handles the transfer of data between the data source and the data-bound controls on the Form. Nonvisual components such as the BindingSource and the non-visual aspects of the BindingNavigator appear in the component tray—the gray region below the Form in **Design** view. We use the default names for automatically generated components throughout this chapter to show exactly what the IDE creates. To make the **DataGridView** occupy the entire window, select the DataGridView, then use the **Properties** window to set the Dock property to Fill.

Step 3: Connecting the BooksDataContext to the authorBindingSource
The final step is to connect the BooksDataContext (created with the LINQ to SQL classes in Section 18.5.1) to the authorBindingSource (created earlier in this section), so that the application can interact with the database. Figure 18.18 shows the small amount of code needed to obtain data from the database and to save any changes that the user makes to the data back into the database.

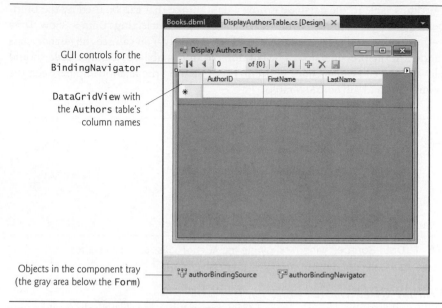

GUI controls for the
BindingNavigator

DataGridView with
the Authors table's
column names

Objects in the component tray
(the gray area below the Form)

Fig. 18.17 | Component tray holds nonvisual components in **Design** view.

```
 1   // Fig. 18.18: DisplayAuthorsTable.cs
 2   // Displaying data from a database table in a DataGridView.
 3   using System;
 4   using System.Linq;
 5   using System.Windows.Forms;
 6
 7   namespace DisplayTable
 8   {
 9      public partial class DisplayAuthorsTable : Form
10      {
11         // constructor
12         public DisplayAuthorsTable()
13         {
14            InitializeComponent();
15         } // end constructor
16
17         // LINQ to SQL data context
18         private BooksDataContext database = new BooksDataContext();
19
20         // load data from database into DataGridView
21         private void DisplayAuthorsTable_Load( object sender, EventArgs e )
22         {
23            // use LINQ to order the data for display
24            authorBindingSource.DataSource =
25               from author in database.Authors
26               orderby author.AuthorID
27               select author;
28         } // end method DisplayAuthorsTable_Load
```

Fig. 18.18 | Displaying data from a database table in a DataGridView. (Part 1 of 2.)

```
29
30          // click event handler for the Save Button in the
31          // BindingNavigator saves the changes made to the data
32          private void authorBindingNavigatorSaveItem_Click(
33             object sender, EventArgs e )
34          {
35             Validate(); // validate input fields
36             authorBindingSource.EndEdit(); // indicate edits are complete
37             database.SubmitChanges(); // write changes to database file
38          } // end method authorBindingNavigatorSaveItem_Click
39       } // end class DisplayAuthorsTable
40    } // end namespace DisplayTable
```

Fig. 18.18 | Displaying data from a database table in a `DataGridView`. (Part 2 of 2.)

As mentioned in Section 18.4, a `DataContext` object is used to interact with the database. The `BooksDataContext` class was automatically generated by the IDE when you created the LINQ to SQL classes to allow access to the Books database. Line 18 creates an object of this class named `database`.

Create the Form's `Load` handler by double clicking the Form's title bar in **Design** view. We allow data to move between the `DataContext` and the `BindingSource` by creating a LINQ query that extracts data from the `BooksDataContext`'s `Authors` property (lines 25–27), which corresponds to the `Authors` table in the database. The `authorBindingSource`'s **DataSource property** (line 24) is set to the results of this query. The `authorBinding-Source` uses the `DataSource` to extract data from the database and to populate the `DataGridView`.

Step 4: Saving Modifications Back to the Database
If the user modifies the data in the `DataGridView`, we'd also like to save the modifications in the database. By default, the `BindingNavigator`'s **Save Data** Button (■) is disabled. To enable it, right click this `Button`'s icon and select **Enabled**. Then, double click the icon to create its `Click` event handler.

Saving the data entered into the `DataGridView` back to the database is a three-step process (lines 35–37). First, all controls on the form are validated (line 35)—if any of the controls have event handlers for the `Validating` event, those execute. You typically handle this event to determine whether a control's contents are valid. Second, line 36 calls **EndEdit** on the `authorBindingSource`, which forces it to save any pending changes in the `BooksDataContext`. Finally, line 37 calls `SubmitChanges` on the `BooksDataContext` to store the changes in the database. For efficiency, LINQ to SQL saves only data that has changed.

Step 5: Configuring the Database File to Persist Changes

When you run the program in debug mode, the database file is overwritten with the original database file each time you execute the program. This allows you to test your program with the original content until it works correctly. When you run the program in release mode (*Ctrl + F5*), changes you make to the database persist automatically; however, if you change the code, the next time you run the program, the database will be restored to its original version. To persist changes for all executions, select the database in the **Solution Explorer** and set the **Copy to Output Directory** property in the **Properties** window to **Copy if newer**.

18.6 Dynamically Binding Query Results

Now that you've seen how to display an entire database table in a `DataGridView`, we show how to perform several different queries and display the results in a `DataGridView`. The **Display Query Results** application (Fig. 18.19) allows the user to select a query from the `ComboBox` at the bottom of the window, then displays the results of the query.

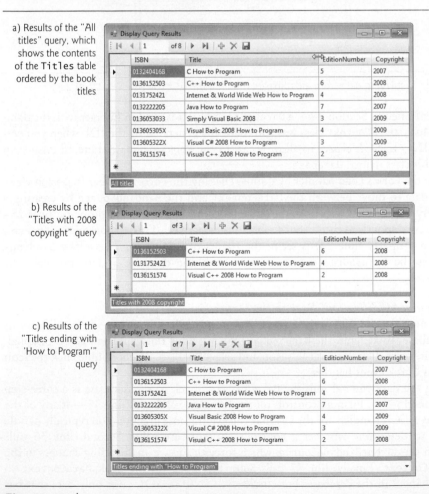

a) Results of the "All titles" query, which shows the contents of the `Titles` table ordered by the book titles

b) Results of the "Titles with 2008 copyright" query

c) Results of the "Titles ending with 'How to Program'" query

Fig. 18.19 | Sample execution of the Display Query Results application.

18.6.1 Creating the Display Query Results GUI

Perform the following steps to build the Display Query Results application's GUI.

Step 1: Creating the Project

First, create a new **Windows Forms Application** named `DisplayQueryResult`. Rename the source file to `TitleQueries.cs`. Set the Form's **Text** property to `Display Query Results`.

Step 2: Creating the LINQ to SQL Classes

Follow the steps in Section 18.5.1 to add the Books database to the project and generate the LINQ to SQL classes.

Step 3: Creating a `DataGridView` to Display the `Titles` Table

Follow *Steps 1* and *2* in Section 18.5.2 to create the data source and the `DataGridView`. In this example, select the `Title` class (rather than the `Author` class) as the data source, and drag the **Title** node from the **Data Sources** window onto the form.

Step 4: Adding a ComboBox to the Form

In **Design** view, add a `ComboBox` named `queriesComboBox` below the `DataGridView` on the Form. Users will select which query to execute from this control. Set the `ComboBox`'s **Dock** property to **Bottom** and the `DataGridView`'s **Dock** property to **Fill**.

Next, you'll add the names of the queries to the `ComboBox`. Open the `ComboBox`'s **String Collection Editor** by right clicking the `ComboBox` and selecting **Edit Items**. You can also access the **String Collection Editor** from the `ComboBox`'s smart tag menu. A **smart tag menu** provides you with quick access to common properties you might set for a control (such as the `Multiline` property of a `TextBox`), so you can set these properties directly in **Design** view, rather than in the **Properties** window. You can open a control's smart tag menu by clicking the small arrowhead (▣) that appears in the control's upper-right corner in **Design** view when the control is selected. In the **String Collection Editor**, add the following three items to `queriesComboBox`—one for each of the queries we'll create:

1. `All titles`

2. `Titles with 2008 copyright`

3. `Titles ending with "How to Program"`

18.6.2 Coding the Display Query Results Application

Next you must write code that executes the appropriate query each time the user chooses a different item from `queriesComboBox`. Double click `queriesComboBox` in **Design** view to generate a `queriesComboBox_SelectedIndexChanged` event handler (Fig. 18.20, lines 44–78) in the `TitleQueries.cs` file. In the event handler, add a `switch` statement (lines 48–75) to change the `titleBindingSource`'s `DataSource` property to a LINQ query that returns the correct set of data. The data bindings created by the IDE *automatically* update the `titleDataGridView` *each time* we change its `DataSource`. The **MoveFirst** method of the `BindingSource` (line 77) moves to the first row of the result each time a query executes. The results of the queries in lines 53–55, 61–64 and 70–73 are shown in Fig. 18.19(a), (b) and (c), respectively. [*Note:* As we mentioned previously, in the generated LINQ to SQL classes, the IDE renamed the `Title` column of the `Titles` table as `Title1` to avoid a naming conflict with the class `Title`.]

Customizing the Form's Load Event Handler

Create the `TitleQueries_Load` event handler (lines 20–28) by double clicking the title bar in **Design** view. Line 23 sets the `Log` property of the `BooksDataContext` to `Console.Out`. This causes the program to output to the console the SQL query that is sent to the database for each LINQ query. When the `Form` loads, it should display the complete list of books from the `Titles` table, sorted by title. Rather than defining the same LINQ query as in lines 53–55, we can programmatically cause the `queriesComboBox_SelectedIndexChanged` event handler to execute simply by setting the `queriesComboBox`'s `SelectedIndex` to 0 (line 27).

```
 1   // Fig. 18.20: TitleQueries.cs
 2   // Displaying the result of a user-selected query in a DataGridView.
 3   using System;
 4   using System.Linq;
 5   using System.Windows.Forms;
 6
 7   namespace DisplayQueryResult
 8   {
 9      public partial class TitleQueries : Form
10      {
11         public TitleQueries()
12         {
13            InitializeComponent();
14         } // end constructor
15
16         // LINQ to SQL data context
17         private BooksDataContext database = new BooksDataContext();
18
19         // load data from database into DataGridView
20         private void TitleQueries_Load( object sender, EventArgs e )
21         {
22            // write SQL to standard output stream
23            database.Log = Console.Out;
24
25            // set the ComboBox to show the default query that
26            // selects all books from the Titles table
27            queriesComboBox.SelectedIndex = 0;
28         } // end method TitleQueries_Load
29
30         // Click event handler for the Save Button in the
31         // BindingNavigator saves the changes made to the data
32         private void titleBindingNavigatorSaveItem_Click(
33            object sender, EventArgs e )
34         {
35            Validate(); // validate input fields
36            titleBindingSource.EndEdit(); // indicate edits are complete
37            database.SubmitChanges(); // write changes to database file
38
39            // when saving, return to "all titles" query
40            queriesComboBox.SelectedIndex = 0;
41         } // end method titleBindingNavigatorSaveItem_Click
42
```

Fig. 18.20 | Displaying the result of a user-selected query in a `DataGridView`. (Part 1 of 2.)

```
43      // loads data into titleBindingSource based on user-selected query
44      private void queriesComboBox_SelectedIndexChanged(
45         object sender, EventArgs e )
46      {
47         // set the data displayed according to what is selected
48         switch ( queriesComboBox.SelectedIndex )
49         {
50            case 0: // all titles
51               // use LINQ to order the books by title
52               titleBindingSource.DataSource =
53                  from book in database.Titles
54                  orderby book.Title1
55                  select book;
56               break;
57            case 1: // titles with 2008 copyright
58               // use LINQ to get titles with 2008
59               // copyright and sort them by title
60               titleBindingSource.DataSource =
61                  from book in database.Titles
62                  where book.Copyright == "2008"
63                  orderby book.Title1
64                  select book;
65               break;
66            case 2: // titles ending with "How to Program"
67               // use LINQ to get titles ending with
68               // "How to Program" and sort them by title
69               titleBindingSource.DataSource =
70                  from book in database.Titles
71                  where book.Title1.EndsWith( "How to Program" )
72                  orderby book.Title1
73                  select book;
74               break;
75         } // end switch
76
77         titleBindingSource.MoveFirst(); // move to first entry
78      } // end method queriesComboBox_SelectedIndexChanged
79   } // end class TitleQueries
80 } // end namespace DisplayQueryResult
```

Fig. 18.20 | Displaying the result of a user-selected query in a `DataGridView`. (Part 2 of 2.)

Saving Changes

Follow the instructions in the previous example to add a handler for the `BindingNavigator`'s **Save Data** Button (lines 32–41). Note that, except for changes to the names, the three lines are identical. The last statement (line 40) displays the results of the **All titles** query in the `DataGridView`.

18.7 Retrieving Data from Multiple Tables with LINQ

In this section, we concentrate on LINQ to SQL features that simplify querying and combining data from multiple tables. The **Joining Tables with LINQ** application (Fig. 18.21) uses LINQ to SQL to combine and organize data from multiple tables, and shows the results of queries that perform the following tasks:

- Get a list of all the authors and the ISBNs of the books they've authored, sorted by last name then first name (Fig. 18.21(a)).

- Get a list of all the authors and the titles of the books they've authored, sorted by last name then first; for each author sort the titles alphabetically (Fig. 18.21(b)).

- Get a list of all the book titles grouped by author, sorted by last name then first; for a given author sort the titles alphabetically (Fig. 18.21(c)).

a) List of authors and the ISBNs of the books they've authored; sort the authors by last name then first name

b) List of authors and the titles of the book's they've authored; sort the authors by last name then first name; for a given author, sort the titles alphabetically

c) List of titles grouped by author; sort the authors by last name then first name; for a given author, sort the titles alphabetically

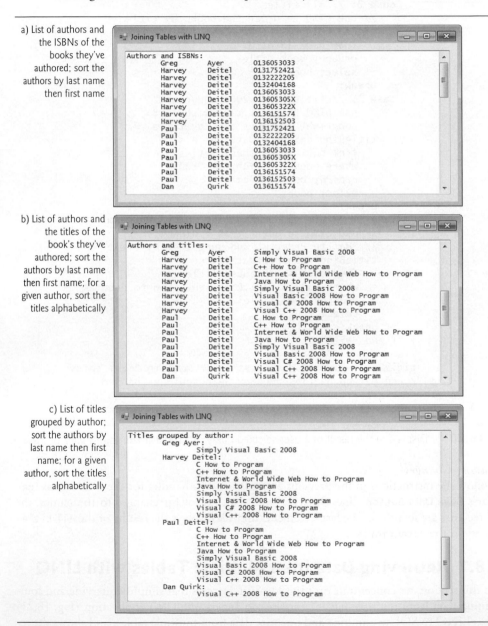

Fig. 18.21 | Outputs from the **Joining Tables with LINQ** application.

GUI for the Joining Tables with LINQ Application
For this example (Fig. 18.22–Fig. 18.25), create a Windows Forms application named
JoinQueries and rename the Form.cs file as JoiningTableData.cs. We set the following
properties for the outputTextBox:

- Font property: Set to Lucida Console to display the output in a fixed-width font.

- Anchor property: Set to Top, Bottom, Left, Right so that you can resize the window and the outputTextBox will resize accordingly.

- Scrollbars property: Set to Vertical, so that you can scroll through the output.

Follow the steps from previous sections to set up the connection to the database and the
LINQ to SQL classes.

Creating the BooksDataContext
The code combines data from the three tables in the Books database and displays the relationships between the book titles and authors in three different ways. It uses LINQ to SQL
classes that have been created using the same steps as the first two examples. As in previous
examples, the BooksDataContext object (Fig. 18.22, line 19) allows the program to interact with the database.

```
1   // Fig. 18.22: JoiningTableData.cs
2   // Using LINQ to perform a join and aggregate data across tables.
3   using System;
4   using System.Linq;
5   using System.Windows.Forms;
6
7   namespace JoinQueries
8   {
9      public partial class JoiningTableData : Form
10     {
11        public JoiningTableData()
12        {
13           InitializeComponent();
14        } // end constructor
15
16        private void JoiningTableData_Load(object sender, EventArgs e)
17        {
18           // create database connection
19           BooksDataContext database = new BooksDataContext();
20
```

Fig. 18.22 | Creating the BooksDataContext for querying the Books database.

Combining Author Names with the ISBNs of the Books They've Written
The first query (Fig. 18.23, lines 23–26) joins data from two tables and returns a list of
author names and the ISBNs representing the books they've written, sorted by LastName
then FirstName. The query takes advantage of the properties that LINQ to SQL creates
based on foreign-key relationships between the database's tables. These properties enable
you to easily combine data from related rows in multiple tables.

```
21              // get authors and ISBNs of each book they co-authored
22              var authorsAndISBNs =
23                  from author in database.Authors
24                  from book in author.AuthorISBNs
25                  orderby author.LastName, author.FirstName
26                  select new { author.FirstName, author.LastName, book.ISBN };
27
28              outputTextBox.AppendText( "Authors and ISBNs:" );
29
30              // display authors and ISBNs in tabular format
31              foreach ( var element in authorsAndISBNs )
32              {
33                  outputTextBox.AppendText(
34                      String.Format( "\r\n\t{0,-10} {1,-10} {2,-10}",
35                          element.FirstName, element.LastName, element.ISBN ) );
36              } // end foreach
37
```

Fig. 18.23 | Getting a list of authors and the ISBNs of the books they've authored.

The first from clause (line 23) gets one author from the Authors table. The second from clause (line 24) uses the generated AuthorISBNs property of the Author class to get only the rows in the AuthorISBN table that link to the current author—that is, the ones that have the same AuthorID as the current author. The combined result of the two from clauses is a collection of all the authors and the ISBNs of the books they've authored. The two from clauses introduce two range variables into the scope of this query—other clauses can access both range variables to combine data from multiple tables. Line 26 combines the FirstName and LastName of an author from the Authors table with a corresponding ISBN from the AuthorISBNs table. This line creates a new anonymous type that contains these three properties.

Anonymous Types
As you know, anonymous types allow you to create simple classes used to store data without writing a class definition. An anonymous type declaration (line 26)—known formally as an anonymous object-creation expression—is similar to an object initializer (Section 10.13). The anonymous type declaration begins with the keyword new followed by a member-initializer list in braces ({}). No class name is specified after the new keyword. The compiler generates a class definition based on the anonymous object-creation expression. This class contains the properties specified in the member-initializer list—First-Name, LastName and ISBN. All properties of an anonymous type are public. Anonymous type properties are read-only—you cannot modify a property's value once the object is created. Each property's type is inferred from the values assigned to it. The class definition is generated automatically by the compiler, so you don't know the class's type name (hence the term anonymous type). Thus, you must use implicitly typed local variables to store references to objects of anonymous types (e.g., line 31). Though we are not using it here, the compiler defines a ToString method when creating the anonymous type's class definition. The method returns a string in curly braces containing a comma-separated list of *PropertyName* = *value* pairs. The compiler also provides an Equals method, which com-

pares the properties of the anonymous object that calls the method and the anonymous object that it receives as an argument.

Combining Author Names with the Titles of the Books They've Written
The second query (Fig. 18.24, lines 40–45) gives similar output, but uses the foreign-key relationships to go one step further and get the title of each book that an author wrote. The first `from` clause (line 40) gets one `title` from the `Titles` table. The second `from` clause (line 41) uses the generated `AuthorISBNs` property of the `Title` class to get only the rows in the `AuthorISBN` table that link to the current `title`—that is, the ones that have the same `ISBN` as the current `title`. Each of those book objects contains an `Author` property that represents the foreign-key relationship between the `AuthorISBNs` table and the `Authors` table. This `Author` property gives us access to the names of the authors for the current book.

```
38          // get authors and titles of each book they co-authored
39          var authorsAndTitles =
40              from title in database.Titles
41              from book in title.AuthorISBNs
42              let author = book.Author
43              orderby author.LastName, author.FirstName, title.Title1
44              select new { author.FirstName, author.LastName,
45                  title.Title1 };
46
47          outputTextBox.AppendText( "\r\n\r\nAuthors and titles:" );
48
49          // display authors and titles in tabular format
50          foreach ( var element in authorsAndTitles )
51          {
52              outputTextBox.AppendText(
53                  String.Format( "\r\n\t{0,-10} {1,-10} {2}",
54                      element.FirstName, element.LastName, element.Title1 ) );
55          } // end foreach
56
```

Fig. 18.24 | Getting a list of authors and the titles of the books they've authored.

Line 42 uses the `let` query operator, which allows you to declare a new variable in a LINQ query—usually to create a shorter name for an expression. The variable can be accessed in later statements just like a range variable. The `author` variable created in the `let` clause refers to `book.Author`. The `select` clause (lines 44–45) uses the `author` and `title` variables introduced earlier in the query to get the `FirstName` and `LastName` of each author from the `Authors` table and the title of each book from the `Titles` table.

Organizing Book Titles by Author
Most queries return results with data arranged in a relational-style table of rows and columns. The last query (Fig. 18.25, lines 60–66) returns hierarchical results. Each element in the results contains the name of an `Author` and a list of `Titles` that the author wrote. The LINQ query does this by using a nested query in the `select` clause. The outer query iterates over the authors in the database. The inner query takes a specific author and retrieves all titles that the author worked on. The `select` clause (lines 62–66) creates an anonymous type with two properties:

- The property Name (line 62) combines each author's name, separating the first and last names by a space.

- The property Titles (line 63) receives the result of the nested query, which returns the title of each book written by the current author.

In this case, we're providing names for each property in the new anonymous type. When you create an anonymous type, you can specify the name for each property by using the format *name = value*.

```
57        // get authors and titles of each book
58        // they co-authored; group by author
59        var titlesByAuthor =
60            from author in database.Authors
61            orderby author.LastName, author.FirstName
62            select new { Name = author.FirstName + " " + author.LastName,
63                Titles =
64                    from book in author.AuthorISBNs
65                    orderby book.Title.Title1
66                    select book.Title.Title1 };
67
68        outputTextBox.AppendText( "\r\n\r\nTitles grouped by author:" );
69
70        // display titles written by each author, grouped by author
71        foreach ( var author in titlesByAuthor )
72        {
73            // display author's name
74            outputTextBox.AppendText( "\r\n\t" + author.Name + ":" );
75
76            // display titles written by that author
77            foreach ( var title in author.Titles )
78            {
79                outputTextBox.AppendText( "\r\n\t\t" + title );
80            } // end inner foreach
81        } // end outer foreach
82     } // end method JoiningTableData_Load
83  } // end class JoiningTableData
84 } // end namespace JoinQueries
```

Fig. 18.25 | Getting a list of titles grouped by authors.

The nested foreach statements (lines 71–81) use the properties of the anonymous type created by the query to output the hierarchical results. The outer loop displays the author's name and the inner loop displays the titles of all the books written by that author.

Notice the expression book.Title.Title1 used in the inner orderby and select clauses (lines 65–66). This is due to the database having a Title column in the Titles table, and is another example of following foreign-key relationships. (Recall that the IDE renamed the Title column in the LINQ to SQL classes to avoid a naming conflict with the generated Title class.) The range variable book iterates over the rows of the Author-ISBN for the current author's books. Each book's Title property contains the corresponding row from the Titles table for that book. The Title1 in the expression returns the Title column (the title of the book) from that row of the Titles table in the database.

18.8 Creating a Master/Detail View Application

Figure 18.26 demonstrates a so-called **master/detail view**—one part of the GUI (the master) allows you to select an entry, and another part (the details) displays detailed information about that entry. In this example, if you select an author from the **Author:** ComboBox, the application displays the details of the books written by that author (Fig. 18.26(b)). If you select a book title from the **Title:** ComboBox, the application displays the co-authors of that book (Fig. 18.26(c)).

a) **Master/Detail** application when it begins execution before an author or title is selected; no results are displayed in the DataGridView until the user makes a selection from one of the ComboBoxes

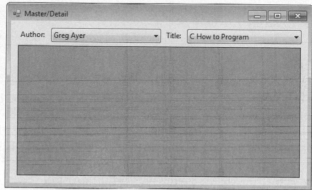

b) Select **Harvey Deitel** from the **Author:** drop-down list to view books he's co-authored

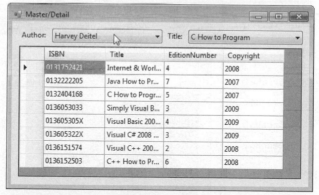

c) Select **C++ How to Program** from the **Title:** drop-down to view the authors who wrote that book

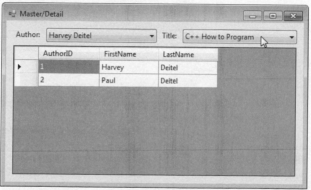

Fig. 18.26 | Master/Detail application.

18.8.1 Creating the Master/Detail GUI

You've seen that the IDE can automatically generate the BindingSource, BindingNavigator and GUI elements when you drag a data source onto the Form. While this works for simple applications, those with more complex operations involve writing more substantial amounts of code. Before explaining the code, we list the steps required to create the GUI.

Step 1: Creating the Project
Create a new **Windows Forms Application** called MasterDetail. Name the source file Details.cs and set the Form's Text property to **Master/Detail**.

Step 2: Creating LINQ to SQL Classes
Follow the instructions in Section 18.5.1 to add the Books database and create the LINQ to SQL classes to interact with the database.

Step 3: Creating GUI Elements
Add two Labels and two ComboBoxes to the top of the Form. Position them as shown in Fig. 18.27. The Label and ComboBox on the left should be named authorLabel and authorComboBox, respectively. The Label and ComboBox on the right should be named titleLabel and titleComboBox. Set the Text properties of the Labels to Author: and Title:, respectively. Also change the DropDownStyle properties of the ComboBoxes from DropDown to DropDownList—this prevents the user from being able to type in the control.

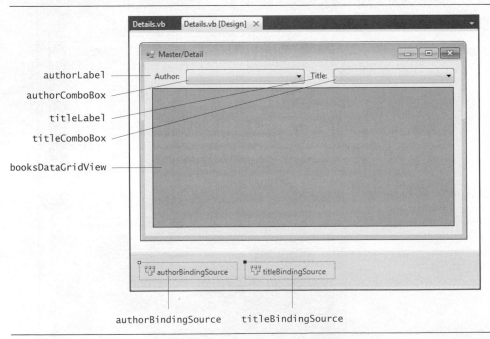

Fig. 18.27 | Finished design of **Master/Detail** application.

Next, create a DataGridView called booksDataGridView to hold the details that are displayed. Unlike previous examples, do not automatically create it by dragging a data source from the **Data Sources** window—this example sets the data source programmatically. Instead, drag the DataGridView from the **Toolbox**. Resize the DataGridView so that it fills the remainder of the Form. Because this control is only for *viewing* data, set its Read-Only property to True using the **Properties** window.

Finally, we need to add two BindingSources from the **Data** section of the **Toolbox**, one for information from the Titles table and one for information from the Authors table. Name these titleBindingSource and authorBindingSource, respectively. As in the previous examples, these appear in the component tray. These BindingSources are used as data sources for the DataGridView—the data source switches between them, depending on whether we want to view a list of Titles or a list of Authors. With the GUI creation complete, we can now write the code to provide the master/detail functionality.

18.8.2 Coding the Master/Detail Application

Nested Class *AuthorBinding*

As you saw in Fig. 18.26, the **Author:** ComboBox displays each author's full name. This example uses data binding to display the names in the ComboBox. When you bind a collection of objects to a ComboBox's DataSource property, the ComboBox normally displays the result of calling ToString on each object in the collection. If the String representation is not appropriate, you can specify *one* property of each object in the collection that should be displayed. In this example, we want to display each author's first and last name.

Recall that the author's name is stored as *two* separate fields in the database, so the auto-generated Author class does not have single property that returns the full name. For this reason, we use a class called AuthorBinding (Fig. 18.28, lines 21–25) to help display the author's full name. Class AuthorBinding's Name property stores an author's full name, and the Author property stores the Author object that contains the author's information from the database. Class AuthorBinding is intended for use only in this example, so we defined it inside class Details—it's a so-called **nested class**. Class definitions may be nested inside other classes when they're intended to be used only by their enclosing classes—that is, they're not meant for use by other programs.

```
 1   // Fig. 18.28: Details.cs
 2   // Using a DataGridView to display details based on a selection.
 3   using System;
 4   using System.Linq;
 5   using System.Windows.Forms;
 6
 7   namespace MasterDetail
 8   {
 9      public partial class Details : Form
10      {
11         public Details()
12         {
13            InitializeComponent();
14         } // end constructor
15
```

Fig. 18.28 | Nested class AuthorBinding in class Details. (Part 1 of 2.)

```
16        // connection to database
17        private BooksDataContext database = new BooksDataContext();
18
19        // this class helps us display each author's first
20        // and last name in the authors drop-down list
21        private class AuthorBinding
22        {
23           public Author Author { get; set; } // contained Author object
24           public string Name { get; set; } // author's full name
25        } // end class AuthorBinding
26
```

Fig. 18.28 | Nested class `AuthorBinding` in class `Details`. (Part 2 of 2.)

Configuring the Data Sources

The `ComboBox`'s **DisplayMember** property is set to the `String` "Name" (Fig. 18.29, line 31), which tells the `ComboBox` to use the `Name` property of the objects in its `DataSource` to determine what text to display for each item. The `DataSource` in this case is the result of the LINQ query in lines 35–38, which creates an `AuthorBinding` object for each author. The `authorComboBox` will contain the `Name` of each author in the query result. Recall from Section 10.13 that object initializers (like lines 37–38) can initialize an object without explicitly calling a constructor.

```
27        // initialize data sources when the Form is loaded
28        private void Details_Load( object sender, EventArgs e )
29        {
30           // display AuthorBinding.Name
31           authorComboBox.DisplayMember = "Name";
32
33           // set authorComboBox's DataSource to the list of authors
34           authorComboBox.DataSource =
35              from author in database.Authors
36              orderby author.LastName, author.FirstName
37              select new AuthorBinding { Author = author,
38                 Name = author.FirstName + " " + author.LastName };
39
40           // display Title.Title1
41           titleComboBox.DisplayMember = "Title1";
42
43           // set titleComboBox's DataSource to the list of titles
44           titleComboBox.DataSource =
45              from title in database.Titles
46              orderby title.Title1
47              select title;
48
49           // initially, display no "detail" data
50           booksDataGridView.DataSource = null;
51        } // end method Details_Load
52
```

Fig. 18.29 | Configuring the `ComboBox`es' and `DataGridView`'s data sources.

For the `titleComboBox`, we specify that each book's title should be displayed (line 41). The LINQ query in lines 45–47 returns a sorted list of `Title` objects and assigns it to the `titleComboBox`'s `DataSource`.

Initially, we don't want to display any data in the `DataGridView`. However, when you set a `ComboBox`'s `DataSource`, the control's `SelectedIndexChanged` event handler is called. To prevent this data from being displayed when the program first loads, we explicitly set the `DataGridView`'s `DataSource` property to `null` (line 50).

The *BindingSource* of a *DataGridView*

Simple GUI elements like `ComboBox`es can work directly from a data source, such as the result of a LINQ to SQL query. However, a `DataGridView` requires a `BindingSource` as its `DataSource`. While building the GUI, you created two `BindingSource` objects—one for displaying a list of `Author`s and one for displaying a list of `Title`s. You can change the columns and data displayed in the `DataGridView` merely by changing its `DataSource` between the two `BindingSource` objects. The `DataGridView` automatically determines the column names it needs to display from its `BindingSource` and refreshes itself when the `BindingSource` changes.

Method *authorComboBox_SelectedIndexChanged*

The `authorComboBox_SelectedIndexChanged` event handler (Fig. 18.30) performs three distinct operations. First, it retrieves the selected `Author` (lines 58–59) from the `author-ComboBox`. The `ComboBox`'s `SelectedItem` property returns an `object`, so we convert the `SelectedItem` property's value to the type `AuthorBinding`—recall that the `ComboBox`'s `DataSource` was set to a collection of `AuthorBinding` objects. Then, the event handler accesses the `AuthorBinding`'s `Author` property to retrieve the wrapped `Author` object.

```
53        // display titles that were co-authored by the selected author
54        private void authorComboBox_SelectedIndexChanged(
55           object sender, EventArgs e )
56        {
57           // get the selected Author object from the ComboBox
58           Author currentAuthor =
59              ( ( AuthorBinding ) authorComboBox.SelectedItem ).Author;
60
61           // set titleBindingSource's DataSource to the
62           // list of titles written by the selected author
63           titleBindingSource.DataSource =
64              from book in currentAuthor.AuthorISBNs
65              select book.Title;
66
67           // display the titles in the DataGridView
68           booksDataGridView.DataSource = titleBindingSource;
69        } // end method authorComboBox_SelectedIndexChanged
70
```

Fig. 18.30 | Displaying the books for the selected author.

Next, the event handler uses LINQ to retrieve the `Title` objects representing books that the `currentAuthor` worked on (lines 64–65). The results of the LINQ query are assigned to the `DataSource` property of `titleBindingSource` (line 63). The event handler sets the titleBindingSource because we want to display Title objects associated with the currentAuthor. Finally, the DataGridView's DataSource is assigned titleBinding-Source to display the books this author wrote (line 68).

Method *titleComboBox_SelectedIndexChanged*

The titleComboBox_SelectedIndexChanged event handler (Fig. 18.31) is nearly identical to authorComboBox_SelectedIndexChanged. Line 76 gets the selected Title from the ComboBox. Lines 80–82 set the authorsBindingSource's DataSource to the list of Authors for the current book. Finally, the DataGridView's DataSource is assigned authorBinding-Source to display the authors who wrote this book (line 85).

```
71          // display the authors of the selected title
72          private void titleComboBox_SelectedIndexChanged(
73             object sender, EventArgs e )
74          {
75             // get the selected Title object from the ComboBox
76             Title currentTitle = ( Title ) titleComboBox.SelectedItem;
77
78             // set authorBindingSource's DataSource to the
79             // list of authors for the selected title
80             authorBindingSource.DataSource =
81                from book in currentTitle.AuthorISBNs
82                select book.Author;
83
84             // display the authors in the DataGridView
85             booksDataGridView.DataSource = authorBindingSource;
86          } // end method titleComboBox_SelectedIndexChanged
87       } // end class Details
88    } // end namespace MasterDetail
```

Fig. 18.31 | Displaying the authors of the selected book.

18.9 Address Book Case Study

Our next example (Fig. 18.32) implements a simple AddressBook application that enables users to perform the following tasks on the database AddressBook.mdf (which is included in the directory with this chapter's examples):

- Insert new contacts
- Find contacts whose last names begin with the specified letters
- Update existing contacts
- Delete contacts

We populated the database with six fictional contacts.

Rather than displaying a database table in a DataGridView, this application presents the details of one contact at a time in several TextBoxes. The BindingNavigator at the top of the window allows you to control which *row* of the table is displayed at any given time. The BindingNavigator also allows you to add a contact, delete a contact and save changes to a contact. When you run the application, experiment with the BindingNavigator's controls. The CD- or DVD-like buttons of the BindingNavigator allow you to change the currently displayed row. Adding a row clears the TextBoxes and sets the TextBox to the right of **Address ID** to zero. When you save a new entry, the **Address ID** field is automatically changed from zero to a unique number by the database.

Recall from Section 18.5 that to allow changes to the database to *persist* between executions of the application, you can run the program in release mode (*Ctrl + F5*).

a) Use the BindingNavigator's controls at the top of the window to navigate through the contacts in the database; initially there are six contacts in the database

b) Type a search String in the **Last Name:** TextBox then press **Find** to locate contacts whose last names begin with that String; only two names start with "Br" so the BindingNavigator indicates two matching records

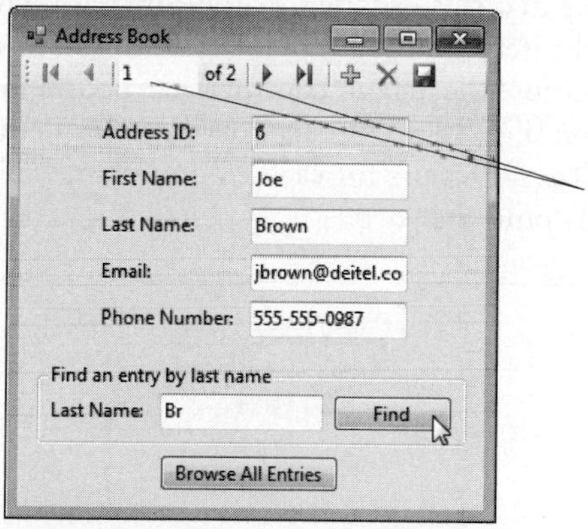

Displaying the first of two matching contacts for the current search

c) Click the **Browse All Entries** Button to clear the search String and to allow browsing of all contacts in the database.

You can now browse through all six contacts

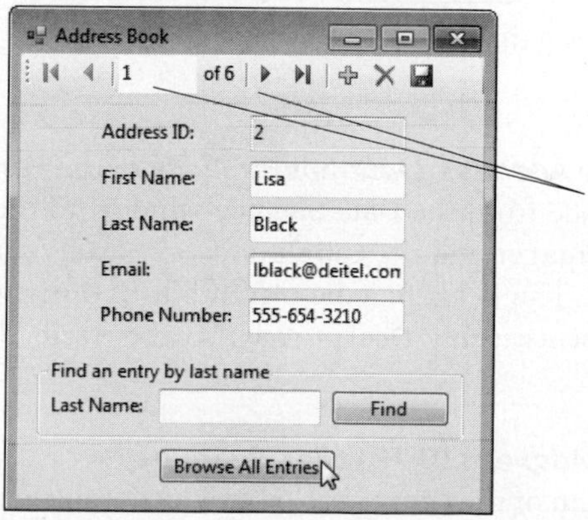

Fig. 18.32 | Manipulating an address book.

18.9.1 Creating the Address Book Application's GUI

We discuss the application's code momentarily. First we show the steps to create this application.

Step 1: Creating the Project
Create a new **Windows Forms Application** named AddressBook, set the Form's filename to Contacts.cs, then set the Form's **Text** property to Address Book.

Step 2: Creating LINQ to SQL Classes and Data Source
Follow the instructions in Section 18.5.1 to add a database to the project and generate the LINQ to SQL classes. For this example, add the AddressBook database and name the file AddressBook.dbml. You must also add the Address table as a data source, as we did with the Authors table in *Step 1* of Section 18.5.2.

Step 3: Displaying the Details of Each Row
In the earlier sections, you dragged an object from the **Data Sources** window to the Form to create a DataGridView that was bound to the data in that object. The IDE allows you to specify the type of control(s) that it will create when you drag and drop an object from the **Data Sources** window onto a Form. In **Design** view, click the Address node in the **Data Sources** window. Note that this becomes a drop-down list when you select it. Click the down arrow to view the items in the list. The item to the left of **DataGridView** is initially highlighted in blue, because the default control that's bound to a table is a DataGridView. Select the **Details** option (Fig. 18.33) in the drop-down list to indicate that the IDE should create a set of Label/TextBox pairs for each column-name/column-value pair when you drag and drop Address onto the Form.

Fig. 18.33 | Specifying that an Address should be displayed as a set of Labels and TextBoxes.

Step 4: Dragging the Address Data-Source Node to the Form
Drag the Address node from the **Data Sources** window to the Form. This automatically creates a BindingNavigator and the Labels and TextBoxes corresponding to the columns of the database table. The fields may be placed out of order, with the Email at the top. Reorder the components, using **Design** view, so they're in the proper order shown in Fig. 18.32.

Step 5: Making the AddressID TextBox ReadOnly
The AddressID column of the Addresses table is an autoincremented identity column, so users should not be allowed to edit the values in this column. Select the TextBox for the AddressID and set its ReadOnly property to True using the **Properties** window.

Step 6: Adding Controls to Allow Users to Specify a Last Name to Locate
While the BindingNavigator allows you to browse the address book, it would be more convenient to be able to find a specific entry by last name. To add this functionality to the application, we must create controls to allow the user to enter a last name and provide event handlers to perform the search.

Add a Label named findLabel, a TextBox named findTextBox, and a Button named findButton. Place these controls in a GroupBox named findGroupBox, then set its Text property to **Find an entry by last name**. Set the Text property of the Label to Last Name: and set the Text property of the Button to Find.

Step 7: Allowing the User to Return to Browsing All Rows of the Database
To allow users to return to browsing all the contacts after searching for contacts with a specific last name, add a Button named browseAllButton below the findGroupBox. Set the Text property of browseAllButton to **Browse All Entries**.

18.9.2 Coding the Address Book Application

Method RefreshContacts
As we showed in previous examples, we must connect the addressBindingSource that controls the GUI with the AddressBookDataContext that interacts with the database. In this example, we do this in the RefreshContacts method (Fig. 18.34, lines 21–31), which is called from several other methods in the application. Method RefreshContacts sets the addressBindingSource's DataSource property to the result of a LINQ query on the Addresses table. We created a private method in this example, because there are three locations in the program where we need to update the addressBindingSource's DataSource property.

```
1   // Fig. 18.34: Contact.cs
2   // Manipulating an address book.
3   using System;
4   using System.Linq;
5   using System.Windows.Forms;
6
7   namespace AddressBook
8   {
9      public partial class Contacts : Form
10     {
11        public Contacts()
12        {
13           InitializeComponent();
14        } // end constructor
15
16        // LINQ to SQL data context
17        private AddressBookDataContext database =
18           new AddressBookDataContext();
19
```

Fig. 18.34 | Creating the BooksDataContext and defining method RefreshContacts for use in other methods. (Part 1 of 2.)

```
20      // fill our addressBindingSource with all rows, ordered by name
21      private void RefreshContacts()
22      {
23         // use LINQ to create a data source from the database
24         addressBindingSource.DataSource =
25            from address in database.Addresses
26            orderby address.LastName, address.FirstName
27            select address;
28
29         addressBindingSource.MoveFirst(); // go to the first result
30         findTextBox.Clear(); // clear the Find TextBox
31      } // end method RefreshContacts
32
```

Fig. 18.34 | Creating the BooksDataContext and defining method RefreshContacts for use in other methods. (Part 2 of 2.)

Method Contacts_Load

Method Contacts_Load (Fig. 18.35) calls RefreshContacts (line 36) so that the first record is displayed when the application starts. As before, you create the Load event handler by double clicking the Form's title bar.

```
33      // when the form loads, fill it with data from the database
34      private void Contacts_Load( object sender, EventArgs e )
35      {
36         RefreshContacts(); // fill binding with data from database
37      } // end method Contacts_Load
38
```

Fig. 18.35 | Calling RefreshContacts to fill the TextBoxes when the application loads.

Method addressBindingNavigatorSaveItem_Click

Method addressBindingNavigatorSaveItem_Click (Fig. 18.36) saves the changes to the database when the BindingNavigator's save Button is clicked. (Remember to enable this button in the BindingNavigator.) We call RefreshContacts after saving to re-sort the data and move back to the first element.

```
39      // Click event handler for the Save Button in the
40      // BindingNavigator saves the changes made to the data
41      private void addressBindingNavigatorSaveItem_Click(
42         object sender, EventArgs e )
43      {
44         Validate(); // validate input fields
45         addressBindingSource.EndEdit(); // indicate edits are complete
46         database.SubmitChanges(); // write changes to database file
47
48         RefreshContacts(); // change back to initial unfiltered data
49      } // end method addressBindingNavigatorSaveItem_Click
50
```

Fig. 18.36 | Saving changes to the database when the user clicks the **Save Data** Button.

The AddressBook database requires values for the first name, last name, phone number and e-mail. We did not check for errors to simplify the code—if a field is empty when you attempt to save, a SqlException exception (namespace System.Data.SqlClient) occurs.

Method findButton_Click

Method findButton_Click (Fig. 18.37) uses LINQ (lines 57–60) to select only people whose last names start with the characters entered in the findTextBox. The query sorts the results by last name then first name. When you enter a last name and click **Find**, the BindingNavigator allows the user to browse only the rows containing the matching last names. This is because the data source bound to the Form's controls (the result of the LINQ query) has changed and now contains only a limited number of rows.

```
51    // use LINQ to create a data source that contains only people
52    // with last names that start with the specified text
53    private void findButton_Click( object sender, EventArgs e )
54    {
55       // use LINQ to create a data source from the database
56       addressBindingSource.DataSource =
57          from address in database.Addresses
58          where address.LastName.StartsWith( findTextBox.Text )
59          orderby address.LastName, address.FirstName
60          select address;
61
62       addressBindingSource.MoveFirst(); // go to first result
63    } // end method findButton_Click
64
```

Fig. 18.37 | Finding the contacts whose last names begin with a specified String.

Method browseAllButton_Click

Method browseAllButton_Click (Fig. 18.38) allows users to return to browsing all the rows after searching for specific rows. Double click browseAllButton to create a Click event handler. Have the event handler call RefreshContacts (line 68) to restore the data source to the full list of people and clear the findTextBox.

```
65       // reload addressBindingSource with all rows
66       private void browseButton_Click( object sender, EventArgs e )
67       {
68          RefreshContacts(); // change back to initial unfiltered data
69       } // end method browseButton_Click
70    } // end class Contacts
71  } // end namespace AddressBook
```

Fig. 18.38 | Allowing the user to browse all contacts.

18.10 Tools and Web Resources

Our extensive LINQ Resource Center at www.deitel.com/LINQ contains many links to additional information, including blogs by Microsoft LINQ team members, sample chapters, tutorials, videos, downloads, FAQs, forums, webcasts and other resource sites.

A useful tool for learning LINQ is LINQPad (www.linqpad.net), which allows you to execute and view the results of any C# or Visual Basic expression, including LINQ queries. It also supports connecting to a SQL Server database and querying it using SQL and LINQ to SQL.

18.11 Wrap-Up

This chapter introduced the relational database model, LINQ to SQL and the IDE's visual programming tools for working with databases. You examined the contents of a simple Books database and learned about the relationships among the tables in the database. You used LINQ and the LINQ to SQL classes generated by the IDE to retrieve data from, add new data to, delete data from and update data in a SQL Server Express database.

We discussed the LINQ to SQL classes automatically generated by the IDE, such as the DataContext class that controls interactions with the database. You learned how to use the IDE's tools to connect to databases and to generate LINQ to SQL classes based on a database's schema. You then used the IDE's drag-and-drop capabilities to automatically generate GUIs for displaying and manipulating database data.

In the next chapter, we demonstrate how to build web applications using Microsoft's ASP.NET technology. We introduce the concept of a three-tier application, which is divided into three pieces that can reside on the same computer or be distributed among separate computers across a network such as the Internet. One of these tiers—the information tier—typically stores data in a database.

Summary

Section 18.1 Introduction
- A database is an organized collection of data.
- A database management system (DBMS) provides mechanisms for storing, organizing, retrieving and modifying data.
- SQL Server Express provides most of the features of Microsoft's full (fee-based) SQL Server product, but has some limitations, such as a maximum database size .
- A SQL Server Express database can be easily migrated to a full version of SQL Server.
- LINQ to SQL allows you to manipulate relational data stored in a SQL Server or SQL Server Express database.

Section 18.2 Relational Databases
- A relational database organizes data simply in tables.
- Tables are composed of rows and columns (also called fields) in which values are stored.
- A column (or group of columns) of each row is the table's primary key—a column (or group of columns) requiring a unique value that cannot be duplicated in other rows. This guarantees that a primary key value can be used to uniquely identify a row.
- A primary key composed of two or more columns is known as a composite key.
- Each column represents a different data attribute.
- Rows are unique (by primary key) within a table, but some column values may be duplicated between rows.

Section 18.3 A Books Database

- A database's tables, their fields and the relationships between them are collectively known as a database schema.
- LINQ to SQL uses a database's schema to define classes that enable you to interact with the database.
- A foreign key is a column in one table that matches the primary-key column in another table.
- Foreign keys, which are specified when a database table is created, link the data in multiple tables.
- Every foreign-key value must appear as another table's primary-key value so the DBMS can ensure that the foreign-key value is valid.
- Foreign keys also allow related data in multiple tables to be selected from those tables—this is known as joining the data.
- There's a one-to-many relationship between a primary key and a corresponding foreign key—a foreign key can appear many times in its own table but only once (as the primary key) in another table.
- An entity-relationship (ER) diagram shows the tables in a database and their relationships.
- Every row must have a value in the primary-key column, and the value of the key must be unique in the table.

Section 18.4 LINQ to SQL

- LINQ to SQL enables you to access data in SQL Server databases using LINQ syntax.
- You interact with LINQ to SQL via classes that are automatically generated by the IDE's LINQ to SQL Designer based on the database schema.
- LINQ to SQL requires every table to have a primary key to support modifying the database data.
- The IDE creates a class for each table. Objects of these classes represent the collections of rows in the corresponding tables.
- The IDE also creates a class for a row of each table with a property for each column in the table. Objects of these classes (row objects) hold the data from individual rows in the database's tables.
- In the class for a row object, an additional property is created for each foreign key. This property returns the row object of the corresponding primary key in another table.
- In the class for a row object, an additional property is created for the collection of row objects with foreign-keys that reference the row object's primary key.
- Once generated, the LINQ to SQL classes have full *IntelliSense* support in the IDE.

Section 18.5 Querying a Database with LINQ

- The IDE provides visual programming tools and wizards that simplify accessing data in your projects. These tools establish database connections and create the objects necessary to view and manipulate the data through the GUI—a technique known as data binding.
- A DataGridView (namespace System.Windows.Forms) displays data from a data source in tabular format.
- A BindingNavigator is a collection of controls that allow you to navigate through the records displayed in a GUI. The BindingNavigator controls also allow you to add records, delete records and save your changes to the database.

Section 18.5.1 Creating LINQ to SQL Classes

- To interact with a database, you must create a connection to the database.
- In Visual C# 2010 Express, use the **Database Explorer** window to connect to the database. In full versions of Visual Studio 2010, use the **Server Explorer** window.

- After connecting to the database, you can generate the LINQ to SQL classes by adding a new **LINQ to SQL Classes** item to your project, then dragging the tables you wish to use from the **Database Explorer** onto the **Object Relational Designer**. When you save the .dbml file, the IDE generates the LINQ to SQL classes.

Section 18.5.2 Data Bindings Between Controls and the LINQ to SQL Classes
- To use the LINQ to SQL classes for data binding, you must first add them as a data source.

- Select **Data > Add New Data Source…** to display the **Data Source Configuration Wizard**. Use an **Object** data source. Select the LINQ to SQL object to use as a data source. Drag that data source from the **Data Sources** window onto the Form to create controls that can display the table's data.

- By default, the IDE creates a DataGridView with the correct column names and a BindingNavigator that contains Buttons for moving between entries, adding entries, deleting entries and saving changes to the database.

- The IDE also generates a BindingSource, which handles the transfer of data between the data source and the data-bound controls on the Form.

- The result of a LINQ query on the DataContext can be assigned to the BindingSource's DataSource property. The BindingSource uses the DataSource to extract data from the database and to populate the DataGridView.

- To save the user's changes to the data in the DataGridView, enable the BindingNavigator's **Save Data** Button (🖫). Then, double click the icon to create its Click event handler. In the event handler, you must validate the data, call EndEdit on the BindingSource to save pending changes in the DataContext, and call SubmitChanges on the DataContext to store the changes in the database. For efficiency, LINQ to SQL saves only data that has changed.

Section 18.6 Dynamically Binding Query Results
- The IDE displays smart tag menus for many GUI controls to provide you with quick access to common properties you might set for a control, so you can set these properties directly in **Design** view. You can open a control's smart tag menu by clicking the small arrowhead (▶) that appears in the control's upper-right corner in **Design** view.

- The MoveFirst method of the BindingSource moves to the first row of the result.

Section 18.7 Retrieving Data from Multiple Tables with LINQ
- To join data from multiple tables you use the properties that LINQ to SQL creates based on foreign-key relationships between the database's tables. These properties enable you to easily access related rows in other tables.

- The Let query operator allows you to declare a new variable in a query—usually to create a shorter name for an expression. The variable can be accessed in later clauses just like a range variable.

- Most queries return result with data arranged in relational-style rows and columns. With LINQ to SQL you can create queries that return hierarchical results in which each item in the result contains a collection of other items.

- Use anonymous types to create simple classes used to store data without writing a class definition.

- An anonymous type declaration—also called an anonymous object-creation expression—begins with the keyword new followed by a member-initializer list.

- The compiler generates a new class definition based on the anonymous object-creation expression, containing the properties specified in the member-initializer list.

- All properties of an anonymous type are public.

- Properties of anonymous types are read-only.

- Each property's type is inferred from the value assigned to it.

- Objects of anonymous types are stored in implicitly typed local variables.

- The compiler defines the ToString method when creating the anonymous type's class definition. The method returns a string of comma-separated *PropertyName* = *value* pairs in curly braces.

- The Equals method, generated for any anonymous type, compares the properties of the anonymous object that calls the method and the anonymous object that it receives as an argument.

Section 18.8 Creating a Master/Detail View Application
- In a master/detail view, one part of the GUI (the master) allows you to select an entry, and another part (the details) displays detailed information about that entry.

- Class definitions may be nested inside other classes.

- A ComboBox's DisplayMember property indicates which property to display in the ComboBox from each object in its DataSource.

- You can change the columns and data displayed in a DataGridView by changing its DataSource. The DataGridView determines the column names it needs to display from the BindingSource.

Section 18.9 Address Book Case Study
- The IDE allows you to specify the type of control(s) that it creates when you drag and drop a data-source member onto a Form. The **Details** option indicates that the IDE should create a set of Label/TextBox pairs for each column-name/column-value pair in the data source.

Terminology

Add Connection dialog	field in a database table
autoincremented database column	foreign key
BindingNavigator class	identity column in a database table
BindingSource class	IQueryable interface
Choose Data Source dialog	joining database tables
column of a database table	LINQ to SQL
composite key	LINQ to SQL Designer
connection to a database	many-to-many relationship
data binding	master/detail view
Data Source Configuration Wizard	Microsoft SQL Server Express
Data Sources window	MoveFirst method of class BindingSource
database	**Object** data source
Database Explorer window	**Object Relational Designer** window
database management system (DBMS)	one-to-many relationship
database schema	primary key
DataContext class	relational database
DataGridView class	row object
DataSource property of class BindingSource	row of a database table
DisplayMember property of the ComboBox control	smart tag menu
EndEdit method of class BindingSource	SubmitChanges method of a DataContext
entity-relationship (ER) diagram	table in a database

Self-Review Exercises

18.1   Fill in the blanks in each of the following statements:
   a) A table in a relational database consists of _____ and _____ in which values are stored.
   b) The _____ uniquely identifies each row in a relational database table.

c) A relational database can be manipulated in LINQ to SQL via a(n) _____ object, which contains properties for accessing each table in the database.

d) The _____ control (presented in this chapter) displays data in rows and columns that correspond to the rows and columns of a data source.

e) Merging data from multiple relational database tables is called _____ the data.

f) A(n) _____ is a column (or group of columns) in a relational database table that matches the primary-key column (or group of columns) in another table.

g) A(n) _____ object serves as an intermediary between a data source and its corresponding data-bound GUI control.

h) The _____ property of a control specifies where it gets the data it displays.

i) The _____ clause declares a new temporary variable within a LINQ query.

18.2 State whether each of the following is *true* or *false*. If *false*, explain why.

a) Providing the same value for a foreign key in multiple rows causes the DBMS to report an error.

b) Providing a foreign-key value that does not appear as a primary-key value in another table is an error.

c) The result of a query can be sorted in ascending or descending order.

d) A BindingNavigator object can extract data from a database.

e) LINQ to SQL automatically saves changes made back to the database.

Answers to Self-Review Exercises

18.1 a) rows, columns. b) primary key. c) DataContext. d) DataGridView. e) joining. f) foreign key. g) BindingSource. h) DataSource. i) Let.

18.2 a) False. Multiple rows can have the same value for a foreign key. Providing the same value for the primary key in multiple rows causes the DBMS to report an error, because duplicate primary keys would prevent each row from being identified uniquely. b) True. c) True. d) False. A BindingNavigator allows users to browse and manipulate data displayed by another GUI control. A DataContext can extract data from a database. e) False. You must call the SubmitChanges method of the DataContext to save the changes made back to the database.

Exercises

18.3 *(Display Authors Table Application Modification)* Modify the **DisplayTable** application in Section 18.5 to contain a TextBox and a Button that allow the user to search for specific authors by last name. Include a Label to identify the TextBox. Using the techniques presented in Section 18.9, create a LINQ query that changes the DataSource property of AuthorBindingSource to contain only the specified authors.

18.4 *(Display Query Results Application Modification)* Modify the **Display Query Results** application in Section 18.6 to contain a TextBox and a Button that allow the user to perform a search of the book titles in the Titles table of the Books database. Use a Label to identify the TextBox. When the user clicks the Button, the application should execute and display the result of a query that selects all the rows in which the search term entered by the user in the TextBox appears anywhere in the Title column. For example, if the user enters the search term "Visual," the DataGridView should display the rows for *Simply Visual Basic 2008*, *Visual Basic 2008 How to Program*, *Visual C# 2008 How to Program* and *Visual C++ 2008 How to Program*. If the user enters "Simply," the DataGridView should display only the row for *Simply Visual Basic 2008*. [*Hint:* Use the Contains method of the String class.]

18.5 *(Baseball Database Application)* Build an application that executes a query against the Players table of the Baseball database included in the Databases folder with this chapter's examples. Display the table in a DataGridView, and add a TextBox and Button to allow the user to search for a specific player by last name. Use a Label to identify the TextBox. Clicking the Button should execute the appropriate query.

18.6   *(Baseball Database Application Modification)* Modify Exercise 18.5 to allow the user to locate players with batting averages in a specific range. Add a minimumTextBox for the minimum batting average (0.000 by default) and a maximumTextBox for the maximum batting average (1.000 by default). Use a Label to identify each TextBox. Add a Button for executing a query that selects rows from the Players table in which the BattingAverage column is greater than or equal to the specified minimum value and less than or equal to the specified maximum value.

18.7   *(Project: AdventureWorks Sample Database)* In this exercise, use Microsoft's sample AdventureWorks database. There are several versions available, depending on what version of SQL Server you're using and your operating system. We used the AdventureWorks LT version of the database—a smaller version with fewer tables and less data than the full version. The files for SQL Server 2008 can be downloaded from

> msftdbprodsamples.codeplex.com/releases/view/37109

The installer allows you to select which version of the database to install.

Use the AdventureWorks database in an application that runs multiple queries on the database and displays the results. First, it should list customers and their addresses. As this is a large list, limit the number of results to ten. [*Hint:* Use LINQ's Take clause at the end of the query to return a limited number of results. The Take clause consists of the Take operator, then an Integer specifying how many rows to take.] Second, if a category has subcategories, the output should show the category with its subcategories indented below it. The queries described here require the Adventure-Works tables Address, Customer, CustomerAddress and ProductCategory.

18.8   *(Project: AdventureWorks Master/Detail view)* Use the Microsoft AdventureWorks database from Exercise 18.7 to create a master/detail view. One master list should be customers, and the other should be products—these should show the details of products the customers purchased, and customers who purchased those products, respectively. Note that there are many customers in the database who did not order any products, and many products that no one ordered. Restrict the drop-down lists so that only customers that have submitted at least one order and products that have been included in at least one order are displayed. The queries in this exercise require the Customer, Product, SalesOrderHeader and SalesOrderDetail tables.

19

Web App Development with ASP.NET

... the challenges are for the designers of these applications: to forget what we think we know about the limitations of the Web, and begin to imagine a wider, richer range of possibilities. It's going to be fun.
—Jesse James Garrett

If any man will draw up his case, and put his name at the foot of the first page, I will give him an immediate reply. Where he compels me to turn over the sheet, he must wait my leisure.
—Lord Sandwich

Objectives

In this chapter you'll learn:

- Web application development using ASP.NET.

- To handle the events from a Web Form's controls.

- To use validation controls to ensure that data is in the correct format before it's sent from a client to the server.

- To maintain user-specific information.

- To create a data-driven web application using ASP.NET and LINQ to SQL.

19.1 Introduction

In this chapter, we introduce **web-application development** with Microsoft's **ASP.NET** technology. Web-based applications create web content for web-browser clients.

We present several examples that demonstrate web-application development using **Web Forms, web controls** (also called **ASP.NET server controls**) and Visual C# programming. Web Form files have the file-name extension **.aspx** and contain the web page's GUI. You customize Web Forms by adding web controls including labels, textboxes, images, buttons and other GUI components. The Web Form file represents the web page that is sent to the client browser. We often refer to Web Form files as **ASPX files**.

An ASPX file created in Visual Studio has a corresponding class written in a .NET language—we use Visual C# in this book. This class contains event handlers, initialization code, utility methods and other supporting code. The file that contains this class is called the **code-behind file** and provides the ASPX file's programmatic implementation.

To develop the code and GUIs in this chapter, we used Microsoft's **Visual Web Developer 2010 Express**—a free IDE designed for developing ASP.NET web applications. The full version of Visual Studio 2010 includes the functionality of Visual Web Developer, so the instructions we present for Visual Web Developer also apply to Visual Studio 2010. The database example (Section 19.8) also requires SQL Server 2008 Express. See the *Before You Begin* section of the book for additional information on this software.

In the online chapter, Web App Development with ASP.NET: A Deeper Look, we present several additional web-application development topics, including:

- master pages to maintain a uniform look-and-feel across the Web Forms in a web application

- creating password-protected websites with registration and login capabilities

- using the **Web Site Administration Tool** to specify which parts of a website are password protected

- using ASP.NET AJAX to quickly and easily improve the user experience for your web applications, giving them responsiveness comparable to that of desktop applications.

19.2 Web Basics

In this section, we discuss what occurs when a user requests a web page in a browser. In its simplest form, a *web page* is nothing more than an *HTML (HyperText Markup Language) document* (with the extension .html or .htm) that describes to a web browser the document's content and how to format it.

HTML documents normally contain *hyperlinks* that link to different pages or to other parts of the same page. When the user clicks a hyperlink, a **web server** locates the requested web page and sends it to the user's web browser. Similarly, the user can type the *address of a web page* into the browser's *address field* and press *Enter* to view the specified page.

Web development tools like Visual Web Developer typically use a "stricter" version of HTML called *XHTML (Extensible HyperText Markup Language)*, which is based on XML (Chapter 26). ASP.NET produces web pages as XHTML documents.

URIs and URLs

URIs (Uniform Resource Identifiers) identify resources on the Internet. URIs that start with http:// are called *URLs (Uniform Resource Locators)*. Common URLs refer to files, directories or server-side code that performs tasks such as database lookups, Internet searches and business application processing. If you know the URL of a publicly available resource anywhere on the web, you can enter that URL into a web browser's address field and the browser can access that resource.

Parts of a URL

A URL contains information that directs a browser to the resource that the user wishes to access. Web servers make such resources available to web clients. Popular web servers include Microsoft's Internet Information Services (IIS) and Apache's HTTP Server.

Let's examine the components of the URL

```
http://www.deitel.com/books/downloads.html
```

The http:// indicates that the HyperText Transfer Protocol (HTTP) should be used to obtain the resource. HTTP is the web protocol that enables clients and servers to communicate. Next in the URL is the server's fully qualified **hostname** (www.deitel.com)—the name of the web server computer on which the resource resides. This computer is referred to as the **host**, because it houses and maintains resources. The hostname www.deitel.com is translated into an **IP (Internet Protocol) address**—a numerical value that uniquely identifies the server on the Internet. A **Domain Name System (DNS) server** maintains a database of hostnames and their corresponding IP addresses, and performs the translations automatically.

The remainder of the URL (/books/downloads.html) specifies the resource's location (/books) and name (downloads.html) on the web server. The location could represent an actual directory on the web server's file system. For *security* reasons, however, the location is typically a *virtual directory*. The web server translates the virtual directory into a real location on the server, thus hiding the resource's true location.

Making a Request and Receiving a Response
When given a URL, a web browser uses HTTP to retrieve the web page found at that address. Figure 19.1 shows a web browser sending a request to a web server. Figure 19.2 shows the web server responding to that request.

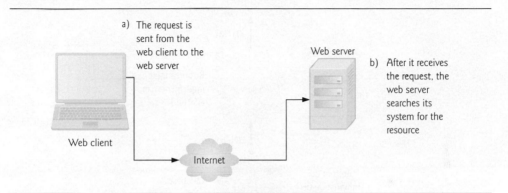

Fig. 19.1 | Client requesting a resource from a web server.

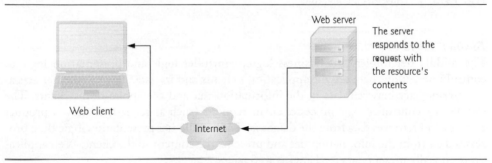

Fig. 19.2 | Client receiving a response from the web server.

19.3 Multitier Application Architecture

Web-based applications are **multitier applications** (sometimes referred to as *n*-**tier applications**). Multitier applications divide functionality into separate **tiers** (that is, logical groupings of functionality). Although tiers can be located on the *same* computer, the tiers of web-based applications commonly reside on *separate* computers for security and scalability. Figure 19.3 presents the basic architecture of a three-tier web-based application.

Information Tier
The **information tier** (also called the **bottom tier**) maintains the application's data. This tier typically stores data in a relational database management system. For example, a retail store might have a database for storing product information, such as descriptions, prices and quantities in stock. The same database also might contain customer information, such as user names, billing addresses and credit card numbers. This tier can contain multiple databases, which together comprise the data needed for an application.

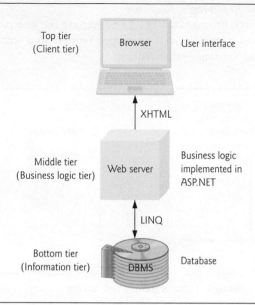

Fig. 19.3 | Three-tier architecture.

Business Logic

The **middle tier** implements **business logic**, **controller logic** and **presentation logic** to control interactions between the application's clients and its data. The middle tier acts as an intermediary between data in the information tier and the application's clients. The middle-tier controller logic processes client requests (such as requests to view a product catalog) and retrieves data from the database. The middle-tier presentation logic then processes data from the information tier and presents the content to the client. Web applications typically present data to clients as web pages.

Business logic in the middle tier enforces *business rules* and ensures that data is reliable before the server application updates the database or presents the data to users. Business rules dictate how clients can and cannot access application data, and how applications process data. For example, a business rule in the middle tier of a retail store's web-based application might ensure that all product quantities remain positive. A client request to set a negative quantity in the bottom tier's product information database would be rejected by the middle tier's business logic.

Client Tier

The **client tier**, or **top tier**, is the application's user interface, which gathers input and displays output. Users interact directly with the application through the user interface (typically viewed in a web browser), keyboard and mouse. In response to user actions (for example, clicking a hyperlink), the client tier interacts with the middle tier to make requests and to retrieve data from the information tier. The client tier then displays to the user the data retrieved from the middle tier. The client tier never directly interacts with the information tier.

19.4 Your First Web Application

Our first example displays the web server's time of day in a browser window (Fig. 19.4). When this application executes—that is, a web browser requests the application's web page—the web server executes the application's code, which gets the current time and displays it in a Label. The web server then returns the result to the web browser that made the request, and the web browser renders the web page containing the time. We executed this application in both the Internet Explorer and Firefox web browsers to show you that the web page renders identically in each.

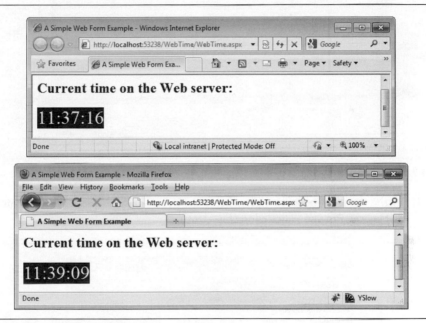

Fig. 19.4 | WebTime web application running in both Internet Explorer and Firefox.

Testing the Application in Your Default Web Browser
To test this application in your default web browser, perform the following steps:

1. Open Visual Web Developer.

2. Select **Open Web Site...** from the **File** menu.

3. In the **Open Web Site** dialog (Fig. 19.5), ensure that **File System** is selected, then navigate to this chapter's examples, select the WebTime folder and click the **Open Button**.

4. Select WebTime.aspx in the **Solution Explorer**, then type *Ctrl + F5* to execute the web application.

Testing the Application in a Selected Web Browser
If you wish to execute the application in another web browser, you can copy the web page's address from your default browser's address field and paste it into another browser's address field, or you can perform the following steps:

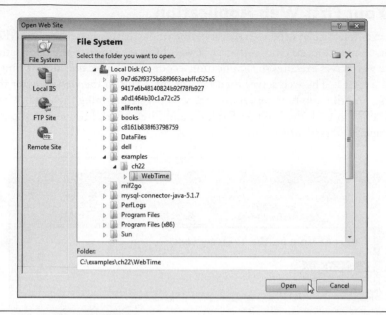

Fig. 19.5 | Open Web Site dialog.

1. In the **Solution Explorer**, right click WebTime.aspx and select **Browse With...** to display the **Browse With** dialog (Fig. 19.6).

Fig. 19.6 | Selecting another web browser to execute the web application.

2. From the **Browsers** list, select the browser in which you'd like to test the web application and click the **Browse** Button.

If the browser you wish to use is not listed, you can use the **Browse With** dialog to add items to or remove items from the list of web browsers.

19.4.1 Building the WebTime Application

Now that you've tested the application, let's create it in Visual Web Developer.

Step 1: Creating the Web Site Project
Select **File > New Web Site...** to display the **New Web Site** dialog (Fig. 19.7). In the left column of this dialog, ensure that **Visual C#** is selected, then select **ASP.NET** Empty Web Site in the middle column. At the bottom of the dialog you can specify the location and name of the web application.

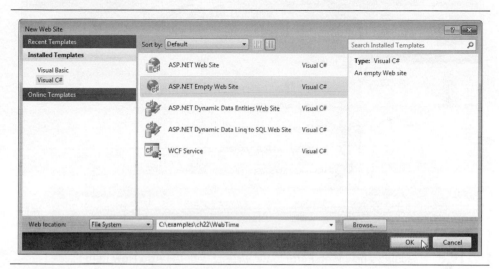

Fig. 19.7 | Creating an **ASP.NET Web Site** in Visual Web Developer.

The **Web location:** ComboBox provides the following options:

- **File System:** Creates a new website for testing on your local computer. Such websites execute in Visual Web Developer's built-in ASP.NET Development Server and can be accessed only by web browsers running on the same computer. You can later "publish" your website to a production web server for access via a local network or the Internet. Each example in this chapter uses the **File System** option, so select it now.

- **HTTP:** Creates a new website on an IIS web server and uses HTTP to allow you to put your website's files on the server. IIS is Microsoft's software that is used to run production websites. If you own a website and have your own web server, you might use this to build a new website directly on that server computer. You must be an Administrator on the computer running IIS to use this option.

- **FTP:** Uses File Transfer Protocol (FTP) to allow you to put your website's files on the server. The server administrator must first create the website on the server for you. FTP is commonly used by so-called "hosting providers" to allow website owners to share a server computer that runs many websites.

Change the name of the web application from WebSite1 to WebTime, then click **OK** to create the website.

Step 2: Adding a Web Form to the Website and Examining the Solution Explorer
A **Web Form** represents one page in a web application—we'll often use the terms "page" and "Web Form" interchangeably. A Web Form contains a web application's GUI. To create the WebTime.aspx Web Form:

1. Right click the project name in the **Solution Explorer** and select **Add New Item...** to display the **Add New Item** dialog (Fig. 19.8).

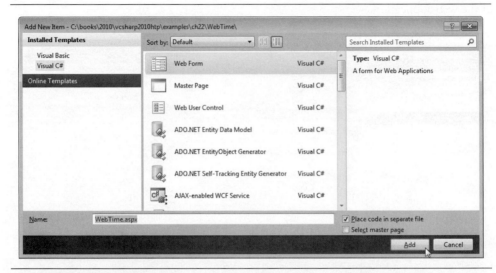

Fig. 19.8 | Adding a new **Web Form** to the website with the **Add New Item** dialog.

2. In the left column, ensure that **Visual C#** is selected, then select **Web Form** in the middle column.

3. In the **Name:** TextBox, change the file name to WebTime.aspx, then click the **Add** Button.

After you add the Web Form, the IDE opens it in **Source** view by default (Fig. 19.9). This view displays the markup for the Web Form. As you become more familiar with ASP.NET and building web sites in general, you might use **Source** view to perform high precision adjustments to your design or to program in the JavaScript language that executes in web browsers. For the purposes of this chapter, we'll keep things simple by working exclusively in **Design** mode. To switch to **Design** mode, you can click the **Design** Button at the bottom of the code editor window.

The Solution Explorer
The **Solution Explorer** (Fig. 19.10) shows the contents of the website. We expanded the node for WebTime.aspx to show you its code-behind file WebTime.aspx.cs. Visual Web Developer's **Solution Explorer** contains several buttons that differ from Visual C# Express. The **Copy Web Site** button opens a dialog that allows you to move the files in this project to another location, such as a remote web server. This is useful if you're developing the application on your local computer but want to make it available to the public from a different location. The **ASP.NET Configuration** button takes you to a web page called the **Web Site Administra-**

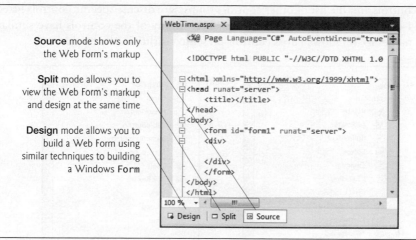

Source mode shows only the Web Form's markup

Split mode allows you to view the Web Form's markup and design at the same time

Design mode allows you to build a Web Form using similar techniques to building a Windows Form

Fig. 19.9 | Web Form in **Source** view.

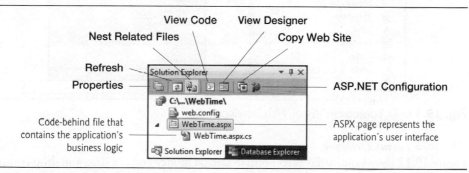

View Code   View Designer

Nest Related Files   Copy Web Site

Refresh

Properties

ASP.NET Configuration

Code-behind file that contains the application's business logic

ASPX page represents the application's user interface

Fig. 19.10 | **Solution Explorer** window for an **Empty Web Site** project after adding the Web Form WebTime.aspx.

tion Tool, where you can manipulate various settings and security options for your application. The **Nest Related Files** button organizes each Web Form and its code-behind file.

If the ASPX file is not open in the IDE, you can open it in **Design** mode three ways:

- double click it in the **Solution Explorer** then select the **Design** tab
- select it in the **Solution Explorer** and click the **View Designer** (🔲) Button
- right click it in the **Solution Explorer** and select **View Designer**

To open the code-behind file in the code editor, you can

- double click it in the **Solution Explorer**
- select the ASPX file in the **Solution Explorer**, then click the **View Code** (🔲) Button
- right click the code-behind file in the **Solution Explorer** and select **Open**

The Toolbox
Figure 19.11 shows the **Toolbox** displayed in the IDE when the project loads. Part (a) displays the beginning of the **Standard** list of web controls, and part (b) displays the remain-

ing web controls and the list of other control groups. We discuss specific controls listed in Fig. 19.11 as they're used throughout the chapter. Many of the controls have similar or identical names to Windows Forms controls presented earlier in the book.

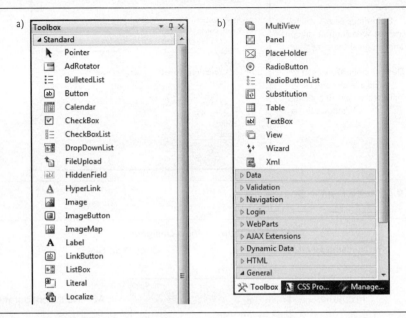

Fig. 19.11 | **Toolbox** in Visual Web Developer.

The Web Forms Designer

Figure 19.12 shows the initial Web Form in **Design** mode. You can drag and drop controls from the **Toolbox** onto the Web Form. You can also type at the current cursor location to add so-called static text to the web page. In response to such actions, the IDE generates the appropriate markup in the ASPX file.

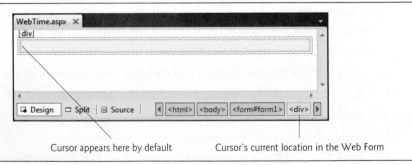

Cursor appears here by default   Cursor's current location in the Web Form

Fig. 19.12 | **Design** mode of the Web Forms Designer.

Step 3: Changing the Title of the Page

Before designing the Web Form's content, you'll change its title to A Simple Web Form Example. This title will be displayed in the web browser's title bar (see Fig. 19.4). It's typically also used by search engines like Google and Bing when they index real websites for searching. Every page should have a title. To change the title:

1. Ensure that the ASPX file is open in **Design** view.

2. View the Web Form's properties by selecting **DOCUMENT**, which represents the Web Form, from the drop-down list in the **Properties** window.

3. Modify the **Title** property in the **Properties** window by setting it to A Simple Web Form Example.

Designing a Page

Designing a Web Form is similar to designing a Windows Form. To add controls to the page, drag-and-drop them from the **Toolbox** onto the Web Form in **Design** view. The Web Form and each control are objects that have properties, methods and events. You can set these properties visually using the **Properties** window or programmatically in the code-behind file. You can also type text directly on a Web Form at the cursor location.

Controls and other elements are placed sequentially on a Web Form one after another in the order in which you drag-and-drop them onto the Web Form. The cursor indicates the insertion point in the page. If you want to position a control between existing text or controls, you can drop the control at a specific position between existing page elements. You can also rearrange controls with drag-and-drop actions in **Design** view. The positions of controls and other elements are relative to the Web Form's upper-left corner. This type of layout is known as relative positioning and it allows the browser to move elements and resize them based on the size of the browser window. Relative positioning is the default, and we'll use it throughout this chapter.

For precise control over the location and size of elements, you can use absolute positioning in which controls are located exactly where you drop them on the Web Form. If you wish to use absolute positioning:

1. Select **Tools > Options....**, to display the **Options** dialog.

2. If it isn't checked already, check the **Show all settings** checkbox.

3. Next, expand the **HTML Designer > CSS Styling** node and ensure that the checkbox labeled **Change positioning to absolute for controls added using Toolbox, paste or drag and drop** is selected.

Step 4: Adding Text and a **Label**

You'll now add some text and a **Label** to the Web Form. Perform the following steps to add the text:

1. Ensure that the Web Form is open in **Design** mode.

2. Type the following text at the current cursor location:

```
Current time on the Web server:
```

3. Select the text you just typed, then select **Heading 2** from the **Block Format** Combo-Box (Fig. 19.13) to format this text as a heading that will appear in a larger bold font. In more complex pages, headings help you specify the relative importance of parts of that content—like sections in a book chapter.

Block Format ComboBox

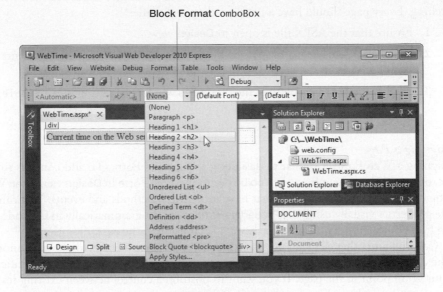

Fig. 19.13 | Changing the text to **Heading 2** heading.

4. Click to the right of the text you just typed and press the *Enter* key to start a new paragraph in the page. The Web Form should now appear as in Fig. 19.14.

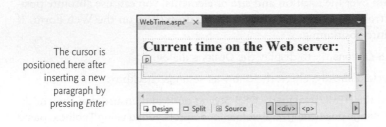

The cursor is positioned here after inserting a new paragraph by pressing *Enter*

Fig. 19.14 | WebTime.aspx after inserting text and a new paragraph.

5. Next, drag a Label control from the **Toolbox** into the new paragraph or double click the Label control in the **Toolbox** to insert the Label at the current cursor position.

6. Using the **Properties** window, set the Label's (ID) property to timeLabel. This specifies the variable name that will be used to programmatically change the Label's Text.

7. Because, the Label's Text will be set programmatically, delete the current value of the Label's Text property. When a Label does not contain text, its name is displayed in square brackets in **Design** view (Fig. 19.15) as a placeholder for design and layout purposes. This text is not displayed at execution time.

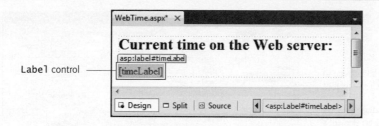

Label control ──────

Fig. 19.15 | WebTime.aspx after adding a Label.

Step 5: Formatting the Label

Formatting in a web page is performed with CSS (Cascading Style Sheets). The details of CSS are beyond the scope of this book. However, it's easy to use CSS to format text and elements in a Web Form via the tools built into Visual Web Developer. In this example, we'd like to change the Label's background color to black, its foreground color yellow and make its text size larger. To format the Label, perform the following steps:

1. Click the Label in **Design** view to ensure that it's selected.

2. Select **View > Other Windows > CSS Properties** to display the **CSS Properties** window at the left side of the IDE (Fig. 19.16).

Fig. 19.16 | CSS Properties window.

3. Right click in the **Applied Rules** box and select **New Style...** to display the **New Style** dialog (Fig. 19.17).

4. Type the new style's name—.timeStyle—in the **Selector:** ComboBox. Styles that apply to specific elements must be named with a dot (.) preceding the name. Such a style is called a CSS class.

5. Each item you can set in the **New Style** dialog is known as a CSS attribute. To change timeLabel's foreground color, select the **Font** category from the **Category** list, then select the yellow color swatch for the **color** attribute.

6. Next, change the **font-size** attribute to xx-large.

7. To change timeLabel's background color, select the **Background** category, then select the black color swatch for the **background-color** attribute.

New style's name

Font category allows you to style an element's font

Background category allows you to specify an element's background color or background image

The new style will be applied to the currently selected element in the page

Preview of what the style will look like

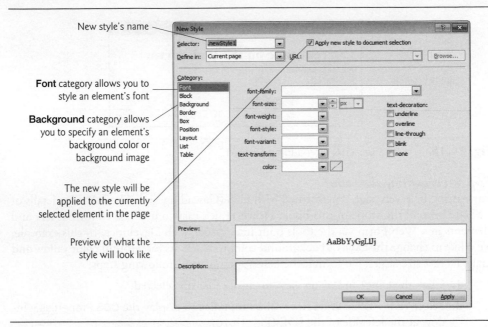

Fig. 19.17 | **New Style** dialog.

The **New Style** dialog should now appear as shown in (Fig. 19.18). Click the **OK Button** to apply the style to the `timeLabel` so that it appears as shown in Fig. 19.19. Also, notice that the `Label`'s `CssClass` property is now set to `timeStyle` in the **Properties** window.

Bold category names indicate the categories in which CSS attribute values have been changed

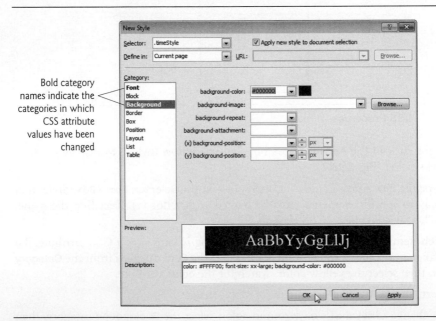

Fig. 19.18 | **New Style** dialog after changing the Label's style.

Fig. 19.19 | **Design** view after changing the Label's style.

Step 6: Adding Page Logic

Now that you've designed the GUI, you'll write code in the code-behind file to obtain the server's time and display it on the Label. Open WebTime.aspx.cs by double clicking it in the **Solution Explorer**. In this example, you'll add an event handler to the code-behind file to handle the Web Form's **Init event**, which occurs when the page is requested by a web browser. The event handler for this event—named **Page_Init**—initialize the page. The only initialization required for this example is to set the timeLabel's Text property to the time on the web server computer. The code-behind file initally contains a Page_Load event handler. To create the Page_Init event handler, simply rename Page_Load as Page_Init. Then complete the event handler by inserting the following code in its body:

```
// display the server's current time in timeLabel
timeLabel.Text = DateTime.Now.ToString("hh:mm:ss");
```

Step 7: Setting the Start Page and Running the Program

To ensure that WebTime.aspx loads when you execute this application, right click it in the **Solution Explorer** and select **Set As Start Page**. You can now run the program in one of several ways. At the beginning of Fig. 19.4, you learned how to view the Web Form by typing *Ctrl + F5*. You can also right click an ASPX file in the **Solution Explorer** and select **View in Browser**. Both of these techniques execute the ASP.NET Development Server, open your default web browser and load the page into the browser, thus running the web application. The development server stops when you exit Visual Web Developer.

If problems occur when running your application, you can run it in debug mode by selecting **Debug > Start Debugging**, by clicking the **Start Debugging** Button (▶) or by typing *F5* to view the web page in a web browser with debugging enabled. You cannot debug a web application unless debugging is explicitly enabled in the application's **Web.config** file—a file that is generated when you create an ASP.NET web application. This file stores the application's configuration settings. You'll rarely need to manually modify Web.config. The first time you select **Debug > Start Debugging** in a project, a dialog appears and asks whether you want the IDE to modify the Web.config file to enable debugging. After you click **OK**, the IDE executes the application. You can stop debugging by selecting **Debug > Stop Debugging**.

Regardless of how you execute the web application, the IDE will compile the project before it executes. In fact, ASP.NET compiles your web page whenever it changes between HTTP requests. For example, suppose you browse the page, then modify the ASPX file or add code to the code-behind file. When you reload the page, ASP.NET recompiles the page on the server before returning the response to the browser. This important behavior ensures that clients always see the latest version of the page. You can manually compile an entire website by selecting **Build Web Site** from the **Debug** menu in Visual Web Developer.

19.4.2 Examining WebTime.aspx's Code-Behind File

Figure 19.20 presents the code-behind file WebTime.aspx.cs. Line 5 begins the declaration of class WebTime. In Visual C#, a class declaration can span multiple source-code files—the separate portions of the class declaration in each file are known as **partial classes**. The **partial modifier** indicates that the code-behind file is part of a larger class. Like Windows Forms applications, the rest of the class's code is generated for you based on your visual interactions to create the application's GUI in **Design** mode. That code is stored in other source code files as partial classes with the same name. The compiler assembles all the partial classes that have the same into a single class declaration.

Line 5 indicates that WebTime inherits from class **Page** in namespace **System.Web.UI**. This namespace contains classes and controls for building web-based applications. Class Page represents the default capabilities of each page in a web application—all pages inherit directly or indirectly from this class.

Lines 8–12 define the Page_Init event handler, which initializes the page in response to the page's Init event. The only initialization required for this page is to set the time-Label's Text property to the time on the web server computer. The statement in line 11 retrieves the current time (DateTime.Now) and formats it as *hh*:*mm*:*ss*. For example, 9 AM is formatted as 09:00:00, and 2:30 PM is formatted as 02:30:00. As you'll see, variable timeLabel represents an ASP.NET Label control. The ASP.NET controls are defined in namespace **System.Web.UI.WebControls**.

```
1   // Fig. 19.20: WebTime.aspx.cs
2   // Code-behind file for a page that displays the web server's time.
3   using System;
4
5   public partial class WebTime : System.Web.UI.Page
6   {
7       // initializes the contents of the page
8       protected void Page_Init( object sender, EventArgs e )
9       {
10          // display the server's current time in timeLabel
11          timeLabel.Text = DateTime.Now.ToString( "hh:mm:ss" );
12      } // end method Page_Init
13  } // end class WebTime
```

Fig. 19.20 | Code-behind file for a page that displays the web server's time.

19.5 Standard Web Controls: Designing a Form

This section introduces some of the web controls located in the **Standard** section of the **Toolbox** (Fig. 19.11). Figure 19.21 summarizes the controls used in the next example.

A Form Gathering User Input
Figure 19.22 depicts a form for gathering user input. This example does not perform any tasks—that is, no action occurs when the user clicks **Register**. As an exercise, we ask you

Web control	Description
TextBox	Gathers user input and displays text.
Button	Triggers an event when clicked.
HyperLink	Displays a hyperlink.
DropDownList	Displays a drop-down list of choices from which a user can select an item.
RadioButtonList	Groups radio buttons.
Image	Displays images (for example, PNG, GIF and JPG).

Fig. 19.21 | Commonly used web controls.

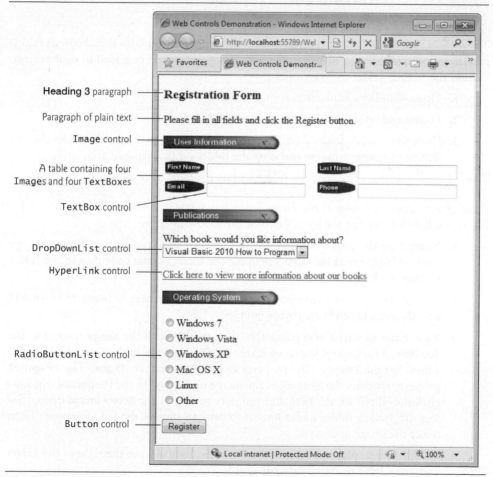

Fig. 19.22 | Web Form that demonstrates web controls.

to provide the functionality. Here we focus on the steps for adding these controls to a Web Form and for setting their properties. Subsequent examples demonstrate how to handle the events of many of these controls. To execute this application:

1. Select **Open Web Site...** from the **File** menu.

2. In the **Open Web Site** dialog, ensure that **File System** is selected, then navigate to this chapter's examples, select the WebControls folder and click the **Open** Button.

3. Select WebControls.aspx in the **Solution Explorer**, then type *Ctrl* + *F5* to execute the web application in your default web browser.

Creating the Web Site

To begin, follow the steps in Section 19.4.1 to create an **Empty Web Site** named WebControls, then add a Web Form named WebControls.aspx to the project. Set the document's Title property to "Web Controls Demonstration". To ensure that WebControls.aspx loads when you execute this application, right click it in the **Solution Explorer** and select **Set As Start Page**.

Adding the Images to the Project

The images used in this example are located in the images folder with this chapter's examples. Before you can display images in the Web Form, they must be added to your project. To add the images folder to your project:

1. Open Windows Explorer.

2. Locate and open this chapter's examples folder (ch22).

3. Drag the images folder from Windows Explorer into Visual Web Developer's **Solution Explorer** window and drop the folder on the name of your project.

The IDE will automatically copy the folder and its contents into your project.

Adding Text and an Image to the Form

Next, you'll begin creating the page. Perform the following steps:

1. First create the page's heading. At the current cursor position on the page, type the text "Registration Form", then use the **Block Format** ComboBox in the IDE's toolbar to change the text to **Heading 3** format.

2. Press *Enter* to start a new paragraph, then type the text "Please fill in all fields and click the Register button".

3. Press *Enter* to start a new paragraph, then double click the **Image** control in the Toolbox. This control inserts an image into a web page, at the current cursor position. Set the Image's (ID) property to userInformationImage. The **ImageUrl** property specifies the location of the image to display. In the **Properties** window, click the ellipsis for the ImageUrl property to display the **Select Image** dialog. Select the images folder under **Project folders:** to display the list of images. Then select the image user.png.

4. Click **OK** to display the image in **Design** view, then click to the right of the Image and press *Enter* to start a new paragraph.

Adding a Table to the Form

Form elements are often placed in tables for layout purposes—like the elements that represent the first name, last name, e-mail and phone information in Fig. 19.22. Next, you'll create a table with two rows and two columns in **Design** mode.

1. Select **Table > Insert Table** to display the **Insert Table** dialog (Fig. 19.23). This dialog allows you to configure the table's options.

2. Under **Size**, ensure that the values of **Rows** and **Columns** are both 2—these are the default values.

3. Click **OK** to close the **Insert Table** dialog and create the table.

By default, the contents of a table cell are aligned vertically in the middle of the cell. We changed the vertical alignment of all cells in the table by setting the valign property to top in the **Properties** window. This causes the content in each table cell to align with the top of the cell. You can set the valign property for each table cell individually or by selecting all the cells in the table at once, then changing the valign property's value.

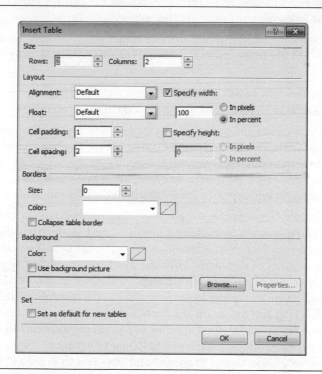

Fig. 19.23 | **Insert Table** dialog.

After creating the table, controls and text can be added to particular cells to create a neatly organized layout. Next, add Image and TextBox controls to each the four table cells as follows:

1. Click the table cell in the first row and first column of the table, then double click the Image control in the **Toolbox**. Set its (ID) property to firstNameImage and set its ImageUrl property to the image fname.png.

2. Next, double click the TextBox control in the **Toolbox**. Set its (ID) property to firstNameTextBox. As in Windows Forms, a **TextBox** control allows you to obtain text from the user and display text to the user

3. Repeat this process in the first row and second column, but set the Image's (ID) property to `lastNameImage` and its ImageUrl property to the image `lname.png`, and set the TextBox's (ID) property to `lastNameTextBox`.

4. Repeat *Steps 1* and *2* in the second row and first column, but set the Image's (ID) property to `emailImage` and its ImageUrl property to the image `email.png`, and set the TextBox's (ID) property to `emailTextBox`.

5. Repeat *Steps 1* and *2* in the second row and second column, but set the Image's (ID) property to `phoneImage` and its ImageUrl property to the image `phone.png`, and set the TextBox's (ID) property to `phoneTextBox`.

Creating the Publications Section of the Page

This section contains an Image, some text, a DropDownList control and a HyperLink control. Perform the following steps to create this section:

1. Click below the table, then use the techniques you've already learned in this section to add an Image named `publicationsImage` that displays the `publications.png` image.

2. Click to the right of the Image, then press *Enter* and type the text "`Which book would you like information about?`" in the new paragraph.

3. Hold the *Shift* key and press *Enter* to create a new line in the current paragraph, then double click the **DropDownList** control in the **Toolbox**. Set its (ID) property to `booksDropDownList`. This control is similar to the Windows Forms ComboBox control, but doesn't allow users to type text. When a user clicks the drop-down list, it expands and displays a list from which the user can make a selection.

4. You can add items to the DropDownList using the **ListItem Collection Editor**, which you can access by clicking the ellipsis next to the DropDownList's Items property in the **Properties** window, or by using the **DropDownList Tasks** smart-tag menu. To open this menu, click the small arrowhead that appears in the upper-right corner of the control in **Design** mode (Fig. 19.24). Visual Web Developer displays smart-tag menus for many ASP.NET controls to facilitate common tasks. Clicking **Edit Items...** in the **DropDownList Tasks** menu opens the **ListItem Collection Editor**, which allows you to add ListItem elements to the DropDownList. Add items for "`Visual Basic 2010 How to Program`", "`Visual C# 2010 How to Program`", "`Java How to Program`" and "`C++ How to Program`" by clicking the **Add** Button four times. For each item, select it, then set its Text property to one of the four book titles.

5. Click to the right of the DropDownList and press *Enter* to start a new paragraph, then double click the **HyperLink** control in the **Toolbox** to add a hyperlink to the

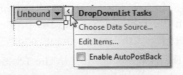

Fig. 19.24 | **DropDownList Tasks** smart-tag menu.

web page. Set its (ID) property to booksHyperLink and its Text property to "Click here to view more information about our books". Set the **NavigateUrl** property to http://www.deitel.com. This specifies the resource or web page that will be requested when the user clicks the HyperLink. Setting the **Target** property to _blank specifies that the requested web page should open in a new browser window. By default, HyperLink controls cause pages to open in the same browser window.

Completing the Page

Next you'll create the **Operating System** section of the page and the **Register** Button. This section contains a **RadioButtonList** control, which provides a series of radio buttons from which the user can select only one. The **RadioButtonList Tasks** smart-tag menu provides an **Edit Items...** link to open the **ListItem Collection Editor** so that you can create the items in the list. Perform the following steps:

1. Click to the right of the HyperLink control and press *Enter* to create a new paragraph, then add an Image named osImage that displays the os.png image.

2. Click to the right of the Image and press *Enter* to create a new paragraph, then add a RadioButtonList. Set its (ID) property to osRadioButtonList. Use the **ListItem Collection Editor** to add the items shown in Fig. 19.22.

3. Finally, click to the right of the RadioButtonList and press *Enter* to create a new paragraph, then add a **Button**. A Button web control represents a button that triggers an action when clicked. Set its (ID) property to registerButton and its Text property to Register. As stated earlier, clicking the **Register** button in this example does not do anything.

You can now execute the application (*Ctrl + F5*) to see the Web Form in your browser.

19.6 Validation Controls

This section introduces a different type of web control, called a **validation control** or **validator**, which determines whether the data in another web control is in the proper format. For example, validators can determine whether a user has provided information in a required field or whether a zip-code field contains exactly five digits. Validators provide a mechanism for validating user input on the client. When the page is sent to the client, the validator is converted into JavaScript that performs the validation in the client web browser. JavaScript is a scripting language that enhances the functionality of web pages and is typically executed on the client. Unfortunately, some client browsers might not support scripting or the user might disable it. For this reason, you should always perform validation on the server. ASP.NET validation controls can function on the client, on the server or both.

Validating Input in a Web Form

The Web Form in Fig. 19.25 prompts the user to enter a name, e-mail address and phone number. A website could use a form like this to collect contact information from visitors. After the user enters any data, but before the data is sent to the web server, validators ensure that the user *entered a value in each field* and that the e-mail address and phone-number values are in an acceptable format. In this example, (555) 123-4567, 555-123-4567 and 123-4567 are all considered valid phone numbers. Once the data is submitted, the web server responds by displaying a message that repeats the submitted information. A real business application would typically store the submitted data in a database or in a file on the server. We simply send the data back to the client to demonstrate that the server received the data. To execute this application:

1. Select **Open Web Site...** from the **File** menu.

2. In the **Open Web Site** dialog, ensure that **File System** is selected, then navigate to this chapter's examples, select the `Validation` folder and click the **Open** Button.

3. Select `Validation.aspx` in the **Solution Explorer**, then type *Ctrl* + *F5* to execute the web application in your default web browser.

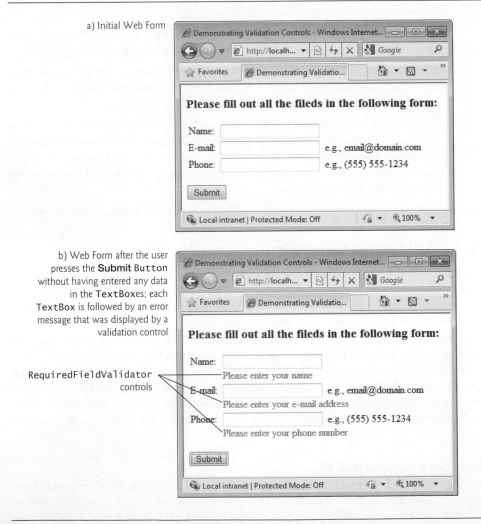

a) Initial Web Form

b) Web Form after the user presses the **Submit** Button without having entered any data in the TextBoxes; each TextBox is followed by an error message that was displayed by a validation control

`RequiredFieldValidator` controls

Fig. 19.25 | Validators in a Web Form that retrieves user contact information. (Part 1 of 2.)

c) Web Form after the user enters a name, an invalid e-mail address and an invalid phone number in the TextBoxes, then presses the **Submit Button**; the validation controls display error messages in response to the invalid e-mail and phone number values

RegularExpressionValidator controls

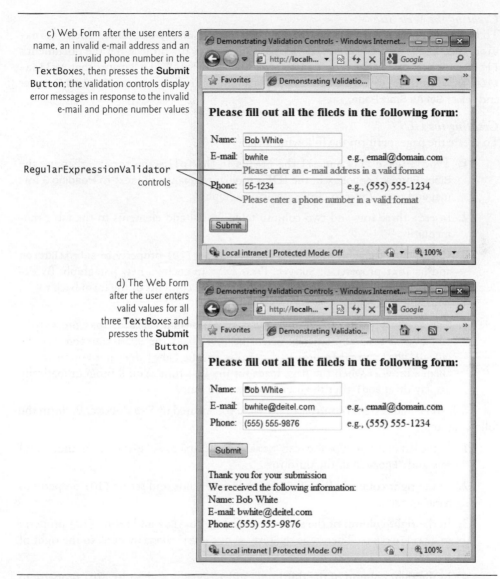

d) The Web Form after the user enters valid values for all three TextBoxes and presses the **Submit Button**

Fig. 19.25 | Validators in a Web Form that retrieves user contact information. (Part 2 of 2.)

In the sample output:

- Fig. 19.25(a) shows the initial Web Form
- Fig. 19.25(b) shows the result of submitting the form before typing any data in the TextBoxes
- Fig. 19.25(c) shows the results after entering data in each TextBox, but specifying an invalid e-mail address and invalid phone number
- Fig. 19.25(d) shows the results after entering valid values for all three TextBoxes and submitting the form.

Creating the Web Site

To begin, follow the steps in Section 19.4.1 to create an **Empty Web Site** named Validation, then add a Web Form named Validation.aspx to the project. Set the document's Title property to "Demonstrating Validation Controls". To ensure that Validation.aspx loads when you execute this application, right click it in the **Solution Explorer** and select **Set As Start Page.**

Creating the GUI

To create the page, perform the following steps:

1. Type "Please fill out all the fields in the following form:", then use the **Block Format** ComboBox in the IDE's toolbar to change the text to **Heading 3** format and press *Enter* to create a new paragraph.

2. Insert a three row and two column table. You'll add elements to the table momentarily.

3. Click below the table and add a Button. Set its (ID) property to submitButton and its Text property to Submit. Press *Enter* to create a new paragraph. By default, a Button control in a Web Form sends the contents of the form back to the server for processing.

4. Add a Label. Set its (ID) property to outputLabel and clear its Text property—you'll set it programmatically when the user clicks the submitButton. Set the outputLabel's **Visible** property to false, so the Label does not appear in the client's browser when the page loads for the first time. You'll programmatically display this Label after the user submits valid data.

Next you'll add text and controls to the table you created in *Step 2* above. Perform the following steps:

1. In the left column, type the text "Name:" in the first row, "E-mail:" in the second row and "Phone:" in the third row.

2. In the right column of the first row, add a TextBox and set its (ID) property to nameTextBox.

3. In the right column of the second row, add a TextBox and set its (ID) property to emailTextBox. Then type the text "e.g., email@domain.com" to the right of the TextBox.

4. In the right column of the third row, add a TextBox and set its (ID) property to phoneTextBox. Then type the text "e.g., (555) 555-1234" to the right of the TextBox.

Using *RequiredFieldValidator* Controls

We use three **RequiredFieldValidator** controls (found in the **Validation** section of the **Toolbox**) to ensure that the name, e-mail address and phone number TextBoxes are not empty when the form is submitted. A RequiredFieldValidator makes an input control a required field. If such a field is empty, validation fails. Add a RequiredFieldValidator as follows:

1. Click to the right of the nameTextBox in the table and press *Enter* to move to the next line.

2. Add a RequiredFieldValidator, set its (ID) to nameRequiredFieldValidator and set the ForeColor property to Red.

3. Set the validator's **ControlToValidate** property to nameTextBox to indicate that this validator verifies the nameTextBox's contents.

4. Set the validator's **ErrorMessage** property to "Please enter your name". This is displayed on the Web Form only if the validation fails.

5. Set the validator's **Display** property to Dynamic, so the validator occupies space on the Web Form only when validation fails. When this occurs, space is allocated dynamically, causing the controls below the validator to shift downward to accommodate the ErrorMessage, as seen in Fig. 19.25(a)–(c).

Repeat these steps to add two more RequiredFieldValidators in the second and third rows of the table. Set their (ID) properties to emailRequiredFieldValidator and phone-RequiredFieldValidator, respectively, and set their ErrorMessage properties to "Please enter your email address" and "Please enter your phone number", respectively.

Using *RegularExpressionValidator* Controls

This example also uses two **RegularExpressionValidator** controls to ensure that the e-mail address and phone number entered by the user are in a valid format. Visual Web Developer provides several *predefined* regular expressions that you can simply select to take advantage of this powerful validation control. Add a RegularExpressionValidator as follows:

1. Click to the right of the emailRequiredFieldValidator in the second row of the table and add a RegularExpressionValidator, then set its (ID) to emailRegularExpressionValidator and its ForeColor property to Red.

2. Set the ControlToValidate property to emailTextBox to indicate that this validator verifies the emailTextBox's contents.

3. Set the validator's ErrorMessage property to "Please enter an e-mail address in a valid format".

4. Set the validator's Display property to Dynamic, so the validator occupies space on the Web Form only when validation fails.

Repeat the preceding steps to add another RegularExpressionValidator in the third row of the table. Set its (ID) property to phoneRegularExpressionValidator and its ErrorMessage property to "Please enter a phone number in a valid format", respectively.

A RegularExpressionValidator's **ValidationExpression** property specifies the regular expression that validates the ControlToValidate's contents. Clicking the ellipsis next to property ValidationExpression in the **Properties** window displays the **Regular Expression Editor** dialog, which contains a list of **Standard expressions** for phone numbers, zip codes and other formatted information. For the emailRegularExpressionValidator, we selected the standard expression **Internet e-mail address**. If the user enters text in the emailTextBox that does not have the correct format and either clicks in a different text box or attempts to submit the form, the ErrorMessage text is displayed in red.

For the phoneRegularExpressionValidator, we selected **U.S. phone number** to ensure that a phone number contains an optional three-digit area code either in parentheses and followed by an optional space or without parentheses and followed by a required hyphen. After an optional area code, a phone number must contain three digits, a hyphen and another four digits. For example, (555) 123-4567, 555-123-4567 and 123-4567 are all valid phone numbers.

Submitting the Web Form's Contents to the Server
If all five validators are successful (that is, each TextBox is filled in, and the e-mail address and phone number provided are valid), clicking the **Submit** button sends the form's data to the server. As shown in Fig. 19.25(d), the server then responds by displaying the submitted data in the outputLabel.

Examining the Code-Behind File for a Web Form That Receives User Input
Figure 19.26 shows the code-behind file for this application. Notice that this code-behind file does not contain any implementation related to the validators. We say more about this soon. In this example, we respond to the page's **Load** event to process the data submitted by the user. Like the Init event, the Load event occurs each time the page loads into a web browser—the difference is that on a postback, you cannot access the posted data in the controls. The event handler for this event is **Page_Load** (lines 8–33). The event handler for the Load event is created for you when you add a new Web Form. To complete the event handler, insert the code from Fig. 19.26.

```
 1    // Fig. 19.26: Validation.aspx.cs
 2    // Code-behind file for the form demonstrating validation controls.
 3    using System;
 4
 5    public partial class Validation : System.Web.UI.Page
 6    {
 7       // Page_Load event handler executes when the page is loaded
 8       protected void Page_Load( object sender, EventArgs e )
 9       {
10          // if this is not the first time the page is loading
11          // (i.e., the user has already submitted form data)
12          if ( IsPostBack )
13          {
14             Validate(); // validate the form
15
16             // if the form is valid
17             if ( IsValid )
18             {
19                // retrieve the values submitted by the user
20                string name = nameTextBox.Text;
21                string email = emailTextBox.Text;
22                string phone = phoneTextBox.Text;
23
24                // show the the submitted values
25                outputLabel.Text = "Thank you for your submission<br/>" +
26                   "We received the following information:<br/>";
27                outputLabel.Text +=
28                   String.Format( "Name: {0}{1}E-mail:{2}{1}Phone:{3}",
29                      name, "<br/>", email, phone);
```

Fig. 19.26 | Code-behind file for the form demonstrating validation controls. (Part 1 of 2.)

```
30                    outputLabel.Visible = true; // display the output message
31              } // end if
32           } // end if
33       } // end method Page_Load
34   } // end class Validation
```

Fig. 19.26 | Code-behind file for the form demonstrating validation controls. (Part 2 of 2.)

Differentiating Between the First Request to a Page and a Postback
Web programmers using ASP.NET often design their web pages so that the current page reloads when the user submits the form; this enables the program to receive input, process it as necessary and display the results in the same page when it's loaded the second time. These pages usually contain a form that, when submitted, sends the values of all the controls to the server and causes the current page to be requested again. This event is known as a **postback**. Line 12 uses the **IsPostBack** property of class Page to determine whether the page is being loaded due to a postback. The first time that the web page is requested, IsPostBack is false, and the page displays only the form for user input. When the postback occurs (from the user clicking **Submit**), IsPostBack is true.

Server-Side Web Form Validation
Server-side Web Form validation must be implemented programmatically. Line 14 calls the current Page's **Validate** method to validate the information in the request. This validates the information as specified by the validation controls in the Web Form. Line 17 uses the **IsValid** property of class Page to check whether the validation succeeded. If this property is set to true (that is, validation succeeded and the Web Form is valid), then we display the Web Form's information. Otherwise, the web page loads without any changes, except any validator that failed now displays its ErrorMessage.

Processing the Data Entered by the User
Lines 20–22 retrieve the values of nameTextBox, emailTextBox and phoneTextBox. When data is posted to the web server, the data that the user entered is accessible to the web application through the web controls' properties. Next, lines 25–29 set outputLabel's Text to display a message that includes the name, e-mail and phone information that was submitted to the server. In lines 25, 26 and 29, notice the use of <br/> rather than \n to start new lines in the outputLabel—
 is the markup for a line break in a web page. Line 30 sets the outputLabel's Visible property to true, so the user can see the thank-you message and submitted data when the page reloads in the client web browser.

19.7 Session Tracking
Originally, critics accused the Internet and e-business of failing to provide the customized service typically experienced in "brick-and-mortar" stores. To address this problem, businesses established mechanisms by which they could *personalize* users' browsing experiences, tailoring content to individual users. Businesses achieve this level of service by tracking each customer's movement through the Internet and combining the collected data with information provided by the consumer, including billing information, personal preferences, interests and hobbies.

Personalization

Personalization makes it possible for businesses to communicate effectively with their customers and also improves users' ability to locate desired products and services. Companies that provide content of particular interest to users can establish relationships with customers and build on those relationships over time. Furthermore, by targeting consumers with personal offers, recommendations, advertisements, promotions and services, businesses create customer loyalty. Websites can use sophisticated technology to allow visitors to customize home pages to suit their individual needs and preferences. Similarly, online shopping sites often store personal information for customers, tailoring notifications and special offers to their interests. Such services encourage customers to visit sites more frequently and make purchases more regularly.

Privacy

A trade-off exists between personalized business service and protection of privacy. Some consumers embrace tailored content, but others fear the possible adverse consequences if the info they provide to businesses is released or collected by tracking technologies. Consumers and privacy advocates ask: What if the business to which we give personal data sells or gives that information to another organization without our knowledge? What if we do not want our actions on the Internet—a supposedly anonymous medium—to be tracked and recorded by unknown parties? What if unauthorized parties gain access to sensitive private data, such as credit-card numbers or medical history? These are questions that must be addressed by programmers, consumers, businesses and lawmakers alike.

Recognizing Clients

To provide personalized services to consumers, businesses must be able to recognize clients when they request information from a site. As we have discussed, the request/response system on which the web operates is facilitated by HTTP. Unfortunately, HTTP is a *stateless protocol*—it *does not* provide information that would enable web servers to maintain state information regarding particular clients. This means that web servers cannot determine whether a request comes from a particular client or whether the same or different clients generate a series of requests.

To circumvent this problem, sites can provide mechanisms by which they identify individual clients. A session represents a unique client on a website. If the client leaves a site and then returns later, the client will still be recognized as the same user. When the user closes the browser, the session typically ends. To help the server distinguish among clients, each client must identify itself to the server. Tracking individual clients is known as **session tracking**. One popular session-tracking technique uses cookies (discussed in Section 19.7.1); another uses ASP.NET's HttpSessionState object (used in Section 19.7.2). Additional session-tracking techniques are beyond this book's scope.

19.7.1 Cookies

Cookies provide you with a tool for personalizing web pages. A cookie is a piece of data stored by web browsers in a small text file on the user's computer. A cookie maintains information about the client during and between browser sessions. The first time a user visits the website, the user's computer might receive a cookie from the server; this cookie is then reactivated each time the user revisits that site. The collected information is intended to be an anonymous record containing data that is used to personalize the user's future visits to the site. For example, cookies in a shopping application might store unique identifiers for users. When a user adds items to an online shopping cart or performs another task resulting in a request to the web server, the server receives a cookie containing the user's unique identifier. The server then uses the unique identifier to locate the shopping cart and perform any necessary processing.

In addition to identifying users, cookies also can indicate users' shopping preferences. When a Web Form receives a request from a client, the Web Form can examine the cookie(s) it sent to the client during previous communications, identify the user's preferences and immediately display products of interest to the client.

Every HTTP-based interaction between a client and a server includes a header containing information either about the request (when the communication is from the client to the server) or about the response (when the communication is from the server to the client). When a Web Form receives a request, the header includes information such as the request type and any cookies that have been sent previously from the server to be stored on the client machine. When the server formulates its response, the header information contains any cookies the server wants to store on the client computer and other information, such as the MIME type of the response.

The **expiration date** of a cookie determines how long the cookie remains on the client's computer. If you do not set an expiration date for a cookie, the web browser maintains the cookie for the duration of the browsing session. Otherwise, the web browser maintains the cookie until the expiration date occurs. Cookies are deleted when they expire.

> **Portability Tip 19.1**
>
> *Users may disable cookies in their web browsers to help ensure their privacy. Such users will experience difficulty using web applications that depend on cookies to maintain state information.*

19.7.2 Session Tracking with `HttpSessionState`

The next web application demonstrates session tracking using the .NET class **Http-SessionState**. When you execute this application, the `Options.aspx` page (Fig. 19.27(a)), which is the application's **Start Page**, allows the user to select a programming language from a group of radio buttons. [Note: You might need to right click `Options.aspx` in the **Solution Explorer** and select **Set As Start Page** before running this application.] When the user clicks **Submit**, the selection is sent to the web server for processing. The web server uses an `HttpSessionState` object to store the chosen language and the ISBN number for one of our books on that topic. Each user that visits the site has a unique `HttpSessionState` object, so the selections made by one user are maintained separately from all other users. After storing the selection, the server returns the page to the browser (Fig. 19.27(b)) and displays the user's selection and some information about the user's unique session (which we show just for demonstration purposes). The page also includes links that allow the user to choose between selecting another programming language or viewing the `Recommenda-tions.aspx` page (Fig. 19.27(e)), which lists recommended books pertaining to the programming language(s) that the user selected previously. If the user clicks the link for book recommendations, the information stored in the user's unique `HttpSessionState` object is read and used to form the list of recommendations. To test this application:

1. Select **Open Web Site...** from the **File** menu.

2. In the **Open Web Site** dialog, ensure that **File System** is selected, then navigate to this chapter's examples, select the `Sessions` folder and click the **Open Button**.

3. Select `Options.aspx` in the **Solution Explorer**, then type *Ctrl + F5* to execute the web application in your default web browser.

Creating the Web Site

To begin, follow the steps in Section 19.4.1 to create an **Empty Web Site** named `Sessions`, then add two Web Forms named `Options.aspx` and `Recommendations.aspx` to the project. Set the `Options.aspx` document's `Title` property to `"Sessions"` and the `Recommendations.aspx` document's `Title` property to `"Book Recommendations"`. To ensure that `Options.aspx` is the first page to load for this application, right click it in the **Solution Explorer** and select **Set As Start Page**.

a) User selects a language from the `Options.aspx` page, then presses **Submit** to send the selection to the server

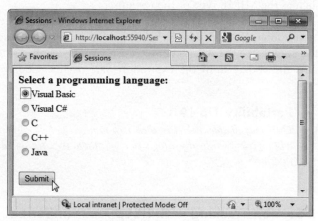

b) `Options.aspx` page is updated to hide the controls for selecting a language and to display the user's selection; the user clicks the hyperlink to return to the list of languages and make another selection

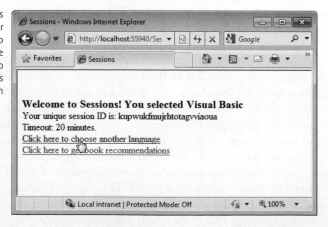

Fig. 19.27 | ASPX file that presents a list of programming languages. (Part 1 of 2.)

c) User selects another language from the `Options.aspx` page, then presses **Submit** to send the selection to the server

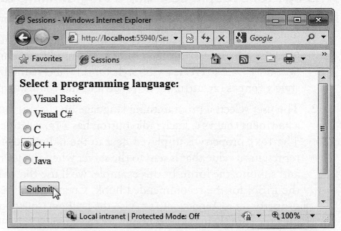

d) `Options.aspx` page is updated to hide the controls for selecting a language and to display the user's selection; the user clicks the hyperlink to get a list of book recommendations

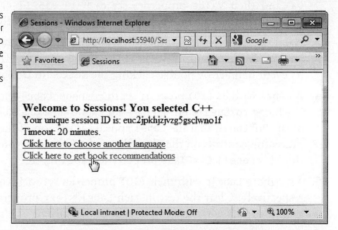

e) `Recommendations.aspx` displays the list of recommended books based on the user's selections

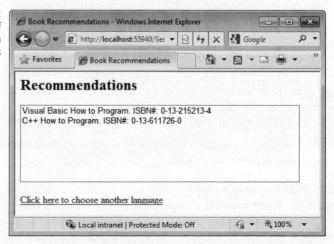

Fig. 19.27 | ASPX file that presents a list of programming languages. (Part 2 of 2.)

19.7.3 Options.aspx: Selecting a Programming Language

The Options.aspx page Fig. 19.27(a) contains the following controls arranged vertically:

1. A Label with its (ID) property set to promptLabel and its Text property set to "Select a programming language:". We used the techniques shown in *Step 5* of Section 19.4.1 to create a CSS style for this label named .labelStyle, and set the style's font-size attribute to large and the font-weight attribute to bold.

2. The user selects a programming language by clicking one of the radio buttons in a RadioButtonList. Each radio button has a Text property and a Value property. The Text property is displayed next to the radio button and the Value property represents a value that is sent to the server when the user selects that radio button and submits the form. In this example, we'll use the Value property to represent the ISBN for the recommended book. Create a RadioButtonList with its (ID) property set to languageList. Use the **ListItem Collection Editor** to add five radio buttons with their Text properties set to Visual Basic, Visual C#, C, C++ and Java, and their Value properties set to 0-13-215213-4, 0-13-605322-X, 0-13-512356-2, 0-13-611726-0 and 0-13-605306-8, respectively

3. A Button with its (ID) property set to submitButton and its Text property set to Submit. In this example, we'll handle this Button's Click event. You can create its event handler by double clicking the Button in **Design** view.

4. A Label with its (ID) property set to responseLabel and its Text property set to "Welcome to Sessions!". This Label should be placed immediately to the right of the Button so that the Label appears at the top of the page when we hide the preceding controls on the page. Reuse the CSS style you created in *Step 1* by setting this Label's CssClass property to labelStyle.

5. Two more Labels with their (ID) properties set to idLabel and timeoutLabel, respectively. Clear the text in each Label's Text property—you'll set these programmatically with information about the current user's session.

6. A HyperLink with its (ID) property set to languageLink and its Text property set to "Click here to choose another language". Set its NavigateUrl property by clicking the ellipsis next to the property in the **Properties** window and selecting Options.aspx from the **Select URL** dialog.

7. A HyperLink with its (ID) property set to recommendationsLink and its Text property set to "Click here to get book recommendations". Set its NavigateUrl property by clicking the ellipsis next to the property in the **Properties** window and selecting Recommendations.aspx from the **Select URL** dialog.

8. Initially, the controls in *Steps 4–7* will not be displayed, so set each control's Visible property to false.

Session Property of a **Page**

Every Web Form includes a user-specific HttpSessionState object, which is accessible through property **Session** of class Page. Throughout this section, we use this property to manipulate the current user's HttpSessionState object. When a page is first requested, a unique HttpSessionState object is created by ASP.NET and assigned to the Page's Session property.

Code-Behind File for **Options.aspx**
Fig. 19.28 presents the code-behind file for the Options.aspx page. When this page is requested, the Page_Load event handler (lines 10–40) executes before the response is sent to the client. Since the first request to a page is not a postback, the code in lines 16–39 *does not* execute the first time the page loads.

```
1   // Fig. 19.28: Options.aspx.cs
2   // Processes user's selection of a programming language by displaying
3   // links and writing information in a Session object.
4   using System;
5
6   public partial class Options : System.Web.UI.Page
7   {
8      // if postback, hide form and display links to make additional
9      // selections or view recommendations
10     protected void Page_Load( object sender, EventArgs e )
11     {
12        if ( IsPostBack )
13        {
14           // user has submitted information, so display message
15           // and appropriate hyperlinks
16           responseLabel.Visible = true;
17           idLabel.Visible = true;
18           timeoutLabel.Visible = true;
19           languageLink.Visible = true;
20           recommendationsLink.Visible = true;
21
22           // hide other controls used to make language selection
23           promptLabel.Visible = false;
24           languageList.Visible = false;
25           submitButton.Visible = false;
26
27           // if the user made a selection, display it in responseLabel
28           if ( languageList.SelectedItem != null )
29              responseLabel.Text += " You selected " +
30                 languageList.SelectedItem.Text;
31           else
32              responseLabel.Text += " You did not select a language.";
33
34           // display session ID
35           idLabel.Text = "Your unique session ID is: " + Session.SessionID;
36
37           // display the timeout
38           timeoutLabel.Text = "Timeout: " + Session.Timeout + " minutes.";
39        } // end if
40     } // end method Page_Load
41
42     // record the user's selection in the Session
43     protected void submitButton_Click( object sender, EventArgs e )
44     {
```

Fig. 19.28 | Process user's selection of a programming language by displaying links and writing information in an HttpSessionState object. (Part 1 of 2.)

```
45          // if the user made a selection
46          if ( languageList.SelectedItem != null )
47             // add name/value pair to Session
48             Session.Add( languageList.SelectedItem.Text,
49                languageList.SelectedItem.Value );
50       } // end method submitButton_Click
51    } // end class Options
```

Fig. 19.28 | Process user's selection of a programming language by displaying links and writing information in an `HttpSessionState` object. (Part 2 of 2.)

Postback Processing

When the user presses **Submit**, a postback occurs. The form is submitted to the server and `Page_Load` executes. Lines 16–20 display the controls shown in Fig. 19.27(b) and lines 23–25 hide the controls shown in Fig. 19.27(a). Next, lines 28–32 ensure that the user selected a language and, if so, display a message in the `responseLabel` indicating the selection. Otherwise, the message "You did not select a language" is displayed.

The ASP.NET application contains information about the `HttpSessionState` object (property `Session` of the `Page` object) for the current client. The object's **SessionID** property (displayed in line 35) contains the **unique session ID**—a sequence of random letters and numbers. The first time a client connects to the web server, a unique session ID is created for that client and a temporary cookie is written to the client so the server can identify the client on subsequent requests. When the client makes additional requests, the client's session ID from that temporary cookie is compared with the session IDs stored in the web server's memory to retrieve the client's `HttpSessionState` object. `HttpSessionState` property **Timeout** (displayed in line 38) specifies the maximum amount of time that an `HttpSessionState` object can be inactive before it's discarded. By default, if the user does not interact with this web application for 20 minutes, the `HttpSessionState` object is discarded by the server and a new one will be created if the user interacts with the application again. Figure 19.29 lists some common `HttpSessionState` properties.

Properties	Description
Count	Specifies the number of key/value pairs in the Session object.
IsNewSession	Indicates whether this is a new session (that is, whether the session was created during loading of this page).
Keys	Returns a collection containing the Session object's keys.
SessionID	Returns the session's unique ID.
Timeout	Specifies the maximum number of minutes during which a session can be inactive (that is, no requests are made) before the session expires. By default, this property is set to 20 minutes.

Fig. 19.29 | `HttpSessionState` properties.

Method `submitButton_Click`

In this example, we wish to store the user's selection in an `HttpSessionState` object when the user clicks the **Submit** Button. The `submitButton_Click` event handler (lines 43–50) adds a key/value pair to the HttpSessionState object for the current user, specifying the language chosen and the ISBN number for a book on that language. The HttpSession-State object is a dictionary—a data structure that stores **key/value pairs**. A program uses the key to store and retrieve the associated value in the dictionary. We cover dictionaries in more depth in Chapter 23.

The key/value pairs in an HttpSessionState object are often referred to as **session items**. They're placed in an HttpSessionState object by calling its **Add** method. If the user made a selection (line 46), lines 48–49 get the selection and its corresponding value from the languageList by accessing its SelectedItem's Text and Value properties, respectively, then call HttpSessionState method Add to add this name/value pair as a session item in the HttpSessionState object (Session).

If the application adds a session item that has the same name as an item previously stored in the HttpSessionState object, the session item is replaced—session item names *must* be unique. Another common syntax for placing a session item in the HttpSessionState object is Session[*Name*] = *Value*. For example, we could have replaced lines 48–49 with

```
Session[ languageList.SelectedItem.Text ] =
    languageList.SelectedItem.Value
```

Software Engineering Observation 19.1

A Web Form should not use instance variables to maintain client state information, because each new request or postback is handled by a new instance of the page. Instead, maintain client state information in HttpSessionState objects, because such objects are specific to each client.

Software Engineering Observation 19.2

A benefit of using HttpSessionState objects (rather than cookies) is that they can store any type of object (not just Strings) as attribute values. This provides you with increased flexibility in determining the type of state information to maintain for clients.

19.7.4 Recommendations.aspx: Displaying Recommendations Based on Session Values

After the postback of Options.aspx, the user may request book recommendations. The book-recommendations hyperlink forwards the user to the page Recommendations.aspx (Fig. 19.27(e)) to display the recommendations based on the user's language selections. The page contains the following controls arranged vertically:

1. A Label with its (ID) property set to recommendationsLabel and its Text property set to "Recommendations". We created a CSS style for this label named .label-Style, and set the font-size attribute to x-large and the font-weight attribute to bold. (See *Step 5* in Section 19.4.1 for information on creating a CSS style.)

2. A ListBox with its (ID) property set to booksListBox. We created a CSS style for this label named .listBoxStyle. In the **Position** category, we set the width attribute to 450px and the height attribute to 125px. The px indicates that the measurement is in pixels.

3. A HyperLink with its (ID) property set to languageLink and its Text property set to "Click here to choose another language". Set its NavigateUrl property

by clicking the ellipsis next to the property in the **Properties** window and selecting Options.aspx from the **Select URL** dialog. When the user clicks this link, the Options.aspx page will be reloaded. Requesting the page in this manner *is not* considered a postback, so the original form in Fig. 19.27(a) will be displayed.

*Code-Behind File for **Recommendations.aspx***

Figure 19.30 presents the code-behind file for Recommendations.aspx. Event handler Page_Init (lines 8–29) retrieves the session information. If a user has not selected a language in the Options.aspx page, the HttpSessionState object's **Count** property will be 0 (line 11). This property provides the number of session items contained in a HttpSessionState object. If the Count is 0, then we display the text **No Recommendations** (line 22), clear the ListBox and hide it (lines 23–24), and update the Text of the HyperLink back to Options.aspx (line 27).

```
 1   // Fig. 19.30: Recommendations.aspx.cs
 2   // Creates book recommendations based on a Session object.
 3   using System;
 4
 5   public partial class Recommendations : System.Web.UI.Page
 6   {
 7      // read Session items and populate ListBox with recommendations
 8      protected void Page_Init( object sender, EventArgs e )
 9      {
10         // determine whether Session contains any information
11         if ( Session.Count != 0 )
12         {
13            // display Session's name-value pairs
14            foreach ( string keyName in Session.Keys )
15               booksListBox.Items.Add( keyName +
16                  " How to Program. ISBN#: " + Session[ keyName ] );
17         } // end if
18         else
19         {
20            // if there are no session items, no language was chosen, so
21            // display appropriate message and clear and hide booksListBox
22            recommendationsLabel.Text = "No Recommendations";
23            booksListBox.Items.Clear();
24            booksListBox.Visible = false;
25
26            // modify languageLink because no language was selected
27            languageLink.Text = "Click here to choose a language";
28         } // end else
29      } // end method Page_Init
30   } // end class Recommendations
```

Fig. 19.30 | Session data used to provide book recommendations to the user.

If the user chose at least one language, the loop in lines 14–16 iterates through the HttpSessionState object's keys (line 14) by accessing the HttpSessionState's **Keys** property, which returns a collection containing all the keys in the session. Lines 15–16 concatenate the keyName, the String " How to Program. ISBN#: " and the key's corresponding value, which is returned by Session(keyName). This String is the recommendation that is added to the ListBox.

19.8 Case Study: Database-Driven ASP.NET Guestbook

Many websites allow users to provide feedback about the website in a guestbook. Typically, users click a link on the website's home page to request the guestbook page. This page usually consists of a form that contains fields for the user's name, e-mail address, message/feedback and so on. Data submitted on the guestbook form is then stored in a database located on the server.

In this section, we create a guestbook Web Form application. The GUI (Fig. 19.31) contains a **GridView** data control, which displays all the entries in the guestbook in tabular format. This control is located in the **Toolbox**'s **Data** section. We explain how to create and configure this data control shortly. The GridView displays **abc** in **Design** mode to indicate data that will be retrieved from a data source at runtime. You'll learn how to create and configure the GridView shortly.

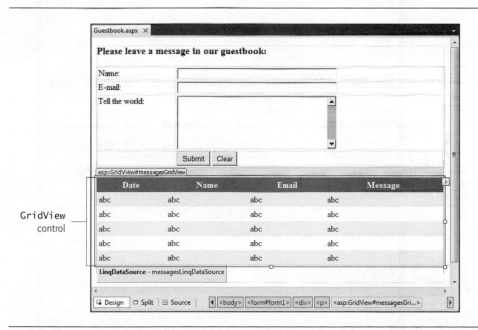

Fig. 19.31 | Guestbook application GUI in **Design** mode.

The Guestbook Database
The application stores the guestbook information in a SQL Server database called Guestbook.mdf located on the web server. (We provide this database in the databases folder with this chapter's examples.) The database contains a single table named Messages.

Testing the Application
To test this application:

1. Select **Open Web Site...** from the **File** menu.

2. In the **Open Web Site** dialog, ensure that **File System** is selected, then navigate to this chapter's examples, select the Guestbook folder and click the **Open** Button.

3. Select Guestbook.aspx in the **Solution Explorer**, then type *Ctrl + F5* to execute the web application in your default web browser.

Figure 19.32(a) shows the user submitting a new entry. Figure 19.32(b) shows the new entry as the last row in the GridView.

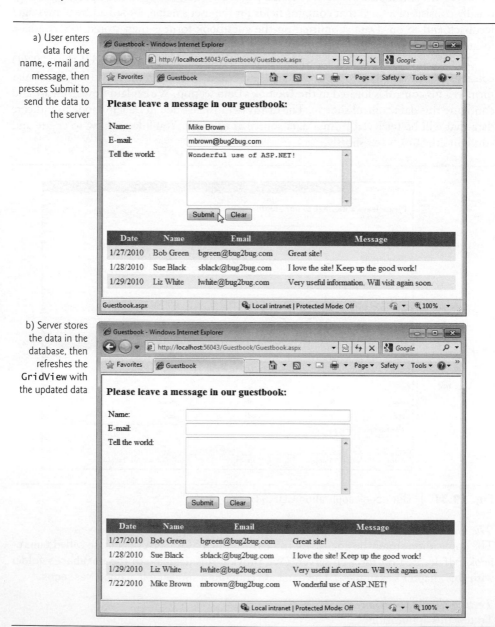

a) User enters data for the name, e-mail and message, then presses Submit to send the data to the server

b) Server stores the data in the database, then refreshes the GridView with the updated data

Fig. 19.32 | Sample execution of the **Guestbook** application.

19.8.1 Building a Web Form that Displays Data from a Database

You'll now build this GUI and set up the data binding between the GridView control and the database. Many of these steps are similar to those performed in Chapter 18 to access and interact with a database in a Windows application. We discuss the code-behind file in Section 19.8.2. To build the guestbook application, perform the following steps:

Step 1: Creating the Web Site
To begin, follow the steps in Section 19.4.1 to create an **Empty Web Site** named Guestbook then add a Web Form named Guestbook.aspx to the project. Set the document's Title property to "Guestbook". To ensure that Guestobook.aspx loads when you execute this application, right click it in the **Solution Explorer** and select **Set As Start Page**.

Step 2: Creating the Form for User Input
In **Design** mode, add the text Please leave a message in our guestbook:, then use the **Block Format** ComboBox in the IDE's toolbar to change the text to **Heading 3** format. Insert a table with four rows and two columns, configured so that the text in each cell aligns with the top of the cell. Place the appropriate text (see Fig. 19.31) in the top three cells in the table's left column. Then place TextBoxes named nameTextBox, emailTextBox and messageText-Box in the top three table cells in the right column. Configure the TextBoxes as follows:

- Set the nameTextBox's width to 300px.

- Set the emailTextBox's width to 300px.

- Set the messageTextBox's width to 300px and height to 100px. Also set this control's TextMode property to MultiLine so the user can type a message containing multiple lines of text.

Finally, add Buttons named submitButton and clearButton to the bottom-right table cell. Set the buttons' Text properties to Submit and Clear, respectively. We discuss the buttons' event handlers when we present the code-behind file. You can create these event handlers now by double clicking each Button in **Design** view.

Step 3: Adding a GridView Control to the Web Form
Add a GridView named messagesGridView that will display the guestbook entries. This control appears in the **Data** section of the **Toolbox**. The colors for the GridView are specified through the **Auto Format...** link in the **GridView Tasks** smart-tag menu that opens when you place the GridView on the page. Clicking this link displays an **AutoFormat** dialog with several choices. In this example, we chose **Professional**. We show how to set the GridView's data source (that is, where it gets the data to display in its rows and columns) shortly.

Step 4: Adding a Database to an ASP.NET Web Application
To use a SQL Server Express database file in an ASP.NET web application, you must first add the file to the project's App_Data folder. For security reasons, this folder can be accessed only by the web application on the server—clients cannot access this folder over a network. The web application interacts with the database on behalf of the client.

The **Empty Web Site** template does not create the App_Data folder. To create it, right click the project's name in the **Solution Explorer**, then select **Add ASP.NET Folder > App_Data**. Next, add the Guestbook.mdf file to the App_Data folder. You can do this in one of two ways:

- Drag the file from Windows Explorer and drop it on the App_Data folder.

- Right click the App_Data folder in the **Solution Explorer** and select **Add Existing Item...** to display the **Add Existing Item** dialog, then navigate to the databases folder with this chapter's examples, select the Guestbook.mdf file and click **Add**. [*Note:* Ensure that **Data Files** is selected in the ComboBox above or next to the **Add Button** in the dialog; otherwise, the database file will not be displayed in the list of files.]

Step 5: Creating the LINQ to SQL Classes

As in Chapter 18, you'll use LINQ to interact with the database. To create the LINQ to SQL classes for the Guestbook database:

1. Right click the project in the **Solution Explorer** and select **Add New Item...** to display the **Add New Item** dialog.

2. In the dialog, select **LINQ to SQL Classes**, enter Guestbook.dbml as the **Name**, and click **Add**. A dialog appears asking if you would like to put your new LINQ to SQL classes in the App_Code folder; click **Yes**. The IDE will create an App_Code folder and place the LINQ to SQL classes information in that folder.

3. In the **Database Explorer** window, drag the Guestbook database's Messages table from the **Database Explorer** onto the **Object Relational Designer**. Finally, save your project by selecting **File > Save All**.

Step 6: Binding the GridView to the Messages Table of the Guestbook Database

You can now configure the GridView to display the database's data.

1. In the **GridView Tasks** smart-tag menu, select **<New data source...>** from the **Choose Data Source** ComboBox to display the **Data Source Configuration Wizard** dialog.

2. In this example, we use a **LinqDataSource** control that allows the application to interact with the Guestbook.mdf database through LINQ. Select **LINQ**, then set the ID of the data source to messagesLinqDataSource and click **OK** to begin the **Configure Data Source** wizard.

3. In the **Choose a Context Object** screen, ensure that GuestbookDataContext is selected in the ComboBox, then click **Next >**.

4. The **Configure Data Selection** screen (Fig. 19.33) allows you to specify which data the LinqDataSource should retrieve from the data context. Your choices on this page design a Select LINQ query. The **Table** drop-down list identifies a table in the data context. The Guestbook data context contains one table named Messages, which is selected by default. *If you haven't saved your project* since creating your LINQ to SQL classes (*Step 5*), the list of tables *will not appear*. In the **Select** pane, ensure that the checkbox marked with an asterisk (*) is selected to indicate that you want to retrieve all the columns in the Messages table.

5. Click the **Advanced...** button, then select the **Enable the LinqDataSource to perform automatic inserts** CheckBox and click **OK**. This configures the LinqDataSource control to automatically insert new data into the database when new data is inserted in the data context. We discuss inserting new guestbook entries based on users' form submissions shortly.

6. Click **Finish** to complete the wizard.

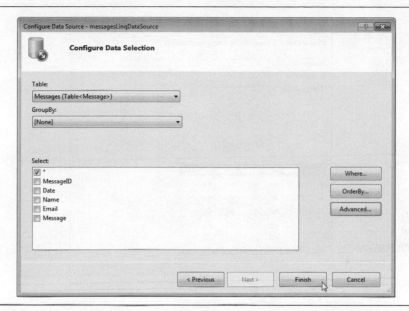

Fig. 19.33 | Configuring the query used by the `LinqDataSource` to retrieve data.

A control named `messagesLinqDataSource` now appears on the Web Form directly below the `GridView` (Fig. 19.34). It's represented in **Design** mode as a gray box containing its type and name. It will *not* appear on the web page—the gray box simply provides a way to manipulate the control visually through **Design** mode—similar to how the objects in the component tray are used in **Design** mode for a Windows Forms application.

The `GridView` now has column headers that correspond to the columns in the Messages table. The rows each contain either a number (which signifies an autoincremented column) or **abc** (which indicates string data). The actual data from the `Guestbook.mdf` database file will appear in these rows when you view the ASPX file in a web browser.

Step 7: Modifying the Columns of the Data Source Displayed in the `GridView`
It's not necessary for site visitors to see the `MessageID` column when viewing past guestbook entries—this column is merely a unique primary key required by the `Messages` table within the database. So, let's modify the `GridView` to prevent this column from displaying on the Web Form. We'll also modify the column **Message1** to read **Message**.

1. In the **GridView Tasks** smart tag menu, click **Edit Columns** to display the **Fields** dialog (Fig. 19.35).

2. Select **MessageID** in the **Selected fields** pane, then click the ⊠ Button. This removes the `MessageID` column from the `GridView`.

3. Next select **Message1** in the **Selected fields** pane and change its `HeaderText` property to `Message`. The IDE renamed this field to prevent a naming conflict in the LINQ to SQL classes.

4. Click **OK** to return to the main IDE window, then set the `Width` property of the `GridView` to 650px.

The `GridView` should now appear as shown in Fig. 19.31.

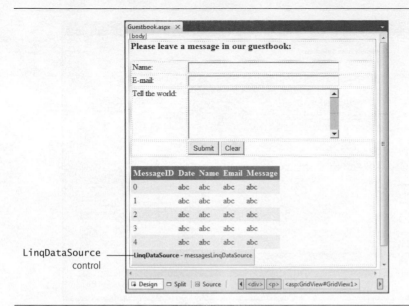

Fig. 19.34 | **Design** mode displaying LinqDataSource control for a GridView.

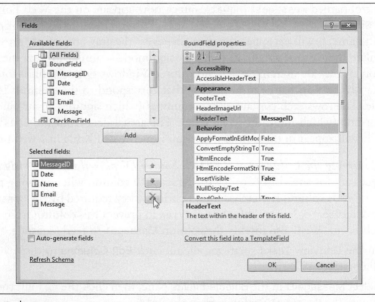

Fig. 19.35 | Removing the MessageID column from the GridView.

19.8.2 Modifying the Code-Behind File for the Guestbook Application

After building the Web Form and configuring the data controls used in this example, double click the **Submit** and **Clear** buttons in **Design** view to create their corresponding Click event handlers in the code-behind file (Fig. 19.36). The IDE generates empty event handlers, so we must add the appropriate code to make these buttons work properly. The event handler for clearButton (lines 37–42) clears each TextBox by setting its Text property to an empty string. This resets the form for a new guestbook submission.

```
1   // Fig. 19.36: Guestbook.aspx.cs
2   // Code-behind file that defines event handlers for the guestbook.
3   using System;
4   using System.Collections.Specialized; // for class ListDictionary
5
6   public partial class Guestbook : System.Web.UI.Page
7   {
8      // Submit Button adds a new guestbook entry to the database,
9      // clears the form and displays the updated list of guestbook entries
10     protected void submitButton_Click( object sender, EventArgs e )
11     {
12        // create dictionary of parameters for inserting
13        ListDictionary insertParameters = new ListDictionary();
14
15        // add current date and the user's name, e-mail address
16        // and message to dictionary of insert parameters
17        insertParameters.Add( "Date", DateTime.Now.ToShortDateString() );
18        insertParameters.Add( "Name", nameTextBox.Text );
19        insertParameters.Add( "Email", emailTextBox.Text );
20        insertParameters.Add( "Message1", messageTextBox.Text );
21
22        // execute an INSERT LINQ statement to add a new entry to the
23        // Messages table in the Guestbook data context that contains the
24        // current date and the user's name, e-mail address and message
25        messagesLinqDataSource.Insert( insertParameters );
26
27        // clear the TextBoxes
28        nameTextBox.Text = String.Empty;
29        emailTextBox.Text = String.Empty;
30        messageTextBox.Text = String.Empty;
31
32        // update the GridView with the new database table contents
33        messagesGridView.DataBind();
34     } // submitButton_Click
35
36     // Clear Button clears the Web Form's TextBoxes
37     protected void clearButton_Click( object sender, EventArgs e )
38     {
39        nameTextBox.Text = String.Empty;
40        emailTextBox.Text = String.Empty;
41        messageTextBox.Text = String.Empty;
42     } // clearButton_Click
43  } // end class Guestbook
```

Fig. 19.36 | Code-behind file for the guestbook application.

Lines 10–34 contain submitButton's event-handling code, which adds the user's information to the Guestbook database's Messages table. To use the values of the Text-Boxes on the Web Form as the parameter values inserted into the database, we must create a **ListDictionary** of insert parameters that are key/value pairs.

Line 13 creates a `ListDictionary` object—a set of key/value pairs that is implemented as a linked list and is intended for dictionaries that store 10 or fewer keys. Lines 17–20 use the `ListDictionary`'s `Add` method to store key/value pairs that represent each of the four insert parameters—the current date and the user's name, e-mail address, and message. The keys must match the names of the columns of the `Messages` table in the `.dbml` file. Invoking the `LinqDataSource` method `Insert` (line 25) inserts the data in the data context, adding a row to the `Messages` table and automatically updating the database. We pass the `ListDictionary` object as an argument to the `Insert` method to specify the insert parameters. After the data is inserted into the database, lines 28–30 clear the Text-Boxes, and line 33 invokes `messagesGridView`'s **DataBind method** to refresh the data that the `GridView` displays. This causes `messagesLinqDataSource` (the `GridView`'s source) to execute its `Select` command to obtain the `Messages` table's newly updated data.

19.9 Online Case Study: ASP.NET AJAX

In the online chapter, Web App Development with ASP.NET: A Deeper Look, you learn the difference between a traditional web application and an **Ajax (Asynchronous JavaScript and XML) web application**. You also learn how to use **ASP.NET AJAX** to quickly and easily improve the user experience for your web applications, giving them responsiveness comparable to that of desktop applications. To demonstrate ASP.NET AJAX capabilities, you enhance the validation example by displaying the submitted form information without reloading the entire page. The only modifications to this web application appear in `Validation.aspx` file. You use Ajax-enabled controls to add this feature.

19.10 Online Case Study: Password-Protected Books Database Application

In the online chapter, Web App Development with ASP.NET: A Deeper Look, we include a web application case study in which a user logs into a password-protected website to view a list of publications by a selected author. The application consists of several pages and provides website registration and login capabilities. You'll learn about ASP.NET master pages, which allow you to specify a common look-and-feel for all the pages in your app. We also introduce the **Web Site Administration Tool** and use it to configure the portions of the application that can be accessed only by users who are logged into the website.

19.11 Wrap-Up

In this chapter, we introduced web-application development using ASP.NET and Visual Web Developer 2010 Express. We began by discussing the simple HTTP transactions that take place when you request and receive a web page through a web browser. You then learned about the three tiers (that is, the client or top tier, the business logic or middle tier and the information or bottom tier) that comprise most web applications.

Next, we explained the role of ASPX files (that is, Web Form files) and code-behind files, and the relationship between them. We discussed how ASP.NET compiles and executes web applications so that they can be displayed in a web browser. You also learned how to build an ASP.NET web application using Visual Web Developer.

The chapter demonstrated several common ASP.NET web controls used for displaying text and images on a Web Form. We also discussed validation controls, which allow you to ensure that user input on a web page satisfies certain requirements.

We discussed the benefits of maintaining a user's state information across multiple pages of a website. We then demonstrated how you can include such functionality in a web application by using session tracking with `HttpSessionState` objects.

Finally, we built a guestbook application that allows users to submit comments about a website. You learned how to save the user input in a SQL Server database and how to display past submissions on the web page. In Chapter 20, we discuss how to create methods that can order array elements in ascending or descending order, and that can search for values in arrays.

Summary

Section 19.1 Introduction

- ASP.NET technology is Microsoft's technology for web-application development.

- Web Form files have the file-name extension .aspx and contain the web page's GUI. A Web Form file represents the web page that is sent to the client browser.

- The file that contains the programming logic of a Web Form is called the code-behind file.

Section 19.2 Web Basics

- URIs (Uniform Resource Identifiers) identify resources on the Internet. URIs that start with http:// are called URLs (Uniform Resource Locators).

- A URL contains information that directs a browser to the resource that the user wishes to access. Computers that run web server software make such resources available.

- In a URL, the hostname is the name of the server on which the resource resides. This computer usually is referred to as the host, because it houses and maintains resources.

- A hostname is translated into a unique IP address that identifies the server. This translation is performed by a domain-name system (DNS) server.

- The remainder of a URL specifies the location and name of a requested resource. For security reasons, the location is normally a virtual directory. The server translates the virtual directory into a real location on the server.

- When given a URL, a web browser uses HTTP to retrieve the web page found at that address.

Section 19.3 Multitier Application Architecture

- Multitier applications divide functionality into separate tiers—logical groupings of functionality—that commonly reside on separate computers for security and scalability.

- The information tier (also called the bottom tier) maintains data pertaining to the application. This tier typically stores data in a relational database management system.

- The middle tier implements business logic, controller logic and presentation logic to control interactions between the application's clients and the application's data. The middle tier acts as an intermediary between data in the information tier and the application's clients.

- Business logic in the middle tier enforces business rules and ensures that data is reliable before the server application updates the database or presents the data to users.

- The client tier, or top tier, is the application's user interface, which gathers input and displays output. Users interact directly with the application through the user interface (typically viewed in a web browser), keyboard and mouse. In response to user actions, the client tier interacts with the middle tier to make requests and to retrieve data from the information tier. The client tier then displays to the user the data retrieved from the middle tier.

Section 19.4.1 Building the WebTime Application

- **File System** websites are created and tested on your local computer. Such websites execute in Visual Web Developer's built-in ASP.NET Development Server and can be accessed only by web browsers running on the same computer. You can later "publish" your website to a production web server for access via a local network or the Internet.

- **HTTP** websites are created and tested on an IIS web server and use HTTP to allow you to put your website's files on the server. If you own a website and have your own web server computer, you might use this to build a new website directly on that server computer.

- **FTP** websites use File Transfer Protocol (FTP) to allow you to put your website's files on the server. The server administrator must first create the website on the server for you. FTP is commonly used by so called "hosting providers" to allow website owners to share a server computer that runs many websites.

- A Web Form represents one page in a web application and contains a web application's GUI.

- You can view the Web Form's properties by selecting DOCUMENT in the **Properties** window. The Title property specifies the title that will be displayed in the web browser's title bar when the page is loaded.

- Controls and other elements are placed sequentially on a Web Form one after another in the order in which you drag-and-drop them onto the Web Form. The cursor indicates the insertion point in the page. This type of layout is known as relative positioning. You can also use absolute positioning in which controls are located exactly where you drop them on the Web Form.

- When a Label does not contain text, its name is displayed in square brackets in **Design** view as a placeholder for design and layout purposes. This text is not displayed at execution time.

- Formatting in a web page is performed with Cascading Style Sheets (CSS).

- A Web Form's Init event occurs when the page is requested by a web browser. The event handler for this event—named Page_Init—initialize the page.

Section 19.4.2 Examining WebTime.aspx's Code-Behind File

- A class declaration can span multiple source-code files—the separate portions of the class declaration in each file are known as partial classes. The partial modifier indicates that the class in a particular file is part of a larger class.

- Every Web Form class inherits from class Page in namespace System.Web.UI. Class Page represents the default capabilities of each page in a web application.

- The ASP.NET controls are defined in namespace System.Web.UI.WebControls.

Section 19.5 Standard Web Controls: Designing a Form

- An Image control's ImageUrl property specifies the location of the image to display.

- By default, the contents of a table cell are aligned vertically in the middle of the cell. You can change this with the cell's valign property.

- A TextBox control allows you to obtain text from the user and display text to the user.

- A DropDownList control is similar to the Windows Forms ComboBox control, but doesn't allow users to type text. You can add items to the DropDownList using the **ListItem Collection Editor**, which you can access by clicking the ellipsis next to the DropDownList's Items property in the **Properties** window, or by using the **DropDownList Tasks** menu.

- A HyperLink control adds a hyperlink to a Web Form. The NavigateUrl property specifies the resource or web page that will be requested when the user clicks the HyperLink.

- A RadioButtonList control provides a series of radio buttons from which the user can select only one. The **RadioButtonList Tasks** smart-tag menu provides an **Edit Items...** link to open the **ListItem Collection Editor** so that you can create the items in the list.

- A Button control triggers an action when clicked.

Section 19.6 Validation Controls

- A validation control determines whether the data in another web control is in the proper format.

- When the page is sent to the client, the validator is converted into JavaScript that performs the validation in the client web browser.

- Some client browsers might not support scripting or the user might disable it. For this reason, you should always perform validation on the server.

- A RequiredFieldValidator control ensures that its ControlToValidate is not empty when the form is submitted. The validator's ErrorMessage property specifies what to display on the Web Form if the validation fails. When the validator's Display property is set to Dynamic, the validator occupies space on the Web Form only when validation fails.

- A RegularExpressionValidator uses a regular expression to ensure data entered by the user is in a valid format. Visual Web Developer provides several predefined regular expressions that you can simply select to validate e-mail addresses, phone numbers and more. A RegularExpressionValidator's ValidationExpression property specifies the regular expression to use for validation.

- A Web Form's Load event occurs each time the page loads into a web browser. The event handler for this event is Page_Load.

- ASP.NET pages are often designed so that the current page reloads when the user submits the form; this enables the program to receive input, process it as necessary and display the results in the same page when it's loaded the second time.

- Submitting a web form is known as a postback. Class Page's IsPostBack property returns true if the page is being loaded due to a postback.

- Server-side Web Form validation must be implemented programmatically. Class Page's Validate method validates the information in the request as specified by the Web Form's validation controls. Class Page's IsValid property returns true if validation succeeded.

Section 19.7 Session Tracking

- Personalization makes it possible for e-businesses to communicate effectively with their customers and also improves users' ability to locate desired products and services.

- To provide personalized services to consumers, e-businesses must be able to recognize clients when they request information from a site.

- HTTP is a stateless protocol—it does not provide information regarding particular clients.

- Tracking individual clients is known as session tracking.

Section 19.7.1 Cookies

- A cookie is a piece of data stored in a small text file on the user's computer. A cookie maintains information about the client during and between browser sessions.

- The expiration date of a cookie determines how long the cookie remains on the client's computer. If you do not set an expiration date for a cookie, the web browser maintains the cookie for the duration of the browsing session.

Section 19.7.2 Session Tracking with **HttpSessionState**
- Session tracking is implemented with class HttpSessionState.

Section 19.7.3 **Options.aspx**: Selecting a Programming Language
- Each radio button in a RadioButtonList has a Text property and a Value property. The Text property is displayed next to the radio button and the Value property represents a value that is sent to the server when the user selects that radio button and submits the form.
- Every Web Form includes a user-specific HttpSessionState object, which is accessible through property Session of class Page.
- HttpSessionState property SessionID contains a client's unique session ID. The first time a client connects to the web server, a unique session ID is created for that client and a temporary cookie is written to the client so the server can identify the client on subsequent requests. When the client makes additional requests, the client's session ID from that temporary cookie is compared with the session IDs stored in the web server's memory to retrieve the client's HttpSessionState object.
- HttpSessionState property Timeout specifies the maximum amount of time that an HttpSessionState object can be inactive before it's discarded. Twenty minutes is the default.
- The HttpSessionState object is a dictionary—a data structure that stores key/value pairs. A program uses the key to store and retrieve the associated value in the dictionary.
- The key/value pairs in an HttpSessionState object are often referred to as session items. They're placed in an HttpSessionState object by calling its Add method. Another common syntax for placing a session item in the HttpSessionState object is Session(*Key*) = *Value*.
- If an application adds a session item that has the same name as an item previously stored in the HttpSessionState object, the session item is replaced—session items names *must* be unique.

Section 19.7.4 **Recommendations.aspx**: Displaying Recommendations Based on Session Values
- The Count property returns the number of session items stored in an HttpSessionState object.
- HttpSessionState's Keys property returns a collection containing all the keys in the session.

Section 19.8 Case Study: Database-Driven ASP.NET Guestbook
- A GridView data control displays data in tabular format. This control is located in the **Toolbox**'s **Data** section.

Section 19.8.1 Building a Web Form that Displays Data from a Database
- To use a SQL Server Express database file in an ASP.NET web application, you must first add the file to the project's App_Data folder. For security reasons, this folder can be accessed only by the web application on the server—clients cannot access this folder over a network. The web application interacts with the database on behalf of the client.
- A LinqDataSource control allows a web application to interact with a database through LINQ.

Section 19.8.2 Modifying the Code-Behind File for the Guestbook Application
- To insert data into a database using a LinqDataSource, you must create a ListDictionary of insert parameters that are formatted as key/value pairs.
- A ListDictionary's Add method stores key/value pairs that represent each insert parameter.
- A GridView's DataBind method refreshes the data that the GridView displays.

Terminology

Add method of class `HttpSessionState`
AJAX (Asynchronous Javascript and XML)
ASP.NET
ASP.NET AJAX
ASP.NET server control
ASPX file
`.aspx` filename extension
bottom tier
business logic
`Button` control
client tier
code-behind file
controller logic
`ControlToValidate` property of a validation
    control
cookie
`Count` property of class `HttpSessionState`
`DataBind` method of a `GridView`
`Display` property of a validation control
DNS (domain name system) server
`DOCUMENT` in the **Properties** window
`DropDownList` control
`ErrorMessage` property of a validation control
expiration date of a cookie
`GridView` control
host
hostname
`HttpSessionState` class
`HyperLink` control
`Image` control
`ImageUrl` property of an `Image` web control
information tier
`Init` event of a Web Form
IP (Internet Protocol) address
`IsPostBack` property of `Page` class
`IsValid` property of `Page` class
key/value pair
`Keys` property of `HttpSessionState` class
`LinqDataSource` control
`ListDictionary` class
`Load` event of Web Form

middle tier
multitier application
n-tier application
`NavigateUrl` property of a `HyperLink` control
`Page` class
`Page_Init` event handler
`Page_Load` event handler
partial class
`partial` modifier
personalization
postback
presentation logic
`RadioButtonList` control
`RegularExpressionValidator` validation con-
    trol
`RequiredFieldValidator` control
session item
`Session` property of `Page` class
session tracking
`SessionID` property of `HttpSessionState` class
`System.Web.UI` namespace
`System.Web.UI.WebControls` namespace
`Target` property of a `HyperLink` control
`TextBox` control
tier in a multitier application
`Timeout` property of `HttpSessionState` class
`Title` property of a Web Form
top tier
unique session ID of an ASP.NET client
`Validate` property of `Page` class
validation control
`ValidationExpression` property of a `Regular-`
    `ExpressionValidator` control
validator
`Visible` property of an ASP.NET control
Visual Web Developer 2010 Express
web-application development
web control
Web Form
web server
`Web.config` ASP.NET configuration file

Self-Review Exercises

19.1 State whether each of the following is *true* or *false*. If *false*, explain why.
    a) Web Form file names end in `.aspx`.
    b) `App.config` is a file that stores configuration settings for an ASP.NET web application.
    c) A maximum of one validation control can be placed on a Web Form.
    d) A `LinqDataSource` control allows a web application to interact with a database.

19.2 Fill in the blanks in each of the following statements:

a) Web applications contain three basic tiers: _____, _____, and _____.

b) The _____ web control is similar to the ComboBox Windows control.

c) A control which ensures that the data in another control is in the correct format is called a(n) _____.

d) A(n) _____ occurs when a page requests itself.

e) Every ASP.NET page inherits from class _____.

f) The _____ file contains the functionality for an ASP.NET page.

Answers to Self-Review Exercises

19.1 a) True. b) False. Web.config is the file that stores configuration settings for an ASP.NET web application. c) False. An unlimited number of validation controls can be placed on a Web Form. d) True.

19.2 a) bottom (information), middle (business logic), top (client). b) DropDownList. c) validator. d) postback. e) Page. f) code-behind.

Exercises

19.3 *(WebTime Modification)* Modify the WebTime example to contain drop-down lists that allow the user to modify such Label properties as BackColor, ForeColor and Font-Size. Configure these drop-down lists so that a postback occurs whenever the user makes a selection—to do this, set their AutoPostBack properties to true. When the page reloads, it should reflect the specified changes to the properties of the Label displaying the time.

19.4 *(Page Hit Counter)* Create an ASP.NET page that uses session tracking to keep track of how many times the client computer has visited the page. Set the HttpSessionState object's Timeout property to 1440 (the number of minutes in one day) to keep the session in effect for one day into the future. Display the number of page hits every time the page loads.

19.5 *(Guestbook Application Modification)* Add validation to the guestbook application in Section 19.8. Use validation controls to ensure that the user provides a name, a valid e-mail address and a message.

19.6 *(Project: WebControls Modification)* Modify the example of Section 19.5 to add functionality to the **Register** Button. When the user clicks the Button, validate all of the input fields to ensure that the user has filled out the form completely, and entered a valid email address and phone number. If any of the fields are not valid, appropriate messages should be displayed by validation controls. If the fields are all valid, direct the user to another page that displays a message indicating that the registration was successful followed by the registration information that was submitted from the form.

19.7 *(Project: Web-Based Address Book)* Using the techniques you learned in Section 19.8, create a web-based Address book with similar functionality to the **Address Book** application that you created in Section 18.9. Display the address book's contents in a GridView. Allow the user to search for entries with a particular last name.

Searching and Sorting

With sobs and tears
he sorted out
Those of the largest size …
—Lewis Carroll

Attempt the end, and never
stand to doubt;
Nothing's so hard, but search
will find it out.
—Robert Herrick

It is an immutable law in
business that words are words,
explanations are explanations,
promises are promises — but
only performance is reality.
—Harold S. Green

Objectives

In this chapter you'll learn:

- To search for a given value in an array using the linear search and binary search algorithm.

- To sort arrays using the iterative selection and insertion sort algorithms.

- To sort arrays using the recursive merge sort algorithm.

- To determine the efficiency of searching and sorting algorithms.

20.1 Introduction

Searching data involves determining whether a value (referred to as the **search key**) is present in the data and, if so, finding the value's location. Two popular search algorithms are the simple linear search and the faster, but more complex, binary search. **Sorting** places data in order, based on one or more **sort keys**. A list of names could be sorted alphabetically, bank accounts could be sorted by account number, employee payroll records could be sorted by social security number and so on. This chapter introduces two simple sorting algorithms, the selection sort and the insertion sort, along with the more efficient, but more complex, merge sort. Figure 20.1 summarizes the searching and sorting algorithms discussed in this book.

Chapter	Algorithm	Location
Searching Algorithms:		
20	Linear Search	Section 20.2.1
	Binary Search	Section 20.2.2
	Recursive Linear Search	Exercise 20.8
	Recursive Binary Search	Exercise 20.9
23	BinarySearch method of class Array	Fig. 23.3
	Contains method of classes List<T> and Stack<T>	Fig. 23.4
	ContainsKey method of class Dictionary<K, T>	Fig. 23.7
Sorting Algorithms:		
20	Selection Sort	Section 20.3.1
	Insertion Sort	Section 20.3.2
	Recursive Merge Sort	Section 20.3.3
	Bubble Sort	Exercises 20.5–20.6
	Bucket Sort	Exercise 20.7
	Recursive Quicksort	Exercise 20.10
20, 23	Sort method of classes Array and List<T>	Figs. 20.4, 23.3–23.4

Fig. 20.1 | Searching and sorting capabilities in this text.

20.2 Searching Algorithms

Looking up a phone number, accessing a website and checking the definition of a word in a dictionary all involve searching large amounts of data. The next two sections discuss two common search algorithms—one that is easy to program yet relatively inefficient and one that is relatively efficient but more complex to program.

20.2.1 Linear Search

The **linear search algorithm** searches each element in an array sequentially. If the search key does not match an element in the array, the algorithm tests each element and, when the end of the array is reached, informs the user that the search key is not present. If the search key is in the array, the algorithm tests each element until it finds one that matches the search key and returns the index of that element.

As an example, consider an array containing the following values

| 34 | 56 | 2 | 10 | 77 | 51 | 93 | 30 | 5 | 52 |

and a method that is searching for 51. Using the linear search algorithm, the method first checks whether 34 matches the search key. It does not, so the algorithm checks whether 56 matches the search key. The method continues moving through the array sequentially, testing 2, then 10, then 77. When the method tests 51, which matches the search key, the method returns the index 5, which is the location of 51 in the array. If, after checking every array element, the method determines that the search key does not match any element in the array, the method returns a sentinel value (e.g., -1). If there are duplicate values in the array, linear search returns the index of the first element in the array that matches the search key.

Figure 20.2 declares class LinearArray. This class has a private instance variable data (an array of ints), and a static Random object named generator to fill the array with randomly generated ints. When an object of class LinearArray is instantiated, the constructor (lines 12–19) creates and initializes the array data with random ints in the range 10–99.

```
1   // Fig. 20.2: LinearArray.cs
2   // Class that contains an array of random integers and a method
3   // that searches that array sequentially.
4   using System;
5
6   public class LinearArray
7   {
8      private int[] data; // array of values
9      private static Random generator = new Random();
10
11     // create array of given size and fill with random integers
12     public LinearArray( int size )
13     {
14        data = new int[ size ]; // create space for array
15
```

Fig. 20.2 | Class that contains an array of random integers and a method that searches that array sequentially. (Part 1 of 2.)

```
16          // fill array with random ints in range 10-99
17          for ( int i = 0; i < size; i++ )
18             data[ i ] = generator.Next( 10, 100 );
19       } // end LinearArray constructor
20
21       // perform a linear search on the data
22       public int LinearSearch( int searchKey )
23       {
24          // loop through array sequentially
25          for ( int index = 0; index < data.Length; index++ )
26             if ( data[ index ] == searchKey )
27                return index; // return index of integer
28
29          return -1; // integer was not found
30       } // end method LinearSearch
31
32       // method to output values in array
33       public override string ToString()
34       {
35          string temporary = string.Empty;
36
37          // iterate through array
38          foreach ( int element in data )
39             temporary += element + " ";
40
41          temporary += "\n"; // add newline character
42          return temporary;
43       } // end method ToString
44    } // end class LinearArray
```

Fig. 20.2 | Class that contains an array of random integers and a method that searches that array sequentially. (Part 2 of 2.)

Lines 22–30 perform the linear search. The search key is passed to parameter searchKey. Lines 25–27 loop through the elements in the array. Line 26 compares each element in the array with searchKey. If the values are equal, line 27 returns the index of the element. If the loop ends without finding the value, line 29 returns -1. Lines 33–43 declare method ToString, which returns a string representation of the array for printing.

Figure 20.3 creates LinearArray object searchArray containing an array of 10 ints (line 13) and allows the user to search the array for specific elements. Lines 17–18 prompt the user for the search key and store it in searchInt. Lines 21–37 loop until the user enters the sentinel value -1. The array holds ints from 10–99 (line 18 of Fig. 20.2). Line 24 calls the LinearSearch method to determine whether searchInt is in the array. If searchInt is found, LinearSearch returns the position of the element, which the method outputs in lines 27–29. If searchInt is not in the array, LinearSearch returns -1, and the method notifies the user (lines 31–32). Lines 35–36 retrieve the next integer from the user.

Efficiency of Linear Search

Searching algorithms all accomplish the same goal—finding an element that matches a given search key, if such an element exists. Many things, however, differentiate search algorithms from one another. The major difference is the amount of effort required to

```
 1   // Fig. 20.3: LinearSearchTest.cs
 2   // Sequentially search an array for an item.
 3   using System;
 4
 5   public class LinearSearchTest
 6   {
 7      public static void Main( string[] args )
 8      {
 9         int searchInt; // search key
10         int position; // location of search key in array
11
12         // create array and output it
13         LinearArray searchArray = new LinearArray( 10 );
14         Console.WriteLine( searchArray ); // print array
15
16         // input first int from user
17         Console.Write( "Please enter an integer value (-1 to quit): " );
18         searchInt = Convert.ToInt32( Console.ReadLine() );
19
20         // repeatedly input an integer; -1 terminates the application
21         while ( searchInt != -1 )
22         {
23            // perform linear search
24            position = searchArray.LinearSearch( searchInt );
25
26            if ( position != -1 ) // integer was not found
27               Console.WriteLine(
28                  "The integer {0} was found in position {1}.\n",
29                  searchInt, position );
30            else // integer was found
31               Console.WriteLine( "The integer {0} was not found.\n",
32                  searchInt );
33
34            // input next int from user
35            Console.Write( "Please enter an integer value (-1 to quit): " );
36            searchInt = Convert.ToInt32( Console.ReadLine() );
37         } // end while
38      } // end Main
39   } // end class LinearSearchTest
```

```
64 90 84 62 28 68 55 27 78 73

Please enter an integer value (-1 to quit): 78
The integer 78 was found in position 8.

Please enter an integer value (-1 to quit): 64
The integer 64 was found in position 0.

Please enter an integer value (-1 to quit): 65
The integer 65 was not found.

Please enter an integer value (-1 to quit): -1
```

Fig. 20.3 | Sequentially search an array for an item.

complete the search. One way to describe this effort is with **Big O notation**, which is a measure of the worst-case runtime for an algorithm—that is, how hard an algorithm may have to work to solve a problem. For searching and sorting algorithms, this is particularly dependent on how many elements there are in the data set and the algorithm used.

Suppose an algorithm is designed to test whether the first element of an array is equal to the second element. If the array has 10 elements, this algorithm requires one comparison. If the array has 1,000 elements, this algorithm still requires one comparison. In fact, this algorithm is completely independent of the number of elements in the array, and is thus said to have a **constant runtime**, which is represented in Big O notation as $O(1)$. An algorithm that is $O(1)$ does not necessarily require only one comparison. $O(1)$ just means that the number of comparisons is *constant*—it does not grow as the size of the array increases. An algorithm that tests whether the first element of an array is equal to any of the next three elements is still $O(1)$, even though it requires three comparisons.

An algorithm that tests whether the first element of an array is equal to *any* of the other elements of the array will require at most $n - 1$ comparisons, where n is the number of elements in the array. If the array has 10 elements, this algorithm requires up to nine comparisons. If the array has 1,000 elements, this algorithm requires up to 999 comparisons. As n grows larger, the n part of the expression "dominates," and subtracting one becomes inconsequential. Big O is designed to highlight these dominant terms and ignore terms that become unimportant as n grows. For this reason, an algorithm that requires a total of $n - 1$ comparisons (such as the one we described earlier) is said to be $O(n)$. An $O(n)$ algorithm is referred to as having a **linear runtime**. $O(n)$ is often pronounced "on the order of n" or more simply "order n."

Now suppose you have an algorithm that tests whether *any* element of an array is duplicated elsewhere in the array. The first element must be compared with every other element in the array. The second element must be compared with every other element except the first (it was already compared to the first). The third element must be compared with every other element except the first two. In the end, this algorithm will end up making $(n - 1) + (n - 2) + \ldots + 2 + 1$ or $n^2/2 - n/2$ comparisons. As n increases, the n^2 term dominates and the n term becomes inconsequential. Again, Big O notation highlights the n^2 term, leaving $n^2/2$. But as we'll soon see, constant factors are omitted in Big O notation.

Big O is concerned with how an algorithm's runtime grows in relation to the number of items processed. Suppose an algorithm requires n^2 comparisons. With four elements, the algorithm will require 16 comparisons; with eight elements, the algorithm will require 64 comparisons. With this algorithm, doubling the number of elements quadruples the number of comparisons. Consider a similar algorithm requiring $n^2/2$ comparisons. With four elements, the algorithm will require eight comparisons; with eight elements, 32 comparisons. Again, doubling the number of elements quadruples the number of comparisons. Both of these algorithms grow as the square of n, so Big O ignores the constant, and both algorithms are considered to be $O(n^2)$, referred to as **quadratic runtime** and pronounced "on the order of n-squared" or more simply "order n-squared."

When n is small, $O(n^2)$ algorithms (running on today's billions-of-operations-per-second personal computers) will not noticeably affect performance. But as n grows, you'll start to notice the performance degradation. An $O(n^2)$ algorithm running on a million-element array would require a trillion "operations" (where each could actually require several machine instructions to execute). This could require many minutes to execute. A billion-element array would require a quintillion operations, a number so large that the algorithm could take decades! $O(n^2)$ algorithms are easy to write, as you'll see shortly. You'll also see algorithms with more favorable Big O measures. These efficient algorithms often take more cleverness and effort to create, but their superior performance can be well worth the extra effort, especially as n gets large and algorithms are compounded into larger applications.

The linear search algorithm runs in $O(n)$ time. The worst case in this algorithm is that every element must be checked to determine whether the search item exists in the array. If the size of the array is doubled, the number of comparisons that the algorithm must perform is also doubled. Linear search can provide outstanding performance if the element matching the search key happens to be at or near the front of the array. But we seek algorithms that perform well, on average, across all searches, including those where the element matching the search key is near the end of the array.

Linear search is the easiest search algorithm to program, but it can be slow compared to other search algorithms. If an application needs to perform many searches on large arrays, it may be better to implement a different, more efficient algorithm, such as the binary search, which we present in the next section.

Performance Tip 20.1

Sometimes the simplest algorithms perform poorly. Their virtue is that they're easy to program, test and debug. Sometimes more complex algorithms are required to realize maximum performance.

20.2.2 Binary Search

The **binary search algorithm** is more efficient than the linear search algorithm, but it requires that the array be sorted. The first iteration of this algorithm tests the middle element in the array. If this matches the search key, the algorithm ends. Assuming the array is sorted in ascending order, if the search key is less than the middle element, the search key cannot match any element in the second half of the array and the algorithm continues with only the first half of the array (i.e., the first element up to, but not including, the middle element). If the search key is greater than the middle element, the search key cannot match any element in the first half of the array, and the algorithm continues with only the second half of the array (i.e., the element after the middle element through the last element). Each iteration tests the middle value of the remaining portion of the array, called a **subarray**. A subarray can have no elements, or it can encompass the entire array. If the search key does not match the element, the algorithm eliminates half of the remaining elements. The algorithm ends by either finding an element that matches the search key or reducing the subarray to zero size.

As an example, consider the sorted 15-element array

| 2 | 3 | 5 | 10 | 27 | 30 | 34 | 51 | 56 | 65 | 77 | 81 | 82 | 93 | 99 |

and a search key of 65. An application implementing the binary search algorithm would first check whether 51 is the search key (because 51 is the middle element of the array). The search key (65) is larger than 51, so 51 is "discarded" (i.e., eliminated from consideration) along with the first half of the array (all elements smaller than 51.) Next, the algorithm checks whether 81 (the middle element of the remainder of the array) matches the search key. The search key (65) is smaller than 81, so 81 is discarded along with the elements larger than 81. After just two tests, the algorithm has narrowed the number of values to check to three (56, 65 and 77). The algorithm then checks 65 (which indeed matches the search key) and returns the index of the array element containing 65. This algorithm required just three comparisons to determine whether the search key matched an element of the array. Using a linear search algorithm would have required 10 comparisons. [*Note:* In this example, we have chosen to use an array with 15 elements so that there will always be an obvious middle element in the array. With an even number of elements, the middle of the array lies between two elements. We implement the algorithm to choose the higher of the two elements.]

Figure 20.4 declares class `BinaryArray`. This class is similar to `LinearArray`—it has a `private` instance variable data (an array of ints), a `static Random` object named generator to fill the array with randomly generated ints, a constructor, a search method (`BinarySearch`), a `RemainingElements` method (which creates a `string` containing the elements not yet searched) and a `ToString` method. Lines 12–21 declare the constructor. After initializing the array with random ints from 10–99 (lines 17–18), line 20 calls method `Array.Sort` on the array data. Method **Sort** is a `static` method of class `Array` that sorts the elements in an array in ascending order. Recall that the binary search algorithm works only on sorted arrays.

```
1   // Fig. 20.4: BinaryArray.cs
2   // Class that contains an array of random integers and a method
3   // that uses binary search to find an integer.
4   using System;
5
6   public class BinaryArray
7   {
8      private int[] data; // array of values
9      private static Random generator = new Random();
10
11     // create array of given size and fill with random integers
12     public BinaryArray( int size )
13     {
14        data = new int[ size ]; // create space for array
15
16        // fill array with random ints in range 10-99
17        for ( int i = 0; i < size; i++ )
18           data[ i ] = generator.Next( 10, 100 );
19
20        Array.Sort( data );
21     } // end BinaryArray constructor
22
23     // perform a binary search on the data
24     public int BinarySearch( int searchElement )
25     {
26        int low = 0; // low end of the search area
27        int high = data.Length - 1; // high end of the search area
28        int middle = ( low + high + 1 ) / 2; // middle element
29        int location = -1; // return value; -1 if not found
```

Fig. 20.4 | Class that contains an array of random integers and a method that uses binary search to find an integer. (Part 1 of 2.)

```
30
31        do // loop to search for element
32        {
33           // print remaining elements of array
34           Console.Write( RemainingElements( low, high ) );
35
36           // output spaces for alignment
37           for ( int i = 0; i < middle; i++ )
38              Console.Write( "   " );
39
40           Console.WriteLine( " * " ); // indicate current middle
41
42           // if the element is found at the middle
43           if ( searchElement == data[ middle ] )
44              location = middle; // location is the current middle
45
46           // middle element is too high
47           else if ( searchElement < data[ middle ] )
48              high = middle - 1; // eliminate the higher half
49           else // middle element is too low
50              low = middle + 1; // eliminate the lower half
51
52           middle = ( low + high + 1 ) / 2; // recalculate the middle
53        } while ( ( low <= high ) && ( location == -1 ) );
54
55        return location; // return location of search key
56     } // end method BinarySearch
57
58     // method to output certain values in array
59     public string RemainingElements( int low, int high )
60     {
61        string temporary = string.Empty;
62
63        // output spaces for alignment
64        for ( int i = 0; i < low; i++ )
65           temporary += "   ";
66
67        // output elements left in array
68        for ( int i = low; i <= high; i++ )
69           temporary += data[ i ] + " ";
70
71        temporary += "\n";
72        return temporary;
73     } // end method RemainingElements
74
75     // method to output values in array
76     public override string ToString()
77     {
78        return RemainingElements( 0, data.Length - 1 );
79     } // end method ToString
80  } // end class BinaryArray
```

Fig. 20.4 | Class that contains an array of random integers and a method that uses binary search to find an integer. (Part 2 of 2.)

Lines 24–56 declare method `BinarySearch`. The search key is passed into parameter `searchElement` (line 24). Lines 26–28 calculate the `low` end index, `high` end index and `middle` index of the portion of the array that the application is currently searching. At the beginning of the method, the `low` end is 0, the `high` end is the length of the array minus 1 and the `middle` is the average of these two values. Line 29 initializes the `location` of the element to -1—the value that will be returned if the element is not found. Lines 31–53 loop until `low` is greater than `high` (this occurs when the element is not found) or `location` does not equal -1 (indicating that the search key was found). Line 43 tests whether the value in the `middle` element is equal to `searchElement`. If this is true, line 44 assigns `middle` to `location`. Then the loop terminates, and `location` is returned to the caller. Each iteration of the loop tests a single value (line 43) and eliminates half of the remaining values in the array (line 48 or 50).

Lines 22–40 of Fig. 20.5 loop until the user enters -1. For each other number the user enters, the application performs a binary search to determine whether the number matches an element in the array. The first line of output from this application is the array of `int`s, in increasing order. When the user instructs the application to search for 72, the application first tests the middle element (indicated by * in the sample output of Fig. 20.5), which is 52. The search key is greater than 52, so the application eliminates from consideration the first half of the array and tests the middle element from the second half. The search key is smaller than 82, so the application eliminates from consideration the second half of the subarray, leaving only three elements. Finally, the application checks 72 (which matches the search key) and returns the index 9.

```
 1   // Fig. 20.5: BinarySearchTest.cs
 2   // Using binary search to locate an item in an array.
 3   using System;
 4
 5   public class BinarySearchTest
 6   {
 7      public static void Main( string[] args )
 8      {
 9         int searchInt; // search key
10         int position; // location of search key in array
11
12         // create array and output it
13         BinaryArray searchArray = new BinaryArray( 15 );
14         Console.WriteLine( searchArray );
15
16         // prompt and input first int from user
17         Console.Write( "Please enter an integer value (-1 to quit): " );
18         searchInt = Convert.ToInt32( Console.ReadLine() );
19         Console.WriteLine();
20
21         // repeatedly input an integer; -1 terminates the application
22         while ( searchInt != -1 )
23         {
24            // use binary search to try to find integer
25            position = searchArray.BinarySearch( searchInt );
```

Fig. 20.5 | Using binary search to locate an item in an array. (Part 1 of 2.)

```
26
27              // return value of -1 indicates integer was not found
28              if ( position == -1 )
29                  Console.WriteLine( "The integer {0} was not found.\n",
30                      searchInt );
31              else
32                  Console.WriteLine(
33                      "The integer {0} was found in position {1}.\n",
34                      searchInt, position);
35
36              // prompt and input next int from user
37              Console.Write( "Please enter an integer value (-1 to quit): " );
38              searchInt = Convert.ToInt32( Console.ReadLine() );
39              Console.WriteLine();
40          } // end while
41      } // end Main
42  } // end class BinarySearchTest
```

```
12 17 22 25 30 39 40 52 56 72 76 82 84 91 93

Please enter an integer value (-1 to quit): 72

12 17 22 25 30 39 40 52 56 72 76 82 84 91 93
                        *
                        56 72 76 82 84 91 93
                                    *
                        56 72 76
                           *
The integer 72 was found in position 9.

Please enter an integer value (-1 to quit): 13

12 17 22 25 30 39 40 52 56 72 76 82 84 91 93
                     *
12 17 22 25 30 39 40
           *
12 17 22
   *
12
*
The integer 13 was not found.

Please enter an integer value (-1 to quit): -1
```

Fig. 20.5 | Using binary search to locate an item in an array. (Part 2 of 2.)

Efficiency of Binary Search

In the worst-case scenario, searching a sorted array of 1,023 elements will take only 10 comparisons when using a binary search. Repeatedly dividing 1,023 by 2 (because after each comparison, we are able to eliminate half of the array) and rounding down (because we also remove the middle element) yields the values 511, 255, 127, 63, 31, 15, 7, 3, 1 and 0. The number 1023 ($2^{10} - 1$) is divided by 2 only 10 times to get the value 0, which indicates that there are no more elements to test. Dividing by 2 is equivalent to one comparison in the binary search algorithm. Thus, an array of 1,048,575 ($2^{20} - 1$) elements takes a maximum of 20 comparisons to find the key, and an array of one billion elements (which is less than $2^{30} - 1$) takes a maximum of 30 comparisons to find the key. This is a tremendous improvement in performance over the linear search. For a one-billion-element array, this is a difference between an average of 500 million comparisons for the linear search and a maximum of only 30 comparisons for the binary search! The maximum number of comparisons needed for the binary search of any sorted array is the exponent of the first power of 2 greater than the number of elements in the array, which is represented as $\log_2 n$. All logarithms grow at roughly the same rate, so in Big O notation the base can be omitted. This results in a big O of *O(log n)* for a binary search, which is also known as **logarithmic runtime**.

20.3 Sorting Algorithms

Sorting data (i.e., placing the data in some particular order, such as ascending or descending) is one of the most important computing applications. A bank sorts all checks by account number so that it can prepare individual bank statements at the end of each month. Telephone companies sort their lists of accounts by last name and, further, by first name to make it easy to find phone numbers. Virtually every organization must sort some data—often, massive amounts of it. Sorting data is an intriguing, compute-intensive problem that has attracted substantial research efforts.

It's important to understand about sorting that the end result—the sorted array—will be the same no matter which (correct) algorithm you use to sort the array. The choice of algorithm affects only the runtime and memory use of the application. The rest of the chapter introduces three common sorting algorithms. The first two—selection sort and insertion sort—are simple to program, but inefficient. The last—merge sort—is much faster than selection sort and insertion sort but more difficult to program. We focus on sorting arrays of simple-type data, namely `int`s. It's possible to sort arrays of objects as well—we discuss this in Chapter 23, Collections.

20.3.1 Selection Sort

Selection sort is a simple, but inefficient, sorting algorithm. The first iteration of the algorithm selects the smallest element in the array and swaps it with the first element. The second iteration selects the second-smallest element (which is the smallest of the remaining elements) and swaps it with the second element. The algorithm continues until the last iteration selects the second-largest element and, if necessary, swaps it with the second-to-last element, leaving the largest element in the last position. After the *i*th iteration, the smallest *i* elements of the array will be sorted in increasing order in the first *i* positions of the array.

As an example, consider the array

| 34 | 56 | 4 | 10 | 77 | 51 | 93 | 30 | 5 | 52 |

An application that implements selection sort first determines the smallest element (4) of this array, which is contained in index 2 (i.e., position 3). The application swaps 4 with 34, resulting in

| 4 | 56 | 34 | 10 | 77 | 51 | 93 | 30 | 5 | 52 |

The application then determines the smallest value of the remaining elements (all elements except 4), which is 5, contained in index 8. The application swaps 5 with 56, resulting in

| 4 | 5 | 34 | 10 | 77 | 51 | 93 | 30 | 56 | 52 |

On the third iteration, the application determines the next smallest value (10) and swaps it with 34.

4	5	10	34	77	51	93	30	56	52

The process continues until the array is fully sorted.

4	5	10	30	34	51	52	56	77	93

After the first iteration, the smallest element is in the first position. After the second iteration, the two smallest elements are in order in the first two positions. After the third iteration, the three smallest elements are in order in the first three positions.

Figure 20.6 declares class SelectionSort, which has an instance variable data (an array of ints) and a static Random object generator to generate random integers to fill the array. When an object of class SelectionSort is instantiated, the constructor (lines 12–19) creates and initializes array data with random ints in the range 10–99.

```
1   // Fig. 20.6: SelectionSort.cs
2   // Class that creates an array filled with random integers.
3   // Provides a method to sort the array with selection sort.
4   using System;
5
6   public class SelectionSort
7   {
8      private int[] data; // array of values
9      private static Random generator = new Random();
10
11     // create array of given size and fill with random integers
12     public SelectionSort( int size )
13     {
14        data = new int[ size ]; // create space for array
15
16        // fill array with random ints in range 10-99
17        for ( int i = 0; i < size; i++ )
18           data[ i ] = generator.Next( 10, 100 );
19     } // end SelectionSort constructor
20
21     // sort array using selection sort
22     public void Sort()
23     {
24        int smallest; // index of smallest element
25
26        // loop over data.Length - 1 elements
27        for ( int i = 0; i < data.Length - 1; i++ )
28        {
29           smallest = i; // first index of remaining array
30
31           // loop to find index of smallest element
32           for ( int index = i + 1; index < data.Length; index++ )
33              if ( data[ index ] < data[ smallest ] )
34                 smallest = index;
```

Fig. 20.6 | Class that creates an array filled with random integers. Provides a method to sort the array with selection sort. (Part 1 of 2.)

```
35
36            Swap( i, smallest ); // swap smallest element into position
37            PrintPass( i + 1, smallest ); // output pass of algorithm
38         } // end outer for
39      } // end method Sort
40
41      // helper method to swap values in two elements
42      public void Swap( int first, int second )
43      {
44         int temporary = data[ first ]; // store first in temporary
45         data[ first ] = data[ second ]; // replace first with second
46         data[ second ] = temporary; // put temporary in second
47      } // end method Swap
48
49      // print a pass of the algorithm
50      public void PrintPass( int pass, int index )
51      {
52         Console.Write( "after pass {0}: ", pass );
53
54         // output elements through the selected item
55         for ( int i = 0; i < index; i++ )
56            Console.Write( data[ i ] + "  " );
57
58         Console.Write( data[ index ] + "* " ); // indicate swap
59
60         // finish outputting array
61         for ( int i = index + 1; i < data.Length; i++ )
62            Console.Write( data[ i ] + "  " );
63
64         Console.Write( "\n                " ); // for alignment
65
66         // indicate amount of array that is sorted
67         for( int j = 0; j < pass; j++ )
68            Console.Write( "--  " );
69         Console.WriteLine( "\n" ); // skip a line in output
70      } // end method PrintPass
71
72      // method to output values in array
73      public override string ToString()
74      {
75         string temporary = string.Empty;
76
77         // iterate through array
78         foreach ( int element in data )
79            temporary += element + "   ";
80
81         temporary += "\n"; // add newline character
82         return temporary;
83      } // end method ToString
84   } // end class SelectionSort
```

Fig. 20.6 | Class that creates an array filled with random integers. Provides a method to sort the array with selection sort. (Part 2 of 2.)

Lines 22–39 declare the Sort method. Line 24 declares variable smallest, which will store the index of the smallest element in the remaining array. Lines 27–38 loop data.Length - 1 times. Line 29 initializes the index of the smallest element to the current item. Lines 32–34 loop over the remaining elements in the array. For each of these elements, line 33 compares its value to the value of the smallest element. If the current element is smaller than the smallest element, line 34 assigns the current element's index to smallest. When this loop finishes, smallest will contain the index of the smallest element in the remaining array. Line 36 calls method Swap (lines 42–47) to place the smallest remaining element in the next spot in the array.

Line 10 of Fig. 20.7 creates a SelectionSort object with 10 elements. Line 13 implicitly calls method ToString to output the unsorted object. Line 15 calls method Sort (lines 22–39 of Fig. 20.6), which sorts the elements using selection sort. Then lines 17–18 output the sorted object. The output uses dashes to indicate the portion of the array that is sorted after each pass (lines 67–68). An asterisk is placed next to the position of the element that was swapped with the smallest element on that pass. On each pass, the element next to the asterisk and the element above the rightmost set of dashes were the two values that were swapped.

```
1   // Fig. 20.7: SelectionSortTest.cs
2   // Testing the selection sort class.
3   using System;
4
5   public class SelectionSortTest
6   {
7      public static void Main( string[] args )
8      {
9         // create object to perform selection sort
10        SelectionSort sortArray = new SelectionSort( 10 );
11
12        Console.WriteLine( "Unsorted array:" );
13        Console.WriteLine( sortArray ); // print unsorted array
14
15        sortArray.Sort(); // sort array
16
17        Console.WriteLine( "Sorted array:" );
18        Console.WriteLine( sortArray ); // print sorted array
19     } // end Main
20  } // end class SelectionSortTest
```

```
Unsorted array:
86  97  83  45  19  31  86  13  57  61

after pass 1: 13  97  83  45  19  31  86  86* 57  61
              --

after pass 2: 13  19  83  45  97* 31  86  86  57  61
              --  --

after pass 3: 13  19  31  45  97  83* 86  86  57  61
              --  --  --
```

Fig. 20.7 | Testing the selection sort class. (Part I of 2.)

```
after pass 4: 13   19   31   45*  97   83   86   86   57   61
              --   --   --   --

after pass 5: 13   19   31   45   57   83   86   86   97*  61
              --   --   --   --   --

after pass 6: 13   19   31   45   57   61   86   86   97   83*
              --   --   --   --   --   --

after pass 7: 13   19   31   45   57   61   83   86   97   86*
              --   --   --   --   --   --   --

after pass 8: 13   19   31   45   57   61   83   86*  97   86
              --   --   --   --   --   --   --   --

after pass 9: 13   19   31   45   57   61   83   86   86   97*
              --   --   --   --   --   --   --   --   --

Sorted array:
13   19   31   45   57   61   83   86   86   97
```

Fig. 20.7 | Testing the selection sort class. (Part 2 of 2.)

Efficiency of Selection Sort

The selection sort algorithm runs in $O(n^2)$ time. Method Sort in lines 22–39 of Fig. 20.6, which implements the selection sort algorithm, contains nested for loops. The outer for loop (lines 27–38) iterates over the first $n - 1$ elements in the array, swapping the smallest remaining element to its sorted position. The inner for loop (lines 32–34) iterates over each element in the remaining array, searching for the smallest. This loop executes $n - 1$ times during the first iteration of the outer loop, $n - 2$ times during the second iteration, then $n - 3, \ldots, 3, 2, 1$. This inner loop will iterate a total of $n(n - 1) / 2$ or $(n^2 - n)/2$. In Big O notation, smaller terms drop out and constants are ignored, leaving a final Big O of $O(n^2)$.

20.3.2 Insertion Sort

Insertion sort is another simple, but inefficient, sorting algorithm. Its first iteration takes the second element in the array and, if it's less than the first, swaps them. The second iteration looks at the third element and inserts it in the correct position with respect to the first two elements, so all three elements are in order. At the ith iteration of this algorithm, the first i elements in the original array will be sorted.

Consider as an example the following array, which is identical to the array used in the discussions of selection sort and merge sort.

| 34 | 56 | 4 | 10 | 77 | 51 | 93 | 30 | 5 | 52 |

An application that implements the insertion sort algorithm first looks at the first two elements of the array, 34 and 56. These are already in order, so the application continues (if they were out of order, it would swap them).

In the next iteration, the application looks at the third value, 4. This value is less than 56, so the application stores 4 in a temporary variable and moves 56 one element to the right. The application then checks and determines that 4 is less than 34, so it moves 34 one element to the right. The application has now reached the beginning of the array, so it places 4 in the zeroth position. The array now is

| 4 | 34 | 56 | 10 | 77 | 51 | 93 | 30 | 5 | 52 |

In the next iteration, the application stores the value 10 in a temporary variable. Then the application compares 10 to 56 and moves 56 one element to the right because it's larger than 10. The application then compares 10 to 34, moving 34 one element to the right. When the application compares 10 to 4, it observes that 10 is larger than 4 and places 10 in element 1. The array now is

| 4 | 10 | 34 | 56 | 77 | 51 | 93 | 30 | 5 | 52 |

Using this algorithm, at the ith iteration, the original array's first i elements are sorted, but they may not be in their final locations—smaller values may be located later in the array.

Figure 20.8 declares the `InsertionSort` class. Lines 22–46 declare the `Sort` method. Line 24 declares variable `insert`, which holds the element to be inserted while the other elements are moved. Lines 27–45 loop through `data.Length - 1` items in the array. In each iteration, line 30 stores in variable `insert` the value of the element that will be inserted in the sorted portion of the array. Line 33 declares and initializes variable `moveItem`, which keeps track of where to insert the element. Lines 36–41 loop to locate the correct position to insert the element. The loop will terminate either when the application reaches the front of the array or when it reaches an element that is less than the value to be inserted. Line 39 moves an element to the right, and line 40 decrements the position at which to insert the next element. After the loop ends, line 43 inserts the element in place. Figure 20.9 is the same as Fig. 20.7 except that it creates and uses an `InsertionSort` object. The output of this application uses dashes to indicate the portion of the array that is sorted after each pass (lines 66–67 of Fig. 20.8). An asterisk is placed next to the element that was inserted in place on that pass.

```
1   // Fig. 20.8: InsertionSort.cs
2   // Class that creates an array filled with random integers.
3   // Provides a method to sort the array with insertion sort.
4   using System;
5
6   public class InsertionSort
7   {
8      private int[] data; // array of values
9      private static Random generator = new Random();
10
11      // create array of given size and fill with random integers
12      public InsertionSort( int size )
13      {
14         data = new int[ size ]; // create space for array
15
16         // fill array with random ints in range 10-99
17         for ( int i = 0; i < size; i++ )
18            data[ i ] = generator.Next( 10, 100 );
19      } // end InsertionSort constructor
20
21      // sort array using insertion sort
22      public void Sort()
23      {
```

Fig. 20.8 | Class that creates an array filled with random integers. Provides a method to sort the array with insertion sort. (Part 1 of 3.)

```
24        int insert; // temporary variable to hold element to insert
25
26        // loop over data.Length - 1 elements
27        for ( int next = 1; next < data.Length; next++ )
28        {
29           // store value in current element
30           insert = data[ next ];
31
32           // initialize location to place element
33           int moveItem = next;
34
35           // search for place to put current element
36           while ( moveItem > 0 && data[ moveItem - 1 ] > insert )
37           {
38              // shift element right one slot
39              data[ moveItem ] = data[ moveItem - 1 ];
40              moveItem--;
41           } // end while
42
43           data[ moveItem ] = insert; // place inserted element
44           PrintPass( next, moveItem ); // output pass of algorithm
45        } // end for
46     } // end method Sort
47
48     // print a pass of the algorithm
49     public void PrintPass( int pass, int index )
50     {
51        Console.Write( "after pass {0}: ", pass );
52
53        // output elements till swapped item
54        for ( int i = 0; i < index; i++ )
55           Console.Write( data[ i ] + "  " );
56
57        Console.Write( data[ index ] + "* " ); // indicate swap
58
59        // finish outputting array
60        for ( int i = index + 1; i < data.Length; i++ )
61           Console.Write( data[ i ] + "  " );
62
63        Console.Write( "\n                " ); // for alignment
64
65        // indicate amount of array that is sorted
66        for( int i = 0; i <= pass; i++ )
67           Console.Write( "--  " );
68        Console.WriteLine( "\n" ); // skip a line in output
69     } // end method PrintPass
70
71     // method to output values in array
72     public override string ToString()
73     {
74        string temporary = string.Empty;
```

Fig. 20.8 | Class that creates an array filled with random integers. Provides a method to sort the array with insertion sort. (Part 2 of 3.)

```
75
76          // iterate through array
77          foreach ( int element in data )
78             temporary += element + "   ";
79
80          temporary += "\n"; // add newline character
81          return temporary;
82      } // end method ToString
83  } // end class InsertionSort
```

Fig. 20.8 | Class that creates an array filled with random integers. Provides a method to sort the array with insertion sort. (Part 3 of 3.)

```
 1  // Fig. 20.9: InsertionSortTest.cs
 2  // Testing the insertion sort class.
 3  using System;
 4
 5  public class InsertionSortTest
 6  {
 7     public static void Main( string[] args )
 8     {
 9        // create object to perform insertion sort
10        InsertionSort sortArray = new InsertionSort( 10 );
11
12        Console.WriteLine( "Unsorted array:" );
13        Console.WriteLine( sortArray ); // print unsorted array
14
15        sortArray.Sort(); // sort array
16
17        Console.WriteLine( "Sorted array:" );
18        Console.WriteLine( sortArray ); // print sorted array
19     } // end Main
20  } // end class InsertionSortTest
```

```
Unsorted array:
12   27   36   28   33   92   11   93   59   62

after pass 1: 12   27*  36   28   33   92   11   93   59   62
                   --   --

after pass 2: 12   27   36*  28   33   92   11   93   59   62
                   --   --   --

after pass 3: 12   27   28*  36   33   92   11   93   59   62
                   --   --   --   --

after pass 4: 12   27   28   33*  36   92   11   93   59   62
                   --   --   --   --   --

after pass 5: 12   27   28   33   36   92*  11   93   59   62
                   --   --   --   --   --   --
```

Fig. 20.9 | Testing the insertion sort class. (Part 1 of 2.)

```
after pass 6: 11* 12  27  28  33  36  92  93  59  62
              --  --  --  --  --  --  --

after pass 7: 11  12  27  28  33  36  92  93* 59  62
              --  --  --  --  --  --  --  --

after pass 8: 11  12  27  28  33  36  59* 92  93  62
              --  --  --  --  --  --  --  --  --

after pass 9: 11  12  27  28  33  36  59  62* 92  93
              --  --  --  --  --  --  --  --  --  --

Sorted array:
11  12  27  28  33  36  59  62  92  93
```

Fig. 20.9 | Testing the insertion sort class. (Part 2 of 2.)

Efficiency of Insertion Sort

The insertion sort algorithm also runs in $O(n^2)$ time. Like selection sort, the implementation of insertion sort (lines 22–46 of Fig. 20.8) contains nested loops. The for loop (lines 27–45) iterates data.Length - 1 times, inserting an element in the appropriate position in the elements sorted so far. For the purposes of this application, data.Length - 1 is equivalent to $n - 1$ (as data.Length is the size of the array). The while loop (lines 36–41) iterates over the preceding elements in the array. In the worst case, this while loop will require $n - 1$ comparisons. Each individual loop runs in $O(n)$ time. In Big O notation, nested loops mean that you must multiply the number of iterations of each loop. For each iteration of an outer loop, there will be a certain number of iterations of the inner loop. In this algorithm, for each $O(n)$ iterations of the outer loop, there will be $O(n)$ iterations of the inner loop. Multiplying these values results in a Big O of $O(n^2)$.

20.3.3 Merge Sort

Merge sort is an efficient sorting algorithm but is conceptually more complex than selection sort and insertion sort. The merge sort algorithm sorts an array by splitting it into two equal-sized subarrays, sorting each subarray and merging them in one larger array. With an odd number of elements, the algorithm creates the two subarrays such that one has one more element than the other.

The implementation of merge sort in this example is recursive. The base case is an array with one element. A one-element array is, of course, sorted, so merge sort immediately returns when it's called with a one-element array. The recursion step splits an array in two approximately equal-length pieces, recursively sorts them and merges the two sorted arrays in one larger, sorted array.

Suppose the algorithm has already merged smaller arrays to create sorted arrays A:

```
    4   10   34   56   77
```

and B:

```
    5   30   51   52   93
```

Merge sort combines these two arrays in one larger, sorted array. The smallest element in A is 4 (located in the zeroth element of A). The smallest element in B is 5 (located in the zeroth element of B). In order to determine the smallest element in the larger array, the algorithm compares 4 and 5. The value from A is smaller, so 4 becomes the first element in the merged array. The algorithm continues by comparing 10 (the second element in A) to 5 (the first element in B). The value from B is smaller, so 5 becomes the second element in the larger array. The algorithm continues by comparing 10 to 30, with 10 becoming the third element in the array, and so on.

Lines 22–25 of Fig. 20.10 declare the Sort method. Line 24 calls method SortArray with 0 and data.Length - 1 as the arguments—these are the beginning and ending indices of the array to be sorted. These values tell method SortArray to operate on the entire array.

```
 1   // Fig. 20.10: MergeSort.cs
 2   // Class that creates an array filled with random integers.
 3   // Provides a method to sort the array with merge sort.
 4   using System;
 5
 6   public class MergeSort
 7   {
 8      private int[] data; // array of values
 9      private static Random generator = new Random();
10
11      // create array of given size and fill with random integers
12      public MergeSort( int size )
13      {
14         data = new int[ size ]; // create space for array
15
16         // fill array with random ints in range 10-99
17         for ( int i = 0; i < size; i++ )
18            data[ i ] = generator.Next( 10, 100 );
19      } // end MergeSort constructor
20
21      // calls recursive SortArray method to begin merge sorting
22      public void Sort()
23      {
24         SortArray( 0, data.Length - 1 ); // sort entire array
25      } // end method Sort
26
27      // splits array, sorts subarrays and merges subarrays into sorted array
28      private void SortArray( int low, int high )
29      {
30         // test base case; size of array equals 1
31         if ( ( high - low ) >= 1 ) // if not base case
32         {
33            int middle1 = ( low + high ) / 2; // calculate middle of array
34            int middle2 = middle1 + 1; // calculate next element over
35
36            // output split step
37            Console.WriteLine( "split:   " + Subarray( low, high ) );
38            Console.WriteLine( "         " + Subarray( low, middle1 ) );
39            Console.WriteLine( "         " + Subarray( middle2, high ) );
40            Console.WriteLine();
```

Fig. 20.10 | Class that creates an array filled with random integers. Provides a method to sort the array with merge sort. (Part I of 3.)

```
41
42          // split array in half; sort each half (recursive calls)
43          SortArray( low, middle1 ); // first half of array
44          SortArray( middle2, high ); // second half of array
45
46          // merge two sorted arrays after split calls return
47          Merge( low, middle1, middle2, high );
48       } // end if
49    } // end method SortArray
50
51    // merge two sorted subarrays into one sorted subarray
52    private void Merge( int left, int middle1, int middle2, int right )
53    {
54       int leftIndex = left; // index into left subarray
55       int rightIndex = middle2; // index into right subarray
56       int combinedIndex = left; // index into temporary working array
57       int[] combined = new int[ data.Length ]; // working array
58
59       // output two subarrays before merging
60       Console.WriteLine( "merge:   " + Subarray( left, middle1 ) );
61       Console.WriteLine( "         " + Subarray( middle2, right ) );
62
63       // merge arrays until reaching end of either
64       while ( leftIndex <= middle1 && rightIndex <= right )
65       {
66          // place smaller of two current elements into result
67          // and move to next space in arrays
68          if ( data[ leftIndex ] <= data[ rightIndex ] )
69             combined[ combinedIndex++ ] = data[ leftIndex++ ];
70          else
71             combined[ combinedIndex++ ] = data[ rightIndex++ ];
72       } // end while
73
74       // if left array is empty
75       if ( leftIndex == middle2 )
76          // copy in rest of right array
77          while ( rightIndex <= right )
78             combined[ combinedIndex++ ] = data[ rightIndex++ ];
79       else // right array is empty
80          // copy in rest of left array
81          while ( leftIndex <= middle1 )
82             combined[ combinedIndex++ ] = data[ leftIndex++ ];
83
84       // copy values back into original array
85       for ( int i = left; i <= right; i++ )
86          data[ i ] = combined[ i ];
87
88       // output merged array
89       Console.WriteLine( "            " + Subarray( left, right ) );
90       Console.WriteLine();
91    } // end method Merge
```

Fig. 20.10 | Class that creates an array filled with random integers. Provides a method to sort the array with merge sort. (Part 2 of 3.)

```
 92
 93        // method to output certain values in array
 94        public string Subarray( int low, int high )
 95        {
 96           string temporary = string.Empty;
 97
 98           // output spaces for alignment
 99           for ( int i = 0; i < low; i++ )
100              temporary += "    ";
101
102           // output elements left in array
103           for ( int i = low; i <= high; i++ )
104              temporary += " " + data[ i ];
105
106           return temporary;
107        } // end method Subarray
108
109        // method to output values in array
110        public override string ToString()
111        {
112           return Subarray( 0, data.Length - 1 );
113        } // end method ToString
114     } // end class MergeSort
```

Fig. 20.10 | Class that creates an array filled with random integers. Provides a method to sort the array with merge sort. (Part 3 of 3.)

Method SortArray is declared in lines 28–49. Line 31 tests the base case. If the size of the array is 1, the array is already sorted, so the method simply returns immediately. If the size of the array is greater than 1, the method splits the array in two, recursively calls method SortArray to sort the two subarrays and merges them. Line 43 recursively calls method SortArray on the first half of the array, and line 44 recursively calls method Sort-Array on the second half of the array. When these two method calls return, each half of the array has been sorted. Line 47 calls method Merge (lines 52–91) on the two halves of the array to combine the two sorted arrays in one larger sorted array.

Lines 64–72 in method Merge loop until the application reaches the end of either subarray. Line 68 tests which element at the beginning of the arrays is smaller. If the element in the left array is smaller or equal, line 69 places it in position in the combined array. If the element in the right array is smaller, line 71 places it in position in the combined array. When the while loop has completed (line 72), one entire subarray is placed in the combined array, but the other subarray still contains data. Line 75 tests whether the left array has reached the end. If so, lines 77–78 fill the combined array with the remaining elements of the right array. If the left array has not reached the end, then the right array has, and lines 81–82 fill the combined array with the remaining elements of the left array. Finally, lines 85–86 copy the combined array into the original array. Figure 20.11 creates and uses a MergeSort object. The output from this application displays the splits and merges performed by merge sort, showing the progress of the sort at each step of the algorithm.

```
 1   // Fig. 20.11: MergeSortTest.cs
 2   // Testing the merge sort class.
 3   using System;
 4
 5   public class MergeSortTest
 6   {
 7      public static void Main( string[] args )
 8      {
 9         // create object to perform merge sort
10         MergeSort sortArray = new MergeSort( 10 );
11
12         // print unsorted array
13         Console.WriteLine( "Unsorted: {0}\n", sortArray );
14
15         sortArray.Sort(); // sort array
16
17         // print sorted array
18         Console.WriteLine( "Sorted: {0}", sortArray );
19      } // end Main
20   } // end class MergeSortTest
```

```
Unsorted:  36 38 81 93 85 72 31 11 33 74

split:     36 38 81 93 85 72 31 11 33 74
           36 38 81 93 85
                         72 31 11 33 74

split:     36 38 81 93 85
           36 38 81
                   93 85

split:     36 38 81
           36 38
                 81

split:     36 38
           36
              38

merge:     36
              38
           36 38

merge:     36 38
                 81
           36 38 81

split:           93 85
                 93
                    85

merge:           93
                    85
                 85 93

merge:     36 38 81
                    85 93
           36 38 81 85 93
```

Fig. 20.11 | Testing the merge sort class. (Part 1 of 2.)

```
split:                    72 31 11 33 74
                          72 31 11
                                   33 74

split:                    72 31 11
                          72 31
                                11

split:                    72 31
                          72
                             31

merge:                    72
                             31
                          31 72

merge:                    31 72
                                11
                          11 31 72

split:                             33 74
                                   33
                                      74

merge:                             33
                                      74
                                   33 74

merge:                    11 31 72
                                   33 74
                          11 31 33 72 74

merge:       36 38 81 85 93
                          11 31 33 72 74
             11 31 33 36 38 72 74 81 85 93

Sorted:      11 31 33 36 38 72 74 81 85 93
```

Fig. 20.11 | Testing the merge sort class. (Part 2 of 2.)

Efficiency of Merge Sort

Merge sort is a far more efficient algorithm than either insertion sort or selection sort when sorting large sets of data. Consider the first (nonrecursive) call to method SortArray. This results in two recursive calls to method SortArray with subarrays each approximately half the size of the original array, and a single call to method Merge. This call to method Merge requires, at worst, $n - 1$ comparisons to fill the original array, which is $O(n)$. (Recall that each element in the array can be chosen by comparing one element from each of the subarrays.) The two calls to method SortArray result in four more recursive calls to SortArray, each with a subarray approximately a quarter the size of the original array, along with two calls to method Merge. These two calls to method Merge each require, at worst, $n/2 - 1$ comparisons for a total number of comparisons of $(n/2 - 1) + (n/2 - 1) = n - 2$, which is $O(n)$. This process continues, each call to SortArray generating two additional calls to method SortArray and a call to Merge, until the algorithm has split the array into one-element subarrays. At each level, $O(n)$ comparisons are required to merge the subarrays. Each level splits the size of the arrays in half, so doubling the size of the array requires only one more level. Quadrupling the size of the array requires only two more levels. This pattern is logarithmic and results in $\log_2 n$ levels. This results in a total efficiency of $O(n \log n)$.

20.4 Summary of the Efficiency of Searching and Sorting Algorithms

Figure 20.12 summarizes many of the searching and sorting algorithms covered in this book and lists the Big O of each. Figure 20.13 lists the Big O values covered in this chapter, along with a number of values for n to highlight the differences in the growth rates.

Algorithm	Location	Big O
Searching Algorithms:		
Linear Search	Section 20.2.1	$O(n)$
Binary Search	Section 20.2.2	$O(\log n)$
Recursive Linear Search	Exercise 20.8	$O(n)$
Recursive Binary Search	Exercise 20.9	$O(\log n)$
Sorting Algorithms:		
Selection Sort	Section 20.3.1	$O(n^2)$
Insertion Sort	Section 20.3.2	$O(n^2)$
Merge Sort	Section 20.3.3	$O(n \log n)$
Bubble Sort	Exercises 20.5–20.6	$O(n^2)$

Fig. 20.12 | Searching and sorting algorithms with Big O values.

$n =$	$O(\log n)$	$O(n)$	$O(n \log n)$	$O(n^2)$
1	0	1	0	1
2	1	2	2	4
3	1	3	3	9
4	1	4	4	16
5	1	5	5	25
10	1	10	10	100
100	2	100	200	10000
1,000	3	1000	3000	10^6
1,000,000	6	1000000	6000000	10^{12}
1,000,000,000	9	1000000000	9000000000	10^{18}

Fig. 20.13 | Number of comparisons for common Big O notations.

20.5 Wrap-Up

In this chapter, you learned how to search for items in arrays and how to sort arrays so that their elements are arranged in order. We discussed linear search and binary search, and selection sort, insertion sort and merge sort. You learned that linear search can operate on any set of data, but that binary search requires the data to be sorted first. You also learned that the simplest searching and sorting algorithms can exhibit poor performance. We introduced Big O notation—a measure of the efficiency of algorithms—and used it to compare the efficiency of the algorithms we discussed. In the next chapter, you'll learn about dynamic data structures that can grow or shrink at execution time.

Summary

Section 20.1 Introduction
- Searching involves determining if a search key is present in the data and, if so, finding its location.
- Sorting involves arranging data in order.

Section 20.2.1 Linear Search
- The linear search algorithm searches each element in an array sequentially until it finds the element that matches the search key. If the search key is not in the array, the algorithm tests each element in the array, and when the end of the array is reached, informs the user that the search key is not present, usually by means of a sentinel value.
- One way to describe the efficiency of an algorithm is with Big O notation (O), which indicates how hard an algorithm may have to work to solve a problem.
- In searching and sorting algorithms, Big O is dependent on how many elements are in the data.
- An $O(n)$ algorithm is referred to as having a linear runtime.
- Big O is designed to highlight dominant factors and ignore terms that become unimportant with high n values. Big O notation is concerned with the growth rate of algorithm runtimes, so constants are ignored.
- The linear search algorithm runs in $O(n)$ time.
- The worst case in linear search is that every element must be checked to determine whether the search item exists. This occurs if the search key is the last element in the array or is not present.

Section 20.2.2 Binary Search
- The binary search algorithm is more efficient than the linear search algorithm, but it requires that the array be sorted.
- The first iteration of binary search tests the middle array element. If this is the search key, the algorithm returns its location. If the search key is less than the middle element, the search continues with the first half of the array. If the search key is greater than the middle element, the search continues with the second half of the array. Each iteration of binary search tests the middle value of the remaining array and, if the element is not found, eliminates half of the remaining elements.
- Binary search is a more efficient searching algorithm than linear search because with each comparison it eliminates from consideration half of the elements in the array.
- Binary search runs in $O(\log n)$ time, because each step removes half of the remaining elements.

Section 20.3.1 Selection Sort
- The selection sort is a simple, but inefficient, sorting algorithm.
- The first iteration of the selection sort selects the smallest element in the array and swaps it with the first element. The second iteration selects the second-smallest element (which is the smallest remaining element) and swaps it with the second element. Selection sort continues until the largest element is in the last position. After the ith iteration of selection sort, the smallest i elements of the whole array are sorted into the first i positions.
- The selection sort algorithm runs in $O(n^2)$ time.

Section 20.3.2 Insertion Sort

- The first iteration of insertion sort takes the second element in the array and, if it's less than the first, swaps them. The second iteration looks at the third element and inserts it in the correct position with respect to the first two. After the ith iteration of insertion sort, the first i elements in the original array are sorted.

- The insertion sort algorithm runs in $O(n^2)$ time.

Section 20.3.3 Merge Sort

- Merge sort is a sorting algorithm that is faster, but more complex to implement, than selection sort and insertion sort.

- The merge sort algorithm sorts an array by splitting it into two equal-sized subarrays, sorting each recursively and merging them into one larger array.

- Merge sort's base case is an array with one element. A one-element array is already sorted.

- Merge sort performs the merge by looking at the first element in each array, which is also the smallest. Merge sort takes the smallest of these and places it in the first element of the larger array. If there are still elements in the subarray, merge sort looks at the second element in that subarray (which is now the smallest element remaining) and compares it to the first element in the other subarray. Merge sort continues this process until the larger array is filled.

- In the worst case, the first call to merge sort has to make $O(n)$ comparisons to fill the n slots in the final array.

- The merging portion of the merge sort algorithm is performed on two subarrays, each of approximately size $n/2$. Creating each of these subarrays requires $n/2 - 1$ comparisons for each subarray, or $O(n)$ comparisons total. This pattern continues as each level works on twice as many arrays, but each is half the size of the previous array. Similar to binary search, this halving results in log n levels for a total efficiency of $O(n \log n)$.

Terminology

Big O notation	$O(n)$
binary search	$O(n^2)$
constant runtime	search key
efficiency of algorithms	quadratic runtime
insertion sort	search key
linear runtime	searching
linear search	selection sort
logarithmic runtime	sort key
merge sort	Sort method of class Array
$O(1)$	sorting
$O(\log n)$	subarray
$O(n \log n)$	swapping values

Self-Review Exercises

20.1 Fill in the blanks in each of the following statements:
   a) A selection sort application would take approximately _____ times as long to run on a 128-element array as on a 32-element array.
   b) The efficiency of merge sort is _____.

20.2 What key aspect of both the binary search and the merge sort accounts for the logarithmic portion of their respective Big Os?

20.3   In what sense is the insertion sort superior to the merge sort? In what sense is the merge sort superior to the insertion sort?

20.4   In the text, we say that after the merge sort splits the array into two subarrays, it then sorts these two subarrays and merges them. Why might someone be puzzled by our statement that "it then sorts these two subarrays"?

Answers to Self-Review Exercises

20.1   a) 16, because an $O(n^2)$ algorithm takes 16 times as long to sort four times as much information. b) $O(n \log n)$.

20.2   Both of these algorithms incorporate "halving"—somehow reducing something by half. The binary search eliminates from consideration one half of the array after each comparison. The merge sort splits the array in half each time it's called.

20.3   The insertion sort is easier to understand and to program than the merge sort. The merge sort is far more efficient ($O(n \log n)$) than the insertion sort ($O(n^2)$).

20.4   In a sense, it does not really sort these two subarrays. It simply keeps splitting the original array in half until it provides a one-element subarray, which is, of course, sorted. It then builds up the original two subarrays by merging these one-element arrays to form larger subarrays, which are then merged until the whole array has been sorted.

Exercises

20.5   *(Bubble Sort)* Implement the bubble sort—another simple, yet inefficient, sorting technique. It's called bubble sort or sinking sort because smaller values gradually "bubble" their way to the top of the array (i.e., toward the first element) like air bubbles rising in water, while the larger values sink to the bottom (end) of the array. The technique uses nested loops to make several passes through the array. Each pass compares successive overlapping pairs of elements (i.e., elements 0 and 1, 1 and 2, 2 and 3, etc.). If a pair is in increasing order (or the values are equal), the bubble sort leaves the values as they are. If a pair is in decreasing order, the bubble sort swaps their values in the array.

The first pass compares the first two elements of the array and swaps them if necessary. It then compares the second and third elements. The end of this pass compares the last two elements in the array and swaps them if necessary. After one pass, the largest element will be in the last position. After two passes, the largest two elements will be in the last two positions. Explain why bubble sort is an $O(n^2)$ algorithm.

20.6   *(Enhanced Bubble Sort)* Make the following simple modifications to improve the performance of the bubble sort you developed in Exercise 20.5:

     a) After the first pass, the largest number is guaranteed to be in the highest-numbered element of the array; after the second pass, the two highest numbers are "in place"; and so on. Instead of making nine comparisons on every pass, modify the bubble sort to make eight comparisons on the second pass, seven on the third pass and so on.

     b) The data in the array may already be in the proper order or near-proper order, so why make nine passes if fewer will suffice? Modify the sort to check at the end of each pass whether any swaps have been made. If none have been made, the data must already be in the proper order, so the application should terminate. If swaps have been made, at least one more pass is needed.

20.7   *(Bucket Sort)* A bucket sort begins with a one-dimensional array of positive integers to be sorted and a two-dimensional array of integers with rows indexed from 0 to 9 and columns indexed from 0 to $n-1$, where n is the number of values to be sorted. Each row of the two-dimensional array is referred to as a *bucket*. Write a class named BucketSort containing a method called Sort that operates as follows:

a) Place each value of the one-dimensional array into a row of the bucket array, based on the value's "ones" (rightmost) digit. For example, 97 is placed in row 7, 3 is placed in row 3 and 100 is placed in row 0. This procedure is called a *distribution pass*.

b) Loop through the bucket array row by row, and copy the values back to the original array. This procedure is called a *gathering pass*. The new order of the preceding values in the one-dimensional array is 100, 3 and 97.

c) Repeat this process for each subsequent digit position (tens, hundreds, thousands, etc.).

On the second (tens digit) pass, 100 is placed in row 0, 3 is placed in row 0 (because 3 has no tens digit) and 97 is placed in row 9. After the gathering pass, the order of the values in the one-dimensional array is 100, 3 and 97. On the third (hundreds digit) pass, 100 is placed in row 1, 3 is placed in row 0 and 97 is placed in row 0 (after the 3). After the last gathering pass, the original array is in sorted order.

The two-dimensional array of buckets is 10 times the length of the integer array being sorted. This sorting technique provides better performance than a bubble sort, but requires much more memory—the bubble sort requires space for only one additional element of data. This comparison is an example of the space/time trade-off: The bucket sort uses more memory than the bubble sort, but performs better. This version of the bucket sort requires copying all the data back to the original array on each pass. Another possibility is to create a second two-dimensional bucket array and repeatedly swap the data between the two bucket arrays.

20.8 *(Recursive Linear Search)* Modify Fig. 20.2 to use recursive method `RecursiveLinearSearch` to perform a linear search of the array. The method should receive the search key and starting index as arguments. If the search key is found, return its index in the array; otherwise, return –1. Each call to the recursive method should check one index in the array.

20.9 *(Recursive Binary Search)* Modify Fig. 20.4 to use recursive method `RecursiveBinarySearch` to perform a binary search of the array. The method should receive the search key, starting index and ending index as arguments. If the search key is found, return its index in the array. If the search key is not found, return –1.

20.10 *(Quicksort)* The recursive sorting technique called quicksort uses the following basic algorithm for a one-dimensional array of values:

a) *Partitioning Step*: Take the first element of the unsorted array and determine its final location in the sorted array (i.e., all values to the left of the element in the array are less than the element, and all values to the right of the element in the array are greater than the element—we show how to do this below). We now have one element in its proper location and two unsorted subarrays.

b) *Recursive Step*: Perform *Step a* on each unsorted subarray.

Each time *Step a* is performed on a subarray, another element is placed in its final location in the sorted array, and two unsorted subarrays are created. When a subarray consists of one element, that element is in its final location (because a one-element array is already sorted).

The basic algorithm seems simple enough, but how do we determine the final position of the first element of each subarray? As an example, consider the following set of values (the element in bold is the partitioning element—it will be placed in its final location in the sorted array):

$$37 \quad 2 \quad 6 \quad 4 \quad 89 \quad 8 \quad 10 \quad 12 \quad 68 \quad 45$$

a) Starting from the rightmost element of the array, compare each element with **37** until an element less than **37** is found, then swap **37** and that element. The first element less than **37** is 12, so **37** and 12 are swapped. The new array is

$$12 \quad 2 \quad 6 \quad 4 \quad 89 \quad 8 \quad 10 \quad 37 \quad 68 \quad 45$$

Element 12 is in italics to indicate that it was just swapped with **37**.

b) Starting from the left of the array, but beginning with the element after 12, compare each element with 37 until an element greater than 37 is found—then swap 37 and that element. The first element greater than 37 is 89, so 37 and 89 are swapped. The new array is

12 2 6 4 *37* 8 10 *89* 68 45

c) Starting from the right, but beginning with the element before 89, compare each element with 37 until an element less than 37 is found—then swap 37 and that element. The first element less than 37 is 10, so 37 and 10 are swapped. The new array is

12 2 6 4 *10* 8 *37* 89 68 45

d) Starting from the left, but beginning with the element after 10, compare each element with 37 until an element greater than 37 is found—then swap 37 and that element. There are no more elements greater than 37, so when we compare 37 with itself, we know that 37 has been placed in its final location of the sorted array. Every value to the left of 37 is smaller than it, and every value to the right of 37 is larger than it.

Once the partition has been applied on the previous array, there are two unsorted subarrays. The subarray with values less than 37 contains 12, 2, 6, 4, 10 and 8. The subarray with values greater than 37 contains 89, 68 and 45. The sort continues recursively, with both subarrays being partitioned in the same manner as the original array.

Based on the preceding discussion, write recursive method `QuickSortHelper` to sort a one-dimensional integer array. The method should receive as arguments a starting index and an ending index in the original array being sorted.

21

Data Structures

Much that I bound,
I could not free;
Much that I freed
returned to me.
—Lee Wilson Dodd

There is always room at the top.
—Daniel Webster

I think that I shall never see
A poem lovely as a tree.
—Joyce Kilmer

Objectives

In this chapter you'll learn:

■ To form linked data structures using references, self-referential classes and recursion.

■ How boxing and unboxing enable simple-type values to be used where **object**s are expected in a program.

■ To create and manipulate dynamic data structures, such as linked lists, queues, stacks and binary trees.

■ Various important applications of linked data structures.

■ To create reusable data structures with classes, inheritance and composition.

21.1 Introduction

This chapter continues our four-chapter treatment of data structures. Most of the **data structures** that we have studied thus far have had fixed sizes, such as one- and two-dimensional arrays. Previously, we also introduced the dynamically resizable `List<T>` collection (Chapter 9). This chapter enhances our discussion of **dynamic data structures** that grow and shrink at execution time. Linked lists are collections of data items "lined up in a row" or "chained together"—users can make insertions and deletions anywhere in a linked list. Stacks are important in compilers and operating systems; insertions and deletions are made at only one end—its **top**. Queues represent waiting lines; insertions are made at the back (also referred to as the **tail**) of a queue, and deletions are made from the front (also referred to as the **head**) of a queue. **Binary trees** facilitate high-speed searching and sorting of data, efficient elimination of duplicate data items, representation of file-system directories and compilation of expressions into machine language. These data structures have many other interesting applications as well.

We'll discuss each of these major types of data structures and implement programs that create and manipulate them. We use classes, inheritance and composition to create and package these data structures for reusability and maintainability. In Chapter 22, we introduce generics, which allow you to declare data structures that can be automatically adapted to contain data of any type. In Chapter 23, we discuss C#'s predefined collection classes that implement various data structures.

The chapter examples are practical programs that will be useful in more advanced courses and in industrial applications. The programs focus on reference manipulation. The exercises offer a rich collection of useful applications.

21.2 Simple-Type `struct`s, Boxing and Unboxing

The data structures we discuss in this chapter store `object` references. However, as you'll soon see, we're able to store both simple- and reference-type values in these data structures. This section discusses the mechanisms that enable simple-type values to be manipulated as objects.

Simple-Type `struct`s

Each simple type (see Appendix B, Simple Types) has a corresponding **struct** in namespace `System` that declares the simple type. These structs are called `Boolean`, `Byte`, `SByte`, `Char`, `Decimal`, `Double`, `Single`, `Int32`, `UInt32`, `Int64`, `UInt64`, `Int16` and `UInt16`. Types declared with keyword **struct** are implicitly value types.

Simple types are actually aliases for their corresponding structs, so a variable of a simple type can be declared using either the keyword for that simple type or the struct name—e.g., int and Int32 are interchangeable. The methods related to a simple type are located in the corresponding struct (e.g., method Parse, which converts a string to an int value, is located in struct Int32). Refer to the documentation for the corresponding struct type to see the methods available for manipulating values of that type.

Boxing and Unboxing Conversions

Simple types and other structs inherit from class **ValueType** in namespace System. Class ValueType inherits from class object. Thus, any simple-type value can be assigned to an object variable; this is referred to as a **boxing conversion** and enables simple types to be used anywhere objects are expected. In a boxing conversion, the simple-type value is copied into an object so that the simple-type value can be manipulated as an object. Boxing conversions can be performed either *explicitly* or *implicitly* as shown in the following statements:

```
int i = 5; // create an int value
object object1 = ( object ) i; // explicitly box the int value
object object2 = i; // implicitly box the int value
```

After executing the preceding code, both object1 and object2 refer to two different objects that contain a copy of the integer value in int variable i.

An **unboxing conversion** can be used to explicitly convert an object reference to a simple value, as shown in the following statement:

```
int int1 = ( int ) object1; // explicitly unbox the int value
```

Explicitly attempting to unbox an object reference that does not refer to the correct simple value type causes an **InvalidCastException**.

In Chapters 22 and 23, we discuss C#'s generics and generic collections. As you'll see, generics eliminate the overhead of boxing and unboxing conversions by enabling us to create and use collections of specific value types.

21.3 Self-Referential Classes

A **self-referential class** contains a reference member that refers to an object of the same class type. For example, the class declaration in Fig. 21.1 defines the shell of a self-referential class named Node. This type has two properties—integer Data and Node reference Next. Next references an object of type Node, an object of the same type as the one being declared here—hence, the term "self-referential class." Next is referred to as a **link** (i.e., Next can be used to "tie" an object of type Node to another object of the same type).

```
1   // Fig. 21.1: Fig21_01.cs
2   // Self-referential Node class declaration.
3   class Node
4   {
5      public int Data { get; set; } // store integer data
6      public Node Next { get; set; } // store reference to next Node
7
```

Fig. 21.1 | Self-referential Node class declaration. (Part I of 2.)

```
 8        public Node( int dataValue )
 9        {
10           Data = dataValue;
11        } // end constructor
12     } // end class node
```

Fig. 21.1 | Self-referential Node class declaration. (Part 2 of 2.)

Self-referential objects can be linked together to form useful data structures, such as lists, queues, stacks and trees. Figure 21.2 illustrates two self-referential objects linked together to form a linked list. A backslash (representing a null reference) is placed in the link member of the second self-referential object to indicate that the link does not refer to another object. The backslash is for illustration purposes; it does *not* correspond to the backslash character in C#. A null link normally indicates the end of a data structure.

Fig. 21.2 | Self-referential class objects linked together.

Common Programming Error 21.1
Not setting the link in the last node of a list to null is a logic error.

Creating and maintaining dynamic data structures requires **dynamic memory allocation**—a program's ability to obtain more memory space at execution time to hold new nodes and to release space no longer needed. As you learned in Section 10.8, C# programs do not explicitly release dynamically allocated memory—rather, the CLR performs automatic garbage collection.

The new operator is essential to dynamic memory allocation. Operator new takes as an operand the type of the object being dynamically allocated and returns a reference to an object of that type. For example, the statement

```
Node nodeToAdd = new Node( 10 );
```

allocates the appropriate amount of memory to store a Node and stores a reference to this object in nodeToAdd. If no memory is available, new throws an OutOfMemoryException. The constructor argument 10 specifies the Node object's data.

The following sections discuss lists, stacks, queues and trees. These data structures are created and maintained with dynamic memory allocation and self-referential classes.

Good Programming Practice 21.1
When creating a large number of objects, test for an OutOfMemoryException. Perform appropriate error processing if the requested memory is not allocated.

21.4 Linked Lists

A **linked list** is a linear collection (i.e., a sequence) of self-referential class objects, called **nodes**, connected by reference links—hence, the term "linked" list. A program accesses a linked list via a reference to the first node of the list. Each subsequent node is accessed via the link-reference member stored in the previous node. By convention, the link reference in the last node of a list is set to null to mark the end of the list. Data is stored in a linked list dynamically—that is, each node is created as necessary. A node can contain data of any type, including references to objects of other classes. Stacks and queues are also linear data structures—in fact, they're constrained versions of linked lists. Trees are nonlinear data structures.

Lists of data can be stored in arrays, but linked lists provide several advantages. A linked list is appropriate when the number of data elements to be represented in the data structure is unpredictable. Unlike a linked list, the size of a conventional C# array cannot be altered, because the array size is fixed at creation time. Conventional arrays can become full, but linked lists become full only when the system has insufficient memory to satisfy dynamic memory allocation requests.

Performance Tip 21.1

An array can be declared to contain more elements than the number of items expected, possibly wasting memory. Linked lists provide better memory utilization in these situations, because they can grow and shrink at execution time.

Programmers can maintain linked lists in sorted order simply by inserting each new element at the proper point in the list (locating the proper insertion point does take time). They do not need to move existing list elements.

Performance Tip 21.2

The elements of an array are stored contiguously in memory to allow immediate access to any array element—the address of any element can be calculated directly from its index. Linked lists do not afford such immediate access to their elements—an element can be accessed only by traversing the list from the front.

Normally linked-list nodes are not stored contiguously in memory. Rather, the nodes are logically contiguous. Figure 21.3 illustrates a linked list with several nodes.

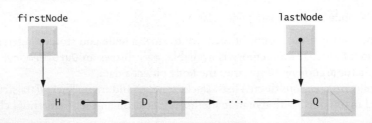

Fig. 21.3 | Linked list graphical representation.

Performance Tip 21.3

Using linked data structures and dynamic memory allocation (instead of arrays) for data structures that grow and shrink at execution time can save memory. Keep in mind, however, that reference links occupy space, and dynamic memory allocation incurs the overhead of method calls.

Linked-List Implementation

Figures 21.4–21.5 use an object of our List class to manipulate a list of miscellaneous object types. Class ListTest's Main method (Fig. 21.5) creates a list of objects, inserts objects at the beginning of the list using List method InsertAtFront, inserts objects at the end of the list using List method InsertAtBack, deletes objects from the front of the list using List method RemoveFromFront and deletes objects from the end of the list using List method RemoveFromBack. After each insert and delete operation, the program invokes List method Display to output the current list contents. If an attempt is made to remove an item from an empty list, an EmptyListException occurs. A detailed discussion of the program follows.

Performance Tip 21.4

Insertion and deletion in a sorted array can be time consuming—all the elements following the inserted or deleted element must be shifted appropriately.

The program consists of four classes—ListNode (Fig. 21.4, lines 8–30), List (lines 33–147), EmptyListException (lines 150–172) and ListTest (Fig. 21.5). The classes in Fig. 21.4 create a linked-list library (defined in namespace LinkedListLibrary) that can be reused throughout this chapter. You should place the code of Fig. 21.4 in its own class library project, as we described in Section 15.13.

```
1   // Fig. 21.4: LinkedListLibrary.cs
2   // ListNode, List and EmptyListException class declarations.
3   using System;
4
5   namespace LinkedListLibrary
6   {
7      // class to represent one node in a list
8      class ListNode
9      {
10        // automatic read-only property Data
11        public object Data { get; private set; }
12
13        // automatic property Next
14        public ListNode Next { get; set; }
15
16        // constructor to create ListNode that refers to dataValue
17        // and is last node in list
18        public ListNode( object dataValue )
19           : this( dataValue, null )
20        {
21        } // end default constructor
22
23        // constructor to create ListNode that refers to dataValue
24        // and refers to next ListNode in List
25        public ListNode( object dataValue, ListNode nextNode )
26        {
27           Data = dataValue;
28           Next = nextNode;
29        } // end constructor
30     } // end class ListNode
```

Fig. 21.4 | ListNode, List and EmptyListException class declarations. (Part 1 of 4.)

```
31
32     // class List declaration
33     public class List
34     {
35        private ListNode firstNode;
36        private ListNode lastNode;
37        private string name; // string like "list" to display
38
39        // construct empty List with specified name
40        public List( string listName )
41        {
42           name = listName;
43           firstNode = lastNode = null;
44        } // end constructor
45
46        // construct empty List with "list" as its name
47        public List()
48           : this( "list" )
49        {
50        } // end default constructor
51
52        // Insert object at front of List. If List is empty,
53        // firstNode and lastNode will refer to same object.
54        // Otherwise, firstNode refers to new node.
55        public void InsertAtFront( object insertItem )
56        {
57           if ( IsEmpty() )
58              firstNode = lastNode = new ListNode( insertItem );
59           else
60              firstNode = new ListNode( insertItem, firstNode );
61        } // end method InsertAtFront
62
63        // Insert object at end of List. If List is empty,
64        // firstNode and lastNode will refer to same object.
65        // Otherwise, lastNode's Next property refers to new node.
66        public void InsertAtBack( object insertItem )
67        {
68           if ( IsEmpty() )
69              firstNode = lastNode = new ListNode( insertItem );
70           else
71              lastNode = lastNode.Next = new ListNode( insertItem );
72        } // end method InsertAtBack
73
74        // remove first node from List
75        public object RemoveFromFront()
76        {
77           if ( IsEmpty() )
78              throw new EmptyListException( name );
79
80           object removeItem = firstNode.Data; // retrieve data
81
```

Fig. 21.4 | ListNode, List and EmptyListException class declarations. (Part 2 of 4.)

```
82              // reset firstNode and lastNode references
83              if ( firstNode == lastNode )
84                 firstNode = lastNode = null;
85              else
86                 firstNode = firstNode.Next;
87
88              return removeItem; // return removed data
89           } // end method RemoveFromFront
90
91           // remove last node from List
92           public object RemoveFromBack()
93           {
94              if ( IsEmpty() )
95                 throw new EmptyListException( name );
96
97              object removeItem = lastNode.Data; // retrieve data
98
99              // reset firstNode and lastNode references
100             if ( firstNode == lastNode )
101                firstNode = lastNode = null;
102             else
103             {
104                ListNode current = firstNode;
105
106                // loop while current node is not lastNode
107                while ( current.Next != lastNode )
108                   current = current.Next; // move to next node
109
110                // current is new lastNode
111                lastNode = current;
112                current.Next = null;
113             } // end else
114
115             return removeItem; // return removed data
116          } // end method RemoveFromBack
117
118          // return true if List is empty
119          public bool IsEmpty()
120          {
121             return firstNode == null;
122          } // end method IsEmpty
123
124          // output List contents
125          public void Display()
126          {
127             if ( IsEmpty() )
128             {
129                Console.WriteLine( "Empty " + name );
130             } // end if
131             else
132             {
133                Console.Write( "The " + name + " is: " );
```

Fig. 21.4 | ListNode, List and EmptyListException class declarations. (Part 3 of 4.)

```
134
135            ListNode current = firstNode;
136
137            // output current node data while not at end of list
138            while ( current != null )
139            {
140               Console.Write( current.Data + " " );
141               current = current.Next;
142            } // end while
143
144            Console.WriteLine( "\n" );
145         } // end else
146      } // end method Display
147   } // end class List
148
149   // class EmptyListException declaration
150   public class EmptyListException : Exception
151   {
152      // parameterless constructor
153      public EmptyListException()
154         : base( "The list is empty" )
155      {
156         // empty constructor
157      } // end EmptyListException constructor
158
159      // one-parameter constructor
160      public EmptyListException( string name )
161         : base( "The " + name + " is empty" )
162      {
163         // empty constructor
164      } // end EmptyListException constructor
165
166      // two-parameter constructor
167      public EmptyListException( string exception, Exception inner )
168         : base( exception, inner )
169      {
170         // empty constructor
171      } // end EmptyListException constructor
172   } // end class EmptyListException
173 } // end namespace LinkedListLibrary
```

Fig. 21.4 | ListNode, List and EmptyListException class declarations. (Part 4 of 4.)

Class ListNode

Encapsulated in each List object is a linked list of ListNode objects. Class ListNode (Fig. 21.4, lines 8–30) contains two properties—Data and Next. Data can refer to any object. [*Note:* Typically, a data structure will contain data of only one type, or data of any type derived from one base type.] In this example, we use data of various types derived from object to demonstrate that our List class can store data of any type. Next stores a reference to the next ListNode object in the linked list. The ListNode constructors (lines 18–21 and 25–29) enable us to initialize a ListNode that will be placed at the end of a List or before a specific ListNode in a List, respectively.

Class *List*

Class List (lines 33–147) contains private instance variables firstNode (a reference to the first ListNode in a List) and lastNode (a reference to the last ListNode in a List). The constructors (lines 40–44 and 47–50) initialize both references to null and enable us to specify the List's name for output purposes. InsertAtFront (lines 55–61), InsertAt-Back (lines 66–72), RemoveFromFront (lines 75–89) and RemoveFromBack (lines 92–116) are the primary methods of class List. Method IsEmpty (lines 119–122) is a **predicate method** that determines whether the list is empty (i.e., the reference to the first node of the list is null). Predicate methods typically test a condition and do not modify the object on which they're called. If the list is empty, method IsEmpty returns true; otherwise, it returns false. Method Display (lines 125–146) displays the list's contents. A detailed discussion of class List's methods follows Fig. 21.5.

Class *EmptyListException*

Class EmptyListException (lines 150–172) defines an exception class that we use to indicate illegal operations on an empty List.

Class *ListTest*

Class ListTest (Fig. 21.5) uses the linked-list library to create and manipulate a linked list. [*Note:* In the project containing Fig. 21.5, you must add a reference to the class library containing the classes in Fig. 21.4. If you use our existing example, you may need to update this reference.] Line 11 creates a new List object and assigns it to variable list. Lines 14–17 create data to add to the list. Lines 20–27 use List insertion methods to insert these values and use List method Display to output the contents of list after each insertion. The values of the simple-type variables are implicitly boxed in lines 20, 22 and 24 where object references are expected. The code inside the try block (lines 33–50) removes objects via List deletion methods, outputs each removed object and outputs list after every deletion. If there's an attempt to remove an object from an empty list, the catch at lines 51–54 catches the EmptyListException and displays an error message.

```
1   // Fig. 21.5: ListTest.cs
2   // Testing class List.
3   using System;
4   using LinkedListLibrary;
5
6   // class to test List class functionality
7   class ListTest
8   {
9      public static void Main( string[] args )
10     {
11        List list = new List(); // create List container
12
13        // create data to store in List
14        bool aBoolean = true;
15        char aCharacter = '$';
16        int anInteger = 34567;
17        string aString = "hello";
18
```

Fig. 21.5 | Testing class List. (Part I of 3.)

```
19          // use List insert methods
20          list.InsertAtFront( aBoolean );
21          list.Display();
22          list.InsertAtFront( aCharacter );
23          list.Display();
24          list.InsertAtBack( anInteger );
25          list.Display();
26          list.InsertAtBack( aString );
27          list.Display();
28
29          // use List remove methods
30          object removedObject;
31
32          // remove data from list and display after each removal
33          try
34          {
35              removedObject = list.RemoveFromFront();
36              Console.WriteLine( removedObject + " removed" );
37              list.Display();
38
39              removedObject = list.RemoveFromFront();
40              Console.WriteLine( removedObject + " removed" );
41              list.Display();
42
43              removedObject = list.RemoveFromBack();
44              Console.WriteLine( removedObject + " removed" );
45              list.Display();
46
47              removedObject = list.RemoveFromBack();
48              Console.WriteLine( removedObject + " removed" );
49              list.Display();
50          } // end try
51          catch ( EmptyListException emptyListException )
52          {
53              Console.Error.WriteLine( "\n" + emptyListException );
54          } // end catch
55      } // end Main
56  } // end class ListTest
```

```
The list is: True

The list is: $ True

The list is: $ True 34567

The list is: $ True 34567 hello

$ removed
The list is: True 34567 hello

True removed
The list is: 34567 hello
```

Fig. 21.5 | Testing class List. (Part 2 of 3.)

```
hello removed
The list is: 34567

34567 removed
Empty list
```

Fig. 21.5 | Testing class List. (Part 3 of 3.)

Method InsertAtFront

Over the next several pages, we discuss each of the methods of class List in detail. Method InsertAtFront (Fig. 21.4, lines 55–61) places a new node at the front of the list. The method consists of three steps:

1. Call IsEmpty to determine whether the list is empty (line 57).

2. If the list is empty, set both firstNode and lastNode to refer to a new ListNode initialized with insertItem (line 58). The ListNode constructor at lines 18–21 of Fig. 21.4 calls the ListNode constructor at lines 25–29, which sets property Data to refer to the object passed as the first argument and sets the Next property's reference to null.

3. If the list is not empty, the new node is "linked" into the list by setting firstNode to refer to a new ListNode object initialized with insertItem and firstNode (line 60). When the ListNode constructor (lines 25–29) executes, it sets property Data to refer to the object passed as the first argument and performs the insertion by setting the Next reference to the ListNode passed as the second argument.

In Fig. 21.6, part (a) shows a list and a new node during the InsertAtFront operation before the new node is linked into the list. The dashed lines and arrows in part (b) illustrate *Step 3* of the InsertAtFront operation, which enables the node containing 12 to become the new list front.

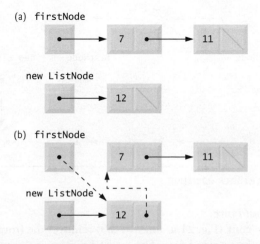

Fig. 21.6 | InsertAtFront operation.

Performance Tip 21.5

After locating the insertion point for a new item in a sorted linked list, inserting an element in the list is fast—only two references have to be modified. All existing nodes remain at their current locations in memory.

Method *InsertAtBack*

Method InsertAtBack (Fig. 21.4, lines 66–72) places a new node at the back of the list. The method consists of three steps:

1. Call IsEmpty to determine whether the list is empty (line 68).

2. If the list is empty, set both firstNode and lastNode to refer to a new ListNode initialized with insertItem (lines 68–69). The ListNode constructor at lines 18–21 calls the ListNode constructor at lines 25–29, which sets property Data to refer to the object passed as the first argument and sets the Next reference to null.

3. If the list is not empty, link the new node into the list by setting lastNode and lastNode.Next to refer to a new ListNode object initialized with insertItem (line 71). When the ListNode constructor (lines 18–21) executes, it calls the constructor at lines 25–29, which sets property Data to refer to the object passed as an argument and sets the Next reference to null.

In Fig. 21.7, part (a) shows a list and a new node during the InsertAtBack operation before the new node has been linked into the list. The dashed lines and arrows in part (b) illustrate *Step 3* of method InsertAtBack, which enables a new node to be added to the end of a list that is not empty.

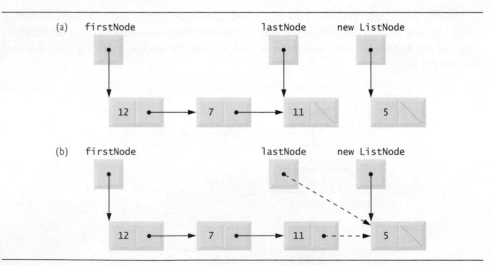

Fig. 21.7 | InsertAtBack operation.

Method *RemoveFromFront*

Method RemoveFromFront (Fig. 21.4, lines 75–89) removes the front node of the list and returns a reference to the removed data. The method throws an EmptyListException (line 78) if the programmer tries to remove a node from an empty list. Otherwise, the method returns a reference to the removed data. After determining that a List is not empty, the method consists of four steps to remove the first node:

1. Assign firstNode.Data (the data being removed from the list) to variable re-moveItem (line 80).

2. If the objects to which firstNode and lastNode refer are the same object, the list has only one element, so the method sets firstNode and lastNode to null (line 84) to remove the node from the list (leaving the list empty).

3. If the list has more than one node, the method leaves reference lastNode as is and assigns firstNode.Next to firstNode (line 86). Thus, firstNode references the node that was previously the second node in the List.

4. Return the removeItem reference (line 88).

In Fig. 21.8, part (a) illustrates a list before a removal operation. The dashed lines and arrows in part (b) show the reference manipulations.

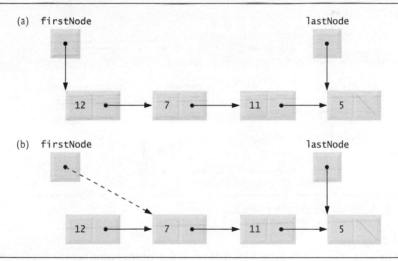

Fig. 21.8 | RemoveFromFront operation.

Method *RemoveFromBack*

Method RemoveFromBack (Fig. 21.4, lines 92–116) removes the last node of a list and returns a reference to the removed data. The method throws an EmptyListException (line 95) if the program attempts to remove a node from an empty list. The method consists of several steps:

1. Assign lastNode.Data (the data being removed from the list) to variable re-moveItem (line 97).

2. If firstNode and lastNode refer to the same object (line 100), the list has only one element, so the method sets firstNode and lastNode to null (line 101) to remove that node from the list (leaving the list empty).

3. If the list has more than one node, create ListNode variable current and assign it firstNode (line 104).

4. Now "walk the list" with `current` until it references the node before the last node. The `while` loop (lines 107–108) assigns `current.Next` to `current` as long as `current.Next` is not equal to `lastNode`.

5. After locating the second-to-last node, assign `current` to `lastNode` (line 111) to update which node is last in the list.

6. Set `current.Next` to `null` (line 112) to remove the last node from the list and terminate the list at the current node.

7. Return the `removeItem` reference (line 115).

In Fig. 21.9, part (a) illustrates a list before a removal operation. The dashed lines and arrows in part (b) show the reference manipulations.

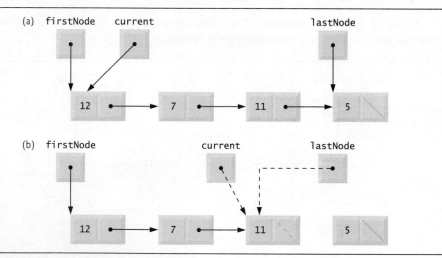

Fig. 21.9 | RemoveFromBack operation.

Method `Display`

Method `Display` (Fig. 21.4, lines 125–146) first determines whether the list is empty (line 127). If so, `Display` displays a `string` consisting of the string `"Empty "` and the list's `name`, then returns control to the calling method. Otherwise, `Display` outputs the data in the list. The method writes a `string` consisting of the string `"The "`, the list's `name` and the string `" is: "`. Then line 135 creates `ListNode` variable `current` and initializes it with `firstNode`. While `current` is not `null`, there are more items in the list. Therefore, the method displays `current.Data` (line 140), then assigns `current.Next` to `current` (line 141) to move to the next node in the list.

Linear and Circular Singly Linked and Doubly Linked Lists

The kind of linked list we have been discussing is a **singly linked list**—it begins with a reference to the first node, and each node contains a reference to the next node "in sequence." This list terminates with a node whose reference member has the value `null`. A singly linked list may be traversed in only one direction.

A **circular, singly linked list** (Fig. 21.10) begins with a reference to the first node, and each node contains a reference to the next node. The "last node" does not contain a `null`

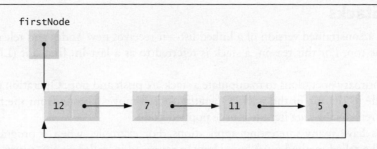

Fig. 21.10 | Circular, singly linked list.

reference; rather, the reference in the last node points back to the first node, thus closing the "circle."

A **doubly linked list** (Fig. 21.11) allows traversals both forward and backward. Such a list is often implemented with two "start references"—one that refers to the first element of the list to allow front-to-back traversal of the list and one that refers to the last element to allow back-to-front traversal. Each node has both a forward reference to the next node in the list and a backward reference to the previous node. If your list contains an alphabetized telephone directory, for example, a search for someone whose name begins with a letter near the front of the alphabet might begin from the front of the list. A search for someone whose name begins with a letter near the end of the alphabet might begin from the back.

In a **circular, doubly linked list** (Fig. 21.12), the forward reference of the last node refers to the first node, and the backward reference of the first node refers to the last node, thus closing the "circle."

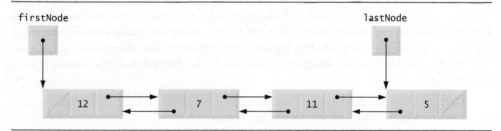

Fig. 21.11 | Doubly linked list.

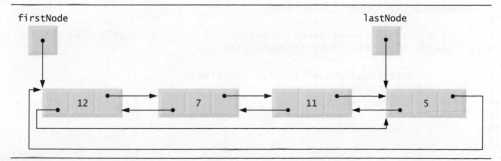

Fig. 21.12 | Circular, doubly linked list.

21.5 Stacks

A **stack** is a constrained version of a linked list—it receives new nodes and releases nodes only at the top. For this reason, a stack is referred to as a **last-in, first-out (LIFO)** data structure.

The primary operations to manipulate a stack are **push** and **pop**. Operation push adds a new node to the top of the stack. Operation pop removes a node from the top of the stack and returns the data item from the popped node.

Stacks have many interesting applications. For example, when a program calls a method, the called method must know how to return to its caller, so the return address is pushed onto the method-call stack. If a series of method calls occurs, the successive return values are pushed onto the stack in last-in, first-out order so that each method can return to its caller. Stacks support recursive method calls in the same manner that they do conventional nonrecursive method calls.

The System.Collections namespace contains class Stack for implementing and manipulating stacks that can grow and shrink during program execution.

In our next example, we take advantage of the close relationship between lists and stacks to implement a stack class by reusing a list class. We demonstrate two different forms of reusability. First, we implement the stack class by inheriting from class List of Fig. 21.4. Then we implement an identically performing stack class through composition by including a List object as a private member of a stack class.

Stack Class That Inherits from List

The program of Figs. 21.13 and 21.14 creates a stack class by inheriting from class List of Fig. 21.4 (line 8 of Fig. 21.3). We want the stack to have methods Push, Pop, IsEmpty and Display. Essentially, these are the methods InsertAtFront, RemoveFromFront, IsEmpty and Display of class List. Of course, class List contains other methods (such as InsertAtBack and RemoveFromBack) that we would rather not make accessible through the public interface of the stack. It is important to remember that all methods in the public interface of class List are also public methods of the derived class StackInheritance (Fig. 21.13).

```
1   // Fig. 21.13: StackInheritanceLibrary.cs
2   // Implementing a stack by inheriting from class List.
3   using LinkedListLibrary;
4
5   namespace StackInheritanceLibrary
6   {
7      // class StackInheritance inherits class List's capabilities
8      public class StackInheritance : List
9      {
10        // pass name "stack" to List constructor
11        public StackInheritance()
12           : base( "stack" )
13        {
14        } // end constructor
15
```

Fig. 21.13 | Implementing a stack by inheriting from class List. (Part 1 of 2.)

```
16              // place dataValue at top of stack by inserting
17              // dataValue at front of linked list
18              public void Push( object dataValue )
19              {
20                  InsertAtFront( dataValue );
21              } // end method Push
22
23              // remove item from top of stack by removing
24              // item at front of linked list
25              public object Pop()
26              {
27                  return RemoveFromFront();
28              } // end method Pop
29          } // end class StackInheritance
30      } // end namespace StackInheritanceLibrary
```

Fig. 21.13 | Implementing a stack by inheriting from class List. (Part 2 of 2.)

The implementation of each StackInheritance method calls the appropriate List method—method Push calls InsertAtFront, method Pop calls RemoveFromFront. Class StackInheritance does not define methods IsEmpty and Display, because StackInheritance inherits these methods from class List into StackInheritance's public interface. Class StackInheritance uses namespace LinkedListLibrary (Fig. 21.4); thus, the class library that defines StackInheritance must have a reference to the LinkedListLibrary class library.

StackInheritanceTest's Main method (Fig. 21.14) uses class StackInheritance to create a stack of objects called stack (line 12). Lines 15–18 define four values that will be pushed onto the stack and popped off it. The program pushes onto the stack (lines 21, 23, 25 and 27) a bool containing true, a char containing '$', an int containing 34567 and a string containing "hello". An infinite while loop (lines 33–38) pops the elements from the stack. When the stack is empty, method Pop throws an EmptyListException, and the program displays the exception's stack trace, which shows the program-execution stack at the time the exception occurred. The program uses method Display (inherited by StackInheritance from class List) to output the contents of the stack after each operation. Class StackInheritanceTest uses namespace LinkedListLibrary (Fig. 21.4) and namespace StackInheritanceLibrary (Fig. 21.13); thus, the solution for class StackInheritanceTest must have references to both class libraries.

```
1   // Fig. 21.14: StackInheritanceTest.cs
2   // Testing class StackInheritance.
3   using System;
4   using StackInheritanceLibrary;
5   using LinkedListLibrary;
6
7   // demonstrate functionality of class StackInheritance
8   class StackInheritanceTest
9   {
```

Fig. 21.14 | Testing class StackInheritance. (Part 1 of 3.)

```
10      public static void Main( string[] args )
11      {
12          StackInheritance stack = new StackInheritance();
13
14          // create objects to store in the stack
15          bool aBoolean = true;
16          char aCharacter = '$';
17          int anInteger = 34567;
18          string aString = "hello";
19
20          // use method Push to add items to stack
21          stack.Push( aBoolean );
22          stack.Display();
23          stack.Push( aCharacter );
24          stack.Display();
25          stack.Push( anInteger );
26          stack.Display();
27          stack.Push( aString );
28          stack.Display();
29
30          // remove items from stack
31          try
32          {
33              while ( true )
34              {
35                  object removedObject = stack.Pop();
36                  Console.WriteLine( removedObject + " popped" );
37                  stack.Display();
38              } // end while
39          } // end try
40          catch ( EmptyListException emptyListException )
41          {
42              // if exception occurs, write stack trace
43              Console.Error.WriteLine( emptyListException.StackTrace );
44          } // end catch
45      } // end Main
46  } // end class StackInheritanceTest
```

```
The stack is: True

The stack is: $ True

The stack is: 34567 $ True

The stack is: hello 34567 $ True

hello popped
The stack is: 34567 $ True

34567 popped
The stack is: $ True

$ popped
The stack is: True
```

Fig. 21.14 | Testing class StackInheritance. (Part 2 of 3.)

```
True popped
Empty stack
   at LinkedListLibrary.List.RemoveFromFront()
      in C:\examples\ch21\Fig21_04\LinkedListLibrary\
      LinkedListLibrary\LinkedListLibrary.cs:line 78
   at StackInheritanceLibrary.StackInheritance.Pop()
      in C:\examples\ch21\Fig21_13\StackInheritanceLibrary\
      StackInheritanceLibrary\StackInheritance.cs:line 27
   at StackInheritanceTest.Main(String[] args)
      in C:\examples\ch21\Fig21_14\StackInheritanceTest\
      StackInheritanceTest\StackInheritanceTest.cs:line 35
```

Fig. 21.14 | Testing class StackInheritance. (Part 3 of 3.)

Stack Class That Contains a Reference to a List

Another way to implement a stack class is by reusing a list class through composition. The class in Fig. 21.15 uses a private object of class List (line 10) in the declaration of class StackComposition. Composition enables us to hide the methods of class List that should not be in our stack's public interface by providing public interface methods only to the required List methods. This class implements each stack method by delegating its work to an appropriate List method. StackComposition's methods call List methods Insert-AtFront, RemoveFromFront, IsEmpty and Display. In this example, we do not show class StackCompositionTest, because the only difference in this example is that we change the name of the stack class from StackInheritance to StackComposition.

```
1   // Fig. 21.15: StackCompositionLibrary.cs
2   // StackComposition declaration with composed List object.
3   using LinkedListLibrary;
4
5   namespace StackCompositionLibrary
6   {
7      // class StackComposition encapsulates List's capabilities
8      public class StackComposition
9      {
10        private List stack;
11
12        // construct empty stack
13        public StackComposition()
14        {
15           stack = new List( "stack" );
16        } // end constructor
17
18        // add object to stack
19        public void Push( object dataValue )
20        {
21           stack.InsertAtFront( dataValue );
22        } // end method Push
23
```

Fig. 21.15 | StackComposition class encapsulates functionality of class List. (Part 1 of 2.)

```
24         // remove object from stack
25         public object Pop()
26         {
27             return stack.RemoveFromFront();
28         } // end method Pop
29
30         // determine whether stack is empty
31         public bool IsEmpty()
32         {
33             return stack.IsEmpty();
34         } // end method IsEmpty
35
36         // output stack contents
37         public void Display()
38         {
39             stack.Display();
40         } // end method Display
41     } // end class StackComposition
42 } // end namespace StackCompositionLibrary
```

Fig. 21.15 | StackComposition class encapsulates functionality of class List. (Part 2 of 2.)

21.6 Queues

Another commonly used data structure is the queue. A queue is similar to a checkout line in a supermarket—the cashier services the person at the beginning of the line first. Other customers enter the line only at the end and wait for service. Queue nodes are removed only from the head (or front) of the queue and are inserted only at the tail (or end). For this reason, a queue is a **first-in, first-out** (**FIFO**) data structure. The insert and remove operations are known as **enqueue** and **dequeue**.

Queues have many uses in computer systems. Computers with only a single processor can service only one application at a time. Each application requiring processor time is placed in a queue. The application at the front of the queue is the next to receive service. Each application gradually advances to the front as the applications before it receive service.

Queues are also used to support **print spooling**. For example, a single printer might be shared by all users of a network. Many users can send print jobs to the printer, even when the printer is already busy. These print jobs are placed in a queue until the printer becomes available. A program called a **spooler** manages the queue to ensure that as each print job completes, the next one is sent to the printer.

Information packets also wait in queues in computer networks. Each time a packet arrives at a network node, it must be routed to the next node along the path to the packet's final destination. The routing node routes one packet at a time, so additional packets are enqueued until the router can route them.

A file server in a computer network handles file-access requests from many clients throughout the network. Servers have a limited capacity to service requests from clients. When that capacity is exceeded, client requests wait in queues.

Queue Class That Inherits from List
The program of Figs. 21.16 and 21.17 creates a queue class by inheriting from a list class. We want the QueueInheritance class (Fig. 21.16) to have methods Enqueue, Dequeue,

IsEmpty and Display. Essentially, these are the methods InsertAtBack, RemoveFrom-Front, IsEmpty and Display of class List. Of course, the list class contains other methods (such as InsertAtFront and RemoveFromBack) that we would rather not make accessible through the public interface to the queue class. Remember that all methods in the public interface of the List class are also public methods of the derived class QueueInheritance.

The implementation of each QueueInheritance method calls the appropriate List method—method Enqueue calls InsertAtBack and method Dequeue calls RemoveFrom-Front. Calls to IsEmpty and Display invoke the base-class versions that were inherited from class List into QueueInheritance's public interface. Class QueueInheritance uses namespace LinkedListLibrary (Fig. 21.4); thus, the class library for QueueInheritance must have a reference to the LinkedListLibrary class library.

```csharp
 1   // Fig. 21.16: QueueInheritanceLibrary.cs
 2   // Implementing a queue by inheriting from class List.
 3   using LinkedListLibrary;
 4
 5   namespace QueueInheritanceLibrary
 6   {
 7      // class QueueInheritance inherits List's capabilities
 8      public class QueueInheritance : List
 9      {
10         // pass name "queue" to List constructor
11         public QueueInheritance()
12            : base( "queue" )
13         {
14         } // end constructor
15
16         // place dataValue at end of queue by inserting
17         // dataValue at end of linked list
18         public void Enqueue( object dataValue )
19         {
20            InsertAtBack( dataValue );
21         } // end method Enqueue
22
23         // remove item from front of queue by removing
24         // item at front of linked list
25         public object Dequeue()
26         {
27            return RemoveFromFront();
28         } // end method Dequeue
29      } // end class QueueInheritance
30   } // end namespace QueueInheritanceLibrary
```

Fig. 21.16 | Implementing a queue by inheriting from class List.

Class QueueInheritanceTest's Main method (Fig. 21.17) creates a QueueInheritance object called queue. Lines 15–18 define four values that will be enqueued and dequeued. The program enqueues (lines 21, 23, 25 and 27) a bool containing true, a char containing '$', an int containing 34567 and a string containing "hello". Class QueueInheritanceTest uses namespace LinkedListLibrary and namespace QueueInheritanceLibrary; thus, the solution for class StackInheritanceTest must have references to both class libraries.

```csharp
1   // Fig. 21.17: QueueTest.cs
2   // Testing class QueueInheritance.
3   using System;
4   using QueueInheritanceLibrary;
5   using LinkedListLibrary;
6
7   // demonstrate functionality of class QueueInheritance
8   class QueueTest
9   {
10     public static void Main( string[] args )
11     {
12        QueueInheritance queue = new QueueInheritance();
13
14        // create objects to store in the queue
15        bool aBoolean = true;
16        char aCharacter = '$';
17        int anInteger = 34567;
18        string aString = "hello";
19
20        // use method Enqueue to add items to queue
21        queue.Enqueue( aBoolean );
22        queue.Display();
23        queue.Enqueue( aCharacter );
24        queue.Display();
25        queue.Enqueue( anInteger );
26        queue.Display();
27        queue.Enqueue( aString );
28        queue.Display();
29
30        // use method Dequeue to remove items from queue
31        object removedObject = null;
32
33        // remove items from queue
34        try
35        {
36           while ( true )
37           {
38              removedObject = queue.Dequeue();
39              Console.WriteLine( removedObject + " dequeued" );
40              queue.Display();
41           } // end while
42        } // end try
43        catch ( EmptyListException emptyListException )
44        {
45           // if exception occurs, write stack trace
46           Console.Error.WriteLine( emptyListException.StackTrace );
47        } // end catch
48     } // end Main
49  } // end class QueueTest
```

Fig. 21.17 | Testing class QueueInheritance. (Part 1 of 2.)

```
The queue is: True

The queue is: True $

The queue is: True $ 34567

The queue is: True $ 34567 hello

True dequeued
The queue is: $ 34567 hello

$ dequeued
The queue is: 34567 hello

34567 dequeued
The queue is: hello

hello dequeued
Empty queue
   at LinkedListLibrary.List.RemoveFromFront()
      in C:\examples\ch21\Fig21_04\LinkedListLibrary\
      LinkedListLibrary\LinkedListLibrary.cs:line 78
   at QueueInheritanceLibrary.QueueInheritance.Dequeue()
      in C:\examples\ch21\Fig21_16\QueueInheritanceLibrary\
      QueueInheritanceLibrary\QueueInheritance.cs:line 28
   at QueueTest.Main(String[] args)
      in C:\examples\ch21\Fig21_17\QueueTest\
      QueueTest\QueueTest.cs:line 38
```

Fig. 21.17 | Testing class `QueueInheritance`. (Part 2 of 2.)

An infinite `while` loop (lines 36–41) dequeues the elements from the queue in FIFO order. When there are no objects left to dequeue, method `Dequeue` throws an `Empty-ListException`, and the program displays the exception's stack trace, which shows the program-execution stack at the time the exception occurred. The program uses method `Display` (inherited from class `List`) to output the contents of the queue after each operation. Class `QueueInheritanceTest` uses namespace `LinkedListLibrary` (Fig. 21.4) and namespace `QueueInheritanceLibrary` (Fig. 21.16); thus, the solution for class `QueueInheritanceTest` must have references to both class libraries.

21.7 Trees

Linked lists, stacks and queues are **linear data structures** (i.e., **sequences**). A **tree** is a nonlinear, two-dimensional data structure with special properties. Tree nodes contain two or more links.

Basic Terminology

With binary trees (Fig. 21.18), each tree node contains two links (none, one or both of which may be `null`). The **root node** is the first node in a tree. Each link in the root node refers to a **child**. The **left child** is the first node in the **left subtree**, and the **right child** is the first node in the **right subtree**. The children of a specific node are called **siblings**. A node with no children is called a **leaf node**. Computer scientists normally draw trees from the root node down—exactly the opposite of the way most trees grow in nature.

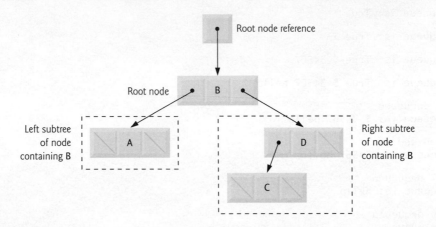

Fig. 21.18 | Binary-tree graphical representation.

 Common Programming Error 21.2
Not setting to null the links in leaf nodes of a tree is a common logic error.

Binary Search Trees

In our binary-tree example, we create a special binary tree called a **binary search tree**. A binary search tree (with no duplicate node values) has the characteristic that the values in any left subtree are less than the value in the subtree's **parent node**, and the values in any right subtree are greater than the value in the subtree's parent node. Figure 21.19 illustrates a binary search tree with 9 integer values. The shape of the binary search tree that corresponds to a set of data can depend on the order in which the values are inserted into the tree.

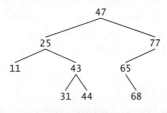

Fig. 21.19 | Binary search tree containing 9 values.

21.7.1 Binary Search Tree of Integer Values

The application of Figs. 21.20 and 21.21 creates a binary search tree of integers and traverses it (i.e., walks through all its nodes) in three ways—using recursive **inorder, preorder** and **postorder** traversals. The program generates 10 random numbers and inserts each into the tree. Figure 21.20 defines class Tree in namespace BinaryTreeLibrary for reuse purposes. Figure 21.21 defines class TreeTest to demonstrate class Tree's functionality. Method Main of class TreeTest instantiates an empty Tree object, then randomly generates 10 integers and inserts each value in the binary tree by calling Tree method Insert-Node. The program then performs preorder, inorder and postorder traversals of the tree. We'll discuss these traversals shortly.

```csharp
1   // Fig. 21.20: BinaryTreeLibrary.cs
2   // Declaration of class TreeNode and class Tree.
3   using System;
4
5   namespace BinaryTreeLibrary
6   {
7      // class TreeNode declaration
8      class TreeNode
9      {
10        // automatic property LeftNode
11        public TreeNode LeftNode { get; set; }
12
13        // automatic property Data
14        public int Data { get; set; }
15
16        // automatic property RightNode
17        public TreeNode RightNode { get; set; }
18
19        // initialize Data and make this a leaf node
20        public TreeNode( int nodeData )
21        {
22           Data = nodeData;
23           LeftNode = RightNode = null; // node has no children
24        } // end constructor
25
26        // insert TreeNode into Tree that contains nodes;
27        // ignore duplicate values
28        public void Insert( int insertValue )
29        {
30           if ( insertValue < Data ) // insert in left subtree
31           {
32              // insert new TreeNode
33              if ( LeftNode == null )
34                 LeftNode = new TreeNode( insertValue );
35              else // continue traversing left subtree
36                 LeftNode.Insert( insertValue );
37           } // end if
38           else if ( insertValue > Data ) // insert in right subtree
39           {
40              // insert new TreeNode
41              if ( RightNode == null )
42                 RightNode = new TreeNode( insertValue );
43              else // continue traversing right subtree
44                 RightNode.Insert( insertValue );
45           } // end else if
46        } // end method Insert
47     } // end class TreeNode
48
```

Fig. 21.20 | Declaration of class TreeNode and class Tree. (Part 1 of 3.)

```
49    // class Tree declaration
50    public class Tree
51    {
52       private TreeNode root;
53
54       // construct an empty Tree of integers
55       public Tree()
56       {
57          root = null;
58       } // end constructor
59
60       // Insert a new node in the binary search tree.
61       // If the root node is null, create the root node here.
62       // Otherwise, call the insert method of class TreeNode.
63       public void InsertNode( int insertValue )
64       {
65          if ( root == null )
66             root = new TreeNode( insertValue );
67          else
68             root.Insert( insertValue );
69       } // end method InsertNode
70
71       // begin preorder traversal
72       public void PreorderTraversal()
73       {
74          PreorderHelper( root );
75       } // end method PreorderTraversal
76
77       // recursive method to perform preorder traversal
78       private void PreorderHelper( TreeNode node )
79       {
80          if ( node != null )
81          {
82             // output node Data
83             Console.Write( node.Data + " " );
84
85             // traverse left subtree
86             PreorderHelper( node.LeftNode );
87
88             // traverse right subtree
89             PreorderHelper( node.RightNode );
90          } // end if
91       } // end method PreorderHelper
92
93       // begin inorder traversal
94       public void InorderTraversal()
95       {
96          InorderHelper( root );
97       } // end method InorderTraversal
98
99       // recursive method to perform inorder traversal
100      private void InorderHelper( TreeNode node )
101      {
```

Fig. 21.20 | Declaration of class TreeNode and class Tree. (Part 2 of 3.)

```
102              if ( node != null )
103              {
104                  // traverse left subtree
105                  InorderHelper( node.LeftNode );
106
107                  // output node data
108                  Console.Write( node.Data + " " );
109
110                  // traverse right subtree
111                  InorderHelper( node.RightNode );
112              } // end if
113          } // end method InorderHelper
114
115          // begin postorder traversal
116          public void PostorderTraversal()
117          {
118              PostorderHelper( root );
119          } // end method PostorderTraversal
120
121          // recursive method to perform postorder traversal
122          private void PostorderHelper( TreeNode node )
123          {
124              if ( node != null )
125              {
126                  // traverse left subtree
127                  PostorderHelper( node.LeftNode );
128
129                  // traverse right subtree
130                  PostorderHelper( node.RightNode );
131
132                  // output node Data
133                  Console.Write( node.Data + " " );
134              } // end if
135          } // end method PostorderHelper
136      } // end class Tree
137  } // end namespace BinaryTreeLibrary
```

Fig. 21.20 | Declaration of class TreeNode and class Tree. (Part 3 of 3.)

```
1   // Fig. 21.21: TreeTest.cs
2   // Testing class Tree with a binary tree.
3   using System;
4   using BinaryTreeLibrary;
5
6   // class TreeTest declaration
7   public class TreeTest
8   {
9       // test class Tree
10      public static void Main( string[] args )
11      {
12          Tree tree = new Tree();
13          int insertValue;
```

Fig. 21.21 | Testing class Tree with a binary tree. (Part 1 of 2.)

```
14
15          Console.WriteLine( "Inserting values: " );
16          Random random = new Random();
17
18          // insert 10 random integers from 0-99 in tree
19          for ( int i = 1; i <= 10; i++ )
20          {
21             insertValue = random.Next( 100 );
22             Console.Write( insertValue + " " );
23
24             tree.InsertNode( insertValue );
25          } // end for
26
27          // perform preorder traversal of tree
28          Console.WriteLine( "\n\nPreorder traversal" );
29          tree.PreorderTraversal();
30
31          // perform inorder traversal of tree
32          Console.WriteLine( "\n\nInorder traversal" );
33          tree.InorderTraversal();
34
35          // perform postorder traversal of tree
36          Console.WriteLine( "\n\nPostorder traversal" );
37          tree.PostorderTraversal();
38          Console.WriteLine();
39       } // end Main
40    } // end class TreeTest
```

```
Inserting values:
39 69 94 47 50 72 55 41 97 73

Preorder traversal
39 69 47 41 50 55 94 72 73 97

Inorder traversal
39 41 47 50 55 69 72 73 94 97

Postorder traversal
41 55 50 47 73 72 97 94 69 39
```

Fig. 21.21 | Testing class Tree with a binary tree. (Part 2 of 2.)

Class TreeNode (lines 8–47 of Fig. 21.20) is a self-referential class containing three properties—LeftNode and RightNode of type TreeNode and Data of type int. Initially, every TreeNode is a leaf node, so the constructor (lines 20–24) initializes references Left-Node and RightNode to null. We discuss TreeNode method Insert (lines 28–46) shortly.

Class Tree (lines 50–136 of Fig. 21.20) manipulates objects of class TreeNode. Class Tree has as private data root (line 52)—a reference to the root node of the tree. The class contains public method InsertNode (lines 63–69) to insert a new node in the tree and public methods PreorderTraversal (lines 72–75), InorderTraversal (lines 94–97) and PostorderTraversal (lines 116–119) to begin traversals of the tree. Each of these methods calls a separate recursive utility method to perform the traversal operations on the internal representation of the tree. The Tree constructor (lines 55–58) initializes root to null to indicate that the tree initially is empty.

Tree method InsertNode (lines 63–69) first determines whether the tree is empty. If so, line 66 allocates a new TreeNode, initializes the node with the integer being inserted in the tree and assigns the new node to root. If the tree is not empty, InsertNode calls TreeNode method Insert (lines 28–46), which recursively determines the location for the new node in the tree and inserts the node at that location. *A node can be inserted only as a leaf node in a binary search tree.*

The TreeNode method Insert compares the value to insert with the data value in the root node. If the insert value is less than the root-node data, the program determines whether the left subtree is empty (line 33). If so, line 34 allocates a new TreeNode, initializes it with the integer being inserted and assigns the new node to reference LeftNode. Otherwise, line 36 recursively calls Insert for the left subtree to insert the value into the left subtree. If the insert value is greater than the root-node data, the program determines whether the right subtree is empty (line 41). If so, line 42 allocates a new TreeNode, initializes it with the integer being inserted and assigns the new node to reference RightNode. Otherwise, line 44 recursively calls Insert for the right subtree to insert the value in the right subtree.

Methods InorderTraversal, PreorderTraversal and PostorderTraversal call helper methods InorderHelper (lines 100–113), PreorderHelper (lines 78–91) and PostorderHelper (lines 122–135), respectively, to traverse the tree and display the node values. The purpose of the helper methods in class Tree is to allow the programmer to start a traversal without needing to obtain a reference to the root node first, then call the recursive method with that reference. Methods InorderTraversal, PreorderTraversal and PostorderTraversal simply take private variable root and pass it to the appropriate helper method to initiate a traversal of the tree. For the following discussion, we use the binary search tree shown in Fig. 21.22.

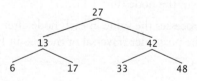

Fig. 21.22 | Binary search tree.

Inorder Traversal Algorithm

Method InorderHelper (lines 100–113) defines the steps for an inorder traversal. Those steps are as follows:

1. If the argument is null, do not process the tree.

2. Traverse the left subtree with a call to InorderHelper (line 105).

3. Process the value in the node (line 108).

4. Traverse the right subtree with a call to InorderHelper (line 111).

The inorder traversal does not process the value in a node until the values in that node's left subtree are processed. The inorder traversal of the tree in Fig. 21.22 is

```
6 13 17 27 33 42 48
```

The inorder traversal of a binary search tree displays the node values in ascending order. The process of creating a binary search tree actually sorts the data (when coupled with an inorder traversal)—thus, this process is called the **binary-tree sort**.

Preorder Traversal Algorithm

Method PreorderHelper (lines 78–91) defines the steps for a preorder traversal. Those steps are as follows:

1. If the argument is null, do not process the tree.
2. Process the value in the node (line 83).
3. Traverse the left subtree with a call to PreorderHelper (line 86).
4. Traverse the right subtree with a call to PreorderHelper (line 89).

The preorder traversal processes the value in each node as the node is visited. After processing the value in a given node, the preorder traversal processes the values in the left subtree, then the values in the right subtree. The preorder traversal of the tree in Fig. 21.22 is

```
27 13 6 17 42 33 48
```

Postorder Traversal Algorithm

Method PostorderHelper (lines 122–135) defines the steps for a postorder traversal. Those steps are as follows:

1. If the argument is null, do not process the tree.
2. Traverse the left subtree with a call to PostorderHelper (line 127).
3. Traverse the right subtree with a call to PostorderHelper (line 130).
4. Process the value in the node (line 133).

The postorder traversal processes the value in each node after the values of all that node's children are processed. The postorder traversal of the tree in Fig. 21.22 is

```
6 17 13 33 48 42 27
```

Duplicate Elimination

A binary search tree facilitates **duplicate elimination.** While building a tree, the insertion operation recognizes attempts to insert a duplicate value, because a duplicate follows the same "go left" or "go right" decisions on each comparison as the original value did. Thus, the insertion operation eventually compares the duplicate with a node containing the same value. At this point, the insertion operation might simply discard the duplicate value.

Searching a binary tree for a value that matches a key value is fast, especially for **tightly packed** binary trees. In a tightly packed binary tree, each level contains about twice as many elements as the previous level. Figure 21.22 is a tightly packed binary tree. A binary search tree with n elements has a minimum of $\log_2 n$ levels. Thus, at most $\log_2 n$ comparisons are required either to find a match or to determine that no match exists. Searching a (tightly packed) 1000-element binary search tree requires at most 10 comparisons, because $2^{10} > 1000$. Searching a (tightly packed) 1,000,000-element binary search tree requires at most 20 comparisons, because $2^{20} > 1,000,000$.

Overview of the Binary-Tree Exercises

The chapter exercises present algorithms for other binary-tree operations, such as performing a **level-order traversal of a binary tree**. The level-order traversal of a binary tree visits the nodes of the tree row by row, starting at the root-node level. On each level of the tree, a level-order traversal visits the nodes from left to right.

21.7.2 Binary Search Tree of IComparable Objects

The binary-tree example in Section 21.7.1 works nicely when all the data is of type int. Suppose that you want to manipulate a binary tree of doubles. You could rewrite the TreeNode and Tree classes with different names and customize the classes to manipulate doubles. Similarly, for each data type you could create customized versions of classes TreeNode and Tree. This proliferates code, and can become difficult to manage and maintain.

Ideally, we'd like to define the binary tree's functionality once and reuse it for many types. Languages like C# provide polymorphic capabilities that enable all objects to be manipulated in a uniform manner. Using such capabilities enables us to design a more flexible data structure. C# provides these capabilities with generics (Chapter 22).

In our next example, we take advantage of C#'s polymorphic capabilities by implementing TreeNode and Tree classes that manipulate objects of any type that implements interface **IComparable** (namespace System). It is imperative that we be able to compare objects stored in a binary search, so we can determine the path to the insertion point of a new node. Classes that implement IComparable define method **CompareTo**, which compares the object that invokes the method with the object that the method receives as an argument. The method returns an int value less than zero if the calling object is less than the argument object, zero if the objects are equal and a positive value if the calling object is greater than the argument object. Also, both the calling and argument objects must be of the same data type; otherwise, the method throws an ArgumentException.

Figures 21.23–21.24 enhance the program of Section 21.7.1 to manipulate IComparable objects. One restriction on the new versions of classes TreeNode and Tree is that each Tree object can contain objects of only one type (e.g., all strings or all doubles). If a program attempts to insert multiple types in the same Tree object, ArgumentExceptions will occur. We modified only five lines of code in class TreeNode (lines 14, 20, 28, 30 and 38) and one line of code in class Tree (line 63) to enable processing of IComparable objects. Except for lines 30 and 38, all other changes simply replaced int with IComparable. Lines 30 and 38 previously used the < and > operators to compare the value being inserted with the value in a given node. These lines now compare IComparable objects via the interface's CompareTo method, then test the method's return value to determine whether it is less than zero (the calling object is less than the argument object) or greater than zero (the calling object is greater than the argument object), respectively. [*Note:* If this class were written using generics, the type of data, int or IComparable, could be replaced at compile time by any other type that implements the necessary operators and methods.]

```
1   // Fig. 21.23: BinaryTreeLibrary2.cs
2   // Declaration of class TreeNode and class Tree.
3   using System;
```

Fig. 21.23 | Declaration of class TreeNode and class Tree. (Part 1 of 4.)

```
4
5   namespace BinaryTreeLibrary2
6   {
7      // class TreeNode declaration
8      class TreeNode
9      {
10        // automatic property LeftNode
11        public TreeNode LeftNode { get; set; }
12
13        // automatic property Data
14        public IComparable Data { get; set; }
15
16        // automatic property RightNode
17        public TreeNode RightNode { get; set; }
18
19        // initialize Data and make this a leaf node
20        public TreeNode( IComparable nodeData )
21        {
22           Data = nodeData;
23           LeftNode = RightNode = null; // node has no children
24        } // end constructor
25
26        // insert TreeNode into Tree that contains nodes;
27        // ignore duplicate values
28        public void Insert( IComparable insertValue )
29        {
30           if ( insertValue.CompareTo(Data) < 0 ) // insert in left subtree
31           {
32              // insert new TreeNode
33              if ( LeftNode == null )
34                 LeftNode = new TreeNode( insertValue );
35              else // continue traversing left subtree
36                 LeftNode.Insert( insertValue );
37           } // end if
38           else if ( insertValue.CompareTo( Data ) > 0 ) // insert in right
39           {
40              // insert new TreeNode
41              if ( RightNode == null )
42                 RightNode = new TreeNode( insertValue );
43              else // continue traversing right subtree
44                 RightNode.Insert( insertValue );
45           } // end else if
46        } // end method Insert
47      } // end class TreeNode
48
49      // class Tree declaration
50      public class Tree
51      {
52         private TreeNode root;
53
54         // construct an empty Tree of IComparable objects
55         public Tree()
56         {
```

Fig. 21.23 | Declaration of class `TreeNode` and class `Tree`. (Part 2 of 4.)

```
57          root = null;
58       } // end constructor
59
60       // Insert a new node in the binary search tree.
61       // If the root node is null, create the root node here.
62       // Otherwise, call the insert method of class TreeNode.
63       public void InsertNode( IComparable insertValue )
64       {
65          if ( root == null )
66             root = new TreeNode( insertValue );
67          else
68             root.Insert( insertValue );
69       } // end method InsertNode
70
71       // begin preorder traversal
72       public void PreorderTraversal()
73       {
74          PreorderHelper( root );
75       } // end method PreorderTraversal
76
77       // recursive method to perform preorder traversal
78       private void PreorderHelper( TreeNode node )
79       {
80          if ( node != null )
81          {
82             // output node Data
83             Console.Write( node.Data + " " );
84
85             // traverse left subtree
86             PreorderHelper( node.LeftNode );
87
88             // traverse right subtree
89             PreorderHelper( node.RightNode );
90          } // end if
91       } // end method PreorderHelper
92
93       // begin inorder traversal
94       public void InorderTraversal()
95       {
96          InorderHelper( root );
97       } // end method InorderTraversal
98
99       // recursive method to perform inorder traversal
100      private void InorderHelper( TreeNode node )
101      {
102         if ( node != null )
103         {
104            // traverse left subtree
105            InorderHelper( node.LeftNode );
106
107            // output node data
108            Console.Write( node.Data + " " );
109
```

Fig. 21.23 | Declaration of class TreeNode and class Tree. (Part 3 of 4.)

```
110                    // traverse right subtree
111                    InorderHelper( node.RightNode );
112                 } // end if
113              } // end method InorderHelper
114
115              // begin postorder traversal
116              public void PostorderTraversal()
117              {
118                 PostorderHelper( root );
119              } // end method PostorderTraversal
120
121              // recursive method to perform postorder traversal
122              private void PostorderHelper( TreeNode node )
123              {
124                 if ( node != null )
125                 {
126                    // traverse left subtree
127                    PostorderHelper( node.LeftNode );
128
129                    // traverse right subtree
130                    PostorderHelper( node.RightNode );
131
132                    // output node Data
133                    Console.Write( node.Data + " " );
134                 } // end if
135              } // end method PostorderHelper
136           } // end class Tree
137        } // end namespace BinaryTreeLibrary
```

Fig. 21.23 | Declaration of class `TreeNode` and class `Tree`. (Part 4 of 4.)

Class `TreeTest` (Fig. 21.24) creates three `Tree` objects to store `int`, `double` and `string` values, all of which the .NET Framework defines as `IComparable` types. The program populates the trees with the values in arrays `intArray` (line 12), `doubleArray` (line 13) and `stringArray` (lines 14–15), respectively.

```
1    // Fig. 21.24: TreeTest.cs
2    // Testing class Tree with IComparable objects.
3    using System;
4    using BinaryTreeLibrary2;
5
6    // class TreeTest declaration
7    public class TreeTest
8    {
9       // test class Tree
10      public static void Main( string[] args )
11      {
12         int[] intArray = { 8, 2, 4, 3, 1, 7, 5, 6 };
13         double[] doubleArray = { 8.8, 2.2, 4.4, 3.3, 1.1, 7.7, 5.5, 6.6 };
14         string[] stringArray = { "eight", "two", "four",
15            "three", "one", "seven", "five", "six" };
```

Fig. 21.24 | Testing class `Tree` with `IComparable` objects. (Part 1 of 3.)

```
16
17        // create int Tree
18        Tree intTree = new Tree();
19        PopulateTree( intArray, intTree, "intTree" );
20        TraverseTree( intTree, "intTree" );
21
22        // create double Tree
23        Tree doubleTree = new Tree();
24        PopulateTree( doubleArray, doubleTree, "doubleTree" );
25        TraverseTree( doubleTree, "doubleTree" );
26
27        // create string Tree
28        Tree stringTree = new Tree();
29        PopulateTree( stringArray, stringTree, "stringTree" );
30        TraverseTree( stringTree, "stringTree" );
31     } // end Main
32
33     // populate Tree with array elements
34     private static void PopulateTree( Array array, Tree tree, string name )
35     {
36        Console.WriteLine( "\n\n\nInserting into " + name + ":" );
37
38        foreach ( IComparable data in array )
39        {
40           Console.Write( data + " " );
41           tree.InsertNode( data );
42        } // end foreach
43     } // end method PopulateTree
44
45     // perform traversals
46     private static void TraverseTree( Tree tree, string treeType )
47     {
48        // perform preorder traversal of tree
49        Console.WriteLine( "\n\nPreorder traversal of " + treeType );
50        tree.PreorderTraversal();
51
52        // perform inorder traversal of tree
53        Console.WriteLine( "\n\nInorder traversal of " + treeType );
54        tree.InorderTraversal();
55
56        // perform postorder traversal of tree
57        Console.WriteLine( "\n\nPostorder traversal of " + treeType );
58        tree.PostorderTraversal();
59     } // end method TraverseTree
60  } // end class TreeTest
```

```
Inserting into intTree:
8 2 4 3 1 7 5 6

Preorder traversal of intTree
8 2 1 4 3 7 5 6

Inorder traversal of intTree
1 2 3 4 5 6 7 8
```

Fig. 21.24 | Testing class Tree with IComparable objects. (Part 2 of 3.)

```
Postorder traversal of intTree
1 3 6 5 7 4 2 8


Inserting into doubleTree:
8.8 2.2 4.4 3.3 1.1 7.7 5.5 6.6

Preorder traversal of doubleTree
8.8 2.2 1.1 4.4 3.3 7.7 5.5 6.6

Inorder traversal of doubleTree
1.1 2.2 3.3 4.4 5.5 6.6 7.7 8.8

Postorder traversal of doubleTree
1.1 3.3 6.6 5.5 7.7 4.4 2.2 8.8


Inserting into stringTree:
eight two four three one seven five six

Preorder traversal of stringTree
eight two four five three one seven six

Inorder traversal of stringTree
eight five four one seven six three two

Postorder traversal of stringTree
five six seven one three four two eight
```

Fig. 21.24 | Testing class `Tree` with `IComparable` objects. (Part 3 of 3.)

Method `PopulateTree` (lines 34–43) receives as arguments an `Array` containing the initializer values for the `Tree`, a `Tree` in which the array elements will be placed and a `string` representing the `Tree` name, then inserts each `Array` element into the `Tree`. Method `TraverseTree` (lines 46–59) receives as arguments a `Tree` and a `string` representing the `Tree` name, then outputs the preorder, inorder and postorder traversals of the `Tree`. The inorder traversal of each `Tree` outputs the data in sorted order regardless of the data type stored in the `Tree`. Our polymorphic implementation of class `Tree` invokes the appropriate data type's `CompareTo` method to determine the path to each value's insertion point by using the standard binary-search-tree insertion rules. Also, notice that the `Tree` of `string`s appears in alphabetical order.

21.8 Wrap-Up

In this chapter, you learned that simple types are value-type `struct`s but can still be used anywhere `object`s are expected in a program due to boxing and unboxing conversions. You learned that linked lists are collections of data items that are "linked together in a chain." You also learned that a program can perform insertions and deletions anywhere in a linked list (though our implementation performed insertions and deletions only at the ends of the list). We demonstrated that the stack and queue data structures are constrained versions of lists. For stacks, you saw that insertions and deletions are made only at the top—so stacks are known as last-in, first out (LIFO) data structures. For queues, which represent waiting lines, you saw that insertions are made at the tail and deletions are made from the head—so queues are known as first-in, first out (FIFO) data structures. We also presented the binary tree data structure. You saw a binary search tree that facilitated high-speed searching and sorting of data and efficient duplicate elimination. In the next chapter, we introduce generics, which allow you to declare a family of classes and methods that implement the same functionality on *any* type.

Summary

Section 21.1 Introduction
- Dynamic data structures can grow and shrink at execution time.

Section 21.2 Simple-Type `struct`s, Boxing and Unboxing
- All simple-type names are aliases for corresponding `struct`s in namespace `System`.
- Each simple type `struct` declares methods for manipulating the corresponding simple-type values.
- Each struct that represents a simple type inherits from class `ValueType` in namespace `System`.
- A boxing conversion creates an object that contains a copy of a simple-type value.
- An unboxing conversion retrieves a simple-type value from an object.

Section 21.3 Self-Referential Classes
- A self-referential class contains a data member that refers to an object of the same class type. Self-referential objects can be linked to form data structures, such as lists, queues, stacks and trees.
- Creating and maintaining dynamic data structures requires dynamic memory allocation—a program's ability to obtain more memory at execution time (to hold new nodes) and to release memory no longer needed.
- Operator `new` takes as an operand the type of the object being dynamically allocated, calls the appropriate constructor to initialize the object and returns a reference to the new object. If no memory is available, `new` throws an `OutOfMemoryException`.

Section 21.4 Linked Lists
- A linked list is a linear collection (i.e., a sequence) of self-referential class objects called nodes, connected by reference links.
- A node can contain properties of any type, including references to objects of other classes.
- A linked list is accessed via a reference to the first node of the list. Each subsequent node is accessed via the link-reference member stored in the previous node.
- By convention, the link reference in the last node of a list is set to `null` to mark the end of the list.
- A circular, singly linked list begins with a reference to the first node, and each node contains a reference to the next node. The "last node" does not contain a null reference; rather, the reference in the last node points back to the first node, thus closing the "circle."
- A doubly linked list allows traversals both forward and backward. Such a list is often implemented with two "start references"—one that refers to the first element of the list to allow front-to-back traversal of the list and one that refers to the last element to allow back-to-front traversal. Each node has both a forward reference to the next node in the list and a backward reference to the previous node.

- In a circular, doubly linked list, the forward reference of the last node refers to the first node, and the backward reference of the first node refers to the last node, thus closing the "circle."

Section 21.5 Stacks
- Stacks are important in compilers and operating systems.
- A stack is a constrained version of a linked list—new nodes can be added to and removed from a stack only at the top. A stack is referred to as a last-in, first-out (LIFO) data structure.
- The primary stack operations are push and pop. Operation push adds a new node to the top of the stack. Operation pop removes a node from the top of the stack and returns the data object from the popped node.

Section 21.6 Queues
- Queues represent waiting lines. Insertions occur at the back (also referred to as the tail) of a queue, and deletions occur from the front (also referred to as the head) of a queue.
- A queue is similar to a checkout line in a supermarket: The first person in line is served first; other customers enter the line at the end and wait to be served.
- Queue nodes are removed only from the head of the queue and are inserted only at the tail of the queue. For this reason, a queue is referred to as a first-in, first-out (FIFO) data structure.
- The insert and remove operations for a queue are known as enqueue and dequeue.

Section 21.7 Trees
- Binary trees facilitate high-speed searching and sorting of data.
- Tree nodes contain two or more links.
- A binary tree is a tree whose nodes all contain two links. The root node is the first node in a tree.
- Each link in the root node refers to a child. The left child is the root node of the left subtree, and the right child is the root node of the right subtree.
- The children of a node are called siblings. A node with no children is called a leaf node.
- A binary search tree (with no duplicate node values) has the characteristic that the values in any left subtree are less than the value in that subtree's parent node, and the values in any right subtree are greater than the value in that subtree's parent node.
- A node can be inserted only as a leaf node in a binary search tree.
- In a preorder traversal, the value in each node is processed as the node is visited. After the value in a given node is processed, the values in the left subtree are processed, then the values in the right subtree are processed.
- In a postorder traversal, the value in each node is processed after the node's left and right subtrees are processed.
- In an inorder traversal, the value in each node is processed after the node's left subtree is processed and before the node's right subtree is processed.
- The inorder traversal of a binary search tree processes the node values in ascending order. The process of creating a binary search tree actually sorts the data (when coupled with an inorder traversal)—thus, this process is called the binary-tree sort.
- The binary search tree facilitates duplicate elimination. As the tree is created, attempts to insert a duplicate value are recognized because a duplicate follows the same "go left" or "go right" decisions on each comparison that the original value did. Thus, the duplicate eventually is compared with a node containing the same value. The duplicate value may simply be discarded at this point.

Terminology

`ArgumentException`	linked list
binary search tree	node
binary tree	`OutOfMemoryException`
binary-tree sort	parent node
boxing conversion	pop on a stack
child node	postorder traversal
circular, doubly linked list	predicate method
circular, singly linked list	preorder traversal
collection	print spooling
`CompareTo` method of interface `IComparable`	push on a stack
data structures	queue
dequeue	right child node
doubly linked list	right subtree
duplicate elimination	root node
dynamic data structures	searching
enqueue	self-referential class
first-in, first-out (FIFO) data structure	sibling node
head of a queue	simple type
`IComparable` interface	singly linked list
inorder traversal	sorting
`InvalidCastException`	spooler
last-in, first-out (LIFO) data structure	stack
leaf node	`struct`
left child node	tail of a queue
left subtree	top of a stack
level-order traversal of a binary tree	tightly packed binary tree
linear data structure	unboxing conversion
link	`ValueType` class

Self-Review Exercises

21.1 State whether each of the following is *true* or *false*. If *false*, explain why.
   a) In a queue, the first item to be added is the last item to be removed.
   b) Trees can have no more than two child nodes per node.
   c) A tree node with no children is called a leaf node.
   d) Linked-list nodes are stored contiguously in memory.
   e) The primary operations of the stack data structure are enqueue and dequeue.
   f) Lists, stacks and queues are linear data structures.

21.2 Fill in the blanks in each of the following statements:
   a) A(n) _____ class is used to define nodes that form dynamic data structures, which can grow and shrink at execution time.
   b) Operator _____ allocates memory dynamically; this operator returns a reference to the allocated memory.
   c) A(n) _____ is a constrained version of a linked list in which nodes can be inserted and deleted only from the start of the list; this data structure returns node values in last-in, first-out order.
   d) A queue is a(n) _____ data structure, because the first nodes inserted are the first nodes removed.

e) A(n) _____ is a constrained version of a linked list in which nodes can be inserted only at the end of the list and deleted only from the start of the list.

f) A(n) _____ is a nonlinear, two-dimensional data structure that contains nodes with two or more links.

g) The nodes of a(n) _____ tree contain two link members.

h) The tree-traversal algorithm that processes the node then processes all the nodes to its left followed by all the nodes to its right is called _____.

Answers to Self-Review Exercises

21.1   a) False. A queue is a first-in, first-out data structure—the first item added is the first item removed. b) False. In general, trees may have as many child nodes per node as is necessary. Only binary trees are restricted to no more than two child nodes per node. c) True. d) False. Linked-list nodes are logically contiguous, but they need not be stored in a physically contiguous memory space. e) False. Those are the primary operations of a queue. The primary operations of a stack are push and pop. f) True.

21.2   a) self-referential. b) new. c) stack. d) first-in, first-out (FIFO). e) queue. f) tree. g) binary. h) preorder.

Exercises

21.3   *(Merging Ordered-List Objects)* Write a program that merges two ordered-list objects of integers into a single ordered-list object of integers. Method Merge of class ListMerge should receive references to each of the list objects to be merged and should return a reference to the merged-list object.

21.4   *(Reversing a Line of Text with a Stack)* Write a program that inputs a line of text and uses a stack object to display the line reversed.

21.5   *(Palindromes)* Write a program that uses a stack to determine whether a string is a palindrome (i.e., the string is spelled identically backward and forward). The program should ignore capitalization, spaces and punctuation.

21.6   *(Evaluating Expressions with a Stack)* Stacks are used by compilers to evaluate expressions and generate machine-language code. In this and the next exercise, we investigate how compilers evaluate arithmetic expressions consisting only of constants, operators and parentheses.

Humans generally write expressions like 3 + 4 and 7 / 9, in which the operator (+ or / here) is written between its operands—this is called *infix notation*. Computers "prefer" *postfix notation*, in which the operator is written to the right of its two operands. The preceding infix expressions would appear in postfix notation as 3 4 + and 7 9 /, respectively.

To evaluate a complex infix expression, a compiler would first convert the expression to postfix notation, then evaluate the postfix version of the expression. Each of these algorithms requires only a single left-to-right pass of the expression. Each algorithm uses a stack object in support of its operation, and in each algorithm the stack is used for a different purpose.

Here, you'll implement the infix-to-postfix conversion algorithm. In the next exercise, you'll implement the postfix-expression evaluation algorithm. In a later exercise, you'll discover that code you write in this exercise can help you implement a complete working compiler.

Write class InfixToPostfixConverter to convert an ordinary infix arithmetic expression (assume a valid expression is entered), with single-digit integers, such as

```
(6 + 2) * 5 - 8 / 4
```

to a postfix expression. The postfix version of the preceding infix expression is

```
6 2 + 5 * 8 4 / -
```

The program should read the expression into `StringBuilder infix`, then use class `StackInheritance` (implemented in Fig. 21.13) to help create the postfix expression in `StringBuilder postfix`. The algorithm for creating a postfix expression is as follows:

a) Push a left parenthesis `'('` on the stack.

b) Append a right parenthesis `')'` to the end of `infix`.

c) While the stack is not empty, read `infix` from left to right and do the following:

   If the current character in `infix` is a digit, append it to `postfix`.

   If the current character in `infix` is a left parenthesis, push it onto the stack.

   If the current character in `infix` is an operator:

   Pop operators (if there are any) at the top of the stack while they have equal or higher precedence than the current operator, and append the popped operators to `postfix`.

   Push the current character in `infix` onto the stack.

   If the current character in `infix` is a right parenthesis:

   Pop operators from the top of the stack and append them to `postfix` until a left parenthesis is at the top of the stack.

   Pop (and discard) the left parenthesis from the stack.

The following arithmetic operations are allowed in an expression:

+ addition
- subtraction
* multiplication
/ division
^ exponentiation
% modulus

Some of the methods you may want to provide in your program follow:

a) Method `ConvertToPostfix`, which converts the infix expression to postfix notation.

b) Method `IsOperator`, which determines whether `c` is an operator.

c) Method `Precedence`, which determines whether the precedence of `operator1` (from the infix expression) is less than, equal to or greater than the precedence of `operator2` (from the stack). The method returns `true` if `operator1` has lower precedence than or equal precedence to `operator2`. Otherwise, `false` is returned.

21.7   *(Evaluating a Postfix Expression with a Stack)* Write class `PostfixEvaluator`, which evaluates a postfix expression (assume it is valid) such as

    6 2 + 5 * 8 4 / -

The program should read a postfix expression consisting of digits and operators into a `StringBuilder`. Using the stack class from Exercise 21.6, the program should scan the expression and evaluate it. The algorithm (for single-digit numbers) is as follows:

a) Append a right parenthesis `')'` to the end of the postfix expression. When the right-parenthesis character is encountered, no further processing is necessary.

b) When the right-parenthesis character has not been encountered, read the expression from left to right.

   If the current character is a digit, do the following:

   Push its integer value on the stack (the integer value of a digit character is its value in the computer's character set minus the value of `'0'` in Unicode).

   Otherwise, if the current character is an *operator*:

   Pop the two top elements of the stack into variables `x` and `y`.

   Calculate `y` *operator* `x`.

   Push the result of the calculation onto the stack.

c) When the right parenthesis is encountered in the expression, pop the top value of the stack. This is the result of the postfix expression.

[*Note:* In *Part b* above (based on the sample expression at the beginning of this exercise), if the operator is '/', the top of the stack is 4 and the next element in the stack is 8, then pop 4 into x, pop 8 into y, evaluate 8 / 4 and push the result, 2, back on the stack. This note also applies to operator '-'.] The arithmetic operations allowed in an expression are:

+   addition
-   subtraction
*   multiplication
/   division
^   exponentiation
%   modulus

You may want to provide the following methods:
 a) Method `EvaluatePostfixExpression`, which evaluates the postfix expression.
 b) Method `Calculate`, which evaluates the expression op1 *operator* op2.

21.8 (*Level-Order Binary Tree-Traversal*) The program of Fig. 21.21 illustrated three recursive methods of traversing a binary tree—inorder, preorder, and postorder traversals. This exercise presents the *level-order traversal* of a binary tree, in which the node values are displayed level by level, starting at the root-node level. The nodes on each level are displayed from left to right. The level-order traversal is not a recursive algorithm. It uses a queue object to control the output of the nodes. The algorithm is as follows:
 a) Insert the root node in the queue.
 b) While there are nodes left in the queue, do the following:

      Get the next node in the queue.
      Display the node's value.
      If the reference to the left child of the node is not null:
          Insert the left child node in the queue.
      If the reference to the right child of the node is not null:
          Insert the right child node in the queue.

Write method `LevelOrderTraversal` to perform a level-order traversal of a binary-tree object. Modify the program of Fig. 21.21 to use this method. [*Note:* You also will need to use the queue-processing methods of Fig. 21.16 in this program.]

Generics

22

Objectives

In this chapter you'll learn:

- To create generic methods that perform identical tasks on arguments of different types.

- To create a generic **Stack** class that can be used to store objects of any class or interface type.

- To understand how to overload generic methods with nongeneric methods or with other generic methods.

- To understand the **new()** constraint of a type parameter.

- To apply multiple constraints to a type parameter.

22.1 Introduction

In Chapter 21, we presented data structures that stored and manipulated `object` references. This chapter continues our multi-chapter discussion on data structures. You could store any `object` in our data structures. One inconvenient aspect of storing `object` references occurs when retrieving them from a collection. An application normally needs to process specific types of objects. As a result, the `object` references obtained from a collection typically need to be downcast to an appropriate type to allow the application to process the objects correctly. In addition, data of value types (e.g., `int` and `double`) must be boxed to be manipulated with `object` references, which increases the overhead of processing such data. Most importantly, processing all data as type `object` limits the C# compiler's ability to perform type checking.

Though we can easily create data structures that manipulate any type of data as `objects` (as we did in Chapter 21), it would be nice if we could detect type mismatches at compile time—this is known as **compile-time type safety**. For example, if a `Stack` should store only `int` values, attempting to push a `string` onto that `Stack` should cause a compile-time error. Similarly, a `Sort` method should be able to compare elements that are all guaranteed to have the same type. If we create type-specific versions of class `Stack` class and method `Sort`, the C# compiler would certainly be able to ensure compile-time type safety. However, this would require that we create many copies of the same basic code.

This chapter discusses **generics**, which provide the means to create the general models mentioned above. **Generic methods** enable you to specify, with a single method declaration, a set of related methods. **Generic classes** enable you to specify, with a single class declaration, a set of related classes. Similarly, **generic interfaces** enable you to specify, with a single interface declaration, a set of related interfaces. Generics provide compile-time type safety. [*Note:* You can also implement generic `structs` and `delegates`.] So far in this book, we've used the generic types `List` (Chapter 9) and `Dictionary` (Chapter 17).

We can write a generic method for sorting an array of objects, then invoke the generic method separately with an `int` array, a `double` array, a `string` array and so on, to sort each different type of array. The compiler performs **type checking** to ensure that the array passed to the sorting method contains only elements of the correct type. We can write a single generic `Stack` class that manipulates a stack of objects, then instantiate `Stack` objects for a stack of `int`s, a stack of `double`s, a stack of `string`s and so on. The compiler performs type checking to ensure that the `Stack` stores only elements of the correct type.

This chapter presents examples of generic methods and generic classes. It also considers the relationships between generics and other C# features, such as overloading. Chapter 23, Collections, discusses the .NET Framework's generic and nongeneric collections classes. A collection is a data structure that maintains a group of related objects or values. The .NET Framework collection classes use generics to allow you to specify the exact types of object that a particular collection will store.

22.2 Motivation for Generic Methods

Overloaded methods are often used to perform similar operations on different types of data. To understand the motivation for generic methods, let's begin with an example (Fig. 22.1) that contains three overloaded DisplayArray methods (lines 23–29, lines 32–38 and lines 41–47). These methods display the elements of an int array, a double array and a char array, respectively. Soon, we'll reimplement this program more concisely and elegantly using a single generic method.

```csharp
1   // Fig. 22.1: OverloadedMethods.cs
2   // Using overloaded methods to display arrays of different types.
3   using System;
4
5   class OverloadedMethods
6   {
7      static void Main( string[] args )
8      {
9         // create arrays of int, double and char
10        int[] intArray = { 1, 2, 3, 4, 5, 6 };
11        double[] doubleArray = { 1.1, 2.2, 3.3, 4.4, 5.5, 6.6, 7.7 };
12        char[] charArray = { 'H', 'E', 'L', 'L', 'O' };
13
14        Console.WriteLine( "Array intArray contains:" );
15        DisplayArray( intArray ); // pass an int array argument
16        Console.WriteLine( "Array doubleArray contains:" );
17        DisplayArray( doubleArray ); // pass a double array argument
18        Console.WriteLine( "Array charArray contains:" );
19        DisplayArray( charArray ); // pass a char array argument
20     } // end Main
21
22     // output int array
23     private static void DisplayArray( int[] inputArray )
24     {
25        foreach ( int element in inputArray )
26           Console.Write( element + " " );
27
28        Console.WriteLine( "\n" );
29     } // end method DisplayArray
30
31     // output double array
32     private static void DisplayArray( double[] inputArray )
33     {
34        foreach ( double element in inputArray )
35           Console.Write( element + " " );
36
37        Console.WriteLine( "\n" );
38     } // end method DisplayArray
```

Fig. 22.1 | Using overloaded methods to display arrays of different types. (Part 1 of 2.)

```
39
40       // output char array
41       private static void DisplayArray( char[] inputArray )
42       {
43          foreach ( char element in inputArray )
44             Console.Write( element + " " );
45
46          Console.WriteLine( "\n" );
47       } // end method DisplayArray
48    } // end class OverloadedMethods
```

```
Array intArray contains:
1 2 3 4 5 6

Array doubleArray contains:
1.1 2.2 3.3 4.4 5.5 6.6 7.7

Array charArray contains:
H E L L O
```

Fig. 22.1 | Using overloaded methods to display arrays of different types. (Part 2 of 2.)

The program begins by declaring and initializing three arrays—six-element int array
intArray (line 10), seven-element double array doubleArray (line 11) and five-element
char array charArray (line 12). Then, lines 14–19 output the arrays.

When the compiler encounters a method call, it attempts to locate a method declaration that has the same method name and parameters that match the argument types in the
method call. In this example, each DisplayArray call exactly matches one of the Display-
Array method declarations. For example, line 15 calls DisplayArray with intArray as its
argument. At compile time, the compiler determines argument intArray's type (i.e.,
int[]), attempts to locate a method named DisplayArray that specifies a single int[]
parameter (which it finds at lines 23–29) and sets up a call to that method. Similarly, when
the compiler encounters the DisplayArray call at line 17, it determines argument double-
Array's type (i.e., double[]), then attempts to locate a method named DisplayArray that
specifies a single double[] parameter (which it finds at lines 32–38) and sets up a call to
that method. Finally, when the compiler encounters the DisplayArray call at line 19, it
determines argument charArray's type (i.e., char[]), then attempts to locate a method
named DisplayArray that specifies a single char[] parameter (which it finds at lines 41–
47) and sets up a call to that method.

Study each DisplayArray method. Note that the array element type (int, double or
char) appears in two locations in each method—the method header (lines 23, 32 and 41)
and the foreach statement header (lines 25, 34 and 43). If we replace the element types in
each method with a generic name (such as T for "type") then all three methods would look
like the one in Fig. 22.2. It appears that if we can replace the array element type in each of
the three methods with a single "generic type parameter," then we should be able to declare
one DisplayArray method that can display the elements of *any* array. The method in
Fig. 22.2 will not compile, because its syntax is not correct. We declare a generic Display-
Array method with the proper syntax in Fig. 22.3.

```
1   private static void DisplayArray( T[] inputArray )
2   {
3       foreach ( T element in inputArray )
4           Console.Write( element + " " );
5
6       Console.WriteLine( "\n" );
7   } // end method DisplayArray
```

Fig. 22.2 | `DisplayArray` method in which actual type names are replaced by convention with the generic name T.

22.3 Generic-Method Implementation

If the operations performed by several overloaded methods are identical for each argument type, the overloaded methods can be more compactly and conveniently coded using a generic method. You can write a single generic-method declaration that can be called at different times with arguments of different types. Based on the types of the arguments passed to the generic method, the compiler handles each method call appropriately.

Figure 22.3 reimplements the application of Fig. 22.1 using a generic `DisplayArray` method (lines 24–30). Note that the `DisplayArray` method calls in lines 16, 18 and 20 are identical to those of Fig. 22.1, the outputs of the two applications are identical and the code in Fig. 22.3 is 17 lines shorter than that in Fig. 22.1. As illustrated in Fig. 22.3, generics enable us to create and test our code once, then reuse it for many different types of data. This demonstrates the expressive power of generics.

```
1   // Fig. 22.3: GenericMethod.cs
2   // Using overloaded methods to display arrays of different types.
3   using System;
4   using System.Collections.Generic;
5
6   class GenericMethod
7   {
8       public static void Main( string[] args )
9       {
10          // create arrays of int, double and char
11          int[] intArray = { 1, 2, 3, 4, 5, 6 };
12          double[] doubleArray = { 1.1, 2.2, 3.3, 4.4, 5.5, 6.6, 7.7 };
13          char[] charArray = { 'H', 'E', 'L', 'L', 'O' };
14
15          Console.WriteLine( "Array intArray contains:" );
16          DisplayArray( intArray ); // pass an int array argument
17          Console.WriteLine( "Array doubleArray contains:" );
18          DisplayArray( doubleArray ); // pass a double array argument
19          Console.WriteLine( "Array charArray contains:" );
20          DisplayArray( charArray ); // pass a char array argument
21      } // end Main
22
```

Fig. 22.3 | Using a generic method to display arrays of different types. (Part 1 of 2.)

```
23        // output array of all types
24        private static void DisplayArray< T >( T[] inputArray )
25        {
26           foreach ( T element in inputArray )
27              Console.Write( element + " " );
28
29           Console.WriteLine( "\n" );
30        } // end method DisplayArray
31    } // end class GenericMethod
```

```
Array intArray contains:
1 2 3 4 5 6

Array doubleArray contains:
1.1 2.2 3.3 4.4 5.5 6.6 7.7

Array charArray contains:
H E L L O
```

Fig. 22.3 | Using a generic method to display arrays of different types. (Part 2 of 2.)

Line 24 begins method `DisplayArray`'s declaration. All generic method declarations have a **type-parameter list** delimited by angle brackets (`<T>` in this example) that follows the method's name. Each type-parameter list contains one or more **type parameters**, separated by commas. A type parameter is an identifier that's used in place of actual type names. The type parameters can be used to declare the return type, the parameter types and the local variable types in a generic method declaration; the type parameters act as placeholders for **type arguments** that represent the types of data that will be passed to the generic method. A generic method's body is declared like that of any other method. Note that the type-parameter names throughout the method declaration must match those declared in the type-parameter list. For example, line 26 declares `element` in the `foreach` statement as type `T`, which matches the type parameter (`T`) declared in line 24. Also, a type parameter can be declared only once in the type-parameter list but can appear more than once in the method's parameter list. Type-parameter names need not be unique among different generic methods.

Common Programming Error 22.1

If you forget to include the type-parameter list when declaring a generic method, the compiler will not recognize the type-parameter names when they're encountered in the method. This results in compilation errors.

Method `DisplayArray`'s type-parameter list (line 24) declares type parameter `T` as the placeholder for the array-element type that `DisplayArray` will output. Note that `T` appears in the parameter list as the array-element type (line 24). The `foreach` statement header (line 26) also uses `T` as the `element` type. These are the same two locations where the overloaded `DisplayArray` methods of Fig. 22.1 specified `int`, `double` or `char` as the element type. The remainder of `DisplayArray` is identical to the version presented in Fig. 22.1.

Good Programming Practice 22.1

It's recommended that type parameters be specified as individual capital letters. Typically, a type parameter that represents the type of an element in an array (or other collection) is named E for "element" or T for "type."

As in Fig. 22.1, the program of Fig. 22.3 begins by declaring and initializing six-element `int` array `intArray` (line 11), seven-element `double` array `doubleArray` (line 12) and five-element `char` array `charArray` (line 13). Then each array is output by calling `DisplayArray` (lines 16, 18 and 20)—once with argument `intArray`, once with argument `doubleArray` and once with argument `charArray`.

When the compiler encounters a method call such as line 16, it analyzes the set of methods (both nongeneric and generic) that might match the method call, looking for a method that best matches the call. If there are no matching methods, or if there's more than one best match, the compiler generates an error. If you have any uncertainty on which of your methods will be called, the complete details of method-call resolution can be found in Section 14.5.5.1 of the Ecma C# Language Specification

```
www.ecma-international.org/publications/standards/Ecma-334.htm
```

or Section 7.5.3 of the Microsoft C# Language Specification 4

```
bit.ly/CSharp4Spec
```

In the case of line 16, the compiler determines that the best match occurs if the type parameter `T` in lines 24 and 26 of method `DisplayArray`'s declaration is replaced with the type of the elements in the method call's argument `intArray` (i.e., `int`). Then, the compiler sets up a call to `DisplayArray` with the `int` as the **type argument** for the type parameter `T`. This is known as the **type-inferencing** process. The same process is repeated for the calls to method `DisplayArray` in lines 18 and 20.

Common Programming Error 22.2

If the compiler cannot find a single nongeneric or generic method declaration that's a best match for a method call, or if there are multiple best matches, a compilation error occurs.

You can also use **explicit type arguments** to indicate the exact type that should be used to call a generic function. For example, line 16 could be written as

```
DisplayArray< int >( intArray ); // pass an int array argument
```

The preceding method call explicitly provides the type argument (`int`) that should be used to replace type parameter `T` in lines 24 and 26 of the `DisplayArray` method's declaration.

For each variable declared with a type parameter, the compiler also determines whether the operations performed on such a variable are allowed for all types that the type parameter can assume. The only operation performed on the array elements in this example is to output the `string` representation of the elements. Line 27 performs an implicit boxing conversion for every value-type array element and an implicit `ToString` call on every array element. Since all objects have a `ToString` method, the compiler is satisfied that line 27 performs a valid operation for any array element.

By declaring `DisplayArray` as a generic method in Fig. 22.3, we eliminated the need for the overloaded methods of Fig. 22.1, saving 17 lines of code and creating a reusable method that can output the string representations of the elements in *any* one-dimensional array, not just arrays of int, double or char elements.

22.4 Type Constraints

In this section, we present a generic Maximum method that determines and returns the largest of its three arguments (all of the same type). The generic method in this example uses the type parameter to declare both the method's return type and its parameters. Normally, when comparing values to determine which one is greater, you would use the > operator. However, this operator is not overloaded for use with every type that's built into the Framework Class Library or that might be defined by extending those types. Generic code is restricted to performing operations that are guaranteed to work for every possible type. Thus, an expression like variable1 < variable2 is not allowed unless the compiler can ensure that the operator < is provided for every type that will ever be used in the generic code. Similarly, you cannot call a method on a generic-type variable unless the compiler can ensure that all types that will ever be used in the generic code support that method.

IComparable<T> Interface

It's possible to compare two objects of the same type if that type implements the generic interface **IComparable<T>** (of namespace System). A benefit of implementing interface IComparable<T> is that IComparable<T> objects can be used with the sorting and searching methods of classes in the System.Collections.Generic namespace—we discuss those methods in Chapter 23. The structures in the Framework Class Library that correspond to the simple types all implement this interface. For example, the structure for simple type double is Double and the structure for simple type int is Int32—both Double and Int32 implement the IComparable<T> interface. Types that implement IComparable<T> must declare a CompareTo method for comparing objects. For example, if we have two ints, int1 and int2, they can be compared with the expression:

```
    int1.CompareTo( int2 )
```

Method CompareTo must return 0 if the objects are equal, a negative integer if int1 is less than int2 or a positive integer if int1 is greater than int2. It's the responsibility of the programmer who declares a type that implements IComparable<T> to define method CompareTo such that it compares the contents of two objects of that type and returns the appropriate result.

Specifying Type Constraints

Even though IComparable objects can be compared, they cannot be used with generic code by default, because not all types implement interface IComparable<T>. However, we can restrict the types that can be used with a generic method or class to ensure that they meet certain requirements. This feature—known as a **type constraint**—restricts the type of the argument supplied to a particular type parameter. Figure 22.4 declares method Maximum (lines 20–34) with a type constraint that requires each of the method's arguments to be of type IComparable<T>. This restriction is important, because not all objects can be compared. However, all IComparable<T> objects are guaranteed to have a CompareTo method that can be used in method Maximum to determine the largest of its three arguments.

```
I    // Fig. 22.4: MaximumTest.cs
2    // Generic method Maximum returns the largest of three objects.
3    using System;
4
5    class MaximumTest
6    {
7       public static void Main( string[] args )
8       {
9          Console.WriteLine( "Maximum of {0}, {1} and {2} is {3}\n",
10            3, 4, 5, Maximum( 3, 4, 5 ) );
11         Console.WriteLine( "Maximum of {0}, {1} and {2} is {3}\n",
12            6.6, 8.8, 7.7, Maximum( 6.6, 8.8, 7.7 ) );
13         Console.WriteLine( "Maximum of {0}, {1} and {2} is {3}\n",
14            "pear", "apple", "orange",
15            Maximum( "pear", "apple", "orange" ) );
16      } // end Main
17
18      // generic function determines the
19      // largest of the IComparable objects
20      private static T Maximum< T >( T x, T y, T z )
21         where T : IComparable< T >
22      {
23         T max = x; // assume x is initially the largest
24
25         // compare y with max
26         if ( y.CompareTo( max ) > 0 )
27            max = y; // y is the largest so far
28
29         // compare z with max
30         if ( z.CompareTo( max ) > 0 )
31            max = z; // z is the largest
32
33         return max; // return largest object
34      } // end method Maximum
35   } // end class MaximumTest
```

```
Maximum of 3, 4 and 5 is 5

Maximum of 6.6, 8.8 and 7.7 is 8.8

Maximum of pear, apple and orange is pear
```

Fig. 22.4 | Generic method Maximum returns the largest of three objects.

Generic method Maximum uses type parameter T as the return type of the method (line 20), as the type of method parameters x, y and z (line 20), and as the type of local variable max (line 23). Generic method Maximum's **where** clause (after the parameter list in line 21) specifies the type constraint for type parameter T. In this case, the clause where T : IComparable<T> indicates that this method requires the type argument to implement interface IComparable<T>. If no type constraint is specified, the default type constraint is object.

C# provides several kinds of type constraints. A **class constraint** indicates that the type argument must be an object of a specific base class or one of its subclasses. An **interface**

constraint indicates that the type argument's class must implement a specific interface. The type constraint in line 20 is an interface constraint, because IComparable<T> is an interface. You can specify that the type argument must be a reference type or a value type by using the **reference-type constraint (class)** or the **value-type constraint (struct)**, respectively. Finally, you can specify a **constructor constraint—new()**—to indicate that the generic code can use operator new to create new objects of the type represented by the type parameter. If a type parameter is specified with a constructor constraint, the type argument's class must provide a public parameterless or default constructor to ensure that objects of the class can be created without passing constructor arguments; otherwise, a compilation error occurs.

It's possible to apply **multiple constraints** to a type parameter. To do so, simply provide a comma-separated list of constraints in the where clause. If you have a class constraint, reference-type constraint or value-type constraint, it must be listed first—only one of these types of constraints can be used for each type parameter. Interface constraints (if any) are listed next. The constructor constraint is listed last (if there is one).

Analyzing the Code
Method Maximum assumes that its first argument (x) is the largest and assigns it to local variable max (line 23). Next, the if statement at lines 26–27 determines whether y is greater than max. The condition invokes y's CompareTo method with the expression y.CompareTo(max). If y is greater than max, then y is assigned to variable max (line 27). Similarly, the statement at lines 30–31 determines whether z is greater than max. If so, line 31 assigns z to max. Then, line 33 returns max to the caller.

In Main (lines 7–16), line 10 calls Maximum with the integers 3, 4 and 5. Generic method Maximum is a match for this call, but its arguments must implement interface IComparable<T> to ensure that they can be compared. Type int is a synonym for struct Int32, which implements interface IComparable<int>. Thus, ints (and other simple types) are valid arguments to method Maximum.

Line 12 passes three double arguments to Maximum. Again, this is allowed because double is a synonym for the Double struct, which implements IComparable<double>. Line 15 passes Maximum three strings, which are also IComparable<string> objects. Note that we intentionally placed the largest value in a different position in each method call (lines 10, 12 and 15) to show that the generic method always finds the maximum value, regardless of its position in the argument list and regardless of the inferred type argument.

22.5 Overloading Generic Methods

A generic method may be **overloaded**. Each overloaded method must have a unique signature (as discussed in Chapter 7). A class can provide two or more generic methods with the same name but different method parameters. For example, we could provide a second version of generic method DisplayArray (Fig. 22.3) with the additional parameters lowIndex and highIndex that specify the portion of the array to output (see Exercise 22.8).

A generic method can be overloaded by nongeneric methods with the same method name. When the compiler encounters a method call, it searches for the method declaration that best matches the method name and the argument types specified in the call. For example, generic method DisplayArray of Fig. 22.3 could be overloaded with a version specific to strings that outputs the strings in neat, tabular format (see Exercise 22.9). If the compiler cannot match a method call to either a nongeneric method or a generic method, or if there's ambiguity due to multiple possible matches, the compiler generates an error.

22.6 Generic Classes

The concept of a data structure (e.g., a stack) that contains data elements can be understood independently of the element type it manipulates. A generic class provides a means for describing a class in a type-independent manner. We can then instantiate type-specific versions of the generic class. This capability is an opportunity for software reusability.

With a generic class, you can use a simple, concise notation to indicate the actual type(s) that should be used in place of the class's type parameter(s). At compilation time, the compiler ensures your code's type safety, and the runtime system replaces type parameters with type arguments to enable your client code to interact with the generic class.

One generic Stack class, for example, could be the basis for creating many Stack classes (e.g., "Stack of double," "Stack of int," "Stack of char," "Stack of Employee"). Figure 22.5 presents a generic Stack class declaration. This class should not be confused with the class Stack from namespace System.Collections.Generics. A generic class declaration is similar to a nongeneric class declaration, except that the class name is followed by a type-parameter list (line 5) and, optionally, one or more constraints on its type parameter. Type parameter T represents the element type the Stack will manipulate. As with generic methods, the type-parameter list of a generic class can have one or more type parameters separated by commas. (You'll create a generic class with two type parameters in Exercise 22.11.) Type parameter T is used throughout the Stack class declaration (Fig. 22.5) to represent the element type. Class Stack declares variable elements as an array of type T (line 8). This array (created at line 21) will store the Stack's elements. [*Note:* This example implements a Stack as an array. As you've seen in Chapter 21, Stacks also are commonly implemented as linked lists.]

```
1   // Fig. 22.5: Stack.cs
2   // Generic class Stack.
3   using System;
4
5   class Stack< T >
6   {
7      private int top; // location of the top element
8      private T[] elements; // array that stores stack elements
9
10     // parameterless constructor creates a stack of the default size
11     public Stack()
12        : this( 10 ) // default stack size
13     {
14        // empty constructor; calls constructor at line 18 to perform init
15     } // end stack constructor
16
17     // constructor creates a stack of the specified number of elements
18     public Stack( int stackSize )
19     {
```

Fig. 22.5 | Generic class Stack. (Part 1 of 2.)

```
20          if ( stackSize > 0 ) // validate stackSize
21             elements = new T[ stackSize ]; // create stackSize elements
22          else
23             throw new ArgumentException( "Stack size must be positive." );
24
25          top = -1; // stack initially empty
26       } // end stack constructor
27
28       // push element onto the stack; if unsuccessful,
29       // throw FullStackException
30       public void Push( T pushValue )
31       {
32          if ( top == elements.Length - 1 ) // stack is full
33             throw new FullStackException( string.Format(
34                "Stack is full, cannot push {0}", pushValue ) );
35
36          ++top; // increment top
37          elements[ top ] = pushValue; // place pushValue on stack
38       } // end method Push
39
40       // return the top element if not empty,
41       // else throw EmptyStackException
42       public T Pop()
43       {
44          if ( top == -1 ) // stack is empty
45             throw new EmptyStackException( "Stack is empty, cannot pop" );
46
47          --top; // decrement top
48          return elements[ top + 1 ]; // return top value
49       } // end method Pop
50    } // end class Stack
```

Fig. 22.5 | Generic class Stack. (Part 2 of 2.)

Class Stack has two constructors. The parameterless constructor (lines 11–15) passes the default stack size (10) to the one-argument constructor, using the syntax this (line 12) to invoke another constructor in the same class. The one-argument constructor (lines 18–26) validates the stackSize argument and creates an array of the specified stackSize (if it's greater than 0) or throws an exception, otherwise.

Method Push (lines 30–38) first determines whether an attempt is being made to push an element onto a full Stack. If so, lines 33–34 throw a FullStackException (declared in Fig. 22.6). If the Stack is not full, line 36 increments the top counter to indicate the new top position, and line 37 places the argument in that location of array elements.

Method Pop (lines 42–49) first determines whether an attempt is being made to pop an element from an empty Stack. If so, line 45 throws an EmptyStackException (declared in Fig. 22.7). Otherwise, line 47 decrements the top counter to indicate the new top position, and line 48 returns the original top element of the Stack.

Classes FullStackException (Fig. 22.6) and EmptyStackException (Fig. 22.7) each provide a parameterless constructor, a one-argument constructor of exception classes (as discussed in Section 13.8) and a two-argument constructor for creating a new exception using an existing one. The parameterless constructor sets the default error message while the other two constructors set custom error messages.

```
1   // Fig. 22.6: FullStackException.cs
2   // FullStackException indicates a stack is full.
3   using System;
4
5   class FullStackException : Exception
6   {
7      // parameterless constructor
8      public FullStackException() : base( "Stack is full" )
9      {
10        // empty constructor
11     } // end FullStackException constructor
12
13     // one-parameter constructor
14     public FullStackException( string exception ) : base( exception )
15     {
16        // empty constructor
17     } // end FullStackException constructor
18
19     // two-parameter constructor
20     public FullStackException( string exception, Exception inner )
21        : base( exception, inner )
22     {
23        // empty constructor
24     } // end FullStackException constructor
25  } // end class FullStackException
```

Fig. 22.6 | `FullStackException` indicates a stack is full.

```
1   // Fig. 22.7: EmptyStackException.cs
2   // EmptyStackException indicates a stack is empty.
3   using System;
4
5   class EmptyStackException : Exception
6   {
7      // parameterless constructor
8      public EmptyStackException() : base( "Stack is empty" )
9      {
10        // empty constructor
11     } // end EmptyStackException constructor
12
13     // one-parameter constructor
14     public EmptyStackException( string exception ) : base( exception )
15     {
16        // empty constructor
17     } // end EmptyStackException constructor
18
```

Fig. 22.7 | `EmptyStackException` indicates a stack is empty. (Part 1 of 2.)

```
19      // two-parameter constructor
20      public EmptyStackException( string exception, Exception inner )
21         : base( exception, inner )
22      {
23         // empty constructor
24      } // end EmptyStackException constructor
25  } // end class EmptyStackException
```

Fig. 22.7 | `EmptyStackException` indicates a stack is empty. (Part 2 of 2.)

As with generic methods, when a generic class is compiled, the compiler performs type checking on the class's type parameters to ensure that they can be used with the code in the generic class. The constraints determine the operations that can be performed on the type parameters. The runtime system replaces the type parameters with the actual types at runtime. For class `Stack` (Fig. 22.5), no type constraint is specified, so the default type constraint, `object`, is used. The scope of a generic class's type parameter is the entire class.

Now, let's consider an application (Fig. 22.8) that uses the `Stack` generic class. Lines 13–14 declare variables of type `Stack<double>` (pronounced "`Stack` of `double`") and `Stack<int>` (pronounced "`Stack` of `int`"). The types `double` and `int` are the `Stack`'s type arguments. The compiler replaces the type parameters in the generic class so that the compiler can perform type checking. Method `Main` instantiates objects `doubleStack` of size 5 (line 18) and `intStack` of size 10 (line 19), then calls methods `TestPushDouble` (lines 28–48), `TestPopDouble` (lines 51–73), `TestPushInt` (lines 76–96) and `TestPopInt` (lines 99–121) to manipulate the two `Stack`s in this example.

```
 1  // Fig. 22.8: StackTest.cs
 2  // Testing generic class Stack.
 3  using System;
 4
 5  class StackTest
 6  {
 7     // create arrays of doubles and ints
 8     private static double[] doubleElements =
 9        new double[]{ 1.1, 2.2, 3.3, 4.4, 5.5, 6.6 };
10     private static int[] intElements =
11        new int[]{ 1, 2, 3, 4, 5, 6, 7, 8, 9, 10, 11 };
12
13     private static Stack< double > doubleStack; // stack stores doubles
14     private static Stack< int > intStack; // stack stores int objects
15
16     public static void Main( string[] args )
17     {
18        doubleStack = new Stack< double >( 5 ); // stack of doubles
19        intStack = new Stack< int >( 10 ); // stack of ints
20
21        TestPushDouble(); // push doubles onto doubleStack
22        TestPopDouble(); // pop doubles from doubleStack
23        TestPushInt(); // push ints onto intStack
24        TestPopInt(); // pop ints from intStack
25     } // end Main
```

Fig. 22.8 | Testing generic class `Stack`. (Part 1 of 4.)

```
26
27      // test Push method with doubleStack
28      private static void TestPushDouble()
29      {
30         // push elements onto stack
31         try
32         {
33            Console.WriteLine( "\nPushing elements onto doubleStack" );
34
35            // push elements onto stack
36            foreach ( var element in doubleElements )
37            {
38               Console.Write( "{0:F1} ", element );
39               doubleStack.Push( element ); // push onto doubleStack
40            } // end foreach
41         } // end try
42         catch ( FullStackException exception )
43         {
44            Console.Error.WriteLine();
45            Console.Error.WriteLine( "Message: " + exception.Message );
46            Console.Error.WriteLine( exception.StackTrace );
47         } // end catch
48      } // end method TestPushDouble
49
50      // test Pop method with doubleStack
51      private static void TestPopDouble()
52      {
53         // pop elements from stack
54         try
55         {
56            Console.WriteLine( "\nPopping elements from doubleStack" );
57
58            double popValue; // store element removed from stack
59
60            // remove all elements from stack
61            while ( true )
62            {
63               popValue = doubleStack.Pop(); // pop from doubleStack
64               Console.Write( "{0:F1} ", popValue );
65            } // end while
66         } // end try
67         catch ( EmptyStackException exception )
68         {
69            Console.Error.WriteLine();
70            Console.Error.WriteLine( "Message: " + exception.Message );
71            Console.Error.WriteLine( exception.StackTrace );
72         } // end catch
73      } // end method TestPopDouble
74
75      // test Push method with intStack
76      private static void TestPushInt()
77      {
```

Fig. 22.8 | Testing generic class Stack. (Part 2 of 4.)

```
78          // push elements onto stack
79          try
80          {
81             Console.WriteLine( "\nPushing elements onto intStack" );
82
83             // push elements onto stack
84             foreach ( var element in intElements )
85             {
86                Console.Write( "{0} ", element );
87                intStack.Push( element ); // push onto intStack
88             } // end foreach
89          } // end try
90          catch ( FullStackException exception )
91          {
92             Console.Error.WriteLine();
93             Console.Error.WriteLine( "Message: " + exception.Message );
94             Console.Error.WriteLine( exception.StackTrace );
95          } // end catch
96       } // end method TestPushInt
97
98       // test Pop method with intStack
99       private static void TestPopInt()
100      {
101         // pop elements from stack
102         try
103         {
104            Console.WriteLine( "\nPopping elements from intStack" );
105
106            int popValue; // store element removed from stack
107
108            // remove all elements from stack
109            while ( true )
110            {
111               popValue = intStack.Pop(); // pop from intStack
112               Console.Write( "{0} ", popValue );
113            } // end while
114         } // end try
115         catch ( EmptyStackException exception )
116         {
117            Console.Error.WriteLine();
118            Console.Error.WriteLine( "Message: " + exception.Message );
119            Console.Error.WriteLine( exception.StackTrace );
120         } // end catch
121      } // end method TestPopInt
122   } // end class StackTest
```

```
Pushing elements onto doubleStack
1.1 2.2 3.3 4.4 5.5 6.6
Message: Stack is full, cannot push 6.6
   at Stack`1.Push(T pushValue) in
      C:\Examples\ch22\Fig22_05_08\Stack\Stack\Stack.cs:line 36
   at StackTest.TestPushDouble() in
      C:\Examples\ch22\Fig22_05_08\Stack\Stack\StackTest.cs:line 39
```

Fig. 22.8 | Testing generic class Stack. (Part 3 of 4.)

```
Popping elements from doubleStack
5.5 4.4 3.3 2.2 1.1

Message: Stack is empty, cannot pop
   at Stack`1.Pop() in
      C:\Examples\ch22\Fig22_05_08\Stack\Stack\Stack.cs:line 47
   at StackTest.TestPopDouble() in
      C:\Examples\ch22\Fig22_05_08\Stack\Stack\StackTest.cs:line 63

Pushing elements onto intStack
1 2 3 4 5 6 7 8 9 10 11
Message: Stack is full, cannot push 11
   at Stack`1.Push(T pushValue) in
      C:\Examples\ch22\Fig22_05_08\Stack\Stack\Stack.cs:line 36
   at StackTest.TestPushInt() in
      C:\Examples\ch22\Fig22_05_08\Stack\Stack\StackTest.cs:line 87

Popping elements from intStack
10 9 8 7 6 5 4 3 2 1
Message: Stack is empty, cannot pop
   at Stack`1.Pop() in
      C:\Examples\ch22\Fig22_05_08\Stack\Stack\Stack.cs:line 47
   at StackTest.TestPopInt() in
      C:\Examples\ch22\Fig22_05_08\Stack\Stack\StackTest.cs:line 111
```

Fig. 22.8 | Testing generic class Stack. (Part 4 of 4.)

Method TestPushDouble (lines 28–48) invokes method Push to place the double values 1.1, 2.2, 3.3, 4.4 and 5.5 stored in array doubleElements onto doubleStack. The foreach statement terminates when the test program attempts to Push a sixth value onto doubleStack (which is full, because doubleStack can store only five elements). In this case, the method throws a FullStackException (Fig. 22.6) to indicate that the Stack is full. Lines 42–47 catch this exception and display the message and stack-trace information. The stack trace indicates the exception that occurred and shows that Stack method Push generated the exception at line 36 of the file Stack.cs (Fig. 22.5). The trace also shows that method Push was called by StackTest method TestPushDouble at line 39 of StackTest.cs. This information enables you to determine the methods that were on the method-call stack at the time that the exception occurred. Because the program catches the exception, the C# runtime environment considers the exception to have been handled, and the program can continue executing.

Method TestPopDouble (lines 51–73) invokes Stack method Pop in an infinite while loop to remove all the values from the stack. Note in the output that the values are popped off in last-in, first-out order—this, of course, is the defining characteristic of stacks. The while loop (lines 61–65) continues until the stack is empty. An EmptyStackException occurs when an attempt is made to pop from the empty stack. This causes the program to proceed to the catch block (lines 67–72) and handle the exception, so the program can continue executing. When the test program attempts to Pop a sixth value, the doubleStack is empty, so method Pop throws an EmptyStackException.

Method TestPushInt (lines 76–96) invokes Stack method Push to place values onto intStack until it's full. Method TestPopInt (lines 99–121) invokes Stack method Pop to remove values from `intStack` until it's empty. Once again, note that the values pop off in last-in, first-out order.

Creating Generic Methods to Test Class **Stack< T >**

Note that the code in methods `TestPushDouble` and `TestPushInt` is almost identical for pushing values onto a `Stack<double>` or a `Stack<int>`, respectively. Similarly the code in methods `TestPopDouble` and `TestPopInt` is almost identical for popping values from a `Stack<double>` or a `Stack<int>`, respectively. This presents another opportunity to use generic methods. Figure 22.9 declares generic method `TestPush` (lines 33–54) to perform the same tasks as `TestPushDouble` and `TestPushInt` in Fig. 22.8—that is, `Push` values onto a `Stack<T>`. Similarly, generic method `TestPop` (lines 57–79) performs the same tasks as `TestPopDouble` and `TestPopInt` in Fig. 22.8—that is, `Pop` values off a `Stack<T>`. Note that the output of Fig. 22.9 precisely matches the output of Fig. 22.8.

```csharp
1   // Fig. 22.9: StackTest.cs
2   // Testing generic class Stack.
3   using System;
4   using System.Collections.Generic;
5
6   class StackTest
7   {
8      // create arrays of doubles and ints
9      private static double[] doubleElements =
10        new double[] { 1.1, 2.2, 3.3, 4.4, 5.5, 6.6 };
11     private static int[] intElements =
12        new int[] { 1, 2, 3, 4, 5, 6, 7, 8, 9, 10, 11 };
13
14     private static Stack< double > doubleStack; // stack stores doubles
15     private static Stack< int > intStack; // stack stores int objects
16
17     public static void Main( string[] args )
18     {
19        doubleStack = new Stack< double >( 5 ); // stack of doubles
20        intStack = new Stack< int >( 10 ); // stack of ints
21
22        // push doubles onto doubleStack
23        TestPush( "doubleStack", doubleStack, doubleElements );
24        // pop doubles from doubleStack
25        TestPop( "doubleStack", doubleStack );
26        // push ints onto intStack
27        TestPush( "intStack", intStack, intElements );
28        // pop ints from intStack
29        TestPop( "intStack", intStack );
30     } // end Main
31
32     // test Push method
33     private static void TestPush< T >( string name, Stack< T > stack,
34        IEnumerable< T > elements )
35     {
```

Fig. 22.9 | Testing generic class `Stack`. (Part 1 of 3.)

```
36                // push elements onto stack
37                try
38                {
39                   Console.WriteLine( "\nPushing elements onto " + name );
40
41                   // push elements onto stack
42                   foreach ( var element in elements )
43                   {
44                      Console.Write( "{0} ", element );
45                      stack.Push( element ); // push onto stack
46                   } // end foreach
47                } // end try
48                catch ( FullStackException exception )
49                {
50                   Console.Error.WriteLine();
51                   Console.Error.WriteLine( "Message: " + exception.Message );
52                   Console.Error.WriteLine( exception.StackTrace );
53                } // end catch
54             } // end method TestPush
55
56             // test Pop method
57             private static void TestPop< T >( string name, Stack< T > stack )
58             {
59                // push elements onto stack
60                try
61                {
62                   Console.WriteLine( "\nPopping elements from " + name );
63
64                   T popValue; // store element removed from stack
65
66                   // remove all elements from stack
67                   while ( true )
68                   {
69                      popValue = stack.Pop(); // pop from stack
70                      Console.Write( "{0} ", popValue );
71                   } // end while
72                } // end try
73                catch ( EmptyStackException exception )
74                {
75                   Console.Error.WriteLine();
76                   Console.Error.WriteLine( "Message: " + exception.Message );
77                   Console.Error.WriteLine( exception.StackTrace );
78                } // end catch
79             } // end TestPop
80          } // end class StackTest
```

```
Pushing elements onto doubleStack
1.1 2.2 3.3 4.4 5.5 6.6
Message: Stack is full, cannot push 6.6
   at Stack`1.Push(T pushValue) in
      C:\Examples\ch22\Fig22_09\Stack\Stack\Stack.cs:line 36
   at StackTest.TestPush[T](String name, Stack`1 stack, IEnumerable`1
      elements) in C:\Examples\ch22\Fig22_09\Stack\Stack\StackTest.cs:line 45
```

Fig. 22.9 | Testing generic class Stack. (Part 2 of 3.)

```
Popping elements from doubleStack
5.5 4.4 3.3 2.2 1.1

Message: Stack is empty, cannot pop
   at Stack`1.Pop() in
      C:\Examples\ch22\Fig22_09\Stack\Stack\Stack.cs:line 47
   at StackTest.TestPop[T](String name, Stack`1 stack) in
      C:\Examples\ch22\Fig22_09\Stack\Stack\StackTest.cs:line 69

Pushing elements onto intStack
1 2 3 4 5 6 7 8 9 10 11
Message: Stack is full, cannot push 11
   at Stack`1.Push(T pushValue) in
      C:\Examples\ch22\Fig22_09\Stack\Stack\Stack.cs:line 36
   at StackTest.TestPush[T](String name, Stack`1 stack, IEnumerable`1
      elements) in C:\Examples\ch22\Fig22_09\Stack\Stack\StackTest.cs:line 45

Popping elements from intStack
10 9 8 7 6 5 4 3 2 1
Message: Stack is empty, cannot pop
   at Stack`1.Pop() in
      C:\Examples\ch22\Fig22_09\Stack\Stack\Stack.cs:line 47
   at StackTest.TestPop[T](String name, Stack`1 stack) in
      C:\Examples\ch22\Fig22_09\Stack\Stack\StackTest.cs:line 69
```

Fig. 22.9 | Testing generic class Stack. (Part 3 of 3.)

Method Main (lines 17–30) creates the Stack<double> (line 19) and Stack<int> (line 20) objects. Lines 23–29 invoke generic methods TestPush and TestPop to test the Stack objects.

Generic method TestPush (lines 33–54) uses type parameter T (specified at line 33) to represent the data type stored in the Stack. The generic method takes three arguments—a string that represents the name of the Stack object for output purposes, an object of type Stack<T> and an IEnumerable<T> that contains the elements that will be Pushed onto Stack<T>. Note that the compiler enforces consistency between the type of the Stack and the elements that will be pushed onto the Stack when Push is invoked, which is the type argument of the generic method call. Generic method TestPop (lines 57–79) takes two arguments—a string that represents the name of the Stack object for output purposes and an object of type Stack<T>.

22.7 Wrap-Up

This chapter introduced generics. We discussed how generics ensure compile-time type safety by checking for type mismatches at compile time. You learned that the compiler will allow generic code to compile only if all operations performed on the type parameters in the generic code are supported for all types that could be used with the generic code. You also learned how to declare generic methods and classes using type parameters. We demonstrated how to use a type constraint to specify the requirements for a type parameter—a key component of compile-time type safety. We discussed several kinds of type constraints, including reference-type constraints, value-type constraints, class constraints, interface constraints and constructor constraints. We also discussed how to implement multiple type constraints for a type parameter. Finally, we showed how generics improve code reuse. In the next chapter, we demonstrate the .NET Framework Class Library's collection classes, interfaces and algorithms. Collection classes are pre-built data structures that you can reuse in your applications, saving you time.

Summary

Section 22.1 Introduction

- Generic methods enable you to specify, with a single method declaration, a set of related methods.
- Generic classes enable you to specify, with a single class declaration, a set of related classes.
- Generic interfaces enable you to specify, with a single interface declaration, a set of related interfaces.
- Generics provide compile-time type safety.

Section 22.2 Motivation for Generic Methods

- Overloaded methods are often used to perform similar operations on different types of data.
- When the compiler encounters a method call, it attempts to locate a method declaration that has the same method name and parameters that match the argument types in the method call.

Section 22.3 Generic-Method Implementation

- If the operations performed by several overloaded methods are identical for each argument type, the overloaded methods can be more compactly and conveniently coded using a generic method.
- You can write a single generic-method declaration that can be called at different times with arguments of different types. Based on the types of the arguments passed to the generic method, the compiler handles each method call appropriately.
- All generic-method declarations have a type-parameter list delimited by angle brackets that follows the method's name. Each type-parameter list contains one or more type parameters, separated by commas.
- A type parameter is used in place of actual type names. The type parameters can be used to declare the return type, parameter types and local variable types in a generic-method declaration; the type parameters act as placeholders for type arguments that represent the types of data that will be passed to the generic method.
- A generic method's body is declared like that of any other method. The type-parameter names throughout the method declaration must match those declared in the type-parameter list.
- A type parameter can be declared only once in the type-parameter list but can appear more than once in the method's parameter list. Type-parameter names need not be unique among different generic methods.
- When the compiler encounters a method call, it analyzes the set of methods (both nongeneric and generic) that might match the method call, looking for a method that best matches the call. If there are no matching methods, or if there's more than one best match, the compiler generates an error.
- You can use explicit type arguments to indicate the exact type that should be used to call a generic function. For example, the method call DisplayArray<int>(intArray); explicitly provides the type argument (int) that should be used to replace type parameter T in the DisplayArray method's declaration.
- For each variable declared with a type parameter, the compiler also determines whether the operations performed on such a variable are allowed for all types that the type parameter can assume.

Section 22.4 Type Constraints

- Generic code is restricted to performing operations that are guaranteed to work for every possible type. Thus, an expression like `variable1 < variable2` is not allowed unless the compiler can ensure that the operator `<` is provided for every type that will ever be used in the generic code. Similarly, you cannot call a method on a generic-type variable unless the compiler can ensure that all types that will ever be used in the generic code support that method.

- It's possible to compare two objects of the same type if that type implements the generic interface `IComparable<T>` (of namespace `System`), which declares method `CompareTo`.

- `IComparable<T>` objects can be used with the sorting and searching methods of classes in the `System.Collections.Generic` namespace.

- Simple types all implement interface `IComparable<T>`.

- It's the responsibility of the programmer who declares a type that implements `IComparable<T>` to declare method `CompareTo` such that it compares the contents of two objects of that type and returns the appropriate result.

- You can restrict the types that can be used with a generic method or class to ensure that they meet certain requirements. This feature—known as a type constraint—restricts the type of the argument supplied to a particular type parameter. For example, the clause `where T : IComparable<T>` indicates that the type arguments must implement interface `IComparable<T>`. If no type constraint is specified, the default type constraint is `object`.

- A class constraint indicates that the type argument must be an object of a specific base class or one of its subclasses.

- An interface constraint indicates that the type argument's class must implement a specific interface.

- You can specify that the type argument must be a reference type or a value type by using the reference-type constraint (`class`) or the value-type constraint (`struct`), respectively.

- You can specify a constructor constraint—`new()`—to indicate that the generic code can use operator `new` to create new objects of the type represented by the type parameter. If a type parameter is specified with a constructor constraint, the type argument's class must provide `public` a parameterless or default constructor to ensure that objects of the class can be created without passing constructor arguments; otherwise, a compilation error occurs.

- It's possible to apply multiple constraints to a type parameter by providing a comma-separated list of constraints in the `where` clause.

- If you have a class constraint, reference-type constraint or value-type constraint, it must be listed first—only one of these types of constraints can be used for each type parameter. Interface constraints (if any) are listed next. The constructor constraint is listed last (if there is one).

Section 22.5 Overloading Generic Methods

- A generic method may be overloaded. All methods must contain a unique signature.

- A generic method can be overloaded by nongeneric methods with the same method name. When the compiler encounters a method call, it searches for the method declaration that most precisely matches the method name and the argument types specified in the call.

Section 22.6 Generic Classes

- A generic class provides a means for describing a class in a type-independent manner.

- Once you have a generic class, you can use a simple, concise notation to indicate the actual type(s) that should be used in place of the class's type parameter(s). At compilation time, the compiler ensures the type safety of your code, and the runtime system replaces type parameters with actual arguments to enable your client code to interact with the generic class.

- A generic class declaration is similar to a nongeneric class declaration, except that the class name is followed by a type-parameter list and optional constraints on its type parameter.
- As with generic methods, the type-parameter list of a generic class can have one or more type parameters separated by commas.
- When a generic class is compiled, the compiler performs type checking on the class's type parameters to ensure that they can be used with the code in the generic class. The constraints determine the operations that can be performed on the variables declared with type parameters.

Terminology

class constraint
CompareTo method of interface IComparable<T>
compile-time type safety
constructor constraint (new())
default type constraint (object) of a type parameter
explicit type argument
generic class
generic interface
generic method
generics
IComparable<T> interface
interface constraint

multiple constraints
new() (constructor) constraint
overloading generic methods
reference-type constraint (class)
scope of a type parameter
type argument
type checking
type constraint
type inference
type parameter
type-parameter list
value type constraint (struct)
where clause

Self-Review Exercises

22.1 State whether each of the following is *true* or *false*. If *false*, explain why.
  a) A generic method cannot have the same method name as a nongeneric method.
  b) All generic method declarations have a type-parameter list that immediately precedes the method name.
  c) A generic method can be overloaded by another generic method with the same method name but a different number of type parameters.
  d) A type parameter can be declared only once in the type-parameter list but can appear more than once in the method's parameter list.
  e) Type-parameter names among different generic methods must be unique.
  f) The scope of a generic class's type parameter is the entire class.
  g) A type parameter can have at most one interface constraint, but multiple class constraints.

22.2 Fill in the blanks in each of the following:
  a) _____ enable you to specify, with a single method declaration, a set of related methods; _____ enable you to specify, with a single class declaration, a set of related classes.
  b) A type-parameter list is delimited by _____.
  c) The _____ of a generic method can be used to specify the types of the arguments to the method, to specify the return type of the method and to declare variables within the method.
  d) The statement "Stack<int> objectStack = new Stack<int>();" indicates that object-Stack stores _____.
  e) In a generic class declaration, the class name is followed by a(n) _____.
  f) The _____ constraint requires that the type argument must have a public parameterless constructor.

Answers to Self-Review Exercises

22.1   a) False. A generic method can be overloaded by nongeneric methods with the same or a different number of arguments. b) False. All generic method declarations have a type-parameter list that immediately follows the method's name. c) True. d) True. e) False. Type-parameter names among different generic methods need not be unique. f) True. g) False. A type parameter can have at most one class constraint, but multiple interface constraints.

22.2   a) Generic methods, generic classes. b) angle brackets. c) type parameters. d) `int`s. e) type-parameter list. f) `new`.

Exercises

22.3   *(Generic Notation)* Explain the use of the following notation in a C# program:

```
public class Array<T>
```

22.4   *(Overloading Generic Methods)* How can generic methods be overloaded?

22.5   *(Determining which Method to Call)* The compiler performs a matching process to determine which method to call when a method is invoked. Under what circumstances does an attempt to make a match result in a compile-time error?

22.6   *(What Does this Statement Do?)* Explain why a C# program might use the statement

```
Array< Employee > workerlist = new Array< Employee >();
```

22.7   *(Generic Linear Search Method)* Write a generic method, `Search`, that implements the linear-search algorithm. Method `Search` should compare the search key with each element in the array until the search key is found or until the end of the array is reached. If the search key is found, return its location in the array; otherwise, return `-1`. Write a test application that inputs and searches an `int` array and a `double` array. Provide buttons that the user can click to randomly generate `int` and `double` values. Display the generated values in a `TextBox`, so the user knows what values they can search for [*Hint:* Use (`T : IComparable< T >`) in the `where` clause for method `Search` so that you can use method `CompareTo` to compare the search key to the elements in the array.]

22.8   *(Overloading a Generic Method)* Overload generic method `DisplayArray` of Fig. 22.3 so that it takes two additional `int` arguments: `lowIndex` and `highIndex`. A call to this method displays only the designated portion of the array. Validate `lowIndex` and `highIndex`. If either is out of range, or if `highIndex` is less than or equal to `lowIndex`, the overloaded `DisplayArray` method should throw an `InvalidIndexException`; otherwise, `DisplayArray` should return the number of elements displayed. Then modify `Main` to exercise both versions of `DisplayArray` on arrays `intArray`, `doubleArray` and `charArray`. Test all capabilities of both versions of `DisplayArray`.

22.9   *(Overloading a Generic Method with a Non-Generic Method)* Overload generic method `DisplayArray` of Fig. 22.3 with a nongeneric version that displays an array of strings in neat, tabular format, as shown in the sample output that follows:

```
Array stringArray contains:
one     two     three   four
five    six     seven   eight
```

22.10   *(Generic Method `IsEqualTo`)* Write a simple generic version of method `IsEqualTo` that compares its two arguments with the `Equals` method, and returns `true` if they're equal and `false` otherwise. Use this generic method in a program that calls `IsEqualTo` with a variety of simple types, such as `object` or `int`. What result do you get when you attempt to run this program?

22.11 *(Generic Class Pair)* Write a generic class Pair which has two type parameters, F and S, representing the type of the first and second element of the pair, respectively. Add properties for the first and second elements of the pair. [*Hint:* The class header should be public class Pair<F, S>.]

22.12 *(Generic Classes TreeNode and Tree)* Convert classes TreeNode and Tree from Fig. 21.20 into generic classes. To insert an object in a Tree, the object must be compared to the objects in existing TreeNodes. For this reason, classes TreeNode and Tree should specify IComparable<T> as the interface constraint of each class's type parameter. After modifying classes TreeNode and Tree, write a test application that creates three Tree objects—one that stores ints, one that stores doubles and one that stores strings. Insert 10 values into each tree. Then output the preorder, inorder and postorder traversals for each Tree.

22.13 *(Generic Method TestTree)* Modify your test program from Exercise 22.12 to use generic method TestTree to test the three Tree objects. The method should be called three times—once for each Tree object.

23

Collections

The shapes a bright container can contain!
—Theodore Roethke

I think this is the most extraordinary collection of talent, of human knowledge, that has ever been gathered together at the White House— with the possible exception of when Thomas Jefferson dined alone.
—John F. Kennedy

Objectives

In this chapter you'll learn:

- The nongeneric and generic collections that are provided by the .NET Framework.

- To use class **Array**'s **static** methods to manipulate arrays.

- To use enumerators to "walk through" a collection.

- To use the **foreach** statement with the .NET collections.

- To use nongeneric collection classes **ArrayList**, **Stack**, and **Hashtable**.

- To use generic collection classes **SortedDictionary** and **LinkedList**.

23.1 Introduction

Chapter 21 discussed how to create and manipulate data structures. The discussion was "low level," in the sense that we painstakingly created each element of each data structure dynamically with new and modified the data structures by directly manipulating their elements and references to their elements. For the vast majority of applications, there's no need to build custom data structures. Instead, you can use the prepackaged data-structure classes provided by the .NET Framework. These classes are known as **collection classes**—they store collections of data. Each instance of one of these classes is a **collection** of items. Some examples of collections are the cards you hold in a card game, the songs stored in your computer, the real-estate records in your local registry of deeds (which map book numbers and page numbers to property owners), and the players on your favorite sports team.

Collection classes enable programmers to store sets of items by using existing data structures, without concern for how they're implemented. This is a nice example of code reuse. Programmers can code faster and expect excellent performance, maximizing execution speed and minimizing memory consumption. In this chapter, we discuss the collection interfaces that list the capabilities of each collection type, the implementation classes and the **enumerators** that "walk through" collections.

The .NET Framework provides three namespaces dedicated to collections. Namespace **System.Collections** contains collections that store references to objects. We included these because there's a large amount of legacy code in industry that uses these collections. Most new applications should use the collections in the **System.Collections.Generic** namespace, which contains generic classes—such as the List<T> and Dictionary<K, V> classes you learned previously—to store collections of specific types. The **System.Collections.Specialized** namespace contains several collections that support specific types, such as strings and bits. You can learn more about this namespace at msdn.microsoft.com/en-us/library/system.collections.specialized.aspx. The collections in these namespaces provide standardized, reusable components; you do not need to write your own collection classes. These collections are written for broad reuse. They're tuned for rapid execution and for efficient use of memory. As new data structures and algorithms are developed that fit this framework, a large base of programmers already will be familiar with the interfaces and algorithms implemented by those data structures.

23.2 Collections Overview

All collection classes in the .NET Framework implement some combination of the collection interfaces. These interfaces declare the operations to be performed generically on various types of collections. Figure 23.1 lists some of the interfaces of the .NET Framework collections. All the interfaces in Fig. 23.1 are declared in namespace `System.Collections` and have generic analogs in namespace `System.Collections.Generic`. Implementations of these interfaces are provided within the framework. Programmers may also provide implementations specific to their own requirements.

Interface	Description
ICollection	The interface from which interfaces IList and IDictionary inherit. Contains a Count property to determine the size of a collection and a CopyTo method for copying a collection's contents into a traditional array.
IList	An ordered collection that can be manipulated like an array. Provides an indexer for accessing elements with an int index. Also has methods for searching and modifying a collection, including Add, Remove, Contains and IndexOf.
IDictionary	A collection of values, indexed by an arbitrary "key" object. Provides an indexer for accessing elements with an object index and methods for modifying the collection (e.g., Add, Remove). IDictionary property Keys contains the objects used as indices, and property Values contains all the stored objects.
IEnumerable	An object that can be enumerated. This interface contains exactly one method, GetEnumerator, which returns an IEnumerator object (discussed in Section 23.3). ICollection extends IEnumerable, so all collection classes implement IEnumerable directly or indirectly.

Fig. 23.1 | Some common collection interfaces.

In earlier versions of C#, the .NET Framework primarily provided the collection classes in the `System.Collections` and `System.Collections.Specialized` namespaces. These classes stored and manipulated `object` references. You could store any `object` in a collection. One inconvenient aspect of storing `object` references occurs when retrieving them from a collection. An application normally needs to process specific types of objects. As a result, the `object` references obtained from a collection typically need to be downcast to an appropriate type to allow the application to process the objects correctly.

The .NET Framework also includes the `System.Collections.Generic` namespace, which uses the generics capabilities we introduced in Chapter 22. Many of these classes are simply generic counterparts of the classes in namespace `System.Collections`. This means that you can specify the exact type that will be stored in a collection. You also receive the benefits of compile-time type checking—the compiler ensures that you're using appropriate types with your collection and, if not, issues compile-time error messages. Also, once you specify the type stored in a collection, any item you retrieve from the collection will have the correct type. This eliminates the need for explicit type casts that can throw `InvalidCastExceptions` at execution time if the referenced object is not of the appropriate type. This also eliminates the overhead of explicit casting, improving efficiency and type safety. Generic collections are especially useful for storing `structs`, since they eliminate the overhead of boxing and unboxing.

This chapter demonstrates collection classes **Array**, **ArrayList**, **Stack**, **Hashtable**, generic **SortedDictionary**, and generic **LinkedList**—plus built-in array capabilities. Namespace `System.Collections` provides several other data structures, including **BitArray** (a collection of true/false values), **Queue** and **SortedList** (a collection of key/value pairs that are sorted by key and can be accessed either by key or by index). Figure 23.2 summarizes many of the collection classes. We also discuss the IEnumerator interface. Collection classes can create enumerators that allow programmers to walk through the collections. Although these enumerators have different implementations, they all implement the IEnumerator interface so that they can be processed polymorphically. As we'll soon see, the foreach statement is simply a convenient notation for using an enumerator. In the next section, we begin our discussion by examining enumerators and the capabilities for array manipulation. [*Note:* Collection classes directly or indirectly implement ICollection and IEnumerable (or their generic equivalents ICollection<T> and IEnumerable<T> for generic collections).]

Class	Implements	Description
System namespace:		
Array	IList	The base class of all conventional arrays. See Section 23.3.
System.Collections namespace:		
ArrayList	IList	Mimics conventional arrays, but will grow or shrink as needed to accommodate the number of elements. See Section 23.4.1.
BitArray	ICollection	A memory-efficient array of bools.
Hashtable	IDictionary	An unordered collection of key/value pairs that can be accessed by key. See Section 23.4.3.
Queue	ICollection	A first-in, first-out collection. See Section 21.6.
SortedList	IDictionary	A collection of key/value pairs that are sorted by key and can be accessed either by key or by index.
Stack	ICollection	A last-in, first-out collection. See Section 23.4.2.
System.Collections.Generic namespace:		
Dictionary< K, V >	IDictionary< K, V >	A generic, unordered collection of key/value pairs that can be accessed by key. See Section 17.4.
LinkedList< T >	ICollection< T >	A doubly linked list. See Section 23.5.2.
List< T >	IList< T >	A generic ArrayList. Section 9.4.
Queue< T >	ICollection< T >	A generic Queue.
SortedDictionary< K, V >	IDictionary< K, V >	A Dictionary that sorts the data by the keys in a binary tree. See Section 23.5.1.
SortedList< K, V >	IDictionary< K, V >	A generic SortedList.
Stack< T >	ICollection< T >	A generic Stack. See .

Fig. 23.2 | Some collection classes of the .NET Framework.

23.3 Class Array and Enumerators

Chapter 8 presented basic array-processing capabilities. All arrays implicitly inherit from abstract base class Array (namespace System); this class defines property Length, which specifies the number of elements in the array. In addition, class Array provides static methods that provide algorithms for processing arrays. Typically, class Array overloads these methods—for example, Array method Reverse can reverse the order of the elements in an entire array or can reverse the elements in a specified range of elements in an array. For a complete list of class Array's static methods visit:

msdn.microsoft.com/en-us/library/system.array.aspx

Figure 23.3 demonstrates several static methods of class Array.

```
1   // Fig. 23.3: UsingArray.cs
2   // Array class static methods for common array manipulations.
3   using System;
4   using System.Collections;
5
6   // demonstrate algorithms of class Array
7   public class UsingArray
8   {
9      private static int[] intValues = { 1, 2, 3, 4, 5, 6 };
10     private static double[] doubleValues = { 8.4, 9.3, 0.2, 7.9, 3.4 };
11     private static int[] intValuesCopy;
12
13     // method Main demonstrates class Array's methods
14     public static void Main( string[] args )
15     {
16        intValuesCopy = new int[ intValues.Length ]; // defaults to zeroes
17
18        Console.WriteLine( "Initial array values:\n" );
19        PrintArrays(); // output initial array contents
20
21        // sort doubleValues
22        Array.Sort( doubleValues );
23
24        // copy intValues into intValuesCopy
25        Array.Copy( intValues, intValuesCopy, intValues.Length );
26
27        Console.WriteLine( "\nArray values after Sort and Copy:\n" );
28        PrintArrays(); // output array contents
29        Console.WriteLine();
30
31        // search for 5 in intValues
32        int result = Array.BinarySearch( intValues, 5 );
33        if ( result >= 0 )
34           Console.WriteLine( "5 found at element {0} in intValues",
35              result );
36        else
37           Console.WriteLine( "5 not found in intValues" );
38
```

Fig. 23.3 | Array class used to perform common array manipulations. (Part I of 2.)

```
39          // search for 8763 in intValues
40          result = Array.BinarySearch( intValues, 8763 );
41          if ( result >= 0 )
42             Console.WriteLine( "8763 found at element {0} in intValues",
43                result );
44          else
45             Console.WriteLine( "8763 not found in intValues" );
46       } // end Main
47
48       // output array content with enumerators
49       private static void PrintArrays()
50       {
51          Console.Write( "doubleValues: " );
52
53          // iterate through the double array with an enumerator
54          IEnumerator enumerator = doubleValues.GetEnumerator();
55
56          while ( enumerator.MoveNext() )
57             Console.Write( enumerator.Current + " " );
58
59          Console.Write( "\nintValues: " );
60
61          // iterate through the int array with an enumerator
62          enumerator = intValues.GetEnumerator();
63
64          while ( enumerator.MoveNext() )
65             Console.Write( enumerator.Current + " " );
66
67          Console.Write( "\nintValuesCopy: " );
68
69          // iterate through the second int array with a foreach statement
70          foreach ( var element in intValuesCopy )
71             Console.Write( element + " " );
72
73          Console.WriteLine();
74       } // end method PrintArrays
75    } // end class UsingArray
```

```
Initial array values:

doubleValues: 8.4 9.3 0.2 7.9 3.4
intValues: 1 2 3 4 5 6
intValuesCopy: 0 0 0 0 0 0

Array values after Sort and Copy:

doubleValues: 0.2 3.4 7.9 8.4 9.3
intValues: 1 2 3 4 5 6
intValuesCopy: 1 2 3 4 5 6

5 found at element 4 in intValues
8763 not found in intValues
```

Fig. 23.3 | Array class used to perform common array manipulations. (Part 2 of 2.)

The using directives in lines 3–4 include the namespaces System (for classes Array and Console) and System.Collections (for interface IEnumerator, which we discuss shortly). References to the assemblies for these namespaces are implicitly included in every application, so we do not need to add any new references to the project file.

Our test class declares three static array variables (lines 9–11). The first two lines initialize intValues and doubleValues to an int and double array, respectively. Static variable intValuesCopy is intended to demonstrate the Array's Copy method, so it's left with the default value null—it does not yet refer to an array.

Line 16 initializes intValuesCopy to an int array with the same length as array intValues. Line 19 calls the PrintArrays method (lines 49–74) to output the initial contents of all three arrays. We discuss the PrintArrays method shortly. We can see from the output of Fig. 23.3 that each element of array intValuesCopy is initialized to the default value 0.

Line 22 uses static Array method **Sort** to sort array doubleValues. When this method returns, the array contains its original elements sorted in ascending order. The elements in the array must implement the IComparable interface.

Line 25 uses static Array method **Copy** to copy elements from array intValues to array intValuesCopy. The first argument is the array to copy (intValues), the second argument is the destination array (intValuesCopy) and the third argument is an int representing the number of elements to copy (in this case, intValues.Length specifies all elements).

Lines 32 and 40 invoke static Array method **BinarySearch** to perform binary searches on array intValues. Method BinarySearch receives the *sorted* array in which to search and the key for which to search. The method returns the index in the array at which it finds the key (or a negative number if the key was not found). BinarySearch assumes that it receives a sorted array. Its behavior on an unsorted array is unpredictable. Chapter 20 discussed binary searching in detail.

Method PrintArrays (lines 49–74) uses class Array's methods to loop though each array. The GetEnumerator method (line 54) obtains an enumerator for array doubleValues. Recall that Array implements the **IEnumerable** interface. All arrays inherit implicitly from Array, so both the int[] and double[] array types implement IEnumerable interface method **GetEnumerator**, which returns an enumerator that can iterate over the collection. Interface **IEnumerator** (which all enumerators implement) defines methods **MoveNext** and **Reset** and property **Current**. MoveNext moves the enumerator to the next element in the collection. The first call to MoveNext positions the enumerator at the first element of the collection. MoveNext returns true if there's at least one more element in the collection; otherwise, the method returns false. Method Reset positions the enumerator before the first element of the collection. Methods MoveNext and Reset throw an **InvalidOperationException** if the contents of the collection are modified in any way after the enumerator is created. Property Current returns the object at the current location in the collection.

Common Programming Error 23.1

If a collection is modified after an enumerator is created for that collection, the enumerator immediately becomes invalid—any methods called on the enumerator after this point throw InvalidOperationExceptions. For this reason, enumerators are said to be "fail fast."

When an enumerator is returned by the GetEnumerator method in line 54, it's initially positioned *before* the first element in Array doubleValues. Then when line 56 calls MoveNext in the first iteration of the while loop, the enumerator advances to the first element in doubleValues. The while statement in lines 56–57 loops over each element until the enumerator passes the end of doubleValues and MoveNext returns false. In each iteration, we use the enumerator's Current property to obtain and output the current array element. Lines 62–65 iterate over array intValues.

Notice that PrintArrays is called twice (lines 19 and 28), so GetEnumerator is called twice on doubleValues. The GetEnumerator method (lines 54 and 62) always returns an enumerator positioned before the first element. Also notice that the IEnumerator property Current is read-only. Enumerators cannot be used to modify the contents of collections, only to obtain the contents.

Lines 70–71 use a foreach statement to iterate over the collection elements like an enumerator. In fact, the foreach statement behaves exactly like an enumerator. Both loop over the elements of an array one by one in consecutive order. Neither allows you to modify the elements during the iteration. This is not a coincidence. The foreach statement implicitly obtains an enumerator via the GetEnumerator method and uses the enumerator's MoveNext method and Current property to traverse the collection, just as we did explicitly in lines 54–57. For this reason, we can use the foreach statement to iterate over *any* collection that implements the IEnumerable interface—not just arrays. We demonstrate this functionality in the next section when we discuss class ArrayList.

Other static Array methods include **Clear** (to set a range of elements to 0, false or null, as appropriate), **CreateInstance** (to create a new array of a specified type), **IndexOf** (to locate the first occurrence of an object in an array or portion of an array), **LastIndexOf** (to locate the last occurrence of an object in an array or portion of an array) and **Reverse** (to reverse the contents of an array or portion of an array).

23.4 Nongeneric Collections

The System.Collections namespace in the .NET Framework Class Library is the primary source for nongeneric collections. These classes provide standard implementations of many of the data structures discussed in Chapter 21 with collections that store references of type object. In this section, we demonstrate classes ArrayList, Stack and Hashtable.

23.4.1 Class ArrayList

In most programming languages, conventional arrays have a fixed size—they cannot be changed dynamically to conform to an application's execution-time memory requirements. In some applications, this fixed-size limitation presents a problem for programmers. They must choose between using fixed-size arrays that are large enough to store the maximum number of elements the application may require and using dynamic data structures that can grow and shrink the amount of memory required to store data in response to the changing requirements of an application at execution time.

The .NET Framework's **ArrayList** collection class mimics the functionality of conventional arrays and provides dynamic resizing of the collection through the class's methods. At any time, an ArrayList contains a certain number of elements less than or equal to its **capacity**—the number of elements currently reserved for the ArrayList. An application can manipulate the capacity with ArrayList property Capacity. [*Note:* New applications should use the generic List<T> class introduced in Chapter 9.]

Performance Tip 23.1

As with linked lists, inserting additional elements into an ArrayList whose current size is less than its capacity is a fast operation.

Performance Tip 23.2

It's a slow operation to insert an element into an ArrayList that needs to grow larger to accommodate a new element. An ArrayList that's at its capacity must have its memory reallocated and the existing values copied into it.

Performance Tip 23.3

*If storage is at a premium, use method **TrimToSize** of class ArrayList to trim an Array-List to its exact size. This will optimize an ArrayList's memory use. Be careful—if the application needs to insert additional elements, the process will be slower, because the Ar-rayList must grow dynamically (trimming leaves no room for growth).*

ArrayLists store references to objects. All classes derive from class object, so an ArrayList can contain objects of any type. Figure 23.4 lists some useful methods and properties of class ArrayList.

Method or property	Description
Add	Adds an object to the ArrayList and returns an int specifying the index at which the object was added.
Capacity	Property that gets and sets the number of elements for which space is currently reserved in the ArrayList.
Clear	Removes all the elements from the ArrayList.
Contains	Returns true if the specified object is in the ArrayList; otherwise, returns false.
Count	Read-only property that gets the number of elements stored in the ArrayList.
IndexOf	Returns the index of the first occurrence of the specified object in the ArrayList.
Insert	Inserts an object at the specified index.
Remove	Removes the first occurrence of the specified object.
RemoveAt	Removes an object at the specified index.
RemoveRange	Removes a specified number of elements starting at a specified index in the ArrayList.
Sort	Sorts the ArrayList.
TrimToSize	Sets the Capacity of the ArrayList to the number of elements the ArrayList currently contains (Count).

Fig. 23.4 | Some methods and properties of class ArrayList.

Figure 23.5 demonstrates class ArrayList and several of its methods. Class ArrayList belongs to the System.Collections namespace (line 4). Lines 8–11 declare two arrays of strings (colors and removeColors) that we'll use to fill two ArrayList objects. Recall from Section 10.10 that constants must be initialized at compile time, but readonly variables can be initialized at execution time. Arrays are objects created at execution time, so we declare colors and removeColors with readonly—not const—to make them unmodifiable. When the application begins execution, we create an ArrayList with an initial capacity of one element and store it in variable list (line 16). The foreach statement in lines 19–20 adds the five elements of array colors to list via ArrayList's **Add** method, so list grows to accommodate these new elements. Line 24 uses ArrayList's overloaded constructor to create a new ArrayList initialized with the contents of array removeColors, then assigns it to variable removeList. This constructor can initialize the contents of an ArrayList with the elements of any ICollection passed to it. Many of the collection classes have such a constructor. Notice that the constructor call in line 24 performs the task of lines 19–20.

```
1   // Fig. 23.5: ArrayListTest.cs
2   // Using class ArrayList.
3   using System;
4   using System.Collections;
5
6   public class ArrayListTest
7   {
8      private static readonly string[] colors =
9         { "MAGENTA", "RED", "WHITE", "BLUE", "CYAN" };
10     private static readonly string[] removeColors =
11        { "RED", "WHITE", "BLUE" };
12
13     // create ArrayList, add colors to it and manipulate it
14     public static void Main( string[] args )
15     {
16        ArrayList list = new ArrayList( 1 ); // initial capacity of 1
17
18        // add the elements of the colors array to the ArrayList list
19        foreach ( var color in colors )
20           list.Add( color ); // add color to the ArrayList list
21
22        // add elements in the removeColors array to
23        // the ArrayList removeList with the ArrayList constructor
24        ArrayList removeList = new ArrayList( removeColors );
25
26        Console.WriteLine( "ArrayList: " );
27        DisplayInformation( list ); // output the list
28
29        // remove from ArrayList list the colors in removeList
30        RemoveColors( list, removeList );
31
32        Console.WriteLine( "\nArrayList after calling RemoveColors: " );
33        DisplayInformation( list ); // output list contents
34     } // end Main
35
```

Fig. 23.5 | Using class ArrayList. (Part 1 of 2.)

```
36      // displays information on the contents of an array list
37      private static void DisplayInformation( ArrayList arrayList )
38      {
39         // iterate through array list with a foreach statement
40         foreach ( var element in arrayList )
41            Console.Write( "{0} ", element ); // invokes ToString
42
43         // display the size and capacity
44         Console.WriteLine( "\nSize = {0}; Capacity = {1}",
45            arrayList.Count, arrayList.Capacity );
46
47         int index = arrayList.IndexOf( "BLUE" );
48
49         if ( index != -1 )
50            Console.WriteLine( "The array list contains BLUE at index {0}.",
51               index );
52         else
53            Console.WriteLine( "The array list does not contain BLUE." );
54      } // end method DisplayInformation
55
56      // remove colors specified in secondList from firstList
57      private static void RemoveColors( ArrayList firstList,
58         ArrayList secondList )
59      {
60         // iterate through second ArrayList like an array
61         for ( int count = 0; count < secondList.Count; count++ )
62            firstList.Remove( secondList[ count ] );
63      } // end method RemoveColors
64   } // end class ArrayListTest
```

```
ArrayList:
MAGENTA RED WHITE BLUE CYAN
Size = 5; Capacity = 8
The array list contains BLUE at index 3.

ArrayList after calling RemoveColors:
MAGENTA CYAN
Size = 2; Capacity = 8
The array list does not contain BLUE.
```

Fig. 23.5 | Using class `ArrayList`. (Part 2 of 2.)

Line 27 calls method `DisplayInformation` (lines 37–54) to output the contents of the `list`. This method uses a `foreach` statement to traverse the elements of an `ArrayList`. As we discussed in Section 23.3, the `foreach` statement is a convenient shorthand for calling `ArrayList`'s `GetEnumerator` method and using an enumerator to traverse the elements of the collection. Also, line 40 infers that the iteration variable's type is `object` because class `ArrayList` is nongeneric and stores references to `object`s.

We use properties **Count** and **Capacity** (line 45) to display the current number and the maximum number of elements that can be stored without allocating more memory to the `ArrayList`. The output of Fig. 23.5 indicates that the `ArrayList` has capacity 8.

In line 47, we invoke method **IndexOf** to determine the position of the `string` "BLUE" in `arrayList` and store the result in local variable `index`. `IndexOf` returns -1 if the element is not found. The `if` statement in lines 49–53 checks if `index` is -1 to determine whether `arrayList` contains `"BLUE"`. If it does, we output its index. `ArrayList` also provides method **Contains**, which simply returns `true` if an object is in the `ArrayList`, and `false` otherwise. Method `Contains` is preferred if we do not need the index of the element.

Performance Tip 23.4

ArrayList methods IndexOf and Contains each perform a linear search, which is a costly operation for large ArrayLists. If the ArrayList is sorted, use ArrayList method BinarySearch to perform a more efficient search. Method BinarySearch returns the index of the element, or a negative number if the element is not found.

After method `DisplayInformation` returns, we call method `RemoveColors` (lines 57–63) with the two `ArrayList`s. The `for` statement in lines 61–62 iterates over `ArrayList` `secondList`. Line 62 uses an indexer to access an `ArrayList` element—by following the `ArrayList` reference name with square brackets (`[]`) containing the desired index of the element. An `ArgumentOutOfRangeException` occurs if the specified index is not both greater than 0 and less than the number of elements currently stored in the `ArrayList` (specified by the `ArrayList`'s `Count` property).

We use the indexer to obtain each of `secondList`'s elements, then remove each one from `firstList` with the **Remove** method. This method deletes a specified item from an `ArrayList` by performing a linear search and removing (only) the first occurrence of the specified object. All subsequent elements shift toward the beginning of the `ArrayList` to fill the emptied position.

After the call to `RemoveColors`, line 33 again outputs the contents of `list`, confirming that the elements of `removeList` were, indeed, removed.

23.4.2 Class Stack

The `Stack` class implements a stack data structure and provides much of the functionality that we defined in our own implementation in Section 21.5. Refer to that section for a discussion of stack data-structure concepts. We created a test application in Fig. 21.14 to demonstrate the `StackInheritance` data structure that we developed. We adapt Fig. 21.14 in Fig. 23.6 to demonstrate the .NET Framework collection class `Stack`. [*Note:* New applications requiring a stack class should use the generic `Stack<T>` class.]

```
1    // Fig. 23.6: StackTest.cs
2    // Demonstrating class Stack.
3    using System;
4    using System.Collections;
5
6    public class StackTest
7    {
8       public static void Main( string[] args )
9       {
10          Stack stack = new Stack(); // create an empty Stack
11
12          // create objects to store in the stack
13          bool aBoolean = true;
```

Fig. 23.6 | Demonstrating class `Stack`. (Part 1 of 3.)

```
14              char aCharacter = '$';
15              int anInteger = 34567;
16              string aString = "hello";
17
18              // use method Push to add items to (the top of) the stack
19              stack.Push( aBoolean );
20              PrintStack( stack );
21              stack.Push( aCharacter );
22              PrintStack( stack );
23              stack.Push( anInteger );
24              PrintStack( stack );
25              stack.Push( aString );
26              PrintStack( stack );
27
28              // check the top element of the stack
29              Console.WriteLine( "The top element of the stack is {0}\n",
30                 stack.Peek() );
31
32              // remove items from stack
33              try
34              {
35                 while ( true )
36                 {
37                    object removedObject = stack.Pop();
38                    Console.WriteLine( removedObject + " popped" );
39                    PrintStack( stack );
40                 } // end while
41              } // end try
42              catch ( InvalidOperationException exception )
43              {
44                 // if exception occurs, output stack trace
45                 Console.Error.WriteLine( exception );
46              } // end catch
47           } // end Main
48
49           // display the contents of a stack
50           private static void PrintStack( Stack stack )
51           {
52              if ( stack.Count == 0 )
53                 Console.WriteLine( "stack is empty\n" ); // the stack is empty
54              else
55              {
56                 Console.Write( "The stack is: " );
57
58                 // iterate through the stack with a foreach statement
59                 foreach ( var element in stack )
60                    Console.Write( "{0} ", element ); // invokes ToString
61
62                 Console.WriteLine( "\n" );
63              } // end else
64           } // end method PrintStack
65        } // end class StackTest
```

Fig. 23.6 | Demonstrating class Stack. (Part 2 of 3.)

```
The stack is: True

The stack is: $ True

The stack is: 34567 $ True

The stack is: hello 34567 $ True

The top element of the stack is hello

hello popped
The stack is: 34567 $ True

34567 popped
The stack is: $ True

$ popped
The stack is: True

True popped
stack is empty

System.InvalidOperationException: Stack empty.
   at System.Collections.Stack.Pop()
   at StackTest.Main(String[] args) in C:\examples\ch23\
      fig23_06\StackTest\StackTest.cs:line 37
```

Fig. 23.6 | Demonstrating class Stack. (Part 3 of 3.)

The using directive in line 4 allows us to use the Stack class with its unqualified name from the System.Collections namespace. Line 10 creates a Stack. As one might expect, class Stack has methods **Push** and **Pop** to perform the basic stack operations.

Method Push takes an object as an argument and inserts it at the top of the Stack. If the number of items on the Stack (the Count property) is equal to the capacity at the time of the Push operation, the Stack grows to accommodate more objects. Lines 19–26 use method Push to add four elements (a bool, a char, an int and a string) to the stack and invoke method PrintStack (lines 50–64) after each Push to output the contents of the stack. Notice that this nongeneric Stack class can store only references to objects, so each of the value-type items—the bool, the char and the int—is implicitly boxed before it's added to the Stack. (Namespace System.Collections.Generic provides a generic Stack class that has many of the same methods and properties used in Fig. 23.6. This version eliminates the overhead of boxing and unboxing simple types.)

Method PrintStack (lines 50–64) uses Stack property Count (implemented to fulfill the contract of interface ICollection) to obtain the number of elements in stack. If the stack is not empty (i.e., Count is not equal to 0), we use a foreach statement to iterate over the stack and output its contents by implicitly invoking the ToString method of each element. The foreach statement implicitly invokes Stack's GetEnumerator method, which we could have called explicitly to traverse the stack via an enumerator.

Method **Peek** returns the value of the top stack element but does not remove the element from the Stack. We use Peek at line 30 to obtain the top object of the Stack, then output that object, implicitly invoking the object's ToString method. An InvalidOperationException occurs if the Stack is empty when the application calls Peek. (We do not need an exception-handling block because we know the stack is not empty here.)

Method Pop takes no arguments—it removes and returns the object currently on top of the Stack. An infinite loop (lines 35–40) pops objects off the stack and outputs them until the stack is empty. When the application calls Pop on the empty stack, an Invalid-OperationException is thrown. The catch block (lines 42–46) outputs the exception, implicitly invoking the InvalidOperationException's ToString method to obtain its error message and stack trace.

 Common Programming Error 23.2
Attempting to Peek or Pop an empty Stack (a Stack whose Count property is 0) causes an InvalidOperationException.

Although Fig. 23.6 does not demonstrate it, class Stack also has method **Contains**, which returns true if the Stack contains the specified object, and returns false otherwise.

23.4.3 Class Hashtable

When an application creates objects of new or existing types, it needs to manage those objects efficiently. This includes sorting and retrieving objects. Sorting and retrieving information with arrays is efficient if some aspect of your data directly matches the key value and if those keys are unique and tightly packed. If you have 100 employees with nine-digit social security numbers and you want to store and retrieve employee data by using the social security number as a key, it would nominally require an array with 1,000,000,000 elements, because there are 1,000,000,000 unique nine-digit numbers. If you have an array that large, you could get high performance storing and retrieving employee records by simply using the social security number as the array index, but it would be a large waste of memory.

Many applications have this problem—either the keys are of the wrong type (i.e., not nonnegative integers), or they're of the right type but are sparsely spread over a large range.

What is needed is a high-speed scheme for converting keys such as social security numbers and inventory part numbers to unique array indices. Then, when an application needs to store something, the scheme could convert the application key rapidly to an index and the record of information could be stored at that location in the array. Retrieval occurs the same way—once the application has a key for which it wants to retrieve the data record, the application simply applies the conversion to the key, which produces the array index where the data resides in the array and retrieves the data.

The scheme we describe here is the basis of a technique called **hashing**, in which we store data in a data structure called a **hash table**. Why the name? Because, when we convert a key into an array index, we literally scramble the bits, making a "hash" of the number. The number actually has no real significance beyond its usefulness in storing and retrieving this particular data record.

A glitch in the scheme occurs when there are **collisions** (i.e., two different keys "hash into" the same cell, or element, in the array). Since we cannot sort two different data records to the same space, we need to find an alternative home for all records beyond the first that hash to a particular array index. One scheme for doing this is to "hash again" (i.e., to reapply the hashing transformation to the key to provide a next candidate cell in the array). The hashing process is designed so that with just a few hashes, an available cell will be found.

Another scheme uses one hash to locate the first candidate cell. If the cell is occupied, successive cells are searched linearly until an available cell is found. Retrieval works the same way—the key is hashed once, the resulting cell is checked to determine whether it contains the desired data. If it does, the search is complete. If it does not, successive cells are searched linearly until the desired data is found.

The most popular solution to hash-table collisions is to have each cell of the table be a hash "bucket"—typically, a linked list of all the key/value pairs that hash to that cell. This is the solution that the .NET Framework's **Hashtable** class implements.

The **load factor** affects the performance of hashing schemes. The load factor is the ratio of the number of objects stored in the hash table to the total number of cells of the hash table. As this ratio gets higher, the chance of collisions tends to increase.

Performance Tip 23.5

*The load factor in a hash table is a classic example of a **space/time trade-off**: By increasing the load factor, we get better memory utilization, but the application runs slower due to increased hashing collisions. By decreasing the load factor, we get better application speed because of reduced hashing collisions, but we get poorer memory utilization because a larger portion of the hash table remains empty.*

Computer-science students study hashing schemes in courses called "Data Structures" and "Algorithms." Recognizing the value of hashing, the .NET Framework provides class Hashtable to enable programmers to easily employ hashing in applications.

This concept is profoundly important in our study of object-oriented programming. Classes encapsulate and hide complexity (i.e., implementation details) and offer user-friendly interfaces. Crafting classes to do this properly is one of the most valued skills in the field of object-oriented programming.

A **hash function** performs a calculation that determines where to place data in the hash table. The hash function is applied to the key in a key/value pair of objects. Class Hashtable can accept any object as a key. For this reason, class object defines method **GetHashCode**, which all objects inherit. Most classes that are candidates to be used as keys in a hash table override this method to provide one that performs efficient hash-code calculations for a specific type. For example, a string has a hash-code calculation that's based on the contents of the string. Figure 23.7 uses a Hashtable to count the number of occurrences of each word in a string. [*Note:* New applications should use generic class Dictionary<K, V> (introduced in Section 17.4) rather than Hashtable.]

```
1   // Fig. 23.7: HashtableTest.cs
2   // Application counts the number of occurrences of each word in a string
3   // and stores them in a hash table.
4   using System;
5   using System.Text.RegularExpressions;
6   using System.Collections;
7
8   public class HashtableTest
9   {
```

Fig. 23.7 | Application counts the number of occurrences of each word in a string and stores them in a hash table. (Part 1 of 3.)

```
10      public static void Main( string[] args )
11      {
12         // create hash table based on user input
13         Hashtable table = CollectWords();
14
15         // display hash-table content
16         DisplayHashtable( table );
17      } // end Main
18
19      // create hash table from user input
20      private static Hashtable CollectWords()
21      {
22         Hashtable table = new Hashtable(); // create a new hash table
23
24         Console.WriteLine( "Enter a string: " ); // prompt for user input
25         string input = Console.ReadLine(); // get input
26
27         // split input text into tokens
28         string[] words = Regex.Split( input, @"\s+" );
29
30         // processing input words
31         foreach ( var word in words )
32         {
33            string wordKey = word.ToLower(); // get word in lowercase
34
35            // if the hash table contains the word
36            if ( table.ContainsKey( wordKey ) )
37            {
38               table[ wordKey ] = ( ( int ) table[ wordKey ] ) + 1;
39            } // end if
40            else
41               // add new word with a count of 1 to hash table
42               table.Add( wordKey, 1 );
43         } // end foreach
44
45         return table;
46      } // end method CollectWords
47
48      // display hash-table content
49      private static void DisplayHashtable( Hashtable table )
50      {
51         Console.WriteLine( "\nHashtable contains:\n{0,-12}{1,-12}",
52            "Key:", "Value:" );
53
54         // generate output for each key in hash table
55         // by iterating through the Keys property with a foreach statement
56         foreach ( var key in table.Keys )
57            Console.WriteLine( "{0,-12}{1,-12}", key, table[ key ] );
58
59         Console.WriteLine( "\nsize: {0}", table.Count );
60      } // end method DisplayHashtable
61   } // end class HashtableTest
```

Fig. 23.7 | Application counts the number of occurrences of each word in a `string` and stores them in a hash table. (Part 2 of 3.)

```
Enter a string:
As idle as a painted ship upon a painted ocean

Hashtable contains:
Key:          Value:
ocean         1
a             2
as            2
ship          1
upon          1
painted       2
idle          1

size: 7
```

Fig. 23.7 | Application counts the number of occurrences of each word in a `string` and stores them in a hash table. (Part 3 of 3.)

Lines 4–6 contain using directives for namespaces System (for class Console), System.Text.RegularExpressions (for class Regex) and System.Collections (for class Hashtable). Class HashtableTest declares three static methods. Method CollectWords (lines 20–46) inputs a string and returns a Hashtable in which each value stores the number of times that word appears in the string and the word is used for the key. Method DisplayHashtable (lines 49–60) displays the Hashtable passed to it in column format. The Main method (lines 10–17) simply invokes CollectWords (line 13), then passes the Hashtable returned by CollectWords to DisplayHashtable in line 16.

Method CollectWords (lines 20–46) begins by initializing local variable table with a new Hashtable (line 22) that has a default maximum load factor of 1.0. When the Hashtable reaches the specified load factor, the capacity is increased automatically. (This implementation detail is invisible to clients of the class.) Lines 24–25 prompt the user and input a string. We use static method Split of class Regex in line 28 to divide the string by its whitespace characters. This creates an array of "words," which we then store in local variable words.

Lines 31–43 loop over every element of array words. Each word is converted to lowercase with string method **ToLower**, then stored in variable wordKey (line 33). Then line 36 calls Hashtable method **ContainsKey** to determine whether the word is in the hash table (and thus has occurred previously in the string). If the Hashtable does not contain an entry for the word, line 42 uses Hashtable method **Add** to create a new entry in the hash table, with the lowercase word as the key and an object containing 1 as the value. Autoboxing occurs when the application passes integer 1 to method Add, because the hash table stores both the key and value in references of type object.

Common Programming Error 23.3
Using the Add method to add a key that already exists in the hash table causes an ArgumentException.

If the word is already a key in the hash table, line 38 uses the Hashtable's indexer to obtain and set the key's associated value (the word count) in the hash table. We first downcast the value obtained by the get accessor from an object to an int. This unboxes the value so that we can increment it by 1. Then, when we use the indexer's set accessor to assign the key's associated value, the incremented value is implicitly reboxed so that it can be stored in the hash table.

Notice that invoking the get accessor of a Hashtable indexer with a key that does not exist in the hash table obtains a null reference. Using the set accessor with a key that does not exist in the hash table creates a new entry, as if you had used the Add method.

Line 45 returns the hash table to the Main method, which then passes it to method DisplayHashtable (lines 49–60), which displays all the entries. This method uses read-only property **Keys** (line 56) to get an ICollection that contains all the keys. Because ICollection extends IEnumerable, we can use this collection in the foreach statement in lines 56–57 to iterate over the keys of the hash table. This loop accesses and outputs each key and its value in the hash table using the iteration variable and table's get accessor. Each key and its value is displayed in a field width of -12. The negative field width indicates that the output is left justified. A hash table is not sorted, so the key/value pairs are not displayed in any particular order. Line 59 uses Hashtable property **Count** to get the number of key/value pairs in the Hashtable.

Lines 56–57 could have also used the foreach statement with the Hashtable object itself, instead of using the Keys property. If you use a foreach statement with a Hashtable object, the iteration variable will be of type **DictionaryEntry**. The enumerator of a Hashtable (or any other class that implements **IDictionary**) uses the DictionaryEntry structure to store key/value pairs. This structure provides properties Key and Value for retrieving the key and value of the current element. If you do not need the key, class Hashtable also provides a read-only **Values** property that gets an ICollection of all the values stored in the Hashtable. We can use this property to iterate through the values stored in the Hashtable without regard for where they're stored.

Problems with Nongeneric Collections

In the word-counting application of Fig. 23.7, our Hashtable stores its keys and data as object references, even though we store only string keys and int values by convention. This results in some awkward code. For example, line 38 was forced to unbox and box the int data stored in the Hashtable every time it incremented the count for a particular key. This is inefficient. A similar problem occurs in line 56—the iteration variable of the foreach statement is an object reference. If we need to use any of its string-specific methods, we need an explicit downcast.

This can cause subtle bugs. Suppose we decide to improve the readability of Fig. 23.7 by using the indexer's set accessor instead of the Add method to add a key/value pair in line 42, but accidentally type:

```
table[ wordKey ] = wordKey; // initialize to 1
```

This statement will create a new entry with a string key and string value instead of an int value of 1. Although the application will compile correctly, this is clearly incorrect. If a word appears twice, line 38 will try to downcast this string to an int, causing an InvalidCastException at execution time. The error that appears at execution time will indicate that the problem is at line 38, where the exception occurred, *not* at line 42. This makes the error more difficult to find and debug, especially in large software applications where the exception may occur in a different file—and even in a different assembly.

23.5 Generic Collections

The System.Collections.Generic namespace contains generic classes that allow us to create collections of specific types. As you saw in Fig. 23.2, many of the classes are simply generic versions of nongeneric collections. A couple of classes implement new data structures. Here, we demonstrate generic collections SortedDictionary and LinkedList.

23.5.1 Generic Class SortedDictionary

A **dictionary** is the general term for a collection of key/value pairs. A hash table is one way to implement a dictionary. The .NET Framework provides several implementations of dictionaries, both generic and nongeneric, all of which implement the IDictionary interface (described in Fig. 23.1). The application in Fig. 23.8 is a modification of Fig. 23.7 that uses the generic class **SortedDictionary**. Generic class SortedDictionary does not use a hash table, but instead stores its key/value pairs in a binary search tree. (We discuss binary trees in depth in Section 21.7.) As the class name suggests, the entries in Sorted-Dictionary are sorted in the tree by key. When the key implements generic interface IComparable<T>, the SortedDictionary uses the results of IComparable<T> method Com-pareTo to sort the keys. Notice that despite these implementation details, we use the same public methods, properties and indexers with classes Hashtable and SortedDictionary in the same ways. In fact, except for the generic-specific syntax, Fig. 23.8 looks remarkably similar to Fig. 23.7. This is the beauty of object-oriented programming.

```
1   // Fig. 23.12: SortedDictionaryTest.cs
2   // Application counts the number of occurrences of each word in a string
3   // and stores them in a generic sorted dictionary.
4   using System;
5   using System.Text.RegularExpressions;
6   using System.Collections.Generic;
7
8   public class SortedDictionaryTest
9   {
10     public static void Main( string[] args )
11     {
12        // create sorted dictionary based on user input
13        SortedDictionary< string, int > dictionary = CollectWords();
14
15        // display sorted dictionary content
16        DisplayDictionary( dictionary );
17     } // end Main
18
19     // create sorted dictionary from user input
20     private static SortedDictionary< string, int > CollectWords()
21     {
22        // create a new sorted dictionary
23        SortedDictionary< string, int > dictionary =
24           new SortedDictionary< string, int >();
25
```

Fig. 23.8 | Application counts the number of occurrences of each word in a string and stores them in a generic sorted dictionary. (Part 1 of 2.)

```
26          Console.WriteLine( "Enter a string: " ); // prompt for user input
27          string input = Console.ReadLine(); // get input
28
29          // split input text into tokens
30          string[] words = Regex.Split( input, @"\s+" );
31
32          // processing input words
33          foreach ( var word in words )
34          {
35              string wordKey = word.ToLower(); // get word in lowercase
36
37              // if the dictionary contains the word
38              if ( dictionary.ContainsKey( wordKey ) )
39              {
40                  ++dictionary[ wordKey ];
41              } // end if
42              else
43                  // add new word with a count of 1 to the dictionary
44                  dictionary.Add( wordKey, 1 );
45          } // end foreach
46
47          return dictionary;
48      } // end method CollectWords
49
50      // display dictionary content
51      private static void DisplayDictionary< K, V >(
52          SortedDictionary< K, V > dictionary )
53      {
54          Console.WriteLine( "\nSorted dictionary contains:\n{0,-12}{1,-12}",
55              "Key:", "Value:" );
56
57          // generate output for each key in the sorted dictionary
58          // by iterating through the Keys property with a foreach statement
59          foreach ( K key in dictionary.Keys )
60              Console.WriteLine( "{0,-12}{1,-12}", key, dictionary[ key ] );
61
62          Console.WriteLine( "\nsize: {0}", dictionary.Count );
63      } // end method DisplayDictionary
64  } // end class SortedDictionaryTest
```

```
Enter a string:
We few, we happy few, we band of brothers

Sorted dictionary contains:
Key:        Value:
band        1
brothers    1
few,        2
happy       1
of          1
we          3

size: 6
```

Fig. 23.8 | Application counts the number of occurrences of each word in a `string` and stores them in a generic sorted dictionary. (Part 2 of 2.)

Line 6 contains a using directive for the System.Collections.Generic namespace, which contains class SortedDictionary. The generic class SortedDictionary takes two type arguments—the first specifies the type of key (i.e., string) and the second the type of value (i.e., int). We have simply replaced the word Hashtable in line 13 and lines 23–24 with SortedDictionary<string, int> to create a dictionary of int values keyed with strings. Now, the compiler can check and notify us if we attempt to store an object of the wrong type in the dictionary. Also, because the compiler now knows that the data structure contains int values, there's no longer any need for the downcast in line 40. This allows line 40 to use the much more concise prefix increment (++) notation. These changes result in code that can be checked for type safety at compile time.

Static method DisplayDictionary (lines 51–63) has been modified to be completely generic. It takes type parameters K and V. These parameters are used in line 52 to indicate that DisplayDictionary takes a SortedDictionary with keys of type K and values of type V. We use type parameter K again in line 59 as the type of the iteration key. This use of generics is a marvelous example of code reuse. If we decide to change the application to count the number of times each character appears in a string, method DisplayDictionary could receive an argument of type SortedDictionary<char, int> without modification. This is precisely what you'll do in Exercise 23.12. The key-value pairs displayed are now ordered by key, as shown in Fig. 23.8.

Performance Tip 23.6

Because class SortedDictionary keeps its elements sorted in a binary tree, obtaining or inserting a key/value pair takes O(log n) time, which is fast compared to linear searching, then inserting.

Common Programming Error 23.4

*Invoking the get accessor of a SortedDictionary indexer with a key that does not exist in the collection causes a **KeyNotFoundException**. This behavior is different from that of the Hashtable indexer's get accessor, which would return null.*

23.5.2 Generic Class LinkedList

The generic **LinkedList** class is a doubly linked list—we can navigate the list both backward and forward with nodes of generic class **LinkedListNode**. Each node contains property **Value** and read-only properties **Previous** and **Next**. The Value property's type matches LinkedList's single type parameter because it contains the data stored in the node. The Previous property gets a reference to the preceding node in the linked list (or null if the node is the first of the list). Similarly, the Next property gets a reference to the subsequent reference in the linked list (or null if the node is the last of the list). We demonstrate a few linked-list manipulations in Fig. 23.9.

```
1   // Fig. 23.9: LinkedListTest.cs
2   // Using LinkedLists.
3   using System;
4   using System.Collections.Generic;
5
```

Fig. 23.9 | Using LinkedLists. (Part 1 of 4.)

```
6    public class LinkedListTest
7    {
8       private static readonly string[] colors = { "black", "yellow",
9          "green", "blue", "violet", "silver" };
10      private static readonly string[] colors2 = { "gold", "white",
11         "brown", "blue", "gray" };
12
13      // set up and manipulate LinkedList objects
14      public static void Main( string[] args )
15      {
16         LinkedList< string > list1 = new LinkedList< string >();
17
18         // add elements to first linked list
19         foreach ( var color in colors )
20            list1.AddLast( color );
21
22         // add elements to second linked list via constructor
23         LinkedList< string > list2 = new LinkedList< string >( colors2 );
24
25         Concatenate( list1, list2 ); // concatenate list2 onto list1
26         PrintList( list1 ); // display list1 elements
27
28         Console.WriteLine( "\nConverting strings in list1 to uppercase\n" );
29         ToUppercaseStrings( list1 ); // convert to uppercase string
30         PrintList( list1 ); // display list1 elements
31
32         Console.WriteLine( "\nDeleting strings between BLACK and BROWN\n" );
33         RemoveItemsBetween( list1, "BLACK", "BROWN" );
34
35         PrintList( list1 ); // display list1 elements
36         PrintReversedList( list1 ); // display list in reverse order
37      } // end Main
38
39      // display list contents
40      private static void PrintList< T >( LinkedList< T > list )
41      {
42         Console.WriteLine( "Linked list: " );
43
44         foreach ( T value in list )
45            Console.Write( "{0} ", value );
46
47         Console.WriteLine();
48      } // end method PrintList
49
50      // concatenate the second list on the end of the first list
51      private static void Concatenate< T >( LinkedList< T > list1,
52         LinkedList< T > list2 )
53      {
54         // concatenate lists by copying element values
55         // in order from the second list to the first list
56         foreach ( T value in list2 )
57            list1.AddLast( value ); // add new node
58      } // end method Concatenate
```

Fig. 23.9 | Using LinkedLists. (Part 2 of 4.)

```
59
60      // locate string objects and convert to uppercase
61      private static void ToUppercaseStrings( LinkedList< string > list )
62      {
63         // iterate over the list by using the nodes
64         LinkedListNode< string > currentNode = list.First;
65
66         while ( currentNode != null )
67         {
68            string color = currentNode.Value; // get value in node
69            currentNode.Value = color.ToUpper(); // convert to uppercase
70
71            currentNode = currentNode.Next; // get next node
72         } // end while
73      } // end method ToUppercaseStrings
74
75      // delete list items between two given items
76      private static void RemoveItemsBetween< T >( LinkedList< T > list,
77         T startItem, T endItem )
78      {
79         // get the nodes corresponding to the start and end item
80         LinkedListNode< T > currentNode = list.Find( startItem );
81         LinkedListNode< T > endNode = list.Find( endItem );
82
83         // remove items after the start item
84         // until we find the last item or the end of the linked list
85         while ( ( currentNode.Next != null ) &&
86            ( currentNode.Next != endNode ) )
87         {
88            list.Remove( currentNode.Next ); // remove next node
89         } // end while
90      } // end method RemoveItemsBetween
91
92      // display reversed list
93      private static void PrintReversedList< T >( LinkedList< T > list )
94      {
95         Console.WriteLine( "Reversed List:" );
96
97         // iterate over the list by using the nodes
98         LinkedListNode< T > currentNode = list.Last;
99
100        while ( currentNode != null )
101        {
102           Console.Write( "{0} ", currentNode.Value );
103           currentNode = currentNode.Previous; // get previous node
104        } // end while
105
106        Console.WriteLine();
107     } // end method PrintReversedList
108  } // end class LinkedListTest
```

Fig. 23.9 | Using LinkedLists. (Part 3 of 4.)

```
Linked list:
black yellow green blue violet silver gold white brown blue gray

Converting strings in list1 to uppercase

Linked list:
BLACK YELLOW GREEN BLUE VIOLET SILVER GOLD WHITE BROWN BLUE GRAY

Deleting strings between BLACK and BROWN

Linked list:
BLACK BROWN BLUE GRAY
Reversed List:
GRAY BLUE BROWN BLACK
```

Fig. 23.9 | Using LinkedLists. (Part 4 of 4.)

The using directive in line 4 allows us to use the LinkedList class by its unqualified name. Lines 16–23 create LinkedLists list1 and list2 of strings and fill them with the contents of arrays colors and colors2, respectively. LinkedList is a generic class that has one type parameter for which we specify the type argument string in this example (lines 16 and 23). We demonstrate two ways to fill the lists. In lines 19–20, we use the foreach statement and method **AddLast** to fill list1. The AddLast method creates a new LinkedListNode (with the given value available via the Value property) and appends this node to the end of the list. There's also an **AddFirst** method that inserts a node at the beginning of the list. Line 23 invokes the constructor that takes an IEnumerable<string> parameter. All arrays implicitly inherit from the generic interfaces IList and IEnumerable with the type of the array as the type argument, so the string array colors2 implements IEnumerable<string>. The type parameter of this generic IEnumerable matches the type parameter of the generic LinkedList object. This constructor call copies the contents of the array colors2 to list2.

Line 25 calls generic method Concatenate (lines 51–58) to append all elements of list2 to the end of list1. Line 26 calls method PrintList (lines 40–48) to output list1's contents. Line 29 calls method ToUppercaseStrings (lines 61–73) to convert each string element to uppercase, then line 30 calls PrintList again to display the modified strings. Line 33 calls method RemoveItemsBetween (lines 76–90) to remove the elements between "BLACK" and "BROWN"—not including either. Line 35 outputs the list again, then line 36 invokes method PrintReversedList (lines 93–107) to display the list in reverse order.

Generic method Concatenate (lines 51–58) iterates over list2 with a foreach statement and calls method AddLast to append each value to the end of list1. The LinkedList class's enumerator loops over the values of the nodes, not the nodes themselves, so the iteration variable has type T. Notice that this creates a new node in list1 for each node in list2. One LinkedListNode cannot be a member of more than one LinkedList. If you want the same data to belong to more than one LinkedList, you must make a copy of the node for each list to avoid InvalidOperationExceptions.

Generic method PrintList (lines 40–48) similarly uses a foreach statement to iterate over the values in a LinkedList, and outputs them. Method ToUppercaseStrings (lines 61–73) takes a linked list of strings and converts each string value to uppercase. This method replaces the strings stored in the list, so we cannot use an enumerator (via a foreach statement) as in the previous two methods. Instead, we obtain the first LinkedListNode via the First property (line 64), and use a while statement to loop through the list (lines 66–72). Each iteration of the while statement obtains and updates the contents of currentNode via property Value, using string method **ToUpper** to create an uppercase version of string color. At the end of each iteration, we move the current node to the next node in the list by assigning currentNode to the node obtained by its own Next property (line 71). The Next property of the last node of the list gets null, so when the while statement iterates past the end of the list, the loop exits.

Notice that it does not make sense to declare ToUppercaseStrings as a generic method, because it uses the string-specific methods of the values in the nodes. Methods PrintList (lines 40–48) and Concatenate (lines 51–58) do not need to use any string-specific methods, so they can be declared with generic type parameters to promote maximal code reuse.

Generic method RemoveItemsBetween (lines 76–90) removes a range of items between two nodes. Lines 80–81 obtain the two "boundary" nodes of the range by using method **Find**. This method performs a linear search on the list and returns the first node that contains a value equal to the passed argument. Method Find returns null if the value is not found. We store the node preceding the range in local variable currentNode and the node following the range in endNode.

The while statement in lines 85–89 removes all the elements between currentNode and endNode. On each iteration of the loop, we remove the node following currentNode by invoking method **Remove** (line 88). Method Remove takes a LinkedListNode, splices that node out of the LinkedList, and fixes the references of the surrounding nodes. After the Remove call, currentNode's Next property now gets the node *following* the node just removed, and that node's Previous property now gets currentNode. The while statement continues to loop until there are no nodes left between currentNode and endNode, or until currentNode is the last node in the list. (There's also an overloaded version of method Remove that performs a linear search for the specified value and removes the first node in the list that contains it.)

Method PrintReversedList (lines 93–107) displays the list backward by navigating the nodes manually. Line 98 obtains the last element of the list via the **Last** property and stores it in currentNode. The while statement in lines 100–104 iterates through the list backward by moving the currentNode reference to the previous node at the end of each iteration, then exiting when we move past the beginning of the list. Note how similar this code is to lines 64–72, which iterated through the list from the beginning to the end.

23.6 Covariance and Contravariance for Generic Types

A new feature in Visual C# 2010 is *covariance* and *contravariance* of generic interface and delegate types. To understand these concepts, we'll consider them in the context of arrays, which have always been covariant and contravariant in C#.

Covariance in Arrays
Recall our Employee class hierarchy from Section 12.5, which consisted of the base class Employee and the derived classes SalariedEmployee, CommissionEmployee and Base-PlusCommissionEmployee. Assuming the declarations

```
SalariedEmployee[] salariedEmployees = {
    new SalariedEmployee( "Bob", "Blue", "111-11-1111", 800M ),
    new SalariedEmployee( "Rachel", "Red", "222-22-2222", 1234M ) };
Employee[] employees;
```

we can write the following statement:

```
employees = salariedEmployees;
```

Even though the array type `SalariedEmployee[]` does *not* derive from the array type `Employee[]`, the preceding assignment *is* allowed because class `SalariedEmployee` is a derived class of `Employee`.

Similarly, suppose we have the following method, which displays the `string` representation of each `Employee` in its `employees` array parameter:

```
void PrintEmployees( Employee[] employees )
```

We can call this method with the array of `SalariedEmployees`, as in:

```
PrintEmployees( salariedEmployees );
```

and the method will correctly display the `string` representation of each `SalariedEmployee` object in the argument array. Assigning an array of a derived-class type to an array variable of a base-class type is an example of **covariance**.

Covariance in Generic Types

Covariance now also works with several *generic interface and delegate types*, including `IEnumerable<T>`. Arrays and generic collections implement the `IEnumerable<T>` interface. Using the `salariedEmployees` array declared previously, consider the following statement:

```
IEnumerable< Employee > employees = salariedEmployees;
```

Prior to Visual C# 2010, this generated a compilation error. Interface `IEnumerable<T>` is now covariant, so the preceding statement *is* allowed. If we modify method `PrintEmployees` as in:

```
void PrintEmployees( IEnumerable< Employee > employees )
```

we can call `PrintEmployees` with the array of `SalariedEmployee` objects, because that array implements the interface `IEnumerable<SalariedEmployee>` and because a `SalariedEmployee` *is an* `Employee` and because `IEnumerable<T>` is covariant. Covariance like this works *only* with *reference* types that are related by a class hierarchy.

Contravariance in Arrays

Previously, we showed that an array of a derived-class type (`salariedEmployees`) can be assigned to an array variable of a base-class type (`employees`). Now, consider the following statement, which has *always* worked in C#:

```
SalariedEmployee[] salariedEmployees2 =
    ( SalariedEmployee[] ) employees;
```

Based on the previous statements, we know that the `Employee` array variable `employees` currently refers to an array of `SalariedEmployees`. Using a cast operator to assign `employees`—an array of base-class-type elements—to `salariedEmployees2`—an array of derived-class-type elements—is an example of contravariance. The preceding cast will fail at runtime if `employees` is *not* an array of `SalariedEmployees`.

Contravariance in Generic Types

To understand **contravariance** in generic types, consider a SortedSet of SalariedEmployees. Class **SortedSet<T>** maintains a set of objects in sorted order—no duplicates are allowed. The objects placed in a SortedSet *must* implement the **IComparable<T> interface**. For classes that *do not* implement this interface, you can still compare their objects using an object that implements the **IComparer<T> interface**. This interface's *Compare* method compares its two arguments and returns 0 if they're equal, a negative integer if the first object is less than the second, or a positive integer if the first object is greater than the second.

Our Employee hierarchy classes do not implement IComparable<T>. Let's assume we wish to sort Employees by social security number. We can implement the following class to compare any two Employees:

```
class EmployeeComparer : IComparer< Employee >
{
    int IComparer< Employee >.Compare( Employee a, Employee b)
    {
        return a.SocialSecurityNumber.CompareTo(
            b.SocialSecurityNumber );
    } // end method Compare
} // end class EmployeeComparer
```

Method Compare returns the result of comparing the two Employees social security numbers using string method CompareTo.

Now consider the following statement, which creates a SortedSet:

```
SortedSet< SalariedEmployee > set =
    new SortedSet< SalariedEmployee >( new EmployeeComparer() );
```

When the type argument does not implement IComparable<T>, you must supply an appropriate IComparer<T> object to compare the objects that will be placed in the Sorted-Set. Since, we're creating a SortedSet of SalariedEmployees, the compiler expects the IComparer<T> object to implement the IComparer<SalariedEmployee>. Instead, we provided an object that implements IComparer<Employee>. The compiler allows us to provide an IComparer for a base-class type where an IComparer for a derived-class type is expected because interface IComparer<T> supports contravariance.

Web Resources

For a list of covariant and contravariant interface types in .NET 4, visit

> msdn.microsoft.com/en-us/library/dd799517.aspx#VariantList

It's also possible to create your own variant types. For information on this, visit

> msdn.microsoft.com/en-us/library/dd997386.aspx

23.7 Wrap-Up

This chapter introduced the .NET Framework collection classes. You learned about the hierarchy of interfaces that many of the collection classes implement. You saw how to use class Array to perform array manipulations. You learned that the System.Collections and System.Collections.Generic namespaces contain many nongeneric and generic collection classes, respectively. We presented the nongeneric classes ArrayList, Stack and

Hashtable as well as generic classes SortedDictionary and LinkedList. In doing so, we discussed data structures in greater depth. We discussed dynamically expanding collections, hashing schemes, and two implementations of a dictionary. You saw the advantages of generic collections over their nongeneric counterparts.

You also learned how to use enumerators to traverse these data structures and obtain their contents. We demonstrated the foreach statement with many of the classes of the Framework Class Library, and explained that this works by using enumerators "behind-the-scenes" to traverse the collections.

Summary

Section 23.1 Introduction
- The prepackaged data-structure classes provided by the .NET Framework are known as collection classes—they store collections of data.
- With collection classes, instead of creating data structures to store these sets of items, the programmer simply uses existing data structures, without concern for how they're implemented.

Section 23.2 Collections Overview
- The .NET Framework collections provide high-performance, high-quality implementations of common data structures and enable effective software reuse.
- In earlier versions of C#, the .NET Framework primarily provided the collection classes in the System.Collections namespace to store and manipulate object references.
- The .NET Framework's System.Collections.Generic namespace contains collection classes that take advantage of .NET's generics capabilities.

Section 23.3 Class **Array** and Enumerators
- All arrays implicitly inherit from abstract base class Array (namespace System).
- The static Array method Sort sorts an array.
- The static Array method Copy copies elements from one array to another.
- The static Array method BinarySearch performs binary searches on an array. This method assumes that it receives a sorted array.
- A collection's GetEnumerator method returns an enumerator that can iterate over the collection.
- All enumerators have methods MoveNext and Reset and property Current.
- MoveNext moves the enumerator to the next element in the collection. MoveNext returns true if there's at least one more element in the collection; otherwise, the method returns false.
- Read-only property Current returns the object at the current location in the collection.
- If a collection is modified after an enumerator is created for that collection, the enumerator immediately becomes invalid.
- The foreach statement implicitly obtains an enumerator via the GetEnumerator method and uses the enumerator's MoveNext method and Current property to traverse the collection. This can be done with any collection that implements the IEnumerable interface—not just arrays.

Section 23.4.1 Class **ArrayList**
- In most programming languages, conventional arrays have a fixed size.
- The .NET Framework's ArrayList collection class enhances the functionality of conventional arrays and provides dynamic resizing of the collection.

- ArrayLists store references to objects.

- ArrayList has a constructor that can initialize the contents of an ArrayList with the elements of any ICollection passed to it. Many of the collection classes have such a constructor.

- The Count and Capacity properties correspond, respectively, to the current number of elements in the ArrayList and the maximum number of elements that can be stored without allocating more memory to the ArrayList.

- Method IndexOf returns the position of a value in an ArrayList, or -1 if the element isn't found.

- We can access an element of an ArrayList by following the ArrayList variable name with square brackets ([]) containing the desired index of the element.

- The Remove method removes the first occurrence of the specified object. All subsequent elements shift toward the beginning of the ArrayList to fill the emptied position.

Section 23.4.2 Class **Stack**
- Class Stack has methods Push and Pop to perform the basic stack operations.

- The non-generic Stack class can store only references to objects, so value-type items are implicitly boxed before they're added to the Stack.

- Method Peek returns the value of the top stack element but does not remove the element.

- Attempting to Peek or Pop an empty Stack causes an InvalidOperationException.

Section 23.4.3 Class **Hashtable**
- Hashing is a high-speed scheme for converting keys to unique array indices. The .NET Framework provides class Hashtable to enable programmers to employ hashing.

- Class Hashtable can accept any object as a key.

- Method ContainsKey determines whether a key is in the hash table.

- Hashtable method Add creates a new entry in the hash table, with the first argument as the key and the second as the value.

- We can use the Hashtable's indexer to obtain and set the key's associated value in the hash table.

- Hashtable property Keys gets an ICollection that contains all the keys.

- If you use a foreach statement with a Hashtable, the iteration variable is of type Dictionary-Entry, which has properties Key and Value for retrieving the key and value of the current element.

Section 23.5.1 Generic Class **SortedDictionary**
- A dictionary is a collection of key/value pairs. A hash table is one way to implement a dictionary.

- Generic class SortedDictionary does not use a hash table, but instead stores its key/value pairs in a binary search tree.

- Generic class SortedDictionary takes two type arguments—the first specifies the type of key and the second the type of value.

- When the compiler knows the type that the data structure contains, there's no need to downcast when we need to use the type-specific methods.

- Invoking the get accessor of a SortedDictionary indexer with a key that does not exist in the collection causes a KeyNotFoundException. This behavior is different from that of the Hashtable indexer's get accessor, which would return null.

Section 23.5.2 Generic Class **LinkedList**
- The LinkedList class is a doubly linked list—we can navigate the list both backward and forward with nodes of generic class LinkedListNode.

- Each node contains property Value and read-only properties Previous and Next.

- The LinkedList class's enumerator loops over the values of the nodes, not the nodes themselves.

- One LinkedListNode cannot be a member of more than one LinkedList. Any attempt to add a node from one LinkedList to another generates an InvalidOperationException.

- Method Find performs a linear search on the list and returns the first node that contains a value equal to the passed argument.

- Method Remove deletes a node from a LinkedList.

Section 23.6 Covariance and Contravariance for Generic Types

- Visual C# 2010 now supports covariance and contravariance of generic interface and delegate types.

- Assigning an array of a derived-class type to an array variable of a base-class type is an example of covariance.

- Covariance now works with several generic interface types, including IEnumerable<T>.

- Covariance in generic collections works *only* with reference types in the same class hierarchy.

- Using a cast operator to assign an array variable of a base-class type to an array variable of a derived-class type is an example of contravariance.

- Class SortedSet maintains a set of objects in sorted order—no duplicates are allowed.

- The objects placed in a SortedSet must be comparable to determine their sorting order. Objects are comparable if their classes implement the IComparable<T> interface.

- For classes that do not implement IComparable<T>, you can compare the objects using an object that implements the IComparer<T> interface. This interface's Compare method compares its two arguments and returns 0 if they are equal, a negative integer if the first object is less than the second, or a positive integer if the first object is greater than the second.

- Providing an IComparer for a base-class type where an IComparer for a derived-class type is expected is allowed because interface IComparer<T> supports contravariance.

Terminology

Add method of class ArrayList
Add method of class Hashtable
AddLast method of class LinkedList
ArgumentException
Array class
ArrayList class
BinarySearch method of class Array
BinarySearch method of class ArrayList
capacity
Capacity property of class ArrayList
Clear method of class Array
Clear method of class ArrayList
collection
collection class
collision
Contains method of class ArrayList
Contains method of class Stack
ContainsKey method of class Hashtable
contravariance
Copy method of interface ICollection

Count property of interface ICollection
covariance
CreateInstance method of class Array
Current property of interface IEnumerator
dictionary
DictionaryEntry structure
enumerator
Find method of class LinkedList
First property of class LinkedList
GetEnumerator method of interface
    IEnumerable
GetHashCode method of class object
hash function
hash table
hashing
Hashtable class
ICollection interface
IComparable<T> interface
IComparer<T> interface
IDictionary interface

IEnumerable interface

IEnumerator interface

IList interface

IndexOf method of class Array

IndexOf method of class ArrayList

int indexer of class ArrayList

InvalidOperationException

KeyNotFoundException

Keys property of interface IDictionary

Last property of class LinkedList

LastIndexOf method of class Array

LinkedList generic class

LinkedListNode generic class

load factor

MoveNext method of interface IEnumerator

Next property of class LinkedListNode

Peek method of class Stack

Pop method of class Stack

Previous property of class LinkedListNode

Push method of class Stack

Queue class

Remove method of class ArrayList

Remove method of class LinkedList

RemoveAt method of class ArrayList

RemoveRange method of class ArrayList

Reset method of interface IEnumerator

Sort method of class Array

Sort method of class ArrayList

SortedDictionary generic class

SortedList class

SortedSet class

space/time trade-off

Stack class

System.Collections namespace

System.Collections.Generic namespace

System.Collections.Specialized namespace

ToLower method of class string

ToUpper method of class string

TrimToSize method of class ArrayList

Value property of class LinkedListNode

Values property of interface IDictionary

Self-Review Exercises

23.1 Fill in the blanks in each of the following statements:

   a) A(n) _____ is used to walk through a collection but cannot remove elements from the collection during the iteration.

   b) Class _____ provides the capabilities of an arraylike data structure that can resize itself dynamically.

   c) An element in an ArrayList can be accessed by using the ArrayList's _____.

   d) IEnumerator method _____ advances the enumerator to the next item.

   e) If the collection it references has been altered since the enumerator's creation, calling method Reset will cause a(n) _____.

23.2 State whether each of the following is *true* or *false*. If *false*, explain why.

   a) Class Stack is in the System.Collections namespace.

   b) A Hashtable stores key/value pairs.

   c) A class implementing interface IEnumerator must define only methods MoveNext and Reset, and no properties.

   d) Values of simple types may be stored directly in an ArrayList.

   e) An ArrayList can contain duplicate values.

   f) A Hashtable can contain duplicate keys.

   g) A LinkedList can contain duplicate values.

   h) Dictionary is an interface.

   i) Enumerators can change the values of elements but cannot remove them.

   j) With hashing, as the load factor increases, the chance of collisions decreases.

Answers to Self-Review Exercises

23.1   a) enumerator (or foreach statement).   b) ArrayList.   c) indexer.   d) MoveNext. e) InvalidOperationException.

23.2 a) True. b) True. c) False. The class must also implement property `Current`. d) False. An `ArrayList` stores only `objects`. Autoboxing occurs when adding a value type to the `ArrayList`. You can prevent boxing by instead using generic class `List` with a value type. e) True. f) False. A `Hashtable` cannot contain duplicate keys. g) True. h) False. `Dictionary` is a class; `IDictionary` is an interface. i) False. An enumerator cannot be used to change the values of elements. j) False. With hashing, as the load factor increases, there are fewer available slots relative to the total number of slots, so the chance of selecting an occupied slot (a collision) with a hashing operation increases.

Exercises

23.3 *(Collections Terminology)* Define each of the following terms:
 a) `ICollection`
 b) `Array`
 c) `IList`
 d) load factor
 e) `Hashtable` collision
 f) space/time trade-off in hashing
 g) `Hashtable`

23.4 *(ArrayList Methods)* Explain briefly the operation of each of the following methods of class `ArrayList`:
 a) `Add`
 b) `Insert`
 c) `Remove`
 d) `Clear`
 e) `RemoveAt`
 f) `Contains`
 g) `IndexOf`
 h) `Count`
 i) `Capacity`

23.5 *(ArrayList Insertion Performance)* Explain why inserting additional elements into an `Array-List` object whose current size is less than its capacity is a relatively fast operation and why inserting additional elements into an `ArrayList` object whose current size is at capacity is relatively slow.

23.6 *(Inheritance Negatives)* In our implementation of a stack in Fig. 21.13, we were able to quickly extend a linked list to create class `StackInheritance`. The .NET Framework designers chose not to use inheritance to create their `Stack` class. What are the negative aspects of inheritance, particularly for class `Stack`?

23.7 *(Collections Short Questions)* Briefly answer the following questions:
 a) What happens when you add a simple type value to a nongeneric collection?
 b) Can you display all the elements in an `IEnumerable` object without explicitly using an enumerator? If yes, how?

23.8 *(Enumerator Members)* Explain briefly the operation of each of the following enumerator-related methods:
 a) `GetEnumerator`
 b) `Current`
 c) `MoveNext`

23.9 *(HashTable Methods an Properties)* Explain briefly the operation of each of the following methods and properties of class `Hashtable`:
 a) `Add`
 b) `Keys`

c) Values
d) ContainsKey

23.10   *(True/False)* Determine whether each of the following statements is *true* or *false*. If *false*, explain why.

    a) Elements in an array must be sorted in ascending order before a BinarySearch may be performed.

    b) Method First gets the first node in a LinkedList.

    c) Class Array provides static method Sort for sorting array elements.

23.11   *(LinkedList without Duplicates)* Write an application that reads in a series of first names and stores them in a LinkedList. Do not store duplicate names. Allow the user to search for a first name.

23.12   *(Generic SortedDictionary)* Modify the application in Fig. 23.8 to count the number of occurrences of each letter rather than of each word. For example, the string "HELLO THERE" contains two Hs, three Es, two Ls, one O, one T and one R. Display the results.

23.13   *(SortedDictionary of Colors)* Use a SortedDictionary to create a reusable class for choosing from some of the predefined colors in class Color (in the System.Drawing namespace). The names of the colors should be used as keys, and the predefined Color objects should be used as values. Place this class in a class library that can be referenced from any C# application. Use your new class in a Windows application that allows the user to select a color, then changes the background color of the Form.

23.14   *(Duplicate Words in a Sentence)* Write an application that determines and displays the number of duplicate words in a sentence. Treat uppercase and lowercase letters the same. Ignore punctuation.

23.15   *(Using a Generic List)* Recall from Fig. 23.2 that class List is the generic equivalent of class ArrayList. Write an application that inserts 25 random integers from 0 to 100 in order into an object of class List. The application should calculate the sum of the elements and the floating-point average of the elements.

23.16   *(Reversing a LinkedList)* Write an application that creates a LinkedList object of 10 characters, then creates a second list object containing a copy of the first list, but in reverse order.

23.17   *(Prime Numbers and Prime Factorization)* Write an application that takes a whole-number input from a user and determines whether it's prime. If the number is not prime, display the unique prime factors of the number. Remember that a prime number's factors are only 1 and the prime number itself. Every number that's not prime has a unique prime factorization. For example, consider the number 54. The prime factors of 54 are 2, 3, 3 and 3. When the values are multiplied together, the result is 54. For the number 54, the prime factors output should be 2 and 3.

23.18   *(Bucket Sort with LinkedList<int>)* In Exercise 20.7, you performed a bucket sort of ints by using a two-dimensional array, where each row of the array represented a bucket. If you use a dynamically expanding data structure to represent each bucket, you do not have to write code that keeps track of the number of ints in each bucket. Rewrite your solution to use a one-dimensional array of LinkedList< int > buckets.

Chapters on the Web

The following chapters are available as PDF documents from this book's Companion Website (www.pearsonhighered.com/deitel/):

- Chapter 24, GUI with Windows Presentation Foundation
- Chapter 25, WPF Graphics and Multimedia
- Chapter 26, XML and LINQ to XML
- Chapter 27, Web App Development with ASP.NET: A Deeper Look
- Chapter 28, Windows Communication Foundation (WCF) Web Services
- Chapter 29, Silverlight and Rich Internet Applications
- Chapter 30, ATM Case Study, Part 1: Object-Oriented Design with the UML
- Chapter 31, ATM Case Study, Part 2: Implementing an Object-Oriented Design

These files can be viewed in Adobe® Reader® (get.adobe.com/reader).

New copies of this book come with a Companion Website access code that is located on the card inside the book's front cover. If the access code is already visible or there is no card, you purchased a used book or an edition that does not come with an access code. In this case, you can purchase access directly from the Companion Website.

A

Operator Precedence Chart

Operators are shown in decreasing order of precedence from top to bottom with each level of precedence separated by a horizontal line. The associativity of the operators is shown in the right column.

Operator	Type	Associativity
.	member access	left-to-right
()	method call	
[]	element access	
++	postfix increment	
--	postfix decrement	
new	object creation	
typeof	get System.Type object for a type	
sizeof	get size in bytes of a type	
checked	checked evaluation	
unchecked	unchecked evaluation	
+	unary plus	right-to-left
-	unary minus	
!	logical negation	
~	bitwise complement	
++	prefix increment	
--	prefix decrement	
(*type*)	cast	
*	multiplication	left-to-right
/	division	
%	remainder	
+	addition	left-to-right
-	subtraction	

Fig. A.1 | Operator precedence chart (Part 1 of 2.).

Operator	Type	Associativity
>>	right shift	left-to-right
<<	left shift	
<	less than	left-to-right
>	greater than	
<=	less than or equal to	
>=	greater than or equal to	
is	type comparison	
as	type conversion	
!=	is not equal to	left-to-right
==	is equal to	
&	logical AND	left-to-right
^	logical XOR	left-to-right
|	logical OR	left-to-right
&&	conditional AND	left-to-right
||	conditional OR	left-to-right
??	null coalescing	right-to-left
?:	conditional	right-to-left
=	assignment	right-to-left
*=	multiplication assignment	
/=	division assignment	
%=	remainder assignment	
+=	addition assignment	
-=	subtraction assignment	
<<=	left shift assignment	
>>=	right shift assignment	
&=	logical AND assignment	
^=	logical XOR assignment	
|=	logical OR assignment	

Fig. A.1 | Operator precedence chart (Part 2 of 2.).

B

Simple Types

Type	Size in bits	Value range	Standard
bool	8	true or false	
byte	8	0 to 255, inclusive	
sbyte	8	–128 to 127, inclusive	
char	16	'\u0000' to '\uFFFF' (0 to 65535), inclusive	Unicode
short	16	–32768 to 32767, inclusive	
ushort	16	0 to 65535, inclusive	
int	32	–2,147,483,648 to 2,147,483,647, inclusive	
uint	32	0 to 4,294,967,295, inclusive	
float	32	*Approximate negative range:* –3.4028234663852886E+38 to –1.40129846432481707E–45 *Approximate positive range:* 1.40129846432481707E–45 to 3.4028234663852886E+38 *Other supported values:* positive and negative zero positive and negative infinity not-a-number (NaN)	IEEE 754 IEC 60559
long	64	–9,223,372,036,854,775,808 to 9,223,372,036,854,775,807, inclusive	
ulong	64	0 to 18,446,744,073,709,551,615, inclusive	

Fig. B.1 | Simple types. (Part 1 of 2.)

Type	Size in bits	Value range	Standard
double	64	*Approximate negative range:* −1.7976931348623157E+308 to −4.94065645841246544E−324 *Approximate positive range:* 4.94065645841246544E−324 to 1.7976931348623157E+308 *Other supported values:* positive and negative zero positive and negative infinity not-a-number (NaN)	IEEE 754 IEC 60559
decimal	128	*Negative range:* −79,228,162,514,264,337,593,543,950,335 (−7.9E+28) to −1.0E−28 *Positive range:* 1.0E−28 to 79,228,162,514,264,337,593,543,950,335 (7.9E+28)	

Fig. B.1 | Simple types. (Part 2 of 2.)

Additional Simple Type Information

- This appendix is based on information from Sections 4.1.4–4.1.8 of Microsoft's version of the *C# Language Specification* and Sections 11.1.4–11.1.8 of the ECMA-334 (the ECMA version of the *C# Language Specification*). These documents are available from the following websites:

  msdn.microsoft.com/en-us/vcsharp/aa336809.aspx
  www.ecma-international.org/publications/standards/Ecma-334.htm

- Values of type float have seven digits of precision.

- Values of type double have 15–16 digits of precision.

- Values of type decimal are represented as integer values that are scaled by a power of 10. Values between −1.0 and 1.0 are represented exactly to 28 digits.

- For more information on IEEE 754 visit grouper.ieee.org/groups/754/. For more information on Unicode, see Appendix F.

C

ASCII Character Set

	0	1	2	3	4	5	6	7	8	9
0	nul	soh	stx	etx	eot	enq	ack	bel	bs	ht
1	nl	vt	ff	cr	so	si	dle	dc1	dc2	dc3
2	dc4	nak	syn	etb	can	em	sub	esc	fs	gs
3	rs	us	sp	!	"	#	$	%	&	'
4	(	)	*	+	,	-	.	/	0	1
5	2	3	4	5	6	7	8	9	:	;
6	<	=	>	?	@	A	B	C	D	E
7	F	G	H	I	J	K	L	M	N	O
8	P	Q	R	S	T	U	V	W	X	Y
9	Z	[	\	]	^	_	'	a	b	c
10	d	e	f	g	h	i	j	k	l	m
11	n	o	p	q	r	s	t	u	v	w
12	x	y	z	{			}	~	del		

Fig. C.1 | ASCII Character Set.

The digits at the left of the table are the left digits of the decimal equivalent (0–127) of the character code, and the digits at the top of the table are the right digits of the character code. For example, the character code for "F" is 70, and the character code for "&" is 38.

Most users of this book are interested in the ASCII character set used to represent English characters on many computers. The ASCII character set is a subset of the Unicode character set used by C# to represent characters from most of the world's languages. For more information on the Unicode character set, see Appendix F.

Appendices on the Web

The following appendices are available as PDF documents from this book's Companion Website (www.pearsonhighered.com/deitel/):

- Appendix D, Number Systems
- Appendix E, UML 2: Additional Diagram Types
- Appendix F, Unicode®
- Appendix G, Using the Visual C# 2010 Debugger

These files can be viewed in Adobe® Reader® (get.adobe.com/reader).

New copies of this book come with a Companion Website access code that is located on the card inside the book's front cover. If the access code is already visible or there is no card, you purchased a used book or an edition that does not come with an access code. In this case, you can purchase access directly from the Companion Website.

Index